DATE DUE

			PRINTED IN U.S.A.

ENCYCLOPEDIA
OF MORMONISM

EDITORIAL BOARD

ENCYCLOPEDIA OF MORMONISM

Edited by
Daniel H. Ludlow

Volume 1

*The History, Scripture, Doctrine, and Procedure
of The Church of Jesus Christ of Latter-day Saints*

Macmillan Publishing Company
New York

Maxwell Macmillan Canada
Toronto

Maxwell Macmillan International
New York   Oxford   Singapore   Sydney

Copyright © 1992 by Macmillan Publishing Company
A Division of Macmillan, Inc.

Macmillan Publishing Company
866 Third Avenue, New York, NY 10022

Maxwell Macmillan Canada, Inc.
1200 Eglinton Avenue East, Suite 200, Don Mills, Ontario M3C 3N1

Library of Congress Catalog Card No.:91–34255

Printed in the United States of America

printing number
    4 5 6 7 8 9 10

Macmillan Inc. is part of the Maxwell Communication
Group of Companies.

Library of Congress Cataloging-in-Publication Data

Encyclopedia of Mormonism/edited by Daniel H. Ludlow.
        p.   cm.
    Includes bibliographical references and index.
    ISBN 0-02-879605-5 (4 vol. set).—ISBN 0-02-904040-X (5 vol.
set).—ISBN 0-02-879600-4 (v. 1)
    1. Church of Jesus Christ of Latter-Day Saints—Encyclopedias.
2. Mormon Church—Encyclopedias.   3. Mormons—Encyclopedias.
I. Ludlow, Daniel H.
    BX8605.5.E62   1992
    289.3'03—dc20   91–34255
                                                          CIP

EDITORIAL AND PRODUCTION STAFF

CONTENTS

LIST OF ARTICLES

LIST OF CONTRIBUTORS

L. LaMar Adams
Brigham Young University
  Seth

Lisa Ramsey Adams
Attorney, Salt Lake City
  Eternal Progression

William J. Adams, Jr.
Granite Community Education, Salt Lake City
  Jeremiah, Prophecies of

Harley K. Adamson
Weber State University, Ogden, UT
  Teachers, Teacher Development

Stan L. Albrecht
Brigham Young University
  Stake

Douglas D. Alder
Dixie College, St. George, UT
  Comprehensive History of the Church
  Ward

Thomas G. Alexander
Brigham Young University
  Salt Lake City, Utah

Frank D. Allan
George Washington Medical School
  Autopsy

James B. Allen
Brigham Young University
  History of the Church: c. 1945–1990
  McKay, David O.

Ruel A. Allred
Brigham Young University
  Instructor, The Juvenile Instructor

Dan W. Andersen
Brigham Young University
  Immortality

Wilson K. Andersen
Brigham Young University
  Spirit Body

A. Gary Anderson
Brigham Young University
  Scripture: Words of Living Prophets
  Smith Family Ancestors
  Smith, Joseph, Sr.

D. Brent Anderson
Business Consultant, Salt Lake City
  Book of Mormon Authorship

Darl Anderson
Businessman, Mesa, AZ
  Non-Mormons, Social Relations with

J. Max Anderson
State of Utah, Salt Lake City
  "Fundamentalists"

Karl Ricks Anderson
Business Consultant, Lyndhurst, OH
  Consecration: Consecration in Ohio and Missouri
  Hiram, Ohio

Paul L. Anderson
Museum of Church History and Art, Salt Lake City
  Building Program
  Tabernacle, Salt Lake City

Richard Lloyd Anderson
Brigham Young University
  Book of Mormon Witnesses
  Cowdery, Oliver
  Smith, Lucy Mack

Gerald S. Argetsinger
Rochester Institute of Technology, Rochester, NY
  Cumorah Pageant

Marilyn Arnold
Brigham Young University
  Book of Mormon: Book of Enos
  Book of Mormon: Book of Jarom
  Book of Mormon: Book of Omni

Harriet Horne Arrington
Historian, Salt Lake City
  Smith, Bathsheba Bigler

Leonard J. Arrington
Brigham Young University
  Economic History of the Church
  History of the Church: c. 1844–1877
  Pioneer Economy
  Young, Brigham: Brigham Young

Wendell J. Ashton
Deseret News, Salt Lake City
  Deseret News

Danel W. Bachman
Church Educational System, Salt Lake City

Anthon Transcript

Plural Marriage

James H. Backman
Brigham Young University

Courts, Ecclesiastical, Nineteenth-Century

Milton V. Backman, Jr.
Brigham Young University

History of the Church: c. 1831–1844

First Vision

Kirtland, Ohio

Howard M. Bahr
Brigham Young University

Individuality

Stephen J. Bahr
Brigham Young University

Social Characteristics

Arthur A. Bailey
Church Educational System, Ephraim, Utah

Adam: LDS Sources

Elect of God

J. Hugh Baird
Brigham Young University

Ballantyne, Richard

Bulletin

Christine Purves Baker
Church Educational System, Peoria, AZ

Helaman₃

Ishmael

Margaret P. Baker
Brigham Young University—Hawaii

Humor

Kenneth W. Baldridge
Brigham Young University—Hawaii

Pearl of Great Price: Contents and Publication

Steven W. Baldridge
Brigham Young University

Granite Mountain Record Vault

Terry B. Ball
Brigham Young University

Book of Mormon: Second Book of Nephi

VerDon W. Ballantyne
Brigham Young University

Aaronic Priesthood: Powers and Offices

Levitical Priesthood

Ariel S. Ballif
Brigham Young University

Patriarch: Stake Patriarch

Jae R. Ballif
Brigham Young University

Melchizedek Priesthood: Powers and Offices in the Melchizedek Priesthood

Melchizedek Priesthood: Restoration of Melchizedek Priesthood

Lowell Bangerter
University of Wyoming

Children: Blessing of Children

Glen E. Barksdale
Pleasant Grove, Utah Jr. High

Sunday

Brent A. Barlow
Brigham Young University

Procreation

Norman J. Barlow
Church Educational System, Los Angeles

David, King

Ivan J. Barrett
Brigham Young University

Church of the Firstborn

Howard H. Barron
Brigham Young University

Hyde, Orson

Roger M. Barrus
Hamden-Sydney College, VA

Politics: Political History

Grant E. Barton
Church Missionary Training Center, Provo, UT

Last Days

Arthur R. Bassett
Brigham Young University

Endless and Eternal

Merrill J. Bateman
Brigham Young University

Conferences: Stake Conference

Jeffrey C. Bateson
Church Finance and Records Dept., Salt Lake City

Clerk

Alexander L. Baugh
Church Educational System, Columbia, SC

First Estate

Patten, David W.

Second Estate

Mary K. Beard
Physician, Salt Lake City

Abortion

Martha Nibley Beck
Writer, Provo, UT

Women, Roles of: Historical and Sociological Development

Maureen Ursenbach Beecher
Brigham Young University

Biography and Autobiography

Snow, Eliza R.

Snow, Lorenzo

Kenneth H. Beesley
LDS Business College, Salt Lake City

LDS Business College

Elouise M. Bell
Brigham Young University

Holiness

James P. Bell
Brigham Young University

Mortality

Purpose of Earth Life: LDS Perspective

Terrell H. Bell
Former U.S. Commissioner of Education

Education: Educational Attainment

Evalyn Darger Bennett
Writer, Lecturer, Salt Lake City

Williams, Clarissa

Richard E. Bennett
University of Manitoba, Winnipeg, Manitoba

Canada, The Church in

Council Bluffs (Kanesville), Iowa

Winter Quarters

Robert F. Bennett
Franklin Institute, Inc., Salt Lake City

Latter-day Saints (LDS)

Alfred Benney
Fairfield College, Fairfield, CT

Catholicism and Mormonism

Francine Russell Bennion
Ricks College, Rexburg, ID

Ruth

Steven D. Bennion
Ricks College, Rexburg, ID

Abel

Reed A. Benson
Brigham Young University

Benson, Ezra Taft

Pride

Sword of Laban

Joseph Ivins Bentley
Attorney, Newport Beach, CA

Martyrdom of Joseph and Hyrum Smith

Smith, Joseph: Legal Trials of Joseph Smith

Allen E. Bergin
Brigham Young University

Mental Health

Visions

Sue Bergin
Writer, Editor, Santa Monica, CA

Life and Death, Spiritual

Lord's Prayer

LaMar C. Berrett
Brigham Young University

Adam-Ondi-Ahman

Endowment Houses

Independence, Missouri

Salt Lake Valley

William E. Berrett
Brigham Young University

Church Educational System (CES)

Jack M. Bethards
Schoenstein Organ Co., San Francisco

Tabernacle Organ

H. George Bickerstaff
Bookcraft Publishing Co., Salt Lake City

Gifts of the Spirit

Susan Easton Black
Brigham Young University

Celestial Kingdom

Name of the Church

Terrestrial Kingdom

Alma R. Blair
Graceland College, Lamoni, IA

Haun's Mill Massacre

Robert W. Blair
Brigham Young University

Vocabulary, Latter-day Saint

Reed H. Blake
Brigham Young University

Calamities and Disasters

Mae Blanch
Brigham Young University

Prayer

V. Ben Bloxham
Brigham Young University

Family History Centers

Law of Adoption

David E. Bohn
Brigham Young University

Freedom

David L. Bolliger
Church Educational System, Salt Lake City

Israel: Lost Tribes of Israel

Paul M. Bons
Church Personnel Dept., Salt Lake City

Organization: Contemporary Organization

David F. Boone
Brigham Young University

Perpetual Emigrating Fund (PEF)

Signs of the Times

R. Wayne Boss
University of Colorado

Home Teaching

Priesthood Interview

Donna Lee Bowen
Brigham Young University

Women in the Book of Mormon

Walter D. Bowen
Brigham Young University

Doctrine and Covenants: Section 107

Spirit World

Marian R. Boyer
Former Counselor in General Presidency, Church Relief Society, Salt Lake City

Visiting Teaching

David C. Bradford
Church Correlation Dept., Salt Lake City

Bishopric

Priesthood Executive Committee, Stake and Ward

M. Gerald Bradford
University of California at Irvine

    Doctrine: Meaning, Source, and History of Doctrine

    Orthodoxy, Heterodoxy, Heresy

Reed H. Bradford
Brigham Young University

    Family: Teachings About the Family

Martha Sonntag Bradley
Brigham Young University

    Folk Art

Merrill Bradshaw
Brigham Young University

    Mormon Youth Symphony and Chorus

William S. Bradshaw
Brigham Young University

    Baptism of Fire and of the Holy Ghost

    Remission of Sins

F. Neil Brady
San Diego State University

    Ethics

    Unity

Rodney H. Brady
Bonneville International Corp., Salt Lake City

    Bonneville International Corporation

    Business: Church Participation in Business

Ronald L. Bramble
Boy Scouts of America, Los Angeles

    Deacon, Aaronic Priesthood

Edward J. Brandt
Church Correlation Dept., Salt Lake City

    Aaron, Brother of Moses

    Ahman

    Wentworth Letter

Hoyt W. Brewster, Jr.
Church Curriculum Dept., Salt Lake City

    Ordination to the Priesthood

Douglas E. Brinley
Brigham Young University

    Faith in Jesus Christ

R. Lanier Britsch
Brigham Young University

    Asia, The Church in: Asia, East

    Asia, The Church in: Asia, South and Southeast

    Hawaii, The Church in

    Oceania, The Church in

Ralph A. Britsch
Brigham Young University

    Prophet: Prophets

Todd A. Britsch
Brigham Young University

    Prophet: Prophets

Carlfred Broderick
University of Southern California

    Suffering in the World

Doris Bayly Brower
Brigham Young University

    World Conferences on Records

Bruce L. Brown
Brigham Young University

    Sin

Cheryl Brown
Brigham Young University

    Book of Mormon: Book of Alma

    Obedience

Gayle Oblad Brown
Writer, Arabic Translator, Orem, UT

    Premortal Life

S. Kent Brown
Brigham Young University

    Apostle

    Gethsemane

    Israel: Overview

    Lehi

Thomas E. Brown
Audio Visual Dept., Salt Lake City

    Membership Records

Victor L. Brown, Jr.
Church Welfare Services, Citrus Heights, CA

    Fathers' Blessings

    Homosexuality

    Men, Roles of

Victor L. Brown, Sr.
General Authority, Salt Lake City

    Doctrine and Covenants: Section 42

Gary L. Browning
Brigham Young University

    Blasphemy

    Thankfulness

Gary C. Bryner
Brigham Young University

    Politics: Political Teachings

Gary L. Bunker
Brigham Young University

    Stereotyping of Latter-day Saints

Glade L. Burgon
Church Educational System, Bountiful, UT

    God the Father: Names and Titles

    Name of God

M. Dallas Burnett
Brigham Young University

    Conferences: General Conference

Alma P. Burton
Church Educational System, Provo, UT

    Doctrine: Distinctive Teachings

    Endowment

    Salvation

H. David Burton
Church Presiding Bishopric's Office, Salt Lake City

    Baptism for the Dead: LDS Practice

    Presiding Bishopric

Marshall T. Burton
Church Educational System, Orem, UT

   Meridian of Time

Richard L. Bushman
Columbia University

   History of the Church:
   c. 1820–1831

   Smith, Joseph: The Prophet

Eliot A. Butler
Brigham Young University

   Brigham Young University:
   Provo, Utah, Campus

L. Reynolds Cahoon
Church Family History Dept., Salt Lake City

   FamilySearch®

Lysle R. Cahoon
Former Church Temple President, Chicago, IL

   Holy of Holies

C. Max Caldwell
Brigham Young University

   Doctrine and Covenants:
   Contents

   Doctrine and Covenants: Section 45

   Revelations, Unpublished

J. LeRoy Caldwell
Brigham Young University

   Messenger and Advocate

Douglas L. Callister
Attorney, Glendale, CA

   Resurrection

Tad R. Callister
Attorney, Glendale, CA

   Dedications

   Jesus Christ: Resurrection of Jesus Christ

J. Elliot Cameron
Church Temple President, Provo, UT

   Priesthood Blessings

Kim S. Cameron
Michigan State University

   Authority

   Stake President, Stake Presidency

Beverly Campbell
Campbell Associates, Washington, DC

   Eve

D. James Cannon
Consultant, Salt Lake City

   Pioneer Day

Donald Q. Cannon
Brigham Young University

   Doctrine and Covenants:
   Section 76

   Kane, Thomas L.

   King Follett Discourse

Elaine Anderson Cannon
Author, St. George, UT

   LDS Student Associations

   Mother in Heaven

   Young Women

Janath Russell Cannon
Church Temple Matron, Frankfurt, Germany

   Relief Society

   Robison, Louise Yates

   Sisterhood

Mark W. Cannon
Consultant, Washington, DC

   Civic Duties

Michael C. Cannon
Church News, Salt Lake City

   Deseret Industries

John K. Carmack
General Authority, Salt Lake City

   Organization of the Church, 1830

John Carr
Former Director Church Internal Communications, Salt Lake City

   Distribution Centers

Barbara R. Carter
Writer, Provo, UT

   Doctrine and Covenants:
   Section 88

K. Codell Carter
Brigham Young University

   Epistemology

   Godhood

Shirley A. Cazier
Writer, Logan, UT

   Rogers, Aurelia Spencer

Bruce A. Chadwick
Brigham Young University

   Native Americans

Jeffrey R. Chadwick
Church Educational System, Ogden UT

   Daniel, Prophecies of

James H. Charlesworth
Princeton Theological Seminary

   Enoch: Ancient Sources

Linda A. Charney
Church Correlation Dept., Salt Lake City

   Joining the Church

   Membership

Lance D. Chase
Brigham Young University—Hawaii

   Spaulding Manuscript

   Zion's Camp

Paul R. Cheesman [deceased]
Brigham Young University

   Book of Mormon: Book of Helaman

   Helaman₂

David J. Cherrington
Brigham Young University

   Poverty, Attitudes Toward

   Societies and Organizations

   Work, Role of

Alan Cherry
Oral History Researcher, Provo, UT

   Blacks

C. Richard Chidester
Church Educational System, Salt Lake City

Worldly, Worldliness

Dong Sull Choi
Brigham Young University

Confession of Sins

Bruce L. Christensen
Public Broadcasting System, Alexandria, VA

Broadcasting

Satellite Communications System

Bryce J. Christensen
Rockford Institute Center on the Family in America, Rockford, IL

Adultery

Chastity, Law of

Christine Quinn Christensen
Writer, Belmont, MA

Blessing on Food

Clayton Christensen
Ceramics Process Systems Corp., Belmont, MA

Testimony Bearing

Horace H. Christensen
IBM, Endwell, NY

Harmony, Pennsylvania

Joe J. Christensen
General Authority, Salt Lake City

Seminaries

Maribeth Christensen
Ricks College, Rexburg, ID

Volunteerism

John R. Christiansen
Brigham Young University

Fear of God

Helen Lance Christianson
Writer, Provo, UT

Birth

Jack R. Christianson
Church Educational System, Orem, UT

Teacher, Aaronic Priesthood

Howard A. Christy
Brigham Young University

Handcart Companies

Richmond Jail

Lewis R. Church
Church Educational System, Pleasant Grove, UT

Enoch: Book of Enoch

Prophet, Seer, and Revelator

Alice T. Clark
University of North Dakota

Humility

Bruce B. Clark
Brigham Young University

Blessings

Carol L. Clark
Church General Relief Society Office, Salt Lake City

Inspiration

Mormon Handicraft

D. Cecil Clark
Brigham Young University

New and Everlasting Covenant

E. Douglas Clark
Attorney, Salt Lake City

Abraham

James R. Clark
Brigham Young University

Joseph of Egypt: Writings of Joseph

John E. Clark
Brigham Young University

Book of Mormon Geography

C. Ross Clement
Church Social Services, Salt Lake City

Social Services

Dean B. Cleverly
Church Missionary Dept., Salt Lake City

Missions

Victor B. Cline
University of Utah

Pornography

Robert A. Cloward
Church Educational System, Cedar City, UT

Dead Sea Scrolls: LDS Perspective

Lost Scripture

Scripture: Forthcoming Scripture

John Cobb, Jr.
Claremont College

Theodicy

Clarissa Katherine Cole
Writer, Provo, UT

Promised Land, Concept of a

Eleanor (Elly) Colton
Writer, Bethesda, MD

Virgin Birth

Don F. Colvin
Church Educational System, Ogden, UT

Nauvoo Temple

Todd Compton
California State University, Northridge

Apostasy

Organization of the Church in New Testament Times

Symbolism

Spencer J. Condie
General Authority, Salt Lake City

Missionary, Missionary Life

Dix S. Coons
Rhode Island College, Warwick, RI

Commandments

Rex E. Cooper
Church Correlation Dept., Salt Lake City

Symbols, Cultural and Artistic

Ralph L. Cottrell, Jr.
Church Educational System, Ogden, UT

Born in the Covenant

Stephen R. Covey
Stephen R. Covey Associates, Provo, UT

Discipleship

Richard O. Cowan
Brigham Young University

Branch, Branch President

History of the Church: c. 1945–1990

Missionary Training Centers

Temples: History of LDS Temples from 1831 to 1990

John H. Cox
Church Ecclesiastical Support System, Salt Lake City

Ward Welfare Committee

Soren F. Cox
Brigham Young University

Interfaith Relationships: Other Faiths

True and Living Church

Richard H. Cracroft
Brigham Young University

Literature, Mormon Writers of: Novels

Lew W. Cramer
U. S. Commerce Dept., Washington, DC

Abinadi

A. Garr Cranney
Brigham Young University

Schools

Rulon G. Craven
General Authority, Salt Lake City

Confirmation

William K. Critchlow III
Attorney, Ogden, UT

Manuscript, Lost 116 Pages

Frank Moore Cross, Jr.
Harvard University

Dead Sea Scrolls: Overview

Perry H. Cunningham
Church Correlation Dept., Salt Lake City

Activity in the Church

Area, Area Presidency

James V. D'Arc
Brigham Young University

Mormons, Image of: Film

Larry E. Dahl
Brigham Young University

Degrees of Glory

Doctrine: Meaning, Source, and History of Doctrine

Lectures on Faith

Paul E. Dahl
Church Educational System, La Mesa, CA

Godhead

Karen Lynn Davidson
Writer, Pasadena, CA

Hymns and Hymnody

LeGrande Davies
Central Davis Jr. High, Layton, UT

Isaiah: Texts in the Book of Mormon

W. D. Davies
Duke University

Scripture: Scriptures

Julio Enrique Dávila
General Authority, Salt Lake City

South America, The Church in: South America, North

Ray Jay Davis
Brigham Young University

Antipolygamy Legislation

Franklin D. Day
Church Educational System, Orem, UT

Elijah: LDS Sources

Gerald J. Day
Snow College, Ephraim, UT

Mission President

Region, Regional Representative

Virgie D. Day
Brigham Young University

Mormons, Image of: The Visual Arts

K. Newell Dayley
Brigham Young University

Mormon Tabernacle Choir

Genevieve DeHoyos
Brigham Young University

Indian Student Placement Services

Ronald D. Dennis
Brigham Young University

Evening and the Morning Star, The

Gathering

Jill Mulvay Derr
Brigham Young University

Relief Society

Sisterhood

Sheri L. Dew
Deseret Book Co., Salt Lake City

Benson, Ezra Taft

John Dillenberger
Graduate Theological Union

Protestantism

Restorationism, Protestant

Donald B. Doty
Physician, Bountiful, UT

Prolonging Life

Colin B. Douglas
Church Curriculum Dept., Salt Lake City

Justification

Josiah W. Douglas
Church Curriculum Dept., Salt Lake City

Blind, Materials for the

Graham W. Doxey
General Authority, Salt Lake City

Garden of Eden

New Jerusalem

Max J. Evans
Utah State Historical Society, Salt Lake City

Forgeries of Historical Documents

Libraries and Archives

Paul H. Evans
Church Public Communications, Salt Lake City

Mormon Tabernacle Choir Broadcast ("The Spoken Word")

William S. Evans
Church Public Communications, Salt Lake City

District, District President

William E. Evenson
Brigham Young University

Evolution

Magnifying One's Calling

Richard M. Eyre
Author, Salt Lake City

Joy

Ze'ev W. Falk
Hebrew University, Jerusalem, Israel

Law of Moses

Gladys Clark Farmer
Brigham Young University

Chastening

Larry C. Farmer
Brigham Young University

Interviews

Dean B. Farnsworth
Brigham Young University

Fulness of the Gospel

James E. Faulconer
Brigham Young University

Foreknowledge of God

Franklin T. Ferguson
Architect, Salt Lake City

Architecture

Isaac C. Ferguson
Church Welfare Services, Salt Lake City

Fast Offerings

Humanitarian Service

William L. Fillmore
Attorney, Provo, UT

Light-Mindedness

Mary Finlayson
Author, Woodside, CA

Elijah, Spirit of

Dennis D. Flake
Church Educational System, Fresno, CA

Buffetings of Satan

Raising the Dead

Joel A. Flake
Church Educational System, Morgantown, WV

Gospel of Abraham

Jesus Christ: Latter-day Appearances of Jesus Christ

Lawrence R. Flake
Church Educational System, Missoula, MT

Holy Spirit of Promise

Liberty Jail

Philip M. Flammer
Brigham Young University

Nauvoo Legion

Robert B. Flanders
Southwest Missouri State University, Springfield, MO

Nauvoo Economy

Donovan E. Fleming
Brigham Young University

High Council

Neil J. Flinders
Brigham Young University

Voice of Warning

Enoc Q. Flores
Brigham Young University

Race, Racism

Rita de Cassia Flores
Writer, Provo, UT

Race, Racism

Charles Jay Fox
Brigham Young University

Polynesian Cultural Center

Christie H. Frandsen
Author, La Canada, CA

Trials

Russell M. Frandsen
Attorney, La Canada, CA

Antichrists

David Noel Freedman
University of Michigan

Prophet: Biblical Prophets

Camille Fronk
LDS Business College, Salt Lake City

Mary, Mother of Jesus

Prophecy in the Book of Mormon

Elma Widdison Fugal
Genealogist, Lindon, UT

Salvation of the Dead

Addie Fuhriman
University of Utah

Charity

David B. Galbraith
Brigham Young University

Brigham Young University: Jerusalem Center for Near Eastern Studies

Messiah: Messiah

Cynthia M. Gardner
Genealogist, Provo, UT

Book of Remembrance

David P. Gardner
University of California, Berkeley, CA

Education: Attitudes Toward Education

Marvin K. Gardner
Ensign, Salt Lake City

General Authorities

Righteousness

R. Quinn Gardner
Business Consultant, Salt Lake City

Bishop's Storehouse

Arnold Kent Garr
Brigham Young University

Brigham Young College

Liahona the Elders' Journal

Lamar E. Garrard
Brigham Young University

Colesville, New York

Fayette, New York

H. Dean Garrett
Brigham Young University

Doctrine and Covenants
Commentaries

Rebaptism

Thomas Garrow
*Social Services, Navajo Nation,
Shiprock, NM*

Native Americans

Crawford Gates
Beloit College, Beloit, WI

Sacrament Meeting

Georgia Gates
Writer, Beloit, WI

Sacrament Meeting

John Gee
*Master's student, University of
California-Berkeley*

Jesus Christ: Forty-Day Ministry
and Other Post-Resurrection
Appearances of Jesus Christ

Leland H. Gentry
*Church Educational System, Salt
Lake City*

Missouri: LDS Communities in
Caldwell and Daviess Counties

Donald B. Gilchrist
*Church Educational System, Sandy,
UT*

Wrath of God

David T. Giles
*Church Educational System, Salt
Lake City*

Joseph Smith—Matthew

Jerry C. Giles
*Church Educational System,
Fairfield, MT*

Angels: Archangels

Jesus Christ: Firstborn in the
Spirit

L. Kay Gillespie
Weber State University, Ogden, UT

Death and Dying

Gary P. Gillum
Brigham Young University

Bible Dictionary

Christology

Creeds

L. Brent Goates
LDS Hospital, Salt Lake City

Lee, Harold B.

H. Wallace Goddard
Utah State University, Logan, UT

Dating and Courtship

Kenneth W. Godfrey
*Church Educational System, Logan,
UT*

Council of Fifty

Freemasonry and the Temple

Freemasonry in Nauvoo

Alan Goff
Cornell University

Book of Mormon: Book of Mosiah

Kristen L. Goodman
*Church Correlation Dept., Salt
Lake City*

Divorce

Bryan J. Grant
*Church Public Communications,
Nuneaton, Warks, England*

British Isles, The Church in

David M. Grant
University of Utah

Matter

Paul G. Grant
*Third District Court, Salt Lake
City*

Doctrine and Covenants: Sections
131–132

Michaelene P. Grassli
*General President, Church Primary,
Salt Lake City*

Children: Roles of Children

Arnold H. Green
Brigham Young University

World Religions (Non-Christian)
and Mormonism: Islam

World Religions (Non-Christian)
and Mormonism: Judaism

C. Wilfred Griggs
Brigham Young University

Apocalyptic Texts

Apocrypha and Pseudepigrapha

John the Beloved

Bruce C. Hafen
Brigham Young University

Disciplinary Procedures

Grace

Justice and Mercy

Marie Kartchner Hafen
Brigham Young University

First Principles of the Gospel

Elizabeth M. Haglund
University of Utah

Public Relations

Richard F. Haglund, Jr.
Vanderbilt University

Intellectual History

Elizabeth H. Hall
Writer, Orem, UT

Silk Culture

John Franklin Hall
Brigham Young University

April 6

Peter

William K. Hamblin
Brigham Young University

Book of Mormon, History of
Warfare in

C. Mark Hamilton
Brigham Young University

Meetinghouse

Annette P. Hampshire
Writer, Upminster, Essex, England

Nauvoo Politics

Ralph C. Hancock
Brigham Young University

Constitution of the United States
of America

Reason and Revelation

Marion D. Hanks
General Authority, Salt Lake City

Salt Lake Temple

Gerald Hansen, Jr.
Ricks College, Rexburg, ID

Jesus Christ: Only Begotten in
the Flesh

H. Reese Hansen
Brigham Young University

Premarital Sex

Louise G. Hanson
Brigham Young University

Columbus, Christopher

Grant R. Hardy
Brigham Young University

Book of Mormon Plates and
Records

Gold Plates

Edwin O. Haroldsen
Brigham Young University

West Indies, The Church in

Bruce T. Harper
*Church Missionary Dept., Salt Lake
City*

Priesthood Offices

Topical Guide

Charles R. Harrell
Brigham Young University

Theogony

James R. Harris, Sr.
Brigham Young University

Cain

Jesus Christ in the Scriptures:
Jesus Christ in the Pearl of Great
Price

Grant Von Harrison
Brigham Young University

Profanity

William G. Hartley
Brigham Young University

Bishop, History of the Office

History of the Church: c. 1878–
1898

Immigration and Emigration

Organization: Organizational and
Administrative History

Leon R. Hartshorn
Brigham Young University

Discernment, Gift of

Doctrine and Covenants: Sections
137–138

Signs of the True Church

Gerald M. Haslam
Brigham Young University

International Genealogical
Index™ (IGI)

Carl S. Hawkins
Brigham Young University

Baptism

Law: Divine and Eternal Law

Carol Lee Hawkins
Brigham Young University

Perfection

John P. Hawkins
Brigham Young University

Ceremonies

Lisa Bolin Hawkins
Brigham Young University

Book of Mormon: Overview

Persecution

T. Glenn Haws
*Church Educational System,
Portland, OR*

Welfare Farms

Welfare Square

D. Arthur Haycock
*Former Church Temple President,
Laie, HI*

Temples: LDS Temple
Dedications

Darwin L. Hayes
Brigham Young University

Nauvoo Neighbor

Harvard S. Heath
Brigham Young University

Smoot Hearings

Tim B. Heaton
Brigham Young University

Vital Statistics

Paul C. Hedengren
Brigham Young University

Bible: LDS Belief in the Bible

Miracles

"J" Malan Heslop
Deseret News, Salt Lake City

Church News

Martin B. Hickman [deceased]
Brigham Young University

Diplomatic Relations

Succession in the Presidency

Michael D. Hicks
Brigham Young University

Music

Ray C. Hillam
Brigham Young University

Secret Combinations

Dawn M. Hills
Surgeon, Pasadena, CA

Fasting

Stuart W. Hinckley
Attorney, Salt Lake City

Capital Punishment

Douglas L. Hind
Church Curriculum Dept., Salt Lake City

Deaf, Materials for the

Frank W. Hirschi
Church Educational System, Centerville, UT

Consecration: Law of Consecration

Celia Hokanson
Writer, Provo, UT

Contention

Jeffrey R. Holland
General Authority, Salt Lake City

Atonement of Jesus Christ

Patricia Terry Holland
Author, Salt Lake City

Motherhood

W. Ladd Hollist
Brigham Young University

Priest, Aaronic Priesthood

Thomas B. Holman
Brigham Young University

Marriage: Social and Behavioral Perspectives

Helene Holt
Brigham Young University

Nauvoo House

Richard Neitzel Holzapfel
Church Educational System, Irvine, CA

Damnation

N. Gaylon Hopkins
Church Educational System, Logan, UT

Heirs: Joint-Heirs with Christ

George A. Horton, Jr.
Brigham Young University

Elias

Malachi, Prophecies of

Paul Y. Hoskisson
Brigham Young University

Book of Mormon Names

Oil, Consecrated

Urim and Thummim

Richard P. Howard
Reorganized Church of Jesus Christ of Latter Day Saints, Independence, MO

Reorganized Church of Jesus Christ of Latter Day Saints (RLDS Church)

Sherwin W. Howard
Weber State University, Ogden, UT

Cursings

Susan Howe
Brigham Young University

Doctrine and Covenants: Sections 121–123

Parables

A. James Hudson
Church Educational System, Boise, ID

Elias, Spirit of

O. Glade Hunsaker
Brigham Young University

Pearl of Great Price: Literature

Mark E. Hurst
Aaronic Priesthood Dept., Salt Lake City

Young Men

Darlene Chidester Hutchison
Church Public Communications, Salt Lake City

Sex Education

Paul Nolan Hyde
Church Educational System, Simi Valley, CA

Intelligences

Paul V. Hyer
Brigham Young University

Sealing: Temple Sealings

Dillon K. Inouye
Brigham Young University

Celibacy

Jeanne B. Inouye
Attorney, Provo, UT

Abuse, Spouse and Child

Stillborn Children

L. Dwight Israelsen
Utah State University, Logan, UT

United Orders

Kent P. Jackson
Brigham Young University

Neum

Scripture: Authority of Scripture

Zenock

Richard H. Jackson
Brigham Young University

City Planning

Community

Historical Sites

Richard W. Jackson
Architect, Salt Lake City

Building Program

Florence Smith Jacobsen
Formerly with Church Arts and Sites, Salt Lake City

Christus Statue

Museums, LDS

Taylor, Elmina Shepard

Cardell K. Jacobson
Brigham Young University

Doctrine and Covenants: Official Declaration–2

Phyllis C. Jacobson
Brigham Young University

Dance

Rhett Stephens James
Church Educational System, Logan, UT

Harris, Martin

Mary Ellen Stewart Jamison
Writer, Glendale, CA

   Christmas

   Easter

Dean Jarman
Church Educational System, Salt Lake City

   Judgment

John C. Jarman
Church Family History Dept., Salt Lake City

   Family Registry™

Donald K. Jarvis
Brigham Young University

   Mormonism, Mormons

Clayne R. Jensen
Brigham Young University

   Sports

De Lamar Jensen
Brigham Young University

   Protestant Reformation

Jay E. Jensen
Church Curriculum Dept., Salt Lake City

   Spirit

Richard L. Jensen
Brigham Young University

   Colonization

   Colorado, Pioneer Settlements in

   Immigration and Emigration

   New Mexico, Pioneer Settlements in

Dean C. Jessee
Brigham Young University

   Smith, Joseph: The Prophet

   Smith, Joseph: Writings of Joseph Smith

   Woodruff, Wilford

Darwin A. John
Church Information Systems, Salt Lake City

   Computer Systems

Clark V. Johnson
Brigham Young University

   Jesus Christ in the Scriptures: Jesus Christ in the Doctrine and Covenants

   Missouri: LDS Communities in Jackson and Clay Counties

David J. Johnson
Brigham Young University

   Archaeology

Hollis R. Johnson
Indiana University

   Worlds

Jeffery Ogden Johnson
Utah State Archives, Salt Lake City

   Deseret, State of

Peter N. Johnson
Brigham Young University

   Man's Search for Happiness

   Motion Pictures, LDS Productions

Mary Jolley
Writer, Salt Lake City

   Fast and Testimony Meeting

Eleanor Park Jones
Writer, Salt Lake City

   Non-Mormons, Social Relations with

Gerald E. Jones
Church Educational System, Concord, CA

   Fate

   Man of Holiness

   Psalms, Messianic Prophecies in

William N. Jones
Intermountain Health Care, Inc., Salt Lake City

   Hospitals

Bruce W. Jorgensen
Brigham Young University

   Literature, Mormon Writers of: Short Stories

Ardeth Greene Kapp
General President, Church Young Women, Salt Lake City

   Youth

Roger R. Keller
Brigham Young University

   Catholicism and Mormonism

   Christians and Christianity

   Clergy

   Cross

   Protestantism

   Restorationism, Protestant

Brian K. Kelly
Church International Magazines, Salt Lake City

   International Magazines

Petrea Gillespie Kelly
Author, Highland, UT

   Contributor

   Young Woman's Journal

William Rolfe Kerr
Utah Commission on Higher Education, Salt Lake City

   Conferences: Conferences

Nephi K. Kezerian
Surgeon, Provo, UT

   Sick, Blessing the

Edward L. Kimball
Brigham Young University

   Kimball, Heber C.

   Kimball, Spencer W.

James L. Kimball, Jr.
Church Historical Dept., Salt Lake City

   Nauvoo Charter

   "This Is the Place" Monument

Stanley B. Kimball
Southern Illinois University, Edwardsville, IL

   Kinderhook Plates

   Mormon Pioneer Trail

Wm. Clayton Kimball
Bentley College, Waltham, MA
  Politics: Political Culture

Eleanor Knowles
Deseret Book Co., Salt Lake City
  Deseret Book Company
  Doctrine: Treatises on Doctrine

Phillip R. Kunz
Brigham Young University
  Family Organizations

Connie Lamb
Brigham Young University
  Immaculate Conception

L. Gary Lambert
Brigham Young University
  Allegory of Zenos
  Alma₁

Neal E. Lambert
Brigham Young University
  Brigham Young University: Provo
  Mormons, Image of: Fiction

John Langeland
*Zions First National Bank, Salt
Lake City*
  Scandinavia, The Church in

Dennis L. Largey
Brigham Young University
  God the Father: Work and Glory
  of God

Dean L. Larsen
General Authority, Salt Lake City
  Seventy: Quorums of Seventy

Courtney J. Lassetter
Businessman, Phoenix, AZ
  Dispensations of the Gospel

Harold R. Laycock
Brigham Young University
  Academies

Robert L. Leake
*Church Melchizedek Priesthood
Dept., Salt Lake City*
  AIDS

E. Dale LeBaron
Brigham Young University
  Africa, The Church in

Rex E. Lee
Brigham Young University
  Constitutional Law

June Leifson
Brigham Young University
  Afterlife

Glen M. Leonard
*Museum of Church History and
Art, Salt Lake City*
  Nauvoo

Tomás F. Lindheimer
Writer, Buenos Aires, Argentina
  South America, the Church in:
  South America, South

Richard P. Lindsay
General Authority, Salt Lake City
  Interfaith Relationships: Christian

Joanne Linnabary
Editor, Provo, UT
  Journals

Daniel H. Ludlow
Brigham Young University
  Zenos

Douglas Kent Ludlow
University of North Dakota
  Liahona

Victor L. Ludlow
Brigham Young University
  Bible: Bible
  David, Prophetic Figure of Last
  Days
  Isaiah: Authorship
  Priesthood in Biblical Times

Gerald N. Lund
*Church Educational System, Salt
Lake City*
  Jesus Christ: Second Coming of
  Jesus Christ
  John, Revelations of
  Plan of Salvation, Plan of
  Redemption

John L. Lund
*Church Educational System,
Fountain Valley, CA*
  Council in Heaven

Immo Luschin
*Church Translation Dept.,
Frankfurt, Germany*
  Ordinances: Administration of
  Ordinances
  Ordinances: Overview
  Temples: LDS Temple Worship
  and Activity

Melvin J. Luthy
Brigham Young University
  Priesthood

Edward Leo Lyman
*Victor Valley College
and California State University,
San Bernardino*
  Utah Statehood

Wayne B. Lynn
*Church Curriculum Dept., Salt
Lake City*
  Curriculum

James K. Lyon
University of California, San Diego
  Hope
  Repentance
  Saints

Joseph Lynn Lyon
*University of Utah Medical School,
Salt Lake City*
  Alcoholic Beverages and
  Alcoholism
  Coffee
  Tea
  Tobacco
  Word of Wisdom

Thomas W. Mackay
Brigham Young University
  Beatitudes
  James, Epistle of

Val Dan MacMurray
Thruler Foundation, Salt Lake City

Self-Sufficiency (Self-Reliance)

Ann N. Madsen
Brigham Young University
Center for Near Eastern Studies,
Jerusalem, Israel

Isaiah: Commentaries on Isaiah

Arch L. Madsen
Bonneville International Corp., Salt
Lake City

KSL Radio

Public Communications

Carol Cornwall Madsen
Brigham Young University

Retrenchment Association

Smith, Emma Hale

Wells, Emmeline B.

Woman Suffrage

Gordon A. Madsen
Attorney, Salt Lake City

South Bainbridge (Afton), New
York

John M. Madsen
Brigham Young University

Enduring to the End

Hope of Israel

Marriage Supper of the Lamb

Susan Arrington Madsen
Author, Hyde Park, UT

Horne, Mary Isabella

Smith, Mary Fielding

Truman G. Madsen
Brigham Young University Center
for Near Eastern Studies,
Jerusalem, Israel

Religious Experience

Scripture: Scriptures

Smith, Joseph: Teachings of
Joseph Smith

Theodicy

Zionism

David B. Magleby
Brigham Young University

Politics: Contemporary American
Politics

Garth L. Mangum
University of Utah

Welfare Services

Robert D. Marcum
Church Educational System,
Rexburg, ID

Idaho, Pioneer Settlements in

Beth M. Marlow
Editor, Orem UT

Meetinghouse Libraries

Robert L. Marrott
Church Educational System,
Bloomington, IN

Dove, Sign of the

Testator

Witnesses, Law of

Evelyn T. Marshall
General Board of the Relief Society,
Salt Lake City

Garments

Richard J. Marshall
Evans Communications, Inc., Salt
Lake City

Exhibitions and World's Fairs

James O. Mason
U.S. Health Education and Welfare
Dept., Washington, DC

Health, Attitudes Toward

Robert J. Matthews
Brigham Young University

Fall of Adam

Jesus Christ in the Scriptures:
Jesus Christ in the Bible

Joseph Smith Translation of the
Bible (JST)

Proclamations of the First
Presidency and the Quorum of
the Twelve Apostles

Cory H. Maxwell
Bookcraft Publishing Co., Salt Lake
City

Angel Moroni Statue

Restoration of All Things

Dean L. May
University of Utah

Agriculture

History of the Church: c. 1844–
1877

Social and Cultural History

Frank O. May, Jr.
Church Curriculum Dept., Salt
Lake City

Artificial Insemination

Correlation of the Church,
Admininistration

General Handbook of Instructions

Policies, Practices, and
Procedures

David M. Mayfield
Family History Dept., Salt
Lake City

Ancestral File™

Personal Ancestral File®

James B. Mayfield
University of Utah

Covenant Israel, Latter-day

Liesel C. McBride
Writer, Orem, UT

Joseph of Egypt: Seed of Joseph

Amelia S. McConkie
Writer, Salt Lake City

Smith, Joseph Fielding

Joseph Fielding McConkie
Brigham Young University

Holy Ghost

Joseph of Egypt: Joseph, Son of
Jacob

Mark L. McConkie
University of Colorado at Colorado
Springs

Following the Brethren

Smith, Joseph Fielding
Translated Beings

Oscar W. McConkie
Attorney, Salt Lake City
Angels: Angels
Angels: Guardian Angels

Daniel B. McKinlay
Writer, Provo, UT
Amen
Strait and Narrow

Lynn A. McKinlay
Brigham Young University
Patriarchal Order of the
Priesthood
Reverence

Kahlile Mehr
*Church Family History Dept., Salt
Lake City*
Name Extraction Program

Byron R. Merrill
Brigham Young University
Assistants to the Twelve
Condescension of God
Original Sin

Keith H. Meservy
Brigham Young University
Book of Mormon, Biblical
Prophecies about
Elohim
Ezekiel, Prophecies of

Charles L. Metten
Brigham Young University
Drama
Salt Lake Theatre

Louis C. Midgley
Brigham Young University
Nature, Law of
Theology

Brent C. Miller
Utah State University, Logan, UT
Dating and Courtship

Harold L. Miller, Jr.
Brigham Young University
Light and Darkness

Robert L. Miller
University of Utah
Science and Scientists

Robert L. Millet
Brigham Young University
Alma$_2$
Jesus Christ: Overview
Jesus Christ, Fatherhood and
Sonship of

Wayne A. Mineer
Physician, Orem, UT
Organ Transplants and Donations

James P. Mitchell
*Church Educational System, Logan,
UT*
Family Home Evening

Terri Tanner Mitchell
Writer, Hyde Park, UT
Family Home Evening

Charles E. Mitchener
*Church Sunday School, Salt Lake
City*
Young Men

Samuel C. Monson
Brigham Young University
Deseret Alphabet

Michael F. Moody
*Church Music Committee, Salt Lake
City*
Musicians

William James Mortimer
Deseret News, Salt Lake City
Bible: LDS Publication of the
Bible
Patriarchal Blessing

James R. Moss
*Former Utah State Superintendent
of Education, Salt Lake City*
[deceased]
Missions of the Twelve to the
British Isles

Dale C. Mouritsen
*Church Educational System,
Sunnyvale, CA*
Mount of Transfiguration
Transfiguration

Maren M. Mouritsen
Brigham Young University
Spafford, Belle Smith

Stephen D. Nadauld
General Authority, Salt Lake City
Business: LDS Attitudes Toward
Business
Financial Contributions

Jack A. Nelson
Brigham Young University
Newspapers, LDS

Robert A. Nelson
Brigham Young University
Literature, Mormon Writers of:
Drama

Robert E. Nelson, Jr.
U.S. Army
Chaplains

William O. Nelson
*Church Correlation Dept., Salt
Lake City*
Anti-Mormon Publications
Quorum of the Twelve Apostles

Hugh W. Nibley
Brigham Young University
Book of Mormon Near Eastern
Background
Temples: Meanings and Functions
of Temples
Young, Brigham: Teachings of
Brigham Young

Terry L. Niederhauser
*Church Educational System, Powell,
WY*
Israel: Gathering of Israel

F. Kent Nielsen
Brigham Young University
Creation, Creation Accounts

Richard A. Nimer
Physician, Pleasant Grove, UT

Blood Transfusions

Keith E. Norman
*Employee Development,
BP America, Solon, OH*

Deification, Early Christian

Infant Baptism: Early Christian
Origins

Leslie Norris
Brigham Young University

Literature, Mormon Writers of:
Poetry

Beverly J. Norton
Brigham Young University

Record Keeping

Don E. Norton
Brigham Young University

Journals

Loui Novak
*Church Educational System,
Pocatello, ID*

John the Baptist

Monte S. Nyman
Brigham Young University

Book of Mormon: Overview

Gentiles, Fulness of

Isaiah: Interpretations in Modern
Scripture

Zoram

Merrill C. Oaks
Physician, Provo, UT

Jesus Christ: Crucifixion of Jesus
Christ

Gen. Robert C. Oaks
U.S. Air Force

Military and the Church

D. Kelly Ogden
Brigham Young University

Bible: King James Version

Jerusalem

Messiah: Messianic Concept and
Hope

Bruce L. Olsen
*Church Public Communications
Dept., Salt Lake City*

Cremation

Family Prayer

Steven L. Olsen
*Museum of Church History and
Art, Salt Lake City*

Celebrations

Centennial Observances

Terrance D. Olson
Brigham Young University

Sexuality

Sin

Richard G. Oman
*Museum of Church History and
Art, Salt Lake City*

Artists, Visual

Beehive Symbol

Sculptors

Allen C. Ostergar, Jr.
*Church Missionary Training
Center, Provo, UT*

Seed of Abraham

C. Eric Ott
*Church Missionary Training
Center, Provo, UT*

Sanctification

Leaun G. Otten
Brigham Young University

Doctrine and Covenants:
Section 84

Immortality and Eternal Life

George W. Pace
Brigham Young University

Doctrine and Covenants:
Section 1

Kingdom of God: in Heaven

Kingdom of God: on Earth

Dennis J. Packard
Brigham Young University

Intelligence

Scripture Study

Sandra Bradford Packard
Brigham Young University

Animals

Rand H. Packer
*Church Educational System, Provo,
UT*

Dispensation of the Fulness of
Times

David A. Palmer
*Amaco Chemicals Corp.,
Naperville, IL*

Cumorah

Howard Palmer
University of Calgary [deceased]

Canada, LDS Pioneer
Settlements in

Martin J. Palmer
Delta Airlines, Salt Lake City

Adam: Ancient Sources

Spencer J. Palmer
Brigham Young University

Reincarnation

World Religions (Non-Christian)
and Mormonism: Overview

World Religions (Non-Christian)
and Mormonism: Buddhism

World Religions (Non-Christian)
and Mormonism: Confucianism

World Religions (Non-Christian)
and Mormonism: Hinduism

World Religions (Non-Christian)
and Mormonism: Shinto

Douglas H. Parker
Brigham Young University

Law of Moses

Law: Divine and Eternal Law

Scott Parker
*Intermountain Health Care, Inc.,
Salt Lake City*

Deseret Hospital

Stephen Parker
*Doctoral Candidate, University of
Chicago*

Deseret

Ed J. Pinegar
Church Educational System, Provo, UT

  Born of God

Max L. Pinegar
Nu Skin International, Provo, UT

  Preaching the Gospel

Brian L. Pitcher
Utah State University, Logan, UT

  Callings

Paul B. Pixton
Brigham Young University

  Communion

  Millennium

  Sacrament: Sacrament

Louise Plummer
Brigham Young University

  Gates, Susa Young

  Spirit of Prophecy

B. Lloyd Poelman
Attorney, Salt Lake City

  Sunday School

Ronald E. Poelman
General Authority, Salt Lake City

  Sealing: Cancellation of Sealings

Richard D. Poll
Western Illinois University, Macomb, Illinois

  Utah Expedition

Margaret McConkie Pope
Brigham Young University

  Exaltation

Bruce Douglas Porter
International Broadcasting, Springfield, VA

  Church of Jesus Christ of Latter-day Saints, The

  Gift of the Holy Ghost

Bruce H. Porter
Church Educational System, San Marcos, CA

  Altar

Larry C. Porter
Brigham Young University

  Aaronic Priesthood: Restoration

  Far West, Missouri

  History of the Church: c. 1820–1831

  Palmyra/Manchester, New York

  Pratt, Parley Parker

  Visions of Joseph Smith

Roger B. Porter
White House, Washington, DC

  United States of America

Allan Kent Powell
Utah State Historical Society, Salt Lake City

  Utah Territory

David H. Pratt
Brigham Young University

  Family History, Genealogy

John P. Pratt
Ashton Research Corporation, Orem, UT

  Book of Mormon Chronology

Paul Alfred Pratte
Brigham Young University

  Press, News Media and the Church

Robert E. Quinn
University of Michigan

  Common Consent

Martin Raish
State University of New York, Binghamton

  Tree of Life

Carolyn J. Rasmus
Brigham Young University

  Temple Square

Dennis Rasmussen
Brigham Young University

  Metaphysics

  Testimony of Jesus Christ

Ellis T. Rasmussen
Brigham Young University

  Abrahamic Covenant

  Deuteronomy

  Old Testament

Tim Rathbone
Lockheed Aircraft Corp., Hesperia, CA

  Book of Mormon Translation by Joseph Smith

Lenet Hadley Read
Author, San Francisco, CA

  Jesus Christ, Types and Shadows of

Rex C. Reeve, Jr.
Brigham Young University

  Book of Mormon: Book of Mormon

  Book of Mormon: Fourth Nephi

  Brother of Jared

Noel B. Reynolds
Brigham Young University

  Book of Mormon, Government and Legal History in

  Gospel of Jesus Christ

  Nephi$_1$

Sydney Smith Reynolds
Author, Orem, UT

  Mother in Israel

  Smith Family

Michael D. Rhodes
Air Force Academy, Colorado Springs, CO

  Book of Abraham: Facsimiles from the Book of Abraham

  Book of Abraham: Studies About the Book of Abraham

A. LeGrand Richards
Businessman, Provo, UT

  High Priest

Cecil O. Samuelson, Jr.
University of Utah Medical School

Medical Practices

Scott Samuelson
Ricks College, Rexburg, ID

Ricks College

Bruce Satterfield
Church Educational System, Iona, ID

Melchizedek: LDS Sources

J. Philip Schaelling
Church Educational System, Austin, TX

Jesus Christ: Baptism of Jesus Christ

Jesus Christ, Sources for Words of

Paul

Gilbert W. Scharffs
Church Educational System, Salt Lake City

Apostate

Ray G. Schwartz
Daily Herald, Provo, UT

Drugs, Abuse of

A. Lynn Scoresby
Brigham Young University

Fatherhood

Howard C. Searle
Church Educational System, Salt Lake City

Historians, Church

History of the Church

Gareth W. Seastrand
Alpine School District, American Fork, UT

Visitors Centers

David R. Seely
Brigham Young University

Jehovah, Jesus Christ

Prophecy

Prophecy in Biblical Times

Gene A. Sessions
Weber State University, Ogden, UT

History of the Church:
c. 1878–1898

Marianne Clark Sharp
Former Counselor in General Presidency, Church Relief Society, Salt Lake City
[deceased]

Relief Society Magazine

William Sheffield
Attorney, San Juan Capistrano, CA

"Voice from the Dust"

Thomas E. Sherry
Oregon State University

Jesus Christ, Second Comforter

Jan Shipps
Indiana University—Purdue University at Indianapolis

Mormonism, An Independent Interpretation

Eric B. Shumway
Brigham Young University—Hawaii

Polynesians

Naomi M. Shumway
Former General President, Church Primary, Salt Lake City

Primary

R. Wayne Shute
Brigham Young University

Restoration of the Gospel of Jesus Christ

Sign Seeking

Signs as Divine Witness

Robert L. Simpson
General Authority, Salt Lake City

New Zealand, The Church in

Temples: Administration of Temples

Andrew C. Skinner
Ricks College, Rexburg, ID

Jesus Christ: Birth of Jesus Christ

Moses

Noah

Royal Skousen
Brigham Young University

Book of Mormon Editions
(1830–1981)

Book of Mormon Manuscripts

Timothy W. Slover
Brigham Young University

Brotherhood

William B. Smart
This People Magazine

Sabbath Day

Barbara B. Smith
Former General President, Church Relief Society, Salt Lake City

Women, Roles of: Gospel Principles and the Roles of Women

Brian L. Smith
Church Educational System, Aloha, OR

Ephraim

Huston Smith
Graduate Theological Union, Berkeley, CA

Purpose of Earth Life: Comparative Perspective

Kay H. Smith
Brigham Young University

Conversion

Paul Thomas Smith
Church Educational System, Salt Lake City

Snow, Lorenzo

Taylor, John

Wells, Junius F.

Robert J. Smith
Brigham Young University

Ward Budget

Timothy L. Smith
Johns Hopkins University

Book of Mormon in a Biblical Culture

Wilford E. Smith
Brigham Young University

"Peculiar" People

Lowell M. Snow
Attorney, Salt Lake City

Blood Atonement

Scouting

R. J. Snow
Brigham Young University

Natural Man

A. D. Sorensen
Brigham Young University

Equality

Zion

Steven R. Sorensen
Church Historical Dept., Salt Lake City

Schools of the Prophets

John L. Sorenson
Brigham Young University

Book of Mormon Peoples

Origin of Man

Krister Stendahl
Harvard Divinity School

Baptism for the Dead: Ancient Sources

Calvin R. Stephens
Church College Curriculum, Salt Lake City

Patriarch: Patriarch to the Church

Joseph Grant Stevenson
Brigham Young University

Heirs: Heirs of God

Joseph Smith—History

Douglas A. Stewart
Church Educational System, Sandy, UT

Israel: Scattering of Israel

Hugh G. Stocks
University of Southern California

Book of Mormon Translations

Brian D. Stubbs
College of Eastern Utah, San Juan Campus, Blanding, UT

Book of Mormon Language

Clyde E. Sullivan
Brigham Young University

Suicide

Howard D. Swainston
Attorney, Los Angeles

Tithing

Terrence L. Szink
Doctoral Candidate, UCLA

Lehi

Oaths

John S. Tanner
Brigham Young University

Jacob, Son of Lehi

Sacrament: Sacrament Prayers

Martin S. Tanner
Attorney, Salt Lake City

Schismatic Groups

Morgan W. Tanner
Doctoral Candidate, UCLA

Book of Mormon: Book of Ether

Jaredites

Charles D. Tate, Jr.
Brigham Young University

Burial

Conference Reports

Conscientious Objection

Gambling

Priestcraft

George S. Tate
Brigham Young University

Covenants in Biblical Times

Prayer Circle

Bruce Thomas Taylor
Physician, Spanish Fork, UT

Book of Moses

J. Lewis Taylor
Church Educational System, Salt Lake City

Book of Life

Stanley A. Taylor
Brigham Young University

Economic Aid

Elaine Thatcher
Consultant, Salt Lake City

Material Culture

Linda Thatcher
Utah Historical Society, Salt Lake City

Fox, Ruth May

Donlu DeWitt Thayer
Brigham Young University

Literature, Mormon Writers of: Personal Essays

Darwin L. Thomas
Brigham Young University

Family: Family Life

Socialization

Gloria Jean Thomas
University of North Dakota

Sacrifice

Janet Thomas
Church Magazines, Salt Lake City

Magic

Satanism

M. Catherine Thomas
Brigham Young University

Hell

Paradise

Scripture, Interpretation Within Scripture

Robert K. Thomas
Brigham Young University

Abuse, Spouse and Child

Ryan L. Thomas
Brigham Young University

Adoption of Children

Shirley W. Thomas
Former Counselor in General Presidency, Church Relief Society, Salt Lake City

Woman's Exponent

Women, Roles of: Gospel

Principles and the Roles of
Women

Gordon C. Thomasson
School for International Training,
Brattleboro, VT

Circumcision

Lamanites

Brent C. Thompson
Church Historical Dept., Salt
Lake City

Prohibition

Dennis L. Thompson
Brigham Young University

Setting Apart

Ward Council

Paul H. Thompson
Weber State University, Ogden, UT

Lay Participation and Leadership

Stephen E. Thompson
Post-Doctoral Fellowship, Brown
University, Providence, RI

Book of Abraham: Contents

Michele Thompson-Holbrook
Writer, Cape Elizabeth, ME

Modesty in Dress

Melvin J. Thorne
F.A.R.M.S., Provo, UT

Ezias

Helaman$_1$

Moroni$_1$

Mosiah$_1$

Nephi$_2$

Nephi$_3$

Nephi$_4$

Clark T. Thorstenson
Brigham Young University

Physical Fitness and Recreation

Richard Tice
Deseret Book Co., Salt Lake City

Magazines

Sherman N. Tingey
Arizona State University, Tempe

Priesthood Quorums

Douglas F. Tobler
Brigham Young University

Europe, The Church in

History, Significance to
Latter-day Saints

Jay M. Todd
Ensign, Salt Lake City

Ensign Magazine

Improvement Era

Papyri, Joseph Smith

Brent L. Top
Brigham Young University

Foreordination

War in Heaven

James A. Toronto
Brigham Young University

Middle East, The Church in

Robert A. Tucker
General Authority Office, Salt Lake
City

Temple Recommend

Richard E. Turley, Jr.
Church Historical Dept., Salt Lake
City

Confidential Records

Mountain Meadows Massacre

Seer Stones

Solemn Assemblies

Rodney Turner
Brigham Young University

Burnings, Everlasting

God the Father: Glory of God

Sons of Perdition

Unpardonable Sin

David K. Udall
Attorney, Mesa, AZ

Non-Mormons, Social Relations
with

Grant Underwood
Church Educational System,
Pomona, CA

Doctrine and Covenants:
Sections 20–22

Millenarianism

Robert Timothy Updegraff
Businessman, North Huntington, PA

Sermon on the Mount

Wouter van Beek
Utrecht University, Netherlands

Covenants

Kent M. Van De Graaff
Brigham Young University

Physical Body

Adrian P. Van Mondfrans
Brigham Young University

Teaching the Gospel

Bruce A. Van Orden
Brigham Young University

Rigdon, Sidney

Smith, Hyrum

Smith, Joseph F.

Dell Van Orden
Church News, Salt Lake City

Almanacs

Bruce T. Verhaaren
Northeastern Illinois University,
Chicago

Ten Commandments

R. Richard Vetterli
Brigham Young University

Elder, Melchizedek Priesthood

Klis Hale Volkening
Author and designer, Salt Lake
City

Doctrine and Covenants:
Section 25

Alton L. Wade
Brigham Young University—Hawaii

Brigham Young University:
Hawaii Campus

Elizabeth Wahlquist
Brigham Young University

Friend, The

Gary Lee Walker
Brigham Young University

Jesus Christ: Prophecies About Jesus Christ

Ronald W. Walker
Brigham Young University

Grant, Heber J.

History of the Church: c. 1898–1945

Pioneer Life and Worship

Steven C. Walker
Brigham Young University

Doctrine and Covenants as Literature

Mankind

Seer

Arthur Wallace
University of California at Los Angeles

Heaven

David A. Wanamaker
LDS Foundation, Orem, UT

LDS Foundation

Douglas A. Wangsgard
Church Educational System, Warrenton, VA

Washing of Feet

C. Terry Warner
Brigham Young University

Accountability

Agency

Truth

Paul R. Warner
Church Educational System, Orem, UT

Jesus Christ, Taking the Name of, Upon Oneself

Ted J. Warner
Brigham Young University

California, Pioneer Settlements in

Nevada, Pioneer Settlements in

Wyoming, Pioneer Settlements in

W. Keith Warner
Brigham Young University

Council of the First Presidency and the Quorum of the Twelve Apostles

First Presidency

President of the Church

Christine Croft Waters
Salt Lake Community College

Maternity and Child Health Care

Ronald G. Watt
Church Historical Dept., Salt Lake City

Journal of Discourses

Clark D. Webb
Brigham Young University

Mysteries of God

L. Robert Webb
Brigham Young University

Ward Organization

Stan E. Weed
Institute for Research and Evaluation, Salt Lake City

Values, Transmission of

John S. Welch
Attorney, Los Angeles

Law: Overview

John W. Welch
Brigham Young University

Book of Mormon Religious Teachings and Practices

Book of Mormon Translation by Joseph Smith

Jesus Christ in the Scriptures: Jesus Christ in the Book of Mormon

R. J. Zvi Werblowsky
Hebrew University, Jerusalem, Israel

Elijah: Ancient Sources

Dale A. Whitman
University of Missouri, Columbia, MO

Extermination Order

David J. Whittaker
Brigham Young University

Articles of Faith

Danites

Intellectual History

Missions of the Twelve to the British Isles

Pratt, Orson

S. Michael Wilcox
Church Educational System, Salt Lake City

Book of Mormon: Book of Moroni

Doctrine and Covenants: Sections 109–110

Samuel the Lamanite

Alan L. Wilkins
Brigham Young University

Organization: Contemporary Organization

Camille S. Williams
Brigham Young University

Women in the Book of Mormon

Clyde J. Williams
Brigham Young University

Book of Mormon: Book of Jacob

Standard Works

Telestial Kingdom

Gerald R. Williams
Brigham Young University

Lawsuits

Richard N. Williams
Brigham Young University

Knowledge

Soul

Jerry A. Wilson
Church Educational System, Logan, UT

Baptismal Covenant

Baptismal Prayer

Holy Spirit

Ted L. Wilson
University of Utah
Salt Lake City, Utah

William A. Wilson
Brigham Young University
Folklore
Three Nephites

Larry T. Wimmer
Brigham Young University
Kirtland Economy

Barbara W. Winder
Former General President, Church Relief Society, Salt Lake City
Relief Society in Nauvoo

Diane E. Wirth
Museum of Ancient Civilizations, Westford, MA
Book of Mormon Authorship

Johann A. Wondra
Vienna Theatre, Vienna, Austria
Worship

Robert S. Wood
Naval War College, Newport, RI
War and Peace

Lael J. Woodbury
Brigham Young University
Hosanna Shout
Pageants
Public Speaking

Robert J. Woodford
Church Educational System, Salt Lake City
Book of Commandments
Doctrine and Covenants Editions

Mary Firmage Woodward
Writer, Provo, UT
Young, Zina D. H.

Dan J. Workman
Church Educational System, Orem, UT
Doctrine and Covenants: Section 93

Dennis A. Wright
Church Educational System, Surrey, British Columbia
Great and Abominable Church

Donald N. Wright
Brigham Young University
Judgment Day, Final

H. Curtis Wright
Brigham Young University
Mulek

Raymond S. Wright, III
Brigham Young University
Family History Library
Utah Genealogical and Historical Magazine

David H. Yarn, Jr.
Brigham Young University
God
Sealing: Sealing Power
Temple President and Matron

Marilyn S. Yarn
Former Temple Matron, Atlanta, GA
Temple President and Matron

Hulda P. Young
Author, Salt Lake City
Compassionate Service

Lawrence A. Young
Brigham Young University
Cult
Sect
Single Adults

Michael K. Young
Columbia University
Oath and Covenant of the Priesthood

John F. Yurtinus
University of Nevada, Carson City
Mormon Battalion

PREFACE

According to a standard definition, an encyclopedia is to "treat comprehensively all the various branches of knowledge" pertaining to a particular subject. The subject of this *Encyclopedia* is The Church of Jesus Christ of Latter-day Saints, widely known as the Mormon church. This is the first major encyclopedia published about the Mormons. It presents the work of hundreds of Latter-day Saint (LDS) lay scholars and others from throughout the world and provides a comprehensive reporting of Mormon history, scripture, doctrines, life, and knowledge, intended for both the non-Mormon and the LDS reader. Readers will find an article on almost any topic conceivably related to the general topic of Mormonism, but no article is exhaustive because of space limitations. Most articles include bibliographic references; cross-references to other articles in the *Encyclopedia* are indicated by small capital letters.

When Macmillan Publishing Company asked authorities at Brigham Young University whether they would be interested in developing an encyclopedia about The Church of Jesus Christ of Latter-day Saints, President Jeffrey R. Holland took the query to his Board of Trustees. They instructed him to proceed. Working closely with Church authorities and Macmillan, President Holland chose an editor in chief and a board of editors. Discussion of possible titles concluded that the work should be called the *Encyclopedia of Mormonism* since that is the term by which the Church is most widely known, though unofficially.

The contract called for a work of one million words in about 1,500 articles in four volumes including pictures, maps, charts, appendixes, indexes, and a glossary. It soon became apparent that references to what the Church calls the standard works—the Bible, the Book of Mormon, the Doctrine and Covenants, and the Pearl of Great Price—would be so frequent that readers who did not have ready access to those works would be at a serious disadvantage in using the *Encyclopedia*. A fifth volume was decided upon to include all the LDS standard works except the Bible, which is readily available everywhere.

The Church does not have a paid clergy or a battery of theologians to write the articles. It functions with a lay ministry, and all members are encouraged to become scholars of the gospel. Over 730 men and women were asked to write articles on topics assigned because of previous interest and study.

Six major articles unfold the history of the Church: (1) the background and founding period in New York; (2) the Ohio, Missouri, and Illinois periods ending with the martyrdom of Joseph Smith; (3) the exodus west and the early pioneer period under Brigham Young; (4) the late pioneer Utah period ending at the turn of the century and statehood; (5) a transitional period during the early twentieth century; and (6) the post–World War II period of international growth. The history of the Church has been dramatic and moving, considering its brief span of just over 160 years. Compared to Catholicism, Judaism, ancient Far East religions, and many Protestant churches, the Church has a very short history.

Nearly 250 articles explain the doctrines of the Church, with special emphasis on basic principles and ordinances of the gospel of Jesus Christ. Twenty-four articles are clustered under the title "Jesus Christ," and another sixteen include his name in the title or relate directly to his divine mission and atonement.

Over 150 articles relate the details on such topics as the First Vision, Zion's Camp, Handcart Companies, Plural Marriage, the Salt Lake Temple, Temple Square, and the Church throughout the world. Biographies cover men and women contemporary in the life of Joseph Smith, Presidents of the Church, and auxiliary founders and past presidents. The only biography of a person living at the time of publication is on the present prophet and President of the Church, Ezra Taft Benson.

And finally, there are over a hundred articles primarily concerned with how Latter-day Saints relate to their families, the Church, and to society in general. It is said there is a "Mormon culture," and several articles explore Mormon lifestyle, folklore, folk art, artists, literature, and other facets that distinguish Latter-day Saints.

It may be that the growth of the Church in the last decades has mandated the encyclopedic account that is presented here. Yet, even as the most recent programs were set down and the latest figures listed, there is an acute awareness that the basic tenet of the Church is that its canon is open-ended. The contemporary President of the Church is sustained as a "prophet, seer, and revelator." While this makes some theological discussion moot, the basic beliefs of the Latter-day Saints, summarized in the Articles of Faith (see Glossary) do not change.

In several areas, the Church shares beliefs held by other Christians, and a number of scholars from other faiths were asked to present articles. However, the most distinctive tenets of the Church—those regarding the premortal and postmortal life, living prophets who receive continuous and current revelation from God, sacred ordinances for deceased ancestors, moral and health codes that provide increasingly well-documented benefits, and the potential within man for progression into an infinite future—are all treated primarily by writers selected from among Latter-day Saints.

Lest the role of the *Encyclopedia* be given more weight than it deserves, the editors make it clear that those who have written and edited have only tried to explain their understanding of Church history, doctrines, and procedures; their statements and opinions remain their own. The *Encyclopedia of Mormonism* is a joint product of Brigham Young University and Macmillan Publishing Company, and its contents do not necessarily represent the official position of The Church of Jesus Christ of Latter-day Saints. In no sense does the *Encyclopedia* have the force and authority of scripture.

DANIEL H. LUDLOW

ACKNOWLEDGMENTS

The support and assistance of many persons and groups are necessary to produce a work as extensive as an encyclopedia. Special thanks are extended to the executives of Macmillan Publishing Company who introduced the idea of the *Encyclopedia of Mormonism* to Brigham Young University. Charles E. Smith made initial contacts on the project, while Philip Friedman, President and Publisher of Macmillan Reference, and Elly Dickason, Editor in Chief of Macmillan Reference, have followed through on the multitudinous details, demonstrating skill and patience in working with us in the preparation of this five-volume work.

The editors also wish to thank the General Authorities of the Church for designating Brigham Young University (BYU) as the contractual Author of the *Encyclopedia*. Two members of the Board of Trustees of the university, who are also members of the Quorum of the Twelve Apostles, were appointed by the First Presidency to serve as advisers to the project: Elder Neal A. Maxwell and Elder Dallin H. Oaks. Other General Authorities who accepted special assignments related to the project include four members of the Quorum of Seventy: Elders Dean L. Larsen, Carlos E. Asay, Marlin K. Jensen, and Jeffrey R. Holland.

Special support also came from the administration of BYU. Jeffrey R. Holland, president of BYU at the time the project was initiated, was instrumental in appointing the Board of Editors and in developing early guidelines. Rex E. Lee, current president of BYU, has continued this support.

The efforts of the Board of Editors and the Project Coordinator, whose names are listed at the front of each volume, have shaped and fashioned every aspect of the project. We offer special thanks to them, and to companions and family members for graciously supporting our efforts over many months. Others who shared in final editing include Bruce B. Clark, Soren F. Cox, Marshall R. Craig, and Ellis T. Rasmussen.

Many others have provided assistance in specialized areas, including Mary Lynn Bahr, Larry E. Dahl, Robert O. Davis, Gary R. Gillespie, Lisa Bolin Hawkins, McRay Magleby, Daniel B. McKinlay, Frank O. May, Robert L. Millet, Don E. Norton, Monte S. Nyman, Bruce A. Patrick, Charlotte A. Pollard, Merle Romer, Amy Rossiter, Evelyn E. Schiess, William W. Slaughter, J. Grant Stevenson, Jay M. Todd, and John Sutton Welch.

Appreciation is gratefully extended to the following individuals and institutions for providing the illustrations for this *Encyclopedia*. Where no credit line appears at the end of a picture's caption, the photograph is used courtesy of The Church of Jesus Christ of Latter-day Saints, Salt Lake City, Utah, or one of its departments or divisions, including Church Education, Church Historical Department, Church Archives, Museum of Church History and Art, Church Public Communications, Visual Resources Library, and Young Women.

As indicated in the captions, specific photographs are used courtesy of the following individuals and institutions: Warren Aston; Robert E. Barrett; LaMar C. Berrett; Brigham Young University; Brigham Young University Museum of Fine Arts; Brigham Young University, Rare Books and Manuscripts; Paul R. Cheesman; Chicago Historical Society, Decorative and Industrial Arts Department; James C. Christensen; Deseret News; Craig Dimond; the government of Egypt; Foundation for Ancient Research and Mormon Studies (F.A.R.M.S.), Provo, Utah; Stephen Fletcher; Frederiksborg Museum, Hillerod, Denmark; C. Wilfred Griggs; Hagen G. Haltern; W. Dee Halverson; Wm. Floyd Holdman; Blaine T. Hudson; Winnifred Cannon Jardine; Peggy Jellinghausen; Edward L. Kimball; Craig Law; Ann Laemmlen Lewis; Library of Congress; Doug Martin; Edith W. Morgan; Peabody Museum of Salem, Massachusetts; Reorganized Church of Jesus Christ of Latter Day Saints, Library-Archives, The Auditorium, Independence, Missouri; Merle Greene Robertson; Alvin E. Rust; Salt Lake Convention and Visitors Bureau; Springville Museum of Art, Springville, Utah; Union Pacific Railroad, Omaha, Nebraska; University of Utah, Special Collections Department, University Libraries; Utah State Historical Society; Utah State University; Nelson Wadsworth; John W. Welch; Frederick G. Williams III; William West Woodland family; Marjorie Woods; and Buddy Youngreen. The maps and charts were produced by Jeffry S. Bird, Brigham Young University Geography Department, under direction of Richard H. Jackson.

Finally, we express appreciation to the 738 authors who contributed their knowledge and insights. The hopes of all who were involved with this project will be realized if the *Encyclopedia* assists readers to come to a greater understanding and appreciation of the history, scriptures, doctrines, practices, and procedures of The Church of Jesus Christ of Latter-day Saints.

SYNOPTIC OUTLINE

The Synoptic Outline is designed to help the reader locate the main articles related to a particular subject. The title of every entry and of every item in the Appendix is listed in the outline at least once. The simple three-tiered outline follows this pattern (with the style of type, capitalization, and emphasis noted here in parentheses):

> I. **(REGULAR TYPE, CAPITAL LETTERS, BOLD)**
>> A. **(Regular type, capital and lower case letters, bold)**
>>> 1. ***(Italic type, capital and lower case letters, bold)***
>>> 2.
>> B.
> II.

The materials in the *Encyclopedia* are organized and listed in this outline under five major headings: (I) History of The Church of Jesus Christ of Latter-day Saints; (II) Scriptures of the Church; (III) Doctrines of the Church; (IV) Organization and government of the Church; and (V) Procedures and practices of the Church and its members as they relate to themselves and to society in general.

I. **HISTORY OF THE CHURCH OF JESUS CHRIST OF LATTER-DAY SAINTS** including references to the (A) major persons associated with the organization and development of the Church, and (B) major events and places associated with the establishment and development of the Church. [See also in the Appendix Biographical Register of General Church Officers; A Chronology of Church History; Church Periodicals; General Church Officers, A Chronology; The Wentworth Letter.]

    A. **Major persons associated with the organization and development of the Church.**

        1. ***Joseph Smith, his forebears and immediate family members***: Smith, Emma Hale; Smith Family; Smith Family Ancestors; Smith, Hyrum; Smith, Joseph* (see also Prophet Joseph Smith); Smith, Joseph, Sr.; Smith, Lucy Mack.

        2. ***Close associates of the Prophet Joseph Smith***: Cowdery, Oliver; Harris, Martin; Hyde, Orson; Kimball, Heber C.; Patten, David W.; Pratt, Orson; Pratt, Parley P.; Rigdon, Sidney; Smith, Mary Fielding; Snow, Eliza R.; Snow, Lorenzo; Taylor, John; Whitmer, David; Woodruff, Wilford; Young, Brigham.

---

*Indicates additional related articles are clustered under that entry title.

3. *Subsequent presidents of the Church* (listed alphabetically): Benson, Ezra Taft; Grant, Heber J.; Kimball, Spencer W.; Lee, Harold B.; McKay, David O.; Smith, George Albert; Smith, Joseph F.; Smith, Joseph Fielding; Snow, Lorenzo; Taylor, John; Woodruff, Wilford; Young, Brigham*.

4. *Biographies of other leaders and of friends of the Church, including some founders and presidents of auxiliary organizations*: Ballantyne, Richard; Fox, Ruth May; Gates, Susa Young; Horne, Mary Isabella; Kane, Thomas L.; Kimball, Sarah Granger; Lyman, Amy Brown; Parmley, LaVern Watts; Robison, Louise Yates; Rogers, Aurelia Spencer; Smith, Bathsheba Bigler; Spafford, Belle Smith; Taylor, Elmina Shepard; Wells, Emmeline B.; Wells, Junius F.; Williams, Clarissa; Young, Zina D. H.

B. **Major events and places associated with the establishment and development of the Church.**

1. *The First Vision (1820)*: First Vision; God*; God the Father*; Jesus Christ*; Revelation; Sacred Grove; Visions; Visions of Joseph Smith.

2. *The acquisition, translation, and publication of the Book of Mormon (1823–1830)*: Anthon Transcript; Book of Mormon*; Book of Mormon Witnesses; Cumorah; Fayette, New York; Harmony, Pennsylvania; Manuscript, Lost 116 pages; Moroni, Visitations of; Native Americans; Palmyra/Manchester, New York; Plates, Metal; Spaulding Manuscript; Stick of Joseph; Urim and Thummim; *View of the Hebrews*; "Voice from the Dust"; Witnesses, Law of.

3. *The establishment and organization of the Church*: Aaronic Priesthood*; April 6; Church of Jesus Christ of Latter-day Saints, The; Fayette, New York; Head of the Church; Keys of the Priesthood; Kingdom of God*; Melchizedek Priesthood*; Name of the Church; Organization of the Church, 1830; Priesthood; Prophet Joseph Smith; Prophet, Seer, and Revelator; True and Living Church.

4. *The development of quorums, groups, and auxiliary organizations of the Church*: Apostle; Area, Area Presidency; Authority; Bishop; Bishop, History of the Office; Bishopric; Branch, Branch President; Callings; Clerk; Council of the First Presidency and the Quorum of the Twelve Apostles; Deacon, Aaronic Priesthood; Elder, Melchizedek Priesthood; Evangelists; First Presidency; General Authorities; High Council; High Priest; Lay Participation and Leadership; Missions; Patriarch*: President of the Church; Presiding Bishopric; Presiding High Priest; Priest, Aaronic Priesthood; Priesthood Councils; Priesthood Offices; Priesthood Quorums; Primary; Quorum of the Twelve Apostles; Region, Regional Representative; Relief Society; Relief Society in Nauvoo; Seventy*; Stake;

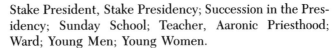

Stake President, Stake Presidency; Succession in the Presidency; Sunday School; Teacher, Aaronic Priesthood; Ward; Young Men; Young Women.

5. *Entries associated with the western New York area around Palmyra (1820–1831)*: Aaronic Priesthood*; Angel Moroni Statue; Anthon Transcript; April 6; Book of Mormon*; Book of Mormon Editions (1830-1981); Book of Mormon Manuscripts; Book of Mormon Plates and Records; Book of Mormon Translation by Joseph Smith; Book of Mormon Witnesses; Book of Moses; Canada, The Church in; Colesville, New York; Conferences*; Cumorah; Cumorah Pageant; Fayette, New York; Gold Plates; Harmony, Pennsylvania; Harris, Martin; Historical Sites; History of the Church*; Joseph Smith Translation of the Bible (JST); Lamanite Mission; Manuscript, Lost 116 Pages; Moroni, Visitations of; New York, Early LDS Sites in; Palmyra/ Manchester, New York; Sacred Grove; Smith, Joseph*; South Bainbridge (Afton), New York.

6. *Entries associated with the Ohio area around Kirtland (1831–1838)*: Book of Abraham*; British Isles, The Church in; Canada, The Church in; Consecration*; Doctrine and Covenants Editions; Hiram, Ohio; Historical Sites; History of the Church*; Joseph Smith Translation of the Bible; Kirtland, Ohio; Kirtland Economy; Kirtland Temple; Lamanite Mission; *Lectures on Faith*; *Messenger and Advocate*; Ohio, LDS Communities in; Schools of the Prophets; Smith, Joseph*; Whitney Store; Zion's Camp.

7. *Entries associated with the Missouri area around Independence, Jackson County (1831–1839)*: Adam-ondi-Ahman; Book of Commandments; Canada, The Church in; City Planning; Consecration*; Danites; *Evening and the Morning Star, The*; Extermination Order; Far West, Missouri; Garden of Eden; Haun's Mill Massacre; Historical Sites; History of the Church*; Independence, Missouri; Lamanite Mission; Liberty Jail; Missouri*; Missouri Conflict; New Jerusalem; Patten, David W.; Reorganized Church of Jesus Christ of Latter Day Saints (RLDS); Richmond Jail; Smith, Joseph*; Zion; Zion's Camp.

8. *Entries associated with the Illinois area around Nauvoo (1839–1846)*: Articles of Faith; Baptism for the Dead*; Book of Abraham*; British Isles, The Church in; Carthage Jail; City Planning; Council of Fifty; Doctrine and Covenants*; Endowment; Freemasonry in Nauvoo; Historical Sites; History of the Church*; Illinois, LDS Communities in; Iowa, LDS Communities in; Kinderhook Plates; King Follett Discourse; Martyrdom of Joseph and Hyrum Smith; Nauvoo; Nauvoo Charter; Nauvoo Economy; *Nauvoo Expositor*; Nauvoo House; Nauvoo Legion; *Nauvoo Neighbor*; Nauvoo Politics; Nauvoo Temple; Plural Marriage; Proclamations of the First Presidency and Council of

the Twelve Apostles; Relief Society in Nauvoo; Succession in the Presidency; *Times and Seasons*; Wentworth Letter.

9. ***Entries associated with the exodus from Nauvoo, Illinois, and the migration to the Great Basin (1846–1869)***: Council Bluffs (Kanesville), Iowa; Council of Fifty; Handcart Companies; Historical Sites; History of the Church*; Immigration and Emigration; Iowa, LDS Communities in; Kane, Thomas L.; Mormon Battalion; Mormon Pioneer Trail; Perpetual Emigrating Fund; "This Is the Place" Monument; Westward Migration, Planning and Prophecy; Winter Quarters.

10. ***Entries associated with the pioneering work of Brigham Young, with the Territory of Deseret, and with the establishment of the State of Utah (1846–1896)***: Academies; Agriculture; Anti-Mormon Publications; Antipolygamy Legislation; Arizona, Pioneer Settlements in; Auxiliary Organizations; Beehive Symbol; Brigham Young College; California, Pioneer Settlements in; Canada, LDS Pioneer Settlements in; Centennial Observances; Church and State; Colonization; Colorado, Pioneer Settlements in; Constitution of the United States of America; Danites; Deseret Alphabet; *Deseret News*; Deseret, State of; Genealogical Society of Utah; Historical Sites; History of the Church*; Home Industries; Idaho, Pioneer Settlements in; Mexico, Pioneer Settlements in; Mountain Meadows Massacre; Nevada, Pioneer Settlements in; New Mexico, Pioneer Settlements in; Pioneer Day; Pioneer Economy; Pioneer Life and Worship; Plural Marriage; Polygamy; Primary; Reformation (LDS) of 1856-1857; Retrenchment Association; Reynolds v. United States; Salt Lake City, Utah; Salt Lake Temple; Salt Lake Theatre; Salt Lake Valley; Seagulls, Miracle of; Silk Culture; Sunday School; Tabernacle Organ; Tabernacle, Salt Lake City; Temple Square; United Orders; University of Deseret; Utah Expedition; Utah Territory; Utah Statehood; Wyoming, Pioneer Settlements in; Young, Brigham*.

11. ***Entries about the growth of the Church in the twentieth century***: Africa, The Church in; Asia, The Church in*; Australia, The Church in; British Isles, The Church in; Canada, The Church in; Church in the World; Europe, The Church in; Granite Mountain Record Vault; Hawaii, The Church in; Historical Sites; History of the Church*; Mexico and Central America, The Church in; Middle East, The Church in; New Zealand, The Church in; Oceania, The Church in; Polynesians; Scandinavia, The Church in; South America, The Church in*; West Indies, The Church in.

12. ***General items pertaining to the history of the Church***: Biography and Autobiography; Blacks; Forgeries of Historical Documents; Historians, Church; History, Significance

to Latter-day Saints; Intellectual History; Legal and Judicial History of the Church; Material Culture; Museums; Newspapers, LDS; Pageants; Persecution; Press, News Media and the Church; Promised Land, Concept of a; Prophet*; Publications; Public Communications; Public Relations; Schismatic Groups; Schools of the Prophets; Social and Cultural History; Social Characteristics; Societies and Organizations; Stereotyping of Mormons; Temples*; Visitors Centers; Women, Roles of.

II. **SCRIPTURES OF THE CHURCH OF JESUS CHRIST OF LATTER-DAY SAINTS** that the Church and its members have accepted as "standard works" include (A) the Bible, both Old Testament and New Testament; (B) the Book of Mormon; (C) the Doctrine and Covenants; and (D) the Pearl of Great Price. [See also in the Appendix JOSEPH SMITH TRANSLATION OF THE BIBLE (SELECTIONS).]

A. **The Bible, both Old Testament and New Testament,** is an extremely important scripture for members of the Church.

1. *Persons, places, and events of the Bible*: Aaron, Brother of Moses; Abel; Abraham; Adam*; Armageddon; Cain; Daniel, Prophecies of; David, King; David, Prophetic Figure of Last Days; Elias; Elijah*; Elohim; Enoch*; Ephraim; Eve; Ezekiel, Prophecies of; Garden of Eden; Gethsemane; Isaiah*; Israel*; James, the Apostle; Jehovah, Jesus Christ; Jeremiah, Prophecies of; Jesus Christ*; John the Baptist; John the Beloved; Joseph of Egypt*; Malachi, Prophecies of; Mary, Mother of Jesus; Melchizedek*; Moses; Noah; Paul; Peter; Ruth; Sarah; Sermon on the Mount; Seth.

2. *Messages and teachings related to the Bible and early Christianity*: Abrahamic Covenant; Angels*; Atonement of Jesus Christ; Baptism; Baptism of Fire and of the Holy Ghost; Beatitudes; Blasphemy; Charity; Christology; Circumcision; Covenants in Biblical Times; Creation, Creation Accounts; Cross; Daniel, Prophecies of; Degrees of Glory; Deification, Early Christian; Discipleship; Doctrine*; Elias, Spirit of; Elijah, Spirit of; Enoch*; Eternal Life; Evangelists; Evil; Ezekiel, Prophecies of; Faith in Jesus Christ; Fall of Adam; Fasting; Fear of God; First Principles of the Gospel; Foreknowledge of God; Foreordination; Fulness of the Gospel; Gift of the Holy Ghost; Gifts of the Spirit; God; God the Father*; Godhead; Godhood; Gospel of Abraham; Gospel of Jesus Christ; Grace; Heaven; Heirs*; Hell; High Priest; Holiness; Holy Ghost; Holy Spirit; Holy Spirit of Promise; Hope of Israel; Humility; Immortality; Immortality and Eternal Life; Isaiah*; Israel*; Jeremiah, Prophecies of; Jesus Christ*; Judgment; Judgment Day, Final; Kingdom of God*; Laying on of Hands; Light of Christ; Lord's Prayer; Love; Prayer; Prophecy*; Prophecy in Biblical Times; Prophet*; Remission of Sins; Repentance; Restoration of All Things; Restoration of the Gospel of

Jesus Christ; Resurrection; Revelation; Sabbath Day; Sacrament*; Sacrifice in Biblical Times; Second Coming of Jesus Christ; Sin; Sons of Perdition; Soul; Spirit; Spirit Body; Spirit of Prophecy; Spirit World; Spiritual Death; Ten Commandments; Tithing; Transfiguration; Unpardonable Sin.

3. *General topics related to the Bible and biblical studies*: Adamic Language; Altar; Apocalyptic Texts; Apocrypha and Pseudepigrapha; Apostle; Armageddon; Bible*; Bible Dictionary; Bible, LDS; Bible Scholarship; Canon; Deuteronomy; Devils; Dispensations of the Gospel; Dove, Sign of the; Epistemology; Foreordination; Gathering; Gentiles; Gentiles, Fulness of; Hebrews, Epistle to the; Holy of Holies; Inspiration; James, Epistle of; Jerusalem; Jesus Christ, Names and Titles of; Jesus Christ, Sources for Words of; Jesus Christ, Taking the Name of, Upon Oneself; Jesus Christ, Types and Shadows of; Jews; John, Revelations of; Joseph Smith Translation of the Bible (JST); Justice and Mercy; Justification; Last Days; Law of Moses; Levitical Priesthood; Marriage Supper of the Lamb; Matthew, Gospel of; Meridian of Time; Messiah*; Millennium; Miracles; Mount of Transfiguration; Mysteries of God; New Heaven and New Earth; New Jerusalem; New Testament; Old Testament; Omnipotent God, Omnipresence of God, Omniscience of God; Original Sin; Parables; Paradise; Perfection; Persecution; Polygamy; Preaching the Gospel; Predestination; Pre-existence (Pre-earthly Existence); Premortal Life; Priesthood in Biblical Times; Promised Land, Concept of a; Psalms, Messianic Prophecies in; Raising the Dead; Saints; Salvation; Sanctification; Scripture*; Scripture, Interpretation within Scripture; Scripture Study; Seed of Abraham; Sermon on the Mount; Seventy*; Sick, Blessing the; Sign Seeking; Signs; Signs as Divine Witness; Signs of the True Church; Stick of Joseph; Stick of Judah; Strait and Narrow; Symbolism; Teaching the Gospel; Temples*; Testimony of Jesus Christ; Theodicy; Theogony; Topical Guide; Urim and Thummim; Virgin Birth; War in Heaven; Washing of Feet; Witnesses, Law of; Works; Worship; Wrath of God.

B. **The Book of Mormon** is recognized by Latter-day Saints as another testament of the divinity of Jesus Christ as it contains an account of the visit of the resurrected Jesus Christ to the peoples of the Western Hemisphere.

1. *Persons, peoples, and places mentioned in the Book of Mormon*: Abinadi; Adam*; Alma$_1$; Alma$_2$; Amulek; Benjamin; Brother of Jared; Cumorah; Ephraim; Ezias; Helaman$_1$; Helaman$_2$; Helaman$_3$; Ishmael; Jacob, Son of Lehi; Jaredites; Jerusalem; Joseph of Egypt*; Laman; Lamanites; Lehi; Mormon; Moroni$_1$; Moroni$_2$; Moses; Mosiah$_1$; Mosiah$_2$; Mulek; Nephi$_1$; Nephi$_2$; Nephi$_3$; Nephi$_4$; Nephites; Neum; Samuel the Lamanite; Smith, Joseph*; Three Nephites; Women in the Book of Mormon; Zenock; Zenos; Zoram.

2. *Messages and teachings of the Book of Mormon*: Agency; Allegory of Zenos; Atonement of Jesus Christ; Baptism; Baptismal Covenant; Baptismal Prayer; Beatitudes; Born of God; Condescension of God; Damnation; Evil; Faith in Jesus Christ; Fall of Adam; Fasting; Foreknowledge of God; Freedom; Fulness of the Gospel; Gathering; Gift of the Holy Ghost; Gifts of the Spirit; God; Gospel of Jesus Christ; Grace; Heaven; Hell; Holiness; Holy Ghost; Holy Spirit; Hope; Humility; Jehovah, Jesus Christ; Jesus Christ*; Jesus Christ, Types and Shadows; Jews; Joy; Justice and Mercy; Justification; Law of Moses; Lord's Prayer; New Heaven and New Earth; New Jerusalem; Oaths; Obedience; Omnipotent God, Omnipresence of God, Omniscience of God; Opposition; Paradise; Persecution; Plan of Salvation, Plan of Redemption; Prayer; Preaching the Gospel; Pride; Priestcraft; Promised Land, Concept of a; Prophecy; Prophecy in the Book of Mormon; Prophet*; Purpose of Earth Life*; Record Keeping; Remission of Sins; Repentance; Resurrection; Revelation; Sacrament*; Salvation; Sanctification; Sign Seeking; Signs; Signs as Divine Witness; Sin; Spiritual Death; Translated Beings; Tree of Life; Unpardonable Sin; Virgin Birth; Visions; Wealth, Attitudes Toward.

3. *General topics related to the Book of Mormon*: Angel Moroni Statue; Angels*; Anthon Transcript; AntiChrists; Blessings; Book of Mormon*; Book of Mormon, Authorship; Book of Mormon, Biblical Prophecies about; Book of Mormon Chronology; Book of Mormon Commentaries; Book of Mormon Economy and Technology; Book of Mormon Editions (1830-1981); Book of Mormon Geography; Book of Mormon, Government and Legal History in; Book of Mormon, History of Warfare in; Book of Mormon in a Biblical Culture; Book of Mormon Language; Book of Mormon Literature; Book of Mormon Manuscripts; Book of Mormon Names; Book of Mormon Near Eastern Background; Book of Mormon Peoples; Book of Mormon Personalities; Book of Mormon Plates and Records; Book of Mormon Religious Teachings and Practices; Book of Mormon Studies; Book of Mormon Translation by Joseph Smith; Book of Mormon Translations; Book of Mormon Witnesses; Canon; Chastening; Columbus, Christopher; Contention; Covenant Israel, Latter-day; Covenants; Cowdery, Oliver; Cumorah Pageant; Dead Sea Scrolls*; Deseret; Fayette, New York; Gentiles; Gold Plates; Grace; Great and Abominable Church; Harmony, Pennsylvania; Harris, Martin; Isaiah*; Israel*; Joseph Smith—History; Judgment; Judgment Day, Final; Kinderhook Plates; Lamanite Mission; Law*; Liahona; Malachi, Prophecies of; Manuscript, Lost 116 Pages; Melchizedek*; Messiah*; Miracles; Moroni, Angel; Moroni, Visitations of; Name of the Church; Native Americans; Natural Man; Palmyra/Manchester, New York; Polynesians; Scripture*; Scripture, Interpretation within Scripture;

Scripture Study; Secret Combinations; Seer; Seer Stones; Smith, Joseph*; Spaulding Manuscript; Standard Works; Stick of Joseph; Suffering in the World; Sword of Laban; Symbolism; Temples*; Temptation; Ten Commandments; Testimony of Jesus Christ; Urim and Thummim; *View of the Hebrews*; "Voice from the Dust"; Whitmer, David; Witnesses, Law of; Women in the Book of Mormon; Works.

C. **The Doctrine and Covenants** contains many revelations from the Lord and other items pertaining to The Church of Jesus Christ of Latter-day Saints and its members.

1. *Persons and places mentioned in the Doctrine and Covenants or associated with it*: Abraham; Adam; Adam-ondi-Ahman; Ahman; Carthage Jail; Colesville, New York; Cowdery, Oliver; Elias; Elijah; Enoch*; Far West, Missouri; Fayette, New York; Harmony, Pennsylvania; Harris, Martin; Hiram, Ohio; Hyde, Orson; Independence, Missouri; John the Baptist; John the Beloved; Kimball, Heber C.; Kirtland, Ohio; Kirtland Temple; Liberty Jail; Malachi, Prophecies of; Melchizedek*; Missouri*; Moses; Nauvoo; Nauvoo House; Nauvoo Temple; New Jerusalem; Noah; Palmyra/Manchester, New York; Pratt, Orson; Pratt, Parley P.; Rigdon, Sidney; Sarah; Smith, Emma Hale; Smith, Hyrum; Smith, Joseph; Smith, Joseph, Sr.; Smith, Joseph F.; Snow, Lorenzo; Taylor, John; Whitmer, David; Woodruff, Wilford; Young, Brigham; Zion.

2. *Messages and teachings of the Doctrine and Covenants*: Aaronic Priesthood*; Abrahamic Covenant; Afterlife; Alcoholic Beverages and Alcoholism; Apostle; April 6; Atonement of Jesus Christ; Baptism; Baptism for the Dead*; Baptism of Fire and of the Holy Ghost; Baptismal Covenant; Baptismal Prayer; Bishop; Born in the Covenant; Born of God; Burnings, Everlasting; Calling and Election; Callings; Celestial Kingdom; Chastening; Chastity, Law of; Children*; Church and State; Church of Jesus Christ of Latter-day Saints, The; Church of the Firstborn; Common Consent; Confirmation; Consecration*; Covenants; Damnation; Deacon, Aaronic Priesthood; Degrees of Glory; Devils; Discernment, Gift of; Discipleship; Dispensation of the Fulness of Times; Dispensations of the Gospel; Divorce; Doctrine*; Elder, Melchizedek Priesthood; Elect of God; Elias, Spirit of; Elijah, Spirit of; Endless and Eternal; Endowment; Eternal Life; Eternal Lives, Eternal Increase; Eternal Progression; Exaltation; Faith in Jesus Christ; Family*; Fast and Testimony Meeting; Fast Offerings; Fasting; Father's Blessings; First Presidency; First Principles of the Gospel; Foreknowledge of God; Foreordination; Fulness of the Gospel; Gift of the Holy Ghost; Gifts of the Spirit; God; God the Father*; Godhead; Godhood; Gospel of Abraham; Gospel of Jesus Christ; Head of the Church; Heirs*; Hell; High Council; High Priest; Holiness; Holy Ghost; Holy

Spirit; Holy Spirit of Promise; Immortality and Eternal Life; Jesus Christ*; John, Revelations of; Justice and Mercy; Justification; Keys of the Priesthood; Lay Participation and Leadership; Laying on of Hands; Levitical Priesthood; Magnifying One's Calling; Man of Holiness; Marriage*; Melchizedek Priesthood*; Millennium; Name of God; Name of the Church; New and Everlasting Covenant; New Heaven and New Earth; Oath and Covenant of the Priesthood; Oaths; Obedience; Ordinances*; Organization*; Patriarch*; Patriarchal Blessings; Patriarchal Order of the Priesthood; Plan of Salvation, Plan of Redemption; Plural Marriage; Prayer; Preaching the Gospel; Pre-existence, Pre-earthly Existence; Premortal Life; Presidency, Concept of; President of the Church; Presiding Bishopric; Presiding High Priest; Priest, Aaronic Priesthood; Priesthood; Priesthood Blessings; Priesthood Offices; Priesthood Quorums; Prophet, Seer, and Revelator; Quorum of the Twelve Apostles; Record Keeping; Remission of Sins; Repentance; Restoration of All Things; Restoration of the Gospel of Jesus Christ; Resurrection; Revelation; Riches of Eternity; Sabbath Day; Sacrament Meeting; Sacrament*; Sacrifice; Saints; Salvation; Salvation of the Dead; Sanctification; Sealing*; Second Coming of Jesus Christ; Seed of Abraham; Setting Apart; Seventy*; Sick, Blessing the; Signs of the True Church; Solemn Assemblies; Sons of Perdition; Soul; Spirit; Spirit Body; Spirit of Prophecy; Spirit Prison; Spirit World; Spiritual Death; Stake; Stake President; Stewardship; Sunday; Teacher, Aaronic Priesthood; Teaching the Gospel; Telestial Kingdom; Temple Ordinances; Temple Recommend; Temples*; Terrestrial Kingdom; Testator; Testimony; Testimony Bearing; Testimony of Jesus Christ; Time and Eternity; Tithing; Tobacco; True and Living Church; Truth; United Orders; Unpardonable Sin; Ward; Ward Organization; Washing and Anointing; Washing of Feet; Welfare; Word of Wisdom; Work, Role of; Works; Zion.

3. *General topics related to the Doctrine and Covenants*: Adam-ondi-Ahman; Agency; Apostasy; Authority; Bishop; Bishop, History of the Office; Bishop's Storehouse; Bishopric; Book of Commandments; Canon; Capital Punishment; Civil War Prophecy; Clerk; Coffee; Commandments; Conferences*; Confession of Sins; Constitution of the United States of America; Constitutional Law; Correlation of the Church, Administration; Council of the First Presidency and the Quorum of the Twelve Apostles; Courts, Ecclesiastical, Nineteenth-Century; Disciplinary Procedures; Doctrine and Covenants*; Doctrine and Covenants Commentaries; Doctrine and Covenants Editions; Doctrine and Covenants as Literature; Drugs, Abuse of; Enduring to the End; Finances of the Church; Financial Contributions; Following the Brethren; Freedom; Freemasonry and the Temple; Freemasonry in Nauvoo; Genealogy; General Authori-

ties; Gentiles; Gentiles, Fulness of; Health, Attitudes toward; Heaven; History of the Church*; Holy of Holies; Home; Home Teaching; Hosanna Shout; Interviews; Israel*; Joining the Church; Judgment Day, Final; Kingdom of God*; Knowledge; Last Days; Latter-day Saints (LDS); Law*; Law of Adoption; Lawsuits; *Lectures on Faith*; Light and Darkness; Light of Christ; Light-Mindedness; Manifesto of 1890; Martyrdom of Joseph and Hyrum Smith; Martyrs; Meetings, Major Church; Membership; Membership Records; Men, Roles of; Meridian of Time; Mission President; Missionary, Missionary Life; Missions; Missouri Conflict; Motherhood; Murder; Mysteries of God; Oil, Consecrated; Organization of the Church in New Testament Times; Orthodoxy, Heterodoxy, and Heresy; Persecution; Policies, Practices, and Procedures; Polygamy; Poverty, Attitudes toward; Prayer Circle; Priesthood Councils; Priesthood Interview; Prophecy*; Prophet*; Purpose of Earth Life*; Reason and Revelation; Righteousness; Sabbath Day; Schools of the Prophets; Scripture*; Scripture, Interpretation within Scripture; Scripture Study; Sign Seeking; Signs; Signs as Divine Witnesses; Signs of the Times; Sin; Succession in the Presidency; Tea; Ten Commandments; Thankfulness; Tolerance; Translated Beings; Trials; Visions of Joseph Smith; Visiting Teaching; Voice of Warning; Wealth, Attitudes toward; Welfare Services; Women, Roles of*; Worldliness; Worship; Wrath of God; Zionism; Zion's Camp.

D. **The Pearl of Great Price** is the shortest of the standard works. However, it contains very important information on several basic principles, doctrines, and ordinances of the Gospel.

1. *Persons, places, and events mentioned in the Pearl of Great Price or associated with this scripture*: Aaronic Priesthood*; Abel; Abraham; Adam*; Cain; Cowdery, Oliver; Creation, Creation Accounts; Cumorah; Elijah*; Enoch*; Eve; First Vision; Garden of Eden; Harmony, Pennsylvania; Harris, Martin; James the Apostle; John the Baptist; John the Beloved; Malachi, Prophecies of; Melchizedek*; Moroni, Angel; Moroni, Visitations of; Moses; Noah; Palmyra/Manchester, New York; Peter; Sacred Grove; Sarah; Seth; Smith, Emma Hale; Smith, Joseph; Smith, Joseph, Sr.; Smith, Lucy Mack; South Bainbridge (Afton), New York; Zion.

2. *Messages and teachings of the Pearl of Great Price*: Abrahamic Covenant; Agency; Atonement of Jesus Christ; Baptism; Baptismal Covenant; Book of Remembrance; Consecration*; Council in Heaven; Covenant Israel, Latter-day; Creation, Creation Accounts; Cursings; Devils; Discernment, Gift of; Dispensations of the Gospel; Doctrine*; Earth; Faith in Jesus Christ; Fall of Adam; Father's Blessings; First Estate; Foreknowledge of God; Foreordination;

God; God the Father*; Godhead; Godhood; Gospel of Abraham; Gospel of Jesus Christ; Heaven; Heirs*; Immortality and Eternal Life; Intelligences; Jehovah, Jesus Christ; Jesus Christ*; Last Days; Millennium; Origin of Man; Plan of Salvation, Plan of Redemption; Prayer; Preaching the Gospel; Pre-existence, Pre-earthly Existence; Premortal Life; Priesthood; Priesthood Blessings: Prophet, Seer, and Revelator; Purpose of Earth Life*; Remission of Sins; Repentance; Revelation; Second Coming of Jesus Christ; Second Estate; Seer; Signs as Divine Witnesses; Sin; Soul; Spirit; Spirit Body; Spiritual Death; Translated Beings; Truth; Visions; Zion.

3. *General topics related to the Pearl of Great Price*: Book of Abraham*; Book of Moses; Elohim; Endless and Eternal; Garden of Eden; Gift of the Holy Ghost; Holiness; Holy Ghost; James, Epistle of; Joseph Smith—History; Joseph Smith—Matthew; Life and Death, Spiritual; Lost Scripture; Mysteries of God; Natural Man; Nature, Law of; New Heaven and New Earth; Obedience; Papyri, Joseph Smith; Patriarchal Order of the Priesthood; Pearl of Great Price*; Priesthood in Biblical Times; Prophecy*; Prophet*; Restoration of the Gospel of Jesus Christ; Resurrection; Righteousness; Sacrifice; Sacrifice in Biblical Times; Salvation; Scripture*; Scripture, Interpretation within Scripture; Sons of Perdition; Spirit of Prophecy; Standard Works; Teaching the Gospel; Testimony; Testimony of Jesus Christ; War in Heaven; Worlds.

III. **DOCTRINES OF THE CHURCH OF JESUS CHRIST OF LATTER-DAY SAINTS** are the essential teachings associated with God's plan of salvation, progression, and eternal life for his children, including the basic principles and ordinances of the gospel of Jesus Christ. The many entries in the Encyclopedia related to these areas are listed under (A) the nature and characteristics of God and of the two other members of the Godhead; (B) the pre-earthly existence; (C) purposes of a mortal, physical, earthly existence; (D) the birth, life, mission and atonement of Jesus Christ; (E) basic principles and ordinances of the gospel of Jesus Christ; (F) other principles and ordinances pertaining to exaltation and eternal life. [See also in the Appendix: DOCTRINAL EXPOSITIONS OF THE FIRST PRESIDENCY; JOSEPH SMITH TRANSLATION OF THE BIBLE (SELECTIONS); LETTERS OF THE FIRST PRESIDENCY; LETTERS OF THE PRESIDING BISHOPRIC; LINES OF PRIESTHOOD AUTHORITY; TEMPLE DEDICATORY PRAYERS (EXCERPTS); THE WENTWORTH LETTER.]

A. **The nature and characteristics of God and of the two other members of the Godhead.**

1. *God the Father*: Ahman; Condescension of God; Elohim; Endless and Eternal; Fear of God; Foreknowledge of God; God; God the Father*; Godhead; Godhood; Heaven; Holiness; Man of Holiness; Name of God; Omnipotent God,

Omnipresence of God, Omniscience of God; Worship; Wrath of God.

2. *Jesus Christ the Son*: Atonement of Jesus Christ; Condescension of God; Faith in Jesus Christ; Godhead; Gospel of Jesus Christ; Head of the Church; Heirs*; Holy Spirit of Promise; Hope of Israel; Jehovah, Jesus Christ; Jesus Christ*; Jesus Christ, Fatherhood and Sonship; Jesus Christ in the Scriptures*; Jesus Christ, Names and Titles of; Jesus Christ, Second Comforter; Jesus Christ, Sources for Words of; Jesus Christ, Taking the Name of, Upon Oneself; Jesus Christ, Types and Shadows of; Light of Christ; Mary, Mother of Jesus; Messiah*; Second Coming of Jesus Christ; Testimony of Jesus Christ; Virgin Birth.

3. *The Holy Ghost (or Holy Spirit)*: Godhead; Holy Ghost; Holy Spirit; Holy Spirit of Promise.

B. **The pre-earthly existence** is one of the least understood stages of the plan of progression and eternal life, although both ancient and modern scriptures refer to this vital period of the existence of all human beings.

1. *The pre-earthly spiritual existence as sons and daughters of our Heavenly Father*: Born of God; Brotherhood; Council in Heaven; First Estate; Intelligences; Kingdom of God*; Mother in Heaven; Origin of Man; Paradise; Pre-existence (Pre-earthly Existence); Premortal life; Sisterhood; Spirit; Spirit Body.

2. *The grand council in heaven and items discussed there*: Accountability; Agency; Atonement of Jesus Christ; Authority; Celestial Kingdom; Council in Heaven; Creation and Creation Accounts; Devils; Doctrine*; Elohim; Fall of Adam; First Estate; Foreknowledge of God; Foreordination; Jehovah; Life and Death, Spiritual; Meridian of Time; Millennium; Mortality; Oaths; Obedience; Perfection; Physical Body; Plan of Salvation, Plan of Redemption; Priesthood; Procreation; Prophet*; Purpose of Earth Life*; Resurrection; Revelation; Reverence; Sacrifice; Salvation; Second Estate; Soul; Telestial Kingdom; Terrestrial Kingdom; War in Heaven.

3. *The devil and other evil spirits*: Antichrists; Buffetings of Satan; Council in Heaven; Damnation; Devils; Evil; Hell; Satanism; Sons of Perdition; Spirit Prison; Spiritual Death; Unpardonable Sin.

C. **Purposes of a mortal, physical, earthly existence.**

1. *The creation of a physical earth*: Adam*; Creation and Creation Accounts; Earth; Jehovah, Jesus Christ; Jesus Christ*.

2. *The importance of a physical body*: Birth; Mankind; Mortality; Physical Body; Physical Fitness, Recreation; Procreation; Purpose of Earth Life*; Second Estate; Work, Role of.

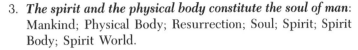

3. *The spirit and the physical body constitute the soul of man*: Mankind; Physical Body; Resurrection; Soul; Spirit; Spirit Body; Spirit World.

D. **The birth, life, ministry, and atonement of Jesus Christ.**

1. *Persons and events associated with the birth of Jesus Christ*: Birth; Condescension of God; God; God the Father*; Heirs*; Holy Ghost; Jesus Christ*; Jesus Christ in the Scriptures*; Mary, Mother of Jesus; Meridian of Time.

2. *Entries associated with the life and ministry of Jesus Christ*: Beatitudes; Dove, Sign of the; Gospel of Jesus Christ; Jesus Christ*; Jesus Christ in the Scriptures*; Jesus Christ, Names and Titles of; Jesus Christ, Second Comforter; Jesus Christ, Sources for Words of; Jesus Christ, Types and Shadows of; John the Baptist; Kingdom of God*; Matthew, Gospel of; Messiah*; Miracles; New Testament; Organization of the Church in New Testament Times; Preaching the Gospel; Sacrament; Sermon on the Mount; Transfiguration; Washing of Feet.

3. *Entries associated with the atonement of Jesus Christ, including his becoming the Savior and Redeemer of all mankind*: Atonement of Jesus Christ; Blood Atonement; Cross; Death and Dying; Gethsemane; Grace; Jesus Christ*; Jesus Christ in the Scriptures*; Resurrection; Second Coming of Jesus Christ.

E. **Basic principles and ordinances of the gospel of Jesus Christ.**

1. *Faith in the Lord Jesus Christ*: Faith in Jesus Christ; Charity; Hope; Jesus Christ*.

2. *Repentance*: Confession; Remission of Sins; Repentance.

3. *Baptism by immersion for the remission of sins*: Baptism; Baptism for the Dead*; Baptismal Covenant; Baptismal Prayer.

4. *Receiving the gift of the Holy Ghost by the laying on of hands*: Baptism of Fire and of the Holy Ghost; Born of God; Confirmation; Discernment, Gift of; Gift of the Holy Ghost; Gifts of the Spirit; Holy Ghost; Laying on of Hands.

5. *Other topics associated with the gospel of Jesus Christ*: Afterlife; Amen; Articles of Faith; Atonement of Jesus Christ; Authority; Beatitudes; Book of Life; Christians and Christianity; Commandments; Conversion; Covenants; Covenants in Biblical Times; Deification, Early Christian; Elect of God; Endless and Eternal; Endowment; Enduring to the End; Fasting; First Principles of the Gospel; Foreordination; Fulness of the Gospel; Gospel of Jesus Christ; Grace; Head of the Church; Jehovah, Jesus Christ; Jesus Christ*; Jesus Christ in the Scriptures*; Jesus Christ, Second Comforter; Judgment; Judgment Day, Final; Justice and Mercy; Justification; Kingdom of God*; Law*; Light of Christ;

Lord's Prayer; Love; Matthew, Gospel of; Messiah; Millennium; Miracles; Mount of Transfiguration; New and Everlasting Covenant; New Testament; Ordinances; Organization of the Church in New Testament Times; Parables; Paradise; Plan of Salvation, Plan of Redemption; Prayer; Preaching the Gospel; Prophecy*; Prophet*; Purpose of Earth Life; Restoration of All Things; Restoration of the Gospel of Jesus Christ; Revelation; Reverence; Righteousness; Sabbath Day; Sacrament*; Sacrifice; Sacrifice in Biblical Times; Sanctification; Second Coming of Jesus Christ; Tithing; Works.

F. **Other principles and ordinances pertaining to exaltation and eternal life.**

1. *Blessing and naming children*: Adoption of Children; Blessings; Born in the Covenant; Children*; Father's Blessings.

2. *Confirmation as a member of the Church*: Common Consent; Confirmation; Gift of the Holy Ghost; Holy Ghost; Holy Spirit; Law of Adoption; Laying on of Hands; Spirit of Prophecy; Testimony; Testimony of Jesus Christ.

3. *Ordination to the priesthood*: Aaronic Priesthood*; Apostle; Bishop; Deacon, Aaronic Priesthood; Elder, Melchizedek Priesthood; High Priest; Keys of the Priesthood; Levitical Priesthood; Melchizedek Priesthood*; Patriarch; Oath and Covenant of the Priesthood; Patriarchal Order of the Priesthood; Priest, Aaronic Priesthood; Priesthood; Priesthood Offices; Priesthood Quorums; Setting Apart; Seventy*; Teacher, Aaronic Priesthood.

4. *The Holy Endowment*: Endowment; Endowment Houses; Salvation for the Dead; Temple Ordinances; Temples*.

5. *Marriage of husband and wife, and the sealing of children to parents*: Eternal Life; Eternal Lives, Eternal Increase; Family*; Fatherhood; Marriage*; Motherhood; New and Everlasting Covenant; Sealing*; Temple Ordinances; Temples*; Time and Eternity.

6. *Other topics associated with exaltation and eternal life and with the eternal nature of the family*: Abrahamic Covenant; Ancestral File™; Book of Remembrance; Brotherhood; Calling and Election; Celestial Kingdom; Dating and Courtship; Degrees of Glory; Eternal Progression; Exaltation; Family*; Family History, Genealogy; Family History Centers; Family History Library; Family Home Evening; Family Organizations; Family Prayer; Family Registry™; FamilySearch™; Feminism; Genealogical Society of Utah; Godhood; Heaven; Heirs*; Immortality; Immortality and Eternal Life; International Genealogical Index™ (IGI); Journals; Joy; Judgment Day, Final; Justification; Magnifying One's Calling; Mysteries of God; Name Extraction Program; Oaths; Obedience; Personal Ancestral File®; Plan of

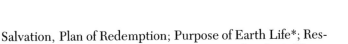

Salvation, Plan of Redemption; Purpose of Earth Life*; Resurrection; Salvation; Sanctification; Sisterhood; Stillborn Children.

IV. **ORGANIZATION AND GOVERNMENT OF THE CHURCH** are listed under the following: (A) the restoration of priesthood authority, keys, and offices; (B) the organization of the Church on April 6, 1830; (C) the development of priesthood quorums and councils; (D) the development of Church units, and the leaders basic to those units; (E) the development of auxiliary organizations (auxiliary to the priesthood), and (F) policies, procedures, and practices in administering the units and activities of the Church. [See also in the Appendix: Biographical Register of General Church Offices; A Chronology of Church History; Church Periodicals; General Church Officers, A Chronology; Lines of Priesthood Authority.]

A. **The restoration of priesthood authority, keys, and offices.**

1. *Restoration of the Aaronic Priesthood, its authority, keys, and offices*: Aaron, Brother of Moses; Aaronic Priesthood*; Harmony, Pennsylvania; John the Baptist; Keys of the Priesthood; Laying on of Hands; Levitical Priesthood; Ordination to the Priesthood; Priesthood; Priesthood Offices; Priesthood Quorums.

2. *Restoration of the Melchizedek Priesthood, its authority, keys, and offices*: James, the Apostle; John the Beloved; Keys of the Priesthood; Melchizedek*; Melchezedek Priesthood*; Oath and Covenant of the Priesthood; Ordination to the Priesthood; Peter; Priesthood; Priesthood Offices; Priesthood Quorums.

B. **The organization of the Church on April 6, 1830.**

1. *Date of the organization*: April 6.

2. *Circumstances of the organization*: Organization of the Church, 1830.

C. **The development of the priesthood quorums and councils.**

1. *The First Presidency*: Council of the First Presidency and the Quorum of the Twelve Apostles; Cowdery, Oliver; First Presidency; Head of the Church; Presidency, Concept of; President of the Church; Presiding High Priest; Prophet, Seer, and Revelator; Prophet*; Smith, Hyrum; Smith, Joseph; Succession in the Presidency.

2. *The Quorum of the Twelve Apostles*: Apostle; Council of the First Presidency and Quorum of the Twelve; Prophet, Seer, and Revelator; Prophet*; Quorum of the Twelve Apostles.

3. *The First Council of the Seventy, The First Quorum of the Seventy, and additional quorums of Seventy*: Area, Area Presidency; Assistants to the Twelve; Seventy*.

4. *The Presiding Bishopric*: Bishop; Bishop, History of the Office; Bishopric; Presiding Bishopric.

5. *The Patriarch to the Church and other patriarchs*: Evangelists; Patriarch*; Patriarchal Blessings.

6. *High Priests, and High Priests Quorums and Groups*: High Priest; Priesthood Quorums.

7. *Elders, and the Elders Quorum*: Elder, Melchizedek Priesthood; Priesthood Quorums.

8. *Bishops, and the calling of a ward bishop*: Bishop; Bishop, History of the Office; Bishopric; Branch, Branch President.

9. *Priests, and the Priests Quorum*: Priest, Aaronic Priesthood; Priesthood Quorums.

10. *Teachers, and the Teachers Quorum*: Priesthood Quorums; Teacher, Aaronic Priesthood.

11. *Deacons, and the Deacons Quorum*: Deacon, Aaronic Priesthood; Priesthood Quorums.

12. *Other topics associated with the restoration and development of priesthood quorums and groups*: Brotherhood; Callings; Church of Jesus Christ of Latter-day Saints, The; Common Consent; Conferences*; Correlation of the Church, Administration; Discipleship; Following the Brethren; General Authorities; *General Handbook of Instructions*; Heirs*; Home Teaching; Keys of the Priesthood; Kingdom of God*; Laying on of Hands; Magnifying One's Calling; Melchizedek Priesthood*; Oath and Covenant of the Priesthood; Ordinances*; Organization*; Patriarchal Order of the Priesthood; Priesthood; Priesthood Blessings; Priesthood Councils; Priesthood Executive Committee, Stake and Ward; Priesthood in Biblical Times; Priesthood Interview; Priesthood Offices; Restoration of All Things; Setting Apart; Spirit of Prophecy; True and Living Church;

D. **The development of Church units, and the leaders basic to those units.**

1. *Missions and Mission Presidents*: Mission President; Missionary, Missionary Life; Missionary Training Centers; Missions; Missions of the Twelve to the British Isles.

2. *Areas and Area Presidencies*: Area, Area Presidency.

3. *Regions and Regional Representatives*: Region, Regional Representative.

4. *Stakes and Stake Presidencies*: High Council; Stake; Stake President, Stake Presidency.

5. *Districts and District Presidencies*: District, District President.

and the Quorum of the Twelve Apostles; First Presidency; Following the Brethren; *General Handbook of Instructions*; High Council; Organization*; Organization of the Church in New Testament Times; Presidency, Concept of; President of the Church; Priesthood Executive Committee, Stake and Ward; Priesthood Quorums; Quorum of Twelve Apostles; Region, Regional Representative; Setting Apart; Seventy*; Stake; Stake President, Stake Presidency; Stewardship; Ward; Ward Council; Ward Organization; Ward Welfare Committee.

3. *Means of communicating with local units and with members of the Church*: Almanacs; *Bulletin*; Callings; *Church News*; Common Consent; Conference Reports; Conferences*; Distribution Centers; *Ensign*; Fast and Testimony Meetings; *Friend, The*; *General Handbook of Instructions*; Home Teaching; Magazines; Meetings, Major Church; Membership Records; *New Era*; Policies, Practices, and Procedures; Proclamations of the First Presidency and Council of the Twelve Apostles; Publications; Public Communications; Sacrament Meeting; Satellite Communication System; Solemn Assemblies; Visiting Teaching.

V. **PROCEDURES AND PRACTICES OF THE CHURCH AND ITS MEMBERS AS THEY RELATE TO THEMSELVES AND TO SOCIETY IN GENERAL** include (A) Church members as they perceive themselves and relate to other members of the Church; (B) Church members as they are perceived by others and as they relate to other churches and groups, and (C) Studies comparing Church members with others, including the vital statistics (demographics) of the Church and its members. [See also in the Appendix: A CHRONOLOGY OF CHURCH HISTORY; CHURCH MEMBERSHIP FIGURES; CHURCH PERIODICALS; DOCTRINAL EXPOSITIONS OF THE FIRST PRESIDENCY; GENERAL CHURCH OFFICERS, A CHRONOLOGY; GLOSSARY; LETTERS OF THE FIRST PRESIDENCY; LETTERS OF THE PRESIDING BISHOPRIC; LINES OF PRIESTHOOD AUTHORITY; A SELECTION OF LDS HYMNS; TEMPLE DEDICATORY PRAYERS (EXCERPTS).]

A. **Church members as they perceive themselves and relate to other members of the Church.**

1. *Emphasis on the importance and eternal nature of the family and on family history (genealogy)*: Adoption of Children; Afterlife; Ancestral File™; Biography and Autobiography; Book of Remembrance; Born in the Covenant; Brotherhood; Children*; Dating and Courtship; Family*; Family History, Genealogy; Family History Centers; Family History Library; Family Home Evening; Family Organizations; Family Prayer; Family Registry™; FamilySearch™; Fatherhood; Feminism; Genealogical Society of Utah; Genealogy; God the Father*; Home; International Genealogical Index™ (IGI); Journals; Librar-

ies and Archives; Maternity and Child Health Care; Men, Roles of; Motherhood; Name Extraction Program; Personal Ancestral File®; Sisterhood; Stillborn Children; *Utah Genealogical and Historical Magazine*; Woman Suffrage; Women, Roles of*; Women's Topics; World Conferences on Records.

2. *Belief in a plan of progression and eternal life leading from a pre-earthly existence to the resurrection and, for the faithful righteous, to Godhood*: Celestial Kingdom; Council in Heaven; Degrees of Glory; Eternal Life; Eternal Lives, Eternal Increase; Eternal Progression; Exaltation; First Estate; God the Father; Godhood; Heaven; Heirs*; Immortality and Eternal Life; Individuality; Intelligences; Judgment Day, Final; Mankind; Marriage*; Mortality; Mother in Heaven; Origin of Man; Perfection; Physical Body; Plan of Salvation, Plan of Redemption; Pre-existence (Pre-earthly Existence); Premortal Life; Purpose of Earth Life*; Resurrection; Salvation of the Dead; Sealing*; Second Estate; Soul; Spirit; Spirit Body; Spirit World; Telestial Kingdom; Terrestrial Kingdom.

3. *Temple ordinances and administration*: Baptism for the Dead; Endowment; Garments; Kirtland Temple; Nauvoo Temple; Salt Lake Temple; Sealing*; Temple Ordinances; Temple President and Matron; Temple Recommend; Temples*.

4. *Missionary service and proselytizing*: Mission President; Missionary, Missionary Life; Missionary Training Centers; Missions; Missions of the Twelve to the British Isles; Preaching the Gospel.

5. *Health codes and care*: Alcoholic Beverages and Alcoholism; Coffee; Deseret Hospital; Health, Attitudes Toward; Hospitals; Maternity and Child Health Care; Medical Practices; Mental Health; Tea; Tobacco; Word of Wisdom.

6. *Principle of continuing revelation to a living prophet*: First Presidency; First Vision; Head of the Church; President of the Church; Presiding High Priest; Prophet Joseph Smith; Prophet, Seer, and Revelator; Prophet*; Revelation; Revelations, Unpublished; Seer; Spirit of Prophecy; Visions; Visions of Joseph Smith.

7. *Principle of the Church [Kingdom of God on the earth] being governed by Apostles with priesthood authority directly from Jesus Christ*: Apostle; Authority; Church of Jesus Christ of Latter-day Saints, The; Church of the First-born; Council of the First Presidency and the Quorum of the Twelve Apostles; Keys of the Priesthood; Latter-day Saints (LDS); Priesthood; Priesthood in Biblical Times; Priesthood Offices; Priesthood Quorums; Quorum of the Twelve Apostles; Restoration of All Things; Restoration of the Gospel of Jesus Christ.

8. *Movies, radio and television programming*: Bonneville International; Broadcasting; KSL Radio; *Man's Search for Happiness*; Mormon Tabernacle Choir; Mormon Tabernacle Choir Broadcast ("The Spoken Word"); Motion Pictures, LDS Productions; Public Communications; Satellite Communication System.

9. *Participation in world's fairs, exhibitions, visitors centers, and development of historical sites*: Christus Statue; Exhibitions and World's Fairs; Historical Sites; Pageants; Polynesian Cultural Center; Sacred Grove; Visitors Centers.

10. *Church educational system and Church curricula*: Academies; Brigham Young College; Brigham Young University*; Church Educational System (CES); Curriculum; Distribution Centers; Education*; Institutes of Religion; Intelligence; Knowledge; LDS Business College; LDS Foundation; LDS Student Associations; Meetinghouse Libraries; Ricks College; Schools; Schools of the Prophets; Seminaries; Teachers, Teacher Development; Teaching the Gospel; University of Deseret; Values, Transmission of.

11. *Libraries and archives*: Brigham Young University*; Family History Centers; Family History Library; Libraries and Archives; Meetinghouse Libraries.

12. *Programs and materials for special groups*: Blind, Materials for the; Deaf, Materials for the; Firesides; Hospitals; Indian Student Placement Services; Lamanite Mission; Leadership Training; Senior Citizens; Single Adults; Social Services; Sports; Welfare Services; Youth.

13. *Arts and music*: Architecture; Art in Mormonism; Artists, Visual; Dance; Drama; Fine Arts; Folk Art; Folklore; Humor; Hymns and Hymnody; Literature, Mormon Writers of*; Mormon Handicraft; Mormon Tabernacle Choir; Mormon Youth Symphony and Chorus; Mormons, Image of*; Motion Pictures, LDS Productions; Museums; Music; Musicians; Pageants; Public Speaking; Sculptors; Symbols, Cultural and Artistic; "This Is the Place" Monument.

14. *Magazines, newspapers, and other periodicals*: Almanacs; *Children's Friend, The*; Church News; *Contributor*; *Deseret News*; *Ensign*; *Evening and the Morning Star, The*; *Friend, The*; *Improvement Era*; *Instructor, The*; International Magazines; *Journal of Discourses*; *Juvenile Instructor*; *Lectures on Faith*; *Liahona The Elders' Journal*; Magazines; *Messenger and Advocate*; *Millennial Star*; *New Era*; *Relief Society Magazine*; *Times and Seasons*; *Utah Genealogical and Historical Magazine*; *Woman's Exponent*; *Young Woman's Journal*.

15. *Official letters, bulletins, and handbooks*: Bulletin; *General Handbook of Instructions*; Policies, Practices, and

Procedures; Proclamations of the First Presidency and Council of the Twelve Apostles; Publications; Wentworth Letter.

16. *Welfare assistance and programs*: Calamities and Disasters; Charity; Deseret Industries; Economic Aid; Economic History of the Church; Emergency Preparedness; Fast Offerings; Humanitarian Services; Self-Sufficiency (Self-Reliance); Social Services; Welfare; Welfare Farms; Welfare Services; Welfare Square; Work, Role of.

17. *Construction and architecture of Church buildings*: Architecture; Building Program; City Planning; Meetinghouses; Temples*.

18. *Books and materials on Church history*: Almanacs; *Comprehensive History of the Church, A*; History of the Church*; *History of the Church* (History of Joseph Smith); History, Significance to LDS: Joseph Smith—History; *Journal of Discourses*; Legal and Judicial History of the Church.

19. *Symbols, celebrations, observances, and dedications*: Angel Moroni Statue; Beehive Symbol; Burial; Celebrations; Centennial Observances; Ceremonies; Christmas; Christus Statue; Dedications; Easter; Pioneer Day; Pioneer Life and Worship; Symbols, Cultural and Artistic; Temple Square; "This Is the Place" Monument; Vocabulary, LDS.

20. *Worship practices and Church activities*: Activity in the Church; Callings; Centennial Observances; Conferences*; Confidential Records; Dedications; Family Home Evening; Fast and Testimony Meeting; Fellowshipping Members; Firesides; Home Teaching; Hymns and Hymnody; Inspiration; Joining the Church; Laying on of Hands; Leadership Training; Meetings, Major Church; Membership; Music; Pioneer Life and Worship; Policies, Practices, and Procedures; Preaching the Gospel; Primary; Public Speaking; Relief Society; Reverence; Sacrament; Sacrament Meeting; Setting Apart; Single Adults; Solemn Assemblies; Sports; Sunday School; Temple Ordinances; Visiting Teaching; Word of Wisdom; Young Men; Young Women.

B. **Church members as they are perceived by others and as they relate to other churches and groups.**

1. *Anti-LDS beliefs, publications, and legal actions*: Anti-Mormon Publications; Antipolygamy Legislation; Cult; "Fundamentalists"; Reynolds v. United States; Sect; Smoot Hearings; Stereotyping of Mormons.

2. *Church beliefs and practices in selected areas shared with other groups in society*: Agency; Animals; Archaeology; Astronomy, Scriptural References to; Blacks; Blessing on

Food; Brotherhood; Catholicism and Mormonism; Chaplains; Children*; Church and State; Church in the World; Civic Duties; Civil Rights; Communion; Community; Compassionate Service; Constitution of the United States of America; Constitutional Law; Diplomatic Relations; Economic Aid; Education*; Emergency Preparedness; Equality; Ethics; Family History, Genealogy; Family Organizations; Fate; Fatherhood; Forgeries of Historical Documents; Freedom; Gentiles; Gentiles, Fulness of; Home; Humanitarian Services; Individuality; Interfaith Relationships*; Jews; Law; Lifestyle; Love; Mankind; Matter; Men, Roles of; Military and the Church; Minorities; Mormonism, An Independent Interpretation; Mormonism, Mormons; Motherhood; Music; Native Americans; Natural Man; Nature, Law of; Non-Mormons, Social Relations with; Origin of Man; "Peculiar" People; Philosophy; Politics*; Poverty, Attitudes toward; Press and Publications; Press, News Media and the Church; Protestant Reformation; Protestantism; Public Communications; Public Relations; Purpose of Earth Life*; Race, Racism; Religious Experience; Religious Freedom; Reorganized Church of Jesus Christ of Latter Day Saints; Restorationism, Protestant; Schismatic Groups; Science and Religion; Science and Scientists; Scouting; Senior Citizens; Single Adults; Social Services: Socialization; Societies and Organizations; Society; United States of America; Unity; Values, Transmission of; Volunteerism; War and Peace; Wealth, Attitudes toward; Welfare Services; Woman Suffrage; Women, Roles of*; Women's Topics; Word of Wisdom; Work, Role of; World Religions*; Worldliness.

3. *The position of the Church on some of the traditional teachings of Christianity*: Aaronic Priesthood; Apocalyptic Texts; Apocrypha and Pseudepigrapha; Apostasy; Apostate; Armageddon; Articles of Faith; Christians and Christianity; Christology; Clergy; Confession of Sins; Creation, Creation Accounts; Creeds; Cross; Cult; Damnation; Deification, Early Christian; Devils; Divorce; Epistemology; Foreknowledge of God; Foreordination; Garden of Eden; Godhead; Grace; Heaven; Hell; Immaculate Conception; Infant Baptism*; Isaiah*; Israel*; James, Epistle of; Jesus Christ*; John, Revelations of; John the Baptist; John the Beloved; Joseph of Egypt*; Judgment Day, Final; Justice and Mercy; Justification; Last Days; Law of Moses; Laying on of Hands; Levitical Priesthood; Light of Christ; Lord's Prayer; Malachi, Prophecies of; Mary, Mother of Jesus; Melchizedek; Melchizedek Priesthood; Metaphysics; Millenarianism; Millennium; Miracles; Moses; Mother in Israel; Mount of Transfiguration; Mysteries of God; Name of God; Name of the Church; New and Everlasting Covenant; Omnipotent God, Omnipresence of God, Omniscience of God; Origin of Man; Original Sin; Orthodoxy, Heterodoxy, and Heresy;

Paradise; Peter; Predestination; Rebaptism; Reincarnation; Sacrament; Sacrifice; Sacrifice in Biblical Times; Saints; Salvation; Salvation of the Dead; Sanctification; Science and Religion; Scripture; Scripture, Interpretation Within Scripture; Second Coming of Jesus Christ; Sect; Sermon on the Mount; Seventy; Sick, Blessing the; Sign Seeking; Signs; Signs as Divine Witness; Signs of the Times; Signs of the True Church; Sin; Sons of Perdition; Soul; Spirit; Spirit Body; Spirit of Prophecy; Spirit World; Spiritual Death; Teaching the Gospel; Ten Commandments; Testimony Bearing; Testimony of Jesus Christ; Theodicy; Theogony; Theology; Transfiguration; Translated Beings; Truth; Unpardonable Sin; Virgin Birth; War in Heaven; Washing of Feet; Works; Worship; Wrath of God; Zion.

4. *The position of the Church on moral and other sensitive issues related directly to society*: Abortion; Abuse, Spouse and Child; Adultery; AIDS; Alcoholic Beverages and Alcoholism; Artificial Insemination; Autopsy; Birth Control; Blacks; Blood Transfusions; Capital Punishment; Celibacy; Chastity, Law of; Coffee; Conscientious Objection; Cremation; Divorce; Drugs, Abuse of; Evolution; Feminism; Gambling; Health, Attitudes Toward; Homosexuality; Lifestyle; Magic; Modesty; Modesty in Dress; Murder; Organ Transplants and Donations; Policies, Practices, and Procedures; Pornography; Poverty, Attitudes Toward; Premarital Sex; Procreation; Profanity; Prohibition; Prolonging Life; Race, Racism; Reincarnation; Satanism; Sex Education; Sexuality; Sterilization; Stillborn Children; Suicide; Tea; Tobacco; Values, Transmission of; War and Peace; Wealth, Attitudes Toward; Welfare Services; Women, Roles of*; Work, Role of.

5. *Business and financial interests of the Church*: Business*; Computer Systems; Deseret Book Company; Economic History of the Church; Finances of the Church; Financial Contributions; LDS Foundation.

C. **Studies comparing Church members with others, including the vital statistics (demographics) of the Church and its members.**

1. *Studies comparing Church members with others*: Activity in the Church; Latter-day Saints (LDS); Medical Practices; Occupational Status; Social and Cultural History; Social Characteristics; Social Services.

2. *Vital statistics (demographics) of the Church and its members*: Vital Statistics.

KEY TO ABBREVIATIONS

AF	Talmage, James E. *Articles of Faith*. Salt Lake City, 1890. (All references are to pagination in printings before 1960).
CHC	*Comprehensive History of the Church*, 6 vols., ed. B. H. Roberts. Salt Lake City, 1930.
CR	*Conference Reports*. Salt Lake City, 1898–.
CWHN	*Collected Works of Hugh Nibley*, ed. S. Ricks, J. Welch, et al. Salt Lake City, 1985–.
Dialogue	*Dialogue: A Journal of Mormon Thought*, 1965–.
DS	Smith, Joseph Fielding. *Doctrines of Salvation*, 3 vols. Salt Lake City, 1954–1956.
ER	*Encyclopedia of Religion*, 16 vols., ed. M. Eliade. New York, 1987.
F.A.R.M.S.	Foundation for Ancient Research and Mormon Studies. Provo, Utah.
HC	*History of the Church*, 7 vols., ed. B. H. Roberts. Salt Lake City, 1st ed., 1902; 2nd ed., 1950. (All references are to pagination in the 2nd edition.)
HDC	Historical Department of the Church, Salt Lake City.
IE	*Improvement Era*, 1897–1970.
JC	Talmage, James E. *Jesus the Christ*. Salt Lake City, 1915.
JD	*Journal of Discourses*, 26 vols., ed. J. Watt. Liverpool, 1854–1886.
JST	*Joseph Smith Translation of the Bible*.
MD	McConkie, Bruce R. *Mormon Doctrine*, 2nd ed. Salt Lake City, 1966.
MFP	*Messages of the First Presidency*, 5 vols., ed. J. Clark. Salt Lake City, 1965–1975.
PJS	*Papers of Joseph Smith*, ed. D. Jessee. Salt Lake City, 1989.
PWJS	*The Personal Writings of Joseph Smith*, ed. D. Jessee. Salt Lake City, 1984.
T&S	*Times and Seasons*, 1839–1846.
TPJS	*Teachings of the Prophet Joseph Smith*, comp. Joseph Fielding Smith. Salt Lake City, 1938.
WJS	*Words of Joseph Smith*, ed. A. Ehat and L. Cook. Provo, Utah, 1980.

A

AARON, BROTHER OF MOSES

Aaron was a son of Amram and Jochebed of the tribe of Levi (Ex. 6:20), and a brother of Moses and Miriam (Ex. 4:14; 15:20). God directed him to meet his brother at the "mount of God" (Ex. 4:27–28), and appointed him spokesman for Moses (Ex. 4:14–16; 7:1–2; 2 Ne. 3:17). The AARONIC PRIEST-HOOD, or lesser priesthood in The Church of Jesus Christ of Latter-day Saints, takes its name from Aaron.

While the Israelites were encamped at Sinai, Aaron, two of his sons, and seventy elders accompanied Moses to the holy mountain, where they saw God (Ex. 24:1, 9–11). Aaron and his sons were called by God through the prophet Moses to serve in the priest's office (Ex. 28:1), Aaron becoming the "high," or chief, priest over the Levitical order (Num. 3:32). His call from God through a prophet is used as an example for all who receive any PRIESTHOOD appointment of God (Heb. 5:4). He held the MELCHIZEDEK PRIESTHOOD, but as chief priest of the lesser priesthood he served in a lesser position equivalent to that of the modern Presiding Bishop (John Taylor, *Items on the Priesthood*, p. 5, Salt Lake City, 1881). Direct descendants of the firstborn son of Aaron have a legal right to the presidency of this priesthood (i.e., BISHOP; D&C 68:15–18; 107:16–17), but such an appointment

requires a call from the FIRST PRESIDENCY of the Church (D&C 68:20).

Aaron was not privileged to enter the land of promise (Num. 20:7–13). Malachi prophesied that, in the latter days, the sons of Levi—which would include Aaron's descendants—would again offer an offering in righteousness (Mal. 3:1–3; cf D&C 13:1). Moreover, all who receive both the Aaronic and Melchizedek priesthoods and magnify their CALLINGS through sacrifice and righteous lives are spoken of as the sons of Moses and of Aaron (D&C 84:18, 27, 30–32, 34).

BIBLIOGRAPHY

Palmer, Lee A. *Aaronic Priesthood Through the Centuries*. Salt Lake City, 1964.

EDWARD J. BRANDT

AARONIC PRIESTHOOD

POWERS AND OFFICES

The two divisions of PRIESTHOOD in The Church of Jesus Christ of Latter-day Saints are the Aaronic and the Melchizedek. Young men twelve to eighteen years of age, and older men who are new converts, are ordained to offices in the Aaronic Priesthood, "which holds the keys [governing or

1

delegating authority] of the ministering of angels, and of the gospel of repentance, and of baptism by immersion for the remission of sins" (D&C 13). It is the priesthood authority by which JOHN THE BAPTIST prepared the way for Jesus Christ, teaching faith, repentance, and baptism for the remission of sins (Matt. 3:1–17; Mark 1:1–11; Luke 1:5–80; John 1:15–34; Acts 8:14–17; D&C 84:25–28). The Aaronic Priesthood does not have the power to confer the Holy Ghost (Matt. 3:11; Mark 1:7–8; John 1:33–34; JS—H 1:70) or to administer totally the affairs of the kingdom of God. It is power and authority God has given to man to prepare him and those to whom he ministers to receive the greater power, authority, and blessings of the MELCHIZEDEK PRIESTHOOD.

Distinctive LDS insights into the origins of the Aaronic Priesthood stem from modern revelations indicating that when Moses led Israel out of Egypt, the Lord purposed to confer upon worthy men of all tribes the higher Melchizedek Priesthood. Disobedience and loss of faith and worthiness, however, caused the Israelites to harden their hearts against the Lord and Moses. Therefore, the Lord eventually

> took Moses out of their midst, and the Holy Priesthood also; and the lesser priesthood continued, which priesthood holdeth the key of the ministering of angels and the preparatory gospel; which gospel is the gospel of repentance and of baptism, and the remission of sins, and the law of carnal commandments, which the Lord in his wrath caused to continue with the house of Aaron among the children of Israel until John [the Baptist], whom God raised up [D&C 84:25–27].

The Israelites, unwilling to abide by the higher law of the fulness of the gospel with its greater priesthood, were given the law of carnal commandments, as a portion of the LAW OF MOSES, with its emphasis on offering symbolic, redemptive sacrifices to prepare them to receive the divine Redeemer, and they were given the lesser priesthood to administer that law. The Lord called AARON and his sons to be the priests and preside over this lesser priesthood (Num. 8). Only direct descendants of Aaron could be ordained priests. The firstborn among the sons of Aaron would preside over the other priests. To assist Aaron and his posterity, particularly with the tabernacle and the preparing and offering of sacrifices, the Lord also called other male members of the tribe of Levi (not of the family of Aaron) to receive and carry out assignments in the lesser priesthood (Num. 3:5–13). The Le-

vites held lesser offices of the Aaronic Priesthood and functioned under the keys or directive authority of that priesthood conferred upon Aaron and his sons (Widtsoe, pp. 12–17). Hence, the lesser priesthood was called the Aaronic Priesthood, after Aaron, but a portion of that priesthood was also called the LEVITICAL PRIESTHOOD because all those to whom it was given belonged to the tribe of Levi. This type of priesthood organization and service continued in Israel until Jesus Christ came.

John the Baptist, a descendant of Aaron through both parents and thus a Levite, was the son of Zacharias, a righteous priest in Israel at the time of the birth of Christ. It was this John whom God chose to prepare the way for Christ's ministry on earth. From John's birth his mission was set and his priesthood functions anticipated (D&C 84:28; Luke 1:5–17).

After being baptized by John, Jesus called his apostles (some of them from among John's disciples) and ordained them (John 15:16); later he conferred upon Peter, James, and John the keys of the kingdom of God and a higher priesthood (see MOUNT OF TRANSFIGURATION). Following his death, resurrection, and ascension, Christ continued to direct his Church by giving commandments to the apostles through the power of the Holy Ghost (Acts 1:2) and through the authority of the higher Melchizedek Priesthood that he had conferred upon them. After the death of the apostles there followed a general apostasy, during which many gospel principles were lost and all the powers of the priesthood were withdrawn from the earth (2 Thes. 2:1–4; 2 Tim. 3:1–5).

On May 15, 1829, John the Baptist appeared to Joseph Smith and Oliver Cowdery as a resurrected messenger from God and conferred the ancient "Priesthood of Aaron" upon them (D&C 13). As the organization of the Church proceeded through the following months and years, many male members received the Aaronic Priesthood and were organized into quorums of priests, teachers, and deacons. In the Restoration, the Aaronic Priesthood has not been restricted to those who are literal descendants of Aaron or of Levi, since those lineages are not at present identified and the priesthood authority that implemented the ordinances of the law of Moses has been replaced by the higher priesthood and laws and ordinances of the gospel of Jesus Christ. Beginning with the reorganization of the priesthood in 1877, the Church established the current practice of ordaining boys to the Aaronic Priesthood during their early teenage years, organizing them at the ward level into PRIESTHOOD QUORUMS by age group and PRIESTHOOD OFFICE, and advancing them periodically to higher offices and eventually to the higher priesthood. The BISHOP of each ward presides over the Aaronic Priesthood in the ward.

Over the Aaronic Priesthood, the "president is to be a bishop; for this is one of the duties of this priesthood" (D&C 107:88), but bishops are also ordained high priests of the Melchizedek Priesthood because they preside and are not literal descendants of Aaron. The other three offices of the Aaronic Priesthood are deacon, teacher, and priest. Under the direction of the bishop, someone with proper authority confers the Aaronic Priesthood upon a worthy young man when he is twelve years old, ordaining him to the office of deacon. If he remains faithful and worthy, he is ordained to the office of teacher when he is fourteen years old and is given additional responsibilities. If he continues to remain faithful and worthy, he is ordained to the office of priest in the Aaronic Priesthood when he is sixteen years old, again receiving increased responsibilities. As young men progress in the priesthood, they retain all the rights and duties of lower offices.

The Lord has instructed the Church that bearers of the priesthood be organized into quorums (D&C 107:85–88). Some reasons for this are to establish order, to facilitate effective instruction in gospel principles and priesthood duties, and to prepare them for greater service and leadership in the Church. In the Aaronic Priesthood, a president and two counselors, chosen from the quorum members, preside over each quorum of deacons and teachers. This presidency is set apart (given powers of presidency) to preside over, sit in council with, and teach the members of the quorum their duty. The bishop is president of the priests quorum. He selects one or more boys as leaders under his presiding leadership and trains them to direct the other members of the quorum. Though the bishop and his two counselors in the bishopric hold all of the keys of the Aaronic Priesthood for the ward, the bishop usually calls an adult adviser to help train the boy leaders and to help instruct quorum members. However, the adviser has no presiding authority.

Thus the Aaronic Priesthood continues in its role as a preparatory priesthood, training young men in gospel principles and priesthood powers as they mature in service related to the preparatory gospel: faith in the Lord Jesus Christ, repentance, baptism for the remission of sins, and love of God and fellow beings. These responsibilities are most evident as the young men prepare, bless, and pass the SACRAMENT of the Lord's Supper each Sabbath day in the SACRAMENT MEETINGS of the Church and as they otherwise assist the bishop in serving the people of the ward.

Today the Aaronic Priesthood gives young men experience and prepares them to receive the Melchizedek Priesthood when they are eighteen years old, with the greater privileges and responsibilities of its oath and covenant (D&C 84:33–40). The Melchizedek Priesthood increases their capacity to serve, perform the saving ordinances of the gospel, and direct the Church when called to do so.

A major activity program for Aaronic Priesthood boys in many areas of the world is SCOUTING. To effectively correlate priesthood and scouting activities, the bishop organizes the YOUNG MEN program in the ward. An adult man is called to serve as president of the Young Men under the bishop's direction. Where scouting is organized, he and his two counselors generally also serve as the scout leaders. In wards with many boys, additional adults may be called to assist in the scouting program.

The bishop also organizes the girls of the ward into a YOUNG WOMEN program, with adult women advisers, and in age groups that correspond with ages of boys in Aaronic Priesthood quorums. Joint activities are planned and carried out regularly with the young men of the Aaronic Priesthood.

[*For a more detailed history of the Aaronic Priesthood, see also* Bishop, History of.]

BIBLIOGRAPHY

Hartley, William G. "The Priesthood Reorganization of 1877: Brigham Young's Last Achievement." *BYU Studies* 20 (Fall 1979):3–36.

McConkie, Oscar W. *Aaronic Priesthood*. Salt Lake City, 1977.

Palmer, Lee A. *Aaronic Priesthood Through the Centuries*. Salt Lake City, 1964.

Widtsoe, John A. *Priesthood and Church Government*, revised ed. Salt Lake City, 1954.

VERDON W. BALLANTYNE

RESTORATION

On May 15, 1829, JOHN THE BAPTIST appeared to Joseph SMITH and Oliver COWDERY near Harmony, Pennsylvania, and bestowed the Aaronic Priesthood on them (*see* AARONIC PRIESTHOOD:

POWERS AND OFFICES). This ordination gave the two men AUTHORITY to baptize (see BAPTISM), and they immediately performed that ORDINANCE for one another in the Susquehannah River. The Prophet Joseph Smith had received no previous REVELATIONS authorizing him to baptize; to perform that ordinance properly required specific authorization from God. The return of John to bestow the Aaronic Priesthood confirmed that divine authority had been lost from the earth and that a heavenly visitation was necessary to restore it.

Joseph Smith and Oliver Cowdery were engaged in translating the Book of Mormon (see BOOK OF MORMON TRANSLATION BY JOSEPH SMITH) at the Prophet's homestead on the Susquehannah River in Harmony when the question of baptism arose. A passage in 3 Nephi 11 (see BOOK OF MORMON: THIRD NEPHI), in which the resurrected Savior instructed the Nephites on the subject, led the two men to wonder about their own baptism. Determining to pray about it, they went to the woods, where, as Oliver later recounted, "on a sudden, as from the midst of eternity, the voice of the Redeemer spake peace to us, while the veil was parted and the angel of God came down clothed with glory, and delivered the anxiously looked for message, and the keys of the Gospel of repentance" (JS—H 1:71n). Joseph said that the angel placed his hands on them and ordained them, saying: "Upon you my fellow servants, in the name of Messiah, I confer the Priesthood of Aaron, which holds the keys of the ministering of angels, and of the gospel of repentance, and of baptism by immersion for the remission of sins; and this shall never be taken again from the earth until the sons of Levi do offer again an offering unto the Lord in righteousness" (JS—H 1:69; D&C 13).

The angel informed them that the Aaronic Priesthood did not have the power of laying on of hands for the GIFT OF THE HOLY GHOST, but that that authority would be given to them later. He told Joseph to baptize Oliver, and Oliver to baptize Joseph, and each to ordain the other to the Aaronic Priesthood. The messenger said "that his name was John, the same that is called John the Baptist in the New Testament, and that he acted under the direction of Peter, James and John, who held the keys of the Priesthood of Melchizedek," which would be conferred later (JS—H 1:72; see MELCHIZEDEK PRIESTHOOD: RESTORATION).

In the time of Jesus, John the Baptist preached repentance to the Jews and baptized in the Jordan River. He baptized Jesus (Matt. 3:13–17; cf. 2 Ne. 31:4–13). John was a direct descendant of AARON, through both his priestly father Zacharias and his mother Elisabeth, one of the "daughters of Aaron" (Luke 1:5). A later revelation to Joseph Smith said that an angel bestowed authority on John to perform his earthly mission when he was eight days old (D&C 84:28).

By ordination and calling, John the Baptist held the KEYS of the Aaronic Priesthood. These include the keys of the "ministering of angels," meaning that holders of the Aaronic Priesthood are eligible to have angels minister to them. This priesthood also has the keys of the preparatory gospel, which embraces the "gospel of repentance and of baptism, and the remission of sins, and the law of carnal commandments" (D&C 84:27).

As others were also to enjoy the blessings associated with baptism for the remission of sins administered under priesthood authority, a revelation was given in 1829 regarding the exact words and procedure that were to be followed in conducting the ordinance for those who repent and ask for baptism.

> Behold ye shall go down & stand in the water & in my name shall ye baptize them. And now behold these are the words which ye shall say calling them by name saying, Having authority given me of Jesus Christ I baptize you in the name of the Father & the Son & of the Holy Ghost Amen. And then shall ye immerse them in water [Cowdery, 1829 Ms.].

In the LDS Church today, only those having either the office of priest in the Aaronic Priesthood or the Melchizedek Priesthood may baptize people.

Monuments commemorating the restoration of the Aaronic Priesthood have been erected at TEMPLE SQUARE, Salt Lake City (1958), and in Harmony, Pennsylvania (1960).

BIBLIOGRAPHY

Cowdery, Oliver. "Written in the year of our Lord & Savior 1829—A True copy of the articles of the Church of Christ." Ms. in handwriting of Oliver Cowdery, LDS Church Archives.

McConkie, Oscar W. *Aaronic Priesthood.* Salt Lake City, 1977.

Palmer, Lee A. *The Aaronic Priesthood Through the Centuries.* Salt Lake City, 1964.

Porter, Larry C. "The Priesthood Restored." In *Studies in Scripture,* ed. R. Millet and K. Jackson, Vol. 2, pp. 389–409. Salt Lake City, 1985.

LARRY C. PORTER

ABEL

Latter-day scripture reveals much about Abel beyond what is contained in the Bible. He and CAIN had older brothers and sisters (Moses 5:2), and Abel "was a keeper of sheep" (Gen. 4:2; Moses 5:17). To his parents, the Lord had given "commandments, that they should worship the Lord their God, and should offer the firstlings of their flocks, for an offering unto the Lord" (Moses 5:5). ADAM and EVE were obedient to the Lord's commands (Moses 5:6), and Abel also "hearkened unto the voice of the Lord. . . . And the Lord had respect unto Abel, and to his offering" (Moses 5:17, 20). On the other hand, Cain specifically at Satan's behest brought an unacceptable offering (Moses 5:18–19, 21; cf. *TPJS*, pp. 58–60).

The book of Moses clarifies the Lord's differing responses to Abel and Cain, and indicates that Adam and Eve had taught their children about the things of God: "And Adam and Eve . . . made all things [of God] known unto their sons and their daughters" (Moses 5:12). Subsequently, Abel "walked in holiness before the Lord" (Moses 5:26), but Cain "loved Satan more than God" (Moses 5:18). When his offering was not accepted, Cain "rejected the greater counsel which was had from God" and "listened not any more to the voice of the Lord, neither to Abel, his brother" (Moses 5:25–26). When Satan promised Cain that "I will deliver thy brother Abel into thine hands," Cain exulted "that I may murder and get gain" (Moses 5:29–31; cf. Hel. 6:27). As a result, Cain "rose up against Abel his brother, and slew him" (Gen. 4:8; Moses 5:32), and said, "I am free; surely the flocks of my brother falleth into my hands" (Moses 5:33). The unconscionable nature of Cain's murder of Abel is underscored by the fact that thereafter "Cain was shut out from the presence of the Lord" (Moses 5:41).

The New Testament affirms Abel's faithfulness and obedience to God: "By faith Abel offered unto God a more excellent sacrifice than Cain, by which he obtained witness that he was righteous, God testifying of his gifts: and by it he being dead yet speaketh" (Heb. 11:4). Joseph SMITH taught that "God spoke to [Abel]: indeed it is said that God talked with him; and if He did, would He not, seeing that Abel was righteous, deliver to him the whole plan of the Gospel? . . . How could Abel offer a sacrifice and look forward with faith on the Son of God, for a remission of his sins, and not

understand the Gospel?" (*TPJS*, p. 59; cf. Moses 5:6–12). Latter-day scripture also states that the priesthood among the ancients had been passed down through Abel, who was ordained by Adam (D&C 84:6–17).

BIBLIOGRAPHY

McConkie, Bruce R. *A New Witness for the Articles of Faith*, pp. 167–68, 340, 658–59. Salt Lake City, 1985.

STEVEN D. BENNION

ABINADI

Abinadi was a courageous prophet (150 B.C.), and the best known martyr in the Book of Mormon. His ministry and execution recounted at the heart of the Book of Mosiah sharpen the contrast between righteous King BENJAMIN and wicked King Noah. ALMA₁, a converted eyewitness, recorded Abinadi's main words shortly after they were spoken (Mosiah 17:4).

Abinadi belonged to a small group of reactionary NEPHITES who had returned from Zarahemla a generation earlier to repossess from the LAMANITES the city of Nephi, the traditional Nephite capital, and its temple. When the excesses of the apostate Nephite king and priests grew intolerable, Abinadi was commanded of the Lord to denounce publicly their abominations; he prophesied their coming captivity and affliction. Abinadi was condemned to death by Noah for this, but escaped.

Where he lived in exile is unknown. Similarities between his and Benjamin's words (cf. Mosiah 16:1; 3:20; 16:5; 2:38; 16:10–11; 3:24–25) could mean that he spent some time in Zarahemla with king Benjamin and his people (W of M 1:16–17), or received similar revelation during this period.

After two years, having been commanded again by the Lord to prophesy, Abinadi reentered the city of Nephi in disguise. Before a crowd, he pronounced a curse in the name of the Lord upon the unrepentant people, their land, and their grain, with forthright predictions of destruction and humiliating bondage, reminiscent of Israel's suffering in Egypt. In a potent curse, like those used in the ancient Near East to condemn covenant breakers, he testified that Noah's life would "be valued even as a garment in a hot furnace" (Mosiah 12:3).

Abinadi was apprehended by the people, bound, delivered to Noah, and accused of lying about the king and prophesying falsely. Both accusations were violations under their law, the LAW OF MOSES (Mosiah 13:23; Ex. 20:16; Deut. 18:20–22). The dual nature of the charges appears to have complicated the ensuing trial, the king typically having jurisdiction over political charges, and the priests over religious matters.

The trial first focused on the charge of false prophecy. The priests challenged Abinadi to interpret Isaiah 52:7–10. They presumably thought this text showed that God had spoken "comfort" to their own people, who had seen the land "redeemed." They contended that whereas Isaiah extolled those who brought "good tidings," Abinadi spoke ill. Under such interpretation, Abinadi's curses conflicted with Isaiah and were held by the priests to be false and unlawful.

Abinadi rebutted the priests in several ways. He accused them of misunderstanding and disobeying the law. He extracted from them an admission that salvation requires obedience to the law and then rehearsed to them the TEN COMMANDMENTS, the basic law of the covenant that they had not kept. He miraculously withstood the king's attempt to silence him, "and his face shone with exceeding luster, even as Moses' did while in the mount of Sinai" (Mosiah 13:5). He then quoted Isaiah 53 and explained its relation to the coming MESSIAH.

Abinadi's prophetic words are among the most powerful in the Book of Mormon. He explained the "form" and coming of God mentioned in Isaiah 52:14 and 53:2 (Mosiah 13:34; 14:2) as the coming of a son in the flesh, thus "being the Father and the Son" (Mosiah 15:1–5). He also taught that God would suffer as the "sheep before her shearers" (Isa. 53:7; Mosiah 14:7). Abinadi was then in a position to answer the priests' question about Isaiah 52:7–10. He proclaimed that those "who shall declare his generation" (cf. Mosiah 15:10) and "publish peace" (Mosiah 15:14) are God's prophets and that they and all who hearken unto their words are his "seed" (Mosiah 15:11, 13). They are the ones who truly bring "good tidings" of salvation, redemption, comfort through Christ, and the reign of God at the Judgment Day.

Using Isaiah's text, Abinadi showed that God could not redeem Noah's people who had willfully rebelled against deity, and that true redemption comes only through repentance and acceptance of Christ. He also showed that his prophecies did not contradict the Isaiah text quoted by the priests.

Noah desired that Abinadi should be put to death, evidently on the charge of bearing false witness against him as the king. A young priest named Alma valiantly attested to the truthfulness of Abinadi's testimony, whereupon he was expelled and the trial recessed for three days while Abinadi was held in prison.

When the trial reconvened, Abinadi was presumably accused of blasphemy (Mosiah 17:8), another capital offense under the law of Moses (Lev. 24:10–16). Noah gave him the opportunity to recant, but Abinadi refused to change God's message, even on threats of death.

Noah was intimidated and desired to release Abinadi. The priests, however, accused Abinadi of a fourth crime, that of reviling against the king (Mosiah 17:12; Ex. 22:28). On this ground Noah condemned Abinadi, and his priestly accusers scourged and burned him. It was normal under Mosaic law for the accusers to inflict the punishment, but burning was an extraordinary form of execution. It mirrored Abinadi's alleged crime: he was burned just as he had said Noah's life would be valued as a garment in a furnace. As Abinadi died, he prophesied that the same fate would befall his accusers. This prophecy was soon fulfilled (Mosiah 17:15–18; 19:20; Alma 25:7–12).

Abinadi was remembered by the Nephites in at least three roles:

1. To Alma, his main convert, Abinadi was a prophet of Christ. Alma taught Abinadi's words concerning the death and resurrection of Christ, the RESURRECTION of the dead, the redemption of God's people (Mosiah 18:1–2), and the mighty change of heart through their conversion (Alma 5:12). Through Alma's descendants, Abinadi influenced the Nephites for centuries.

2. To Ammon, who beheld the martyrdom of 1,005 of his own converts (Alma 24:22), Abinadi was recalled as the prime martyr "because of his belief in God" (Alma 25:11; cf. Mosiah 17:20; see also Mosiah 7:26–28). This was recognized as the real reason for Abinadi's death, since the priests' charge of reviling proved to be a false pretext.

3. To MORMON, who witnessed the decadence and destruction of the Nephites 500 years later, Abinadi was remembered for prophesying that because of wickedness evil would come upon the

land and that the wicked would be utterly destroyed (Morm. 1:19; cf. Mosiah 12:7–8).

BIBLIOGRAPHY

Welch, John W. "Judicial Process in the Trial of Abinadi." Provo, Utah, 1981.

LEW W. CRAMER

ABORTION

The Church of Jesus Christ of Latter-day Saints considers the elective termination of pregnancy "one of the most . . . sinful practices of this day" (*General Handbook of Instructions*, 11-4), although not necessarily murder. The Lord has said, "Thou shalt not . . . kill, nor do *anything* like unto it" (D&C 59:6; emphasis added in Packer, p. 85).

Members of the Church must not "submit to, be a party to, or perform an abortion" (*General Handbook*, 11-4). The only exceptions are where "incest or rape was involved, or where competent medical authorities certify that the life of the mother is in jeopardy, or that a severely defective fetus cannot survive birth" (Packer, p. 85). Even these exceptions do not justify abortion automatically. Church members are counseled that they should consider abortion in such cases only after consulting with their BISHOP and receiving divine confirmation through prayer.

"Church members who encourage, perform, or submit to an abortion are subject to Church discipline as appropriate" to help them repent (*General Handbook*, 11-4). As far as has been revealed, the sin of abortion is one for which a person may repent and gain forgiveness (*General Handbook*, 11-4; Packer, p. 86).

BIBLIOGRAPHY

General Handbook of Instructions. Salt Lake City, 1989.

Packer, Boyd K. "Covenants." *Ensign* 20 (Nov. 90):84–86.

MARY K. BEARD

ABRAHAM

Few biblical characters figure so prominently in LDS faith as does Abraham. Belief that he was a real person is shared by others, but the LDS approach is unique: Revelations received by the Prophet Joseph SMITH confirm the basic historicity of Genesis and add information echoed in ancient sources, many of which have emerged since his day.

The BOOK OF ABRAHAM as restored by Joseph SMITH autobiographically recounts Abraham's early life, explaining why he was singled out as the pivotal recipient of divine promises for the blessing of mankind. Not only had he been foreordained in PREMORTAL LIFE (Abr. 3:23; cf. *Apocalypse of Abraham* 22:1–5), but as a young man in Ur he opposed idolatry and human sacrifice, ironically turning him into an intended victim (Abr. 1:5–20; cf. *Genesis Rabbah* 38:13). The irony increases when God's last-minute rescue of Abraham foreshadowed what would transpire at Abraham's offering of Isaac.

After marrying SARAH and learning of his lineal right to the PATRIARCHAL ORDER OF THE PRIESTHOOD as disclosed in the "records of the fathers" (Abr. 1:2–4, 26, 31; 2:2; *Jubilees* 12:27; cf. D&C 107:40–57), Abraham traveled to Haran, where he apparently received his ORDINATION (Abr. 2:9–11; *WJS*, pp. 245, 303). He also saw the Lord, who gave him remarkable promises: Abraham would be blessed above measure; his posterity would carry the gospel to all nations; and all who received it would bear his name, be accounted his posterity, and bless him as their father (Abr. 2:6–11; cf. Gen. 12:1–3).

Accompanied by their converts, Abraham and Sarah proceeded to Canaan (Abr. 2:15; *Genesis Rabbah* 39:14). Famine soon forced them to Egypt, but not before God commanded Abraham to ask Sarah to pose as his sister (Abr. 2:22–25; *Genesis Apocryphon* 19:14–21), and then showed him a vision of the cosmos and creation so that he could teach these things to the Egyptians (Abr. 3–5; cf. *Sefer Yetsirah*).

The book of Abraham narrative ends here, but the book's last facsimile (no. 3) depicts Pharaoh—who traditionally claimed exclusive possession of priesthood and kingship (Abr. 1:25–27)—honoring Abraham's priesthood by allowing him to occupy the throne and instruct the court in astronomy (cf. *Pseudo-Eupolemus*; Josephus, *Antiquities* 1.viii.2). Pharaoh's recognition of Abraham's priesthood was unknown in any other ancient source until the 1947 discovery of the *Genesis Apocryphon*, purporting, like the book of Abraham, to contain an autobiographical account of Abraham but continuing the narrative into Egypt (*Genesis Apocryphon* 20:8–34): When Pharaoh took Sarah to the palace, Abraham tearfully appealed to God, who immediately protected her by afflicting Pharaoh. The affliction worsened, but Pharaoh finally had a dream of Abraham healing him; the patriarch was then summoned and, laying hands on Pharaoh's head, restored him to health. This is the only known instance in the Old Testament or related pseudepigrapha of a healing by LAYING ON OF HANDS, and it sets the stage for the book of Abraham scene. Together these two sources explain why the ancients considered Abraham's encounter with Pharaoh "a crucial event in the history of mankind" (Nibley, 1981 [citing Wacholder], p. 63).

But it was Sarah who had faced the most difficult dilemma in Egypt: If she honored both Abraham's request (by feigning maidenhood) and her marriage vows (by refusing Pharaoh's advances), she faced certain death. The alternative was simply to accept her new role with its dazzling wealth and influence. Sarah proved her loyalty at the peril of her life, and was—as were Abraham and Isaac—finally rescued by God. Her sacrifice demonstrated her equality with Abraham and their mutual dependence (*CWHN* 1:98; *IE* 73 [Apr. 1970]:79–95).

Later events of Abraham's life are illuminated by other LDS sources, as when Sarah, still childless after returning to Canaan, gave her maid Hagar to Abraham (Gen. 16:1–3) and thereby "administered unto Abraham according to the law" (D&C 132:65; see also verse 34)—congruent with now extant ancient Near Eastern sources describing the legal obligation of a childless wife. Sarah's action demonstrated, says one LDS Apostle, "her love and integrity to her husband" (*JD* 23:228) and was, says Philo, one of "numberless proofs" of her "wifely love. . . . Everywhere and always she was at his side, . . . his true partner in life and life's events, resolved to share alike the good and ill" (*On Abraham*, pp. xlii–xliii).

LDS sources further describe how Abraham was taught about Jesus Christ by MELCHIZEDEK (*TPJS*, pp. 322–23), who, as a prototype of Christ (JST Gen. 14:26–36; Alma 13:17–19), gave Abraham the PRIESTHOOD after the Order of the Son of God (*see* MELCHIZEDEK PRIESTHOOD; D&C 84:14; 107:2–4; cf. *Genesis Rabbah* 43:6) with accompanying temple ORDINANCES foreshadowing Christ (Abraham, Facsimile 2; Alma 13:2, 16; cf. *Cave of Treasures* [Budge], p. 148). Later, Abraham "looked forth and saw the days of the Son of Man,

and was glad" (JST Gen. 15:9–12; Hel. 8:17; John 8:56).

Abraham's supreme test—the offering of Isaac—both recalled Abraham's prior experience and typified things to come. Centuries before Jesus, a Book of Mormon prophet pointed to Abraham's offering of Isaac as "a similitude of God and his Only Begotten Son" (Jacob 4:4–5)—just as many Christian fathers would do retrospectively. Abraham's life thus typified and testified of his preeminent descendant Jesus, who, because he was also the Son of God, could atone for Abraham and all others.

Abraham's life also prefigured that of another descendant, Joseph Smith (D&C 132:30–31), whose prayer at age fourteen echoes young Abraham's prayer at the same age (*Jubilees* 11:16–17; JS—H 1:7–17). Both men had been foreordained; both received the priesthood, preached the gospel, and encountered formidable opposition; both spoke face to face with divine messengers and God himself; both possessed a URIM AND THUMMIM, translated ancient records, and wrote scripture; and both founded an influential community of saints.

But the connection is more direct. John TAYLOR reported that Abraham visited Joseph Smith (*JD* 20:174–75; 21:94), whose mission included revealing lost knowledge about Abraham (cf. 2 Ne. 3:7, 12) and whose entire ministry of RESTORATION helped fulfill Abraham's COVENANT that through his seed all nations would be blessed (2 Ne. 29:14; 3 Ne. 20:27, 29). A central purpose of that restoration is to make Abraham's promises effective for his descendants, who through temple ordinances may receive the blessings of Abraham and be sealed in an ancestral chain back to Abraham and Adam (D&C 2; *TPJS*, pp. 337–38).

To achieve the glory of Abraham, Latter-day Saints are commanded to come to Christ by "do[ing] the works of Abraham," whose life constitutes a pattern (D&C 132:32; cf. Isa. 51:1–2; John 8:39; *Koran* 16:120–23). These works begin with BAPTISM and reception of the HOLY GHOST, whereupon the recipient must "press forward" (2 Ne. 31:19–20) in righteousness, as did Abraham, by obeying God, receiving the priesthood and temple ordinances, honoring covenants, building a family unit, teaching children, keeping sacred records, preaching the gospel, and proving faithful in opposition (Abr. 1–2; Gen. 12–25). Progression along this path brings increased identification with

Abraham and Sarah and the blessings promised to them. For example, anyone who is not a descendant of Abraham but receives the Holy Ghost becomes the SEED OF ABRAHAM (*TPJS*, pp. 149–50; Abr. 2:10; cf. Gal. 3:29), while each man magnifying the Melchizedek Priesthood likewise becomes Abraham's seed (D&C 84:33–34). And each couple married eternally in the temple is promised the blessings of Abraham—posterity as the stars of heaven and sand of the seashore, meaning an eternal increase of posterity in the CELESTIAL KINGDOM (D&C 132:30; *JD* 11:151–52; 15:320).

Such blessings of innumerable posterity were promised to Abraham on several occasions (Abr. 3:13–14; Gen. 13:16; 15:5; 17:2, 6), but it was not until he demonstrated his willingness to offer Isaac as a sacrifice that the Lord guaranteed the promises (Gen. 22:16–18), showing, explains Joseph Smith, that any person who would attain ETERNAL LIFE "must sacrifice all things" (*TPJS*, p. 322). Accordingly, the Lord's people must be "tried, even as Abraham," to become sanctified through Abraham's descendant Christ (D&C 101:4–5; Moro. 10:33) in preparation to "sit down in the kingdom of God, with Abraham" and Sarah (Alma 5:24) on thrones of glory to inherit the same blessings of EXALTATION already enjoyed by that exemplary couple (D&C 132:34–37; cf. *Testament of Isaac* 2:5–7).

BIBLIOGRAPHY

Kimball, Spencer W. "The Example of Abraham." *Ensign* 6 (June 1975):3–7.

Nibley, Hugh. "A New Look at the Pearl of Great Price." *IE* 71–73 (Jan. 1968–May 1970), a series of articles covering two years.

———. *Abraham in Egypt.* Salt Lake City, 1981.

E. DOUGLAS CLARK

ABRAHAM, GOSPEL OF

See: Gospel of Abraham

ABRAHAMIC COVENANT

The divine archetypal covenant, of which Abraham's covenant is an example, is the everlasting covenant of the GOSPEL OF JESUS CHRIST. By accepting the gospel, humankind can be redeemed from the doom of death and the blight of sin to enjoy ETERNAL LIFE with God.

Abraham's mission was not new; it was like the mission of Adam, Enoch, and Noah. The same divine power—or PRIESTHOOD—that gave them authority to promulgate the covenant of divine redemption for God's children in their time was renewed with Abraham and his seed; it was explicitly to be perpetuated by him and his literal and spiritual heirs for all time (Gen. 12:1–3; Abr. 1:18–19; 2:6, 9–11).

ABRAHAM'S IMPLEMENTATION OF THE COVENANT MISSION From the records of his forefathers, Abraham learned of the true and living God and the saving priesthood powers. Although his immediate ancestors had fallen away from the gospel, he desired and received that true priesthood from Melchizedek, with its powers and responsibilities (Abr. 1:1–7, 18, 19, 31; D&C 84:14; Alma 13:14–19; Gen. 14:18–20).

The idolatrous Chaldeans had rejected Abraham and placed him to be sacrificed on an altar (Abr. 1:5–12); but the Lord rescued him and directed him to leave his home in Ur for a new land of promise (Gen. 11:27–32; 12:1–3; Abr. 1:1, 17; 2:1–5). Abraham took other family members with him to a place they named Haran, where he won additional converts to the way of the Lord. With them he departed to undertake his ministry in the land promised to him and to all his descendants who would hearken to the voice of the Lord (Abr. 2:6, 14–20; Gen. 12:4–8).

Abraham and his company settled first in the Bethel area, built an altar, and proclaimed the name of the Lord—a procedure he perpetuated in the homes he established thereafter (Gen. 12:8; 13:4, 18). Near Bethel, the covenant promises and responsibilities were renewed, and CIRCUMCISION was made the token of the covenant, to remind all bearers to keep themselves pure and free from sin (Gen. 17). Abraham became a man of good repute (Gen. 14:13, 18–20; 23:1–16) and was trusted by God, who commended him, saying, "I know him, that he will command his children and his household after him, and they shall keep the way of the Lord, to do justice and judgment" (Gen. 18:19). The ultimate test and a revelation of the meaning of the redemptive covenant came to him in the divine requirement that, in anticipation of the sacrifice of the Savior, he be willing to sacrifice his own birthright son. He passed the test, his son was saved, and he learned how all may be saved by the divine Redeemer (Gen. 22:1–18; John 8:56; Jacob 4:5; Gal. 3:8).

PERPETUATION OF THE MISSION BY ABRAHAM'S HEIRS Abraham's lineal and spiritual successors learned to keep the covenant by the things they suffered. Their efforts sometimes prospered and their neighbors were impressed (Gen. 17:1–7; 26:1–5, 24–28; 28:13–22; 30:25–27; 32:24–29; 35:1–15; 39:1–6, 21–23; 40:8; 41:9–16, 37–42).

A PATRIARCHAL BLESSING given by Abraham's grandson Jacob (Israel) to his twelve sons indicated future covenant roles for his descendants, particularly those through Judah and Joseph (Gen. 49:10, 22–26).

In addition to Jacob's progeny, Abraham had descendants through Ishmael, the son of Hagar—Sarah's handmaiden. Of Ishmael's family, "twelve princes" are named who established "towns" and "nations" (Gen. 25:12–16). Six sons by Abraham's wife Keturah are also named among his families: Zimran, Jokshan, Medan, Midian, Ishbak, and Shuah (Gen. 25:2). To all these, he promised gifts before his death (Gen. 25:1–7), including spiritual gifts. One descendant, Jethro (or Reuel), priest of Midian, provided Moses with a wife, ordained him to the priesthood, and advised him in organizing, governing, and judging Israel (Ex. 2:16–22; 18:12–27; D&C 84:6–16). Scores of descendants of Esau, with their tribal leaders and kings, are also named (Gen. 36).

Today, millions claim Abraham as their father. All may have his covenant privileges if they will but do the works of Abraham. The Lord never told Abraham that he alone would be blessed by the covenant or that it would bless only his birthright seed; the charge was that in him and his seed all families of all nations should be blessed. All who accept the covenant of the divine Redeemer become Abraham's seed spiritually and receive the same blessings as his biological descendants (Gen. 12:1–3; Abr. 2:8–11; Gal. 3:7–9, 26–29; cf. John 8:33, 37, 39; Rom. 9:6–8).

THE ABRAHAMIC HERITAGE THROUGH MOSES AND THE PROPHETS The mission of Moses was to deliver the children of Israel from the bondage of slavery and death in Egypt and return them to the promised land. They were to enter the land only after the iniquity of the prior inhabitants had become so excessive that they were no longer worthy to retain it (1 Ne. 17:35; Gen. 15:13–16; 17:7–9; JST Gen. 17:4–7; Ex. 4:22–23; 6:1–8). Through

Moses, the Lord gave the Israelites laws, ordinances, statutes, and commandments to help them remember their duties to God and to make them a kingdom of priests, a holy people, and a peculiar treasure as God's exemplary servants (Ex. 19:1–6, 20ff; Deut. 4:1–6; Mosiah 13:27–30).

Israel did well in living according to the covenant in the last days of Moses and in the time of his successor, Joshua; but in the days of the judges and beyond, the Israelites lapsed into the ways of neighboring nations instead of following the moral and religious laws of the true God (Judg. 2:7–13; 17:6; 21:25). Because cycles of apostasy were repeated throughout Israel's history, the Israelites were periodically castigated by the prophets for their sins and called to repentance (e.g., Isa. 1:1–4; Hosea 4:1–6; Amos 3; Micah 3; Jer. 2; Ezek. 2).

Two themes dominate the messages of the Old Testament prophets: (1) the promised Redeemer would come, and though he would suffer rejection by many, he would establish the promised way of salvation for all; (2) in the last days the covenant of Abraham would be reestablished (Isa. 2:2–5, 11; 7:14–16; 9:1–7; 52:13–15, 53; Jer. 23:5–8; Ezek. 37:11–28; Dan. 9:21–27; Micah 5:2–5; Zech. 9:9–11; 11:10–13; 13:6; 14:4–9).

FULFILLMENT AND PERPETUATION The Redeemer did come, and the laws and prophecies prepared the faithful to receive him (Gal. 3:16–24, 25–29; Acts 2:47; 5:14; 1 Cor. 15:6). He accomplished his mission of personal teaching and sacrifice on earth and then commissioned the new Christian heirs of the covenant to make it known unto all the world (Matt. 24:14; 28:19–20; Mark 16:15–16). However, over a period of centuries, the priesthood power to administer the proper ordinances of the covenant and some vital facets of doctrine were lost. All these have now been restored in the latter-day dispensation of the gospel (D&C 110:11–16) and are again available to all families and nations of the earth.

BIBLIOGRAPHY

Brandt, Edward J. "The Covenants and Blessings of Abraham." Ensign 3 (Feb. 1973):42–43.

Kimball, Spencer W. Abraham: An Example to Fathers. Salt Lake City, 1977.

Nyman, Monte S. "Abraham, the Father of the Faithful." Sperry Lecture Series. Provo, Utah, 1975.

Topical Guide, "Abrahamic Covenant"; and Dictionary, "Abraham, Covenant of." In LDS Edition of the King James Version of the Bible. Salt Lake City, 1979.

ELLIS T. RASMUSSEN

ABUSE, SPOUSE AND CHILD

Abuse is behavior that deliberately threatens or injures another person. It may be physical, emotional, or sexual. Some forms of physical and emotional abuse include beatings, neglect, and threats of abandonment. While it also may take varied forms, sexual abuse of another adult usually involves the use of force or intimidation to coerce sexual activity. Sexual abuse of a child, on the other hand, includes any sexual behavior between the child and someone in a position of power, trust, or control (see *Child Abuse: Helps for Ecclesiastical Leaders*, Salt Lake City, 1985).

Individuals who abuse their spouses or children violate the laws of both God and society. Church leaders have counseled that even more subtle forms of abuse are evil—among them, shouting at or otherwise demeaning family members and demanding offensive intimate relations from one's spouse (Gordon B. Hinckley, "Keeping the Temple Holy," *Ensign* 20 [May 1990]:52). Church members guilty of abusing others are directed to seek the counsel of their BISHOPS and, where necessary, professional help. Church disciplinary procedures may need to be instituted to help abusers repent and to protect innocent persons.

While the causes of abuse are myriad and complex, all forms of abusive behavior are antithetical to the spirit of service and sacrifice exemplified in the life of the Savior Jesus Christ. Because it is often designed to control another person, abuse is inconsistent with AGENCY, which is central to God's PLAN OF SALVATION. In a revelation given in 1839, the Lord said, "No power or influence can or ought to be maintained by virtue of the priesthood, only by persuasion, by long-suffering, by gentleness and meekness, and by love unfeigned" (D&C 121:41). Abuse is a serious sin and cannot be ignored, but abusers can be forgiven when they truly repent.

BIBLIOGRAPHY

Hinckley, Gordon B. "To Please Our Heavenly Father." *Ensign* 15 (May 1985):48–51.

Monson, Thomas S. "A Little Child Shall Lead Them." *Ensign* 20 (May 1990):53–60.

Peterson, H. Burke. "Unrighteous Dominion." Ensign 19 (July 1989):6–11.

JEANNE B. INOUYE
ROBERT K. THOMAS

ACADEMIES

Between 1875 and 1910, the LDS Church sponsored thirty-three academies for secondary education in seven western states, Canada, and Mexico. Factors contributing to the development of the academy system were (1) the lack of public educational facilities in Utah before 1900; (2) the influx of a non-Mormon population with the accompanying establishment of academies by other denominations, schools that attracted many LDS youth; and (3) the need to provide schools in areas newly settled under the COLONIZATION program that the Church carried out in the western United States, Mexico, and Canada.

A typical academy experienced three phases of curricular development. Until about 1900, elementary subjects predominated, with some piecemeal additions of secondary and normal (teacher-training) courses. The curriculum provided basic academic subjects with an emphasis on vocational and cultural fields, including mechanical and agricultural skills, gymnastics, homemaking, vocal music, and art.

From 1900 to 1910 the academies offered more diversified secondary courses leading to terminal diplomas in preparation for vocations and missionary service. They featured enlarged academic departments and a broader offering including, dramatics, choirs, bands, orchestras, music clubs, debate societies, athletics, and sports. Normal courses were expanded to three and four years, and college-level classes made their appearance in a number of the schools.

After 1910 specialized courses were consolidated into standard four-year high school curricula, including much more extensive music and other cultural offerings than were found in the public high schools of the day. All of the schools served as cultural centers in their communities, sponsoring performances and sports involving much of the adult populace and importing artists, lecturers, and dramatic companies.

Some of these schools succumbed to the widespread economic depression following the Panic of 1893 and to the rise of public schools in UTAH TERRITORY after the free school act of 1890. Twenty-two of the academies, however, continued to thrive during the early twentieth century, constituting the only secondary schools in many LDS communities until after 1911.

By 1927 the Church had closed or turned over to the states all but eight of the academies. Six

Second Emery Stake Academy, c. 1911, in Castle Dale, in central Utah, that area's largest school at the time. The stakes of the Church built and operated about thirty-three academies mainly between 1875 and 1912.

remained as accredited normal schools or two-year colleges, one as a university, and one as a secondary school. By 1934 only three—BRIGHAM YOUNG UNIVERSITY, RICKS COLLEGE, and Juarez Academy—continued under Church sponsorship. All three are presently operating (1991).

Factors leading to closing or transferring the academies to state education systems included the burden of financing two competing systems as public high schools emerged and the success of church-sponsored SEMINARIES and INSTITUTES in supplementing secular education with religious training.

During the mid-twentieth century, schools similar in purpose and scope to the earlier academies were established in the South Pacific and elsewhere administered by the CHURCH EDUCATIONAL SYSTEM.

In 1953 legislation was passed in Utah as part of a cost-reduction effort to return Weber, Snow, and Dixie Colleges to the Church, but in a statewide referendum Utah voters rejected the proposal and the colleges remained with the state.

A list of some of the principal academies with their founding dates, locations, name changes, and 1991 status follows:

- Brigham Young Academy, 1875, Provo, Utah; became Brigham Young University in 1903; continues to the present.
- Brigham Young College, 1877, Logan, Utah; a four-year college briefly in 1903, but closed as a junior college in 1926.
- Salt Lake Stake Academy, 1886, Salt Lake City, Utah; a high school, known at various times as LDS High School, LDS University, and LDS College; closed in 1931 and transformed into LDS Business College, which continues today.
- St. George Stake Academy, 1888, St. George, Utah; Dixie Normal College, 1917; Dixie Junior College, 1923; state-operated Dixie College, 1933 to the present.
- Bannock Stake Academy, 1888, Rexburg, Idaho; Fremont Stake Academy, 1898; Ricks Academy, 1902; Ricks Normal College, 1917; Ricks Col-

lege, 1918; made a four-year college, 1948; a junior college, 1956 to the present.

- Sanpete Stake Academy, 1888, Ephraim, Utah; Snow Academy, 1900; Snow Normal College, 1917; Snow Junior College, 1923; Snow College, a state junior college, 1932 to the present.
- Weber Stake Academy, 1888, Ogden, Utah; Weber Academy, 1908; Weber Normal College, 1918; Weber College, 1922; a state junior college, 1922; a four-year college 1962; Weber State College, 1963; Weber State University, 1991.
- St. Joseph Stake Academy, 1891, Thatcher, Arizona; LDS Academy, 1898; Gila Academy, 1911; Gila Normal College, 1920; Gila Junior College, 1923; Eastern Arizona Junior College, 1932 to the present time.
- Juárez Stake Academy, 1897, Colonia Juárez, Mexico; Academia Juárez, 1963 to the present.

BIBLIOGRAPHY

Bennion, Milton Lynn. *Mormonism and Education*. Salt Lake City, 1939.

Jenson, Andrew. *Encyclopedic History of the Church of Jesus Christ of Latter-day Saints*. Salt Lake City, 1941. (Academies listed under latest titles.)

Laycock, Harold R. "A History of Music in the Academies of the Latter-day Saints Church, 1876–1926." D.M.A. diss., University of Southern California, 1961.

HAROLD R. LAYCOCK

ACCOUNTABILITY

In LDS doctrine, to be "accountable" means that one must answer to God for one's conduct. Answering for the deeds done in mortality is not simply an administrative requirement but an aspect of human nature itself: to be a child of God is to possess AGENCY, which is both the power to choose between OBEDIENCE and rebellion and the accountability for how that power is used.

The scriptures teach that accountability is not limited to public behavior; everyone will be asked to answer for all they do and say and even for what they think (Matt. 12:36; Alma 12:12–14), and for the use they make of every resource and opportunity God gives them (*TPJS*, pp. 68, 227). Joseph Smith taught that strict accounting is represented in the New Testament parable of the talents (Matt. 25:14–30): the master commits a certain sum in talents (an ancient currency) to each of three servants and later calls for an accounting. Two of the three use and double the resources entrusted to them, while the third, out of fear, buries his portion and thereby steals the increase that rightfully belongs to the master: "Where the five talents were bestowed, ten will be required; and he that has made no improvement will be cast out as an unprofitable servant" (*TPJS*, p. 68).

Only those capable of committing sin and of repenting are accountable (D&C 20:71). Children younger than eight and the mentally impaired are not. Satan has no power to tempt little children or other unaccountable individuals (D&C 29:46–50).

While individuals are usually accountable for their own sins, leaders may also be accountable for the sins of their people if they do not "teach them the word of God with all diligence" (Ezek. 3:17–21; Jacob 1:19; *see also* VOICE OF WARNING). Parents may have to answer for the wrongdoing of their children if they do not teach them the gospel (2 Ne. 4:5–6; D&C 68:25; Moses 7:37).

It is sometimes claimed that people cannot help doing some of the things that God calls sin, such as acts of HOMOSEXUALITY and substance abuse. Regarding such conduct, however, Church leaders teach that "we are to control [feelings and impulses], meaning we are to direct them according to the moral law" (Packer, 1990, p. 85). "One's parents may have failed," wrote President Spencer KIMBALL, "our own backgrounds may have been frustrating, but . . . we have within ourselves the power to rise above our circumstances, to change our lives. Man can change human nature" (p. 176).

BIBLIOGRAPHY

Brown, Victor L. "Agency and Accountability." *Ensign* 15 (May 1985):14–17.

Kimball, Spencer W. *Faith Precedes the Miracle*. Salt Lake City, 1972.

Packer, Boyd K. "Atonement, Agency, Accountability." *Ensign* 18 (May 1988):69–72.

———. "Covenants." *Ensign* 20 (Nov. 1990):85.

C. TERRY WARNER

ACTIVITY IN THE CHURCH

For Latter-day Saints, activity in the Church involves a broad range of public and private religious practices intended to enhance the spiritual well-being of the faithful and accomplish good works. When Latter-day Saints speak of being "active in the Church," they have reference to observing a full religious lifestyle of attendance, devotion, service, and learning. As one measure of their rate of activity, 48 percent of adult Latter-day Saints in the United States in 1989 reported that they attended church services weekly, compared to 38 percent of adult members in other denominations.

The religious practices of active Latter-day Saints include attendance at worship services and religious education classes on Sunday; donation of TITHING and other financial contributions; service in a variety of Church CALLINGS; performance of TEMPLE ORDINANCES on behalf of the deceased; personal and FAMILY PRAYER; SCRIPTURE STUDY; religious discussion with other family members; adherence to moral standards of personal honesty and integrity; genealogical research; service in the community; and development of habits of thrift and self-sufficiency. General surveys show that even though private religious practice is strongly encouraged by the Church, only 67 percent of active adult Latter-day Saints pray daily, compared to 83 percent in other denominations; and 41 percent reported reading the scriptures daily or several times a week, compared to 52 percent in other denominations (Research Division; cf. National Opinion Research Center; Princeton Religion Research Center).

Religious activity may fluctuate over the course of a person's lifetime, depending on a number of personal and situational variables. In general, the rates of public and private religious activity are somewhat higher among women than men. This gender difference in religious activity is found within every denomination. In addition, the religious activity of adult Latter-day Saints is influenced by (1) religious background, including parents' religious activity, home religious observance, and religious activity during childhood and adolescent years; and (2) current life situation, including marital status and educational or occupational status. Church members who are most likely to have lower levels of religious activity include adults married outside the faith, adults who are divorced or have never married, adults with less than a high school education working in blue-collar jobs, and adults without a religious background.

Age also has an important effect on religious activity. In the United States, 85 percent of Latter-day Saint children under age ten attend Church meetings three to four times a month, but the percentage of frequent attenders declines over the next fifteen years to 55 percent during their mid-twenties. It then rises to 60 percent at age forty, falls to a low of 50 percent during the mid-fifties, and rises again to 60 percent by age seventy.

The process by which people discontinue active participation in the religious life of their church for a period of time is called "disengagement." Disengaged Mormons are usually referred to as "inactive" or "less active" members. While they do not regularly attend church or participate in other public religious practices, inactive Latter-day Saints usually retain a strong identification with the Church and value that identity (Albrecht, Cornwall, and Cunningham). Research has shown that religious socialization in the family is an important predictor of the likelihood that a person will experience a period of inactivity during adolescence or young adulthood. This finding accurately describes the experience of Latter-day Saints. Church members from homes in which both parents are LDS and attend church frequently, pray, read the scriptures, and discuss religion with their children are much less likely to have a period of inactivity than those from homes in which one or neither parent attends church regularly nor practices religion in the home.

About 75 percent of lifelong Latter-day Saints experience a period of inactivity lasting a year or more. The process of disengagement most commonly begins sometime between the ages of fourteen and twenty. Of those who leave, 60 percent return to active participation between their mid-twenties and late thirties, when they marry and begin a family. Some Latter-day Saints who had stopped attending church were asked to list the reasons why they had left. Lifestyle issues and problems of social integration were mentioned most frequently. More than half said they had found other interests that led them to spend less and less time in Church-related activities; 42 percent reported that they felt their lifestyle was no longer compatible with participation in the Church; 40 percent said they did not feel as if they belonged or fit in; and 25 percent said they felt it did not matter to anyone whether they attended or not. Less frequently mentioned reasons included moving to a new community, work-schedule conflicts, poor health, marriage to an inactive member or marriage outside the Church, and conflicts with Church members, programs, or doctrines.

For those who convert to the Church as teenagers or adults, the period of greatest risk for inactivity is the first year or two after joining the Church (*see* CONVERSION). About 70 percent of the new Latter-day Saint converts in the United States who do become inactive stop attending within three to five years after joining the Church. Of those who drop out, 45 percent return to active participation in five to ten years. Activity among these converts is influenced by (1) the personal characteristics of the convert, such as religious background, age, and marital status; (2) how personally involved the convert was in the investigation process, such as experiencing the Spirit of God and attending Church worship services; and (3) the extent to which the convert developed social relationships with other Latter-day Saints both before and after baptism.

In any religious tradition, social relationships are critical in developing and maintaining religious activity. People's religious lives are acted out in the context of a network of social ties within the family, the congregation, and the community. In addition, social relationships are the means by which religious traditions are transmitted from one generation to the next and the medium through which religious practices are shared and expressed. LDS religious activity is centered in the family and in the congregation (*see* WARD). In these settings, children and new converts learn by instruction and example what it means to be an "active" Latter-day Saint (*see* VALUES, TRANS-MISSION OF).

BIBLIOGRAPHY

Albrecht, Stan L. "The Consequential Dimension of Mormon Religiosity." *BYU Studies* 29 (Spring 1989):57–108.

———, Marie Cornwall, and Perry H. Cunningham. "Religious Leave-Taking: Disengagement and Disaffiliation Among Mormons." In *Falling from the Faith*, ed. David G. Bromley, pp. 62–80. Newbury Park, Calif., 1988.

Center for Demography and Ecology, University of Wisconsin-Madison. *National Survey of Families and Households.* Madison, 1987.

Cornwall, Marie. "The Social Bases of Religion: A Study of Factors Influencing Religious Belief and Commitment." *Review of Religious Research* 29 (Sept. 1987):44–56.

———. "The Influence of Three Agents of Religious Socialization: Family, Church, Peers." In *The Religion and Family Connection: Social Science Perspectives*, ed. Darwin L. Thomas, pp. 207–231. Provo, Utah, 1988.

———. "The Determinants of Religious Behavior: A Theoretical Model and Empirical Test." *Social Forces* 68 (1989):283–99.

National Opinion Research Center. *General Social Survey.* Chicago, 1988.

Princeton Religion Research Center. *Religion in America.* Princeton, N.J., 1982.

Research Division, The Church of Jesus Christ of Latter-day Saints. Surveys of Church Members (1981–1984), unpublished.

PERRY H. CUNNINGHAM

ADAM

[*This entry consists of two parts:*

LDS Sources
Ancient Sources

The first article discusses LDS teachings about Adam. The second one offers several apocryphal and pseudepigraphic sources as points of comparison. For further information on Adam, see Adamic Language, Eve, Fall of Adam, Mortality, Original Sin, *and* Plan of Salvation; *regarding the beginnings of earth life, see* Creation, Earth, Evolution, Garden of Eden, Origin of Man, Purpose of Earth Life, *and* Worlds.]

LDS SOURCES

For Latter-day Saints, Adam stands as one of the noblest and greatest of all men. Information found in the scriptures and in declarations of latter-day apostles and prophets reveals details about Adam and his important roles in the pre-earth life, in Eden, in mortality, and in his postmortal life. They identify Adam by such names and titles as Michael (D&C 27:11; 29:26), archangel (D&C 88:112), and Ancient of Days (D&C 138:38).

The Prophet Joseph SMITH taught that Michael, spoken of in the Bible (Dan. 10:13; Jude 1:9; Rev. 12:7), is Adam. In his PREMORTAL LIFE, Adam received the PRIESTHOOD (*TPJS*, p. 157), was taught the plan of God (*TPJS*, p. 167), and was appointed to be the head of the human family (*TPJS*, p. 158). He participated in the creation of the earth and occupied a position of authority next to Jesus Christ (*TPJS*, p. 158), under whose direction he at all times functions (D&C 78:16). He led the forces of righteousness against the devil "and his angels," who were overcome and expelled from heaven (*see* WAR IN HEAVEN).

Latter-day scriptures attest that Adam is a son of God, that his PHYSICAL BODY was created by the Gods in their own image and placed in the GARDEN

Adam and Eve Cast Out of the Garden of Eden, by Tiffany Studios, New York (1892, leaded stained glass, over 6 feet in diameter), inside the Salt Lake Temple, in the second floor corridor leading from the World Room to the Main Hall. Photograph by C. R. Savage, 1911.

OF EDEN (Moses 6:9, 22; Abr. 5:7–11; *TPJS*, p. 345–53; cf. 2 Ne. 2:14–19). In this physical-spiritual state in Eden, Adam was called the "first man" (Moses 1:34) and given responsibility to dress the garden and "open the way of the world" (*TPJS*, p. 12). He was given dominion and responsibility over the earth, and he gave names to its creatures (Moses 3:19). He was joined with EVE in marriage (Abr. 5:4–19), but in their premortal condition "they would have had no children" (2 Ne. 2:23). Adam received the KEYS OF THE PRIESTHOOD (Abr., Facsimile 2, Fig. 3), and its ordinances were confirmed upon Adam and Eve (cf. *TPJS*, p. 167).

In order to obey the command of God to multiply and people the earth, Adam and Eve transgressed the law. Their deliberate action resulted in their fall (*see* FALL OF ADAM), and they were expelled from the garden. "Adam fell that men might

be; and men are, that they might have joy" (2 Ne. 2:25). Thus, their action precipitated, as God had planned, the mortal phase of the PLAN OF SALVATION.

In their mortal state, Adam and Eve were taught further about the plan of salvation by heavenly messengers (Moses 5:4–9; 6:50–54). They received the priesthood ordinances (Moses 5:59; 6:64–65) and all things necessary to teach their children (Moses 5:12). LDS sources indicate that with Eve, Adam had sons and daughters before Cain and Abel were born (Moses 5:2–3, 16–17). They suffered the effects of the temptations of the devil and experienced the sorrow of family dissension that led to murder and wickedness among some of their children (Moses 5:12–53).

Adam and Eve had a fully developed language and kept written records (Moses 6:5–9). They preserved their genealogical record and an account of the Creation. Three years before his death, Adam called his righteous posterity to ADAM-ONDI-AHMAN and gave them his final blessing (D&C 107:53).

As the first on this earth to receive priesthood keys, Adam continues to dispense authority to others and to watch over priesthood administration on the earth; those to whom keys have been given must return them or account for them to Adam, and he will in turn deliver them or give an accounting of them to Christ (*TPJS*, pp. 157, 167). This will occur when the Ancient of Days (Adam) attends a council at Adam-ondi-Ahman preliminary to the second coming of Christ (Dan. 7:9–10; cf. *TPJS*, p. 122).

At the end of the Millennium, Adam as Michael will again lead the righteous in battle against the devil and his armies. Michael and the hosts of heaven will again prevail (D&C 88:111–15). When Adam then sounds the trumpet, the graves will be opened and the remainder of the dead will come forth to be judged (D&C 29:26–27). Subject to the Father and Christ, Adam will then preside eternally over his posterity (*TPJS*, p. 157).

Adam's various titles relate to particular phases of his mission. In his premortal and postmortal roles, he is known as Michael and as the archangel (D&C 29:26). In Hebrew, *michael* means one "who is like God," and in his powerful and leading role as archangel, Adam serves as the captain of the Lord's hosts in battle against the devil and his forces. Adam was the name given him for mortality (Moses 1:34). In Hebrew, '*adam* means "man" or "mankind." In LDS sources, further meanings of the word include "first man" (D&C 84:16), "many" (Moses 1:34), and "first father" (Abr. 1:3), denoting his historical role as the "grand progenitor" of the entire human family (*TPJS*, p. 167). "Ancient of Days" appears to be his title because he is "the first and oldest of all" (*TPJS*, p. 167).

Adam has been highly esteemed by all the prophets, both ancient and modern. President Brigham YOUNG expressed the idea in 1852 and later years that Adam "is our Father and our God, and the only God with whom we have to do" (*JD* 1:50). This remark has led some to conjecture that Brigham Young meant that Adam, who was on earth as our progenitor, was in reality God the Father. However, this interpretation has been officially rejected as incorrect (Kimball, p. 77). Later in the same speech Brigham Young clearly stated "that the earth was organized by three distinct characters, namely Eloheim, Yahovah, and Michael" (*JD* 1:51). Additional information about Brigham Young's feelings on Adam can also be found in a conference speech given October 8, 1854 (*JD* 1:50), clarifying somewhat his earlier statement. It is there implied that through a process known as divine investiture, God delegates his power to his children. Adam was the first on earth to receive this authority, which includes all essential keys, titles, and dominions possessed by the Father (D&C 84:38; cf. 88:107). Thus, he had conferred upon him all things that were necessary for the accomplishment of his manifold responsibilities, and Adam is a name-title signifying that he is the first man and father of all.

BIBLIOGRAPHY

Broderick, Carl. "Another Look at Adam-God." *Dialogue* 16 (Summer 1983):4–7.

Buerger, David J. "The Adam-God Doctrine." *Dialogue* 15 (Spring 1982):14–58.

Kimball, Spencer W. "Our Own Liahona." *Ensign* 6 (Nov. 1976):77–79.

McConkie, Joseph Fielding, and Robert L. Millet, eds. *The Man Adam*. Salt Lake City, 1990.

Petersen, Mark E. *Adam: Who Is He?* Salt Lake City, 1976.

ARTHUR A. BAILEY

ANCIENT SOURCES

Adam is portrayed in ancient Jewish and Christian sources as the first human and progenitor of the race. Many apocryphal texts rework the Old Testament Adamic narrative and contain or reflect valuable ancient traditions. Some Latter-day Saints have profitably compared a few of these views with certain concepts about Adam given in Latter-day Saint sources.

In Judaism, Genesis 1–2 is used as a basis for understanding mankind's relationship to God. Adam's posterity inherited his fallen nature, yet Adam is regarded as the archetypal model for mankind—as indicated in texts that date back at least to Hellenistic times (second century B.C.) and is amplified in medieval Jewish philosophy. Philo, following a Platonic model, saw in the two creation narratives of Genesis a distinction between a heavenly or spiritual man, created first spiritually in the image of God (Gen. 1:27; cf. Moses 3:5), and a second, earthly man, formed out of the dust (Gen. 2:7). Most early Jewish exegetes accepted the historicity of the biblical account, though Genesis 2:8–3:24 was often interpreted allegorically. The Talmud and the Aggadah supplied rich details to the Adamic story, including an impressive description of how all future generations—and their PROPHETS—passed before Adam and were viewed by him (Sanh. 38b; Av. Zar. 5a; Gen. R. 24:2; cf. D&C 107:55–57). Adam was given the Noachian laws (Sanh. 56b) and the law of the SABBATH (Mid. Ps. to 92:6). He was the first man to offer sacrifice (Av. Zar. 8a; cf. Moses 5:5). The medieval cabalists added mystical interpretations as well, although Adam is never identified here as Michael, as in the Latter-day Saint scripture (see D&C 27:11; 107:54; 128:21).

Orthodox Christian theology, articulated during the second century by Irenaeus and others in response to the challenges posed by gnosticism, faithfully saw the Old Testament through the role of Christ. Early Christianity regarded the incarnation and ATONEMENT OF JESUS CHRIST as the fulfillment of the work begun by Adam. While Adam was the prototype of the old, mortal man, Christ became the prototype of the new man, blessed with the promise of immortality. Jesus became the "second Adam," whose atonement enabled mankind to overcome the effects of the Fall (1 Cor. 15:22, 45).

The creation story and the Adamic narrative in Genesis were especially important in gnosticism, which interpreted the Fall as the downfall of the divine principle into the material world. This contributed to gnosticism's negative attitude toward the physical creation. Several Gnostic writings deal with Adam. One of these, the *Apocalypse of Adam*, found at Nag Hammadi, is heavily dependent upon Jewish apocalyptic traditions and contains no explicit Christian doctrines. It purports to be a revelation given to Adam after the Fall by three heavenly messengers, explaining the nature and extent of the Fall and providing the promise of a future Redeemer. This knowledge is then passed by Adam to SETH and his descendants (cf. D&C 107:41–57).

The Life of Adam and Eve is a significant apocryphal work dealing with the life and death of Adam. It was probably written in Palestine between 100 B.C. and A.D. 200. It has been preserved in Greek, Latin, and Slavonic recensions, each considerably different from the others. This work describes Adam's and Eve's repentance after leaving the Garden of Eden at length (cf. Moses 6:50–68). No clear and central doctrine emerges, but the text stresses the ideas of final JUDGMENT and RESURRECTION. Other eschatological features are missing. It conveys no hint of the traditional doctrine of ORIGINAL SIN. Adam is perfect; EVE, weak but not wicked, deplores her own shortcomings while loving and obeying Adam.

A central feature of the *Cave of Treasures*, a Syriac work, is its story of a cave where Adam lived and was buried. His body was retrieved by Noah, who took it into the ark and afterward reinterred it on Golgotha. By this account, the redemptive blood of Jesus, also called the "last Adam," shed at the Crucifixion first flowed on the grave of Adam, demonstrating an inexorable link between the FALL OF ADAM and the atonement of Christ. Thus, in the *Gospel of Bartholomew* 1:22, Jesus says to Adam, "I was hung upon the cross for thee and for thy children's sake," and in 2 *Enoch* 42, Adam in Paradise is brought out "together with the ancestors . . . so that they may be filled with joy" and eternal riches.

Many ancient texts about Adam exist, notably the Ethiopic *Book of Adam and Eve*, and the Armenian books of *Death of Adam*, *History of Adam's Expulsion from Paradise*, *History of Cain and Abel*, *Adam's Sons*, and *Concerning the Good Tidings of Seth*.

BIBLIOGRAPHY

Ginzberg, Louis. *Legends of the Jews*, Vol. 1, pp. 3–142. Philadelphia, 1937.

Johnson, M. D. "The Life of Adam and Eve." In *The Old Testament Pseudepigrapha*, ed. J. Charlesworth, Vol. 2, pp. 249–95. Garden City, N.Y., 1985.

Robinson, James M., ed. *The Nag Hammadi Library*, 2nd ed. New York, 1989.

Robinson, Stephen E. "The Apocalypse of Adam." *BYU Studies* 17 (Winter 1977):131–53.

———. "The Book of Adam in Judaism and Early Christianity." In *The Man Adam*, ed. J. McConkie and R. Millet, pp. 131–50, listing titles of many ancient works. Salt Lake City, 1990.

MARTIN J. PALMER

ADAM-GOD

See: Young, Brigham: Teachings of Brigham Young

ADAMIC LANGUAGE

The concept of the Adamic language grew among Latter-day Saints out of statements from scripture, comments of early Church leaders, and subsequent tradition. It does not play a central doctrinal role, and there is no official Church position delineating its nature or status.

The scriptures state that this language, written and spoken by ADAM and his children, was "pure and undefiled" (Moses 6:5–6). Brigham YOUNG taught that it continued from Adam to Babel, at which time the Lord "caused the people to forget their own mother tongue, . . . scatter[ing] them abroad upon the face of the whole earth," except possibly for Jared and his family in the Book of Mormon (*JD* 3:100; cf. Gen. 11:1–9; Mosiah 28:17). This statement reflects the widely held Mormon belief that the founding members of the JAREDITE civilization preserved the Adamic language at their immigration to the new world (Ether 1:33–43; 3:24–28). Thus, the description by the brother of Jared of his apocalyptic vision was rendered linguistically inaccessible without divine interpretive help, since "the language which ye shall write I [God] have confounded" (Ether 3:21–28).

In the early years of the Church, some words of the Adamic language may have been revealed to Joseph Smith (*JD* 2:342), and other early Church leaders, including Brigham Young (*HC* 1:297) and Elizabeth Ann Whitney (*Woman's Exponent* 7 [Nov. 1, 1878], p. 83), who were said to have spoken it in tongues. More recently President Ezra Taft BENSON alluded to its possible universal reinstatement to resolve linguistic diversity (*Teachings of Ezra Taft Benson* [Salt Lake City, 1988], p. 93; cf. Brigham Young *JD* 3:100).

Similarly, Zephaniah 3:9, possibly referring to the future of the Adamic language, says, "I will turn to the people a pure language, that they may all call upon the name of the Lord." The word *pure* comes from the Hebrew *berurah*, from *barar*, "to cleanse" or purify; also "to choose."

Because it is generally held that a language reflects its culture, possibly the erosion of the purity of the Adamic culture after Babel led to a concomitant loss of purity of expression in its mirroring language.

JOHN S. ROBERTSON

ADAM-ONDI-AHMAN

Adam-ondi-Ahman, a settlement in Daviess County, Missouri, received its unusual name from the Prophet Joseph SMITH in 1838 when Latter-day Saints were moving into the area. Members of the Church had been forced out of Jackson County, Missouri, in 1833 after three years of tem-

porary asylum, and were subsequently asked to leave Clay County. When they appealed to the state legislature to make a new county "for Mormons," Caldwell and Daviess counties were organized. The Saints immediately moved into Caldwell County with Far West as the county seat, and soon also began settling in adjoining Daviess County. In May 1838 Joseph Smith led surveyors to a horseshoe bend of the Grand River, seventy miles north of present-day Kansas City, and proclaimed a new community, which he named Adam-ondi-Ahman because, said he, "it is the place where Adam shall come to visit his people, or the Ancient of Days shall sit, as spoken of by Daniel the Prophet" (*HC* 3:35; D&C 116). Orson Pratt interpreted the name to mean "Valley of God, where Adam dwelt" (*JD* 18:343).

The Prophet's revelations indicated several things about the area: (1) the GARDEN OF EDEN was located in Jackson County, Missouri, and after ADAM was expelled from the garden, he went north to Adam-ondi-Ahman; (2) three years before Adam's death, he gathered the righteous of his posterity to Adam-ondi-Ahman and bestowed upon them his last blessing; (3) this site would be the location of a future meeting of the Lord with

Lyman Wight's second cabin in the valley of Adam-ondi-Ahman in northwestern Missouri, a Latter-day Saint settlement from 1836 to 1838.

Adam and the Saints, as spoken of by the prophet Daniel (Dan. 7:9–14, 21–27; 12:1–3).

When Joseph Smith arrived in the valley with the survey team, he found three or four Latter-day Saint families already living there and made the log cabin of Lyman Wight his headquarters. From June to October 1838, the population of the two-mile-square Adam-ondi-Ahman increased to about 400 people. Another 600 scattered throughout Daviess County viewed Adam-ondi-Ahman as their capital city.

Approximately 90 percent of the Saints in Daviess County settled on land under "preemption rights," which meant that the government had not yet made the land available for purchase. Believing that they would eventually own the land, the Latter-day Saints worked hard to develop their farms. In June 1838, when the third STAKE of the Church was organized at Adam-ondi-Ahman, with John Smith as stake president, a peaceful atmosphere seemed to prevail. However, in July the settlers were served public notice to leave Daviess County or face serious consequences. The Saints placed their militia in a state of readiness to defend themselves. When hostilities erupted in August, the militia from Church headquarters at Far West went to Adam-ondi-Ahman, but no battle ensued. Similar action occurred in September.

On October 11, mobs forced the Latter-day Saints from DeWitt in Carroll County and then turned to Daviess County, intent on driving them all out of the state. They burned cabins, stole animals, and harassed families. When the Far West militia arrived for the third time, in October 1838, Church members throughout Daviess County gathered to Adam-ondi-Ahman for safety, and the community's population swelled to more than a thousand. Confinement in tents and wagons and a sudden snowstorm added to their miseries.

While Joseph Smith and the Far West militia were in Adam-ondi-Ahman during October, the Church members assembled to witness the dedication of the public square by Brigham YOUNG. At this time, Joseph Smith pointed out a location where Adam had once built an altar. In May the Prophet had identified this same site as one that had also been used by early American Indians.

After the October plundering and burnings by the mobs and retaliatory actions by the Latter-day Saints, who were intent on defending themselves, the state militia forced them to surrender their arms on November 7, 1838, and gave them ten days to move to Far West. Adam-ondi-Ahman was abandoned and fell into the hands of non-Mormon settlers. Church families from Daviess County spent the winter at Far West before being expelled from the state in the spring of 1839.

The Missourians who were responsible for expelling Church members from Daviess County knew that in four days their land would be offered for sale by the U.S. government. With the Mormons gone, these residents purchased the improved land and reaped the benefits of the Saints' labor.

John Cravens purchased most of the central area of the city of Adam-ondi-Ahman and renamed it Cravensville. The town existed for thirty-two years and had enough residents to vie with Gallatin for the county seat of Daviess County, but after 1871 the land was returned to farming and grazing.

In 1944 Wilford C. Wood purchased thirty-eight acres at Adam-ondi-Ahman for the Church, and an additional 3,000 acres have since been purchased. Archival research and archaeological excavation have helped to determine the location, size, nature, and history of the city.

BIBLIOGRAPHY

McConkie, Bruce R. *The Millennial Messiah*, pp. 575–88. Salt Lake City, 1982.

LAMAR C. BERRETT

ADMINISTRATION OF ORDINANCES

See: Ordinances: Administration of Ordinances

ADOPTION OF CHILDREN

The adoption of children is common among members of the Church. This is no doubt in part a concomitant of the Church's opposition to ABORTION and its emphasis on the central importance of the FAMILY. President Ezra Taft Benson, commenting on adoption, stated that many "have prayerfully chosen to adopt children, and . . . [you] wonderful couples we salute . . . for the sacrifices and love you have given to those children you have chosen to be your own" (Benson, p. 11).

There are no doctrinal limitations on the legal adoption of children by members of the Church.

Under most circumstances, adopted children may be sealed to the adoptive parents in an LDS temple (*see* SEALING). However, living children born in the covenant, that is, born to parents who have been sealed to each other in an LDS temple, cannot be sealed to any other parents although they can be adopted for life; and children who have been previously sealed to another couple may not be sealed to adoptive parents without cancellation of the former sealing. The temple sealing of a living adopted child into an eternal family relationship is performed only after legal adoption is finalized in accordance with local law (*General Handbook of Instructions*, Salt Lake City, 1989, 6-6).

Adopted children who have been sealed to adoptive parents are considered as natural children for all doctrinal purposes, including tracing genealogical lineage. All sealed children are entitled to all the blessings promised to children born in the covenant.

The desire to adopt children is strong among Church members, but Church leaders have cautioned them never to become involved in adoption practices that are legally questionable. In a letter dated April 20, 1982, the FIRST PRESIDENCY urged members to "observe strictly all legal requirements of the country or countries involved in the adoption." It was also stated that "the needs of the child must be a paramount concern in adoption." Members considering adoption are counseled to work through the Church's SOCIAL SERVICES agency or through others with the "specialized professional knowledge" necessary to ensure that the child's needs are met.

BIBLIOGRAPHY

Benson, Ezra Taft. Annual Parents Fireside, Feb. 22, 1987. *Church News* (Feb. 28, 1987):3, 10.

RYAN L. THOMAS

ADULTERY

Adultery constitutes a grievous violation of the law of CHASTITY. For Latter-day Saints it is defined as sexual intercourse between a married person and someone other than his or her legal and lawful spouse, while fornication involves two unmarried parties. Both transgressions fall under condemnation in scripture and in the teachings of The Church of Jesus Christ of Latter-day Saints.

The Lord forbids adultery in the TEN COMMANDMENTS and elsewhere in the Law of Moses (see, e.g., Ex. 20:14; Lev. 20:10; Deut. 22:22). Both in Israel and in the Western Hemisphere, Christ commanded his followers not to commit adultery in thought or deed (Matt. 5:27–28; 3 Ne. 12:27–28). In this DISPENSATION, the Lord has again prohibited adultery, and "anything like unto it" (D&C 59:6), while reproving even adulterous thoughts as an offense against the Spirit (D&C 42:23–26). In an official pronouncement in 1942, the FIRST PRESIDENCY of the Church decried sexual sin—including adultery, fornication, and prostitution—as an offense "in its enormity, next to murder" (*IE* 45 [Nov. 1942]:758; *MFP* 6:176).

Because adultery or fornication breaks BAPTISMAL COVENANTS and temple vows and may involve other members of the Church, penitent offenders are to confess the sin to their BISHOP or other Church authority, who may convene a disciplinary council. After prayerful deliberation, the council may excommunicate or disfellowship an adulterer, or implement some type of probation to help the offender repent. The excommunication of an adulterous priesthood leader is almost certain. A disciplinary council usually requires the adulterer to seek forgiveness from the betrayed spouse and from anyone drawn into the sin. By demonstrating an abhorrence for past sin and a commitment to righteousness, the repentant adulterer may, after an adequate period of probation, become fully reconciled to Christ, rebaptized, and reinstated in the Church and find forgiveness from God (D&C 58:47–48).

BIBLIOGRAPHY

Kimball, Spencer W. "The Sin Next to Murder." In *The Miracle of Forgiveness*, pp. 61–75. Salt Lake City, 1969.

BRYCE J. CHRISTENSEN

ADVERSARY

See: Devils

ADVOCATE WITH THE FATHER

See: Jesus Christ, Names and Titles of

AFRICA, THE CHURCH IN

The Church of Jesus Christ of Latter-day Saints has been a presence in Africa since 1853, but for the first 125 years it was established only in southern Africa. Applications by the Church for admittance into central Africa in the 1960s were denied, but those in 1978 were approved, and growth of the Church there has been impressive.

From 1853 until 1978 most of the work of the Church in Africa was with European immigrants and their descendants in South Africa and in Northern and Southern Rhodesia (now Zambia and Zimbabwe, respectively). In June 1978, when the FIRST PRESIDENCY announced the revelation extending the priesthood to all worthy male members of the Church, the way was opened for the Church to extend its full program to all the nations of Africa (see D&C, Official Declaration—2). Missionaries were sent to Nigeria and Ghana at the request of many local people who had already studied the Church SCRIPTURES and literature and had organized themselves into units that they unofficially called The Church of Jesus Christ of Latter-day Saints. Church missions were later organized

in Zaire, Sierra Leone, Liberia, the Ivory Coast, and Mauritius and Reunion islands.

The establishment of the Church in Africa began at a special Church conference in Salt Lake City in August 1852, when President Brigham YOUNG called 106 men to leave their wives in charge of their families, homes, farms, and businesses and go on missions to various lands of the world to proclaim the restored GOSPEL. Three were called to go to South Africa: Jesse Haven, William H. Walker, and Leonard I. Smith, with Elder Haven assigned to preside. Leaving their families in the care of God, they arrived at the Cape of Good Hope on April 18, 1853, and set about to establish the Church in South Africa, encouraging the converts to "gather to Zion" in Utah. The missionaries faced heavy opposition from the local clergy and indifference to their message among the people generally; fewer than 200 people accepted baptism in the two and a half years they served.

One of the first converts in South Africa in 1853 was Nicholas Paul, a thirty-year-old builder who aided and protected missionaries and let them use his home for meetings. He became the presi-

Members of the Eket Branch, in Nigeria (1984). Courtesy Ann Laemmlen Lewis.

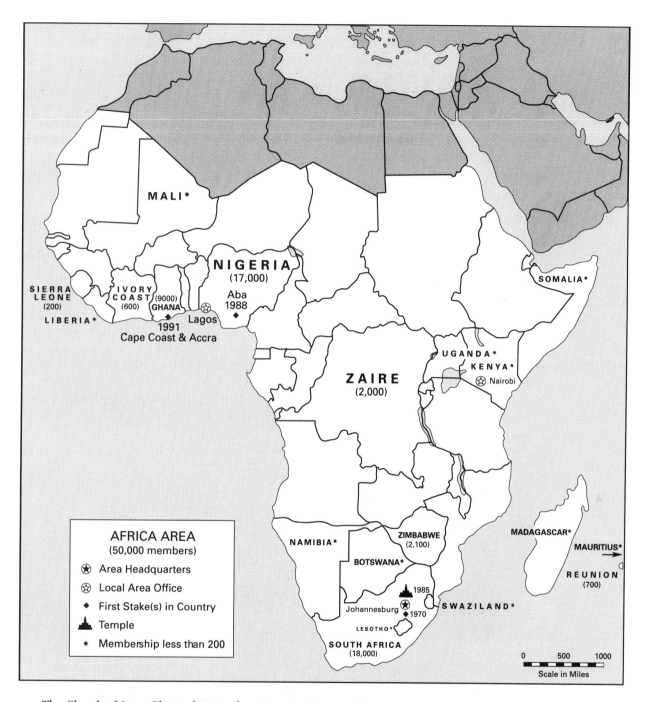

The Church of Jesus Christ of Latter-day Saints in Africa as of January 1, 1991.

dent of the first branch of the Church in Africa, which was organized in his home in Mowbray (Cape Town area). The 1853 missionaries also organized a branch of the Church in Port Elizabeth. When they returned to their families in America in 1855, other missionaries from America and South Africa were called to replace them. Between 1855 and 1865, 278 converts to the Church emigrated from South Africa to Utah.

No LDS missionaries served in South Africa from 1866 to 1903, and the Church grew slowly. Missionaries returned in 1903 and served until 1940, when they were withdrawn because of World War II. During those years 230 missionaries

Helen Bassey Davies Udoeyo, Relief Society President of the Eket Branch, knitting, with her scriptures and Relief Society handbook on her lap (1985).

Spencer W. KIMBALL pronounced a dedicatory prayer upon the land of South Africa which included the promise that WARDS and stakes would dot the land and a TEMPLE would be built there. New stakes were created in Durban (1981) and Cape Town (1984). The first black African stake was organized in 1988 in Aba, Nigeria, with David W. Eka as its president.

Church growth in Africa since 1978 has been much higher in percentage than in the rest of the world. The major challenge is no longer to gain converts but to prepare local priesthood leadership. And as the Church continues to expand into sub-Saharan Africa, it must face the challenges of poverty and illiteracy. In addition to contributing to famine relief programs, the Church is helping its members in Africa to learn and implement the principles of self-reliance and independence.

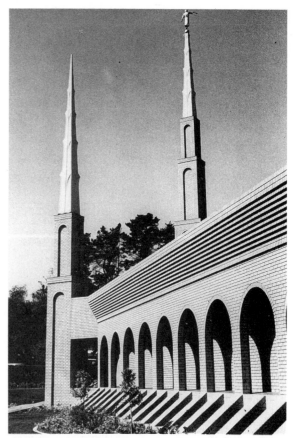

The Johannesburg South Africa Temple is the first LDS temple in Africa (dedicated 1985). In the dedicatory prayer, President Gordon B. Hinckley prayed for blessings on this nation and that its leaders be inspired "to find a basis for reconciliation" among its people. Courtesy Marjorie Woods.

had worked in South Africa. Since the return of LDS missionaries to South Africa in 1944, the Church has grown steadily there and also expanded to other areas of Africa.

In addition to the efforts of foreign missionaries, much of the growth of the Church in Africa has resulted from the service of local members. Johanna Fourie instituted the Primary program for teaching the children in 1932 and spent the rest of her life (thirty-eight years) guiding and building this program throughout South Africa.

In 1954 President David O. MCKAY became the first GENERAL AUTHORITY of the Church to visit South Africa. The first LDS Church STAKE in South Africa was organized in Johannesburg in 1970, with Louis P. Hefer as STAKE PRESIDENT. That stake was divided into two stakes in 1978. In 1972 Church SEMINARIES and INSTITUTES OF RELIGION were introduced into southern Africa. All African countries in which the Church is established now have these programs. The added weekday religious training of the youth has increased local missionary participation. In 1973 President

Elder Neal A. Maxwell of the Quorum of the Twelve presides at the creation of the Aba Nigeria Stake in 1988, the first stake of the Church in Nigeria. Left to right: Lazarus and Sylvia Onitchi, Elder Maxwell, Eugene Nwagbara and his wife Eugene Nnenna, Stake President David W. Eka and wife Eka-Etta, Ephraim S. and Patricia Etete, Elder Robert E. Sackley of the Seventy, and his wife Marjorie Sackley.

The Church has always tried to teach the gospel in the language of the people. As Afrikaans is an official language in South Africa, many missionaries sent there have learned to speak it. The BOOK OF MORMON was published in Afrikaans in 1973, and the DOCTRINE AND COVENANTS and the PEARL OF GREAT PRICE in 1981. The Book of Mormon has also been translated into several African languages: Efik (Nigeria, 1983), Kissi (Kenya, 1983), Malagasy (Madagascar, 1986), Akan (Ghana, 1987), Zulu (South Africa, 1978), and Shona (Zimbabwe, 1988). Local members have helped make these translations possible, such as Pricilla Sampson-Davis, a retired schoolteacher from Cape Coast, Ghana, who translated the Book of Mormon, LDS Hymns, and other Church publications into Akan. Translations into additional African languages continue in process.

One of the most significant events in the history of the Church in Africa was the dedication of the temple in Johannesburg in 1985, which has made it possible for the members to receive locally all the ORDINANCES of the Church and to perform them in proxy for their deceased ancestors. The first TEMPLE PRESIDENT and MATRON of this temple were Harlan W. and Geraldine Merkley Clark. Although the work of the Church in Africa was slow and localized from 1853 until the 1980s, Elder Alexander B. Morrison of the SEVENTY stated in 1987: "The gleaning and gathering of the children of God in Africa is just beginning. In the words of the Prophet Joseph, it will go forward 'boldly, nobly, and independent, till . . . [the truth of God has] swept every country, and sounded in every ear, till the purposes of God shall be accomplished, and the Great Jehovah shall say the work is done'" (p. 26).

BIBLIOGRAPHY

Brigham, Janet. "Nigeria and Ghana: A Miracle Precedes the Messengers." *Ensign* 10 (Feb. 1980):73–76.

LeBaron, E. Dale. "Gospel Pioneers in Africa." *Ensign* 20 (Aug. 1990):40–43.

———. *All Are Alike unto God.* Salt Lake City, 1990.

Lye, William. "From Burundi to Zaire: Taking the Gospel to Africa." *Ensign* 10 (Mar. 1980):10–15.

Mabey, Rendell N., and Gordon T. Allred. *Brother to Brother: The Story of Latter-day Saint Missionaries Who Took the Gospel to Black Africa.* Salt Lake City, 1984.

Morrison, Alexander B. "The Dawning of a New Day in Africa." *Ensign* 17 (Nov. 1987):25–26.

E. DALE LEBARON

AFTERLIFE

[*Other articles related to this topic are:* Degrees of Glory; Heaven; Hell; Immortality and Eternal Life; Paradise; Plan of Salvation; Salvation; Spirit Prison; Translated Beings.]

Latter-day Saints believe that life continues after the death of the mortal body and that death is but a separation of the PHYSICAL BODY and the SPIRIT. The spirits of all individuals, "whether they be good or evil, are taken home to that God who gave them life" (Alma 40:11). President Brigham YOUNG said that the transition from death into the SPIRIT WORLD is "from a state of sorrow, grief, mourning, woe, misery, pain, anguish and disappointment into a state of existence, where I can enjoy life to the fullest extent; . . . my spirit is set free; . . . I go, I come, I do this, I do that; . . . I am full of life, full of vigor, and I enjoy the presence of my heavenly Father" (*JD* 17:142). The desire, personality, and disposition that individuals develop, shape, and mold in this life will continue into the afterlife.

If individuals are evil in their hearts, their spirits will enter the spirit world intent upon doing evil; if individuals are good and strive to do the things of God, that disposition will also continue, only to a greater degree—learning, increasing, growing in grace and in knowledge of truth (see Brigham Young, *JD* 7:333). Amulek explained that the "same spirit which doth possess your bodies at the time that ye go out of this life, that same spirit will have power to possess your body in that eternal world" (Alma 34:34).

Life did not begin at mortal birth, nor will it end at mortal death. God's gift to all individuals is everlasting life. Every person will die physically; every person will receive a literal RESURRECTION of the body and never die again.

JUNE LEIFSON

AGENCY

"Agency" refers both to the capacity of beings "to act for themselves" (2 Ne. 2:26) and their ACCOUNTABILITY for those actions. Exercising agency is a spiritual matter (D&C 29:35); it consists in either receiving the enlightenment and COMMANDMENTS that come from God or resisting and rejecting them by yielding to the devil's temptations (D&C 93:31). Without awareness of alternatives an individual could not choose, and that is why being tempted by evil is as essential to agency as being enticed by the Spirit of God (D&C 29:39). Furthermore, no one is forced either to act virtuously or to sin. "The devil could not compel mankind to do evil; all was voluntary. . . . God would not exert any compulsory means, and the devil could not" (*TPJS*, p. 187).

Agency is an essential ingredient of being human, "inherent in the spirit of man" (McKay, p. 366) both in the premortal spirit existence (D&C 29:36) and in MORTALITY. No being can possess sensibility, rationality, and a capacity for happiness without it (2 Ne. 2:11–13, 23; D&C 93:30). Moreover, it is the specific gift by which God made his children in his image and empowered them to grow to become like him through their own progression of choices (L. Snow, *JD* 20:367). It was because Satan "sought to destroy the agency of man" (Moses 4:3) that the war was fought in heaven before earth life (cf. Rev. 12:7). What was then, and is now, at stake in the battle to preserve agency is nothing less than the possibility of both the continued existence and the divine destiny of every human being. This principle helps explain the Church's strong position against political systems and addictive practices that inhibit the free exercise of agency.

Agency is such that men and women not only *can* choose obedience or rebellion but *must* (B. Young, *JD* 13:282). They cannot avoid being both free and responsible for their choices. Individuals capable of acting for themselves cannot remain on neutral ground, abstaining from both receiving and rejecting light from God. To be an agent means both being able to choose and having to choose either "liberty and eternal life, through the great Mediator" or "captivity and death, according to the captivity and power of the devil" (2 Ne. 2:27–29; 10:23). A being who is "an agent unto himself" is continually committing to be either an agent and servant of God or an agent and servant of Satan. If this consequence of choosing could be overridden or ignored, men and women would not determine their own destiny by their choices and agency would be void.

The captivity resulting from sin is also called "the bondage of sin" (D&C 84:49–51). Sin sets up dispositions in the sinner that empower Satan to control the sinner's thoughts and behavior by means of temptation. As this happens, the individual still possesses agency in name, but his capacity to exercise it is abridged. In this sense, to misuse one's agency is to lose that agency: "Evil, when listened to, begins to rule and overrule the spirit [that] God has placed within man" (B. Young, *JD* 6:332). Conversely, using agency to receive and obey the influence of the spirit of Christ liberates one from this bondage. Thus, though agency, in the sense of the capacity to choose life or death, is a kind of freedom, it differs in quality from the liberty that is inherent in obedience to Christ. Jesus said, "If the Son therefore shall make you free, ye shall be free indeed" (John 8:36). When King Benjamin's people in the Book of Mormon received a REMISSION OF SINS and were spiritually born again, they attested that their affections and desires had been so changed that they had "no more disposition to do evil, but to do good continually" (Mosiah 5:2). Obedience expands agency, and the alternative to obedience is bondage.

Thus, in the LDS concept of agency, obedience and agency are not antithetical. On the one hand, Church leaders consistently stand against all coercion of conscience ("We are not disposed, had we the power, to deprive anyone of exercising . . . free independence of mind" [*TPJS*, p. 49]) and counsel Church members to depend first of all on themselves for decisions about the application of gospel principles. On the other hand, obedience—willing and energetic submission to the will of God even at personal sacrifice—is a central gospel tenet. Far from contradicting freedom, obedience is its highest expression. "But in rendering . . . strict obedience, are we made slaves? No, it is the only way on the face of the earth for you and me to become free. . . . The man who yields strict obedience to the requirements of Heaven, acts upon the volition of his own will and exercises his freedom" (B. Young, *JD* 18:246).

Church leaders consistently call agency a gift of God. Sin abridges the agency of sinners to the point that unless some power releases them from this bondage, they will be "lost and fallen" (Mosiah 16:4). That power is Christ's atonement, which overcomes the effects of sin, not arbitrarily, but on condition of wholehearted REPENTANCE. "Because . . . they are redeemed from the fall they have become free forever . . . to act for themselves" (2 Ne. 2:26). Thus, human agency was purchased with the price of Christ's suffering. This means that to those who blame God for allowing human suffering, Latter-day Saints can respond that suffering is less important than the gift of agency, upon which everything else depends, and that none of us has paid a greater price for this gift than Christ.

BIBLIOGRAPHY

Madsen, Truman G. *Eternal Man*, pp. 63–70. Salt Lake City, 1966.

McKay, David O. *IE* 53 (May 1950):366.

Packer, Boyd K. "Atonement, Agency, Accountability." *Ensign* 18 (May 1988):69–72.

Romney, Marion G. "Decisions and Free Agency." *IE* 71 (Dec. 1968):73–76.

Stapley, Delbert L. "Using Our Free Agency." *Ensign* 5 (May 1975):21–23.

C. TERRY WARNER

AGRAPHA

See: Jesus Christ, Sources for Words of

AGRICULTURE

The Latter-day Saints were pioneers in developing techniques and institutions of irrigated agriculture and dry farming in the Far West, probably because of a particular juxtaposition of modern attitudes toward farming and farm life, skills gained in early industrial Britain and the United States, and the pressing need to increase production on Utah's hardscrabble farms.

Most American-born Latter-day Saints, even if trained in a trade, had some experience with farming in more humid areas before moving into the desert wilderness in 1847. They were joined by a major influx of converts from the British Isles, most from the industrialized regions of England and Wales and therefore with little farming experience. In Utah, virtually all the pioneers had to become farmers to survive. Until the transcontinental railroad was completed in 1869, they had to

Mormon pioneers displayed ingenuity and industry as they brought the valleys of the Inter-mountain West under irrigation. This style of hay derrick (c. 1900 on Blue Creek Ranch, near Brigham City, Utah), introduced into the area by Danish converts, became widely known as the "Mormon hay derrick."

raise enough food for themselves and for the immigrants who would arrive too late to grow anything. Finding Utah's annual rainfall insufficient to raise most crops, they had to irrigate the crops with water diverted from canyon streams. Also, only a small amount of land was situated so that canals could be built above the fields to irrigate the crops below. All of these circumstances—and the LDS ethic of community action—combined to shape the role of Mormons in the agricultural history of the United States.

Unlike many traditional farmers, the Latter-day Saints had a modern view of their lands and farming. Land was necessary for making a living, but it was not imbued with mystical qualities that gave superior virtue, independence, or permanence to farm life. President Brigham YOUNG, himself a craftsman, supported manufacturing and artisan crafts as well as farming and did not impute moral superiority to one over the others. Farming for the Saints was not "a way of life" but a way of making a living, and this attitude freed them from undue reverence for traditional farming practices

and from any reluctance to leave the land to take up ranching, manufacturing, trade, professions, and other pursuits that might assure a better standard of living. Moreover, the paucity of irrigable land kept most farms small, limiting production to barely more than a household subsistence level, in spite of a willingness, even eagerness, to engage in commercial agriculture.

The need to irrigate crops impelled LDS farmers to become innovators in western irrigation. Paradoxically, the high number of people previously skilled in manufacturing may have helped them to do so. The artisan-farmers applied the hydraulic engineering techniques they had learned in factories and workshops powered by water to the task of bringing water to fields. Necessity forced them to do so quickly, if sometimes clumsily. But they demonstrated that irrigated agriculture on a regional scale was possible.

A whole set of cooperative management techniques for building and maintaining dams and canal systems, distributing water to individual farmers, and applying it to the fields evolved into a model for later settlers in the arid West. It was appropriate that the first National Irrigation Congress be held in Salt Lake City in 1891, for many considered Utah a model of what was being accomplished in the West through irrigation. Ordinary farmers from Utah, skilled in irrigation techniques, have been well represented among those who have opened land in Canada and in federally sponsored irrigation projects in Idaho, Arizona, New Mexico, Wyoming, California, Oregon, and Washington, spreading both their farming techniques and their faith throughout the West.

The urgent need to maximize production on Utah's small farms led many Latter-day Saints to study scientific agriculture. Perhaps chief among them was John A. Widtsoe, later an apostle, who, after a Harvard education in physical chemistry, concentrated on expanding agricultural production. Directing the Utah Agricultural Experiment Station, he encouraged studies on soils, climate, fertilizers, and soil-working techniques, which led to publication of his *Principles of Irrigation Practice* (1914). He directed dry-farming experiments for nonirrigable lands, which culminated in *Dry Farming: A System of Agriculture for Countries Under a Low Rainfall* (1910).

Other Latter-day Saints who improved farming practices were Edgar B. Brossard in the economics of farm production; William M. Jardine (secretary of agriculture under President Calvin Coolidge) in agronomy; Phillip V. Cardon (administrator of the Agricultural Research Administration and director general of the United Nations Food and Agriculture Organization) in forage crops and diseases; Franklin S. Harris in agronomy and sugar beet culture; Lowry Nelson in rural sociology; Thomas L. Martin in agronomy; and Willard Gardner in soil physics.

Church President Ezra Taft BENSON (secretary of agriculture under President Dwight D. Eisenhower) devoted much of his life to founding farmer cooperatives. The Ezra Taft Benson Agriculture and Food Institute at Brigham Young University (1975) fosters cooperative agricultural techniques in developing countries.

Latter-day Saints continue as individuals and under Church auspices to work at improving crop yields throughout the world and applying cooperative principles to improving the standard of living in developing regions. Since the early 1970s some Latter-day Saints have been called by the Church as "additional assignment" missionaries to encour-

age practical self-help programs and better farming techniques in regions of Africa, Asia, and the Americas. Gordon Wagner, a Latter-day Saint with a doctorate in economics from Cornell, worked on his own during the 1970s and 1980s to apply LDS cooperative principles to agricultural development problems in impoverished regions of Africa.

BIBLIOGRAPHY

Arrington, Leonard J., and Davis Bitton. *The Mormon Experience: A History of the Latter-day Saints*, pp. 310–19. New York, 1979.

Arrington, Leonard J., and Dean May. "'A Different Mode of Life': Irrigation and Society in Nineteenth-Century Utah." *Agricultural History* 49 (Jan. 1975):3–20.

Mead, Elwood, et al. *Report of Irrigation Investigations in Utah.* Washington, D.C., 1903.

DEAN L. MAY

AHMAN

Ahman is twice mentioned as one of the names of God in the Doctrine and Covenants. In each instance, Jesus Christ is called Son Ahman, suggesting Son God and son of Ahman (D&C 78:20; 95:17). Orson Pratt, an apostle, suggested that this was one of the names of God in the pure language (*JD* 2:342; cf. Zeph. 3:9; *see* ADAMIC LANGUAGE).

Ahman is also an element of the place-name ADAM-ONDI-AHMAN, Missouri, where the Lord visited ADAM and "administered comfort" to him and where Adam prophesied concerning "whatsoever should befall his posterity unto the latest generation" (D&C 107:53–57; cf. D&C 78:15–16). Adam lived in the region of Adam-ondi-Ahman (D&C 117:8), and PROPHECY anticipates a future visit of Adam at this place (D&C 116:1; cf. Dan. 7:13).

BIBLIOGRAPHY

Pratt, Orson. "The Holy Spirit and the Godhead." *JD* 2:334–47.

EDWARD J. BRANDT

AIDS

The FIRST PRESIDENCY statement on AIDS (acquired immune deficiency syndrome) released May 27, 1988, admonishes Church members to become informed about AIDS and to avoid all actions that place themselves or others at risk. Members are also encouraged to become informed about AIDS-related laws and policies in the country where they live and to join in wise and constructive efforts to stem the spread of AIDS.

The statement calls for Church members to extend Christlike sympathy and compassion to all who are infected or ill with AIDS. Particular concern and sympathy are expressed for those having received the virus through blood transfusions, babies infected by their mothers, and marriage partners infected by a spouse. Leaders and members are encouraged to reach out with kindness and comfort to the afflicted, ministering to their needs and assisting them with their problems.

While hope is expressed that medical discoveries will make it possible both to prevent and cure AIDS, the observance of clearly understandable and divinely given guidance regardless of such potential discoveries will do more than all else to check a potential AIDS epidemic: "That guidance is chastity before marriage, total fidelity in marriage, abstinence from all homosexual relations, avoidance of illegal drugs, and reverence and care for the body, which is the temple of God."

The First Presidency statement includes remarks given about AIDS by Gordon B. Hinckley, First Counselor in the First Presidency, in the April 1987 general priesthood meeting: "Prophets of God have repeatedly taught through the ages that practices of homosexual relations, fornication, and adultery are grievous sins. Sexual relations outside the bonds of marriage are forbidden by the Lord. We reaffirm those teachings. . . . Each of us has a choice between right and wrong. But with that choice there inevitably will follow consequences. Those who choose to violate the commandments of God put themselves at great spiritual and physical jeopardy."

In January 1989 a special bulletin on AIDS was sent to Church leaders throughout the world to provide (1) scientific and medical information about AIDS; (2) counsel reaffirming the blessings and protection that come from living God's commandments; and (3) guidelines and policies dealing with interviewing and assisting those infected with the AIDS virus. Some items treated in the four-page special bulletin are:

- Church teachers and activity leaders who on occasion may be involved in cleaning up blood or rendering first aid should become aware of,

and follow, local health department recommendations regarding the prevention of AIDS infection.

- AIDS-infected individuals who may be contemplating marriage are to be encouraged by local Church leaders to be honest with potential marriage partners and to disclose their AIDS infection. For a person to do less would be deceitful, and in violation of one's covenants with God.

- Where transgression of God's laws has resulted in infection, the Church advocates the example of Jesus Christ, who condemned the sin but loved the sinner.

- AIDS victims who seek membership in the Church, temple recommends, or other blessings are treated as all others who express faith in God, repent, request baptism, and are living the teachings of Jesus Christ.

BIBLIOGRAPHY

Public Communications Department. "First Presidency Statement on AIDS." Salt Lake City, May 27, 1988; cf. "News of the Church," *Ensign* 18 (July 1988):79.

Questions and Answers for Priesthood Leaders Regarding AIDS (special bulletin). Salt Lake City, Jan. 1989.

ROBERT L. LEAKE

ALCOHOLIC BEVERAGES AND ALCOHOLISM

Active members of The Church of Jesus Christ of Latter-day Saints abstain from drinking alcoholic beverages. This practice of abstinence derives from an 1833 revelation known as the WORD OF WISDOM, which states "that inasmuch as any man drinketh wine or strong drink among you, behold it is not good, neither meet in the sight of your Father" (D&C 89:5). The harmful effects of ethyl alcohol (the active ingredient in all alcoholic beverages) on human health are also noted in the Bible (Prov. 31:4–5; Isa. 5:11). Although the Word of Wisdom was given originally to show the will of God and not as a commandment, abstinence from alcohol was expected of fully participating Church members by the early twentieth century and faithful observance is virtually prerequisite to temple work and leadership callings in the Church (*see* DOCTRINE AND COVENANTS: SECTION 89).

Ethyl alcohol is produced by yeast fermentation in grains and fibers containing sugar. The amount of alcohol in wine and beer is normally less than 10 percent because fermentation stops when the ethyl alcohol concentration reaches this level. In modern times, however, the amount in alcoholic beverages has been increased by distillation.

The availability of beverages with higher concentrations of alcohol has increased the number of social and medical problems associated with ingesting it. Some conditions that are increased among those who use alcohol include cancers of the oral cavity, larynx, and esophagus; cirrhosis of the liver; degenerative diseases of the central nervous system; and higher accidental death rates (both automobile and pedestrian accidents).

The proscription on alcohol ingestion has reduced the incidence of all of these conditions among Latter-day Saints. The number of alcoholics in any population is usually estimated from the number of deaths caused by cirrhosis of the liver. An unpublished study conducted at the University of Utah in 1978 found that the number of deaths from alcoholic cirrhosis of the liver among LDS people was about half that of the non-LDS in Utah and other areas of the United States. This suggests that while the Word of Wisdom does not prevent alcoholism entirely, it has been effective in reducing its incidence.

[See also Social Services.]

BIBLIOGRAPHY

Gilman, A. G., L. S. Goodman, and A. Gilman, eds. *Goodman and Gilman's The Pharmacological Basis of Therapeutics*, 6th ed., pp. 376–86. New York, 1980.

Hawks, Ricky D. "Alcohol Use Trends Among LDS High School Seniors in America from 1982–1986." *AMCAP Journal* 15, 1 (1989):43–51.

———. "Alcohol Use Among LDS and Other Groups Teaching Abstinence." In *Drug and Alcohol Abuse Reviews*, R. R. Watson, ed., pp. 133–49. Clifton, N.J., 1990.

JOSEPH LYNN LYON

ALLEGORY OF ZENOS

The Allegory of Zenos (Jacob 5) is a lengthy, prophetic declaration made by ZENOS, a Hebrew prophet, about the destiny of the house of ISRAEL. Evidently copied directly from the plates of brass into the Book of Mormon record by JACOB, it was intended (1) to reinforce Jacob's own teachings both about Jesus Christ ("We knew of Christ, and

we had a hope of his glory many hundred years before his coming"—Jacob 4:4) and about the house of Israel's anticipated unresponsiveness toward the coming Redeemer ("I perceive . . . they will reject the stone upon which they might build and have safe foundation"—Jacob 4:15), and (2) to instruct his people about the promised future regathering of Israel, to which Jacob's people belonged.

Framed in the tradition of parables, the allegory "likens" the house of Israel to an olive tree whose owner struggles to keep it from dying. The comparison figuratively illustrates God's bond with his chosen people and with the Gentiles, and underscores the lesson that through patience and compassion God will save and preserve the compliant and obedient.

The narrative contains seventy-six verses, divisible into five parts, all tied together by an overarching theme of good winning over bad, of life triumphing over death. In the first part, an alarmed owner, recognizing threatening signs of death (age and decay) in a beloved tree of superior quality, immediately tries to nurse it back to health (verses 4–5). Even though new growth appears, his ministering does not fully heal the tree; and so, with a servant's help, he removes and destroys waning parts and in their place grafts limbs from a "wild" tree. At the same time, he detaches the old tree's "young and tender" new growth for planting in secluded areas of his property. Though disappointed, he resolves to save his beloved tree (verses 6–14).

Second, following a lengthy interval of conscientious care, the owner's labor is rewarded with a generous harvest of choice fruit, not only from the newly grafted limbs on his old tree but also from the new growth that he planted around the property. These latter trees, however, have produced unequally: the two trees with least natural advantages have the highest, positive yield; while the most advantaged tree's production is only half good, compelling removal of its unprofitable parts. Even so, the owner continues an all-out effort on every tree, even this last one (verses 15–28).

In the third part, a long time passes. The owner and the servant return again to measure and evaluate the fruit, only to learn the worst: the old tree, though healthy, has produced a completely worthless crop; and it is the same for the other trees. Distressed, the owner orders all the trees destroyed. His assistant pleads for him to forbear a little longer. In the fourth segment, the "grieved" owner, accompanied by the servant and other workers, carefully tries again in one last effort. Together they reverse the previous implantation (the "young and tender" plants are returned to the old tree) and splice other old tree limbs into the previously selected trees, appropriately pruning, cultivating, and nurturing each tree as required (verses 29–73). This particular operation of mixing and blending, mingling and merging all the trees together, meets with success in replicating the superior quality crop of "natural fruit" everywhere on his property. Elated, he promises his helpers a share ("joy") in the harvest for as long as it lasts. But he also pledges destruction of all the trees if and when their capacity for a positive yield wanes again (verses 73–77).

In the subsequent chapter Jacob renders a brief interpretation (6:1–4). Conscious that his people, the Nephites, branched from the house of Israel, he is particularly anxious to redirect their increasingly errant behavior, and therefore reads into the allegory a sober caution of repentance for these impenitent New World Israelites: "How merciful is our God unto us, for he remembereth the house of Israel, both roots and branches; and he stretches forth his hands unto them all the day long; . . . but as many as will not harden their hearts shall be saved in the kingdom of God" (6:4).

Modern interpretations of the allegory have emphasized its universality. Accordingly, readers have explored its application to the house of Israel and the stretch of covenant time, that is, beginning with God's pact with Abraham and finishing with the Millennium and the ending of the earth; its doctrinal connection to the ages of spiritual apostasy, the latter-day Restoration, Church membership, present global proselytizing, the return of the Jews, and the final judgment. Other studies have begun to explore its literary and textual correspondences with ancient documents (Hymns from Qumran) and with the Old (Genesis, Isaiah, Jeremiah) and New Testaments (Romans 11:16–24); and even its association with the known laws of botany. Some scholars have declared it one of the most demanding and engaging of all scriptural allegories, if not the most important one.

BIBLIOGRAPHY

Hess, Wilford M. "Botanical Comparisons in the Allegory of the Olive Tree." In *The Book of Mormon: Jacob Through Words of Mormon, To Learn with Joy*, ed. M. Nyman and C. Tate, pp. 87–102. Provo, Utah, 1990.

McConkie, Joseph Fielding, and Robert L. Millet. *Doctrinal Commentary on the Book of Mormon*, Vol. 2, pp. 46–77. Salt Lake City, 1988.

Nibley, Hugh. *Since Cumorah*, pp. 283–85. In *CWHN* 7.

Nyman, Monte S. *An Ensign to All People*, pp. 21–36. Salt Lake City, 1987.

L. GARY LAMBERT

ALMA₁

Alma₁ (c. 174–92 B.C.) was the first of two Almas in the Book of Mormon. He was a descendant of NEPHI₁, son of LEHI, and was the young priest in the court of king Noah who attempted a peaceful release of the prophet ABINADI. For that action, Alma incurred royal vengeance, banishment, and threats upon his life. He had been impressed by Abinadi's accusations of immorality and abuses within the government and society and by his testimony of the gospel of Jesus Christ (Mosiah 17:2). Subsequently forced underground, Alma wrote out Abinadi's teachings, then shared them with others, attracting sufficient adherents—450—to organize a society of believers, or a church. The believers assembled in a remote, undeveloped area called Mormon. Participants in the church pledged to "bear one another's burdens," "mourn with those that mourn," "comfort those that stand in need of comfort," and "stand as witnesses of God at all times and in all things" (Mosiah 18:8–9). This pledge was then sealed by BAPTISM, which was considered "a testimony that ye have entered into a covenant to serve him [Almighty God] until you are dead as to the mortal body" (verse 13). Believers called themselves "the church of God, or the church of Christ, from that time forward" (verse 17).

Alma's leadership included ordaining lay priests—one for every fifty members—whom he instructed to labor for their own support, and to limit their sermons to his teachings and the doctrine "spoken by the mouth of the holy prophets . . . nothing save it were repentance and faith on the Lord" (Mosiah 18:19–20). Alma also required that there be faithful observance of the SABBATH, daily expressions of gratitude to God, and no CONTENTION, "having their hearts knit together in unity and in love" (18:21–23). The priests assembled with and taught the people in a worship meeting at least once weekly (18:25). Through generous donations, everyone cared for one another "according to that which he had" (18:27–28).

Eventually the believers were discovered and king Noah accused Alma of sedition, ordering his army to crush him and his followers. Forced into exile, Alma led the people deeper into the wilderness, where they thrived for twenty years in a region they named Helam (Mosiah 18:32–35; 23:1–5, 20). Alma ardently declined well-intended efforts to make him king, and successfully dissuaded his people from adopting a monarchical government, urging them to enjoy the new "liberty wherewith ye have been made free" and to "trust no man to be a king" (Mosiah 23:13). He did not oppose monarchies as such but, rather, acknowledged their fundamental limitation: "If it were possible that ye could always have just men to be your kings it would be well for you to have a king" (23:8).

Alma and his people afterward suffered oppression at the hands of Amulon, also an ex-priest and deserter from king Noah's court, who, along with the remnant of a LAMANITE army, discovered Alma's people in their wilderness refuge. During their suffering the voice of the Lord promised relief and deliverance because of their covenant with him: "I, the Lord God, do visit my people in their afflictions" (Mosiah 24:14). Once again, in Moses-like fashion, Alma guided his people out of bondage, and led them during a twelve-day journey to a new land—the Land of Zarahemla—where they joined with the people of Zarahemla and exiled NEPHITES to form a new and stronger Nephite nation (Mosiah 24:24–25).

The king of Zarahemla, Mosiah₂, also a descendant of transplanted God-fearing Nephites, sanctioned and even authorized expansion of Alma's church in his kingdom; the church, however, operated separately and independently of the state. The king also assigned the reins of leadership to Alma (Mosiah 25:19; 26:8), who successfully directed the church during twenty years characterized largely by tribulations, with many confrontations between nonbelievers and church members resulting in ordeals for both him and the church (Mosiah 26:1–39). Eventually, widespread antagonism necessitated a royal injunction to lessen the tension (27:1–6). Even one of Alma's sons was among the ranks of the enemies of the church, his agitation and criticism inviting yet worse persecution for church members (27:8–10).

During his lifetime Alma watched king Mosiah dismantle the monarchy and transform it into a system of judges elected by the people (Mosiah 29:2); he also saw his own son, Alma₂—the one who earlier had brought grief to him and the church—become the first chief judge (Mosiah 29:1–44). This political transformation proved pivotal in the history of the Land of Zarahemla. Directly and indirectly Alma had a hand in bringing it about; the record of his and his people's pain under oppressive rulers was widely known throughout the kingdom (25:5–6) and remained distinct in king Mosiah's mind (29:18). Alma's influence, then, can be seen as transcending the immediate spiritual boundaries of his stewardship over the church. Indeed, because of this influence the entire Nephite nation came to know unprecedented changes in almost every dimension of daily living—political, social, and economic, as well as religious. These changes—and all their connected ramifications for the social order and the populace—prepared the backdrop against which the resurrected Christ's visit to the Americas was staged. Loved by his followers for his devotion and faith, and held in esteem by his peers for his effective leadership, Alma will probably always be best known as the founder of the church in Zarahemla. His posterity became the leading Nephite family for over 400 years, down to Ammaron in A.D. 321 (4 Ne. 1:48). Alma died at age eighty-two, less than a hundred years before the birth of Jesus Christ.

L. GARY LAMBERT

ALMA₂

Few individuals have had greater influence upon a civilization than Alma₂, son of Alma₁. He was a key figure in the rise of the Nephite church and republic, serving as the first chief judge in Zarahemla, commander-in-chief of the Nephite army, and high priest (c. 90–73 B.C.). His efforts to protect his people from war, dissension, and wickedness were exceeded only by his single-minded dedication to the Savior, whom he came to know through revelation.

This crusader for righteousness first appears in the Book of Mormon as a rebellious young man. He and four of the sons of King Mosiah₂, described as "the very vilest of sinners" (Mosiah 28:4), rebelled against the teachings of their parents and

Alma the Younger Called to Repentance, by James C. Christensen (1980, leaded stained glass). The angel of the Lord rebukes the young and rebellious Alma: "If thou wilt of thyself be destroyed, seek no more to destroy the church of God" (Alma 36:9). Courtesy Museum of Fine Arts, Brigham Young University.

sought to overthrow the church. As they went about that work (c. 100–92 B.C.), the angel of the Lord appeared to them, spoke with a voice of thunder, calling these wayward young men to repentance, and explaining that he did so because of the prayers of the people and of Alma's father. For three days and three nights Alma lay in a physically comatose state, during which time he spiritually confronted all his sins, "for which," he later said, "I was tormented with the pains of hell" (Alma 36:12–14).

In the depth of his anguish of soul, Alma re-membered his father's words concerning the coming of Jesus Christ to atone for the sins of the world. As Alma cried out in his heart to Christ, pleading for mercy and deliverance from "the gall of bitterness" and "the everlasting chains of death," he stated: "I could remember my pains no more; yea, I was harrowed up by the memory of my sins no more" (Alma 36:17–19). After their conversion, Alma and the sons of Mosiah devoted their lives to preaching repentance and the joyous gospel (Alma 36:24).

For about nine years Alma served as both the high priest over the church and the chief judge or governor over a new political system of judges among the Nephites. He was well educated, the keeper of sacred and civil records, an inspiring orator, and a skillful writer. As a young civil and religious leader, he faced a number of challenges. Several religio-political factions were emerging in Nephite society, notably the Zoramites, Mulekites, members of the church, and an anti-church group, the followers of Nehor (*see* BOOK OF MORMON PEOPLES). Maintaining Nephite leadership over all these groups proved impossible. In a landmark case in his first year as chief judge, Alma held the popular Nehor guilty of enforcing priestcraft with the sword, which resulted in his execution (Alma 1:2–15). This soon led to civil war with Alma himself slaying the new rebel leader, one of Nehor's protégés, in battle (Alma 2–3). There followed a serious epidemic of pride and inequality among many in the church (Alma 4) and the secession of the arrogant Zoramites. "Seeing no way that he might reclaim [the people] save it were in bearing down in pure testimony against them" (Alma 4:19), Alma resigned his position as chief judge and devoted himself completely to the work of the ministry (Alma 4:19; 31:5). His religious work, especially in the Nephite cities of Zarahemla (Alma 5, 30) and Gideon (Alma 7), the Nehorite stronghold of Ammonihah (Alma 8–16), and the Zoramite center in Antionum (Alma 31–35), revitalized the church and set the pattern of administration for the next century down to the coming of Christ.

Alma's most enduring contributions are to be found in his sermons and his blessings upon the heads of his children. No doubt as a result of his own conversion (Mosiah 27), Alma's words frequently center on the atoning sacrifice of the Redeemer and on the necessity for men and women to be BORN OF GOD, changed, and renewed through Christ. To the people of Gideon, Alma delivered a profound prophetic oracle regarding the birth of Jesus and the ATONEMENT he would make, "suffering pains and afflictions and temptations of every kind . . . that he may loose the bands of death which bind his people; and he will take upon him their infirmities, that his bowels may be filled with mercy . . . that he may know according to the flesh how to succor his people according to their infirmities" (Alma 7:11–12). In Zarahemla, Alma stressed the need for the new birth and for acquiring the image and attributes of the Master; in doing so, he provided a series of over forty questions that assess one's depth of conversion and readiness to meet one's Maker (see Alma 5).

In Ammonihah, Alma and his convert Amulek were accused of a crime, taunted, and imprisoned for several weeks without clothing or adequate food. After being forced to witness the burning of several faithful women and children, Alma and Amulek were miraculously delivered and their persecutors annihilated. The discourses of Alma and Amulek on the Creation, the Fall, and the Atonement are among the clearest and most fundamental theological statements on these subjects in scripture (see Alma 11–12, 34, 42). In explaining humility, faith, and prayer to the poor in Antionum (Alma 32–34), Alma and Amulek set forth a pattern whereby those without faith in Christ (or those within the fold who desire to strengthen their belief) would plant the seed of the word of Christ in their hearts and eventually receive the confirming impressions of testimony that come by the power of the HOLY GHOST.

Some of the most penetrating doctrinal information in the Book of Mormon comes through words that Alma spoke to his sons. To HELAMAN₁, his eldest son and successor, Alma eloquently recounted the story of his own conversion, gave him loving fatherly counsel, and entrusted him with custody of the plates of brass, the plates of Nephi, the plates of Ether, and the LIAHONA (Alma 36–37). To Shiblon, he gave wise practical advice (Alma 38). To his errant youngest son, Corianton, who eventually went on to serve valiantly in the church, Alma explained the seriousness of sexual sin, that wickedness never was happiness (Alma 39, 41:10), that all spirits will be judged after death and will eventually stand before God after a perfect resurrection (Alma 40), and that the word "restoration" does not mean that God will restore a sinner to some former state of happiness (Alma 41), for

divine mercy cannot rob justice when the law of God has been violated (Alma 42).

A relatively young man at the time of his conversion, Alma lived fewer than twenty years thereafter. Yet in those two decades he almost singlehandedly invigorated and established the cause of truth and liberty in the Nephite church and society. Never forgetting the thunderous voice of the angel at the time of his conversion, Alma always carried with him this unchanging desire: "O that I were an angel, and could have the wish of mine heart, that I might go forth and speak with the trump of God, with a voice to shake the earth, and cry repentance unto every people! . . . that there might not be more sorrow upon all the face of the earth" (Alma 29:1–2). When he left one day and was never seen or heard again, his sons and the church supposed "that [the Lord] received Alma in the spirit, unto himself," even as Moses (Alma 45:19), drawing an apt comparison between these two great lawgivers, judges, commanders, spiritual leaders, and prophets.

For Latter-day Saints, Alma's life and lessons are rich and timeless. He serves as a hope to parents who have wandering children, and as a beacon to those who stray. He stands as a model public servant, a sterling illustration of the new life in Christ, a fearless preacher, missionary, and gifted theologian. Alma was a prophet who received a prophet's reward.

BIBLIOGRAPHY

Holland, Jeffrey R. "Alma, Son of Alma." *Ensign* 7 (March 1977):79–84.

Perry, L. Tom. "Alma the Younger." *CR* (April 1979):16–17.

ROBERT L. MILLET

ALMANACS

Early Mormon almanacs (1845–1866) first borrowed heavily from standard almanacs being published, but then came to focus on interests of members of The Church of Jesus Christ of Latter-day Saints. Since 1973 the *Church Almanac* has printed only information pertaining to the Church.

Orson Pratt, an apostle, published the first Mormon almanacs in New York City in 1845 and 1846. Basing his *Prophetic Almanac for 1845* on standard American almanacs, Elder Pratt added a few articles about doctrines of the Church. Then

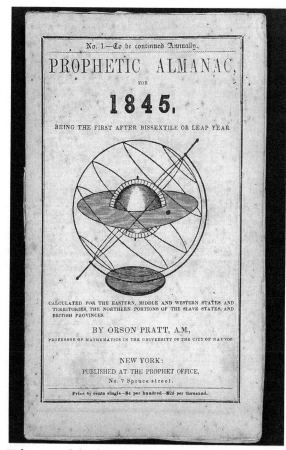

Title page of the first Mormon Almanac, Orson Pratt's *Prophetic Almanac*, published in New York in 1845. It contained standard calendar information, significant historical dates, and a comparison of "the Doctrines of Christ" with "the Doctrines of Men." Recent LDS Church Almanacs have presented statistics and information about Church history and officers. Photographer: William W. Mahler. Courtesy Rare Books and Manuscripts, Brigham Young University.

NEWS, in cooperation with the Historical Department of the Church. It was published annually from 1974 to 1983, but biennially thereafter. Presently it is a 352-page, soft-bound, ready-reference of facts and statistics of the Church. It is intended for use in libraries, schools, and other institutions, as well as private homes. The *Almanac* prints thousands of historical and contemporary items about the Church, such as brief biographical sketches of all past and present GENERAL AUTHORITIES; a year-by-year historical chronology of the Church since the 1820s; a month-by-month chronology of major events in the Church during the past two years; and past and current information about STAKES, MISSIONS, AREAS, and TEMPLES throughout the world, including histories, populations, and numbers of Church units.

Liberal use is made of photographs. In addition to photos of current events, users see photographs of all current and past General Authorities for whom there are pictures available, including an 1853 daguerreotype of the Prophet Joseph SMITH's uncle, John Smith, who was an assistant counselor in the FIRST PRESIDENCY and later the PATRIARCH TO THE CHURCH.

Each biennial issue of the *Almanac* is updated and revised. Copies may be purchased at Church DISTRIBUTION CENTERS or ordered by mail from the *Deseret News*, P.O. Box 1257, Salt Lake City, UT 84110.

BIBLIOGRAPHY

Deseret News Church Almanac. Salt Lake City, 1974–.

Whittaker, David J. "Almanacs in the New England Heritage of Mormonism." *BYU Studies* 29 (Fall 1989):89–113.

DELL VAN ORDEN

his 1846 issue broke from the standard mold and became a distinctively Mormon almanac.

Between 1851 and 1866, William Wine Phelps published fourteen known issues of *Deseret Almanac* (from 1859–1864 entitled *Almanac*) in Salt Lake City. Also borrowing from standard almanacs, he added religious and cultural articles and some notes pertaining to frontier-society needs.

The current *Deseret News Church Almanac* is prepared and edited by the staff of the CHURCH

ALTAR

A focal point of religious worship throughout the ages, and in most cultures, has been the altar—a natural or man-made elevation used for prayer, sacrifice, and related purposes. Sacrifice on the altar was a basic rite. The characteristic worship practice in Old Testament times was sacrificial in nature, and consequently the altar became one of the most important ritual objects described in that book of scripture.

Sacred and symbolic meaning is ascribed to the altar. The stipulations of the "law of the altar" (Ex. 20:24–26) suggest that its construction is associated with the creation of the world and God's COVENANTS with humankind. As the waters of creation receded, dry land appeared and was known as the primordial mound (first hill). Here, according to legend, the gods stood in order to complete the Creation. Because of divine presence, this spot became sacred or holy ground, a point of contact between this world and the heavenly world. The altar was built that people might kneel by it to communicate and make covenants with their God. The altar in Ezekiel 43:15 is named "the mountain of God" (Hebrew term, hahar'el), and becomes the symbolic embodiment of the Creation, the primordial mound, and the presence of God.

At an altar ADAM learned the meaning of sacrifice (Moses 5:5–8). Following the Flood, the patriarch NOAH immediately built an altar and offered his sacrifices to the Most High. When ABRAHAM received the promise and covenant of an inheritance for his posterity, he marked this sacred event with an altar (Gen. 12:6–7). On Mount Moriah the young Isaac was bound upon the sacrificial table or altar in preparation for his father's supreme offering and demonstration of obedience (Gen. 22:9–14). Tradition says the place of this consecrated altar became the locus of the temple in Jerusalem.

The temple complex in Jerusalem had four different altars. In an ascending order of sacral primacy, they were as follows: First, the Altar of Sacrifice, often called the altar of burnt offering or the table of the Lord (Mal. 1:7, 12; 1 Cor. 10:21), was placed outside of the temple itself in the Court of Israel and was more public than the others. Sacrifices for the sins of Israel were offered here, anticipating fulfillment in the sacrifice of Jesus Christ (Heb. 9:25–26; Alma 34:9–10, 14–16). Second, the Altar of Incense stood in the "holy place" before the veil inside the temple proper. John describes the smoke of this altar as the "prayers of all saints upon the golden altar which was before the throne" (Rev. 8:3–4). Third, within the same area of the temple stood the Table of Shewbread, upon which rested twelve loaves of bread, frankincense, and a drink offering. And fourth, the ark of the covenant rested in the HOLY OF HOLIES, the most inner, sacred area within the temple. The ark was to Israel the portable throne or Mercy Seat and symbolized the presence of the Lord. It was here

that the high priest, once a year on the Day of Atonement (Heb. 9:7; Lev. 16:1–17), made covenants with the Lord for all Israel, as though he represented all at the altar.

In LDS TEMPLES, altars of a different sort play a major role. Kneeling by them, Latter-day Saints participate in covenant-making ceremonies. They make these covenants, as was done anciently, in the symbolic presence of God at the altar (Ps. 43:4; cf. Ps. 118:27). Thus, while kneeling at an altar in a temple, a man and woman make covenants with God and each other in a marriage ceremony that is to be binding both in MORTALITY and in the eternal world. Here, if parents were not previously married in a temple, they and their children may be sealed together for time and eternity by the power and AUTHORITY of the priesthood. Likewise, these ORDINANCES may be performed by proxies at an altar within the temple on behalf of people identified in genealogical records as having died without these privileges.

As the ancients came to the altar to communicate and commune with God, so also do members of the Church, in a temple setting, surround the altar in a PRAYER CIRCLE and in supplication. United in heart and mind, the Saints petition God for his blessings upon mankind, his Church, and those who have special needs.

In a more public SACRAMENT MEETING, the Altar of Sacrifice is symbolized by the "sacrament table." On this table are emblems of the sacrifice of Jesus Christ, the bread and the water respectively representing the body and blood of the Savior (Luke 22:19–20). Each week individuals may partake of the SACRAMENT and renew their covenants.

Today members of the Church make sacred covenants with God and consecrate their lives and all that they have been blessed with as they "come unto Christ" and lay all things symbolically upon the altar as a sacrifice. To them a sacred altar is a tangible symbol of the presence of God, before whom they kneel with "a broken heart and contrite spirit" (2 Ne. 2:7; 3 Ne. 11:20).

BIBLIOGRAPHY

Eliade, Mircea. *Patterns in Comparative Religion.* New York, 1974.

Talmage, James E. *The House of the Lord.* Salt Lake City, 1971.

Packer, Boyd K. *The Holy Temple.* Salt Lake City, 1980.

BRUCE H. PORTER

AMEN

Among Latter-day Saints the saying of an audible "amen" is the seal and witness of all forms of worship and of priesthood ordinances. The Hebrew word, meaning "truly," is transliterated into Greek in the New Testament, and thence to the English Bible. It is found many times in the Book of Mormon. The Hebrew infinitive conveys the notions "to confirm, support, uphold, be faithful, firm." In antiquity the expression carried the weight of an oath. By saying "amen" the people solemnly pledged faithfulness and assented to curses upon themselves if found guilty (Deut. 27:14–26). And by saying "amen" the people also sealed their praises of God (1 Chr. 16:36; Ps. 106:48; Rom. 11:36; 1 Pet. 4:11). Nehemiah records a dramatic instance: "And Ezra blessed the Lord. . . . And all the people answered, Amen, Amen, with lifting up their hands: and they bowed their heads, and worshipped the Lord with their faces to the ground" (Neh. 8:6).

By saying "amen," Latter-day Saints officially sustain what is said in formal and private prayer, as also in the words of sermons, official admonition, and testimony (see D&C 88:135). In the sacrament service, by repeating "amen" at the end of prayers on the bread and on the water, they covenant to always remember Christ, "that they may have his Spirit to be with them" (D&C 20:77–79). At temple dedications in solemn assembly they stand with uplifted hands and shout "Hosanna to God and the Lamb," followed by a threefold "amen" (*see* HOSANNA SHOUT).

BIBLIOGRAPHY

Welch, John W. "Amen." *BYU Religious Studies Center Newsletter* 3 (Sep. 1988):3–4.

DANIEL B. MCKINLAY

AMMONITES

See: Book of Mormon Peoples

AMULEK

Amulek (fl. c. 82–74 B.C.), a Nephite inhabitant of the city Ammonihah (Alma 8:20), was a wealthy man in his community (Alma 10:4). Formerly rebellious toward God, he heeded an angel of the Lord and became a missionary companion to ALMA₂ (Alma 10:10). An articulate defender of gospel principles, he displayed virtues of long-suffering and faith, gave up his wealth to teach the gospel, and became a special witness for Christ (see Alma 8–16; 32–34).

Amulek bore powerful testimony to his own city, which earlier had rejected Alma. He confounded opposing lawyers and called upon them to repent—particularly Zeezrom, who had plotted to tempt and destroy him (Alma 11:25). He taught about the nature of the GODHEAD and the role of Christ, emphasizing the resurrection and final judgment (Alma 11:28–45). Touched by the words of Amulek and Alma, Zeezrom recognized the truth, repented, and defended the two missionaries (Alma 14:6–7).

When nonbelievers forced Alma and Amulek to witness the burning of women and children, Amulek desired to save them from the flames. He was restrained, however, by Alma (Alma 14:10–11; *see* MARTYRS). They themselves were bound, were smitten, and endured hunger as they lay naked in prison (Alma 14:14–22). At last, receiving strength according to their faith, they miraculously broke their bonds and walked out of the collapsing prison, while those who had smitten them died in its ruins (Alma 14:26–28).

Because of his faith in Christ, Amulek was rejected by his family and friends (Alma 15:16). When peace was restored after the Lamanite destruction of Ammonihah, Alma, Amulek, and others built up the church among the Nephites (Alma 16:15).

As a special witness for Christ and filled with the Holy Spirit, Amulek testified to the poor of the Zoramites that only in Christ was salvation possible (Alma 34:5–13). He stated that Christ would come into the world and make an infinite atonement for the sins of the people. "Not any man" could accomplish this act, which would be the great and last sacrifice, bringing mercy to satisfy the demands of justice and saving those who believe on his name (Alma 34:8–16). In return, Amulek said, Christ asked for faith unto repentance, charitable deeds, acceptance of the name of Christ, no contending against the Holy Ghost, no reviling of enemies, and bearing one's afflictions patiently (Alma 34:17–41).

BIBLIOGRAPHY

Dahl, Larry E. "The Plan of Redemption—Taught and Rejected." In *Studies in Scripture*, ed. Kent P. Jackson, Vol. 8, pp. 307–320. Salt Lake City, 1987.

NORBERT H. O. DUCKWITZ

ANCESTRAL FILE™

Ancestral File™ is a large genealogical database published on compact disks (CD-ROM) for use in personal computers. Its purpose is to preserve genealogies of families throughout the world, make these genealogies available to researchers of all faiths and nationalities, and help them avoid unnecessary effort and expense. The file is produced and maintained by the FAMILY HISTORY LIBRARY of The Church of Jesus Christ of Latter-day Saints located in Salt Lake City.

By January 1990 Ancestral File contained approximately 7 million lineage-linked names; it is expected that millions more will be added each year. The distinguishing features of this file are that it:

1. displays and prints ancestors' individual records, pedigrees, family groups, and descendancy charts;

2. uses standardized spelling of names, locality cross-references, and other convenient retrieval techniques;

3. facilitates correcting and updating the data;

4. gives a reference number for a microfilm copy of the original information;

5. contains the names and addresses of persons who contributed the information;

6. enables users to copy family-linked data onto diskettes to be matched and merged with their own files.

Open participation in Ancestral File is essential to its purposes. All researchers can contribute their genealogies by providing additional information on entire families, and by using PERSONAL ANCESTRAL FILE® or other genealogical software that accommodates the GEDCOM (Genealogical Data Communication) format. Ancestral File is available at the Family History Library in Salt Lake City and at hundreds of its affiliated FAMILY HISTORY CENTERS in outlying stake centers of the Church. Mail-order printouts may be obtained by correspondence.

Ancestral File and Personal Ancestral File are trademarks of the Corporation of the President of The Church of Jesus Christ of Latter-day Saints.

BIBLIOGRAPHY

Mayfield, David M., and A. Gregory Brown. "Family Search." *Genealogical Computing* (July 1990).

DAVID M. MAYFIELD

ANGEL MORONI STATUE

A monument to the angel Moroni (*see* MORONI, ANGEL) stands atop the hill CUMORAH, four miles south of Palmyra, New York, where MORONI₂ gave

Angel Moroni Monument, by Torlief S. Knaphus (1935, granite and cast bronze, 39'), at the Hill Cumorah, south of Palmyra, New York. This monument stands on the Hill Cumorah where the gold plates containing the Book of Mormon record were deposited and where the Angel Moroni delivered them in 1827 to Joseph Smith.

Joseph Smith the GOLD PLATES from which he translated the Book of Mormon (see MORONI, VISITATIONS OF). Mounted on a 25-foot shaft of white granite, the ten-foot bronze figure of Moroni points toward heaven with the right hand and holds a replica of the plates with the left. Created by Norwegian sculptor Torleif S. Knaphus, the monument was dedicated by Church President Heber J. GRANT on July 21, 1935.

Moroni was the last in a line of prophet-leaders in the Western Hemisphere whose history is recorded in the Book of Mormon. Latter-day Saints believe John the Revelator foretold Moroni's angelic ministry: "And I saw another angel fly in the midst of heaven, having the everlasting gospel to preach unto them that dwell on the earth, and to every nation, and kindred, and tongue, and people" (Rev. 14:6).

Because Moroni's mission was vital to the RESTORATION of the gospel of Jesus Christ and the establishment of The Church of Jesus Christ of Latter-day Saints, a statue of Moroni as a herald sounding a trumpet has been placed on several Latter-day Saint TEMPLES (e.g., Salt Lake City, Los Angeles, and Washington, D.C.).

BIBLIOGRAPHY

Giles, John D. "The Symbolism of the Angel Moroni Monument—Hill Cumorah." *Instructor* 86 (Apr. 1951):98–99.

CORY H. MAXWELL

ANGELS

[*This entry consists of three articles:*

Angels

Archangels

Guardian Angels

The first article discusses the nature of angels as pertaining to their ministry to people on the earth, showing that different classes perform different types of service. The second article examines a hierarchy among angels, and identifies Michael as an archangel. The last article explores the concept of guardian angels, and examines what the scriptures and the Brethren have said. It proposes the Holy Spirit as a type of guardian angel.]

ANGELS

Latter-day Saints accept the reality of angels as messengers for the Lord. Angels are mentioned in the Old and New Testaments, the Book of Mor-

mon, the Doctrine and Covenants, and the Pearl of Great Price and are prominent in the early history of The Church of Jesus Christ of Latter-day Saints. Angels are of various types and perform a variety of functions to implement the work of the Lord on the earth.

The skepticism of the modern age has tended to diminish belief in angels. However, Jesus Christ frequently spoke of angels, both literally and figuratively. When Jesus' disciples asked him to "declare unto us the parable of the tares of the field," he responded, "He that soweth the good seed is the Son of Man; the field is the world . . . and the reapers are the angels" (Matt. 13:36–39). Angels are actual beings participating in many incidents related in scripture (e.g., Luke 1:13, 19; 2:25; John 20:12, etc.). They exist as a part of the "whole family in heaven" (Eph. 3:15). All people, including angels, are the offspring of God.

In form angels are like human beings. They do not, of course, have the wings many artists symbolically show (*TPJS*, p. 162). Concerning the two angels who visited Lot's home in Sodom, the local residents inquired, "Where are the *men* which came in to thee this night?" (Gen. 19:1, 5, emphasis added). Daniel described the angel Gabriel as having "the appearance of a man" (Dan. 8:15). At the sepulcher of the risen Savior "the angel of the Lord descended from heaven" (Matt. 28:2) as "a young man . . . clothed in a long white garment" (Mark 16:5). A quite detailed description of an angel was given by Joseph Smith in recording the visit of the angel Moroni (JS—H 1:30–33, 43).

The angels who visit this earth are persons who have been assigned as messengers to this earth: "There are no angels who minister to this earth but those who do belong or have belonged to it" (D&C 130:5).

There are several types and kinds of beings, in various stages of progression, whom the Lord has used as angels in varying circumstances. One kind is a spirit child of the Eternal Father who has not yet been born on the earth but is intended for earthly mortality. Such is probably the type of angel who appeared to Adam (Moses 5:6–8).

In the early days of the mortal world, many righteous persons were taken from the earth, or translated (see TRANSLATED BEINGS). Enoch and his people (Moses 7:18–21, 31, 63, 69; Heb. 11:5), Moses (Alma 45:19), and Elijah (2 Kgs. 2:11–12) were all translated. The Prophet Joseph SMITH taught that translated beings "are designed for future missions" (*TPJS*, p. 191), and hence can be angelic ministrants.

Another kind of angel may be an individual who completed his mortal existence but whose labors continue in the SPIRIT WORLD while he awaits the RESURRECTION of the body. Such are referred to as "the spirits of just men made perfect" (Heb. 12:22–23; D&C 76:69; *TPJS*, p. 325). "Are they not all ministering spirits, sent forth to minister for them who shall be heirs of salvation?" (Heb. 1:13–14).

Since the resurrection of Jesus Christ, some angels have been "resurrected personages, having bodies of flesh and bones" (D&C 129:1). The Prophet Joseph Smith indicated that resurrected angels have advanced further in light and glory than spirits (*TPJS*, p. 325). Such are the beings who have been instrumental in the RESTORATION OF THE GOSPEL in the DISPENSATION OF THE FULNESS OF TIMES. It was of this type of angel that John wrote, "And I saw another angel fly in the midst of heaven, having the everlasting gospel to preach unto them that dwell on the earth, and to every nation, and kindred, and tongue, and people" (Rev. 14:6). ELIAS, MOSES, ELIJAH, MORONI, JOHN THE BAPTIST, PETER, and JAMES are examples of resurrected angels who ministered to the Prophet Joseph Smith.

Pursuant to John's prophecy in Revelation 14:6, the fulness of the gospel, in word and power, has been restored to the earth through the ministration of angels. The angel MORONI, a resurrected being, revealed the record of the Book of Mormon which contains the fulness of the gospel of Jesus Christ (D&C 20:8–11; *see* MORONI, VISITATIONS OF). Later he who was called John the Baptist in the New Testament, now also a resurrected being, came as an angel and restored the Aaronic Priesthood to Joseph Smith and Oliver COWDERY on May 15, 1829 (D&C 13; JS—H 1:68–72; *see* AARONIC PRIESTHOOD: RESTORATION OF). Likewise, Peter, James, and John, as angelic embodied messengers from God, restored the Melchizedek Priesthood (D&C 27:12–13; *see* MELCHIZEDEK PRIESTHOOD: RESTORATION OF). Moses, Elias, and Elijah each appeared as angels and committed once again the "keys of the gathering of Israel," the "dispensation of the gospel of Abraham" (including celestial or patriarchal marriage), and the keys of the sealing powers to "turn the hearts of the fathers to the children, and the children to the fathers" (D&C 110:11–16).

Other "divers angels" have come to deliver keys, power, priesthood, and glory (D&C 128:18–21); to teach (2 Ne. 10:3; Mosiah 3:2–3; Rev. 1:1), guide, and inspire (Rev. 5:11); and to make the gospel operative in the lives of men and women. However, the work of the angels of the restoration is not complete, and the scriptures indicate that there will yet be other angelic administrations before "the hour of [God's] judgment is come" (D&C 88:103–104; 133:36).

Angelic messengers bring knowledge, priesthood, comfort, and assurances from God to mortals. However, when priesthood or keys are to be conveyed, the ministering angel possesses a body of flesh and bones, either from resurrection or translation. Spirits can convey information, but they cannot confer priesthood upon mortal beings, because spirits do not lay hands on mortals (cf. D&C 129).

The Lord himself may also at times be called an angel, since the term means "messenger." He is the "messenger of salvation" (D&C 93:8), and the "messenger of the covenant" (Mal. 3:1), and is the "Angel which redeemed me" of whom Jacob spoke in Genesis 48:15–16.

Some of the Father's spirit children "kept not their first estate" (Jude 1:6; D&C 29:36–38; Rev. 12:3–9), and, as Peter explained, "God spared not the angels that sinned, but cast them down to hell" (2 Pet. 2:4). These are angels to the devil. Thus, Satan and those who chose to follow him are sometimes referred to as angels (2 Cor. 11:14–15; 2 Ne. 2:17; *see also* FIRST ESTATE; WAR IN HEAVEN).

A different usage of the term "angel" is applied to those who, because they have not obeyed the principles of the new and everlasting covenant of marriage, do not qualify for exaltation but remain separately and singly as ministering angels without EXALTATION in their saved condition for all eternity (D&C 132:16–17).

BIBLIOGRAPHY

McConkie, Bruce R. *Mormon Doctrine.* Salt Lake City, 1966.

McConkie, Oscar W. *Angels.* Salt Lake City, Utah, 1975.

Pratt, Parley P. "Angels and Spirits." In *Key to the Science of Theology,* 10th ed., pp. 112–19. Salt Lake City, 1973.

OSCAR W. MCCONKIE

ARCHANGELS

Traditionally, angels have been viewed as guardians of persons or places, and bearers of God's tidings. The prefix "arch" intensifies this meaning to denote one who rules or is outstanding, principal, or preeminent. Several biblical texts give prominence to four, six, or seven angels (Ezek. 9:2; Rev. 8:2). Dionysius, a sixth-century Christian theologian, purports the existence of nine angelic orders called choirs, one of which is called "archangels." Milton's *Paradise Lost* has the archangels Raphael and Michael appear to and instruct ADAM concerning the fall of the angels, the Creation, and the history of the world. Dante also refers to archangels in *The Divine Comedy*.

In the literature of The Church of Jesus Christ of Latter-day Saints, an archangel is a chief angel, holding a position of PRIESTHOOD authority in the heavenly hierarchy. Michael (Adam) is the only one precisely so designated in scripture (D&C 29:26; 88:112; 107:54; 128:21; 1 Thes. 4:16; Jude 1:9), although others (Gabriel, who is also NOAH; Raphael, Raguel, etc.) are mentioned in scriptural, apocryphal, and pseudepigraphic works. Teachings of Latter-day Saint prophets indicate that a priesthood organization exists among the heavenly hosts (*TPJS*, pp. 157, 208). However, discussion of specific positions or functions in the celestial hierarchy beyond the scriptures cited above is conjectural.

JERRY C. GILES

GUARDIAN ANGELS

One of the functions of angels is to warn and protect mortals. The Lord whispered to David, "There shall no evil befall thee, neither shall any plague come nigh thy dwelling. For he shall give his angels charge over thee, to keep thee in all thy ways. They shall bear thee up in their hands, lest thou dash thy foot against a stone" (Ps. 91:10–12). The angel of the Lord's presence saved Israel (Isa. 63:9). Daniel replied to the King: "My God hath sent his angel, and hath shut the lions' mouths, that they have not hurt me . . . " (Dan. 6:22).

This well-known guardian function of angels has given rise to an assumption on the part of some that all persons, or at least the righteous, have individual angels assigned to them throughout life as guardians. There is no scriptural justification for this tradition, although it has been entertained sometimes among Latter-day Saints and others (*TPJS*, p. 368).

Latter-day Saints believe that every person born into the world is accorded protecting care and direction by God, provided in part by the LIGHT OF CHRIST (D&C 84:44–48; Moro. 7:12–19). Those who have the GIFT OF THE HOLY GHOST may be warned, guarded, or shielded through the spirit of revelation (D&C 8:2–4). The term "guardian angel" may best be viewed as a figure of speech that has to do with God's protecting care and direction or, in special instances, with an angel dispatched to earth in fulfillment of God's purposes.

OSCAR W. MCCONKIE

ANIMALS

Latter-day Saints believe that animals, like humans, have SPIRITS, in the form of their bodies (D&C 77:2). Like humans and plants, animals were created first as spirits in heaven and then physically on the earth (Moses 3:5). Mortal and subject to death, animals will be saved through the ATONEMENT of Christ (*TPJS*, pp. 291–92). Humans and animals will eventually live in peace on this earth (Isa. 11:6–9; 2 Ne. 30:12–15; D&C 101:24–26). The Prophet Joseph SMITH taught that animals will be found in heaven, in myriad forms, from myriad worlds, enjoying eternal felicity, and praising God in languages God understands (*TPJS*, pp. 291–92).

Animals, like other "good things which come of the earth . . . are made for the benefit and the use of man," but are "to be used, with judgment, not to excess, neither by extortion" (D&C 59:16–20). God gave Adam and Eve dominion over the animals (Gen. 1:28), but legitimate dominion is neither coercive nor exploitive (D&C 121:34–46). He sanctions the eating of animal flesh but forbids its waste (Gen. 9:2–5; D&C 49:18–21). The JOSEPH SMITH TRANSLATION OF THE BIBLE (JST) cautions, "Surely, blood shall not be shed, only for meat, to save your lives; and the blood of every beast will I require at your hands" (JST Gen. 9:11).

Destroying animal life merely for sport has been strongly criticized by several Latter-day Saint leaders, including Lorenzo SNOW, Joseph F. SMITH, Joseph Fielding SMITH, and Spencer W. KIMBALL. Lorenzo Snow called it a "murderous amusement."

When the Prophet Joseph Smith saw his associates about to kill three rattlesnakes at their campsite, he said, "Let them alone—don't hurt them! How will the serpent ever lose its venom, while the servants of God possess the same disposition, and continue to make war upon it? Men must become harmless before the brute creation, and when men lose their vicious dispositions and cease to destroy the animal race, the lion and the lamb can dwell together, and the sucking child can play with the serpent in safety" (*TPJS*, p. 71).

Heber C. Kimball criticized the use of spurs and whips, saying, "[Horses] have the same life in them that you have, and we should not hurt them" (*JD* 5:137). Brigham YOUNG called neglect of livestock a "great sin" (*JD* 12:218). So far, no authoritative Church statement on the use of animals in medical research and product testing is available.

BIBLIOGRAPHY

Jones, Gerald E. "The Gospel and Animals." *Ensign* 2 (Aug. 1972):62–65.

Kimball, Spencer W. "Fundamental Principles to Ponder and Live." *Ensign* 8 (Nov. 1978):43–46.

Smith, Joseph Fielding. *Answers to Gospel Questions*, Vol. 4, pp. 42–47. Salt Lake City, 1963.

Snow, Lorenzo. *Teachings of Lorenzo Snow*, Williams, Clyde J., comp., pp. 188–89. Salt Lake City, 1984.

SANDRA BRADFORD PACKARD

ANTHON TRANSCRIPT

The Anthon Transcript was a sheet of paper, thought to be lost, upon which Joseph SMITH copied sample "reformed Egyptian" characters from the plates of the Book of Mormon. In the winter of 1828, Martin HARRIS showed these characters to Dr. Charles Anthon of Columbia College (now Columbia University), and hence the name.

In February 1828, Martin Harris, a farmer from Palmyra, New York, visited the Prophet Joseph Smith, who was then residing in HARMONY, PENNSYLVANIA, where he had just begun to translate the Book of Mormon (*see* BOOK OF MORMON TRANSLATION BY JOSEPH SMITH). Smith had earlier turned to Harris for financial backing for the translation; now Harris came to Harmony to take samples of the reformed Egyptian characters from the GOLD PLATES (cf. Morm. 9:32), thereafter to obtain scholarly opinion about their authenticity. Smith gave Harris a copy of some of the characters, along with a translation, which Harris then presented to at least three scholars in the eastern United States. The most important of these, given the nature of the inquiry, was Charles Anthon, an acclaimed classicist at Columbia College.

The two men's accounts of the meeting differ. Harris said that Professor Anthon gave him a certificate verifying the authenticity of the characters but that when Anthon learned that Joseph Smith claimed to have received the plates from an angel, he took the certificate back and destroyed it. Anthon, for his part, left written accounts in 1834 and 1841 in which he contradicted himself on whether he had given Harris a written opinion about the document. In both accounts, apparently to dissociate himself from appearing to promote the book, he maintained that he told Harris that he (Harris) was a victim of a fraud. Modern research suggests that, given the state of knowledge of Egyptian in 1828, Anthon's views would have been little more than opinion. Whatever the case may be about a written statement from Anthon, Harris returned to Harmony ready to assist Joseph Smith with the translation.

The REORGANIZED CHURCH OF JESUS CHRIST OF LATTER-DAY SAINTS possesses a handwritten

Charles Anthon (1787–1867), a professor of classical languages at Columbia College (now Columbia University) in New York from 1820 to 1867. His library in 1828 included recent works on hieroglyphic and demotic Egyptian.

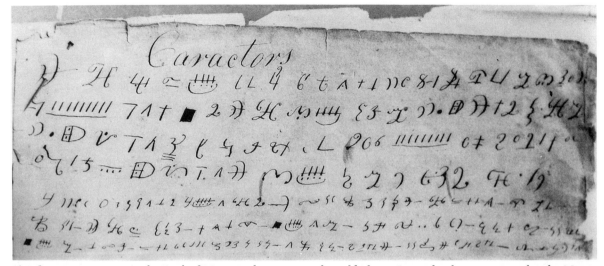

This document represents the Book of Mormon characters on the gold plates. It may be the transcript taken by Martin Harris to Charles Anthon in 1828, or a copy of it. The heirs of David Whitmer sold this document to the Reorganized Church of Jesus Christ of Latter Day Saints. This text is too short to be deciphered. Courtesy Library-Archives, Reorganized Church of Jesus Christ of Latter Day Saints, The Auditorium, Independence, Missouri.

text known as the Anthon Transcript that contains seven horizontal lines of characters apparently copied from the plates. David WHITMER, who once owned the document, said it was this text that Martin Harris showed to Charles Anthon. However, this claim remains uncertain because the transcript does not correspond with Anthon's assertion that the manuscript he saw was arranged in vertical columns. Even if the document is not the original, it almost certainly represents characters either copied from the plates in Joseph Smith's possession or copied from the document carried by Harris. Twice in late 1844, after the Prophet's martyrdom, portions of these symbols were published as characters that Joseph Smith had copied from the gold plates—once as a broadside and once in the December 21 issue of the Mormon newspaper *The Prophet* (*see* MAGAZINES). In 1980 a document surfaced that seemed to match Anthon's description and appeared to be the original Anthon Transcript. But in 1987, Mark W. Hofmann admitted that he had forged it (*see* FORGERIES).

Harris's visit with scholars was more than just an interesting sidelight in the history of Mormonism. By his own report, Harris returned to Harmony convinced that the characters were genuine. Thereafter, he willingly invested his time and resources to see the Book of Mormon published. Moreover, the Prophet, Harris himself, and later generations of Latter-day Saints have viewed his visit as a fulfillment of Isaiah 29:11–12, which

speaks of "a book that is sealed" being delivered to "one that is learned" who could not read it (*PJS* 1:9; cf. 2 Ne. 27:6–24; *see also* BOOK OF MORMON, BIBLICAL PROPHECIES ABOUT). His efforts apparently encouraged Joseph Smith in the initial stages of the translation. The Anthon Transcript is also important to subsequent generations as an authentic sample of characters that were inscribed on the gold plates and thus one of the few tangible evidences of their existence.

[*See also* Book of Mormon Language.]

BIBLIOGRAPHY

Kimball, Stanley B. "I Cannot Read a Sealed Book." *IE* 60 (Feb. 1957):80–82, 104, 106.

———. "The Anthon Transcript: People, Primary Sources, and Problems." *BYU Studies* 10 (Spring 1970):325–52.

"Martin Harris' Visit to Charles Anthon: Collected Documents on Short-hand Egyptian." *F.A.R.M.S. Preliminary Report.* Provo, Utah, 1985.

DANEL W. BACHMAN

ANTICHRISTS

Antichrists are those who deny the divinity of JESUS CHRIST or essential parts of his gospel and actively oppose the followers of Christ or seek to destroy their faith.

The epistles of John explicitly condemn as antichrists those with a lying spirit who deny that Jesus is the Christ and deny the physical resurrection. Antichrists are to be notably active in the last days (1 Jn. 2:18, 22; 4:3; 2 Jn. 1:7).

The Book of Mormon profiles many subtle and sophisticated aspects of antichrist characters, though the text explicitly refers to only one of them as antichrist.

Sherem (c. 540 B.C.) rejected the prophetic Christian teachings of the Nephite prophets, arguing that belief in the coming Christ perverted the law of Moses. He employed several archetypical arguments and methods, claiming that no one could know of things to come, including the coming of Christ. When confronted, Sherem asserted that if there were a Christ he would not deny him, but he knew "there is no Christ, neither has been, nor ever will be," thus contradicting his own argument that no one could "tell of things to come." Demanding a sign of divine power, Sherem was stricken by God, and then confessed that he had been deceived by the DEVIL in denying the Christ (Jacob 7:1–23).

Nehor (c. 91 B.C.), a practitioner of PRIESTCRAFT, preached and established a church to obtain riches and worldly honor and to satisfy his pride. He taught that God had created everyone, had redeemed everyone, and that people need not "fear and tremble" because everyone would be saved. Furthermore, he said priests should be supported by the people. Nehor attacked and killed a defender of the true doctrine of Christ, and was tried before Alma₂ and executed (Alma 1:2–16). He was not executed for being an antichrist, but for having enforced his beliefs "by the sword."

Korihor (c. 74 B.C.) was an extremist, rejecting all religious teachings, even to the point of not posturing either as a defender of traditions or as a reformer of corrupted religious practices. He was labeled "Anti-Christ" because he taught that there was no need for a Christ and that none would come. He described the religious teachings of the church as foolish traditions designed to subject the people to corrupt and lazy priests. In a dramatic confrontation with the Nephite chief judge, and with the prophet Alma₂, Korihor claimed that one cannot know anything that cannot be seen, making knowledge or prophecy of future events impossible. He ridiculed all talk of visions, dreams, and the mysteries of God. He called belief in sin, the atonement of Christ, and the remission of sins a derangement of the mind caused by foolish religious traditions. He denied the existence of God and, after demanding a sign as proof of his existence, was struck dumb. After Alma accused him of possessing a lying spirit, Korihor confessed that he had been deceived by Satan, had taught words and doctrines pleasing to the carnal mind, and had even begun to believe them himself (Alma 30:6–60).

BIBLIOGRAPHY

Riddle, Chauncey C. "Korihor: The Arguments of Apostasy." *Ensign* 7 (Sept. 1977):18–21.

RUSSELL M. FRANDSEN

ANTI-MORMON PUBLICATIONS

Anti-Mormonism includes any hostile or polemic opposition to Mormonism or to the Latter-day Saints, such as maligning the founding prophet, his successors, or the doctrines or practices of the Church. Though sometimes well intended, anti-Mormon publications have often taken the form of invective, falsehood, demeaning caricature, prejudice, and legal harassment, leading to both verbal and physical assault. From its beginnings, The Church of Jesus Christ of Latter-day Saints and its members have been targets of anti-Mormon publications. Apart from collecting them for historical purposes and in response to divine direction, the Church has largely ignored these materials, for they strike most members as irresponsible misrepresentations.

Few other religious groups in the United States have been subjected to such sustained, vitriolic criticism and hostility. From the organization of the Church in 1830 to 1989, at least 1,931 anti-Mormon books, novels, pamphlets, tracts, and flyers have been published in English. Numerous other newsletters, articles, and letters have been circulated. Since 1960 these publications have increased dramatically.

A major reason for hostility against the Church has been its belief in extrabiblical REVELATION. The theological foundation of the Church rests on the claim by the Prophet Joseph SMITH that God the Father, Jesus Christ, and angels appeared to him and instructed him to restore a DISPENSATION of the gospel.

Initial skepticism toward Joseph Smith's testimony was understandable because others had made similar claims to receiving revelation from

God. Moreover, Joseph Smith had brought forth the Book of Mormon, giving tangible evidence of his claim to revelation, and this invited testing. His testimony that the book originated from an ancient record engraved on metal PLATES that he translated by the gift and power of God was considered preposterous by disbelievers. Hostile anti-Mormon writing and other abuses grew largely out of the perceived need to supply an alternative explanation for the origin of the Book of Mormon. The early critics focused initially on discrediting the SMITH FAMILY, particularly Joseph Smith, Jr., and attempted to show that the Book of Mormon was entirely of nineteenth-century origin. Later critics have focused more on points of doctrine, individual leaders, and Church operation.

EARLY CRITICISMS (1829–1846). Joseph Smith's disclosure that heavenly messengers had visited him was met with derision, particularly by some local clergymen. When efforts to dissuade him failed, he became the object of ridicule. From the time of the FIRST VISION (1820) to the first visit by the ANGEL MORONI (1823), Joseph "suffered every kind of opposition and persecution from the different orders of religionists" (Lucy Mack Smith, *History of Joseph Smith*, p. 74).

The first serious attempt to discredit Joseph Smith and the Book of Mormon was by Abner Cole, editor of the *Reflector*, a local paper in Palmyra, New York. Writing under the pseudonym Obadiah Dogberry, Cole published in his paper extracts from two pirated chapters of the 1830 edition of the Book of Mormon, but was compelled to desist because he was violating copyright law. Cole resorted to satire. He attempted to malign Joseph Smith by associating him with money digging, and he claimed that Joseph was influenced by a magician named Walters.

Alexander Campbell, founder of the Disciples of Christ, wrote the first published anti-Mormon pamphlet. The text appeared first as articles in his own paper, the *Millennial Harbinger* (1831), and then in a pamphlet entitled *Delusions* (1832). Campbell concluded, "I cannot doubt for a single moment that [Joseph Smith] is the sole author and proprietor of [the Book of Mormon]." Two years later he recanted this conclusion and accepted a new theory for the origin of the Book of Mormon, namely that Joseph Smith had somehow collaborated with Sidney RIGDON to produce the Book of Mormon from the SPAULDING MANUSCRIPT (see below).

The most notable anti-Mormon work of this period, *Mormonism Unvailed* (sic), was published by Eber D. Howe in 1834. Howe collaborated with apostate Philastus Hurlbut, twice excommunicated from the Church for immorality. Hurlbut was hired by an anti-Mormon committee to find those who would attest to Smith's dishonesty. He "collected" affidavits from seventy-two contemporaries who professed to know Joseph Smith and were willing to speak against him. *Mormonism Unvailed* attempted to discredit Joseph Smith and his family by assembling these affidavits and nine letters written by Ezra Booth, also an apostate from the Church. These documents allege that the Smiths were money diggers and irresponsible people. Howe advanced the theory that Sidney Rigdon obtained a manuscript written by Solomon Spaulding, rewrote it into the Book of Mormon, and then convinced Joseph Smith to tell the public that he had translated the book from plates received from an angel. This theory served as an alternative to Joseph Smith's account until the Spaulding Manuscript was discovered in 1884 and was found to be unrelated to the Book of Mormon.

The Hurlbut-Howe collection and Campbell's *Delusions* were the major sources for nearly all other nineteenth- and some twentieth-century anti-Mormon writings, notably the works of Henry Caswall, John C. Bennett, Pomeroy Tucker, Thomas Gregg, William Linn, and George Arbaugh. Most of these writers drew routinely from the same body of anti-Mormon lore (see H. Nibley, "How to Write an Anti-Mormon Book," *Brigham Young University Extension Publications*, Feb. 17, 1962, p. 30).

Perhaps the most infamous manifestation of anti-Mormonism came in the MISSOURI CONFLICT, during which Governor Lilburn W. Boggs issued an EXTERMINATION ORDER. "The Mormons," he wrote, "must be treated as enemies and must be exterminated or driven from the state, if necessary for the public good" (*HC* 3:175). This order led to the expulsion of the Mormons from Missouri and their resettlement in Illinois.

While incarcerated in LIBERTY JAIL in 1839, Joseph Smith wrote to the Saints and instructed them not to respond polemically but to "gather up the libelous publications that are afloat; and all that are in the magazines, and in the encyclopedias, and all the libelous histories that are published, and are writing, and by whom" so that they could bring to light all misleading and untruthful reports about the Church (D&C 123:4–5, 12–13). This

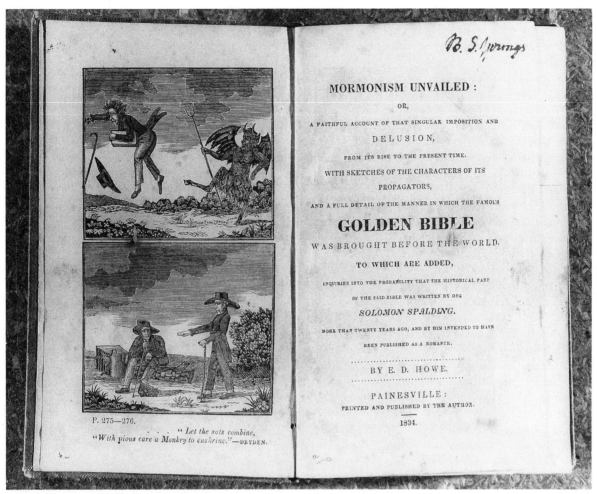

Title page of E. D. Howe's *Mormonism Unvailed* (1834), one of the earliest anti-Mormon publications. It advanced the theory that the historical part of the Book of Mormon "was written by one Solomon Spalding." Courtesy Rare Books and Manuscripts, Brigham Young University.

procedure has been followed by Latter-day Saints over the years.

After the Saints moved to NAUVOO, Illinois, a principal antagonist was Thomas C. Sharp, editor of the *Warsaw Signal*. Alarmed over the Church's secular power, he used his paper to oppose it. In 1841 he published *Mormonism Portrayed*, by William Harris.

Six notable anti-Mormon books were published in 1842. The first was *The History of the Saints*; or, *An Exposé of Joe Smith and Mormonism*, by John C. Bennett, who had served as Joseph Smith's counselor in the First Presidency and was also the first mayor of Nauvoo. After he was excommunicated from the Church for immorality, he turned against the Mormons and published a series of letters in a Springfield, Missouri, newspaper. He charged that Joseph Smith was "one of the

grossest and most infamous impostors that ever appeared upon the face of the earth." Bennett's history borrowed heavily from *Mormonism Portrayed*.

That same year, Joshua V. Himes published *Mormon Delusions and Monstrosities*, which incorporated much of Alexander Campbell's *Delusions*. The Reverend John A. Clark published *Gleanings by the Way*, and Jonathan B. Turner, *Mormonism in All Ages*. Both books relied heavily on Howe and Hurlbut's *Mormonism Unvailed*. Daniel P. Kidder's *Mormonism and the Mormons* expanded the Spalding theory of Book of Mormon origins to include Oliver COWDERY in addition to Joseph Smith and Sidney Rigdon.

Called the "Anti-Mormon Extraordinaire," the Reverend Henry Caswall published *The City of the Mormons*, or *Three Days at Nauvoo*. He claimed that he gave Joseph Smith a copy of a Greek manuscript of the Psalms and that Smith identified it as a dictionary of Egyptian hieroglyphics. Caswall invented dialogue between himself and Smith to portray Joseph Smith as ignorant, uncouth, and deceptive. In 1843 Caswall published *The Prophet of the Nineteenth Century* in London, borrowing most of his material from Clark and Turner.

By 1844 Joseph Smith also faced serious dissension within the Church. Several of his closest associates disagreed with him over the PLURAL MARRIAGE revelation and other doctrines. Among the principal dissenters were William and Wilson Law, Austin Cowles, Charles Foster, Francis and Chauncey Higbee, Charles Ivins, and Robert Foster. They became allied with local anti-Mormon elements and published one issue of a newspaper, the *Nauvoo Expositor*. In it they charged that Joseph Smith was a fallen prophet, guilty of whoredoms, and dishonest in financial matters.

The Nauvoo City Council and Mayor Joseph Smith declared the newspaper an illegal "nuisance" and directed the town marshal to destroy the press. This destruction inflamed the hostile anti-Mormons around Nauvoo. On June 12, 1844, Thomas Sharp's newspaper, the *Warsaw Signal*, called for the extermination of the Latter-day Saints: "War and extermination is inevitable! Citizens arise, one and all!!! Can you *stand* by, and suffer such infernal devils! to rob men of their property and rights, without avenging them. . . . Let [your comment] be made with powder and ball!!!" Two weeks later Joseph Smith and his brother Hyrum were assassinated in CARTHAGE JAIL while awaiting trial on charges of treason.

Sharp defended the killing on the grounds that "the most respectable citizens" had called for it. Sharp and four others eventually were tried for the murders, but were acquitted for lack of evidence.

Many felt that the Church would die with its founders. When the members united under the leadership of the Twelve Apostles, anti-Mormon attacks began with new vigor. Sharp renewed his call for the removal of the Mormons from Illinois. By September 1845, more than 200 Church members' homes were burned in the outlying areas of Nauvoo. In February 1846, the Saints crossed the Mississippi and began the exodus to the West.

Revenge was possibly a motive of some anti-Mormons, especially apostates. Philastus Hurlbut,

Simonds Ryder, Ezra Booth, and John C. Bennett sought revenge because the Church had disciplined them. Alexander Campbell was angered because he lost many of his Campbellite followers when they joined the Latter-day Saints. Mark Aldrich had invested in a real-estate development that failed because Mormon immigrants did not support it, and Thomas Sharp had lost many of his general business prospects.

MORMON STEREOTYPING AND THE CRUSADE AGAINST POLYGAMY (1847–1896). Settlement in the West provided welcome isolation for the Church, but public disclosure of the practice of POLYGAMY in 1852 brought a new barrage of ridicule and a confrontation with the federal government.

The years from 1850 to 1890 were turbulent ones for the Church because reformers, ministers, and the press openly attacked the practice of polygamy. Opponents founded antipolygamy societies, and Congress passed ANTIPOLYGAMY LEGISLATION. Mormons were stereotyped as people who defied the law and were immoral. The clear aim of the judicial and political crusade against the Mormons was to destroy the Church. Only the 1890 MANIFESTO, a statement by Church President Wilford WOODRUFF that abolished polygamy officially, pacified the government, allowing the return of confiscated Church property. Voluminous anti-Mormon writings, lectures, and cartoons at this time stereotyped the Church as a theocracy that defied the laws of conventional society; many portrayed its members as deluded and fanatical; and they alleged that polygamy, secret rituals, and BLOOD ATONEMENT were the theological underpinnings of the Church. The main motives were to discredit LDS belief, morally to reform a perceived evil, or to exploit the controversy for financial and political profit. The maligning tactics that were used included verbal attacks against Church leaders; caricatures in periodicals, magazines, and lectures; fictional inventions; and outright falsehoods.

Probably the most influential anti-Mormon work in this period was Pomeroy Tucker's *Origin, Rise, and Progress of Mormonism* (1867). A printer employed by E. B. Grandin, publisher of the *Wayne Sentinel* and printer of the first edition of the Book of Mormon, Tucker claimed to have been associated closely with Joseph Smith. He supported the Hurlbut-Howe charge that the Smiths were dishonest and alleged that they stole from their neighbors. However, he acknowledged that his insinuations were not "sustained by judicial investigation."

The Reverend M. T. Lamb's *The Golden Bible or the Book of Mormon: Is It from God?* (1887) ridiculed the Book of Mormon as "verbose, blundering, stupid, . . . improbable, . . . impossible, . . . [and] a foolish guess." He described the book as unnecessary and far inferior to the Bible, and he characterized those who believe the Book of Mormon as being misinformed.

Of fifty-six anti-Mormon novels published during the nineteenth century, four established a pattern for all of the others. The four were sensational, erotic novels focusing on the supposed plight of women in the Church. Alfreda Eva Bell's *Boadicea, the Mormon Wife* (1855) depicted Church members as "murderers, forgers, swindlers, gamblers, thieves, and adulterers!" Orvilla S. Belisle's *Mormonism Unveiled* (1855) had the heroine hopelessly trapped in a Mormon harem. Metta Victoria Fuller Victor's *Mormon Wives* (1856) characterized Mormons as a "horrid" and deluded people. Maria Ward (a pseudonym) depicted Mormon torture of women in *Female Life Among the Mormons* (1855). Authors wrote lurid passages designed to sell the publications. Excommunicated members tried to capitalize on their former membership in the Church to sell their stories. Fanny Stenhouse's *Tell It All* (1874) and Ann Eliza Young's *Wife No. 19* (1876) sensationalized the polygamy theme. William Hickman sold his story to John H. Beadle, who exaggerated the DANITE myth in *Brigham's Destroying Angel* (1872) to caricature Mormons as a violent people.

Church leaders responded to these attacks and adverse publicity only through sermons and admonitions. They defended the Church's fundamental doctrine of revelation and authority from God. During the period of federal prosecution, the First Presidency condemned the acts against the Church by the U.S. Congress and Supreme Court as violations of the United States Constitution.

THE SEARCH FOR A PSYCHOLOGICAL EXPLANATION (1897–1945). After the Church officially discontinued polygamy in 1890, the public image of Mormonism improved and became moderately favorable. However, in 1898 Utah elected to the U.S. Congress B. H. Roberts, who had entered into plural marriages before the Manifesto. His

election revived polygamy charges and further exposés by magazine muckrakers, and Congress refused to seat him. During the congressional debate, the Order of Presbytery in Utah issued a publication, *Ten Reasons Why Christians Cannot Fellowship the Mormon Church*, mainly objecting to the doctrine of modern revelation.

The election of Reed Smoot to the U.S. Senate (January 20, 1903) prompted additional controversy. Although he was not a polygamist, Smoot was a member of the QUORUM OF THE TWELVE APOSTLES. Ten months after he had been sworn in as a senator, his case was reviewed by the Senate Committee on Privileges and Elections. The SMOOT HEARINGS lasted from January 1904 to February 1907. Finally, in 1907 the Senate voted to allow him to take his seat. The First Presidency then published *An Address to the World*, explaining the Church's doctrines and answering charges. The Salt Lake Ministerial Association rebutted that address in the *Salt Lake Tribune* on June 4, 1907.

During 1910 and 1911, *Pearson's, Collier's, Cosmopolitan, McClure's,* and *Everybody's* magazines published vicious anti-Mormon articles. *McClure's* charged that the Mormons still practiced polygamy. *Cosmopolitan* compared Mormonism to a viper with tentacles reaching for wealth and power. The editors called the Church a "loathsome institution" whose "slimy grip" had served political and economic power in a dozen western states. These articles are classified by Church historians as the "magazine crusade."

The advent of the motion picture brought a repetition of the anti-Mormon stereotype. From 1905 to 1936, at least twenty-one anti-Mormon films were produced. The most sordid of them were *A Mormon Maid* (1917) and *Trapped by the Mormons* (1922). The films depicted polygamous leaders seeking women converts to satisfy their lusts, and Mormons murdering innocent travelers in secret rites. Some of the most virulent anti-Mormon writings at this time came from Britain. Winifred Graham (Mrs. Theodore Cory), a professional anti-Mormon novelist, charged that Mormon missionaries were taking advantage of World War I by proselytizing women whose husbands were away to war. The film *Trapped by the Mormons* was based on one of her novels.

When the Spaulding theory of Book of Mormon origins was discredited, anti-Mormon proponents turned to psychology to explain Joseph Smith's visions and revelations. Walter F. Prince

One of many political cartoons from the late nineteenth century, depicting Mormonism as a despotic, ignorant, adulterous threat to society. Charles W. Carter Collection.

and Theodore Schroeder offered explanations for BOOK OF MORMON NAMES by way of imaginative but remote psychological associations. I. Woodbridge Riley claimed in *The Founder of Mormonism* (New York, 1903) that "Joseph Smith, Junior was an epileptic." He was the first to suggest that Ethan Smith's *View of the Hebrews* (1823) and Josiah Priest's *The Wonders of Nature and Providence, Displayed* (1825) were the sources for the Book of Mormon.

At the time the Church commemorated its centennial in 1930, American historian Bernard De Voto asserted in the *American Mercury,* "Unquestionably, Joseph Smith was a paranoid." He later admitted that the *Mercury* article was a "dishonest attack" (*IE* 49 [Mar. 1946]:154).

Harry M. Beardsley, in *Joseph Smith and His Mormon Empire* (1931), advanced the theory that Joseph Smith's visions, revelations, and the Book of Mormon were by-products of his subconscious mind. Vardis Fisher, a popular novelist with Mormon roots in Idaho, published *Children of God: An American Epic* (1939). The work is somewhat sympathetic to the Mormon heritage, while offering a naturalistic origin for the Mormon practice of polygamy, and describes Joseph Smith in terms of "neurotic impulses."

In 1945 Fawn Brodie published *No Man Knows My History,* a psychobiographical account of Joseph Smith. She portrayed him as a "prodigious mythmaker" who absorbed his theological ideas from his New York environment. The book repudiated the Rigdon-Spaulding theory, revived the Alexander Campbell thesis that Joseph Smith alone was the author of the book, and postulated that *View of the Hebrews* (following Riley, 1903) provided the basic source material for the Book of Mormon. Brodie's interpretations have been followed by several other writers.

Church scholars have criticized Brodie's methods for several reasons. First, she ignored valuable manuscript material in the Church archives that was accessible to her. Second, her sources were mainly biased anti-Mormon documents collected primarily in the New York Public Library, Yale Library, and Chicago Historical Library. Third, she began with a predetermined conclusion that shaped her work: "I was convinced," she wrote, "before I ever began writing that Joseph Smith was not a true prophet," and felt compelled to supply an alternative explanation for his works (quoted in Newell G. Bringhurst, "Applause, Attack, and Ambivalence—Varied Responses to Fawn M. Brodie's *No Man Knows My History,*" *Utah Historical Quarterly* 57 [Winter 1989]:47–48). Fourth, by using a psychobiographical approach, she imputed thoughts and motives to Joseph Smith. Even Vardis Fisher criticized her book, writing that it was "almost more a novel than a biography because she rarely hesitates to give the content of a mind or to explain motives which at best can only be surmised" (p. 57).

REVIVAL OF OLD THEORIES AND ALLEGATIONS (1946–1990). Anti-Mormon writers were most prolific during the post-Brodie era. Despite a generally favorable press toward the Church during many of these years, of all anti-Mormon books, novels, pamphlets, tracts, and flyers published in English before 1990, more than half were published between 1960 and 1990 and a third of them between 1970 and 1990.

Networks of anti-Mormon organizations operate in the United States. The *1987 Directory of Cult Research Organizations* contains more than a hundred anti-Mormon listings. These networks distribute anti-Mormon literature, provide lectures that attack the Church publicly, and proselytize Mormons. Pacific Publishing House in California lists more than a hundred anti-Mormon publications.

A broad spectrum of anti-Mormon authors has produced the invective literature of this period. Evangelicals and some apostate Mormons assert that Latter-day Saints are not Christians. The main basis for this judgment is that the Mormon belief in the Christian GODHEAD is different from the traditional Christian doctrine of the Trinity. They contend that Latter-day Saints worship a "different Jesus" and that their scriptures are contrary to the Bible. Another common tactic is to attempt to show how statements by past Church leaders contradict those by current leaders on such points as Adam as God, blood atonement, and plural marriage.

A current example of ridicule and distortion of Latter-day Saint beliefs comes from Edward Decker, an excommunicated Mormon and cofounder of Ex-Mormons for Jesus, now known as Saints Alive in Jesus. Professing love for the Saints, Decker has waged an attack on their beliefs. Latter-day Saints see his film and book, both entitled *The Godmakers*, as a gross misrepresentation of their beliefs, especially the TEMPLE ORDINANCES. A regional director of the Anti-Defamation League of B'nai B'rith and the Arizona Regional Board of the National Conference of Christians and Jews are among those who have condemned the film.

Though anti-Mormon criticisms, misrepresentations, and falsehoods are offensive to Church members, the First Presidency has counseled members not to react to or debate those who sponsor them and has urged them to keep their responses "in the form of a positive explanation of the doctrines and practices of the Church" (*Church News*, Dec. 18, 1983, p. 2).

Two prolific anti-Mormon researchers are Jerald and Sandra Tanner. They commenced writing in 1959 and now offer more than 200 publications.

Their main approach is to demonstrate discrepancies, many of which Latter-day Saints consider contrived or trivial, between current and past Church teachings. They operate and publish under the name of the Utah Lighthouse Ministry, Inc. Their most notable work, *Mormonism—Shadow or Reality?* (1964, revised 1972, 1987), contains the essence of their claims against the Church.

During the 1950s, 1960s, and early 1970s, the Church had a generally favorable public image as reflected in the news media. That image became more negative in the later 1970s and the early 1980s. Church opposition to the equal rights amendment and the excommunication of Sonia Johnson for apostasy, the Church's position with respect to priesthood and BLACKS (changed in 1978), a First Presidency statement opposing the MX missile, the John Singer episode including the bombing of an LDS meetinghouse, tensions between some historians and Church leaders, the forged "Salamander" letter, and the other Mark Hofmann FORGERIES and murders have provided grist for negative press and television commentary. The political leverage of the Church and its financial holdings have also been subjects of articles with a strong negative orientation.

A widely circulated anti-Mormon book, *The Mormon Murders*, by Steven Naifeh and Gregory White Smith (1988), employs several strategies reminiscent of old-style anti-Semitism. The authors use the Hofmann forgeries and murders as a springboard and follow the stock anti-Mormon themes and methods found in earlier works. They explain Mormonism in terms of wealth, power, deception, and fear of the past.

Church leaders have consistently appealed to the fairness of readers and urged them to examine the Book of Mormon and other latter-day SCRIPTURES and records for themselves rather than to prejudge the Church based on anti-Mormon publications. In 1972 the Church established the Public Communications Department, headquartered in Salt Lake City, to release public information about the Church.

BIBLIOGRAPHY

No definitive history of anti-Mormon activities has been written. A sample of LDS sources on anti-Mormonism follows:

Allen, James B., and Leonard J. Arrington. "Mormon Origins in New York: An Introductory Analysis." *BYU Studies* 9 (1969):241–74. Analyzes pro-Mormon and anti-Mormon approaches.

Anderson, Richard Lloyd. "Joseph Smith's New York Reputation Reappraised." *BYU Studies* 10 (1970):283–314. Analyzes the Hurlbut-Howe affidavits published in *Mormonism Unvailed*.

Bunker, Gary L., and Davis Bitton. *The Mormon Graphic Image 1834–1914*. Salt Lake City, 1983. Traces the history of anti-Mormon caricature.

Bushman, Richard L. *Joseph Smith and the Beginnings of Mormonism*. Urbana, Ill., 1984. Discusses the early anti-Mormonism writings of Campbell, Howe, and Hurlbut.

Kirkham, Francis W. *A New Witness for Christ in America*, 2 vols. Independence, Mo., 1942, and Salt Lake City, 1952. Examines the early newspaper articles and anti-Mormon explanations for the origin of the Book of Mormon.

Nibley, Hugh W. *The Mythmakers*. Salt Lake City, 1961. Surveys the anti-Mormon writers during the Joseph Smith period.

———. "Censoring the Joseph Smith Story," *IE* 64 (July, Aug., Oct., Nov. 1961). Serialized articles examining how fifty anti-Mormon works treat the Joseph Smith story.

———. *Sounding Brass*. Salt Lake City, 1963. Surveys the anti-Mormon writers during the Brigham Young period.

———. *The Prophetic Book of Mormon*, CWHN 8 chaps. 4–8, 10–12, examines anti-Mormon arguments.

Scharffs, Gilbert W. *The Truth About the Godmakers*. Salt Lake City, 1986. Treats the film *The Godmakers*.

WILLIAM O. NELSON

ANTIPOLYGAMY LEGISLATION

Bigamy is the crime of marrying while an undivorced spouse from a valid prior marriage is living. Because many prominent nineteenth-century Mormon men became polygamists under Church mandate, both their vulnerability to prosecution for bigamy and the legal attacks on the Church and its members for supporting PLURAL MARRIAGE created a crisis for Mormonism during the 1870s and 1880s.

Bigamy was recognized as an offense by the early English ecclesiastical courts, which considered it an affront to the marriage sacrament. Parliament enacted a statute in 1604 that made bigamy a felony cognizable in the English common law courts. After American independence, the states adopted antibigamy laws, but they received little attention until the nineteenth century in Utah.

The United States government has constitutional power to enact laws governing territories, and under that authority Congress enacted the Morrill Act (1862), making bigamy in a territory a crime punishable by a fine and five years in prison. The statute was upheld in REYNOLDS V. UNITED STATES (1879), although the defendant argued that the law violated the First Amendment guarantee of the free exercise of religion.

Few Mormons were prosecuted for bigamy because the government had difficulty obtaining testimony about plural wedding ceremonies. Rather, they were charged with bigamous cohabitation, a misdemeanor created by the Edmunds Act (1882). Proving cohabitation was easy enough, and over 1,300 Latter-day Saints were jailed as "cohabs" in the 1880s.

Antipolygamy legislation also put pressure on the Church by threatening members' civil rights and Church property rights. The Edmunds Act barred persons living in POLYGAMY from jury service, public office, and voting. The Edmunds-Tucker Act (1887) disincorporated both the Church and the Perpetual Emigrating Fund on the ground that they fostered polygamy. Furthermore, it authorized seizure of Church real estate not directly used for religious purposes, and acquired in excess of a $50,000 limitation imposed by the Morrill Act. In the Idaho Territory a test oath adopted in 1885 was used to ban all Mormons (and former Mormons) from voting because of the Church's position on polygamy.

In 1890 after the U.S. Supreme Court upheld the seizure of Church property under the Edmunds-Tucker Act in *The Late Corporation of the Mormon Church v. United States* and the Idaho test oath in *Davis v. Beason*, it became clear that plural marriage was leading toward the economic and political destruction of the Church. Shortly after these decisions, a revelation was received by President Wilford WOODRUFF, who then withdrew the requirement for worthy males to take plural wives and announced the MANIFESTO, formally stating his counsel to Latter-day Saints to abide by antibigamy laws (see D&C Official Declaration—1). The Manifesto ended the legal confrontation between the U.S. government and the Church.

Congress passed a final federal antibigamy provision in 1892, which excluded polygamists from immigration into the United States. This exclusion remains part of the U.S. Immigration and Naturalization Code.

Utah, Oklahoma, New Mexico, and Arizona incorporated antibigamy provisions into their turn-of-the-century state constitutions as required by Congress for admission to the Union. Idaho's constitution not only outlaws bigamy but also bars polygamists and persons "celestially married" from public office and voting. However, that was interpreted in *Budge v. Toncray* by the Idaho court not

About 1,300 LDS men who had practiced plural marriage were jailed by federal officers pursuant to the Edmunds Act (1882), and many women were found "in contempt of court" and jailed for refusing to testify against their husbands. In the Utah penitentiary in 1885 are (from left to right) Francis A. Brown, Freddy Self, Moroni Brown, Amos Milton Musser, George H. Kellogg, Parley P. Pratt, Jr., Rudger Clawson, and Job Pingree. Photographer: John P. Soule.

to include monogamous Mormons married in an LDS temple.

During the twentieth century, federal and state governments have prosecuted other polygamists under a variety of general statutes. For example, federal officials have filed cases against polygamists charging unlawful use of the mails to proselytize for polygamy and alleging that moving plural wives across state boundaries violates laws against interstate kidnapping and interstate transportation of women for immoral purposes. Because of their practice of plural marriage, polygamists have also had legal troubles with state laws about adoption, inheritance, and government employment. Changing social attitudes about unconventional personal relationships may undermine the use of legislation in this way. For example, in 1988 an Arizona court held that it was illegal to deny a law enforcement security bond to an admitted polygamist merely because of his marital status.

Laws against plural marriage and its practitioners were enacted with reforming zeal. Congress and party platforms considered Mormon polygamy and southern slavery the "twin relics of barbarism." However, the lawmakers were not so forthcoming about their own religious bigotry: their aim was to destroy the Church's economic and political power, and bigamy was their tool. The Church's temporal position was eroded, but it survived the crisis.

BIBLIOGRAPHY

American Law Institute. *Model Penal Code and Commentaries*, Sec. 230.1. Philadelphia, 1980.

Davis, Ray Jay. "The Polygamous Prelude." *American Journal of Legal History* 6 (1962):1–27.

Driggs, Ken. "The Prosecutions Begin." *Dialogue* 21 (1988):109–125.

RAY JAY DAVIS

APOCALYPTIC TEXTS

Apocalypse is a Greek word meaning REVELATION, and *apocalyptic* as an adjective describes the genre of literature that contains visionary or revelatory experiences. Although such writings have been known from ancient times (examples include sections of ISAIAH, EZEKIEL, DANIEL, and the New Testament Revelation of JOHN), discoveries since the late nineteenth century of apocalyptic texts have increased scholarly interest in the subject. The apocalyptic tradition was one of those the early Christian church rejected in the third through the fifth centuries, only to be recovered in modern times through these discoveries. The importance of revelation in the RESTORATION of the gospel through the Prophet Joseph SMITH makes the study of apocalyptic texts as worthwhile to Latter-day Saints as it is interesting to scholars.

The relationship between the canonical prophetic and the apocalyptic in Jewish and Christian sources is acknowledged to be very close. Some of the major characteristics of revelation literature are as follows:

1. The seer often gives a brief autobiographical account in which he recounts his initial experiences and important personal events.

2. The recipient of a vision is often, but not always, ecstatic (the spirit apparently leaving the body during the vision).

3. The prophet may be taken on a journey through the heavens.

4. Visits to the SPIRIT WORLD, HEAVEN, and HELL are common.

5. The teachings imparted during such experiences are secrets that the prophet is counseled to keep to himself or share only with the community of believers (the experience may be shared, but most of what is learned cannot be disclosed).

6. Usually an account of the suffering that the righteous must endure is given.

7. The descent from heaven of a new order of society in the LAST DAYS is described.

8. Commonly an *angelus interpres*, a heavenly messenger, is sent to explain and interpret the vision.

9. After receiving such visions, the prophet is almost always overcome and has to wait some time before receiving back his strength or perhaps is raised up quickly by the right hand of divinity.

Although scholars have specifically identified and studied the genre of apocalyptic literature mainly since the 1950s, students of the Restoration will recognize every aspect of this ancient literary form in the life and writings of Joseph Smith before 1844. Accounts of the FIRST VISION contain an autobiographical introduction, as do visions of NEPHI₁ in the Book of Mormon and of Abraham in the Pearl of Great Price. In 1 Nephi 11, Nephi is taken in the spirit to a high mountain (a very popular theme in revelation), and Moses, ALMA₂, Joseph Smith, and others speak of being overcome by the visions they received (Moses 1:10; Mosiah 27:19; JS—H 1:20). Enoch (Moses 7; see also 1 Enoch), Moses (Moses 1), and Joseph Smith (e.g., D&C 76) describe journeys into and through eternal realms, recording the infinite creations of God and numerous places where men may ultimately dwell. Those same prophets, and others whose accounts are found in the Book of Mormon, report visions of the last days, the wars and destructions among men, and the ultimate victory of God. In keeping with apocalyptic tradition, the details of such visions are sealed up with a promise that they will be given to the righteous in a time determined by the Lord. Angels appeared to Joseph Smith to instruct him and explain such things as how to find and recover PLATES seen in a vision and how to baptize properly and with the authority given by a messenger from God. In the Book of Mormon, Nephi saw a vision more completely through the assistance of an angel who pointed out and explained details of the apocalypse to him. These representative examples show how the apocalyptic tradition is as interwoven in the fabric of the Restoration as it was in the traditions of ancient Judaism or early Christianity.

BIBLIOGRAPHY

Hellholm, David, ed. *International Colloquium on Apocalypticism (1979: Uppsala, Sweden)*. Tübingen, 1983.

Koch, Klaus. *Ratlos vor der Apokalyptik*. Gutersloh, 1970. Translated by M. Kohl as *The Rediscovery of Apocalyptic*. London, 1972.

Nibley, Hugh W. "Last Call: An Apocalyptic Warning from the Book of Mormon." In *CWHN* 8:498–532.

C. WILFRED GRIGGS

APOCRYPHA AND PSEUDEPIGRAPHA

These two terms are often found together in modern scholarly writings, although they had quite different meanings in ancient times. "Apocrypha" in its various forms refers to something hidden or concealed, usually because of its special or sacred value to the one hiding it. "Pseudepigrapha" refers to writings falsely ascribed to some important or famous figure or to writings with a false title. Such writings are not considered genuine, at least in the sense of originating with the falsely ascribed name.

During the second century A.D., some Christian authors (for example, Irenaeus and Tertullian) began to use *apocryphon* (singular form) to designate a forged or false writing. Both authors, and those who followed them in this practice, were trying to discredit the secret and sacred writings of their opponents, whom they considered heretics. In time, therefore, many writings once kept hidden from the general public for reasons of their sacredness and holiness were rejected and branded as unreliable or false by church fathers who disliked them.

After Jerome translated the Bible into Latin (c. A.D. 400), the books known from the Greek version of the Old Testament but not contained in the Hebrew version became known as the Apocrypha, or writings of uncertain accuracy. This collection of writings was accepted as scripture by most Christians before the Council of Nicaea, but only by some following that council. In recent centuries, Catholics have generally accepted these books with the rest of the Old Testament, and Protestants have generally denied them scriptural status. In Joseph SMITH's day, some editions of the King James Version of the Bible placed the Apocrypha between the Old and New Testaments, and some other Protestant versions included the Apocrypha either with the Old Testament or as an appendix to the Bible.

When Joseph Smith was engaged in translating the Old Testament (*see* JOSEPH SMITH TRANSLATION OF THE BIBLE [JST]), he came to the Apocrypha and sought divine counsel on what to do with it. The revelation given in response to his prayer informed him that the Apocrypha contains both truth and error, but was "mostly translated correctly" (D&C 91:1). Although he was counseled not to translate the Apocrypha, the revelation states that any who read those writings with the HOLY SPIRIT as a guide "shall obtain benefit therefrom"; without the HOLY GHOST, a man "cannot be benefited" spiritually by reading the Apocrypha (D&C 91:5-6).

Since the nineteenth century, increased understanding of intertestamental Judaism and Hellenistic culture has shown the Apocrypha to be historically important and religiously valuable. These writings display a belief in resurrection, eternal life, and eschatological teachings concerning the LAST DAYS. The fall of Adam (*see* ADAM: ANCIENT SOURCES), sin, the Jewish Law, and the need for righteousness are topics also found in the Apocrypha.

Additionally, during the past two centuries many writings have been discovered that were purportedly written by ancient prophets or apostles, or were otherwise related to biblical texts (*see* LOST SCRIPTURE). Many of these writings were considered sacred to certain groups of Jews or Christians, but were rejected in the long process of biblical canonization (primarily from the second to the fifth centuries A.D.). Scholars routinely add these discoveries to the corpus of apocryphal and pseudepigraphical writings. The application of these terms in their modern sense (i.e., writings forged or falsely ascribed to an ancient religious figure) to ancient texts displays a modern bias against their spiritual or historical authenticity, but one should also note that often modern scholars do not consider most biblical books to be inspired by God or written by the authors associated with them.

One important aspect of the expanded collection of the Apocrypha has to do with the canon itself. Centuries after it was determined which books were to be included in the Bible, people began to believe and teach that the Bible was both complete (containing all that God had given through ancient prophets and apostles) and infallible (having been transmitted without any errors). Joseph Smith received correctives to both ideas, being given additional scripture originally written by ancient prophets and being inspired to make corrections in the texts of the Bible. Among the ancient writings he restored are the BOOK OF ABRAHAM and the writings of Moses (canonized as the BOOK OF MOSES, itself including a restoration to Moses of an older Enoch writing; see Moses 6–7; quotations from ancient biblical prophets in the Book of Mormon (such as JOSEPH OF EGYPT and four otherwise unknown writers named

ZENOS, ZENOCK, NEUM, and EZIAS); and writings from the New Testament apostle John (see D&C 7 and 93). Corrections to the biblical text include an expanded version of Matthew 24 and alternate readings in Isaiah.

Not only has modern revelation resulted in the restoration of ancient prophetic records and opened the canon in modern times, but the recovery of many ancient texts shows how open and diverse the canon was in earlier times. One ancient religious tradition, repeated in different settings and at different times, attests to two levels of sacred writings, one for public discourse and the other for more restricted use within the community of believers. One might note in this regard that a similar injunction to keep some writings within a restricted community is found in the book of Moses revealed to Joseph Smith: "Show [these words] not unto any except them that believe" (Moses 1:42; cf. 4:32). Some recently found texts bear the title "Apocryphon," used in the ancient sense of secret or hidden writing. It was this "advanced" level of instruction that was rejected by the church fathers, and the negative meaning of "apocryphal" began to replace the positive or sacred sense. Because in ancient times many such writings were not made public by those who accepted them and because they were distorted and maligned by those who rejected them, scholars lack definitive methods by which to determine if these writings have been transmitted accurately.

In this large collection of writings, relating to both Old and New Testaments, many diverse subjects are discussed, and a few are found repeatedly. Revelation, in the form of APOCALYPTIC TEXTS, is perhaps the most common element: numerous apocryphal texts claim to contain the mysteries, or secrets, of heaven revealed to man. Testaments of patriarchs frequently occur in the Old Testament apocryphal writings; and instructions, eschatological warnings, ritual passages, and cosmic visions are transmitted by the resurrected Jesus to his disciples in many of the New Testament Apocrypha. The type of literature that encompasses these themes is often called Gnostic literature, and scholars generally view the gnosticism seen in apocryphal texts as a fusion of many diverse elements (Hellenism, Judaism, mystery religions, and Christianity, to name a few) into a complex and mystical religious movement. Considerable study will be necessary before all the questions relating to the origin, accuracy, meaning, and significance

of apocryphal literature can be answered. Numerous versions of the fourteen books of the Old Testament Apocrypha known in Joseph Smith's time are available, either in separate publications or in modern printings of the Bible, such as the Jerusalem Bible or the New English Bible.

Joseph Smith was well in advance of modern perceptions concerning the Apocrypha when he was given the revelation warning the Saints to seek spiritual guidance when reading such works, alerting them to truths to be obtained therein.

BIBLIOGRAPHY

Charlesworth, James H., ed. *Old Testament Pseudepigrapha*, 2 vols. New York, 1983, 1985.

Cloward, Robert A. *Old Testament Apocrypha and Pseudepigrapha and the Dead Sea Scrolls: A Selected Bibliography of the Text Editions and English Translations.* F.A.R.M.S. Reports. Provo, Utah, 1988.

Griggs, C. Wilfred, ed. *Apocryphal Writings and the Latter-day Saints.* Provo, Utah, 1986.

Hennecke, Edgar, and Wilhelm Schneenelcher, eds. *New Testament Apocrypha*, 2 vols. Translated by R. McL. Wilson. Philadelphia, 1963, 1965.

C. WILFRED GRIGGS

APOSTASY

Latter-day Saints believe that apostasy occurs whenever an individual or community rejects the revelations and ordinances of God, changes the gospel of Jesus Christ, or rebels against the commandments of God, thereby losing the blessings of the Holy Ghost and of divine AUTHORITY. The rise of revelatory communities, apostasies, and restorations has happened cyclically throughout the history of mankind, in a series of DISPENSATIONS from the time of Adam and Enoch (Moses 7) to the present. Latter-day Saints see a historical "great apostasy" and subsequent loss of authority beginning in the New Testament era and spreading in the centuries immediately following that era. Though Latter-day Saints have not emphasized the great apostasy as much as they have the concept that the Church is a revelatory RESTORATION, the need of a restoration implies that something important was lost after the departure of the primitive Christian church.

The English word "apostasy" derives from the Greek *apostasía* or *apóstasis* ("defection, revolt"; used in a political sense by Herodotus and Thucydides); it is mentioned in a religious context in the Septuagint and the New Testament (e.g., Josh. 22:22 and 2 Chr. 29:19; 2 Thes. 2:3 states that an *apostasía* must come before the second coming of Christ). It can mean the intransitive "to stand away from," or the active "to cause to stand away from." Thus an apostasy can be an active, collective rebellion or a "falling away."

Joseph SMITH in his FIRST VISION (1820) was told by Christ that all existing churches had gone astray, both in their teachings and in their practice, although they had "a form of godliness" (JS—H 1:18–19). Thus it was necessary for a "restoration" of the gospel to take place.

In addition, in the Book of Mormon (1 Ne. 11–14; 2 Ne. 28; cf. Morm. 8), the prophet NEPHI₁ had a vision of the early Christian church and its twelve apostles, against whom the "multitudes of the earth" and the house of Israel fought (1 Ne. 11:34–35). He foresaw a "great and abominable church" that persecuted true Christians and the poor, and whose members were motivated by such things as pride, clothing themselves in precious raiment, and indulging in sexual immorality (*see* GREAT AND ABOMINABLE CHURCH). It altered the simplicity of the gospel insidiously, did away with covenants, excised important scriptures, and denied the existence of miracles. This apostasy can be linked, in the ALLEGORY OF ZENOS, with the scattering of Israel when all the trees in the Lord's vineyard had become corrupt (Jacob 5:39–48), and it was paralleled by the calamitous apostasy of the Nephites in the New World (1 Ne. 12:15–19; 4 Ne. 1:24–46).

However, this "great church" was not any one specific church, according to Nephi; in his apocalyptic vision there are only two churches, and "whoso belongeth not to the church of the Lamb of God belongeth to that great church" (1 Ne. 14:10). It is typological, symbolic of many historical and social movements (2 Ne. 27:1); even nominal adherents to Christ's church, if driven by pride, wealth, prestige, and their appurtenances, may find themselves members of that "great church" (cf. 1 Ne. 8:27–28).

All through their history, Latter-day Saints have written and theorized about historical events involved in the "great apostasy," a theme discussed in several Restorationist writings of the late eighteenth and early nineteenth centuries (*see* RESTORATIONISM, PROTESTANT). In 1833, referring to Mark 16:17–18 and 1 Corinthians 12, Jo-

seph Smith stated: "By the foregoing testimonies we may look at the Christian world and see [that] the apostasy there has been from the apostolic platform" (*TPJS*, p. 15). Oliver COWDERY wrote on the apostasy in the first issue of the MESSENGER AND ADVOCATE (1834). In 1840 Orson PRATT spoke of "a general and awful apostasy from the religion of the New Testament" (*Listen to the Voice of Truth*, 1.1). He particularly emphasized a lack of binding ordinances because of the absence of PRIESTHOOD authority; baptism was a key example. In Pratt's view all churches before the Restoration were wrong in some ways, doctrinally and ritually, even though they might be right in others. Benjamin Winchester, an early LDS pamphleteer, wrote an extensive treatise using New Testament sources to demonstrate that an apostasy had been prophesied (*A History of Priesthood*, Philadelphia, 1843, pp. 72–96). In the 1850s and 1860s many references were made to "the great apostasy" (O. Pratt, *JD* 12:247) and "the great falling away" (W. Woodruff, *JD* 8:262) in Latter-day Saint sermons.

This idea—breaking off from established religion because it seems out of tune with New Testament Christianity—has obvious Protestant overtones, but the LDS view differs from typical Protestant attitudes in its emphasis on the loss and restoration of exclusive, clear-cut priesthood authority, correct ordinances, and continuing revelation. In contrast, Protestants typically rely primarily on biblical reinterpretation.

In 1909 James E. Talmage wrote *The Great Apostasy*, in which he gathered New Testament passages that Latter-day Saints have cited to show that a great apostasy was predicted by Jesus Christ, Paul, and other apostles and prophets (esp. Matt. 24:4–13, 23–26; Acts 20:29–30; Gal. 1; 2 Thes. 2:7–8; 1 Tim. 4:1–3; 2 Tim. 3:1–6; 4:1–4; Jude 1:3–4; Rev. 13:4–9; 14:6–7; and in the Old Testament, Amos 8:11–12). Talmage also chronicled the persecution of early Christians that hastened the Apostasy and described the primitive Church as changing internally in several respects. He argued that the simple principles of the gospel were mixed with the pagan philosophical systems of the day (Trinitarianism, resulting in the Nicene Creed; false opposition of body and spirit, creating excessive asceticism); that rituals were changed and added to in unauthorized ways (simple early Christian rites were replaced by complex pagan-influenced ceremonies; baptism by immersion was lost; the baptism of infants was introduced [cf. Moro. 8];

communion was changed); and that church organization was altered (the apostles and prophets, the necessary foundation of the church of Christ, were martyred, leaving a void that could not be filled by bishops; thus the medieval church showed little similarity to the organization or practices of the New Testament church).

LDS teachings on the early Christian apostasy have received additional support in the twentieth century as some scholars have argued that the primitive Church began as a centralized Judaic organization, was faced with the challenge of a Hellenized/Oriental, ascetic Gnostic Christianity, and became like its enemy in order to compete. The very idea of a centralized Christianity has given way to a picture of diverse and fragmented early Christianity, where it is hard to determine what is orthodox and what is heretical, what is Gnostic and what is "mainstream." For instance, Peter Brown and William Phipps argue that Augustine's influential doctrine of ORIGINAL SIN, with its concomitant ritual, INFANT BAPTISM, was derived from his Gnostic background and was, in reality, heretical, while Pelagius' opposition to these ideas was orthodox. But Augustine's doctrines prevailed, and continue to influence Western theology and culture. Another early Christian doctrine that did not survive in Western Christianity was DEIFICATION, though it remained central to Eastern Christianity.

A complex religious and cultural milieu both nurtured and transformed early Christianity. Many factors must be taken into consideration in analyzing this transformation of Christianity. For example, some have put the blame exclusively on Greek philosophy and the influence of philosophy on Gnosticism for the rise of the great apostasy. But asceticism (i.e., hatred of the body, of sexuality, of the physical world) played a major role in the apostasy of the early church, and extreme asceticism is characteristically Oriental. Moreover, much of Greek philosophy has been found to be consistent with the gospel; Elder Orson F. Whitney referred to Plato and Socrates as "servants of the Lord," although in a "lesser sense" than the prophets (CR [April 1921]:33).

The concept of a historical apostasy from early Christianity can present a barrier between Latter-day Saints and others concerned with INTERFAITH RELATIONSHIPS. But Latter-day Saints do not view these events judgmentally; much of spiritual value happened during the Middle Ages and in other Christian churches. Brigham Young emphasized that good men before the restoration had "the spirit of revelation" and stated that John Wesley was as good a man "as ever walked on this earth" (JD 7:5; 6:170; 11:126). President Young held that all churches and religions have "more or less truth" (JD 7:283), and he admonished the Saints to seek and accept truths wherever they might be found. In conference talks, General Authorities, including President Spencer W. Kimball and President Thomas S. Monson, have quoted or praised such luminaries as Billy Graham and Mother Teresa.

BIBLIOGRAPHY

Bauer, Walter. *Orthodoxy and Heresy in Earliest Christianity.* Philadelphia, 1971.

Benson, Ezra T. "Apostasy from the Truth." *IE* 52 (Nov. 1949):713, 756–60.

Brown, Peter. *Augustine of Hippo,* pp. 395–400. Berkeley, Calif., 1967.

Brown, S. Kent. "Whither the Early Church?" *Ensign* 18 (Oct. 1988):7–10.

Bushman, Richard L. *Joseph Smith and the Beginnings of Mormonism,* p. 207. Urbana, Ill., 1984.

Dodds, Eric R. *Pagan and Christian in an Age of Anxiety.* Cambridge, 1965.

Nibley, Hugh. *The World and the Prophets.* In *CWHN* 3.

———. *Mormonism and Early Christianity,* in *CWHN* 4, treats the disappearance of Christian baptisms for the dead (1948, pp. 100–167); the reshaping of early Christian texts and histories in light of the failure of the infant church to survive (1955, pp. 168–322); the forgotten teachings of Jesus during his forty-day ministry after his resurrection (1966, pp. 10–44); and the loss of the early Christian prayer circle (1978, pp. 45–99); bibliography (p. xii, n.8).

Peterson, Daniel C., and Stephen D. Ricks. "Comparing LDS Beliefs with First Century Christianity." *Ensign* 18 (Mar. 1988):7–11.

Phipps, William. "The Heresiarch: Pelagius or Augustine?" *Anglican Theological Review* 62 (1980):130–31.

Roberts, B. H. *The "Falling Away."* Salt Lake City, 1931.

———. *Outlines of Ecclesiastical History.* Salt Lake City, 1893.

Robinson, Stephen E. "Early Christianity and 1 Nephi 13–14." In *First Nephi, The Doctrinal Foundation,* ed. M. Nyman and C. Tate, pp. 177–91. Provo, Utah, 1988.

Rudolph, Kurt. *Gnosis: The Nature and History of Gnosticism.* San Francisco, 1983.

Sperry, Sidney B. "New Light on the Great Apostasy." *IE* 53 (Sept. 1950):710–11, 744–51.

Talmage, James. *The Great Apostasy.* Salt Lake City, 1909.

Vogel, Dan. *Religious Seekers and the Advent of Mormonism,* pp. 49–66. Salt Lake City, 1988, contains valuable bibliography; reviewed by Grant Underwood, *BYU Studies* 30 (Winter 1990):120–26.

TODD COMPTON

APOSTATE

Members of the Church vary in their levels of participation or belief (*see* ACTIVITY IN THE CHURCH). Latter-day Saints who have seriously contravened or ignored cardinal Church teachings (publicly or privately) are considered apostates, whether or not they have officially left the Church or affiliated with another religion. By not participating in Church meetings one is not considered apostate. However, when individuals ask to have their names removed from Church records, policy requires such requests to be honored. A Church DISCIPLINARY PROCEDURE may be held for any member who violates important commandments and "will not repent" (Mosiah 26:32; D&C 42:28). Open repudiation of the Church, its leaders, and teachings is one ground for excommunication.

The steps to apostasy are usually gradual. All members are counseled to guard against all manifestations of personal apostasy (*DS* 3:293–312; Asay, pp. 67–68). The most frequent causes of apostasy are failure to maintain strict standards of morality, taking personal offense (real or perceived), marrying someone who is of another faith or who is irreligious, neglecting to pray and maintain spirituality, or misunderstanding of the teachings of the Church.

Apostasy may be accelerated by a faulty assumption that scripture or Church leaders are infallible. Joseph SMITH taught that "a prophet was a prophet only when he was acting as such" (*HC* 5:265). He also declared he "was but a man, and [people] must not expect me to be perfect" (*HC* 5:181). Neither the Church nor its leaders and members claim infallibility.

Above all, the Church affirms that its members should seek personal revelation to know the truth and live in tune with the spirit of God. Those who have not done this may drop by the wayside when their faith is challenged or when difficulties arise.

Apostates sometimes become enemies of the Church. Leaving the Church, which claims to be God's official church, containing the fulness of the gospel, often results in feelings of guilt. While many return, others develop a need to defend their actions, "disprove" the Church, or become hostile enemies. The fruits of apostasy are generally bitter. The Book of Mormon warns of unfavorable conditions that result from transgression contrary to "light and knowledge" (Alma 9:23).

LDS scriptures establish a loving and hopeful attitude toward apostates. Latter-day Saints are strongly counseled to love those who have left the faith, and to encourage, plead, and work with those who have strayed, inviting "the lost sheep" back to the fold (Luke 15:3–7). Of the wayward, the resurrected Savior taught, "Ye shall not cast him out of your . . . places of worship, for unto such shall ye continue to minister; for ye know not but what they will return and repent, and come unto me with full purpose of heart, and I shall heal them; and ye shall be the means of bringing salvation unto them" (3 Ne. 18:32). The desire to return is motivated by the reality of REPENTANCE enabled by the ATONEMENT of Jesus Christ. "He who has repented of his sins, the same is forgiven, and I, the Lord, remember them no more. By this ye may know if a man repenteth of his sins—behold, he will confess them and forsake them" (D&C 58:42–43).

[*See also* Anti-Mormon Publications; Schismatic Groups.]

BIBLIOGRAPHY

Asay, Carlos E. "Opposition to the Work of God." *Ensign* 11 (Nov. 1981):67–68.

Foster, Lawrence. "Career Apostates: Reflections on the Works of Jerald and Sandra Tanner." *Dialogue* 17 (Summer 1984):35–60.

Howard, F. Burton. "Come Back to the Lord." *Ensign* 16 (Nov. 1986):76–78.

GILBERT W. SCHARFFS

APOSTLE

An "apostle" is an ordained leader in the MELCHIZEDEK PRIESTHOOD in The Church of Jesus Christ of Latter-day Saints. Apostles are chosen through inspiration by the PRESIDENT OF THE CHURCH, sustained by the general membership of the Church, and ordained by the FIRST PRESIDENCY and the QUORUM OF THE TWELVE APOSTLES by the laying on of hands. They serve as GENERAL AUTHORITIES—as distinguished from local and regional officers—holding their office as apostle for the duration of their lives. The senior apostle is the President of the Church.

In addition to serving as witnesses of Jesus Christ to all the world (D&C 107:23), as Jesus' apostles did, members of the current Quorum of

Quorum of the Twelve Apostles (1961–1962): Front row (left to right): Joseph Fielding Smith, Harold B. Lee, Spencer W. Kimball, Ezra Taft Benson, Mark E. Petersen, Delbert L. Stapley. Back row (left to right): Marion G. Romney, LeGrand Richards, Richard L. Evans, George Q. Morris, Howard W. Hunter, Gordon B. Hinckley.

the Twelve Apostles hold the KEYS OF THE PRIESTHOOD—that is, the rights of presidency (D&C 107:35; cf. 124:128). Of their priesthood authority, President Brigham Young said, "The keys of the eternal Priesthood, which is after the order of the Son of God, are comprehended by being an Apostle. All the Priesthood, all the keys, all the gifts, all the endowments, and everything preparatory to entering into the presence of the Father and of the Son, are in, composed of, circumscribed by, or I might say incorporated within the circumference of, the Apostleship" (*JD* 1:134–35). As a PRIESTHOOD QUORUM, the Quorum of the Twelve Apostles is next in authority to the Quorum of the First Presidency (D&C 107:24). Further, it directs the domestic and international ministry of the quorums of the SEVENTY (D&C 107:34; cf. 124:139–40), and except in the presence of a member of the First Presidency or a more senior member of the Twelve, an apostle presides wherever he may be in the Church.

In the New Testament, an apostle (from Greek *apostellein*, to send forth [as a representative or agent]) was a divinely chosen envoy (Mark 3:14; John 15:16; Acts 1:21–26) who was a witness to Christ's resurrection and carried a missionary obligation to testify to it.

Jesus himself was an apostle through whom God spoke (Heb. 1:2; 3:1). The Father sent Jesus, and whoever receives him receives the one who sent him (Mark 9:37; John 8:16–19). As the Father sent him, so Jesus sent his apostles (John 20:21). Initially, they were called from those who "companied with us [the Twelve] all the time that the Lord Jesus went in and out among us" (Acts 1:21). The number twelve, associated with the apostles, echoes the number of tribes of Israel whom the apostles are to judge (Matt. 19:28; Luke 22:30). In this connection, they stood as the foundation of the early Christian church (Eph. 2:19–21; 4:11–14).

At times, the term embraces more than the Twelve, as is implied both in the phrase "all the apostles" (1 Cor. 15:7)—which follows particular mention of "the twelve" by PAUL (1 Cor. 15:5)—and in references to persons named as apostles who were known not to be among the Twelve (Acts 14:14; Rom. 16:7). It is probable that by A.D. 54 the Lord's brother James had become one of the Twelve (1 Cor. 15:7; Gal. 1:19). Even so, most New Testament references to apostles refer to members of Jesus' original Twelve or to Paul. They were the guarantors or prime witnesses of Jesus' resurrection, which itself constituted the assurance that he was the expected Messiah and Lord of glory (Acts 1:8–11). In the first century, apostles were traveling witnesses to Jesus' resurrection, sent by him into the world for this purpose (Acts 1:8; cf. Matt. 28:19–20). At the group's core—and the Church's foundation—stood PETER, JAMES, and JOHN, who had been with or near Jesus during critical experiences, including his transfiguration (Mark 9:2–9) and his agony in Gethsemane (Mark 14:32–34).

The significance of Jesus' twelve apostles is underscored in the Book of Mormon. First, about 600 B.C. both Lehi and his son Nephi₁ saw in vision the Twelve as followers of Jesus in Palestine and as victims of persecution (1 Ne. 1:10–11; 11:29, 34–36). Second, these Twelve are to judge the twelve tribes of Israel and the other twelve disciples whom the resurrected Jesus chose during his ministry in the Western Hemisphere about A.D. 34 (1 Ne. 12:9–10; Morm. 3:18–19; cf. D&C 29:12). Third, these latter twelve disciples—as distinguished from Jesus' twelve apostles in Palestine—are to judge their own people who are descended from the house of Israel (3 Ne. 27:27). Fourth, during his visit in the Western Hemisphere, the risen Jesus established the position of the Twelve in his church when he chose and instructed them carefully in his gospel (3 Ne. 11:18–12:1; cf. 13:25–34; 15:11–16:20; 18:36–37; 27:13–21). He conferred on them authority to teach the gospel and administer its ordinances—that is, to baptize both with water and the Spirit—thus making them the transmitters of the Church's doctrine and practices (3 Ne. 11:22; 18:36–37; 19:6–14; 26:17). Fifth, in harmony with the pattern in the New Testament, the Book of Mormon records that Jesus was sent by the Father (3 Ne. 18:27; cf. 16:3) and that he in turn commissioned those twelve disciples to "go forth unto this people, and declare the words which I have spoken" (3 Ne. 11:41).

Modern revelation adds further information. The apostolic office and authority were restored to the Prophet Joseph SMITH and Oliver COWDERY by Peter, James, and John, thus underscoring the continuing significance of this office in the Church (D&C 27:12; *see also* MELCHIZEDEK PRIESTHOOD: RESTORATION OF). As early as June 1829, nearly a year before the Church was organized, Oliver Cowdery and David WHITMER, later joined by Martin HARRIS, were instructed concerning the kinds of men to be chosen as apostles and were commissioned to select the first Twelve in the modern era (D&C 18:26–38). This commission was carried out on February 14–15, 1835, when Cowdery, Whitmer, and Harris selected twelve men to be apostles and ordained the nine who were present (*HC* 2:186–98).

Modern scripture specifies that "every decision . . . must be by the unanimous voice" of the Quorum of the Twelve Apostles (D&C 107:27). Further, its members are empowered to baptize, declare the gospel, and ordain others to the priesthood (D&C 18:26–36). The Lord has instructed that the number of apostles in the Quorum of the Twelve must be maintained (D&C 118:1) and that their keys "have come down from the fathers, . . . being sent down from heaven" (D&C 112:32). Those who serve in this office are to "cleanse [their] hearts and [their] garments, lest the blood of this generation be required at [their] hands" (D&C 112:33).

BIBLIOGRAPHY

Kittel, Gerhard, ed., and Geoffrey W. Bromiley, ed. and transl. *Theological Dictionary of the New Testament*, Vol. 1, pp. 407–447. Grand Rapids, Mich., 1964–1976.

McConkie, Bruce R. *The Mortal Messiah*, Vol. 2, pp. 99–114, 303–326. Salt Lake City, 1980.

S. KENT BROWN

APRIL 6

April 6, 1830, is the date on which The church of Jesus Christ of Latter-day Saints was organized. The Prophet Joseph SMITH was divinely authorized to reestablish the Church of Christ on this day (*see* RESTORATION) and it may be the anniversary of the Lord's birth on earth (D&C 20:1). The Church commemorates the importance of April 6 by scheduling its annual General Conference on or near this day.

Concerning the date of Christ's birth, one of the earliest known references to December 25 was in the third century A.D. (Hippolytus, *Commentarii in Danielem*, 4.23.3). Scholarly consensus recognizes that early Christians probably appropriated December 25 from pagan festivals such as the Dies Natalis Invicti, established by the Emperor Aurelian (cf. Hoehner, pp. 11–27). Controversy, ancient and modern, regarding that date has had little influence in the LDS community (*see* CHRISTMAS). Presidents of the Church, including Harold B. LEE (p. 2) and Spencer W. KIMBALL (p. 54), have reaffirmed that April 6 is the true anniversary of Christ's birth, but have encouraged Church members to join with other Christians in observing Christmas as a special day for remembering Jesus' birth and teachings.

Some discussion has centered on the actual year of Jesus' nativity. Some argue that the phrase "one thousand eight hundred and thirty years since the coming of our Lord and Savior Jesus Christ in the flesh" (D&C 20:1) should be interpreted to mean that Christ was born exactly 1,830 years before April 6, 1830 (Lefgren). This view has been both challenged (Brown et al., pp. 375–83) and supported (Pratt, pp. 252–54). Others assert that the phrase was not intended to fix the year of Christ's birth but was simply an oratorical mode of expressing the current year.

Attempts to determine the exact date of Christ's birth or death are complicated by a dearth of pertinent historical information and multiple dating systems. The present dating system derives from the determination that Christ was born in 753 A.U.C. (*ab urbe condita*—from the founding of the city [of Rome]), made by the Scythian monk Dionysius, commissioned by Pope John 1 in A.D. 525 (1278 A.U.C.). The accuracy of Dionysius' system stands at the center of all discussion concerning the date of Christ's birth (Hoehner, p. 11).

John the Baptist's ministry began in the fifteenth year of the reign of Tiberius Caesar (Luke 3:1), the only precise date in the New Testament. The fifteenth year would have begun in September A.D. 28 and ended in September A.D. 29. On this basis alone the dates of Christ's life can be reckoned from the New Testament.

The LDS Church has not taken an official position on the issue of the year of Christ's birth. Bruce R. McConkie, an apostle, offers what for the present appears to be the most definitive word on the question: "We do not believe it is possible with the present state of our knowledge—including that which is known both in and out of the Church—to state with finality when the natal day of the Lord Jesus actually occurred" (Vol. 1, p. 349, n. 2).

BIBLIOGRAPHY

Brown, S. Kent, et al. Book Review of Lefgren's *April 6*. *BYU Studies* 22 (Summer 1982):375–83.

Filmer, W. E. "The Chronology of the Reign of Herod the Great." *Journal of Theological Studies* 17 (1966):283–98.

Hoehner, H. W. *Chronological Aspects of the Life of Christ*. Grand Rapids, Mich., 1977.

Kimball, Spencer W. "Remarks and Dedication of the Fayette, New York, Buildings." *Ensign* 10 (May 1980):54.

Lee, Harold B. "Strengthening the Stakes of Zion." *Ensign* 3 (July 1973):2.

Lefgren, J. *April Sixth*, Salt Lake City, 1980.

McConkie, Bruce R. *Mortal Messiah*, Vol. 1, p. 349, n. 2. Salt Lake City, 1979.

Pratt, J. "Afterwords" (Letter to the Editor). *BYU Studies* 23 (Spring 1983):252–54.

JOHN FRANKLIN HALL

ARCHAEOLOGY

Archaeology is the study and interpretation of past human cultures based on known material remains. Biblical and Mesoamerican archaeological research is of special interest to Latter-day Saints.

Archaeological data from the ancient Near East and the Americas have been used both to support and to discredit the Book of Mormon. Many scholars see no support for the Book of Mormon in the archaeological records, since no one has found any inscriptional evidence for, or material remains that can be tied directly to, any of the persons, places, or things mentioned in the book (Smithsonian Institution).

Several types of indirect archaeological evidence, however, have been used in support of the Book of Mormon. For example, John L. Sorenson and M. Wells Jakeman tentatively identified the Olmec (2000–600 B.C.) and Late Pre-Classic Maya (300 B.C.–A.D. 250) cultures in Central America with the JAREDITE and NEPHITE cultures, based on correspondences between periods of cultural development in these areas and the pattern of cultural change in the Book of Mormon.

Likewise, parallels between cultural traits of the ancient Near East and Mesoamerica perhaps indicate transoceanic contacts between the two regions. Among these are such minor secondary traits as horned incense burners, models of house types, wheel-made pottery, cement, the true arch, and the use of stone boxes. All of these may, however, represent independent inventions. Stronger evidence for contacts may be found in the TREE OF LIFE motif, a common religious theme, on Stela 5 from Izapa in Chiapas, Mexico. Jakeman, in 1959, studied Stela 5 in detail and concluded that it represented the sons of a legendary ancestral couple absorbing and perhaps recording their knowledge of a munificent Tree of Life. This can be compared favorably to the account of Lehi's vision in the Book of Mormon (1 Ne. 8).

The presence of a bearded white deity, Quetzalcoatl or Kukulcan, in the pantheon of the Aztec, Toltec, and Maya has also been advanced as indirect evidence of Christ's visit to the New World. The deity is represented as a feathered serpent, and elements of his worship may have similarities to those associated with Christ's atonement.

Recent work by LDS professional archaeologists such as Ray Matheny at El Mirador and by the New World Archaeological Foundation in Chiapas has been directed toward an understanding of the factors that led to the development of complex societies in Mesoamerica in general. Under C. Wilfred Griggs, a team of Brigham Young University scholars has sponsored excavations in Egypt, and other LDS archaeologists have been involved in projects in Israel and Jordan.

Another area of archaeological investigation is in LDS history. Dale Berge's excavations at Nauvoo; the Whitmer farm in New York; the early Mormon settlement of Goshen (Utah); the Utah mining town of Mercur; and, most recently, Camp Floyd, the headquarters of Johnston's army in Utah, have provided information about the economic and social interactions between early Mormon and non-Mormon communities.

BIBLIOGRAPHY

Griggs, C. Wilfred, ed. *Excavations at Seila, Egypt.* Provo, Utah, 1988.

Jakeman, M. Wells. "The Main Challenge of the Book of Mormon to Archaeology; and a Summary of Archaeological Research to Date Giving a Preliminary Test of Book-of-Mormon Claims." In *Progress in Archaeology, An Anthology,* ed. R. Christensen, pp. 99–103. Provo, Utah, 1963.

———. "Stela 5, Izapa, as The Lehi Tree-of-Life Stone.'" In *The Tree of Life in Ancient America,* ed. R. Christensen. Provo, Utah, 1968.

Matheny, Ray T. "An Early Maya Metropolis Uncovered, Elmirador." *National Geographic* 172, no. 3 (1987):316–39.

Smithsonian Institution. "Statement Regarding the Book of Mormon." Department of Anthropology, National Museum of Natural History, SIL–76, 1982.

Sorenson, John L. "An Evaluation of the Smithsonian Institution's 'Statement' Regarding the Book of Mormon" *F.A.R.M.S. Paper.* Provo, Utah, 1982.

———. *An Ancient American Setting for the Book of Mormon.* Salt Lake City, 1985.

An Egyptian gold-covered mummy, excavated in Egypt by Brigham Young University archaeologists in 1988. Courtesy C. Wilfred Griggs.

DAVID J. JOHNSON

ARCHITECTURE

In the first generation the architecture of The Church of Jesus Christ of Latter-day Saints bore the stamp of individuality and originality. With a membership of less than fifteen thousand, Latter-day Saints undertook three daring projects: the KIRTLAND TEMPLE in Ohio, the master plan for the city of NAUVOO, Illinois, and the NAUVOO TEMPLE.

The Kirtland Temple, designed by the Prophet Joseph SMITH and Artemis Millett, has a pristine exterior free of extraneous detail and a well-planned interior bathed in natural light. The master plan for Nauvoo, created by Joseph Smith and others, was similar in concept to Smith's "plat for the City of Zion." It consisted of a grid of streets with gardens adjoining each dwelling. The highest hill was reserved for the temple, which rose above all other structures and made Nauvoo, as originally planned, a clear visual statement of the religious

This stake center in Bountiful, Utah, is typical of an architectural style used in the 1950s.

and social priorities of Mormon life. The Nauvoo Temple, designed by William Weeks, was similar to the Kirtland Temple but larger and more ornate.

After the westward migration to the Great Basin, other demanding projects were undertaken. CITY PLANNING for Salt Lake City was similar to the master plan for Nauvoo, with the temple as the dominant feature. Four temples were commissioned to be built in four Utah cities: in Salt Lake City, St. George, and Logan under architect Truman O. Angell, and in Manti under architect William H. Folsom. The block and bulwark form of the earlier temples was retained but, except for St. George, the facades were elaborate. The tower scheme of the Salt Lake Temple became the symbol of the new dispensation and embodied the growing proclivity of the Church to prefer complexity rather than simplicity in its architecture.

In addition to temples, the Church continued to produce other important buildings that were architecturally impressive, notably its tabernacles. Among the most distinguished were the Coleville, Logan, and Brigham City tabernacles. The SALT LAKE TABERNACLE, designed by Truman O. Angell assisted by William H. Folsom and Henry Grow, remains the ideal of architectural integrity and is the zenith of Mormon architecture.

After 1900 the rapidly growing Church continued to produce a wide variety of religious structures, including temples, meetinghouses, and educational buildings, especially at BRIGHAM YOUNG UNIVERSITY. Meetinghouses typically incorporated an axially organized chapel with pews arranged before an elevated central pulpit and an off-center sacrament table. Works of art and natural light were used sparingly (see MEETINGHOUSES). Early buildings in Salt Lake City included the classically detailed Church headquarters building, whose architect was Joseph Don Carlos Young, and the adjacent Hotel Utah. These structures, with the temple and tabernacle, became the architectural center of the Latter-day Saints and of Salt Lake City.

In the early decades of the twentieth century the Church commissioned temples in the western United States, Canada, Europe, and the South Pacific. The form of these structures differed from the earlier temples. Most were designed by Edward O. Anderson, and each featured a large, rectangular, flat-roofed assembly hall surmounted by a tower and enclosed by a lower mass of ancillary spaces. Natural light was admitted to the interior sparingly. The opaque character became the hallmark of future temples, including the Alberta Temple in Cardston, designed by Harold W. Burton. Its design received architectural commendation from outside the Church.

In response to worldwide growth and changes in organization, new buildings were added to the Church headquarters enclave. On Temple Square an annex was added to the temple, altering its symmetry. A 28-story office tower and plaza were constructed, designed by architect George Cannon Young. Restoration of the Lion and Beehive houses, originally Brigham Young's residences, was completed.

Burgeoning growth led to a centralized Church Building Committee. Standard plans were developed, first for meetinghouses or chapels and then for temples. The meetinghouses, categorized by size, phases, and configuration, were uniformly designed for wards and stakes regardless of location. The standard-plan temples, initially the work of architect Emil Fetzer, and first built in Ogden and Provo, were designed to accommodate up to 100 ENDOWMENT sessions a day with maximum mobility. These single-towered edifices, of which more than a dozen have been built, all followed the same basic plan but employed changes and decoration in an attempt to capture a sense of individuality. After 1980 a second generation of standard-plan temples, credited to the Church architectural staff, was commissioned. These small, slightly differenti-

The Assembly Hall (c. 1888), on Temple Square in Salt Lake City, has been used for over a century for Church meetings, conferences, firesides, public lectures, and concerts. Photographer: C. R. Savage.

ated structures, built in large urban centers worldwide, typically featured a broad, low roof with various tower arrangements which, by replicating the most obvious elements of the Salt Lake Temple, announced the Church's presence.

Throughout its history Mormon architecture has been more functional than experimental, more temperate than ornate, more restrained than innovative. There is a marked tendency to avoid any distraction from direct and personal spirituality. Latter-day Saints' concern for uniting heavenly principles with earthly practices has been adequately expressed in practical, durable, and extraordinarily well-maintained buildings and grounds.

FRANKLIN T. FERGUSON

AREA, AREA PRESIDENCY

An area is the largest geographical administrative subdivision of the Church and is presided over by an area presidency, composed of three members of the quorums of the SEVENTY.

An area presidency consists of a president and two counselors who provide spiritual guidance and administrative direction to leaders and members of the Church in their area. As members of the quorums of the Seventy, area presidencies are also called to preach the gospel, to be special witnesses of Jesus Christ, and to build up and regulate the affairs of the Church as assigned under the direction of the FIRST PRESIDENCY and the QUORUM OF THE TWELVE APOSTLES.

The specific duties of an area presidency include implementing the policies and instructions of the General Authorities presiding over them; instructing area leaders and members in the principles of the gospel; selecting and training REGIONAL REPRESENTATIVES, stake presidencies, and mission leaders; counseling with local leaders, members, and missionaries about Church-related, personal, and spiritual problems; establishing priorities for a broad range of Church activities; supervising the work of area staff personnel; conferring with community and religious leaders on social and moral issues of common concern; and making regular reports to higher Church leaders on conditions and progress in their area.

Area presidencies in the United States and Canada live in Salt Lake City. On weekends they often travel to their assigned areas and meet with leaders and members in stake CONFERENCES and various regional and stake training meetings. They also spend several weeks a year touring MISSIONS and training missionaries and mission leaders. In addition, members of area presidencies in the United States have assignments at Church headquarters in Salt Lake City that occupy a large portion of their time during the week. Area presidencies in other parts of the world live in their assigned areas. They spend their full time directing the work of the Church in their area.

BIBLIOGRAPHY

"Area Presidencies Called as Church Modifies Geographical Administration." *Ensign* 14 (Aug. 1984):75.

Hinckley, Gordon B. "The Sustaining of Church Officers." *Ensign* 15 (May 1985):4–6.

PERRY H. CUNNINGHAM

ARIZONA, PIONEER SETTLEMENTS IN

Mormon pioneering in Arizona began in the mid-1800s and continued until well after 1900, and was especially active from 1873 until 1890. Latter-day Saints first came to Arizona in 1846, with the march of the MORMON BATTALION from Santa Fe to southern California. Later missionaries such as Alfred Billings, Jacob Hamblin, Ira Hatch, and Thales Haskell explored the territory in the 1850s and 1860s. By 1870 interest in transportation on the Colorado River, in grazing, in border control, and in the desert as a refuge led to the establishment of Callsville and Lees Ferry on the Colorado River and Pipe Spring on the Arizona Strip.

In 1873 COLONIZATION began in earnest. Brigham YOUNG, with Thomas L. KANE, planned a colonizing thrust that would eventually extend from Salt Lake City to a Mormon seaport at Guaymas, Mexico. A party of scouts under Lorenzo Roundy examined the San Francisco Mountains and the Little Colorado River drainages for town sites. Brigham Young called 200 colonizing and Indian missionaries who, without adequate preparation, hurried south in the winter and spring of 1873. This mission foundered in the desert country north of the Little Colorado, and the missionaries retreated to Utah. Only John D. Lee and a few others held on at Lees Ferry and Moenkopi.

The southward movement lay dormant for two years. When it revived, plans focused on UNITED ORDER settlements and Indian missions. Missionaries James S. Brown and Daniel W. Jones led expeditions south, and four colonizing companies were dispatched under Lot Smith, a tough Mormon Battalion veteran known for his exploits against the UTAH EXPEDITION. During 1876 these colonists established united order towns at Sunset, Brigham City, Obed, and Joseph City on the lower Little Colorado. By 1878 Latter-day Saints had settled farther upstream, at Snowflake, Taylor, St. Johns, Concho, and Eagar, as well as at several sites in western New Mexico. Colonists also moved farther south into the Salt River Valley, where several towns were established, including Mesa and Lehi. Others settled at Pima, Thatcher, and Safford in the Gila River country, and at St. David on the San Pedro River.

The intense united order impulse of the earliest companies soon diminished, and towns established after 1877 were organized on a less communal basis. Even the strongest orders at Sunset and Joseph City gave up communal organization by 1886. The proselytization of Indians also lapsed as economic competition created tensions between NNATIVE AMERICANS and whites. Although irrigation was a continuing struggle, prosperous agricultural villages soon flourished in all the Mormon districts. Led by John W. Young, Arizona Latter-day Saints became a major force in building the Santa Fe railroad and in ranching on the Arizona Strip and near Flagstaff. Establishing a branch of Zion's Cooperative Mercantile Institution (ZCMI), they also engaged in commerce, freighting, and banking.

At first Latter-day Saints found political life in Arizona difficult. In Apache County, friction among Mexicans, ranchers, and traders escalated into fierce struggles by 1880. In 1884 David K. Udall and a few others were imprisoned for practicing PLURAL MARRIAGE; many fled to Mexico. But after the MANIFESTO was issued in 1890, two-party politics were embraced and Church members found a place in Arizona's political institutions.

The 1890 federal census counted 6,500 Latter-day Saints in Arizona. Although Church settlement continued well into the twentieth century, the pioneer period ended by 1900. By that time Latter-day Saints, firmly established Arizonans both in their own minds and in the eyes of others, comprised a distinctive cultural element in Arizona.

The erection of a temple at Mesa, dedicated in 1927, reflected the significance of Arizona to the

Church, and provided Native American members and other Church members in Mexico with closer access to temple ordinances. Among twentieth-century Church leaders with Arizona roots was Spencer W. KIMBALL, President of the Church from 1973 to 1985. By 1990 there were 236,000 Latter-day Saints in Arizona, most of them residing in urban areas.

BIBLIOGRAPHY

Fish, Joseph. *The Life and Times of Joseph Fish, Mormon Pioneer.* Danville, Ill., 1970.

McClintock, James H. *Mormon Settlement in Arizona: Record of Peaceful Conquest of the Desert.* Phoenix, Ariz., 1921.

Peterson, Charles S. *Take Up Your Mission: Mormon Colonizing Along the Little Colorado River 1870–1900.* Tucson, Ariz., 1973.

Smith, Jesse N. *Journal of Jesse Nathaniel Smith.* Salt Lake City, 1953.

CHARLES S. PETERSON

ARMAGEDDON

The name Armageddon is a Greek transliteration of the Hebrew *har megiddo*, mountain of Megiddo, and is used by John the Revelator to symbolize the assembling of a vast world army in the last days (Rev. 16:16). Sixty miles north of Jerusalem, the site of the ancient city of Har Megiddo overlooks the Plain of Esdraelon or the valley of Jezreel, forming a natural entrance to the heart of the land from the Mediterranean Sea.

Anciently the valley was the scene of violent and crucial battles. It was here, during the period of the Judges, that Deborah and Barak defeated the Canaanite general Sisera and delivered Israel from Canaanite rule (Judg. 4–5). Around 640 B.C., King Josiah of Judah was killed at Har Megiddo by the army of Pharaoh Necho, resulting in Judah's subjugation to Egypt (2 Chr. 35:20–23; 2 Kgs. 23:29).

Armageddon is destined to play a future role in world events. It is LDS belief that the prophecies of the scriptures will be fulfilled and that armies representing the nations of the earth will be gathered in the valley of Megiddo. It may be that given the extent of the conflict, Armageddon is a symbolic representation of worldwide conflict centered in this geographic area. The scriptures state that when the battle is at its zenith, Christ, the

King of Kings, will appear on the Mount of Olives accompanied by dramatic upheavals. Subsequently, the armies spoken of by John will be destroyed, followed by Christ's millennial reign (cf. Zech. 11–14; Rev. 16:14–21; D&C 45:42–53; *JD* 7:189; *MD*, p. 71). How long it will take to bring about these events is not revealed. The name Armageddon does not occur in latter-day scripture, nor is there a known mention of it by the Prophet Joseph Smith.

V. DANIEL ROGERS

ARTICLES OF FAITH

In 1842, in response to a specific request from John Wentworth (editor of the *Chicago Democrat*), Joseph SMITH sent a succinct overview of his own religious experiences and the history of the Church over which he presided (*see* WENTWORTH LETTER). At the end of the historical sketch, he appended a list summarizing the "faith of the Latter-day Saints." Later titled "Articles of Faith," these thirteen items were first published in the Nauvoo *Times and Seasons* in March 1842 and were later included in the 1851 British Mission pamphlet *The Pearl of Great Price*, compiled by Elder Franklin D. Richards. That pamphlet was revised in 1878 and again in 1880. In 1880, a general conference of the Church voted to add the Pearl of Great Price to the STANDARD WORKS of the Church, thus including the thirteen articles. The Articles of Faith do not constitute a summation of all LDS beliefs, and they are not a creed in the traditional Christian sense, but they do provide a useful authoritative summary of fundamental LDS scriptures and beliefs.

The articles begin with an affirmative declaration that the GODHEAD is composed of three personages: the Father, his Son Jesus Christ, and the Holy Ghost (cf. Acts 7:55–56; 2 Cor. 13:14; 2 Ne. 31:21; JS—H 1:17).

The second item focuses attention on the beginning of mortal history and affirms that human beings have moral AGENCY and therefore accountability for their own acts: "Men will be punished for their own sins, and not for Adam's transgression" (cf. Deut. 24:16; 2 Ne. 2:27).

The third article directs attention to the centrality of the ATONEMENT of Christ and how mankind benefits in relationship to it: "Through the

Atonement of Christ, all mankind may be saved, by obedience to the laws and ordinances of the Gospel" (Mosiah 3:7–12; D&C 138:4).

The fourth article spells out the foundational principles and ordinances: faith in Jesus Christ, repentance, baptism by immersion for the remission of sins, and the laying on of hands for the GIFT OF THE HOLY GHOST (cf. Acts 8:14–19; Heb. 6:1–2; 3 Ne. 11:32–37).

The next two articles address issues of authority and organization: A man must be called of God, confirmed by divine inspiration and by the laying on of hands by those in authority, in order to preach the gospel and administer its ordinances (cf. 1 Tim. 4:14; D&C 42:11); further, the Church is essentially "the same organization that existed in the Primitive Church, namely, apostles, prophets, pastors, teachers, evangelists, and so forth" (cf. Eph. 4:11).

The seventh item affirms the LDS belief in the GIFTS OF THE SPIRIT, specifically naming several: the gift of tongues, prophecy, revelation, visions, healing, and the interpretation of tongues (cf. 1 Cor. 12:10; D&C 46:10–26).

The place of sacred scripture is addressed in the eighth article: Latter-day Saints "believe the Bible to be the word of God as far as it is translated correctly"; they also "believe the Book of Mormon to be the word of God" (cf. Ezek. 37:16; John 10:16; 2 Tim. 3:16).

The ninth article states that the restored gospel is not bound up in a closed set of books, but rather declares the principle of continuing REVELATION, and therefore an open canon. Latter-day Saints affirm belief in all past and present revelation, and they look forward to many future revelations (cf. Amos 3:7; D&C 76:7).

Article ten summarizes four great events of the last days: the literal gathering of Israel and the restoration of the Ten Tribes; the building of ZION, the New Jerusalem, in the Western Hemisphere; Christ's personal reign on earth; and the eventual renewal of the earth itself, when it will receive its paradisiacal glory, the state of purity it had before the Fall of Adam (see 3 Ne. 21–22).

The eleventh article declares the LDS belief in freedom of worship and of conscience for both themselves and all others. It states: "We claim the privilege of worshipping Almighty God according to the dictates of our own conscience, and allow all men the same privilege, let them worship how, where, or what they may." And the twelfth article states the political stance of the Latter-day Saints as law-abiding citizens (D&C 134; *see* POLITICS: POLITICAL TEACHINGS; TOLERANCE).

The final declaration provides a broad perspective for life and an invitation to the LDS approach to life: "We believe in being honest, true, chaste, benevolent, virtuous, and in doing good to all men; indeed, we may say that we follow the admonition of Paul—We believe all things, we hope all things, we have endured many things, and hope to be able to endure all things. If there is anything virtuous, lovely, or of good report or praiseworthy, we seek after these things" (cf. 1 Cor. 13:7; Philip. 4:8).

The Wentworth Letter was not the first attempt to summarize basic LDS beliefs. Earlier lists, some of which may have influenced the Wentworth listing, had appeared prior to 1842. As early as June 1829, Joseph Smith and Oliver COWDERY were committing to paper the "Articles and Covenants" of the soon-to-be-organized Church. Later known as Doctrine and Covenants Section 20, this text enumerates a number of basic beliefs, including the existence of God; the creation and fall of man; the centrality of Jesus Christ; the fundamental ordinances of the gospel, including baptism; and the basic duties of members (20:17–36). This document, the first accepted by a Church conference vote, was not an exhaustive listing of all beliefs but rather a basic charter for the infant organization, rooted in the Bible and the Book of Mormon.

In the first issue of the *LDS Messenger and Advocate* (Oct. 1834), published in Kirtland, Ohio, Oliver Cowdery enumerated eight "principles," all of which had their parallel in section 20.

Other early lists that summarized the leading principles of Latter-day Saint beliefs prior to the Wentworth Letter include one prepared by Joseph Young for publication by John Hayward in *The Religious Creeds and Statistics of Every Christian Denomination in the United States* (Boston, 1836, pp. 139–40). In five paragraphs, he outlined the doctrines of (1) the Godhead and atonement of Jesus Christ; (2) the first principles and ordinances of the gospel performed by apostolic authority as in the ancient Church of Christ; (3) the gathering of lost Israel and the restoration of spiritual gifts to her; (4) the Second Coming of Christ; and (5) the resurrection and judgment of all mankind.

Another list of eighteen "principles and doctrines" was included by Parley P. Pratt in the introduction to his *Late Persecution of the Church of Jesus Christ of Latter-day Saints* (New York, 1840, pp. iii–xiii). For example, "The first principle of Theology as held by this Church, is Faith in God the eternal Father, and in his Son Jesus Christ, who verily was crucified for the sins of the world . . . and in the Holy Ghost who bears record of them" (pp. iii–iv). Many phrases in Pratt's list are similar to those in the Wentworth Letter.

Orson Pratt offers an expansive and eloquent "sketch of the faith and doctrine" of the Church in his *Interesting Account of Several Remarkable Visions* (Edinburgh, 1840, pp. 24–31). The order in which it presents its themes in nineteen paragraphs (many of which begin, "We believe that . . .") is nearly identical to that of the thirteen points of the Wentworth Letter. Orson Pratt's explanations include biblical references and personal testimony of the truth and divine origins of these teachings.

Orson Hyde published in German a history of the Church that included a chapter of sixteen articles (actually essays) on such topics as the Godhead, the use of scripture, faith, repentance, baptism, confirmation, sacrament of bread and wine, confession of sins and Church discipline, children, revelations, lay priesthood, baptism for the dead, prayer, holidays, washing of the feet, and patriarchal blessings (*A Cry from the Wilderness* [Frankfurt, 1842]).

Even after the Wentworth Letter was published in March 1842, many other lists of LDS beliefs continued to appear for the next generation. In April 1849, James H. Flanigan included a list of fourteen statements in a pamphlet published in England, and this list was quoted and sometimes modified in various publications throughout the nineteenth century. For example, it was quoted in Charles MacKay's popular book *The Mormons; or the Latter-day Saints* (London, 1851, pp. 46–47). This list follows the Wentworth Letter almost verbatim, adding such points as "the Lord's supper" to Article 4; including "wisdom, charity, [and] brotherly love" among the gifts of the spirit in Article 7; and inserting a fourteenth article regarding the literal resurrection of the body. Other lists (usually composed by missionaries) were published in various parts of the world throughout this era.

The canonization of the Wentworth letter as part of the Pearl of Great Price in 1880 reflected and assured its undisputed priority. And when James E. Talmage was asked by the First Presidency in 1891 to prepare a work on theology for use as a textbook in Church schools, it was to these Articles of Faith that he turned for the outline of his volume. First published in 1899 and still in use today, Talmage's *Articles of Faith* greatly elaborate on the themes of Joseph Smith's Wentworth list. In twenty-four chapters, Talmage provides extensive commentary and scriptural references regarding each of the concepts mentioned in the thirteen articles, plus sections on the sacrament of the Lord's Supper and resurrection (as in Flanigan's listing), and finally a section on practical religion (benevolence, tithes and offerings, consecration, social order within the Church, eternal marriage, sanctity of the body, and keeping the Sabbath day holy).

As early as the 1850s, LDS missionaries printed broadsides that contained the Articles of Faith. In time, these missionary placards were reduced to wallet size and are still used by missionaries throughout the world. In the PRIMARY classes of the Church, children memorize the Articles of Faith as a requirement for graduation at age twelve, and adults have also been encouraged to learn and use them for personal study and in missionary work.

Although not a formal creed, the Articles of Faith are a marvelously abridged summary (less than 400 words) of the basic beliefs of The Church of Jesus Christ of Latter-day Saints. While there have been many variations published since Joseph Smith's day, a central core of beliefs stated in all these articles comes from the earliest years of the Restoration—a fact that testifies both to its internal consistency and its constancy.

BIBLIOGRAPHY

Lyon, T. Edgar. "Origin and Purpose of the Articles of Faith." *Instructor* 87 (Aug.–Oct. 1952):230–31, 264–65, 275, 298–99, 319.

McConkie, Bruce R. *A New Witness for the Articles of Faith.* Salt Lake City, 1985.

Sondrup, Steven P. "On Confessing Faith: Thoughts on the Language of the Articles of Faith." In *Literature of Belief,* ed. N. Lambert, pp. 197–215. Provo, Utah, 1981.

Talmage, James E. *AF.* Salt Lake City, 1899.

Welch, John W. "[Joseph Smith and Paul:] Co-Authors of the Articles of Faith?" *Instructor* 114 (Nov. 1969):422–26.

Whittaker, David J. "The 'Articles of Faith' in Early Mormon Literature and Thought." In *New Views of Mormon History, A Collection of Essays in Honor of Leonard J. Arrington,* ed. D. Bitton and M. Beecher, pp. 63–92. Salt Lake City, 1987.

DAVID J. WHITTAKER

ARTIFICIAL INSEMINATION

Artificial insemination is defined as placing semen into the uterus or oviduct by artificial rather than natural means. The Church does not approve of artificial insemination of single women. It also discourages artificial insemination of married women using semen from anyone but the husband. "However, this is a personal matter that ultimately must be left to the husband and wife, with the responsibility for the decision resting solely upon them" (*General Handbook of Instructions*, 11-4). Children conceived by artificial insemination have the same family ties as children who are conceived naturally. The *General Handbook of Instructions* (1989) states: "A child conceived by artificial insemination and born after the parents are sealed in the temple is born in the covenant. A child conceived by artificial insemination before the parents are sealed may be sealed to them after they are sealed."

BIBLIOGRAPHY

General Handbook of Instructions, 11–4. Salt Lake City, 1989.

FRANK O. MAY, JR.

ARTISTS, VISUAL

While the work of LDS artists encompasses many historical and cultural styles, its unity derives from their shared religious beliefs and from recurring LDS religious themes in their works. The absence of an official liturgical art has kept the Church from directing its artists into specified stylistic traditions. This has been especially conducive to variety in art as the Church has expanded into many different cultures, with differing artistic styles and traditions. Some of the aesthetic constants of LDS artists are the narrative tradition in painting, a reverence for nature, absence of nihilism, support of traditional societal values, respect for the human body, a strong sense of aesthetic structure, and rigorous craftsmanship.

The history of LDS painters begins in NAUVOO in the 1840s, in the second decade following the establishment of the LDS Church (1830). Two factors especially influenced the early development of an artistic tradition within this small, new church on the American frontier: missionary work abroad and the desire of new converts to join the main body of the members.

The first two LDS painters, both English converts, were Sutcliffe Maudsley (1809–1881), from Lancashire, and William W. Major (1804–1854), from Bristol. Maudsley painted the earliest portraits among the Latter-day Saints—primitive but accurate profiles of members of the SMITH FAMILY in Nauvoo. Major, who crossed the plains in 1848, was the earliest painter in the Utah territory. His most famous painting, begun in WINTER QUARTERS and completed in the Salt Lake Valley, depicts Brigham YOUNG and his family in the stage-like interior of an imaginary English mansion, an attempt to transplant to the American frontier a British art tradition that goes back to Gainsborough.

In 1853 another English convert painter, Frederick H. Piercy (1830–1891), journeyed to Utah, making detailed sketches and watercolor drawings along the way to illustrate an LDS emigrant guide book, *Route from Liverpool to Great Salt Lake Valley*. This visual record is the earliest extant series showing the Mormon route. Many of its original paintings and drawings are in the Boston Museum of Fine Arts.

Over the next quarter of a century, many more British converts who were artists, most with limited formal education and modest art training in England, migrated to Utah. Almost all of them painted the mountains and the Great Salt Lake in the exaggerated and romantic styles then popular in England. Romantic landscapes were linked to their religious faith. They saw the face of the Lord in nature and ZION in the purity of the western wilderness. Very few of these early works by British converts depict genre or historical subjects. A major exception is the huge painting of Joseph SMITH preaching to the Indians done for the SALT LAKE TEMPLE by London-born William Armitage (1817–1890).

Other prominent English convert painters from this period were Alfred Lambourne (1850–1926) and Henry Lavender Adolphus Culmer (1854–1914). Culmer received the most national recognition, primarily through his large paintings of the canyons and deserts of southern Utah published in the March 1907 issue of the *National Geographic Magazine*.

Contemporaneous Scandinavian convert painters included C. C. A. (Carl Christian Anton) Christensen (1831–1912), from Denmark, and

C. C. A. Christensen (1831–1912), a Danish convert trained at the Royal Academy of Fine Arts in Copenhagen, created a series of Mormon history panoramas and used them to give missionary lectures. He also painted murals in the Manti and St. George temples. From the Brigham Young University photograph collection. Courtesy Nelson Wadsworth.

Danquart A. Weggeland (1827–1918), from Norway. Both were trained at the Royal Academy of Art in Copenhagen and favored historical and genre paintings. Christensen's *Mormon Panorama* is the most significant series of LDS historical paintings from the nineteenth century. It includes twenty-three tempera paintings, each six feet by ten feet, recounting the pre-Utah history of the Church in epic dimensions. These paintings have been widely published (*Art in America* 58 [May-June 1970]:52–65) and exhibited (Whitney Museum of American Art, 1970).

An American-born painter in this early period was George M. Ottinger (1833–1917), from Phila-

delphia. His art includes both historical and landscape painting.

In 1890 the Church called some of the most skilled younger LDS painters to study in Paris. These "art missionaries," John Hafen (1856–1910), Lorus Pratt (1855–1923), John B. Fairbanks (1855–1940), Edwin Evans (1860–1946), and Herman H. Haag (1871–1895), studied art to prepare to paint the murals in the Salt Lake Temple. They studied academic figure drawing formally and impressionism informally. Other artists who also studied in Paris in this early period were James T. Harwood (1860–1940) and John W. Clawson (1858–1936), a grandson of Brigham Young.

These artists returned to Utah to paint and teach, and then sent their best students to Paris to study. This second wave included Mahonri M. Young (1877–1957), also a grandson of Brigham Young, and Donald Beauregard (1884–1914). Young returned to Utah and then went to New York City, where he taught at the Art Students League. In his lifetime he developed a national reputation as a sculptor and graphic artist. Beauregard spent most of his short artistic life in New Mexico, contributing to the early Santa Fe art tradition.

With the coming of World War I, the center of training for Utah painters shifted from Paris to New York City. The two most significant LDS artists of this period were Minerva K. Teichert (1888–1976) and LeConte Stewart (1891–1990). Both sought to celebrate their faith and tradition artistically, but in different ways. Teichert painted historical and genre scenes from LDS and western history and religious scenes from the Book of Mormon, while Stewart celebrated the pioneer landscape of Utah.

The next major leaders in LDS painting were Arnold Friberg (b. 1913) from Illinois, and Alvin Gittens (1921–1981), a convert from England. Both taught at the University of Utah. Friberg's most significant commissions included work for Cecil B. DeMille's *Ten Commandments* (for which he was nominated for an Academy Award), a series of scenes from the Book of Mormon, and portraits of Great Britain's Prince Charles and Queen Elizabeth II. Gittens was best known as a portrait painter and a teacher. He put his students through rigorous courses in anatomy and perspective when other art schools were emphasizing expressionism. Gittens was the region's preeminent portrait painter until his death.

Self-Portrait, by Minerva Kohlhepp Teichert (1937, graphite). Raised in Pocatello, Idaho, Minerva Teichert (1889-1976) studied art at the Art Institute of Chicago and the Art Students League in New York, then came home in 1917 to marry a Wyoming rancher. Throughout her life she painted scenes from the West and its people and from LDS history and scripture. Her impressionistic style is reflected in this self-portrait. Courtesy Museum of Fine Arts, Brigham Young University.

In the early 1970s a new group of LDS painters began to form around Brigham Young University. These artists were particularly interested in exploring the interface between their religious faith and their art. The leading artists of the group were Gary E. Smith (b. 1942), a convert from Oregon; Dennis Smith (b. 1942) and William F. Whitaker, Jr. (b. 1943) from Utah; James Christensen (b. 1943) from California; and Trevor Southey (b. 1940), a convert from Zimbabwe. The Mormon Arts Festival, held annually at BYU from 1969 to 1984, served as a showplace for some of their best religious work.

Utah continues to attract LDS convert artists from outside the United States, and BYU has become a focus for this artistic immigration. Two of the most recent immigrant faculty are Wulf Barsch (b. 1943) from Germany and Soren Edsberg (b. 1945) from Denmark. Barsch, a winner of the 1975–1976 Prix de Rome, has built a national repu-

tation from his strong semiabstract paintings, which often include LDS themes. Edsberg, the son of Knud Edsberg (b. 1911), a prominent Danish portrait and genre painter, has built a European reputation for his geometric paintings.

There are many other LDS painters who have not come to Utah. Giovanna Lacerti (b. 1935) and Pino Drago (b. 1947) from Italy and Johan Bentin (b. 1936) from Copenhagen are notable European LDS artists. Some of the most prominent Latin American and Caribbean LDS painters are Jorge Cocco (b. 1936) of Mexico, Antonio Madrid (b. 1949) of Panama, and Henri-Robert Bresil (b. 1952) from Haiti. They have produced important LDS paintings using artistic approaches totally different from their fellow LDS artists in Utah. Cocco and Madrid look to Spain for stylistic models. Bresil draws on the bright and exuberant folk tradition of Haiti.

In the South Pacific, Rei Hamon (b. around 1915), a part-Maori member of the Church from New Zealand, is an environmental artist. His tight stipple drawings celebrate his profoundly religious attachment to the land, plants, and animals of New Zealand.

In the American Southwest, many Native Americans have joined the Church as a result of missionary work going back to the 1850s. Some of the finest Hopi artists are LDS. Among the most prominent are Fannie Nampeyo Polacca (c. 1900–1987), her son Thomas (b. 1935), and Helen Naha (b. 1922), potters; Lowell Talishoma (b. 1950) and Emil Pooley (1908–1980), kachina carvers; and Wayne Sekaquaptewa (1923–1979) and Michael Sockyma (b. 1942), silversmiths. Among the Navajo, Lucy McKelvey (b. 1946) has a national reputation as a potter. Ida Redbird (1888–1971) is perhaps the most famous Maricopa potter. Among the Santa Clara, Christina (1892–1980) and Terrisita Naranjo (b. 1919) have national and international reputations as potters.

In Indonesia, where batik is the preeminent art form, Hadi Pranoto (b. 1937), from Java, is a respected batik artist. In Guatemala, where textile weaving is the main national art form, Juan Zarate (b. 1930), is an accomplished weaver.

Many Latter-day Saint women are fine quilters. Those with national reputations include Charlotte Anderson (b. 1952), from Kearns, Utah; Joyce Stewart (b. 1940), from Rexburg, Idaho; and Marva Dalebout (b. 1928), from St. George, Utah.

In the mountain West many LDS painters are

known for their western and wildlife art. The rise of this art is part of a new self-confidence in a growing region of the country that is beginning to come of age. Jackson Hole, Wyoming; Santa Fe, New Mexico; and Scottsdale, Arizona, are significant centers of the American art market. The West, with its landscape, people, and animals, has become the wellspring of American mythology, and because many LDS people live in the West and have experienced much of the western heroic experience, western art has been a natural area of interest for them. Some of the leading LDS artists in this genre are Michael Coleman (b. 1946), Robert Duncan (b. 1941), Valoy Eaton (b. 1938), and Jim Norton (b. 1953), from Utah; Nancy Glazier (b. 1947) and Gary Carter (b. 1939), living in Montana; and Jim Wilcox (b. 1941), Harold Hopkinson (b. 1918), and Mel Fillerup (b. 1924), from Wyoming. Most paint in either a realist or an impressionist manner. In theme and intention, they are philosophical descendants of the early British and Scandinavian LDS immigrant artists who came west and were awed by the land but held to the epic tradition of which they were a part.

The geographical and cultural diversity of the LDS people has brought aesthetic variety to the LDS art tradition. The artists' shared religious faith and values have constantly infused that tradition with meaning.

Many works by LDS artists are displayed in the Museum of Church History and Art in Salt Lake City, which plays an important role in sharing LDS art with the world.

[*See also* Art in Mormonism; Musicians; Sculptors.]

BIBLIOGRAPHY

Gibbs, Linda Jones. *Masterworks*. Salt Lake City, 1984.

———. *Harvesting the Light: The Paris Art Mission and Beginnings of Utah Impressionism*. Salt Lake City, 1987.

Haseltine, James L. *100 Years of Utah Painting*. Salt Lake City, 1965.

Horne, Alice Merrill. *Devotees and Their Shrines: A Hand Book of Utah Art*. Salt Lake City, 1914.

Olpin, Robert S. *Dictionary of Utah Art*. Salt Lake City, 1980.

Oman, Richard G. "LDS Southwest Indian Art." *Ensign* 12 (Sept. 1982):33–48.

———, and Richard L. Jensen. *C. C. A. Christensen, 1831–1912: Mormon Immigrant Artist*. Salt Lake City, 1984.

Piercy, Frederick H. *Route from Liverpool to Great Salt Lake Valley*. Liverpool, 1855.

RICHARD G. OMAN

ART IN MORMONISM

From the earliest days of the Church, its leaders have recognized the significant role art plays in enlightening and inspiring Church members. For this reason, the First Presidency encouraged a group of young artists to study in France in the 1880s. They brought back both new artistic skills and an enthusiasm for the art they had seen in Europe. The many temple murals and other paintings done by these artists continue to educate, encourage, and inspire generations of Latter-day Saints. Because Mormon art has been primarily oriented toward service in the Church, much of it has been didactic. Artworks have been used to help teach gospel principles. Images illustrating Book of Mormon and Church history events have become familiar reminders of them. Artworks are also used to teach non-Mormons about Church history and doctrine.

Lux Aeterna, pencil and graphite drawing, by Hagen G. Haltern (1989). An LDS artist, Haltern strives to integrate artistic representation of eternal reality based on five levels of meaning detectable in Exodus 31:1-4 (the anagogical, allegorical, legal, literal, and practical). Courtesy Hagen G. Haltern.

The Church has supported the production of art vocally by pronouncement from the pulpit and financially by purchasing artwork for most of its buildings other than meetinghouses. It has established a Church art museum, which provides exhi-

Alpha and Omega: On My Way Home, by Wulf Barsch (1985, oil on paper, 24″ × 50″). This LDS artist uses images from Utah landscapes and a stylized Alpha and Omega to depict a sense of mankind's eternal journey homeward to God. Courtesy Church Museum of History and Art.

The Miracle of the Gulls, by Minerva K. Teichert (1936, oil on canvas, 40″ × 46″). In the early years following the arrival of the Mormon pioneers in the Salt Lake Valley, infestations of crickets threatened their badly needed crops. The arrival of seagulls, who ate the crickets, saved much of the harvest. The event has become known as the "miracle of the gulls."

bition space for past and present LDS artists. Additionally, it sponsors an annual art competition. Many of its leaders, especially President Spencer W. Kimball (1972–1985), have challenged Church members to develop their artistic talents so that they can tell the story of the Church in art. Many LDS artists have accepted the challenge and are trying to create art that is both instructive and spiritually inspiring. Consequently, much LDS art has to do with things peculiar to the heritage of the Church and the LDS experience.

The purposes of inspiration and encouragement are equally important to the purpose of instruction in LDS art. Whether it is conveyed through a painted landscape or a sculpted human figure in solitary prayer, the spirit of LDS art is essentially the same: it evokes a sense of the goodness of God and of a belief in his eternal plan for mankind. It is this overarching philosophy, this spiritual perspective, that binds LDS artists together.

Even though LDS artists have been aware of contemporary trends in art, they have generally chosen not to follow the current avant-garde fashion. They have tried to relate their art in a pervasive, eternal sense to concerns that continually affect mankind. Their quest consists of the attempt to translate their religious ideals into their various mediums. Their search thus takes them on a different path from that of many other artists and attempts to lead them to the spiritual sources of their beliefs. Feeling that they will reach their goals only through direct access to this spiritual source, LDS artists seek inspiration as a means of attaining this quality in their art. For them, painting or sculpting is a private activity imbued with purpose that affects more than their artistic lives. By conducting their lives with a sense of truth and integrity, they hope to be brought closer to this spiritual core.

Much discussion about a "Mormon aesthetic" has taken place in recent years, but it seems that the very personal nature of this spiritual artistic quest prevents the attainment of a prevalent aesthetic. LDS artists are now found in many parts of the world, and their diverse cultures are providing the input of a wide variety of heritages. While LDS art is characterized by stylistic diversity, it also shows certain common features because of the shared faith of the artists.

BIBLIOGRAPHY

Bradshaw, Merrill K. "Toward a Mormon Aesthetic." *BYU Studies* 21 (Winter 1981):91–99.

Carmer, Carl. "A Panorama of Mormon Life." *Art in America* 58 (May–June 1970):52–65.

Packer, Boyd K. "The Arts and the Spirit of the Lord." *BYU Studies* 16 (Summer 1976):575–88.

"A Portfolio of Mormon Painters." *Ensign* 7 (July 1977):39–57.

Wheelwright, Lorin F., and Lael J. Woodbury, eds. *Mormon Arts*. Provo, Utah, 1972.

Young, Mahonri Sharp. "Mormon Art and Architecture." *Art in America* 58 (May–June 1970):66–69.

MARTHA MOFFIT PEACOCK

ASIA, THE CHURCH IN

[*This entry is made up of two articles:*

    Asia, East

    Asia, South and Southeast

Asia, East *discusses the growth and development of the Church in China, Japan, South Korea, Hong Kong, and Taiwan.* Asia, South and Southeast *discusses Church growth in the Philippines, Thailand, Singapore, Indonesia, Vietnam, India, and Sri Lanka.*]

ASIA, EAST

EARLY LDS MISSIONARY ATTEMPTS IN CHINA AND JAPAN. President Brigham YOUNG sent Hosea Stout, James Lewis, and Chapman Duncan to China in August 1852. They reached Hong Kong on April 28, 1853. Although they preached the gospel to the people, they could not gain a foothold

Latter-day Saints in Osaka, Japan, in 1917, where missionaries taught an English Bible class every Tuesday evening. Photographer: Joseph H. Stimpson.

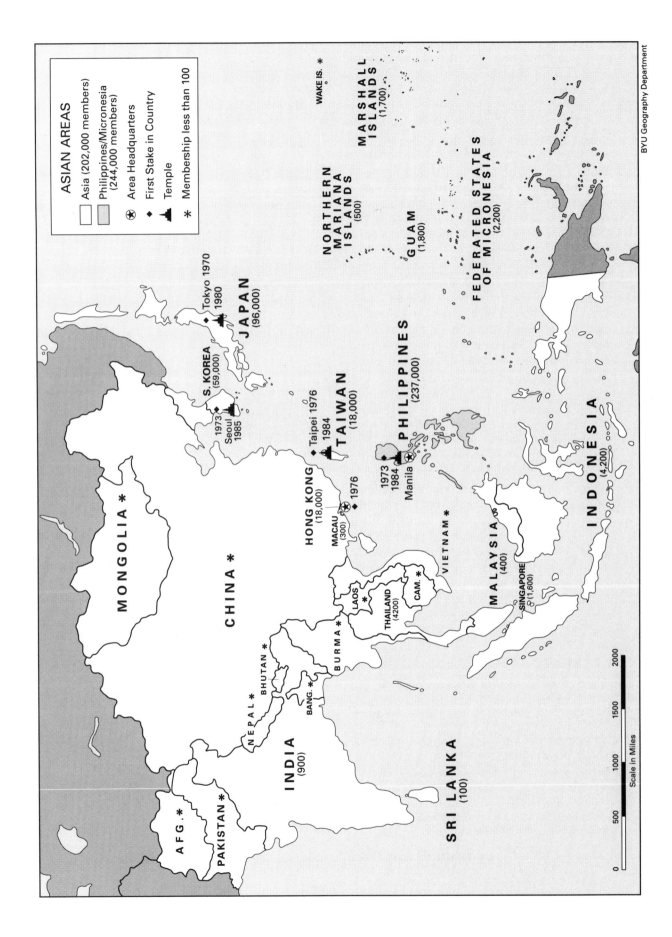

ASIAN AREAS

Asia (202,000 members)
Philippines/Micronesia (244,000 members)
⊛ Area Headquarters
◆ First Stake in Country
🏛 Temple
* Membership less than 100

WAKE IS. *

MARSHALL ISLANDS (1,700)

NORTHERN MARIANA ISLANDS (500)

GUAM (1,800)

FEDERATED STATES OF MICRONESIA (2,200)

Tokyo 1970
1980

JAPAN (96,000)

S. KOREA (59,000)

1973
Seoul 1985

Taipei 1976
1984

TAIWAN (18,000)

PHILIPPINES (237,000)

1973
1984
Manila

INDONESIA (4,200)

HONG KONG (18,000)

1976

MACAU (300)

MONGOLIA *

CHINA *

VIETNAM *

MALAYSIA (400)

SINGAPORE (1,600)

LAOS *

THAILAND (4200)

CAM. *

BURMA *

BHUTAN *

NEPAL *

BANG. *

INDIA (900)

SRI LANKA (100)

AFG. *

PAKISTAN *

Scale in Miles

0   500   1000   1500   2000

BYU Geography Department

and sailed home after fifty-six days. On January 9, 1921, David O. MCKAY, an apostle, visited Beijing and dedicated the Chinese realm to missionary work, but the Church did not attempt to go to China until 1949.

Efforts to establish the Church in Japan came almost fifty years after the unsuccessful first Chinese attempt. In February 1901, President Lorenzo SNOW announced plans to open a mission in Japan, with Heber J. GRANT, an apostle, as president and Louis A. Kelsch, Horace S. Ensign, and eighteen-year-old Alma O. Taylor also to serve. Elder Grant dedicated Japan to the preaching of the gospel on September 1, 1901, at Yokohama. Learning the language, customs, and traditions was so difficult, however, that the new missionaries spent eighteen months studying before they ventured out among the Japanese people. The slow start was symptomatic of the entire mission until its closure in August 1924. Although they had baptized only 166 people in 23 years, they did publish a Japanese translation of the Book of Mormon (1909), several tracts, and a hymnal.

THE CHURCH IN JAPAN SINCE WORLD WAR II. In the spring of 1947, the First Presidency assigned Edward L. Clissold to reopen the Japanese mission, and missionary work was resumed in Japan in 1948. President Clissold had served in the U.S. occupation forces in Japan and was acquainted with government offices and procedures. The first group of missionaries arrived on June 26, 1948. They were helped by LDS service personnel, who contributed much to the success of the postwar mission. For example, Sato Tatsuo, the first Japanese to join the Church after World War II, was taught the gospel by Boyd K. Packer, later an apostle, and three of his fellow servicemen. Sato organized the first Sunday School in Nagoya in 1946. He later translated the Doctrine and Covenants and the Pearl of Great Price, and retranslated the Book of Mormon into contemporary Japanese. By August 1949, missionaries were proselytizing in at least ten major cities and Japanese members numbered 211.

The Church has grown steadily in Japan, and native Japanese serve in all levels of leadership in the Church. When the Tokyo stake was organized on March 15, 1970, the president was Tanaka

Kenji, and all the stake officers were Japanese. Most of the mission presidents have been either native Japanese or Americans of Japanese ancestry, and by 1990 almost one-third of the more than two thousand LDS missionaries in Japan were local Japanese. In 1977, Yoshihiko Kikuchi became the first Japanese and Asian called as a GENERAL AUTHORITY of the Church.

Members of the Church in Japan have access to the full program of the Church: for example, SEMINARIES and INSTITUTES (started in 1972); a translation services department to provide Church written materials in the Japanese language; and genealogy services through the microfilming of registers at civic and Buddhist repositories. At an area conference held in Tokyo in August 1975, President Spencer W. KIMBALL announced to the 12,300 participants plans to build a temple in Tokyo. He returned to dedicate the completed structure on October 27–29, 1980.

By 1955, the Japanese mission included South Korea and Okinawa, and the name of the mission was changed to the Northern Far East Mission. At the same time, the Church organized the Southern Far East Mission with H. Grant Heaton as its first president. That mission included Hong Kong, Taiwan, the Philippines, and Guam. For several years during the Korean conflict, the successive Japan mission presidents, Vinal G. Mauss and Hilton A. Robertson, supervised proselytizing as well as Church organizations for military people throughout East Asia, Guam, and the Philippines. With the truce in Korea, it became possible to establish missionary work there.

CHURCH GROWTH IN SOUTH KOREA. Although the Church did not officially move into Korea until 1955, LDS military personnel had taught and baptized some twenty Koreans by May 1953. Kim Ho Jik, a Korean who had studied for a doctorate at Cornell University, joined the Church in New York in 1951. On returning home he became an influential member of the Church and of the Korean government. Until his death in 1959, Kim facilitated the founding of the Church in South Korea. As in Japan, the Church in Korea is in the hands of local leaders.

The newly appointed mission president, Paul Andrus, sent the first two elders from Japan to

←——The Church of Jesus Christ of Latter-day Saints in Asia and the Far East, as of January 1, 1991.

Seoul in April 1956. By the summer of 1962, when Korea became a separate mission with Gail E. Carr as president, there were over 1,600 members. In 1968, the Church was established in every major city and all provincial capitals. Unlike most other areas of the world, the majority of Koreans baptized were men, and even in the late 1970s, 55 percent of converts were male. Korea has remained the most fruitful Asian mission other than the Christian Philippines.

The second and third mission presidents, Spencer J. Palmer and Robert H. Slover, did much to enlarge the Church in Korea. Both men emphasized public relations, translation work (the Book of Mormon was published in Korean in 1967 and the Doctrine and Covenants and Pearl of Great Price in 1968), leadership training, the purchase of property for chapels and other uses, and preparation for stakes. President Edward Brown later supervised the beginning of the seminary and institute program. In March 1973, Rhee Ho Nam was sustained as president of the first Korean stake. Two years later, in 1975, the Korea Seoul Mission was divided and a new mission was organized in Pusan with Han In Sang as president. On December 14–15, 1985, President Gordon B. Hinckley dedicated the Seoul Korea Temple.

CHURCH DEVELOPMENT IN THE CHINESE REALM. The Chinese-speaking area of Asia has over a billion inhabitants, but the Church has had access only to Taiwan (twenty million), Hong Kong (five million), and Macao. Political conditions in the People's Republic of China have not allowed proselytizing. Church growth in Hong Kong and Taiwan has, however, been significant.

In 1949, the Church briefly opened missionary work in Hong Kong, but because of the Chinese civil war between the Nationalists and the Communists (which ended in October 1949) and the Korean conflict, the Hong Kong colony had many problems. Although nine missionaries served and fourteen Chinese joined the Church, the Hong Kong Mission was closed on February 6, 1951. After the end of the Korean conflict, when missionary numbers had increased, Church leaders reopened the Chinese area mission in August 1955. It was comprised of Hong Kong, Taiwan, Guam, the Philippines and other parts of Southeast Asia, and the People's Republic of China, even though the latter was still closed to missionary work. By June 1956, there were forty missionaries in Hong Kong and three hundred Chinese had been baptized.

On June 4, 1956, four elders flew from Hong Kong to Taipei, Taiwan, to commence missionary work in the Mandarin Chinese language. LDS military people gave considerable support during the founding stages in Taiwan. By mid-1958 there were 286 Chinese members there. On June 1, 1959, Mark E. Petersen, an apostle, dedicated Taiwan to the preaching of the gospel, reinvoking Elder McKay's 1921 dedication of the entire Chinese realm.

The founding of LDS missionary work in the Philippines and other parts of Southeast Asia was

CHURCH IN ASIA as of December 31, 1989 (For more recent figures see Appendix 13.)

Area	Members	Missions	Stakes/Districts	Wards and Branches
China	NA	0	0/0	3
Hong Kong	17,000	1	4/0	26
India	800	0	0/3	9
Indonesia	4,100	0	0/3	18
Japan	91,000	9	23/15	264
Korea, Republic	50,000	4	14/4	146
Macao	200	0	0/0	1
Malaysia	300	0	0/1	3
Pakistan	NA	0	0/0	2
Papua New Guinea	2,100	0	0/1	13
Philippines	213,000	9	38/39	638
Singapore	1,400	1	0/1	5
Sri Lanka	100	0	0/0	1
Taiwan	17,000	2	3/2	47
Thailand	3,600	1	0/3	16
Asia Total:	400,600	27	82/72	1,192

directed by the presidents of the Southern Far East Mission during the 1960s. Because various countries were broken off to form new missions, the name and scope of the Southern Far East Mission were changed to the Hong Kong-Taiwan Mission on November 1, 1969. Fourteen months later, on January 11, 1971, a separate mission was established in Taiwan.

Since then, development has been separate but quite parallel. On April 22, 1976, Chang I-Ch'ing was sustained as president of the Taiwan Taipei Stake. Three days later, Poon Shiu-Tat (Sheldon) was sustained as Hong Kong's first stake president. The founding of seminaries and institutes in 1975 and the development of translation work were also parallel. In 1990 each region had multiple missions and stakes. The Taipei Taiwan Temple was dedicated November 17-18, 1984, by Gordon B. Hinckley of the First Presidency.

MAINLAND CHINA. Formal missionary work has not been undertaken in the People's Republic of China. Three branches of the Church were organized on the Chinese mainland in 1990, but they were restricted to expatriates. Since 1979, a number of Brigham Young University performance groups have toured the People's Republic of China, garnering high praise and great popularity.

ASIA, SOUTH AND SOUTHEAST

EARLY HISTORY. The first two Latter-day Saints to reach India were George Barber and Benjamin Richey, British sailors who in 1849 visited Calcutta and made friends who asked for missionaries. In June 1851, Elder Joseph Richards arrived. He baptized eight people, ordained Maurice White an elder, and appointed him branch president of the "Wanderer's Branch," the first unit of the Church in Asia. That December, William Willes, a second missionary, arrived in Calcutta. By mid-May, when he counted 19 Europeans and 170 Indian farmers as Church members, he wrote to Utah for more missionaries. However, his branch withered quickly when the Indian farmers learned that there would be no immediate, direct material gain from joining the Church. Meanwhile, President Brigham Young dispatched nine additional missionaries from Utah to India and four to Siam (Thailand) in August 1852. After a difficult trip, they arrived in Calcutta on April 23, 1853.

Although they and some of their converts traversed thousands of miles of dusty or muddy In-

LDS chapel in Taiwan. The first four LDS missionaries were transferred from Hong Kong to Taipei in 1956. Large meetinghouses were completed in Taipei and Kaohsiung in the 1960s.

dian and Burmese roads, preached in notable and humble surroundings, published tracts in five languages (and had the Book of Mormon translated into Urdu), and bore a witness to the peoples of India, Burma, and Siam that the gospel had been restored, they had little success, and the Church was not established in India or Southeast Asia until after World War II.

THE CHURCH IN THE PHILIPPINES. Joseph Fielding SMITH, an apostle, dedicated the Philippines for the preaching of the gospel on August 21, 1955, and the first four missionaries arrived from Hong Kong in June 1961. Establishing the Church in the Philippines progressed more smoothly than in any other part of Asia because over 90 percent of the population were Christian, almost 50 percent used English to some degree, and Americans who were teaching a religion with American origins were generally popular. By 1967, the Philippines was made a separate mission with Paul Rose as president, and by 1973, over 13,000 Filipinos had been baptized. On May 20, 1973, Ezra Taft BENSON, an apostle, organized the Manila Philippines Stake with Agusto A. Lim as president. Four years later the Manila stake was divided into three stakes. The developing of experienced leadership and building of adequate meetinghouses have been a challenge, but members have had the full program of the Church, including seminaries and institutes since 1972. Selections from the Book of Mormon were published in Tagalog (1987); a missionary training center was established in Manila (1986); and on September 25–27, 1984, President Gordon B. Hinckley dedicated the Manila Philippines Temple. In 1988 the First Presidency made Manila the headquarters for the Philippines/Micronesia area of the Church and assigned an area president to live there. Church growth in the Philippines has been the most rapid of all Asian countries, and over 80 percent of the missionaries in 1990 were local Filipinos.

THE CHURCH IN THAILAND. Church growth in Thailand has progressed slowly because the Thais' devotion to king, country, the Buddhist religion (94 percent), and tradition appears to form a seamless whole. The Church entered Thailand when Latter-day Saints were part of the U.S. military personnel sent there in 1961. In July 1966, an LDS servicemen's branch was organized with two hundred members. On November 2, 1966, Gordon B. Hinckley, then an apostle, dedicated Thailand for the preaching of the gospel. By late 1967, the first six elders were sent to Bangkok from Hong Kong. In July 1973, the Thailand Bangkok Mission was organized, and the Book of Mormon was published in Thai in 1976.

THE SINGAPORE MISSION AREA. Missionary activity began in Singapore in 1968, the first branch of the Church being organized on October 13. Earlier that year, on March 19, two missionaries had been assigned there from Hong Kong. Elder Ezra Taft Benson dedicated Singapore for the preaching of the gospel on April 14, 1969, and on November 1, it became the headquarters for the Southeast Asia Mission with G. Carlos Smith, Jr., as president. He was responsible for missionary work in all the nations of South and Southeast Asia except the Philippines.

LDS expansion in Singapore has not been easy because the government banned all foreign missionaries from Singapore and prohibited open proselytizing in 1970. The Church is allowed only a limited number of visas, including those of the mission president and his wife, at any one time, but through the efforts of young local missionaries the growth of the Church has been steady.

INDONESIAN CHURCH GROWTH. Since 1980, virtually all LDS missionary work in Indonesia has been performed by local members. Indonesia is the only Muslim country where Church proselytizing has succeeded. The Church officially entered Indonesia when Elder Ezra Taft Benson dedicated that country for the teaching of the gospel on October 26, 1969. G. Carlos Smith, Jr., the newly called president of the Southeast Asia Mission, sent six elders from Singapore on January 5, 1970. But on April 11, the Indonesian government halted door-to-door proselytizing and church meetings until the Church obtained official recognition. Although government recognition came nine days later, relations between the Church and various departments of the Indonesian government have not been smooth.

In April 1975, the First Presidency organized the Indonesia Jakarta Mission with Hendrik Gout as president. He had the Book of Mormon translated and published in Bahasa Indonesian (1977), fostered the work of welfare services missionaries, and facilitated the establishment of an elementary school in Jakarta in 1976. (It closed in 1988.)

In 1978, government regulations required that Indonesian nationals hold all missionary (and ministerial) positions, and by late 1980 all non-Indonesian LDS missionaries were removed from the country. It was necessary to recombine the Indonesia Jakarta Mission with the Singapore Mission until 1985, when Effian Kadarusman, an Indonesian, was appointed president over the reestablished mission. By 1988, close to one hundred Indonesians were serving full-time missions in their country. In 1989 the Indonesia Jakarta Mission was again made a part of the Singapore Mission.

THE CHURCH'S BRIEF ENCOUNTER WITH VIETNAM. The first Latter-day Saints in Vietnam were military advisers in the early 1960s, and by 1968 more than five thousand LDS servicemen were assigned there. The first servicemen's group was organized in Saigon on June 30, 1963. In December 1965, Vietnam became a district of the Southern Far East Mission with headquarters in Hong Kong. At the same time, six servicemen were called to serve as part-time missionaries. By February 1966, several U.S. servicemen and thirty Vietnamese had been baptized. On October 30, 1966, Elder Gordon B. Hinckley dedicated Vietnam for the preaching of the gospel.

On April 6, 1973, four full-time missionaries were transferred to Saigon from Hong Kong. The Vietnamese Book of Mormon was distributed to members in photocopy form in May 1974. By March 1975, the Church had fifteen missionaries and more than three thousand Vietnamese members. At that point the missionaries were withdrawn, and a month later, Saigon fell. Almost all of the LDS members eventually left Vietnam and migrated to the United States.

CHURCH GROWTH IN INDIA AND SRI LANKA. India and Sri Lanka have laws prohibiting proselytizing by foreigners, and the Church respects those laws. Most of the growth within India and Sri Lanka has been the result of efforts of local members who have conveyed the gospel message to their friends. For example, in 1965, S. Paul Thiruthuvadoss was baptized after an individual search for the gospel of Jesus Christ. He was briefly assisted by foreign missionaries, and his efforts resulted in the baptism of more than two hundred Tamil-speaking South Indians.

In December 1978, Edwin Dharmaraju and his wife, both of whom had been baptized in Western Samoa, served a short mission in their home city of Hyderabad, India. Before returning to Samoa, Dharmaraju baptized twenty-two family members, ordained four men to the Aaronic Priesthood, and organized a group of the Church. Also, Sister Dharmaraju's father, a Baptist minister, had found such interest in the Book of Mormon that he translated it into the Telugu language (48 million speakers). It was published in 1982, as was the complete Hindi (175 million speakers) version and selections in Tamil (42 million speakers). Bengali (48 million speakers) selections of the Book of Mormon were published in 1985.

Another important Indian missionary was Raj Kumar, who strengthened new members and branches as they were established. By 1986 local missionaries were serving full-time missions for the Church in India and Sri Lanka, assisted by North American friendship-missionary couples sent from the Singapore Mission to make friends for the Church in various cities. They and other expatriates, such as business and government personnel stationed in India, did not proselytize, but answered questions and taught the gospel to those who sought them out.

BIBLIOGRAPHY

Britsch, R. Lanier. "The Latter-day Saint Mission to India: 1851–1856." *BYU Studies* 12 (Spring 1972):262–78.

———. "The Closing of the Early Japan Mission." *BYU Studies* 15 (Winter 1975):171–90.

———. "From Bhutan to Wangts'ang: Taking the Gospel to Asia." *Ensign* 10 (June 1980):6–10.

———. "The Church's Years in Vietnam." *Ensign* 10 (Aug. 1980):25–30.

Moss, James R.; R. Lanier Britsch; James R. Christianson; and Richard O. Cowan. *The International Church.* Provo, Utah, 1982.

Palmer, Spencer J. *The Church Encounters Asia.* Salt Lake City, 1970.

R. LANIER BRITSCH

ASSISTANTS TO THE TWELVE

In 1941 five men were called as Assistants to the Quorum of the Twelve Apostles. J. Reuben Clark, Jr., of the First Presidency explained at the conference that they had been called because of the rapid growth of the Church and the ever-expanding demands upon the Quorum of the Twelve. A total of thirty-eight men served the Church as Assistants to the Twelve before the office was merged with the SEVENTY in 1976.

As General Authorities, Assistants to the Twelve had the authority to minister throughout the Church and to fulfill assignments as directed by the Quorum of the Twelve. They presided over, and spoke at, stake conferences; helped organize stakes; toured missions; and directed missionary work in many parts of the world.

A number of men who first served as Assistants to the Twelve were later called to be members of the Quorum of the Twelve Apostles: George Q. Morris, Boyd K. Packer, Marvin J. Ashton, L. Tom Perry, David B. Haight, James E. Faust, Neal A. Maxwell, and Joseph B. Wirthlin. Several others who had served as Assistants to the Twelve also served in the Quorum of the Twelve and later as Counselors in the First Presidency, including Hugh B. Brown, N. Eldon Tanner, Marion G. Romney, and Gordon B. Hinckley.

An important 1835 revelation on priesthood describes the Seventy as the quorum standing next in authority to the Twelve, and under their direction, the Seventy share responsibility for the Church throughout the world (D&C 107:25–26, 33–34). According to President Spencer W. KIMBALL in 1976, the calling of the Assistants was "similar to that envisioned by the revelations for the First Quorum of Seventy," but "the scope and demands of the work at that time [1941]" did not yet justify the reconstitution of that quorum (p. 9).

After accelerating growth in many parts of the world led to the organization of the First Quorum of Seventy in 1975, the nearly two dozen Assistants then serving became members of that quorum in 1976.

BIBLIOGRAPHY

Kimball, Spencer W. "The Reconstitution of the First Quorum of the Seventy." *Ensign* (Nov. 1976):9.

Widtsoe, John A. "Assistants to the Twelve." *IE* 44 (May 1941):288.

BYRON R. MERRILL

ASTRONOMY, SCRIPTURAL REFERENCES TO

Latter-day Saint scriptures indicate that both biblical and latter-day prophets and seers were shown visions of the heavenly realms to orient them to God's dominion and eternal purposes. These visions gave information about (1) the governing of systems of WORLDS and stellar objects; (2) a heliocentric, planetary cosmology; (3) the plurality of worlds; (4) the spiritual and physical CREATION of the EARTH and the universe; and (5) the role of Jesus Christ as creator.

The BOOK OF ABRAHAM states that God's physical dominion (throne) is located near a star called Kolob (Abr. 3:2–3). While it might seem reasonable to suppose that this refers to some distinguishing feature of the universe, all efforts to identify it are speculative and not authoritative. Wherever Kolob is located, its purpose is to "govern" all planets that are of the same "order" as the Earth (Abr. 3:9). Since ABRAHAM says no more than that, it is not clear whether he is speaking physically, metaphorically, or allegorically. Thus, "to govern" might mean a physical bonding as with gravity, while "order" could conceivably mean planets similar to the Earth in size, or planets in the same region of this galaxy or even in the entire Milky Way galaxy. Kolob was also said by the Egyptians to provide the light for all stars, including that for our sun (Abr. Facsimile 2). Even so, Latter-day Saints have made no definitive comment on the meaning of these passages.

In contrast to some interpretations of biblical scholars who attribute a geocentric cosmology to the words of Joshua (10:12–14), Job (9:6–7), Isaiah (38:7–8), and other Old Testament passages, the Book of Mormon affirms the sun-centered (heliocentric) view accepted by modern planetary physics. The prophets Nephi$_2$ (Hel. 12:13–15) and Alma$_2$ agree that "surely it is the earth that moveth and not the sun" (Alma 30:44).

Psalm 8:3–4 has been the classic text for discussion of the "plurality of worlds." LDS scriptures give even more direct support for modern astronomers' search for extraterrestrial intelligence. The prophets Enoch, Moses, and Joseph Smith all received revelations dealing with the existence of sentient life on other planets. Moses revealed both the spatial and temporal existence of countless worlds: that God had created "worlds without number," that "many worlds. . . . have [already] passed away," and that other worlds are yet to be created (Moses 1:33–38). Joseph Smith received revelations explaining that through Jesus Christ these worlds are created and inhabited (D&C 76:22–24; 93:9–10; Moses 1:33), that all kingdoms are bound by certain LAWS and conditions (D&C 88:36–38, 42–47), and that resurrected beings reside on celestialized planets (D&C 130:4–7).

The various creation accounts in LDS scripture outline a spirit creation of the heavens and the earth that preceded the physical creation, thus affirming the spiritual nature of the cosmos (Moses 2–3; Abr. 4–5); spirit is indeed "matter" of a different order (D&C 131:7–8). While Moses calls creation periods "days," Abraham speaks of "times" and of thousand-year days (Abr. 3:4; 5:13), suggesting a complex physical creation process.

BIBLIOGRAPHY

Athay, R. Grant. "Worlds Without Number: The Astronomy of Enoch, Abraham, and Moses." *BYU Studies* 8 (Spring 1968):255–69.

Hansen, H. Kimball. "Astronomy and the Scriptures." In *Science and Religion: Toward a More Useful Dialogue*, ed. W. Hess and R. Matheny, Vol. 1, 181–96. Geneva, Ill., 1979.

Salisbury, Frank B. *The Creation*. Salt Lake City, 1976.

ERICH ROBERT PAUL

ATONEMENT OF JESUS CHRIST

The atonement of Jesus Christ is the foreordained but voluntary act of the Only Begotten Son of God. He offered his life, including his innocent body, blood, and spiritual anguish as a redeeming ransom (1) for the effect of the fall of Adam upon all mankind and (2) for the personal sins of all who repent, from Adam to the end of the world. Latter-day Saints believe this is the central fact, the crucial foundation, the chief doctrine, and the greatest expression of divine love in the PLAN OF SALVATION. The Prophet Joseph SMITH declared that all "things which pertain to our religion are only appendages" to the atonement of Christ (*TPJS*, p. 121).

The literal meaning of the word "atonement" is self-evident: at-one-ment, the act of unifying or bringing together what has been separated and estranged. The atonement of Jesus Christ was indispensable because of the separating transgression, or fall, of Adam, which brought death into the world when Adam and Eve partook of the fruit of the tree of knowledge of good and evil (Gen. 2:9; 3:1–24). Latter-day Saints readily acknowledge both the physical and the SPIRITUAL DEATH that Adam and Eve brought upon themselves and all of their posterity, physical death bringing the temporary separation of the spirit from the body, and spiritual death bringing the estrangement of both the spirit and the body from God. But they also believe that the Fall was part of a divine, foreordained plan without which mortal children would not have been born to Adam and Eve. Had not these first parents freely chosen to leave the Garden of Eden via their transgression, there would have been on this earth no human family to experience opposition and growth, moral AGENCY and choice, and the joy of RESURRECTION, redemption, and ETERNAL LIFE (2 Ne. 2:23; Moses 5:11).

The need for a future atonement was explained in a premortal COUNCIL IN HEAVEN at which the spirits of the entire human family were in attendance and over which GOD THE FATHER presided. The two principal associates of God in that council were the premortal Jesus (also known as Jehovah; *see* JESUS CHRIST, JEHOVAH) and the premortal Adam (also known as Michael). It was in this premortal setting that Christ voluntarily entered into a covenant with the Father, agreeing to enhance the moral agency of humankind even as he atoned for their sins, and he returned to the Father all honor and glory for such selflessness. This preordained role of Christ as mediator explains why the book of Revelation describes Christ as "the Lamb slain from the foundation of the world" (Rev. 13:8) and why Old Testament prophets, priests, and kings, including Moses (Deut. 18:15, 17–19), Job (19:25–27), the Psalmist (Ps. 2,

22), Zechariah (9:9; 12:10; 13:6), Isaiah (7:14; 9:6–7; 53), and Micah (5:2), could speak of the Messiah and his divine role many centuries before his physical birth. A Book of Mormon prophet wrote, "I say unto you that none of the prophets have written, nor prophesied, save they have spoken concerning this Christ" (Jacob 4:4; 7:11). To the brother of Jared who lived some two thousand years before the Redeemer's birth, the premortal Christ declared, "Behold, I am he who was prepared from the foundation of the world to redeem my people" (Ether 3:14). Such scriptural foreshadowings are reflected in the conversation Christ had with two of his disciples on the road to Emmaus: "Beginning at Moses and all the prophets, he expounded unto them in all the scriptures the things concerning himself" (Luke 24:27; cf. also 24:44).

For Latter-day Saints, it is crucially important to see the agreed-upon and understood fall of man only in the context of the equally agreed-upon and

Gethsemane, by James C. Christensen (1984, oil on panel, 40″ × 44″). Jesus kneels in the Garden of Gethsemane, strengthened by an angel from heaven, as he suffers and atones for the sins of the world (see Luke 22:43). Courtesy James C. Christensen.

understood redemption of man—redemption provided through the atonement of Jesus Christ. Thus, one of the most important and oft-quoted lines of Latter-day Saint scripture says, "Adam fell that men might be; and men are, that they might have joy. And the Messiah cometh in the fulness of time, that he may redeem the children of men from the fall" (2 Ne. 2:25–26).

LDS scripture teaches that the mission of Christ as Redeemer and the commandment to offer animal sacrifice as an anticipatory reminder and symbol of that divine atonement to come were first taught to Adam and Eve soon after they had been expelled from the Garden of Eden (Moses 5:4–8). The atonement of Christ was taught to the parents of the family of man with the intent that they and their posterity would observe the sacrificial ordinances down through their generations, remembering as they did so the mission and mercy of Christ who was to come. Latter-day Saints emphatically teach that the extent of this atonement is universal, opening the way for the redemption of all mankind—non-Christians as well as Christians, the godless as well as the god-fearing, the untaught infant as well as the fully converted and knowledgeable adult. "It is expedient that there should be a great and last sacrifice," said Amulek in the Book of Mormon, "an infinite and eternal sacrifice. . . . There can be nothing which is short of an infinite atonement which will suffice for the sins of the world" (Alma 34:10, 12).

This infinite atonement of Christ—and of Christ only—was possible because (1) he was the only sinless man ever to live on this earth and therefore was not subject to the spiritual death that comes as a result of sin; (2) he was the Only Begotten of the Father and therefore possessed the attributes of Godhood, which gave him power over physical death (see 2 Ne. 9:5–9; Alma 34:9–12); and (3) he was the only one sufficiently humble and willing in the premortal council to be foreordained there to that service (*JC*, pp. 21–62).

The universal, infinite, and unconditional aspects of the atonement of Jesus Christ are several. They include his ransom for Adam's original transgression so that no member of the human family is held responsible for that sin (A of F 2; *see* ORIGINAL SIN). Another universal gift is the resurrection from the dead of every man, woman, and child who lives, has ever lived, or ever will live, on the earth. Thus, the Atonement is not only universal in the sense that it saves the entire human family from physical death, but it is also infinite in the sense that its impact and efficacy in making redemption possible for all reach back in one direction to the beginning of time and forward in the other direction throughout all eternity. In short, the Atonement has universal, infinite, and unconditional consequences for all mankind throughout the duration of all eternity.

Emphasizing these unconditional gifts arising out of Christ's atoning sacrifice, Latter-day Saints believe that other aspects of Christ's gift are conditional upon obedience and diligence in keeping God's commandments. For example, while members of the human family are freely and universally given a reprieve from Adam's sin through no effort or action of their own, they are not freely and universally given a reprieve of their own sins unless they pledge faith in Christ, repent of those sins, are baptized in his name, receive the GIFT OF THE HOLY GHOST and confirmation into Christ's church, and press forward with a brightness of hope and faithful endurance for the remainder of life's journey. Of this personal challenge, Christ said, "For behold, I, God, have suffered these things for all, that they might not suffer if they would repent; but if they would not repent they must suffer even as I; which suffering caused myself, even God, the greatest of all, to tremble because of pain, and to bleed at every pore, and to suffer both body and spirit—and would that I might not drink the bitter cup, and shrink" (D&C 19:16–18).

Furthermore, although the breaking of the bonds of mortal death by the resurrection of the body is a free and universal gift from Christ, a product of his victory over death and the grave, the kind or nature of the body (or "degree of glory" of the body), as well as the time of one's resurrection, is affected very directly by the extent of one's faithfulness in this life (*see* DEGREES OF GLORY). The apostle Paul made clear, for example, that those most fully committed to Christ will "rise first" in the resurrection (1 Thes. 4:16). Paul also speaks of different orders of resurrected bodies (1 Cor. 15:40). The bodies of the highest orders or degrees of glory in the Resurrection are promised to those who faithfully adhere to the principles and ordinances of the gospel of Jesus Christ; they will not only enjoy IMMORTALITY (a universal gift to everyone) but also ETERNAL LIVES in the celestial kingdom of glory (D&C 88:4; 132:24; *see also* RESURRECTION).

Latter-day Saints stress that neither the unconditional nor the conditional blessings of the Atonement would be available to mankind except through the grace and goodness of Christ. Obviously the unconditional blessings of the Atonement are unearned, but the conditional ones are also not fully merited. By living faithfully and keeping the commandments of God, one can receive additional privileges; but they are still given freely, not fully earned. They are always and ever a product of God's grace. Latter-day Saint scripture is emphatic in its declaration that "there is no flesh that can dwell in the presence of God, save it be through the merits, and mercy, and grace of the Holy Messiah" (2 Ne. 2:8).

The Church is also emphatic about the salvation of little children, the mentally impaired, those who lived without ever hearing the gospel of Jesus Christ, and so forth: these are redeemed by the universal power of the atonement of Christ and will have the opportunity to receive the fulness of the gospel in the SPIRIT WORLD (see SALVATION FOR THE DEAD).

To meet the demands of the Atonement, the sinless Christ went first into the Garden of GETHSEMANE, there to bear the spiritual agony of soul only he could bear. He "began to be sorrowful and very heavy," saying to his three chief disciples, "My soul is exceeding sorrowful, unto death" (Mark 14:34). Leaving them to keep watch, he went further into the garden, where he would suffer "the pains of all men, yea, the pains of every living creature, both men, women, and children, who belong to the family of Adam" (2 Ne. 9:21). There he "struggled and groaned under a burden such as no other being who has lived on earth might even conceive as possible" (*JC*, p. 613).

Christ's atonement satisfied the demands of justice and thereby ransomed and redeemed the souls of all men, women, and children "that his bowels may be filled with mercy, according to the flesh, that he may know according to the flesh how to succor his people according to their infirmities" (Alma 7:12). Thus, Latter-day Saints teach that Christ "descended below all things"—including every kind of sickness, infirmity, and dark despair experienced by every mortal being—in order that he might "comprehend all things, that he might be in all and through all things, the light of truth" (D&C 88:6). This spiritual anguish of plumbing the depths of human suffering and sorrow was experienced primarily in the Garden of Gethsemane. It

was there that he was "in an agony" and "prayed more earnestly." It was there that his sweat was "as it were great drops of blood falling down to the ground" (Luke 22:44) for he bled "at every pore" (D&C 19:18). It was there that he began the final march to Calvary.

The majesty and triumph of the Atonement reached its zenith when, after unspeakable abuse at the hands of the Roman soldiers and others, Christ appealed from the cross, "Father, forgive them; for they know not what they do" (Luke 23:34). Forgiveness was the key to the meaning of all the suffering he had come to endure.

Such an utterly lonely and excruciating mission is piercingly expressed in that near-final and most agonizing cry of all, "Eli, Eli, lama sabachthani? that is to say, My God, my God, why hast thou forsaken me?" (Matt. 27:46). In the depths of that anguish, even nature itself convulsed, "and there was a darkness over all the earth. . . . The sun was darkened. . . . And, behold, the veil of the temple was rent in twain from the top to the bottom; and the earth did quake, and the rocks rent" (Luke 23:43–45; Matt. 27:51–52). Finally, even the seemingly unbearable had been borne and Jesus said, "It is finished" (John 19:30), and then, saying "Father, into thy hands I commend my spirit," he "gave up the ghost" (Luke 23:46). Latter-day Saints believe that every tongue will someday, somewhere confess as did a Roman centurion at the Crucifixion, "Truly this was the Son of God" (Matt. 27:54).

"The Savior thus becomes master of the situation—the debt is paid, the redemption made, the covenant fulfilled, justice satisfied, the will of God done, and all power is now given into the hands of the Son of God—the power of the resurrection, the power of the redemption, the power of salvation. . . . He becomes the author of eternal life and exaltation. He is the Redeemer, the Resurrector, the Savior of man and the world" (Taylor, p. 171). Furthermore, his atonement extends to all life—beasts, fish, fowl, and the earth itself.

To the thoughtful woman and man, it is "a matter of surpassing wonder" (*AF*, p. 77) that the voluntary and merciful sacrifice of a single being could satisfy the infinite and eternal demands of justice, atone for every human transgression and misdeed, and thereby sweep all mankind into the encompassing arms of his merciful embrace. A President and prophet of the LDS Church writing on this subject said:

In some mysterious, incomprehensible way, Jesus assumed the responsibility which naturally would have devolved upon Adam; but which could only be accomplished through the mediation of Himself, and by taking upon Himself their sorrows, assuming their responsibilities, and bearing their transgressions or sins. In a manner to us incomprehensible and inexplicable, He bore the weight of the sins of the whole world, not only of Adam, but of his posterity; and in doing that opened the kingdom of heaven, not only to all believers and all who obeyed the law of God, but to more than one-half of the human family who die before they come to years of maturity as well as to the heathen, who having died without law, will, through His mediation, be resurrected without law, and be judged without law, and thus participate . . . in the blessings of His atonement [Taylor, pp. 148–49].

Latter-day Saints sing a favorite hymn, written by Charles H. Gabriel, that expresses their deepest feelings regarding this greatest of all gifts:

I stand all amazed at the love Jesus offers me,

Confused at the grace that so fully he proffers me.

I tremble to know that for me he was crucified,

That for me, a sinner, he suffered, He bled and died.

Oh, it is wonderful that he should care for me

Enough to die for me!

Oh, it is wonderful, wonderful to me! [*Hymns*, No. 193].

BIBLIOGRAPHY

McConkie, Bruce R. *The Promised Messiah*. Salt Lake City, 1978.

Nibley, Hugh W. "The Atonement of Jesus Christ," *Ensign* 20 (July 1990):18–23; (Aug. 1990):30–34; (Sept. 1990):22–26; (Oct. 1990):26–31.

Taylor, John. *The Mediation and Atonement*. Salt Lake City, 1882.

JEFFREY R. HOLLAND

AUSTRALIA, THE CHURCH IN

The Church of Jesus Christ of Latter-day Saints was introduced into Australia when a seventeen-year-old British convert, William James Barratt, emigrated from England to Adelaide in November 1840. He had been ordained an elder by George A. Smith, a member of the Quorum of the Twelve Apostles, who instructed him to share the gospel whenever he could. Barratt, whose descendants still live in the Adelaide area, eventually drifted away from the Church, but not until after he had baptized Robert Beauchamp, probably the first Australian convert. Beauchamp later became president of the Australian mission. Andrew and Elizabeth Anderson, also British converts, immigrated to Wellington, near Dubbo, New South Wales, with their three children in 1841. Anderson baptized several converts and in 1844 organized the first Australian BRANCH of the Church, in Wellington.

Official LDS missionary work did not begin in Australia until John Murdock and Charles W. Wandell arrived in Sydney from Utah on October 30, 1851. Thereafter, the Church grew slowly in Australia until President David O. MCKAY visited the area in 1955 and authorized construction of meetinghouses for the branches. The first Austra-

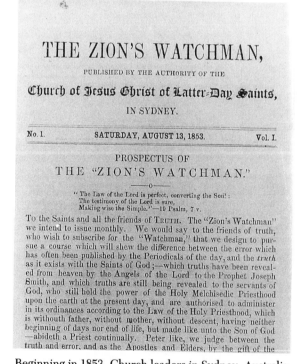

Beginning in 1853, Church leaders in Sydney, Australia, published a monthly periodical entitled *The Zion's Watchman*, addressed "To the Saints and all the friends of Truth." Courtesy Rare Books and Manuscripts, Brigham Young University.

lian STAKES were organized in 1960 in Sydney, Brisbane, and Melbourne. Significant growth has continued since then, leading to the building of a temple in Sydney. It was dedicated in September 1984. By 1990 the Church was strong throughout Australia, with the Pacific Area presidency based in Sydney, and with a temple, 5 missions, 18 stakes, and 205 wards and branches serving 73,200 members in the country as a whole. Australian members of the Church appear to have successfully blended their cultural values of ruggedness and individualism with gospel teachings, creating a uniquely Australian Church culture.

The early days of the Church in Australia were difficult. Prompted by the public preaching of the LDS missionaries, newspapers published articles attacking the Church's doctrines. The missionaries countered with articles, tracts, and spirited defenses of the Church and its teachings in public meetings, many of which were held at the Sydney racecourse. Many of the early converts immigrated to Utah in the spirit of gathering to Zion, some dying en route in the wreck of the *Julia Ann* in 1852 (Devitry-Smith, 1989). This spirit of migration also brought to Australia a significant number of British Saints who were hoping to find gold in the newly discovered goldfields in order to fund their further travel to Utah. Most were unsuccessful in reaching their monetary goal. After 1900 Church leaders encouraged members to stay in their own nations to strengthen the local membership.

When the American missionaries were called home during the UTAH EXPEDITION in 1857, the Church branches in Australia were left to the few members who had not emigrated. When the missionaries returned to the region a few years later, much of their effort was directed toward New Zealand, where many Maoris were joining the Church. During the 1880s the Sydney Branch was discontinued, but the Melbourne Branch remained strong. In 1896, the Sydney Branch was reestablished, and in 1898 the Australian Mission, which then also included New Zealand, was divided, making New Zealand a separate mission. In 1904, with Church assistance in funding, the Brisbane Saints built the first LDS meetinghouse in Australia at Wooloongabba.

Most members of the Church in Australia live in large cities and towns, but many branches also thrive in small rural towns and communities throughout the Australian bush and outback. A

LDS chapel in Sydney, Australia (c. 1962). Missionary work progressed slowly in Australia from 1840 until the 1950s. The first LDS meetinghouse was built in Brisbane in 1906. New meetinghouses authorized by David O. McKay in the 1950s accelerated Church growth.

small meetinghouse to accommodate aboriginal members of the Church was erected in 1984 at Elliott, about 450 miles south of Darwin. Many Australian members travel considerable distances to attend Church meetings; for example, members of the Alice Springs Branch travel more than 900 miles to attend district conferences in Darwin. Other members live in outback communities totally isolated from personal contact with organized branches. In 1929, recognizing the need for better communication among members scattered over such a large area as Australia, mission president Clarence Tingey began publication of *Austral Star*, which provided members with local and international news of the Church and messages and instructions from Church leaders.

Among prominent Church members with Australian connections are Joseph Ridges, the designer of the original Mormon Tabernacle organ; William Fowler, author of the LDS hymn "We Thank Thee, O God, for a Prophet"; and Robert E. Sackley of the Quorums of the Seventy. Both Marion G. Romney and Bruce R. McConkie, later of the Council of the Twelve, served missions in Australia.

BIBLIOGRAPHY

Britsch, R. Lanier. *Unto the Islands of the Sea: A History of the Latter-day Saints in the Pacific.* Salt Lake City, 1986.

Devitry-Smith, John. "William James Barratt: The First Mormon Down Under." *BYU Studies* 28 (Summer 1988):53–66.

———. "The Wreck of the *Julia Ann*." *BYU Studies* 29 (Spring 1989):5–29.

Newton, Marjorie. "The Gathering of the Australian Saints in the 1850s." *BYU Studies* 27 (Spring 1987):67–78.

WILLIAM G. EGGINGTON

AUTHORITY

The claim of The Church of Jesus Christ of Latter-day Saints to be the only TRUE AND LIVING CHURCH on the earth is centered on the concept of authority. The LDS belief has been well stated by President Joseph F. SMITH: "As to the question of authority, nearly everything depends upon it. No ordinance can be performed to the acceptance of God without divine authority. No matter how fervently men may believe or pray, unless they are endowed with divine authority they can only act in their own name, and not legally nor acceptably in the name of Jesus Christ, in whose name all things must be done" (Smith, p. 102).

Because several different definitions are associated with authority in the scriptures, this doctrine has often been misunderstood:

1. Authority refers to formalized power associated with position, function, or legal designation as exemplified by the authority given Joseph in Egypt by Pharaoh (Gen. 41:40–41), by the man who gave his servants authority over his house when he departed (Mark 13:34), and by Church officers designated to have authority over members (Matt. 8:9; D&C 107:8). Authority in these cases presumes control by virtue of assigned position.

2. Authority is strength, might, or control of resources. This is exemplified by the power established by the Philistines over the Jews (Judg. 15) and by Rome's control of Judea at the time of Christ (Matt. 27:2). Authority in this sense connotes superiority or stature above another resulting from acquisitions, possessions, or physical strength.

3. Authority is expertise, as in the case of an expert on a subject. Examples include the authority ascribed to the twelve-year-old Jesus as a result of his teachings in the temple (Luke 2:42, 46–47), and the authority associated with the preaching of prophets such as NEPHI₁, LEHI, ABINADI, and the sons of MOSIAH₂ (Mosiah 13:6; Alma 17:3; Hel. 5:18).

4. Authority is a divine commission or calling from God. For example, Jesus gave his apostles specific authority to preach and to administer his gospel (Matt. 10:1; John 15:16; 3 Ne. 12:1), and certain individuals were empowered to baptize and perform miracles by this authority (Acts 5:12–16; 8:5–17; Alma 5:3; Mosiah 18:13, 18; Moro. 2:1–3). As conveyed by Jesus Christ, this authority meant that ORDINANCES performed on earth would be honored in heaven and, conversely, to loose (dissolve an ordinance) on earth would mean it was loosed in heaven (Matt. 16:19). The name given to this kind of authority in the scriptures is PRIESTHOOD (Heb. 7:11–12, 14, 24; 1 Pet. 2:5, 9; D&C 84:107).

That these meanings have often been confused is exemplified by the scribes' query of Jesus regarding his own basis of authority: "By what authority doest thou these things?" (Matt. 21:23–27). Is your authority political (definition 1) or power from on high (definition 4)? they asked.

As Christ's authority was based on power from on high, so does the Church rest its claim as the only true and living church upon possessing the divine authority to act for God. This authority differentiates the Church from all others. Other systems and organizations may possess other types of authority, but the divine authority associated with Christ's church, the priesthood, resides only in this one.

An explanation of the characteristics of divine authority helps clarify the claims of the Church. First, "no man taketh this honour unto himself, but he that is called of God, as was Aaron" (Heb. 5:4). Divine authority cannot be obtained by study, graduation from school, or mere desire (Acts 19:13–16). It must be obtained in the divinely appointed way, as was the case with AARON (Ex. 28:41).

Second, obtaining the authority to act in the name of God comes by the LAYING ON OF HANDS by one already holding this authority or priesthood (1 Tim. 4:14; 2 Tim. 1:6; Moro. 2:1–3; Deut. 34:9). Simon, for example, desired to purchase the apostles' authority, as he might have done with other types of authority. He was condemned by Peter for desiring to obtain the "gift of God" with money (Acts 8:14–20), and purchasing authority carries his name, simony.

Third, ordinances performed in the Church are spiritually binding only when performed under this divinely commissioned authority, received in the proper way (Mosiah 23:17; D&C 20:73; 132:13; 2 Sam. 6:6–7). For example, Paul rebaptized certain Ephesians who had been previously baptized by an unauthorized person (Acts 19:1–6). King Limhi and many of his followers were converted to Christ and were desirous of being baptized, but they waited to receive that ordinance because the one with authority did not feel worthy (Mosiah 21:33–35).

A fourth fact concerning divine authority is that it was lost from the earth sometime after the resurrection and ascension of Christ into heaven (*see* APOSTASY), so a restoration of divine authority was needed (2 Thes. 2:1–4; 1 Tim. 4:1–3; 2 Tim. 3:1–7). In 1829 heavenly messengers, previously endowed with divine authority by Christ himself, conferred authority upon Joseph Smith and Oliver COWDERY as part of the RESTORATION of The Church of Jesus Christ of Latter-day Saints (*see* AARONIC PRIESTHOOD: RESTORATION OF; MELCHIZEDEK PRIESTHOOD: RESTORATION OF). Members of the Church ordained to this authority now record their personal "line of authority." This record indicates the path of ordinations connecting their priesthood authority to Jesus Christ himself.

Fifth, the authority to preside is efficacious for an individual only when it is accompanied by the COMMON CONSENT of the members of the Church over whom that person will preside (D&C 20:65; 26:2; 42:11).

Abuses of authority and authoritarianism are inherent in any organized system, and such abuses are especially associated with authority based solely on position, strength, or knowledge. Organizations such as the Church are sometimes perceived by outsiders as authoritarian, primarily because of confusion over the meanings of authority. If authority in the Church were based on politics, personal attributes, or expertise, then a charge of authoritarianism might have some validity. However, divine authority (definition 4) is inseparably connected to principles of righteousness, and when we "undertake to cover our sins, or to gratify our pride, our vain ambition, or to exercise control or dominion or compulsion upon the souls of the children of men, in any degree of unrighteousness, behold, the heavens withdraw themselves; the Spirit of the Lord is grieved; and when it is withdrawn, Amen to the priesthood or the authority of that man" (D&C 121:37).

Members of the Church understand that the exercise of divine authority includes the responsibility to bless people and minister to their well-

being. Proper use of this authority is inconsistent with authoritarianism and the abuses of authority, so the negative connotations sometimes associated with authority are not generally present in the Church.

BIBLIOGRAPHY

Ehat, Andrew F., and Lyndon W. Cook, eds. *The Words of Joseph Smith*. Provo, Utah, 1980.

Richards, LeGrand. *A Marvelous Work and a Wonder*. Salt Lake City, 1968.

Smith, Joseph F. *Gospel Doctrine*. Salt Lake City, 1977.

Talmage, James E. *AF*. Salt Lake City, 1977.

KIM S. CAMERON

AUTOPSY

The Church of Jesus Christ of Latter-day Saints holds that an autopsy may be performed if the family of the deceased gives consent and if the autopsy complies with the law of the community. The purpose of an autopsy is, where possible, to examine the results of trauma or disease recorded in the vital organs of the body so as to define the specific cause of death for the family, the community, and the professionals who attended the deceased. It also permits the training and instruction of those who continue the search for better ways of coping with disease. It is one of the methods whereby both those who die and those who examine them contribute to improving the quality of life and health of their fellow human beings.

FRANK D. ALLAN

AUXILIARY ORGANIZATIONS

The LDS Church is characterized by two types of organizational entities: PRIESTHOOD QUORUMS and organizations auxiliary to the priesthood. Members of priesthood quorums, or groups of priesthood holders, along with those called to priesthood leadership positions, have the ecclesiastical responsibility and authority for carrying out the missions of the Church. The auxiliary organizations are complementary to priesthood line organization and exist primarily to assist the priesthood. The auxiliaries are the RELIEF SOCIETY (women, eighteen and older), SUNDAY SCHOOL (all members twelve and older), YOUNG WOMEN (twelve through eighteen),

YOUNG MEN (twelve through eighteen), and PRIMARY (all children eighteen months through eleven years).

Auxiliary organizations seek to provide gospel instruction, wholesome activities, the sharing of resources, settings where supportive friendships can form, and formal and informal opportunities for the sharing of faith and values. Each organization tailors its program to a specific age group and gender and provides members with opportunities for Christian service. Each has a set of leaders functioning at the ward, stake, and general levels of the Church organization, and ward and stake auxiliary leaders receive training each year at an auxiliary training meeting.

Although the Relief Society (1842) had roots in the early years of the Church's development, the auxiliary organizations developed as formal parts of Church structure after it moved to Utah in 1847. The Relief Society and the Sunday School were established Churchwide in the early 1860s by President Brigham YOUNG, followed by the Cooperative Retrenchment Association in 1869 (forerunner of the Young Women organization), and the Young Men's Mutual Improvement Association in 1875 (forerunner to the Young Men organization). The Primary Association, emphasizing religious activities for children, began in 1878; weekday religion classes for children, emphasizing religious instruction, were instituted in 1890. These two entities were merged in 1929 to form the present-day Primary.

During the opening decades of the twentieth century, each auxiliary organization developed in its own way into a major facet of the Church programs for its members. Under the leadership of a presidency and board called at the general level of the Church to provide resources and direction to the local congregations, each auxiliary developed its own Churchwide curriculum, magazine, and set of regular meetings and activities. In addition, there was a general movement to structure classes and activities by age groupings. As each auxiliary expanded its program, it also developed a leadership structure staffed by the lay membership. Today, a presidency and board or staff are called at the ward level to implement the program and serve the members; at the stake level to provide leadership training and support and combine resources and activities; and at the general Church level to establish program guidelines and policies, develop materials and provide leadership.

In the early 1970s, an organization for SINGLE ADULTS was established at the general Church level under the direction of the Melchizedek Priesthood Committee. Its purpose was to develop programs and policies to address the needs and concerns of single adult members. Activities were instituted at the ward and stake level, and leaders were called to plan such activities. The general level was not continued beyond the 1970s, and local leaders and activities function under the direction of local priesthood and Relief Society leaders.

As the auxiliary programs expanded in the first half of the twentieth century, one of the challenges became coordinating and maintaining the relationship between the priesthood line of ultimate responsibility for the work of the Church and the auxiliaries as agents of the priesthood in accomplishing it. This challenge was recognized by President Joseph F. SMITH as early as 1906. In the latter part of the twentieth century, the Church has made significant efforts to structure and define its work so that the principle of priesthood governance can be fully realized (see CORRELATION OF THE CHURCH, ADMINISTRATION). The thrust has been to link the efforts of priesthood leaders and auxiliary leaders more closely and to align them with the priesthood channel of decision making and action. Specifically, at each level of the Church organization, auxiliary leaders are accountable to priesthood leaders rather than to the auxiliary organization.

Priesthood correlation provides more direct representation of the needs of all Church members in Church government. When properly implemented, it is the process through which women participate in the governance of the Church. Female leaders express their views, represent their concerns, and share in the decision-making process in partnership with men holding priesthood offices.

BIBLIOGRAPHY

Cowan, Richard O. *The Church in the Twentieth Century.* Salt Lake City, 1985.

Jenson, Andrew. *Encyclopedic History of the Church of Jesus Christ of Latter-day Saints.* Salt Lake City, 1941.

Smith, Joseph Fielding. *Essentials in Church History.* Salt Lake City, 1950.

IRENE HEWETTE ERICKSEN

B

BABYLON

See: Worldly, Worldliness

BALLANTYNE, RICHARD

Richard Ballantyne was born in Whitridgebog, Roxburgshire, Scotland, on August 26, 1817, to David Ballantyne and Ann Bannerman. He was strong-minded, and ever worked for justice for the oppressed and mercy for the sinner and the weak. In his early days, Richard was frugal, somewhat austere, and honest in his business; in later years, he displayed sympathy and affection. His concern for the moral and spiritual welfare of children led him to establish the first LDS SUNDAY SCHOOL, in 1849, in Salt Lake City.

Ballantyne was brought up in the Relief Presbyterian Church. As a youth he worked on his parents' farm. Between the ages of nine and fourteen he occasionally attended school during the winter. At fourteen he was apprenticed to a baker; subsequently, he bought the business and managed it until he left Scotland.

In December 1842, at age twenty-five, Ballantyne was baptized into the Church at Leith, in the waters of the Firth of Forth. The following year

he, his mother, two sisters, and a brother immigrated to NAUVOO, where he managed several businesses and engaged in farming along the Mississippi River. In Nauvoo he suffered persecution along with many of the Saints. In the summer of 1846, he and four other men were kidnapped by a mob, held hostage, and threatened with death. After two weeks, the mob bargained with Church leaders and returned the men to Nauvoo to avoid being charged with the kidnapping.

That same year, Ballantyne was ordained a SEVENTY and, soon after, a HIGH PRIEST. At the exodus from Nauvoo in 1846, he remained behind to help settle the Saints' affairs. In September of that year, having completed his assignment, he moved to WINTER QUARTERS. On February 17, 1847, he married Hulda Meriah Clark. They entered Utah in 1848, their first son having been born while they were crossing the plains.

Upon arriving in Salt Lake City, Ballantyne immediately considered the possibilities of schooling for the children. He asked for and received his bishop's permission to establish a Sunday School. Because no suitable meeting place was available, he added a room onto his home and held the first Sunday School in the Church on December 9, 1849. Approximately fifty students attended. Later this Sunday School was moved to the Fourteenth

Richard Ballantyne (1817–1898) was a native of Scotland, where he taught Sunday School in the Presbyterian Church. He began Sunday Sabbath instruction for LDS children in his Salt Lake City home in 1849. He later organized Sunday Schools in other communities where he lived. His success inspired a churchwide movement. Courtesy the Utah State Historical Society.

Ward meetinghouse. When asked why he had been so desirous of organizing a Sunday School, he replied:

> I was early called to this work by the voice of the spirit, and I have felt many times that I have been ordained to this work before I was born, for even before I joined the church I was moved upon to work for the young. Surely no more joyful nor profitable labor can be performed by an Elder [Jenson, Vol. 1, p. 705].

In the fall of 1852, Ballantyne was called on a mission to India, and arrived in Calcutta on July 24, 1853. Although the work was very discouraging, he worked hard until his release and return to Utah in September 1855 (*see* ASIA: SOUTH AND SOUTHEAST).

He married Mary Pierce on November 27, 1855, as a plural wife, and about two years later married Caroline Sanderson. He and his three wives had twenty-two children and more than one hundred grandchildren.

During his life in Utah, Ballantyne managed several businesses, including two railroads, a newspaper, and several merchandising companies.

He was a member of the Weber County Court for fourteen years. At the time of his death, November 8, 1898, he was a senior member of the HIGH COUNCIL of the Ogden Utah Stake.

BIBLIOGRAPHY

Ashton, Wendell J. *Theirs in the Kingdom*, 2nd ed., pp. 235–58. Salt Lake City, 1970.

Cannon, Donald Q., and David J. Whittaker, eds. *Supporting Saints: Life Stories of Nineteenth-Century Mormons.* Provo, Utah, 1985.

CHC, 3:6–9; 4:72–73; 5:478–80.

Jenson, Andrew, ed. *Latter-Day Saint Biographical Encyclopedia*, Vol. 1, pp. 703–706. Salt Lake City, 1971.

J. HUGH BAIRD

BAPTISM

The fourth ARTICLE OF FAITH of The Church of Jesus Christ of Latter-day Saints declares that "baptism by immersion for the remission of sins" is one of the "first principles and ordinances of the Gospel." Latter-day Saints believe, as do many Christians, that baptism is an essential initiatory ordinance for all persons who are joining the Church, as it admits them to Christ's church on earth (John 3:3–5; D&C 20:37, 68–74). It is a primary step in the process, which includes faith, repentance, BAPTISM OF FIRE AND OF THE HOLY GHOST, and enduring to the end, whereby members may receive remission of their sins and gain access to the CELESTIAL KINGDOM and ETERNAL LIFE (e.g., Mark 16:15–16; 2 Ne. 31:13–21; D&C 22:1–4; 84:64, 74; *MD*, pp. 69–72).

Latter-day Saint baptisms are performed for converts who have been properly instructed, and are at least eight years of age (the age of accountability). Baptism must be performed by one who has proper priesthood AUTHORITY. The major features of the ordinance include the raising of the right hand, the reciting of the prescribed BAPTISMAL PRAYER by the one performing the baptism, and the complete immersion of the candidate (3 Ne. 11:23–26; D&C 20:71–74; 68:27). Baptism symbolizes the covenant by which people promise to come into the fold of God, to take upon themselves the name of Christ, to stand as a witness for God, to keep his commandments, and to bear one another's burdens, manifesting a determination to serve him to the end, and to prepare to receive the spirit of Christ for the remission of sins. The Lord, as his part of the covenant, is to pour out his spirit upon them, redeem them from their sins, raise them in the first resurrection, and give them eternal life (Mosiah 18:7–10; D&C 20:37).

The rich symbolism of the ordinance invites candidates and observers to reflect on its meanings. Burial in the water and arising out of the water symbolize the candidate's faith in the death, burial, and resurrection of Jesus Christ, as well as the future resurrection of all people. It also represents the candidate's new birth to a life in Christ, being BORN OF GOD, thus born again of the water and of the spirit (Rom. 6:3–6; Mosiah 18:13–14; Moses 6:59–60; D&C 128:12–13).

Latter-day Saint scriptures indicate that the history of this ordinance predates the ministry of John the Baptist. Beginning with Adam (Moses 6:64–66), baptism by immersion in water was introduced as standard practice, and has been observed in all subsequent dispensations of the gospel when priesthood authority was on the earth (D&C 20:25–27; 84:27–28). For variants of such precedents, Latter-day Saints trace the baptismal initiations in many pre-Christian religions (see Meslin, 1987). As recorded in the Book of Mormon, LEHI and NEPHI₁ foresaw the baptism of Jesus Christ in vision and taught their people to follow his righteous example (1 Ne. 10:7–10; 11:27; 2 Ne. 31:4–9). Moreover, before the time of Jesus Christ, ALMA₁ initiated converts into the church of God by baptism as a sign of their covenant (Mosiah 18:8–17; Alma 4:4–5).

According to the account of his appearance to the Nephites, Jesus taught the necessity of faith, repentance, baptism, and the GIFT OF THE HOLY GHOST, and he authorized twelve disciples to baptize (3 Ne. 11:18–41; 19:11–13; 26:17–21). The Book of Mormon provides adequate instructions for baptism and proper words for the baptismal prayer (3 Ne. 11:23–28; Moro. 6:1–4; cf. D&C 20:73).

In addition to relying on information in the Book of Mormon, Latter-day Saints follow the New Testament teachings on baptism. Jesus taught that baptism is necessary for salvation. He told Nicodemus, "Except a man be born of water and of the Spirit, he cannot enter into the kingdom of God" (John 3:1–5). He required baptism of those who professed to become his disciples (John 4:1–2). His farewell commission to his apostles was that they should go to all nations, teaching and baptizing

A boy is baptized a member of The Church of Jesus Christ of Latter-day Saints. Jesus said, "Ye shall go down and stand in the water, and in my name shall ye baptize them" (3 Ne. 11:23); "and he commandeth all men that they must repent, and be baptized in his name" (2 Ne. 9:23). A person who is baptized covenants with God to serve him and keep his commandments.

(Matt. 28:19), and he declared, "He that believeth *and is baptized* shall be saved; but he that believeth not shall be damned" (Mark 16:16; emphasis added). Paul, after his miraculous vision on the road to Damascus, was taught the gospel by Ananias who told him to "arise, and be baptized, and wash away thy sins" (Acts 22:16). To the penitent multitude on the day of Pentecost, Peter proclaimed, "Repent, and be baptized every one of you in the name of Jesus Christ for the remission of sins" (Acts 2:38).

Latter-day Saints do not accept baptismal practices and teachings that arose among some Christian groups in the centuries after the death of the apostles, including INFANT BAPTISM, baptism by means other than immersion, and the idea that baptism is not necessary for salvation. The Nephite prophet MORMON denounced the practice of infant baptism, which had apparently crept in among his people, and declared that anyone who supposed that little children need baptism would deny the mercies of Christ, setting at naught the value of his atonement and the power of his redemption (Moro. 8:4–20).

The authority to baptize was restored by John the Baptist to Joseph Smith and Oliver COWDERY on May 15, 1829 (JS—H 1:68–72). From the early days of the restored Church, missionaries have been sent to "declare repentance and faith on the Savior, and remission of sins by baptism" (D&C 19:31; 55:2; 84:27, 74). "He that believeth and is baptized shall be saved, and he that believeth not, and is not baptized, shall be damned" (D&C 112:29). This is the central teaching of the GOSPEL OF JESUS CHRIST (3 Ne. 11:31–40).

Consequently, persons coming into The Church of Jesus Christ of Latter-day Saints at age eight or older are required to submit to baptism, even though they may have been previously baptized in other churches (D&C 22). Likewise, excommunicants undergo baptism again once they have qualified for readmission into the Church.

The form of the ordinance is prescribed in latter-day revelation, which makes clear that the baptism must be performed by a person who has priesthood authority and that it requires completely immersing the penitent candidate below the water and then bringing the person out of the water (3 Ne. 11:25–26; D&C 20:72–74). Baptism is followed by the LAYING ON OF HANDS for the gift of the Holy Ghost.

Contemporary Church practice provides for the candidate to be interviewed and approved by an authorized priesthood official (usually the BISHOP or other officer presiding over the congregation or a MISSION official), who determines whether the applicant meets the qualifying conditions of repentance, faith in the Lord Jesus Christ, and an understanding of and willingness to obey the laws and ordinances of the gospel. It is also necessary that an official record of each baptism be kept by the Church.

Baptism may be performed in the font provided in many meetinghouses or in any body of water that is suitable for the sacred occasion and deep enough for complete immersion. The candidate and the person performing the ordinance will be dressed in plain and modest white clothing. The ceremony is unpretentious, typically attended by the candidate's family, close friends, and interested members of the congregation. A speaker or two may offer a few words of instruction and joyous welcome to the candidate.

The earlier practice of rebaptism to manifest repentance and recommitment, or for a restoration of health in time of sickness, is no longer practiced in the Church.

Belief that baptism is necessary for the salvation of all persons who reach the age of accountability (D&C 84:64, 74) does not condemn persons who have died without the opportunity to hear the true gospel of Jesus Christ or to receive baptism from proper priesthood authority. Latter-day Saints believe that proxy BAPTISM FOR THE DEAD should be performed vicariously (1 Cor. 15:29; D&C 124:28–35, 127–128), and that it becomes effective if the deceased beneficiary accepts the gospel while in the spirit world awaiting resurrection (see 1 Pet. 3:18–20; 4:6; cf. D&C 45:54). This vicarious work for the benefit of previous generations, binding the hearts of the children to their fathers (Mal. 4:5–6), is one of the sacred ordinances performed in Latter-day Saint TEMPLES (D&C 128:12–13).

BIBLIOGRAPHY

Meslin, Michel. "Baptism." In *Encyclopedia of Religion*, Mircea Eliade, ed. Vol. 2, pp. 59–63. New York, 1987.

Smith, Joseph Fielding. *Doctrines of Salvation*, Vol. 2, pp. 323–37. Salt Lake City, 1955.

Talmage, James E. *AF*, pp. 109–42. Salt Lake City, 1984.

CARL S. HAWKINS

BAPTISMAL COVENANT

When a person enters into a Latter-day Saint baptism, he or she makes a covenant with God. Baptism is a "sign . . . that we will do the will of God, and there is no other way beneath the heavens whereby God hath ordained for man to come to Him to be saved" (*TPJS*, p. 198).

Candidates promise to "come into the fold of God, and to be called his people, . . . to bear one another's burdens, . . . to mourn with those that mourn, and . . . to stand as witnesses of God . . . even until death" (Mosiah 18:8–9). A person must enter this covenant with the proper attitudes of HUMILITY, REPENTANCE, and determination to keep the Lord's commandments, and serve God to the end (2 Ne. 31:6–17; Moro. 6:2–4; D&C 20:37). In turn, God promises remission of sins, redemption, and cleansing by the Holy Ghost (Acts 22:16; 3 Ne. 30:2). This covenant is made in the name of the Father, the Son, and the Holy Ghost.

The baptized can renew this covenant at each SACRAMENT MEETING by partaking of the SACRAMENT. This continual willingness to remember Christ and to keep his commandments brings the Lord's promise of his Spirit and produces the "fruits" (Gal. 5:22) and "gifts" (D&C 46) that lead to ETERNAL LIFE.

BIBLIOGRAPHY

Tripp, Robert M. *Oaths, Covenants and Promises*, pp. 11–19. Salt Lake City, 1973.

JERRY A. WILSON

BAPTISMAL PRAYER

The wording of the baptismal prayer used in The Church of Jesus Christ of Latter-day Saints is prescribed in the earliest compilation of instructions for Church operations (D&C 20). When an individual is baptized, the person with the proper priesthood AUTHORITY goes down into the water with the candidate, raises his right arm to the square, calls the individual by the full legal name, and says, "Having been commissioned of Jesus Christ, I baptize you in the name of the Father, and of the Son, and of the Holy Ghost. Amen," and then immerses the candidate (D&C 20:73). A version of the prayer that differs only slightly from this was given by Jesus Christ to the NEPHITES and is recorded in the Book of Mormon (3 Ne. 11:25).

Earlier in the Book of Mormon there is a somewhat different account of the baptismal prayer that was spoken. When ALMA₁ in the second century B.C. established the Church among the Nephites, he prayed: "O Lord, pour out thy Spirit upon thy servant, that he may do this work with holiness of heart" (Mosiah 18:12). The baptismal prayer that followed emphasized the COVENANT represented in BAPTISM and the need for a subsequent baptism of the Spirit: "I baptize thee, having authority from the Almighty God, as a testimony that ye have entered into a covenant to serve him until you are dead as to the mortal body; and may the Spirit of the Lord be poured out upon you; and may he grant unto you eternal life, through the redemption of Christ, whom he has prepared from the foundation of the world" (Mosiah 18:13; *see* BAPTISM OF FIRE AND OF THE HOLY GHOST).

BIBLIOGRAPHY

It is informative to compare LDS practice and scriptural accounts with the Christian tradition as reported in E. C. Whitaker, *Documents of the Baptismal Liturgy*, London, 1970.

JERRY A. WILSON

BAPTISM FOR THE DEAD

[*This entry consists of two articles:*

LDS Practice
Ancient Sources

The first article traces the development of the LDS doctrine of baptizing for the dead. In the second article, the dean of the Harvard School of Theology discusses the practice in ancient times.]

LDS PRACTICE

Baptism for the dead is the proxy performance of the ORDINANCE of baptism for one deceased. Joseph SMITH taught, "If we can baptize a man in the name of the Father [and] of the Son and of the Holy Ghost for the remission of sins it is just as much our privilege to act as an agent and be baptized for the remission of sins for and in behalf of our dead kindred who have not heard the gospel or fulness of it" (Kenney, p. 165).

The first public affirmation of the ordinance of baptism for the dead in the Church was Joseph Smith's funeral sermon for Seymour Brunson in NAUVOO in August 1840. Addressing a widow who had lost a son who had not been baptized, he called the principle "glad tidings of great joy," in contrast to the prevailing tradition that all unbaptized are damned. The first baptisms for the dead in modern times were done in the Mississippi River near Nauvoo.

Revelations clarifying the doctrine and practice have been given from time to time:

1. This was a New Testament practice (1 Cor. 15:29; cf. D&C 128; *see* BAPTISM FOR THE DEAD: ANCIENT SOURCES).

2. The ministry of Christ in the SPIRIT WORLD was for the benefit of those who had died without hearing the gospel or the fulness of it (1 Pet. 4:6; *see* SALVATION FOR THE DEAD).

3. Such baptisms are to be performed in temple fonts dedicated to the purpose (*TPJS*, p. 308; cf. D&C 124:29–35). In November 1841 the font

Baptismal font in the Salt Lake Temple. In such fonts, Latter-day Saints perform proxy baptisms on behalf of people who have died without being baptized. In the ancient Temple of Solomon, a deep brass basin similarly "stood upon twelve oxen . . . and the sea was set above them, and all their hinder parts were inward" (1 Kings 7:25).

in the unfinished NAUVOO TEMPLE was so dedicated.

4. The language of the BAPTISMAL PRAYER is the same as for the living, with the addition of "for and in behalf of" the deceased.

5. Witnesses are to be present for proxy baptisms and a record is to be kept in Church archives (D&C 128:3, 8).

6. Women are to be baptized for women and men for men.

7. Not only baptism but CONFIRMATION and the higher TEMPLE ORDINANCES may also be performed by proxy (*TPJS*, pp. 362–63).

8. The law of AGENCY is inviolate in this world and the world to come. Thus, those served by proxy have the right to accept or reject the ordinances.

In the early years of the Church, proxy baptisms were performed only for direct blood ancestors, usually no more than four generations back.

Today, Latter-day Saints are baptized not only for their own forebears but also for other persons, unrelated to them, identified through the NAME EXTRACTION PROGRAM. The practice reflects the yearning of children for their parents and of parents for their children, and charitable feelings for others as well, that they receive the fulness of the blessings of the gospel of Jesus Christ. In LDS perspective, whatever else one may do to mourn, give honorable burial to, cherish, or memorialize the dead, this divinely authorized ordinance of baptism is a demonstration of love and has eternal implications.

BIBLIOGRAPHY

Kenney, Scott G., ed. *Wilford Woodruff's Journal*, Vol. 2. Midvale, Utah, 1983.

Widtsoe, John A. "Fundamentals of Temple Doctrine." *Utah Genealogical and Historical Magazine* 13 (July 1922):129–35.

H. DAVID BURTON

ANCIENT SOURCES

In his first epistle to the Corinthians Paul wrote: "Otherwise, what shall they do who are being baptized for the dead? If the dead are not raised at all, why are they being baptized for them" (Conzelmann, *1 Corinthians* 15:29).

This verse is part of Paul's argumentation against those who denied a future resurrection (cf. 2 Tim. 2:18, Justin, Dial. 80). He refers to a practice of vicarious baptism, a practice for which we have no other evidence in the Pauline or other New Testament or early Christian writings. Interpreters have puzzled over the fact that Paul seems to accept this practice. At least he does not see fit to condemn it as heretical, but Paul clearly refers to a distinct group within the Church, a group that he accuses of inconsistency between ritual and doctrine.

A practice of vicarious baptism for the dead (for example among the Marcionites, A.D. 150) was known and seen as heretical by the ancient commentators. Thus they interpreted Paul's words in 1 Corinthians 15:29 so as not to lend support to such practices or to any theology implicit in it. Through the ages their interpretations have persisted and multiplied (B. M. Foschini reports and evaluates forty distinct explanations of this verse). Most of the Greek fathers understood "the dead" to refer to one's own body; others have interpreted the verse as referring to pagans seeking baptism "for the sake of joining" lost Christian relatives. Still others have suggested different sentence structures: "Otherwise what will they achieve who are being baptized? Something merely for their dead bodies?"

Once the theological pressures from later possible developments of practice and doctrine are felt less constricting, the text seems to speak plainly enough about a practice within the Church of vicarious baptism for the dead. This is the view of most contemporary critical exegetes. Such a practice can be understood in partial analogy with Paul's reference to how the pagan spouses and joint children in mixed marriages are sanctified and cleansed by the Christian partners (1 Cor. 7:14). Reference has often been made to 2 Maccabees 12:39–46, where Judas Maccabeus, "taking account of the resurrection," makes atonement for his dead comrades. (This was the very passage which Dr. Eck used in favor of purgatory in his 1519 Leipzig debate with Martin Luther. So it be- came part of the reason why Protestant Bibles excluded the Apocrypha or relegated them to an Appendix.)

To this could be added that the next link in Paul's argument for a future resurrection is his own exposure to martyrdom (1 Cor. 15:30–32), a martyrdom that Paul certainly thinks of as having a vicarious effect (Phil. 2:17, Rom. 15:16, cf. Col. 1:24).

Such a connection may be conscious or unconscious. In either case it makes it quite reasonable that Paul's remark refers to a practice of a vicarious baptism for the dead.

BIBLIOGRAPHY

Conzelmann, H. *1 Corinthians*. Hermeneia Series. Philadelphia, 1975.

Foschini, B. "Those Who Are Baptized for the Dead; 1 Cor. 15:29." *Catholic Biblical Quarterly* 12 (1950):260–76, 378–88; 13 (1951):46–78, 172–98, 276–85.

KRISTER STENDAHL

BAPTISM OF FIRE AND OF THE HOLY GHOST

Baptism of fire and the Holy Ghost refers to the experience of an individual who receives the ordinance of the LAYING ON OF HANDS for the GIFT OF THE HOLY GHOST. It is the second in a two-part sequence following baptism by immersion in water through which a repentant person committed to Christ and his gospel is BORN OF GOD or born again. As Jesus explained to Nicodemus, "Except a man be born of water and of the Spirit, he cannot enter into the kingdom of God" (John 3:5). Commenting on this passage, Joseph Smith remarked, "Baptism by water is but half a baptism, and is good for nothing without . . . the baptism of the Holy Ghost" (*TPJS*, p. 314). The baptism of fire, ministered by the Holy Ghost, is manifested through a set of personal sensations, impressions, and insights that constitute a spiritual witness from deity that one has received a remission of sins (2 Ne. 31:17). The baptism of fire inaugurates the transmission of spiritual gifts to the faithful to assist them throughout life in remaining true to their baptismal COVENANT (1 Cor. 12; Moro. 10:8–23; D&C 46:10–33).

The doctrine of the two baptisms was taught by John the Baptist: "I indeed baptize you with water, . . . but he that cometh after me . . . shall baptize you with the Holy Ghost, and with fire" (Matt. 3:11). At Christ's baptism the Holy Ghost was manifested in the sign of a DOVE (Luke 3:22), and he appeared to the disciples on the day of Pentecost as cloven tongues of fire (Acts 2:3; see JESUS CHRIST). The ordinance of conferring the Holy Ghost initiated early Christian converts into the Church (Acts 8:12–17; 3 Ne. 18; Moro. 2–3; 6), and is a practice (often referred to as CONFIRMATION) restored to the latter-day Church and administered by the MELCHIZEDEK PRIESTHOOD (D&C 20:38–41).

As symbols for baptism, both water (used for washing) and fire (used in the smelting of metals, hence a "refiner's fire," Mal. 3:2–3) represent agents that cleanse and purify, the former externally, the latter internally, leading to SANCTIFICATION (Alma 13:12; Moro. 6:4). In addition, fire suggests warmth and light, realized in tangible sensations such as a burning in the bosom and an awareness of enlightenment accompanying the reception of the divine spirit (D&C 9:8; 88:49).

For Latter-day Saints, baptism by fire and the Holy Ghost is a real phenomenon in literal fulfillment of God's covenant to those who repent and are baptized (2 Ne. 31:10–21). Through this experience a person may realize the promises Jesus made with regard to how the Holy Ghost would function as a Comforter, a witness of the ATONEMENT, a teacher, and a guide to truth (John 14:16, 26; 15:26).

BIBLIOGRAPHY

Cannon, Elaine, and Ed J. Pinegar. *The Mighty Change*. Salt Lake City, 1978.

WILLIAM S. BRADSHAW

BEATITUDES

The Beatitudes, or promises of blessings in Jesus' SERMON ON THE MOUNT (Matt. 5:3–12), hold a particular significance for Latter-day Saints because the resurrected Lord gave essentially that same sermon to the Nephites and the Lamanites in the Western Hemisphere, as recorded in 3 Nephi 12–14. The words in the Beatitudes echo Isaiah 61:1–2 and Psalm 107:4–7, 9. Church members cite the setting of the Book of Mormon sermon as well as a few notable verbal differences (such as "Blessed are the poor in spirit *who come unto me*," and the phrase "for they shall be filled *with the Holy Ghost*") as examples of how the Book of Mormon complements the Bible, attesting to its message while clarifying and expanding it (cf. 1 Ne. 13 [esp. verses 39–42]; 2 Ne. 27, 29).

In the Book of Mormon, most of the sermon is addressed to baptized members of the Church (cf. 3 Ne. 11 and 12:1–2). Thus, the expectations in the sermon concern those living the law of the gospel as taught by Christ. Other parts of the sermon are directed specifically to leaders.

Some significant differences appear in the wording of the biblical and Book of Mormon versions of the Beatitudes. In the Book of Mormon, two new "beatitudes" precede those in Matthew: baptized members are blessed if they give heed to their leaders and have faith in Christ (3 Ne. 12:1), and "more blessed" are those who receive the testimony of emissaries whom Christ has called (3 Ne. 12:2). These two additional beatitudes are incorporated into the biblical sermon in the JOSEPH SMITH TRANSLATION OF THE BIBLE (JST). Matthew 5:3 is elaborated as noted above (cf. D&C 84:49–53). Matthew 5:4 is virtually unchanged at 3 Nephi 12:4 but is somewhat developed at 3 Nephi 12:19 (cf. Morm. 2:11–13). The words "shall be filled with the Holy Ghost" (3 Ne. 12:6) express on a spiritual level (cf. Ps. 17:15, Septuagint) the implicit meaning of cattle feeding upon grass (Matt. 5:6; Greek, *chortasthêsontai*; cf. the grass [*chortos*] where the disciples are miraculously fed at Matt. 14:19 and the verb "filled" at Matt. 15:33, 37). Matthew 5:5 is unchanged, as are Matthew 5:7–9; but Matthew 5:10 reads "which are persecuted for righteousness' sake," while 3 Nephi 12:10 has "who are persecuted for my name's sake," reflecting the Christ-centered theme throughout the Nephite version of the sermon. For the first two verbs of Matthew 5:12, which the KJV takes as imperatives, 3 Nephi 12:12 has "For ye shall have great joy and be exceeding glad."

Church leaders often refer to the Beatitudes as the Lord's promises of blessings and happiness to those who follow him and as the result of obedience or the "fruit of the Spirit" (Gal. 5:22–23). Those who would be obedient have the individual responsibilities of turning to the Lord and of implementing the principles inherent in the qualities described in the Beatitudes (cf. D&C 88:63–65 and 97:16, which adapt the sixth beatitude to temple worship).

BIBLIOGRAPHY

Thomas, Catherine. "The Sermon on the Mount: The Sacrifice of the Human Heart (Matthew 5–7; Luke 6:17–49)." In *Studies in Scripture*, ed. R. Millet, Vol. 5, pp. 236–50. Salt Lake City, 1986.

Welch, John W. *The Sermon at the Temple and the Sermon on the Mount*. Salt Lake City, 1990.

Wilcox, S. Michael. "The Beatitudes—Pathway to the Savior." *Ensign* 21 (Jan. 1991):19–23.

THOMAS W. MACKAY

BEEHIVE SYMBOL

Nineteenth-century leaders of The Church of Jesus Christ of Latter-day Saints consciously created symbols to buttress their community. The most persistent of these pioneer symbols was the beehive.

Its origin may relate to the statement in the Book of Mormon that the JAREDITES carried "with them deseret, which, by interpretation, is a honey bee" (Ether 2:3). The *Deseret News* (Oct. 11, 1881) described the symbol of the beehive in this way: "The hive and honey bees form our communal coat of arms. . . . It is a significant representation of the industry, harmony, order and frugality of the people, and of the sweet results of their toil, union and intelligent cooperation."

Working together during this early period, individuals contributed specialized talents and skills for building an integrated and well-planned community in a hostile environment. Community, not individuality, created this persistent symbol. The beehive has appeared on public and private Mormon buildings (such as temples, tabernacles, and meetinghouses, Brigham Young's Beehive House, and the mercantile institution ZCMI) as well as in folk art and on furniture.

Today it appears as a logo of some Church-related organizations, on the seals of the state of Utah and of two universities, on Church WELFARE products, and on some commercial signs in Utah.

It links the Mormon community across time while symbolizing the Mormon pioneer past.

BIBLIOGRAPHY

Cannon, Hal. *The Grand Beehive*. Salt Lake City, 1980.

Oman, Richard, and Susan Oman. "Mormon Iconography." In *Utah Folk Art: A Catalog of Material Culture*, ed. H. Cannon. Provo, Utah, 1980.

RICHARD G. OMAN

BENJAMIN

Benjamin, son of MOSIAH₁, was an important king in Nephite history (d. c. 121 B.C.). His reign came at a crucial juncture in the history of the NEPHITES and was important both culturally and politically. His father, Mosiah₁, "being warned of the Lord," had led the Nephites out of the land of Nephi to the land of Zarahemla (Omni 1:12, 19). Thereafter, during his own reign, Benjamin fought, as was customary for kings in the ancient world (cf. Mosiah 10:10), with his "own arm" against invading LAMANITES (W of M 1:13), keeping his people "from falling into the hands of [their] enemies" (Mosiah 2:31). He succeeded in consolidating Nephite rule over the land of Zarahemla (Omni 1:19) and reigned there "in righteousness" over his people (W of M 1:17).

Benjamin, described as a "holy man" (W of M 1:17) and "a just man before the Lord," also led his people as a prophet (Omni 1:25) and was, with the assistance of other prophets and holy men, able to overcome the contentions among his people and to "once more establish peace in the land" (W of M 1:18). Accordingly, Amaleki, who was himself "without seed," entrusted Benjamin with the record on the "small plates" (Omni 1:25). Keenly interested in the preservation of sacred records, Benjamin taught his sons "in all the language of his fathers" and "concerning the records . . . on the plates of brass" (Mosiah 1:2–3).

Mosiah 2–6 records Benjamin's farewell address, designed primarily to effect a "change in heart" in his people and to bring them to Jesus Christ. He deals with man's obligations to his fellow men and to God, punishment for rebellion against God, gratitude, faith, and service. This address is as relevant now as it was when first presented. In addition, reporting the words spoken to him by an angel, Benjamin prophesied that "the Lord Omnipotent . . . shall come down from heaven among the children of men" as the Messiah, "working mighty miracles" (Mosiah 3:5). Further, Benjamin declared that the Messiah would "be called Jesus Christ, the Son of God, . . . and his mother shall be called Mary" (3:8)—the earliest mention of her name in the Book of Mormon. Moreover, Jesus would "suffer temptations, and pain of body, hunger, thirst, and fatigue, even more than man can suffer" (3:7). After being crucified, Jesus would "rise the third day from the dead; and behold, he standeth to judge the world" (3:10). Significantly, Benjamin taught that the power of the atonement of Jesus Christ was in effect for him and his people, "as though he had already come" to earth (3:13).

The impact of Benjamin's address on subsequent Nephite generations can be gauged by how much it is mentioned later in the Book of Mormon. Following Benjamin's death, his son and successor, MOSIAH₂, sent Ammon and fifteen other representatives from Zarahemla to the land of Nephi (Mosiah 7:1–6), where they found the Nephite king Limhi and his people in bondage to the Lamanites. After the representatives had identified themselves, Limhi caused his people to gather at the local temple, where he addressed them. Thereafter, Ammon "rehearsed unto them the last words which king Benjamin had taught them, and explained them to the people of king Limhi, so that they might understand all the words which he spake" (Mosiah 8:3). Similarly, HELAMAN₂ (c. 30 B.C.) admonished his sons LEHI₄ and NEPHI₂ to "remember . . . the words which king Benjamin spake unto his people; yea, remember that there is no other way nor means whereby man can be saved, only through the atoning blood of Jesus Christ" (Hel. 5:9). These words mirror one of the central themes of Benjamin's address: "Salvation was, and is, and is to come, in and through the atoning blood of Christ" (Mosiah 3:18–19; cf. Hel. 14:12).

After a long and prosperous reign, Benjamin died about 121 B.C. No higher tribute was paid to his greatness than that given by his son Mosiah₂. In a discourse given at the end of his own reign, in which he considers the advantages and pitfalls of various forms of government, Mosiah says, "If ye could have men for your kings who would do even as my father Benjamin did for this people, . . . then it would be expedient that ye should always have kings to rule over you" (Mosiah 29:13).

BIBLIOGRAPHY

Nibley, Hugh W. *An Approach to the Book of Mormon.* In *CWHN* 4:295–310.

STEPHEN D. RICKS

BENSON, EZRA TAFT

Ezra Taft Benson (1899–), thirteenth President of The Church of Jesus Christ of Latter-day Saints, is noted for his extensive Church service and his distinguished career in government. He served forty-two years as a member of the Quorum of the Twelve Apostles and was U.S. secretary of agriculture for eight years in the administration of President Dwight D. Eisenhower. As President of the Church, he repeatedly bore witness that the Book of Mormon is the major instrument to bring the members of the Church and the world to Christ, and he admonished the Saints to strengthen their families and to preserve their God-given freedoms.

President Benson was born August 4, 1899, in the small rural community of Whitney, Idaho, the oldest of eleven children born to George Taft Benson, Jr., and Sarah Dunkley. He was named after his great-grandfather, Ezra T. (Taft) Benson, an APOSTLE, who entered the Salt Lake Valley with the first Mormon pioneer company in July 1847. The pioneer Ezra T. was the son of John Benson, Jr., and Chloe Taft of Mendon, Massachusetts. John Benson, Sr., was an officer during the American Revolution.

Ezra Taft Benson was reared on the family farm in Whitney, driving a team of horses at the age of five, milking cows, and thinning sugar beets. He entered grade school at the age of eight. "Be as careful of the books you read as of the company you keep" was the counsel that governed his reading habits (Dew, p. 24). In addition to the scriptures, he read Bunyan's *Pilgrim's Progress*; biographies of George Washington, Benjamin Franklin, and Abraham Lincoln, and success stories by Horatio Alger. His grandparents gave him a two-volume set by Orison S. Marden, *Little Visits with Great Americans* (1905), which he devoured.

Increased responsibility was thrust on him as a youth when his father was called as a missionary to the Northern States Mission, leaving behind his wife and seven children; the eighth was born while he was in the mission field. A spirit of missionary work enveloped the home, and all eleven children eventually served at least one full-time mission.

In 1914, Ezra entered the Church-sponsored Oneida Academy in Preston, Idaho, graduating in 1918. That year as Scoutmaster, he led his Scouts into choral competition and won the Cache Valley chorus championship. Also during that year he enlisted in the military service just before the close of World War I.

As a young man, he developed a love for the land and for the Lord, two fundamental influences in his ensuing life. He felt that the basic ingredient for successful farming was intelligent, hard work. To increase his agricultural skills, he took correspondence courses and began attending the Utah State Agricultural College (now Utah State University). He accepted a mission call to England in 1921, where he served as Newcastle Conference clerk, Sunderland Branch president, and president of the Newcastle Conference, which included all of northern England. Upon his return, he soon enrolled at Brigham Young University, where he was president of the Agriculture Club and Men's Glee Club and was named the most popular man on campus. He graduated with honors, majoring in animal husbandry with a minor in agronomy.

He married Flora Smith Amussen in the Salt Lake Temple on September 10, 1926. She was the youngest child of Carl Christian Amussen, a Danish convert who crossed the plains and became a prominent Utah jeweler, and Barbara McIsaac Smith. Flora attended Utah State Agricultural College, where she served as vice-president of the student body, took the lead in a Shakespearean play, and won the women's singles tennis championship. She served a mission in the Hawaiian Islands.

Of his wife, President Benson said, "She had more faith in me than I had in myself" (Dew, p. 96). One Church leader commented that if there were more women in the Church like Sister Benson, there would be more men in the Church like Brother Benson. They became the parents of six children—Reed, Mark, Barbara, Beverly, Bonnie, and Beth.

Benson received a research scholarship to Iowa State College, where he obtained his master's degree in agricultural economics on June 13, 1927. He returned to the family farm, which he and his

brother Orval had purchased from their father, and on March 4, 1929, was appointed Franklin County agricultural agent. He helped farmers solve their problems by setting up demonstration farms, inviting in specialists, teaching crop rotation, and introducing improved varieties of grains.

In 1930, he was promoted to agricultural economist and marketing specialist for the University of Idaho, with offices in the state capitol in Boise. Traveling throughout Idaho, he encouraged farmers to work cooperatively in producing and marketing their goods. For five years, he served as the executive secretary of the Idaho Cooperative Council. He took a leave in 1936 for additional graduate study, attending the University of California in Berkeley on a fellowship awarded by the Giannini Foundation for Agricultural Economics. Soon after his return to Boise, he was called by the Church in November 1938 to serve as stake president. In April 1939, he became executive secretary of the National Council of Farmer Cooperatives at its headquarters in Washington, D.C. The council represented some 4,000 cooperative purchasing and marketing organizations involving almost 1.6 million farmers. Ezra Benson represented cooperatives before committees of Congress and served on a four-man national agriculture advisory committee to President Franklin D. Roosevelt during World War II.

On June 30, 1940, the Church called him as the first president of the Washington, D.C., stake,

The Benson family in 1943 at the time of Elder Benson's call to the apostleship: Ezra and his wife, Flora Amussen Benson, with their children (left to right) Bonnie, Mark, Barbara, Beverly, and (standing) Reed.

and on July 26, 1943, he was called to the QUORUM OF THE TWELVE APOSTLES. He was sustained in that position at the October general conference and was ordained an apostle by President Heber J. GRANT on October 7, 1943.

In December 1945, following the devastation of World War II, President George Albert SMITH called Elder Benson to be the European mission president. His faith in the Lord, administrative skills, and experience in dealing with government helped him accomplish the four-point charge given to him by the First Presidency: "First, to attend to the spiritual affairs of the Church in Europe; second, to work to make available food, clothing, and bedding to our suffering Saints in all parts of Europe; third, to direct the reorganization of the missions of Europe; and, fourth, to prepare for the return of missionaries to those countries" (*IE* 50 [May 1947]:293). He was among the first American civilians to administer relief in many of the devastated areas. During his first five months in Europe, he visited over one hundred cities in thirteen countries. Within ten months, he completed his mission, having distributed ninety-two boxcar loads of food, clothing, bedding, and medical supplies; reopened missions with new mission presidents and full-time missionaries; and given the Latter-day Saints in Europe a renewed spirit of hope.

U.S. President Dwight D. Eisenhower looks on as Chief Justice Fred M. Vinson administers the oath of office to Secretary of Agriculture Ezra Taft Benson in January 1953.

In 1952, following the counsel of President David O. McKay, Ezra Taft Benson accepted the Cabinet position of secretary of agriculture in the Eisenhower administration. His selection was greeted with widespread approval. In his "General Statement on Agricultural Policy," he said, "The supreme test of any government policy, agricultural or other, should be 'How will it affect the character, morale, and well-being of our people?'. . . A completely planned and subsidized economy weakens initiative, discourages industry, destroys character, and demoralizes the people" (Benson, 1962, p. 602).

He assumed office when farm income was declining and wartime legislation was piling up surpluses in government warehouses, inviting increased government controls of agriculture. He worked to reverse that course, winning significant legislative victories in spite of intense political opposition.

He became known for his integrity, and friend and foe alike acknowledged that he was a man of religious principles who stood by his convictions despite political pressures. He traveled hundreds of thousands of miles, carrying his farm message throughout the nation and the world, and aggressively encouraged consumption of U.S. farm products. He authored three books, *Farmers at the Crossroads* (1956), *Freedom to Farm* (1960), and *Crossfire: The Eight Years with Eisenhower* (1962).

He served eight years in the Cabinet, meeting with heads of state and agriculture leaders and farmers in over forty nations. He had discussions with such leaders as Chiang Kai-shek, Nehru, Khrushchev, King Hussein, and David Ben-Gurion. During this time, his example and activities brought positive and widespread attention to the Church. President David O. McKay said that Secretary Benson's work in the Cabinet would "stand for all time as a credit to the Church and the nation" (Benson, 1962, p. 519).

With the encouragement of President David O. McKay, a major thrust of Elder Benson's many Church and civic addresses pertained to freedom and the threats to it. The substance of those messages is found in his books *The Red Carpet* (1962), *Title of Liberty* (1964), and *An Enemy Hath Done This* (1969). In Church general conference in April 1965, he warned, "To have been on the wrong side of the freedom issue during the war in heaven meant eternal damnation. How then can Latter-

Elder Benson, with LDS Scout leader Bertram Stokes, greets Scouts from throughout the British Mission at a gathering in the Birmingham District (c. 1946).

day Saints expect to be on the wrong side in this life and escape the eternal consequences?" (*IE* 68 [June 1965]:537).

President Benson's international stature helped to facilitate the acceptance and growth of the Church throughout the world. He dedicated several nations to the preaching of the gospel, established the first stakes in many countries, and supervised various areas of the world. He served as chairman of Quorum of the Twelve committees and sat on numerous boards.

In December 1973, Ezra Taft Benson became president of the Quorum of the Twelve Apostles. His executive abilities were again demonstrated in this calling. A great spirit of unity was manifest, and he measured proposed policies or procedures by the yardstick "What is best for the kingdom?" (Petersen, p. 3).

Brigham Young University honored him by

establishing the Ezra Taft Benson Agriculture and Food Institute in 1975 to help relieve world food problems and raise the quality of global life through improved nutrition and enlightened agriculture practices.

Many national and international citations and awards, including a number of honorary doctorate degrees, were bestowed on him. From the Boy Scouts of America he received the Silver Beaver, Silver Antelope, and Silver Buffalo; he served on their National Executive Board. On April 1, 1989, he was presented world Scouting's highest award, the Bronze Wolf. During his ninetieth birthday celebration, the President of the United States conferred upon him the Presidential Citizens Medal, naming him "one of the most distinguished Americans of his time" (*Church News*, Aug. 5, 1989, p. 4).

Upon the death of President Spencer W. Kimball, Ezra Taft Benson became President of the Church on November 10, 1985, at the age of eighty-six. At that time he delivered a statement reiterating the mission of the Church—to preach the gospel, perfect the Saints, and redeem the dead—and reaffirming that the Church is led by the Lord Jesus Christ. He selected as his counselors in the First Presidency Gordon B. Hinckley and Thomas S. Monson. The new First Presidency soon issued a special invitation to those members who had ceased activity or become critical of the Church to "come back" (*Church News*, Dec. 22, 1985, p. 3), and they opened the temples to worthy members married to unendowed spouses.

In a solemn assembly at general conference April 6, 1986, he was sustained by Church members as the PROPHET, SEER, AND REVELATOR, and President of the Church. In his opening address at that conference, President Benson stressed the need to "cleanse the inner vessel (see Alma 60:23), beginning first with ourselves, then with our families, and finally with the Church" (*Ensign* 16 [May 1986]:4). In commencing that cleansing, he declared, "The Book of Mormon has not been, nor is it yet, the center of our personal study, family teaching, preaching, and missionary work. Of this we must repent" (*Ensign* 16 [May 1986]:5–6).

In his concluding address of the conference, he said, "The Lord inspired His servant Lorenzo Snow to reemphasize the principle of tithing to redeem the Church from financial bondage. . . . Now, in our day, the Lord has revealed the need to reemphasize the Book of Mormon to get the

Ezra Taft Benson was ordained and set apart as the thirteenth President of the Church on November 10, 1985.
During his administration he emphasized the Book of
Mormon and the theme "Come Unto Christ" in
strengthening missionary work and families.

Church and all the children of Zion out from under
condemnation—the scourge and judgment" (*Ensign* 16 [May 1986]:78; see D&C 84:54–58). To that
end, his address "The Book of Mormon Is the
Word of God" was repeated in regional conferences throughout the Church. This emphasis
greatly accelerated the distribution and reading of
the Book of Mormon and "brought more souls to
Christ, both within and without the Church, than
ever before" (*Ensign* 18 [Nov. 1988]:4).

Continuing to help set the Church in order
and perfect the Saints, he delivered another landmark address entitled "Beware of Pride" and gave
separate messages to the children, young men,
young women, single adult brethren, single adult
sisters, fathers, mothers, and the elderly.

Throughout the years, the home and family
were the center of many of President Benson's
conference messages, such as his widely broadcast
address "Our Homes—Divinely Ordained" (*IE* 52
[May 1949]:278–79, 332–33) and his frequent reference to his goal that there be "no empty chairs"

in the family circle in the next life (Dew, p. 363).
He has manifested a great love for the children and
youth of the Church.

He was President during the Bicentennial of
the U.S. Constitution and, as one of its greatest
defenders, he delivered messages honoring this
divine document and its inspired framers (*The
Constitution: A Heavenly Banner*, Salt Lake City,
1986).

During his presidency, new temples were
announced and several were dedicated, and missionary work expanded around the world with special opportunities being afforded, particularly in
Eastern Europe, in countries previously closed.

For nearly fifty years his thousands of
speeches stressed mankind's three great loyalties—
loyalty to God, loyalty to family, and loyalty to
country. His life has been exemplary in striving to
live those loyalties as a prophet, a patriarch, and a
patriot.

BIBLIOGRAPHY

Benson, Ezra Taft. *A Witness and a Warning*. Salt Lake City,
1988.

——. *Come, Listen to a Prophet's Voice*. Salt Lake City,
1990.

——. *Crossfire: The Eight Years With Eisenhower*. New
York, 1962.

——. *God, Family, Country*. Salt Lake City, 1974.

——. *The Teachings of Ezra Taft Benson*. Salt Lake City,
1988.

Dew, Sheri L. *Ezra Taft Benson: A Biography*. Salt Lake City,
1987.

Petersen, Mark E. "President Ezra Taft Benson." *Ensign* 16
[Jan. 1986]:2–4.

REED A. BENSON
SHERI L. DEW

BIBLE

*[The entry on the Bible is designed as an overview of the
positive LDS appraisal and extensive use of this scriptural collection. Articles under this entry are:*

Bible

LDS Belief in the Bible

King James Version

LDS Publication of the Bible

*The first article explains the importance of the Bible
among the standard works of the Church. The second*

article explores the depth of belief in the Bible. The third article examines the use by the Church of the King James Version of the Bible. The concluding article gives information contained in the Bible published by the Church in 1979 and details of the publication. Articles that address related issues include Old Testament and New Testament. For discussions of the range of matters associated with the LDS view of scripture in general, see Standard Works and particularly the set of articles under the general heading Scripture.]

BIBLE

The Bible stands at the foundation of The Church of Jesus Christ of Latter-day Saints, constitutes one of its standard works, and is accepted as the word of God. In 1820 a New Testament passage in the epistle of James prompted the young Joseph Smith to ask God about the religions of his time, and thereupon he received his FIRST VISION, in which he saw God the Father and Jesus Christ (James 1:5; JS—H 1:11–12, 17–18). Three years later, Old Testament and New Testament passages provided the principal scriptural foundation of Joseph's second major spiritual experience when the angel MORONI appeared to him and taught him from Malachi, Isaiah, Joel, Daniel, and other scriptures (JS—H 1:36–41; JD 24:241; *Messenger and Advocate* 1 [Apr. 1835]:109). After completing the Book of Mormon translation and organizing the restored Church of Jesus Christ in 1830, the Prophet Joseph Smith thoroughly studied the Bible as instructed by the Lord and prepared the JOSEPH SMITH TRANSLATION OF THE BIBLE (JST).

From childhood, Latter-day Saints are introduced to the teachings of the Bible. Certain passages are emphasized in teaching children. Most children in PRIMARY—and particularly those in families who hold FAMILY HOME EVENING and follow scripture reading programs—become familiar with the events recorded in Genesis, including stories of Adam and Eve, Noah, Abraham, Jacob, and Joseph. Later episodes of the prophets, judges, and kings (such as Moses, Samson, Samuel, David, Solomon, Jonah, and Daniel), as well as those of New Testament personalities (e.g., Peter, Paul, and Stephen), are also favorites. The stories of Deborah, Ruth, Esther, and Mary are especially loved by girls. However, the life and teachings of Jesus Christ are the most studied and appreciated (*see* JESUS CHRIST: MINISTRY OF JESUS CHRIST).

Richer gospel teachings come into focus in repeated study of the Bible by Latter-day Saints.

In addition to Sunday School instruction, teenagers attending SEMINARY classes spend two years of their four-year curriculum on the Bible. A similar emphasis is found in college-level religion classes in the universities and colleges of the Church educational system and in INSTITUTE OF RELIGION classes at other universities and colleges. LDS missionaries often refer to Bible passages as they teach investigators of the Church. One of the strongest demonstrations of the importance of Bible study to the Latter-day Saints is found in the adult Sunday School program. In the Gospel Doctrine classes, two of every four years are devoted to reading, studying, and discussing the Bible. Another strong evidence of LDS commitment to the Bible is the effort and expense incurred to produce the LDS PUBLICATION OF THE BIBLE in 1979. The General Authorities of the Church frequently quote from the Bible in their writings and general and stake conference addresses. Thus, the Bible forms an important gospel foundation for all Church members, from the newly baptized to the presiding leaders.

PREVALENT BIBLICAL TEACHINGS AND PRACTICES. Among the teachings found in the Bible, some concepts receive special emphasis. For example, Latter-day Saints readily identify with the Old Testament pattern of God speaking through living prophets (Amos 3:7), a pattern visible in the Church today. They also relate to the house of Israel through their individual PATRIARCHAL BLESSINGS, which usually identify a genealogical line back to one of the tribes of Israel. The concept of a covenant people, as taught in Genesis, Exodus, and Deuteronomy, conforms to LDS beliefs about being a covenant people today. Many laws and commandments, in particular a health code, distinguish both ancient Israel and its modern spiritual counterpart in the Church (Lev. 11; D&C 89; *see* WORD OF WISDOM). The wanderings of ancient Israel and the challenges in settling the PROMISED LAND also parallel early LDS history, so much so that Brigham YOUNG has been called a modern Moses (e.g., Arrington, 1985; *see also* PERSECUTION; PIONEERS).

New Testament teachings that are emphasized among Latter-day Saints include the teachings of the Savior and the apostles on basic gospel principles, especially faith and repentance, and covenant ordinances, particularly baptism and the GIFT OF THE HOLY GHOST (*see* FIRST PRINCIPLES

OF THE GOSPEL). Latter-day parallels to the New Testament Church organization, PRIESTHOOD offices, and missionary work have their counterparts in contemporary LDS beliefs, practices, and Church organization (*see* ORGANIZATION OF THE CHURCH IN NEW TESTAMENT TIMES).

BIBLICAL EMPHASIS WITHIN THE BOOK OF MORMON. Among Old Testament writings, those of Moses, Isaiah, and Malachi receive special attention from Latter-day Saints because of their prominence within the Book of Mormon. The teachings of Moses as found in the Pentateuch (an expanded portion of Genesis 1–6 being available also in the PEARL OF GREAT PRICE) provide the foundation for understanding the Mosaic DISPENSATION of the house of Israel. The Book of Mormon record, which originated with LEHI and with the people of Zarahemla (see MULEK), came mostly out of this Israelite setting. The record includes Adam and Eve and events in the Garden of Eden (e.g., 2 Ne. 2:15–25), and references to the flood at the time of Noah (e.g., Alma 10:22), to people divinely led to the Americas at the time of the Tower of Babel (Ether 1:3–5, 33), to events in the lives of the patriarchs (e.g., 2 Ne. 3:4–16), and to the calling, works, and words of Moses (e.g., 1 Ne. 17:23–31; 2 Ne. 3:16–17; *see also* LAW OF MOSES). The fifth chapter of 1 Nephi reviews the biblical records that Lehi's family brought out of Jerusalem (*see* BOOK OF MORMON PLATES AND RECORDS) and, along with 1 Nephi 17, highlights key biblical events, particularly the Israelite exodus from Egypt, although without the details found in the Pentateuch. The examples and teachings of Old Testament prophets, judges, and kings were also part of the biblical records of the community of Lehi. Because this group lived under the law of Moses (2 Ne. 25:24), Old Testament religious practices are continued in the Book of Mormon.

Fully one-third of the writings of Isaiah are found in the Book of Mormon, making Isaiah the most frequently quoted biblical book there. Twenty-two of the sixty-six chapters of Isaiah are quoted in whole or in part in the Book of Mormon (a total of 433 of Isaiah's 1,292 verses). Book of Mormon prophets and writers typically selected those chapters highlighting God's covenant relationships and his promises to Israel, the role and calling of the MESSIAH, and prophecies concerning the LAST DAYS. These themes are prevalent in contemporary LDS theology as well (A of F 3, 4, 9, 10).

Malachi's teachings in the Book of Mormon are important because the resurrected Jesus quoted them and thus emphasized them (cf. 3 Ne. 24–25; Mal. 3–4; D&C 2:1–3). Malachi's words concerning a messenger sent to prepare the way for Christ's second coming, the payment of tithes and offerings, and the latter-day mission of ELIJAH thus form another important nucleus of Old Testament teachings within LDS society.

Because the main Book of Mormon colony left Jerusalem approximately six hundred years before the beginning of the New Testament period, Book of Mormon writers did not have access to New Testament records. However, they had access to two important sources of doctrines paralleling some of the New Testament: the resurrected Christ and divine revelation. The resurrected Christ delivered to his hearers in the Americas a sermon essentially the same as the one he had delivered near the Sea of Galilee. He also gave important additions and clarifications that focus on him as the Redeemer and Lord, on the fulfillment of the law of Moses, and on the latter days (3 Ne. 11–18; *see also* BEATITUDES; SERMON ON THE MOUNT). In addition, he amplified teachings recorded in John 10, especially verse 16, about his role as the Good Shepherd of the scattered sheep of Israel (3 Ne. 15:12–24). MORMON'S important teachings about baptism and about faith, hope, and charity parallel New Testament teachings, especially those of Paul in 1 Corinthians 13.

IS THE BIBLE COMPLETE? Latter-day Saints revere the Bible as the word of God revealed to humankind. However, Joseph Smith recognized that translations do not reflect totally and exactly the original words and intentions of the ancient prophets and other biblical writers. Thus, in the WENTWORTH LETTER he wrote, "We believe the Bible to be the word of God as far as it is translated correctly" (A of F 8). Joseph Smith observed that "our latitude and longitude can be determined in the original Hebrew with far greater accuracy than in the English version. There is a grand distinction between the actual meaning of the prophets and the present translation" (*TPJS*, pp. 290–91). While Latter-day Saints accept rather explicitly what the Bible now says, they realize that more is to be accounted for than is available in the extant biblical record.

In addition to difficulties associated with translating from ancient to modern languages, other scriptures also declare that some parts of the original biblical text have been lost or corrupted (e.g., 1 Ne. 13:28–29; D&C 6:26–27; 93:6–18). Joseph Smith commented on the Bible's incompleteness: "It was apparent that many important points touching the salvation of men, had been taken from the Bible, or lost before it was compiled" (*TPJS*, pp. 10–11). He later said, "Much instruction has been given to man since the beginning which we do not possess now. . . . We have what we have, and the Bible contains what it does contain" (*TPJS*, p. 61). The Prophet Joseph further stated, "I believe the Bible as it read when it came from the pen of the original writers. Ignorant translators, careless transcribers, or designing and corrupt priests have committed many errors" (*TPJS*, p. 327). Thus, the elements of mistranslation, incompleteness, and other errors weaken the Bible; but the spirit of its messages still reveals enough of God's word to fulfill his appointed purposes. Joseph Smith summarized thus: "Through the kind providence of our Father a portion of His word which He delivered to His ancient saints, has fallen into our hands [and] is presented to us with a promise of a reward if obeyed, and with a penalty if disobeyed" (*TPJS*, p. 61). Latter-day Saints have continued to trust in the general accuracy of the biblical texts even though they know that that text may not always be correct. Thus, they study and revere the Bible, especially in the context of other scriptures and modern revelation, which have much to say about the Bible and how it is to be interpreted, and as they study they ponder and pray that they may receive inspiration from God and come to understand the Bible's messages as they need to be applied in their lives (cf. Moro. 10:3–5).

FIRST PRESIDENCY'S ENDORSEMENT OF BIBLE READING.   Each of the Presidents of the Church has encouraged Latter-day Saints to read the scriptures and to apply scriptural teachings in their lives, as the scriptures also admonish (cf. 2 Tim. 3:16; 1 Ne. 19:23). As a demonstration of this emphasis, in 1983, a year proclaimed as the "Year of the Bible" in the United States, the members of the FIRST PRESIDENCY of the Church issued a strong statement in support of Bible reading and application: "We commend to all people everywhere the daily reading, pondering and heeding of the divine truths of the Holy Bible." They also declared the Church's attitude toward the Bible by saying that "the Church of Jesus Christ of Latter-day Saints accepts the Holy Bible as essential to faith and doctrine" and that the Church is committed to Bible reading and scholarship as demonstrated by the publishing of an enhanced edition of the King James Version. "Moreover," they continued, "the Holy Bible is the textbook for adult, youth and children's classes throughout the Church each year."

In the same statement, the First Presidency highlighted the role and value of the Bible in the lives of individuals. They observed that when "read reverently and prayerfully, the Holy Bible becomes a priceless volume, converting the soul to righteousness. Principal among its virtues is the declaration that Jesus is the Christ, the Son of God, through whom eternal salvation may come to all." They continued with the promise that "as we read the scripture, we avail ourselves of the better part of this world's literature" and they encouraged all to "go to the fountain of truth, searching the scriptures, reading them in our homes, and teaching our families what the Lord has said through the inspired and inspiring passages of the Holy Bible" ("Statement of the First Presidency," p. 3).

The Latter-day Saint use of the Bible differs from the Judeo-Christian norm because it is not the sole LDS source of authority (*see* SCRIPTURE: AUTHORITY OF SCRIPTURE). The Bible is interpreted and understood by Latter-day Saints through four important means: (1) other LDS scriptures, which enrich and give perspective to an understanding of biblical teachings; (2) statements of modern prophets and apostles on the meaning of some biblical passages; (3) the Joseph Smith Translation of the Bible; and (4) personal revelation through the gift of the Holy Ghost enhancing the comprehension of the scriptures. Consequently, Latter-day Saints are not left without information about the meaning of many difficult passages that have divided the entire Christian world for two millennia.

The LDS perspective on the Bible is summarized well in the statement of the seventh Church president, Heber J. GRANT, who said, "All my life I have been finding additional evidences that the Bible is the Book of books, and that the Book of Mormon is the greatest witness for the truth of the Bible that has ever been published" (*IE* 39 [Nov. 1936]:660).

BIBLIOGRAPHY

Anderson, Richard L. *Understanding Paul.* Salt Lake City, 1983.

Arrington, Leonard. *Brigham Young: American Moses.* New York, 1985.

Barlow, Philip L. *Mormons and the Bible.* New York, 1990.

Harrison, Roland Kenneth. *Introduction to the Old Testament.* Grand Rapids, Mich., 1969.

Ludlow, Daniel H. *A Companion to Your Study of the Old Testament.* Salt Lake City, 1981.

Ludlow, Victor L. *Unlocking the Old Testament.* Salt Lake City, 1981.

———. *Isaiah: Prophet, Seer, and Poet.* Salt Lake City, 1982.

Matthews, Robert J. *A Bible! A Bible!.* Salt Lake City, Utah, 1990.

McConkie, Bruce R. *The Mortal Messiah.* Salt Lake City, 1979.

Nyman, Monte S., ed. *Isaiah and the Prophets.* Provo, Utah, 1984.

Reynolds, Noel B. "The Brass Plates Version of Genesis." In *By Study and Also by Faith,* ed. J. Lundquist and S. Ricks, Vol. 2, pp. 136–73. Salt Lake City, 1990.

Sperry, Sidney B. *Paul's Life and Letters.* Salt Lake City, 1955.

———. *The Voice of Israel's Prophets.* Salt Lake City, 1965.

———. *The Spirit of the Old Testament.* Salt Lake City, 1970.

"Statement of the First Presidency." *Church News,* Mar. 20, 1983, p. 3.

Talmage, James E. *Jesus the Christ.* Salt Lake City, 1915.

Welch, John W. *The Sermon at the Temple and the Sermon on the Mount.* Salt Lake City, 1990.

VICTOR L. LUDLOW

LDS BELIEF IN THE BIBLE

The Church believes the word of God contained in the Bible. It accepts the Bible "as the foremost of [the Church's] standard works, first among the books which have been proclaimed as . . . written guides in faith and doctrine. In the respect and sanctity with which the Latter-day Saints regard the Bible they are of like profession with Christian denominations in general" (*AF,* 1966 ed., p. 236).

Latter-day Saints value the Bible for many reasons. The Bible presents the revelations of God in several DISPENSATIONS or eras, each headed by prophets. They also read and follow the Bible for the instructional and spiritual value of the events it describes. While some of the Old Testament describes the law of Moses that Latter-day Saints believe was fulfilled with the atonement of Christ (3 Ne. 9:17), nevertheless the Old Testament stories, commandments, ordinances, proverbs, and prophetic writings still express the basic patterns of God's will toward his children and how they should act toward him.

Latter-day Saints revere the New Testament for its account of the birth, ministry, atonement, and resurrection of the Savior, Jesus Christ. The teachings of Jesus in the New Testament comprise the core of LDS doctrine, and their preeminence is evidenced by their frequent appearance in other LDS STANDARD WORKS accepted as scripture and in LDS speaking and writing.

The writings of the New Testament apostles are accepted and appreciated for their doctrine and wise and inspired counsel and for documenting the apostolic challenge of proclaiming the gospel, adhering to the original teachings of Christ, establishing the unity of the faith, and promoting the righteousness of believers in a rapidly growing Church. Latter-day Saints also find references in several letters of the early apostles of the falling away (*see* APOSTASY) that necessitated the RESTORATION, alerting the faithful to remain fervent and active in the faith and to stay true to the love of Jesus Christ.

While Latter-day Saints devoutly regard the Bible, they do not consider it the sole authoritative source of religious instruction and personal guidance. They also study accounts of God's dealings with other ancient peoples such as those found in the Book of Mormon along with the teachings of the Prophet Joseph SMITH and the latter-day prophets and apostles (*see* DOCTRINE AND COVENANTS; GENERAL AUTHORITIES; JOSEPH SMITH TRANSLATION OF THE BIBLE [JST]; PEARL OF GREAT PRICE). Latter-day Saints consider personal revelation the individual's ultimate source for understanding scripture and knowing God's will.

Viewed as being harmonious with each other, all these sources enhance and clarify one another, and aid modern readers in correctly comprehending and translating these texts.

Latter-day Saints believe all that God has revealed. They seek to know and do the word of God wherever it has been made known in truth and authority. They believe that salvation is in Jesus Christ and not in any combination of words or books. They believe in God and in his son Jesus Christ, whose words and ways can be known through a lifetime of SCRIPTURE STUDY, service, and prayer, and by personal revelation through the power of the Holy Ghost.

BIBLIOGRAPHY

Matthews, Robert J. *A Bible! A Bible!* Salt Lake City, 1990.

PAUL HEDENGREN

KING JAMES VERSION

In various lands where The Church of Jesus Christ of Latter-day Saints has been established, it uses a translation of the Bible in the local language. In English-speaking areas, the Church uses the King James (or Authorized) Version (KJV), mainly because it was the basic English text used by the Prophet Joseph Smith and because subsequent Church leaders have approved its use. The Church does not claim that the KJV is perfect, but it is currently the preferred English version and was used in the Church's 1979 edition and later printings of the Bible.

The books of the Bible were originally written in Hebrew, Aramaic, or Greek. No original biblical manuscripts exist today, but they were copied and translated into many languages in antiquity. Many early papyri and parchments have survived. From those records, numerous modern translations have been made.

From 1604 to 1611, some fifty-four scholars worked to produce the KJV of the Bible. This was not the first English translation. In 1382, John Wycliffe translated the Bible from the Latin Vulgate; a revised edition was published in 1388. From 1523 to 1530, William Tyndale translated the Pentateuch from Hebrew and the New Testament from Greek. Still later in the 1500s, other translations appeared, including the Protestant Geneva Bible in 1560 and the Bishops' Bible in 1568. The former became popular with the laity and the latter with Protestant bishops. The Catholic Rheims-Douai Bible was finished in 1609 (1582 New Testament, 1609 Old Testament), based on the Latin Vulgate.

In an attempt to heal differences between Anglicans and Puritans, King James I appointed a body of scholars to produce a version of the Bible to be authorized for use in the English churches. They used the best texts available to them, mainly the "Received Text of the New Testament in the multilanguage ("polyglot") editions, presenting the Old and New Testaments in Hebrew and Greek respectively, and other languages. The long and respected line of English Bibles was also diligently compared and used.

The resulting King James Version was published in 1611. Various editions of the KJV appeared throughout the 1600s, which resulted in many printing inaccuracies. The Cambridge (1762) and Oxford (1769) editions featured a revised text, updated spelling, corrected punctuation, increased italics, and changed marginal notes.

Many other English versions have appeared, especially in light of the discovery of additional early manuscripts, beginning with Constantin von Tischendorf's first find at St. Catherine's Monastery in the Sinai peninsula in 1844. These translations have generally endeavored to render the ancient texts into contemporary usage while reflecting the form of the oldest available manuscripts as much as possible.

Latter-day Saints have not made extensive use of these other translations. Many feel that popularization tends to dilute the sacred nature of the Bible. They also find the ancient textual variants to be relatively insignificant, usually not changing the important messages of the Bible, most of which, in any event, are corroborated elsewhere in LDS scripture.

Although the KJV was Joseph Smith's English Bible, he did not regard it as a perfect or official translation; this is why he studied Hebrew and undertook the task of producing an inspired revision of the scriptures. He commented that he preferred some aspects of the Martin Luther translation (*HC* 6:307, 364), and several other nineteenth-century Church leaders stressed the need for greater accuracy and truth in Bible translations.

Twentieth-century Church leaders have given a variety of reasons for the continued use of the KJV: it was the common translation in use in the English-speaking world at the time of the Restoration; its language prevails in all the STANDARD WORKS; a large number of passages in the Book of Mormon, which parallel the Bible, were translated into the English style of the KJV; the JOSEPH SMITH TRANSLATION OF THE BIBLE (JST) was based on the KJV, with 90 percent of the verses unchanged. All latter-day prophets have used the KJV, and using the KJV in all Church publications has made it possible to standardize annotations and indices.

The KJV is viewed by many as a masterpiece of English literature. It has been called "the noblest monument of English prose," and it is certainly the most influential; its translators "showed great sensitivity," and the result was "destined for extraordinary influence and acclaim" (Speiser, pp. lxxiii–iv). H. L. Mencken praised it as "probably the most beautiful piece of writing in all the literature of the world" (Paine, p. viii).

The KJV is a relatively conservative translation. This is generally a strength, although at times it produces obscure renderings. Moreover, some of its diction is now archaic and ungrammatical in current usage, and it is not consistent in the spelling of names in the Old and New Testaments (for example, Isaiah/Esaias and Elijah/Elias). Identical words in the synoptic Gospels are sometimes translated differently, and some misprints were never corrected (for instance, in Matt. 23:24, "strain *at* a gnat" should have been rendered "strain *out* a gnat").

After studying many modern English translations, however, President J. Reuben Clark, Jr., a counselor in the First Presidency, said in 1956 that the KJV was "the best version of any yet produced" (Clark, p. 33). For example, he felt that the KJV translators clearly portrayed Jesus as the promised Messiah and as the Son of God, and accepted the gift of prophecy, the reality of miracles, and the uniqueness of the love of Christ; whereas modern translations have tended to promote naturalistic explanations for divine action, preferred the word "sign" instead of "miracle," and used "love" in place of "charity," and "appoint" instead of "ordain." His views have been influential among most Latter-day Saints. Not all alternative translations, of course, suffer from the problems identified by President Clark.

BIBLIOGRAPHY

Barlow, Philip L. *Mormons and the Bible*, pp. 132–62. New York, 1990.

Bruce, F. F. *History of the Bible in English*, 3rd ed. New York, 1978.

Clark, J. Reuben, Jr. *Why the King James Version*. Salt Lake City, 1956.

Daiches, David. *The King James Version of the English Bible*. Chicago, 1941.

Metzger, Bruce M. *The Text of the New Testament*. New York, 1968.

Paine, G. *The Learned Men*, p. viii. New York, 1959.

Speiser, E. *Genesis*, pp. lxiii–iv. Garden City, N.Y., 1964.

D. KELLY OGDEN

LDS PUBLICATION OF THE BIBLE

An edition of the King James Version of the Bible with new Bible study aids was published by The Church of Jesus Christ of Latter-day Saints in 1979, culminating seven years' work by Church leaders and scholars. The goals were to make Bible study more meaningful for Church members by supplying maps, charts, definitions, headnotes, footnotes, and cross-references to all of the four STANDARD WORKS, and also to provide a single Bible edition for use in the Church curriculum.

This project began in 1972, about the time the study of the scriptures became the primary goal for the adult curriculum of the Church. Previously Church teachers had relied mainly on lesson manuals prepared by individuals or committees. The work was commissioned by the FIRST PRESIDENCY, who appointed a Bible Aids committee to oversee the project. This committee (later called the Scriptures Publications Committee) consisted initially of Thomas S. Monson, Boyd K. Packer, and Marvin J. Ashton of the QUORUM OF THE TWELVE APOSTLES. Ashton was later given another assignment and Bruce R. McConkie was appointed.

The committee called scholars, editors, and publication specialists from BRIGHAM YOUNG UNIVERSITY, the CHURCH EDUCATIONAL SYSTEM, and DESERET BOOK COMPANY to prepare Latter-day Saint-oriented aids to help readers better understand the King James text. Early in the project the First Presidency determined that the King James text would be used without change. This text of the Bible, along with the Book of Mormon, the Doctrine and Covenants and the Pearl of Great Price, was entered into a computer data base. Each verse was reviewed, and key topics and terms identified. Computer printouts were generated comprising long lists of possible cross-references from which useful citations were then selected. Emphasis was given to references from the Book of Mormon, Doctrine and Covenants, and Pearl of Great Price that helped clarify Bible passages along with abundant interbiblical cross-references. These now appear in the footnotes and in the TOPICAL GUIDE (an extensive subject index and modified concordance). A BIBLE DICTIONARY, 24 pages of full-color maps, and a complete gazetteer were included. The Bible Dictionary provides concise explanations of biblical items and often adds points of interest to Latter-day Saints. Brief explanations of some words or phrases from Hebrew and Greek were also included as footnotes, along with about 600 passages from the JOSEPH SMITH TRANSLATION OF THE BIBLE (JST). Unique summaries at the beginning of each chapter in this edition of the King James Bible suggest the doctrinal and historical content of each chapter from an LDS point of view.

The footnote system organizes all the aids available in this publication of the Bible. Some earlier Bible editions place cross-references in a center column on the page, but this format limits the amount of material that can be included. A flexible system of three footnote columns at the bottom of each page was designed, with "callout" letters (*a*, *b*, *c*, etc.) allocated separately for each verse placed in the text as needed. Included in the footnotes are cross-references to other scriptures, the Topical Guide, and the Bible Dictionary; also explanatory Greek and Hebrew idioms and other clarifying information.

Once the scholarly and editorial work was completed in early 1978, typesetting began. Cambridge University Press in Cambridge, England, was selected as typesetter, because that press, one of the early printers of the King James Version after it was first issued in 1611, has been continuously involved in Bible publications since the late 1500s. Its expert staff proved invaluable to Church members who worked with them in editing the copy for typesetting and preparing the final pages. All the type was set in Monotype hot metal. Each page was prepared so that every footnote was contained on the same page as the verse to which it pertained. To serve the needs of programs in the Church Educational System, a self-imposed delivery deadline of September 1979 for the first copies of the Bible loomed over those involved in this production. The formidable task of typesetting and paginating 2,423 pages of complex text was completed in May 1979 after fifteen months of intense effort.

Printing and binding were first contracted with University Press and Publishers Book Bindery of Winchester, Massachusetts, who subcontracted some of the work to National Bible Press in Philadelphia, Pennsylvania. What at first seemed impossible production deadlines all came together and the first copies were delivered August 8, 1979. Many Latter-day Saints acknowledged the hand of God at work in this monumental publication.

This edition of the King James Version of the Bible has stimulated further interest in Bible study throughout the Church. It has extended and deepened members' understanding of and appreciation for the Bible as the word of God. It has also demonstrated that all the Latter-day Saint books of sacred scripture are correlated in many mutually supportive and enriching ways.

BIBLIOGRAPHY

Anderson, Lavina Fielding. "Church Publishes First LDS Edition of the Bible." *Ensign* 9 (Oct. 1979):8–18.

Matthews, Robert J. "The New Publications of the Standard Works—1979, 1981." *BYU Studies* 22 (Fall 1982):387–424.

Mortimer, William James. "The Coming Forth of the LDS Editions of Scripture." *Ensign* 13 (Aug. 1983):35–41.

Packer, Boyd K. "Scriptures." *Ensign* 12 (Nov. 1982):51–53.

WILLIAM JAMES MORTIMER

BIBLE, LDS

[The Church of Jesus Christ of Latter-day Saints reveres the Bible as the word of God given through ancient prophets and apostles, though it recognizes that the current text is not identical with the original. The Church has consistently used the King James Version (KJV) for formal classes, missionary work, and personal study among English-speaking peoples, utilizing KJV editions issued by the major Bible publishing houses. However, because latter-day revelation offers insight, interpretation, and supplemental material to thousands of biblical passages and in order to make the message of the Bible more readily accessible to LDS readers, the Church published in 1979 an edition of the KJV with multiple study helps. These include chapter headings, cross-references to other LDS scriptural works, explanatory footnotes, clarification of Greek and Hebrew terms and idioms, a subject-matter guide, a dictionary, maps, and excerpts from an inspired translation of the Bible by the Prophet Joseph Smith.

Articles directly related to this subject are Bible: LDS Publication of the Bible; Bible Dictionary; Joseph Smith Translation of the Bible (JST); *and* Topical Guide. *Other relevant articles are* Bible: LDS Belief in the Bible; Bible: King James Version; Scripture; Scripture Study; Standard Works.]

BIBLE DICTIONARY

In 1979 The Church of Jesus Christ of Latter-day Saints published its own edition of the King James Version of the Bible with many reader's aids, including a new Bible dictionary. This dictionary contains much information relevant to the Bible that is unique to Mormonism. Bible dictionaries have traditionally been geographic and cultural word books, dating back to works such as Langenstein's *Vocabularius Bibliae* (1476) and Heyden's *Biblisches Namen Buch* (1567), which surveyed biblical history and archaeology then known. The increase in biblical scholarship since World War II has seen both a proliferation of linguistic materials and changes in dictionaries to include doctrinal concepts as well as people and places. Many denominations have published Bible dictionaries each reflecting a unique theological stance.

Cambridge University Press granted the Church permission to use its Bible dictionary as a base, to be amended as needed. It was changed in three major ways: 1. Entries considered to be in error or of insufficient value were omitted. 2. Entries that were incomplete, because they were based on the Bible alone, were complemented by information from the BOOK OF MORMON, the DOCTRINE AND COVENANTS, the PEARL OF GREAT PRICE, and the teachings of the Prophet Joseph SMITH. This affected such entries as the FALL, ZION, URIM AND THUMMIM, ADAM, SACRIFICE, CIRCUMCISION, and TEMPLE. 3. New entries were added, including discussions on such matters as DISPENSATION OF THE FULNESS OF TIMES, AARONIC PRIESTHOOD, MELCHIZEDEK PRIESTHOOD, writing, and the family.

The dictionary provides new information in the light of such discoveries as the Dead Sea Scrolls, and explains language and cultural items, including several English words used in the Bible whose meanings have changed. Another major help is a harmony of the events in the life of Christ that includes not only the four Gospels but also 3 Nephi in the Book of Mormon and other references to latter-day REVELATION. The dictionary also contains an eleven-page world history chart of the major events that pertain to the Old and New Testaments and a chart of the main New Testament quotations that have Old Testament origins. The work totals 196 pages with 1,285 entries. It is not a declaration of the official position of the Church, but represents LDS perspectives as related to the products of ongoing scholarship that may be modified by further discovery and by future revelation.

BIBLIOGRAPHY

Brewster, Hoyt W., Jr. "Discovering the LDS Editions of Scripture." *Ensign* 13 (Oct. 1983):55–58.

Matthews, Robert J. "The New Publications of the Standard Works—1979, 1981." *BYU Studies* 22 (Fall 1982):387–424.

GARY P. GILLUM

BIBLE SCHOLARSHIP

Latter-day Saints recognize Bible scholarship and intellectual study of the biblical text. Joseph Smith and his associates studied Greek and Hebrew and taught that religious knowledge is to be obtained by study as well as by faith (D&C 88:118). However, Latter-day Saints prefer to use Bible scholarship rather than be driven or controlled by it.

The Prophet Joseph Smith suggested certain broad parameters for any LDS critical study of the Bible: "We believe the Bible to be the word of God as far as it is translated correctly; we also believe the Book of Mormon to be the word of God" (A of F 8). Because Latter-day Saints prefer PROPHETS to scholars as spiritual guides, and the inspiration of SCRIPTURE and the Holy Ghost to the reasoning of secondary texts, Bible scholarship plays a smaller role in LDS spirituality than it does in some denominations.

A fundamental operating principle of "revealed" religions is that all truth cannot be completely discovered through human reason alone. Without God's aid, no one can obtain the vital data, proper perspectives, and interpretive keys for knowing him (*see* REASON AND REVELATION). Because Latter-day Saints believe that their religion is revealed through living prophets of God, they subordinate human reason to revealed truth.

In this latter connection, Latter-day Saints show some affinities with contemporary conservative Roman Catholic and evangelical Bible scholarship. They accept and use most objective results of Bible scholarship, such as linguistics, history, and archaeology, while rejecting many of the discipline's naturalistic assumptions and its more subjective methods and theories. In those instances where Bible scholarship and revealed religion conflict, Latter-day Saints hold to interpretations of the Bible that appear in the other LDS scriptures and in the teachings of latter-day prophets.

These observations suggest three basic operating principles for Bible scholarship among Latter-day Saints:

1. Approaches to the Bible must accept divine inspiration and revelation in the original biblical text: it presents the word of God and is not a merely human production. Therefore, any critical methodology that implicitly or explicitly ignores or denies the significant involvement of God in the biblical text is rejected. With minor exceptions, such as the Song of Solomon, which Joseph Smith judged not to be inspired (cf. *IE* 18 [Mar. 1915]:389), the text is not to be treated in an ultimately naturalistic manner. God's participation is seen to be significant both in the events them-

selves and in the process of their being recorded. His activity is thus one of the effects to be reckoned with in interpreting the events and in understanding the texts that record them.

2. Despite divine inspiration, the biblical text is not uninfluenced by human language and not immune to negative influences from its human environment, and there is no guarantee that the revelations given to ancient prophets have been perfectly preserved (cf. 1 Ne. 13:20–27). Thus, critical study of the Bible is warranted to help allow for, and suggest corrections of, human errors of formulation, transmission, translation, and interpretation of the ancient records.

3. Such critical scholarship, in addition to recognizing the divine origins of the Bible, must in its conclusions take account of the teachings of the BOOK OF MORMON and the other revelations to modern prophets included in the DOCTRINE AND COVENANTS and the PEARL OF GREAT PRICE, since for Latter-day Saints such sources not only have priority over revelations recorded in antiquity (cf. D&C 5:10) but also aid in interpreting the biblical text.

Latter-day Saints insist on objective hermeneutics, that is, they maintain that the biblical text has a specific, objective meaning and that the intent of the original author is both important and largely recoverable. For this reason, LDS scholars, like other conservatives, have tended toward the more objective tools of Bible scholarship, such as linguistics, history, and archaeology—recognizing that these tools themselves have to be evaluated critically—and have generally avoided the more subjective methods of literary criticism.

The most influential LDS Bible commentators include James E. Talmage, Bruce R. McConkie, Sidney B. Sperry, and Hugh W. Nibley, though Talmage's work was completed prior to many important discoveries, and McConkie's work is concerned less with critical exegesis than with understanding the New Testament within the overall body of LDS doctrine.

BIBLIOGRAPHY

Anderson, Richard L. *Understanding Paul.* Salt Lake City, 1983.

McConkie, Bruce R. *Doctrinal New Testament Commentary,* 3 vols. Salt Lake City, 1965–1973.

Nibley, Hugh W. *Collected Works of Hugh Nibley.* Salt Lake City, 1986–.

Sperry, Sidney B. *Paul's Life and Letters.* Salt Lake City, 1955.

———. *The Voice of Israel's Prophets.* Salt Lake City, 1961.

———. *The Spirit of the Old Testament.* Salt Lake City, 1970.

Talmage, James E. *Jesus the Christ.* Salt Lake City, 1915.

STEPHEN E. ROBINSON

BIOGRAPHY AND AUTOBIOGRAPHY

From the earliest decades members of the Church have adhered to the Puritan tradition of writing spiritual autobiographies, often for reasons similar to those of their forebears, namely, to express their faith and to justify their actions in the light of that faith. New models and counsel also influenced the Latter-day Saints in this regard: the Book of Mormon, one of the first documents of the Church, begins autobiographically—"I, Nephi, having been born of goodly parents . . ." (1 Ne. 1:1)—and it contains long sections of both biography and autobiography. A version of Joseph SMITH's autobiography is canonized in the PEARL OF GREAT PRICE (*see* JOSEPH SMITH—HISTORY), and the Doctrine and Covenants injunction that "a record [be] kept among you" (D&C 21:1) has been interpreted in practice to apply to Latter-day Saints individually as well as institutionally.

In 1977 the annotated *Guide to Mormon Diaries and Autobiographies* listed nearly 3,000 such documents published or available in various libraries and archives. About half are retrospective autobiographies, as distinguished from journals of daily entries. As a result of the general LDS interest in FAMILY HISTORY, encouraged especially by President Spencer W. KIMBALL, that number multiplied in the 1980s. In addition, countless personal accounts and family histories remain in family possession throughout the Church.

The variety of Mormon autobiographies is vast, ranging "from conscious virtuosity to self-conscious artifice, from unconscious brilliance to dull-minded monotony" (Lambert, p. 69). In the classic *Autobiography of Parley Parker Pratt* (1874), Pratt artistically portrays himself variously as mystic, recluse, proselyte, jokester, preacher, acolyte, and apostle, each presented in form and language suited to the posture. In contrast, the equally well-known *A Mormon Mother: An Autobiography*, by Annie Clark Tanner, is less artful but more introspective, revealing a complexity of unresolved questions in its author. Mary Goble Pay's short autobiography (in Cracroft and Lambert, pp. 145–53) well represents the life-writing of a comparatively unlettered Latter-day Saint. In stark simplicity and with convincing sincerity, it tells her story as if to a child.

Biography is likewise a frequent LDS literary form (*see* LITERATURE, MORMON WRITERS OF: PERSONAL ESSAYS). Drawing on the literary tradition of the previous three centuries, early LDS biographers took as models the "life and times" forms, depicting the public achievements of Church leaders. Usually the works reflected the double value placed on Latter-day Saint individuality and community by merging the life of the individual with the history of the movement. Often didactic, these works were defensive in tone, tending to conceal as much as they revealed about the character and experience of the subject. Sensitive facts were either omitted or passed over lightly: a man's excommunication, his plural wives, an altercation with a fellow churchman, or an unsuccessful venture. Sometimes, of course, such facts were already known; in that case, the biographer's role often became one of explaining them away.

A half-century after Lytton Strachey, the eminent Victorian biography writer, altered the fashion of biography by insisting on telling the whole truth about his subjects, Latter-day Saint writers began to include more in their accounts about the private lives of Church leaders. Marion G. Romney's much-quoted directive, printed in the foreword of a jointly authored biography of J. Reuben Clark, Jr. (Fox, 1980; Quinn, 1983), states that "any biographer of President Clark must write the truth about him; to tell more than or less than the truth would violate a governing principle of his life." Romney, a counselor in the FIRST PRESIDENCY, advised the authors not to produce "a mere collection of uplifting experiences" or "a detailed defense of his beliefs." He required of them "a biography of the man himself, as he was, written with the same kind of courage, honesty, and frankness that J. Reuben Clark himself would have shown," including "his decisions and indecisions, sorrows and joys, regrets and aspirations, reverses and accomplishments" (Fox, p. xi). That statement, exemplified in the biography of Spencer W. KIMBALL (Kimball and Kimball, 1977), indicates a turn of tide in Mormon biography, wherein the bland, impeccably moral, and defensive biographies were replaced by studies reflecting flesh-and-blood reality.

Many have attempted to write the life of the Prophet Joseph Smith. His mother, Lucy Mack SMITH, dictated the first serious study, *Biographical Sketches of Joseph Smith the Prophet* (1853), but it was as much her own autobiography as her son's biography. On both counts, the book has held up as accurate source material, though not as a finished prose study. Subsequent Joseph Smith biographies by George Q. Cannon (1888), John Henry Evans (1933), Preston Nibley (1944), Leon Hartshorn (1970), and Francis M. Gibbons (1977), while appropriate to LDS audiences of the time, do not satisfy the recent taste for a complete embodiment of the subject.

In a more scholarly mode, though less than thorough or accurate in its use of sources, was Fawn M. Brodie's *No Man Knows My History* (1945). Its appearance caused a furor among Latter-day Saints and issued a challenge to answering scholars, which contributed to historians paying increased attention to serious research in their writing of Church history. An alternative to Brodie is Donna Hill's *Joseph Smith, the First Mormon* (1977), and her brother Marvin's review "Secular or Sectarian History? A Critique of *No Man Knows My History*" (1974) in *Church History*.

None, however, has totally succeeded in vivifying Mormonism's founder. Richard L. Bushman's *Joseph Smith and the Beginnings of Mormonism* comes close, but it deals only with the first years of the Prophet's life. Nevertheless, it is a promising re-creation, striving to see people and events as the participants would have understood them. With the commencement of Dean Jessee's publication of the *Papers of Joseph Smith* in 1989, it became possible for biographers to be even more rigorous and complete in their presentation of the full man in all his complexity.

With the growing interest in social history has come an increase in biographies of members of the Church other than General Authorities. People such as those covered in Leonard Arrington and Davis Bitton's *Saints Without Halos: The Human Side of Mormon History* and Donald Q. Cannon and David J. Whittaker's *Supporting Saints: Life Stories of Nineteenth-Century Mormons* are being featured in separate biographical volumes. Juanita Brooks's *John D. Lee* (rev. ed., 1972), for many years the exemplar of Mormon biography, and Leonard Arrington's *From Quaker to Latter-day Saint: Bishop Edwin D. Woolley* (1976) demonstrate how universally interesting the drama of life can be when it is well written.

Latter-day Saint women have seldom been subjects of full-length biographies. The 1984 Newell-Avery study of Emma Hale SMITH stands alone as a full-length treatment of a woman leader, but biographies of Eliza R. SNOW and Emmeline B. WELLS are in progress. Of a lay Mormon woman, one biography of significance has been published, that of historian Juanita Brooks by Levi Peterson (1988).

A few autobiographical accounts of Latter-day Saint women are already available. Besides *A Mormon Mother*, there are the self-told lives of such people as Ellis R. Shipp, Mary Jane Mount Tanner, Sarah Studevant Leavitt, and Aurelia Spencer ROGERS, though it must be recognized that few of these accounts were written for distribution beyond the author's family. Another nineteenth-century woman, Fanny Stenhouse, used the autobiographical mode to produce her *Exposé of Polygamy in Utah* (1872), later revised and widely published as *Tell It All* (1874).

Modern female novelists such as Virginia Sorenson, author of *Where Nothing Is Long Ago* (1963), and Rodello Hunter, author of *Daughter of Zion* (1972), have published autobiographical material combined with some of the trappings of fiction. Several handwritten lives, such as that of Martha Cragun Cox, and others published to limited audiences, such as that of Louisa Barnes Pratt and Mary Ann Weston Maughan, remain largely untapped in obscure archives.

To encourage the writing of Latter-day Saint biographies, the David Woolley and Beatrice Cannon Evans family endowed a prize that has been awarded annually since 1983. It is now administered by the Mountain West Center for Regional Studies at Utah State University. Winners of that award are marked with an asterisk in the following selected main LDS biographies: Allen, James B. *Trials of Discipleship: The Story of William Clayton, A Mormon*. Urbana, Ill., 1987*; Arrington, Leonard J. *Brigham Young: American Moses*. New York, 1985*; Brodie, Fawn M. *No Man Knows My History: The Life of Joseph Smith, the Mormon Prophet*, 2nd rev. ed. New York, 1971; Brooks, Juanita. *John D. Lee: Zealot, Pioneer Builder, Scapegoat*, rev. ed. Glendale, Calif., 1985; Bushman, Richard. *Joseph Smith and the Beginnings of Mormonism*. Urbana, Ill., 1984*; Fox, Frank W. *J. Reuben Clark: The Public Years*. Provo, Utah, 1980; Hill, Donna. *Joseph Smith: The First Mormon*. New York, 1977; Hoopes, David S., and Roy H. Hoopes. *The Making of a Mormon Apostle: The Story of Rudger Clawson*. Lanham, Maryland, 1990; Kimball, Edward L., and Andrew E. Kimball, Jr. *Spencer W. Kimball: Twelfth President of* *the Church of Jesus Christ of Latter-day Saints*. Salt Lake City, 1977; Kimball, Stanley B. *Heber C. Kimball: Mormon Patriarch and Pioneer*. Urbana, Ill., 1981; Larson, Andrew Karl. *Erastus Snow: The Life of a Missionary and Pioneer for the Early Mormon Church*. Salt Lake City, 1971; Launius, Roger D. *Joseph Smith III: Pragmatic Prophet*. Urbana, Ill., 1988*; Lyon, T. Edgar, Jr. *John Lyon: The Life of a Pioneer Poet*. Provo, Utah, 1989; Madsen, Truman G. *Defender of the Faith: The B. H. Roberts Story*. Salt Lake City, 1980; Merrill, Milton R. *Reed Smoot: Apostle in Politics*. Logan, Utah, 1989; Newell, Linda King, and Valeen Tippetts Avery. *Mormon Enigma: Emma Hale Smith*. New York, 1984*; Peterson, Levi S. *Juanita Brooks: Mormon Woman Historian*. Salt Lake City, 1988*; Quinn, D. Michael. *J. Reuben Clark: The Church Years*. Provo, Utah, 1983; Schindler, Harold. *Orrin Porter Rockwell: Man of God, Son of Thunder*, 2nd ed. Salt Lake City, 1966; Yarn, David H. *Young Reuben*. Provo, Utah, 1973.

BIBLIOGRAPHY

Allen, James B. "Writing Mormon Biographies." In *World Conference on Records: Preserving Our Heritage*, ser. 116, pp. 1–15. Salt Lake City, 1980.

Bitton, Davis. *Guide to Mormon Diaries and Autobiographies*. Provo, Utah, 1977.

———. "Mormon Biography." *Biography: An Interdisciplinary Quarterly* 4 (Winter 1981):1–16.

Cracroft, Richard, and Neal Lambert, eds. *A Believing People*, pp. 145–53. Provo, Utah, 1974.

Lambert, Neal. "The Representation of Reality in Nineteenth-Century Mormon Autobiography." *Dialogue* 11 (Summer 1978):63–74.

Sondrup, Steven P. "Literary Dimensions of Mormon Autobiography." *Dialogue* 11 (Summer 1978):75–80.

Walker, Ronald W. "The Challenge and Craft of Mormon Biography." *BYU Studies* 22 (Spring 1982):179–92.

Whittaker, David J. "The Heritage and Tasks of Mormon Biography." In *Supporting Saints*, ed. D. Cannon and D. Whittaker, pp. 1–16. Salt Lake City, 1985.

MAUREEN URSENBACH BEECHER

BIRTH

The Church of Jesus Christ of Latter-day Saints teaches that every person experiences a series of "births." All were born as spirit children of God in a PREMORTAL LIFE. Second, these individual spirit children received a mortal, physical body when they were born on earth. Third, those who accept and live the GOSPEL OF JESUS CHRIST go through a process of being born again in a spiritual sense (see BORN OF GOD). Although these births are real, they do not in any way constitute any type of REINCARNATION.

Men and women become conscious of their divine origin and birthright when they recognize their relationship with the Supreme Being, address him as Father, and become aware that in scripture God addresses mankind as his children (1 Jn. 3:1–2; Matt. 6:9).

In the COUNCIL IN HEAVEN, God the Father offered his spirit children the opportunity to progress toward becoming like he is by leaving his presence and being born on earth in a mortal, physical body and learning to live by faith (Abr. 3:22–28). Mortal birth is the event by which one's SPIRIT BODY is temporarily joined with a mortal tabernacle begotten by earthly parents. The exact time when the premortal spirit enters the unborn physical tabernacle is not specified in divine revelation. Through the FALL OF ADAM, and birth into mortality, mankind becomes subject to two deaths: the physical or temporal death, which is a death of the body, and the spiritual death, which is being shut out of God's presence (see LIFE AND DEATH; PLAN OF SALVATION).

Through the ATONEMENT of Jesus Christ all people are given opportunity to be born again in a spiritual sense as his sons and daughters so as to return to God's presence as his spiritually begotten children (Mosiah 5:7–9; Alma 5:14). The process of being born of the spirit begins when one is baptized and receives the GIFT OF THE HOLY GHOST. Since the HOLY GHOST is a member of the GODHEAD, the effects of the spiritual death, or separation between man and God, is lessened individually when one is truly born of the Spirit.

Birth as spirit beings and birth as mortals have already occurred to all of mankind on the earth. The spiritual rebirth necessary for salvation in the presence of God requires considerable additional individual effort through obedience to the gospel of Jesus Christ.

BIBLIOGRAPHY

Clark, J. Reuben, Jr. *Man—God's Greatest Miracle.* Salt Lake City, 1956.

Smith, Joseph Fielding. *Man, His Origin and Destiny,* p. 354. Salt Lake City, 1954.

HELEN LANCE CHRISTIANSON

BIRTH, SPIRITUAL

See: Born of God; Premortal Life

BIRTH CONTROL

The GENERAL HANDBOOK OF INSTRUCTIONS for Church leaders has the following instructions concerning birth control: "Husbands must be considerate of their wives, who have a great responsibility not only for bearing children but also for caring for them through childhood. . . . Married couples should seek inspiration from the Lord in meeting their marital challenges and rearing their children according to the teachings of the gospel" (*General Handbook,* 11-4).

Interpretation of these general instructions is left to the AGENCY of Church members. One of the basic teachings of the Church, however, is that spirit children of God come to earth to obtain a physical body, to grow, and to be tested. In that process, adults should marry and provide temporal bodies for those spirit children. For Latter-day Saints, it is a blessing, a joy, and also an obligation to bear children and to raise a family.

One of the cornerstones of the gospel is agency or choice. Latter-day Saints believe that everyone will be held responsible for the choices they make. Many decisions involve the application of principles where precise instructions are not given in the *General Handbook of Instructions* or in the scriptures. The exercise of individual agency is therefore required, and Latter-day Saints believe that personal growth results from weighing the alternatives, studying matters carefully, counseling with appropriate Church leaders, and then seeking inspiration from the Lord before making a decision.

Church members are taught to study the question of family planning, including such important aspects as the physical and mental health of the mother and father and their capacity to provide the basic necessities of life. If, for personal reasons, a couple prayerfully decides that having another child immediately is unwise, birth control may be appropriate. Abstinence, of course, is a form of contraception. Like any other method, however, it has its side effects, some of which may be harmful to the marriage relationship.

Prophets past and present have never stipulated that bearing children was the sole function of the marriage relationship. They have taught that physical intimacy is a strong force in expressing and strengthening the love bond in marriage, enhancing and reinforcing marital unity.

Decisions regarding the number and spacing of children are to be made by husband and wife together, in righteousness, and through empathetic communication, and with prayer for the Lord's inspiration. Latter-day Saints believe that persons are accountable not only for what they do but for why they do it. Thus, regarding family size and attendant questions, members should desire to multiply and replenish the earth as the Lord has commanded. In that process, God intends that his children use the agency that he has given them in charting a wise course for themselves and their families.

BIBLIOGRAPHY

The Church of Jesus Christ of Latter-day Saints. *General Handbook of Instructions*, 11-4. Salt Lake City, 1989.

"I Have a Question." *Ensign* 9 (Aug. 1979):23–24.

HOMER S. ELLSWORTH

BIRTH RATES

See: Vital Statistics

BISHOP

A bishop is the ecclesiastical leader of a Latter-day Saint congregation or WARD, and has comprehensive pastoral and administrative responsibility at that level. This differs from other Christian churches in which bishops administer large geographical areas involving a number of congregations.

The word "bishop" comes from the Greek word *episkopos*, meaning "overseer." He is the pastor or shepherd, and is charged with the care of his flock. In the apostolic period, PAUL wrote to the bishops in Philippi (Phil. 1:1), and other letters speak of the bishop's duties and of his sacred role in caring for the Church of God (1 Tim. 3:1–7; Titus 1:7–9).

The bishop's office is a complex priesthood calling. The bishop is president of the ward's AARONIC PRIESTHOOD holders and is responsible for all their activities. He is also an ordained HIGH PRIEST in the MELCHIZEDEK PRIESTHOOD and is the presiding high priest in the ward, responsible

for all ward activities and functions (D&C 107:15–17). As the common judge and the presiding high priest, he determines the worthiness of all members of his ward and directs the performance of sacred ordinances (D&C 107:68–76). He is assisted by two counselors, usually high priests, who with the bishop constitute the BISHOPRIC and share responsibility for all ward organizations. The bishop and his counselors extend calls to ward members as needed to fill the numerous assignments in the many programs of the ward, encompassing activities for ward members at all ages.

A bishop holds his official position for an indefinite time period. A new bishop is called when an existing bishop is replaced or when a new ward is organized. After prayerful deliberation, the STAKE PRESIDENCY proposes a new bishop to the FIRST PRESIDENCY and QUORUM OF THE TWELVE APOSTLES. The individual nominated must be a member of the priesthood body of the ward. He does not seek nor apply for this position and no theological degree is necessary. A bishop is a lay minister and receives no monetary compensation for his services. Like other local Church officers, he must maintain himself and his family through normal employment. In selecting a bishop, a stake presidency ordinarily considers testimony, judgment, commitment, and charity toward ward members, as well as the virtues of sobriety and integrity and the administrative and teaching skills identified in the New Testament description of bishops:

A bishop then must be blameless, the husband of one wife, vigilant, sober, of good behavior, given to hospitality, apt to teach. Not given to wine, no striker, not greedy of filthy lucre; but patient, not a brawler, not covetous. One that ruleth well his own house, having his children in subjection with all gravity; (for if a man know not how to rule his own house, how shall he take care of the church of God?) Not a novice, lest being lifted up with pride he fall into the condemnation of the devil [1 Tim. 3:2–6].

Receiving a call to be a bishop is often a powerfully spiritual experience for a man as he realizes the awesome responsibility and feels the spirit confirm the importance of the call.

The bishop is sustained by a vote of the congregation, after which he is ordained and set apart to this holy office by the laying-on of hands generally by the stake president under assignment from the First Presidency. After a bishop is released from active duty, he will often be called "bishop" throughout his life because of the love and respect that ward members have for him.

The bishop has overall responsibility for all functions of the ward, which are designed to lead each individual member to Christ and eternal life. He is to "watch over the Church" (D&C 46:27). With other ward leaders, he is concerned for the daily physical needs of each ward member, especially the sick, elderly, and handicapped. He is like a father to the ward.

As the PRESIDING HIGH PRIEST of the ward, the bishop presides at sacrament, priesthood, and ward council meetings, and at all other ward services or activities. By these and other means he watches over both the spiritual and temporal affairs of the ward and its individual members and organizes the activities for preaching the gospel, serving in the temple, and helping ward members become more Christlike.

The bishop is the common judge of his ward. He spends much time visiting with or interviewing ward members. He determines their worthiness to participate in sacred ordinances, to receive the priesthood, to receive calls to serve in the ward and on missions, and to do temple work. He spends many hours interviewing and counseling youth as they become prospective missionaries.

Besides determining worthiness, the bishop must see that all Church ordinances are performed and recorded correctly. His direction or approval is necessary for baptism, confirmation, administration of the sacrament, blessing and naming of babies, priesthood ordinations, and all temple ordinances for members of his ward.

Where there is need, the bishop may be involved in counseling on a regular basis. He may help ward members establish goals for improvement, or he may impose appropriate discipline. In cases of serious transgression, he may initiate formal DISCIPLINARY PROCEDURES, which can affect membership, and may be necessary to bring some back to full fellowship.

As the president of the Aaronic Priesthood, a bishop has a specific responsibility to the YOUNG MEN and YOUNG WOMEN of the ward, ages twelve to eighteen. He is to see that all youth are instructed not only in scriptures and doctrine but also in the principles of charity and honesty, with special training of the young men in the duties of the priesthood, including administration of the sacrament, HOME TEACHING, baptizing, and missionary work. The bishop is automatically president of the quorum of priests in his ward, which generally consists of young men ages sixteen through eighteen. Bishops have similar responsibility for the young women of the ward. He meets monthly with a Bishop's Youth Committee, composed of adult and youth leaders for the young men and women.

Other duties of the bishop include receiving and accounting for the FINANCIAL CONTRIBUTIONS of ward members and caring of the needy through the BISHOP'S STOREHOUSE and the FAST OFFERING fund. He sees that all necessary supplies are at hand for ward functions. He arranges for and conducts funeral services. When it is appropriate and civil laws permit, he may perform marriages.

The bishop, as a father in his own home, as a family provider with a normal occupation, and as a member of the community in which he lives, has many time demands beyond his ecclesiastical calling. He must organize well and delegate and supervise effectively to accomplish all his duties.

The bishop's Sunday schedule usually involves a twelve or more hour day, including attending and conducting organizational meetings, worship services, training sessions; counseling and interviewing ward members; extending invitations or calls to participate in Church service in the ward; visiting the sick in hospitals; and visiting ward members in their homes as needed. He spends many additional hours during the week in meeting ward needs. His counselors and priesthood and auxiliary leaders also spend many hours helping him with these ward responsibilities. However, the overall responsibility for ward members and certain specific duties, such as annual interviewing of individuals for temple recommends and tithing settlement, are not in ordinary circumstances delegated.

Ward members believe that a man called of God, as the bishop is, will be endowed with wisdom, understanding, and spiritual discernment (D&C 46:27). Thus they frequently seek and greatly appreciate his advice and assistance.

BIBLIOGRAPHY

Beecher, Dale. "The Office of Bishop." *Dialogue* 15 (Winter 1982):103–115.

Brandt, Edward J. "The Office of Bishop in The Church of Jesus Christ of Latter-day Saints—A Sesquicentennial Review." In *A Sesquicentennial Look at Church History*, pp. 57–70. Provo, Utah, 1980.

DON M. PEARSON

BISHOP, HISTORY OF THE OFFICE

The work of the office of bishop in The Church of Jesus Christ of Latter-day Saints has evolved over 160 years to accommodate changing Church needs. When the Church was small, bishops were concerned primarily with the temporal needs of the Church, and spiritual needs were left to the Prophet. At the 1846 exodus from NAUVOO, three kinds of bishops functioned: general bishops, WARD bishops, and traveling or regional bishops. In 1847 the first presiding bishop was called, and was assigned Church-wide temporal and administrative duties. Ward bishops worked under the supervision of the presiding bishop, traveling or regional bishops, and STAKE PRESIDENTS. In the late 1800s ward bishops were assigned greater responsibility for ward members, seeing to their spiritual as well as temporal needs. Thus the need for traveling or regional bishops gradually diminished and the office soon ceased altogether. Contemporary Church organization includes ward bishops and a presiding bishop who is a General Authority (*see* PRESIDING BISHOPRIC).

BEFORE NAUVOO, 1830–1839. Revelation to Joseph Smith restored the office of bishop in February 1831 (D&C 41:9; cf. 1 Tim. 3:1–7). Edward Partridge was called as the Church's first bishop, and was made responsible for operating a storehouse to help the poor (D&C 42:30–39) and for administering property transactions connected with the LAW OF CONSECRATION (D&C 42; 58:17). In December 1831 Newel K. Whitney was also called as a bishop (D&C 72). The two served as regional or traveling bishops (D&C 20:66), Whitney for Ohio and the eastern states and Partridge for MISSOURI (*Latter-day Saint Biographical Encyclopedia* 1:219–20, 224). The First Presidency ordained them and called two counselors to assist each one. In November 1831, the Lord had revealed the AARONIC PRIESTHOOD organization, designating bishops as the presidents of the Aaronic Priesthood to preside over quorums of up to forty-eight PRIESTS (D&C 107:87–88). Bishops Partridge and Whitney helped organize these priesthood quorums and selected and set apart quorum presidents. After the organization of the first STAKES in 1834, bishops functioned much like stake officers.

In response to additional revelations (D&C 42:30–39; 51:1–20; 84:103–104), bishops Partridge and Whitney managed such Church temporal matters as paying bills, buying and selling lands and goods, helping with construction projects, printing, and assisting the poor. In Missouri, where members consecrated and pooled belongings, Bishop Partridge signed the consecration deeds, received donations into a BISHOP'S STOREHOUSE, and deeded back donated and purchased properties based on members' needs. He was remunerated for his full-time service.

NAUVOO PERIOD, 1839–1846. In 1841, when the law of TITHING replaced deeding all of one's property to the Church, bishops helped receive and disburse tithes. However, the Prophet Joseph Smith as Church President and trustee-in-trust held title to Church properties and established Church financial policies.

The office of ward bishops began with the establishment of the first wards in Nauvoo. There, bishops Newel K. Whitney and George Miller, who replaced Bishop Partridge (who had died in 1840), had general jurisdictions and also served in an assigned municipal ward. By 1842 Nauvoo's thirteen wards each had a bishop with two counselors. Their main tasks were to process tithes and to assist newcomers and aid the poor, which they accomplished with donated FAST OFFERINGS. Bishops also carried a major responsibility for dealing with ward members in cases of wrongdoing. However, bishops rarely conducted Sunday WORSHIP meetings; such services were held outdoors on a citywide or stake basis or in individual homes. Nauvoo bishops collectively organized and directed the work of deacons, teachers, and priests quorums in the city.

By the time of the exodus from Nauvoo, the Church had three types of bishops: general bishops, who in 1845 became trustees for the Church; ward bishops; and traveling bishops sent beyond Nauvoo to receive Church funds.

EXODUS AND EARLY UTAH, 1846–1900. During the exodus, ordained and acting bishops cared for the needy through tithes, offerings, and labor. WINTER QUARTERS was divided into twenty-two wards, each with a bishop. By 1848 bishops in KANESVILLE, IOWA, exercised civil as well as ecclesiastical authority. On April 6, 1847, Bishop Newel K. Whitney became the first presiding bishop for the entire Church.

When Latter-day Saints first settled in Utah, the norm was for each settlement to have a president and at least one bishop (the nucleus of an embryonic stake). Salt Lake City, the largest settlement, was divided into nineteen wards in 1849, each with a bishop and two counselors. When Presiding Bishop Whitney died in 1850, he was replaced by Bishop Edward Hunter, who was given two counselors, thereby creating the first PRESIDING BISHOPRIC. They were responsible for Church temporal affairs, for local bishops, and for stake Aaronic Priesthood quorums. Bishop Hunter met every two weeks with northern Utah bishops to coordinate efforts regarding public works, tithes, resources, immigration and immigrants, and the needy. However, the First Presidency, not the Presiding Bishopric, made finance and resource policy and called and released bishops.

In each stake, bishops called men, and later, boys, to fill stake-level deacons' quorums, teachers' quorums, and priests' quorums, and gave them responsibilities in their wards. The basic ward officers for the pioneer Utah period were the BISHOPRIC and the teachers' quorum, then called block teachers or ward teachers (see HOME TEACHING). Under direction of the bishop, teachers visited members in their homes, settled disputes, and helped the needy. Teachers and bishoprics heard charges of wrongdoing and decided guilt or innocence. Bishops, as Church judges, conducted inquiries regarding sin and held bishops' courts, if necessary, to excommunicate, disfellowship, or exonerate (see DISCIPLINARY PROCEDURES). During the REFORMATION (LDS) OF 1856–1857, bishops and teachers saw to the catechizations interviews, and rebaptism of members.

Bishops spent much of their time managing tithing. Most tithes were "in kind," necessitating the creation of bishop's storehouses, which included corrals for animals and bins for farm products. Tithing houses sometimes became commerce centers, serving as trading posts, banks issuing and receiving tithing scrip, wayside inns, and transportation and mail hubs. The Presiding Bishopric issued price valuations for donated and traded products, creating uniform prices for the territory. In the largely cashless PIONEER ECONOMY, bishops used two-thirds of the local tithes to help the poor and to pay for public improvements. They forwarded one-third of the tithing commodities to Salt Lake City to pay laborers on the Salt Lake Temple and various public works projects. Bishops received a small percentage of the tithes to cover personal expenses incurred while managing the

donations. By the mid-1850s, ward bishops had taken over the Presiding Bishopric's task of conducting annual tithing settlements with members.

During the consecration movement in the 1850s and the UNITED ORDER efforts in the 1870s, bishops received, recorded, and dispersed donated properties. Ward bishops recruited resources for use elsewhere, such as products in short supply, special funds, supplies for the militia, and teamsters and wagons to take immigrants west from staging points and supply depots in Nebraska, Iowa, and, later, Wyoming (see IMMIGRATION AND EMIGRATION).

The First Presidency and the Presiding Bishopric supervised local bishops through visits to wards, two annual general conferences requiring the attendance of bishops, distribution of circular letters, and the reports of traveling and regional bishops. Stake presidents served as the bishops' ecclesiastical superior line officers. In the Salt Lake, Cache, and Utah valleys, stake presidents held regular bishops' quorum meetings.

During this period, bishops had both temporal and spiritual responsibility for their wards and communities. They called ward officers, conducted meetings and presided over funerals, supervised ORDINANCES, and gave BLESSINGS. They assisted the needy through the use of tithes, fast offerings, and volunteer labor. During the 1856 famine, bishops requisitioned foodstuffs to distribute within a ward and to share with other wards. In the mid-1850s some wards created RELIEF SOCIETIES to aid needy Indians. Ward Relief Societies became widespread in the 1870s, and the bishops relied on them to seek out and help the needy.

Elders, seventies, and high priests met in stake quorums and were not directly subject to the bishops. In the 1860s and 1870s bishops helped organize and supervise Relief Societies for women, and other ward AUXILIARY ORGANIZATIONS, such as Mutual Improvement Associations for youth and adults, Sunday Schools, and Primaries for children.

In 1877 bishops presided over wards varying in size from 171 members in Morgan Stake wards (northern Utah) to 808 members in Utah Stake wards (central Utah). Each stake contained an average of twelve wards. An average ward had 432 members, 81 families, 13 high priests, 19 seventies, 38 elders, 6 priests, 6 teachers, and 10 deacons. During a thorough reorganization of the priesthood in 1877, President Brigham Young added 140 wards to the existing 101, retaining 56 bishops and ordaining 185 new ones. Most bishopric counselors were newly called, too, and were required to be high priests. Thus in 1877 new personnel comprised about 80 percent of the Church's bishoprics.

New instructions directed bishops to account for their ward members; keep Aaronic Priesthood units staffed; attend weekly Aaronic Priesthood meetings and monthly stake priesthood meetings; operate an effective ward teaching program; conduct the sacrament during Sunday School; turn in monthly and quarterly reports of membership, finances, and ward activities; keep accurate records of disciplinary proceedings; support temple laborers; and hold proper Sabbath meetings, thus setting basic patterns for ward organization and procedures today. Bishops' agents replaced regional presiding bishops. In response to instructions to involve boys eleven to nineteen years old in an Aaronic Priesthood office, bishops called them to be deacons in their wards, beginning the shift of Aaronic Priesthood work to the youth. Bishops continued to call elders and high priests as acting priests and acting teachers to do the ward teaching.

Nineteenth-century Utah bishops were the civic leaders in their communities. They encouraged immigrants to become citizens and to vote. They discussed political matters at Church meetings; backed the development of the telegraph, railroad, mines, canals, and cooperative stores; and established and superintended local schools. The average length of service for all nineteenth-century Utah bishops was eleven years, but 15 percent served for more than twenty years. Bishops had above-average incomes. They entered into plural marriage more than other male members; at least 60 percent of bishops had one or more plural wives.

Because of federal antipolygamy efforts during the 1880s, many bishops were prosecuted or were forced into hiding, thus virtually halting their political involvement. Their wards were incorporated so that they, rather than the general Church, owned meetinghouses, saving them from confiscation by the federal government. The tithing system was disrupted and tithe paying declined. In 1889, stake tithing clerks replaced the bishops' agents.

1900–1930. Beginning about 1900, after Utah had gained statehood (1896), the economic prac-

tices of the Church were modified. By the early 1900s tithing had changed from donations of commodities primarily to cash; tithing houses gradually disappeared and the collection task became simpler. Fast offerings also were most often donated in cash rather than food.

A priesthood reform movement from 1908 to 1922 designated the Aaronic Priesthood for boys, with ordination ages of twelve for deacons, fifteen for teachers, and seventeen for priests. Each age group received new duties and standardized lesson manuals. Bishops supervised the ward-level quorums and became presidents of the wards' Aaronic Priesthood.

Another change in 1908 required that all ward priesthood quorums cease meeting at separate times and instead meet together weekly in a ward priesthood meeting on Monday nights. For the first time bishops regularly met with and presided over all ward priesthood groups at once. In the 1930s ward priesthood meetings shifted from Monday nights to Sunday mornings.

1930–1960. Stakes and wards continued to spread beyond the Rocky Mountain region. Bishops in outlying areas with LDS minorities faced new problems not found in the predominantly LDS state of Utah. Away from the Intermountain West, Church meetinghouses were few in number, and members often lived long distances from one another.

Changes during this period include the creation by the Presiding Bishopric of a central membership file so bishops could receive or send membership records more efficiently, a uniform WARD BUDGET system, achievement award programs for the youth, the regular publication of a bulletin from the Presiding Bishopric to be disseminated to all bishops, arrangement of funds for bishops to attend general conferences, and the improvement of the handbook for bishops. Since ward teachers were ward officers and personal representatives of the bishop, the bishopric personally selected and interviewed the ward teachers, and conducted monthly report meetings with them.

With the introduction of the welfare services program in the late 1930s, bishops established and operated ward welfare projects and mobilized ward support for stake projects. They introduced more efficient methods of collecting and utilizing fast offerings and allocated food and clothing from the new bishop's storehouses to the needy.

DEVELOPMENTS SINCE 1960. The postwar "baby boom" and rapid increases in convert baptisms produced sudden and steep growth in Church membership during the 1960s, which required more wards, bishops, and meetinghouses. The Church established stakes and wards internationally, producing a growing number of non-English-speaking bishops.

To help new bishops, the Church published a wide array of instruction manuals for the various organizations and activities of the Church. By the 1980s new bishops in the United States received several such manuals, a GENERAL HANDBOOK OF INSTRUCTIONS, and various priesthood guidebooks. Because the bishop's tasks became so numerous that many bishops in the 1950s and 1960s were spending most weeknights as well as all day Sunday attending to Church duties, the Church moved to ease and simplify the nature of the bishop's assignment.

In 1964, as part of a new Church emphasis on CORRELATION, "ward teaching," now known as home teaching, became a responsibility of Melchizedek Priesthood quorum leaders, thus removing a major supervisory assignment from the bishops, though bishops continued to visit members in their homes and conduct funerals, visit the sick, and bestow blessings. In the 1970s and 1980s the bishop's service tenure was generally shortened, although length of service was not set; and ward sizes were reduced. Computerization of membership and financial records simplified bishops' record-keeping tasks. LDS SOCIAL SERVICES became a counseling resource to which bishops could refer members with difficult problems. Monday nights were reserved for FAMILY HOME EVENINGS, when no ward activities were to be held, thus giving both bishops and members more time for their families. By the 1980s the Church had consolidated all ward meetings, previously spread throughout the week, into one three-hour block on Sunday, saving bishops and members much travel and meeting time, particularly in wards that covered large areas. In 1990 Church headquarters began a quarterly allotment from the general tithing fund to cover ward expenses for wards in North America. This eliminated the bishop's need to solicit ward budget money through donations and fund-raising activities. The Church also simplified its disciplinary procedures.

[See also Bishop; Bishopric.]

BIBLIOGRAPHY

Arrington, Leonard J. Great Basin Kingdom. Lincoln, Neb., 1966.

Beecher, Dale F. "The Office of Bishop." Dialogue 15 (Winter 1982):103–15.

Hartley, William G. "The Priesthood Reform Movement, 1908–1922." BYU Studies 13 (Winter 1973):137–56.

Pace, Donald G. "Community Leadership on the Mormon Frontier: Mormon Bishops and the Political, Economic, and Social Development of Utah Before Statehood." Ph.D. diss., Ohio State University, 1983.

Widtsoe, John A. Priesthood and Church Government. Salt Lake City, 1939.

WILLIAM G. HARTLEY

BISHOPRIC

The bishopric, consisting of the BISHOP and two counselors, is the presiding or governing council in a WARD (congregation). These three men oversee all Church programs in the ward. They are assisted in the clerical, financial, and other administrative work by an executive secretary, a ward CLERK, and assistant clerks as needed. (See also PRESIDING BISHOPRIC.)

A bishop is called by the Lord to this office through the STAKE PRESIDENT, who presents the prospective bishop's name to the GENERAL AUTHORITIES for clearance and approval. The bishop selects two adult men to serve as his counselors and submits their names to the stake president for approval. Upon approval, the STAKE PRESIDENCY presents the names of the complete bishopric in a meeting of ward members for their sustaining vote. The stake president or a visiting General Authority ordains the bishop by the LAYING ON OF HANDS and sets him and his counselors apart in their positions.

The bishopric selects other men to serve as ward executive secretary, ward clerk, and assistant clerks; they are likewise approved by the stake president and priesthood executive committee, sustained by the members of the ward, and set apart by the stake president or his representative. The bishop and his counselors are ordained high priests (except in student wards, where elders may be called as counselors in the bishopric). All give voluntary, unpaid service.

The bishopric is charged to (1) promote the spiritual and temporal welfare of the members of the ward, with a primary focus on youth; (2) supervise the performance of priesthood ordinances and sacraments; (3) extend CALLINGS to members to staff ward organizations; (4) administer the programs of the Church in the ward, conduct meetings and maintain order in the Church organization and structure; (5) manage the financial affairs of the ward (including receiving local donations to the Church and transferring funds to Church headquarters, and supervising all expenditures of Church funds); (6) oversee the care and protection of the ward meetinghouse and other ward physical facilities that the Church owns or leases; (7) carry out Church DISCIPLINARY PROCEDURES for serious violations of moral law and Church standards; (8) foster a sense of community among ward members, with a special emphasis on fellowshipping new members; and (9) encourage members to perform their religious responsibilities. Bishoprics are requested to do whatever is needed to encourage Church participation and religious activity among all ward members.

The bishopric is responsible for calling and conducting all of the executive meetings of the ward, including a weekly bishopric meeting, a weekly priesthood executive committee meeting, and various meetings to plan and coordinate youth activities and train youth leaders. Bishopric members also divide responsibility and attend the leadership and training meetings of each AUXILIARY ORGANIZATION they supervise (see PRIMARY; RELIEF SOCIETY; SUNDAY SCHOOL; YOUNG MEN; YOUNG WOMEN).

After prayerfully considering recommendations from ward organization leaders who request members to serve in teaching, leadership, and other service callings, the bishopric decides whom to call, and issues the invitation to serve. The bishop delegates supervisory responsibility for the various auxiliary organizations, maintenance of membership records, receipting of financial contributions to the Church, and certain matters pertaining to Church education. The bishop cannot delegate such duties as counseling members involved in serious transgressions, convening disciplinary councils, presiding over the PRIEST quorum in the ward, performing civil marriages for members of the ward, and conducting TITHING settlement (an annual, personal report by ward members concerning the donations they have made).

The bishopric has the primary responsibility for developmental programs involving the youth in the ward. This entails promoting and attending activities for the youth, interviewing young men and women regularly, and overseeing the work of adults called to assist in teaching or planning activities. Activities are designed to provide youth with opportunities for recreation, service, and the application of religious principles to everyday life. The bishop focuses his efforts on the young men and women aged sixteen through eighteen, and assigns his counselors to work with youth aged twelve through thirteen and fourteen through fifteen. The bishop is to interview all young persons in the ward individually at least once each year (usually near their birthdays), and the counselors are to interview those twelve through sixteen years old at least annually. The bishop is the only member of the bishopric who discusses individual matters of personal worthiness with the youth.

Those who serve in a bishopric are expected to live with honesty, integrity, and devotion to their spiritual commitment. Their example of Christian service is essential to the quality of their influence among all ward members.

BIBLIOGRAPHY

Hinckley, Gordon B. "To the Bishops of the Church." *Ensign* 18 (Nov. 1988):48–51.

———. "In . . . Counsellors There Is Safety." *Ensign* 20 (Nov. 1990):48–51.

DAVID C. BRADFORD

BISHOP'S STOREHOUSE

The bishop's storehouse system is a network of Church-owned and -operated commodity resource centers that function much like retail stores, with the major difference that goods cannot be purchased but are given to needy individuals whom local LDS bishops judge to be worthy and deserving of Church assistance. Recipients are invited to work or render service in various ways in exchange for goods to avoid allowing the goods given to be a form of dole.

The storehouse stocks basic food and essential household items, produced largely from Church agricultural properties, canneries, and light manufacturing operations. The entire system, where practical, is vertically integrated, from farming and harvesting through processing and distributing. All work is performed by Church volunteers and re-

Between 1889 and 1898, little United States money was available in Utah. Many tithing storehouses of the Church paid workers and aided the poor by issuing notes payable in local goods and merchandise. This five-cent note, printed black on light pink in St. Louis, was issued by the Cache Stake, in Logan, Utah. Reprinted by permission from Alvin Rust, *Mormon and Utah Coin and Currency* (Salt Lake City, 1984).

cipients and is largely independent of the commercial economy. The contribution of time, talents, and resources of the membership of the Church in various areas sustains the storehouse.

The concept of the storehouse and the Church WELFARE SERVICES emerged from scriptural principles, elucidated by a series of revelations given to the Prophet Joseph SMITH beginning in 1831, a year after the Church was organized. In one revelation, Church members were directed to "remember the poor, and consecrate [their] properties for [the poor's] support" (D&C 42:30). The goods and money thus contributed were to be "kept in [the Lord's] storehouse, to administer to the poor and the needy" under the direction of the local presiding leader, the bishop (verse 34). Bishops were charged to seek donations as well (D&C 104:15–16; *Welfare Services Resource Handbook*, p. 9).

As defined by Church doctrine, the concept of the bishop's storehouse is founded on the belief that members of the Church should care for themselves and for each other. This is done, first, in families and, second, through the Church. Members are discouraged from seeking assistance from governmental or other social agencies.

The implementation of the mutual help program has varied considerably according to the economic conditions of the members and the organizational structure of the Church. At various times, distribution of goods has occurred through bishops, tithing offices, or bishop's storehouses. Utilization of the storehouse concept received intense emphasis during the UNITED ORDER effort of the 1870s. From that time forward, most WARDS maintained their own storehouse until the introduction of regional storehouses (1934–1936). Storehouses figured prominently in the Church's effort to care for its people during the economic depression of the 1930s and formed the basis for a more systematic approach to shared assistance.

After World War II, the Church welfare system, centered in the storehouse, evolved into an integrated and complex Church-wide production and distribution system. A higher level of coordi-

Food and many other necessities are given to needy members, upon recommendation of a local bishop, from over 110 Bishop's Storehouse facilities.

nation between welfare farms, dairies, and canneries was established, and a wider range of goods became available. The Church established central storehouses to supply regional storehouses. In the 1970s, with the maturing of the storehouse system, the Church selectively introduced local production and storehouses in areas outside the United States where need and resources warranted. The storehouse system is also available for assistance in cases of disaster (*see* CALAMITIES AND DISASTERS; EMERGENCY PREPAREDNESS).

Presently, the entire Bishop's Storehouse Resource System operates with efficiency and quality equal to commercial commodity activities, but maintains its spirit of volunteer service and local administration. While the bishop's storehouse system effectively assists thousands of people every year with material necessities, its additional value lies in the character development and spiritual growth of both givers and receivers.

BIBLIOGRAPHY

Arrington, Leonard J. *Great Basin Kingdom.* Cambridge, Mass., 1958.

———; Feramorz Y. Fox; and Dean L. May. *Building the City of God*, pp. 337–58. Salt Lake City, 1976.

Cook, Lyndon W. *Joseph Smith and the Law of Consecration.* Provo, Utah, 1985.

Stewart, George; Dilworth Walker; and E. Cecil McGavin. *Priesthood and Church Welfare*, 2nd ed. pp. 49–61. Salt Lake City, 1939.

Welfare Services Resource Handbook. Salt Lake City, 1980.

R. QUINN GARDNER

BLACKS

The history of black membership in The Church of Jesus Christ of Latter-day Saints can be divided between the era from 1830 to June 1978 and the period since then.

HISTORY. Though few in number, blacks have been attracted to the Church since its organization. Early converts (such as Elijah Abel) joined during the 1830s; others (such as Jane Manning James) joined after the Saints moved to Illinois. Among those who came to Utah as pioneers were Green Flake, who drove Brigham Young's wagon into the Salt Lake Valley; and Samuel Chambers, who joined in Virginia as a slave and went west after being freed. Throughout the twentieth cen-

tury, small numbers of blacks continued to join the Church, such as the Sargent family of Carolina County, Virginia, who joined in 1906; Len and Mary Hope, who joined in Alabama during the 1920s; Ruffin Bridgeforth, a railroad worker in Utah, converted in 1953; and Helvécio Martins, a black Brazilian businessman, baptized in 1972 (he became a GENERAL AUTHORITY in 1990). These members remained committed to their testimonies and Church activities even though during this period prior to 1978 black members could not hold the PRIESTHOOD or participate in TEMPLE ORDINANCES.

The reasons for these restrictions have not been revealed. Church leaders and members have explained them in different ways over time. Although several blacks were ordained to the priesthood in the 1830s, there is no evidence that Joseph Smith authorized new ordinations in the 1840s, and between 1847 and 1852 Church leaders maintained that blacks should be denied the priesthood

Samuel D. Chambers (1831–1929) and his wife Amanda Leggroan (c. 1908). Chambers was converted in Mississippi in 1844 and came to Utah in 1870 after the Civil War. For eighty-five years he was faithful and loyal to the Church. He served joyfully and was deeply respected.

because of their lineage. According to the BOOK OF ABRAHAM (now part of the PEARL OF GREAT PRICE), the descendants of Cain were to be denied the priesthood of God (Abr. 1:23–26). Some Latter-day Saints theorized that blacks would be restricted throughout mortality. As early as 1852, however, Brigham Young said that the "time will come when they will have the privilege of all we have the privilege of and more" (Brigham Young Papers, Church Archives, Feb. 5, 1852), and increasingly in the 1960s, Presidents of the Church taught that denial of entry to the priesthood was a current commandment of God, but would not prevent blacks from eventually possessing all eternal blessings.

Missionaries avoided proselytizing blacks, and General Authorities decided not to send missionaries to Africa, much of the Caribbean, or other regions inhabited by large populations of blacks. Before World War II, only German-speaking missionaries were sent to Brazil, where they sought out German immigrants. When government war regulations curtailed proselytizing among Germans, missionary work was expanded to include Portuguese-speaking Brazilians. Determining genealogically who was to be granted and who denied the priesthood became increasingly a sensitive and complex issue.

During the civil rights era in the United States, denial of the priesthood to blacks drew increasing criticism, culminating in athletic boycotts of Brigham Young University, threatened lawsuits, and public condemnation of the Church in the late 1960s. When questioned about the Church and blacks, Church officials stated that removal of the priesthood restriction would require revelation from God—not policy changes by men.

RECENT DEVELOPMENTS. On June 9, 1978, President Spencer W. KIMBALL announced the revelation that all worthy males could hold the priesthood (see DOCTRINE AND COVENANTS: DECLARATION 2). Following this official revelation, proselytizing was expanded worldwide to include people of African descent. Between 1977 and 1987, Church membership grew from 3,969,000 to 6,440,000, an increase of 62 percent. Because LDS membership records do not identify race, it is impossible to measure accurately the growth of black membership, except in areas where people are largely or exclusively of African descent. In the

Caribbean, excepting Puerto Rico, membership grew from 836 to 18,614 and in Brazil from 51,000 to 250,000 during that decade.

In other areas of Latin America, such as Colombia and Venezuela, increasing numbers of blacks also joined the Church. In Europe, blacks, including African immigrants to Portugal, joined the Church. Moreover, in Ghana, Nigeria, and throughout west and central Africa, missionary work expanded at a phenomenal rate. Excluding South Africa, where the membership was predominantly white, membership grew from 136 in 1977 to 14,347 in 1988, almost all in west Africa (see AFRICA, THE CHURCH IN).

The LDS Afro-American Oral History Project, conducted by the Charles Redd Center for Western Studies at Brigham Young University, demonstrated the increasing number of black members in the United States. Through interviews with black Latter-day Saints throughout the country, a symposium on LDS Afro-Americans held at Brigham Young University, and responses to a mailed survey, a more reliable flow of data was generated about the thoughts, feelings, convictions, and experiences of LDS Afro-Americans. The study found that within the Church Afro-Americans experience both high acceptance and, paradoxically, cultural miscommunications. For example, in response to the survey, 81 percent felt their future as blacks in the Church was hopeful. They explained that they experienced more social interactions and more meaningful relationships with Church members of all races, especially whites. At the same time, however, 46 percent said white members were not aware of the "needs and problems of black members." Some felt a lack of fellowship as well as economic and racial prejudice from white members.

Black Latter-day Saints are a nonhomogeneous mix of various "kindreds, tongues, and peoples" emerging from thousands of years of unprecedented religious and cultural exclusions. As with LDS Afro-Americans, many black members outside the United States encounter contrasting circumstances of full ecclesiastical involvement, on the one hand, and general Church ignorance of their respective cultures, on the other hand. Local leaders and members (primarily white Latter-day Saints) often lack a good working knowledge of black members' needs, concerns, and circumstances. Despite the 1978 priesthood revelation

Helvécio Martins, from Brazil, sustained as a General Authority on March 31, 1990.

and expanded missionary work among blacks, unexplored challenges to their growth and retention remain in counterpoint to their happiness with priesthood inclusion.

Despite the cultural miscommunications that remain, black Latter-day Saints enjoy opportunities in all phases of Church activity, including missionary work, quorum leadership, BISHOPRICS, and STAKE PRESIDENCIES, along with other members. The first entirely black African stake was organized in 1988. Indeed, black Latter-day Saints may be an LDS historical enigma that has emerged as a prime example of success in LDS brotherhood and sisterhood.

BIBLIOGRAPHY

Bringhurst, Newell G. *Saints, Slaves, and Blacks.* Westport, Conn., 1981.

Carter, Kate B. "The Negro Pioneer." In *Our Pioneer Heritage*, Vol. 8, pp. 497–580. Salt Lake City, 1965.

Embry, Jessie L. "Separate but Equal? Black Branches, Genesis Groups, or Integrated Wards?" *Dialogue* 23 (Spring 1990):11–37.

LDS Afro-American Oral History Project. Brigham Young University, Provo, Utah, 1985–1988.

ALAN CHERRY

JESSIE L. EMBRY

BLASPHEMY

Blasphemy denotes sacrilegious actions, speech, or thoughts that mock or revile God. A person blasphemes who, understanding the gravity of this behavior, willfully belittles or maligns God, the Godhead, or that which is of them, such as the commandments, covenants, ordinances, revelation, scriptures, and prophets.

Under the LAW OF MOSES, blasphemy—understood anciently to be mainly the unauthorized uttering of the ineffable name of Jehovah (YHWH)—was a heinous offense punishable by stoning (Ex. 20:7; Lev. 24:10–16). Charges of blasphemy figure twice in the Book of Mormon—in Sherem's false accusations against Jacob (Jacob 7:7) and in Korihor's insolent speech before the chief judge (Alma 30:30). In these cases, and generally, blasphemy embraced many forms of impiety, whether directed against God, against his servants (Acts 13:45), against the king (1 Kgs. 21:10), or in some cases against holy places or things, including the law (Acts 6:13). However, when blasphemies were spoken in relative ignorance, the gift of mercy could mitigate the requirements of justice (1 Tim. 1:13).

If a person with spiritual knowledge intentionally blasphemes God or the divine, the sin is most serious. For those who have entered into the NEW AND EVERLASTING COVENANT, blasphemy in extreme form is a sin against the HOLY GHOST wherein one assents anew unto the death of Christ and the shedding of his innocent blood. This is called the UNPARDONABLE SIN against the Holy Ghost (Matt. 12:31–32; D&C 132:27).

Emphasizing the gravity of the sin of blasphemy for those who claim to be his followers, Christ revealed that when he comes to purge the world he will commence with those "who have professed to know my name and have not known me, and have blasphemed against me in the midst of my house" (D&C 112:26).

Latter-day Saints are to refrain from blasphemy and the taking of the name of God in vain. Profanity and acrimony diminish spirituality and must be avoided: "But now ye also put off all these; anger, wrath, malice, blasphemy, filthy communication out of your mouth" (Col. 3:8). People are not defiled, Jesus emphasized, by what goes into the mouth, but by what comes from the heart: "For out of the heart proceed evil thoughts, murders, adulteries, fornications, thefts, false witness, blasphemies" (Matt. 15:19). Accordingly, Latter-day Saints are enjoined to avoid all forms of evil speaking of God, of the Lord's anointed, and, by implication, of all that is his, for "in nothing doth man offend God, or against none is his wrath kindled, save those who confess not his hand in all things, and obey not his commandments" (D&C 59:21).

[See also Profanity.]

BIBLIOGRAPHY

Hinckley, Gordon B. "Take Not the Name of God in Vain." *Ensign* 17 (Nov. 1987):44–48.

GARY L. BROWNING

BLESSING ON FOOD

Blessings on food are prayers to thank God for providing sustenance and to ask his blessings both on the food and on those who share it. In Mormon homes such blessings precede each meal and may be given by any member of a dining party, adult or child. In private these prayers are spoken orally, but may be spoken silently by individuals dining in public. All blessings on the food are addressed to God in the name of Jesus Christ. They are spoken from the heart as there is no prescribed prayer.

Latter-day Saints follow the patterns established by Christ and his disciples in blessings on food. When feeding the multitudes, Christ gave thanks for sustenance (Matt. 15:35–36) and blessed it (Matt. 14:19). Paul taught that food was to be received with prayer and thanksgiving (1 Tim. 4:3–5).

Biblical examples of praying over food are the basis for the Jewish, Catholic, and Protestant traditions of blessings on food or saying grace. Converts to Mormonism tended to continue these traditions from their prior faiths, and to be bolstered by the Latter-day Saint instruction on prayer: All things are to be done "with prayer and thanksgiving." Food and all "good things which come of the earth . . . are made for the benefit and the use of man, both to please the eye and to gladden the heart, . . . to strengthen the body and enliven the soul . . . . And in nothing doth man offend God, or against none is his wrath kindled, save those who confess not his hand in all things" (D&C 59:7, 17–19, 21).

Petitioning God for blessings on the food to be eaten is typical of Mormon table blessings. This may include requests for nourishment and good health, for strength to do one's work and God's will and to be of service. Other blessings on the diners or on those who prepared the meal are also deemed appropriate.

In many cultures, breaking bread or sharing a meal with others is an act of hospitality. According to Latter-day scripture such sharing may also be a foretaste of the future Messianic banquet (D&C 58:8). Because family meals provide opportunities for sharing the deepest spiritual concerns and rejoicings, it is especially appropriate to begin such occasions with prayer and the invocation of the Spirit. In LDS families this prayer is customarily spoken at the beginning of the meal only, and not also following the meal, as is the custom among some people of other religions. Because there is no prescribed form for Latter-day Saint blessings on food, such blessings enable families daily to express their own feelings, thoughts, and words in intimate prayer and fellowship two or three times a day.

CHRISTINE QUINN CHRISTENSEN

BLESSINGS

The term "blessings" is used in two different ways in The Church of Jesus Christ of Latter-day Saints. In a broad traditional sense as used in many cultures, the word applies to all good things that come in a person's life—the wonders of nature, the joys of family, the benefits of liberty and education—anything and everything that enriches life. Such blessings are often pointed to as a manifestation of God's love for his children. Latter-day Saint writings are interspersed with this usage. In more specific terminology, blessings refer to ORDINANCES performed under PRIESTHOOD AUTHORITY.

A PRIESTHOOD BLESSING may be given only

by those who have been ordained to the MELCHIZEDEK PRIESTHOOD. In the Church, most boys at the age of twelve have the AARONIC PRIESTHOOD conferred upon them and are ordained to the office of DEACON. At age fourteen, they are usually ordained TEACHERS, and at age sixteen, PRIESTS. If the priesthood bearer continues to show faithfulness and worthiness, then at age eighteen, or anytime thereafter, he may receive the Melchizedek Priesthood with ordination to the priesthood office of ELDER. An elder in the Melchizedek Priesthood has authority to perform most priesthood functions in the Church, including giving priesthood blessings.

Each priesthood ordination, from deacon to apostle, is a type of priesthood blessing and is characterized, as are all priesthood blessings, by (1) the LAYING-ON OF HANDS by those in authority, (2) an invocation of the authority of the priesthood and the name of Jesus Christ, and (3) such words of blessing as follow the impressions of the Spirit.

This third element, that of spiritual impressions, is vital for any priesthood blessing. A fundamental doctrine of the Church is a belief that a worthy priesthood bearer, when giving a priesthood blessing, will receive promptings from the HOLY SPIRIT regarding what is to be spoken—not necessarily the exact words, but ideas or thoughts that he will then express as clearly as he can in his own words. This is the essence of a priesthood blessing, and distinguishes it from a PRAYER. A prayer seeks to communicate with God, either vocally or silently, and is rooted in the faith that God will hear the words or the thoughts and feelings and then, in his infinite wisdom and power, will respond. A priesthood blessing is based on trust that the priesthood holder, while speaking the blessing, will receive spiritual promptings regarding what is to be spoken and thus his words represent the will of God.

In the Church, formal priesthood blessings include the following:

BLESSING OF CHILDREN. When babies are just a few weeks old, they are usually given a priesthood blessing for the special purpose of conferring a name by which the baby will be known and bestowing promises based on spiritual impressions regarding the baby's future life. A quality of prophecy attends this process. If a baby's father is a worthy holder of the Melchizedek Priesthood, he will usually pronounce the blessing, but it may be given by a grandfather, a family friend, or any other qualified priesthood holder chosen by the baby's parents. Babies are usually blessed in the presence of the congregation at a FAST AND TESTIMONY MEETING. However, the blessing may be given at other times and places, such as in a hospital or home, if there is a special need.

CONFIRMATION FOLLOWING BAPTISM. Two ordinances are required for admission to Church MEMBERSHIP. The first is BAPTISM. The second, CONFIRMATION, is performed shortly following baptism and is a type of priesthood blessing. Two or more men who hold the Melchizedek Priesthood place their hands on the head of the person who has been baptized and, with one of the men serving as voice, the baptized person is confirmed a member of the Church and given the GIFT OF THE HOLY GHOST. Additional words of counsel or admonition are then expressed according to spiritual promptings.

SETTING APART TO CHURCH ASSIGNMENTS. Customarily, whenever any person is called to serve as a teacher or officer in any of the Church organizations, and always when a person is called to be a MISSIONARY or TEMPLE worker, persons holding proper priesthood authority place their hands on the person's head and the individual is set apart to the assignment. One of the priesthood bearers pronounces the blessing and expresses whatever counsel or thoughts he is impressed to say.

ADMINISTERING TO THE SICK. Blessings of health or comfort are given to one who is sick or injured. Two Melchizedek Priesthood men normally give this blessing in accord with James 5:14. The head of the sick person is anointed with a few drops of olive oil consecrated for this purpose. The two priesthood bearers then gently place their hands on the head of the afflicted person and the one sealing the anointing expresses promises of healing or comfort as he is impressed. Many incidents of dramatic and even miraculous healings have been recorded in Church history. Any worthy Melchizedek Priesthood bearer, when requested, may give such a blessing.

PATRIARCHAL BLESSINGS. Each organized STAKE in the Church has one or more PATRIARCHS called to give patriarchal blessings to stake members. Normally this blessing is given just once in a person's life, usually when a person is young, most often in the teenage years. However, the blessing may be given at any age from childhood to advanced years. The patriarchal blessing is a lifetime blessing of guidance, warning, encouragement, and reassurance. Men serving as patriarchs are spiritually mature high priests in the Melchizedek Priesthood who have been ordained especially for the sacred CALLING of giving patriarchal blessings.

FATHER'S AND HUSBAND'S BLESSINGS. Every Melchizedek Priesthood bearer who is a husband or father has the authority, through worthiness, to give a priesthood blessing on special occasions or in times of special need to members of his family—a husband's blessing to his wife or a father's blessing to a son or daughter. Such blessings may be suggested by the husband or father or requested by the one desiring the blessing. They are blessings of love, counsel, and encouragement. Like all priesthood blessings, these are given by the laying on of hands on the head of the one receiving the blessing.

SPECIAL BLESSINGS OF COUNSEL AND COMFORT. All priesthood officers in the Church, from GENERAL AUTHORITIES through STAKE PRESIDENCIES and WARD BISHOPRICS to home teachers, have authority to give blessings of counsel or comfort to Church members within their jurisdiction. These are official priesthood blessings given in the same manner and with similar spiritual promptings as other priesthood blessings. Persons desiring such a blessing usually request it of one of the local priesthood officers in the area where they reside.

BIBLIOGRAPHY

Brockbank, Bernard P. *Commandments and Promises of God.* Salt Lake City, 1983.

Kimball, Spencer W. *Faith Precedes the Miracle.* Salt Lake City, 1972.

McKay, David O. *Gospel Ideals.* Salt Lake City, 1976.

Monson, Thomas A. *Pathways to Perfection.* Salt Lake City, 1973.

BRUCE B. CLARK

BLIND, MATERIALS FOR THE

During his earthly ministry, Jesus was always sensitive to individuals and their personal needs. He paid particular attention to those with handicaps

In 1941, Helen Keller was given a Braille copy of the Book of Mormon by President Heber J. Grant in the president's office. The Church produces a wide variety of materials for the blind. Courtesy University of Utah.

and healed many of their infirmities (e.g., Matt. 11:5). Today, The Church of Jesus Christ of Latter-day Saints teaches similar sensitivity to people with special needs.

Since 1904, the Church has produced gospel materials for the blind and the visually impaired, and now all such people may obtain these materials in a wide variety of helpful formats.

Access to printed material is often inadequate for the visually impaired. To help overcome this lack, the Church produces materials on audiocassettes, in Braille, and in large-print versions. Audiocassettes are available at both standard and half-speed. Half-speed cassettes require the type of slow-speed cassette player that the Library of Congress lends to visually impaired persons in the United States.

The Church provides the scriptures on audiocassettes, in large type, and in Braille. It also produces courses of study and selected Church books in Braille and on audiocassettes. The words to Church hymns are available in Braille and on recordings.

The *Ensign* magazine and selections from the *New Era* and *Friend* magazines are recorded on half-speed, four-track audiocassettes each month and mailed as the *Ensign Talking Book* to several thousand subscribers worldwide. The FIRST PRESIDENCY Message and the *Friend* are also produced in Braille each month.

JOSIAH W. DOUGLAS

BLOOD ATONEMENT

The doctrines of the Church affirm that the ATONEMENT wrought by the shedding of the blood of Jesus Christ, the Son of God, is efficacious for the sins of all who believe, repent, are baptized by one having authority, and receive the Holy Ghost by the laying on of hands. However, if a person thereafter commits a grievous sin such as the shedding of innocent blood, the Savior's sacrifice alone will not absolve the person of the consequences of the sin. Only by voluntarily submitting to whatever penalty the Lord may require can that person benefit from the atonement of Christ.

Several early Church leaders, most notably Brigham YOUNG, taught that in a complete theocracy the Lord could require the voluntary shedding of a murderer's blood—presumably by CAPITAL PUNISHMENT—as part of the process of atonement for such grievous sin. This was referred to as "blood atonement." Since such a theocracy has not been operative in modern times, the practical effect of the idea was its use as a rhetorical device to heighten the awareness of Latter-day Saints of the seriousness of murder and other major sins. This view is not a doctrine of the Church and has never been practiced by the Church at any time.

Early anti-Mormon writers charged that under Brigham Young the Church practiced "blood atonement," by which they meant Church-instigated violence directed at dissenters, enemies, and strangers. This claim distorted the whole idea of blood atonement—which was based on voluntary submission by an offender—into a supposed justification of involuntary punishment. Occasional isolated acts of violence that occurred in areas where Latter-day Saints lived were typical of that period in the history of the American West, but they were not instances of Church-sanctioned blood atonement.

BIBLIOGRAPHY

McConkie, Bruce R. "Blood Atonement Doctrine." In *Mormon Doctrine*, 2nd ed. Salt Lake City, 1966.

Penrose, Charles W. *Blood Atonement, As Taught by Leading Elders of The Church of Jesus Christ of Latter-day Saints.* Salt Lake City, 1884.

Peterson, Paul H. "The Mormon Reformation," pp. 176–99. Ph.D. diss., Brigham Young University, 1981.

Smith, Joseph Fielding. "The Doctrine of Blood Atonement." In *Answers to Gospel Questions*, Vol. 1, pp. 180–91. Salt Lake City, 1957.

LOWELL M. SNOW

BLOOD TRANSFUSIONS

Although there are references in scripture to the sacredness of blood, the Church does not hold that any scripture or revelation prohibits giving or receiving blood or blood products, such as gamma globulin, the antihemophilic factor, and antibodies through transfusion or injection, and it is therefore not opposed to its members engaging in such practices. In fact, individual wards sometimes have blood drives to increase a supply on hand when a ward member might need a transfusion. The Church, however, leaves the decision of whether to be a donor or a recipient of a blood transfusion or blood products to the individual member or family concerned.

The Church recognizes that the use of blood transfusions and blood products often saves lives by replacing blood serum volume, red and white cells, platelets, and other substances that may have been lost or damaged by disease, accident, or surgical operation. It is also aware that many operative procedures, such as open-heart surgery and organ transplantation, could not be as safely performed and that many diseases, such as leukemia, aplastic anemia, and certain types of cancers, could not be adequately treated without blood and blood-product transfusions.

Blood transfusions can carry very harmful and life-threatening diseases, such as acquired immunodeficiency syndrome (AIDS), hepatitis, and other infectious diseases, and therefore may be a hazard. However, these hazards may be completely eliminated in nonemergency operations by the process of autotransfusion, whereby a patient's own blood is donated, stored, and given back when needed. This practice is feasible because blood can be stored for a number of months. However, the

Church leaves all decisions about the use or non-use of blood to the member or family concerned in consultation with their physician.

RICHARD A. NIMER

BONNEVILLE INTERNATIONAL CORPORATION

In 1964 KSL and other Church-owned commercial broadcasting stations and operations were consolidated into Bonneville International Corporation (BIC), headquartered in Salt Lake City. The founding president of BIC was Arch L. Madsen. He was succeeded by Rodney H. Brady in 1985. Historically, its board of directors has included a member of the FIRST PRESIDENCY.

In addition to KSL Radio and Television, Bonneville has acquired and founded several other units: (1) a television station in Seattle, (2) radio stations in Seattle, New York City, Kansas City, Los Angeles, Chicago, San Francisco, Dallas, and Phoenix; (3) Bonneville Media Communications, a full-service production and advertising company located in Salt Lake City; (4) Bonneville Washington News Bureau, in the nation's capital; (5) Bonneville Broadcasting System (BBS), a music programming service in Northbrook, Illinois, that provides "easy listening" and "soft adult contemporary" music programming to radio stations throughout the United States and abroad; (6) Bonneville Satellite Corporation, which was formed in Salt Lake City in 1980 and much of which was sold in 1987, with BIC retaining interest as a limited partner; and (7) Bonneville Entertainment Company, incorporated in 1981.

Bonneville programming reaches an international audience through placement of programs, public service messages, and other services on stations throughout the world, with emphasis on values-oriented programming. Bonneville stations do not proselytize for the Church, and religious programming (generally confined to Sunday morning) includes representation from all major religions. Neither BIC nor its divisions use their facilities to solicit funds for the Church. Bonneville and its divisions are taxpaying, commercial enterprises.

The philosophy of BIC is summarized in this excerpt from the company's statement of "Mission and Commitments": "We are a values-driven company composed of values-driven people. We are committed to serving and improving individuals, communities, and society through providing quality broadcast entertainment, information, news, and values-oriented programming."

BIBLIOGRAPHY

"Bonneville International Corporation." Brochure, Salt Lake City, 1989.

Wolsey, Heber G. "The History of Radio Station KSL from 1922 to Television." Ph.D. diss., Michigan State University, 1967.

RODNEY H. BRADY

BOOK OF ABRAHAM

[*This entry includes five articles:*

> Origin of the Book of Abraham
>
> Translation and Publication of the Book of Abraham
>
> Contents of the Book of Abraham
>
> Facsimiles from the Book of Abraham
>
> Studies About the Book of Abraham

The Book of Abraham autobiographically recounts Abraham's early years and is one of the texts in the LDS scriptural collection titled Pearl of Great Price. The article Origin of the Book of Abraham *recounts the discovery and purchase of the Joseph Smith Papyri and events leading up to the publication of the Book of Abraham itself. The article* Translation and Publication of the Book of Abraham *details briefly both the process by which Joseph Smith produced the text of the Book of Abraham and the history of its appearance in print. The article* Contents of the Book of Abraham *surveys generally the events narrated in the book, including Abraham's miraculous rescue from death and God's covenant with him before he departed his homeland.* Facsimiles from the Book of Abraham *introduces the ancient Egyptian illustrations that are currently published with the work and assesses their relationship to the text. A review of studies published to date on the Book of Abraham appears in* Studies about the Book of Abraham.]

ORIGIN OF THE BOOK OF ABRAHAM

In July 1835, while living in Kirtland, Ohio, the Prophet Joseph SMITH purchased, on behalf of the Church, four Egyptian mummies and accompanying papyri from Michael H. Chandler, a traveling entrepreneur from Pennsylvania. The price was $2,400. Chandler had acquired eleven mummies in early 1833 and had sold the other seven in the eastern United States prior to meeting Joseph Smith. Shortly after obtaining the antiquities, Joseph Smith announced that the papyri contained some writings of the patriarchs ABRAHAM and JOSEPH, both of whom had lived in Egypt (Gen. 12:37, 39–50).

These antiquities had been exhumed by Antonio Lebolo on the west bank of the Nile River opposite the ancient city of Thebes (present-day Luxor), probably between 1817 and 1821. Lebolo, born in Castellamonte, Piedmont (northern Italy), had been a gendarme during Napoleon's occupation of the Italian peninsula. When Napoleon was defeated, Lebolo chose voluntary exile rather than face imprisonment under the reemerging Sardinian monarchy. He moved to Egypt, where he was employed by Bernardino Drovetti, former consul general of France in Egypt, to oversee his excavations in Upper Egypt. Drovetti also allowed Lebolo to excavate on his own. Lebolo discovered eleven well-preserved mummies in a large tomb. Because Lebolo directed several hundred men excavating at different sites, the exact location has not been identified. The mummies were shipped to Trieste, where Lebolo authorized Albano Oblasser, a shipping magnate, to sell them on his behalf. Lebolo died February 19, 1830, in Castellamonte. Oblasser forwarded the eleven mummies to two shipping companies in New York City—McLeod and Gillespie, and Maitland and Kennedy—to sell them to anybody who would pay an appropriate sum. The proceeds were to be sent to Lebolo's heirs. Chandler acquired them in the winter or early spring of 1833. He claimed that Lebolo was his uncle, but that relationship has not been confirmed.

It has become clear that some Abrahamic literature exhibits links with Egypt. For example,

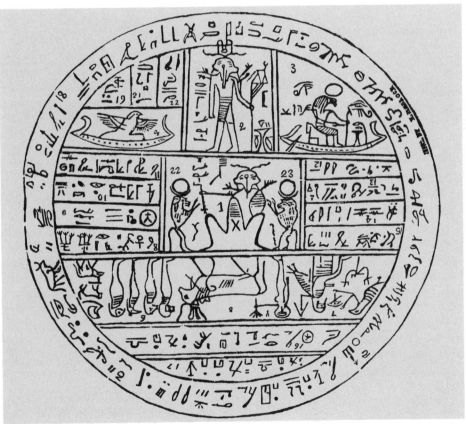

Facsimile 2 from the Book of Abraham, first published in *Times and Seasons* in 1842. This hypocephalus (a round papyrus placed under the head of a mummy by the Egyptians) is a richly symbolic expression of the deceased person's desire for resurrection, eternal life, procreation, dominion, and stability. Over 100 such hyocephali are known, first appearing during the Saite Dynasty (663–525 B.C.). Courtesy Rare Books and Manuscripts, Brigham Young University.

the *Testament of Abraham*—likely first written in Greek—almost certainly derives from Egypt. Substituting a biblical figure such as Abraham in Egyptian hieroglyphic scenes is a Jewish technique known from the Hellenistic period (Grobel, pp. 373–82). Thus, it is not surprising that Egyptian texts are somehow linked to the appearance of the Book of Abraham.

According to some Egyptologists, the writings of Abraham acquired by Joseph Smith are to be dated to the early Christian era. Such dating is not without precedent. The *Testament of Abraham*, edited initially by M. R. James in 1892, was described by him as "a second century Jewish-Christian writing composed in Egypt" (Nibley, pp. 20–21).

The identity of the mummies is not known, since there are no primary sources that identify them.

BIBLIOGRAPHY

Grobel, K. ". . . Whose Name Was Neves." *New Testament Studies* 10 (1963–1964):373–82.

Nibley, Hugh W. *Abraham in Egypt*. Salt Lake City, 1981.

Peterson, H. Donl. *The Pearl of Great Price: A History and Commentary*. Salt Lake City, 1987.

H. DONL PETERSON

TRANSLATION AND PUBLICATION OF THE BOOK OF ABRAHAM

On October 10, 1880, in a general conference, members of The Church of Jesus Christ of Latter-day Saints voted to accept the book of Abraham as a scriptural work. Several views have been advanced concerning the process whereby the Prophet Joseph SMITH produced the work. Although he and his associates began an "Egyptian Alphabet and Grammar" while they studied the papyri, the purpose of that work is obscure. It was not completed, explained, or published by Joseph Smith or any of his successors. However, it is certain that he began working in KIRTLAND, OHIO, on the relevant Egyptian papyri soon after purchasing them from Michael H. Chandler in 1835.

Probably no one in the United States in 1835 could interpret Egyptian hieroglyphics through ordinary translation techniques. When he translated the gold plates of the Book of Mormon from the "reformed Egyptian" text (1827–1829), the Prophet stated that he did it "by the gift and power of God." Likewise, it was principally divine inspiration rather than his knowledge of languages that produced the English text of the book of Abraham. His precise methodology remains unknown.

On July 5, 1835, the Prophet recorded, "I commenced the translation of some of the characters or hieroglyphics, and much to our joy found that one of the rolls contained the writings of Abraham. . . . Truly we can say, the Lord is beginning to reveal the abundance of peace and truth" (*HC* 2:236). After delays, Joseph Smith appointed two men on November 2, 1837, to raise funds to help translate and print the book of Abraham. But because of further difficulties, he was unable to begin publishing for four more years. The book of Abraham was first printed in three issues of the *Times and Seasons* on March 1, March 15, and May 16, 1842. These installments contained the entire current book of Abraham, including the three facsimiles. In February 1843, Joseph Smith promised that more of the book of Abraham would be published. However, continued harassment by enemies kept the Prophet from ever publishing more of the record. It did receive considerable notoriety when several prominent eastern newspapers in the United States reprinted Facsimile 1 and part of the text from the *Times and Seasons* publication.

In 1851 the writings of Abraham were published in England as a part of the Pearl of Great Price, a small compilation by Franklin D. Richards containing some of Joseph Smith's translations and revelations. It was this compilation that was canonized in 1880, in SALT LAKE CITY, thereby placing it alongside three other sacred collections or standard works: the Bible, the Book of Mormon, and the Doctrine and Covenants.

In 1856 the papyri were sold by Joseph's widow to Abel Combs. With the exception of a few fragments returned to the Church in 1967, the present location of the papyri is unknown.

[See also PAPYRI, JOSEPH SMITH.]

BIBLIOGRAPHY

Nibley, Hugh. "The Meaning of the Kirtland Egyptian Papers." *BYU Studies* 11, no. 4 (Summer 1971):350–99.

Peterson, H. Donl. *The Pearl of Great Price: A History and Commentary*. Salt Lake City, 1987.

H. DONL PETERSON

CONTENTS OF THE BOOK OF ABRAHAM
The book of Abraham in the Pearl of Great Price consists of an account of Abraham's experiences with the Lord in four lands: Chaldea, Haran, Canaan, and Egypt. This observation is consistent with the work's opening phrase, "In the land of." Except for events chronicled in the first chapter, Sarai (Sarah) shared fully the vicissitudes and triumphs of her husband.

As the work opens, Abraham is living among an idolatrous people in Chaldea (Abr. 1:1, 5–7). But because of severe persecution (1:12, 15) after having preached against their wickedness, he decides to emigrate. Resulting official opposition almost costs Abraham his life, as a human sacrifice (1:12–15). When he prays for divine help, an angel rescues him, promising that he will be led to a new land and receive the priesthood (1:15–19).

When the famine prophesied by the angel comes to Chaldea (1:29–30), Abraham departs with Sarai, his nephew Lot, and his family, with his father, Terah, following the company (2:4). After they settle in Haran, the Lord commands Abraham to continue on to Canaan and reveals to him the founding elements of the ABRAHAMIC COVENANT (2:6–11). Because of famine, Abraham goes to Egypt, where the Lord commands him—a feature absent from Genesis 12:11–13—to introduce Sarai as his sister so that the Egyptians will not kill him (2:21–25).

In the third chapter, Abraham describes a vision that he received through a URIM AND THUMMIM concerning the worlds created by God, the premortal spirits of people, and the COUNCIL IN HEAVEN wherein the gods (cf. John 1:1–4, 14; Heb. 1:1–3) planned the creation of the earth and humankind. The fourth and fifth chapters recount the completion of these plans and the placing of Adam and Eve in the GARDEN OF EDEN.

By the book's account, Chaldea was under Egyptian hegemony during Abraham's lifetime. Local religion included Egyptian solar worship, the worship of Pharaoh, and human sacrifice. The discovery of the land of Egypt is attributed to Egyptus, daughter of Ham and Egyptus; her eldest son, whose name was Pharaoh, established its first government.

Doctrinal contributions of the book include a fuller explanation of Abraham's covenant and its relationship to the gospel (2:6–11), and a better understanding of premortal life (3:22–28). Con-

cerning ASTRONOMY, it names the celestial body nearest God's abode, Kolob (3:2–4), and details the creation of the earth by a council of Gods in the fourth chapter. Abraham 1:26–27 has been interpreted by some as the scriptural basis for previously withholding the priesthood from BLACKS.

Concerning biblical connections, the idolatry of Terah (cf. Josh. 24:2) and the Lord's rescue of Abraham (cf. Isa. 29:22) are spelled out in the book of Abraham and in other ancient Abraham texts.

Many themes of the book appear in other ancient literatures, including Abraham's struggle against idolatry (*Jubilees* 12; Charlesworth, Vol. 2, pp. 79–80), the attempted sacrifice of Abraham (*Pseudo-Philo* 6; Charlesworth, Vol. 2, pp. 310–12), and Abraham's vision of God's dwelling place, events in the Garden of Eden, and premortal spirits (*Apocalypse of Abraham* 22–23; Charlesworth, Vol. 1, p. 700). God's instruction to Abraham to introduce Sarai as his sister is echoed in the *Genesis Apocryphon* (column 19) as having come through a dream. Abraham's teaching astronomy to Egyptians (Book of Abraham Facsimile 3) is described in *Pseudo-Eupolemus* 9.17.8 and 9.18.2 (Charlesworth, Vol. 2, pp. 881–82) and in Josephus (*Antiquities* 1.8.2).

BIBLIOGRAPHY

Charlesworth, James H., ed. *The Old Testament Pseudepigrapha*, 2 vols. Garden City, N.Y., 1983, 1985.

Millet, Robert L., and Kent P. Jackson, eds. *Studies in Scripture*, Vol. 2. Salt Lake City, 1985.

Peterson, H. Donl, and Charles D. Tate, eds. *The Pearl of Great Price: Revelations from God*. Provo, Utah, 1989.

STEPHEN E. THOMPSON

FACSIMILES FROM THE BOOK OF ABRAHAM

Three facsimiles are published with the text of the book of Abraham in the Pearl of Great Price. All are similar to Egyptian illustrations known from other sources.

FACSIMILE NUMBER 1. Representations similar to Facsimile 1 abound in Egyptian religious texts. A typical example appears in the 151st chapter of the *Book of the Dead*, showing the god Anubis embalming Osiris, who is lying on a lion couch. In some details, such as the posture of the reclining figure, Facsimile 1 differs from other Egyptian texts.

Only for Facsimile 1 is the original document known to be extant. Comparisons of the papyrus fragments as well as the hieroglyphic text accompanying this drawing demonstrate that it formed a part of an Egyptian religious text known as the *Book of Breathings*. Based on paleographic and historical evidence, this text can be reliably dated to about the first century A.D. Since reference is made to this illustration in the book of Abraham (Abr. 1:12), many have concluded that the *Book of Breathings* must be the text that the Prophet Joseph SMITH used in his translation. Because the *Book of Breathings* is clearly not the book of Abraham, critics claim this is conclusive evidence that Joseph Smith was unable to translate the ancient documents.

In the historical documents currently possessed by the Church, Joseph Smith never described fully the actual process he used in translating ancient documents. In reference to the Book of Mormon, he said that it was "not expedient" for him to relate all the particulars of its coming forth (*HC* 1:220; *see* BOOK OF MORMON: TRANSLATION BY JOSEPH SMITH). He did, in several instances, refer to the book of Abraham as a translation (*HC* 4:543, 548); and when the installments of the book of Abraham were published in the *Millennial Star*, it was described as being "translated by Joseph Smith" (July 1842, p. 34). Both Wilford WOODRUFF (in his journal) and Parley P. Pratt (in the July 1842 *Millennial Star*) maintained that the translation was done by means of the URIM AND THUMMIM, although Joseph Smith himself does not mention using this instrument anywhere in the translation.

One must consider, however, what Joseph Smith meant by translation. Section 7 of the DOCTRINE AND COVENANTS offers one standard measure. Here, the Prophet, using the Urim and Thummim, translated a "record made on parchment by John the Revelator." Although it is not known whether Joseph Smith actually had this document, he provided a translation of it. Since it is not known just how Joseph Smith translated, it is reasonable to postulate that, when studying the Egyptian papyri purchased from Michael Chandler, Joseph Smith sought revelation from the Lord concerning them and received in that process the book of Abraham. He might then have searched through the papyri in his possession to find illustrations similar to those he had learned by revelation. This forms one possible explanation of

how drawings done about the first century A.D. were used to illustrate the book of Abraham.

FACSIMILE NUMBER 2. Egyptologists call Facsimile 2 a hypocephalus (Greek for "under the head"), and numerous examples are preserved in museums around the world. Their stated purpose was to keep the body warm (i.e., ready for resurrection) and to transform the deceased into a god in the hereafter. Joseph Smith explained that Facsimile 2 contained representations of God, the earth, the Holy Ghost, etc. His explanations are, in general, reasonable in light of modern Egyptological knowledge. For example, the four standing figures in the lower portion of the facsimile are said by Joseph Smith to represent "earth in its four quarters." The Egyptians called these the four sons of Horus and, among other things, they were gods of the four quarters of the earth.

FACSIMILE NUMBER 3. Facsimile 3 presents a constantly recurring scene in Egyptian literature, best known from the 125th chapter of the *Book of the Dead*. It represents the judgment of the dead before the throne of Osiris. It is likely that it came at the end of the *Book of Breathings* text, of which Facsimile 1 formed the beginning, since other examples contain vignettes similar to this. Moreover, the name of Hor, owner of the papyrus, appears in the hieroglyphs at the bottom of this facsimile.

Joseph Smith explained that Facsimile 3 represents Abraham sitting on the pharaoh's throne teaching principles of astronomy to the Egyptian court. Critics have pointed out that the second figure, which Joseph Smith says is the king, is the goddess Hathor (or Isis). There are, however, examples in other papyri, not in the possession of Joseph Smith, in which the pharaoh is portrayed as Hathor. In fact, the whole scene is typical of Egyptian ritual drama in which costumed actors played the parts of various gods and goddesses.

In summary, Facsimile 1 formed the beginning, and Facsimile 3 the end of a document known as the *Book of Breathings*, an Egyptian religious text dated paleographically to the time of Jesus. Facsimile 2, the hypocephalus, is also a late Egyptian religious text. The association of these facsimiles with the book of Abraham might be explained as Joseph Smith's attempt to find illustrations from the papyri he owned that most closely matched what he had received in revelation when translating the Book of Abraham. Moreover, the Prophet's explanations of each of the facsimiles accord with present understanding of Egyptian religious practices.

BIBLIOGRAPHY

Harris, James R. "The Book of Abraham Facsimiles." In *Studies in Scripture*, Vol. 2, ed. R. Millet and K. Jackson. Salt Lake City, 1985.

Nibley, Hugh. *Abraham in Egypt.* Salt Lake City, 1981.

Rhodes, Michael D. "A Translation and Commentary of the Joseph Smith Hypocephalus." *BYU Studies* 17 (Spring 1977):259–74.

MICHAEL D. RHODES

STUDIES ABOUT THE BOOK OF ABRAHAM

DOCTRINAL COMMENTARIES. Doctrinal studies of the book of Abraham have usually been components of general commentaries on the Pearl of Great Price without focusing on the book of Abraham in particular. George Reynolds and Janne Sjodahl's *Commentary on the Pearl of Great Price* (Salt Lake City, 1965) is a typical example. The most comprehensive study of this sort is *Doctrinal Commentary on the Pearl of Great Price* (Salt Lake City, 1969) by Hyrum Andrus.

HISTORICAL STUDIES. In 1912 the pamphlet *Joseph Smith, Jr., as a Translator* by F. S. Spaulding, Episcopal bishop of Utah, attempted the first formal non-LDS study of the book of Abraham. It contained letters from eight leading Egyptologists concerning the three book of Abraham facsimiles and commenting on the "accuracy" of their interpretation by the Prophet Joseph SMITH. The scholars unanimously agreed that the Prophet was wrong. At the time, no Latter-day Saint scholar was capable of refuting their claims. It was not until 1936 that J. E. Homans, a non-Latter-day Saint writing under the pseudonym R. C. Webb, published *Joseph Smith as a Translator*, defending the Prophet's abilities as a translator, but not directly addressing the points that were made by the Egyptologists.

In 1967 eleven fragments of the Egyptian papyri once owned by Joseph Smith were rediscovered by Aziz S. Atiya and were then presented to the Church by the New York Metropolitan Museum of Art. Several pieces were determined to be from an Egyptian religious text known as the *Book of Breathings*. Three noted Egyptologists soon made translations of and commentaries on the fragments, which resulted in new attacks on Joseph

Smith's "inabilities" as a translator. The critics argued that the *Book of Breathings* bore no relationship to the book of Abraham, which Joseph Smith apparently claimed to have translated from these very papyri. Indeed, the *Book of Breathings* is a late text, originating about the first century A.D., some 2000 years after the time of Abraham. Against criticisms such as these, Hugh Nibley has consistently and ably defended Joseph Smith, maintaining that the book of Abraham should be evaluated on the basis of what it claims to be—Abraham's own account of his life. Nibley's research has shown that a significant number of links exist between the book of Abraham and ancient texts related to Abraham. These similarities seem too numerous and subtle to be attributed to mere coincidence.

In his explanation of Facsimile 2 in the book of Abraham, Joseph Smith maintained that certain information contained therein was not to be revealed to the world, "but is to be had in the Holy Temple of God." Studies of Egyptian temple ritual since the time of Joseph Smith have revealed parallels with Latter-day Saint temple celebrations and doctrine, including a portrayal of the creation and fall of mankind, WASHINGS AND ANOINTINGS, and the ultimate return of individuals to God's presence. Moreover, husband, wife, and children are sealed together for eternity, GENEALOGY is taken seriously; people will be judged according to their deeds in this life, and the reward for a just life is to live in the presence of God forever with one's family. It seems unreasonable to suggest that all such parallels occurred by mere chance.

A number of pseudepigraphic texts purporting to be accounts from the life of Abraham have come to light since Joseph Smith's day, such as the *Apocalypse of Abraham* and the *Testament of Abraham*, documents that exhibit notable similarities with the book of Abraham. For example, in chapter 12 of the *Testament of Abraham* there is a description of the judgment of the dead that matches in minute detail the scene depicted in Facsimile 3 of the book of Abraham and, incidentally, chapter 125 of the Egyptian *Book of the Dead*. In fact, parallels to almost every verse in the book of Abraham can be found in the pseudepigraphical writings about Abraham.

In summary, the numerous similarities that the book of Abraham and associated Latter-day Saint doctrines share with both Egyptian religious texts and recently discovered pseudepigraphical writings may confirm further the authenticity of the Joseph Smith translation known as the book of Abraham. A major question about its authenticity continues to revolve around whether Joseph Smith translated the work from the papyrus fragments the Church now has in its possession or whether he used the URIM AND THUMMIM to receive the text of the book of Abraham by revelation, as is the case with the translation of the scroll of John the Revelator, found in Doctrine and Covenants section 7, or the BOOK OF MOSES, which is excerpted from the JOSEPH SMITH TRANSLATION OF THE BIBLE and is also found in the Pearl of Great Price. From these examples, it is evident that for Joseph Smith it was not necessary to possess an original text in order to have its translation revealed to him. In his function as PROPHET, SEER, and REVELATOR, many channels were open to him to receive information by divine inspiration.

[See also Book of Abraham Facsimiles.]

BIBLIOGRAPHY

Ashment, Edward H. "The Facsimiles of the Book of Abraham: A Reappraisal." *Sunstone* 4, nos. 5–6 (Dec. 1979):33–48.

Baer, Klaus. "The Breathing Permit of Hor." *Dialogue* 3, no. 3 (1968):109–134.

Homans, J. E. *Joseph Smith as a Translator*. Salt Lake City, 1936.

Nibley, Hugh. *The Message of the Joseph Smith Papyri*. Salt Lake City, 1975.

———. *Abraham in Egypt*. Salt Lake City, 1981.

Parker, Richard. "The Joseph Smith Papyri: A Preliminary Report." *Dialogue* 3, no. 2 (1968):86–92, 98–99.

Rhodes, Michael D. "A Translation and Commentary on the Joseph Smith Hypocephalus." *BYU Studies* 17 (Spring 1977): 259–74.

Spaulding, F. S. *Joseph Smith, Jr., as a Translator*. Pamphlet. Salt Lake City, 1912.

Wilson, John. "A Summary Report." *Dialogue* 3, no. 2 (1968):67–85.

MICHAEL D. RHODES

BOOK OF COMMANDMENTS

The Prophet Joseph SMITH and a council of HIGH PRIESTS collected the Prophet's early revelations in November 1831, into the Book of Commandments. They originally decided to print 10,000 copies of the book at Independence, Missouri, but later reduced this number to 3,000. As editor of the Church's newspaper called *The Evening and* *The Morning Star* and of the Book of Commandments, William W. Phelps also printed some of the major revelations in that paper during 1832–1833.

Publication plans were frustrated when a mob destroyed the printing establishment on July 20, 1833, when Phelps had printed only five 32-page signatures. These 160 pages contained sixty-five revelations, the last of which was not completely typeset. Although fire destroyed most of these uncut pages, Church members salvaged enough to put together about a hundred copies, only a few of which survive today. The revelations in the Book of Commandments became part of a larger collection titled the Doctrine and Covenants, first printed in 1835.

BIBLIOGRAPHY

Petersen, Melvin J. "A Study of the Nature of and the Significance of the Changes in the Revelations as Found in a Comparison of the Book of Commandments and Subsequent Editions of the Doctrine and Covenants." Master's thesis, Brigham Young University, 1955.

Woodford, Robert J. "The Historical Development of the Doctrine and Covenants, Volume 1." Ph.D. diss., Brigham Young University, 1974.

ROBERT J. WOODFORD

BOOK OF JOSEPH OF EGYPT

See: Joseph of Egypt: Writings of Joseph

BOOK OF LIFE

In a figurative sense, the book of life is the complete record of one's life, the sum total of thoughts, words, and deeds written in the soul, of which the Lord will take account in the day of judgment (Rev. 20:12; Alma 12:14).

The scriptures also speak of a book of life, or "the Lamb's book of life," as "the record . . . kept in heaven" (D&C 128:7) in which are written both the names and deeds of the faithful. It is also the heavenly register of those who inherit eternal life (Heb. 12:23; Alma 5:58; D&C 76:68), "the book of the names of the sanctified, even them of the celestial world" (D&C 88:2; cf. Mal. 3:16–17).

In the Bible, the phrase "book of the living" appears first in Psalm 69:28, and the notion of a heavenly ledger is alluded to often (Ex. 32:32–33;

Dan. 7:10; 12:1; Isa. 4:3; 65:6; see also Phil. 4:3; Rev. 3:5; 13:8; 21:27). Names of faithful Saints may be recorded in the book of life conditionally while they are in mortality (Luke 10:20) or "from the foundation of the world" (Rev. 17:8), but may be "blotted out" because of unrepented transgression (Rev. 3:5; 22:19; Alma 5:57; D&C 85:5, 11). Ultimately, only the names of those who qualify for eternal life remain written or "sealed" (*TPJS*, p. 9) in the Lamb's book of life.

Latter-day Saints believe that essential items written in the "books yet to be opened" are linked to proper Church records, including those of essential gospel ordinances performed by priesthood authority for individuals and attested by authorized witnesses. In ancient covenant ceremonies, the names of the righteous were solemnly recorded, thus numbering them among "the living" (e.g., Num. 1:1–46; Mosiah 6:1–2). What is properly recorded on earth is recorded in heaven (D&C 128:7–8). Final sealing in the Lamb's book requires, further, the approval of the Holy Spirit of Promise (D&C 132:19).

J. LEWIS TAYLOR

BOOK OF MORMON

[*This entry introduces the Book of Mormon, with the* Overview *describing its basic nature, contents, and purposes; a brief article follows on the* Title Page *from the* Book of Mormon; *and the remaining articles are devoted to a brief explanation of each book in the Book of Mormon.*

Overview
Title Page from Book of Mormon
First Book of Nephi
Second Book of Nephi
Book of Jacob
Book of Enos
Book of Jarom
Book of Omni
The Words of Mormon
Book of Mosiah
Book of Alma
Book of Helaman
Third Nephi
Fourth Nephi
Book of Mormon

Book of Ether
Book of Moroni

The teachings of the Book of Mormon are discussed in doctrinal articles throughout the Encyclopedia; see Doctrine; Gospel of Jesus Christ. *See also* Book of Mormon Religious Teachings and Practices; Jesus Christ in the Scriptures: the Book of Mormon; Prophecy: Prophecy in the Book of Mormon.

Concerning its essential relationship with the Bible and other scripture, see Bible; Book of Mormon, Biblical Prophecies about; Book of Mormon in a Biblical Culture; Isaiah; Scripture; Standard Works.

On the writing and composition of the Book of Mormon, see Book of Mormon Authorship; Book of Mormon Language; Book of Mormon Literature; Book of Mormon Plates and Records.

For information about its origin and publication, see Book of Mormon Editions; Book of Mormon Manuscripts; Book of Mormon Translation by Joseph Smith; Book of Mormon Translations; Book of Mormon Witnesses; Manuscript, Lost 116 Pages; Moroni, Visitations of. *See, generally,* Book of Mormon Studies.

Separate articles can be found on Book of Mormon Peoples; Jaredites; Lamanites; Nephites; Women in the Book of Mormon; *articles on the main individuals in this scripture are listed under* Book of Mormon Personalities.

Internal aspects of Book of Mormon culture and civilization are discussed in such entries as Book of Mormon Chronology; Book of Mormon Economy and Technology; Book of Mormon Geography; Book of Mormon, Government and Legal History in; Book of Mormon, History of Warfare in; Jesus Christ: Forty-Day Ministry and Other Post-Resurrection Appearances of Jesus Christ; Liahona; Secret Combinations; Sword of Laban; Three Nephites; Tree of Life.]

OVERVIEW

The Prophet Joseph SMITH called the Book of Mormon "the most correct of any book on earth, and the keystone of our religion" and said that a person "would get nearer to God by abiding by its precepts, than by any other book" (*TPJS*, p. 194), for it contains the fulness of the GOSPEL OF JESUS CHRIST (D&C 20:8–9). To members of The Church of Jesus Christ of Latter-day Saints, the Book of Mormon forms the doctrinal foundation of the Church and speaks the word of God to all the world.

The Book of Mormon both confirms and supplements the Bible: "Behold, this [the Book of Mormon] is written for the intent that ye may believe that [the Bible]; and if ye believe [the Bible] ye will believe [the Book of Mormon] also" (Morm.

Jesus Christ Is the God of That Land, by Minerva K. Teichert (1949, oil on board, 36″ × 48″). Superimposed on the western hemisphere and flanked by Quetzal birds, native American symbols of liberty and freedom, this painting conveys the central message of the Book of Mormon "that Jesus is the Christ, the Eternal God, manifesting himself unto all nations." Courtesy Springville Museum of Art.

7:9). The Bible is primarily a record of God's dealings with the forebears and descendants of Jacob or Israel in the ancient Near East. Latter-day Saints believe the Book of Mormon to be a record of God's dealings principally with another group of Israelites he brought to the Western Hemisphere from Jerusalem about 600 B.C. (*see* LEHI). They anticipated the birth and coming of Jesus Christ and believed in his ATONEMENT and gospel. Their complex, lengthy records were abridged by a prophet named MORMON, inscribed on plates of gold, and buried by his son, MORONI$_2$, after internecine wars destroyed all of the believers in Christ in the New World except Moroni (A.D. 385).

JOSEPH SMITH AND THE BOOK OF MORMON. In his short lifetime, Joseph Smith brought forth many scriptures (*see* DOCTRINE AND COVENANTS; PEARL OF GREAT PRICE). His first prophetic calling was to bring forth the Book of Mormon. In 1823, at age seventeen, he was shown the hidden record by Moroni, then a resurrected angelic messenger from God (JS—H 1:27–54). After several visitations during the next four years, Joseph was allowed to remove the sacred record from its resting place in the hill CUMORAH, near Palmyra, New York. Despite many interruptions and persistent persecutions (JS—H 1:57–60), Joseph Smith trans-

lated the lengthy record in about sixty working days. Latter-day Saints bear testimony that he did this "through the mercy of God, by the power of God" (D&C 1:29), "by the inspiration of heaven" (*Messenger and Advocate* [Oct. 1834]:14–16; JS—H 1:71, n.). He had the assistance of several scribes, chiefly Oliver COWDERY, who wrote what Joseph Smith dictated. The book was published in Palmyra in 1830. At least eleven witnesses, in addition to Joseph Smith, saw and/or hefted the Book of Mormon plates before he returned them to Moroni (*see* BOOK OF MORMON WITNESSES).

PURPOSES AND CONTENTS. The Book of Mormon, as its modern subtitle states, stands with the Bible as "Another Testament of Jesus Christ." Its main purposes are summarized on its title page: to show the remnants of the Book of Mormon people what great things God did for their forefathers, to make known the covenants of the Lord, and to convince "Jew and Gentile that Jesus is the Christ, the Eternal God, manifesting himself unto all nations." The central event in the Book of Mormon is the appearance of the resurrected Christ to righteous inhabitants of the Western Hemisphere after his ascension into heaven at Jerusalem. During his visit, Christ delivered a sermon that is similar to the SERMON ON THE MOUNT recorded in the New Testament, but with certain vital clarifications and additions. He declared his doctrine, the fulness of his gospel necessary to enter the kingdom of God; and he established his Church with its essential ordinances, and ordained disciples to preside over the Church. At this time, Christ also explained the promises of God to Israel; healed the sick and disabled; blessed the children and their parents; and expressed his great love, allowing each individual to come forward and touch the wounds he had received during his crucifixion (see 3 Ne. 11–26). The record of Jesus' visit and many other passages in the Book of Mormon verify the divine sonship, ministry, atonement, resurrection, and eternal status of the Lord Jesus Christ and show that the fulness of his gospel is the same for all people, whenever and wherever they have lived.

The ancestors of these people to whom Jesus appeared had been in the Western Hemisphere for about 600 years. The Book of Mormon opens with the family of Lehi in Jerusalem at the time of the biblical prophet Jeremiah. Lehi was warned by God about 600 B.C. to take his family and flee Jerusalem before it was destroyed by Babylon (1 Ne. 1:1–2). The account, written by Lehi's son NEPHI$_1$,

In this wooden box, Joseph Smith kept the Book of Mormon plates. The inside of the box measures 14″ × 16″. The depth is 6 1/4″ sloping to 4″. The lid and bottom are walnut, and the sides are made from boxwood. The box was also used as a lap desk. In the possession of emeritus Church Patriarch Eldred G. Smith.

first tells of his family's departure from Jerusalem and of his dangerous return to the city with his brothers to obtain sacred records that contained their lineage, the five books of Moses, and a history of the Jews and writings of prophets down to Jeremiah's time (1 Ne. 3–5).

The group traveled in the wilderness until they reached a pleasant land by the sea where Nephi, with God's instruction, built a ship that took them to the New World (1 Ne. 17–18). Nephi's older brothers, LAMAN and Lemuel, expressed resentment at Nephi's closeness to the Lord and did not want him to rule over them (1 Ne. 16:37–39; 18:10). When the family reached the New World, this antagonism led to a schism between the NEPHITES and LAMANITES that pervades the Book of Mormon.

As the Nephite sermons, prophecies, and historical records were compiled and handed down, the writers emphasized that those who keep God's commandments prosper. Unfortunately, many who prospered became proud and persecuted others, with war as the eventual result. The desolation of war humbled the people, who began again to call upon God.

Ancient American prophets, like biblical prophets such as Moses, Isaiah, and Daniel, were shown visions of the future of various nations. For example, Nephi foresaw Christopher COLUMBUS' discovery of America, the influx of Gentiles into the New World, and the American Revolution

(1 Ne. 13:12–15, 18–19), as well as the birth and earthly ministry of Jesus Christ. Christ's birth, ministry, and death were prophesied by Lehi, Nephi, BENJAMIN, SAMUEL THE LAMANITE, and other prophets. When MOSIAH₁ discovered a people who had left Jerusalem with MULEK, a son of Zedekiah (see Jer. 52:10; Omni 1:12–15; Hel. 8:21), and King Limhi's messengers found a record of the extinct JAREDITES, the Nephites learned that they were not the only people God had brought to the Western Hemisphere.

After the appearance of Jesus Christ, the Nephites and Lamanites enjoyed peace for more than 160 years (4 Ne. 1:18–24). Then, many who had been righteous broke their covenants with God, and the Church and their civilization began to collapse. At last, in A.D. 385, the few remaining Nephites were hunted and killed by Lamanites. The book ends with Moroni, the last Nephite, writing to the people of modern times, admonishing them to "come unto Christ, and be perfected in him" (Moro. 10:32).

MODERN APPLICATIONS. Latter-day Saints embrace the Book of Mormon as a record for all people. In addition to instructing their contemporaries and descendants, the prophets who wrote these ancient records foresaw modern conditions and selected lessons needed to meet the challenges of this world (Morm. 8:34–35). Their book is a record of a fallen people, urging all people to live righteously and prevent a similar fall today.

The Book of Mormon has had a profound effect on the Church and its members. It is so fundamental that Joseph Smith said, "Take away the Book of Mormon and the revelations and where is our religion? We have none" (TPJS, p. 71).

The Book of Mormon teaches that the living God has spoken to several peoples throughout the earth who have written sacred records as he has commanded (2 Ne. 29:11–12). The Book of Mormon is one such record.

It also stands as evidence to Latter-day Saints that God restored his true and living Church through Joseph Smith. The importance of this belief for Latter-day Saints cannot be overestimated, for they are confident that God watches over the people of the earth and loves them, and that he continues to speak to them through contemporary prophets who apply unchanging gospel principles to today's challenges.

The Book of Mormon also is important to Latter-day Saints as an aid in understanding the

Bible and the will of God. Nephi prophesied that many "plain and precious" truths and covenants would be taken from the gospel and the Bible after the deaths of the apostles (1 Ne. 13:26–27). Many questions that have arisen from the Bible are answered for Latter-day Saints by the Book of Mormon, such as the mode of and reasons for baptism (2 Ne. 31; 3 Ne. 11:23–26); the proper way to administer the sacrament of the Lord's Supper (Moro. 4–5); the nature of the Resurrection (Alma 40); the effects of the FALL OF ADAM, and the reasons for evil and suffering in the world (2 Ne. 2). The Book of Mormon reinforces the LDS doctrine that the gospel of Jesus Christ existed before the Creation and has been revealed to prophets and believers throughout time.

Also sacred to Latter-day Saints is the Book of Mormon as a tutor in discerning the promptings of the Holy Ghost. Many Latter-day Saints, including those born into LDS families, trace their conversion to Jesus Christ and their commitment toward the Church to prayerful study of the Book of Mormon, and through it they learn to recognize the Holy Spirit. Thus, the book becomes a continuing symbol of personal revelation and of God's love for and attention to the needs of each person. It also declares that all mankind will be judged by its precepts and commandments (Mosiah 3:24; Moro. 10:27; *see* JUDGMENT). It is evidence that God remembers every creature he has created (Mosiah 27:30) and every covenant he has made (1 Ne. 19:15; 3 Ne. 16:11). The Book of Mormon is the base from which millions have begun a personal journey of spiritual growth and of service to others.

For LDS children, the Book of Mormon is a source of stories and heroes to equal those of the Bible—Joseph in Egypt, Daniel in the lions' den, the faithful Ruth, and brave Queen Esther. They tell and sing with enthusiasm about the army of faithful young men led by HELAMAN₁ (Alma 56:41–50); of the prophet ABINADI's courage before wicked King Noah (Mosiah 11–17); of Nephi and his unwavering faithfulness (1 Ne. 3–18); of Abish, a Lamanite woman who for many years appears to be the lone believer in Christ in King Lamoni's court until the missionary Ammon taught the gospel to the king and queen (Alma 19); and of Jesus' appearances to the Nephites (3 Ne. 11–28). There are many favorites. The book is used to teach children doctrines, provide examples of the Christlike life, and remind them of God's great love and hope for all his children.

The book is central to missionary work. It is the Church's most important missionary tool and is destined to go to every nation, kindred, tongue, and people (Rev. 14:6–7). All LDS missionaries encourage those they contact to read and pray about the book as a means of receiving their own testimony from God about the truthfulness of the Book of Mormon, a witness of Jesus Christ.

Latter-day Saints are regularly admonished to make fuller use of the Book of Mormon. In 1832, two and one-half years after the book was published, the word of the Lord warned the Saints that they had treated the revelations too lightly and had neglected to "remember the new covenant, even the Book of Mormon" (D&C 84:57). Church leaders repeatedly encourage members to make the Book of Mormon a greater part of their lives. President Ezra Taft BENSON has counseled Latter-day Saints to read the book daily and to share it and the gospel message with all the world.

READING THE BOOK OF MORMON. This sacred record asks the reader to approach its words with faith and prayer. One of its teachings is that readers will "receive no witness until after the trial of [their] faith" (Ether 12:6). Therefore, although aspects of the book may seem unusual or improbable at first, it invites its readers to entertain them as possibilities until the whole picture becomes clear and other feelings are experienced and thoughts considered. Moreover, the final inscription of Moroni₂ on the title page asks readers to look beyond human weaknesses in the book: "If there are faults they are the mistakes of men; wherefore, condemn not the things of God." He closed his own book within the Book of Mormon by exhorting all who receive these things to ask God, with a sincere heart and with real intent, having faith in Christ, if they are not true, and promises that God will manifest the truth of it (Moro. 10:4).

Latter-day Saints of all ages and interests find rewards in reading the Book of Mormon. At first, people tend to focus attention on its main messages and story lines. With further reading and pondering, they discover numerous themes, meaningful nuances, interesting details, and profound spiritual expressions.

The first-time reader may find the Book of Mormon difficult at times. Its style, as translated into English, is somewhat similar to that of the King James Version of the Bible, and the reader who is not familiar with the Bible will encounter some unfamiliar word usages. The 1981 edition of the Book of Mormon is annotated with many Bible references and aids to facilitate a more detailed comparison.

Book of Mormon prophets Nephi, JACOB, and Abinadi quote extensively from Isaiah (see, e.g., 2 Ne. 6–8 [Isa. 49–51]; 2 Ne. 12–24 [Isa. 2–14]; Mosiah 14 [Isa. 53]), an Old Testament prophet whose poetic style and allusions have challenged readers of the Bible and also have proved difficult to many who study the Book of Mormon. Initially, some Church leaders encourage first-time readers to move through these chapters, understanding what is accessible and saving the rest for later study. In Isaiah's writings, Latter-day Saints find an important testimony of Christ and of the fulfillment of God's covenants with the house of Israel. Christ admonished his followers to "search these things diligently, for great are the words of Isaiah" (3 Ne. 23:11).

Another possible hurdle for readers is the book's nonchronological insertions. Nephi and Jacob and Jacob's descendants wrote first-person accounts from about 590 B.C. until about 150 B.C., and then Mormon (about A.D. 385) inserted a shorter chapter to explain his role as abridger of another record. Then the reader is returned via Mormon's abridgment to the history of Nephi's successors and of the descendants of ALMA₁. As groups of people break away from and return to the main body, parts of their records are incorporated into the book, causing the reader to jump back to earlier events. Likewise, Moroni's abridgment of the very ancient book of Ether appears out of chronological order near the end. In addition, the Book of Mormon, like the Old Testament, describes events from widely separated intervals. As an abridgment, it contains only a small part of the proceedings of these ancient peoples.

APPROACHING THE TEXT. The arrangement of the Book of Mormon lends itself to many approaches. Three mutually supportive avenues are most often followed. First, the book serves as a source of guidance and doctrine, yielding lessons and wisdom applicable to contemporary life. This approach is recommended in the writings of Nephi, who wrote that he "did liken the scriptures unto [his people], that it might be for [their] profit and learning" (1 Ne. 19:23). Latter-day Saints find its pages rich with ennobling narratives, clear doctrines, eternal truths, memorable sayings, and principles. Knowing the conditions of the latter days, the ancient prophets periodically address the individual reader directly. Latter-day Saints emphasize the need to read the Book of Mormon prayerfully, with faith in God, to benefit personally from its teachings and to come unto Christ.

A second approach to the Book of Mormon, adding historical dimension to the first approach, is to study the book as an ancient text. The reader who accepts the Book of Mormon as an ancient Hebrew lineage history written by prophets in the New World will find the book consistent with that description and setting. The book is a repository of ancient cultures that are as far removed from modern readers as are those of the Old and New Testaments. Continuing research has found Hebrew poetic forms, rhetorical patterns, and idioms, together with many Mesoamerican symbols, traditions, and artifacts, to be implicit in the book or consistent with it.

Finally, one may enjoy the Book of Mormon as a work of literature. Although the style may seem tedious or repetitive at times, there are order, purpose, and clarity in its language. Its words are often as beautiful and as memorable as passages in the Psalms, the Gospel of John, and other notable religious works of prose and poetry.

Most faithful readers of the Book of Mormon, however, do not define or limit themselves to any single approach or methodology, for these approaches are all transcended by the overriding implications of the book's divine origins and eternal purposes. Study and faith, reflection and application, all help a person know and comprehend the messages of the Book of Mormon. But for millions of Latter-day Saints, their most important experience with the Book of Mormon has been the spiritual knowledge that they have received of its truth. It has changed and enriched their lives and has brought Jesus Christ and his teachings closer to them.

BIBLIOGRAPHY

Benson, Ezra Taft. *A Witness and a Warning*. Salt Lake City, 1988.

Downs, Robert B. *Books That Changed America*. London, 1970.

Faust, James E. "The Keystone of Our Religion." *Ensign* 13 (Nov. 1983):9.

Nibley, Hugh W. "The Mormon View of the Book of Mormon." *Concilium* 10 (Dec. 1967):82–83; reprinted, *CWHN* 8:259–64.

MONTE S. NYMAN
LISA BOLIN HAWKINS

TITLE PAGE FROM THE BOOK OF MORMON
Joseph SMITH once wrote, "I wish to mention here that the title-page of the Book of Mormon is a literal translation, taken from the very last leaf, on the left hand side of the collection or book of plates, which contained the record which has been translated; . . . and that said title-page is not . . . a modern composition, either of mine or of any other man who has lived or does live in this generation" (*HC* 1:71.).

The title page is therefore the translation of an ancient document, at least partially written by MORONI₂, son of Mormon, in the fifth century A.D. It describes the volume as an "abridgment of the record of the people of Nephi, and also of the Lamanites" and "an abridgment taken from the Book of Ether also, which is a record of the people of Jared" (*see* BOOK OF MORMON PLATES AND RECORDS).

According to the title page, the Book of Mormon is addressed to LAMANITES, Jews, and GENTILES and is designed to inform Lamanites of promises made to their forebears and to convince "Jew and Gentile that Jesus is the Christ, the Eternal God, manifesting himself unto all nations."

The title page was used as the description of the Book of Mormon on the federal copyright application filed June 11, 1829, with R. R. Lansing, Clerk of the District Court of the United States for the Northern District of New York, at Albany.

BIBLIOGRAPHY

Ludlow, Daniel H. "The title page." In *The Book of Mormon: First Nephi, The Doctrinal Foundation*, ed. Monte S. Nyman and Charles D. Tate, pp. 19–33. Provo, Utah, 1988.

ELDIN RICKS

FIRST BOOK OF NEPHI
Written by NEPHI₁, an ancient prophet who fled Jerusalem with his father, LEHI, and Lehi's family shortly after 600 B.C., this book tells of their travels

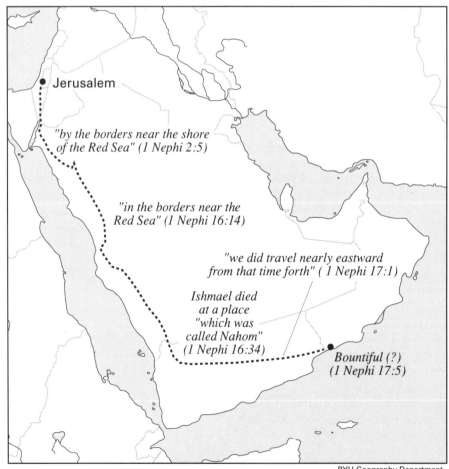

BYU Geography Department

Possible route of Lehi in the Old World, from Jerusalem to the ocean, c. 600–587 B.C.

under divine guidance to the Western Hemisphere. With its detailed testimony of the mission of Jesus Christ and its panoramic view of sacred history, 1 Nephi is the doctrinal and historical foundation for all of the Book of Mormon. Its stated intent is to testify that the God of Israel can save all who repent and exercise faith in him (1 Ne. 1:20; 6:4).

Composed several years after Nephi arrived in the "promised land," the record, of which the First Book of Nephi was a part, contained prophesying and sacred preaching "for Christ's sake, and for the sake of [his] people" (Jacob 1:4). Its fundamental message is that the God of Israel is merciful and has the power to save those who obey him (1 Ne. 1:20; 6:4; 22:30–31). Nephi supports this thesis with historical and prophetic evidence. He cites Israel's exodus from Egypt twice as evidence of God's redeeming power, and saw the same power at work in his family's exodus from a doomed Jerusalem. A seer of remarkable spiritual stature, Nephi testified that greater acts of redemption lay in the future: God himself would come to earth to ransom man from death and sin (1 Ne. 11:33; 19:10), and before the end of the world, Israel would be redeemed.

The narrative of 1 Nephi is vivid and dramatic; acts of divine intervention dominate this account. It begins in the first year of the Judean King Zedekiah (1 Ne. 1:4; cf. 2 Kgs. 24:8–18; dated by Babylonian documents at 597 B.C.). Jerusalem had just capitulated after a brief Babylonian siege, and King Jehoiachin, together with many of Judah's prominent citizens, had been deported. When Jerusalem persisted in its arrogance, a host of prophets, including Jeremiah and Lehi, warned of destruction. As people conspired to kill Lehi, he was warned by the Lord and escaped south into the desert. Twice his four sons returned to the region, once to obtain a copy of the scriptures written on plates of brass and again to convince Ishmael and his family to flee with them (chaps. 3–7). Guided by a miraculous brass compass (*see* LIAHONA), Lehi's group then completed a grueling odyssey that covered eight years in the wilderness, arriving at a verdant spot on the southern coast of the Arabian Peninsula. There, Nephi was summoned by the Lord to a mountain where he was instructed to build a ship to carry the group to a land of promise. Through God's frequent inspiration and protection, the ship was finished and the treacherous voyage completed (chaps. 16–18).

Through all these events, Lehi and Nephi were opposed by the oldest sons in the family,

Wadi Sayq, near the border between Yemen and Oman on the Gulf of Aden (1989). Areas with vegetation such as this along the southern coast of the Arabian peninsula match the description of the place where Lehi and his group built their ship (1 Nephi 17:5), but they were unknown to Westerners until after the Book of Mormon was published. Courtesy Warren Aston.

LAMAN and Lemuel, who were not only skeptical but sometimes violent in their opposition. The record vindicates Nephi in many ways. An angel once intervened to protect Nephi from his brothers; twice he escaped from them, being filled with the power of God. Several times, by his faith, he succeeded where they failed.

Records of powerful visions are interspersed throughout the narrative. Lehi received his prophetic commission in a vision as he prayed on Jerusalem's behalf: He saw a pillar of fire dwelling upon a rock and God seated upon his throne and was given a book to read that decreed judgment upon the city (chap. 1). Soon after, Nephi heard the voice of the Lord, saying that Nephi would teach and rule over his elder brothers (chap. 2); and Lehi had a dream that centered around a magnificent tree, a river, an iron rod, and a great and spacious building (chap. 8; *see also* TREE OF LIFE). The family's escape from a proud and materialistic Jerusalem and their subsequent quest for salvation in the wilderness are vividly reflected in the imagery of this dream. Lehi also prophesied about the Babylonian captivity of the Jews, their eventual return to Palestine, and the coming of a Messiah who would redeem mankind from its lost and fallen state (chap. 10).

Inspired by Lehi's spiritual experiences and wanting to know the meaning of his father's dream, Nephi sought and received the same vision, together with its interpretation. This revelation puts the experiences of Lehi and his posterity into the context of God's redemptive plan and provides much of the historical and doctrinal framework for subsequent Book of Mormon prophecy: (1) Nephi saw the birth, ministry, and atoning sacrifice of the Son of God, and the rejection of his apostles by Israel; (2) he witnessed the division of Lehi's family, followed by the rise, decline, and destruction of his own posterity by the descendants of his brothers, and saw that the Lamb of God would visit various branches of Israel, including Nephi's posterity; (3) he saw a GREAT AND ABOMINABLE CHURCH among the Gentiles, as well as a dispensation of the gospel to the Gentiles and their crucial role in gathering Israel and a remnant of Nephi's seed; and (4) he was shown the final victory of God over the powers of evil at the end of the world (chaps. 11–14).

Citing other corroborating prophecies, 1 Nephi 19–22 reinforces those four themes, the mainstays of the Nephite outlook on world history. Nephi first gives a detailed testimony of the atoning sacrifice of the God of Israel, his rejection, and the scattering of God's covenant people, quoting ZENOS, ZENOCK, and NEUM (chap. 19); he then quoted ISAIAH to show that God will defer his anger and will eventually gather his people through the assistance of gentile kings and queens (chaps. 20–21); and, finally, he exhorts all to obey God's commandments and be saved, for in the last days the wicked shall burn and the Holy One of Israel shall reign (chap. 22).

BIBLIOGRAPHY

Axelgard, Frederick W. "1 and 2 Nephi: An Inspiring Whole." *BYU Studies* 26 (Fall 1986):53–65.

Nibley, Hugh. *Lehi in the Desert.* In CWHN 5.

Nyman, Monte S., and Charles D. Tate, Jr., eds. *The Book of Mormon: First Nephi, the Doctrinal Foundation.* Provo, Utah, 1988.

RULON D. EAMES

SECOND BOOK OF NEPHI

The Second Book of Nephi (2 Nephi) is a work written about 550 B.C. by the same author who wrote 1 Nephi and included it on his small PLATES. The second book contains four prophetic discourses and treatises from three Book of Mormon prophets, LEHI, JACOB, and Nephi$_1$, as well as substantial excerpts of the prophecies of Isaiah from the brass plates. Additionally, 2 Nephi briefly records the difficult transition from the founding generation of Lehi's colony to the succeeding generation in their new homeland.

The first segment of the book consists of Lehi's admonitions and testament to his posterity before his death (1:1–4:11). He directed his opening words to his older sons, Laman, Lemuel, and Sam, as well as to the sons of Ishmael. He reminded them of God's mercy in leading them to a promised land, taught them concerning the COVENANT of righteousness that belongs to the land, warned of the loss of liberty and prosperity that will follow disobedience to God, and urged them to become reconciled to their brother Nephi as their leader (1:1–27).

Following this admonition, Lehi pronounced specific blessings on all of his descendants, either as individuals or as family groups. His blessings contain prophecies and promises concerning the future of each individual or group in the covenant land and are followed by counsel "according to the workings of the Spirit" (1:6). His instructions to his youngest sons, Jacob and Joseph, are doctrinally significant. He spoke to Jacob concerning God's plan of salvation for his children, teaching principles that are fundamental to understanding the gospel of Jesus Christ, including the doctrine of redemption through the Messiah, the necessity of opposition and agency, the role of Satan, and the importance of the fall of Adam and Eve (2:1–30). Lehi taught his son Joseph concerning the prophecies of his ancestor Joseph of Egypt, who foretold the latter-day mission of another Joseph (the Prophet Joseph SMITH) and of the coming forth of the Book of Mormon (3:1–25).

Nephi$_1$, son of Lehi, is author of the next section, the only historical segment in the record (4:12–5:34). After recounting the death of Lehi and the subsequent rebellion of Laman, Lemuel, and the sons of Ishmael (4:12–13), Nephi noted that he was keeping two records: the large plates on which he wrote his people's secular history and the small plates on which he recorded "that which is pleasing unto God," including many excerpts from the plates of brass (4:14–15; 5:29–33).

As Nephi wrote of his delight in pondering the scriptures and "the things of the Lord," he was moved to compose a beautiful psalm (4:16–35). In these verses, much like the biblical psalmist, Nephi used inspiring imagery and poetic parallelism to praise God for his goodness, to lament his own weaknesses, and to declare his devotion to the Lord.

Nephi closed this segment by telling of the partitioning of Lehi's posterity into two distinct peoples, the NEPHITES (the believers) and the LAMANITES (the unbelievers). He described the theological, cultural, and geographical divisions that developed between the brother nations, lamenting that within forty years of separating they were at war one with another (5:1–34).

A sermon by Jacob constitutes the third entry in 2 Nephi (chaps. 6–10), followed by the fourth and final part, a long written discourse from Nephi (chaps. 11–33). Quoting substantial portions of Isaiah, both Nephi and Jacob emphasized two major themes: the history and future of God's covenant people, and the mission of the Messiah. For his discourse on these topics, Nephi first quoted the text of Isaiah 2–14 in 2 Nephi 12–24 and then commented on them in chapters 25–30, incorporating portions of Isaiah 29 in his discussion. Jacob quoted Isaiah 50:1–52:2 in chapters 7–8. Apparently, Joseph Smith put these quotations from Isaiah in King James English, but with many variant readings reflecting the Nephite source.

Citing and reflecting on Isaiah, Jacob, and Nephi focused on such events as the Babylonian captivity and return (6:8–9; 25:10–11); the apostasy, scattering, and oppression of the house of Israel; and the latter-day gathering of their descendants, their restoration by conversion to the gospel of Christ, and the establishment of Zion—themes that concerned them because of their own Israelite ancestry (6:6–18; 8:1–25; 10:1–25; 25:14–17; 26:14–30:18). They further prophesied the destruction of the wicked before the second coming of the Savior followed by the subsequent era of peace (12:1–22; 21:1–24:3).

In their discourses, Jacob and Nephi taught of the Messiah's earthly ministry, rejection, and crucifixion (6:9; 7:1–11; 9:1–54; 10:3–5; 17–19) and his gospel fundamentals of faith, repentance, baptism, and obedience (9:23–24; 31:1–21; see GOSPEL OF JESUS CHRIST); they then prophesied

his baptism, atoning sacrifice, and resurrection, followed by his ministry among the Nephites, his ultimate second coming, and the final judgment (9:5–27; 26:1–9; 31:4–12).

In chapter 29, Nephi made special mention of the Lord's desire that the Book of Mormon be used as "a standard" by his people, along with the Bible (29:2), noting that other books will come forth. In closing the record, Nephi testified that the words therein are the words of Christ, the words by which readers shall be judged (33:10–15).

BIBLIOGRAPHY

Jackson, Kent P., ed. *Studies in Scripture*, Vol. 7, pp. 86–174. Salt Lake City, 1987.

McConkie, Joseph Fielding, and Robert L. Millet. *Doctrinal Commentary on the Book of Mormon*, Vol. 1, pp. 182–376. Salt Lake City, 1987.

Nyman, Monte S., and Charles D. Tate, eds. *The Book of Mormon: Second Nephi, The Doctrinal Structure*. Provo, Utah, 1989.

TERRY B. BALL

BOOK OF JACOB

Written by JACOB, fifth son of LEHI, sometime after 545 B.C., the work follows the pattern outlined by NEPHI₁ for making entries on the small PLATES by including sacred sermons, significant revelations, prophecies, and some historical information. Jacob, a Nephite prophet, wrote to persuade all men to "come unto Christ" (Jacob 1:7).

The book appears to have been written in three stages. The first constitutes an important discourse by Jacob at the temple, in which he called his people to repent from immorality, materialism, and pride (chaps. 2–3). He counseled men and women to be generous with their possessions, promising that, if they sought the KINGDOM OF GOD before seeking riches, they would be blessed with sufficient wealth to assist others (2:17–19). Jacob strongly warned his people against sins of immorality because many had transgressed the law of CHASTITY, including practicing polygamy not authorized by the Lord (2:30). He reminded his hearers that the Lord "delight[s] in the chastity of women" and that the sins of the men had broken the hearts of their wives and children (2:22–35).

The second part contains prophecies concerning the ATONEMENT of Christ, the rejection of Jesus of Nazareth by many Jews, and the scattering and gathering of ISRAEL (chaps. 4–6). Jacob desired that later generations would "know that we knew of Christ, and we had a hope of his glory many hundred years before his coming" (4:4). The major component of this section is Jacob's quoting of the allegory of the tame and wild olive trees (chap. 5). Written by ZENOS, an Israelite prophet whose writings were preserved on the brass plates, this allegory outlines in symbolic narrative the prophetic story of the scattering and gathering of Israel, including Lehi's descendants, from the establishment of Israel to the end of the earth.

The third segment recounts Jacob's experience with an ANTI-CHRIST named Sherem, who with skill and power of language endeavored to flatter and deceive people away from belief in Christ (7:1–4). Sherem had accused Jacob of blasphemy and false prophecy and had tried to convince people that there would be no Christ. In the end, Sherem was confounded by Jacob and, after seeking for a sign, was smitten by God and died shortly thereafter (7:7–8, 13–20). Recovering from Sherem's divisive teachings through searching the scriptures, Jacob's people were able to experience anew the peace and love of God (7:23).

BIBLIOGRAPHY

Matthews, Robert J. "Jacob: Prophet, Theologian, Historian." In *The Book of Mormon: Jacob Through Words of Mormon*, ed. M. Nyman and C. Tate, Provo, Utah, 1990.

CLYDE J. WILLIAMS

BOOK OF ENOS

Following the pattern set by his father and predecessors (Jacob 1:2–4; cf. Enos 1:13–16), Enos, son of JACOB, personally recorded the TESTIMONY and prophetic promises granted to him. Enos (c. 515–417 B.C.) is a figure who touches the heart. He typifies conversion, compassion, and confidence before the Lord. While he was hunting beasts, the words of his father "concerning eternal life, and the joy of the saints, sunk deep into [his] heart," and his "soul hungered" (1:3–4). All day and into the night he "wrestle[d] . . . before God" in "mighty prayer" until he received a remission of his sins. He successively prayed for his own welfare, for the welfare of his brethren the NEPHITES, who strayed too easily from righteousness, and then for his brethren the LAMANITES, who had become increasingly ferocious and wild. Enos received a COVENANT declaration from the Lord that the Nephite records would be brought forth to the Lamanites. He knew with a surety that he would see his Redeemer's face with pleasure and would receive a place in the mansions of the Father (1:27).

MARILYN ARNOLD

BOOK OF JAROM

Jarom, son of ENOS, recorded a brief summary of the fortunes of the NEPHITES during his lifetime (c. 440–355 B.C.). Twice he justified the brevity of his account, pleading limited space and little new doctrine to add to the words of his predecessors. Reflecting an era of strict conservatism in the flourishing colony, Jarom recounted great Nephite efforts to observe the LAW OF MOSES and to anticipate the coming MESSIAH. Despite their larger numbers, the LAMANITES were unsuccessful in their frequent attacks on the prospering Nephites, and Jarom attributed the Nephite successes to the prophets, priests, and teachers who stirred them continually to repentance.

MARILYN ARNOLD

BOOK OF OMNI

This book concluded and filled the small PLATES of Nephi. It contains brief statements by a succession of record keepers who were descendants of JACOB but apparently not spiritual leaders: Omni, Amaron, Chemish, Abinadom, and Amaleki (fourth–second centuries B.C.). Amaleki, whose account is the longest of the five, described the important transition that occurred in Book of Mormon history when MOSIAH₁ led the escape of a band of faithful NEPHITES from the land of Nephi to Zarahemla (c. 200 B.C.). Here they discovered descendants of a group that had left Jerusalem with MULEK but had lost their religion and language. Amaleki connected the corruption of their language with the absence of written records, establishing the importance of record preservation. Mosiah brought with him the plates of brass containing "the record of the Jews" (Omni 1:14), including the laws that kings were required to have under the LAW OF MOSES (see Deut. 17:18–19). He was accepted as king over both these peoples and ruled for a generation. Amaleki survived Mosiah but had no heirs, so he transmitted his records to Mosiah's son, King BENJAMIN.

MARILYN ARNOLD

THE WORDS OF MORMON

MORMON was at work on his abridgment of the large PLATES of NEPHI₁ when he discovered the small plates of Nephi, a prophetic record from early NEPHITE history (W of M 1:3). Because he was deeply impressed with the messianic PROPHECIES that he read on the small plates, and in response to "the workings of the Spirit," Mormon included that set of plates with his digest (W of M 1:4–7). But because that record ended a few years before the book of Mosiah began (c. A.D. 130), Mormon assumed the prerogative of an editor and appended this historical postscript to the small plates to bring its conclusion into correlation with the opening of the book of Mosiah. This appendage, called the Words of Mormon, was composed about A.D. 385.

ELDIN RICKS

BOOK OF MOSIAH

The book of Mosiah is religiously rich, symbolically meaningful, chronologically complex, and politically significant. Although its disparate events range from 200 to 91 B.C., they are unified particularly by the theme of deliverance and by the reign of the Nephite king MOSIAH₂.

Several groups figure prominently in this history: (1) the main body of Nephites under King BENJAMIN and his son Mosiah₂, together with the people of Zarahemla (Mulekites), who outnumbered their Nephite rulers and neighbors; (2) the people of Zeniff, who failed in their attempt to reoccupy the Nephites' homeland, the land of Nephi; and (3) the people of ALMA₁, who broke away from the people of Zeniff and became the people of Alma, followers of the martyred prophet ABINADI. The last two groups returned to Zarahemla shortly after Mosiah became king.

The book of Mosiah is drawn from several underlying textual sources: Benjamin's speech (124 B.C.); the record of Zeniff (c. 200–120 B.C.), including Alma's record of Abinadi's trial (c. 150 B.C.) and of his people (c. 150–118 B.C.); and the annals of Mosiah (124–91 B.C.).

BENJAMIN'S SPEECH (CHAPS. 1–6). The coronation of Mosiah occurred in a setting similar to the traditional Israelite assembly at the temple, together with sacrifices, covenant renewal, confessions, pronouncements regarding Christ's atoning blood, and admonitions to serve God and help the poor. Benjamin died, and Mosiah reigned. He sponsored Ammon's expedition to find the people of Zeniff (7:1–8:21).

RECORD OF ZENIFF (CHAPS. 9–22). About seventy-five years earlier, Zeniff had established his colony; he fought two wars, and his wicked son Noah succeeded him. Twice, the prophet Abinadi delivered a condemnation of Noah; Abinadi rehearsed the Ten Commandments, quoted Isaiah 53, and discoursed on the atonement of Jesus Christ and the resurrection. As he was suffering death by fire, Abinadi prophesied that his death would prefigure Noah's. One of Noah's priests, Alma₁, believed Abinadi's preaching, fled into the wilderness, and assembled a group of converts who escaped together from Noah's soldiers. Meanwhile, a military officer named Gideon opposed Noah, the Lamanites attacked, and Noah fled and was subsequently executed by his own people in the manner that Abinadi had predicted. Noah's son, Limhi, was left to reign for many years as a vassal king in servitude to the Lamanites. At length, Limhi and his people were delivered and escaped to Zarahemla.

ALMA'S RECORD (CHAPS. 23–24). The followers of Alma₁ practiced baptism and placed strong emphasis on unity, loving one another, and avoiding contention. In a speech that presaged Mosiah's final words establishing the reign of the judges, Alma₁ refused to become a king, wanting his people to be in bondage to no person. Nevertheless, they came under cruel bondage to the Lamanites, now led by some of Alma's former associates, the evil priests of Noah. Several years later, the people of Alma were miraculously delivered.

THE ANNALS OF MOSIAH (CHAPS. 25–29). The Nephites, the people of Zarahemla (Mulekites), the people of Limhi, and the people of Alma₁ were unified under Mosiah as king, with Alma as high priest. Alma was given authority to organize and regulate churches, but many members apostasized and persecuted the righteous. Among the wicked were his son ALMA₂ and the four sons of Mosiah. When they were confronted by an angel of the Lord, they repented and were converted. Mosiah translated the Jaredite record, passed the Nephite records and sacred artifacts to Alma₂, and installed Alma₂ as the first chief judge according to the voice of the people.

The narratives in the book of Mosiah emphasize the theme of deliverance from bondage, whether physical or spiritual. In his address, Benjamin speaks of spiritual deliverance through the atoning blood of Christ, emphasizing mankind's dependence on God and its responsibility to the poor (both themes or typologies are similarly shaped in the Bible by the Exodus tradition). The account of the conversion of Alma$_2$ is a notable case of deliverance from spiritual bondage by calling upon the name of Jesus Christ (Mosiah 27; Alma 36). Two groups are delivered from physical bondage and oppression: Limhi's people and the converts of Alma after their enslavement by the Lamanites. As in the Exodus pattern, they "cried" to the Lord, who heard and delivered them from bondage. An emissary named Ammon expressly compared the deliverance of the people of Zeniff to the exodus of Israel from Egypt and of Lehi from Jerusalem (Mosiah 7:19–22, 33).

The book of Mosiah establishes several pairs of comparisons in a manner similar to a literary technique often used in the Bible: Alma$_1$ and Amulon are examples of good and bad priests; Benjamin and Noah are contrasting exemplars of noble and corrupt kingship. The extreme contrast between these kings is cited by Mosiah at the end of his reign to explain the wisdom in shifting the government of the Nephites from kingship to a reign of judges (Mosiah 29).

The Jaredite record is mentioned three times (Mosiah 8:9; 21:27; 28:11–19). In an attempt to get help from Mosiah's settlement, Limhi dispatched a search party; it did not find Mosiah, but found human remains, weapons of war, and twenty-four gold plates. The party returned this record to Limhi, who gave it to Mosiah, who translated it using two stones called "interpreters" (see URIM AND THUMMIM). The record told of the rise and fall of the Jaredites (see BOOK OF MORMON: BOOK OF ETHER).

BIBLIOGRAPHY

Tate, George S. "The Typology of the Exodus Pattern in the Book of Mormon." In *Literature of Belief*, ed. N. Lambert, pp. 245–66. Provo, Utah, 1981.

Thomasson, Gordon C. "Mosiah: The Complex Symbolism and the Symbolic Complex of Kingship in the Book of Mormon." *F.A.R.M.S. Paper.* Provo, Utah, 1982.

Tvedtnes, John A. "King Benjamin and the Feast of Tabernacles." In *By Study and Also by Faith*, ed. J. Lundquist and S. Ricks, Vol. 2, pp. 197–237. Salt Lake City, 1990.

ALAN GOFF

BOOK OF ALMA

The book of Alma is the longest book in the Book of Mormon. It was abridged by MORMON, principally from the records of three men, ALMA$_2$ (chaps. 1–16, 27–44), Ammon (chaps. 17–26), and Alma's son HELAMAN$_1$ (chaps. 45–62), and concludes with remarks by Mormon (chap. 63). Its broad theme is that the preaching of the word of God in pure testimony is mightier than politics or the sword in establishing peace, justice, equality, and goodness (Alma 4:19; 31:5). The book demonstrates this theme through repeated examples of individuals who were converted to faith in the anticipated Savior, Jesus Christ, and examples of people who were given victory by God over their wicked and ambitious enemies.

The book of Alma covers thirty-nine years (91–52 B.C.). The first fourteen years are covered by two concurrent accounts—one encompassing the teachings and activities of Alma$_2$, who resigned his judgeship in order to engage in missionary work in the land of Zarahemla (chaps. 1–16), and the other containing the words and deeds of the sons of King MOSIAH$_2$ and their companions as they made considerable personal sacrifice in their efforts to preach the gospel among the LAMANITES (chaps. 17–26).

The first section begins with the trial of Nehor before the chief judge Alma; Nehor was convicted and executed for the crime of enforcing PRIESTCRAFT with the sword (chap. 1). Alma then fought a civil war against Nehor's followers and prevailed (chaps. 2–4), but he soon relinquished the judgeship to devote full time to the ministry. He preached powerful sermons at the cities of Zarahemla (chaps. 5–6), Gideon (chap. 7), and Melek (chap. 8), and went to the wicked city of Ammonihah, where he was cast out, but ordered by an angel to return. In Ammonihah the second time, he met and was assisted by Amulek, who was instructed by an angel to find Alma (chap. 8). Although they were opposed by a skilled lawyer named Zeezrom, eventually they converted many, including Zeezrom. However, their male converts were expelled from the city, and Alma and Amulek were imprisoned and forced to watch the wives and children of their converts being burned to death. Eventually, Alma and Amulek were delivered when an earthquake destroyed the prison and killed their captors (chaps. 9–14). Shortly thereafter, this apostate city was annihilated by invading Lamanites (chap. 16).

During the same fourteen years, the sons of Mosiah and their companions were in the land southward. Ammon went to the land of Ishmael, and through his service to, and love of, King Lamoni, he converted the king and many of his people (chaps. 17–19), whom he taught to live the LAW OF MOSES in anticipation of the coming of Christ (Alma 25:15). Ammon and Lamoni then went to the land of Middoni to free his fellow missionaries from prison. En route they were confronted by Lamoni's father, the king of all the Lamanites, who took to the sword. Ammon withstood his blows, gained control over the king, and made him promise freedom for his brothers and autonomy for Lamoni and his people (chap. 20). Once Ammon's brother, Aaron, and his companions were free, they went to Lamoni's father, and taught and converted him, his household, and many of his people. These converted Lamanites, concerned about the return of prior blood guilt, made an oath never to shed blood again (chap. 23). Other Lamanites and dissident Nephites attacked these converts and killed 1,005, who would not defend themselves because of that oath. Many of the attacking Lamanites (but not the Nephite dissenters) felt remorse for their actions and laid down their arms and also became converted (chaps. 24–25). Eventually, Ammon led these converts, called Anti-Nephi-Lehies, to Nephite territory, where they settled in the land of Jershon (chap. 27). The Lamanites who were left behind become angry at the Nephites and then attacked and destroyed Ammonihah (Alma 25:1–2; described more fully in Alma 16:1–11).

After these developments, Korihor, an ANTICHRIST and advocate of blasphemous doctrines, confronted Alma as high priest in the court of the chief judge, where he asked for a sign from God, was struck dumb, and died shortly thereafter (chap. 30). Next, Alma led a delegation to preach to the Zoramites, a group that had defected from the Nephites. Many poverty-stricken Zoramites were reconverted and cast out by the other Zoramites. The unconverted promptly allied with the Lamanites, attacked the Nephites, and were defeated (chaps. 31–35, 43–44).

The chapters focusing on Alma also contain his blessings and instructions to his three sons (chaps. 36–42) and an account of his disappearance (being taken to heaven; chap. 45). The book of Alma ends with the detailed accounts by HELAMAN₁ of further wars between the Nephites and Lamanites (chaps.

43–62; see BOOK OF MORMON, HISTORY OF WARFARE IN). The final chapter (chap. 63) notes the deaths of Pahoran, Moroni, Helaman, and his brother Shiblon, marking the end of this era of righteous Nephite control of Zarahemla. It also tells of Hagoth, a shipbuilder who transported people to the north, but he was never heard from again after a second departure.

The book of Alma covers a critical period in Nephite history, the opening years of the Nephite judgeship (see BOOK OF MORMON, GOVERNMENT AND LEGAL HISTORY IN). The survival of this popularly based form of government was threatened several times in the course of the book, starting when Nehor's follower Amlici sought to become king. It was threatened again when the Zoramites (described above) defected. Further trouble arose when Amlickiah, a Zoramite, persuaded many of the lower judges to support him as king. A general named Moroni rallied the Nephite troops by raising a banner that he called the Title of Liberty; it proclaimed the need to remember and defend their God, their religion, their freedom, their peace, their wives, and their children. Amalickiah and a few of his men fled to the Lamanites, where he, through treachery and murder, established himself as king and led the Lamanites in a prolonged war against the Nephites. Amalickiah was killed after seven years of war, but the wars continued under his brother Ammoron for six more years. Those years became particularly perilous for the Nephites when "kingmen" arose in Zarahemla and expelled the Nephite government from the capital (discussed in CWHN 8:328–79). Moroni was forced to leave the battlefront to regain control of the capital before he could turn his full attention to defeating the Lamanites. In each case, the Nephites ultimately prevailed and gave thanks and praise to God.

In the book of Alma, the delineation of the Nephite and Lamanite nations along ancestral lines becomes blurred. Several groups of Nephites—Amlicites (chaps. 2–3), Zoramites (chaps. 31–35, 43), Amalickiahites (chaps. 46–62), and kingmen (chaps. 51, 61)—rejected Nephite religious principles and joined the Lamanites in an attempt to overthrow the Nephite government. Several groups of Lamanites—Anti-Nephi-Lehies (chaps. 17–27), converts from the army that marched against the Anti-Nephi-Lehies (chap. 25), and some Lamanite soldiers captured by Moroni (chap. 62)—embraced the gospel and Nephite way of life and went to live among the Nephites. By the end of the book, these populations are distinguished more by ideology than by lineage. Those who desired government by the "voice of the people" and embraced the teachings of the gospel are numbered among the Nephites, while those who opposed them are called Lamanites.

Many important religious teachings are found in the book of Alma. Alma 5 is a speech given by Alma calling the people of the city of Zarahemla to repent and teaching all followers of Christ to judge the state of their former spiritual rebirth and present well-being. Alma 7, delivered to the righteous city of Gideon, teaches believers to make the ATONEMENT of Christ a reality in their lives. Chapters 12 and 13 elucidate the mysteries of redemption, RESURRECTION, and the PRIESTHOOD after the order of the Son of God. Alma 32 and 33 are a sermon given by Alma to the Zoramite poor, explaining the correct manner of prayer, the relationship between humility and faith in Jesus Christ, and the process of increasing faith. Alma 34 is Amulek's talk on the need for the "infinite and eternal sacrifice" made by the Son of God. In it Amulek also teaches the people how to pray and tells them how to live so that their prayers will not be vain.

Alma teaches his sons trust in God by telling of his personal CONVERSION (chap. 36). He also gives instructions about the keeping of sacred records and explains how God's purposes are accomplished through small means (chap. 37). He teaches the evil of sexual sin (chap. 39), the nature of resurrection and restoration (chaps. 40–41), the purpose and consequences of the FALL OF ADAM, including spiritual and temporal death), and the relationship between JUSTICE AND MERCY (see chap. 42).

The war chapters include instances of, and statements about, justifiable reasons for war (chap. 48), along with the example of the protective power of faith exercised by the young warriors who fought under Helaman, none of whom died in battle, for they believed their mothers' teachings that "God would deliver them" (Alma 56:47–48).

Overall, the book of Alma teaches through vivid, detailed narratives how personal ambition can lead to APOSTASY and war, and shows how the Lord gathers his people through the preaching of the gospel of Christ and delivers them in righteousness against aggression.

BIBLIOGRAPHY

For essays on Alma the Younger, Ammon, King Lamoni, Ammonihah, Korihor's sophistry, Amlici, several dissenters, Captain Moroni, the Nephite chief judges, and other figures in the book of Alma, see Jeffrey R. Holland, *The Book of Mormon: It Begins with a Family*, pp. 79–170. Salt Lake City, 1983.

CHERYL BROWN

BOOK OF HELAMAN

The book of Helaman chronicles one of the most tumultuous periods in the history of the NEPHITES and LAMANITES (52–1 B.C.). The narrative focuses on the unexpected difficulties (e.g., the Lamanites' invasion and unprecedented occupation of the land of Zarahemla narrated in chaps. 4 and 5) and unexpected resolutions that came from God (e.g., the withdrawal of the Lamanite occupation forces as the direct result of the missionary work of two sons of Helaman, NEPHI$_2$ and Lehi, in 5:49–52).

This book takes its name from its first author, HELAMAN$_2$, son of HELAMAN$_1$. Other contributors to the record were Nephi and Lehi, sons of Helaman$_2$ (16:25), and MORMON, the principal editor of the Book of Mormon, who added political and religious commentary.

The account opens after Helaman had received custody of the Nephite records from his uncle Shiblon (Alma 63:11) in the fortieth year of the reign of the judges (c. 52 B.C.; Hel. 1:1). The narrative falls into six major segments: the record of Helaman (chaps. 1–3); the record of Nephi (chaps. 4–6); the prophecy of Nephi (chaps. 7–11); Mormon's editorial observations on God's power (chap. 12); the prophecy of SAMUEL THE LAMANITE (chaps. 13–15); and a brief statement about the five-year period before Jesus' birth (chap. 16). Several religious discourses are woven into the narrative, including Helaman's admonition to his sons (5:6–12), Nephi's psalm (7:7–9), Nephi's sermon from the tower in his garden (7:13–29; 8:11–28), Nephi's prayer (11:10–16), and Samuel's long speech atop the walls of Zarahemla (13:5–39; 14:2–15:17).

Perhaps the most prominent person mentioned in the book is Nephi$_2$. After Nephi resigned from the office of chief judge, he and his brother Lehi devoted themselves fully to preaching the message of the gospel (5:1–4). His defense of God's providence affirmed the power of prophecy (8:11–

28) and, on a practical level, led to the conviction of the murderer of the chief judge (9:21–38). The Lord entrusted him with the power to seal the heavens so that no rain would fall (10:4–11), a power that Nephi used to bring about the cessation of civil strife and wickedness (11:1–18).

The rise of the GADIANTON ROBBERS (1:9–12; 2:3–11), a hostile and secret society within the Nephite and Lamanite polities, was perhaps the most disheartening and ominous occurrence during those fifty-one years. Mormon informs readers of both the organization's character (6:17–30) and its debilitating impact on society (2:13–14; 6:38–39; 11:24–34).

In contrast to these despairing observations is one of the book's central themes: the surprising ascendancy of the Lamanites in spiritual matters. After the Nephites were overrun by a Lamanite army led by Nephite dissidents in 35 B.C. and failed to regain lost territories (4:5–10), Nephi and Lehi went among the Lamanites to preach the gospel (5:16–20). Their remarkable success in converting listeners to Christ led to their imprisonment (5:21). But in an extraordinary outpouring of the Spirit of God, all in the prison were converted, an event that led to a spiritual reversal among the Lamanites and the eventual withdrawal of Lamanite military forces from Nephite lands (5:22–52). Thereafter, Lamanites carried out the work of the Church, preaching to both their own people and the Nephites (6:1–8, 34–36).

Almost thirty years later (c. 6 B.C.), a Lamanite prophet named Samuel prophesied at Zarahemla. He condemned the decadence of Nephite society, warning of destruction of both individuals and society (13:5–39, esp. 38; 14:20–15:3). He also prophesied that signs to be seen in the Western Hemisphere would accompany both the birth and death of Jesus (14:2–25). He declared the power of the Atonement in redeeming mankind from the fall of Adam and in bringing about the Resurrection. Finally, he spoke of the Lamanites' righteousness and the promises of God to them in the latter days (15:4–16).

BIBLIOGRAPHY

Jackson, Kent P., ed. *Studies in Scripture*, Vol. 8, pp 92–124. Salt Lake City, 1988.

PAUL R. CHEESMAN

THIRD NEPHI

The book of 3 Nephi is the dramatic and spiritual climax of the Book of Mormon. It focuses on three advents of Jesus: first, as the child born in Bethlehem; second, as the resurrected Lord visiting the Nephites; and third, at his SECOND COMING as the final judge at the end of the world. Within a year of the devastating destructions at the time of his crucifixion, the resurrected Jesus descended among a group of righteous people in the Nephite city of Bountiful. He revealed himself unmistakably as the Lord and Savior of the world, expounded his gospel, and established his Church.

The book's author, NEPHI₃, was the religious leader of an ethnically mixed group of Nephites and Lamanites at the time of Christ's birth. His book covers events from that time to A.D. 34. It appears Mormon copied much of Nephi's text verbatim into his abridgment.

Nephi's record begins at the time when the fulfillment of the messianic prophecies of SAMUEL THE LAMANITE miraculously saved believers from a threatened antimessianic persecution. The signs of Jesus' birth appeared—a night of daylight and a new star—vindicating the faith of those who believed the prophecies that Jesus would be born into the world (chap. 1).

After these signs, many were converted to the Church led by Nephi. On the other hand, greed, pleasure-seeking, and pride increased drastically, and the government was soon infiltrated with organized corruption that caused complete anarchy and a breakdown of the people into family tribes and robber bands. Prolonged attacks by these bands plagued the Nephites, who finally abandoned their own properties and formed a single body with enough provisions to subsist for seven years. The Nephites eventually prevailed, but these disruptions and wickedness brought on the collapse of the central government. Although most rejected Nephi₃'s warnings and miracles, he baptized and ordained those who would believe and follow (chaps. 2–7).

The believers began looking for the calamitous signs of Christ's death, also prophesied by Samuel. A violent storm arose and massive earthquakes occurred demolishing many cities, killing thousands of the wicked, and leaving the more righteous survivors in a thick vapor of darkness for three days of mourning. After the tumult settled, the voice of Jesus Christ spoke out of the darkness,

Jesus Christ Visits the Americas, by John Scott (1969, oil on canvas, 47″ × 121″). The resurrected Jesus Christ appeared to 2,500 men, women, and children who had gathered at their temple in Bountiful. He instructed them for three days (see 3 Ne. 11–28).

expressing his sadness over the unrepentant dead and his hope that those who were spared would receive him and his redemption. He announced that his sacrifice had ended the need for blood sacrifice as practiced under the law of Moses (chaps. 8–10).

Later, in radiant white, the resurrected Christ descended to show his wounds, to heal, to teach, and to ordain leaders for his Church. On the first day of several such visits, Jesus appeared to a group of 2,500 men, women, and children assembled at the temple in Bountiful. He ordained twelve disciples and gave them the power to baptize and bestow the gift of the Holy Ghost; he instructed the people in the principles, ordinances, and commandments of his gospel (*see* SERMON ON THE MOUNT); he explained that he had fulfilled the law of Moses; he healed the sick and blessed their families. He announced his plan to show himself to still other people not then known by the Jews or the Nephites. Finally, he entered into a covenant with them. The people promised to keep the commandments he had given them, and he administered to them the sacrament of bread and wine, in remembrance of his resurrected body that he had shown to them and of the blood through which he had wrought the Atonement (chaps. 11–18).

On the morning of the second day, the disciples baptized the faithful and gave them the gift of the Holy Ghost, and they were encircled by angels and fire from heaven. Jesus appeared again and offered three marvelous prayers, explained God's covenant with Israel and its promised fulfillment, reviewed and corrected some items in the Nephite scriptures, and foretold events of the future world, quoting prophesies from Isaiah, Micah, and Malachi. He inspired even babes to reveal "marvelous things" (3 Ne. 26:16). Then he explained the past and future history of the world, emphasizing that salvation will extend to all who follow him (chaps. 19–26).

A third time, Jesus appeared to the twelve Nephite disciples alone. He named his Church and explained the principles of the final judgment. Three of the disciples were transfigured and beheld heavenly visions. Jesus granted these three disciples their wish to remain on earth as special servants until the end of the world (chaps. 27–28; *see also* THREE NEPHITES; TRANSLATED BEINGS).

Christ revisited the Nephites over an extended period, and told them that he would also visit the lost tribes of Israel.

His Church grew having all things common, with neither rich nor poor. This peaceful condition lasted nearly 180 years, and "surely there could not be a happier people" (4 Ne. 1:16).

Mormon wrote his abridgment of 3 Nephi more than three hundred years after the actual events. By then, the descendants of the Nephites who had been so blessed had degenerated into terminal warfare. Mormon's final, sober testimony to his future readers speaks of the Lord's coming in the last days, which, like his coming to the land Bountiful, would be disastrous for the ungodly but glorious for the righteous (chaps. 29–30).

The text of 3 Nephi fits several categories. First, it is a Christian testament, a Christian gospel. It contains many direct quotations from Jesus and establishes his new covenant. Recorded in a touching personal tone by a participating eyewitness of awesomely tragic and beautiful events, the account convincingly invites the reader to believe the gospel of Jesus Christ and to feel the love he has for all people.

The text also has been compared to the pseudepigraphic forty-day literature that describes Christ's ministry to the faithful in the Holy Land after his resurrection (see JESUS CHRIST: FORTY-DAY MINISTRY AND OTHER POST-RESURRECTION APPEARANCES OF JESUS CHRIST; CWHN 8:407–34). Others have seen in chapters 11–18 a covenant ritual that profoundly expands the meaning of the Sermon on the Mount in the Gospel of Matthew (Welch, pp. 34–83). The account also resembles the apocalyptic message of the books of Enoch: From the type and purpose of the initial cataclysm, to the sublimity of its revelations to the faithful, to the creation of a righteous society, 3 Nephi is a story of theodicy, theophany, and theocracy.

The text yields practical instructions for sainthood. It is not a wishful utopian piece but a practical handbook of commandments to be accepted in covenantal ordinances and obeyed strictly, with devotion and pure dedication to God. This is not the genre of wisdom literature, not merely a book of moral suggestions for the good life. It explains Christ's gospel plainly, and makes the lofty ideals of the Sermon on the Mount livable by all who receive the Holy Ghost. Empowered by true Christian ordinances and the gifts of the Holy Spirit, the Nephites established a paradise surpassed in righteousness only by Enoch's Zion.

This Zion welcomes everyone, from every place and every time. It promises blessings to "*all* the pure in heart" who come unto Christ (3 Ne. 12:3–9, emphasis added). Thus, 3 Nephi urges all to accept and live Christ's gospel to perfect earthly society, and to join with the Zion of all the former and future righteous peoples so that, as Malachi states, the earth will not be "utterly wasted" at Christ's second coming (JS—H 1:39). This was Enoch's ancient achievement and Joseph SMITH's modern hope. The text does not discuss God's mil-lennial kingdom; nor does Christ here pray, "Thy kingdom come." For among those happy Nephites, it had come already.

[*See also* Jesus Christ in the Scriptures: the Book of Mormon.]

BIBLIOGRAPHY

Anderson, Richard L. "Religious Validity: The Sacrament Covenant in Third Nephi." In *By Study and Also by Faith*, ed. J. Lunquist and S. Ricks, Vol. 2, pp.1–51. Salt Lake City, 1990.

Ludlow, Victor L. *Jesus' "Covenant People Discourse" in 3 Nephi*. Religious Education Lecture Series. Provo, Utah, 1988.

Stendahl, Krister. "The Sermon on the Mount and Third Nephi." In *Reflections on Mormonism*, ed. T. Madsen. Provo, Utah, 1978.

Welch, John W. *The Sermon at the Temple and the Sermon on the Mount*. Salt Lake City, 1990.

CHARLES RANDALL PAUL

FOURTH NEPHI

Abridged by MORMON, this brief work contains the writings of four Nephite prophets (A.D. 34–320): NEPHI4, son of NEPHI3, who was a disciple of the risen Jesus; Amos, son of Nephi4; and Amos and Ammaron, two sons of Amos. The first section of 4 Nephi briefly summarizes four generations of peace, righteousness, and equality that resulted from the conversion of the people to the GOSPEL OF JESUS CHRIST after the visit of the resurrected Savior. In contrast, the last section foreshadows the later destruction of the Nephite nation that followed a gradual and conscious rejection of the gospel message.

Fourth Nephi narrates an unparalleled epoch in human society when all the people followed the teachings of Christ for nearly two centuries. The book is best known for its account of the social and religious power of the love of God that overcame contention and other social and political ills (4 Ne. 1:15–16). The people experienced urban renewal, stable family life, unity in the Church, and social and economic equality, as well as divine miracles (1:3–13, 15–17). "Surely there could not [have been] a happier people . . . created by the hand of God" (1:16).

The book also previews the ensuing APOSTASY of most of the population from the teachings of Christ, introducing a state of wickedness and chaos that eventually led to total destruction. According to the account the individual and collective decline was gradual and sequential, with the loss of social and religious order manifested in contention, PRIDE in prosperity, class distinctions with widening social divisions, rejection of Christ and his gospel, and persecution of the Church (1:24–46).

BIBLIOGRAPHY

Skinner, Andrew C. "The Course of Peace and Apostasy." In *Studies in Scripture*, ed. K. Jackson, Vol. 8. Salt Lake City, 1988.

REX C. REEVE, JR.

BOOK OF MORMON

The short book of Mormon (A.D. 320–400/421), within the Book of Mormon, documents the extraordinary collapse of Nephite civilization, as had been foretold (1 Ne. 12:19–20; Alma 45:10–14). It consists of MORMON's abridgment of his larger and more complete history (Morm. 1–6), his final admonition both to future LAMANITES and to other remnants of the house of ISRAEL (chap. 7), and the prophetic warnings of Mormon's son MORONI₂ to future readers of the record (chaps. 8–9). Because Nephites of Mormon's day had rejected JESUS CHRIST and his gospel, superstition and magic replaced divine REVELATION (Morm. 1:13–19). A border skirmish (1:10) escalated into a major war, driving the Nephites from their traditional lands (2:3–7, 16, 20–21). Following a ten-year negotiated peace, they repulsed a Lamanite attack, which Mormon, former commander of the Nephite army, refused to lead. As conditions worsened, Mormon reluctantly agreed to command the Nephite army at CUMORAH, where they were destroyed (chaps. 3–6). With poignant anguish, Mormon lamented over his slain people: "O ye fair ones, how could ye have rejected that Jesus, who stood with open arms to receive you!" (6:17–22).

Mormon concluded his record by inviting Lamanites and other remnants of the house of Israel to learn of their forefathers, to lay down their weapons of war, and to repent of their SINS and believe that Jesus Christ is the Son of God. His final words are, "If it so be that ye believe in Christ, and are baptized, first with water, then with fire and with the Holy Ghost, . . . it shall be well with you in the day of judgment. Amen" (7:10).

After the final battle (A.D. 385), Moroni₂—alone and unsure of his own survival—noted his father's death and concluded his father's record

(8:1–5). Fifteen years later (A.D. 400), Moroni recorded that survivors of his people had been hunted from place to place until they were no more except for himself. He also observed that the Lamanites were at war with one another and that the whole country witnessed continual bloodshed. For a second time he closed the work, promising that those who would receive this record in the future and not condemn it would learn of greater spiritual matters (8:6–13).

Moroni apparently returned to the record a third time (between A.D. 400 and 421). Having seen a vision of the future (8:35), he testified that the PLATES of the Book of Mormon would come forth by the power of God in a day when people would not believe in miracles. SECRET COMBINATIONS would abound, churches be defiled, and wars, rumors of wars, earthquakes, and pollutions be upon the earth. Moroni also spoke warnings to those in the latter days who do not believe in Christ and who deny the revelations of God, thus standing against the works of the Lord (8:14–9:27). He mentioned the difficulty of keeping records, written as they were in "reformed Egyptian" (9:31–33; cf. Ether 12:23–25). Moroni closed his father's volume with a testimony of the truth of his words (9:35–37).

BIBLIOGRAPHY

Mackay, Thomas W. "Mormon and the Destruction of Nephite Civilization." In *Studies in Scripture*, ed. K. Jackson, Vol. 8. Salt Lake City, 1988.

REX C. REEVE, JR.

BOOK OF ETHER

The book of Ether is MORONI₂'s abbreviated account of the history of the JAREDITES, who came to the Western Hemisphere at the time of the "great tower" of Babel and lived in the area later known as the Nephite "land northward," much earlier than Lehi's colony. Moroni retold their account, recorded on twenty-four plates of gold found by the people of Limhi and translated by MOSIAH₂ (Mosiah 28:11–19). Ether, the last prophet of the Jaredites and a survivor of their annihilation, inscribed those plates soon after the final destruction of his people. It is not known whether Moroni relied on Mosiah's translation or retranslated the Jaredite record in whole or in part. Moroni humbly claims not to have written "the hundredth part" of the record by Ether (Ether 15:33).

The structure of the book of Ether is much like the rest of the Book of Mormon. It tells of the emigration of people by land and sea from the Near East, the Lord's prophetic guidance of these people, and their rise, prosperity, and fall, all in direct relation to their obedience to the Lord's commandments in their promised land. Moroni included the book of Ether because his father MORMON had planned to do so (Mosiah 28:19) but for some reason did not complete the project. Both knew the value of this record and could see that the Jaredite history closely paralleled certain Nephite events.

Moroni appended this history to the Nephite account as a second witness against the evils and SECRET COMBINATIONS that led to the annihilation of both the Jaredites and the Nephites. Several of its themes reinforce the messages in the Nephite section of the Book of Mormon: the necessity to follow the prophets away from persistent and pernicious wickedness, the power of faith in the Lord demonstrated by Jared and the BROTHER OF JARED, the testimony that Jesus Christ is the eternal saving God, and the collapse of a nation when its people determinedly choose wickedness. Nevertheless, there are notable cultural differences between the Jaredite and the Nephite civilizations; for example, the Jaredites were ruled solely by kings, and they lacked Israelite law and customs, since they were pre-Mosaic.

Although condensed, the book reflects an epic style (see *CWHN* 5:153–449; 6:329–58). It begins with the emigration of the Jaredites from "the great tower" (Ether 1:33, cf. Gen. 11:9) and the valley of "Nimrod" (Ether 2:1; cf. Gen. 10:8) to a new land of promise in the Western Hemisphere. It then abridges a history of the Jaredite kings and wars, and concludes with the destruction of the Jaredite civilization. A brief outline of the book follows: Ether's royal lineage is given (chap. 1); the premortal Jesus appears to the brother of Jared in response to his prayers and touches sixteen small stones, causing them to shine to provide light as the Jaredite barges cross the sea (chaps. 2–6); the generations of Jaredite kings live, hunt, quarrel, enter into secret combinations, and Jaredite prophets warn of impending destruction (chaps. 7–11); Moroni attests that Ether was a prophet of great faith and knowledge (chaps. 12–13); Ether witnesses and records the annihilation of the Jaredite armies (chaps. 14–15).

The main figures and doctrinal statements appear mostly at the beginning and end of the book of Ether. Moroni's editing is of key importance, for he infuses the story with major insights, admonitions, and comparisons. Jared is mentioned at the outset as the founder of the Jaredite people. The revelations and faith of the brother of Jared are given special significance at the beginning and end of the book. Shiz and Coriantumr are crucial historical and symbolic figures because they become the instruments of annihilation. Ether, the author of the underlying text, was an eyewitness to the final battles, and Moroni esteemed his prophecies as "great and marvelous" (Ether 13:13). The middle of the book recounts the more mundane events associated with the reigns of the Jaredite kings.

Several doctrines taught within the book of Ether are greatly valued among Latter-day Saints, namely, that prosperity in the promised land (the Americas) is conditioned on serving "the God of the land who is Jesus Christ" (Ether 2:12), that the premortal Christ had a SPIRIT BODY "like unto flesh and blood" (3:6), that God is a God of power and truth (3:4, 12), that three witnesses would verify the truth of the Book of Mormon (5:3), that the corruption and downfall of society can come because of secret combinations (8:22), that the Lord will show mankind its weakness so that through humility weak things may become strengths (12:27), and that a NEW JERUSALEM will eventually be built in the Western Hemisphere (13:3–12).

BIBLIOGRAPHY

Sperry, Sidney B. *Book of Mormon Compendium*, pp. 460–81. Salt Lake City, 1968.

Welch, John W. "Sources Behind the Book of Ether." *F.A.R.M.S. Paper.* Provo, Utah, 1986.

MORGAN W. TANNER

BOOK OF MORONI

Between A.D. 400 and 421, MORONI₂, the last custodian of the GOLD PLATES, compiled the final book in the Book of Mormon record. He wrote: "I had supposed not to have written any more; but I write a few more things, that perhaps they may be of worth unto my brethren" (Moro. 1:4). He then brought together loosely related but important items, including ORDINANCES performed both in the church of his day and in The Church of Jesus Christ of Latter-day Saints today (chaps. 2–6), one of his father's sermons (chap. 7), and two of his father's letters (chap. 9). He concluded with his own testimony and exhortations to readers (chap. 10).

ORDINANCES (CHAPS. 2–6). Chapter 2 contains instructions given by the resurrected Jesus Christ to his twelve disciples in the Western Hemisphere at the time when he bestowed upon them the GIFT OF THE HOLY GHOST. This gift is conferred in the name of Jesus Christ and by the LAYING ON OF HANDS from one who has received authority. Chapter 3 explains that priests and teachers were ordained in the name of Jesus Christ by the laying-on of hands by one holding proper authority. The main function of priests and teachers was to teach repentance and faith in Jesus Christ. Chapters 4 and 5 contain the set prayers for blessing the SACRAMENT of the Lord's Supper, prayers currentltly used in the Church. Chapter 6 outlines the requirements for BAPTISM, which include a "broken heart," contrite spirit, and true repentance. Moroni then detailed how Church members recorded the names of all members, taught one another, met together in fasting and prayer, and partook of the sacrament often.

MORMON'S SERMON AND LETTERS (CHAPS. 7–9). Mormon's sermon (chap. 7) deals with faith, hope, and charity and includes teachings on how to distinguish between good and evil, the necessity of spiritual gifts, the nature of miracles, and instruction on how to obtain charity, "the pure love of Christ" (7:47).

The first letter (chap. 8) condemns INFANT BAPTISM. Mormon taught that children are made pure through the atonement of Christ and do not need the cleansing power of baptism until they are old enough to be accountable for their actions and can repent of their sins.

The second letter (chap. 9) recites the level of depravity to which the Nephites and LAMANITES had fallen (before A.D. 385), offering reasons for their prophesied destruction ("they are without principle, and past feeling"—verse 20), along with Mormon's charge to his son to remain faithful to Christ in spite of their society's wickedness.

EXHORTATION AND FAREWELL (CHAP. 10). Moroni exhorts all who read the Book of Mormon to ponder and pray for a divine witness of its truthfulness (verses 3–5) and urges his readers not to deny the gifts of the Holy Ghost, which he enumerates (verses 8–19). He bears his personal

TESTIMONY of Jesus Christ and urges all to "come unto Christ, and be perfected in him, and deny yourselves of all ungodliness" (verse 32). He bids his readers farewell until he meets them on the final JUDGMENT DAY at "the pleasing bar of the great Jehovah" (verse 34).

BIBLIOGRAPHY

Jackson, Kent P., ed. *Studies in Scripture*, Vol. 8, pp. 282–312. Salt Lake City, 1988.

S. MICHAEL WILCOX

BOOK OF MORMON, BIBLICAL PROPHECIES ABOUT

Latter-day Saints believe that the coming forth of the Book of Mormon as an instrument in God's hand for bringing his latter-day work to fruition was revealed to biblical prophets such as ISAIAH and EZEKIEL (cf. 1 Ne. 19:21; *see* FOREKNOWLEDGE OF GOD). Their prophecies about these matters, like those about the coming of Jesus Christ, are better understood when some of the historical events that surround them are known.

JOSEPH'S PROPHECY. Allusions are made to a branch that would be broken off in Jacob's blessing to Joseph, promising that he would become a fruitful bough whose "branches" would run "over the wall" and that his posterity would be heir to divine blessings (Gen. 49:22–26; 1 Ne. 19:24; cf. Deut. 33:13–17). A further prophecy in the Book of Mormon aids in interpreting Genesis 49.

According to a prophecy of Joseph in Egypt, preserved in the Book of Mormon (2 Ne. 3:4–21), two sets of records would be kept by two tribes of Israel—one (the Bible) written by the tribe of Judah and the other (Book of Mormon) kept by the tribe of Joseph (2 Ne. 3:12; cf. Ezek. 37:15–19). Those kept by the tribe of Joseph were written on PLATES of brass and largely parallel the biblical records (1 Ne. 5:10–16; 13:23). They were carried to a promised land in the Western Hemisphere by LEHI, a prophet and descendant of Joseph, who fled Jerusalem about 600 B.C. Lehi exclaimed, "Joseph truly saw our day. And he obtained a promise of the Lord, that out of the fruit of his loins the Lord God would raise up a righteous branch unto the house of Israel; not the Messiah, but a branch which was to be broken off" (2 Ne. 3:5).

VISIT OF RESURRECTED JESUS. A succession of prophets taught the gospel of Jesus Christ to Lehi's "branch" of Joseph's descendants and prophesied that after Jesus was resurrected, he would visit them (e.g., 2 Ne. 26:1). Regarding this circumstance, Jesus told his hearers in Palestine that he had "other sheep . . . which are not of this fold: them also I must bring, and they shall hear my voice; and there shall be one fold, and one shepherd" (John 10:16). When he appeared in the Western Hemisphere (c. A.D. 34), he allowed the multitude to touch the wounds in his hands and side and feet so that they would understand the reality of his resurrection (3 Ne. 11:10–15). Later, he specifically referred to his words recorded in John's gospel (3 Ne. 15:16–24; John 10:16), saying, "Ye are they of whom I said: Other sheep I have which are not of this fold" (3 Ne. 15:21). Further, he taught them his gospel, called twelve disciples (*see* APOSTLE), announced the fulfillment of the LAW OF MOSES, instituted the SACRAMENT, and organized his church—causing them to become of one fold with his disciples in Palestine, having him as their common shepherd (3 Ne. 11–29).

RECORD FROM THE GROUND. Latter-day Saints teach that Isaiah foresaw that part of this branch of Joseph's family would eventually be destroyed. He likened it to David's city Ariel, that would also be destroyed when hostile forces "camped against" or laid siege to it (Isa. 29:3). But despite the fact that many of the people of this branch would be slain, both Isaiah and Nephi explained that the voice of Joseph's descendants would be heard again as a voice "out of the ground"; their speech would "whisper out of the dust" (Isa. 29:4; 2 Ne. 26:16). For "the words of the faithful should speak as if it were from the dead" (2 Ne. 27:13; cf. 26:15–16; *see* "VOICE FROM THE DUST").

Perceiving how this would take place, NEPHI₁, the first writer in the Book of Mormon, wrote about 570 B.C. to unborn generations: "My beloved brethren, all those who are of the house of Israel, and all ye ends of the earth, I speak unto you as the voice of one crying from the dust" (2 Ne. 33:13). Similarly, the last writer in the Book of Mormon, MORONI₂, wrote about A.D. 400: "I speak unto you as though I spake from the dead; for I know that ye shall have my words" (Morm. 9:30; cf. Moro. 10:27). As he was about to bury the records, he wrote: "No one need say [the records] shall not come, for they surely shall, for the Lord

hath spoken it; for out of the earth shall they come, by the hand of the Lord, and none can stay it" (Morm. 8:26; cf. *TPJS*, p. 98).

The phrase "out of the ground" is thus a metaphor for the voice of those who have died, but it also refers to records being buried in the earth until they come forth. The overall connection between Isaiah, chapter 29, and the Book of Mormon people is discussed in 2 Nephi, chapters 26–29 (cf. Morm. 8:23–26).

THE RECORD APPEARS. Parts of the GOLD PLATES were sealed when Joseph Smith received them. Isaiah spoke of "the words of a book that is sealed" that would be delivered to a "learned" person (Isa. 29:11). Latter-day Saints see the role of the "learned" person fulfilled by Professor Charles Anthon of Columbia College (New York), and these "words of a book" constitute the ANTHON TRANSCRIPT. The book itself, however, would be delivered to another (Joseph Smith) who would simply acknowledge, "I am not learned" (Isa. 29:12), but would be divinely empowered to translate it.

Isaiah foresaw that when the book would appear, people would be contending over God's word (Isa. 29:13). This circumstance would provide the context wherein God could perform his "marvelous work and a wonder," causing the "wisdom of their wise men" to perish and the "understanding of their prudent men [to] be hid" while the meek would "increase their joy in the Lord" and the "poor among men shall rejoice in the Holy One of Israel" (Isa. 29:14, 19). Meanwhile, those who had "erred in spirit shall come to understanding, and they that murmured shall learn doctrine" (Isa. 29:22–24; cf. 2 Ne. 27:6–26).

TWO RECORDS. Ezekiel also prophesied concerning the two records—that of Joseph or Ephraim (i.e., the Book of Mormon) and that of Judah (i.e., the Bible)—that would be joined in the last days as an instrument provided by the Lord to gather his people back to himself (Ezek. 37:15–22; cf. 2 Ne. 3:11–12; *see* EZEKIEL, PROPHECIES OF; ISRAEL: GATHERING OF ISRAEL).

For Latter-day Saints, when Ezekiel spoke of "sticks" (probably waxed writing boards), he was illustrating the instruments by which God would bring peoples together in the latter days, just as he used the concept of the Resurrection to illustrate the gathering of God's people, which is the theme of chapters 34–37. Just as bodies are reconstituted in the Resurrection, so will Israel be reconstituted in the gathering; and the formerly divided nations will become one (Ezek. 37:1–14). Thus, the publication of the Book of Mormon in 1830 was a sign that the divided tribes of Israel were to become one under God and that God's latter-day work was beginning to be implemented (Ezek. 37:21–28; cf. 1 Ne. 13:34–41; 3 Ne. 20:46–21:11).

BIBLIOGRAPHY

McConkie, Bruce R. *A New Witness for the Articles of Faith*, pp. 422–58. Salt Lake City, 1985.

Meservy, Keith H. "Ezekiel's Sticks and the Gathering of Israel." *Ensign* 17 (Feb. 1987):4–13.

Robison, Parley Parker, comp. *Orson Pratt's Works on the Doctrines of the Gospel*, pp. 269–84. Salt Lake City, 1945.

KEITH H. MESERVY

BOOK OF MORMON, GOVERNMENT AND LEGAL HISTORY IN THE

Because the Book of Mormon focuses on religious themes, information about political and legal institutions appears only as background for the religious account. Even so, it is apparent that several different political institutions characterized NEPHITE, LAMANITE, and JAREDITE society.

The Nephites were ruled by hereditary kings from c. 550 to 91 B.C., when the rule changed to a reign of judges. After the coming of Christ, two centuries of peace under the government of his Church were followed by a breakdown of society into tribal units and finally by the destruction of the Nephites.

From the beginning, the Nephite legal system was based on the LAW OF MOSES as it was written in the scriptures, as it was possibly practiced by Israel in the seventh century B.C., and as it was modified (slightly) over the years until the coming of Jesus Christ. As the Nephite prophets had long predicted (2 Ne. 25:24), Jesus fulfilled the law of Moses. After his coming, Nephite law consisted of the commandments of Christ.

GOVERNMENT. After leading his family and a few others out of Jerusalem, Lehi established his colony in the Western Hemisphere as a branch of Israel in a new promised land, but its organization was inherently unstable, for it seems to have given no clear principle for resolving political disputes. The seven lineage groups established at Lehi's death and mentioned consistently in the Book of Mormon were Nephites, Jacobites, Josephites, Zoramites, Lamanites, Lemuelites, and Ishmaelites (Jacob 1:13; 4 Ne. 1:36–38; Morm. 1:8; Welch, 1989, p. 69). When this system proved unable to keep the peace, NEPHI₁ led away the first four of these family groups, who believed the revelations of God; established a new city; and accepted the position of Nephite king by popular acclamation. The other three groups eventually developed a monarchical system, with a Lamanite king receiving tribute from other Ishmaelite, Lamanite, and Lemuelite vassal kings.

This original split provides the basic political theme for much of Nephite and Lamanite history. Laman and Lemuel were Lehi's oldest sons, and they naturally claimed a right to rule. But a younger brother, Nephi, was chosen by the Lord to be their ruler and teacher (1 Ne. 2:22), and Nephi's account of this early history was written in part to document his calling as ruler (Reynolds). The conflict over the right to rule continued, providing much of the rhetorical base for the recurring wars between Lamanites and Nephites hundreds of years later.

Possibly because of the controversial circumstances in which Nephite kingship was established, its ideology was clear from earliest times. Nephite kings were popularly acclaimed (2 Ne. 5:18). They had a temple as their religious center (2 Ne. 5:16) and were careful to maintain venerable symbols of divinely appointed kingship in the sword of Laban, the Liahona, and ancient records (2 Ne. 5:12–14; cf. Ricks).

Only the first Nephite king (Nephi₁) and the last three kings (MOSIAH₁, BENJAMIN, and MOSIAH₂) are named in the Book of Mormon. These four kings served as military leaders and prophets, and worked closely with other prophets in reminding people of their obligations to God and to one another. For example, in his final address to his people, King Benjamin reported to the people a revelation from God and put them under covenant to take the name of Christ upon them and to keep God's and the king's commandments.

Some Nephite kings were unrighteous. Noah, a king of one Nephite subgroup (the people of Zeniff), exploited the weaknesses of the Nephite system, sustaining himself and his council of corrupt priests in riotous living from the labors of the people. Doubts about the institution of kingship became acute when the oppressions of Noah were reported to the main body of Nephites. King Mosiah$_2$, when his sons declined the monarchy, resolved the succession crisis by proposing to change the kingship into a system of lower and higher judges. This form of government was accepted by the people in 91 B.C. (Mosiah 29) and lasted, in spite of several crises and corruptions, for approximately a hundred years. Though the position of chief judge continued to have military and religious preeminence and was frequently passed from father to son, it differed from the kingship pattern in that the higher judges could be judged by lower judges if they broke the law or oppressed the people (Mosiah 29:29).

ALMA$_2$ became the first chief judge and served simultaneously as high priest, governor, and military chief captain. Because these offices required the approval of the people, who had rejected monarchy, critics have tended to confuse the Nephite system with the democracy of the United States. However, there was no representative legislature, the essential institution in American republican ideology. Also, the major offices were typically passed from father to son, without elections (Bushman, pp. 14–17); "the voice of the people" is reported many times as authorizing or confirming leadership appointments and other civic or political actions.

It appears that during the first two centuries after the coming of Christ, the Nephites operated under an ecclesiastical system without judges or kings, with courts constituted only of the church elders (4 Ne. 1:1–23; Moro. 6:7). With the eventual apostasy and collapse of the Nephite church, no civil institutions were in place to preserve law and order. Attempts to organize and conduct public affairs by reversion to a tribal system and, later, to military rule did not prevent the final destruction of the civilization.

The Book of Mormon also gives a brief account of the Jaredites, a much earlier civilization that began at the time of the great tower and was monarchical from beginning to end. Jaredite kings seem to have been autocrats, and succession was more often determined through political and military adventurism than through legal procedures.

LAW. Until the coming of Christ, the Nephites and converted Lamanites strictly observed the law of Moses as they knew and understood it (2 Ne.

5:10; 25:24–26; Jarom 1:5; Jacob 4:4–5; Alma 25:15; 30:3; Hel. 13:1; 3 Ne. 1:24–25). Preserved on the brass plates, the law of Moses was the basis of their criminal and civil law, as well as of the rules of purity, temple sacrifice, and festival observances of the Nephites; they knew, however, that the law of Moses would be superseded in the future messianic age (2 Ne. 25:24–27).

Recent publications (Welch, 1984, 1987, 1988, 1989, 1990) have identified a rich array of legal information in the text of the Book of Mormon. Procedural and administrative aspects of Nephite law developed from one century to another, while the substance of the customary law changed very little. Nephite leaders seem to have viewed new legislation as presumptuous and generally evil (Mosiah 29:23) and any change of God's law without authority as blasphemous (Jacob 7:7). Their religious laws included many humanitarian provisions and protections for persons and their religious freedom and property. These rules were grounded in a strong principle of legal equality (Alma 1:32; 16:18; Hel. 4:12).

In two early incidents, Jacob, the brother of Nephi$_1$, was involved in controversies concerning the law. The first involved the claimed right of some Nephites to have concubines (Jacob 2:23–3:11), and the second arose when Sherem accused Jacob of desecrating the law of Moses (Jacob 7:7).

The trial of ABINADI (Mosiah 11–17) indicates that, at least in the case of Noah, the king had jurisdiction over political issues but took counsel on religious matters from a body of priests: Causes of action were brought against Abinadi for cursing the ruler, testifying falsely, giving a false prophecy, and committing blasphemy (Mosiah 12:9–10, 14; 17:7–8, 12). Legal punishments in the Book of Mormon were often fashioned so as to match the nature of the crime; thus, Abinadi was burned for reviling the king, whose life he had said would be valued as a garment in a furnace (Mosiah 12:3; 17:3).

At the time the Nephites abandoned monarchy, Mosiah$_2$ instituted a major reform of Nephite procedural law. A system of judges and other officers was instituted; lower judges were judged by a higher judge (Mosiah 29:28); judges were paid for the time spent in public service (Alma 11:3); a standardized system of weights and measures was instituted (Alma 11:4–19); slavery was formally prohibited (Alma 27:9); and defaulting debtors faced banishment (Alma 11:2). There were officers (Alma 11:2) and lawyers who assisted, but their official functions are not clear. It appears that ordinary citizens had sole power to initiate lawsuits (otherwise, the judges would have brought the action against Nephi₂ in Helaman 8:1).

The trial of Nehor was an important precedent, establishing the plenary and original jurisdiction of the chief judge (Alma 1:1–15). It appears that under the terms of Mosiah 29, the higher judges were intended only to judge if the lower judges judged falsely. But in the trial of Nehor, Alma₂ took the case directly, enhancing the power of the chief judge.

The reform also protected freedom of belief, but certain overt conduct was punished (Alma 1:17–18; 30:9–11). The case of Korihor established the rule that certain forms of speech (blasphemy, inciting people to sin) were punishable under the Nephite law even after the reform of Mosiah.

All this time, the underlying Nephite law remained the law of Moses as interpreted in light of a knowledge of the gospel. Public decrees regularly prohibited murder, plunder, theft, adultery, and all iniquity (Mosiah 2:13; Alma 23:3). Murder was defined as "deliberately killing" (2 Ne. 9:35), which excluded cases where one did not lie in wait (on Nephi's slaying of Laban, cf. Ex. 21:13–14 and 1 Ne. 4:6–18). Theft was typically a minor offense, but robbery was a capital crime (Hel. 11:28), usually committed by organized outsiders and violent and politically motivated brigands, who were dealt with by military force (as they were typically in the ancient Near East).

Evidently, technical principles of the law of Moses were consistently observed in Nephite civilization. For example, the legal resolution of an unobserved murder in the case of Seantum in Helaman 9 shows that a technical exception to the rule against self-incrimination was recognized by the Nephites in the same way that it was by later Jewish jurists, as when divination detected a corpus delicti (Welch, Feb. 1990). The execution of Zemnarihah by the Nephites adumbrated an obscure point attested in later Jewish law that required the tree from which a criminal was hanged to be chopped down (3 Ne. 4:28; Welch, 1984). The case of the Ammonite exemption from military duty suggests that the rabbinic understanding of Deuteronomy 20 in this regard was probably the same as the Nephites' (Welch, 1990, pp. 63–65).

One may also infer from circumstantial evidence that the Nephites observed the traditional ritual laws of Israelite festivals. One example might be the assembly of Benjamin's people in tents around the temple and tower from which he spoke. There are things in the account that are similar to the New Year festivals surrounding the Feast of Tabernacles and the Day of Atonement (Tvedtnes, in Lundquist and Ricks, *By Study and Also by Faith*, Salt Lake City, 1990, 2:197–237).

With the coming of the resurrected Christ, recorded in 3 Nephi, the law of Moses was fulfilled and was given new meaning. The Ten Commandments still applied in a new form (3 Ne. 12); the "performances and ordinances" of the law became obsolete (4 Ne. 1:12), but not the "law" or the "commandments" as Jesus had reformulated them in 3 Nephi 12–14.

BIBLIOGRAPHY

Bushman, Richard L. "The Book of Mormon and the American Revolution." *BYU Studies* 17 (Autumn 1976):3–20.

Reynolds, Noel B. "The Political Dimension in Nephi's Small Plates." *BYU Studies* 27 (Fall 1987):15–37.

Ricks, Stephen D. "The Ideology of Kingship in Mosiah 1–6." *F.A.R.M.S. Update*, Aug. 1987.

Welch, John W. "The Execution of Zemnarihah." *F.A.R.M.S. Update*, Nov. 1984.

———. "The Law of Mosiah." *F.A.R.M.S. Update*, Mar. 1987.

———. "Statutes, Judgments, Ordinances and Commandments." *F.A.R.M.S. Update*, June 1988.

———. "Lehi's Last Will and Testament: A Legal Approach." In *The Book of Mormon: Second Nephi, the Doctrinal Structure*, ed. M. Nyman and C. Tate, pp. 61–82. Provo, Utah, 1989.

———. "The Case of an Unobserved Murder." *F.A.R.M.S. Update*, Feb. 1990.

———. "Law and War in the Book of Mormon." In *Warfare in the Book of Mormon*, ed. S. Ricks and W. Hamblin, pp. 46–102. Salt Lake City, 1990.

NOEL B. REYNOLDS

BOOK OF MORMON, HISTORY OF WARFARE IN

Much of the Book of Mormon deals with military conflict. In diverse, informative, and morally instructive accounts, the Book of Mormon reports a wide variety of military customs, technologies, and tactics similar to those found in many premodern societies (before A.D. 1600–1700), especially some distinctive Israelite beliefs and conventions as adapted to the region of Mesoamerica.

The Book of Mormon teaches that war is a result of iniquity. Wars and destructions were brought upon the Nephites because of the contentions, murderings, idolatry, whoredoms, and abominations "which were among themselves," while those who were "faithful in keeping the commandments of the Lord were delivered at all times" from captivity, death, or unbelief (Alma 50:21–22).

The Book of Mormon implicitly condemns wars of aggression. Until their final calamity, all Nephite military objectives were strictly defensive. It was a mandatory, sacred obligation of all able-bodied Nephite men to defend their families, country, and religious freedoms (Alma 43:47; 46:12), but only as God commanded them (see WAR AND PEACE).

WARFARE. In the Book of Mormon, aside from the Ammonite converts who swore an oath against bloodshed and a remarkable period of peace following the visitation of Christ, armed conflict at different levels of intensity was a nearly constant phenomenon. Several prophets and heroes of the Book of Mormon were military men who fought in defense of their people, reflecting the grim realities of warfare in ancient history.

Religion and warfare were closely connected in the Book of Mormon. Certain elements of the Israelite patterns of "holy war" were continued in the Book of Mormon, such as the important ancient idea that success in war was due fundamentally to the will of God and the righteousness of the people (Alma 2:28; 44:4–5; 50:21; 56:47; 57:36; 58:33; Morm. 2:26). Nephite armies consulted prophets before going to battle (Alma 16:5; 43:23–24; 3 Ne. 3:19) and entered into covenants with God before battle. On one occasion, the Nephite soldiers swore a solemn oath, covenanting to obey God's commandments and to fight valiantly for the cause of righteousness; casting their garments on the ground at the feet of their leader and inviting God to cast themselves likewise at the feet of their enemies if they should violate their oath (Alma 46:22; cf. 53:17). A purity code for warriors may be seen in the account of the stripling warriors of Helaman (Alma 56–58).

As was the case in all premodern situations, warfare in the Book of Mormon was closely bound to the natural environment and ecology: weather, altitude, terrain, food supply, seasonality, and agricultural cycles. Geography determined some of the strategy and tactics in Book of Mormon warfare (Sorenson, 1985, pp. 239–76). The favorable times for campaigns in the Book of Mormon appear to have been between the eleventh and the fourth months, which has been compared with the fact that military action often took place during the cool and dry post-harvest months from November through April in Mesoamerica (see Alma 16:1; 49:1; 52:1; 56:27; Ricks and Hamblin, pp. 445–77).

Animals, either used as beasts of burden or ridden into battle, evidently were not widely available or practical in the Nephite world: No animal is ever mentioned as being used for military purposes in the Book of Mormon.

Technologically, Nephite soldiers fought, in one way or other, with missile or melee weapons in face-to-face, hand-to-hand encounters, frequently wearing armor. They used metallurgy for making weapons and armor, and engineering for building fortifications. In the Book of Mormon, Nephi taught his people to make swords modeled after the sword of Laban (2 Ne. 5:14–15). Innovations described include a proliferation of fortifications (once thought absent in ancient America) and Nephite armor in the first century B.C. (Alma 43:19; 48), soon copied by the Lamanites (Alma 49:24). It has been pointed out that the weapons (swords, scimitars, bows, and arrows) and armor (breastplates, shields, armshields, bucklers, and headplates) mentioned in the Book of Mormon are comparable to those found in Mesoamerica; coats of mail, helmets, battle chariots, cavalry, and sophisticated siege engines are absent from the Book of Mormon and Mesoamerica, despite their importance in biblical descriptions (Ricks and Hamblin, pp. 329–424).

The ability to recruit, equip, train, supply, and move large groups of soldiers represented a major undertaking for these societies, often pressing them beyond their limits and thereby ultimately contributing to their collapse. As the story of MORONI₁ and Pahoran illustrates, warfare exerted terrible social and economic pressure on Nephite society (Alma 58–61). Nephite army sizes coincided with general demographic growth: Armies numbered in the thousands in the first century B.C. and in the tens of thousands in the fourth century A.D.

It appears that Book of Mormon military organization was aristocratic and dominated by a highly trained hereditary elite. Thus, for example, military leaders such as Moroni₁, his son Moronihah, and MORMON each became the chief captain at a young age (Alma 43:17; 62:39; Morm. 2:1).

Book of Mormon armies were organized on a decimal system of hundreds, thousands, and ten thousands, as they typically were in ancient Israel and many other ancient military organizations.

The book of Alma chronicles the grim realities, strain, and pain of war, vividly and realistically (*CWHN* 7:291–333). Preparations for war were complex; provisioning, marching, and countermarching are frequently mentioned. Manpower was recruited from the ordinary ranks of the citizenry; soldiers had to be equipped and organized into units for marching and tactics and mobilized at central locations.

Some battles were fought at prearranged times and places, as when Mormon met the Lamanites at Cumorah (Morm. 6:2; cf. 3 Ne. 3:8). But much was typified by guerrilla warfare or surprise attacks: The Gadianton robbers typically raided towns, avoided open conflict, made terrorizing demands, and secretly assassinated government officials.

Actual battlefield operations usually represented only a small portion of a campaign. Scouts and spies reconnoitered for food, trails, and the location of enemy troops. Battle plans were generally made shortly before the enemy was encountered and frequently took the form of a council, as Moroni held in Alma 52:19.

When actual fighting began, controlling the army undoubtedly proved difficult. Soldiers generally fought in units distinguished by banners held by an officer. Moroni's banner, or "title of liberty," apparently served such functions (Alma 43:26, 30; 46:19–21, 36).

As far as one can determine, attacks typically began with an exchange of missiles to wound and demoralize the enemy; then hand-to-hand combat ensued. The battle described in Alma 49 offers a good description of archery duels preceding hand-to-hand melees. When panic began to spread in the ranks, complete collapse could be sudden and devastating. The death of the king or commander typically led to immediate defeat or surrender, as happened in Alma 49:25. The death of one Lamanite king during the night before the New Year proved particularly demoralizing (Alma 52:1–2). Most casualties occurred during the flight and pursuit after the disintegration of the main units; there are several examples in the Book of Mormon

of the rout, flight, and destruction of an army (e.g., Alma 52:28; 62:31).

Laws and customary behavior also regulated military relations and diplomacy. Military oaths were taken very seriously. Oaths of loyalty from troops and oaths of surrender from prisoners are mentioned frequently in the Book of Mormon, and treaties were concluded principally with oaths of nonaggression (Alma 44:6–10, 20; 50:36; 62:16; 3 Ne. 5:4–5). Legally, robbers or brigands were considered to be military targets, not common offenders (Hel. 11:28). Further elements of martial law in the Book of Mormon included the suspension of normal judicial processes and transferral of legal authority to commanding military officers (Alma 46:34), restrictions on travel, warnings before the commencement of hostilities (3 Ne. 3; cf. Deut. 20:10–13), the extraordinary granting of military exemption on condition that those exempted supply provisions and support (Alma 27:24; cf. Deut. 20:8; Babylonian Talmud, *Sotah* 43a–44a), and requirements of humanitarian treatment for captives and women.

WARS. Eighty-five instances of armed conflict can be identified in the Book of Mormon (Ricks and Hamblin, pp. 463–74). Some were brief skirmishes; others, prolonged campaigns. Some were civil wars; others, intersectional. Causes of war varied, and alliances shifted accordingly. The main wars include the following:

In the early tribal conflicts (c. 550–200 B.C.), social, religious, and cultural conflicts led to repeated Lamanite aggression after the Nephites separated from the Lamanites. The Nephites did not flourish under these circumstances, and to escape further attacks they eventually left the land of Nephi, moving northward to Zarahemla.

King Laman's son (c. 160–150 B.C.), envious of Nephite prosperity and angry at them for taking the records (especially the plates of brass, Mosiah 10:16), attacked both the people of Zeniff (Nephites who had returned to the land of Nephi) and the people of BENJAMIN (Nephites and Mulekites in the land of Zarahemla). As a result of these campaigns, Zeniff became a tributary to the Lamanites; Benjamin's victory more firmly united the land of Zarahemla under his rule (W of M; Mosiah 9–10).

The war of Amlici (87 B.C.) was a civil war in Zarahemla, sparked by the shift of government from a kingship to judgeship and by the execution of Nehor. Amlici, a follower of Nehor, militated in favor of returning to a kingship. This civil war was the first recorded time Nephite dissenters allied themselves with Lamanites; it resulted in an unstable peace (Alma 2–3).

The sudden destruction of Ammonihah (81 B.C.), a center of the recalcitrant followers of Nehor, was triggered by Lamanite anger toward certain Nephites who had caused some Lamanites to kill other Lamanites (Alma 16; 24–25).

The Ammonite move (77 B.C.) from Lamanite territory to the land of Jershon to join the Nephites led to a major Lamanite invasion of Nephite lands (Alma 28).

Three years later, many Zoramite poor were converted by the Nehpites and moved from Antionum (the Zoramite capital) to Jershon (the land given to the Ammonites with guarantees of protection by the Nephites). The loss of these workers ignited the Zoramite attack allied with Lamanites and others against the Nephites (Alma 43–44). New forms of armor introduced by the Nephites figured prominently in this war.

During this turbulent decade, a politically ambitious man named Amalickiah, with Lamanite allies, sought to reestablish a kingship in Zarahemla after the disappearance of ALMA$_2$. Amalickiah was defeated (72 B.C.), but he swore to return and kill Moroni$_1$ (Alma 46–50). A seven-year campaign ensued (67–61 B.C.), fought in two arenas, one southwest of Zarahemla and the other in the seaboard north of Zarahemla. Outlying towns fell, and the capital city was plagued with civil strife. At length, a costly victory was won by the Nephites (Alma 51–62).

In the short war of Tubaloth (51 B.C.), Ammoron's son Tubaloth and Coriantumr (a descendant of King Zarahemla) captured but could not hold the land of Zarahemla during the political chaos that followed the rebellion of Paanchi after the death of the chief judge Pahoran (Hel. 1). In the aftermath, the Gadianton robbers rose to power, and some Nephites began migrating to the north.

The war of Moronihah (38, 35–30 B.C.) followed the appointment of NEPHI$_2$ as chief judge (Hel. 4). Nephite dissenters, together with Lamanites, occupied half of the Nephite lands, and Nephi$_2$ resigned the judgment seat.

The wars of Gadianton and Kishkumen (26–19

B.C.) began with the assassinations of two consecutive chief judges, Cezoram and his son; greed and struggles for power brought on conflicts with the Gadianton robbers around Zarahemla. Lamanites joined with Nephites against these robbers until a famine, called down from heaven by the prophet Nephi$_2$, brought a temporary Nephite victory (Hel. 6-11).

Giddianhi and Zemnarihah (A.D. 13–22) led menacing campaigns against the few righteous Nephites and Lamanites who remained and joined forces at this time (3 Ne. 2–4). Low on supplies, the Gadianton robbers became more open and aggressive; they claimed rights to Nephite lands and government. The coalition of Nephites and Lamanites eventually defeated the robbers.

The final Nephite wars (A.D. 322, 327–328, 346–350) began after heavy population growth and infestation of robbers led to a border dispute, and the Nephites were driven to a narrow neck of land. The Nephites fortified the city of Shem and managed to win a ten-year peace treaty (Morm. 1–2), but the Nephites eventually counterattacked in the south. Gross wickedness existed on both sides (Morm 6; Moro. 9), until at a prearranged battleground the Nephites met the Lamanites and were annihilated (c. A.D. 385).

Many chapters in the Book of Mormon deal with war, and for several reasons.

1. The inevitability of war was a fundamental concern in virtually all ancient civilizations. Disposable economic resources were often largely devoted to maintaining a military force; conquest was a major factor in the transformation and development of Book of Mormon societies, as it was in the growth of most world civilizations.

2. The Book of Mormon is a religious record, and for the people of the Book of Mormon, as in nearly all ancient cultures, warfare was fundamentally sacral. It was carried out in a complex mixture of religious ritual and ideology.

3. Mormon, the compiler and abridger of the Book of Mormon, was himself a military commander. Many political and religious rulers in the Book of Mormon were closely associated with, if not the same as, their military commanders or elites.

4. Important religious messages are conveyed through these accounts. Wars in Nephite history

verify the words of their prophets such as ABINADI and SAMUEL THE LAMANITE (Morm. 1:19). Wars were instruments of God's judgment (Morm. 4:5) and of God's deliverance (Alma 56:46–56). Ultimately they stand as a compelling witness to warn people today against falling victim to the same fate that the Nephites and Jaredites finally brought upon themselves (Morm. 9:31; Ether 2:11–12).

BIBLIOGRAPHY

de Vaux, Roland. *Ancient Israel.* New York, 1965.

Hillam, Ray. "The Gadianton Robbers and Protracted War." *BYU Studies* 15 (1975):215–24.

Ricks, Stephen D., and William J. Hamblin, eds. *Warfare in the Book of Mormon.* Salt Lake City, 1990. (Further bibliography is listed on pp. 22–24.)

Sorenson, John L. *An Ancient American Setting for the Book of Mormon,* pp. 239–76. Salt Lake City, 1985.

WILLIAM J. HAMBLIN

BOOK OF MORMON AUTHORSHIP

Many studies have investigated Book of Mormon authorship because the book presents itself as a composite work of many ancient authors. Those who reject Joseph SMITH's claim that he translated the book through divine power assume that he or one of his contemporaries wrote the book. Various claims or arguments have been advanced to support or discount these competing positions.

Disputes about the book's authorship arose as soon as its existence became public knowledge. The first general reaction was ridicule. Modern minds do not easily accept the idea that an angel can deliver ancient records to be translated by an untrained young man. Moreover, most Christians in 1830 viewed the CANON of scripture as complete with the Bible; hence, the possibility of additional scripture violated a basic assumption of their faith. Opponents of Joseph Smith, such as Alexander Campbell, also argued that the Book of Mormon was heavily plagiarized from the Bible and that it reflected themes and phraseology current in New York in the 1820s. Many critics have speculated that Sidney RIGDON or Solomon Spaulding played a role in writing the book (*see* SPAULDING MANUSCRIPT). It has also been suggested that Joseph Smith borrowed ideas from another book (*see* VIEW OF THE HEBREWS). Though these varieties of objections and theories are still defended in many

quarters, they are not supported by modern authorship studies and continue to raise as many questions as they try to answer (e.g., *CWHN* 8:54–206).

Some have suggested that Joseph Smith admitted that he was the author of the Book of Mormon because the title page of the first edition lists him as "Author and Proprietor." This language, however, comes from the federal copyright statutes and legal forms in use in 1829 (1 *Stat.* 125 [1790], amended 2 *Stat.* 171 [1802]). In the preface to the same 1830 edition, Joseph Smith stated that he translated Mormon's handwriting "by the gift and power of God" (*see* BOOK OF MORMON TRANSLATION). The position of The Church of Jesus Christ of Latter-day Saints has invariably been that the truth of Joseph Smith's testimony can be validated through the witness of the HOLY GHOST.

Scholarly work has produced a variety of evidence in support of the claim that the texts of the Book of Mormon were written by multiple ancient authors. These studies significantly increase the plausibility of Joseph Smith's account of the origin of the book.

The internal complexity of the Book of Mormon is often cited as a strong indication of multiple authorship. The many writings reportedly abridged by MORMON are intricately interwoven and often expressly identified (*see* BOOK OF MORMON PLATES AND RECORDS). The various books within the Book of Mormon differ from each other in historical background, style, and distinctive characteristics, yet are accurate and consistent in numerous minute details.

Historical studies have demonstrated that many things either not known or not readily knowable in 1829 about the ancient Near East are accurately reflected in the Book of Mormon. This body of historical research was expanded by the work of Hugh W. Nibley (*see* BOOK OF MORMON STUDIES), who has recently discovered that ancient communities, such as Qumran, have many characteristics parallel to those of Book of Mormon peoples (*CWHN* 5–8). The Jews at Qumran were "sectaries," purists who left Jerusalem to avoid corruption of their covenants; they practiced ablutions (a type of baptism) before the time of Christ and wrote one of their records on a copper scroll that they sealed and hid up to come forth at a future time. One of Nibley's analyses demonstrates that King BENJAMIN's farewell speech to his people

(Mosiah 2–5) is a good example of the ancient year-rite festival (*CWHN* 6:295–310). Subsequent studies have suggested that King Benjamin's people might have been celebrating the Israelite festival of Sukkoth and doing things required by Jewish laws not translated into English until after the Book of Mormon was published (Tvedtnes, 1990).

Structural studies have identified an artistic literary form, chiasmus, that appears in rich diversity in both the Bible and the Book of Mormon (*see* BOOK OF MORMON LITERATURE). The most significant structural studies of the Book of Mormon derive from John W. Welch's analysis (Reynolds, pp. 33–52). Little known in 1829, this literary form creates inverted parallelism such as is found in this biblical passage in Leviticus 24:17–21:

> He that killeth any man . . .
> He that killeth a beast . . .
> If a man cause a blemish . . .
> Breach for breach,
> Eye for eye
> Tooth for tooth.
> As he hath caused a blemish . . .
> He that killeth a beast . . .
> He that killeth a man. . . .

And from the Book of Mormon, in Alma 41:13–14 (cf. Welch, pp. 5–22):

> Good for that which is good
> Righteous for that which is righteous
> Just for that which is just
> Merciful for that which is merciful
> Therefore my son
> See that you are merciful
> Deal justly
> Judge righteously
> And do good continually.

Although chiasmus can appear in almost any language or literature, it was prevalent in the biblical period around the early seventh century B.C., the time of the Book of Mormon prophets LEHI and NEPHI[1]. The especially precise and beautiful crafting of several Book of Mormon texts further supports the idea that their authors deliberately and painstakingly followed ancient literary conventions, which is inconsistent with seeing the New England born Joseph Smith as the author of these passages.

Other stylistic studies have examined the frequency of Hebrew root words, idioms, and syntax in the Book of Mormon (Tvedtnes, 1970). Some Book of Mormon names that have no English equivalents have Hebrew cognates (Hoskisson; *CWHN* 6:281–94). There are also discernible differences between the vocabularies and abridging techniques of Mormon and his son Moroni (see Keller).

Extensive statistical studies, including stylometry (or wordprinting), have been conducted on the Book of Mormon (Reynolds, pp. 157–88; cf. Hilton). Blocks of writing were analyzed to identify the writers' near-subconscious tendencies to use noncontextual word patterns in peculiar ratios and combinations. Wordprinting has been used to ascertain the authorship of such works as twelve disputed *Federalist Papers* and a posthumously published novel by Jane Austen. When applied to the Book of Mormon, wordprinting reveals that the word patterns of the Book of Mormon differ significantly from the personal writings of Joseph Smith, Solomon Spaulding, Sidney Rigdon, and Oliver COWDERY, who served as Joseph Smith's scribe. Furthermore, patterns of Nephi[1] are consistent among themselves but different from those of ALMA[2]. The results of objectively measuring these phenomena indicate an extremely low statistical probability that the Book of Mormon could have been written by one author. The introduction of new vocabulary into the text is at a low rate, which is consistent with the uniform role of Joseph Smith as translator.

BIBLIOGRAPHY

Hilton, John L. "On Verifying Wordprint Studies: Book of Mormon Authorship." *BYU Studies* 30 (Summer 1990):89–108.

Hoskisson, Paul. "An Introduction to the Relevance of and a Methodology for a Study of the Proper Names of the Book of Mormon." In *By Study and Also by Faith*, ed. J. Lundquist and S. Ricks, Vol. 2, pp. 126–35. Salt Lake City, 1990.

Keller, Roger R. "Mormon and Moroni as Authors and Abridgers." *F.A.R.M.S Update*, Apr. 1988.

Reynolds, Noel B., ed. *Book of Mormon Authorship: New Light on Ancient Origins*. Provo, Utah, 1982.

Tvedtnes, John. "Hebraisms in the Book of Mormon: A Preliminary Survey." *BYU Studies* 2 (Autumn 1970):50–60.

———. "King Benjamin and the Feast of Tabernacles." In *By Study and Also by Faith*, ed. J. Lundquist and S. Ricks, Vol. 2, pp. 197–237. Salt Lake City, 1990.

Welch, John W. "Chiasmus in Biblical Law." In *Jewish Law Association Studies IV*, ed. B. Jackson, pp. 5–22. Atlanta, 1990.

Wirth, Diane E. *A Challenge to the Critics: Scholarly Evidences of the Book of Mormon*. Bountiful, Utah, 1986.

D. BRENT ANDERSON

DIANE E. WIRTH

BOOK OF MORMON IN A BIBLICAL CULTURE

One does not need to look beyond the prevailing revivalist sects in America to discover why the earliest Mormon elders won an immediate hearing for their sacred book. Firm calls for personal righteousness and obedience to the moral requirements of the Judeo-Christian scriptures were by 1830 the dominant motifs in all Protestant communions. Moreover, each of the American sects shared speculations about the ancient and future history of Indians and Jews.

These interests and beliefs were also predominant among Methodist, Congregational, and Baptist ministers serving congregations in and around Cheshire, in northern England. Heber C. Kimball's *Journal*, giving an account of his mission to Great Britain, shows how the flowering of biblical study and of millennial speculation prepared the soil for early Mormon evangelization there. He reported that even clergymen in the Church of England told their congregations that the teachings of the Latter-day Saints reveal the same principles taught by the apostles of old.

The Book of Mormon also gives clear direction on several matters that the Christian scriptures seem to have left unclear, including baptism by immersion and the promises that all believers, and not just the apostles, might be "filled with the Holy Ghost"; that Christian believers can be made pure in heart (as John Wesley had insisted in the previous century); that the experience of salvation received by a free response to free grace is available to all persons, and not simply to the "elect"; and that obedience and works of righteousness are the fruit of that experience. The book also affirms the veracity of the biblical accounts of the scattering of Israel by affirming that Native Americans originated from descendants of Joseph and Judah.

The persuasive power of the new scriptures and of the missionaries who expounded them, therefore, lay in their testimony to beliefs that were central to evangelical Protestant sects in both Jacksonian America and early Victorian England. An early LDS missionary, Parley P. PRATT, told his English hearers that two errors in interpretation of the Bible had produced widespread uncertainty. One was the belief that direct inspiration by the Holy Ghost was not intended for all ages of the Church; and the other was that the Jewish and Christian scriptures contained all truth necessary

to salvation and comprised a sufficient rule of faith and practice.

Some nineteenth-century deacons and elders and a few evangelical pastors struggled with grave temptations to doubt the truth and relevance of large portions of the book upon which they had been taught to stake their eternal destiny. True, the details of the histories recounted in the two sacred books were radically different. But they fit together wondrously. And their moral structure, the story they told of Jesus, their promise of salvation, and their description of humankind's last days were remarkably similar. Though the new scriptures had similarities with evangelical Arminianism, at the expense of the Calvinist views long dominant in colonial America, the same was true of the early nineteenth-century teachings of many Protestants, even Presbyterians, to say nothing of Methodists and Disciples of Christ. In the voice of two witnesses, the Bible and the Book of Mormon, Latter-day Saints declared the truth confirmed, just as the prophet NEPHI₁ had predicted (cf. 2 Ne. 29:8).

In five important ways, the Book of Mormon seems to some who are not members of the Church to strengthen the authority of Holy Scripture. First in importance is the volume's affirmation that the Christian religion is grounded upon both the Old and New Testaments. The book affirms what recent biblical scholarship is now making plain: the continuity of the theology, ethics, and spirituality that the two Testaments proclaimed. In the Book of Mormon, Jesus is the Lord who gave the law to Moses, and the risen Christ is identical to the prophet Isaiah's MESSIAH. He delivers exactly the same message of redemption, faith, and a new life of righteousness through the Holy Spirit that the New Testament attributes to him.

Second, the Book of Mormon reinforces the unifying vision of biblical religion, grounding it in the conviction of a common humanity that the stories of creation declared, God's promise to Abraham implied, and Jesus affirmed. Puritan MILLENARIANISM may have inspired an ethnocentric view of Anglo-Saxon destiny, but the image of the future in the Book of Mormon is a wholly opposite one. It envisions a worldwide conversion of believers and their final gathering into the kingdom of God. This begins where John Wesley's "world parish" leaves off.

Third, the biblical bond linking holiness to hope for salvation, both individual and social, also finds confirmation in the Book of Mormon. Certainly, Methodists had no corner on that linkage, for Baptist preachers, Charles G. Finney's Congregationalists, Alexander Campbell's Disciples of Christ, and Unitarians like William E. Channing affirmed it. Ancient Nephites heeded the word of their prophets and looked forward to the second coming of Jesus Christ, the Son of Righteousness. When he appeared to their descendants in the New World, Jesus repeated even more understandably the words of the SERMON ON THE MOUNT that he had proclaimed in the Old.

Fourth, Joseph Smith's translation of an ancient sacred book helped bring to fruition another movement, long growing among Puritans, Pietists, Quakers, and Methodists, to restore to Christian doctrine the idea of the presence of the Holy Spirit in the lives of believers. Charles G. Finney came eventually to believe, for example, that the baptism of the Holy Spirit, or the experience of entire SANCTIFICATION, would remedy the inadequacies of righteousness and love that he saw in his converts. So, of course, did almost all Methodists. Observers from both inside and outside the restored Church testified that in the early years something akin to modern pentecostal phenomena took place among at least the inner circle of the Saints. By the 1830s, evangelicals in several traditions were greatly expanding their use of the example of the Day of Pentecost to declare that God's power is at work in the world.

Fifth, the Book of Mormon shared in the restoration of some Christian expectations that in the LAST DAYS biblical prophecies will be literally fulfilled. Those who by faith and baptism become Saints will be included among God's people, chosen in "the eleventh hour." They, too, should gather in ZION, a NEW JERUSALEM for the New World, and a restored Jerusalem in the Old; and Christ will indeed return.

Whatever LDS interpretations of the King James Version of the Holy Scriptures developed later, the mutually supportive role of the Bible and the Book of Mormon was central to the thinking of Joseph Smith, the early missionaries, and their converts.

BIBLIOGRAPHY

Kimball, Heber C. *Journal.* Nauvoo, Ill., 1840.

Smith, Timothy L. "The Book of Mormon in a Biblical Culture." *Journal of Mormon History* 7 (1980):3–21.

TIMOTHY L. SMITH

BOOK OF MORMON CHRONOLOGY

The Book of Mormon contains a chronology that is internally consistent over the thousand-year NEPHITE history, with precise Nephite dates for several events, including the crucifixion of Jesus Christ. However, its chronology has not been unequivocally tied to other calendars because of uncertainties in biblical dates and lack of details about the Nephite calendars. Even less information exists about JAREDITE chronology (Sorenson, 1969).

INTERNAL NEPHITE CHRONOLOGY. Nephites kept careful track of time from at least three reference points:

1. Years were counted from the time LEHI left Jerusalem (Enos 1:25; Mosiah 6:4); not only was this an important date of origin, but also an angel had said that the Savior would come "in 600 years" from that time (1 Ne. 19:8).
2. Time was also measured from the commencement of the reign of the judges (c. 91 B.C.; cf. 3 Ne. 1:1), which marked a major political reform ending five centuries of Nephite kingship (Jacob 1:9–11; Alma 1:1), during which the years of each king's reign were probably counted according to typical ancient practices (1 Ne. 1:4; Mosiah 29:46).
3. The Nephites later reckoned time from the sign of the birth of Christ (3 Ne. 2:8).

The Book of Mormon links all three systems in several passages that are apparently consistent. Table 1 lists several events using the Nephite systems.

Most of the Nephite record pertains to three historical periods: the time of Lehi and his sons (c. 600–500 B.C.), the events preceding and following the coming of Christ (c. 150 B.C.–A.D. 34), and the destruction of the Nephites (c. A.D. 300–420). Thus, the relatively large book of Alma covers only thirty-nine years, while the much smaller books of Omni and 4 Nephi each cover more than two hundred years.

LDS editions of the Book of Mormon show dates in Nephite years, deduced from the text, at the bottom of the pages. The exact nature of the Nephite year, however, is not described. The Nephite year began with the "first day" of the "first month" (Alma 51:37–52:1; 56:1), and it probably had twelve months because the eleventh month was at "the latter end" of the year (Alma 48:2, 21;

TABLE 1 SELECTED EVENTS IN NEPHITE HISTORY

Lehi	Nephite Years Judges	Christ	Event	Reference
1		(−600)	Lehi departs from Jerusalem	1 Ne. 10:4; 19:8
9		(−592)	Lehi's group arrives in Bountiful	1 Ne. 17:4–5
56		(−545)	Jacob receives plates from Nephi	Jacob 1:1
200		(−401)	Law of Moses strictly observed	Jarom 1:5
477		(−124)	King Benjamin's speech	Mosiah 6:3–4
510	1	(−91)	Alma₁, Mosiah die; Alma₂ first judge	Mosiah 29:44–46
	9	(−83)	Nephihah becomes judge	Alma 4:20–8:2
	15	(−77)	The return of the sons of Mosiah	Alma 17:1–6
	18	(−74)	Korihor refuted	Alma 30
			Alma's Mission to the Zoramites	Alma 31:6–35:12
	18	(−74)	War because of Zoramites	Alma 35:13; 43:3–4
			Moroni leads army	Alma 43:17
	37	(−55)	Nephites begin migrating northward	Alma 63:4–6
	42	(−50)	Helaman₂ becomes judge; Gadianton	Hel. 2:1–5
	53	(−39)	Helaman₂ dies; Nephi₂ chief judge	Hel. 3:37
	58	(−34)	Zarahemla captured	Hel. 4:5
	67	(−25)	Most Nephites join Gadianton	Hel. 6:16, 21
	73	(−19)	Nephi invokes a famine	Hel. 11:2–5
	75	(−17)	Gadianton robbers expelled	Hel. 11:6-17
	77	(−15)	Most Nephites reconverted	Hel. 11:21
	80	(−12)	Robbers return	Hel. 11:24–29
	86	(−6)	Samuel the Lamanite prophesies	Hel. 13:1–16:9
601	92	(1)	Sign of the birth of Christ	3 Ne. 1:1,4,19
609	100	9	Begin to reckon time from Christ	3 Ne. 2:5–8
		13	Severe war with robbers begins	3 Ne. 2:11–13
		19	Major Nephite victory	3 Ne. 4:5, 11–15
		26	Nephites prosper	3 Ne. 6:1–4
		30	Nephite society disintegrates	3 Ne. 6:14–7:13
		34	Destruction; Christ appears	3 Ne. 8:2–28:12
		36	All converted; property held in common	4 Ne. 1:2–3
		201	Private ownership reinstituted	4 Ne. 1:24–25
		231	Tribalization reemerges	4 Ne. 1:35–38
		245	The wicked outnumber righteous	4 Ne. 1:40
		300	Nephites as wicked as Lamanites	4 Ne. 1:45
		326	Mormon leads army	Morm. 2:2
		350	Treaty with Lamanites and Robbers	Morm. 2:28
		362	Mormon refuses to lead Nephites	Morm. 3:8–11
		385	Nephites destroyed; Mormon dies	Morm. 6:5–8:3
		421	Moroni seals up the record	Moro. 10:1–2

NOTE: Years in parentheses are calculated, with the year −600 beginning just over 600 Nephite years before the birth of Christ.

49:1), but the lengths of the months and of the year itself are not mentioned.

Until the coming of Christ, the Nephites observed the LAW OF MOSES (2 Ne. 25:24; Alma 25:15), which generally used lunar months (new moon to new moon). The Savior was crucified on the *fourteenth* day of the first lunar month of the Jewish calendar (John 19:14; Lev. 23:5), but on the *fourth* day of the first Nephite month (3 Ne. 8:5). This may imply that Nephite months at that time were not lunar and that their civil calendar may have differed from their religious calendar.

John L. Sorenson (1990) has observed that during the reign of the judges warfare was mostly limited to four consecutive Nephite months. These months can be approximately correlated with our calendar because even today warfare in Mesoamerica (the probable area of BOOK OF MORMON GEOGRAPHY for most of Nephite history) is conducted mostly during the dry season after the fall harvest. This correlation implies that the Nephite year at that time began in December (*see* BOOK OF MORMON, HISTORY OF WARFARE IN). This would mean that because the crucifixion of Christ (presumably in early April) occurred in the first Nephite month, the Nephites probably shifted their calendar to begin the first month in April at the same time they began reckoning time from the birth of Christ. This conclusion is consistent with the Nephite record that Christ was born some time after the end of the Nephite year (3 Ne. 1:1–9).

EXTERNAL CHRONOLOGY. Evidence supports two possible lengths for Nephite years: 365 days and 360 days. Each can be correlated to external history. The internal chronology is consistent, so that if the exact nature of the Nephite calendar were known, only one reference point in external history would be needed to fix the entire Nephite chronology. However, at least two such dates would be required to determine the length of the Nephite year. Three principal events are common to both Nephite and Old World sources: (1) the first year of the reign of Zedekiah, King of Judah; (2) the birth of Christ; and (3) the death of Christ. Because there are varying degrees of uncertainty about these three reference points, alternative correlation methods have been proposed, each using two of these dates.

First, Orson PRATT proposed that the Nephites used a 365-day year, as had the Egyptians previously and as did the Mesoamericans afterward (*Millennial Star* 28 [Dec. 22, 1866]:810). It has been noted (Lefgren) that such a year agrees, to the very day, with one choice for the birth and death dates of Christ—namely, Thursday, APRIL 6, 1 B.C., and Friday, April 1, A.D. 33, respectively (Gregorian calendar). Both of these dates are supported by other arguments (J. Pratt, 1985 and 1990). This theory assumes that the third system of Nephite reckoning began on the very day of the birth of Christ, which is not explicitly stated in the Book of Mormon but is consistent with Sorenson's conclusions above.

Second, most historians believe that the first year of King Zedekiah began in 598–96 B.C. Lehi left Jerusalem shortly afterward (1 Ne. 1:4; 2:4). The date of the birth of Christ is not known directly from historical sources, but it is believed that King Herod died in 5–4 B.C., implying that Christ was born shortly before (Matt. 2:1). Using these two events as reference points, Huber has proposed a 360-day Nephite year because 600 such years fit the interval from Lehi to Christ (3 Ne. 1:1); such a system has historical precedent, and apparently underlies certain prophecies in which the word "time" may equal 360 days (e.g., Rev. 12:6, 14).

BIBLIOGRAPHY

Brown, S. Kent; C. Wilfred Griggs; and H. Kimball Hansen. "Review of *April Sixth* by John C. Lefgren." *BYU Studies* 22 (Summer 1982):375–83. See rebuttal and response in *BYU Studies* 23 (Spring 1983):252–55.

Huber, Jay H. "Lehi's 600 Year Prophecy and the Birth of Christ." *F.A.R.M.S. Paper.* Provo, Utah, 1982.

Lefgren, John C. *April Sixth.* Salt Lake City, 1980.

Pratt, John P. "The Restoration of Priesthood Keys on Easter 1836. Part 1: Dating the First Easter." *Ensign* 15 (June 1985):59–68.

———. "Yet Another Eclipse for Herod." *The Planetarian* 19 (Dec. 1990):8–14.

Sorenson, John L. "The Years of the Jaredites." *F.A.R.M.S. Paper.* Provo, Utah, 1969.

———. "Seasonality of Warfare in the Book of Mormon and in Mesoamerica." In *Warfare in the Book of Mormon*, ed. S. Ricks and W. Hamblin, pp. 445–77. Salt Lake City, 1990.

JOHN P. PRATT

BOOK OF MORMON COMMENTARIES

Because the Book of Mormon is the best known and most widely circulated LDS book, many commentaries on and reference books about it have been written to assist readers. Inasmuch as its historical timeline spans from c. 2200 B.C. to A.D. 421 and its doctrinal content is extensive, it is difficult for a one-volume work to meet the many needs and interests. The references cited herein contain bibliographies that will provide readers with additional sources.

George Reynolds and Janne M. Sjodahl coauthored a *Commentary on the Book of Mormon* (1955–1961), a seven-volume work (published posthumously to both authors) that has been widely circulated. Hugh Nibley's *Lehi in the*

Desert and the World of the Jaredites (1952; rev. 1988) provides insightful historical material on the travels of Lehi's party from Jerusalem, which occurred about c. 600 B.C., through the Arabian Peninsula, to the Western Hemisphere, and also on the journey of the Jaredite colony at about c. 2200 B.C. from the Near East to the Western Hemisphere. Francis W. Kirkham wrote a two-volume work entitled *A New Witness for Christ in America* (rev. ed. 1959–1960) that discusses the coming forth and the translation and printing of the Book of Mormon and non-LDS explanations of the same topics. B. H. Roberts authored a three-volume work titled *New Witnesses for God* (1909). Volumes 2 and 3 addressed four topics: the Book of Mormon as a witness of the Bible; the discovery, translation, and people of the Book of Mormon; evidence of its truth; and Roberts's responses to various objections to the book. Sidney B. Sperry authored *Our Book of Mormon* (1947); *The Book of Mormon Testifies* (1952); and *Book of Mormon Compendium* (1968). Daniel H. Ludlow wrote a popular one-volume work, *A Companion to Your Study of the Book of Mormon* (1976).

The Religious Studies Center at Brigham Young University sponsors an annual symposium on the Book of Mormon. Beginning in 1985, it has published a volume of selected lectures for each symposium. Both doctrinal and historical materials are included. Other volumes are planned as additional symposia are held. A volume entitled *A Book of Mormon Treasury* (1959), taken from the pages of the *Improvement Era*, contains thirty-six articles by General Authorities and other respected students of the Book of Mormon on historical, geographical, and doctrinal matters, as well as biblical relationships. Following a similar format, Kent P. Jackson compiled a two-volume work, *Studies in Scripture Volume Seven—1st Nephi—Alma 29* (1987) and *Studies in Scripture Volume Eight—Alma 30—Moroni* (1988). Jackson also edited a special Book of Mormon issue of *BYU Studies* 30 (Summer 1990):1–140. Other scholarly materials related to Book of Mormon topics are available through F.A.R.M.S. (Foundation for Ancient Research and Mormon Studies).

Others who have contributed to the literature about the Book of Mormon are Paul R. Cheesman, whose works include *The World of the Book of Mormon* (1984), and Monte S. Nyman, whose publications include *An Ensign to All People: The Sacred Message and Mission of the Book of Mormon* (1987).

Church headquarters publishes materials for use in weekly priesthood quorum meetings, Relief Society meetings, Sunday School classes, and Institute and Seminary classes to assist members in better understanding the Book of Mormon.

Several authors have written on Book of Mormon archaeology and geology. Two popular books with an archaeological approach are Dewey and Edith Farnsworth, *The Americas Before Columbus* (1947), and Milton R. Hunter and Thomas Stuart Ferguson, *Ancient America and the Book of Mormon* (1950). More recent studies on Book of Mormon geography include John L. Sorenson, *An Ancient American Setting for the Book of Mormon* (1985); F. Richard Hauck, *Deciphering the Geography of the Book of Mormon* (1988); and Joseph L. Allen, *Exploring the Lands of the Book of Mormon* (1989). The Nephites, Lamanites, Mulekites, and Jaredites were historical cultures that occupied time and space; however, Church leaders have declared no official position as to where the Book of Mormon civilizations were situated other than that they were in the Western Hemisphere.

[*See also* other Book of Mormon entries.]

H. DONL PETERSON

BOOK OF MORMON ECONOMY AND TECHNOLOGY

The Book of Mormon reports information about three pre-Hispanic American peoples. Although its writers do not offer a detailed picture of the economic and material culture of their societies, numerous incidental details are preserved in the account. In many cases, though not in every instance, archaeology confirms the general details. The problems that remain in matching the Book of Mormon to its presumed ancient setting are no doubt due both to the scant information given in the book itself and to incompleteness in the archaeological record.

Testing what the Book of Mormon says about pre-Columbian material culture is more difficult than it might at first appear to be. For instance, it is a historically well-established fact that craft techniques can be lost; thus one cannot confidently assume that technologies mentioned for limited

Book of Mormon populations survived after the destruction of the Nephites. Nor can one assume what Old World technologies were successfully transferred to the New. Many crafts would not have been known to the small colonist parties, and even among the skills that were transported across the sea, many may not have proved useful or adaptable in the new environment. For that matter, items attested in early portions of the Book of Mormon may not safely be assumed to have survived into subsequent history within the record itself.

The economy of Book of Mormon peoples seems, on the whole, to have been relatively simple. Although many Nephites and Jaredites lived in cities of modest size (a point whose plausibility has been enhanced by recent research), their societies were agriculturally based. Trade was mentioned for some periods, but was constrained by frequent wars. In the infrequently mentioned times of free travel, trade barriers fell, and Lamanites and Nephites predictably prospered (e.g., Hel. 6:7–9).

Despite the economy's agrarian base, wealth was manifested in terms of movable flocks, herds, costly clothing, gold, silver, and "precious things" rather than land (Jacob 2:12–13; Enos 1:21; Jarom 1:8; Mosiah 9:12; Alma 1:6, 29; 17:25; 32:2; Ether 10:12). The ideology of the leading Book of Mormon peoples undoubtedly contributed to this phenomenon: They referred to themselves as a righteous remnant obliged to abandon their comfortable dwellings and depart into the wilderness because of their religious convictions. Since entire populations seem to have moved often, land may not have been a stable source of wealth (2 Ne. 5:5–11; Omni 12–13, 27–30; Mosiah 9; 18:34–35; 22; 24:16–25; Alma 27; 35:6–14; 63:4–10; Hel. 2:11; 3:3–12; 4:5–6, 19; 3 Ne. 3:21–4:1; 7:1–2). Ideally, wealth was to be shared with the poor and for the common good, but strong contrasts between rich and poor are evident more often than not.

Agriculture in the Book of Mormon involved livestock and sown crops. For example, in the fifth century B.C., the Nephites "did till the land, and raise all manner of grain, and of fruit, and flocks of herds, and flocks of all manner of cattle of every kind, and goats, and wild goats, and also many horses" (Enos 1:21). In the second century B.C., the people of Zeniff cultivated corn, wheat, barley,

"neas," and "sheum" (Mosiah 9:9; cf. Alma 11:7). Early nineteenth-century American language usage suggests that Book of Mormon "corn" may denote maize or "Indian corn," which was and is a staple in diets in most parts of native America. Some of the other listed items remain less certain. Only in 1982 was evidence published demonstrating the presence of cultivated pre-Columbian barley in the New World (Sorenson, 1985, p. 184). "Neas" is not identifiable; but the word "sheum" appears to be cognate with early Akkadian *she-um*, a grain probably of the barley type (*see* F.A.R.M.S. Staff, "Weights and Measures").

Book of Mormon mention of horses in pre-Columbian America has drawn much criticism, and no definitive answer to this question is at present available. Linguistic data suggest that Book of Mormon "horse" need not refer to *equus*, but could indicate some other quadruped suitable for human riding, as Mesoamerican art suggests (Sorenson, 1985, p. 295). Moreover, some little-noticed archaeological evidence indicates that in certain areas the American Pleistocene horse could have survived into Book of Mormon times (*Update*, June 1984).

Most transportation was evidently on human backs; in the two contexts that the Book of Mormon mentions "chariots," it appears that their use was quite limited (Alma 18:9–12; 20:6; 3 Ne. 3:22). Chariots are never mentioned in military settings. Wheels are nowhere mentioned in the Book of Mormon (except in a quote from Isaiah). Thus, it is unknown what Nephite "chariots" may have been. "Highways" and "roads" are mentioned as used by the Nephites (3 Ne. 6:8). Some Latter-day Saints consider these to be reflected in the extensively documented road systems of ancient Mexico. "Ships" of unknown form were used during the middle of the first century B.C. for travel on the "west sea" coast (Alma 63:6) and for shipping timber to the north (Hel. 3:10), and at times maritime travel was evidently extensive (Hel. 3:14). Fine pearls are also mentioned as costly items (4 Ne. 1:24).

"Silk and fine-twined linen" are mentioned (e.g., Alma 1:29; Ether 10:24) along with common (cotton?) cloth. The "silk" is unlikely to have been produced from silkworms as in China, but similar fabrics were known, at least in Mesoamerica. For example, in Guatemala fiber from the wild pineapple plant, and among the Aztecs rabbit hair, served

The use of cement appears extensively in Mesoamerican archaeology around the first century A.D., as, for example, in these cement buildings at Teotihuacan in the Valley of Mexico. The Book of Mormon states that some Nephite dissenters who moved into a land northward "became exceeding expert in the working of cement" and built "cities both of wood and of cement" beginning in 46 B.C. (Hel. 3:7, 11). Courtesy John W. Welch.

to make silklike fabrics. Although flax apparently was not known in America prior to the arrival of the Spaniards (linen was made from flax in the Old World), several vegetable-based fabrics with similar characteristics are well attested in ancient America (*Update*, Nov. 1988).

Care must be exercised when reading the Book of Mormon, or any other text originating in a foreign or ancient culture, to avoid misunderstanding unfamiliar things in light of what is familiar. For instance, the Nephites are said to have used "money," but since the Israelites in Lehi's day lacked minted coinage, Nephite "money" was probably noncoined.

A well-integrated system of dry measures and metal-weight units is outlined in Alma 11; some analysts have pointed out that the system sketched is strikingly simple, efficient, and rational (Smith). In its binary mathematical configuration and its use of barley and silver as basic media of exchange, the Nephite system recalls similar systems known in Egypt and in the Babylonian laws of Eshnunna (F.A.R.M.S. Staff, "Weights and Measures"; *Update*, March 1987).

Making weapons of "steel" and "iron" is mentioned by the Nephites only during their first few generations (2 Ne. 5:15; Jarom 1:8; iron is mentioned only as a "precious" ornamental metal during the time of Mosiah 11:8). Just what these terms originally meant may not be clear. Jaredite "steel" and "iron" and other metals are mentioned twice

but are not described (Ether 7:9; 10:23). The weapons of the common soldier were distinctly simpler: stones, clubs, spears, and the bow and arrow (e.g., Alma 49:18–22).

The relative simplicity of Book of Mormon society does not imply lack of sophistication by ancient standards. For example, it would seem that literacy was not uncommon among either Nephites or Jaredites. The founding leaders of the migrations were definitely literate, and the Nephites in their middle era are said to have produced "many books and many records of every kind" (Hel. 3:15). The Lamanites and Mulekites, on the other hand, were less consistent record keepers (Omni 1:17–18; Mosiah 24:4–6; Hel. 3:15). The Jaredites and Nephites kept their most sacred records on almost imperishable metal PLATES, although some of their books were on flammable material (Alma 14:8). The plates that Joseph Smith had in his possession, and that he and other contemporary eyewitnesses described, seem well within the skill of pre-Hispanic metallurgists (Putnam; Sorenson, 1985, pp. 278–88), and the manner of their burial has rich precedent in the Eastern Hemisphere (Wright).

BIBLIOGRAPHY

Cheesman, Paul R. *Ancient Writing on Metal Plates*. Bountiful, Utah, 1985.

F.A.R.M.S. *Updates* (Provo, Utah), contain useful discussions, including bibliographies, of pre-Columbian horses (June

1984), metallurgy of golden plates (Oct. 1984), pre-Hispanic domesticated barley (Dec. 1984), the loss of technologies (July 1985), the legal implementation of the Nephite system of weights and measures (Mar. 1987), and possible silks and linens (Nov. 1988).

F.A.R.M.S. Staff. "Weights and Measures in the Time of Mosiah II." Provo, Utah, 1983.

Nibley, Hugh W. *The Prophetic Book of Mormon*, in *CWHN* 8:245–46, 385–86, and *Since Cumorah*, in *CWHN* 7:220–27. Discusses metallic plates, steel, cement, money, and fauna.

Putnam, Reed. "Were the Golden Plates Made of Tumbaga?" *IE* (Sept. 1966):788–89, 828–31.

Smith, R. P. "The Nephite Monetary System." *IE* 57 (May 1954):316–17.

Sorenson, John L. "A Reconsideration of Early Metal in Mesoamerica." *Katunob* 9 (Mar. 1976):1–18.

———. *An Ancient American Setting for the Book of Mormon.* Salt Lake City, 1985.

Wright, H. Curtis. "Ancient Burials of Metallic Foundation Documents in Stone Boxes." In *Occasional Papers, University of Illinois Graduate School of Library and Information Science* 157 (1982):1–42.

DANIEL C. PETERSON

BOOK OF MORMON EDITIONS (1830–1981)

Two major goals of each published edition of the Book of Mormon have been (1) to faithfully reproduce the text; and (2) to make the text accessible to the reader. The goal of textual accuracy has led later editors to earlier editions and, when available, to the original and printer's manuscripts (*see* BOOK OF MORMON MANUSCRIPTS). The goal of accessibility has led to some modernization and standardization of the text itself and the addition of reader's helps (introductory material, versification, footnotes, chapter summaries, dates, pronunciation guides, and indexes).

Four editions were published during Joseph SMITH's lifetime:

1. 1830: 5,000 copies; published by E. B. Grandin in Palmyra, New York. In general, the first edition is a faithful copy of the printer's manuscript (although on one occasion the original manuscript rather than the printer's was used for typesetting). For the most part, this edition reproduces what the compositor, John H. Gilbert, considered grammatical "errors." Gilbert added punctuation and determined the paragraphing for the first edition. In the Preface, Joseph Smith explains the loss of the Book of Lehi—116 pages of manuscript (*see*

MANUSCRIPT, LOST 116 PAGES). The testimonies of the Three and the Eight Witnesses were placed at the end of the book. In this and all other early editions, there is no versification.

2. 1837: Either 3,000 or 5,000 copies; published by Parley P. PRATT and John Goodson, Kirtland, Ohio. For this edition, hundreds of grammatical changes and a few emendations were made in the text. The 1830 edition and the printer's manuscript were used as the basis for this edition.

3. 1840: 2,000 copies; published for Ebenezer Robinson and Don Carlos Smith (by Shepard and Stearns, Cincinnati, Ohio), Nauvoo, Illinois. Joseph Smith compared the printed text with the original manuscript and discovered a number of errors made in copying the printer's manuscript from the original. Thus the 1840 edition restores some of the readings of the original manuscript.

4. 1841: 4,050 copies (5,000 contracted); published for Brigham YOUNG, Heber C. KIMBALL, and Parley P. Pratt (by J. Tompkins, Liverpool, England). This first European edition was printed with the permission of Joseph Smith; it is essentially a reprinting of the 1837 edition with British spellings.

Two additional British editions, one in 1849 (edited by Orson PRATT) and the other in 1852 (edited by Franklin D. Richards), show minor editing of the text. In the 1852 edition, Richards added numbers to the paragraphs to aid in finding passages, thereby creating the first—although primitive—versification for the Book of Mormon.

Three other important LDS editions have involved major changes in format as well as minor editing:

1. 1879: Edited by Orson Pratt. Major changes in the format of the text included division of the long chapters in the original text, a true versification system (which has been followed in all subsequent LDS editions), and footnotes (mostly scriptural references).

2. 1920: Edited by James E. Talmage. Further changes in format included introductory material, double columns, chapter summaries, and new footnotes. Some of the minor editing found in this edition appeared earlier in the 1905 and 1911 editions, also under the editorship of Talmage.

3. 1981: Edited by a committee headed by members of the Quorum of the Twelve. This edition is a

major reworking of the 1920 edition: The text appears again in double columns, but new introductory material, chapter summaries, and footnotes are provided. About twenty significant textual errors that had entered the printer's manuscript are corrected by reference to the original manuscript. Other corrections were made from comparison with the printer's manuscript and the 1840 Nauvoo edition.

The REORGANIZED CHURCH OF JESUS CHRIST OF LATTER DAY SAINTS (RLDS) also has its own textual tradition. Prior to 1874, the RLDS used an edition of the Book of Mormon published by James O. Wright (1858, New York), basically a reprinting of the 1840 Nauvoo edition. The first and second RLDS editions (1874, Plano, Illinois; and 1892, Lamoni, Iowa) followed the 1840 text and had their own system of versification. Unlike the later LDS editions, all RLDS editions have retained the original longer chapters.

In 1903 the RLDS obtained the printer's manuscript and used it to produce their third edition (1908, Lamoni, Iowa). The text of the 1908 edition restored many of the readings found in that manuscript, but generally did not alter the grammatical changes made in the 1837 Kirtland edition. This edition also included a new versification, which has remained unchanged in all subsequent RLDS editions. In 1966 the RLDS published a thoroughly modernized Book of Mormon text. Both the 1908 (with minor editing) and the 1966 texts are available, but only the 1908 edition is authorized for use in the RLDS Church.

A critical text of the Book of Mormon was published in 1984–1987 by the Foundation for Ancient Research and Mormon Studies. This is the first published text of the Book of Mormon to show the precise history of many textual variants. Although this textual study of the editions and manuscripts of the Book of Mormon is incomplete and preliminary, it is helpful for a general overview of the textual history of the Book of Mormon.

BIBLIOGRAPHY

Anderson, Richard L. "Gold Plates and Printer's Ink." *Ensign*, 6 (Sept. 1976):71–76.

Heater, Shirley R. "Gold Plates, Foolscap, & Printer's Ink; Part II: Editions of the Book of Mormon." *Zarahemla Record* 37–38 (1987):2–15.

Larson, Stanley R. "A Study of Some Textual Variations in the Book of Mormon Comparing the Original and the Printer's Manuscripts and the 1830, the 1837, and the 1840 Editions." Master's thesis, Brigham Young University, 1974.

Matthews, Robert J. "The New Publication of the Standard Works 1979, 1981." *BYU Studies* 22 (1982):387–424.

Skousen, Royal. "Towards a Critical Edition of the Book of Mormon." *BYU Studies* 30 (1990):41–69.

Stocks, Hugh G. "The Book of Mormon, 1830–1879: A Publishing History." Master's thesis, UCLA, 1979.

———. "The Book of Mormon in English, 1870–1920: A Publishing History and Analytical Bibliography." Ph.D. diss., UCLA, 1986.

ROYAL SKOUSEN

BOOK OF MORMON GEOGRAPHY

Although the Book of Mormon is primarily a religious record of the NEPHITES, LAMANITES, and JAREDITES, enough geographic details are embedded in the narrative to allow reconstruction of at least a rudimentary geography of Book of Mormon lands. In the technical usage of the term "geography" (e.g., physical, economic, cultural, or political), no Book of Mormon geography has yet been written. Most Latter-day Saints who write geographies have in mind one or both of two activities: first, internal reconstruction of the relative size and configuration of Book of Mormon lands based upon textual statements and allusions; second, speculative attempts to match an internal geography to a location within North or South America. Three questions relating to Book of Mormon geography are discussed here: (1) How can one reconstruct a Book of Mormon geography? (2) What does a Book of Mormon geography look like? (3) What hypothetical locations have been suggested for Book of Mormon lands?

RECONSTRUCTING INTERNAL BOOK OF MORMON GEOGRAPHY. Although Church leadership officially and consistently distances itself from issues regarding Book of Mormon geography in order to focus attention on the spiritual message of the book, private speculation and scholarship in this area have been abundant. Using textual clues, laymen and scholars have formulated over sixty possible geographies. Dissimilarities among them stem from differences in (1) the interpretation of scriptural passages and statements of General Authorities; (2) procedures for reconciling scriptural information; (3) initial assumptions concerning the text and traditional LDS identification of certain features mentioned (especially the hill CUMORAH and the "narrow neck of land," which figure prominently in the text); and (4) personal penchants and disciplinary training.

Those who believe that reconstructing a Book of Mormon geography is possible must first deal with the usual problems of interpreting historical texts. Different weights must be given to various passages, depending upon the amount and precision of the information conveyed. Many Book of Mormon cities cannot be situated because of insufficient textual information; this is especially true for Lamanite and Jaredite cities. The Book of Mormon is essentially a Nephite record, and most geographic elements mentioned are in Nephite territory.

From textual evidence, one can approximate some spatial relationships of various natural features and cities. Distances in the Book of Mormon are recorded in terms of the time required to travel from place to place. The best information for reconstructing internal geography comes from the accounts of wars between Nephites and Lamanites during the first century B.C., with more limited information from Nephite missionary journeys. Travel distance can be standardized to a degree by controlling, where possible, for the nature of the terrain (e.g., mountains versus plains) and the relative velocity (e.g., an army's march versus travel with children or animals). The elementary internal geography presented below is based on an interpretation of distances thus standardized and directions based on the text.

AN INTERNAL BOOK OF MORMON GEOGRAPHY. Numerous attempts have been made to diagram physical and political geographies depicting features mentioned in the text, but this requires many additional assumptions and is difficult to accomplish without making approximate relationships appear precise (Sorenson, 1991). The description presented below of the size and configuration of Book of Mormon lands and the locations of settlements within it summarizes the least ambiguous evidence.

Book of Mormon lands were longer from north to south than from east to west. They consisted of two land masses connected by an isthmus ("a narrow neck of land") flanked by an "east sea" and a "west sea" (Alma 22:27, 32). The land north of the narrow neck was known as the "land northward" and that to the south as the "land south-ward" (Alma 22:32). The Jaredite narrative took place entirely in the land northward (Omni 1:22; Ether 10:21), but details are insufficient to place their cities relative to one another. Most of the Nephite narrative, on the other hand, took place in the land southward. Travel accounts for the land southward indicate that the Nephites and Lamanites occupied an area that could be traversed north to south by normal travel in perhaps thirty days.

The land southward was divided by a "narrow strip of wilderness" that ran from the "sea east" to the "sea west" (Alma 22:27). Nephites occupied the land to the north of this wilderness, and the Lamanites, that to the south. Sidon, the only river mentioned by name, ran northward between eastern and western wildernesses from headwaters in the narrow strip of wilderness (Alma 22:29). The Sidon probably emptied into the east sea—based on the description of the east wilderness as a rather wide, coastal zone—but its mouth is nowhere specified.

The relative locations of some important Nephite cities can be inferred from the text. Zarahemla was the Nephite capital in the first century B.C. That portion of the land southward occupied by the Nephites was known as the "land of Zarahemla" (Hel. 1:18). The city of Nephi, the original Nephite colony, by this time had been occupied by Lamanites and served at times as one of their capitals for the land south of the narrow wilderness divide (Alma 47:20). Based upon the migration account of Alma$_1$, the distance between the cities of Zarahemla and Nephi can be estimated to be about twenty-two days' travel by a company that includes children and flocks, mostly through mountainous terrain (cf. Mosiah 23:3; 24:20, 25).

The distance from Zarahemla to the narrow neck was probably less than that between Zarahemla and Nephi. The principal settlement near the narrow neck was the city of Bountiful, located near the east sea (Alma 52:17–23). This lowland city was of key military importance in controlling access to the land northward from the east-sea side.

The relative location of the hill Cumorah is most tenuous, since travel time from Bountiful, or the narrow neck, to Cumorah is nowhere specified. Cumorah was near the east sea in the land northward, and the limited evidence suggests that it was probably not many days' travel from the narrow neck of land (Mosiah 8:8; Ether 9:3). It is also probable that the portion of the land northward occupied by the Jaredites was smaller than the Nephite-Lamanite land southward.

Book of Mormon lands encompassed mountainous wildernesses, coastal plains, valleys, a large river, a highland lake, and lowland wetlands. The land also apparently experienced occasional volcanic eruptions and earthquakes (3 Ne. 8:5–18). Culturally, the Book of Mormon describes an urbanized, agrarian people having metallurgy (Hel. 6:11), writing (1 Ne. 1:1–3), lunar and solar calendars (2 Ne. 5:28; Omni 1:21), domestic animals (2 Ne. 5:11), various grains (1 Ne. 8:1), gold, silver, pearls, and "costly apparel" (Alma 1:29; 4 Ne. 1:24). Based upon these criteria, many scholars currently see northern Central America and southern Mexico (Mesoamerica) as the most likely location of Book of Mormon lands. However, such views are private and do not represent an official position of the Church.

HYPOTHESIZED LOCATIONS OF BOOK OF MORMON LANDS.   Two issues merit consideration in relation to possible external correlations of Book of Mormon geography. What is the official position of the Church, and what are the pervading opinions of its members?

In early Church history, the most common opinion among members and Church leaders was that Book of Mormon lands encompassed all of North and South America, although at least one more limited alternative view was also held for a time by some. The official position of the Church is that the events narrated in the Book of Mormon occurred somewhere in the Americas, but that the specific location has not been revealed. This position applies both to internal geographies and to external correlations. No internal geography has yet been proposed or approved by the Church, and none of the internal or external geographies proposed by individual members (including that proposed above) has received approval. Efforts in that direction by members are neither encouraged nor discouraged. In the words of John A. Widtsoe, an apostle, "All such studies are legitimate, but the conclusions drawn from them, though they may be correct, must at the best be held as intelligent conjectures" (Vol. 3, p. 93).

Three statements sometimes attributed to the Prophet Joseph Smith are often cited as evidence of an official Church position. An 1836 statement asserts that "Lehi and his company . . . landed on the continent of South America, in Chili [sic],

thirty degrees, south latitude" (Richards, Little, p. 272). This view was accepted by Orson Pratt and printed in the footnotes to the 1879 edition of the Book of Mormon, but insufficient evidence exists to clearly attribute it to Joseph Smith ("Did Lehi Land in Chili [sic]?"; cf. Roberts, Vol. 3, pp. 501–503, and Widtsoe, Vol. 3, pp. 93–98).

In 1842 an editorial in the Church newspaper claimed that "Lehi . . . landed a little south of the Isthmus of Darien [Panama]" (T&S 3 [Sept. 15, 1842]:921–22). This would move the location of Lehi's landing some 3,000 miles north of the proposed site in Chile. Although Joseph Smith had assumed editorial responsibility for the paper by this time, it is not known whether this statement originated with him or even represented his views. Two weeks later, another editorial appeared in the Times and Seasons that, in effect, constituted a book review of Incidents of Travel in Central America, Chiapas and Yucatan, by John Lloyd Stephens. This was the first accessible book in English containing detailed descriptions and drawings of ancient Mayan ruins. Excerpts from it were included in the Times and Seasons, along with the comment that "it will not be a bad plan to compare Mr. Stephens' ruined cities with those in the Book of Mormon: light cleaves to light, and facts are supported by facts. The truth injures no one" (T&S 3 [Oct. 1, 1842]:927).

In statements since then, Church leaders have generally declined to give any opinion on issues of Book of Mormon geography. When asked to review a map showing the supposed landing place of Lehi's company, President Joseph F. Smith declared that the "Lord had not yet revealed it" (Cannon, p. 160 n.). In 1929, Anthony W. Ivins, counselor in the First Presidency, added, "There has never been anything yet set forth that definitely settles that question [of Book of Mormon geography]. . . . We are just waiting until we discover the truth" (CR, Apr. 1929, p. 16). While the Church has not taken an official position with regard to location of geographical places, the authorities do not discourage private efforts to deal with the subject (Cannon).

The unidentified Times and Seasons editorialist seems to have favored modern Central America as the setting for Book of Mormon events. As noted, recent geographies by some Church members promote this identification, but others consider upstate New York or South America the correct setting. Considerable diversity of opinion remains among Church members regarding Book of Mormon geography; however, most students of the problem agree that the hundreds of geographical references in the Book of Mormon are remarkably consistent—even if the students cannot always agree upon precise locations.

Of the numerous proposed external Book of Mormon geographies, none has been positively and unambiguously confirmed by archaeology. More fundamentally, there is no agreement on whether such positive identification could be made or, if so, what form a "proof" would take; nor is it clear what would constitute "falsification" or "disproof" of various proposed geographies. Until these methodological issues have been resolved, all internal and external geographies—including supposed archaeological tests of them—should, at best, be considered only intelligent conjectures.

BIBLIOGRAPHY

Allen, Joseph L. *Exploring the Lands of the Book of Mormon.* Orem, Utah, 1989.

Cannon, George Q. "Book of Mormon Geography." *Juvenile Instructor* 25 (Jan. 1, 1890):18–19; repr., *Instructor* 73 (Apr. 1938):159–60.

Clark, John E. "A Key for Evaluating Nephite Geographies." *Review of Books on the Book of Mormon* 1 (1989):20–70.

Hauck, F. Richard. *Deciphering the Geography of the Book of Mormon.* Salt Lake City, 1988.

Palmer, David A. *In Search of Cumorah: New Evidences for the Book of Mormon from Ancient Mexico.* Bountiful, Utah, 1981.

Richards, F., and J. Little, eds. *Compendium of the Doctrines of the Gospel,* rev. ed. Salt Lake City, 1925.

Roberts, B. H. *New Witnesses for God,* 3 vols. Salt Lake City, 1909.

Sorenson, John L. *An Ancient American Setting for the Book of Mormon.* Salt Lake City, 1985.

——. *A Hundred and Fifty Years of Book of Mormon Geographies: A History of the Ideas.* Salt Lake City, 1991.

Warren, Bruce W., and Thomas Stuart Ferguson. *The Messiah in Ancient America.* Provo, Utah, 1987.

Washburn, J. Nile. *Book of Mormon Lands and Times.* Salt Lake City, 1974.

Widtsoe, John A. *Evidences and Reconciliations,* 3 vols. Salt Lake City, 1951.

JOHN E. CLARK

BOOK OF MORMON LANGUAGE

The language of the Book of Mormon exhibits features typical of a translation from an ancient Near Eastern text as well as the stamp of nineteenth-century English and the style of the King James Version (KJV) of the Bible. That the language of the Book of Mormon should resemble that of the KJV seems only natural, since in the time of the Prophet Joseph SMITH, the KJV was the most widely read book in America and formed the standard of religious language for most English-speaking people (see *CWHN* 8:212–18). Furthermore, the Book of Mormon shares certain affinities with the KJV: both include works of ancient PROPHETS of ISRAEL as well as accounts of part of the ministry of Jesus Christ, both are translations into English, and both are to become "one" in God's hand as collections of his word to his children (Ezek. 37:16–17; 1 Ne. 13:41; D&C 42:12).

LANGUAGES USED BY THE NEPHITES. Statements in the Book of Mormon have spawned differing views about the language in which the book was originally written. In approximately 600 B.C., NEPHI$_1$—the first Book of Mormon author and one who had spent his youth in JERUSALEM—wrote, "I make a record [the small plates of Nephi] in the language of my father, which consists of the learning of the Jews and the language of the Egyptians" (1 Ne. 1:2). One thousand years later, MORONI$_2$, the last Nephite prophet, noted concerning the PLATES of Mormon that "we have written this record . . . in the characters which are called among us the reformed Egyptian, being handed down and altered by us, according to our manner of speech. And if our plates [metal leaves] had been sufficiently large we should have written in Hebrew; but the Hebrew hath been altered by us also. . . . But the Lord knoweth . . . that none other people knoweth our language" (Morm. 9:32–34). In light of these two passages, it is evident that Nephite record keepers knew Hebrew and something of Egyptian. It is unknown whether Nephi, Mormon, or Moroni wrote Hebrew in modified Egyptian characters or inscribed their plates in both the Egyptian language and Egyptian characters or whether Nephi wrote in one language and Mormon and Moroni, who lived some nine hundred years later, in another. The mention of "characters" called "reformed Egyptian" tends to support the hypothesis of Hebrew in Egyptian script. Although Nephi's observation (1 Ne. 1:2) is troublesome for that view, the statement is ambiguous and inconclusive for both views.

Nephite authors seem to have patterned their writing after the plates of brass, a record containing biblical texts composed before 600 B.C. that was in the possession of descendants of JOSEPH OF

EGYPT (1 Ne. 5:11–16). At least portions of this record were written in Egyptian, since knowledge of "the language of the Egyptians" enabled LEHI, father of Nephi, to "read these engravings" (Mosiah 1:2–4). But whether it was the Egyptian language or Hebrew written in Egyptian script is again not clear. Egyptian was widely used in Lehi's day, but because poetic writings are skewed in translation, because prophetic writings were generally esteemed as sacred, and because Hebrew was the language of the Israelites in the seventh century B.C., it would have been unusual for the writings of Isaiah and Jeremiah—substantially preserved on the brass plates (1 Ne. 5:13; 19:23)—to have been translated from Hebrew into a foreign tongue at this early date. Thus, Hebrew portions written in Hebrew script, Egyptian portions in Egyptian script, and Hebrew portions in Egyptian script are all possibilities. If the brass plates came into being while the Israelites were still in Egypt, then earlier portions (e.g., prophecies of Joseph in Egypt) were possibly written in Egyptian and later portions (e.g., words of Jeremiah) in Hebrew.

Concerning Book of Mormon composition, Mormon 9:33 indicates that limited space on the GOLD PLATES dictated using Egyptian characters rather than Hebrew. In Lehi's day, both Hebrew and Egyptian were written with consonants only. Unlike Hebrew, Egyptian had bi-consonantal and even triconsonantal signs. Employing such characters—particularly in modified form—would save space.

Written characters were handed down and altered according to Nephite speech (Morm. 9:32). This observation suggests that at least later generations of Nephites used Egyptian characters to write their contemporary spoken language, an altered form of Hebrew. It is extremely unlikely that a people isolated from simultaneous contact with the two languages could have maintained a conversational distinction between, and fluency in the two languages over a thousand-year period. Thus, if Egyptian characters were altered as the living language changed, then the Nephites were probably using such characters to write their spoken language, which was largely Hebrew.

Though some of Lehi's group that left Jerusalem may have spoken Egyptian, a reading knowledge of the script on the brass plates would have allowed them to "read these engravings" (Mosiah 1:4). But the possibility that Lehi's colony could maintain spoken Egyptian as a second language through a thousand years without merging it with Hebrew or losing it is beyond probability. Therefore, the fact that the Nephites had "altered" the Egyptian characters according to their "manner of speech" underscores the probability that they were writing Hebrew with Egyptian characters. In addition, Moroni's language (c. A.D. 400) was probably different enough from that of Lehi (c. 600 B.C.) that reading Lehi's language may have required as much study in Moroni's day as Old English requires of modern English-speaking people.

LANGUAGE AMONG NATIVE AMERICANS. Because Moroni's time represents a near midpoint between Lehi and the present, a consideration of the near end of the continuum could be helpful. The vague picture presented by statements in the text might be brought into focus by examining American Indian languages. The time depth from Latin to modern Romance languages is only slightly less than that from Lehi to the present. Similarities among Romance languages are plentiful and obvious, while language similarities between Native American languages and Hebrew or Egyptian are generally viewed as neither plentiful nor obvious. Though some professionals have alluded to similarities, no study has yet convinced scholars of Near Eastern links with any pre-Columbian American language.

One study, however, holds promise for demonstrating links to the Uto-Aztecan language family (Stubbs, 1988). Though other language groups offer suggestive leads, Uto-Aztecan yields more than seven hundred similarities to Hebrew, in phonological, morphological, and semantic patterns consistent with modern linguistic methods. While a handful of Egyptian words are identifiable, they are minimal compared to their Hebrew correspondents.

HEBRAISMS IN THE BOOK OF MORMON. Many typical Hebrew language patterns have been identified in the Book of Mormon, though several are also characteristic of other Near Eastern languages. For example, the cognate accusative, literarily redundant in English, is used in Hebrew for emphasis: "They feared a fear" (Ps. 14:5, Hebrew text). Similar structures appear in the Book of Mormon: "to fear exceedingly, with fear" (Alma 18:5), another possible translation of the same cognate accusative (cf. 1 Ne. 3:2; 8:2; Enos 1:13).

Hebrew employs prepositional phrases as adverbs more often than individual adverbs, a feature typical of Book of Mormon language: "in haste" (3 Ne. 21:29) instead of "hastily" and "with gladness" (2 Ne. 28:28) instead of "gladly."

Tvedtnes has noted a possible example of Hebrew agreement: "This people *is* a free people" (Alma 30:24; emphasis added). In English, "people" is usually considered grammatically plural, but in Hebrew it is often singular. While this phrase in Alma may have been verbless, it may also have contained the third-person singular pronoun /hu/ placed between the two noun phrases or at the end as an anaphoric demonstrative functioning as a copula verb. Uto-Aztecan Indian languages also have the word /hu/, which is a third-person singular pronoun in some languages but a "be" verb in others.

Possession in English is shown in two constructs—"the man's house" and "the house of the man"—but only the latter construct is employed in Hebrew. The lack of apostrophe possession in the Book of Mormon is consistent with a translation from the Hebrew construct. Further, the "of" construct is common for adjectival relationships in Hebrew. Correspondingly, the Book of Mormon consistently employs phrases such as "plates of brass" (1 Ne. 3:12) instead of "brass plates" and "walls of stone" (Alma 48:8) rather than "stone walls."

Sentence structures and clause-combining mechanisms in Hebrew differ from those in English. Long strings of subordinate clauses and verbal expressions, such as those in Helaman 1:16–17 and Mosiah 2:20–21 and 7:21–22, are acceptable in Hebrew, though unorthodox and discouraged in English: "Ye all are witnesses . . . that Zeniff, who was made king, . . . he being over-zealous, . . . therefore being deceived by . . . king Laman, who having entered into a treaty, . . . and having yielded up [various cities], . . . and the land round about—and all this he did, for the sole purpose of bringing this people . . . into bondage" (Mosiah 7:21–22).

Frequent phrases such as "from before" and "by the hand of" represent rather literal translations from Hebrew. For example, "he fled from before them" (Mosiah 17:4), instead of the more typically English "he fled from them," portrays the common Hebrew compound preposition /millifne/.

While many words and names found in the Book of Mormon have exact equivalents in the Hebrew Bible, certain others exhibit Semitic characteristics, though their spelling does not always match known Hebrew forms. For example, "Rabbanah" as "great king" (Alma 18:13) may have affin-

ities with the Hebrew root /rbb/, meaning "to be great or many." "Rameumptom" (Alma 31:21), meaning "holy stand," contains consonantal patterns suggesting the stems /rmm/ramah/, "to be high," and /tmm/tam/tom/, "to be complete, perfect, holy." The /p/ between the /m/ and /t/ is a linguistically natural outgrowth of a bilabial /m/ in cluster with a stop /t/, such as the /p/ in /assumption/ from /assume + tion/, and the /b/ in Spanish /hombre/ from Latin /homere/.

Claims that Joseph Smith composed the Book of Mormon by merely imitating King James English, using biblical names and inventing others, typically exhibit insensitivities about its linguistic character. Names such as "Alma" have been thought peculiar inventions. However, the discovery of the name "Alma" in a Jewish text (second century A.D.), the seven hundred observed similarities between Hebrew and Uto-Aztecan, literary patterns such as chiasmus, and numerous other features noted in studies since 1830 combine to make the fabrication of the book an overwhelming challenge for anyone in Joseph Smith's day.

[*See also* Book of Mormon Authorship; Book of Mormon Literature; Book of Mormon Names; Book of Mormon, Near Eastern Background; Book of Mormon Translation by Joseph Smith.]

BIBLIOGRAPHY

Hoskisson, Paul Y. "Ancient Near Eastern Background of the Book of Mormon." *F.A.R.M.S. Reprint.* Provo, Utah, 1982.

Nibley, Hugh. *Lehi in the Desert and the World of the Jaredites.* CWHN 5.

———. *An Approach to the Book of Mormon.* CWHN 6.

Sperry, Sidney B. "The Book of Mormon as Translation English." *IE* 38 (Mar. 1935):141, 187–88.

———. "Hebrew Idioms in the Book of Mormon." *IE* 57 (Oct. 1954):703, 728–29.

———. *Book of Mormon Compendium.* Salt Lake City, 1968.

Stubbs, Brian D. "A Creolized Base in Uto-Aztecan." *F.A.R.M.S. Paper.* Provo, Utah, 1988.

Tvedtnes, John A. "Hebraisms in the Book of Mormon: A Preliminary Survey." *BYU Studies* 11 (Autumn 1970):50–60.

BRIAN D. STUBBS

BOOK OF MORMON LITERATURE

Although understated as literature in its clear and plain language, the Book of Mormon exhibits a wide variety of literary forms, including intricate Hebraic poetry, memorable narratives, rhetorically effective sermons, diverse letters, allegory, figurative language, imagery, symbolic types, and wisdom literature. In recent years these aspects of Joseph Smith's 1829 English translation have been increasingly appreciated, especially when compared with biblical and other ancient forms of literature.

There are many reasons to study the Book of Mormon as literature. Rather than being "formless," as claimed by one critic (Bernard DeVoto, *American Mercury* 19 [1930]:5), the Book of Mormon is both coherent and polished (although not obtrusively so). It tells "a densely compact and rapidly moving story that interweaves dozens of plots with an inexhaustible fertility of invention and an uncanny consistency that is never caught in a slip or contradiction" (*CWHN* 7:138).

Despite its small working vocabulary of about 2,225 root words in English, the book distills much human experience and contact with the divine. It presents its themes artfully through simple yet profound imagery, direct yet complex discourses, and straightforward yet intricate structures. To read the Book of Mormon as literature is to discover how such literary devices are used to convey the messages of its content. Attention to form, diction, figurative language, and rhetorical techniques increases sensitivity to the structure of the text and appreciation of the work of the various authors. The stated purpose of the Book of Mormon is to show the LAMANITES, a remnant of the House of ISRAEL, the covenants made with their fathers, and to convince Jew and Gentile that Jesus is the Christ (see Book of Mormon title page). MORMON selected materials and literarily shaped the book to present these messages in a stirring and memorable way.

While the discipline of identifying and evaluating literary features in the Book of Mormon is very young and does not supplant a spiritual reading of the text, those analyzing the book from this perspective find it a work of immediacy that shows as well as tells as great literature usually does. It no longer fits Mark Twain's definition of a classic essentially as a book everyone talks about but no one reads; rather, it is a work that "wears you out before you wear it out" (J. Welch, "Study, Faith, and the Book of Mormon," *BYU 1987–88 Devotional and Fireside Speeches*, p. 148. [Provo, Utah, 1988]). It is increasingly seen as a unique work that beautifully and compellingly reveals and speaks to the essential human condition.

POETRY. Found embedded in the narrative of the Book of Mormon, poetry provides the best examples of the essential connection between form and content in the Book of Mormon. When many inspired words of the Lord, angels, and prophets are analyzed according to ancient verse forms, their meaning can be more readily perceived. These forms include line forms, symmetry, parallelism, and chiastic patterns, as defined by Adele Berlin (*The Dynamics of Biblical Parallelism* [Bloomington, Ind., 1985]) and Wilford Watson (*Classical Hebrew Poetry* [Sheffield, 1984]). Book of Mormon texts shift smoothly from narrative to poetry, as in this intensifying passage:

> But behold, the Spirit hath said this much unto me, saying: Cry unto this people, saying—
>> Repent ye, and prepare the way of the Lord, and walk in his paths, which are straight; for behold, the kingdom of heaven is at hand, and the Son of God cometh upon the face of the earth [Alma 7:9].

The style of the Book of Mormon has been criticized by some as being verbose and redundant, but in most cases these repetitions are orderly and effective. For example, parallelisms, which abound in the Book of Mormon, serve many functions. They add emphasis to twice-repeated concepts and give definition to sharply drawn contrasts. A typical synonymous parallelism is in 2 Nephi 9:52:

> *Pray* unto him continually *by day*,
> and *give thanks* unto his holy name *by night*.

Nephi's discourse aimed at his obstinate brothers includes a sharply antithetical parallelism:

> Ye are *swift* to do *iniquity*
> But *slow* to *remember* the Lord your God. [1 Ne. 17:45.]

Several fine examples of chiasmus (an a–b–b–a pattern) are also found in the Book of Mormon. In the Psalm of Nephi (2 Ne. 4:15–35), the initial appeals to the *soul* and *heart* are accompanied by negations, while the subsequent mirror uses of *heart* and *soul* are conjoined with strong affirmations, making the contrasts literarily effective and climactic:

> Awake, my *soul*! No longer droop in sin.
>> Rejoice, O my *heart*, and give place no more for the enemy of my soul.
>> Do not anger again because of mine enemies.

Do not slacken my strength because of mine afflictions.
Rejoice, O my *heart*, and cry unto the Lord, and say:
O Lord, I will praise thee forever;
yea, my *soul* will rejoice in thee, my God, and the rock of my salvation. [2 Ne. 4:28–30.]

Other precise examples of extended chiasmus (a–b–c—c–b–a) are readily discernible in Mosiah 5:10–12 and Alma 36:1–30 and 41:13–15. This literary form in Alma 36 effectively focuses attention on the central passage of the chapter (Alma 36:17–18); in Alma 41, it fittingly conveys the very notion of restorative justice expressed in the passage (cf. Lev. 24:13–23, which likewise uses chiasmus to convey a similar notion of justice).

Another figure known as *a fortiori* is used to communicate an exaggerated sense of multitude, as in Alma 60:22, where a "number parallelism" is chiastically enclosed by a twice-repeated phrase:

Yea, will ye sit in idleness
while ye are surrounded with *thousands* of those,
yea, and *tens of thousands*,
who do also sit in idleness?

Scores of Book of Mormon passages can be analyzed as poetry. They range from Lehi's brief desert poems (1 Ne. 2:9–10, a form Hugh Nibley identifies as an Arabic *qasida*) [*CWHN* 6:270–75] to extensive sermons of Jacob, Abinadi, and the risen Jesus (2 Ne. 6–10; Mosiah 12–16; and 3 Ne. 27).

NARRATIVE TEXTS. In the Book of Mormon, narrative texts are often given vitality by vigorous conflict and impassioned dialogue or personal narration. Nephi relates his heroic actions in obtaining the brass plates from Laban; Jacob resists the false accusations of Sherem, upon whom the judgment of the Lord falls; Ammon fights off plunderers at the waters of Sebus and wins the confidence of king Lamoni; Amulek is confronted by the smooth-tongued lawyer Zeezrom; Alma$_2$ and Amulek are preserved while their accusers are crushed by collapsing prison walls; Captain Moroni$_1$ engages in a showdown with the Lamanite chieftain Zerahemnah; Amalickiah rises to power through treachery and malevolence; a later prophet named NEPHI$_2$ reveals to an unbelieving crowd the murder of their chief judge by the judge's own brother; and the last two Jaredite kings fight to the mutual destruction of their people.

Seen as a whole, the Book of Mormon is an epic account of the history of the NEPHITE nation. Extensive in scope with an eponymic hero, it presents action involving long and arduous journeys and heroic deeds, with supernatural beings taking an active part. Encapsulated within this one-thousand-year account of the establishment, development, and destruction of the Nephites is the concentrated epic of the rise and fall of the Jaredites, who preceded them in type and time. (For its epic milieu, see *CWHN* 5:285–394.) The climax of the book is the dramatic account of the visit of the resurrected Jesus to an assemblage of righteous Nephites.

SERMONS AND SPEECHES. Prophetic discourse is a dominant literary form in the Book of Mormon. Speeches such as King BENJAMIN's address (Mosiah 1–6), Alma$_2$'s challenge to the people of Zarahemla (Alma 5), and Mormon's teachings on faith, hope, and charity (Moro. 7) are crafted artistically and have great rhetorical effectiveness in conveying their religious purposes. The public oration of SAMUEL THE LAMANITE (Hel. 13–15) is a classic prophetic judgment speech. Taking rhetorical criticism as a guide, one can see how Benjamin's ritual address first aims to persuade the audience to reaffirm a present point of view and then turns to deliberative rhetoric—"which aims at effecting a decision about future action, often the very immediate future" (Kennedy, *New Testament Interpretation Through Rhetorical Criticism* [1984], p. 36). King Benjamin's speech is also chiastic as a whole and in several of its parts (Welch, pp. 202–205).

LETTERS. The eight epistles in the Book of Mormon are conversational in tone, revealing the diverse personalities of their writers. These letters are from Captain Moroni$_1$ (Alma 54:5–14; 60:1–36), Ammoron (Alma 54:16–24), Helaman$_1$ (Alma 56:2–58:41), Pahoran (Alma 61:2–21), Giddianhi (3 Ne. 3:2–10), and Mormon (Moro. 8:2–30; 9:1–26).

ALLEGORY, METAPHOR, IMAGERY, AND TYPOLOGY. These forms are also prevalent in the Book of Mormon. ZENOS's allegory of the olive tree (Jacob 5) vividly incorporates dozens of horticultural details as it depicts the history of God's dealings with Israel. A striking simile curse, with Near Eastern parallels, appears in Abinadi's prophetic denunciation: The life of King Noah shall be "as a garment in a furnace of fire, . . . as a stalk, even as a dry stalk of the field, which is run over by the beasts and trodden under foot" (Mosiah 12:10–11).

An effective extended metaphor is Alma's comparison of the word of God to a seed planted in one's heart and then growing into a fruitful TREE OF LIFE (Alma 32:28–43). In developing this metaphor, Alma uses a striking example of synesthesia: As the word enlightens their minds, his listeners can know it is real—"ye have *tasted* this *light*" (Alma 32:35).

Iteration of archetypes such as tree, river, darkness, and fire graphically confirms Lehi's understanding "that there is an opposition in all things" (2 Ne. 2:11) and that opposition will be beneficial to the righteous.

A figural interpretation of God-given words and God-directed persons or events is insisted on, although not always developed, in the Book of Mormon. "All things which have been given of God from the beginning of the world, unto man, are the typifying of [Christ]" (2 Ne. 11:4); all performances and ordinances of the law of Moses "were types of things to come" (Mosiah 13:31); and the LIAHONA, or compass, was seen as a type: "For just as surely as this director did bring our fathers, by following its course, to the promised land, shall the words of Christ, if we follow their course, carry us beyond this vale of sorrow into a far better land of promise" (Alma 37:45). In its largest typological structure, the Book of Mormon fits well the seven phases of revelation posited by Northrop Frye: creation, revolution or exodus, law, wisdom, prophecy, gospel, and apocalypse (*The Great Code: The Bible and Literature* [New York, 1982]).

WISDOM LITERATURE. Transmitted sayings of the wise are scattered throughout the Book of Mormon, especially in counsel given by fathers to their sons. Alma counsels, "O remember, my son, and learn wisdom in thy youth; yea, learn in thy youth, to keep the commandments of God" (Alma 37:35; see also 38:9–15). Benjamin says, "I tell you these things that ye may learn wisdom; that ye may learn that when ye are in the service of your fellow beings ye are only in the service of your God" (Mosiah 2:17). A memorable aphorism is given by Lehi: "Adam fell that men might be; and men are, that they might have joy" (2 Ne. 2:25). Pithy sayings such as "fools mock, but they shall mourn" (Ether 12:26) and "wickedness never was happiness" (Alma 41:10) are often repeated by Latter-day Saints.

APOCALYPTIC LITERATURE. The vision in 1 Nephi 11–15 (sixth century B.C.) is comparable in form with early APOCALYPTIC literature. It contains a vision, is delivered in dialogue form, has an otherworldly mediator or escort, includes a commandment to write, treats the disposition of the recipient, prophesies persecution, foretells the judgment of the wicked and of the world, contains cosmic transformations, and has an otherworldly place as its spatial axis. Later Jewish developments of complex angelology, mystic numerology, and symbolism are absent.

STYLE AND TONE. Book of Mormon writers show an intense concern for style and tone. Alma desires to be able to "speak with the trump of God, with a voice to shake the earth," yet realizes that "I am a man, and do sin in my wish; for I ought to be content with the things which the Lord hath allotted unto me" (Alma 29:1–3). Moroni$_2$ expresses a feeling of inadequacy in writing: "Lord, the Gentiles will mock at these things, because of our weakness in writing. . . . Thou hast also made our words powerful and great, even that we cannot write them; wherefore, when we write we behold our weakness, and stumble because of the placing of our words" (Ether 12:23–25; cf. 2 Ne. 33:1). Moroni's written words, however, are not weak. In cadences of ascending strength he boldly declares:

O ye pollutions, ye hypocrites, ye teachers, who sell yourselves for that which will canker, why have ye polluted the holy church of God? Why are ye ashamed to take upon you the name of Christ? . . . Who will despise the works of the Lord? Who will despise the children of Christ? Behold, all ye who are despisers of the works of the Lord, for ye shall wonder and perish [Morm. 8:38, 9:26].

The styles employed by the different writers in the Book of Mormon vary from the unadorned to the sublime. The tones range from Moroni's strident condemnations to Jesus' humblest pleading: "Behold, mine arm of mercy is extended towards you, and whosoever will come, him will I receive" (3 Ne. 9:14).

A model for communication is Jesus, who, Moroni reports, "told me in plain humility, even as a man telleth another in mine own language, concerning these things; and only a few have I written, because of my weakness in writing" (Ether 12:39–40). Two concepts in this report are repeated throughout the Book of Mormon—plain speech and inability to write about some things. "I have spoken plainly unto you," Nephi says, "that ye cannot misunderstand" (2 Ne. 25:28). "My soul delighteth in plainness," he continues, "for after this manner doth the Lord God work among the children of men" (2 Ne. 31:3). Yet Nephi also delights in the words of Isaiah, which "are not plain unto you" although "they are plain unto all those that are filled with the spirit of prophecy" (2 Ne. 25:4). Containing both plain and veiled language, the Book of Mormon is a spiritually and literarily powerful book that is direct yet complex, simple yet profound.

BIBLIOGRAPHY

England, Eugene. "A Second Witness for the Logos: The Book of Mormon and Contemporary Literary Criticism." In *By Study and Also by Faith*, 2 vols., ed. J. Lundquist and S. Ricks, Vol. 2, pp. 91–125. Salt Lake City, 1990.

Jorgensen, Bruce W.; Richard Dilworth Rust; and George S. Tate. Essays on typology in *Literature of Belief*, ed. Neal E. Lambert. Provo, Utah, 1981.

Nichols, Robert E., Jr. "Beowulf and Nephi: A Literary View of the Book of Mormon." *Dialogue* 4 (Autumn 1969):40–47.

Parry, Donald W. "Hebrew Literary Patterns in the Book of Mormon." *Ensign* 19 (Oct. 1989):58–61.

Rust, Richard Dilworth. "Book of Mormon Poetry." *New Era* (Mar. 1983):46–50.

Welch, John W. "Chiasmus in the Book of Mormon." In *Chiasmus in Antiquity*, ed J. Welch, pp. 198–210. Hildesheim, 1981.

RICHARD DILWORTH RUST
DONALD W. PARRY

BOOK OF MORMON MANUSCRIPTS

The printed versions of the Book of Mormon derive from two manuscripts. The first, called the original manuscript (O), was written by at least three scribes as Joseph SMITH translated and dictated. The most important scribe was Oliver COWDERY. This manuscript was begun no later than April 1829 and finished in June 1829.

A copy of the original was then made by Oliver Cowdery and two other scribes. This copy is called the printer's manuscript (P), since it was the one normally used to set the type for the first (1830) edition of the Book of Mormon. It was begun in July 1829 and finished early in 1830.

The printer's manuscript is not an exact copy of the original manuscript. There are on the average three changes per original manuscript page.

A page from the original Book of Mormon manuscript, covering 1 Nephi 4:38–5:14. It shows how fluent Joseph Smith's dictation was. He did not change or revise the text as he dictated. Oliver Cowdery, one of his scribes, stated, "Day after day I continued, uninterrupted, to write from his mouth . . . a voice dictated by the inspiration of heaven."

These changes appear to be natural scribal errors; there is little or no evidence of conscious editing. Most of the changes are minor, and about one in five produce a discernible difference in meaning. Because they were all relatively minor, most of the errors thus introduced into the text have remained in the printed editions of the Book of Mormon and have not been detected and corrected except by reference to the original manuscript. About twenty of these errors were corrected in the 1981 edition.

The compositor for the 1830 edition added punctuation, paragraphing, and other printing marks to about one-third of the pages of the printer's manuscript. These same marks appear on one fragment of the original, indicating that it was used at least once in typesetting the 1830 edition.

In preparation for the second (1837) edition, hundreds of grammatical changes and a few textual emendations were made in P. After the publication of this edition, P was retained by Oliver Cowdery. After his death in 1850, his brother-in-law, David WHITMER, kept P until his death in 1888. In 1903 Whitmer's grandson sold P to the REORGANIZED CHURCH OF JESUS CHRIST OF LATTER DAY SAINTS, which owns it today. It is wholly extant except for two lines at the bottom of the first leaf.

The original manuscript was not consulted for the editing of the 1837 edition. However, in producing the 1840 edition, Joseph Smith used O to restore some of its original readings. In October 1841, Joseph Smith placed O in the cornerstone of the NAUVOO HOUSE. Over forty years later, Lewis Bidamon, Emma SMITH's second husband, opened the cornerstone and found that water seepage had destroyed most of O. The surviving pages were handed out to various individuals during the 1880s.

Today approximately 25 percent of the text of O survives: 1 Nephi 2 through 2 Nephi 1, with gaps; Alma 22 through Helaman 3, with gaps; and a few other fragments. All but one of the authentic pages and fragments of O are housed in the archives of the LDS Historical Department; one-half of a sheet (from 1 Nephi 14) is owned by the University of Utah.

BIBLIOGRAPHY

Heater, Shirley R. "Gold Plates, Foolscap, & Printer's Ink, Part I: Manuscripts of the Book of Mormon." *Zarahemla Record* 35-36 (1987):3–15.

Jessee, Dean C. "The Original Book of Mormon Manuscript." *BYU Studies* 10 (1970):259–78.

ROYAL SKOUSEN

BOOK OF MORMON NAMES

The Book of Mormon contains 337 proper names and 21 gentilics (or analogous forms) based on proper names. Included in this count are names that normally would not be called proper, such as kinds of animals, if they appear as transliterations in the English text and not as translations. Conversely, proper names that appear only in translation are not included, such as Bountiful and Desolation. Of these 337 proper names, 188 are unique to the Book of Mormon, while 149 are common to the Book of Mormon and the Bible. If the textual passages common to the Book of Mormon and the Bible are excluded, 53 names occur in both books.

It would seem convenient to divide the Book of Mormon collection or listing of names (onomasticon) into three groups because it mentions (1) JAREDITES, (2) the community founded by LEHI (which might be termed "Lehites"), and (3) the people referred to as the people of Zarahemla (who might be called "Mulekites"), each of which contributed to the history of the Book of Mormon and therefore to the list of proper names (*see* BOOK OF MORMON PEOPLES). While this grouping can be made with some degree of accuracy for Jaredite names, it is not easy to maintain the distinction between Lehite and Mulekite, because a portion of the Lehites united with the Mulekites sometime before 130 B.C.; practically nothing is known about Mulekite names before that time. For the present, Lehite and Mulekite names must be treated together. Given this grouping of the Book of Mormon onomasticon, 142 of the 188 unique Book of Mormon names are Lehite-Mulekite, 41 are Jaredite, and 5 are common to both groups.

Much preliminary work remains to be done on the Book of Mormon onomasticon. The transliteration system of the English text must be clarified: does the j of the text indicate only the Nephite phoneme /y/ or can it also represent /h/ in the name "Job," as it does once in the King James Version? A reliable critical analysis of the text is needed: what is the range of possible spellings of Cumorah that might indicate phonemic values? Linguistic phenomena beg explanation: there are no exclusively Book of Mormon names that begin with /b/; but several begin with /p/. Q and x do not occur in any Book of Mormon name. V, w, and y do not occur in any exclusively Book of Mormon name. D, f, and u do not begin any exclusively Book of Mormon name.

The Lehite-Mulekite names often show greatest affinity with Semitic languages (*CWHN* 6:281–94). For instance, Abish and Abinadi resemble *ab*, father, names in Hebrew; Alma appears in a Bar Kokhba letter (c. A.D. 130) found in the Judean desert; Mulek could be a diminutive of West Semitic *mlk*, king; Omni and Limhi appear to have the same morphology as Old Testament Omri and Zimri; Jershon is remarkably close to a noun form of the Hebrew root *yrš* (see below). Some Lehite-Mulekite names more closely resemble Egyptian: Ammon, Korihor, Pahoran, and Paanchi (*CWHN* 5:25–34). Jaredite names exhibit no consistently obvious linguistic affinity.

Like proper names in most languages, the proper names of the Book of Mormon probably had semantic meanings for Book of Mormon peoples. Such meanings are evident from several instances wherein the Book of Mormon provides a translation for a proper name. For example, Irreantum means "many waters" (1 Ne. 17:5), and Rabbanah is interpreted as "powerful or great king" (Alma 18:13). The single greatest impediment to understanding the semantic possibilities for the Book of Mormon proper names remains the lack of the original Nephite text. The transliterations of the English text allow only educated conjectures and approximations about the nature of the names and their possible semantic range. In addition, such postulations, if to be of any value, must be based on a knowledge of the possible linguistic origins of the names, such as Iron Age Hebrew and Egyptian for Lehite and Mulekite names.

The proper names of the Book of Mormon can provide information about the text and the language(s) used to compose it. When studied with apposite methodology, these names testify to the ancient origin of the Book of Mormon. For example, Jershon is the toponym for a land given by the Nephites to a group of Lamanites as an inheritance; based on the usual correspondence in the King James Version of j for the Hebrew phoneme /y/, Book of Mormon Jershon could correspond to the Hebrew root *yrš* meaning "to inherit," thus providing an appropriate play on words in Alma 27:22: "and this land Jershon is the land which we will give unto our brethren for an inheritance." Similarly, one Book of Mormon name used for a man that might have seemed awkward, Alma, now is known from two second-century A.D. Hebrew documents of the Bar Kokhba period (Yadin, p. 176) and thus speaks for a strong and continuing Hebrew presence among Book of Mormon peoples.

BIBLIOGRAPHY

Hoskisson, Paul Y. "An Introduction to the Relevance of and a Methodology for a Study of the Proper Names of the Book of Mormon." In *By Study and Also by Faith*, ed. J. Lundquist and S. Ricks, Vol. 2, pp. 126–35. Salt Lake City, 1990.

Tvedtnes, John A. "A Phonemic Analysis of Nephite and Jaredite Proper Names." *F.A.R.M.S. Paper*. Provo, Utah, 1977.

Yadin, Y. *Bar Kokhba*, p. 176. Jerusalem, 1971.

PAUL Y. HOSKISSON

BOOK OF MORMON NEAR EASTERN BACKGROUND

According to the Book of Mormon, the JAREDITES, the NEPHITES, and the "Mulekites" (*see* MULEK) migrated to the Western Hemisphere from the Near East in antiquity, a claim that has been challenged. While Book of Mormon students readily admit that no direct, concrete evidence currently exists substantiating the links with the ancient Near East that are noted in the book, evidence can be adduced—largely external and circumstantial—that commands respect for the claims of the Book of Mormon concerning its ancient Near Eastern background (*CWHN* 8:65–72). A few examples will indicate the nature and strength of these ties, particularly because such details were not available to Joseph Smith, the translator of the Book of Mormon, from any sources that existed in the early nineteenth century (*see* BOOK OF MORMON TRANSLATION BY JOSEPH SMITH).

1. LEHI (c. 600 B.C.) was a righteous, wellborn, and prosperous man of the tribe of Manasseh who lived in or near Jerusalem. He traveled much, had a rich estate in the country, and had an eye for fine metalwork. His family was strongly influenced by the contemporary Egyptian culture. At a time of mounting tensions in Jerusalem (the officials were holding secret meetings by night), he favored the religious reform party of Jeremiah, while members of his family were torn by divided loyalties. One of many prophets of doom in the land, "a visionary man," he was forced to flee with his family, fearing pursuit by the troops of one Laban, a high military official of the city. Important records that Lehi needed were kept in the house of Laban (1 Ne. 1–5; *CWHN* 6:46–131; 8:534–35). This closely parallels the situation in Lachish at the time, as described in contemporary records discovered in 1934–1935 (H. Torczyner, *The Lachish Letters*, 2

vols., Oxford, 1938; cf. *CWHN* 8:380–406). The Bar Kokhba letters, discovered in 1965–1966, recount the manner in which the wealthy escaped from Jerusalem under like circumstances in both earlier and later centuries (Y. Yadin, *Bar Kokhba*, Chaps. 10 and 16, Jerusalem, 1971; cf. *CWHN* 8:274–88).

2. Lehi's flight recalls the later retreat of the Desert Sectaries of the Dead Sea, both parties being bent on "keeping the commandments of the Lord" (cf. 1 Ne. 4:33–37; *Battle Scroll* [1QM] x.7–8). Among the Desert Sectaries, all volunteers were sworn in by covenant (*Battle Scroll* [1QM] vii.5–6). In the case of NEPHI₁, son of Lehi, he is charged with having "taken it upon him to be our ruler and our teacher. . . . He says that the Lord has talked with him . . . [to] lead us away into some strange wilderness" (1 Ne. 16:37–38). Later in the New World, Nephi, then MOSIAH₁, and then ALMA₁ (c. 150 B.C.) led out more devotees, for example, the last-named, to a place of trees by "the waters of Mormon" (2 Ne. 5:11–10; Omni 1:12–13; Mosiah 18). The organization and practices instigated by Alma are like those in the Old World communities: swearing in, baptism, one priest to fifty members, traveling teachers or inspectors, a special day for assembly, all labor and share alike, called "the children of God," all defer to one preeminent Teacher, and so on (Mosiah 18; 25). Parallels with the Dead Sea Scroll communities are striking, even to the rival Dead Sea colonies led by the False Teacher (*CWHN* 6:135–44, 157–67, 183–93; 7:264–70; 8:289–327).

3. "And my father dwelt in a tent" (1 Ne. 2:15). Mentioned fourteen times in 1 Nephi, the sheikh's tent is the center of everything. When Lehi's sons returned from Jerusalem safely after fleeing Laban's men and hiding in caves, "they did rejoice . . . and did offer sacrifices . . . on an altar of stones . . . and gave thanks" (1 Ne. 2:7; 5:9). Taking "seeds of every kind" for a protracted settlement, "keeping to the more fertile parts of the wilderness," they hunt along the way, making "not much fire," living on raw meat, guided at times by a "Liahona"—a brass ball "of curious workmanship" with two divination arrows that show the way. One long camping was "at a place we call Shazer" (cf. Arabic *shajer*, trees or place of trees); and they buried Ishmael at Nahom, where his daughters mourned and chided Lehi (1 Ne. 16; cf. Arabic *Nahm*, a moaning or sighing together, a chiding).

Canaanite horned altar or incense burner from Megiddo in ancient Palestine (c. 1900 B.C.) in the Rockefeller Museum, Jerusalem. This distinctive style of altar was also used by the Israelites (see Lev. 4:7; 1 Kings 1:50; 2:28). Courtesy LaMar C. Berrett.

Lehi vividly describes a *sayl*, a flash flood of "filthy water" out of a wadi or stream bed that can sweep one's camp away (1 Ne. 8:13, 32; 12:16), a common event in the area where he was traveling. At their first "river of water" Lehi recited a formal "*qasida*," an old form of desert poetry, to his sons Laman and Lemuel, urging them to be like the stream and the valley in keeping God's commands (1 Ne. 2). He describes the terror of those who in "a mist of darkness . . . did lose their way, wandered off and were lost." He sees "a great and spacious building," appearing to stand high "in the air . . . filled with people, . . . and their manner of dress was exceeding fine" (1 Ne. 8; cf. the "skyscrapers" of southern Arabia, e.g., the town of Shibam). The building fell in all its pride like the fabled Castle of Ghumdan. Other desert imagery abounds (*CWHN* 5:43–92).

4. Among lengthier connected accounts, MORONI₁ (c. 75 B.C.), leading an uprising against an oppressor, "went forth among the people waving

the rent part of his garment" to show the writing on it (Alma 46:19–20). The legendary Persian hero Kawe did the same thing with his garment. The men of Moroni "came running, . . . rending their garments. . . as a covenant [saying] . . . may [God] cast us at the feet of our enemies . . . to be trodden underfoot" (Alma 46:21–22). Both the rending of and the treading on the garments were ancient practices (*CWHN* 6:216–18; 7:198–202; 8:92–95). The inscription on the banner, "in memory of our God, our religion, and our peace, our wives, and our children" (Alma 46:12), is similar to the banners and trumpets of the armies in the Dead Sea *Battle Scroll* ([1QM] iii.1–iv.2). Before the battle Moroni goes before the army and dedicates the land southward as Desolation, and the rest he named "a chosen land, and the land of liberty" (Alma 46:17). In the *Battle Scroll* ([1QM] vii.8ff.) the high priest similarly goes before the army and dedicates the land of the enemy to destruction and that of Israel to salvation (*CWHN* 6:213–16). Moroni compares his torn garment-banner to the coat of Joseph, half of which was preserved and half decayed: "Let us remember the words of Jacob, before his death . . . as this remnant of [the coat] hath been preserved, so shall a remnant of [Joseph] be preserved." So Jacob had both "sorrow . . . [and] joy" at the same time (Alma 46:24–25). An almost identical story is told by the tenth-century savant Tha'labi, the collector of traditions from Jewish refugees in Persia (*CWHN* 6:209–21; 8:249, 280–81).

5. There is a detailed description of a coronation in the Book of Mormon that is paralleled only in ancient nonbiblical sources, notably Nathan ha-Babli's description of the coronation of the Prince of the Captivity. The Book of Mormon version in Mosiah 2–6 (c. 125 B.C.) is a classic account of the well-documented ancient "Year Rite": (a) The people gather at the temple, (b) bringing firstfruits and offerings (Mosiah 2:3–4); (c) they camp by families, all tent doors facing the temple; (d) a special tower is erected, (e) from which the king addresses the people, (f) unfolding unto them "the mysteries" (the real ruler is God, etc.); (g) all accept the covenant in a great acclamation; (h) it is the universal birthday, all are reborn; (i) they receive a new name, are duly sealed, and registered in a national census; (j) there is stirring choral music (cf. Mosiah 2:28; 5:2–5); (k) they feast by families (cf. Mosiah 2:5) and return to their homes (*CWHN* 6:295–310).

This "patternism" has been recognized only since the 1930s.

6. The literary evidence of Old World ties with the Book of Mormon is centered on Egyptian influences, requiring special treatment. The opening colophon to Nephi's autobiography in the Book of Mormon is characteristic: "I, Nephi . . . I make it with mine own hand" (1 Ne. 1:1, 3). The characters of the original Book of Mormon writing most closely resemble Meroitic, a "reformed Egyptian" known from an Egyptian colony established on the upper Nile River in the same period (*see* ANTHON TRANSCRIPT; BOOK OF MORMON LANGUAGE). Proper names in the Book of Mormon include Ammon (the most common name in both 26th Dynasty Egypt [664–525 B.C.] and the Book of Mormon); Alma, which has long been derided for its usage as a man's name (now found in the Bar Kokhba letters as "Alma, son of Judah"); Aha, a

Similar to the horn altar from Israel is this four-cornered altar or incense burner from Oaxaca, Mexico, dating to the Monte Alban 1 period (c. 500–100 B.C.) Specimen in Museo-Frissell, Oaxaca, Mexico. Courtesy F.A.R.M.S.

Nephite general (cf. Egyptian *aha*, "warrior"); Paankhi (an important royal name of the Egyptian Late Period [525–332 B.C.]); Hermounts, a country of wild beasts (cf. Egyptian Hermonthis, god of wild places); Laman and Lemuel, "pendant names" commonly given to eldest sons (cf. Qabil and Habil, Harut and Marut); Lehi, a proper name (found on an ancient potsherd in Ebion Gezer about 1938); Manti, a form of the Egyptian god Month; Korihor (cf. Egyptian Herhor, Horihor); and Giddianhi (cf. Egyptian Djhwti-ankhi, "Thoth is my life"), etc. (*CWNH* 5:25–34; 6:281–94; 7:149–52, 168–72; 8:281–82; *see* BOOK OF MORMON NAMES).

7. The authenticity of the GOLD PLATES on which the Book of Mormon was inscribed has often been questioned until the finding of the Darius Plates in 1938. Many other examples of sacred and historical writing on metal plates have been found since (C. Wright in *By Study and Also by Faith*, 2:273–334, ed. J. Lundquist and S. Ricks, Salt Lake City, 1990). The brass (bronze) plates recall the Copper Scroll of the Dead Sea Scrolls, the metal being used to preserve particularly valuable information, namely the hiding places of treasures—scrolls, money, sacred utensils—concealed from the enemy. The Nephites were commanded, "They shall hide up their treasures . . . when they shall flee before their enemies;" but if such treasures are used for private purposes thereafter, "because they will not hide them up unto [God], cursed be they and also their treasures" (Hel. 13:19–20; *CWHN* 5:105–107; 6:21–28; 7:56–57, 220–21, 272–74).

8. In sharp contrast to other cultures in the book, the JAREDITES carried on the warring ways of the steppes of Asia "upon this north country" (Ether 1, 3–6). Issuing forth from the well-known dispersion center of the great migrations in western Asia, they accepted all volunteers in a mass migration (Ether 1:41–42). Moving across central Asia they crossed shallow seas in barges (Ether 2:5–6). Such great inland seas were left over from the last ice age (*CWHN* 5:183–85, 194–96). Reaching the "great sea" (possibly the Pacific), they built ships with covered decks and peaked ends, "after the manner of Noah's ark" (Ether 6:7), closely resembling the prehistoric "magur boats" of Mesopotamia. The eight ships were lit by shining stones, as was Noah's Ark according to the Palestinian Tal-

mud, the stones mentioned in the Talmud and elsewhere being produced by a peculiar process described in ancient legends. Such arrangements were necessary because of "the furious wind . . . [that] did never cease to blow" (Ether 6:5, 8). In this connection, there are many ancient accounts of the "windflood"—tremendous winds sustained over a period of time—that followed the Flood and destroyed the Tower (*CWHN* 5:359–79; 6:329–34; 7:208–10).

9. The society of the Book of Ether is that of the "Epic Milieu" or "Heroic Age," a product of world upheaval and forced migrations (cf. descriptions in H. M. Chadwick, *The Growth of Literature*, 3 vols., Cambridge, 1932–1940). On the boundless plains loyalty must be secured by oaths, which are broken as individuals seek ever more power and gain. Kings' sons or brothers rebel to form new armies and empires, sometimes putting the king and his family under lifelong house arrest, while "drawing off" followers by gifts and lands in feudal fashion. Regal splendor is built on prison labor; there are plots and counterplots, feuds, and vendettas. War is played like a chess game with times and places set for battle and challenges by trumpet and messenger, all culminating in the personal duel of the rulers, winner take all. This makes for wars of extermination and total social breakdown with "every man with his band fighting for that which he desired" (Ether 7–15; *CWHN* 5:231–37, 285–307).

10. Elements of the archaic matriarchy were brought from the Old World by Book of Mormon peoples (Ether 8:9–10). For instance, a Jaredite queen plots to put a young successor on the throne by treachery or a duel, and then supplants him with another, remaining in charge like the ancient perennial Great Mother in a royal court (cf. *CWHN* 5:210–13). The mother-goddess apparently turns up also among the Nephites in a cult-place (Siron), where the harlot Isabel and her associates were visited by crowds of devotees (Alma 39:3–4, 11); Isabel was the name of the great hierodule of the Phoenicians (*CWHN* 8:542).

BIBLIOGRAPHY

Nibley, Hugh W. *CWHN*, Vols. 5–8. Salt Lake City, 1988–1989.

HUGH W. NIBLEY

BOOK OF MORMON PEOPLES

At least fifteen distinct groups of people are mentioned in the Book of Mormon. Four (NEPHITES, LAMANITES, JAREDITES, and the people of Zarahemla [Mulekites]) played a primary role; five were of secondary concern; and six more were tertiary elements.

NEPHITES. The core of this group were direct descendants of NEPHI₁, the son of founding father LEHI. Political leadership within the Nephite wing of the colony was "conferred upon none but those who were descendants of Nephi" (Mosiah 25:13). Not only the early kings and judges but even the last military commander of the Nephites, MORMON, qualified in this regard (he explicitly notes that he was "a pure descendant of Lehi" [3 Ne. 5:20] and "a descendant of Nephi" [Morm. 1:5]).

In a broader sense, "Nephites" was a label given all those governed by a Nephite ruler, as in Jacob 1:13: "The people which were not Lamanites were Nephites; nevertheless, they were called [when specified according to descent] Nephites, Jacobites, Josephites, Zoramites, Lamanites, Lemuelites, and Ishmaelites." It is interesting to note that groups without direct ancestral connections could come under the Nephite sociopolitical umbrella. Thus, "all the people of Zarahemla were numbered with the Nephites" (Mosiah 25:13). This process of political amalgamation had kinship overtones in many instances, as when a body of converted Lamanites "took upon themselves the name of Nephi, that they might be called the children of Nephi and be numbered among those who were called Nephites" (Mosiah 25:12). The odd phrase "the people of the Nephites" in such places as Alma 54:14 and Helaman 1:1 suggests a social structure where possibly varied populations ("the people") were controlled by an elite ("the Nephites").

Being a Nephite could also entail a set of religious beliefs and practices (Alma 48:9–10; 4 Ne. 1:36–37) as well as participation in a cultural tradition (Enos 1:21; Hel. 3:16). Most Nephites seem to have been physically distinguishable from the Lamanites (Jacob 3:5; Alma 55:4, 8; 3 Ne. 2:15).

The sociocultural and political unity implied by the use of the general title "Nephites" is belied by the historical record, which documents a long series of "dissensions" within and from Nephite rule, with large numbers periodically leaving to join the Lamanites (Alma 31:8; 43:13; Hel. 1:15).

The Book of Mormon—a religiously oriented lineage history—is primarily a record of events kept by and centrally involving the Nephites. Since the account was written from the perspective of this people (actually, of its leaders), all other groups are understood and represented from the point of view of Nephite elites. There are only fragments in the Nephite record that indicate directly the perspectives of other groups, or even of Nephite commoners.

LAMANITES. This name, too, was applied in several ways. Direct descendants of Laman, Lehi's eldest son, constituted the backbone of the Lamanites, broadly speaking (Jacob 1:13–14; 4 Ne. 1:38–39). The "Lemuelites" and "Ishmaelites," who allied themselves with the descendants of Laman in belief and behavior, were also called Lamanites (Jacob 1:13–14). So were "all the dissenters of [from] the Nephites" (Alma 47:35). This terminology was used in the Nephite record, although one cannot be sure that all dissenters applied the term to themselves. However, at least one such dissenter, Ammoron, a Zoramite, bragged, "I am a bold Lamanite" (Alma 54:24).

Rulers in the Lamanite system appear to have had more difficulty than Nephite rulers in binding component social groups into a common polity (Alma 17:27–35; 20:4, 7, 9, 14–15; 47:1–3). They seem to have depended more on charisma or compulsion than on shared tradition, ideals, or an apparatus of officials. Whether a rule existed that Lamanite kings be descendants of Laman is unclear. Early in the second century B.C. two successive Lamanite kings were called Laman (Mosiah 7:21; 24:3); since this designation was being interpreted across a cultural boundary by a record keeper of Nephite culture, it is possible that "Laman" was really a title of office, in the same manner that Nephite kings bore the title "Nephi" (Jacob 1:9–11). Later, however, Lamoni, a local Lamanite ruler, is described as "a descendant of Ishmael," not of Laman (Alma 17:21), and his father, king over the entire land of Nephi (originally a homeland of the Nephites, but taken and occupied by the Lamanites throughout much of the remainder of Book of Mormon history), would have had the same ancestry. Evidently, if there was a rule that Laman's descendants inherit the throne, it was inconsistently applied. Moreover, Amalickiah and his brother, both Nephite dissenters, gained the Lamanite throne and claimed legitimacy (Alma 47:35; 52:3).

Repeatedly, the Lamanites are said to have been far more numerous than the Nephites (Jarom 1:6; Mosiah 25:3; Hel. 4:25), a fact that might appear to be inconsistent with the early Nephite characterization of them as savage hunters, which normally require much more land per person than farmers require (Enos 1:20; Jarom 1:6). The expression "people of the Lamanites" (Alma 23:9–12) may indicate that Lamanite elites dominated a disparate peasantry.

The few direct glimpses that Nephite history allows of the Lamanites indicate a level well beyond "savage" culture, though short of the "civilization" claimed for the Nephites. Perhaps their sophistication was due somewhat to the influence of Nephite dissenters among them (see Mosiah 24:3–7). Apparently some Lamanites proved apt learners from this source; moreover, those converted to the prophetic religion taught by Nephite missionaries are usually described as exemplary (Alma 23:5–7; 56; Hel. 6:1).

THE PEOPLE OF ZARAHEMLA (MULEKITES). In the third century B.C., when the Nephite leader Mosiah₁ and his company moved from the land of Nephi down to the Sidon river, "they discovered a people, who were called the people of Zarahemla" (Omni 1:13–14) because their ruler bore that name. These people were descendants of a party that fled the Babylonian conquest of Jerusalem in 586 B.C., among whom was a son of the Jewish king Zedekiah, MULEK. Hence Latter-day Saints often refer to the descendants of this group of people as Mulekites, although the Book of Mormon never uses the term. When discovered by the Nephites around 200 B.C., this people was "exceedingly numerous," although culturally degenerate due to illiteracy and warfare (Omni 1:16–17). The Nephite account says the combined population welcomed Mosiah as king.

Mosiah found that the people of Zarahemla had discovered the last known survivor of the Jaredites shortly before his death. By that means, or through survivors not mentioned, elements of Jaredite culture seem to have been brought to the Nephites by the people of Zarahemla (*CWHN* 5:238–47). The fact that the people of Zarahemla

spoke a language unintelligible to the Nephites further hints at an ethnic makeup more diverse than the brief text suggests, which assumes a solely Jewish origin.

The Mulekites are little referred to later, probably because they were amalgamated thoroughly into eclectic Nephite society (Mosiah 25:13). However, as late as 51 B.C., a Lamanite affiliate who was a descendant of king Zarahemla attacked and gained brief control over the Nephite capital (Hel. 1:15–34).

JAREDITES. This earliest people referred to in the Book of Mormon originated in Mesopotamia at the "great tower" referred to in Genesis 11. From there a group of probably eight families journeyed to America under divine guidance.

The existing record is a summary by MORONI₂, last custodian of the Nephite records, of a history written on gold plates by Ether, the final Jaredite prophet, around the middle of the first millennium B.C. Shaped by the editorial hands of Ether, Moroni₂, and MOSIAH₂ (Mosiah 28:11–17), and by the demand for brevity, the account gives but a skeletal narrative covering more than two millennia of Jaredite history. Most of it concerns just one of the eight lineages, Jared's, the ruling line to which Ether belonged, hence the name Jaredites (*see* BOOK OF MORMON PLATES AND RECORDS).

Eventually a flourishing cultural tradition developed (Ether 10:21–27), although maintaining a viable population seems to have been a struggle at times (Ether 9:30–34; 11:6–7). By the end, millions were reported victims of wars of extermination witnessed by the prophet Ether (Ether 15:2). A single survivor, Coriantumr, the last king, was encountered by the people of Zarahemla sometime before 200 B.C., although it is plausible that several remote groups also could have survived to meld unnoticed by historians into the successor Mulekite and Lamanite populations.

SECONDARY GROUPS. The same seven lineage groups are mentioned among Lehi's descendants near the beginning of the Nephite record and again 900 years later (Jacob 1:13; Morm. 1:8). Each was named after a first-generation ancestor and presumably consisted of his descendants. Among the Nephites there were four: Nephites proper, Jacobites, Josephites, and Zoramites. Within the Lamanite faction, Laman's own descendants were joined by the Lemuelites and Ishmaelites. These divisions disappeared after the appearance of

Christ at Bountiful (there were neither "Lamanites, nor any manner of -ites" [4 Ne. 1:17]), but that descent was not forgotten, for the old lineages later reappeared (4 Ne. 1:20, 36–37). What might have happened was that some public functions that the groups had filled were taken over for several generations by the Christian church, which they all had joined. Based on analogy to social systems in related lands, it is possible that membership in these seven groups governed marriage selection and property inheritance, and perhaps residence (Alma 31:3). The Lemuelites evidently had their own city (Alma 23:12–13), and descent determined where the Nephites and the people of Zarahemla sat during Mosiah₂'s politico-religious assembly (Mosiah 25:4; cf. 25:21–23). Such functions may also have been filled by groups other than the seven lineages.

The seven lineage groups may be referred to as "tribes," as in 3 Nephi 7:2–4. Immediately before the natural disasters that signaled the crucifixion of Jesus Christ, Nephite social unity collapsed, and they "did separate one from another into tribes, every man according to his family and his kindred and friends; . . . therefore their tribes became exceedingly great" (3 Ne. 7:2–4).

The **Jacobites** are always listed first of the three secondary peoples among the Nephites. They were descendants of Nephi's younger brother, Jacob. Nothing is said of them as a group except that they were counted as Nephites politically and culturally. Since Jacob himself was chief priest under the kingship of his brother Nephi, and since he and his descendants maintained the religious records begun by Nephi, it is possible that the Jacobites as a lineage group bore some special priestly responsibilities.

The **Josephites** are implied to have been descendants of Joseph, Nephi's youngest brother. The text is silent on any distinctive characteristics.

The **Zoramites** descended from Zoram, Laban's servant who agreed under duress to join the party of Lehi following the slaying of Laban in Jerusalem (1 Ne. 4:31–37). Both early and late in the account (Jacob 1:13 and 4 Ne. 1:36), the Zoramites are listed in alignment with Nephi's descendants, although around 75 B.C. at least some of them dissented for a time and joined the Lamanite alliance (Alma 43:4). As they were then "appointed . . . chief captains" over the Lamanite armies (Alma 48:5), they may earlier have played a formal military role among the Nephites. A reason for

their split with the Nephites was evidently recollection of what had happened to their founding ancestor: Ammoron, dissenter from the Nephites and king of the Lamanites in the first century B.C., recalled: "I am . . . a descendant of Zoram, whom your fathers pressed and brought out of Jerusalem" (Alma 54:23).

During their dissidence, their worship, characterized as idolatrous yet directed to a god of spirit, was conducted in "synagogues" from which the wealthy drove out the poor (Alma 31:1, 9–11; 32:5). Their practices departed from both Nephite ways and the LAW OF MOSES (Alma 31:9–12). Shortly after the signs marking the birth of Christ and almost eight years after the earliest mention of their separation from the Nephites, these Zoramites were still dissident and were luring naive Nephites to join the Gadianton robbers by means of "lyings" and "flattering words" (3 Ne. 1:29). Yet two centuries later they were back in the Nephite fold (4 Ne. 1:36).

The list of secondary peoples among the Lamanites starts with the **Lemuelites**. Presumably they were the posterity of Lehi's second eldest son, Lemuel. Nothing is said of the group as a separate entity other than routine listings among the Nephites' enemies (Jacob 1:13–14; Morm. 1:8–9), although a "city of Lemuel" is mentioned in Alma 23:12.

The **Ishmaelites** were descendants of the father-in-law of Nephi and his brothers (1 Ne. 7:2–5). Why Ishmael's sons (1 Ne. 7:6) did not found separate lineages of their own is nowhere indicated. As with the other secondary groups, there is little to go on in characterizing the Ishmaelites. At one time they occupied a particular land of Ishmael within the greater land of Nephi, where one of their number, Lamoni, ruled (Alma 17:21).

Somehow, by the days of Ammon and his fellow missionaries (first century B.C.), the Ishmaelites had gained the throne over the entire land of Nephi as well as kingship over some component kingdoms. (Alma 20:9 has the grand king implying that Lamoni's brothers, too, were rulers.) Yet the king recited the familiar Lamanite litany of complaint about how in the first generation Nephi had "robbed our fathers" of the right to rule (Alma 20:13). Evidently he was a culturally loyal Lamanite even though of a minor lineage.

The final information known about both Ishmaelites and Lemuelites is their presence in the combined armies fighting against the Nephites in

Mormon's day (Morm. 1:8). Presumably their contingents were involved in the final slaughter of the Nephites at CUMORAH.

TERTIARY GROUPS. Six other groups qualify as peoples, even though they did not exhibit the staying power of the seven lineages.

The earliest described are the **people of Zeniff** (Zeniffites). Zeniff, a Nephite, about half a century after Mosiah had first discovered the people and land of Zarahemla, led a group out of Zarahemla who were anxious to resettle "the land of Nephi, or . . . the land of our fathers' first inheritance" (Mosiah 9:1). Welcomed at first by the Lamanites there, in time they found themselves forced to pay a high tax to their overlords. A long section on them in the book of Mosiah (Mosiah 9–24) relates their dramatic temporal and spiritual experiences over three generations until they were able to escape back to Zarahemla. There they became Nephites again, although perhaps they retained some residential and religious autonomy as one of the "seven churches" (Mosiah 25:23).

Two groups splintered off from the people of Zeniff. The **people of Alma₁** were religious refugees who believed in the words of the prophet Abinadi and fled from oppression and wickedness under King Noah, the second Zeniffite king (Mosiah 18, 23–24). Numbering in the hundreds, they maintained independent social and political status for less than twenty-five years before escaping from Lamanite control and returning to Nephite territory, where they established the "church of God" in Zarahemla (Mosiah 25:18) but soon disappeared from the record as an identifiable group.

The second Zeniffite fragment started when the priests of King Noah, headed by Amulon, fled into the wilderness to avoid execution by their rebellious subjects. In the course of their escape, they kidnapped Lamanite women and took them as wives, thus founding the **Amulonites** in a land where they established their own version of Nephite culture (Mosiah 24:1). In time, they adopted the religious "order of Nehor" (see below), usurped political and military leadership, and "stirred up" the Lamanites to attack the Nephites (Alma 21:4; 24:1–2; 25:1–5). They and the Amalekites (see below) helped the Lamanites construct a city named Jerusalem in the land of Nephi. Judging from brief statements by the Nephites (Mosiah 12–13; Alma 21:5–10), both Amulonites and Amalekites saw themselves as defenders of a belief system based on the Old Testament, which no doubt explains the naming of their city.

One of the earliest groups of Nephite dissenters was the **Amlicites.** Ambitious Amlici, a disciple of Nehor, likely claiming noble birth (Alma 51:8), gathered a large body of followers and challenged the innovative Nephite system of rule by judges instituted by Mosiah₂; Amlici wished to be king. When his aim was defeated by "the voice of the people," he plotted an attack coordinated with the Lamanites that nearly succeeded in capturing Zarahemla, the Nephite capital. Loyal forces under ALMA₂ finally succeeded in destroying or scattering the enemy (Alma 2:1–31). Amlici was slain, but the fate of his forces is unclear. Likely, elements of them went with the defeated Lamanite army to the land of Nephi. The name Amlicite is not used thereafter.

Another group of Nephite dissenters, the **Amalekites,** lived in the land of Nephi (Alma 21:2–3; 43:13). Their origin is never explained. However, based on the names and dates, it is possible that they constituted the Amlicite remnant previously mentioned, their new name possibly arising by "lamanitization" of the original. They were better armed than common Lamanites (Alma 43:20) and, like some Zoramites, were made military leaders within the Lamanite army because of their "more wicked and murderous disposition" (Alma 43:6). From the record of the Nephite missionaries, we learn that they believed in a god (Alma 22:7). Many of them, like the Amlicites, belonged to the religious order of Nehor and built sanctuaries or synagogues where they worshipped (Alma 21:4, 6). Like the Amulonites, they adamantly resisted accepting Nephite orthodox religion (Alma 23:14). Instead, they believed that God would save all people. From their first mention to the last, only about fifteen years elapsed.

During a fourteen-year mission in the land of Nephi, the Nephite missionaries Ammon and his brothers gained many Lamanite converts (Alma 17–26). A Lamanite king, Lamoni, who was among these converts, gave the Lamanite converts the name **Anti-Nephi-Lehies.** These people were singularly distinguished by their firm commitment to the gospel of Jesus Christ, including, most prominently, the Savior's injunctions to love one's enemies and not to resist evil (3 Ne. 12:39, 44; Matt. 5:39, 44). Ammon maintained that in Christlike love this people exceeded the Nephites (Alma 26:33). After their conversion, the Book of Mormon says, they "had no more desire to do evil" (Alma 19:33) and "did not fight against God any more, neither against any of their brethren" (Alma 23:7). Having previously shed human blood, they covenanted as a people never again to take human life (Alma 24:6) and even buried all their weapons (Alma 24:17). They would not defend themselves when attacked by Lamanites, and 1,005 of them were killed (Alma 24:22). Ammon urged the vulnerable Anti-Nephi-Lehies to flee to Nephite territory. Among the Nephites they became known as the **people of Ammon** (or **Ammonites**; see Alma 56:57). They ended up in a separate locale within the Nephite domain, the land of Jershon (Alma 27:26). Later, they moved en masse to the land of Melek (Alma 35:13), where they were joined from time to time by other Lamanite refugees.

Some years later, desiring to assist the Nephite armies in defending the land but not wishing to break their covenant (Alma 53:13), the people of Ammon sent 2,000 of their willing sons to be soldiers, since their sons had not taken the covenant of nonviolence that they had. These "two thousand stripling soldiers" (Alma 53:22) became known as the sons of Helaman, their Nephite leader, and had much success in battle (Alma 56:56). Although they were all wounded, none were ever killed, a remarkable blessing ascribed "to the miraculous power of God, because of their exceeding faith" (Alma 57:26; cf. 56:47).

According to Helaman 3:11, a generation later some of the people of Ammon migrated into "the land northward." This is the last mention of them in the Book of Mormon.

OTHER GROUPS. Among the other groups mentioned in the Book of Mormon are the widespread secret combinations or "robbers." Yet these groups do not qualify as "peoples" but as associations, which individuals could join or leave on their own volition.

Another group, the "order of Nehor," was a cult centered around the ideas that priests should be paid and that God would redeem all people. They were not really a "people" in the technical sense—the term implies a biological continuity that a cult lacks.

The inhabitants of separate cities were also sometimes called peoples. Local beliefs and customs no doubt distinguished them from each other, but insufficient detail prohibits describing units of this scale.

BIBLIOGRAPHY

Nibley, Hugh W. *Lehi in the Desert; The World of the Jaredites; There Were Jaredites.* CWHN 5. Salt Lake City, 1988.

Sorenson, John L. *An Ancient American Setting for the Book of Mormon.* Salt Lake City, 1985.

Welch, John W. "Lehi's Last Will and Testament: A Legal Approach." In *The Book of Mormon: Second Nephi, The Doctrinal Structure,* ed. M. Nyman and C. Tate, pp. 61–82. Provo, Utah, 1989.

JOHN L. SORENSON

BOOK OF MORMON PERSONALITIES

[*The experiences, thoughts, feelings, and personalities of several individuals are brought to light in the Book of Mormon. Jesus Christ is central in the book; see* Jesus Christ in the Book of Mormon.

The founding prophet was Lehi. For articles concerning him and members of his family, see Lehi; Laman; Nephi₁; Jacob; *and* Ishmael. *Concerning Lehi's wife, Sariah, and the other women of the Book of Mormon, see* Women in the Book of Mormon.

The last Nephite king (153–90 B.C.) was Mosiah₂. For articles on his grandfather, father, and brother, see Mosiah₁, Benjamin, Helaman₁. *From 90 B.C. to A.D. 321 the Nephite records were kept by descendants of Alma₁; see* Alma₁; Alma₂; Helaman₂; Helaman₃; Nephi₂; Nephi₃; Nephi₄. *The last Nephite prophets, military leaders, and historians were* Mormon *and his son,* Moroni₂, *named after an earlier chief captain* Moroni₁.

Four other prophets figure prominently in the Book of Mormon; see Abinadi; Amulek; Samuel the Lamanite; *and* Brother of Jared. *Prophets from the Old World quoted in the Book of Mormon include* Ezias; Isaiah; Joseph; Moses; Neum; Zenock; *and* Zenos. *Regarding the various groups of people in the Book of Mormon, see* Book of Mormon Peoples; Jaredites; Lamanites; Mulek; *and* Nephites. *See also* Book of Mormon Names.]

BOOK OF MORMON PLATES AND RECORDS

The Book of Mormon is a complex text with a complicated history. It is primarily an abridgment of several earlier records by its chief editor and namesake, MORMON. All these records are referred to as "plates" because they were engraved on thin

Original manuscript from Joseph Smith's dictation 1829

Printer's manuscript (working copy) 1829-1830

The Book of Mormon 1830

Translated by Joseph Smith

Book of Lehi (Lost 116 manuscript pages)

Plates of Mormon

Sealed Plates (not translated)

Small Plates of Nephi
c. 580-200 BC.

Large Plates of Nephi
c.580 BC - 321 AD

Translated by Mosiah and Abridged by Moroni

Abridged by Mormon

1 NEPHI
2 NEPHI
JACOB
ENOS
JAROM
OMNI

WORDS OF MORMON

LEHI
MOSIAH
ALMA
HELAMAN
3 NEPHI
4 NEPHI

MORMON

ETHER

MORONI

Title Page - 421 AD

Abridged by Nephi

Isaiah 48-49
Isa 2-14,29,50-51
Zenos

Isaiah 53 and other texts

Priesthood and Sacrament Prayers

Abridged by Ether

Record of Lehi

Plates of Brass

Benjamin's Speech 124 BC (Mosiah 2-5)

Record of Zeniff c. 200-120 BC (Mosiah 9-11, 19-22)

Records of Alma c. 150-120 BC (Mosiah 12-18, 23-24)

Records of Sons of Mosiah c. 90-77 BC (Alma 17-26)

Epistles of Helaman, Pahoran and Moroni c. 64-62 BC (Alma 56-58,60-61)

Records of Nephi - 34 AD

Records of the Jaredites c. 2200-300 BC

Documents from Mormon c.355 AD

Indicates abridging

Indicates quoting

John W. Welch and the BYU Geography Department

sheets of metal. Various source documents were used by Mormon in his compilation, leading to abrupt transitions and chronological disjunctions that can confuse readers. However, when one is aware of the history of the text, these are consistent and make good sense. The various plates and records referred to in the Book of Mormon and used in making it are (1) the plates of brass; (2) the record of LEHI; (3) the large plates of NEPHI$_1$; (4) the small plates of Nephi; (5) the plates of Mormon; and (6) the twenty-four gold plates of Ether.

THE GOLD PLATES.   The GOLD PLATES that the Prophet Joseph SMITH received and translated were the plates of Mormon on which Mormon and his son MORONI$_2$ made their abridgment. Mormon, a prophet and military leader who lived at the end of the NEPHITE era (c. A.D. 385), was the penultimate custodian of the records of earlier Nephite prophets and rulers. In particular, he had the large plates of Nephi, which were the official Nephite chronicle and which he was commanded to continue (Morm. 1:4). He later made his own plates of Mormon, on which he compiled an abridgment of the large plates of Nephi (W of M 1:3–5; 3 Ne. 5:9–10), which covered 985 years of Nephite history, from Lehi's day to his. The large plates drew on still earlier records and the writings of various prophets and frequently included various source materials such as letters, blessings, discourses, and memoirs.

   After Mormon had completed his abridgment through the reign of King BENJAMIN (c. 130 B.C.), he discovered the small plates of Nephi, a separate history of the same time period focusing on the spiritual events of those years and quoting extensively from the plates of brass. Inspired to add the small plates of Nephi to his own record, Mormon inserted a brief explanation for the double account of early Nephite history (W of M 1:2–9).

   Mormon continued his abridgment, selecting from the large plates, paraphrasing, and often adding his own comments, extending the account down to his time. Anticipating death, he passed the plates to his son Moroni. Over the next few decades, Moroni wandered alone, making additions to his father's record, including two chapters now included in a book previously abridged by his

This gold plate of Darius proclaims his majesty and the vast extent of his Persian empire. It was buried in a neatly made stone box in 516–515 B.C. at Persepolis. This gold plate and its duplicate silver tablet were discovered in 1933. Similarly, the Nephites of the sixth century B.C. kept two sets of records on gold plates, one of which was buried in a stone box in 421 A.D. Courtesy Paul R. Cheesman.

father (Morm. 7–8) and an account of the JAREDITES that he had abridged from the twenty-four gold plates of Ether. He also copied an extensive vision of the last days that had been recorded by an early Jaredite prophet, the BROTHER OF JARED, and which Moroni was commanded to seal (Ether 4:4–5). He also added brief notes on church rituals (Moro. 1–6), a sermon and two letters from his father (Moro. 7–9), and an exhortation to future readers (Moro. 10). Finally, Moroni took this somewhat heterogeneous collection of records—the plates of Mormon, the small plates of Nephi, his abridgment of the plates of Ether, and the sealed portion containing the vision of the brother of Jared—and buried them in the earth. About 1,400 years later, in 1823, Moroni, now resurrected, appeared to the Prophet Joseph Smith and revealed the location of these records. The plates

---

←——Origin of the Book of Mormon.

of Mormon, which, except for the sealed portion, were subsequently translated by Joseph Smith, are known today as the gold plates.

The present English Book of Mormon, however, is not simply a translation of all those gold plates. Joseph Smith and Martin HARRIS began by translating the plates of Mormon, and when they had reached the reign of King Benjamin, they had 116 pages of translation. Harris borrowed these pages to show to his wife, then lost them, and they were never recovered (see MANUSCRIPT, LOST 116 PAGES). Joseph was commanded not to retranslate this material (D&C 10:30–46), but instead to substitute a translation of the parallel small plates of Nephi, which includes the books of 1 Nephi, 2 Nephi, Jacob, Enos, Jarom, and Omni. Thus, the present Book of Mormon contains only the second account of early Nephite history.

The translation continues from the rest of the plates of Mormon, which were abridged from the large plates of Nephi, and includes the books of Mosiah, Alma, Helaman, 3 Nephi, 4 Nephi, and Mormon (the last two chapters of which were written by Moroni). Next follow Moroni's abridgment of Jaredite history (the book of Ether) and his closing notes (the book of Moroni). Joseph Smith was commanded not to translate the sealed vision of the brother of Jared, which apparently made up a substantial portion of the gold plates (Ludlow, p. 320). Although Joseph Smith translated only from the gold plates, he and his associates saw many other records (JD 19:38; *Millennial Star* 40 [1878]:771–72).

THE PLATES OF BRASS. It is now known that many ancients of the Mediterranean area wrote on metal plates. "Where the record was one of real importance, plates of copper, bronze, or even more precious metal were used instead of the usual wooden, lead, or clay tablets" (CWHN 5:119; see also H. C. Wright, in *Journal of Library History* 16 [1981]:48–70). Such a metal record was in the possession of one Laban, a leader in Jerusalem in 600 B.C. How Laban obtained these plates and where they originally came from are not known. Several theories have been advanced, including the possibility that the plates of brass originated in the days of JOSEPH OF EGYPT (Ludlow, p. 56). The Book of Mormon indicates that Laban and his father had inherited and preserved the record because they were descendants of this Joseph (1 Ne. 5:16).

The Book of Mormon does tell how the prophet Lehi came to possess the plates of brass. After fleeing Jerusalem, Lehi was commanded by God to send his sons back to the city to obtain the plates from Laban. When he received them, Lehi found that they contained the five books of Moses, a record of the Jews from the beginning down to the reign of Zedekiah, the prophecies of the holy prophets for that same time period (including some of JEREMIAH's prophecies), and a genealogy of Lehi's fathers (1 Ne. 3–5).

Nephi and succeeding spiritual leaders highly valued the plates of brass. They were passed down by major prophets from Nephi to Mormon, and since they were written in an adapted form of Egyptian (see BOOK OF MORMON LANGUAGE), their keepers were taught to read that language (Mosiah 1:2–4). The plates of brass were the basic scriptures of the Nephite nation, and for centuries their prophets read them, quoted them in sermons, and excerpted material from them to enrich their own writings. For example, when the prophet ABINADI cited the Ten Commandments in a disputation with the priests of Noah, his knowledge of the Ten Commandments was due, at least indirectly, to the plates of brass (Mosiah 12–13). As MOSIAH$_2$ stated, "For it were not possible that our father, Lehi, could have remembered all these things, to have taught them to his children, except it were for the help of these plates" (Mosiah 1:4).

Book of Mormon records, particularly the small plates of Nephi, occasionally quote at length from the plates of brass, and these quotations include twenty-one complete chapters from Isaiah. Although the translation of these quotations generally follows the wording of the King James Version of the Bible, there are many significant differences, which may indicate the existence of older textual sources (Tvedtnes, pp. 165–77). It is also evident from the scriptural quotations in the Book of Mormon that the plates of brass contained a more extensive record of the writings of Hebrew prophets than does the present Old Testament. For example, the Book of Mormon includes prophecies of Joseph of Egypt that are not found in the Bible, as well as writings of ZENOS, ZENOCK, NEUM, and EZIAS, prophets who are not specifically named in the Old Testament.

THE RECORD OF LEHI. Unfortunately, Mormon's abridgment of the record of Lehi was the material translated in the 116 manuscript pages that were lost, and consequently it is not available in the present Book of Mormon. Lehi wrote an account of his life and spiritual experiences that was included in the large plates of Nephi (1 Ne. 19:1). Mormon abridged this record in his plates, and Joseph Smith translated it, but since it was lost by Martin Harris, very little is now known about it except what can be inferred from references in other texts (Brown, pp. 25–32; see also the preface to the first edition [1830] of the Book of Mormon). When Nephi and JACOB cite the words of Lehi, they seem to be quoting from this now-lost text, and at least the first eight chapters of 1 Nephi (part of the small plates) appear to be based on the record of Lehi. Other passages in the small plates may also have been derived from that record.

THE LARGE PLATES OF NEPHI.   Nephi began the large plates soon after his arrival in the New World. They were the official continuous chronicle of the Nephites from the time they left Jerusalem (c. 600 B.C.) until they were destroyed (A.D. 385). Apparently the large plates were divided into books, each named for its primary author. These plates "contained a 'full account of the history of [Nephi's] people' (1 Ne. 9:2, 4; 2 Ne. 4:14; Jacob 1:2–3), the genealogy of Lehi (1 Ne. 19:2) and the 'more part' of the teachings of the resurrected Jesus Christ to the Nephite nation (3 Ne. 26:7)" (Ludlow, p. 57). Begun as basically a secular history, they later became a combined record, mingling a thousand years of Nephite history and religious experiences.

The large plates emphasize the covenants made with the house of Israel and quote messianic prophecies of Old World prophets not found in the Old Testament. This information was excerpted from the plates of brass that Lehi's colony brought with it from Jerusalem. They also record wars and contentions, correspondence between military leaders, and information on various missionary journeys. The interventions and miraculous power of God permeate this history. The recorded sermons of King Benjamin, Abinadi, and ALMA$_2$ are indicative of these individuals' deep understanding of the gospel of Jesus Christ and of their faith in his prophesied coming. These plates feature an account of the post-Resurrection ministry and teachings of Christ to the people of the western world (3 Ne. 11–28).

The large plates of Nephi were passed down from king to king until they came into the posses-sion of Mosiah$_2$. He added such records as those of Zeniff and ALMA$_1$ to the large plates and then gave them to Alma$_2$. The plates subsequently passed through a line of prophets until Ammaron's day in the early fourth century A.D. Ammaron chose Mormon, then only a child, to continue the record when he was mature. Mormon recorded the events of his day on the large plates and then used them as the source for his abridgment, which was later buried in the hill CUMORAH. Joseph Smith did not receive the large plates, but the Book of Mormon suggests that they may yet be published to the world (3 Ne. 26:6–10).

THE SMALL PLATES OF NEPHI.   Approximately twenty years after beginning the large plates, Nephi was commanded to make another set of plates. This second set was to be reserved for an account of the ministry of his people (1 Ne. 9; 2 Ne. 5:28–33). They were to contain the things considered most precious—"preaching which was sacred, or revelation which was great, or prophesying" (Jacob 1:2–4).

The small plates were kept for over four centuries, not quite half the time covered by the large plates, by nine writers: Nephi, Jacob, Enos, Jarom, Omni, Amaron, Chemish, Abinadom, and Amaleki. All of these authors were the sons or brothers of their predecessors. Though these plates include the writings of many over a long time period, 80 percent of the text was written by Nephi, the first writer, and an additional 12 percent by his brother Jacob.

Mormon included the small plates with his record when he delivered the plates of Mormon to his son Moroni because their witness of Christ pleased him and because he was impressed by the Spirit of the Lord to include them "for a wise purpose" (W of M 1:3–7). However, since the small plates covered the historical period already recorded in his abridgment of the record of Lehi (namely, from Lehi down to the reign of King Benjamin) and since the book of Mosiah began with the end of King Benjamin's reign, Mormon found it necessary to write a brief explanation to show how the small plates of Nephi connect with the book of Mosiah. He entitled this explanation "Words of Mormon."

While the writers of the small plates recognized the need to provide a historical narrative, their main purpose was to talk of Christ, to preach of Christ, and to prophesy of Christ (2 Ne. 25:26).

Because Nephi was concerned with teaching his people the covenants and promises made to ancient Israel, he extracted these teachings from earlier prophets as recorded on the plates of brass. He quoted extensively from the prophet Isaiah (2 Ne. 12–24; cf. Isa. 2–14) and then wrote a commentary on it, predicting the future of Jews, Lamanites, and Gentiles and prophesying much that would happen in the latter days (2 Ne. 25–30).

Jacob continued his brother's approach by recording his own sermons and a long quotation from and explanation of a prophecy of Zenos. The writings of later authors in the small plates are much briefer and less concerned with spiritual matters.

Amaleki noted in his writings that the small plates were full and turned them over to King Benjamin (Omni 1:25, 30), who then possessed both the large and the small plates of Nephi, as well as the plates of brass. All these sets of plates were handed down from generation to generation until they were entrusted to Mormon.

THE PLATES OF MORMON. After Mormon received the plates, he made a new set on which he engraved his abridgment of the large plates of Nephi (3 Ne. 5:10–11). It is this abridgment plus some additions by Mormon's son Moroni that constitute the gold plates given to Joseph Smith. He described them as follows:

> These records were engraven on plates which had the appearance of gold, each plate was six inches wide and eight inches long and not quite so thick as common tin. They were filled with engravings, in Egyptian characters and bound together in a volume, as the leaves of a book with three rings running through the whole. The volume was something near six inches in thickness, a part of which was sealed. The characters on the unsealed part were small, and beautifully engraved [Jessee, p. 214].

The descriptions reported by other witnesses add details which suggest that the plates were composed of a gold alloy (possibly tumbaga) and that they weighed about fifty pounds (Putnam, pp. 788–89, 829–31). Each plate was as thick as parchment or thick paper.

Most of the time, Mormon relied on the large plates of Nephi for his information. Much of the historical narrative in the Book of Mormon appears to be his paraphrase of earlier records, but occasionally first-person documents are worked into the text. For example, in Mosiah 9 and 10 the narrative suddenly includes a first-person account of Zeniff (apparently an earlier document that Mormon simply copied), and then in chapter 11 Mormon's paraphrase resumes. In addition, many sermons, blessings, and letters appear to be reproduced intact.

Nevertheless, some passages can definitely be ascribed to Mormon: the abridgment of his contributions to the large plates (Morm. 1–7), his sermon and letters recorded by Moroni (Moro. 7–9), and the explanatory comments that he inserted into his narrative. In some of these interpolations he identifies himself (W of M; 3 Ne. 5:8–26; 26:6–12; 28:24; 4 Ne. 1:23), but it seems likely that the frequent "thus we see" comments are also Mormon attempting to stress matters of particular spiritual importance to his readers (e.g., Alma 24:19, 27; 50:19–23; Hel. 3:27–30; 12:1–2).

THE TWENTY-FOUR GOLD PLATES OF ETHER. These twenty-four gold plates were a record of ancient Jaredites, inhabitants of the Americas before the Nephites. This particular people left the Tower of Babel at the time of the confusion of tongues. Their prophet-leaders were led to the ocean, where they constructed eight peculiar barges. These were driven by the wind across the waters to America, where the Jaredites became a large and powerful nation. After many centuries, wickedness and wars led to a final war of annihilation. During that final war, Ether, a prophet of God, wrote their history and spiritual experiences on twenty-four gold plates, perhaps relying on earlier Jaredite records (see J. Welch, "Preliminary Comments on the Sources behind the Book of Ether," in *F.A.R.M.S. Manuscript Collection*, pp. 3–7. Provo, Utah, 1986).

After witnessing the destruction of his people, Ether hid the twenty-four gold plates. Many years later (c. 121 B.C.) they were discovered by a small Nephite exploring party and given to Mosiah₂, a prophet-king, who translated them into the Nephite language through the use of SEER STONES (Mosiah 8:8–9; 28:11–16). Much later (c. A.D. 400) Moroni abridged this history of the Jaredites as his father Mormon had intended, concentrating on spiritual matters and adding inspired commentaries. Moroni included this abridgment, now known as the book of Ether, with what he and his father had already written. (The twenty-four gold plates of Ether were not among the plates received by Joseph Smith.)

CHARACTERISTICS OF MORMON'S EDITING. The Book of Mormon is quite complicated. The foregoing summary of the plates and other records from which the book was derived is drawn from a number of scattered but consistent comments included in the present text. The narrative itself is often complex. For instance, in Mosiah 1–25, Mormon narrates the stories of three separate groups and subgroups of people—principally the people of Mosiah, of Limhi, and of Alma—with their respective histories and interactions with each other and with the Lamanites (*see* BOOK OF MORMON PEOPLES). The story might have been quite confusing, as it jumps from one people to another, and back and forth in time, but Mormon has kept it remarkably clear. Alma 17–26 is a lengthy flashback recounting the histories of several missionaries on the occasion of their reunion with old friends, and Alma 43–63 narrates the history of a war with the Lamanites, keeping straight the events that happened on two fronts.

Mormon's account might have been much more complex. He emphasizes that he is presenting less than one hundredth of the material available to him (e.g., W of M 1:5; 3 Ne. 26:6–7). Furthermore, his source materials give a lineage history of one family, Lehi and his descendants, and do not encompass all events in the ancient western world (Sorenson, 1985, pp. 50–56). Mormon further simplifies his record by continuing Jacob's practice of lumping diverse peoples into two major groups:

> Now the people which were not Lamanites were Nephites; nevertheless, they were called Nephites, Jacobites, Josephites, Zoramites, Lamanites, Lemuelites, and Ishmaelites. But I, Jacob, shall not hereafter distinguish them by these names, but I shall call them Lamanites that seek to destroy the people of Nephi, and those who are friendly to Nephi I shall call Nephites, or the people of Nephi, according to the reigns of the kings [Jacob 1:13–14; see also Morm. 1:8–9].

The vast editing project that produced the Book of Mormon would require clear guidelines for selecting materials for inclusion. Mormon is quite explicit about the purpose of his abridgment. Like Nephi, he is writing a history to lead people to Christ, and he is writing specifically for the people of later times (2 Ne. 25:23; Morm. 7). The plates of Mormon were created to come forth in the latter days. Mormon is interested in pointing out the principles that will be of most use to such people, and his careful editing and his "thus" and "thus we see" passages are all directed at making the moral lessons easier to identify and understand.

Finally, Mormon took his job as record keeper and abridger very seriously. He was commanded by God to make his record (title page to the Book of Mormon; 3 Ne. 26:12). Also, Nephite society had a strong tradition of the importance of written records, and this was one of the criteria by which they distinguished themselves from the more numerous Mulekites (Omni 1:14–19). Furthermore, the various plates seem to have been handed down from one prophet or king to another as sacred relics and symbols of authority (Mosiah 28:20; 3 Ne. 1:2). In addition, the Nephites had a ceremonial record exchange when different branches of the family were reunited (Mosiah 8:1–5; 22:14). Most important, the Nephites knew that they would be held responsible for and would be judged by what was written in the records, just as all people will be (2 Ne. 25:21–22; 33:10–15; Morm. 8:12).

BIBLIOGRAPHY

Brown, S. Kent. "Lehi's Personal Record: Quest for a Missing Source." *BYU Studies* 24 (winter 1984):19–42.

Doxey, Roy W. "What is the Approximate Weight of the Gold Plates from Which the Book of Mormon Was Translated?" In *A Sure Foundation: Answers to Difficult Gospel Questions*, pp. 50–52. Salt Lake City, 1988.

Jessee, Dean C. *Personal Writings of Joseph Smith*. Salt Lake City, 1984.

Ludlow, Daniel H. *A Companion to Your Study of the Book of Mormon*. Salt Lake City, 1976.

Putnam, Read H. "Were the Golden Plates Made of Tumbaga?" *IE* 69 (Sept. 1966):788–89, 828.

Sorenson, John L. "The 'Brass Plates' and Biblical Scholarship." *Dialogue* 10 (Autumn 1977):31–39.

———. *An Ancient American Setting for the Book of Mormon*. Salt Lake City, 1985.

Sperry, Sidney B. *Our Book of Mormon*. Salt Lake City, 1950.

Tvedtnes, J. "Isaiah Variants in the Book of Mormon." In *Isaiah and the Prophets*, ed. M. Nyman, pp. 165–77. Provo, Utah, 1984.

GRANT R. HARDY
ROBERT E. PARSONS

BOOK OF MORMON RELIGIOUS TEACHINGS AND PRACTICES

Most of the Book of Mormon is about a group of Israelites who were guided by prophets, had the doctrines and ordinances of the gospel of Jesus

Christ, but lived the law of Moses until the coming of Christ. After his resurrection, Jesus appeared to some of them, and organized his church, and for four generations they lived in peace and happiness. Many details about the religious teachings and practices of these people are found in the Book of Mormon. Latter-day Saints believe that these Christian teachings are applicable in the world today, both because the eternal DOCTRINE of God is as binding on one generation as on the next and because the contents of the Book of Mormon were selected and preserved by prophets with the modern world in mind. These teachings are also found in the revelations that established contemporary LDS practices and ordinances.

In 3 Nephi and Moroni, documents recorded by firsthand witnesses preserve many words of the resurrected Jesus and give the basic doctrines, covenants, and ordinances of his church. Some of the main points follow:

1. Jesus defined his doctrine. Ye must "repent, and believe in me . . . and be baptized in my name, and become as a little child. . . . This is my doctrine" (3 Ne. 11:32, 38–39). The promise is given that God will visit such people "with fire and with the Holy Ghost" (3 Ne. 11:35).

2. Jesus instructed the people to be baptized by immersion, and gave the words of the BAPTISMAL PRAYER (3 Ne. 11:26–27). Only those who were "accountable and capable of committing sin" were baptized (Moro. 8:9–15; cf. 6:3).

3. Jesus ordained twelve disciples and gave them AUTHORITY to baptize (3 Ne. 11:21–22). Moroni 2:2 preserves the words that Jesus spoke when he laid his hands on these disciples and gave them power to give the Holy Ghost (3 Ne. 18:36–37). The words the disciples used in subsequent ordinations of priests and teachers are found in Moroni 3:1–4.

4. The SACRAMENT PRAYERS are recorded in Moroni 4–5. The words of these prayers derive from the first-person expressions that Jesus spoke when he administered the sacrament in 3 Nephi 18:6–11.

5. The Nephite church met together often "to fast and to pray, and to speak one with another concerning the welfare of their souls, and . . . to partake of bread and wine, in remembrance of the Lord Jesus" (Moro. 6:5–6).

6. These Christians regularly renewed their covenant to keep the commandments Jesus had given them: for instance, to have no contention, anger, or derision; to offer a sacrifice of a broken heart and contrite spirit; to keep the law of chastity in thought and in deed; to love their enemies; to give sustenance to the poor; to do secret acts of charity; to pray alone and with others; to serve only God, not the things of the world; and to strive to become perfected like God and Jesus (3 Ne. 11–14; *see* SERMON ON THE MOUNT). They were promised that Jesus' spirit would continue with them and that they would be raised up at the last day.

7. This church was led by Nephi₃, one of the twelve disciples chosen by Jesus and sent out to preach the things they had heard him say and had seen him do (3 Ne. 27:1). The people were admonished to "give heed unto the words of these twelve" (3 Ne. 12:1).

8. At the Lord's instruction, the church was called by the name of Jesus Christ, and members called on the Father in the name of Christ in all things (3 Ne. 27:8–9; *see* NAME OF THE CHURCH).

9. The disciples healed the sick and worked miracles in the name of Jesus (4 Ne. 1:5; *see* SICK, BLESSING THE).

10. They followed Jesus' examples in prayer, reverencing and praising God, asking for forgiveness, and praying that the will of God would be done (3 Ne. 13:9–13; 19:16–35). The people were commanded to "pray in [their] families" (3 Ne. 18:21; *see* FAMILY PRAYER).

11. They had "all things common among them, every man dealing justly, one with another. . . . Therefore there were not rich and poor" (3 Ne. 26:19; 4 Ne. 1:3; *see* CONSECRATION).

12. As Jesus had instructed, his followers were strict in keeping iniquity out of their communities and synagogues, with "three witnesses of the church" being required to excommunicate offenders; nevertheless, all were helped, and those who sincerely repented were forgiven (3 Ne. 18:28–32; Moro. 6:7–8; *see* DISCIPLINARY PROCEDURES).

During the centuries before Christ, Nephite prophets had taught the fulness of the gospel and prepared the people for the coming of Jesus Christ. With respect to the points mentioned above, compare the following antecedents in Nephite history. Some can be traced back into ancient Israel; others were introduced at various times through inspiration or revelation:

1. The doctrine of Christ—faith in the Lord Jesus Christ, repentance, baptism, and the purging of sin by the fire of the Holy Ghost—was taught in the Book of Mormon as early as the time of Nephi₁ (2 Ne. 31). Nephite prophets frequently spoke about the "plan of redemption" or, as Alma called it, "the great plan of happiness" (Alma 42:8). They looked forward to the coming of God himself to earth to redeem mankind from their lost and fallen state. They knew that he would atone for the transgression of Adam and for all the sins of those who would "not procrastinate the day of [their] repentance" (Alma 34:33), and that all mankind would be physically resurrected and then judged according to the JUSTICE AND MERCY of God (Alma 40–42).

2. Covenantal baptisms were performed from the beginning of the record, notably by Alma₁ at the waters of Mormon (Mosiah 18). His baptismal prayer sought sanctification of the heart as the covenantor promised to serve God "even until death" so that he or she might be granted eternal life through the redemption of Christ (Mosiah 18:12–13). Alma's group remained intact even after they took up residence among other Nephites, and those Nephites who submitted to baptism "after the manner he [had baptized] his brethren in the waters of Mormon" belonged to this church (Mosiah 25:18).

3. Centuries before the time of Christ, Nephite priests and teachers were consecrated (2 Ne. 5:26), appointed (Mosiah 6:3; Alma 45:22–23), or ordained by the laying-on of hands (Alma 6:1; cf. Num. 27:23). They watched over the church, stirred the people to remember their covenants (Mosiah 6:3), preached the law and the coming of the Son of God (Alma 16:18–19), and offered their firstlings in "sacrifice and burnt offerings according to the law of Moses" (Mosiah 2:3; cf. Deut. 15:19–23), which they understood to be a type of Christ (2 Ne. 11:4). Nephites and Lamanites had temples, the first one being built "after the manner of the temple of Solomon" (2 Ne. 5:16). The altar was a place of worship where the people assembled, "watching and praying continually, that they might be delivered from Satan, and from death, and from destruction" (Alma 15:17). Nephite priests also taught in synagogues, or gathering places, and ideally no one was excluded (2 Ne. 26:26; Alma 32:2–

12). Because they held the Melchizedek Priesthood (Alma 13:6–19), they could function in the ordinances of the Aaronic Priesthood even though they were not Levites. Nephite priests were ordained in a manner that looked "forward on the Son of God, [the ordination] being a type of his order" (Alma 13:16).

4. The covenantal language used by King BENJAMIN (c. 124 B.C.) was similar to the language of the Nephite sacrament prayers. Benjamin's people witnessed that they were willing to keep God's commandments, took upon them the name of Christ, and promised to "remember to retain the name written always in [their] hearts" (Mosiah 5:5–12; cf. Num. 6:27).

5. The Nephites gathered to fast and pray for spiritual blessings (Mosiah 27:22; Hel. 3:35). In addition, like their Israelite ancestors, they fasted in connection with mourning for the dead (Hel. 9:10; cf. 2 Sam. 3:35).

6. Covenant renewals were a long-standing part of the law of Moses, pursuant to which all men, women, and children were required to gather around the temple at appointed times to hear and recommit themselves to keep the law of God (Deut. 31:10–13; cf. Mosiah 2:5). Nephite religious law at the time of Alma₂ prohibited sorcery, idol worship, idleness, babbling, envy, strife, wearing costly apparel, pride, lying, deceit, malice, reviling, stealing, robbing, whoredom, adultery, murder, and all manner of wickedness (Alma 1:32; 16:18). In addition, Nephi₂ counseled against oppressing the poor, withholding food from the hungry, sacrilege, denying the spirit of prophecy, and deserting to the Lamanites (Hel. 4:12).

7. The righteous Nephites were accustomed to being led by prophets, inspired kings, high priests, and chief judges. These leaders kept the sacred records that were frequently cited in Nephite religious observances. The institutions of Nephite prophecy varied from time to time: some prophets were also kings; subsidiary prophets worked under King Benjamin (W of M 1:17–18); others, like ABINADI, were lone voices crying repentance. Their surviving messages, however, were constant and accurate: they preached the gospel and the coming of Christ, and they knew that when he came he would ordain twelve authorized leaders both in the East (1 Ne. 1:10; 11:29) and in the West (1 Ne. 12:7–10).

8. The name of Jesus Christ was revealed to the early Nephite prophets (2 Ne. 10:3; 25:19), and thereafter the Nephites prayed and acted in the name of Jesus Christ (2 Ne. 32:9; Jacob 4:6). Alma₁ called his followers "the church of Christ" (Mosiah 18:17).

9. Like the Israelite prophets, the Nephite prophets performed miracles in the name of the Lord. As had Elijah (1 Kgs. 17), for example, Nephi₂ closed the heavens and caused a famine (Hel. 11:4), and Nephi₃ raised the dead and healed the sick (3 Ne. 7:19–22).

10. The Nephites watched and prayed continually (Alma 15:17). They were counseled to pray three times a day—morning, noon, and night—for mercy, for deliverance from the power of the devil, for prosperity, and for the welfare of their families (Alma 34:18–25; cf. Ps. 55:17). They taught that effective prayer had to be coupled with charitable actions (Alma 34:26–29), which are necessary to retain a remission of sin (Mosiah 4:26).

11. Regarding wealth and possessions, many early Book of Mormon prophets condemned the evils of seeking power and riches. The cycle leading from prosperity to pride, wickedness, and then catastrophe was often repeated, echoing formulas characteristic of DEUTERONOMY. The righteous Nephites covenanted to give liberally to the poor and to bear one another's burdens.

12. Typically, those who entered into the required covenant became "numbered" among the Nephites. If they transgressed, their names were "blotted out," presumably being removed from a roster (Mosiah 5:11; 6:1). Detailed procedures for excommunicating transgressors were established by Alma₁, who was given authority by King MOSIAH₂ to judge members of the church. Forgiveness was to be extended "as often as [the] people repent" (Mosiah 26:29–30).

Teachings and practices such as these specifically prepared the way for the personal coming of Jesus Christ after his resurrection. Despite years of preparation, the immediate reaction of some of the Nephite multitude to the initial words of the resurrected Christ was still to wonder "what he would concerning the law of Moses" (3 Ne. 15:2). Even though the prophets had long explained the limited function of the law, it remained a sacred and integral part of their lives until it was fulfilled by Jesus (e.g., 2 Ne. 25:24–25; Alma 30:3; 3 Ne. 1:24).

When Jesus spoke, it became evident how old things "had become new" (3 Ne. 15:2).

The diversity of religious experience in the Book of Mormon is further seen in the great number of religious communities it mentions in varying situations. Outside of orthodox Nephite circles (whose own success varied from time to time), there were an extravagant royal cult of King Noah and his temple priests (Mosiah 11); a false, rivaling church in Zarahemla formed by Nehor (Alma 1); centers of worship among the Lamanites (Alma 23:2); the wicked and agnostic Korihor (Alma 30); an astounding aristocratic and apostate prayer stand (an elevated platform for a single worshipper) of the Zoramites (Alma 31:13–14); and secret combinations or societies with staunch oath-swearing adherents intent on murder and gain (3 Ne. 3:9). Frequent efforts were made by Nephite missionaries, such as Alma₂, Ammon, and Nephi₂, to convert people from these groups to the gospel of Jesus Christ and to organize them into righteous churches and communities. On occasion, the converts became more righteous than all their contemporaries. Even among the righteous, there were varying degrees of comprehension and knowledge, for the mysteries of God were imparted by God and his prophets according to the diligence of the hearers (Alma 12:9–11).

Many doctrinal points and practical insights fill the pages of the Book of Mormon. A few of them are the following: Alma₂ explains that by his suffering Jesus came to "know according to the flesh how to succor his people" (Alma 7:12). Alma₂ describes how faith may be nurtured into knowledge (Alma 32). Benjamin identifies sin as "rebellion against God" (Mosiah 2:36–37) and presents a hopeful outlook for all who will "yield to the enticings of the Holy Spirit and put off the natural man" (Mosiah 3:19). Alma₂ depicts the condition of spirits after death as they return to God, "who gave them life" (Alma 40:11). Jacob speaks poignantly of the nakedness of the unrepentant, who will stand filthy before the judgment of God (2 Ne. 9:14). Benjamin extols the "blessed and happy state" of the righteous who taste the love and goodness of God (Mosiah 2:41; 4:11). And Lehi states the purpose of existence: "Men are that they might have joy" (2 Ne. 2:25). The Book of Mormon teaches the one pathway to eternal happiness by numerous inspiring images, instructions, and examples.

Many Book of Mormon prophetic teachings have already been fulfilled (e.g., 1 Ne. 13; 2 Ne. 3;

Hel. 14), but several still look to the future. One reason some people were puzzled when Jesus declared he had fulfilled the law and the prophets was that many prophecies of Isaiah, Nephi₁, and others remained open—in particular, the Nephites had not yet been reunited with a redeemed people of Israel. Jesus explained: "I do not destroy that which hath been spoken concerning things which are to come" (3 Ne. 15:7). Yet to be fulfilled in the prophetic view of the Book of Mormon are promises that the branches of scattered Israel will be gathered in Christ and will combine their records into one (2 Ne. 29:13–14), that the remnants of Lehi's descendants will be greatly strengthened in the Lord (2 Ne. 30:3–6; 3 Ne. 21:7–13), and that a great division will occur: a New Jerusalem will be built in the Western Hemisphere by the righteous (3 Ne. 21:23; Ether 13:1–9), while the wicked will be destroyed (1 Ne. 30:10). "Then," Jesus said, "shall the power of heaven come down among them; and I also will be in the midst" (3 Ne. 21:25).

[*See also* Jesus Christ in the Book of Mormon.]

BIBLIOGRAPHY

Most Latter-day Saint doctrinal writings refer to the Book of Mormon on particular topics, but no comprehensive analysis of Nephite religious experience as such has been written.

In general, see Sidney B. Sperry, *Book of Mormon Compendium* (Salt Lake City, 1968); and Rodney Turner, "The Three Nephite Churches of Christ," in *The Keystone Scripture*, ed. P. Cheesman, pp. 100–126 (Provo, Utah, 1988).

For a cultural anthropologist's approach to Nephite religious institutions and practices, see John L. Sorenson, *An Ancient American Setting for the Book of Mormon* (Salt Lake City, 1985).

JOHN W. WELCH

BOOK OF MORMON STUDIES

Since the publication of the BOOK OF MORMON in 1830, a substantial amount of material analyzing, defending, and attacking it has been published. Studies of this complex record have taken various approaches, for the book itself invites close scrutiny and rewards patient and reflective research.

For most Latter-day Saints the primary purpose of scripture study is not to prove to themselves the truth of scriptural records—which they already accept—but to gain wisdom and understanding about the teachings of these sacred writings and to apply in daily life gospel principles learned there. Because of the origins of the Book of Mormon, however, many people have also explored the secondary features of this document: its vocabulary, style, factual assertions, main themes, and subtle nuances.

Book of Mormon research has generally followed many of the same forms as biblical research. In both fields, writings range from expository texts to doctrinal, historical, geographical, textual, literary, and comparative commentaries. But there are also several salient differences. For example, unlike the authors of the Bible, the prophets, compilers, and abridgers of the Book of Mormon frequently state explicitly the dates when they worked, their purposes in writing, and the sources from which they drew, thus clarifying many compositional and interpretive issues; furthermore, academic and archaeological studies of the Book of Mormon are more limited than in biblical research because the earliest extant text is Joseph SMITH's 1829 English translation and the precise locations of Book of Mormon settlements are unknown. Nevertheless, a significant number of internal and comparative analyses have been pursued. The works of the following individuals are most notable.

ALEXANDER CAMPBELL. The founder of the Disciples of Christ and a colleague of Sidney RIGDON before Rigdon converted to Mormonism, Alexander Campbell (1788–1866) composed a response to the Book of Mormon that he published on February 7, 1831, in his paper the *Millennial Harbinger* (reprinted as a pamphlet called *Delusions*). In it, Campbell challenged the idea that the Book of Mormon had been written by multiple ancient prophets and attacked the character of Joseph Smith. He said that the book was solely the product of Joseph Smith, written by him alone and "certainly conceived in one cranium" (p. 13). Campbell claimed that the book simply represents the reflections of Joseph Smith on the social, political, and religious controversies of his day: "infant baptism, ordination, the trinity, regeneration, repentance, justification, the fall of man, the atonement, transubstantiation, fasting, penance, church government, religious experience, the call to the ministry, the general resurrection, eternal punishment, who may baptize, and even the question of freemasonry, republican government, and the rights of man" (p. 13). He also asserted that the Book of Mormon misunderstands Israelite and Jewish history (portraying the Nephites as Christians hundreds of years before the birth of Christ) and is written in abysmal English grammar. Campbell characterized Joseph Smith as a "knave" who was "ignorant" and "impudent" (p. 11; *see also* ANTI-MORMON PUBLICATIONS). *Delusions* is significant among Book of Mormon studies because in many ways it set the agenda for most subsequent critiques of the Book of Mormon (e.g., that the book derives from, or responds to, various trends in early-nineteenth-century upstate New York). Subsequently, however, Campbell changed his position, adopting the Spaulding-Rigdon theory, according to which Sidney Rigdon purloined a copy of a manuscript by Solomon Spaulding, developed from it what became the Book of Mormon, which he passed on to Joseph Smith in the late 1820s, and later pretended to have met Joseph for the first time in 1830 (*see* SPAULDING MANUSCRIPT).

ORSON PRATT. In *Divine Authenticity of the Book of Mormon* (1850–1851), a series of six pamphlets, Orson Pratt (1811–1881), a member of the Quorum of the Twelve Apostles, drew together early Latter-day Saint thinking about the Book of Mormon. He argued on logical grounds for the divine authenticity of the Book of Mormon, confronted criticisms of it, and presented evidence in favor of its truth, relying heavily on biblical and historical evidences. He did not discuss the contents of the Book of Mormon directly, but addressed ideas of other churches that hindered their acceptance, or even serious consideration, of the Book of Mormon.

The first three pamphlets discussed the nature of revelation, giving evidence to support Pratt's claim that continued communication from God is both necessary and scriptural. The final three pamphlets reported on many witnesses who received heavenly visions substantiating Joseph Smith's claims (*see* BOOK OF MORMON WITNESSES), and asserted that the divinity of the Book of Mormon is confirmed by many miracles, similar to those recorded in the Bible, experienced by Latter-day Saints. Finally, he appealed to prophetic evidence for the Book of Mormon, taken from Daniel and Isaiah. In an 1872 discourse, Pratt proposed a geography for the Book of Mormon that

George Reynolds (1842–1909) held many Church positions in England before coming to America in 1865. He served as secretary to the First Presidency until the end of his life and was called as one of the First Seven Presidents of the Seventy in 1890. He was the first to write extensive commentaries on the Book of Mormon. His Book of Mormon concordance required twenty-one years to produce. Courtesy University of Utah.

has greatly influenced LDS thinking (*see* BOOK OF MORMON GEOGRAPHY).

GEORGE REYNOLDS AND JANNE M. SJODAHL. During the nineteenth century, most defenses of, and attacks on, the Book of Mormon were based primarily on reason, on examinations of the environment contemporary with the book, or on the Bible. But George Reynolds (1842–1909) and Janne M. Sjodahl (1853–1939), in their seven-volume *Commentary on the Book of Mormon* (reissued 1955–1961), investigated the plausibility of the claims of the Book of Mormon by examining external evidences of a historical, cultural, linguistic, or religious nature from the Old World and the New. Although their examples and explanations are often not heavily documented and were sometimes mistaken, this work was the first major effort to study the cultural and historical contexts of the Book of Mormon (i.e., to place the book in a historical context by adducing relevant materials from the ancient world).

Whereas in *The Story of the Book of Mormon*, an earlier work, Reynolds had agreed with Orson Pratt on Book of Mormon geography, in their *Commentary* he and Sjodahl placed geography at a low level of priority and were interested primarily in establishing an internally consistent map of all Book of Mormon sites, without attempting to identify those sites with modern locations (Reynolds, pp. 19, 49, 301–330; Reynolds and Sjodahl, Vol. 1, pp. ix–xi). Reynolds eventually authored nearly three hundred articles and several Book of Mormon resource works. Sjodahl published *An Introduction to the Study of the Book of Mormon*, featuring a wide variety of cultural and linguistic theories.

B. H. ROBERTS. Among the most influential Latter-day Saint writers of his time, B. H. Roberts (1857–1933) wrote widely on a variety of Church-related topics, including the Book of Mormon. Like Reynolds and Sjodahl, he was interested not only in the theological implications of the Book of Mormon but also in its historical, geographical, and cultural setting (1909, Vol. 2, pp. 143–44, 162, 347–458; Vol. 3, pp. 3–92). Roberts was not afraid to ask difficult—and, for him, sometimes unanswerable—questions about the Book of Mormon, but affirmed his faith in the Book of Mormon to the end of his life (1985, pp. 61–148; J. Welch, *Ensign* 16 [Mar. 1986]:58–62).

FRANCIS KIRKHAM. In his two-volume study *A New Witness for Christ in America* (1942), Francis Kirkham (1877–1972) examined the 1820s historical evidence relating to the coming forth of the Book of Mormon. Kirkham showed that the testimonies of Joseph Smith and his friends are consistent and coherent, while those of his enemies are frequently inconsistent and contradictory. He carefully documented how alternative explanations for the origin of the Book of Mormon sometimes changed or were abandoned. While favoring the traditional view of Book of Mormon origins, Kirkham allowed all to speak for themselves with little commentary. He liberally presented the primary materials, published and unpublished, from libraries and archives across the United States. His use of the widest available range of primary sources set a new standard in the study of the origins of the Book of Mormon.

Kirkham's second volume of *A New Witness*

for Christ in America (1951) examined the alternative explanations of Book of Mormon origins. Regarding the assertion that Joseph Smith wrote the book personally, Kirkham presented statements of some who knew Joseph well, with views representing both sides of the issue of whether he was capable of writing such a book. Kirkham also gave extensive evidence to show that the Spaulding hypothesis was fraught with difficulties. The theory provides only the most circumstantial and dubious evidence for Rigdon's theft of the manuscript and for his passing it on to Joseph Smith with no one else's knowledge. Even though the Spaulding hypothesis has fallen into disfavor as an explanation of the Book of Mormon during the past several decades, it is still occasionally revived.

HUGH W. NIBLEY. In his considerable corpus of writings on the Book of Mormon, written over a period of some forty years, Hugh W. Nibley (b. 1910) has taken several approaches, mainly historical contextualization based on the internal claims of the Book of Mormon as a document of people who come from the ancient Near East, but also testing the book for authenticity on the basis of internal evidence alone, and seeing the fateful collapse of mighty civilizations as an ominous warning to people today.

In *Lehi in the Desert* (1949–1952), after reviewing the great American archaeologist William F. Albright's criteria for determining the historical plausibility of ancient accounts, Nibley asks these questions about the story of Lehi: "Does it correctly reflect 'the cultural horizon and religious and social ideas and practices of the time'? Does it have authentic historical and geographical background? Is the *mise-en-scène* mythical, highly imaginative, or extravagantly improbable? Is its local color correct, and are its proper names convincing?" (*CWHN* 5:4). The proper approach to the Book of Mormon, according to Nibley, is simply to give the book the benefit of the doubt, granting that it is what it claims to be (a historically authentic ancient document of a people who originated in ancient Israel) and then testing the internal evidence of the book itself (names, cultural and religious ideas) against what can be known about the ancient Near East. When this is done, a picture emerges that is strikingly consistent with what can be determined about the ancient Near East. Most of Nibley's examples come from the Arabs, Egyptians, and Israelites.

Hugh W. Nibley (1910–), noted linguist and historian of religion, was one of the first to detect and explore numerous cultural similarities between ancient Near Eastern literatures and Book of Mormon texts. His candid wit and wide-ranging insights emphasize the relevance of the Book of Mormon to modern world circumstances (1989). Photographer: Mark A. Philbrick. Courtesy F.A.R.M.S.

With wit and erudition, Nibley argues against alternative explanations of the Book of Mormon. For example, in discussing Thomas O'Dea's environmentalist assertion that the book is obviously an American work, Nibley calls for greater specificity and uniqueness of the American sentiments that allegedly permeate the work (*CWHN* 8:185–86). With skillful parry and thrust, Nibley proceeds in his studies on the Book of Mormon, sometimes defending points in the book, sometimes taking the offensive against those who attack it, always enriching the reader's understanding of its setting. As a teacher, lecturer, and writer, Nibley has been widely influential on subsequent studies of the Book of Mormon.

JOHN L. SORENSON. Devoting his attention to Mesoamerica in an effort to understand better the geographical, anthropological, and cultural setting of BOOK OF MORMON PEOPLES, John L. Sorenson (b. 1924) examines the text of the Book of Mormon. He carefully analyzes the Mesoamerican evidence, particularly the geography, climatic conditions, modes of life and warfare, and archaeological remains in *An Ancient American Setting for the Book of Mormon*, in order to create a plausible, coherent matrix for understanding the book. With regard to Book of Mormon geography, Sorenson concludes that the events recorded in the Book of Mormon occurred in a fairly restricted area of southern Mexico and Guatemala:

> The narrow neck of land is the Isthmus of Tehuantepec. The east sea is the Gulf of Mexico or its component, the Gulf of Campeche. The west sea is the Pacific Ocean to the west of Mexico and Guatemala. The land southward comprises that portion of Mexico east and south of the Isthmus of Tehuantepec. . . . The land northward consists of part of Mexico west and north of the Isthmus of Tehuantepec. . . . The final battleground where both Jaredite and Nephite peoples met their end was around the Tuxtla Mountains of south-central Veracruz [pp. 46–47].

An Ancient American Setting for the Book of Mormon has placed the study of the ancient American background of the Book of Mormon on a scholarly footing as no previous work (*see* BOOK OF MORMON GEOGRAPHY).

CURRENT DIRECTIONS IN BOOK OF MORMON STUDIES. Much of the scholarly work on the Book of Mormon has been devoted to a fuller understanding of its theological riches or concerned with applying the Book of Mormon principle to "liken all scriptures unto us" (1 Ne. 19:23). Some of the recent publications of the Religious Studies Center at Brigham Young University have focused on various theological aspects of the Book of Mormon and on seeking life applications from the book (e.g., essays by various authors in Cheesman, in McConkie and Millet, and in Nyman and Tate).

Following the lead of Nibley, Sorenson, and others, several recent studies on the Book of Mormon have been concerned with enhancing an understanding of its Old World background and American setting. The research and publications of the Foundation for Ancient Research and Mormon

Studies (F.A.R.M.S.), the Society for Early Historic Archaeology (SEHA), and the Archaeological Research Institute have been particularly concerned with the historical and geographic context of the Book of Mormon.

In certain circles, one of the major focuses in current Book of Mormon studies is concerned with its historicity. Whereas in the past, positions on the Book of Mormon divided themselves roughly between those who accepted it as an inspired and historically authentic ancient document and those who rejected it in both these regards, several different lines of approach have developed.

According to one view—a position that has existed since even before its first publication—the Book of Mormon is a conscious fabrication of Joseph Smith. Those holding to this view see the book as reflecting no inspiration and having no historical value, although they may see some religious value in it as a statement of Joseph Smith's religious feelings. The assumption underlying this view may be either a doctrinaire rejection of divine intervention in human affairs or a specific rejection of Joseph Smith's claims to experience with the divine. Those maintaining this position may accept either the Spaulding theory or, more commonly, various environmentalist explanations for the contents of the book (*see* VIEW OF THE HEBREWS). One environmentalist explanation that has attracted some interest in the recent past among both believers and nonbelievers is based on the purported "magic worldview" that suffused the environment in which Joseph Smith grew up. However, this position has been heavily criticized and has not been widely received.

Another view of the Book of Mormon accepts its inspiration but rejects its historical authenticity, seeing it as in some sense inspired but not the product of antiquity, coming rather from the pen of Joseph Smith.

A third position accepts parts of the Book of Mormon as ancient, but views other parts of the book as inspired expansions on the text. This view has suffered because a concession that any part of the book is authentically ancient (and beyond the powers of Joseph Smith to have established through research) seems an admission that the Book of Mormon is what it claims to be and what has traditionally been claimed for it: that it is ancient.

While these views have been articulated by some members in the LDS community, the majority of LDS students of the Book of Mormon accept the traditional view of its divine authenticity and study it as both an ancient document and a tract for modern days, thereby enhancing their appreciation of, and benefit from, the book.

BIBLIOGRAPHY

For bibliographies, see annual issues of the *Review of Books on the Book of Mormon* and John W. Welch, Gary P. Gillum, and DeeAnn Hofer, *Comprehensive Bibliography of the Book of Mormon*, *F.A.R.M.S. Report*, Provo, Utah, 1982. For essays on Pratt, Reynolds, Roberts, Kirkham, Sperry, and Nibley, see articles in the *Ensign*, 1984–1986.

Bush, Lester E., Jr. "The Spalding Theory Then and Now." *Dialogue* 10 (Autumn 1977):40–69.

Cheesman, Paul R., ed. *The Book of Mormon: The Keystone Scripture*. Provo, Utah, 1988.

Clark, John. "A Key for Evaluating Nephite Geographies" (review of F. Richard Hauck, *Deciphering the Geography of the Book of Mormon*). *Review of Books on the Book of Mormon*, 1 (1989):20–70.

Kirkham, Francis W. *A New Witness for Christ in America*, rev. ed., 2 vols. Salt Lake City, 1959–1960.

McConkie, Joseph Fielding, and Robert L. Millet. *Doctrinal Commentary on the Book of Mormon*, 2 vols. Salt Lake City, 1987–1988.

Nibley, Hugh. *Lehi in the Desert/The World of the Jaredites/There Were Jaredites; An Approach to the Book of Mormon; Since Cumorah;* and *The Prophetic Book of Mormon*. In *CWHN* 5–8.

Nyman, Monte S., and Charles D. Tate, eds. *The Book of Mormon: First Nephi, The Doctrinal Foundation; Second Nephi, The Doctrinal Structure; Jacob Through Words of Mormon, to Learn with Joy*. Provo, Utah, 1988–1990.

Reynolds, George. *The Story of the Book of Mormon*. Salt Lake City, 1888.

———, and Janne M. Sjodahl. *Commentary on the Book of Mormon*, 5th ed., 7 vols. Salt Lake City, 1972.

Reynolds, Noel B., ed. *Book of Mormon Authorship: New Light on Ancient Origins*. Provo, Utah, 1982.

Ricks, Stephen D., and William J. Hamblin, eds. *Warfare in the Book of Mormon*. Salt Lake City, 1990.

Roberts, B. H. *New Witnesses for God*, Vols. 2–3. Salt Lake City, 1909.

———. *Studies of the Book of Mormon*, ed. B. Madsen. Urbana, Ill., 1985.

Sjodahl, Janne M. *An Introduction to the Study of the Book of Mormon*. Salt Lake City, 1927.

Sorenson, John L. *An Ancient American Setting for the Book of Mormon*. Salt Lake City, 1985.

Sperry, Sidney B. *Book of Mormon Compendium*. Salt Lake City, 1968.

STEPHEN D. RICKS

BOOK OF MORMON TRANSLATION BY JOSEPH SMITH

By its own terms, the Book of Mormon is a translation of an ancient book; yet Joseph SMITH knew no ancient languages at the time he dictated this text to his scribes. He and several of his close associates testified that the translation was accomplished "by the gift and power of God" (HC 1:315; see also D&C 1:29; 20:8).

Little is known about the translation process itself. Few details can be gleaned from comments made by Joseph's scribes and close associates. Only Joseph Smith knew the actual process, and he declined to describe it in public. At a Church conference in 1831, Hyrum Smith invited the Prophet to explain more fully how the Book of Mormon came forth. Joseph Smith responded that "it was not intended to tell the world all the particulars of the coming forth of the Book of Mormon; and . . . it was not expedient for him to relate these things" (HC 1:220).

Much is known, however, about when and where the work of translation occurred. The events are documented by several independent firsthand witnesses. Joseph Smith first obtained the GOLD PLATES at the hill CUMORAH in New York, in the early morning hours of September 22, 1827. To avoid local harassment and mobs, he moved to HARMONY, PENNSYLVANIA, in December 1827. There he copied and translated some of the characters from the plates, with his wife Emma and her brother Reuben Hale acting as scribes. In 1856, Emma recalled that Joseph dictated the translation to her word for word, spelled out the proper names, and would correct her scribal errors even though he could not see what she had written. At one point while translating, Joseph was surprised to learn that Jerusalem had walls around it (E. C. Briggs, "Interview with David Whitmer," *Saints' Herald* 31 [June 21, 1884]:396–97). Emma was once asked in a later interview if Joseph had read from any books or notes while dictating. She answered, "He had neither," and when pressed, added: "If he had anything of the kind he could not have concealed it from me" (*Saints' Herald* 26 [Oct. 1, 1879]:290).

Martin HARRIS came to Harmony in February 1828, and shortly afterward took a transcript and translation of some of the characters to New York City, where he showed them to Professor Charles Anthon at Columbia College (see ANTHON TRANSCRIPT). He returned fully satisfied that Joseph was telling the truth, and from April 12 to June 14, 1828, Harris acted as scribe while Joseph Smith translated the book of Lehi.

On June 15, 1828, Joseph and Emma's first son was born but died a few hours later. About July 15, Joseph learned that Martin Harris had lost the 116 pages they had translated (see MANUSCRIPT, LOST 116 PAGES), and subsequently the angel MORONI took the plates and the interpreters temporarily from Joseph, who was chastened but reassured by the Lord that the work would go forth (D&C 3:15–16).

On September 22, 1828, the plates and translation tools were returned to Joseph Smith, and during that winter he translated "a few more pages" (D&C 5:30). The work progressed slowly until April 5, 1829, when Oliver COWDERY, a school teacher who had seen the Lord and the plates in a vision (*PWJS*, p. 8), arrived in Harmony and offered his scribal services to Joseph. Virtually all of the English text of the Book of Mormon was then translated between April 7 and the last week of June, less than sixty working days.

The dictation flowed smoothly. From the surviving portions of the Original Manuscript it appears that Joseph dictated about a dozen words at a time. Oliver would read those words back for verification, and then they would go on. Emma later added that after a meal or a night's rest, Joseph would begin, without prompting, where he had previously left off (*The Saints' Herald* 26 [Oct. 1, 1879]:290). No time was taken for research, internal cross-checking, or editorial rewriting. In 1834 Oliver wrote: "These were days never to be forgotten—to sit under the sound of a voice dictated by the inspiration of heaven, awakened the utmost gratitude of this bosom! Day after day I continued, uninterrupted, to write from his mouth as he translated" (*Messenger and Advocate* 1 [Oct. 1834]:14).

During April, May, and June 1829, many events occurred in concert with the translation of the Book of Mormon. By May 15, the account of Christ's ministry in 3 Nephi had been translated. That text explicitly mentions the necessity of being baptized by proper authority, and this injunction inspired Joseph Smith and Oliver Cowdery to pray, leading to the restoration of the Aaronic Priesthood on May 15 (JS—H 1:68–74) and of the Melchizedek Priesthood soon afterward (see AARONIC PRIESTHOOD: RESTORATION OF;

MELCHIZEDEK PRIESTHOOD: RESTORATION OF). Time was also required for trips to Colesville, New York, for supplies (thirty miles away); to earn money to purchase paper; to obtain a federal copyright on June 11, 1829; to baptize Samuel and Hyrum Smith; to preach to several interested people; and, during the first week of June, to move by buckboard over 100 miles to the Peter Whitmer farm in Fayette, New York, where about 150 final pages were translated, with some of the Whitmers also acting as scribes. The work was completed before the end of June, at which time the Three and the Eight Witnesses were allowed to see the plates (see BOOK OF MORMON WITNESSES).

The original manuscript for Helaman 1:15–16 shows how the name "Coriantumr" was first written by Oliver Cowdery phonetically but was then crossed out and spelled correctly on the same line as the translation progressed. Witnesses stated that Joseph Smith spelled the proper names that he translated.

Most evidence supports the idea that Joseph and Oliver began their work in April 1829 with the speech of BENJAMIN (Mosiah 1–6), translated to the end of the book of Moroni in May, then translated the Title Page, and finally translated the small plates of Nephi (1 Nephi–Omni) and the Words of Mormon before the end of June (Welch and Rathbone). The text of the Title Page, "the last leaf" of the plates of Mormon (*HC* 1:71), was used as the book's description on the copyright form filed on June 11, 1829.

Many factors, including divine sources of knowledge and Joseph's own spiritual efforts and personal vocabulary, apparently played their roles in producing the English text of the Book of Mormon. Some accounts emphasize the divine factor. Years later, David WHITMER indicated that words would appear to Joseph on something resembling a piece of parchment and that he would read the words off to his scribe (*An Address to All Believers in Christ*, 1887, p. 12). Other accounts indicate that human effort was also involved. When Oliver Cowdery attempted to translate in April 1829, he was told by the Lord: "You must study it out in your mind; then you must ask me if it be right" (D&C 9:8). According to David Whitmer, Joseph could only translate when he was humble and faithful. One morning something had gone wrong about the house; Joseph could not translate a single syllable until he went into an orchard, prayed, and then he and Emma made amends (*CHC* 1:131). Joseph's ability to translate apparently increased as the work progressed.

Most reports state that throughout the project Joseph used the "Nephite interpreters" or, for convenience, he would use a SEER STONE (see *CHC* 1:128–30). Both instruments were sometimes called by others the URIM AND THUMMIM. In 1830, Oliver Cowdery is reported to have testified in court that these tools enabled Joseph "to read in English, the reformed Egyptian characters, which were engraved on the plates" (Benton, *Evangelical Magazine and Gospel Advocate* 2 [Apr. 9, 1831]:15). In an 1891 interview, William Smith indicated that when his brother Joseph used the "interpreters" (which were like a silver bow twisted into the shape of a figure eight with two stones between the rims of the bow connected by a rod to a breastplate), his hands were left free to hold the plates. Other late reports mention a variety of further details, but they cannot be historically confirmed or denied.

Regarding the nature of the English translation, its language is unambiguous and straightforward. Joseph once commented that the book was "translated into our own language" (*TPJS*, p. 17; cf. D&C 1:24). In several chapters, for good and useful reasons, this meant that the language would follow the King James idiom of the day (*see CWHN* 8:212–16; Welch, 1990, pp. 134–63). It also assured that the manuscript would contain human misspellings and grammatical oddities, implying that if it had been translated in another decade its phraseology and vocabulary might have been slightly different.

At the same time, circumstantial evidence in the English text suggests that the translation was quite precise. For example, the independent and identical translations of 1 Nephi 1:8 and of Alma 36:22 (precisely quoting twenty-one of Lehi's words in 1 Nephi 1:8) typify the internal accuracy manifested in this long and complex record. Moreover, several formulaic terms, Hebraisms, stylistic indications of multiple authorship, varieties of parallelism and extended chiasmus (*see* BOOK OF MORMON AUTHORSHIP; BOOK OF MORMON LITERATURE), as well as certain Semitic proper names and some textual variants, not at all evident from the King James Bible, corroborate the claim that the translation was faithful to a consistent underlying text.

Naturally, it is rarely possible to translate exactly the same range of meanings, word for word, from one language into another, and thus opinions have varied about the nature of the correspondence of the ancient text to the English translation. David Whitmer is quoted as saying that "frequently one character would make two lines of manuscript while others made but a word or two words" (*Deseret News*, Nov. 10, 1881). Nevertheless, the linguistic relationship between the English translation and the characters on the plates cannot be determined without consulting the Nephite original, which was returned to the angel Moroni in 1829 (*see* MORONI, VISITATIONS OF).

BIBLIOGRAPHY

Roberts, B. H. "Translation of the Book of Mormon." *IE* 9 (Apr. 1906):706–136.

Ricks, Stephen D. "Joseph Smith's Means and Methods of Translating the Book of Mormon." *F.A.R.M.S. Paper.* Provo, Utah, 1984.

Welch, John W. "How Long Did It Take Joseph Smith to Translate the Book of Mormon?" *Ensign* 18 (Jan. 1988):46.

———. *The Sermon at the Temple and the Sermon on the Mount*, pp. 130–63. Salt Lake City, 1990.

Welch, John W., and Tim Rathbone. "The Translation of the Book of Mormon: Basic Historical Information." *F.A.R.M.S. Paper*. Provo, Utah, 1986.

JOHN W. WELCH
TIM RATHBONE

BOOK OF MORMON TRANSLATIONS

After the Prophet Joseph SMITH's original translation of the Book of Mormon from the gold plates into English in 1829 and the return of those plates to the angel Moroni, no translations from English into other languages appeared until the 1850s. During the late nineteenth and early twentieth centuries, the Church produced translations of the Book of Mormon irregularly, often in groups of languages, and at widely separated intervals. However, in the 1970s and later, translations from the English text of the Book of Mormon became systematic and frequent.

Making the Book of Mormon and other STANDARD WORKS available in many languages is foreshadowed by the divine injunction "that every man shall hear the fulness of the gospel in his own tongue, and in his own language" (D&C 90:11). As missions were opened on the continent of Europe in 1850 and 1851, Church leaders in many of the newly opened missions mounted simultaneous translation efforts. The Danish edition (1851), produced by Erastus Snow for the Scandinavian Mission from a Danish translation by Peter Olsen Hansen, was the first printed (*see* SCANDINAVIA, THE CHURCH IN). At the same time, John TAYLOR supervised translations into French by Curtis E. Bolton and German by George P. Dykes, while Lorenzo SNOW was working on the Italian edition and John Davis on a Welsh one. All of these appeared in 1852, and culminated with George Q. Cannon's translation of the Book of Mormon into Hawaiian in 1855. No further translations were published for twenty years.

In 1875 Meliton G. Trejo and Daniel W. Jones produced the first translation of selections from the Book of Mormon into Spanish. This ninety-six-page document, comprising only the books of 1 and 2 Nephi, Omni, 3 Nephi, and Mormon, was the first partial translation and one of only two partial printings of the Book of Mormon in book form at the time. (The other was the publication of 1 Nephi–Words of Mormon in the DESERET ALPHABET.) Trejo and James Z. Stewart completed a translation of the entire book into Spanish in 1886. The remainder of the nineteenth century produced three further translations: Swedish (1878), Maori (1889), and Dutch (1890). Sixteen more, including the first in Asian languages and several in South Pacific tongues, appeared between 1903 and 1977.

In 1971, in support of an expanding missionary program, the Church organized a Translation Services Department (*see* ORGANIZATION) to direct a systematic program of scripture translation. They began with the production of a large number of translations of *Selections from the Book of Mormon*, designed to place selected chapters in the hands of missionaries, general readers, and members as quickly as possible and to train translators. The *Selections*, chosen and approved by the FIRST PRESIDENCY and the QUORUM OF THE TWELVE APOSTLES, were the same in all languages, and consisted of the following:

Book	Chapters
1 Nephi	1–7, 16–18
2 Nephi	1–4; 5:1–20; 9, 29, 31–33
Enos	all
Mosiah	2–5, 17, 18
Alma	5, 11, 12, 32, 34, 39–42
Helaman	13–16
3 Nephi	1, 8, 11–30
4 Nephi	all
Mormon	1, 4, 6–9
Moroni	all

This *Selections* volume is being progressively replaced by full translations. As of 1990, the entire Book of Mormon was available in 36 languages (including English), while *Selections* was available in 44 additional languages.

Retranslations of early editions began in 1952 with the second translation into Spanish. Subsequently, the Japanese, Italian, and German editions were retranslated; other retranslations appeared as *Selections* from 1980 on. With the issuance of the 1981 English edition of the Book of Mormon (*see* BOOK OF MORMON EDITIONS), the Church Translation Department began systematically reviewing all existing translations, setting priorities for retranslation, and producing new editions more in conformity with the English format.

BIBLIOGRAPHY

"Book of Mormon Editions, Translated and Published." *Deseret News 1989–90 Church Almanac*. Salt Lake City, 1988.

The Millennial Star, Vols. 13–14 (1850–1851).

HUGH G. STOCKS

BOOK OF MORMON WITNESSES

Beginning with the first edition of 1830, the Book of Mormon has generally contained two sets of testimonies—the "Testimony of Three Witnesses" and the "Testimony of Eight Witnesses." When Joseph SMITH first obtained the GOLD PLATES, he was told to show them to no one. As translation progressed, he and those assisting him learned, both in the pages of the Book and by additional revelation, that three special witnesses would know, by the power of God, "that these things are true" and that several besides himself would see the plates and testify to their existence (Ether 5:2–4; 2 Ne. 27:12–13; D&C 5:11–13). The testimonies of the witnesses affirm that these things occurred.

The witnesses were men known for truthfulness and sobriety. Though each of the Three Witnesses was eventually excommunicated from the Church (two returned), none ever denied or retracted his published testimony. Each reaffirmed at every opportunity the veracity of his testimony and the reality of what he had seen and experienced.

A June 1829 revelation confirmed that Oliver COWDERY, David WHITMER, and Martin HARRIS would be the Three Witnesses (D&C 17). Soon thereafter, they, with Joseph Smith, retired to the woods near FAYETTE, NEW YORK, and prayed for the promised divine manifestation. The "Testimony of Three Witnesses" summarizes the supernatural event that followed, when an angel appeared and showed them the plates and engravings and they heard the Lord declare that the Book of Mormon was "translated by the gift and power of God." They said that the same divine voice "commanded us that we should bear record of it."

Joseph Smith's mother later recounted Joseph's great relief at no longer being the sole witness of the divine experiences of the restoration (*see* LAW OF WITNESSES). That others had also seen an angel and "will have to testify to the truth of what I have said for now they know for themselves" relieved him of a great burden (Lucy Smith Preliminary Manuscript, Church Archives).

Soon afterward, at the Smith farm in New York, eight others were allowed to view and handle the plates: Christian Whitmer, Jacob Whitmer, Peter Whitmer, Jr., John Whitmer, Hiram Page, Joseph Smith, Sr., Hyrum Smith, and Samuel H. Smith. Their signed "Testimony of Eight Witnesses" reports that Joseph Smith showed these eight men the metal plates, which they "hefted" while turning the individual "leaves" and examining the engravings of "curious workmanship." In 1829 the word *curious* carried the meaning of the Latin word for "careful," suggesting that the plates were wrought "with care and art." Five of these Eight Witnesses remained solidly with the Church; John Whitmer was excommunicated in 1838, and his brother Jacob Whitmer and brother-in-law Hiram Page then became inactive.

Most of these eleven witnesses were members of the large Smith and Whitmer families—families who had assisted in guarding and in translating the ancient record. Not surprisingly, other family members reported indirect contact with the plates and the translation. Young William Smith once helped his brother Joseph carry the plates wrapped in a work frock. Joseph's wife Emma SMITH felt the pliable plates as she dusted around the cloth-covered record on her husband's translating table. Burdened with daily chores and caring for her family and visitors working on the translation, Mother Whitmer (Peter Whitmer, Sr.'s, wife) was shown the plates by a heavenly messenger to assure her that the work was of God.

Martin Harris, a prosperous farmer of Palmyra, New York, who had long sought a religion fulfilling biblical prophecy, assisted with the translation previous to his experience as a witness. In 1828 he spent two months transcribing as Joseph Smith dictated the first major segment of Book of Mormon translation—116 handwritten pages. After Martin lost these pages, he wrote no more for the Prophet, but he later financed the publication of the book.

Oliver Cowdery was the main scribe for the Book of Mormon. A schoolteacher, he learned of the gold plates and the translation while boarding with Joseph Smith's parents near Palmyra, New York. In early April 1829, Oliver walked from the

Smith home to HARMONY, PENNSYLVANIA, where Joseph Smith was translating. On the way Oliver visited his friend David Whitmer, who also developed an intense interest in the new scripture. When persecution increased in Harmony, David came as requested and moved Joseph and Oliver to his family farm near Fayette (more than 100 miles away), about June 1.

Joseph Smith later recalled the insistent pleading of Harris, Whitmer, and Cowdery after they learned that three would be permitted to see the plates. The June 1829 revelation confirmed that they would be the Three Witnesses—and that they would then testify both from firsthand knowledge and "by the power of God" to the end "that my servant Joseph Smith, Jr., may not be destroyed" (D&C 17:3–4). Of the perhaps 200 recorded interviews with the Three Witnesses, a significant percentage stress the spiritual intensity of the witnesses as they described the angel and the plates. By themselves, the Prophet's reputation and claims were vulnerable, but the testimony of additional reputable, solemn witnesses who shared a divine experience added credibility.

Lucy Smith's autobiography records the overwhelming gratitude of the Three Witnesses as they returned to the Whitmer house after sharing this experience. Joseph Smith's own history gives the fullest details of the event: repeated prayers followed by a vision given simultaneously to the Prophet, Cowdery, and Whitmer, and soon after a nearly identical vision experienced by the Prophet with Harris. According to Joseph, the intense glory of God enveloped the natural surroundings, and in this divine light the angel appeared, carefully displayed the plates, specifically counseled David Whitmer—the only one of the three who did not eventually return to the Church—to endure to the end, and the voice of God declared the book divine (HC 1:54–56).

By early 1838, disagreements on Church policies brought disaffection and excommunication for each of the Three Witnesses, and they separated; Cowdery died in 1850, Harris in 1875, and Whitmer in 1888. Throughout their lives, each witness freely answered questions about his firsthand experience with the angel and the plates. Obviously not relying on Joseph Smith's account, which was not written until the months following their excommunication, each spoke spontaneously and independently; yet the details harmonized with each other and with Joseph Smith's history.

Joseph Smith and the Eight Witnesses, by Harold T. (Dale) Kilbourn (1984), illustrates Joseph Smith allowing the eight witnesses to touch the gold plates from which the Book of Mormon was translated. "We did handle with our hands; and we also saw the engravings thereon, all of which has the appearance of ancient work, and of curious workmanship. And this we bear record with words of soberness."

The alienation of the witnesses from the Church stemmed largely from conflicts regarding authority. After receiving revelation, the Three Witnesses felt they shared equally with Joseph Smith in foundational experiences, and their certainty about a past vision contributed to their inflexibility concerning future revelations. They sided with the Prophet's critics who reacted negatively to the failure of the Kirtland Safety Society (*see* KIRTLAND ECONOMY), and they opposed Joseph Smith's vigorous doctrinal and administrative leadership. After their excommunication, each felt deep rejection, resulting, predictably, in their harsh criticisms of Church leadership. Even in these circumstances, each of the Three Witnesses continued to maintain vigorously the authenticity of their published testimony. None expressed any doubt as to what they had testified. Both Oliver Cowdery and Martin Harris returned to the Church at the end of their lives; David Whitmer retained religious independence but to the end aggressively defended the Book of Mormon.

Skeptics have discounted the "Testimony of Three Witnesses" on the ground of collusion or deception. Yet each of the three was a respected and independent member of non-Mormon society, active in his community. Their lives, fully documented, clearly demonstrate their honesty and intelligence. David Whitmer repeatedly reacted against charges of possible "delusion." To one skeptic, he responded: "Of course we were in the spirit when we had the view . . . but we were in the body also, and everything was as natural to us, as it is at any time" (Anderson, p. 87). Perhaps their later alienation makes them even more credible as witnesses, for no collusion could have withstood their years of separation from the Church and from each other.

The testimonies of the Three and Eight Witnesses balance the supernatural and the natural, the one stressing the angel and heavenly voice, the other the existence of a tangible record on gold plates. To the end of their lives, each of the Three said he had seen the plates, and each of the Eight insisted that he had handled them. Most of the Eight and all of the Three Witnesses reiterated their Book of Mormon testimonies just before death. Together with Joseph Smith they fulfill Nephi's prophecy: "They shall testify to the truth of the book and the things therein" (2 Ne. 27:12).

BIBLIOGRAPHY

Contributions of the Three Witnesses to the translation of the Book of Mormon are detailed in Lucy Mack Smith, *Biographical Sketches of Joseph Smith the Prophet and His Progenitors for Many Generations* (Liverpool, 1853 [reprinted Salt Lake City, 1902 under the title *History of the Prophet Joseph by His Mother Lucy Mack Smith*]). Joseph Smith's recollections of the events of June 1829 are found in Dean C. Jessee, ed., *The Papers of Joseph Smith*, Vol. 1 (Salt Lake City, 1989) (see transcriptions of the 1839 draft and 1839 manuscript history). See also Joseph Smith's published *History of the Church*.

For the Witnesses' testimonies, and their lives outside the Church, see Richard Lloyd Anderson, *Investigating the Book of Mormon Witnesses* (corr. ed.; Salt Lake City, 1989). Primary documents concerning their testimonies appear in Preston Nibley, *Witnesses of the Book of Mormon* (Salt Lake City, 1953). For life sketches, see Andrew Jenson, *Latter-day Saints Biographical Encyclopedia*, Vol. 1 (Salt Lake City, 1901). Profiles for most of the Witnesses are also in Lyndon Cook, *Revelations of the Prophet Joseph Smith* (Salt Lake City, 1985).

RICHARD LLOYD ANDERSON

BOOK OF MOSES

The book of Moses is an extract of several chapters from Genesis in the JOSEPH SMITH TRANSLATION OF THE BIBLE (JST) and constitutes one of the texts in the PEARL OF GREAT PRICE. The Prophet Joseph SMITH began an inspired revision of the Old Testament in June 1830 to restore and clarify vital points of history and doctrine missing from the Bible.

As for other ancient books, the original title of the first chapter of Moses may have been its opening line, "The words of God" (Moses 1:1). The account deals with Moses' revelation, and beginning with chapter 2 largely parallels Genesis 1:1–6:13. The revelation came to Moses after his call to deliver the Israelites from bondage in Egypt (Moses 1:26). Much of it concerns God's dealings with Adam and Eve and their immediate posterity following their expulsion from the GARDEN OF EDEN, a topic on which the current text of Genesis is silent. Structurally, a series of orienting visions (chap. 1) is followed by a revelation of the Creation and its aftermath (2:1–8:1). Embedded within this revelation is an extended account of ENOCH (6:25–51; 7:1–8:1), which itself quotes from a record of Adam (6:51–68). A narrative concerning Enoch's descendants, chiefly Noah, appears next (8:2–30).

An outline of the book of Moses follows:

Chapter 1. God reveals himself and his creations to Moses; Satan tries to deceive Moses; God's work and glory are characterized.

Chapter 2. God reveals to Moses—and commands him to write—the creation of the HEAVENS and the EARTH; man has dominion over other living things.

Chapter 3. All things were created in a spirit state before being created naturally on the earth; man and woman are created in God's image.

Chapter 4. Satan, who had rebelled in the pre-earthly council, tempts Eve; Adam and Eve transgress and are expelled from the Garden, becoming subject to death (*see* DEVIL).

Chapter 5. Children are born to Adam and Eve; Adam offers animal sacrifice as a type and shadow of the anticipated Savior's atoning sacrifice; the gospel of the future Jesus Christ is preached; Cain rebels, and wickedness spreads.

Chapter 6. Adam and his faithful posterity have a "pure and undefiled" language, both written and spoken, and keep records (*see* ADAMIC LANGUAGE); Enoch preaches the word of God and proclaims that the plan of salvation was revealed to Adam; faith, repentance, baptism, and the gift of the Holy Ghost are taught.

Chapter 7. God reveals himself to Enoch, who preaches and establishes the city of ZION; Enoch foresees the coming of Christ, his atonement and his resurrection; Enoch foresees the

RESTORATION of the gospel in the LAST DAYS, the NEW JERUSALEM, and the second coming of the Savior.

Chapter 8. Great wickedness arises at the time of Noah; he and his sons preach the gospel, but it goes unheeded; all flesh is destroyed by the flood.

A comparison of the book of Moses with Old Testament pseudepigraphic texts shows parallels not found in the present text of Genesis. For example, Adam and Eve were to offer sacrifices to God after being driven from the Garden (Moses 5:5–7; cf. *Life of Adam and Eve*, 29.4), and Satan rebelled against God and was expelled from heaven (Moses 4:3–4; cf. *Life*, 12–16).

A major point of doctrine restored by the book of Moses is that the gospel of salvation was preached "from the beginning" (Moses 5:58), an idea echoed both by Paul's statement that the gospel was preached to Abraham (Gal. 3:8) and by the Book of Mormon (Jacob 4:4–5; 7:10–11; cf. D&C 29:41–42). Similarly, Eusebius (c. A.D. 263–339) maintained that the teaching of Christianity was neither new nor strange and that the religion of the patriarchs was identical with that of the Christians (*Ecclesiastical History* 1.2.1–22).

In this connection, the book of Moses clarifies the fact that Adam and Eve understood the coming mission of Jesus Christ (Moses 6:51–63). Sacrificial offerings, Adam learned, were "a similitude of the sacrifice of the Only Begotten" (5:6–8). Further, Adam was baptized in water, received the Holy Ghost (5:9; 6:64–68), and was taught the plan of salvation (6:62). Adam and Eve and their posterity were also taught the purpose of the Fall and rejoiced in the Lord's plan for redemption (5:10–12).

The book of Moses augments the biblical account of Enoch, who is briefly referred to in Genesis 5:22–24 as one who "walked with God." This restoration of Moses' account includes the fact that Enoch beheld in a vision the Savior's ministry (Moses 7:55–57), the SPIRIT WORLD (6:35–36; 7:56–57), the restoration of the gospel in the last days (7:62), and the second advent of the Savior (7:60, 65). Enoch's importance in the book of Moses parallels his significant role in other Enoch texts (Nibley, p. vii).

BIBLIOGRAPHY

Charlesworth, James H. *The Old Testament Pseudepigrapha*, Vol. 2, p. 285. Garden City, N.Y., 1983, 1985.

Nibley, Hugh. *Enoch The Prophet*. In *CWHN*, 2. Salt Lake City, 1986.

Reynolds, Noel B. "The Brass Plates Version of Genesis." In *By Study and Also by Faith*, ed. J. Lundquist and S. Ricks, Vol. 2, pp. 136–73. Salt Lake City, 1990.

BRUCE T. TAYLOR

BOOK OF REMEMBRANCE

From antiquity God has commanded his people to keep records. In the days of Adam the people wrote a book of remembrance "by the spirit of inspiration" (Moses 6:5) to identify the faithful, to "know" their fathers (Moses 6:45–46), to define "the right of priesthood" (Abr. 1:31), and to promote literacy (see Moses 6:6). Biblical records indicate similar practices (see Ezra 2:62; Neh. 7:5; Ezek. 13:9; Mal. 3:16). NEPHI₁, in the Book of Mormon, stressed the importance of family history. In 1 Nephi 3–5, the Lord commanded LEHI to obtain the brass plates containing a history of his ancestors before leaving Jerusalem, to "enlarge their memory" (Alma 37:8) so that his posterity might know whence and from whom they came and might not lose the language of their fathers. Later, the Savior admonished the Nephites to be accurate and complete in their record keeping (3 Ne. 23:7–13). He also quoted Malachi 3:16–18, which includes a statement about keeping a book of remembrance (3 Ne. 24:16–18).

Latter-day Saints are encouraged to prepare family records as a Book of Remembrance, containing patriarchal blessings, records of ordinations and other sacred information, as well as personal and family histories, spiritual experiences, and other evidences of God's goodness and love (D&C 85:9; 128:7–8, 24). As a latter-day prophet said, "Those who keep a book of remembrance are more likely to keep the Lord in remembrance in their daily lives. Journals are a way of counting our blessings and of leaving an inventory of these blessings for our posterity" (Kimball, p. 76).

BIBLIOGRAPHY

Kimball, Spencer W. "Listen to the Prophets." *Ensign* (May 1978):76.

CYNTHIA M. GARDNER

BORN IN THE COVENANT

Latter-day Saints make several formal COVENANTS with God such as baptism, confirmation, ordination to the priesthood, and eternal marriage, commonly called temple marriage. A temple marriage or SEALING refers to the ceremony in which a man and a woman are married (sealed) to each other for TIME AND ETERNITY in a temple by the AUTHORITY of the holy priesthood. Children born to the couple after this marriage are automatically sealed to their parents eternally and are spoken of as having been born in the covenant.

Children born to parents not members of the Church or to members who have not been married (sealed) in a temple by priesthood authority are not born in the covenant. However, if these parents subsequently are sealed in temple covenants they can have their children sealed to them, and can secure the same eternal family ties as if all were born in the covenant.

For the eternal blessings of being sealed as a family member to be valid, each must remain faithful to his or her covenants.

[*See also* Salvation of the Dead.]

RALPH L. COTTRELL, JR.

BORN OF GOD

Born of God or "born again" refers to the personal spiritual experience in which repentant individuals receive a forgiveness of sins and a witness from God that if they continue to live the COMMANDMENTS and endure to the end, they will inherit ETERNAL LIFE. The scriptures teach that just as each individual is "born into the world by water, and blood, and the spirit," so must one be "born again" of water and the Spirit and be cleansed by the blood of Christ (John 3:5; Moses 6:59). To be born of God implies a sanctifying process by which the old or NATURAL MAN is supplanted by the new spiritual man who enjoys the companionship of the Holy Ghost and hence is no longer disposed to commit sin (Col. 3:9–10; Mosiah 3:19; *TPJS*, p. 51). When individuals are born again they are spiritually begotten sons and daughters of God and more specifically of Jesus Christ (Mosiah 5:7; 27:25). The Book of Mormon prophet ALMA₁ calls this inner transformation a "mighty change in your hearts" (Alma 5:14).

LDS scripture and literature contain numerous examples of individuals who have undergone this process of spiritual rebirth. Enos relates that after "mighty prayer and supplication" the Lord declared that his sins had been forgiven (Enos 1:1–8). After King Benjamin's discourse, the people said that the Spirit had "wrought a mighty change in us, or in our hearts," and that they had "no more disposition to do evil, but to do good continually" (Mosiah 5:2). Of his conversion experience, Alma₂ says, "Nevertheless, after wading through much tribulation, repenting nigh unto death, the Lord in mercy hath seen fit to snatch me out of an everlasting burning, and I am born of God" (Mosiah 27:28). Similar experiences are recounted about King Lamoni and his father (Alma 19, 22). In an account written in 1832, the Prophet Joseph Smith describes his FIRST VISION as being significant not only for opening a new DISPENSATION of the gospel, but also for his personal conversion. He writes, "The Lord opened the heavens upon me and I saw the Lord and he spake unto me saying Joseph my son thy sins are forgiven thee. [A]nd my soul was filled with love and for many days I could rejoice with great joy and the Lord was with me" (PJS 1:6–7).

MORMON explains the "mighty change" that must occur if one is to be born of God. The first fruit of repentance is the BAPTISM of water and fire, which baptism "cometh by faith unto the fulfilling of the commandments." Then comes a REMISSION OF SINS that brings a meekness and lowliness of heart. Such a transformation results in one's becoming worthy of the companionship of the Holy Ghost, who "filleth with hope and perfect love, which love endureth by diligence unto prayer" (Moro. 8:25–26).

LDS scriptures teach that spiritual rebirth comes by the GRACE of God to those who adhere to the principles and ordinances of the gospel of Jesus Christ, namely, faith, repentance, baptism, and reception of the GIFT OF THE HOLY GHOST. For the process to be genuine, however, one must be diligently engaged in good works, for as James says, "faith without works is dead; . . . by works [is] faith made perfect" (James 2:20, 22). A mere confession of change, or receiving baptism or another ordinance, does not necessarily mean that one has been born of God.

Other Christian faiths also emphasize the

importance of being "born again." Unlike many of these, Latter-day Saints do not believe this experience alone is sufficient for SALVATION. Instead, the process of spiritual rebirth signals to Latter-day Saints the beginning of a new life abounding with faith, grace, and good works. Only by ENDURING TO THE END may the individual return to the presence of God. Those who receive the ordinance of baptism and are faithful in keeping the commandments may enjoy the constant presence of the Holy Ghost who, like fire, will act as a sanctifier, and will witness to the hearts of the righteous that their sins are forgiven, imparting hope for eternal life.

Persons who have experienced this mighty change manifest attitudinal and behavioral changes. Feeling their hearts riveted to the Lord, their obedience extends beyond performance of duty. President Harold B. LEE taught, "Conversion must mean more than just being a 'card-carrying' member of the Church with a tithing receipt, a membership card, a temple recommend, etc. It means to overcome the tendencies to criticize and to strive continually to improve inward weaknesses and not merely the outward appearances" (*Ensign*, June 1971, p. 8). Latter-day Saints believe that individuals who are truly born of God gladly give a life of service to their fellow beings—they share the gospel message, sacrifice their own time, energy, and resources for the benefit of others, and in general hold high the light of Christ, being faithful to all the commandments.

BIBLIOGRAPHY

Cannon, Elaine, and Ed J. Pinegar. *The Mighty Change.* Salt Lake City, 1978.

ED J. PINEGAR

BRANCH, BRANCH PRESIDENT

A branch is generally the smallest organized congregation of the Church (normally fewer than two hundred members). At first, local Latter-day Saint congregations were known as "churches" (D&C 24:3; 26:1). Soon these units were more commonly called "branches" (D&C 72:23; 107:39), reflecting the manner in which they were formed—members sharing the gospel and creating new congregations in neighboring communities.

As the Church has grown, STAKES, composed of several large congregations known as WARDS,

are formed in centers of strength. In MISSION areas, DISTRICTS are composed of smaller congregations known as branches. Branches may also be found in stakes, typically in outlying communities where a smaller number of Church members can support only a less complete organization. In recent years a new kind of branch has emerged. In large urban centers an increasing number of ethnic minorities, isolated from the majority because of language and too small as a group to form a ward, have been organized as a branch. Furthermore, the Church has outlined programs that may be followed by isolated families or groups that are too small to form even a branch.

A branch is headed by a branch president, whereas a WARD is presided over by a BISHOP. Unlike the bishop, who must hold the office of HIGH PRIEST, the branch president need not be a high priest, but must be an ELDER in the MELCHIZEDEK PRIESTHOOD. The branch president and his two counselors have responsibilities similar to, and function like, a BISHOPRIC.

In the United States in 1990 there were 72 missions, 1,112 stakes, 7,750 wards, and 1,286 branches. Elsewhere there were 156 missions, 627 stakes, 2,786 wards, and 4,483 branches (*Ensign* 20 [May 1990]:22; *Deseret News 1991–1992*; Church Almanac, p. 94).

RICHARD O. COWAN

BRIGHAM YOUNG COLLEGE

President Brigham YOUNG founded Brigham Young College (BYC) in Logan, Utah, on July 24, 1877, just two years after he founded Brigham Young Academy (Brigham Young University from 1903) in Provo, Utah. Established to train the youth of the Church in northern Utah, southern Idaho, and western Wyoming, BYC had nearly 40,000 students in its forty-nine years of operation (1877–1926). At first a normal school primarily preparing elementary teachers (1877–1894), it then inaugurated college courses and for fifteen years granted bachelors' degrees (1894–1909). During its final period (1910–1926), the school operated as a high school and junior college. With the Church Board of Education decision to discontinue its schools except Brigham Young University, Brigham Young College closed its doors in May 1926; gave its library to Utah State Agricultural College, also in Logan; and sold its buildings and land to Logan City to be used as a high school. The old BYC buildings were demolished in the 1960s, and the new Logan High School was built on the site.

Four alumni of Brigham Young College became members of the Quorum of the Twelve Apostles: Richard R. Lyman, Melvin J. Ballard, John A. Widtsoe, and Albert E. Bowen.

BIBLIOGRAPHY

Garr, Arnold Kent. "A History of Brigham Young College, Logan, Utah." Master's thesis, Utah State University, 1973.

Sorensen, A. N. "Brigham Young College." In *The History of a Valley: Cache Valley, Utah-Idaho*, ed. Joel E. Ricks, pp. 349–69. Logan, Utah, 1956.

ARNOLD K. GARR

BRIGHAM YOUNG UNIVERSITY

PROVO, UTAH, CAMPUS

Brigham Young University (BYU) is a four-year private institution located in Provo, Utah, owned and operated by The Church of Jesus Christ of Latter-day Saints as part of the CHURCH EDUCATIONAL SYSTEM. Twenty-seven thousand students from all fifty states and many other countries study under the direction of approximately 1,500 full-time faculty in the ten colleges and two professional schools. Approximately 80 percent of the students are enrolled in one of the 130 different undergraduate programs. Along with these extensive undergraduate programs, BYU offers master's and doctoral degrees in a variety of disciplines through fifty-seven graduate departments as well as the Law School and the Graduate School of Management. BYU awarded 6,421 degrees in the 1989–1990 school year. With its close ties to the sponsoring Church, BYU has been committed to providing the best possible postsecondary education for the youth of the Church in an atmosphere that emphasizes both teaching and scholarly research—both reasoned and revealed learning.

BYU functions under the direction of the Church through a board of trustees that includes the First Presidency, the general presidents of the

This aerial view of Brigham Young University from the south shows the Provo, Utah, campus with Mt. Timpanogos to the north (c. 1985). Courtesy Brigham Young University.

women's AUXILIARY ORGANIZATIONS, and selected General Authorities. The university operates on a budget provided by the Church, one-third of which is derived from student tuition.

STUDENTS. About 9,000 of BYU's 27,000 students are from Utah, 16,000 from other states, and 2,000 from countries outside the United States. Approximately 49 percent of the students are women, and 51 percent, men. About 25 percent of the students are married. Approximately 40 percent have served as MISSIONARIES for the Church. Most students live in apartments or dormitories on or near campus, and many work to support themselves while at school; about one-third of the students are employed part-time by the university.

In 1989, entering freshmen had an average American College Test (ACT) composite score of 24.7 (of a possible 36; the national average for all freshmen that year was 18.6) and an average high school grade point average (GPA) of 3.43 (of a possible 4.0). At that time BYU was fifth among the nation's private universities in the number of undergraduates who went on to earn doctoral degrees and eighteenth among all universities in the United States in the number of entering National Merit scholars.

Most students at BYU are members of The Church of Jesus Christ of Latter-day Saints; members of other faiths who will accept and observe its standards of conduct are welcome.

FACULTY. The 1,500 faculty members at Brigham Young University have degrees from most of the major universities of the United States, and most are members of the Church. This is the natural result of an expectation that the faculty member should be involved fully in the work of the university and should be able to exert influence on students in the full breadth of the mission of BYU, including teaching of religious education courses. Realizing that students are influenced religiously in all their classes, the university officers have sought to attract the best-qualified members of the Church to faculty positions; however, well-qualified persons of other faiths are also employed on the faculty.

MISSION OF THE UNIVERSITY. The religious focus of BYU is evident in its *Bulletin's* declaration of purpose: "The mission of Brigham Young University—founded, supported, and guided by The Church of Jesus Christ of Latter-day Saints—is to assist individuals in their quest for perfection and eternal life. That assistance should provide a period of intensive learning in a stimulating setting where a commitment to excellence is expected and the full realization of human potential is pursued" (p. 1).

Latter-day Saints believe that the study of all truth is especially important for those who have received the saving truths of the gospel of Jesus Christ. The Lord has instructed, "Teach ye diligently and my grace shall attend you, that you may be instructed more perfectly in . . . things both in heaven and in the earth, and under the earth; things which have been, things which are, things which must shortly come to pass; . . . a knowledge also of countries and of kingdoms. . . . Seek ye out of the best books words of wisdom; . . . seek learning, even by study and also by faith" (D&C 88:78–79, 118).

On the occasion of his inauguration, Dallin H. Oaks, eighth president of BYU, said, "Our reason for *being* is to be a university. But our reason for *being a university* is to encourage and prepare young men and women to rise to their full spiritual potential as sons and daughters of God" (Inauguration Response of President Dallin H. Oaks, Nov. 1971, p. 18).

HISTORY. By the 1870s the economic state of the Church and its members was tenuous at best as they struggled to establish themselves in the Great Basin. A deep-rooted determination to learn had led them to establish community schools almost as soon as townsites were chosen (*see* ACADEMIES). The vision was higher than the performance, and although attendance was poor in some of the community elementary schools, President Brigham YOUNG and others were planning more consequential and more influential schools, for, as he said, "all science and art belong to the Saints" (*JD* 10:224). "It is the business of the Elders of this Church," President Young said at another time, "to gather up all the truths in the world pertaining to life and salvation, to the Gospel we preach, to mechanism[s] of every kind, to the sciences, and to philosophy, wherever [they] may be found in every nation, kindred, tongue, and people, and bring it to Zion" (*JD* 7:283–84).

Consequently, late in 1875, Brigham Young donated a building and established the Brigham Young Academy in Provo. A preliminary term of instruction was held, beginning in January 1876;

As part of the semicentennial anniversary of Brigham Young University, October 15–17, 1925, a parade passes before the Karl G. Maeser Memorial Building (built 1911).

and in April of that year, Karl G. Maeser, a young, well-educated German immigrant, was appointed to lead the school. Maeser was instructed that "neither the alphabet nor the multiplication tables were to be taught without the Spirit of God" (Wilkinson and Skousen, p. 67). The school began with twenty-nine pupils in the elementary program and one teacher, Karl Maeser. In the words of Ernest L. Wilkinson, seventh president of BYU,

> The school was born in poverty, nurtured in conflict, orphaned by the death of Brigham Young, . . . left homeless when its uninsured building was completely destroyed by fire, threatened with faculty and administrative resignations because of irregular or missed salary payments, and nearly abandoned on many occasions because of lack of funds. . . . [At first the academy] was a private school without a sponsor or means of support. . . . It survived only because of the financial sacrifices made by its faculty and Board of Trustees and voluntary gifts from its friends and from The Church of Jesus Christ of Latter-day Saints. [Finally, after 21 years of struggling existence,] the school was incorporated as an educational subsidiary of the LDS Church, which assumed responsibility for its survival [Wilkinson and Skousen, p. xi].

In 1903 the board of trustees changed the name of the school from Brigham Young Academy to Brigham Young University. Nine years later, the board set enrollment limits at 1,300 for the high school and 250 for the college, with a maximum of fifteen paid teachers for the latter. Forty years

after its founding, BYU awarded its first four-year college degree.

The university grew from 1,500 students in 1945 to 25,000 by 1970. Since 1970, by decision of the board of trustees, enrollment has been limited to between 25,000 and 27,000 students. Growth has continued, but in less visible ways, with improving facilities, students, and faculty and with the university taking a respected place among other institutions in the state, region, and nation. It continues to struggle with significant problems of growth. With the continuing expansion of Church membership, BYU feels pressure to admit more students than it can adequately accommodate.

The following men have led the institution for the past 115 years: Brigham Young Academy was directed initially by Warren N. Dusenberry (1875–1876) and then for a longer period by Karl G. Maeser (1876–1892), whose character and high educational standards had a permanent impact on the fledgling institution. The presidents of the university thereafter have been Benjamin Cluff, Jr. (1892–1903), George H. Brimhall (1904–1921), Franklin S. Harris (1921–1945), Howard S. McDonald (1945–1949), Ernest L. Wilkinson (1949–1971), Dallin H. Oaks (1971–1980), Jeffrey R. Holland (1980–1989), and Rex E. Lee (from 1989).

RELIGION AND RELIGIOUS EDUCATION. LDS students at BYU are assigned to student WARDS, which hold their Sunday services in the academic buildings on campus. About 200 students belong to each ward. In these wards, many of the pastoral functions, including sermons, instruction, friendship, and support, are provided by the students themselves. Weekday social activities for students are organized around Church wards. BYU encourages students of other faiths to be actively associated with wards or with their congregations in the community.

Religious instruction represents the university's commitment to a wide spectrum of learning and is a direct response to such divine declarations as "it is impossible for a man to be saved in ignorance" (D&C 131:6) and "the glory of God is intelligence, or, in other words, light and truth" (D&C 93:36). Religious Education has fifty full-time and eighty part-time faculty who teach over 400 classes daily to approximately 22,000 students. It offers courses in scripture study (including the Old Testament, New Testament, Book of Mormon, Doctrine and Covenants, and Pearl of Great Price), Christian history, LDS Church history, family history (genealogy), comparative religion, biblical languages, and other topics.

GENERAL AND HONORS EDUCATION. Honors and general education are emphasized at BYU. General education both underpins and complements fields of major study. The general education curriculum is designed to inform students of how fields of study have come to the present state of knowledge and to enhance their awareness of the methodological and cognitive constraints on the pursuit of truth. In addition, given BYU's concern that the development of individuals be eternal, general education entails continued inquiry into the gospel of Jesus Christ and its implications for knowledge, society, and truth. General-education courses undergo continuing faculty review and evaluation to consider the integration of material and rigorousness of method for each course.

The university's honors education program links a broad university perspective with the specific concentration of a major. It is open to all students, whether or not they choose to complete all the requirements for the designation "University Honors" at graduation.

COLLEGES AND PROGRAMS (1991). The College of Biology and Agriculture has 100 faculty members and offers degrees in the following areas: agronomy and horticulture, animal science, biology, botany and range science, food science and nutrition, microbiology, and zoology. In addition, the college manages research and student training on an 800-acre farm and a 6,200-acre livestock ranch. The college oversees the Ezra Taft Benson Agriculture and Food Institute, which emphasizes training and research in small-plot agriculture and family nutrition for developing areas of the world. The college also manages a 460-acre wildlife preserve in southern Utah and the M. L. Bean Life Science Museum, which houses the university's extensive botanical and zoological collections.

The College of Education, with ninety-five faculty members, offers degree programs in education leadership, educational psychology, elementary education, and secondary education. In addition to an extensive program in the preparation of public school teachers and administrators on both the elementary and secondary levels, the college offers study in early childhood teaching, special-education teaching (for students who will work with those who have intellectual or emotional handicaps or learning disabilities), and communication sciences and disorders (speech and language pathology and audiology).

The College of Engineering and Technology has ninety-eight faculty in six departments: chemical engineering, civil engineering, electrical and computer engineering, mechanical engineering, industrial education, and technology. Research programs include the Advanced Combustion Engineering Research Center, the CAM (computer-aided manufacturing) Software Research Center, the Catalysis Laboratory, the Engineering Computer Graphics Laboratory, and the Digital Signal Processing program.

The College of Family, Home, and Social Sciences has 200 faculty in fifteen academic departments and centers, including anthropology, clothing and textiles, economics, family sciences, geography, history, home economics, political science, psychology, social work, and sociology. The college supervises several centers and institutes, including the Center for Studies of the Family; the Charles Redd Center for Western Studies, which promotes research and publishing regarding the American West and maintains a large oral history program; the Joseph Fielding Smith Institute for Church History, which is primarily engaged in research and writing of history about The Church of Jesus Christ of Latter-day Saints, for both a professional and a general audience; the Center for Family and Community History, which supervises genealogy, family, community, and public history programs; and the David M. Kennedy Center for International Studies, which sponsors and supervises interdisciplinary programs in American, Asian, Canadian, European, Latin American, and Near Eastern studies.

The College of Fine Arts and Communications, with 135 faculty, offers thirty-seven areas of emphasis in art, communications, design, music, and theatre and film. The college has for its use five speech and drama theaters; two concert halls; two art galleries; a major art museum; and journalism, advertising, and broadcast laboratories, including a campus daily newspaper, and the university radio (KBYU-FM) and television (KBYU-TV) stations. The BYU Motion Picture Studio became part of the Church Audiovisual Department in 1991. In addition, musical ensembles and performing groups from the college tour each summer throughout the United States, Europe, and Asia.

The College of Humanities has 230 full-time faculty and offers majors in Asian, Classical, English, French, Germanic, Near Eastern, Portuguese, Slavic, and Spanish languages and literatures; humanities; comparative literature; library and information sciences; linguistics; and philosophy. As a result of their two-year mission experience in a foreign country, many students at BYU elect to continue language study in addition to their major emphasis, resulting in an unusually high number of students speaking foreign languages at BYU. The college also oversees the work of the Humanities Research Center, with a main emphasis on computer-assisted language and literature research; *BYU Studies*, a quarterly journal for the community of LDS scholars; the Center for the Study of Christian Values in Literature; and almost a dozen different foreign-language houses where students live in residence and carry on daily activities with native teachers.

The College of Nursing has forty faculty. It accepts approximately 120 baccalaureate students and fifteen master's students into its NLN-accredited program annually (National League for Nursing). Its programs offer emphases in family, medical-surgical, child, and psychological nursing.

The College of Physical and Mathematical Sciences, with 155 faculty, has departments of chemistry, computer science, geology, mathematics, physics and astronomy, and statistics. The college has established a number of special facilities and programs, including four State Centers of Excellence: X-ray imagery, chemical separations, com-

puter-aided education, and supercritical fluid-separation technologies. The college also oversees the Center for Thermodynamics, the Center for Statistical and Computing Research, and research programs and special facilities for solid-state physics, astrophysics and astronomy, calorimetry, environmental chemistry, molecular structure studies, chemical separations, earth sciences, and fission-track dating.

The College of Physical Education has ninety faculty members and offers degrees in health sciences; physical education—dance; physical education—sports; recreation management and youth leadership. In intercollegiate athletics, BYU is a member of the Western Athletic Conference and participates in most intercollegiate sports for both men and women. The college oversees, in addition to its own degree programs, a campuswide intramural program consisting of more than sixty events involving thousands of women and men. The university's athletic facilities include not only large intercollegiate facilities for basketball, football, and track but also indoor and outdoor tracks, pools, courts, and playing fields that accommodate the intramural programs and other recreational exercise for students and faculty members.

The J. Willard and Alice S. Marriott School of Management has approximately 110 faculty in its six academic departments, including accountancy, business management, information management, managerial economics, public management, and organizational behavior. The Graduate School of Management offers the master of accountancy, the master of business administration, the executive MBA, the master of organizational behavior, the master of public administration, and the executive MPA programs. In addition, the School of Management coordinates university programs in Air Force and Army ROTC with their sixteen military faculty.

The J. Reuben Clark Law School, with its twenty-eight faculty members, offers a six-semester course of graduate professional study leading to the doctor of jurisprudence degree. The Law School also offers a master of comparative law program.

BYU offers several Study-Abroad Programs, including semesters in several European and Asian countries, Mexico, and Israel (*see* BRIGHAM YOUNG UNIVERSITY: JERUSALEM CENTER FOR NEAR EASTERN STUDIES).

The Division of Continuing Education at BYU enrolls more than 390,000 students yearly in evening classes, independent study, conferences and workshops, travel study, study abroad, and other courses at centers in California; Ogden, Utah; Salt Lake City; and Rexburg, Idaho.

ACCREDITATION. BYU is fully accredited by the Northwest Association of Schools and Colleges. In addition, most professional programs of the university are reviewed, evaluated, and accredited by national and state associations and boards.

BIBLIOGRAPHY

Bergera, Gary James, and Ronald Priddis. *Brigham Young University: A House of Faith.* Salt Lake City, 1985.

Brigham Young University Bulletin (annual catalog). Provo, Utah, 1990.

Butterworth, Edwin. *Brigham Young University: 1,000 Views of 100 Years.* Provo, Utah, 1975.

Clark, Marden J. "On the Mormon Commitment to Education." *Dialogue* 7 (Winter 1972):11–19.

Holland, Jeffery R. *A School in Zion.* Provo, Utah, 1988.

Kimball, Spencer W. "Second Century Address." *BYU Studies* 16 (Summer 1976):445–57.

King, Arthur H. "The Idea of a Mormon University." *BYU Studies* 13 (Winter 1973):115–25.

Pardoe, T. Earl. *The Sons of Brigham.* Provo, Utah, 1969.

Poll, Richard Douglas. *The Honors Program at Brigham Young University, 1960–1985.* Provo, Utah, 1985.

Waterstradt, Jean Anne, ed. *They Gladly Taught: Ten BYU Professors.* Provo, Utah, 1986.

Wilkinson, Ernest L., et al. *Brigham Young University: The First One Hundred Years,* 4 vols. Provo, Utah, 1975–1976.

———, and W. Cleon Skousen. *Brigham Young University: A School of Destiny.* Provo, Utah, 1976.

ELIOT A. BUTLER
NEAL E. LAMBERT

JERUSALEM CENTER FOR NEAR EASTERN STUDIES

The Jerusalem Center for Near Eastern Studies grew out of a Jerusalem "semester abroad" educational program for undergraduates instituted by Brigham Young University (BYU) in 1968. It became popular among Latter-day Saint students because of their commitment to the religious traditions of the Bible. The academic offerings at the Center focus on biblical and contemporary studies, correlated with a study of archaeology, biblical geography, Near Eastern history, Judaism, Islam, Near Eastern languages, and international relations and politics. Studies are enhanced with weekly field trips to biblical and historical sites in

The Brigham Young University Jerusalem Center for Near Eastern Studies is located on a five-acre site on Mount Scopus. First occupied in March 1987, the center was dedicated in May 1989 by Howard W. Hunter. Photographer: John P. Snyder. Courtesy Brigham Young University.

Israel and extended study tours to Jordan and Egypt.

Several academic programs, varying in content and covering periods ranging from a few weeks to six months, are offered at the Center for undergraduates and graduates. Research scholars from Brigham Young University also use these facilities, often in association with scholars and universities in the Middle East. In addition, the Center hosts a variety of continuing education programs or "travel study tours" for youths and adults.

The Center provides students a period of intensive learning in a stimulating setting in which a commitment to excellence is expected. Ideally, students conclude their studies in the Holy Land with deepened spiritual and intellectual appreciation of its history, peoples, and cultures.

The Jerusalem Center facilities are located on the northern half of the Mount of Olives, adjacent to the Mt. Scopus campus of Hebrew University. The eight-floor study center is terraced into the hillside. It is constructed of white Jerusalem limestone and designed with an architectural blend of domes, arches, and straight lines, complemented by flower gardens that feature several species of trees and bushes referred to in the Bible. The interior of the Center, with its cupolas, arches, galleries, and vaulted ceilings, is also congenial to its Near Eastern setting. Large windows and spacious patios offer a magnificent panorama of old and modern Jerusalem.

In the early 1980s the construction of the Center faced resolute opposition from certain religious circles and Israeli nationalist groups who feared that the Center might become a base for Mormon proselytizing of Jews. In the spirit of accommodation and out of a desire for peaceful INTERFAITH RELATIONS, BYU agreed with the government of Israel that the Center would be used exclusively for educational and cultural activities.

The Center also helps to serve the spiritual needs of Latter-day Saints, visiting or residing, in the Holy Land. An ecclesiastical organization consisting of a district and several branches has been established to provide worship services each sabbath (see MIDDLE EAST, THE CHURCH IN).

BIBLIOGRAPHY

"BYU's Jerusalem Center Opens." *Ensign* 17 (June 1987):77.

"David Galbraith Heads BYU Jerusalem Center." *Ensign* 17 (Aug. 1987):79.

DAVID B. GALBRAITH

BRIGHAM YOUNG UNIVERSITY—HAWAII CAMPUS

BYU—Hawaii is a four-year, liberal arts institution located on northeastern Oahu, thirty-seven miles from Honolulu. Its multiracial student body of 2,000 comes from over fifty countries: 60 percent from Hawaii and the U.S. mainland, and 40 percent from the South Pacific and the Asian rim (see OCEANIA, THE CHURCH IN; ASIA, EAST, THE CHURCH IN; ASIA, SOUTH AND SOUTHEAST, THE CHURCH IN; HAWAII, THE CHURCH IN).

In 1865 the Church purchased 6,000 acres of land at Laie, where missionaries had conducted a primary school for many years. In 1921 David O. MCKAY, a member of the QUORUM OF THE TWELVE APOSTLES, visited the islands and became convinced that Church-sponsored higher education in Hawaii was essential to serve the Pacific basin. It was not until the late 1940s, however, that Church leaders of Oahu seriously began to investigate educational needs. In 1954 David O. McKay, then President of the Church, took definite steps to establish a school by appointing Dr. Reuben D. Law to head a proposed junior college in Laie.

In 1955, with a student body of 153—nearly all from Hawaii—and a faculty of 20, the Church College of Hawaii (CCH) was established as a two-year college and began classes in six war-surplus buildings while labor missionaries built a permanent campus. The school quickly expanded into a four-year teacher-training institution for Church schools in the South Pacific, which it remained for its first two decades. Midway through this period, following several years of effort to find a way to provide employment opportunities for the student body, the Church opened the POLYNESIAN CULTURAL CENTER in October 1963, which currently provides employment for nearly half the students.

In the early 1970s, CCH temporarily underwent a change of direction toward becoming a vocational school. A significant drop in enrollment resulted, however, and after careful study and reconsideration—both in Hawaii and in Utah—a decision was made to reestablish the college as a liberal-arts institution.

Major restructuring was initiated in 1974, when Church College of Hawaii was renamed Brigham Young University—Hawaii Campus and came under the direction of the president of BRIGHAM YOUNG UNIVERSITY in Provo, Utah. Since that time, enrollment has increased to 2,000 students.

Located in Laie, Oahu, Hawaii, the Church College of Hawaii (now Brigham Young University—Hawaii Campus) was established in 1954. Photograph, 1960, by Camera Hawaii.

Accredited by the Western Association of Schools and Colleges, the school is organized into seven academic divisions. Although there is no religious requirement for admission, all students and faculty are expected to follow the dress, grooming, and moral standards of the school's honor code. Since the late 1960s, BYU—Hawaii has excelled in various athletic competitions and has won national championships in rugby and men's and women's volleyball.

BIBLIOGRAPHY

Britsch, R. Lanier. *Moramona: The Mormons in Hawaii.* Laie, Hawaii, 1989.

Law, Reuben D. *The Founding and Early Development of The Church College of Hawaii.* St. George, Utah, 1972.

ALTON L. WADE

BRITISH ISLES, THE CHURCH IN

The Church of Jesus Christ of Latter-day Saints came to the British Isles when seven LDS missionaries landed at Liverpool, England, on July 19, 1837. The success of this first mission (more than 1,500 converts by April 1839) set the stage for the even more successful apostolic mission of 1839–1841, which saw nine of the eleven apostles (the twelfth place was vacant at the time) serving as missionaries in England under the direction of Brigham YOUNG. The Church grew rapidly in Great Britain among the working classes of the Northwest, the Midlands, and, especially, Wales. Membership counts at the end of 1851 showed 33,000 members of the Church in the United Kingdom and Ireland and 12,000 in Utah. Although total membership in the British Isles declined after the mid-1850s due to emigration and attrition, substantial additions through baptisms continued through the 1860s. From 1870 to the mid-1950s, the Church did not experience sustained growth in the United Kingdom and Ireland. But the dedication of the London Temple (in Lingfield, Surrey) in September 1958 and the creation of the Manchester England Stake on March 27, 1970, initiated a second growth phase of membership; by 1990 the Church had more than 160,000 members in 9 missions, 40 stakes, and

This building at 42 Islington Street, Liverpool, England (no longer standing), served from 1855 to 1904 as headquarters for the British and European Missions of the Church and as the office of the *Millennial Star*.

more than 330 wards and branches in the British Isles. The strength of the Church in the United Kingdom and Ireland in 1990 is indicated by the number of stakes: thirty-two in England, five in Scotland, two in Wales, and one in Northern Ireland. Branches (congregations) in the Republic of Ireland, whose members are not as numerous as in other areas, are under the jurisdiction of mission districts rather than a stake.

When the missionaries first arrived in the British Isles, they went to Preston, England, where Joseph Fielding's brother, Rev. James Fielding, had invited him and his missionary companions to preach at his Vauxhall Chapel. James's enthusiasm waned when it became apparent that he risked losing his congregation, and he promptly closed the chapel to the missionaries. They then taught in private homes, and a week later baptized the first nine British converts in the river Ribble, at Preston. By Sunday, August 6, there were nearly fifty converts in Preston, and Elder Heber C. Kimball organized the Preston Branch. In two months, membership had reached 140, and the

original branch was divided into five separate branches in October. Missionary work was extended to Bedford, and to Alston, near the Scottish border, where the missionaries had relatives. Elder Kimball preached in the villages of the Ribble Valley.

On Christmas Day of 1837, the members met for the first conference in Britain, and on Sunday, April 8, 1838, another conference held in the Cockpit, Preston, drew down the curtain on the first phase of Mormon missionary work in Britain. There were 1,500–2,000 British members of the Church, and the leadership was transferred to Joseph Fielding as elders Kimball and Orson Hyde set sail for America.

APOSTOLIC MISSION, 1838–1841. The second major LDS missionary thrust in the British Isles began on July 8, 1838, at Far West, Missouri, when the Prophet Joseph SMITH received a revelation instructing the Twelve Apostles to prepare to serve a mission in Great Britain. Brigham Young and six other apostles left from New York for Britain between December 1839 and March 1840. Willard Richards, who had remained there after the 1837 mission, was ordained an apostle in Britain on April 14, 1840, by Brigham Young. The missionaries baptized thousands of converts (Wilford WOODRUFF personally baptized more than a thousand), organized branches and conferences, and directed the work of the Church, including printing scriptures and tracts, and began publishing the MILLENNIAL STAR, the British Church periodical that would have a continuous run from 1840 through 1970. In 1841, shortly before he returned to America, Brigham Young arranged for richly bound copies of the Book of Mormon to be presented to Queen Victoria and Prince Albert. The volume presented to the queen was located in the Royal Library at Windsor in 1986.

The Britain of those days was ripe for a message of hope, and the preaching of a restored gospel of Jesus Christ was timely. By June 1842 there were 8,245 members of the Church in the United Kingdom and Ireland. Six years later there were 18,000, and by the end of 1851 England had 24,199 Latter-day Saints, Wales had 5,244, Scotland had 3,291, and Ireland had 160—a total of almost 33,000—and an additional 11,000 had already emigrated to America. In 1851 there were more members of the Church in the United Kingdom and Ireland than there were in Utah (12,000).

EMIGRATION.   Emigration to the United States to help build the main body of the Church was the recommended pattern for the members during the first century of the Church in the British Isles. The PERPETUAL EMIGRATING FUND was established in September 1849 to assist. Those who emigrated with the help of this revolving fund were to pay back the money as they could, so that others might be helped. The fund was formally discontinued in 1887, after thousands had benefited from it. Additional thousands were assisted by friends and relatives who had already emigrated. From 1847 to 1869, more than 32,000 British and Irish converts to the Church left their homelands for a new life in pioneer America. When the novelist Charles Dickens visited the *Amazon* before it set sail from London on June 4, 1863, to see what the Mormon emigrants were like, he noted: "I . . . had come aboard this Emigrant Ship to see what eight hundred Latter-day Saints were like. . . . Nobody is in an ill-temper, nobody is the worse for drink, nobody swears an oath or uses a coarse word, nobody appears depressed, nobody is weeping, and down upon the deck in every corner where it is possible to find a few square feet to kneel, crouch or lie in, people, in every suitable attitude for writing, are writing letters. Now, I have seen emigrants ships before this day in June. And these people are strikingly different from all other people in like circumstances whom I have ever seen, and I wonder aloud, 'What *would* a stranger suppose these emigrants to be!' . . . I should have said they were in their degree, the pick and flower of England" (Dickens, pp. 223–25).

Dickens set down his impressions of Mormon emigrants in one of a series of essays that appeared at intervals between 1860 and 1869 in his weekly magazine, *All the Year Round*. He later published them in the chapter "Bound for the Great Salt Lake" in *The Uncommercial Traveller*. He concluded with:

I afterwards learned that a dispatch was sent home by the captain before he struck out into the wide Atlantic, highly extolling the behaviour of these emigrants, and the perfect order and propriety of all their social arrangements. . . . I went on board their ship to bear testimony against them if they deserved it, as I fully believed they would; to my great astonishment they did not deserve it; and my predispositions and tendencies must not affect me as an honest witness. I went over the *Amazon's* side, feeling it impossible to deny that, so far, some remarkable

influence had produced a remarkable result, which better known influences have often missed [Dickens, p. 232].

The 895 LDS emigrants under the direction of Elder William Bramall were well organized. The ship's captain explained:

The most of these came aboard yesterday evening. They came from various parts of England in small parties that had never seen one another before. Yet they had not been a couple of hours on board, when they established their own police, made their own regulations, and set their own watches at all the hatchways. Before nine o'clock, the ship was as orderly and quiet as a man-of-war [Dickens, p. 223].

THE CHURCH IN BRITAIN IN THE TWENTIETH CENTURY.   The early years of the twentieth century were troubled times for the Church in the United Kingdom and Ireland. Much of its strength had been drawn away through emigration; between 1870 and 1892 Church membership declined from 9,000 to barely 2,600. Then, against the backdrop of the polygamy issue, and fanned by newspaper exposés and by novels from writers such as Sir Arthur Conan Doyle and Winifred Graham, an "anti-Mormon crusade" reached a peak in 1911. Persecution was rife, violence was threatened, and missionaries were occasionally tarred and feathered, as in Nuneaton, Warwickshire. Nevertheless, the Church grew in this time of trials, more than doubling in membership between 1897 and 1910, and averaging more than 8,000 members in Great Britain from then until after the end of World War I. But with missionary work disrupted by two world wars, a modest decline kept membership at an average of about 6,000 through 1950.

In the mid-1950s, membership in the United Kingdom and Ireland stood at 9,000, when the second major phase of the growth and development of the Church in the British Isles began. Emphasis was given to "staying and building," and steps were taken to ensure that Church members in the United Kingdom did not need to emigrate to enjoy all the blessings of the Church membership.

President David O. McKay dedicated the London Temple, at Lingfield, Surrey, on September 7–9, 1958. The first European stake was created March 17, 1960, in Manchester, and others followed in rapid succession. Where only a handful of LDS chapels existed in Britain before 1960, with most congregations worshiping in rented rooms or

The home of John and Jane Benbow (1832–1840), near Castle Frome, Herefordshire, England (c. 1987). Before his conversion to the LDS Church, Benbow was a prominent member of the United Brethren. Wilford Woodruff preached here in March 1840, baptizing the first of approximately 600 converts from the United Brethren. John and Jane Benbow and Thomas Kington financed the first British edition of the Book of Mormon and LDS hymn book. Courtesy W. Dee Halverson.

halls, by 1970 more than 100 chapels had been completed, and this number rose to around 250 by the end of the 1980s. These manifestations of a permanent presence led to a dramatic reawakening in the British Isles, and an era of increased baptisms and Church growth.

The Public Communications Department was established in 1975 to disseminate information about the Church. The Church Educational System began its work with youth, and missionary and temple work increased. More genealogical records were obtained for microfilming, and a network of family history centers was inaugurated. The Church welfare services program, with its support to the needy based on the principle of work, commenced in 1980 with the purchase of a 305-acre farm at Kington, Worcestershire. In January 1985 the London Missionary Training Center, located near the temple, opened its doors.

THE 150TH ANNIVERSARY. Media attention peaked in 1987, when the Church celebrated its 150th anniversary in the British Isles. Broadcaster and writer Ian Bradley produced a thirty-minute BBC documentary on the Church that aired twice on radio in Britain, and also on the World Service.

At the anniversary dinner at the Savoy Hotel in London, on July 24, and in the presence of dis-

tinguished guests from both sides of the Atlantic, the British contribution to the colonizing of the American Far West was formally recognized in a videotaped message from U.S. President Ronald Reagan: "The Mormon contribution to American life is beyond measuring, and the contribution of the British Isles to the Mormon Church is also immense. They are the contributions of love and joy; of faith and family; of work and community. They are a dedication to the values that are at the heart of free nations—and good ones—and they are a faith in the promise of tomorrow."

THE CHURCH IN THE BRITISH ISLES IN 1990. Britain, like many other parts of Europe, has experienced a decline in religious observance since World War II. Many British churches now have congregations that are predominantly middle-aged to elderly, and largely female. Latter-day Saints in the United Kingdom and Ireland, in contrast, are experiencing the second flowering of the Church there. About 37 percent of British LDS baptisms came between 1837 and 1869, and nearly 50 percent have come since 1950. During the 1970s and 1980s, a new LDS congregation was established in the United Kingdom and Ireland almost every two weeks, and a new chapel was dedicated almost every month.

DEMOGRAPHICS. In demographic terms, the LDS Church in the British Isles at the end of 1989 had a young membership profile. While 43 percent of the British population that year were under thirty, the Church figure was 53 percent. Primary children (ages three to eleven) made up 20 percent of the British Latter-day Saints; 10 percent were teenagers (ages twelve to eighteen); and 25 percent were young adults (ages eighteen to thirty).

EDUCATION. The majority of LDS British youth attended state schools in 1989. Studies showed 13 percent of members of the Church had some form of higher education. Among recent converts this figure was 18 percent.

EMPLOYMENT. In 1989 unemployment was a major social problem in the British Isles, and the rate for LDS men was similar to the national figure of 13 percent. When they were employed, Church males generally showed a higher percentage in white-collar occupations compared with the figure for all British men; fewer LDS women were in the labor force than British women generally.

THE CHALLENGE OF LAY CLERGY. The recent increased growth of the Church in the United Kingdom and Ireland meant that the majority of local Church leaders in 1989 were still first-generation members. This created great need for effective leadership training of its lay clergy.

BRITISH CONTRIBUTIONS TO THE CHURCH. British contributions to the Church have taken two main forms: providing a training ground for many early Church leaders, and helping to build and sustain the fledgling Church through the influx of British immigrants. Of the 1839 apostolic mission, in particular, it is important to note that that group of missionaries contained the next four Presidents of the Church: Brigham Young, John Taylor, Wilford Woodruff, and Lorenzo Snow. They received vital training and experience in the British Isles, and forged a strong unity within the Quorum of the Twelve that sustained the Church through the testing times that followed the martyrdom of the Prophet Joseph Smith in 1844. These men would lead and direct the Church into the twentieth century.

As a young man, David O. McKay was a missionary in Scotland, his ancestral homeland. This picture, on the shores of Loch Lomond, was probably taken during his tour of the European missions in 1952, the year after he was sustained as President of the Church. Courtesy Utah State Historical Society.

All of the men who have served as President of the Church, from Joseph Smith to Ezra Taft Benson, trace their ancestry back to the British Isles. The ancestors of President Benson, for example, came from Caversham, Oxfordshire. All of the Church Presidents except Joseph Smith, Harold B. Lee, and Spencer W. Kimball labored as missionaries in Great Britain.

CHURCH LEADERS BORN IN BRITAIN. John Taylor, the third President of the Church, was born in Milnthorpe, Westmoreland, and joined the Church in Upper Canada. George Q. Cannon and Charles W. Penrose, both of whom became members of the Quorum of the Twelve and later counselors in the First Presidency, came from Liverpool and Camberwell, London, respectively. George Teasdale and James E. Talmage, also apostles, were from London and from Hungerford, Berkshire. John Rex Winder, from Biddenden, Kent, was a counselor in the First Presidency (1887–1910), and George Reynolds, from London, and B. H. Roberts, from Warrington, were presidents of the Seventy.

Other British General Authorities were John Longden, from Oldham, Lancashire, and John Wells, from Carolton, Nottinghamshire. In 1990, Nottingham-born Derek A. Cuthbert was serving in the First Quorum of the Seventy. Ruth May Fox, born in Westbury, Wiltshire, in 1853, was the general president of the Young Women from 1929–1937. May Anderson of Liverpool was editor of the Church's CHILDREN'S FRIEND magazine from 1902 to 1940, first counselor in the General Presidency of the Primary from 1905 to 1925, and its President from 1925 to 1939. She was also the moving force behind the establishment of the Primary Children's Hospital in Salt Lake City (see HOSPITALS). May Green Hinckley, of Brampton, Derbyshire, was General President of the Primary and editor of the *Children's Friend* from 1940 to 1943. The Church's Sunday School organization was founded in 1849 by Scotsman Richard Ballantyne.

Life was not all work. The Saints carried with them a love of music. As the first pioneer party crossed the plains, they did so to the strains of William Pitt's Brass Band, from the English Midlands. One of the best-remembered British converts is William Clayton, from Penwortham, Lancashire. He founded the branch of the Church in Manchester before emigrating, and went on to serve as a clerk to Joseph Smith. While crossing the plains, he kept a meticulous record, and wrote the rallying song, "Come, Come, Ye Saints," which is one of the best-known hymns of the Church.

THE MORMON TABERNACLE CHOIR. The renowned Mormon Tabernacle Choir owes its existence, in no small measure, to British emigrants. It is said that Brigham Young, hearing a group of Welsh converts singing four-part harmony in their native tongue, commented, "I don't understand the words, but you should become the nucleus of a great church choir." The first conductor of the Mormon Tabernacle Choir was John Parry, born in Newmarket, Flintshire, and its first organist was a sixteen-year-old native of Norwich, Joseph Daynes. Other early conductors also came from Britain, including George Careless, from London; Ebenezer Beesley, from Oxfordshire; and Evan Stephens, from Pencader, Carmarthenshire. In fact, seven of the first eight directors of the choir were born in the British Isles. The first Tabernacle pipe organ was designed by an Englishman, Joseph Ridges, who built it in Australia.

In June 1982 the British contribution to the choir—indeed, to the Church itself—was graphically demonstrated at the conclusion of a concert in the Royal Albert Hall, London, when the presenter asked all members of the choir with British ancestry to stand. All but four of the 350-voice choir stood.

At a time when a number of the mainstream churches in the United Kingdom and Ireland are wrestling with some of the fundamental doctrines and practices of Christianity—the nature of resurrection, the virgin birth, ecumenism, and the ordination of women—the unchanging nature of LDS beliefs appeals to many who come into contact with the Church. Mormons seem to have found a way to hold on to the fundamentals of the faith, yet be receptive to the pressures of the present. In his cover story for the November 15, 1987, issue of the Sunday *Times Magazine*, journalist Keith Wheatley wrote: "The phenomenal growth of the Latter-day Saints in recent times shows that they have no need to dilute their doctrines. . . . They seem to be a church whose hour has come."

BIBLIOGRAPHY

Allen, James B., and Thomas G. Alexander, eds. *Manchester Mormons*. Santa Barbara, Calif., 1974.

Bloxham, Ben; James R. Moss; and Larry C. Porter, eds. *Truth Will Prevail: The Rise of The Church of Jesus Christ of Latter-day Saints in the British Isles, 1837–1987*. Solihull, U.K., 1987.

Cannon, Donald Q., and Larry C. Porter, eds. *Mormonism in the British Isles 1837–1987*. *BYU Studies* 27 (Winter and Spring 1987):3–131; 3–135 (two whole issues on the topic).

Cowley, Matthias F., ed. *Wilford Woodruff: History of His Life and Labors, as Recorded in His Daily Journals*. Salt Lake City, 1964.

Cuthbert, Derek A. *The Second Century: Latter-day Saints in Great Britain*, Vol. 1, 1937–1987. Salt Lake City, 1987.

Dickens, Charles. *The Uncommercial Traveller* and *Reprinted Pieces, Etc.* London, 1958.

Evans, Richard L. *A Century of "Mormonism" in Great Britain*. Salt Lake City, 1937.

Jensen, Richard L., and Malcolm R. Thorp, eds. *Mormons in Early Victorian Britain*. Salt Lake City, 1989.

Kimball, Stanley B. *Heber C. Kimball: Mormon Patriarch and Pioneer*. Urbana, Ill., 1986.

Taylor, P. A. M. *Expectations Westward: The Mormons and the Emigration of Their British Converts in the Nineteenth Century*. Edinburgh and London, 1965.

BRYAN J. GRANT

BROADCASTING

The Church of Jesus Christ of Latter-day Saints is a broadcasting entity. Its involvement in radio and television parallels the rapid expansion of those technologies that began during the early 1900s. In 1921 the Latter-day Saints University in Salt Lake City, Utah, received the first U.S. broadcast license issued to an educational institution. Radio in America developed primarily as a commercial rather than an educational service, as did the Church's broadcasting activities. On May 6, 1922, radio station KZN went on the air in Salt Lake City, and the Church began a long and complex involvement in broadcast and programming innovation.

In 1925 the call letters were changed to KSL when the Church assumed majority ownership of the station and hired Earl J. Glade, one of broadcasting's early pioneers, to manage its operation (*see* KSL RADIO).

KSL affiliated with the National Broadcasting Company (NBC) in 1929, which immediately began carrying broadcasts of the MORMON TABERNACLE CHOIR. These broadcasts continued until 1933, when KSL became a Columbia Broadcasting System (CBS) affiliate station. In 1936 the Tabernacle Choir Broadcast program took its present format as "Music and the Spoken Word" with

Richard L. Evans as host. This Sunday morning radio program originating from the Mormon Tabernacle on TEMPLE SQUARE continues today as the longest continuously broadcast network program in America. "Music and the Spoken Word" has been translated for radio distribution into several languages. The format and style of this radio program set the pattern for much of the Church's subsequent programming efforts.

Technical innovation designed to improve signal quality and increase geographic coverage enhanced the Church's broadcast facilities. By 1933 KSL-AM was a Federal Communications Commission (FCC) Class 1-A clear-channel station transmitting at 50,000 watts, the maximum allowable power. During the 1940s and 1950s, FM radio and television stations were added, and the Church also acquired minority interest in two Idaho broadcast properties. FM radio, black-and-white and later color television, stereo sound, cable television, and satellite transmissions have become a major part of the Church's wide-ranging broadcast capabilities.

KSL-AM and its sister FM radio and television stations emerged as the equivalent of a graduate school in broadcast management, programming, engineering, journalism, and advertising. Many, like Arch L. Madsen, who had worked with Glade during KSL's early years, became leaders of international stature and reputation. Under Madsen's leadership in the late 1950s the regional intermountain broadcast activities of the Church were transformed into their present international scope.

In 1961 the Church expanded its international activities with the purchase of WNYW, call letters for five shortwave radio transmitters near Boston. Daily broadcasts to Europe and Latin America, most of them non–Church-related, were made in English, Spanish, Portuguese, French, and German. Church broadcasts included programs on Church news, values, and culture. The Tabernacle Choir broadcast and sessions of general conference were also programmed. In 1974, when the newer technologies of satellites, cable, and videotape were developed, the Church sold WNYW.

On May 6, 1922, President Heber J. Grant began the first radio broadcast over KZN (later KSL), the radio station sponsored by the *Deseret News* in Salt Lake City. Pictured left to right are Nathan O. Fullmer, Anthony W. Ivins, George Albert Smith, two not identified, Augusta Winters Grant, Heber J. Grant, C. Clarence Neslen, and George J. Cannon.

BONNEVILLE INTERNATIONAL CORPORATION was formed in 1964 as the holding company for the Church's broadcast properties. Bonneville acquired radio and television stations in Seattle, Washington, and additional radio facilities throughout the United States, giving it commercial licenses for seven FM, five AM, and two television stations in 1990.

Three more FCC noncommercial, educational licenses are held by the Church's educational institutions in Utah and Idaho. BRIGHAM YOUNG UNIVERSITY operates KBYU-FM and TV. RICKS COLLEGE operates KRIC-FM, primarily for student training. The production capacity of these stations also allows them to serve Church educational objectives that are unfeasible for commercial broadcast activities.

The Church also holds interests in satellite communications and cable television distribution systems. The first intercontinental satellite transmission between North America and Europe included a performance by the Tabernacle Choir.

Early commercial network affiliation with NBC and CBS led to a basic broadcast philosophy grounded in a belief that FCC licenses are held as a public trust and not as preaching tools. The Church has avoided an evangelistic style of radio and television broadcasting and has limited the religious content of its programming. It is felt that the value and contribution of these facilities would diminish if the stations were used exclusively for religious purposes.

Most of the Church's programming efforts in both radio and television have been keyed to creating a favorable image for the Church rather than presenting its doctrine and making converts. "Music and the Spoken Word," public service announcements, BYU basketball and football games, and an assortment of public affairs and cultural programs have dominated the Church's primary programming content.

The Church's semi-annual general conference broadcasts are a significant exception to this rule. The first general conference was broadcast by KSL in 1924. Since then the broadcast reach of general conference has been expanded to cover much of the world. Through broadcast, cable, satellite, and videotape distribution, the conferences are translated into several languages and distributed to stations in many countries through Bonneville International productions.

During the 1970s the Church experimented with a more direct approach to broadcasting a doctrinal message through a prime-time special, "A Christmas Child." Since this broadcast, a number of Church-produced programs have focused on specific doctrinal messages. The production of programs that teach gospel principles directly to the audience has moved higher on the list of Church broadcast priorities.

BIBLIOGRAPHY

Emery, Walter B. *Broadcasting and Government: Responsibilities and Regulations*, pp. 37–38. East Lansing, Mich., 1961.

Kahn, Frank J., ed. *Documents of American Broadcasting*, 3rd ed., pp. xvii, 72–73, 426–27. Englewood Cliffs, N.J., 1978.

Witherspoon, John, and Roselle Kovitz. "The History of Public Broadcasting," pp. 7, 81. Washington, D.C., 1987.

BRUCE L. CHRISTENSEN

BROTHERHOOD

While members of other Christian denominations may speak metaphorically of all humankind being brothers and sisters and children of God, Latter-day Saints believe it literally in the sense that a FATHER IN HEAVEN and a MOTHER IN HEAVEN created spirit children in a PREMORTAL existence. Those spirit children, born into this or other worlds as mortal men and women, are therefore all of the same "generation" and are literally brothers and sisters, children of deity. Among them is Jesus Christ, who is distinct from other men and women in that he is the Firstborn Son of God in the spirit and the Only Begotten of the Father in the flesh.

An important LDS doctrine based on this belief is the concept of equal opportunity for salvation. Since all mortals are offspring of deity, all have equal access to saving grace and may, through good works and moral progression while living as mortals, become saved by that grace. This doctrine of literal kinship is a major driving force behind the Church's proselytizing activities: Latter-day Saints believe that they have an obligation to teach the gospel of Jesus Christ to all the world because all its inhabitants are their brothers and sisters.

Latter-day Saints also believe in the brotherhood of the priesthood, similar to the SISTERHOOD of the Relief Society; a special bond exists among the members of both an individual PRIESTHOOD QUORUM and the entire body of the priesthood. As explained in scripture and instructions from Church leaders, this bond obligates priesthood holders to act as shepherds for one another and to be actively concerned for the welfare of other members and their families. In practice, this obligation is largely discharged through monthly HOME TEACHING, a system whereby quorum members visit one another, assessing needs and delivering a spiritual message.

Because stakes and wards of the LDS Church are operated by a lay clergy, most active members, both men and women, serve in some unpaid Church calling (see LAY PARTICIPATION AND LEADERSHIP). The service rendered by priesthood holders in their ecclesiastical positions is often labor-intensive and provides an opportunity for close interaction. This system fosters a feeling of brotherhood of service among priesthood holders.

The most common title used by Latter-day Saints in referring to themselves and to each other is "Brother" or "Sister," though General Authorities of the Church are most often referred to by their more formal titles of "Elder" or "President."

BIBLIOGRAPHY

Brown, Hugh B. "The Gospel Is for All Men." IE 72 (June 1969):31–34.

Johnson, P. Wendel. "The How of Brotherhood." IE 72 (Sept. 1969):70–75.

Oaks, Dallin H. "Brother's Keeper." Ensign 16 (May 1986):20.

Taylor, Henry D. "Am I My Brother's Keeper?" Ensign 2 (July 1972):74–75.

TIMOTHY W. SLOVER

BROTHER OF JARED

The brother of Jared (c. 2200 B.C.) was the first JAREDITE prophet (see BOOK OF MORMON: BOOK OF ETHER). He led his people from "the great tower" in Mesopotamia to the Western Hemisphere. "A large and mighty man, and a man highly favored of the Lord" (Ether 1:34), he is remembered most for his very great faith that allowed him to see and converse face to face with the premortal Jesus Christ (Ether 3:13; 12:19–21) and to be shown in VISION all the inhabitants and events of the earth from beginning to end (Ether 3:25).

Only a few details are known about the life and revelations of this ancient PROPHET. In response to his prayer of faith, the Lord did not confound his language or that of his family and friends at the time of the Tower of Babel. Instead, the Lord instructed him to lead those people to a land "choice above all the lands of the earth" (Ether 1:42), and he was promised that his descendants would become a great and righteous nation. They were called the Jaredites. The Lord came in a cloud to tell the brother of Jared where they should travel, but he did not see him (Ether 2:4). They gathered flocks and seeds, and journeyed to a place on the sea that they called Moriancumer (Ether 2:13). Although the Book of Mormon does not give this prophet's name, Joseph Smith later identified it as Mahonri Moriancumer (T&S 2 [1841]:362; Juvenile Instructor, Vol. 27 [May 1, 1892]:282).

For four years the Jaredites dwelt in tents on the seashore. During those years, the brother of Jared apparently ceased praying for guidance, and when the Lord appeared again in a cloud, he talked with him for three hours and chastened him, which caused him to repent and return to favor with God. Latter-day Saints see this as evidence of God's concern for his children, of the importance of daily prayer, and of the fact that the Spirit of the Lord will not always strive with man, even with a great prophet, unless he continues to petition the Lord in righteousness (Ether 2:15).

The brother of Jared built eight unique barges (Ether 2:16–25) in which to cross the ocean. Then he prepared sixteen clear molten stones and asked the Lord to make them shine to illuminate the inside of the barges (Ether 3:1–5). As the Lord touched the stones, the brother of Jared saw the finger of the Lord and was "struck with fear" (Ether 3:6). Never before, the record states, had man come before God with such exceeding faith; as a result, he was brought into the presence of the Lord Jesus Christ and saw the premortal SPIRIT BODY of Christ (Ether 3:9–13).

In this vision, the brother of Jared learned many things: he was told that he had been redeemed from the Fall; he saw that human beings were physically created in the image of God and that the spirit body of Jesus looked the same as would his future physical body; he beheld all the inhabitants of the earth from the beginning to the end; and he learned many other sacred things, which he was commanded to record in a cryptic language, sealed up to come forth in the "due time" of the Lord (Ether 3:24; 4:1–2). With that record he included two stones that had been prepared by the Lord to aid future prophets in interpreting the record. For all these reasons, Latter-day Saints esteem the brother of Jared as one of the mightiest prophets who ever lived.

The brother of Jared and his people crossed the sea to the promised land. His great faith, as noted by Moroni, once caused a mountain, Zerin, to be removed (Ether 12:30). He had twenty-two sons and daughters. He lived to see his people begin to prosper and his nephew, Orihah, anointed as their king.

BIBLIOGRAPHY

Eyring, Henry B. "The Brother of Jared." *Ensign* 8 (July 1978):62–65.

REX C. REEVE, JR.

BUFFETINGS OF SATAN

An individual who receives extensive spiritual knowledge, enters into sacred COVENANTS, and then turns away from those promises to the Lord may be left to the buffetings of Satan until complete REPENTANCE has occurred. This sin differs in nature and category from one committed in ignorance. Paul alluded to such in 1 Corinthians 5:1–5, but a clearer understanding of the doctrine is found in latter-day REVELATION (see DS 2:96–98).

To the Prophet Joseph SMITH the Lord revealed the situation of some who had broken the covenants by which they had entered the UNITED ORDER. That revelation reads, "The soul that sins against this covenant, and hardeneth his heart against it, shall be dealt with according to the laws of my church, and shall be delivered over to the buffetings of Satan until the day of redemption" (D&C 82:20–21; cf. 78:12; 104:9–10). The same principle applies to persons whose temple marriage is sealed by the HOLY SPIRIT OF PROMISE, and who later transgress and break their covenants. The revelation states that they "shall be delivered unto the buffetings of Satan unto the day of redemption, saith the Lord God" (D&C 132:26).

Elder Bruce R. McConkie, a latter-day APOSTLE, explained that to be "turned over to the buffetings of Satan is to be given into [Satan's] hands; it is to be turned over to him with all the protective power of the priesthood, of righteousness, and of godliness removed, so that Lucifer is free to torment, persecute, and afflict such a person without let or hindrance. When the bars are down, the cuffs and curses of Satan, both in this world and in the world to come, bring indescribable anguish typified by burning fire and brimstone.

The damned in hell so suffer" (*MD*, "Buffetings of Satan"; see also McConkie, Vol. 2, p. 335).

The term "buffetings of Satan" used in latter-day revelation is associated with punishment for the violation of covenants and is distinct from the "buffet" or "buffeted" used occasionally in the New Testament, which refers to the suffering, maltreatment, and persecution to which the Savior, Paul, and other church members were often subjected by people (Matt. 26:67; 1 Cor. 4:11; 2 Cor. 12:7).

[*See also* Damnation; Hell.]

BIBLIOGRAPHY

McConkie, Bruce R. *Doctrinal New Testament Commentary*, 3 vols. Salt Lake City, 1965–1973.

DENNIS D. FLAKE

BUILDING PROGRAM

Throughout its history the Church has faced the challenge of providing adequate buildings to serve its growing membership for worship and for cultural, educational, and recreational activities. The "building program" is the term given to the Church's system of central direction, design, and financing for the construction of meetinghouses and temples throughout the world. Under the direction of the First Presidency and Presiding Bishopric, a professional staff headquartered in Salt Lake City creates standard building plans and specifications, and establishes procedures for construction and expenditures. Although this program has been extensively developed in the years since World War II, some central direction and planning have existed from the Church's beginnings.

The Church's first two important buildings, the temples at KIRTLAND, Ohio, and NAUVOO, Illinois, were both projects initiated, financed, and supervised by general Church leaders. Members throughout the Church contributed money, and many local Saints contributed every tenth day's labor. Some young men were called for full-time work, and more experienced craftsmen were employed at subsistence wages paid from contributed funds. Similar procedures were followed for the never-completed Nauvoo House and, after the move west, the Salt Lake Temple and Tabernacle.

As Church membership grew and dispersed throughout hundreds of settlements in the West, design and construction of meetinghouses, stake tabernacles, Church schools, and other buildings became a local responsibility. In many cases, Church Presidents or other general leaders encouraged such projects, and occasionally provided designs and financial assistance, but usually the responsibility for raising funds and supervising construction remained with local ecclesiastical officers.

In 1923 the Church Architectural Department in Salt Lake City began furnishing plans for meetinghouses and SEMINARY buildings throughout the Church. Over the next decade, about 350 meetinghouses and 35 seminary buildings were constructed from these plans, most of them red-brick buildings in an adaptation of colonial style. Willard Young, a son of Brigham Young, directed the department, with architect Joseph Don Carlos Young, another son, providing most of the plans. Non-Mormon architects also provided plans for more than 185 buildings during this period, mostly outside of Utah. Funding and construction remained a local responsibility, except for about 50 buildings that received some Church support. This department ceased providing plans around 1933, and local congregations again became responsible for the design of their own buildings, with only general direction from the department.

The decades following the Great Depression and World War II left the Church with pressing needs for many new meetinghouses, because of unprecedented growth, particularly outside the Great Basin. The Church Building Committee, led by Howard J. McKean, was organized in 1946 to fill these needs. The program began with a ratio of 40 percent general Church financing and 60 percent raised locally, but within a few years this ratio changed in most cases to 50–50. Under this program, the Church Building Department supervised the preparation of building plans by independent architects. The local bishop or branch president became the contractor for each project, working with an experienced construction foreman, usually a local member. Local congregations contributed as much labor and skill as possible. The value of their work was credited toward their share of the building cost, usually not more than 10 percent of the total. The local branch or ward was required to raise half of its share of the cost before construction could begin, and all of it before completion. If the cash flow stopped, construction stopped. More than 630 meetinghouses were built between 1945 and 1955 following this procedure, with few delays because of funding. In Utah and

The Provo Utah Edgemont Stake Center, dedicated in 1990, was one of more than 8,000 Church buildings constructed between 1948 and 1990. Courtesy Doug Martin.

most other areas of the United States, these red-brick colonial buildings with white steeples became prominent features of the landscape. After 1950, various standard architectural plans were also provided for seminary and institute buildings.

By the early 1950s the growth of the Church in the South Pacific created need for meetinghouses and schools in areas where money and skilled labor were in short supply. In 1954, Church leaders, including the new Building Committee chairman, Wendell Mendenhall, responded with a building missionary program. Members with construction skills were called to oversee projects in Polynesia. Supervisors took their families with them and received living allowances. They were to train and supervise young building missionaries and other local volunteers while they built the buildings. This program began with the construction of the Church college and temple in New Zealand. In 1956 it expanded to provide meetinghouses and schools throughout the South Pacific and Australia, using plans sent from Salt Lake City. In 1960–1961 the program extended to meetinghouses in the British Isles and continental Europe, with offices in England, Holland, and Germany. Because of differences in language and building procedures in these countries, local architects prepared plans based on standard guidelines. In 1962 the building missionary program was extended to the Far East, Latin America, the United States, and Canada. Difficulties in supervision and financial management caused the discontinuance of this program in 1965. More than 2,000 buildings were constructed under this system.

In the late 1950s, increased construction in the United States and Canada led to the creation of four area offices within the Building Department in Salt Lake City, each supervising property acquisitions, plan refinement, construction, and financial management of projects within a geographical area. These area offices have been divided and extended through the years to include other countries as well. During the late 1950s and early 1960s, building plans evolved toward more diversified styles.

In 1965 a new Church Building Committee, under the chairmanship of Mark B. Garff, instituted more centralized control of the building program. The headquarters office continued to prepare detailed standardized plans and specifications, including color schemes and landscape designs, for virtually all new buildings. Local architects were retained for each project to help in preparing site plans, obtaining competitive bids and building permits, and overseeing construction. In 1978 the Real Estate, Building, and Operations and Maintenance divisions were combined into the Department of Physical Facilities, with Fred A. Baker as managing director. Area offices were expanded, increased in number, extended worldwide, and placed under the direction of General Authorities assigned as area presidencies in 1984, with many offices moved to the regions they served. Plans for meetinghouses were still produced in the headquarters office in Salt Lake City and distributed through these offices. The ratio of Church to local financial participation in building projects changed over these years, to 70–30 in 1960, to 96–4 in 1982, and to 100–0 in 1990. In the United States, nearly all construction is performed by contractors, while in some other countries local members still contribute some labor. Where practical, meetinghouses are shared by two or more wards or branches.

The building of temples throughout the world has remained under the close supervision of the First Presidency. The Temples and Special Projects Division of the Building Department (later the Department of Physical Facilities) in Salt Lake City began supervising the preparation of plans and construction of temples throughout the world in 1965. In 1983 the design of temple standard plans was transferred to the Architectural and Engineering Division. In most cases, local architects have been retained to adapt these standard designs to local conditions and styles and to aid in supervising bidding and construction.

The centrally directed building program has been one of the largest and most costly programs of the Church. While the high degree of central control and standardization may have discouraged architectural innovation and flexibility in meeting local circumstances, the system has provided consistent guidelines and orderly procedures for an enormous undertaking. Between 1948 and 1990, it directed the construction of more than 8,500 buildings, supporting and aiding the growth and development of the Church around the world.

BIBLIOGRAPHY

Allen, James B., and Glen M. Leonard. *The Story of the Latter-day Saints.* Salt Lake City, 1976.

Cowan, Richard O. *The Church in the Twentieth Century.* Salt Lake City, 1985.

Cummings, David W. *Mighty Missionary of the Pacific.* Salt Lake City, 1961.

PAUL L. ANDERSON
RICHARD W. JACKSON

BULLETIN

The *Bulletin* (1980–) constitutes official correspondence from Church headquarters to all general and local-unit Church leaders. It was formerly called the *Messenger* (1956–1964), the *Priesthood Bulletin* (1965–1974), and the *Messages* (1975–1980). Issued as needed by the Correlation Department of the Church under the direction of the FIRST PRESIDENCY and the QUORUM OF THE TWELVE, it communicates or reaffirms current Church policies, practices, procedures, and programs. All previous *Bulletins* are periodically superseded by the issuance of a revised GENERAL HANDBOOK OF INSTRUCTIONS and by policy letters from the First Presidency.

J. HUGH BAIRD

BURIAL

The Church of Jesus Christ of Latter-day Saints counsels its members to bury their dead in the earth to return dust to dust, unless the law of the country requires CREMATION. However, the decision whether to bury or cremate the body is left to the family of the deceased, taking into account any laws governing the matter. Burial of the body usually follows a funeral or graveside service. The body of a deceased member of the Church who has received the temple ENDOWMENT should be dressed in temple clothing. RELIEF SOCIETY sisters dress deceased women, and priesthood brethren the men. When it is not possible to clothe the body, temple clothing may be laid over it.

A member of the BISHOPRIC typically presides at the burial, where a simple, earnest prayer is offered to dedicate the grave, with blessings promised as the Spirit dictates. This prayer may include a dedication of the grave as a sacred resting place until the resurrection if the person giving the prayer holds the MELCHIZEDEK PRIESTHOOD and has been asked to give such a dedication. The grave site often becomes a sacred spot for the family of the deceased to visit and care for.

CHARLES D. TATE, JR.

BURNINGS, EVERLASTING

Moses described God as a "consuming fire" (Deut. 4:24), his glory consuming everything corrupt and unholy (D&C 63:34; 101:23–24). The Prophet Joseph SMITH explained, "God Almighty Himself dwells in eternal fire; flesh and blood cannot go there, for all corruption is devoured by the fire," but a resurrected being, "flesh and bones quickened by the Spirit of God," can (TPJS, pp. 326, 367; cf. Luke 24:36–43; 1 Cor. 15:50). Heaven, not hell, is the realm of everlasting burnings, a view contrasting with the popular conception of hell as a place of fire, brimstone, and searing heat. Heat is a characteristic of God's glory (D&C 133:41–44).

Only those cleansed from physical and moral corruption can endure immortal glory (3 Ne. 27:19; Moses 6:57; TPJS, p. 351). Hence, Isaiah rhetorically asked, "Who among us shall dwell with the devouring fire? who among us shall dwell with everlasting burnings?" (Isa. 33:14). Joseph Smith taught, "All men who are immortal (i.e., resurrected beings in any of the DEGREES OF GLORY) dwell in everlasting burnings" (TPJS, pp. 347, 361, 367). Resurrected bodies are qualitatively different according to their glory (1 Cor. 15:39–44; D&C 88:28–32).

Describing a vision of the CELESTIAL KINGDOM, Joseph Smith reported, "I saw the transcendent beauty of the gate through which the heirs of that kingdom will enter, which was like unto circling flames of fire; also the blazing throne of God, whereon was seated the Father and the Son" (D&C 137:2–3).

RODNEY TURNER

BUSINESS

[This is a two-part entry:

LDS Attitudes Toward Business
Church Participation in Business

The first article explains the Church position toward business in general, and the second article describes the nature of the Church's participation in business activities through recently affiliated corporations. For historical information, see Community; Economic History; Kirtland Economy; Pioneer Economy.]

LDS ATTITUDES TOWARD BUSINESS

Business endeavors hold no mandated interest for the Church or its members. Church members involve themselves in all avenues of life in much the same proportion as the general population of the region or country in which they live (see OCCUPATIONAL STATUS). Church members are urged to be honest in all their dealings with their fellow men, including business and professional activities. Elements of history, theology, and practice combine to form a positive LDS attitude toward honest business endeavors.

Many LDS attitudes toward business are rooted in the Church's frontier heritage. As the Church developed settlements in Ohio, Missouri, Illinois, and the Great Basin, it became necessary and desirable to be involved in business activities. Cooperative business efforts were necessary for success, independence, and survival.

In addition to its spiritual and cultural roles, the Church sponsored economic initiatives that could not be mounted by individual entrepreneurs. For example, when it was determined that sugar would be expensive and difficult to obtain in the Great Basin, the Church in the 1850s sponsored a business venture to cultivate and process sugar beets. Converts brought capital and equipment from Europe, and factories were constructed. After extended difficulties, a thriving sugar beet industry resulted in the 1890s. Similarly, to provide banking services, a Church-sponsored bank was incorporated. A general store—Zion's Cooperative Mercantile Institution (ZCMI)—was begun, as were a newspaper, the DESERET NEWS, and several hospitals; later, radio and television stations were acquired by the Church (*see* BROADCASTING). As the capital needed for these businesses became available from private sources, the Church divested itself of nearly all business activities unrelated to its ecclesiastical mission.

Thus, historically, members of the Church have been integrally involved in business activities. In their pioneer environment, Latter-day Saints developed, out of necessity, traits of self-sufficiency, pragmatism, and resourcefulness. This heritage is reflected in an entrepreneurial spirit and penchant for hard work that lend themselves very well to business endeavors.

The theology of the Church is also supportive of honest business. Church doctrines emphasize individual AGENCY and self-determination, which provide fertile conceptual soil for fostering business attitudes of free enterprise. The Church teaches that property and wealth are STEWARD-SHIPS and that all people will be held accountable to God for what they have done with the time and resources entrusted to them (Young, p. 301). Church leaders continue to encourage members to live within their means, to save and be frugal, and to remain economically independent by avoiding debt. Such principles are harmonious with business success and help prepare Church members to perform well in a business environment.

In addition, the Church's organizational practices provide an opportunity for developing skills that are useful in business. Each member, young and old, is called upon to serve in some CALLING. Young boys and girls give talks in Church and develop public-speaking skills. Church youth are given leadership opportunities, and adult men and women fill numerous leadership and teaching positions in every local congregation (*see* LAY PARTICIPATION AND LEADERSHIP; LEADERSHIP TRAINING). Budgeting, counseling, organizing, and performing administrative tasks are carried out on a regular basis. From these experiences, members develop business-related skills that are useful in many business contexts.

Over the years, Church leaders have spoken forthrightly about maintaining high standards of business ethics and have warned against becoming carried away by business endeavors: "Material blessings are a part of the gospel if they are achieved in the proper way and for the right purpose" (N. Eldon Tanner, *Ensign* 9 [Nov. 1979]:80). Fair business dealing, giving value for value received, is scripturally required (Lev. 19:11, 35–36; 25:14; Deut. 24:14–15). Thus, President Spencer W. KIMBALL distinguished clean money from filthy lucre or compromise money: Clean money is "compensation received for a full day's honest work, . . . reasonable pay for faithful service, . . . fair profit from the sale of goods, commodities, or service; . . . income received from transactions where all parties profit" (Kimball, p. 948), and he counseled against conducting business unnecessarily on the Sabbath.

Employers are admonished to be generous and kind; employees, to be loyal and diligent. President Brigham YOUNG encouraged "every man who has capital [to] create business and give employment and means into the hands of laborers"; he saw economic strength in "the bone and sinew of workingmen and women," and encouraged all to be industrious: "If we all labor a few hours a day, we could then spend the remainder of our time in rest and the improvement of our minds" (Young, pp. 300–302). "Let every man and woman be industrious, prudent, and economical in their acts and feelings, and while gathering to themselves, let each one strive to identify his or her interests with . . . those of their neighbor and neighborhood, let them seek their happiness and welfare in that of all" (Young, p. 303).

[*See also* Consecration; Riches of Eternity; Wealth, Attitudes Toward.]

BIBLIOGRAPHY

Kimball, Spencer W. "Keep Your Money Clean." *IE* 56 (Dec. 1953):948–50.

Young, Brigham. *Discourses of Brigham Young*, comp. J. Widtsoe. Salt Lake City, 1954.

On the business experiences and philosophies of a prominent LDS entrepreneur in the 1930s, see Dean L. May, "Sources of Marriner S. Eccles's Economic Thought," *Journal of Mormon History* 3 (1976):85–99.

STEPHEN D. NADAULD

CHURCH PARTICIPATION IN BUSINESS

Historically, two purposes have characterized Church participation in business: to provide important services to the community that might not otherwise be available, and to provide a reasonable return on the resources of the Church. During the first half century of settlement in Utah, the Church started or helped to start many businesses. Some continue to operate; but as communities became self-sufficient, the Church withdrew from such business activities as banking, health care, commercial printing, sugar processing, and the Hotel Utah.

Most of the business assets of the Church originated in the pioneer era when its people were isolated from other business and commercial centers. When a newspaper was needed to help keep people of Utah informed, the Church established the DESERET NEWS in 1850. In the 1920s, federal officials urged newspapers to develop broadcast operations. In 1922 the *Deseret News* did as requested, and that was the beginning of KSL and BONNEVILLE INTERNATIONAL CORPORATION. To help Utah farmers develop a cash crop that they could sell beyond the borders of the state, the Church helped pioneer the sugar beet industry. ZCMI department stores were the outgrowth of a cooperative movement among the early pioneers. When hotel accommodations were insufficient to provide housing for a growing number of visitors to Temple Square and other points of interest in Salt Lake City shortly after the turn of the century, the Church joined with other community interests to construct Hotel Utah. Over a period of years, the Church bought out other investors to become the sole owner of Hotel Utah. The Church became more involved in Salt Lake City real estate primarily to preserve the beauty and the integrity of the downtown area, especially around Temple Square. That purpose guided Church officials when they decided in the late 1960s to lease to Salt Lake County, for one dollar per year, the property on which Symphony Hall and the Salt Palace Convention Center are now located.

At the beginning of 1990, major commercial businesses owned by the Church included Beneficial Development Company, Beneficial Life Insurance Company, Bonneville International Corporation, DESERET BOOK COMPANY, Deseret News Publishing Company, Deseret Trust Company, Farm Management Company, Temple Square Hotel Corporation, Utah Home Fire Insurance Company, and Zions Securities Corporation. The Church also owns Laie Resorts, Inc., a small motel, restaurant, and service station located adjacent to the POLYNESIAN CULTURAL CENTER in Hawaii. These businesses come under the umbrella of Deseret Management Company, a holding company that receives and distributes profits, performs internal audits, generates consolidated financial statements, files consolidated income tax returns for the group, coordinates activities, and reviews business operations and plans.

The Church of Jesus Christ of Latter-day Saints Foundation receives from Church businesses contributions from their pretax earnings, which in turn are given to the community as contributions to the arts, education, and charitable groups, and other beneficiaries. The LDS FOUNDATION coordinates the distribution of major portions of the charitable contributions designated by Church-owned businesses. In recent years, the Foundation has been a significant contributor to the new LDS Hospital wing, the new Primary Children's Medical Center, the new Holy Cross Hospital, the Salvation Army, Saint Vincent De Paul Center soup kitchen for the homeless, the Salt Lake City Homeless Shelter, the Utah Symphony, Ballet West, the United Way, and related organizations. Income from Church business operations permits participation in local community causes without using the tithing of members from around the world. Those tithes are dedicated to continuing the primary work of the Church, which includes teaching the gospel to the world, building faith and testimony and promoting activity among the membership, and helping members to complete sacred temple ordinances in proxy for the deceased.

Other business activities are under the aegis of the Investment Properties Division of the Church. For example, it oversees Church-owned farmland in several states and Canada, although many of the agricultural activities on the land are managed by Farm Management Companies.

The Church does not publish financial data regarding its privately owned businesses. However, Church officials have indicated that profits from business operations are used to provide living allowances for the General Authorities of the Church. While business profits are not disclosed, President Gordon B. Hinckley, a member of the First Presidency, said in 1985 that the combined income from all these business interests would not keep the work of the Church going for longer than a very brief period (Hinckley, 1985, p. 50).

In addition to its wholly owned businesses, the Church has controlling interest in the chain of

ZCMI department stores. Also, the Church once owned U and I Sugar Company, but many assets of that company have been sold. The company name was changed to U and I, Inc., and, more recently, to AgriNorthwest Company. Its remaining assets are held by Deseret Management Company. The Church also has a significant but noncontrolling interest in Heber J. Grant and Company, a holding company. Other investments include a varied portfolio of stocks and bonds.

Each of the businesses owned by the Church operates in a competitive environment and must succeed or fail according to standard business operating principles. These companies pay taxes to federal, state, and local governments. (The Church is the fourth largest payer of real estate taxes in Salt Lake County.) Church businesses have boards of directors that set policies for the individual companies. In most cases, Church leadership is represented on the boards of directors, but many boards include persons of other faiths.

Operating management is in the hands of professional managers, who need not be Church members. The Church requires them to operate the businesses in harmony with its principles and values of honesty, integrity, sensitivity, and service.

The Church expects its businesses to return something back to the communities from which they derive their revenues, and it encourages managers to participate actively in community activities and in business and professional associations. The Church expects them to set standards of excellence, to be leaders in their particular industries, and always to be conscious of the values of the ownership that they represent.

The major commercial businesses owned by the Church engage in the following activities:

Beneficial Development Company is a property development company dealing primarily with real estate holdings in and around Salt Lake City. In a very few instances, the company has installed roads, water systems, and other amenities for residential developments.

Beneficial Life Insurance Company offers the full range of life insurance protection. The company operates subsidiary insurance companies in Des Moines, Iowa, and Portland, Oregon.

Bonneville International Corporation is a commercial radio and television broadcast company with stations in Salt Lake City, Seattle, San Francisco, Los Angeles, Kansas City, Phoenix,

Dallas, Chicago, and New York. A division, Bonneville Communications, provides promotional services, and produces and distributes the weekly MORMON TABERNACLE CHOIR BROADCAST, the general conferences of the Church, the Homefront Series public service announcements, items for the Missionary Department, and various seasonal programs. The company also provides commercial advertising and promotional services for national businesses and organizations.

Deseret Book Company operates retail book stores in Utah, Idaho, California, Oregon, and Arizona. The company also serves as a publishing arm of the Church to publish books and other materials for and about the Church. In addition, the company operates the Mormon Handicrafts outlet in Salt Lake City.

Deseret News Publishing Company publishes Salt Lake City's afternoon daily, the *Deseret News*, and is a partner in the Newspaper Agency Corporation, which handles printing, advertising, and circulation for the two Salt Lake City dailies.

Deseret Trust Company receives and administers trust funds and trust properties given to the Church.

Farm Management Company manages commercial farms and other agricultural properties owned or leased by the Church, including Deseret Ranches of Florida (Orlando), Deseret Land and Livestock (Rich County, Utah), Deseret Farms of California (Sacramento), Rolling Hills (Emmett, Idaho), West Hills Orchards (Elberta, Utah), and Cactus Lane Ranch (Phoenix, Arizona).

Temple Square Hotel Corporation operates The Inn at Temple Square, a small European-style hotel across from Temple Square; and The Lion House, a historic building in downtown Salt Lake City that is used for luncheons, dinners, wedding receptions, and other social events.

Zions Securities Corporation manages properties owned by the Church, primarily in the downtown area of Salt Lake City, including the ZCMI Mall, the Eagle Gate Plaza office tower, the Eagle Gate Apartments, the Gateway Condominiums, several other apartment buildings, and a number of parking facilities.

BIBLIOGRAPHY

Hinckley, Gordon B. "Questions and Answers." *Ensign* 15 (Nov. 1985):49–52.

——. Untitled address to the Governor's Conference on

Utah's Future, Sept. 7, 1988. (Available upon request from the Church's Public Communications Department.)

Lindsey, Robert. "The Mormons—Growth, Prosperity and Controversy." *New York Times Magazine*, Jan. 12, 1986.

Parrish, Michael. "The Saints Among Us." *Rocky Mountain Magazine* 2 (Jan.–Feb. 1980):17–32.

Turner, Judd. "The Church in Business." *This People* 10 (Summer 1989):50–55.

See also the following series of articles on Church and business:

"*Arizona Republic* Explores LDS Financial Holdings." *Deseret News*, June 30, 1991, pp. A1, A4.

"LDS Revenues Come Primarily from Tithing." *Deseret News*, July 1, 1991, pp. A1, A4.

"LDS Church Real Estate Holdings Include Farms, Ranches, Buildings. *Deseret News*, July 2, 1991, pp. A1, A4, A5.

"LDS Church Uses Media Empire to Set Example in Communities." *Deseret News*, July 3, 1991, pp. A1, A5.

RODNEY H. BRADY

BYU

See: Brigham Young University

C

CAIN

Although the Bible says little about Cain, latter-day scriptures give considerable information. These tell that Cain, son of Adam and Eve, came under the influence of Satan, whom "he loved . . . more than God" (Moses 5:18; see DEVIL), and thereafter became the founder of secret societies whose purposes include to "murder and get gain" (Moses 5:31; cf. 5:49–51).

When Eve bore Cain, she rejoiced in the prospect of a child who would accept his parents' teaching concerning the true Son (Moses 5:7–8) saying, "I have gotten a man from the Lord; wherefore he may not reject his words. But behold, Cain hearkened not, saying: Who is the Lord that I should know him?" (Moses 5:16).

It was Satan who commanded Cain to make an offering to the Lord. When Cain followed Satan's instruction, his offering was rejected by the Lord. In the words of Moses, "Satan commanded him, saying: Make an offering unto the Lord. . . . But unto Cain, and to his offering, [the Lord] had not respect. Now Satan knew this, and it pleased him" (Moses 5:18, 21).

Earlier instructions from an angel to Adam and Eve had emphasized that animal sacrifice "is a similitude of the sacrifice of the Only Begotten of the Father. . . . Wherefore, thou shalt do all that

thou doest in the name of the Son" (Moses 5:7–8). Thus, Cain already knew what was acceptable to God, but he refused to follow counsel (*TPJS*, pp. 58, 169).

In the aftermath of his offering, the Lord assured Cain that "if thou doest well, thou shalt be accepted." However, he warned, "if thou doest not well, sin lieth at the door, and Satan desireth to have thee; and except thou shalt hearken unto my commandments, I will deliver thee up" (Moses 5:23). Cain's course of action, the Lord continued, would have long-lasting, even eternal consequences, for "thou [Cain] shalt rule over him [Satan]; for from this time forth thou shalt be the father of his [Satan's] lies; thou shalt be called Perdition; for thou wast also before the world. And it shall be said in time to come—That these abominations were had from Cain; for he rejected the greater counsel which was had from God" (Moses 5:23–25; cf. *TPJS*, p. 190).

Cain grew up with a knowledge of God and even conversed with him person to person. Yet he rejected the counsel of God and also killed his own brother ABEL. Afterward, the Lord said to Cain, "The voice of thy brother's blood cries unto me from the ground. And now thou shalt be cursed from the earth which hath opened her mouth to receive thy brother's blood from thy hand. . . . And Cain said unto the Lord: Satan tempted me because of my brother's flocks. And I was wroth also; for his offering thou didst accept and not mine" (Moses 5:35–38).

In consequence of Cain's rebellion, the Lord cast him out of his presence (Moses 5:38–39; *see* SPIRITUAL DEATH) and "set a mark upon Cain, lest any finding him should kill him" (Moses 5:40), protecting him from death by the hand of any avenger (cf. also Moses 7:22). Moreover, Satan had convinced Cain that by committing murder he would acquire both power and wealth. "Cain said: Truly I am Mahan, the master of this great secret, that I may murder and get gain" (Moses 5:31). This latter point became the foundation of the SECRET COMBINATIONS instituted by Cain in collusion with Satan and perpetuated by Cain's descendant Lamech (Moses 5:47–52).

In the Book of Mormon, although the origin and even the operating procedures of such secret organizations are mentioned and condemned from time to time (e.g. Hel. 6:22–30), MORONI₂, like others, purposely limits himself to general remarks when discussing their evils.

> And now I, Moroni, do not write the manner of their oaths and combinations, for it hath been made known unto me that they are had among all people. . . . Whoso buildeth it [a secret combination] up seeketh to overthrow the freedom of all lands, nations, and countries; and it bringeth to pass the destruction of all people, for it is built up by the devil, who is the father of all lies; even that same liar . . . who caused man to commit murder from the beginning [Ether 8:20, 25].

BIBLIOGRAPHY

McConkie, Bruce R. *A New Witness for the Articles of Faith,* pp. 167–68, 340, 658–59. Salt Lake City, 1985.

Smith, Joseph Fielding. *DS* 1:49, 61.

JAMES R. HARRIS

CALAMITIES AND DISASTERS

Calamities and disasters are sudden, unexpected events that cause extensive destruction, death, or injury and result in widespread community disruption and individual trauma. From its beginnings, The Church of Jesus Christ of Latter-day Saints has sought to be prepared against natural disasters following admonitions such as "if ye are prepared, ye shall not fear" (D&C 38:30). Preparedness is carried out on both individual and institutional levels.

In their homes, members are encouraged to have food storage sufficient for a year and other essentials of EMERGENCY PREPAREDNESS: clothing, bedding, fuel (where possible), and the like. Church members are also advised to have sufficient supplies to enable them to be completely self-sustaining for at least fourteen days without the benefit of electricity and clean running water.

On the organizational level, the Church response to disasters is administered by the PRESIDING BISHOPRIC at Church headquarters, by the STAKE PRESIDENT, and by the ward BISHOP. Each ward and stake has lay specialists called to assist in welfare and emergency preparedness. Meetinghouses are equipped to shelter people displaced by disasters, and regional storehouses can be drawn on for basic supplies. Large-scale disasters are responded to through the office of the Presiding Bishop.

Historically, Latter-day Saints organized to cope with the handcart crises in 1856, the flu epidemic of 1918, postwar crises in western Europe after both world wars, the Teton Dam disaster in southeast Idaho, mudslides and flooding in many places, and hurricane destruction in the South Pacific. The Church attempts to be in constant readiness to handle such immediate needs as search and rescue, food distribution, and shelter management. In addition, it addresses itself to individual members' needs such as vocational training and emotional therapy, through the WELFARE SERVICES and LDS Social Services Departments of the Church.

REED H. BLAKE

CALIFORNIA, PIONEER SETTLEMENTS IN

Spaniards founded missions, presidios, pueblos, and ranchos in California seventy-seven years before the arrival of the Mormons, but Latter-day Saints were among the first Anglo-Americans to establish settlements there. Brigham YOUNG believed that a seaport on the West Coast was essential to the landlocked community in Utah. He may have thought early of San Francisco as a Mormon seaport, and the ports of San Diego and San Pedro (Los Angeles area) ultimately were included within the boundaries of the proposed state of Deseret (*see* DESERET, STATE OF).

The first Latter-day Saint settlers in California located at Yerba Buena, a port connected with the mission and presidio San Francisco de Asís. Founded in 1776, the Catholic mission had fewer than one hundred people living in the area in 1845. After Elder Sam Brannan and 238 Saints arrived there on the ship *Brooklyn* on July 31, 1846, Latter-day Saints for a time predominated in Yerba Buena. About twelve families of the *Brooklyn* Saints founded the first Mormon colony in California, the short-lived agricultural community of New Hope (1846–1848), on the Stanislaus River in central California. Another of the *Brooklyn* Saints, John M. Horner, became a wealthy farmer at the southern end of San Francisco Bay. He helped found eight towns in the area and made substantial

Charles C. Rich (1809–1883), member of the Quorum of the Twelve, one of many Latter-day Saints in California between 1846 and 1857. In 1851, Rich and Amasa M. Lyman were called to establish a self-sustaining unit of the Church in San Bernardino, California. Land was purchased, the town laid out, and schools and mills established. In 1857, the settlers were recalled to Salt Lake City. Rich, who later settled Bear Lake Valley on the Utah-Idaho border, was known for his goodness, generosity, and physical strength. Photograph, c. 1880, Charles W. Carter.

financial contributions to the Church's missionary work in the 1850s.

Recognizing the rich potential of California, Brannan journeyed east to meet Brigham Young, then traveling west with the original PIONEERS of 1847. At their meeting on the Green River in western Wyoming, Brannan tried to persuade Brigham Young to continue on to California rather than stop in the Great Basin. Failing in this effort, Brannan returned to Yerba Buena, where he headed a prosperous LDS community until the gold rush of 1848–1849 and internal difficulties led to its dissolution. In 1847 Yerba Buena was renamed San Francisco.

Some 340 men of the MORMON BATTALION reached southern California in January 1847. Though they arrived shortly after the California War for Independence, or Bear Flag Revolt, ended, battalion veterans nevertheless had a significant impact on California history. When the battalion came to San Diego, their one-year enlistment was nearly completed. Eighty-one men reenlisted (about fifteen of whom left California on another assignment), and the rest (about 245) were discharged. Though some immediately joined their families in the SALT LAKE VALLEY, others remained in California to obtain funds before traveling to Utah. Some worked in the San Diego and Los Angeles areas, while others moved north to seek employment in San Francisco or at Sutter's Fort, on the American River near present-day Sacramento.

Six recently discharged members of the battalion were at Sutter's Mill when the initial discovery of gold was made on January 24, 1848. Indeed, it is the journal of Mormon Battalion veteran Henry W. Bigler that historians use to set the date for the initial discovery of gold in California. Other battalion veterans were involved in the early 1848 search for gold, and one particularly rich region was called "Mormon Diggings." Probably the most successful Mormon gold miner was Thomas Rhoads, who had taken his large family overland from Missouri to California in 1846. Some of the Mormon miners took an estimated $25,000–$30,000 in gold to Salt Lake City, providing a substantial boost to the infant economy. Brigham Young called a limited number of Latter-day Saints on missions to mine gold in California in 1849 and 1850. Others who were disillusioned with the Great Basin or infected with "gold fever" gravitated to California against his advice.

In 1851, under the direction of Charles C. Rich, an apostle, 437 colonists from Utah were sent to found a settlement near the Cajon Pass. The result was San Bernardino, the principal LDS settlement in California along the "Mormon Corridor" connecting Utah settlements and the West Coast. It was intended to.be a gathering place for immigrants from the Pacific as well as a way station to assist LDS immigration via the Pacific. Latter-day Saints from the gold fields also gathered there. By 1856 about 3,000 settlers lived in San Bernardino, but the colony was plagued by dissension. In 1857, as the U.S. Army approached Utah (*see* UTAH EXPEDITION), Brigham Young instructed the San Bernardino Saints, along with other outlying settlers, to return to Utah. Only a little more than half complied, and many of those who remained drifted from the Church. After the 1857 evacuation, as before, California attracted some Latter-day Saints who were dissatisfied with Brigham Young's relatively authoritarian style of leadership, or with the practice of polygamy, or with the Great Basin itself.

After its official withdrawal from California in 1857–1858, the Church sponsored no further COLONIZATION in the state. Latter-day Saints subsequently moved to California as individuals rather than at the request of the Church. Many migrated there in the 1920s during the southern California land promotion boom. Thousands moved there during World War II for employment opportunities in war industries such as shipping and aircraft. Today California has perhaps the greatest density of Latter-day Saints outside the states of Utah and Idaho. Two LDS temples are located there, in Los Angeles and Oakland, with another under construction in San Diego in 1990.

BIBLIOGRAPHY

Arrington, Leonard J. *Great Basin Kingdom.* Cambridge, Mass., 1958.

———. *Charles C. Rich: Mormon General and Western Frontiersman,* pp. 137–213. Provo, Utah, 1974.

Bailey, Paul. *Sam Brannan and the California Mormons.* Los Angeles, 1943.

Campbell, Eugene E. "The Mormon Gold Mining Mission of 1849." *BYU Studies* 1–2 (Autumn 1959–Winter 1960):19-31.

———. "Brigham Young's Outer Cordon: A Reappraisal." *Utah Historical Quarterly* 41 (Summer 1973):221-53.

Davies, J. Kenneth. *Mormon Gold: The Story of California's Mormon Argonauts.* Salt Lake City, 1984.

Hunter, Milton R. *Brigham Young the Colonizer.* Salt Lake City, 1940.

Orton, Chad M. *More Faith Than Fear: The Los Angeles Stake Story.* Salt Lake City, 1987.

TED J. WARNER

CALLING AND ELECTION

An exhortation to make one's "calling and election sure" is found in Peter's writings (2 Pet. 1:3–10), and is associated with the "more sure word of prophecy" (2 Pet. 1:16–19). The Prophet Joseph SMITH explained that "the more sure word of prophecy means a man's knowing that he is sealed up unto eternal life, by revelation and the spirit of prophecy, through the power of the Holy Priesthood" (D&C 131:5).

Peter said that the acquisition and exercise of faith, virtue, knowledge, temperance, patience, godliness, brotherly kindness, and charity are necessary to make one's "calling and election sure" and to obtain a fulness of the blessings of God (2 Pet. 1:5–7; cf. *TPJS*, p. 305).

In addition to acquiring these qualities of character, those who would have their calling and election made sure must receive the ordinances of the gospel, including the temple ordinances (D&C 131:2–3; 132:19–20).

Having one's calling and election made sure is not attained easily. Speaking of this, the Prophet Joseph Smith taught that "When the Lord has thoroughly proved [a person], and finds that the [person] is determined to serve Him at all hazards, then the [person] will find his[/her] calling and election made sure" (*TPJS*, p. 150). The Prophet indicates that this was the case with ancient prophets such as Isaiah, Ezekiel, John, Paul and others (*TPJS*, p. 151).

BIBLIOGRAPHY

Doxey, Roy W., comp. *The Latter-day Prophets and the Doctrine and Covenants,* Vol. 4, pp. 406–409. Salt Lake City, 1965.

McConkie, Bruce R. *Doctrinal New Testament Commentary,* Vol. 3, pp. 323–53. Salt Lake City, 1973.

ROY W. DOXEY

CALLINGS

The Church of Jesus Christ of Latter-day Saints is organized to benefit all who participate, and all are expected to assist in its labors (*see* ACTIVITY IN THE

CHURCH; LAY PARTICIPATION AND LEADERSHIP; WARD ORGANIZATION). The Church is administered according to the principles of individual involvement, service, and self-government. There is no paid ministry in local WARDS or STAKES, and the work of the Church is carried out through volunteer service by the members, who are called by priesthood leaders to contribute in various capacities. Callings may be general requests or assignments to follow some particular instruction for the benefit of the Church, assignments to serve in the PRIESTHOOD, or requests to fill specific administrative, teaching, or service-oriented positions. They are usually for indefinite periods of time. Committed Latter-day Saints accept and fulfill one or more callings at any given time. Called by Church leaders whom Latter-day Saints support as inspired representatives of the Lord, members serve until they are released, often because they are called to other positions that need their talents, and as the inspiration of the Holy Ghost indicates.

The most frequent callings are charges to Church members to take certain actions or to perform specific functions. Early examples of this are seen in the revelations from God—recorded from 1830 on in the Doctrine and Covenants—that call for the gathering of his people (D&C 29:7–8; 57:1–2). These calls initiated the dynamic missionary effort of the Church, the migration and gathering of Saints to form a new society of those striving to be pure in heart (D&C 97:21), and the development of support organizations to encourage and finance these activities.

Calls to action can be issued by leaders to the members overall, to a congregation, or to an individual. These calls may be permanent or temporary, depending upon the needs of the Church and the members. Another type of calling is the selection of a member to receive the priesthood. Every worthy male member of the Church age twelve or older may be called to receive the Aaronic, and later the Melchizedek Priesthood and is sequentially ordained to an office in each priesthood (D&C 20:60; see also PRIESTHOOD OFFICES). One who holds the priesthood has a permanent calling and obligation to remain worthy to help build the KINGDOM OF GOD on earth, with family responsibilities being central to that call. In a message "To the Home Teachers of the Church" in the May 1989 Ensign, President Ezra Taft BENSON wrote that an essential priesthood calling, equal in importance to any other in the church, is to assist Church families through a HOME TEACHING assignment. All offices and callings in the church derive their "rights, powers, and prerogatives" from the priesthood (McConkie, p. 353).

A third type of calling, and the most typical, involves positions in local congregations in either the priesthood or auxiliary programs of the Church. Latter-day Saints believe that a calling as an officer or teacher is a stewardship, where they are to bless those they have been called to serve (Matt. 20:26–28).

The majority of callings are unpaid and temporary. But callings in certain governing quorums of the Church require full-time service and in some cases are permanent, with financial support if needed (see GENERAL AUTHORITIES). Any worthy member can receive a full-time unpaid call to serve as a missionary, MISSION PRESIDENT, or as a TEMPLE PRESIDENT AND MATRON, but these callings are for a limited number of months or years. As of 1990, for example, every worthy unmarried young man (eligible at age nineteen) is expected to serve a period as a full-time missionary, without reimbursement from the Church. Worthy young women who so choose may receive mission calls at age twenty-one.

One purpose of Church callings is to benefit individual members by letting them do the work of the Church. Responsibility and authority are distributed locally. Leaders delegate to officers and teachers the responsibility of conceiving, planning, preparing, and executing the activities pertinent to their callings (D&C 107:99). This decentralized organization encourages initiative and personal growth among members of local wards and stakes. Through service, members learn their responsibility and their capacity, enlarge their understanding, and increase their commitment to the gospel (D&C 58:26–28; Matt. 10:39).

Calls are issued through an orderly process. The first step involves the selection of those to be called. For example, the presiding authority (the STAKE PRESIDENT or BISHOP) is to thoughtfully and prayerfully evaluate possible candidates for each office or teaching responsibility. Other leaders who eventually will be working closely with the person may be asked to suggest the names of a few candidates they think could serve ably. Newly called presidents of quorums or auxiliaries are given the right and responsibility of submitting the names of those they wish to be their counselors, and unless there are problems of availability or worthiness, such candidates are given priority. Personal worthiness, ability, willingness to serve, individual and family circumstances, whether the calling would benefit those being served, and the possible impact on the lives of the member and the member's family are to be considered carefully. The prime consideration for a leader in selecting a person for a calling is confirmation by the Holy Ghost of the correctness of the final selection. When leaders select members to fulfill callings in this manner, members understand that callings have divine approval.

The second step involved in extending a call requires the authorized leader to hold a private interview with the member to issue and explain the calling. When a wife, husband, or child is to receive a call, it is recommended that the husband, wife, or parents of the candidate be consulted regarding the calling. Support by family members of the one who is receiving a call is an important consideration.

All calls respect individual agency with the decision to accept or decline resting with the member being called. It is considered an opportunity and honor to be asked to serve; however, calls require sacrifice, and they may come at inconvenient times. Therefore, the persons called are counseled to make the decision by examining their circumstances and taking the matter to the Lord in prayer. To accept a calling requires humility, invites personal prayer, and inspires increased commitment. Many of the blessings associated with callings result from the voluntary nature of the service. When the calling is viewed as a sacred stewardship, the dedication to the calling is of high quality. If a member decides, because of an unwillingness to serve, not to accept a call from God, the decision is viewed with regret by those issuing the call (Widtsoe, p. 199).

The third step in the process is the presentation of the name of the person called to a constituent body of members for a sustaining vote. According to the principle of COMMON CONSENT in the Church, no person is to serve in an official calling without the consent of the membership (D&C 20:65). The sustaining vote is not an election, but signifies that members know of no reason why the individual should be disqualified from service and that they are willing to offer cooperation and support (Arrington and Bitton, p. 208). Members are instructed to have faith and be supportive of those called to serve. At least once a year, members have the opportunity in a ward or branch conference to formally sustain their entire general and local Church leadership.

After receiving the consent of the Church, the call is completed by the LAYING ON OF HANDS by authorized priesthood holders. This act of ordination, or SETTING APART, confers the authority of the office or position and testifies "visibly and without question, that the powers or keys or prerogatives are vested in the recipient" (McConkie, p. 326). A priesthood BLESSING is given to the one called, the fulfillment of which is conditional upon faithful service. Generally, members anticipate receiving the ordinance of being set apart and are spiritually uplifted.

Once sustained and set apart in a calling, members receive training in their new responsibilities through their leaders and Church-produced manuals, as well as during in-service meetings and special conferences (see LEADERSHIP TRAINING). It is understood that individuals will serve in particular callings for a time then be released, giving them the opportunity to support others in the position who once supported them. Ordinarily, members do not resign from their callings; they are released by the presiding authority. However, a member may go to the presiding authority to ask that new circumstances be considered and a release extended, if necessary. Releases are announced to the congregation and a vote of appreciation is offered to recognize the member's service.

Duration of service in a calling depends on the member's circumstances, the needs and resources of the Church, and the whisperings of the Spirit to the presiding authority. It is not the practice of the Church to "promote" persons from one position to another. All positions are considered equally necessary (1 Cor. 12:12–31), and positions of high visibility often involve increased responsibility and commitment of time. Similarly, members do not volunteer, campaign, or call themselves to positions. President J. Reuben Clark, Jr., explained that "in the service of the Lord, it is not where you serve but how" (IE 54 [June 1951]:412). The collective strength of the Church is enhanced through every member receiving broad experience in a variety of callings.

BIBLIOGRAPHY

Arrington, Leonard R., and Davis Bitton. *The Mormon Experience*, pp. 207–208. New York City, 1979.

McConkie, Bruce R. *A New Witness for the Articles of Faith*, pp. 305–354. Salt Lake City, 1985.

Widtsoe, John A. *Priesthood and Church Government*, pp. 193–205, 233–45. Salt Lake City, 1939.

BRIAN L. PITCHER

CANADA, THE CHURCH IN

By October 1830, converts to the Church were teaching the gospel to family and friends in Canadian cities and towns less than 200 miles from Palmyra, New York. Between 1830 and 1845, LDS missionaries labored in Upper Canada (now Ontario) and the more easterly Maritime Provinces of British North America. Lower Canada (Quebec), with its Roman Catholic heritage and traditions, was then largely impervious to competing religious influences. Brigham YOUNG, Parley P. PRATT and Orson PRATT, John E. Page, and even the Prophet Joseph SMITH visited and preached in Upper Canada during these early years. Some 2,500 Canadians joined the Church in Kingston, Earnestown, Toronto, Brantford, Mount Pleasant, North and South Crosby, and elsewhere. Yet so many Latter-day Saint Canadian converts migrated to the centers of the Church or fell away that the 1861 census counted only seventy-four Mormons in all of Upper Canada.

The second LDS penetration into Canada came some fifty years later and 2,500 miles farther west, when Church President John TAYLOR, a British-born Canadian convert, sent Charles Ora Card to Canada to find a place of refuge for the Saints from the U.S. government's campaign against PLURAL MARRIAGE. Card's small 1887 settlement on Lee's Creek in southern Alberta be-

came Cardston. The Canadian government also outlawed plural marriage, but most public opposition to the Church declined with the 1890 MANIFESTO, which officially ended the practice.

Taking full advantage of the Canadian government's "National Policy," which encouraged immigration, several thousand skilled and seasoned Latter-day Saints moved north, and soon several other Mormon towns sprung up around Cardston: Raymond (1890), and Sterling and McGrath (1898). The Alberta Stake was organized on June 9, 1895, the first LDS stake outside the United States. Charles O. Card was its president. Skilled in farming, particularly sugar beets, and in irrigating large land acreages, LDS farmers soon earned the admiration of friend and foe. By 1914, more than 10,000 Latter-day Saints were settled in a score of communities in southern Alberta. In 1923 the Church dedicated the Cardston Temple, the first temple outside the United States and its territories.

Gradually the LDS populations in Canada have shifted northward to the larger urban centers of Lethbridge, Calgary, Red Deer, and Edmonton. In the process, many members of the Church have shifted from agricultural to professional careers. Since 1950, Latter-day Saints have been known for their involvement in the oil and gas industry, railroad construction, provincial politics, education, and in many other pursuits. In 1990, more than 50,000 members of the Church lived in Alberta, 12,000 in Calgary alone.

The Alberta Temple, located in Cardston, in southern Alberta, and dedicated in 1923, was the first LDS temple built outside the United States and its territories. Constructed of handhewn white marble from British Columbia, it won architectural acclaim.

From the Latter-day Saint communities in Alberta, members have pursued educational vocational careers in Canadian communities from coast to coast. The ranks of Church members all across Canada have grown steadily, though not spectacularly. The story has often been the same—a few local converts, some Alberta move-ins, a steady stream of missionaries, some more local converts and leaders, rented halls giving way to Church-built meetinghouses, branches becoming wards, districts becoming stakes. The first Canadian stakes outside Alberta were organized in Toronto, Ontario, and Vancouver in 1960. Since then stakes have been organized in Manitoba, Saskatchewan, Nova Scotia, and New Brunswick, characteristically encompassing large land areas. Quebec, once hostile, had two stakes, one English- and one French-speaking, in 1990.

Hugh B. Brown and Nathan Eldon Tanner, who had been successful business, military, and education leaders in Alberta, came to serve as counselors in the FIRST PRESIDENCY of the Church in 1961–1970 and 1963–1982, respectively.

In 1990 more than half the Canadian LDS population of approximately 125,000 lived outside of Alberta, in sixteen of the country's thirty-four stakes. The dedication and opening of the Toronto Temple in 1990 symbolized more than 150 years of achievements by the Church in Canada.

BIBLIOGRAPHY

Bennett, Richard E. "A Study of The Church of Jesus Christ of Latter-day Saints in Upper Canada, 1830–1850." M.A. thesis, Brigham Young University, 1975.

Card, Brigham Young. *The Canadian Mormon Communities in Southwestern Alberta, Canada: Origins, Persistence, and Transformation of an Ethnic Identity.* Canada, 1988.

———— et al., eds. *The Mormon Presence in Canada.* Logan, Utah, 1990.

Tagg, Melvin S. *A History of the Mormon Church in Canada.* Lethbridge, Alta., 1968.

RICHARD E. BENNETT

CANADA, LDS PIONEER SETTLEMENTS IN

LDS experience in Canada provides an important comparison to the study of the Church in the United States. Though the Church settlements of southern Alberta, begun in the late nineteenth century, were an extension of the LDS cultural region in the Great Basin, they gradually developed a unique character because they lay at the frontier intersection of two commonwealths, the Canadian and the Mormon—and as a hinterland of each. Constantly influenced by the exchange of people, ideas, and culture with the Great Basin, LDS settlements in Alberta contributed to the Church several General Authorities, including Hugh B. Brown and N. Eldon Tanner, both of whom served in the First Presidency.

Since most early Church converts from eastern Canada in the 1830s and 1840s soon joined the Saints in the United States (*see* GATHERING), the LDS presence in Canada was fleeting until the late 1880s. The first permanent Church settlements in Canada were built in Alberta by Latter-day Saints from Utah seeking refuge from PERSECUTION that

Charles O. Card (1839–1906), a pioneer leader who helped establish the first permanent LDS settlements in Canada, became president of the Alberta Stake in 1895, the first LDS stake outside the present boundaries of the United States.

followed increasingly harsh ANTIPOLYGAMY LEGISLATION. Led by Charles Ora Card, they established farms in 1887 around present-day Cardston.

Card, a prominent community and Church leader in Cache Valley, Utah, had been arrested in July 1886 for practicing polygamy. After escaping from custody, he visited Church President John TAYLOR, a British-born resident of Canada at the time of his conversion, who directed Card to go to Canada to seek "British justice." President Taylor's son, John W., an apostle, entrepreneur, and visionary, joined Card in leading the early development of Canadian LDS settlements.

In the fall of 1886, Card and two companions selected southwestern Alberta—a region with good land, water for irrigation, accessible timber and coal, and close to the Blood Indian reservation—where they hoped to proselytize. Cardston was established on April 26, 1887, and the Cardston ward of the Cache stake was organized in 1888. By 1891 there were 359 Saints in the area.

Influenced by prolonged conflict between the U.S. government and the Mormons, the press and politicians elsewhere in Canada opposed LDS settlement. But local boosters and Canadian government officials welcomed the arrival of farmers skilled in irrigation in an area known for its aridity. However, official opposition to polygamy was clear. When, in November 1888, Church leaders sought permission to bring existing plural families to Canada, the government quickly outlawed polygamy. Most opposition to the Church in Canada declined after the 1890 MANIFESTO announced the official end of plural marriage.

Previous experience helped the new settlers meet the challenges of pioneering in Canada. The Cardston Company, a joint-stock venture, mobilized capital for community projects, including a flour mill, cheese factory, steam threshing outfit, sawmill, and other enterprises. Some of the capital came from Card's wife, Zina, a daughter of Brigham Young, who was a former college professor, and a suffragette who served as a role model for other Canadian LDS women. The economic success of the Saints broke down barriers that separated them from local society. A series of drought years in the early 1890s showed the necessity of irrigation and highlighted LDS achievements with small-scale irrigation projects.

Beginning in the late 1890s, a second wave of LDS immigrants came primarily for economic reasons. The Galt coal mining interests in Lethbridge, hoping irrigation would allow them to sell sizable tracts of land to agricultural interests, formed a partnership with Card, who saw the potential for a major colonization program for LDS farmers from the United States. The 1898 contract between the Galt Company and the Church attracted LDS subcontractors, laborers, and teamsters to Alberta to build an irrigation system. Most were farmers intent on settling. By 1900 the canal was completed, and Lord Minto, the Canadian governor general, and George Q. Cannon and Joseph F. SMITH of the First Presidency attended the opening.

These new LDS settlers founded several new towns, including Magrath and Stirling. During the late 1890s and early 1900s, population growth in the Cardston area and a continuing influx from the United States prompted Latter-day Saints to settle in Beazer, Kimball, Leavitt, Taylorville, Woolford, Jefferson, and Del Bonita.

A new surge of settlement began in 1902–1903 when wealthy Utah mine owner Jesse Knight established a sugar factory in Raymond. Latter-day Saints played a key role both as growers and as managers of the sugar company in establishing the sugar beet industry, which remains an important part of southern Alberta's economy.

In 1906, E. J. Wood, successor to Charles O. Card as president of the Alberta Stake, bought a large ranch, opening 35,000 acres to colonization and laying out the towns of Glenwood (1908) and Hillspring (1910). Church settlements also developed outside the southwest Alberta core area, at Barnwell, Taber, Orton, and Frankburg. Irrigation, the village settlement pattern (see CITY PLANNING), cooperative economic enterprise, and an active cultural, social, and religious life were transferred from the American Great Basin to southern Alberta. By 1911 Latter-day Saints had established eighteen new communities in southern Alberta, and 10,000 Saints, mostly farmers and their families, lived in the area of southwest Alberta alone.

With the outbreak of World War I, many young Canadian Latter-day Saints showed their loyalty to their homeland by joining the Canadian armed forces. Before the war, in order to offset questions about their patriotism, Church leaders had asked several young men, including Hugh B. Brown, to take officer training and to recruit others. By 1915 more than 200 LDS youth from the Cardston area had been recruited.

Pioneering, wartime nationalism, and the passage of time all contributed to the growing identification of Latter-day Saints with Alberta and Canada. This identity was solidified with the dedication of the temple in Cardston in 1923 by President Heber J. GRANT. A new Alberta-born and educated LDS generation emerged in small towns full of vitality. Cars, roads, and the telephone broke down rural isolation. Amateur sports, music, drama, school fairs, picnics, and rodeos reached their zenith. Alberta Latter-day Saints came into increasing contact with a wide variety of other ethnic and religious groups, including the communal Hutterites and Japanese and eastern Europeans, brought in to labor in the sugar industry.

Intense sports rivalries between the neighboring towns cemented hometown loyalties. The small LDS communities in southern Alberta dominated men's basketball in the province for decades and served as training grounds for several provincial and national basketball championship teams.

While they had an active cultural life, LDS towns did not thrive financially in an era of agricultural boom and bust. Magrath and Raymond grew quickly after their founding: by 1906 Magrath had a population of 884 and Raymond a population of 1,568. But with limited agricultural hinterlands, their growth quickly leveled off, and they grew little after 1911. Both towns developed a small industrial base that lasted until the 1960s: Raymond with its sugar factory and Magrath with a woolen mill and canning factory. With a bigger agricultural hinterland and the temple, Cardston remained the largest predominantly LDS town. Its population grew gradually from 1,000 in 1906 to about 2,000 by the 1920s.

During the 1920s many of the Canadian-born generation began looking for other opportunities. Some left for urban areas in Alberta or elsewhere in Canada, or for the United States. Church growth in other parts of Canada has often depended on leadership provided by Latter-day Saints who had pioneer roots in southern Alberta but migrated elsewhere.

Hard hit by the Great Depression of the 1930s, many Latter-day Saints rallied to the Social Credit party, which swept into power in Alberta in 1935 and retained power until 1971. Several LDS community leaders supported the monetary-reform movement, including Cardston high school principal N. Eldon Tanner, a cabinet minister from the late 1930s until the early 1950s, and school-teachers John Blackmore and Solon Low, who both became national leaders of the party. Several other Church members were elected to the provincial legislature. The three largest cities in Alberta have each elected LDS mayors.

Since 1947 immense oil and gas discoveries have transformed Alberta. With oil-induced prosperity and farm mechanization, many Latter-day Saints moved to the cities, gradually making them the focal point of LDS life. Eventually Latter-day Saints in Calgary numbered more than in all the other Mormon towns of southern Alberta. From a tight-knit, rural, geographically compact group consisting mostly of farmers, Latter-day Saints in Canada have become increasingly urban, middle class, and geographically dispersed. Those in Alberta, however, retain their strong cultural, religious, and kinship links with American Latter-day Saints while serving as full-fledged members of Canadian society.

BIBLIOGRAPHY

Card, Brigham Y., et al., eds. *The Mormon Presence in Canada*. Edmonton and Logan, 1989.

Lethbridge Stake Historical Committee and Melvin S. Tagg. *A History of the Mormon Church in Canada*. Lethbridge, Alberta, 1968.

HOWARD PALMER

CANON

[*In one of its religious senses, the term "canon" refers to the literary works accepted by a religion as* Scripture. *The word derives from the Hebrew* qaneh *(reed), which came to mean "measuring rod" and then "rule." It thus indicates the norm or the standard by which all things are measured. Latter-day Saints accept a more extensive and more open canon of scripture than those accepted by other Christians and by Jews. Latter-day Saints accept, in addition to the* Bible, *the* Book of Mormon, *the* Doctrine and Covenants, *and the* Pearl of Great Price. *These four scriptural collections are called the* Standard Works. *Related topics include* Joseph Smith Translation of the Bible (JST); Jesus Christ, Sources for Words of; New Testament; Old Testament; "Voice from the Dust"; *and the articles assembled under the entry* Jesus Christ in the Scriptures.]

CAPITAL PUNISHMENT

Ancient scriptures indicate that capital punishment is an appropriate penalty for murder. God said to Noah, "And whoso sheddeth man's blood, by man shall his blood be shed; for man shall not shed the blood of man" (JST Gen. 9:12). And to Moses the Lord said: "He that killeth any man shall surely be put to death" (Lev. 24:17). Thus it is clear that when the civil and religious authorities were combined, as in the days of the Old Testament prophets, capital punishment was the directed result.

In modern times with the separation of church and state, the power to take physical life is reserved to the state. Modern revelations do not oppose capital punishment, but they do not direct its imposition to civil government. In the same revelation where the Lord instructed the Prophet Joseph SMITH, "And again, I say, thou shall not kill; but he that killeth shall die," the Lord made the application of capital punishment contingent on the laws of civil government: "And it shall come to pass, that if any persons among you shall kill they shall be delivered up and dealt with according to the laws of the land . . . and it shall be proved according to the laws of the land" (D&C 42:19, 79). In a headnote to the published account of this revelation, the Prophet specified the revelation embraced "the law of the Church," which might indicate that even when capital punishment does not result from murder the murderer dies as to things pertaining to the Spirit.

The FIRST PRESIDENCY and the QUORUM OF THE TWELVE APOSTLES affirmed this position against murder in an official declaration dated December 12, 1889, written in response to rumors perpetrated by enemies of the Church that it taught its members that they were not bound by the laws of the United States. Included in that official declaration is the proclamation "this Church views the shedding of human blood with the utmost abhorrence" (*MFP* 3:183).

Church leaders have frequently made statements consistent with the scriptures and declarations quoted above. Elder Orson F. Whitney said in the October 1910 general conference, "To execute a criminal is not murder" (*CR*, Oct. 1910, p. 51). Elder Bruce R. McConkie wrote, "Mortal man is not authorized, except in imposing the requisite death penalties for crimes, to take the blood of his fellow beings under any circumstances" (McConkie, p. 257).

In summary, capital punishment is viewed in the doctrines of the Church to be an appropriate penalty for murder, but that penalty is proper only after the offender has been found guilty in a lawful public trial by constitutionally authorized civil authorities.

BIBLIOGRAPHY

Clark, James R., ed. *Messages of the First Presidency*, Vol. 3. Salt Lake City, 1966.

Doxey, Roy W. "The Law of Moral Conduct." *Relief Society Magazine* 47 (Aug. 1960):539–46.

McConkie, Bruce R. *The Promised Messiah.* Salt Lake City, 1978.

STUART W. HINCKLEY

CARTHAGE JAIL

The old jail in the town of Carthage, Illinois, seat of Hancock County, was the site of the MARTYRDOM OF JOSEPH AND HYRUM SMITH on June 27, 1844, by a mob of approximately 150 men. Today it is a HISTORICAL SITE of the Church and serves as a memorial to prophets of God who suffered martyrs' deaths.

The jail was built in 1839. Constructed of native red limestone, the two-story rectangular gable-front building measures twenty-nine by thirty-five feet. Like other county jails in Illinois, Carthage Jail was built to incarcerate petty thieves and debtors and to serve as a temporary holding place for violent criminals. It housed a debtor's room in the northwest corner of the first floor, and a dungeon, or "criminal cell" on the second floor, north side. There was also a living area for the jailer's family that included a kitchen, a dining room, and bedrooms. The cells were dark and generally foul-smelling and had only meager makeshift furnishings.

Joseph SMITH, Hyrum SMITH, and several other LDS leaders were incarcerated in Carthage Jail on June 25, 1844, to answer charges stemming from the destruction of the press used to print the anti-Mormon newspaper *Nauvoo Expositor*. During their three-day confinement they sought, through letters and personal appeals—even to the governor, then in Carthage—for an impartial reso-

This etching by Charles B. Hall shows the Carthage Jail (c. 1855), where Joseph and Hyrum Smith were martyred. They were shot by a mob in the upstairs bedroom of the jailor's quarters on June 27, 1844. Courtesy Rare Books and Manuscripts, Brigham Young University.

lution of the charges and for protection from people openly threatening their lives.

They were first placed in "close confinement" in the dungeon. Later they were moved to the debtors' cell and then to the jailer's upstairs bedroom in the southeast corner. By midday of June 27, only the Smiths and John TAYLOR and Willard Richards of the Quorum of the Twelve Apostles remained confined in the jail. The governor had disbanded the militia, left the prisoners under guard of the Carthage Greys (known enemies of the Latter-day Saints), and gone to NAUVOO with a detachment of troops.

Shortly after 5:00 P.M. a large force of armed men with blackened faces rushed the jail. Overcoming token resistance by the Greys, some of the mob entered the building, ascended the stairs to the landing just outside the upstairs bedroom, and commenced shooting into the room through the closed door. Hyrum Smith, PATRIARCH TO THE CHURCH and associate President in the Church's First Presidency, was gunned down. John Taylor was critically wounded, but Willard Richards miraculously escaped injury (*HC* 6:561–622). The Prophet, shot from both inside and outside the jail as he prepared to leap from an upstairs window, fell to the ground dead, near a well.

Carthage Jail served Hancock County until 1866. It was then a private residence, until the Church purchased it in 1903. Assisted by the Illinois Department of Public Works and Buildings, the Church completed a partial restoration of the jail in 1935.

In 1989, on the 145th anniversary of the martyrdom, the Church completed a major renovation of the whole Carthage Jail block. The jail proper was restored to its 1844 condition, and the block was fenced, landscaped, and dressed with walks, monuments, and sculpture. The adjacent visitors center, enlarged to accommodate 150 people, now holds exhibits and a theater showing a film that portrays Joseph Smith's religious and spiritual experiences.

BIBLIOGRAPHY

Baker, LeGrand L. "On to Carthage to Die." *IE* 72 (June 1969):10–13, 15.

McRae, Joseph A., and Eunice McRae. "Carthage Jail: A Physical Description of an Historical Structure." *IE* 45 (June 1942):372–73, 391.

DONALD L. ENDERS

CATHOLICISM AND MORMONISM

Roman Catholicism and Eastern Orthodoxy are grounded in the same theological tradition. They are similar to each other doctrinally and hold teachings that differ from Mormonism.

GOD. Both Catholicism and Orthodoxy believe God to be the Creator of the universe, and that God's being is trinitarian—that the persons of Father, Son, and Holy Spirit exist simultaneously in one divine nature. LDS doctrine is, on the other hand, tritheistic; it is subordinationist. The Son is subordinate to the Father, and the Holy Spirit is "sent forth by the will of the Father through Jesus Christ, his son." Both Catholic traditions teach that God is a self-revealing mystery whose perfect manifestation is in Jesus Christ, who is present to the world in the Church. Latter-day Saints affirm that Jesus Christ has a separate nature and is a separate entity from the Father, and that as Jesus Christ was and is visible, embodied, and glorified, so is the Father (see DOCTRINE: DOCTRINAL DISTINCTIVE TEACHINGS).

CHRIST. According to Catholic belief, Jesus was born of a virgin, and is the "Incarnate Son of God." As both God and man, he is the "Savior of the World." For Latter-day Saints Christ was not, is not now, and never will be united in nature or substance with the Father. His oneness with the Father is spiritual in spirit, purpose, and mind. Jesus, in LDS belief, is the Only Begotten Son of the Father in the flesh. He entered mortality, subject to growth as well as being, and fulfilled the will of the Father as exemplar, savior, and mediator. He was not given all power on earth and in heaven until he received the fulness of the glory of the Father (see GODHEAD).

ATONEMENT. In both Catholic traditions Christ's atonement provides access to salvific grace. Christ's death-resurrection is the saving event and the cross, the symbol of salvation. For Latter-day Saints the atonement of Jesus Christ was a descending below all things in order to rise above all. He suffered "according to the flesh" because in no other way could he know the anguish of sin and sinfulness, exemplify redemptive love, and reconcile justice and mercy. The Atonement reunites man with God both through sanctification and resurrection. All that Christ received from the Father may be received by man from the Father through Christ. This transformation is akin to the Eastern Orthodox view of theosis. The goal of discipleship is to become, through Christ, the image and likeness of God (see ATONEMENT; DEIFICATION).

AUTHORITY. Catholics believe that Jesus bestowed his pastoral authority on Peter, who thus became the first "Vicar of Christ" and head of the church, and that this authority to teach and to sanctify has been passed on in unbroken succession in the institution of the Papacy. Eastern Orthodoxy holds that Peter was first among equals, therefore patriarchs have equal authority. They also ascribe a special authority to the first seven ecumenical councils. Latter-day Saints believe that Peter held the keys of apostolic authority, which were also conferred upon the twelve apostles. Priesthood powers are not indelible but inseparably connected to righteousness. The loss of the full KEYS OF THE PRIESTHOOD was a failure to transmit. Their modern reconferral was under the hands of Peter, James, and John (see AARONIC PRIESTHOOD: RESTORATION OF). Every worthy male in the Church is to receive ordination to the priesthood with authority to perform saving ordinances and every father is to function as a patriarch to his own family.

SCRIPTURE. For Catholics and Orthodox, the Old and New Testament is the "inexhaustible source of Christian belief." The canon is closed. For Latter-day Saints the canon remains open. Scripture is the record of prophetic utterance given under inspiration. There is no final revelation. Revelation in on-going. Neither written scripture, nor natural theology, supersedes the "living oracles" (see RELIGIOUS EXPERIENCE; REVELATION; SCRIPTURE).

CHURCH. Catholicism and Orthodoxy understand the Church as a "communion of saints." The Holy Spirit enlivens the Church with grace empowering it to carry on the work of Christ in history. It is a community of salvation where the gospel is preached and the sacraments received. Latter-day Saints believe that with the restoration of the higher priesthood came three elements lost from the New Testament Church: (1) organizational patterns and their related offices, including a quorum of twelve apostles; (2) the spirit of prophecy, and all the spiritual gifts; and (3) the temple with its essential ordinances and practices (*see* GIFTS OF THE SPIRIT; ORGANIZATION; TEMPLES). Catholics affirm that grace centers in God's free gift offered through Christ in the sacraments and is infused to the soul. Baptism is essential for salvation. All sacraments are the necessary means of the grace needed for salvation. Mormon rites or ordinances are processes of spiritual rebirth in which the powers of godliness are manifest. They are received by all and all the ordinances are essential to salvation, from baptism to the higher ordinances of the temple. Their efficacy requires proper forms, ordained priesthood authority, and the faith and repentance of the person. There are degrees of salvation and the fulness of salvation or exaltation requires the fulness of the ordinances (*see* BAPTISM; CONFIRMATION; ENDOWMENT; TEMPLE ORDINANCES).

EUCHARIST. For both Catholic traditions, the Eucharist is a sacrament in which the true body and blood of Jesus is physically present, that is, the actual saving reality of the Lord. The liturgical act of consecration is a true sacrifice in which, through transubstantiation, the elements of bread and wine become the body and blood of Christ. The Orthodox associates the act of the priest in this liturgy with veneration for icons, which represent their prototype who is Christ. Latter-day Saints understand the sacrament as a remembrance of the body and blood of Christ. Sanctification is from the Spirit and takes place in the recipients who bring a broken heart and contrite spirit to the prayer and the partaking (*see* SACRAMENTS).

MARRIAGE AND FAMILY. Although Catholicism and Orthodoxy understand celibacy to be a spiritual ideal, marriage is a grace-giving sacrament that symbolizes the bond between Christ and the Church. Catholics hold that this is a life-long contract and do not permit divorce. Latter-day Saints teach that the eternal glorification of the family, and of the community of families within the Church, is the highest spiritual possibility. As the high priest who officiated in the ancient temple was married; and as the apostles were married, so today marriage is a high ordinance, to which others are preparatory. The nurture and love of the family of man, which is ultimately the family of God, is the proper work and glory of the saintly life. When sealed and sanctified by the authority of the priesthood, the covenants and relationships and duties of parenthood continue into the next world (*see* CELIBACY; MARRIAGE: ETERNAL).

While honoring Mary, Latter-day Saints have no equivalent of the doctrines of the immaculate conception, perpetual virginity, and bodily assumption of Mary, nor of the Orthodox veneration of icons. Other LDS teachings differ significantly from traditional Catholic teaching: modification of classical readings of the omnipotence and omnipresence of God; the premortal existence of the spirits of all mankind; the affirmation that spirit is refined matter; the Fall as planned, voluntary, and essential to the growth of the soul amid contrast and opposition; the denial of original sin and of pedobaptism; the inclusive nature of the Abrahamic covenant; and the replacement of heaven-hell distinction with the teaching of degrees of glory in the resurrection.

BIBLIOGRAPHY

Florovsky, Georges. *Bible, Church, Tradition: An Eastern Orthodox View.* Belmont, Mass., 1972.

McBrien, Richard P. *Catholicism*, Study Edition. San Francisco, 1981.

McManners, John, ed. *The Oxford Illustrated History of Christianity.* New York, 1990.

Patrinacos, Rev. Nicon D. *A Dictionary of Greek Orthodoxy.* Pleasantville, N.Y., 1984.

Rahner, Karl, and Herbert Vorgrimler. *Dictionary of Theology.* New York, 1981.

ALFRED BENNEY
ROGER R. KELLER

CELEBRATIONS

Through their religious and community celebrations, members of The Church of Jesus Christ of Latter-day Saints express some of their spiritual and social values and expectations. Although events and traditions in families and localities are celebrated often by members throughout the Church, the major celebrations help to define and express the unique religious identity and heritage of Latter-day Saints.

The mortal life cycle of individual Church members is typically marked by the performance of a series of formal PRIESTHOOD ORDINANCES. The most prominent are naming and BLESSING children, BAPTISM and CONFIRMATION, ENDOWMENT, and SEALING (temple MARRIAGE). These ceremonies, usually witnessed or participated in by the person's family and friends, consist of making sacred COVENANTS, and receiving PRIESTHOOD BLESSINGS, and inspired counsel that provide guidance through mortality and prepare the recipient for eternity. These ordinances are often marked by informal celebrations with family and friends.

The family as a unit of both religious worship and eternal association is celebrated by many Latter-day Saints in daily activities and weekly FAMILY HOME EVENINGS. The daily activities may consist of scripture study, gospel discussion, prayers, or singing activities held usually at the beginning or ending of the day. Family home evening generally occupies one night a week. It is designed to strengthen the bonds of family members through a wide variety of spiritual, social, educational, and recreational activities, and thus it augments involvement in traditional holidays such as Christmas, Easter, Thanksgiving, and Mother's Day. Extended LDS families often participate on a larger scale with periodic family reunions.

The identity of Latter-day Saints as "modern Israel" finds its most exuberant expression in PIONEER DAY. This annual celebration commemorates the entrance of the first LDS PIONEERS into the Salt Lake Valley on July 24, 1847. For Latter-day Saints, this commemoration has come to symbolize the establishment of a divinely ordained "promised land" in the American West.

Since 1849, Pioneer Day has given Latter-day Saints an excellent opportunity to express their identity as a covenant people. In the context of devotionals, parades, dances, sporting events, banquets, and a host of other activities, Mormons review the manifestation of God's hand in the course of their history, the creation and sustaining of their mode of life, and the religious dimension of their continuing associations. Although the focus of Pioneer Day is Salt Lake City and the Mormon West, Latter-day Saints throughout the Church memorialize their religious heritage on July 24 with celebrations appropriate to their particular settings and circumstances.

The LDS identification of the Church as the living KINGDOM OF GOD ON EARTH finds its greatest cultural and religious expression at general conferences. These semiannual gatherings in April and October have been observed by Church leaders and members alike almost since the ORGANIZATION OF THE CHURCH on APRIL 6, 1830. The conferences are currently held on the first Sunday of April and October, plus the preceding Saturday. The months symbolically mark the changing of the seasons between winter and summer, and April is also usually the month when Easter comes, commemorating the resurrection of Jesus Christ.

General conference unites the divine authority, organization, doctrine, and spiritual resources of the Church. The salient symbols include the architecture of TEMPLE SQUARE; the hierarchical seating of Church leadership from the FIRST PRESIDENCY through the QUORUM OF THE TWELVE APOSTLES, the quorums of the SEVENTY, and the leading men and women of the AUXILIARY ORGANIZATIONS; the use of the scriptures and revelation in the addresses given; the expression of both diversity and solidarity by the gathered Church membership representing many nations in their sustaining the leadership; and reports heralding significant growth in the rapidly expanding Church membership.

The general conferences also serve as major occasions of personal pilgrimages for thousands of Latter-day Saints to travel to Salt Lake City in April or October. It is likewise an occasion of vicarious involvement for millions of others who follow the conference sessions through various telecommunications media. In addition, the conference proceedings are later printed and distributed. As a result, the general conferences have become an extremely important collective spiritual experience for Latter-day Saints throughout the world.

Through general conferences, and on a smaller scale through the weekly congregational worship services of individual WARDS and STAKES, Latter-day Saints renew and celebrate their membership in the organization that they recognize as the kingdom of God on earth.

BIBLIOGRAPHY

Olsen, Steven L. "Community Celebrations and Cultural Identity: Pioneer Day in Nineteenth Century Mormonism." Unpublished paper, 1987.

Shipps, Jan. *Mormonism: The Story of a New Religious Tradition*, pp. 131–49. Urbana, Ill., 1985.

STEVEN L. OLSEN

CELESTIAL KINGDOM

The Church of Jesus Christ of Latter-day Saints teaches of three degrees of glory in the AFTERLIFE—the celestial, terrestrial, and telestial. Jesus alluded to these when he said, "In my Father's house are many mansions" (John 14:2). Paul likened them to the sun, moon, and stars, with the highest or celestial being typical of the sun (1 Cor. 15:40–41; cf. D&C 76:50–98). The celestial kingdom was seen in vision by JOHN the Revelator, PAUL, and the Prophet Joseph SMITH (Rev. 4:6; 2 Cor. 12:2; *TPJS*, pp. 106–107). This earth in its "sanctified, immortal, and eternal state" will become a celestial sphere (D&C 88:19–20; 130:9).

Celestial glory comes to those "who received the testimony of Jesus, and believed on his name and were baptized after the manner of his burial, . . . and who overcome by faith, and are sealed by the Holy Spirit of promise, which the Father sheds forth upon all those who are just and true" (D&C 76:51–53). Within the celestial glory are three levels, and to obtain the highest requires a temple marriage or SEALING.

Inhabitants of the highest celestial degree inherit "thrones, kingdoms, principalities, and powers," and dwell with God and Jesus Christ forever (D&C 76:54–70; 132:19–20).

[*See also* Degrees of Glory; Telestial Kingdom; Terrestrial Kingdom.]

SUSAN EASTON BLACK

CELIBACY

Celibacy, the deliberate renunciation of marriage, is foreign to LDS life. Like other forms of ascetic withdrawal, it may deprive the participant of crucial life experiences. Spiritual maturity and exaltation in the highest degree of the CELESTIAL KINGDOM require marriage (D&C 131:2–3).

The norm of Latter-day Saint teaching and practice is for individuals to marry, procreate, and foster righteous living in their families as indicated in the scriptures: "Be fruitful, and multiply, and replenish the earth" (Gen. 1:28). "Marriage is honourable in all" (Heb. 13:4). "Whoso forbiddeth to marry is not ordained of God, for marriage is ordained of God unto man" (D&C 49:15). Those who are unable to marry in a temple in mortality through no fault of their own will receive compensatory blessings later (D&C 137:5–8).

The practice of celibacy was not widespread among the Christian clergy until centuries after the death of the apostles. "Forbidding to marry" was, for Paul, a sign of apostasy (1 Tim. 4:3). Because ancient and modern revelation endorses marriage and because most religious leaders in the Old and New Testaments were married, Latter-day Saints reject attempts to interpret the Bible as advocating celibacy.

BIBLIOGRAPHY

Lea, Henry C. *History of Sacerdotal Celibacy in the Christian Church*, 4th ed. London, 1932.

DILLON K. INOUYE

CENSORSHIP

See: Confidential Records

CENTENNIAL OBSERVANCES

The historical consciousness of Latter-day Saints in the twentieth century has been richly expressed in the celebration of centennial anniversaries of important foundational events. Building on the elaborate jubilee (fifty-year) celebrations in 1880 of the ORGANIZATION OF THE CHURCH and in 1897 of the beginnings of the LDS COLONIZATION in the American West, the Church ushered in the twentieth century in 1905 with the centenary of the birth of the Prophet Joseph SMITH. For this occasion, President Joseph F. SMITH led a group of Church leaders and Smith family members to Sharon, Vermont, Joseph Smith's birthplace, and dedicated a memorial cottage and large granite obelisk to his memory. Many LDS congregations held local observances.

The Joseph Smith Memorial became one of the first HISTORICAL SITES of the Church. Following its dedication, the Smith company visited a number of other Mormon historic sites. This tour confirmed a growing interest by Latter-day Saints in preserving their past through the restoration of such historical sites in later commemorations.

Another major centenary was celebrated on September 22, 1927, when President Heber J. GRANT conducted a devotional on the hill CUMORAH at the approximate location where Joseph Smith received the GOLD PLATES of the Book of Mormon from the angel Moroni one hundred years earlier (*see* MORONI, VISITATIONS OF). On

September 25, congregations throughout the Church held commemorative programs as part of their Sunday worship services.

The 1930 centenary of the organization of the Church saw a much more ambitious memorial. The major celebration centered on the week of April 6. Church leaders arranged for participation in the festivities to extend beyond the 100,000 who gathered in Salt Lake City by installing radio receivers in more than a thousand meetinghouses within the broadcasting range of KSL RADIO. For the opening session of general conference, congregations assembled in these chapels and many others not so equipped. At an appointed time, Latter-day Saints throughout the Church stood and gave the sacred HOSANNA SHOUT, normally reserved for the dedication of TEMPLES. As the general conference continued on the following Monday and Tuesday, many speakers reviewed the Church's hundred-year legacy. Each evening of

the week of April 6–12, the Salt Lake TABERNACLE was filled to overflowing for the pageant "Message of the Ages," an ambitious stage production by a thousand actors, singers, and musicians that chronicled a sacred history of the gospel. The Church's seven temples were also dramatically illuminated for the centennial. For PIONEER DAY (July 24) that year, Saints from the eastern United States and Canada and missionaries serving in the area gathered to the hill Cumorah to witness "Footprints on the Sands of Time," the first of the PAGEANTS at that historic site.

The 1947 centennial of the arrival of the first company of Mormon PIONEERS into the SALT LAKE VALLEY was the largest LDS celebration to date. The entire year was one of observances throughout the Church, but it centered on July 24. That day included all the traditional Pioneer Day activities—devotionals, concerts, banquets, parades, rodeos, sports contests, and dances—but on a grander

On September 23, 1923, Church leaders met in Palmyra and Manchester, New York, for the centennial of the angel Moroni's first visitation to Joseph Smith on the hill Cumorah. Pictured here in the Sacred Grove (left to right) are Joseph Fielding Smith (second from left), Rudger Clawson, President Heber J. Grant, Sister Augusta W. Grant, James E. Talmage, and Brigham H. Roberts, president of the Eastern States Mission. Photographer: Antoine LeGrande Bunker.

scale. Particularly memorable was the reenactment of the Mormon exodus from NAUVOO (*see* WESTWARD MIGRATION). This modern "pioneer trek" included many Church leaders and other dignitaries who drove the MORMON PIONEER TRAIL in automobiles decorated as covered wagons and who rehearsed pioneer activities along the way. At the mouth of Emigration Canyon, east of Salt Lake City, President George Albert SMITH dedicated the "THIS IS THE PLACE" MONUMENT, a series of sculptures created by Mahonri M. Young, grandson of Brigham YOUNG.

The 1980 sesquicentennial of the founding of the Church brought another year-long celebration with a variety of observances by Latter-day Saints worldwide. The highlight of this commemoration came April 6 in conjunction with general conference. President Spencer W. KIMBALL dedicated the reconstructed Peter Whitmer, Sr., log home on the original site, in the township of FAYETTE, NEW YORK, where the Church had been organized in 1830. Millions witnessed the occasion via the Church's first satellite broadcast (*see* SATELLITE BROADCAST SYSTEM).

Featured in an expanded Pioneer Day parade that year was the display of hundreds of banners made by the YOUNG WOMEN from throughout the Church expressing their basic values through an artistic tradition dating back to Pioneer Day parades of the nineteenth century.

A number of smaller-scale sesquicentennials have since commemorated both the historical roots of the Church and its early geographical spread beyond the borders of the United States. The most memorable of these were the sesquicentennials anniversaries of the first Latter-day Saint mission to Great Britain (1987)—the first outside North America (*see* MISSIONS OF THE TWELVE TO THE BRITISH ISLES)—and the founding of Nauvoo, Illinois (1989).

BIBLIOGRAPHY

Anderson, Paul. "Heroic Nostalgia: Enshrining the Mormon Past." *Sunstone* 5 (July–Aug. 1980):47–55.

Belding, Patricia. "A Monumental Race with Winter: The Dedication of the Joseph Smith Birthplace." *Vermont Life* 38 (Fall 1983):45–48.

Bitton, Davis. "The Ritualization of Mormon History." *Utah Historical Quarterly* 43 (1975):67–85.

STEVEN L. OLSEN

CEREMONIES

Ceremony and ritual are key concepts for understanding religious behavior. In LDS parlance the word ordinance embraces most official observances. Latter-day Saints often use the word "ceremony" in reference to worship in the temple. They speak of temple dedication ceremonies, with SOLEMN ASSEMBLIES, dedicatory prayers, and the HOSANNA SHOUT.

In LDS self-awareness, a sequence of ORDINANCES, with temple ceremonies as the apex, constitute the main axis of religious existence. These ordinances are called by Joseph SMITH the "rites of salvation," (TPJS, p. 191). They define the character and interactions of priesthood, Church organization, authority, living revelation, family structure, kinship linkages, and moral responsibility.

In the discourse of social science, by contrast, ceremony usually refers to any cultural performance that identifies or changes one's social status. Ceremony that concerns the divine or sacred is called ritual.

Comparative study of diverse cultures and peoples suggest several generalizations on ritual that Latter-day Saints would call ordinances or sacred ceremonies.

First, ritual is symbolic. The central values, premises, and assumptions of a way of life are encoded in ceremony. A whole system of thought may be expressed in a simple gesture, a placement of hands, a posture. For Latter-day Saints the blessing and passing of the sacrament, beginning with the presiding priesthood authorities, reactivates each member's covenant relationship with Jesus Christ and the entire complex of living prophets, priesthood authority, revelation, and the influences of the Holy Spirit.

Second, it identifies sacred or set-apart space and time and marks fundamental transformations of social relationships. For Latter-day Saints the Sabbath is sacred time when even the preparation of food should be done with an eye single to the glory of God and with "singleness of heart" (D&C 59:13). The temple stands as the epitome of sacred space and time, the place of the divine name and presence, and embodies the enduring covenants of marriage, family, and SEALING.

Third, ritual perpetuates the community through sacred drama. It marks and engenders spiritual birth and rebirth. Regular participation regenerates sentiments of attachment. In this view ceremony is to the reproduction of family and community what DNA is to the biological individual. Among Latter-day Saints such ceremonies include the blessing and naming of infants, priesthood ordinations, PATRIARCHAL BLESSINGS and FATHER'S BLESSINGS by the laying-on of hands, administering to the sick with consecrated olive oil, and the setting apart of persons to a variety of callings of teaching and service.

Fourth, ritual and other LDS social ceremonies memorialize key events in their historical formation. The historical consciousness of Latter-day Saints is celebrated in periodic commemorations, pageants, dedications, and group memorial services of key events in the restoration (see CENTENNIAL OBSERVANCES; CUMORAH PAGEANT; GENERAL CONFERENCE; PIONEER DAY).

Fifth, ritual is often countercultural, defining and contrasting the principles of the religious community with those of surrounding societies. LDS emphasis on the "gathering" of disciples to a geographic and spiritual Zion, and the ceremonial renewal of responsibilities in periodic testimony bearing enhance discipleship, and are counterbalances to the disruptions of a secular world of increasingly fragile and fleeting relationships.

Sixth, ritual provides moral authority and constancy to cope with rapid change and social upheaval. It is the cement that unites individuals in common cause. As the Church undergoes geometric expansion, it draws together peoples of all backgrounds and provides the basis for communication and trust amid national, cultural, and ethnic diversity.

No society or group exists without both social and sacred ceremony. Among Latter-day Saints the fundamental importance of ceremony, and of divine authority in its performance, are given expression in a unique latter-day scripture: "In the ordinances . . . the power of godliness is manifest. And without the ordinances thereof, and the authority of the priesthood, the power of godliness is not manifest unto men in the flesh" (D&C 84: 20–21).

BIBLIOGRAPHY

Alexander, Bobby C. "Ceremony." In *The Encyclopedia of Religion*, ed. Mircea Eliade, Vol. 3, pp. 179–83. New York, 1987.

Morris, Brian. *Anthropological Studies of Religion: An Introductory Text*. New York, 1987.

JOHN P. HAWKINS

CHAPLAINS

The Church of Jesus Christ of Latter-day Saints endorses a corps of chaplains who serve in the U.S. armed forces. The history of LDS chaplains began in the Spanish-American War. Then Elder B. H. Roberts of the Seventy, at age sixty, and two others were appointed to the U.S. Army chaplaincy in 1917. The first LDS Naval chaplains served in World War II, and the first LDS Air Force chaplain was appointed in 1948.

By the beginning of the Vietnam War in Southeast Asia, most LDS chaplains who served during the Korean War had been released and new eligibility requirements precluded the appointment of most lay ministers, including Latter-day Saints. In 1965, however, the requirements were altered to allow for the lay ministry background of many LDS applicants. As with other religious groups, a person must be endorsed by a church before applying to the government for appointment as a chaplain. Prerequisites for an LDS chaplain include the MELCHIZEDEK PRIESTHOOD, an honorable MISSION, temple MARRIAGE, and a master's degree in counseling.

LDS chaplains have contributed to the development of military chaplaincy policy. For example,

Elder Brigham H. Roberts (far right) served in World War I as one of the first LDS chaplains. Enlisting at age sixty and having orders to report from Bordeaux to Verdun as peace was won, Roberts became a model of dedication and service to LDS chaplains. Courtesy University of Utah.

an LDS chaplain played a significant research role in the constitutional defense of the U.S. chaplaincy in federal court in 1979 and 1985.

LDS chaplains conduct religious services comparable to those led by chaplains of the Protestant faiths, and they provide counseling, classroom instruction, and other support activities to military personnel and their families. They provide such services through coordination with other chaplains or ministers. LDS chaplains are approved and supervised by the Church's Military Relations Committee.

BIBLIOGRAPHY

Boone, Joseph F. *The Roles of The Church of Jesus Christ of Latter-day Saints in Relation to the United States Military 1900–1975.* Ph.D. diss., Brigham Young University, 1975.

Maher, Richard T. *For God and Country: Memorable Stories from the Lives of Mormon Chaplains.* Bountiful, Utah, 1975.

ROBERT E. NELSON, JR.

CHARITY

Charity is a concept found in many cultures, its meaning ranging from a general selfless love of humanity to the specific alms-giving that is often its focus in modern times. Latter-day Saints take their understanding of charity from the Book of Mormon: "Charity is the pure love of Christ, and it endureth forever; and whoso is found possessed of it at the last day, it shall be well with him" (Moro. 7:47; cf. Ether 12:34; 2 Ne. 26:30).

As the love of Christ, charity is characterized as selfless and self-sacrificing (1 Cor. 13:5), emanating from a pure heart, a good conscience, and faith unfeigned (1 Tim. 1:5). Thus, more than an act, charity is an attitude, a state of heart and mind (1 Cor. 13:4–7) that accompanies one's works and is proffered unconditionally (D&C 121:45). It follows, but surpasses in importance, faith and hope (1 Cor. 13:13).

This may have been what Jesus was trying to teach Peter in John 21:15–17, wherein he asks Peter three times if he "loves" him, and, to Peter's affirmative answers, responds, "Feed my sheep" and "Feed my lambs," teaching that the true love of Christ always goes out to others. Loving all of God's children and being willing to sacrifice for them are the depth and breadth of the pure love of Christ. This "bond of perfectness and peace"

(D&C 88:125; Col. 3:14) becomes the foundation of all human relationships (cf. 1 Cor. 13). The everlasting love of charity is intended to be an integral part of one's nature: one is to cleave unto it (Moro. 7:46) and be clothed in it (D&C 88:125). In fact, *all* things are to be done in charity. Charity is everlasting; it covers sins (1 Pet. 4:8), it casts out all fears (Moro. 8:17), and it is a prerequisite for entering the kingdom of Heaven (Ether 12:34; Moro. 10:21).

Throughout its history, the law of the LDS Church has been that its members are to do all things with charity. Since its inception in 1842, the LDS Relief Society has had the motto Charity Never Faileth (1 Cor. 13:8; Moro. 7:46). The concept of charity is fundamental to the teachings and the procedures of the Church, being the very core of all it does, including missionary work, welfare services, temple work, tithes and offerings, and home and visiting teaching. As the spiritual welfare of the individual member of the Church is contingent upon charity, so is the welfare of Zion dependent upon the charity in the hearts of Latter-day Saints (2 Ne. 26:28).

BIBLIOGRAPHY

Benson, Ezra Taft. "To the Elderly in the Church." *Ensign* 19 (Nov. 1989):4–8.

Hansen, W. Eugene. "Love." *Ensign* 19 (Nov. 1989):23–24.

Holland, Jeffrey R. "He Loved Them unto the End." *Ensign* 19 (Nov. 1989):25–26.

ADDIE FUHRIMAN

CHASTENING

Latter-day Saints view chastening as a manifestation of God's love and concern. "For whom the Lord loveth he chasteneth, and scourgeth every son whom he receiveth" (Heb. 12:6). Like other religious peoples, they sometimes see death, famine, pestilence, and other human calamities as "acts of God" because he allows them to happen as functions of natural forces. However, Latter-day Saints tend to focus less on the punitive nature of such events and more on the possible positive results, such as HUMILITY, REPENTANCE, instruction, and spiritual change. To "chasten" denotes "to make chaste."

God loves all mankind and works to bring his children back to dwell with him. No one can endure God's presence who has not been purified to become like him. For this reason, Latter-day Saints view life on this earth as a period of testing and training, a time to instruct, refine, and purify the individual, making the child of God more like the Father.

The Book of Mormon tells of God allowing natural disasters to chasten people because whole communities had forgotten him, broken his commandments, and desecrated holy things (Hel. 12:3). The Doctrine and Covenants teaches that many will be blessed if they willingly turn their hearts to God and accept the call to repent and put their lives in order (D&C 93:38–52; cf. Heb. 12:5–11).

The Prophet Joseph SMITH stands as an example to Latter-day Saints as one loved, yet chastened by the Lord. To carry out his mission effectively, he had to learn many lessons. Sometimes the Lord merely reminded him to humble himself and become more submissive. Other times, as when he allowed Martin Harris to take the first 116 manuscript pages of the Book of Mormon, which were subsequently lost, the Lord withdrew the power of translation and allowed Joseph to suffer the oppression of darkness. When Joseph was incarcerated in the LIBERTY JAIL, the Lord counseled that all his experiences would be for his good (D&C 122:7). It was, indeed, during and after this difficult period that Joseph received some very significant revelations.

GLADYS CLARK FARMER

CHASTITY, LAW OF

In the law of chastity, the Lord commands restraint in exercising the body's sexual and procreative powers. As revealed in scripture, this law forbids all sexual relationships outside of marriage. Authorities of The Church of Jesus Christ of Latter-day Saints also condemn perverse or coercive sexual acts within marriage.

"Thou shalt not commit adultery," declares the Lord in the Decalogue (Ex. 20:14). Elsewhere in scripture, he prohibits fornication, HOMOSEXUALITY, incest, and bestiality (Ex. 22:16; Lev. 18:6-23). Teaching in both the eastern and western hemispheres, Jesus denounced unchastity in thought as well as deed (Matt. 5:27–28; 3 Ne. 12:27–28). The apostle Paul warned that if the Saints succumbed to sexual sin they would not "re-

tain God in their knowledge" (Rom. 1:26–29). The Lord affirmed in the Book of Mormon that he "delight[s] in the chastity of women," condemning infidelity of husbands as an offense against wives and children (Jacob 2:28, 31–35). The prophet ABINADI indicted the priests of King Noah for harlotry and for failure to live and teach the Mosaic law that prohibits adultery (Mosiah 12:29; 13:22). Corianton was taught by his father, ALMA₂, that sexual sin is "most abominable above all sins save it be the shedding of innocent blood or denying the Holy Ghost" (Alma 39:5). Mormon lamented the utter degeneracy of soldiers who raped female prisoners, "depriving them of that which was most dear and precious above all things, which is chastity and virtue" (Moro. 9:9).

In latter-day revelation, Church leaders are directed to excommunicate adulterers if they refuse to repent. The Doctrine and Covenants reproves adulterous desires as a denial of the faith, disqualifying offenders from the companionship of the Spirit (D&C 42:23–26; 63:16). The Prophet Joseph SMITH beheld in vision that unrepentant adulterers and whoremongers will be with liars and sorcerers in the TELESTIAL KINGDOM (D&C 76:103).

Church leaders have repeatedly stressed obedience to the law of chastity. In an official pronouncement in 1942, the FIRST PRESIDENCY promised "the exaltations of eternities" to those who remain chaste, deploring sexual immorality as a destroyer of individuals and nations. "The doctrine of this Church," they stated, "is that sexual sin— the illicit sexual relations of men and women— stands, in its enormity, next to murder. The Lord has drawn no essential distinctions between fornication, adultery, and harlotry or prostitution. Each has fallen under His solemn and awful condemnation" (CR 112 [Oct. 1942]:10–12). Sexual violations desecrate much that is holy, including divinely given procreative powers, the sanctity of life, marriage, and family. President David O. MCKAY said chastity is "the most vital part of the foundation of a happy marriage and . . . the source of strength and perpetuity of the race" (CR 137 [Apr. 1967]:8). Church leaders recognize only one standard of chastity for both men and women. Speaking in 1980, President Spencer W. KIMBALL affirmed: "Total chastity before marriage and total fidelity after are still the standard from which there can be no deviation without sin, misery, and unhappiness" (CR 150 [Oct. 1980]:4).

The law of chastity applies not only to behavior but also to dress, speech, and thought. Latter-day Saints are counseled to dress modestly, to use dignified language in speaking of bodily functions, and to cultivate virtuous thoughts. Accordingly, they are to avoid anything pornographic in literature, movies, television, and conversation. Though many outside the Church regard masturbation as normal, LDS leaders teach that the practice is wrong, one that feeds base appetites and may lead to other sinful conduct. Similarly, unmarried couples who engage in petting or fondling are breaking the law of chastity, and stimulating impulses that may lead to other sin.

Chastity fosters personal peace and confidence (see D&C 121:45). Referring specifically to unchastity, Alma wrote that "wickedness never was happiness" (Alma 41:10). The Church teaches that those guilty of infidelity lose the Spirit of the Lord, and bring upon themselves and their families jealousy, grief, anger, and distrust.

Persons guilty of unchastity may receive forgiveness through full REPENTANCE. Because unchastity violates baptismal and explicit temple vows, penitent offenders must confess such sins to their BISHOP, branch president, or other appropriate Church leader. After prayerfully considering the transgression, the Church leader may—especially in cases of adultery, fornication, or homosexuality—convene a DISCIPLINARY COUNCIL to help the transgressor through repentance and to protect the integrity of the Church. Depending on the offense and the spiritual maturity of the offender, a disciplinary council may excommunicate, disfellowship, place on probation, or exonerate the person.

Disciplinary councils usually require transgressors to seek forgiveness from individuals whom they have drawn into sexual sin and from spouses betrayed through infidelity. Transgressors are also to seek forgiveness from God through prayerful reformation of their lives, forsaking unchaste actions and thoughts. God promises that he will not remember the sins of those who repent fully (Isa. 1:18; D&C 58:42–43). However, recurrence of the transgression can cause the weight of the former sin to return (D&C 82:7), and more serious consequences to follow (D&C 42:26).

Living the law of chastity does not mean asceticism. Rather, it means to "bridle all [our] passions, that [we] may be filled with love" (Alma 38:12). Within marriage, physical intimacy strengthens the divinely ordained bond between husband and wife. By protecting the soul against carnality, chastity safeguards the joys of marriage in this life and exaltation in the life to come. Only the morally clean may enter the temple, where Latter-day Saints solemnly covenant to keep themselves chaste so that they may receive God's greatest blessing, eternal life (D&C 14:7). Through receiving temple ordinances and remaining worthy, a husband and wife may reach a perfect union sealed by the HOLY SPIRIT OF PROMISE, thus achieving a marriage that endures beyond the grave, blessed with spirit offspring in the eternities (D&C 132:19; cf. 131:1–4).

BIBLIOGRAPHY

Benson, Ezra Taft. *The Teachings of Ezra Taft Benson*, pp. 277–86. Salt Lake City, 1988.

Kimball, Spencer W. *The Miracle of Forgiveness*, pp. 61–89. Salt Lake City, 1969.

McKay, David O. *Gospel Ideals*, pp. 458–76. Salt Lake City, 1953.

BRYCE J. CHRISTENSEN

CHILDREN

[*This entry consists of three articles:*

Roles of Children
Blessing of Children
Salvation of Children

The first article explores the roles of children from leaving their heavenly parents to their roles and activities within an earthly family. The second article relates to an ordinance within the Church usually performed a few weeks after the birth of children when they are given the names by which they shall be known on the records of the Church and normally a blessing is given at the same time. The last article discusses the innocence of children until they reach the age of accountability; that their salvation is assured until that time.]

ROLES OF CHILDREN

Latter-day Saints believe that children are SPIRIT sons and daughters of God who have come to earth with their own divine inheritances and identities. Parents, with the support of the Church, are responsible for nurturing the divine and righteous attributes of their children and for helping them develop love for God and fellow beings. Through

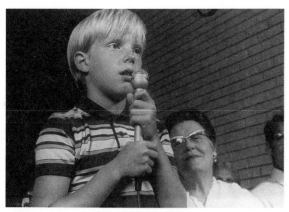

Children, like adults, express their beliefs and feelings about the gospel of Jesus Christ during monthly testimony meetings (Orem, Utah, 1982). Courtesy Floyd Holdman.

love and prayerful guidance, parents can help children learn that they have a potential for greatness and goodness, and that life on earth has purpose and eternal consequences. Parents and children can establish family bonds that may endure forever (*see* MARRIAGE: ETERNAL MARRIAGE).

God has commanded parents to teach their children "to understand the doctrine of repentance, faith in Christ the son of the living God, and of baptism and the gift of the Holy Ghost"; they are also to "teach their children to pray, and to walk uprightly before the Lord" (D&C 68:25, 28). Childhood is a period of preparation and practice in which children must learn to distinguish good from evil, so that when they reach the age of ACCOUNTABILITY and are baptized (usually at eight years), they will be ready to exercise their AGENCY wisely and assume the responsibilities of membership in the Church. Children should learn to serve God and other people, and should prepare for responsibilities they will have as adults.

The Church teaches that children learn gospel values, doctrines, and behavioral applications most effectively in the home. They learn at a very young age to pray individually and as part of the family. In many homes during FAMILY PRAYER, families kneel together while one member prays, and small children take their turn with the help of their parents. In addition to regular individual and family prayers and blessings on the food at each meal, children learn that they can pray whenever they want to express gratitude or need divine help. They can receive priesthood BLESSINGS from their fathers or home teachers when they need inspirational help or guidance.

Latter-day Saints are encouraged to help their children read and study the SCRIPTURES daily, and many do this as a family activity at a specified time each day. LDS families are also counseled to hold a FAMILY HOME EVENING once each week. All family members, including young children, can be given opportunities to conduct these meetings, prepare and present lessons, lead music, read scriptures, answer questions, offer prayers, and provide refreshments. Within this framework of support and cooperation, children take part in making decisions and solving family problems, and they learn to internalize values as they develop autonomy, initiative, and competence. LDS children also learn the gospel in less formal settings as families work, play, and eat together. These activities provide occasions to teach gospel values and create bonds of trust.

Through its programs the Church supports the parents and the home. It provides training, materials, and other adult role models for children, thereby reinforcing gospel principles taught by the family. Children participate with their families during weekly worship services called SACRAMENT MEETINGS, at which they may partake of the SACRAMENT, participate in congregational singing, and give as well as listen to gospel-related talks. During the monthly FAST AND TESTIMONY MEETING, members, including children, may bear individual TESTIMONY to the ward congregation.

PRIMARY is an organized program of religious instruction and activity in the Church for children ages eighteen months to twelve years. Its purpose is to teach children the gospel of Jesus Christ and help them learn to live it. Participating in Primary helps children prepare for BAPTISM and other ORDINANCES.

In Primary, held each Sunday, children develop skills and gain competence in communication, leadership, gospel scholarship, and social relationships through many gospel-centered activities. They offer prayers, recite scriptures, and give gospel-related talks. They sing songs written specifically for children, listen to stories, and participate in activities such as dramatizations, role plays, and games. In smaller age-grouped classes, they receive scripturally based lessons designed for their level of understanding. Primary leaders and teachers encourage the children to study and learn the ARTICLES OF FAITH. Each year the Primary children prepare a sacrament meeting presentation in which they share with the congregation the scriptural concepts they have studied.

Periodic weekday activities help children apply the gospel principles they learn on Sunday and encourage them to interact informally with their peers and leaders. The Primary sponsors quarterly activity days for all children that provide wholesome fun by involving them in physical, creative, cultural, and service activities. Ten- and eleven-year-old girls and boys participate in achievement days twice a month during which they set goals and are recognized as they learn skills in hospitality, arts and crafts, sports and physical fitness, health and personal grooming, outdoor fun and skills, service and citizenship, family skills, and safety and emergency preparedness. In some areas, boys participate in Church-sponsored SCOUTING programs for their achievement day activities.

The Church provides resources specifically designed to teach children. Age-appropriate scripture-based lesson manuals, a children's songbook, teaching guides, and training videos are available for leaders and teachers. The FRIEND, a monthly magazine written specifically for children, is available through subscription in most English-speaking countries. Excerpts are translated and compiled in INTERNATIONAL MAGAZINES for children living in other parts of the world.

[See also Family; Fatherhood; Motherhood; Primary.]

BIBLIOGRAPHY
Family Guidebook. Salt Lake City, 1980.
Primary Handbook. Salt Lake City, 1985.

MICHAELENE P. GRASSLI

BLESSING OF CHILDREN
The blessing of infants is normally performed during a FAST AND TESTIMONY MEETING. The father who holds the MELCHIZEDEK PRIESTHOOD, or another bearer of that priesthood selected by the family, usually pronounces a name and blessing upon a child within a few weeks after its birth. Either may be assisted by other Melchizedek Priesthood bearers. Older children may be blessed at the time of the conversion of their family. Under special circumstances children may be blessed at home or in a hospital.

The precedent for blessing children was set by the Savior in both Palestine and the New World. Both the New Testament (Mark 10:16) and the Book of Mormon (3 Ne. 17:21) describe Jesus blessing little children. In a revelation concerning the government of the Church, the Prophet Joseph SMITH received specific directions on this ORDINANCE: "Every member of the Church of Christ having children is to bring them unto the elders before the church, who are to lay their hands upon them in the name of Jesus Christ, and bless them in his name" (D&C 20:70).

The blessing ordinance thus described is neither the infant baptism performed in many other Christian churches nor simply a christening and prayer on the child's behalf. Instead, the priesthood bearer seeks to exercise his right to receive revelation from God in the child's behalf. The fixed portions of the ordinance are the addressing of Heavenly Father, the invoking of the Melchizedek Priesthood authority by which the blessing is spoken, giving the child its name, and closing in the name of Jesus Christ. The giving of the name formally identifies the child on the records of the Church as part of what may become an eternal family unit.

The blessing itself is to be given as dictated by the Spirit and may contain prophecy concerning the child's future, a statement of gifts or promises, and instruction or promises to the parents or siblings of the child.

BIBLIOGRAPHY
Smith, Joseph F. "Blessing and Naming Infants." Gospel Doctrine, 12th ed. pp. 191–92. Salt Lake City, 1961.

LOWELL BANGERTER

SALVATION OF CHILDREN
In Latter-day Saint doctrine children are to be instructed in the principles of the gospel and baptized when eight years of age (D&C 68:25–27). They are then responsible to adhere to the teachings of the Church relative to obtaining SALVATION. Before that time they are considered "infants" or "little children" and are not required to be baptized. They are considered "alive in Christ" and are "whole" (Moro. 8:8–12; JST, Matt. 18:10–11).

Although children, with all the rest of mankind, feel the mortal "effects" of ADAM's transgres-

Religious instruction in the LDS family centers around teaching gospel principles to the children. This nativity reenactment was part of a joint family gathering at Christmas in Logan, Utah, 1982. Courtesy Craig Law.

sion, they (and all others) do not have any mystical stain of original sin upon them. Adults must have their own personal sins remitted by repentance and baptism (John 3:5; Acts 2:38; Moses 6:57–62), but "the Son of God hath atoned for original guilt, wherein the sins of the parents [both Adam's and their mortal parents'] cannot be answered upon the heads of the children, for they are whole from the foundation of the world" (Moses 6:54).

The prophet MORMON taught: "Listen to the words of Christ; . . . the curse of Adam is taken from them in me, that it hath no power over them. . . . It is solemn mockery before God, that ye should baptize little children" (Moro. 8:8–9). The Lord instructed Joseph SMITH that "little children are redeemed from the foundation of the world through mine Only Begotten; wherefore, they cannot sin, for power is not given unto Satan to tempt little children, until they begin to become accountable before me" (D&C 29:46–47).

This unconditional benefit of Christ's atonement saves all little children regardless of race, color, or nationality, for "all children are alike unto me" (Moro. 8:17). They all begin their mortal lives pure and innocent (D&C 93:38), and "little children also have eternal life" (Mosiah 15:25).

If they die while in this state of innocence and purity, they return to that God who gave them life,

saved, and fit for his company. They are in a "blessed" condition, for God's "judgment is just; and the infant perisheth not that dieth in his infancy" (Mosiah 3:16, 18). The Prophet Joseph Smith saw in vision "that all children who die before they arrive at the years of accountability are saved in the celestial kingdom of heaven" (D&C 137:10; *TPJS*, p. 200).

All that is said of infants and little children applies also to those who may be adults in physical body but are not accountable mentally (D&C 29:49–50).

Concepts outlined in scripture and by the prophets clearly demonstrate the marvelous uniting of the laws of justice and mercy because of the Atonement: none are eternally disadvantaged by noncompliance to gospel laws or ordinances they do not know or are not capable of understanding and thus cannot comply.

CALVIN P. RUDD

CHILDREN'S FRIEND, THE

Published by the PRIMARY, *The Children's Friend* was the children's magazine of the Church from 1902 through 1970. Reflecting its pioneer heritage, the January 1902 first issue (2,000 copies) was mailed out hand-wrapped in used but ironed wrapping paper and tied with string collected from nearby homes. May Anderson, editor of the magazine from 1902 until 1940, wrote in the first issue, "The basis of all our work will be to make the children want to live better lives." The first attempt to accomplish this was made by printing materials for the leaders and teachers of children: lesson guides, stories from the lives of outstanding men and women, stories about children, songs, memory work, handiwork projects, and specific instructions to Primary workers. Later a section for parents was added, and in 1909 a more direct approach was attempted by including materials for the children themselves in girls' and boys' departments. Later, pictures, riddles, continued stories, and a "Just for Fun" page were added (1913). In 1923 the size of the pages was doubled and the contents were directed more toward the children. Some of its stories were dramatized on "The Children's Friend of the Air" program over a local radio station in Salt Lake City.

Sister Anderson was succeeded as editor by May Green Hinckley (1940–1943), Adele Cannon Howells (1943–1951), and LaVern W. Parmley (1951–1970). In January 1971, as the Church consolidated its magazines, *The Children's Friend* was replaced by the FRIEND magazine, the current publication designed expressly for the children of the Church.

BIBLIOGRAPHY

Kerr, Marion Belnap. "*The Children's Friend* for Fifty Years." *The Children's Friend* 51 (Jan.–Feb. 1952):29, 76.

VIVIAN PAULSEN

CHOIRS

See: Mormon Tabernacle Choir; Music

CHRIST

See: Jesus Christ

CHRISTIANS AND CHRISTIANITY

The Old World origin of the word "Christian" is obscure. Possibly it was first used by pagans in Antioch to identify those who followed Christ.

However, by the end of the first century A.D., it was an accepted self-designation among Church members as reflected in the writings of Ignatius (c. 35–c. 107 A.D.). The word is used three times in the New Testament (Acts 11:26; 26:28; 1 Pet. 4:16).

In the new world (Book of Mormon world), there was a similar designation for Church members (Mosiah 18:12–17; Alma 46:13–16; 48:10). "Christian" designated those who were "true believers in Christ" and who "took upon them, gladly, the name of Christ, or Christians as they were called, because of their belief in Christ who should come" (Alma 46:15). Here the term "Christian" referred to those who believed Christ *would* come, and not only, as in the New Testament, to those who believed he *had* come.

Perhaps the term first used by Old World Christians for themselves was the Greek word *hagioi*, meaning "holy ones" or "saints." Latter-day Saints have taken upon themselves this New Testament designation (Acts 9:13; 32, 41; Rom. 1:7; 1 Cor. 1:2; Phil. 1:1). Such terminology is seen in the Book of Mormon (1 Ne. 13:5, 9; 14:12, 14; 2 Ne. 9:18–19; Morm. 8:23; Moro. 8:26), the Doctrine and Covenants (1:36; 84:2; 88:114; 104:15), and the Pearl of Great Price (Moses 7:56).

The Church of Jesus Christ of Latter-day Saints does not see itself as one Christian denomination among many, but rather as God's latter-day RESTORATION of the fulness of Christian faith and practice. Thus, from its earliest days LDS Christians sought to distinguish themselves from Christians of other traditions. Other forms of Christianity, while bearing much truth and doing much good under the guidance of the HOLY SPIRIT, are viewed as incomplete, lacking the AUTHORITY of the priesthood of God, the temple ORDINANCES, the comprehensive understanding of the PLAN OF SALVATION, and the nonparadoxical understanding of the GODHEAD. Therefore, the designation "saint" reflects attachment to the New Testament church, and also designates a difference from Catholic, Eastern Orthodox, and Protestant Christianity in the current DISPENSATION.

In response, and for a variety of other reasons, some Catholic, Orthodox, and Protestant Christians have been reticent to apply the term "Christian" to Latter-day Saints. One reason is that the Latter-day Saints claim the only divinely established line of authority is within the Church. If that divine authority was not transmitted after the death of the first Apostles, then the sacrament, ordinations, credal formulations, and ecclesiastical structures of other Christian groups lack divine sanction. Many traditional Christians see this stance as placing Latter-day Saints outside the Christian family as defined by some confessions of faith and accepted ordinances.

Further, Latter-day Saints claim that God spoke and manifested himself not only to persons of biblical times, but also to the people in the Book of Mormon, and that he continues to speak to his people through REVELATION today. Thus, Latter-day Saints are not always viewed as "biblical Christians," when that term requires the belief that the canon of scripture is complete in the Bible. To the Mormons, God is still a God of continuing revelation, which means that credal and confessional statements are not final. No one confession, or even all of them together, can fully comprehend the dynamism of God. He is to be heard and his words are to be recorded as he gives continuing divine guidance through revelation. Hence, the LDS canon is open; the Doctrine and Covenants becomes an official, open-ended locus for revelations that affect the whole Church; and revelations continue to come to the living prophets, seers, and revelators of the Church, to be communicated to the members.

Latter-day Saints hold that Christians in the broadest sense are those who base their beliefs on the teachings of Jesus and who have a personal relationship with him. Within that definition they recognize Catholic, Eastern Orthodox, Protestant, and Latter-day Saint Christians, with the understanding that Latter-day Saint Christianity is the restored fulness of Christ's gospel. The lives of Latter-day Saints are their affirmations of their Christian faith. As President Brigham YOUNG stated, "If we are not Christlike we are not Christian" (Watson).

Traditional Christianity often defines Christian affiliation as the acceptance of certain beliefs and dogmas. Because Latter-day Saints do not accept certain extrascriptural dogmas—especially those bearing the philosophical overlay of much post–New Testament Christian teaching—some in other churches feel that Latter-day Saints cannot be Christian. They are not "orthodox" in this sense. But for the Mormon, right beliefs (orthodoxy) and right behaviors (orthopraxy) are those congruent with the revealed mind and will of the Lord. Some of the misunderstandings between traditional communities and the Latter-day Saints arise from this issue: whether Christians must first believe traditional, especially credal, dogmas in order to live "correct Christian lives."

An inclusive definition of Latter-day Saint Christianity is in the Book of Mormon: "And we talk of Christ, we rejoice in Christ, we preach of Christ, we prophesy of Christ, and we write according to our prophecies, that our children may know to what source they may look for a remission of their sins" (2 Ne. 25:26). Christ and his atoning sacrifice have been the undergirding message of The Church of Jesus Christ of Latter-day Saints from its inception. Christ has been the central message of all the latter-day PROPHETS and APOSTLES. They understand that Old Testament prophets anticipated him, New Testament apostles preached and testified of him, Book of Mormon prophets heralded him, and the Doctrine and Covenants presents his word to this generation. Jesus Christ is the living Lord of the Church. Apart from him there is no salvation.

President Spencer W. KIMBALL said, "There can be no real and true Christianity, even with good works, unless we are deeply and personally committed to the reality of Jesus Christ as the Only Begotten Son of the Father who bought us, who purchased us in the great act of atonement" (Kimball, p. 68). He also expressed the hope that all would come to realize that every LDS prayer, hymn, and sermon is centered in the Lord Jesus Christ. "We are true followers of Jesus Christ; and we hope the world will finally come to the conclusion that we are Christians, if there are any in the world" (Kimball, p. 434).

BIBLIOGRAPHY

Gealy, F. D. "Christian." In *The Interpreter's Dictionary of the Bible*, Vol. 1, pp. 571–72. Nashville, Tenn., 1962.

Grundmann, Walter. "Chiro." *Theological Dictionary of the New Testament*, Vol. 9, pp. 27–580. Grand Rapids, Mich., 1964–1974.

Kimball, Edward L., ed. *The Teachings of Spencer W. Kimball.* Salt Lake City, 1982.

Watson, Eldon J., comp. *Brigham Young Addresses*, Vol. 4, p. 5 for July 14, 1861. Unpublished, March 1980.

ROGER R. KELLER

CHRISTMAS

Christmas is the holiday when Latter-day Saints and other Christians celebrate the birth of Jesus Christ. This epochal event, seen in vision by ancient prophets, heralded the entry into mortality of the Son of God, the JEHOVAH of the Old Testament, and the promised Messiah. Even though Latter-day Saints believe that the birth of Jesus actually occurred in the spring of the year (D&C 20:1; *see* APRIL 6), they observe the December celebration when, more than at any other time of year, the Christian world unites in remembering Christ's birth and practicing his teachings of love, charity, self-sacrifice, and tolerance.

Most Latter-day Saints include some of the traditions, games, decorations, music, and food associated with the Christmas customs of their homelands in their family celebrations. Such items as Christmas trees, stockings, gifts, and greeting cards add to the beauty of the holiday and are not discouraged. But the recommended focus is religious. The Church encourages family closeness, concern for neighbors, thoughtfulness for fellow workers, renewal of friendships, and acts of Christ-like love, giving, and celebration. Appropriate sermons, lessons, songs, and programs are presented in Sabbath services during the Christmas season. Latter-day Saints are cautioned that holiday shopping, decorating, and festivities should not obscure the remembrance of Christ nor hinder the quest for peace on earth.

BIBLIOGRAPHY

Packer, Boyd K. "Keeping Christmas." In *BYU Speeches of the Year, 1966–1967*. Provo, Utah, 1967.

MARY ELLEN STEWART JAMISON

CHRISTOLOGY

Christology is the theological study of the human and divine natures and roles of Jesus Christ.

It developed soon after the death of the apostles in the first century, as conflicting teachings arose over the proper understanding of Christ. Christology served both as a response to heresies and as a development of a systematic theology that orthodox Christians could accept. Eventually these teachings were discussed in councils and formulated into CREEDS, for instance, at Nicaea (A.D. 325), Constantinople (A.D. 381), and Chalcedon (A.D. 451). These creeds insisted upon a full communion of Christ's divine and human natures, as opposed to the teaching that he was either divine or human, or part one and part the other. In every sense, the councils concluded, Christ is God and of the same substance (*homoousios*).

Various Christologies competed in the early Christian church. Docetists taught that Jesus Christ only seemed to suffer on the cross, since he only appeared to have a body. Modalists taught that there is only one God in three modes; Arianism, that there are three persons united in purpose. Nestorianism insisted upon two separate wills in a dyadic unity, while Apollonarianism taught that Jesus' human body was inhabited by a divine soul.

Over the years, others have insisted that Jesus Christ is merely the ideal man for humanity, since Jesus often called himself "the Son of man." They have felt that he seldom drew attention to his divinity, as Albert Schweitzer argues in his famous *Quest of the Historical Jesus* (1911).

Some modern Lutheran theologians believe that Jesus was not simultaneously on the earth as a human and in heaven as God. Under this view, Jesus was divine in the PREEXISTENCE but gave up his godly status and divine properties, except moral attributes, and took upon himself flesh and became a man. This is called the "kenotic" theory.

John Hick, a British philosopher-theologian, feels that Christianity should return to the earliest Christology, the "grace" theory, which teaches that Christ was transformed into a being sharing the divine properties by being infused with his Father's grace.

Although the term "Christology" is not frequently used by Latter-day Saints, the doctrine of the Church can be described in the following manner: Jesus Christ descended from his high preexistent station as a God when he came to earth to die for mankind's sins (*see* JESUS CHRIST: FIRST BORN IN THE SPIRIT; CONDESCENSION OF GOD). He was JEHOVAH come to earth in a physical body as the Only Begotten of the Father in the flesh (*see* JESUS CHRIST: ONLY BEGOTTEN IN THE FLESH). While on earth he was still God, but he received from his Father "grace for grace," as do God's other children (D&C 93:12; *see* JESUS CHRIST: MINISTRY OF). The Book of Mormon and Doctrine and Covenants speak forcefully of the divine sonship of Christ and also of his humanity (Mosiah 15:2–3; Alma 6:8; 11:38; 13:16; 34:2; 3 Ne. 11:7, 28:10; D&C 93; *see* JESUS CHRIST, FATHERHOOD AND SONSHIP).

Like Jesus Christ, all mortals live in a state of humiliation, but through the mediation of the Christ they may progress to a state of EXALTATION (*see* DEIFICATION; GODHOOD). There is no ultimate disparity between the divine and human natures; Joseph SMITH asserted that mankind is of the same species as God, having been made in God's image (theomorphism) and being eternal, with unlimited capacity (*TPJS*, pp. 345–46). One early LDS leader proclaimed, "As man now is, God once was. As God now is, man may be" (Lorenzo SNOW). Latter-day Saints speak of man as a god in embryo and of Jesus Christ as mankind's elder brother. A favorite LDS children's hymn is titled "I Am a Child of God."

Latter-day Saint doctrine can be understood to have appreciation for Christ and applications for man that go beyond traditional Christology. It is LDS teaching that all the Father's children possess the potential to strive toward the same godhood that the GODHEAD already has; because in their humanity there is a divinity that is progressing and growing according to the faith, intelligence, and love that abound in their souls. Like the attribute of perfection, divinity is not a static absolute but a dynamic progression (*see* ETERNAL PROGRESSION).

BIBLIOGRAPHY

Brown, Raymond E. "Christology." In *The New Jerome Biblical Commentary*, ed. R. Brown, J. Fitzmyer, and R. Murphy. Englewood Cliffs, N.J., 1990.

Hick, John. "An Inspiration Christology for a Religiously Plural World." In *Encountering Jesus: A Debate on Christology*, ed. Stephen T. Davis, pp. 5–22. Atlanta, 1988.

O'Collins, Gerald. "Jesus." *ER* 8:19–23.

GARY P. GILLUM

CHRISTUS STATUE

Replicas of the Christus statue by Danish sculptor Bertel Thorvaldsen (1768–1844) are located in several LDS VISITORS CENTERS. These white carrara marble statues of Christ, with his hands outstretched, inviting all to come to him, help present the central doctrine of the Church: that Jesus of Nazareth is the Son of God and the Savior and Redeemer of the world.

The first such statue acquired by the Church was a gift of Stephen L Richards, First Counselor to President David O. McKay (1951–1959). In 1966 this heroic-size (11 feet, 1 inch) Christus was placed in the North Visitors Center on TEMPLE SQUARE in Salt Lake City.

The second Christus was commissioned for

Christus, by Bertel Thorvaldsen (c. 1965, carrara marble replica of 1821 original, 3.36 m), in the North Visitors Center, Temple Square, Salt Lake City. Thorvaldsen's statue of the resurrected Christ helps present LDS belief in Jesus Christ, the son of God and redeemer of the world. It stands in a rotunda before a mural of the universe to show that "by him, and through him, and of him, the worlds are and were created" (D&C 76:24).

display in the Church's pavilion at the New York World's Fair (1964–1965) and was sculpted by Aldo Rebachi of Florence, Italy. It was intended to help visitors understand that Latter-day Saints (or Mormons) are Christians. This statue was later placed in the Visitors Center on the grounds of the Los Angeles Temple.

Additional Christus statues are currently located at visitors centers adjacent to temples in New Zealand; Hawaii; Mexico City; Washington, D.C.; and Mesa, Arizona.

BIBLIOGRAPHY

Marshall, Richard J. "Mormon Pavilion at the New York World's Fair . . . A Progress Report." *IE* 68 (Apr. 1965):290–97, 334–35.

Sheridan, Luise. "Bertel Thorvaldsen: Creator of Christus." *IE* 67 (Apr. 1964):272–75, 307.

Top, Brent L. "Legacy of the Mormon Pavilion New York World's Fair." *Ensign* 19 (Oct. 1989):22–28.

FLORENCE SMITH JACOBSEN

CHURCH EDUCATIONAL SYSTEM (CES)

The Church of Jesus Christ of Latter-day Saints has established educational programs throughout the United States and in some ninety other countries to provide an effective combination of religious and secular education to its members. The primary aim shared by these programs is to assist students in gaining an understanding and personal witness of the restored gospel of Jesus Christ at the same time as they pursue their secular studies. Latter-day Saints are taught by their leaders and their scriptures to seek after truth in every sphere.

CES comprises the various educational programs of the Church. BRIGHAM YOUNG UNIVERSITY, BRIGHAM YOUNG UNIVERSITY—HAWAII CAMPUS, RICKS COLLEGE, and LDS BUSINESS COLLEGE provide higher education balanced with religious instruction for students attending these Church-owned institutions. SEMINARIES offer weekday religious instruction for high school students, and INSTITUTES offer similar instruction for college students attending non-LDS colleges and universities. Exensive adult and continuing education programs with headquarters at BYU provide educational opportunities for those not officially enrolled in the formal institutions. In addition, the Church maintains a few elementary and secondary schools in less developed nations.

EDUCATIONAL PHILOSOPHY. Since the early days of the Church, leaders have placed a strong emphasis on education. The Prophet Joseph SMITH, in discussing the PURPOSE OF EARTH LIFE, consistently stressed learning. He said that one of the fundamental principles of Mormonism is to "receive truth let it come from where it may" (*WJS*, p. 229). Revelations given to Joseph Smith state that "the glory of God is intelligence" (D&C 93:36) and that "whatever principle of intelligence we attain unto in this life, it will rise with us in the resurrection" (D&C 130:18). Other revelations further emphasize the importance of both religious and secular learning:

Teach ye diligently and my grace shall attend you, that you may be instructed more perfectly . . . in all things that pertain unto the kingdom of God, that are expedient for you to understand; of things both in heaven and in the earth, and under the earth; things which have been, things which are, things which must shortly come to pass; things which are at home, things which are abroad; the wars and the perplexities of the nations, and the judgments which are on the land; and a knowledge also of countries and of kingdoms [D&C 88:78–79].

Brigham YOUNG, the second president of the Church, advanced the same concept, teaching that "all wisdom, and all the arts and sciences in the world are from God, and are designed for the good of His people" (*JD* 12:147). These ideas and scriptures have become the foundation of the educational philosophy of the Church (*see* EDUCATION: ATTITUDES TOWARD EDUCATION).

HISTORY OF EARLY EDUCATIONAL INSTITUTIONS. As the Saints moved to Ohio, Missouri, and Illinois, they established elementary and secondary schools in each settlement. SCHOOLS OF THE PROPHETS were organized for adult leaders beginning in Kirtland, Ohio, in 1833. In 1840, a university was established in Nauvoo. During their trek to the Rocky Mountains the Saints conducted elementary classes in the temporary camps. In the fall of 1847, just three months after the first company of PIONEERS arrived in the SALT LAKE VALLEY, schools were organized. Three years following, in 1850, the UNIVERSITY OF DESERET was founded. (In 1892 the territorial legislature changed the name to the University of Utah.)

Beginning in 1875, the Church established ACADEMIES throughout the intermountain United States and some in Canada and Mexico to provide elementary and secondary secular and religious education. To coordinate the programs and growth of the academies, a General Church Board of Education was organized in 1888, consisting of selected Church leaders. Karl G. Maeser was named the first superintendent of Church schools, a position that later became the Commissioner of Church Education. By 1907 the Church Board of Education was responsible for the administration of some thirty-five academies.

About 1890, with the increased availability of free public high schools, attendance at Church academies declined. Some closed their doors, and others were reorganized as junior colleges. By 1931 only Juárez Academy in Mexico remained as an academy. At that time the Church began transferring its junior colleges to state governments. However, it retained Ricks College in Rexburg, Idaho, and Brigham Young Academy in Provo, Utah, which developed into Brigham Young University.

As an increasing number of LDS youth began to attend public secondary schools, Church leaders recognized the need to provide a religious curriculum to complement regular secular studies. In 1912 the Church began building seminaries on Church-owned property adjacent to public high schools, where students could take a daily class in religion. Some public districts released students for an hour for this purpose; other students attended early morning classes before school started. To facilitate the religious training of students attending non-LDS colleges and universities, the Church established institutes of religion adjacent to college campuses beginning in 1926. The success of seminaries and institutes resulted in the spread of these programs to many parts of the world.

ORGANIZATION. In 1989 the Church Board of Education decided to decentralize the administration of all CES programs and the position of commissioner was abolished. Direct administration of Brigham Young University, Brigham Young University—Hawaii Campus, Ricks College, and LDS Business College was taken over by the boards of trustees legally established for each institution. These boards all have the same membership as the Church Board of Education. They are comprised of the First Presidency and other General Authorities and officers of the Church as assigned, including specifically the presidents of the two women's AUXILIARY ORGANIZATIONS. By virtue of their assignments to each of these boards, these officers serve each institution concurrently. Also, the operation of seminaries, institutes of religion, religious education in adult and continuing education programs, and the operation of elementary and secondary schools of the Church is guided by the general Church Board of Education.

CHURCH SCHOOLS, SEMINARIES, AND INSTITUTES. Members of the Church are encouraged to take full advantage of public education opportunities where available. However, in some areas where there is a high concentration of members and few public education opportunities, the Church Board of Education has established elementary, middle, or secondary schools in which both secular and religious instruction is offered. Some 9,300 students attend Church schools located in Mexico, Kiribati, Fiji, Tonga, Western Samoa, and New Zealand. While serving as Commissioner of Church Education, Neal A. Maxwell explained the objectives of these schools: "Literacy and basic education are gospel needs. Without literacy individuals are handicapped—spiritually, intellectually, physically, socially and economically. Education is often not only the key to the individual member's economic future, but also to his opportunities for self-realization, for full Church service and for contributing to the world around him—spiritually, politically, culturally and socially" (*Annual Report*, 1971).

Where public education is readily available, CES offers seminary and institute programs to supplement secular education with religious teachings. During the 1988–1989 school year, 255,361 high school students participated in seminary, constituting 55 percent of all eligible LDS youth. Institute enrollment was 125,534—54 percent of those eligible. Courses in seminaries and institutes center around the reading and study of the Old Testament, New Testament, Book of Mormon, Doctrine and Covenants and Church history, and Pearl of Great Price. The teachings of these courses emphasize the reality of a living God, the resurrected Christ, the visitation of heavenly beings in restoring the gospel and Church of Jesus Christ to Joseph Smith, the continuing nature of revelation, the teachings of living prophets, and the GIFTS OF THE SPIRIT. Students in seminary and institute are taught that personal religious knowledge can be obtained by seeking individual revelation, living the principles taught by Christ, and witnessing the results of doing the will of God.

The CES Salt Lake office is responsible for maintaining the quality of the curriculum and teaching staff of seminaries and institutes. Full-time teachers within the United States and Canada are required to have a bachelor's degree and to participate in an intensive training course at BYU or at one of the approved institutes. The training procedure varies somewhat in areas outside the United States and Canada where there are fewer Church members.

BIBLIOGRAPHY

Arrington, Leonard J. "The Founding of the L.D.S. Institutes of Religion." *Dialogue* 2 (Summer 1967):137–47.

Backman, Milton V., Jr. *The Heavens Resound*, pp. 264–75. Salt Lake City, 1983.

Bennion, M. Lynn. *Mormonism and Education*. Salt Lake City, 1939.

Berrett, William E. *A Miracle in Weekday Religious Education.* Salt Lake City, 1988.

Buchanan, Frederick S. "Education Among the Mormons: Brigham Young and the Schools of Utah." *History of Education Quarterly* 22 (Winter 1982):435–59.

Chamberlin, Ralph V. *The University of Utah, A History of Its First Hundred Years 1850 to 1950.* Salt Lake City, 1960.

French, Calvin V. "Organization and Administration of the Latter-day Saint School System of Free Education, Common School Through University at Nauvoo, Illinois, 1840–1845." Master's thesis, Temple University, 1965.

Monnett, John Daniel. "The Mormon Church and Its Private School System in Utah: The Emergence of the Academies, 1880–1892." Ph.D. diss., University of Utah, 1984.

Quinn, D. Michael. "Utah's Educational Innovation: LDS Religion Classes, 1890–1929." *Utah Historical Quarterly* 43 (Fall 1975):379–89.

Tuttle, A. Theodore. "Released Time Religious Education Program of the Church of Jesus Christ of Latter-day Saints." Master's thesis, Stanford University, 1949.

WILLIAM E. BERRETT

CHURCH OF THE FIRSTBORN

The church of the Firstborn is Christ's heavenly church, and its members are exalted beings who gain an inheritance in the highest heaven of the celestial world and for whom the family continues in eternity.

In the scriptures Jesus Christ is called the Firstborn. He was the first spirit child born of God the Father in the premortal existence and was in the beginning with God (John 1:1–5, 14). Christ also became the Firstborn from the dead, the first person resurrected, "that in all things he might have the preeminence" (Col. 1:18; Acts 26:23; 1 Cor. 15:23; Rev. 1:5). Even as the FIRST PRINCIPLES and ORDINANCES, including baptism in water and the reception of the Holy Ghost, constitute the gate into the earthly Church of Jesus Christ, so higher ordinances of the priesthood constitute the gate into the church of the Firstborn. To secure the blessings that pertain to the church of the Firstborn, one must obey the gospel from the heart, receive all of the ordinances that pertain to the house of the Lord, and be sealed by the HOLY SPIRIT OF PROMISE in the celestial kingdom of God (D&C 76:67, 71, 94; 77:11; 78:21; 88:1–5; *TPJS*, p. 237).

Revelations to the Prophet Joseph SMITH supplement those of the New Testament to indicate that the church of the Firstborn consists of those who have the inheritance of the Firstborn and become joint-heirs with Christ in receiving all that the Father has (Rom. 8:14–17; D&C 84:33–38; *see* HEIRS OF GOD). The Lord said, "If you keep my commandments you shall receive of his fulness, and be glorified in me as I am in the Father; . . . I . . . am the Firstborn; . . . And all those who are begotten through me are partakers of the glory of the same, and are the church of the Firstborn" (D&C 93:20–22). The church of the Firstborn is the divine patriarchal order in its eternal form. Building the priesthood family order on this earth by receiving sealings in the temple is a preparation and foundation for this blessing in eternity (*see* GOSPEL OF ABRAHAM).

When persons have proved themselves faithful in all things required by the Lord, it is their privilege to receive covenants and obligations that will enable them to be heirs of God as members of the church of the Firstborn. They are "sealed by the Holy Spirit of promise" and are those "into whose hands the Father has given all things" (D&C 76:51–55). They will be priests and priestesses, kings and queens, receiving the Father's glory, having the fulness of knowledge, wisdom, power, and dominion (D&C 76:56–62; cf. 107:19). At the second coming of Jesus Christ, the "general assembly of the church of the firstborn" will descend with him (Heb. 12:22–23; JST Gen. 9:23; D&C 76:54, 63).

BIBLIOGRAPHY

Smith, Joseph Fielding. *DS*, Vol. 2, pp. 8–9, 41–49. Salt Lake City, 1973.

IVAN J. BARRETT

CHURCH GROWTH

See: Vital Statistics

CHURCH OF JESUS CHRIST OF LATTER-DAY SAINTS, THE

The Church of Jesus Christ of Latter-day Saints is the official name of the Church established on April 6, 1830, at Fayette, New York, under the direction of the Prophet Joseph SMITH. It is commonly referred to as the Mormon Church because of its belief in the Book of Mormon, and members are often called Mormons or Latter-day Saints. Originally chartered with six members, the Church has grown into an international organization encompassing millions of members in many countries in the world.

From 1830 until 1838, members of the Church referred to it as "The Church of the Latter-day Saints" or "The Church of Christ." On April 26, 1838, the official title of the Church was given by revelation: "For thus shall my church be called in the last days, even The Church of Jesus Christ of Latter-day Saints" (D&C 115:4).

Each phrase in this name is significant. "The Church of Jesus Christ" indicates that Jesus Christ stands at the head of the Church, and that his gospel, teachings, and divine AUTHORITY constitute the fundamental basis of the Church. The term "Saints" is in accord with New Testament usage connoting a member of the covenant group (Acts 9:13, 32, 41; Rom. 1:7; Phil. 1:1; see LATTER-DAY SAINTS.) It has no direct relationship to the connotation of "saints" as used in Roman Catholic or Orthodox traditions. The term "Latter-day" indicates that the Church was restored in the last era of human history prior to the second coming of Christ and also distinguishes today's Church from the "Former-day" organization established by Christ during his mortal ministry in Palestine. The Church of Jesus Christ of Latter-day Saints is a divinely restored embodiment of the original Church of Jesus Christ, and the appointed guardian of its doctrine, authority, and divine mission (see ORGANIZATION: CONTEMPORARY).

The Church is the kingdom of God on the earth, a divinely established institution through which God accomplishes his purposes pertaining to the salvation of his children. President Spencer W. KIMBALL suggested that the Church has three primary objectives to help people come unto Christ, sometimes identified as its three principal missions. The first is to *proclaim the gospel* to all mankind. The Church does this through a large missionary force, as well as through the efforts of individual Church members. The second mission is to *perfect the Saints*, which includes teaching them the gospel of Christ, administering the essential ORDINANCES OF SALVATION, and assisting them in a lifelong process of repentance, discipleship, and preparation for eternal life. The third

mission of the Church is *redeeming the dead*, making it possible for generations of the deceased, who had no opportunity to accept the gospel in mortality, to receive the truths and ordinances of salvation. This work is accomplished by proxy ordinances performed in the temples of the Church. It leads to Church encouragement of family history research. Later, Church Presidents may alter or add to these missions as directed or inspired by the Lord.

The Church is also a society of believers to provide a framework for cooperative effort, mutual support, and temporal assistance as needed. The bonds of love among the Saints are a vital prerequisite to the accomplishment of the Church's purposes and are identified in the scriptures as one sign of the true church of God (John 13:35; see SIGNS OF THE TRUE CHURCH). Latter-day Saints regard themselves as the "covenant people" of the Lord, heirs to the ancient covenant between God and Abraham, and, by birth or adoption, members of the house of Israel. The Church is the instrument through which God is gathering the dispersed tribes of Israel in the latter days in accordance with his promises to Abraham and other biblical PROPHETS.

The Church of Jesus Christ of Latter-day Saints is distinguished from other Christian

Go Ye Therefore and Teach All Nations, by Grant Romney Clawson, after a work by Harry Anderson (1973, detail from a mural in the Church Office Building, Salt Lake City, Utah). Jesus Christ is the head of the Church. Here he sends his disciples to go "and teach all nations, baptizing them in the name of the Father, and of the Son, and of the Holy Ghost" (Matt. 28:19). Courtesy Floyd Holdman.

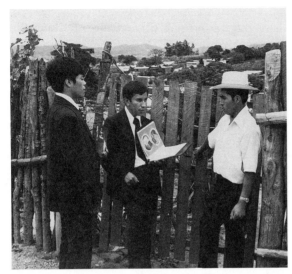

One of the main functions of the Church is to proclaim the gospel. As of March 1991, about 44,000 full-time missionaries were teaching the gospel in 257 missions throughout the world.

churches in several fundamental ways. Most of these differences stem from the Church's essential belief in continuing revelation. Thus, Latter-day Saints accept the Holy Bible as the word of God, and also accept the Book of Mormon, Doctrine and Covenants, and Pearl of Great Price as scripture and as standard works. They accept the calling of modern prophets and APOSTLES, beginning with Joseph Smith, and continuing to the present. LDS doctrines regarding the nature of the Godhead, the plan of salvation, vitality of priesthood authority, and the interpretation of scriptural prophecies also differ in various ways from those of the Roman Catholic, Orthodox, or Protestant branches of Christianity. Latter-day Saints emphasize religious freedom and tolerance. The Church does not typically participate in formal ecumenical activities; however, it is committed to cooperate with other religious, civic, and educational organizations in advancing common moral and social purposes (*see* INTERFAITH RELATIONS).

The Church is governed by priesthood authority. The term "priesthood" among Latter-day Saints refers not only to the body of men who hold ecclesiastical offices in the Church, but also to the actual authority or power given them by ordination to the priesthood. There are two divisions within the priesthood, a lesser or Aaronic Priesthood, and a higher priesthood or Melchizedek Priesthood. All worthy male members of the Church from age

twelve onward are ordained to the priesthood, normally holding offices within the Aaronic Priesthood from ages 12 to 18, and offices in the Melchizedek Priesthood thereafter. Offices in the Aaronic Priesthood include: DEACON, TEACHER, PRIEST, and BISHOP. The Melchizedek Priesthood offices are ELDER, HIGH PRIEST, PATRIARCH, SEVENTY, and apostle.

The Church sees itself as organized after the basic pattern of the first century Church of Christ and in accordance with a series of revelations to Joseph Smith (D&C 20 and 107; A of F 6). Successive Presidents of the Church have refined the organization to meet changing needs and demands of an expanding international organization but have not altered the fundamental structure of the Church as it was first organized. The Church is presided over by a president, who generally has two counselors; together with him, they constitute the First Presidency of the Church.

A second governing body, the QUORUM OF THE TWELVE APOSTLES, consists of twelve men called to be "special witnesses of the name of Christ in all the world" (D&C 107:23). The Quorum of the Twelve collectively holds in latent form the same priesthood authority as the President of the Church, and in the event of his death is the body that governs the Church and installs a new president. Members of the First Presidency and the Quorum of the Twelve Apostles are regarded and sustained by vote of Latter-day Saints as PROPHETS, SEERS, AND REVELATORS, receiving direct revelation from Jesus Christ. These brethren are assisted by members of the quorums of the Seventy and the Presiding Bishopric.

The quorums of the Seventy, each consisting of up to seventy men, have special responsibility for missionary work and also supervise Church activities in geographic areas under the direction of the Twelve. The Presiding Bishopric is responsible for the temporal affairs of the Church, including finances, records, buildings, and administration of the Church welfare services program. All these men are designated by Latter-day Saints as General Authorities because their authority extends over the entire Church. The headquarters and central administrative offices of the Church are located in Salt Lake City, Utah.

The President of the Church receives revelation from God that relates to the whole Church, but all leaders and members are entitled to divine inspiration within the scope of their responsibilities and regarding their personal lives. Such revelation helps bring UNITY and common purpose to the Church, making it like a living organism, the "body of Christ" (1 Cor. 12:12–28; Col. 1:18).

General Authorities preside over the Church throughout the world, overseeing those who administer geographical units known as wards, stakes, regions, and areas. A stake is a cluster of wards, a region is a group of stakes, and an area is a group of regions. A ward is a congregation of Saints, usually numbering between 200 and 600 members. Wards are usually organized according to geographical boundaries, and all members living within those boundaries belong to the same ward. A ward is led by a bishop who serves usually about five years and is called from among the membership of the congregation; under the direction of the bishop, the ward is usually staffed entirely by its own members. Several wards together, usually no more than ten, constitute a stake, led by a stake president, also called from among the members of the stake. The term "stake" was given by revelation (D&C 101:21) and is linked to Old Testament imagery of Zion as a great tent upheld by lengthened cords and stakes (Isa. 33:20; 54:2). In areas where Church population is too small for wards and stakes to be formed, it is administered through missions, districts, and branches. While the main function of missions is to proclaim the gospel, in some areas of the world they also administer smaller units of the Church known as districts, which are made up of branches, usually consisting of fewer than 200 members. Branches can also exist under stakes if the units are too small to constitute a ward.

Within the wards and branches of the Church, there are specialized auxiliary organizations intended to meet specific needs of groups within the Church. They provide important support to the quorums of the priesthood. The largest of these is the Relief Society, the women's organization established in 1842 under the direction of the Prophet Joseph Smith. It provides cultural, social, and spiritual enrichment to the women of the Church and also renders compassionate service to families in need, hence the name Relief Society.

Other auxiliaries of the Church are the Primary, responsible for the instruction of children under the age of twelve; the Young Men organization, for young men between the ages of twelve and eighteen; the Young Women organization, for young women of the same age group; and the Sun-

day School organization, which administers Sunday instruction in gospel doctrine to youth and adults.

Local officers and teachers throughout the Church receive no financial compensation. Formal training is not required for holding positions in the Church, nor is there a ministerial career track of any kind (*see* LAY PARTICIPATION AND LEADERSHIP). An individual receives a calling, like a formal invitation, to serve in a specific position by Church authorities responsible for that unit of the Church; such callings are believed to be made under divine inspiration.

Regular worship services in the Church are conducted in individual wards. Members of the ward meet together each Sunday for a general worship service known as SACRAMENT MEETING. The sacrament, or the Lord's Supper, is administered, ward business is conducted, hymns are sung, and members of the congregation give inspirational talks on gospel subjects. Members also meet each Sunday in smaller priesthood or auxiliary groups. In all, formal Sunday meetings may last up to three hours. Latter-day Saint communities are involved in an entire way of life, and a typical family is likely to spend many hours each week in Church-related activities, meetings, and service (*see* MEETINGS, MAJOR CHURCH). Regular CONFERENCES—ward, stake, regional, area, and general—provide continuity and association with the larger community of the Church.

The twenty-eight-story Church Office Building in Salt Lake City, Utah, shown here in an aerial view from the southeast, at the time it was dedicated on July 24, 1975. The maps of the world, in relief on the building, signify this as the world headquarters of the Church.

The Washington Temple was dedicated in 1974. As of 1990, there were forty-four temples, where Church members participate in ordinances necessary for their own exaltation and for the salvation and exaltation of others who have died without these ordinances.

Latter-day Saints regard the family as the basic unit of the Church, and of society, and emphasize the sanctity of marriage and the importance of family ties. Mormons believe that marriage and family relationships can continue beyond this life into the eternities, that men and women are equal in the sight of God, and that the blessings of the gospel revolve around the family.

Observers in the past may have regarded the Church as largely a western U.S. phenomenon, or at least as an American church. However, as of 1990, nearly 40 percent of the members lived outside the United States. Church growth internationally has been rapid since the end of World War II, especially in Latin America, the South Pacific, Australia, and parts of Asia and Africa. This growth has been perhaps the greatest challenge facing the Church in recent decades. By the end of 1990, nearly 50,000 members were serving as missionaries for one to three years, the majority outside the United States. This missionary corps, becoming skilled in many languages, imparts a cosmopolitan dimension to the contemporary Church.

To the Prophet Joseph Smith, the Lord described The Church of Jesus Christ of Latter-day Saints as "the only true and living church upon the face of the whole earth, with which I, the Lord, am well pleased" (D&C 1:30).

BRUCE DOUGLAS PORTER

CHURCH NEWS

The *Church News* is a weekly supplement to the daily *Deseret News* of Salt Lake City, Utah. It reports the worldwide happenings of The Church of Jesus Christ of Latter-day Saints.

Coverage includes official Church announcements, appointments, conferences, and activities. Regular features are: Messages of Inspiration, Church News Viewpoint, LDS Calendar, current gospel study information, Mormon Forum on timely topics, and This Week in Church History. A staff of reporter-photographers travels worldwide to report on Church events and people. They are aided by an international corps of *Church News* correspondents.

The aim of the *Church News* is to inform readers of happenings in the Church by publishing well-edited stories, colorful graphics and photographs, and attractive displays in a readable format.

News of the Church had been covered previously in the regular issues of the *Deseret News* from 1850 to April 1931, when a separate Saturday "Church Section" appeared. It proved popular and the name was changed to *Church News* in 1943. The *Church News* is circulated as part of the *Deseret News* in home delivery areas and mailed separately to subscribers elsewhere.

"J" MALAN HESLOP

CHURCH AND STATE

Latter-day Saints believe that the separation of church and state is essential in modern societies prior to the Millennium. LDS scriptures teach that civic laws should not interfere with religious practices, nor should religious institutions manipulate governments to their advantage. Many LDS teachings emphasize the role of governments in preserving individual freedom of conscience. The Church is active in countries with various types of governments and encourages its members to be involved in civic affairs and to honor the laws of the land (*see* CIVIC DUTIES). LDS practice tended to be more integrationist and theocratic in the isolated early Utah period and has been more separationist in the twentieth century.

Discourse within the Church on issues of church and state proceeds on at least two planes: (1) in discussions of historical and contemporary church-state relations, and (2) in discussions of ideal settings, such as will exist in the Millennium, when "Christ will reign personally upon the earth" (A of F 10), or in the CELESTIAL KINGDOM.

The principles of free AGENCY and freedom of conscience, which are fundamental to LDS church–state theory, are consistent on both planes of discourse. However, the institutional implications of these principles are different in the two settings. In the present world, where believers are subject to the imperfections of human government, separation of church and state is vital to the protection of religious liberty. On the ideal plane, in contrast, Latter-day Saints anticipate more inte-

grated theocratic, or what Joseph SMITH called "theodemocratic" institutions (*T&S* 5 [Apr. 15, 1844]:510), both because of the inherent legitimacy of divine rule and because the participants in millennial or celestial societies willingly accept such rule. Nevertheless, LDS prophets have consistently taught that even in the millennial society freedom of conscience will be respected. For example, Brigham YOUNG stated, "In the Millennium men will have the privilege of their own belief" (*JD* 12:274; cf. *DS* 3:63–64). The Church does not advocate theocracy for the premillennial world. It instructs members to "be subject to the powers that be, until he reigns whose right it is to reign" (D&C 58:22)—that is, until Christ comes.

In the meantime, several principles apply. As noted above, the fundamental assumption is that human beings have free agency and a number of inherent human rights, most notably "the free exercise of conscience" (D&C 134:2). The Church declares, "We believe that religion is instituted of God; and that men are amenable . . . to him only, for the exercise of it, unless their religious opinions prompt them to infringe upon the rights and liberties of others; . . . that the civil magistrate should restrain crime, but never control conscience; should punish guilt, but never suppress the freedom of the soul" (D&C 134:4). This recognition of freedom of conscience includes a commitment to toleration, as is emphasized in the Church's eleventh Article of Faith: "We claim the privilege of worshiping Almighty God according to the dictates of our own conscience, and allow all men the same privilege, let them worship how, where, or what they may."

A corollary of freedom of conscience is that human law does not have the right "to interfere in prescribing rules of worship to bind the consciences of men, nor dictate forms for public or private devotion" (D&C 134:4). This principle of nonintervention by the state in religious affairs is understood to proscribe not only interference with individual practice but also interference with the autonomy of the Church as an institution pursuing its religious mission. The position of the Church in this regard was vindicated in the U.S. Supreme Court in *Corporation of the Presiding Bishop of the Church of Jesus Christ of Latter-day Saints et al. v. Amos et al.* (483 U.S. 327 [1987]) and is consistent with international understanding of religious liberty (e.g., Principle 16 of the Concluding Document of the Vienna Meeting of the Conference on Security and Co-operation in Europe [1989]). Consistent with this position, the Church believes in maintaining strict independence for itself and affiliated institutions, such as Church-sponsored schools and universities, and accordingly does not accept direct aid or subsidies from governmental sources because of the actual or potential regulatory interference this might entail.

The Church is also committed to separation of church and state from the religious side. "We do not believe it just to mingle religious influence with civil government, whereby one religious society is fostered and another proscribed in its spiritual privileges, and the individual rights of its members, as citizens, denied" (D&C 134:9). This does not mean that the Church is precluded from taking a stand on moral or other issues when it is religiously motivated to do so or that religious values must be pushed to the margin of public life; nor does it mean that the Church cannot have indirect influence on the state as a result of the Church's efforts to teach religious principles and to make positive contributions in its members' lives. It does mean that it is inappropriate for a religious organization to manipulate the machinery of secular power to procure advantages for itself or disadvantages for others.

The Church is not viewed as a worldly organization. It avails itself of legal structures, such as corporate or other organizational entities available to it in various countries, to arrange its temporal affairs, and it complies with all legal requirements this may entail, but it is not dependent for its spiritual authority on any worldly institution. Latter-day Saints believe that their Church is established and guided by God through a prophet and apostles who hold the keys and priesthood authority needed to teach gospel truths and to officiate in the ordinances necessary for salvation and exaltation.

The Church teaches the importance of government and encourages its members to obey the law of the land wherever they live. Human governments and laws are admittedly imperfect, but they play an important role in preserving order and providing stable contexts within which individuals can seek truth and strive to live in accordance with the dictates of conscience. Governmental leaders are accountable to God "for their acts . . . both in making laws and administering them, for the good and safety of society" (D&C 134:1; cf. 124:49–50).

Implementation of the foregoing principles in history has moved through a number of phases. In the earliest phase, the Church was essentially a small, persecuted religious group seeking religious liberty and a place to settle, first in western New York and then in Ohio, Missouri, and Illinois. During much of this period, the Church relied heavily on its own organization to manage its social structure. The NAUVOO CHARTER permitted some overlap of church and state. Toward the end of the Nauvoo period, Joseph Smith organized the COUNCIL OF FIFTY, which was intended to provide a potential framework within which Christ's millennial reign could be organized.

During the mid-nineteenth-century exodus from Nauvoo to the Great Basin, social, political, and economic organization was managed by the Church, since no other effective organization was available. Church leaders worked to establish separate governmental institutions, first in the form of a state of DESERET, then in the Territory of Utah, and in continuing efforts to secure Utah's statehood. During much of the nineteenth century, however, the federal government in particular was a hostile rather than a neutral force in the community. This reinforced the tendency for the Church to manage society through its own channels. Dreams of building Zion also contributed to tendencies to work through the Church.

After the MANIFESTO officially ended PLURAL MARRIAGE in 1890 and Utah attained statehood in 1896, tension between the Church and state institutions gradually abated and reciprocal trust grew. During the twentieth century, therefore, the Church has pursued a more consistently separationist policy and has been free to emphasize its primarily spiritual mission. The Church is now established in well over 100 countries, and this internationalization has further reinforced the idea that the essential mission of the Church can be accomplished within a wide range of legal and political systems as long as there is sufficient separation of church and state to afford effective protection for religious liberty. Church teachings reinforce a constellation of values in its members that most governments welcome: family stability, honesty, hard work, avoidance of drug dependency, loyalty to country, and obedience to law. The result is that while the Church contributes to religious pluralism wherever it is found, it simultaneously contributes to social stability and the improvement of diverse societies.

[*See also* Civic Duties; Constitutional Law; Legal and Judicial History; Politics: Political History; Politics: Political Teachings.]

BIBLIOGRAPHY

Firmage, Edwin Brown, and Richard Collin Mangrum. *Zion in the Courts: A Legal History of the Church of Jesus Christ of Latter-day Saints, 1830–1900.* Urbana, Ill., 1988.

Jensen, Therald N. "Mormon Theory of Church and State." Ph.D. diss., University of Chicago, 1938.

Mangrum, Richard Collin. "Mormonism, Philosophical Liberalism, and the Constitution." *BYU Studies* 27 (Summer 1987):119–37.

Melville, J. Keith. "Theory and Practice of Church and State During the Brigham Young Era." *BYU Studies* 3 (Autumn 1960):33–55.

Taylor, John. *The Government of God.* Liverpool, 1852.

W. COLE DURHAM, JR.

CHURCH IN THE WORLD

[*Since it was organized with six members in Fayette, New York, in 1830, The Church of Jesus Christ of Latter-day Saints has spread throughout the United States and to many countries of the world. The history and development of the Church in the United States are discussed in six major articles found under the heading* History of the Church. *The history and development of the Church outside the United States are discussed in different articles under the headings* Africa; Asia, East; Asia, South and Southeast; Australia; British Isles; Canada; Europe; Hawaii; Mexico and Central America; Middle East; New Zealand; Oceania; Scandinavia; South America; *and* West Indies.]

CIRCUMCISION

Circumcision (Gen. 17:9–14) was the sign of the covenant Abram made with God (Gen. 17:10), in token of which his name was changed to Abraham (Gen. 17:5; cf. Luke 1:59, 2:21). Joseph SMITH's translation of the Bible indicates that the performance of circumcision on the eighth day after birth symbolized "that children are not accountable before me until they are eight years old" (JST Gen. 17:4–20; cf. D&C 68:25; 74:1–7). The rite is attested in the intertestamental period (1 Macc. 1:15, 60–61; 2 Macc. 6:10) and is still observed in Judaism and Islam. Circumcision as a necessity for salvation became a major controversy in early Christianity (Acts 10:45; 11:2; 15:1–31), since it had become associated with the law of Moses.

The Book of Mormon seems to imply the continuing practice of circumcision among its peoples from about 600 B.C. They "were strict in observing the ordinances of God, according to the law of Moses" (e.g., Alma 30:3), apparently including the practice of circumcision. Near the end of Nephite history the Lord revealed to the prophet Mormon that "the law of circumcision is done away in me" (Moro. 8:8).

In modern times, Joseph Smith affirmed the perpetuity of the Abrahamic covenant and defended the integrity of Judaism. Today, however, if Latter-day Saint males are circumcised, it is for cleanliness and health, not religious, reasons. From the beginning of the modern Church, the emphasis has been on circumcision of heart (cf. Deut. 10:16; 30:6; Jer. 4:4; Ezek. 44:9). Such a heart is taken as a sign or token of one's covenants with Christ. This may be the understanding of "broken heart and contrite spirit" among Book of Mormon prophets (2 Ne. 2:7; 3 Ne. 12:19; Moro. 6:2) and in modern revelation (e.g., D&C 59:8).

GORDON C. THOMASSON

CITY PLANNING

For Latter-day Saints, city planning began with the Prophet Joseph Smith, who emphasized the advantages of living in compact COMMUNITIES rather than on isolated farms. Many of his ideas were adopted in modified form in LDS settlements in Missouri, Illinois, and the Great Basin of the American West. These communities always provided opportunities for education, cooperation, fine arts, and worship.

Joseph Smith's ideas about city planning are contained in a document known as the City of Zion plan, which he prepared in 1833. The characteristics of this Zion plan include a regular grid pattern with square blocks, wide streets (132 feet), alternating half-acre lots so that houses face alternate streets on each block, uniform brick or stone construction, homes set back 25 feet from the street, frontyard landscaping, gardens in the backyard, the location of farms outside of town, and the designation of central blocks as a site for TEMPLES, schools, and other public buildings.

Though Joseph Smith did not identify the sources behind the plan, perhaps he was influenced by the biblical pattern of Moses arranging the tribes around the tabernacle (Num. 2), as well as by towns in his own experience. Clearly his goal was to design communities that enhanced the cooperation and religious unity envisioned in the revelations about Zion.

LDS portions of KIRTLAND, OHIO, which was surveyed shortly after this plan was presented, followed it closely. Other cities influenced by Joseph Smith were somewhat different. The Saints at Far West, Missouri (1836–1839), surveyed their city into square blocks of four acres with only four one-acre lots on each. Four 132-feet-wide streets bounded a central square, but other streets were narrower. NAUVOO, Illinois (1839–1846), was similar to Far West, but only the two main streets were wider than 50 feet.

Immediately after the pioneers arrived in the Salt Lake Valley in 1847, President Brigham YOUNG issued instructions for establishing Salt Lake City. His plan reflected elements of the City of Zion plan, with blocks the same size, but instead of twenty half-acre lots in each block, each contained eight lots, 1.25 acres in size. As in Joseph

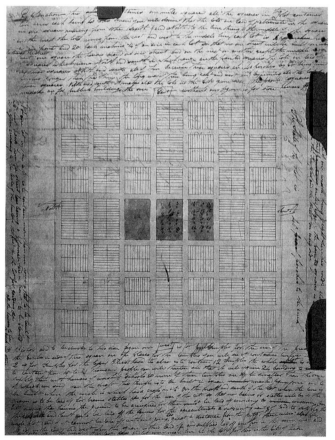

The original plat of Independence, Missouri, on paper. Designed by Joseph Smith, 1833. Using variations of this pattern, each town that was established by the Latter-day Saints was laid out in rectangular plots of land in town blocks allotted for residences and farms.

Smith's plan, all streets were 132 feet wide and the houses on each block faced alternate streets, with each set 20 feet back from the sidewalk. The most important difference was that the lots were much larger. Each city lot became a minifarm with animals, barns, and gardens. The rapid influx of settlers into Salt Lake City led to the early subdivision of the large lots.

Other settlements (see COLONIZATION) followed the same general pattern as Salt Lake City, but the actual lot, block, and street sizes varied from community to community. While most communities adhered to the rigid grid pattern oriented to the cardinal directions, street widths ranged from 66 to 172 feet, block sizes from four to ten acres, and lot sizes from one-half to more than one acre. Though differing in details, Mormon towns were characterized by large lots, wide streets, and large blocks, features that still distinguish these communities of America's Intermountain West. This expansive pattern later enhanced urbanization, providing space for four lanes of traffic and for large-scale downtown development.

The emphasis on large scale has also created a distinctive landscape in the small Mormon agricultural communities of the Intermountain West. Typically, the wide streets have only a narrow two-lane strip of pavement, flanked by twenty- to thirty-foot unimproved shoulders of weeds or gravel. Most residents of these villages use the large lots only for small gardens; barns, corrals, and outbuildings of the nineteenth century often remain as landscape relics. Where population growth has led to subdivision of the street frontage of the large lots, the center of the blocks has often remained open. The interior of these large blocks may be devoted to household gardens or simply allowed to remain vacant until land prices justify higher density apartment buildings or other uses for the space.

City planning in the Mormon culture region incorporates the experiences of the Mormons in their migration across the American frontier. Joseph Smith's plan combined his New England village background with the rectangular blocks and lots typical of Philadelphia. Brigham Young adopted this rectangular pattern and added to it an emphasis on subsistence agriculture, which led to large blocks and lots for minifarms within the community. Joseph Smith's requirement to build of brick or stone was paralleled by Brigham Young's encouragement to build of adobe (unfired clay bricks). Old Mormon villages are currently dominated by adobe, brick, and stone homes, and even the modern suburbs in Mormon communities have a high concentration of brick construction. The large scale of both Joseph Smith's and Brigham Young's visions of the ideal city and the emphasis on uniform setback, landscaping, and brick or stone construction combine to make the Mormon village a distinctive pattern of city planning in America.

BIBLIOGRAPHY

Jackson, Richard H. "The Mormon Village: Genesis and Antecedents of the City of Zion Plan." *BYU Studies* 17 (Winter 1977):223–40.

Nelson, Lowry. *The Mormon Village: A Pattern and Techniques of Land Settlement.* Salt Lake City, 1954.

Ricks, Joel Edward. *Forms and Methods of Early Mormon Settlement in Utah and Surrounding Regions, 1847–1877.* Logan, Utah, 1964.

RICHARD H. JACKSON

CIVIC DUTIES

Latter-day Saint teachings emphasize many aspects of civic duty, including responsible self-government; an informed, public-spirited citizenry; and obedience to LAW. LDS scriptures and leaders also encourage activity in organizations that build and maintain COMMUNITY life, making oneself available for public and military service, and avoidance of government welfare dependency. LDS teaching stresses EDUCATION and a healthy lifestyle, both of which contribute to a strong citizenry (*see* WORD OF WISDOM).

In September 1968 the First Presidency urged members "to do their civic duty and to assume their responsibilities as individual citizens in seeking solutions to the problems which beset our cities and communities" (*see* PROCLAMATIONS OF FIRST PRESIDENCY). Members are obligated to respect governmental authority. The twelfth Article of Faith states, "We believe in being subject to kings, presidents, rulers, and magistrates, in obeying, honoring, and sustaining the law." This commitment to good citizenship is further elucidated in scripture: "We believe that all men are bound to sustain and uphold the respective governments in which they reside, while protected in their inherent and inalienable rights by the laws of such governments; and that sedition and rebellion are unbecoming every citizen thus protected" (D&C 134:5).

LDS emphasis on civic duty stems from Christian commitment to community service and individual FREEDOM. The CONSTITUTION OF THE UNITED STATES, which also promotes these values, was established by God through "wise men" for the "protection of all flesh" (D&C 101:77–80). Latter-day Saints are to strive to elect "honest" and "wise" leaders who will support constitutional freedoms, particularly freedom of religion (D&C 98:10). The Christian tradition of civic virtue that underlay the American founding has been documented by LDS scholars (Vetterli and Bryner). Latter-day Saints tend to take seriously their responsibility to participate in the political process. Since World War II, Utah has been the state with the highest percentage of eligible voters who do in fact vote in presidential elections (72 percent). Latter-day Saints are also strongly encouraged to be patriotic and share in the responsibility of defending their homelands through military service, if necessary, wherever they might live ("First Presidency Statement," *Church News*, May 24, 1969, p. 12).

Latter-day Saint women were involved in public life long before women in other parts of the United States. They have always voted in Church congregations. The University of Deseret, founded in Salt Lake City in 1850, was the first coeducational university west of the Mississippi. H. H. Bancroft's *History of Utah* reported that women voted in the provisional government before territorial status in 1850 (p. 272, San Francisco, 1890). The first documented women voters in modern times were in Salt Lake City on February 14, 1870. Mary W. Chamberlain was elected mayor of Kanab, Utah, with an all-female town board, in 1912. The first woman state senator elected in the United States (Dr. Mattie Hughes Paul Cannon, 1896) and the first woman elected to the U.S. Senate who was neither the wife nor the daughter of a politician (Paula Hawkins, Florida, 1980) were Latter-day Saints.

The Church encourages its members to make themselves available for public office, and many have responded. Latter-day Saints have served as governors of such states as California (Culbert Olson and Goodwin Knight) and Michigan (George Romney). In 1952 two Latter-day Saints were serving in the U.S. House of Representatives and two in the U.S. Senate. In 1991 there were nine LDS representatives and one nonvoting territorial delegate in the House and three Latter-day Saints in the Senate. There have been five LDS cabinet members (Ezra Taft BENSON, Agriculture; Stewart L. Udall, Interior; George W. Romney, Housing and Urban Development; David M. Kennedy, Treasury; and Terrell H. Bell, Education). Latter-day Saints have served as both domestic and national security advisers in the Bush administration. Prior to 1952, no Latter-day Saint had served as a federal judge. Since then, eleven have been appointed to federal district courts and four to appeals courts.

Church members are encouraged to help their communities through VOLUNTEERISM. The LDS Church is one of the most active sponsors of the SCOUTING movement in the United States. Concern for the international community was evident when members fasted in 1985 and contributed nearly $11 million for Ethiopian and other famine relief and agricultural development for distribution largely through other agencies (see HUMANITARIAN SERVICE).

In times of increasing dependence on government programs and assistance, Latter-day Saints as a group consciously try to live in such a way as to reduce their burden on government. Their lifestyle, teachings, and youth programs are often cited as explanations for low rates of crime, drug abuse, alcoholism, illness, and unemployment in the areas where they live. Through these and other means, they invest in, and promote, education, moral behavior, and leadership—and with some success. For example, medical studies now document the healthiness of the Mormon lifestyle (*USA Today*, Dec. 6, 1989, p. 1), which presumably contributes to a stronger and less dependent citizenry. LDS SOCIAL SERVICES and employment and welfare programs save governments millions of dollars annually. The predominantly LDS state of Utah regularly ranks first in the proportion of high school graduates who take advanced placement courses. *Fortune* magazine ranked metropolitan Salt Lake City first in the availability of intelligent, enthusiastic, and loyal workers (Oct. 22, 1990, p. 49), and *Financial World* ranked Utah the second best-governed state (Apr. 17, 1990, p. 31).

[*See also* Politics: Political Teachings; Politics: Contemporary; United States of America.]

BIBLIOGRAPHY

Vetterli, Richard, and Gary Bryner. *In Search of the Republic: Public Virtue and the Roots of American Government.* Totowa, N.J., 1987.

MARK W. CANNON

CIVIL RIGHTS

Civil rights are legal guarantees designed to protect persons from arbitrary or discriminatory treatment. Common examples are those protecting freedom of speech, freedom of worship, freedom of assembly, the right to due process of law, the right to vote, the right to equal protection of the law, and safeguards for persons accused of crime, such as the right against self-incrimination, the right to confront one's accuser, the right to a jury trial, the right to counsel, and the right to a speedy trial. These and other rights are declared in the Constitution of the United States of America and in the constitutions of many other countries (see CONSTITUTIONAL LAW). Civil rights are found in statutes as well as in constitutions and may provide, for example, detailed guarantees against public and private discrimination on the basis of such characteristics as race, gender, age, and religion. Civil rights issues arise when people disagree about the rights that are, or ought to be, guaranteed by law.

The Church of Jesus Christ of Latter-day Saints and its members have an obvious interest in securing their own rights. Beyond this, several strands of doctrine and belief—sometimes competing—shape the views of members and leaders regarding civil rights in general. The principle of free AGENCY seems most compatible with a legal system guaranteeing wide latitude for individual choice and decision. With respect to religious liberties, agency is reinforced by individual and institutional interests in freedom from governmental restraint. In the UNITED STATES OF AMERICA, commitment to individual rights is further reinforced by allegiance to the personal liberties guaranteed by the U.S. Constitution, which Latter-day Saints regard as an inspired document. On the other hand, the Church teaches its members to obey properly constituted governmental authority (D&C 134:5; 98:6; A of F 12), which may lead to accommodation and submission when core religious interests are not threatened. In addition, Church teachings on moral questions sometimes predispose members, as well as the institutional Church, to take positions on political issues (ABORTION, for example) that run counter to the rights claimed by others. As a result, the position of the Church and its members toward current civil rights issues is complex.

A Church statement of belief regarding government, adopted in 1835, singled out "free exercise of conscience, the right and control of property, and the protection of life" as rights essential to the peace of society (D&C 134:2; see POLITICS: POLITICAL TEACHINGS). This 1835 statement repeatedly stressed the importance of RELIGIOUS FREEDOM, and the Church and its members have sometimes found it necessary to take legal action to vindicate free exercise rights. In *Corporation of the Presiding Bishop of The Church of Jesus Christ of Latter-day Saints et al. v. Amos et al.* (483 U.S. 327 [1987]), for example, the Church successfully defended its right to impose a religious test for employment in certain Church-owned establishments. The Church as an institution has avoided legal action where possible, but has been willing to defend its rights in court when necessary.

Apart from its special legal interests, the Church is publicly committed to a broad range of civil rights for all. An oft-cited 1963 statement by a member of the Church First Presidency, Hugh B. Brown, called for "full civil equality for all of God's children," saying "it is a moral evil . . . to deny any human being the right to gainful employment, to full educational opportunity, and to every privilege of citizenship, just as it is a moral evil to deny him the right to worship" (p. 1058).

In the political arena, where competing claims to civil rights are frequently debated, the Church participates indirectly by encouraging members to vote and to foster a society congenial to Christian teaching and righteous living. Occasionally, when public issues implicate important matters of doctrine and morals, the Church publishes recommended positions on disputed issues and encourages members and others to follow their counsel. Thus, the Church has urged restrictions on the sale of alcoholic beverages, opposed the legalization of gambling and lotteries, favored right-to-work legislation (no closed or union shop), advocated the defeat of the equal rights amendment (ERA), and spoken out against pornography, abortion, and child abuse.

Within the Church, individual rights play a muted role as compared with secular society. Love and duty are stressed far more than individual claims of right. Moreover, the Church is a voluntary organization whose sanctions extend only to rights of membership and participation within the group, so fewer safeguards are necessary. Thus, Church disciplinary proceedings do not provide the full set of procedural protections the accused would receive in secular courts. Although due process notices and appeal rights are given, service

of process is not strictly enforced and there is no right to confront one's accuser, no jury trial, and no right to counsel. Indeed, confession of sin by the repentant sinner may be at odds with the right against self-incrimination (see DISCIPLINARY PROCEDURES). Free speech is another illustration of the contrast with secular society. Members are free to say or publish what they wish. Yet, Church etiquette and policies, obligations of confidentiality, respect for divine and holy things, and the need to avoid offending others impose restraints upon freedom of expression. Likewise, voting within the Church involves the concept of common consent, but has none of the trappings of democratic elections and in most instances amounts to ratification of leadership callings and decisions. As for gender equality and children's rights, the relationships of men, women, and children are governed by religious principles, freely adopted by members, which teach EQUALITY but emphasize differences in roles. These principles are taught as eternal patterns, not derived from prevailing attitudes toward civil rights in any secular society, past or present.

BIBLIOGRAPHY

Allen, James B., and Glen M. Leonard. *The Story of the Latter-day Saints.* Salt Lake City, 1976.

Brown, Hugh B. *IE* 66 (Dec. 1963):1058.

Cowan, Richard O. *The Church in the Twentieth Century.* Salt Lake City, 1985.

Firmage, Edwin Brown, and Richard Collin Mangrum. *Zion in the Courts: A Legal History of the Church of Jesus Christ of Latter-day Saints, 1830–1900.* Urbana, Ill., 1988.

Mangrum, R. Collin. "Mormonism, Philosophical Liberalism, and the Constitution." *BYU Studies* 27 (Summer 1987):119–37.

McAffee, Thomas B. "Constitutional Interpretation and the American Tradition of Individual Rights." *BYU Studies* 27 (Summer 1987):139–69.

Melville, J. Keith. "Joseph Smith, the Constitution, and Individual Liberties." *BYU Studies* 28 (Spring 1988):65–74.

ROBERT E. RIGGS

CIVIL WAR PROPHECY

Joseph SMITH's Civil War prophecy is contained in sections 87 and 130 of the Doctrine and Covenants. He prophesied on December 25, 1832, that a war would begin in South Carolina; that the southern states would divide against the northern states; that the South would seek support from other nations, including Great Britain; and that the war would lead to the death and misery of many souls. These items in the prophecy were all fulfilled in the Civil War (1861–1865). In 1843 the Prophet noted (D&C 130:12–13) that he had also learned by revelation in 1832 that slavery would be the probable cause of the upcoming crisis. These matters are all history now, but certain verses in the Civil War prophecy have broader applications and it appears that portions of the revelation are yet to be fulfilled.

Section 87 was not published by the Church until 1851 and was not canonized until 1876. It was, however, copied and circulated by some Church leaders and missionaries in the 1830s. The Civil War prophecy became one of the most widely published revelations in the Doctrine and Covenants. Not surprisingly, it received greatest attention during the Civil War, as many viewed the conflict as a vindication of the prophetic powers of Joseph Smith.

BIBLIOGRAPHY

Cannon, Donald Q. "A Prophecy of War." In *Studies in Scripture*, ed. R. Millet and K. Jackson, Vol. 1, pp. 335–39. Salt Lake City, 1989.

PAUL H. PETERSON

CLERGY

The word "clergy" generally designates those who are priests or ministers within the Catholic, Eastern Orthodox, or Protestant traditions. Since the term refers to full-time paid professionals, it is not used by Latter-day Saints. They refer to their Church officers as BRANCH PRESIDENTS, BISHOPS, or STAKE PRESIDENTS. These individuals are laypersons who, without professional training in theology, are called to these positions for limited periods of time by those having AUTHORITY.

Some Latter-day Saints have ambivalent feelings about the clergy of other Christian traditions, in part because some professional ministers participated in the early PERSECUTION of the Saints and others in current times continue to produce ANTI-MORMON PUBLICATIONS. Also, because Latter-day Saints believe that the Lord has revealed the fulness of the gospel through his modern prophets, the professional clergy have been viewed as teaching only part of the truth. However, The Church of Jesus Christ of Latter-day Saints readily acknowledges the extensive contributions of Jewish, Catholic, Eastern Orthodox, Protestant, and other clergy to the spiritual and moral well-being of their communities and their parishioners.

BIBLIOGRAPHY

Bangerter, William Grant. "'Tis a Two-Way Street." *Ensign* 10 (July 1986):66–71.

ROGER R. KELLER

CLERK

Almost since the Church was organized in 1830, clerks have been divinely charged with the sacred responsibility of RECORD KEEPING. Although STAKE PRESIDENTS and BISHOPS have overall responsibility for the records kept in their STAKES and WARDS, clerks are charged with the stewardship of creating and maintaining membership, historical, and financial records. Clerks are lay members of the Church called by stake presidents to serve on a volunteer basis between three and ten hours a week in a stake or ward. Most serve for two to three years, but some have served for as many as thirty years in different clerk roles.

LDS scriptures speak of the calling of clerks and the importance of making a record of ordinances and other significant events in the Church and in the lives of members:

> It is the duty of the Lord's clerk, whom he has appointed, to keep a history, and a general church record of all things that transpire in Zion, and of all those who consecrate properties, and receive inheritances legally from the bishop; and also their manner of life, their faith, and works [D&C 85:1–2].

Clerks record ordinances performed for both the living and the dead, tithes and offerings given, minutes of Church meetings, and historical events. They are encouraged to be accurate and thorough in gathering information and reporting details. They must keep strict confidence and guard the privacy rights of Church members because they keep personal and sensitive information about them.

The stake clerk and assistant stake clerks perform record-keeping activities at the stake level and often are invited to supervise the training and work of ward clerks. The ward clerk and his assistant clerks have responsibility for gathering most statistical data about members that enable the Church to function properly.

To ensure accurate and complete Church records, clerks coordinate the gathering of information, train assistant clerks, supervise record keeping, and make certain that proper financial controls and procedures are followed. They also ensure compliance with audit findings and oversee the use and support of computer information systems. Clerks keep the financial records, recording the expenditure of funds to support Church programs and making it possible for bishops to provide members with information regarding their personal tithes and offerings.

Clerks maintain MEMBERSHIP RECORDS that include demographic information and ordinance information for each member. They record the participation of members in some Church services. Stake and ward priesthood leaders use this information to help members prepare to receive the ordinances and covenants of the gospel. Modern technology has simplified record keeping in the Church. Most stake and ward clerks in the United States and Canada use computer systems that enable them to produce information quickly for stake presidents and bishops and to send information to Church headquarters.

JEFFREY C. BATESON

COFFEE

Active Latter-day Saints abstain from drinking coffee. This practice derives from an 1833 revelation known as the WORD OF WISDOM, which states that "hot drinks are not for the body or the belly" (D&C 89:9). Hyrum Smith, Assistant President of the Church, later defined "hot drinks" as coffee and TEA (T&S 3 [June 1, 1842]:800), establishing the official interpretation for subsequent generations. The Word of Wisdom was given originally to show the will of God, though not as a commandment. Abstinence from coffee has been expected of fully participating members since the early twentieth century (see DOCTRINE AND COVENANTS: SECTION 89).

The main chemical in coffee that has caused health concerns is caffeine, a cerebral and cardiovascular stimulant. A large number of other sub-

stances are also found in coffee, and their effects on health are not yet well understood.

BIBLIOGRAPHY

Gilman, A. G.; L. S. Goodman; and A. Gilman, eds. *Goodman and Gilman's The Pharmacological Basis of Therapeutics*, 6th ed., pp. 592–604. New York, 1980.

Stratton, Clifford J. "The Xanthines: Coffee, Cola, Cocoa, and Tea." *BYU Studies* 20 (Summer 1980):371–88.

JOSEPH LYNN LYON

COLESVILLE, NEW YORK

Colesville, New York, is a township located in Broome County, in the south central part of the state, where one of the earliest BRANCHES of the Church was organized in 1830. The central part of the township lies approximately ten miles northeast of the present city of Binghamton. In October 1825 Joseph Smith went to the area to work intermittently for Josiah Stowell for a little over a year. Stowell lived just south of the village of South Bainbridge in adjoining Bainbridge Township, Chenango County (since 1857 the village of Afton, Afton Township). Sometime during 1826 Joseph Smith also worked for Joseph Knight, Sr., who with his family resided on a farm located on Pickerel Pond, immediately east of Nineveh, a village in Colesville Township on the Susquehanna River.

Joseph Smith maintained a friendly relationship with the Knight family and others in the Colesville area. In 1829, when Joseph and Oliver COWDERY were translating the Book of Mormon in HARMONY, PENNSYLVANIA, Joseph Knight, Sr., came from Colesville to visit and to give them food and writing materials. At other times, Joseph traveled the thirty miles from Harmony to Colesville for supplies. Joseph Smith related that the Melchizedek Priesthood was bestowed upon him and Oliver Cowdery by Peter, James, and John along the banks of the Susquehanna River between Colesville and Harmony (D&C 128:20; *see* MELCHIZEDEK PRIESTHOOD: RESTORATION OF).

After the Church was organized on April 6, 1830, in FAYETTE, NEW YORK, Joseph made several visits to the Knight family in Colesville to preach the gospel. On one of these visits, he cast an evil spirit out of Newel Knight, a son of Joseph Knight, Sr. This was the first miracle performed in the Church after its organization (*HC* 1:82–83).

Numerous converts were baptized in the area, despite strong opposition from enemies of the Church. Joseph was brought to trial during July 1830 in both Chenango and Broome counties on charges related to his religious activities, but was acquitted in both instances. The Colesville Branch, often spoken of as the first branch of the Church, was organized in October 1830, with Hyrum SMITH as branch president. He was followed in this office by Newel Knight. The membership of the branch was approximately sixty-five members.

The Saints in the Colesville area, following instruction of the Prophet (D&C 38), migrated to Kirtland and then Thompson, Ohio, in April–May 1831, and subsequently on to Kaw Township, Jackson County, Missouri, during June–July 1831. Through all their moves they stayed together and were known as the Colesville Branch.

BIBLIOGRAPHY

Porter, Larry C. "A Study of the Origins of The Church of Jesus Christ of Latter-day Saints in the States of New York and Pennsylvania, 1816–1831." Ph.D. diss., Brigham Young University, 1971.

LAMAR E. GARRARD

COLONIZATION

[*This entry is an overview of Latter-day Saint colonization in the Great Basin. Articles on* City Planning; Community; Gathering; *and* Immigration and Emigration *discuss principles guiding colonization decisions. For further discussion of colonization outside Utah, see entries on LDS pioneer settlements in* Arizona; California; Canada; Colorado; Idaho; Mexico; Nevada; New Mexico; *and* Wyoming. *Related articles are* Economic History of the Church; Native Americans; *and* Young, Brigham.]

Latter-day Saints were industrious colonizers of the American West. During the Brigham YOUNG administration alone, they founded nearly four hundred settlements, with three hundred more thereafter. Though some were distant from Salt Lake City, they were not isolated villages but maintained close communication with adjacent settlements and Church headquarters. Following a pattern that emerged in the Church's first decade, each was founded to provide protection and promote unity and shared values.

Between 1830 and 1846, Latter-day Saints settled in or near a series of Church headquarters. After conflict and persecution in New York, Ohio, Missouri, and Illinois, they sought refuge in a virtual no-man's-land in the West. After establishing a new headquarters in the heretofore largely uninhabited SALT LAKE VALLEY, Latter-day Saints sought to ensure self-rule by establishing a dominant influence over a vast territory including present-day Utah and Nevada and parts of Idaho, Wyoming, and California. Immigrant converts, first from the United States and the British Isles and after 1852 from continental Europe, swelled the ranks of colonists. Under the direction of President Brigham Young, exploring parties were sent out and settlements were established in a corridor extending from the Salt Lake Valley southwest to Las Vegas, Nevada, and San Bernardino, California. Missions to Native Americans prompted the establishment of several settlements around the perimeter of the Mormon sphere of influence: Fort Limhi, Idaho, on the Salmon River to the northwest; the Elk Mountain Mission to the southeast (near present-day Moab, Utah); and Harmony and Santa Clara, Utah, and Las Vegas to the southwest. Settlements in Carson Valley, Nevada, on the west were an outgrowth of individual LDS enterprise along the route of gold-seekers traveling to California, reinforced at the direction of Church leaders. To the northeast, Fort Bridger and Fort Supply, Wyoming, were to anchor a series of way stations between Salt Lake City and the Missouri River along the MORMON TRAIL to facilitate immigration and trade. San Bernardino was to be a temporary gathering place for Saints from the Pacific Coast.

For various reasons, most of these outer colonies proved less than successful and were discontinued by 1858. The march of the UTAH EXPEDITION toward Utah and hostility provoked by the MOUNTAIN MEADOWS MASSACRE prompted a withdrawal from most distant outposts. After the conclusion of the so-called Utah War, colonization resumed, but within a more compact territory. St. George, Utah, the focal point of the 1861 Cotton Mission, became a key settlement in the Southwest. With President Young's persistent support, that settlement survived the demise of its cotton industry after America's Civil War and the abandonment of LDS efforts to establish a route for trade and immigration via the Gulf of California and the lower Colorado River. With the addition of settlements in northern Utah and southern Idaho,

This view of Logan, Utah, c. 1890, with the Logan Temple above the town and grist mill in the foreground, shows the broad streets and typical layout of a thriving "Mormon village." Courtesy University of Utah.

the population came to be most heavily concentrated in the territory's northern region.

Meanwhile, the extension of settlement beyond the Salt Lake Valley deprived Native Americans of prime hunting and fishing lands. After initial conflicts, President Young established a policy of feeding the Indians rather than fighting them, but still advised villages to build fortifications against possible attack. Latter-day Saints sought to convert the Indians both to their religion and to the pursuit of agriculture. Even with the assistance of federally sponsored farms, however, few Indians made successful transitions. The continued influx of LDS immigrants and the failure of Church and government efforts to reverse the gradual impoverishment of the Native American population led to the Walker War of the 1850s and to the Black Hawk War of the 1860s. The subsequent resettlement of the surviving Indians to reservations removed one of the major obstacles to further colonization.

Before Brigham Young's death in 1877, additional settlements were planted along the Little Colorado River in Arizona, followed by more in Colorado, New Mexico, Canada, and Mexico. Elsewhere, the Palawai Valley on the island of Lanai and, later, Laie on Oahu became gathering places for Saints in Hawaii, the first such settlements outside western North America.

Colonization was generally directed and coordinated from Church headquarters. Church leaders selected key sites and handpicked leaders to direct the founding of new villages. Some settlers volunteered, while others received a CALLING to relocate. When LDS families established new locations on their own initiative, Church leaders usually visited soon afterward to ensure that the settlement was properly organized. Thus, each settlement was effectively a colony of the mother settlement in Salt Lake City. From initial sites, Latter-day Saints spread out to occupy most of the arable land nearby and founded new towns.

Beginning in 1880, Mormon villages spread along the route of the Utah and Northern Railway and the Upper Snake River Valley in Idaho. Many of these were settled through individual initiative rather than Church direction, and Church leaders labored with some difficulty to encourage the location of homes in the customary compact Mormon villages rather than scattered throughout the surrounding farmland.

Colonies in Alberta, Canada, and in Chihua-

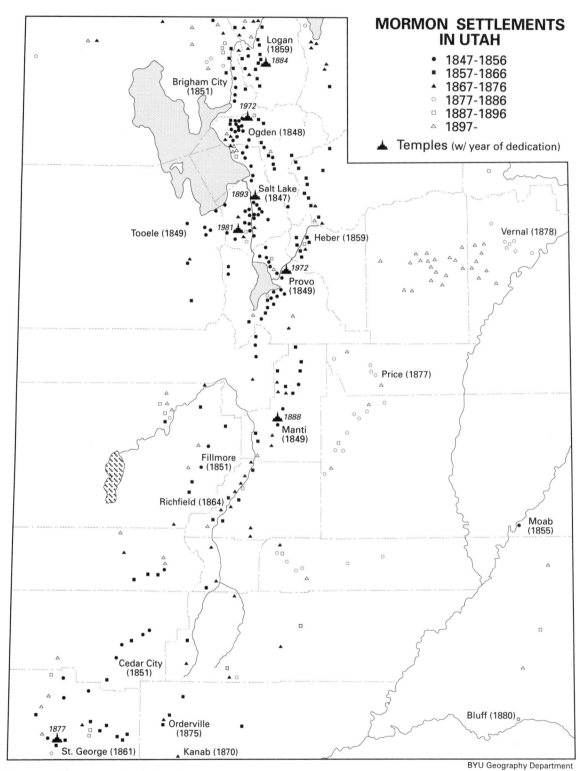

MORMON SETTLEMENTS IN UTAH

- • 1847-1856
- ▪ 1857-1866
- ▲ 1867-1876
- ○ 1877-1886
- □ 1887-1896
- △ 1897-

▲ Temples (w/ year of dedication)

Logan (1859) *1884*

Brigham City (1851)

1972

Ogden (1848)

Salt Lake (1847) *1893*

Tooele (1849) *1981*

Heber (1859)

1972

Provo (1849)

Vernal (1878)

Price (1877)

Manti (1849) *1888*

Fillmore (1851)

Richfield (1864)

Moab (1855)

Cedar City (1851)

Orderville (1875)

Bluff (1880)

1877

St. George (1861)

Kanab (1870)

BYU Geography Department

Mormon settlements in Utah, 1847–1906.

Cardston (1886)

C A N A D A

W A S H I N G T O N

M O N T A N A

Summerville (1892)

O R E G O N

Limhi (1855)

I D A H O

Lovell (1900-1901)

Rexburg (1883)

W Y O M I N G

Franklin (1860)   Afton (1885)
Paris (1863)
Brigham City (1851)   Logan (1859)
Fort Supply (1853)
Ogden (1848)

N E V A D A

Salt Lake City (1847)

Genoa (1849)

Provo (1849)

U T A H

Fillmore (1851)

Richfield (1864)

C O L O R A D O

Parowan (1851)   Moab (1855)
Pueblo (1846)
Cedar City (1851)

St. George (1861)   Kanab (1870)
Bluff (1880)
Pipe Springs (1863)
Manassa (1879)

Las Vegas (1855)
Kirtland (1899)

C A L I F O R N I A   Callville (1864)

Brigham City (1876)   Ramah (1882)

Joseph City (1876)

San Bernardino
(1851)   Woodruff (1876)

N E W
Snowflake (1877)
M E X I C O

Lehi (1877)
Mesa (1878)   Thatcher (1882)

A R I Z O N A

Saint David (1877)

M E X I C O

Colonia Juarez (1885)

BYU Geography Department

Selected Mormon settlements in the West, 1847–1890.

hua, Mexico, largely resulted from the Church's attempts to find refuge for polygamists under threat of prosecution during the 1880s (*see* ANTIPOLYGAMY LEGISLATION). Later efforts included the Big Horn Basin of Wyoming by 1900 and Kelsey, Texas, in 1901. Though Kelsey was one of only a handful of LDS settlements established outside the larger sphere of Latter-day Saint influence, the town still exhibited many of the characteristics of a planned Mormon village.

Early in the twentieth century, new colonization ceased and emphasis was placed on strengthening congregations throughout the world rather than on gathering to already predominantly LDS communities.

BIBLIOGRAPHY

Arrington, Leonard J. *Great Basin Kingdom.* Cambridge, Mass., 1958.

Campbell, Eugene E. "Brigham Young's Outer Cordon—A Reappraisal." *Utah Historical Quarterly* 41 (Summer 1973):220–53.

Hunter, Milton R. *Brigham Young the Colonizer.* Santa Barbara, Calif., 1973.

Sherlock, Richard. "Mormon Migration and Settlement After 1875." *Journal of Mormon History* 2 (1975):53–68.

RICHARD L. JENSEN

COLORADO, PIONEER SETTLEMENTS IN

The first Latter-day Saints in Colorado were predominantly from the American South. In 1846, converts from Mississippi, expecting to join Brigham Young and the pioneer company en route to the Great Basin, wintered at the site of present-day Pueblo after learning that the first company of Nauvoo emigrants would not leave the Missouri River until the next spring. A group of sick members of the MORMON BATTALION, including women and children, joined these Mississippi Saints, and all left Pueblo in time to reach the Great Salt Lake Valley in July 1847.

Southern converts also formed the nucleus of permanent LDS colonization in Colorado, wintering in Pueblo in 1877–1878 and settling in 1878 in the San Luis Valley. Joined by settlers from Sanpete County and elsewhere in Utah and by two families from New Mexico, they founded several settlements in the following decade. The San Luis

Stake, with headquarters at Manassa, was organized in 1883 and consisted of LDS colonists in Conejos County. Jack Dempsey, a son of expatriate southern Latter-day Saints, was born in Manassa and, as world heavyweight boxing champion, bore the nickname "Manassa Mauler."

Beginning as early as 1880, LDS settlers began to establish farms along the Mancos River in southwest Colorado. In 1901, after land in the nearby Fort Lewis Indian Reservation was made available for settlement, Latter-day Saints began to establish farms on the Fort Lewis Mesa. They constituted a majority of the settlers in that area, though Mancos itself was not a predominantly Mormon town. The Young Stake, organized in 1912, consisted of Latter-day Saints in Mancos, the Fort Lewis Mesa, and northwestern New Mexico.

Early growth of the Church along the eastern slope of the Rocky Mountains came largely through the proselytizing of the Western States Mission, long headquartered in Denver; branches of the Church were established there and in Englewood, Fort Collins, and Pueblo by 1930. Farther west, additional growth came in Alamosa and Grand Junction in the first third of the twentieth century. By 1990, after continued proselytizing and in-migration, there were 87,000 Latter-day Saints in Colorado.

BIBLIOGRAPHY

Anderson, Carleton Q.; Betty Shawcroft; and Robert Compton. *The Mormons: 100 Years in the San Luis Valley of Colorado 1883–1983.* La Jara, Colo., 1982.

Jenson, Andrew. *Encyclopedic History of The Church of Jesus Christ of Latter-day Saints.* Salt Lake City, 1941.

The Stone Rolls Forth: A History of The Church of Jesus Christ of Latter-day Saints in Southeastern Colorado 1846–1986. Compiled by the Colorado Springs, Colorado North Stake, 1988.

RICHARD L. JENSEN

COLUMBUS, CHRISTOPHER

Latter-day Saints generally regard Columbus as having fulfilled a prophecy contained early in the Book of Mormon. NEPHI₁ recorded a vision of the future of his father's descendants. After foreseeing the destruction of his own seed, Nephi beheld a GENTILE "separated from the seed of my brethren by the many waters," and saw that the Spirit of

Latter-day Saints attending classes in the San Luis Stake Academy, in Manassa, Colorado, December 1909. Each stake, wherever located, was counseled to appoint an academy principal and to operate a school for the general education of the Saints.

God "came down and wrought upon the man; and he went forth upon the many waters, even unto the seed of my brethren, who were in the promised land" (1 Ne. 13:12).

Nephi appears to give an accurate account of Columbus's motives. Even though he was well-acquainted with the sciences of his day and his voyages have been viewed by some historians as primarily an economic triumph of Spain over Portugal, Columbus apparently had bigger motives for his voyage and felt himself spiritually driven to discover new lands. Newly acknowledged documents show that medieval eschatology, the scriptures, and divine inspiration were the main forces compelling him to sail. His notes in the works of Pierre d'Ailly and his own unfinished *Book of Prophecies* substantiate his apocalyptic view of the world and his feelings about his own prophetic role.

Among the themes of this book was the conversion of the heathen. Columbus quoted Seneca, "The years will come . . . when the Ocean will loose the bonds by which we have been confined, when an immense land shall lie revealed" (Watts, p. 94). He believed himself chosen by God to find that land and deliver the light of Christianity to the natives there. He was called *Christoferens* (the Christ-bearer). A map contemporaneous with his voyages depicts him bearing the Christ child on his shoulders across the waters. He believed that he was to help usher in the age of "one fold, and one shepherd," citing John 10:16 (cf. 3 Ne. 15:21), and spoke of finding "the new heaven and new earth."

Writing to King Ferdinand and Queen Isabella to gain financial support, Columbus testified that a voice had told him he had been watched over from infancy to prepare him for discovering the Indies. He felt that he was given divine keys to ocean barriers that only he could unlock (Merrill, p. 135). In a second letter, he emphasized his prophetic role: "Reason, mathematics, and maps of the world were of no use to me in the execution of the enterprise of the Indies. What Isaiah said [e.g., Isa. 24:15] was completely fulfilled" (Watts, p. 96). Unknowingly, Columbus also fulfilled Nephi's prophecy.

BIBLIOGRAPHY

Merrill, Hyde M. "Christopher Columbus and the Book of Mormon." *IE* 69 (1966):97–98, 135–36.

Nibley, Hugh W. "Columbus and Revelation." *Instructor* 88 (1953):319–20; reprinted in *CWHN* 8:49–53.

Watts, Pauline Moffitt. "Prophecy and Discovery: On the Spiritual Origins of Christopher Columbus's 'Enterprise of the Indies.'" *American Historical Review* 90 (1985):73–102.

LOUISE G. HANSON

COMFORTER

See: Holy Ghost

COMMANDMENTS

Latter-day Saints believe that commandments are divine directives for righteous living; bring happiness and spiritual and temporal blessings; and are part of God's way to redeem his children and endow them with ETERNAL LIFE. Therefore, commandments provide not only a test of faith, obedience, and love for God and Jesus Christ but also an opportunity to experience love from God and joy both in this life and in the life to come. Commandments are received by REVELATION directly from deity or through his prophets. Written accounts of such revelations are contained in the scriptures, which include the BIBLE, the BOOK OF MORMON, the DOCTRINE AND COVENANTS, and the PEARL OF GREAT PRICE.

At the organization of the Church on April 6, 1830, Joseph SMITH was designated a seer, translator, prophet, apostle, and elder. On that occasion, the Lord said to the Church, "Thou shalt give heed unto all [Joseph Smith's] words and commandments which he shall give unto you as he receiveth them, walking in all holiness before me; for his word ye shall receive, as if from mine own mouth, in all patience and faith" (D&C 21:4–5; cf. D&C 1:37–38; 5:10; 68:34). Based upon these admonitions, members of the Church accept righteous instruction from those authorized by God as commandments binding upon the Church and upon individuals.

To the Church in 1831 the Lord restated the "first and great" commandment (cf. Matt. 22:37–38): "Wherefore, I give unto them a commandment, saying thus: Thou shalt love the Lord thy God with all thy heart, with all thy might, mind,

and strength; and in the name of Jesus Christ thou shalt serve him" (D&C 59:5). This reiteration was followed by the previously established divine injunctions not to steal, commit adultery, or kill (D&C 59:6).

In the Doctrine and Covenants, section 42, which the Lord identified as the "law of the Church" (D&C 42:2, 59), verses 19–27 reaffirm many admonitions from the TEN COMMANDMENTS. These basic commandments have been reiterated in successive DISPENSATIONS, or eras, in essentially the same form (Ex. 20:3–17; Deut. 5:6–21; Mosiah 12:34–36; D&C 42:19–27; cf. Matt. 5:17–48).

In Old Testament times, because the prohibition of certain outward acts was emphasized, the consequences of disobedience were seemingly stressed more than spiritual and physical redemption through obedience (see LAW OF MOSES). With a different emphasis the New Testament and the Book of Mormon accentuate the purifying process of obedience. Christ made it clear that the commandments were to include not only the deeds of men and women but also their thoughts and motives. In the SERMON ON THE MOUNT, he contrasted the old law and the new. For instance, to look upon a woman with lust in one's heart was defined as a type of adultery (Matt. 5:28). To become angry with neighbors placed one in danger of judgment (Matt. 5:21–22). Rather than seeking vengeance and "an eye for an eye," Jesus' followers were to turn the other cheek and go the extra mile (Matt. 5:38–42). To sum up the new law, Christ said, "Ye have heard that it hath been said, Thou shall love thy neighbour, and hate thine enemy. But I say unto you, love your enemies, bless them that curse you, do good to them that hate you, and pray for them which despitefully use you, and persecute you; . . . Be ye therefore perfect, even as your Father which is in heaven is perfect" (Matt. 5:43–44, 48; cf. 3 Ne. 12:43–48).

To those listeners in the Western Hemisphere who survived the destruction of A.D. 34, the resurrected Christ explained the relationship between the law and the gospel: "Think not that I am come to destroy the law or the prophets. I am not come to destroy but to fulfil; for verily I say unto you, one jot nor one tittle hath not passed away from the law, but in me it hath all been fulfilled. And behold, I have given you the law and the commandments of my Father, that ye shall believe in me, and that ye shall repent of your sins, and come unto me with a broken heart and a contrite spirit" (3 Ne. 12:17–19). Christ's new law clearly requires that not only outward acts but also inner thoughts and feelings conform to the spirit of the law (cf. Alma 12:12–14; D&C 88:109).

In the Church today, the Lord has emphasized that his commandments include the responsibility of self-direction: "Behold, it is not meet that I should command in all things; for he that is compelled in all things, the same is a slothful and not a wise servant; wherefore he receiveth no reward. Verily I say, men should be anxiously engaged in a good cause, and do many things of their own free will, and bring to pass much righteousness; for the power is in them, wherein they are agents unto themselves" (D&C 58:26–28). When the "law of the Church" was received in 1831 (D&C 42), this individual responsibility was also stressed: "Thou shalt love thy wife with all thy heart" (42:22), and "Thou shalt not speak evil of thy neighbor, nor do him any harm" (42:27). Later, the Lord said, "Thou shalt not steal; neither commit adultery, nor kill, nor do anything like unto it" (D&C 59:6). It is apparent that God requires an awareness of one's AGENCY and in effect grants each the power to direct oneself. As one lives in accord with the commandments and thereby becomes more sensitive to the promptings of the HOLY GHOST, outward observances become less important and the perfection of one's thoughts and motives comes to occupy one's attention.

Thus is it that Latter-day Saints find fulfillment and happiness in obedience not only to specific commandments such as the WORD OF WISDOM (D&C 89) and the law of TITHING (D&C 119) but also to the counsel from inspired leaders given in Church conferences and in approved written sources, such as official Church publications.

BIBLIOGRAPHY

Richards, Stephen L. "Keep the Commandments." *IE* 52 (May 1949):273, 345–48.

Sill, Sterling W. "Keep the Commandments." *Ensign* 3 (Jan. 1973):82–83.

DIX S. COONS

COMMON CONSENT

Common consent is a fundamental principle of decision making at all levels in The Church of Jesus Christ of Latter-day Saints. In selecting new officers and making administrative decisions, Church leaders are instructed to seek the will of God. Once the Lord makes his will known and a decision is reached, the matter is brought before the appropriate quorum or body of Church members, who are asked to sustain or oppose the action. This process provides for direction of the Church by revelation, while protecting the AGENCY of the members to verify in their own minds whether decisions have been proper and made according to the will of God.

The principle of common consent has functioned in the Church since its inception, though the actual practices incorporating this principle have evolved significantly. The revelation on LDS Church government, received when it was organized in April 1830, states: "No person is to be ordained to any office in this church, where there is a regularly organized branch of the same, without the vote of that church" (D&C 20:65). This instruction was reemphasized three months later: "All things shall be done by common consent in the church" (D&C 26:2). LDS practices may have been influenced in these earliest years by the Book of Mormon model of theocratic government that conducted its "business by the voice of the people" (Mosiah 29:25–26), and by biblical example (e.g., Ex. 24:3; Num. 27:19).

Evidence from accounts of some early meetings and conferences indicates that many of the New England leaders of the Church felt that the membership should be directly involved in decision-making meetings, including making motions on policy issues, following standard parliamentary procedure for public meetings, and voting to finalize decisions. Individual members sometimes exercised the prerogative to call a meeting, and once it was in session, anyone had the right to address the group. The conduct of their meetings followed the congregational model that was familiar to them. However, before long early Latter-day Saints began to realize that having a prophet as their leader was a reality that must be recognized in decision making, and that they could not follow the traditional congregational model without denying the authority and revelations that God had bestowed on Joseph SMITH, these being the essential features of the Restoration that brought them together in the Church.

An incident in September 1830, wherein Hiram Page claimed to have received revelations for the direction of the Church, brought the issue

Church members gathered in the Salt Lake Tabernacle raise their right hands to signify their support of a proposition to sustain Church leaders (1987).

into focus. The confusion of Oliver Cowdery and other Church members that was caused by Page's claim to be a second revelator provided the occasion for a revelation through Joseph Smith clarifying the distinctive role of Joseph as the prophet. This revelation also indicated that "all things must be done in order, and by common consent in the church" (D&C 28:13). As the authority of Joseph Smith and his successors in the office of President of the Church was clarified over the following years by subsequent revelations (D&C 107:65–67, 91–92), the principle that the sustaining voice of the members of the Church should be sought was also repeatedly reaffirmed (D&C 38:34; 42:11; 102:9; 124:144). As priesthood councils and priesthood quorums were introduced into the Church organization, general discussion of policy issues and decision making became more their responsibility in council meetings, and less an agenda item for conferences, which in turn focused more on preaching the gospel.

Today the Church continues to operate by divine revelation and common consent. CALLINGS to positions of Church service at all levels of the organization and ordination to the priesthood are made by the inspiration of authorized leaders and are then brought before the appropriate body of members to be sustained or opposed. Members do not nominate persons to office, but are asked to give their sustaining vote to decisions of presiding councils by raising their right hand, and anyone may give an opposing vote in the same way. This procedure is also followed in accepting important revelations and scriptural additions.

In a much less visible but equally important practice, decision makers at all levels present policy decisions and callings to priesthood councils for their comment and approval. At the local level a BISHOP will ordinarily discuss decisions with his counselors in the bishopric before presenting a matter to the ward membership for a sustaining vote. On many policy and program decisions the bishopric will consult with the ward council and work for consensus in that group before taking action. Following the same pattern, the stake president consults with his counselors in the stake presidency and then with the high council. The First Presidency consults in this same way on matters of general Church policy and action in regular meetings with the Quorum of the Twelve Apostles.

Unanimity is the ideal for all these decision processes because of the importance of UNITY in the Church: "If ye are not one ye are not mine" (D&C 38:27). The three presiding quorums over the whole Church are of equal authority within their own spheres (D&C 107:22–26), but their decisions are of "the same power or validity" only when made "by the unanimous voice" of the quorum (D&C 107:27). Many important decisions take shape over what seem like long periods because achieving unanimity is highly valued by the quorums.

Because of the emphasis on divine and prophetic leadership and because of well-established norms and values in decision-making procedures, public dissent on a proposed calling or policy is unusual. There are, however, mechanisms for accommodating dissent. Normally, if one or more members find the proposed action objectionable, the dissenting member or members are asked to meet with the presiding officer privately to make known the reason for the question or objection. After considering the objections, presiding officers are free to pursue whatever decision they believe to be right.

BIBLIOGRAPHY

Cannon, Donald Q., and Lyndon W. Cook, eds. *Far West Record: Minutes of The Church of Jesus Christ of Latter-day Saints, 1830–1844.* Salt Lake City, 1983.

Quinn, D. Michael. "The Evolution of the Presiding Quorums of the LDS Church." *Journal of Mormon History* 1 (1974):21–38.

Widtsoe, John A. *Evidences and Reconciliations*, pp. 269–75. Salt Lake City, 1960.

Zuckerman, Michael. *Peaceable Kingdoms.* New York, 1970.

ROBERT E. QUINN

COMMUNION

Communion refers to partaking of the Lord's Supper. The more common term among members of The Church of Jesus Christ of Latter-day Saints is SACRAMENT (D&C 59:9). *Eucharistia* is the Greek term that meant "thanksgiving" among early Christians.

Partaking of the sacrament is the central act of worship and COVENANT renewal and resembles the simple commemorative meal described in the New Testament (cf. Matt. 26:26–28; Mark 14:22–24; Luke 22:19–20; Acts 2:42, 46). Postbiblical doctrines of transubstantiation (real presence) and of a "mere sign" are absent from the LDS teachings. All members of the Church, including unbaptized children, are encouraged to partake of the bread and water as emblems in remembrance of the body and blood of Jesus Christ (see D&C 27). The communion sought is a communion of spirit as envisioned in the SACRAMENT PRAYERS (Moro. 4–5; 3 Ne. 18; D&C 20:77, 79).

[*See also* Sacraments.]

PAUL B. PIXTON

COMMUNITY

For Latter-day Saints, community is an essential and eternal part of life in this world and in the world to come. From the time the Church was established (1830), its teachings have placed emphasis on principles of unity, cooperation, mutual assistance, and beautification of one's surroundings. The community of believers envisioned by the Prophet Joseph SMITH continues today, based essentially on the principles he established. Changes, however, occurred as the Church moved to the Intermountain West, where Mormon towns and cities rose, and later as the Church spread to many parts of the world. As the Church has grown, the community embodied in the WARD has become a special focus of spiritual and social life among Church members, however small or isolated the congregation. Wherever Latter-day Saints find themselves, they form a community of believers based on human relationships that are expected to endure forever.

TEACHINGS OF JOSEPH SMITH AND BRIGHAM YOUNG. The advantages of village life described by Joseph Smith are an extension of life in a New England town. The Smiths brought to the frontier their New England background, emphasizing the importance of the community in providing education, mutual assistance, and political and economic organization. Joseph Smith's ideas about the importance of community life were an application of a revelation received in February 1831 on the law of CONSECRATION and STEWARDSHIP (D&C 42). This revelation encouraged the members of the Church to band together and live a communitarian life in which the wealthy would voluntarily share their surplus with the poor. These ideas about community were partially implemented in Kirtland, Ohio, in 1831. Participants soon moved to Jackson County, Missouri, to be involved with Joseph Smith's City of Zion plan, through which he envisioned many social, educational, intellectual, economic, and professional advantages to the Saints from living together in communities, each containing 15,000 to 20,000 people, rather than being scattered on farms, as was the custom on the frontier at that time (*CHC* 1:311–12; *see also* CITY PLANNING).

However, persecution drove the Saints from Missouri in 1838–1839, and some 12,000 of them fled to the NAUVOO area in Illinois. Based on a modified plan of the City of Zion, Nauvoo became a general model for community development later used by the Latter-day Saints in settling the Intermountain West.

An essential element of the organization of the communities established by the Latter-day Saints between 1830 and 1846 was the division of the larger communities into wards and STAKES, each with its own leaders. The BISHOP of each ward was a major figure in this organization. Nauvoo was eventually divided into a number of wards, each representing a geographic area of the city and the countryside beyond it. The bishop, with his counselors, was involved in supervising both the temporal and the spiritual affairs of the families within his ward's boundaries.

The guidelines left by Joseph Smith and fifteen years of experience in community building in Ohio, Missouri, and Illinois provided the basis for the principles that President Brigham YOUNG followed during the migration to Utah and the establishment and development of the LDS settlements of the Intermountain West.

The first principle was based on Joseph Smith's belief that the Latter-day Saints should live in a village and commute to rural farming areas around the community.

Second, property rights of residents of LDS communities were to be held under the principle of stewardship, which suggested that the interest of the group was more important than that of the individual. This principle was later implemented by Brigham Young, who tried for thirty years to incorporate these communitarian teachings into the settlement of the Intermountain West.

Third, the duty of the Saints was to care for, and beautify, the earth (Nibley, pp. 3–29). The belief that the earth could be improved through the efforts of an industrious and dedicated community of Saints was of particular importance as the Church migrated to the arid Great Basin.

The fourth principle advocated frugality and the economic independence of the Saints.

The fifth principle emphasized the importance of unity and cooperation among Church members. Community cooperation allowed them to establish hundreds of settlements in the arid West, based on principles of faith, love, charity, kindness, service, and sharing one another's burdens.

SETTLEMENT OF THE INTERMOUNTAIN WEST. The communitarian principles established and developed during the formative years of the Church were institutionalized in the settlement of the Great Basin. One of the distinguishing characteristics of the Intermountain West is the presence of LDS communities based on these principles. Historically, these settlements ranged through southern Idaho, southwestern Wyoming, Utah, Nevada, California, Arizona, northwestern New Mexico, and southern Colorado. The role of religion was unique in their establishment.

The ward became the main base for organizing cooperation, economic development, spiritual and temporal welfare, and even the administration of justice in the new settlements. Salt Lake City, for example, was divided geographically into wards, with the bishop of each responsible for the well-being of the members within his jurisdiction. In each ward unit, believers unified their efforts in such prosaic activities as building a fence to protect the ward's newly sown crops, digging irrigation ditches to provide water for the land within the ward's boundary, caring for widows or the families of men who were absent on missions for the Church, assisting with births, burying the dead, and being involved in every other aspect of life within the ward. Disputes over water or land also were handled by the priesthood within the ward boundaries.

The importance of concerted efforts in LDS communities is still obvious to any observer of these small western towns. Many have only one ward. Thus, the Meadow Utah Ward is also the town of Meadow, Utah. The activities of the ward

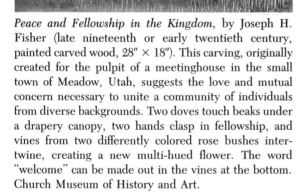

Peace and Fellowship in the Kingdom, by Joseph H. Fisher (late nineteenth or early twentieth century, painted carved wood, 28″ × 18″). This carving, originally created for the pulpit of a meetinghouse in the small town of Meadow, Utah, suggests the love and mutual concern necessary to unite a community of individuals from diverse backgrounds. Two doves touch beaks under a drapery canopy, two hands clasp in fellowship, and vines from two differently colored rose bushes intertwine, creating a new multi-hued flower. The word "welcome" can be made out in the vines at the bottom. Church Museum of History and Art.

are the focus of the social, political, and economic life of the community, involving even the few non-Mormons who reside there. In larger cities and in places where there are fewer Latter-day Saints, the ward remains the focus of activity for believers.

THE TWENTIETH CENTURY. The modern LDS community operates in basically the same manner as the earliest communities founded under the direction of Joseph Smith. The fundamental principles of cooperation, equality, beautifying the earth, frugality and independence, unity and cooperation, and stewardship of material possessions

are modified only in emphasis, not in principle. The continued reliance on an unpaid leadership allows the majority of ward members to be involved in providing services for the local congregation. From the bishop to the home teachers and visiting teachers who regularly visit each LDS home, all members are invited to become actively involved with the well-being of the entire community. The ward provides not only worship services but friends, economic assistance, and a support group that can be relied upon to provide the assistance any family might need, particularly in a society in which extended family members may not be nearby to provide such assistance. In this way, for many the ward becomes a surrogate family, and the common practice of addressing fellow Saints as "Brother" and "Sister" takes on enhanced and spiritually literal meaning. One belongs in the community of Saints regardless of one's other affiliations or lack of them; one is welcome in the ward however outcast one may feel elsewhere.

The effectiveness of the individual ward varies from place to place as a function of the ability and commitment of the leaders and members. The extent of unity among ward members and their commitment to the principles of mutual assistance and concern for one another also affect the effectiveness of the individual ward; yet, in general, the wards function as an instant community for the Latter-day Saint wherever he or she may move.

Membership in the LDS community is not restricted to those who have been longtime members of the Church. The Church is actively involved in proselytizing, with nearly 50,000 missionaries throughout the world who introduce prospective members to the ward or branch community, where they are encouraged to attend and become involved. The Church organizations are the structures used to fellowship them into the community.

The ward community strives to operate on what Joseph Smith said was the basis of governance in the Church: teach the members correct principles and let them govern themselves (*JD* 10:57–58). While the principle of equality of resources is not now practiced as it was in the 1830s or 1870s, members of the Church still dedicate their time and talents to the welfare of the community as a whole and are encouraged to tithe and to contribute to the assistance of the poor.

LIFE IN THE MORMON COMMUNITY. The importance of the Church in the lives of its members cannot be overstated (*see* MEMBERSHIP). Not only are its principles and practices a part of everyday life in such matters as dress, food, personal habits, and financial and time management, but the involvement of the entire ward in helping one another also creates a strong bond among ward members. The Church emphasizes the integrity of the family and teaches that a fundamental purpose of the Church is to strengthen the family. In addition to formal and informal family religious observances, Church meetings consist (as of 1990) of a three-hour block of time on Sundays, the focus of which is an hour-long general meeting in which members of the congregation deliver talks on gospel principles and partake of the SACRAMENT of the Lord's Supper; following the SACRAMENT MEETING, sessions for SUNDAY SCHOOL, PRIESTHOOD, RELIEF SOCIETY, YOUNG WOMEN, and PRIMARY are held. In earlier decades various auxiliary meetings, youth activities, and ward events were held during the week, and the meetinghouse was a bustling center of ward and stake activities and classes nearly every day.

Members also have contact with one another through the HOME TEACHING and VISITING TEACHING programs, through assisting one another as needs arise, and through the other meetings and activities associated with the various Church AUXILIARY ORGANIZATIONS. Members of wards and stakes may participate in sports activities. The ward sponsors periodic socials, Scouting activities, and cultural events that involve the members of the community, both LDS and others. The cooperation of members of the ward in helping widows, the poor, the ill, the aged, and others with special needs provides additional opportunities for interaction. In combination, the activities and opportunities for service among members of the ward strengthen the ties of the LDS community and enhance their commitment to "love one another," as Christ commanded (John 13:34–35).

ETERNAL PERSPECTIVES. The attitudes of Latter-day Saints regarding community are influenced by the belief that human relationships are eternal. People are by nature social beings whose lives and feelings are eternally intertwined with those of others. In premortal life, all human beings were born as spirit children in the family of God and therefore became members of an eternal and divine society. In the present life, people can become members of the Church by entering into the new and everlasting covenant of baptism, which binds people together as members of the kingdom of God. The Latter-day Saint view of the kingdoms of glory yet to come anticipates immortal beings living together forever. In other words, heaven includes life with other people and with God. In the highest degree of the celestial glory, a fulness of joy is found in ETERNAL MARRIAGE and familial relationships. Indeed, the nature of GODHOOD itself and the composition of the GODHEAD as three personages eternally united in a common cause demonstrate the divine prototype for personal relationships.

Latter-day Saints have faith that all people will come forth at the day of judgment and continue at various levels thereafter. This expectation gives a permanent and sensitive dimension to friendships, companionships, and virtually all contacts with other people in local and worldwide communities, both religious and civic. The ideal of human existence looks toward the creation of a people of ZION modeled after the city of Enoch and the establishment of a perfected community, a NEW JERUSALEM, under the personal governance of Jesus Christ.

[See also Brotherhood; Sisterhood; Society; Unity.]

BIBLIOGRAPHY

Alder, Douglas D. "The Mormon Ward: Congregation or Community?" *Journal of Mormon History* 5 (1978):61–78.

Arrington, Leonard J. *Great Basin Kingdom.* Cambridge, Mass., 1958.

———. *Brigham Young: American Moses.* New York, 1985.

Arrington, Leonard J., et al. *Building the City of God.* Salt Lake City, 1976.

Embry, Jessie L., and Howard A. Christy, eds. *Community Development in the American West: Past and Present, Nineteenth- and Twentieth-Century Frontiers.* Provo, Utah, 1985.

Hine, Robert V. *Community on the American Frontier.* Norman, Okla., 1980.

Hunter, Milton R. *Brigham Young the Colonizer.* Salt Lake City, 1940.

Jackson, Richard H., ed. *The Mormon Role in the Settlement of the West.* Provo, Utah, 1978.

Nibley, Hugh. "Brigham Young on the Environment." In *To the Glory of God,* ed. T. Madsen and C. Tate, pp. 3–29. Salt Lake City, 1972.

O'Dea, Thomas F. *The Mormons.* Chicago, 1957.

Peterson, Charles S. "A Mormon Town: One Man's West." *Journal of Mormon History* 3 (1976):3–12.

Poll, Richard D., et al., eds. *Utah's History,* rev. ed., pp. 133–52, 275–335. Logan, Utah, 1989.

RICHARD H. JACKSON

COMPASSIONATE SERVICE

The term "compassionate service" is used in the Church to refer to love-inspired assistance willingly given to meet physical, spiritual, and emotional needs. It requires a sensitivity that perceives human distress beyond spoken words (Luke 10:30–37; cf. 8:43–48), an eye that recognizes the good in people (Mosiah 4:16–18), and an understanding heart attuned to the HOLY SPIRIT to discern what is appropriate to say and do (3 Ne. 17:5–8; John 19:25–27). A call to Christlike service undergirded the Prophet Joseph SMITH's formal charge to the Female RELIEF SOCIETY organized in 1842. Aware of the dire needs of the Saints, he said that "the object of the society [is to search] after objects of charity and [administer] to their wants" (Minutes of the Female Relief Society of Nauvoo, p. 7). A Necessity Committee of sixteen sisters was appointed "to search out the poor and suffering, to call upon the rich for aid, and thus, as far as possible, relieve the wants of all" (*History of Relief Society*, p. 68). Since that time, not only Relief Society members but also other Church members have been involved in formal and informal acts of compassionate service.

Present-day Relief Society visiting teachers continue to carry out Joseph Smith's commission with regular visits to each LDS family, discerning needs and providing caring support. Ezra Taft BENSON stated, "We urge you, particularly priesthood brethren and Relief Society sisters, to be sensitive to the needs of the poor, the sick, and the needy . . . [and] see that the widows and fatherless are assisted" (p. 7). Through appropriate channels of the PRIESTHOOD and Relief Society, assistance is to be given to the poor, sick, bereaved, homeless, and members with special personal problems and burdens (Mosiah 18:8–9; D&C 52:40).

When compassionate service is clothed in the true spirit of charity—which the Book of Mormon defines as the pure love of Christ—it becomes an all-encompassing and rewarding experience for the giver as well as the receiver (1 Cor. 13:4–8; Moro. 7:6–8, 45–47).

[*See also* Visiting Teaching.]

BIBLIOGRAPHY

A Centenary of Relief Society, 1842–1942. Salt Lake City, 1942.

Benson, Ezra Taft. "Council to the Saints." *Ensign* 14 (May 1984):6–8.

History of Relief Society, 1842–1966. Salt Lake City, 1966.

Minutes of the Female Relief Society of Nauvoo, March 17, 1842, p. 7.

HULDA PARKER YOUNG

Relief Society sisters and their families provide compassionate watchcare for each other, make themselves aware of one another's needs, and give loving service to individuals and families (c. 1985).

COMPREHENSIVE HISTORY OF THE CHURCH

Intended as a centennial history of the LDS Church (1830–1930), Elder B. H. Roberts's six-volume *Comprehensive History of the Church* stands as a high point in the publication of Church history to that time. Most earlier works were either attacks upon or defenses of the Church. Although Roberts's study was a kind of defense, he set a more even tone, a degree of uncommon objectivity.

Like several historians preceding him (Bancroft, Whitney, Tullidge), Roberts set out to produce a multivolume work. Originally a periodical series prepared for the *Americana* magazine, Roberts's articles appeared in forty-two-page installments between July 1909 and July 1915 (*CHC* 1:v–vi). As the centennial year of 1930 approached, Elder George Albert Smith suggested that Roberts bring his work up to date and that the Church publish it for the centennial.

Published in handsome bindings with numerous illustrations, the work was impressive. But to the reader of today its importance lies beyond its format. Roberts was pointing the way to a new approach; he wanted Church history to avoid apology and undiscriminating defense of the faith. For example, he was skeptical of including any myths parading as history: "I find my own heart strengthened in the truth by getting rid of the untruth, the spectacular, the bizarre, as soon as I learn that it is based on worthless testimony" (Madsen, p. 363). He treated the difficulties of the Saints in Missouri objectively, assigning some elements of blame to both sides.

Roberts was willing to deal with sensitive topics. His analysis of the MOUNTAIN MEADOWS MASSACRE was fairly exacting. He was also willing to press his editors to get what he felt was fairness; he insisted on including Joseph Smith's KING FOLLETT DISCOURSE despite urgings to the contrary by some members. In some ways Roberts's *Comprehensive History* was an act of courage; certainly it was his magnum opus.

Though not trained as a historian, Roberts was well known as an orator and as a theologian. He read widely and was a vibrant politician, a noted missionary, and a popular Church leader. His theological writings continue to attract attention. All of this energy, even charisma, flows into his writing, producing rhapsodic prose that sometimes overshoots the mark. He wrote in the Romantic style, accepting Prescott and Parkman as his models.

The *Comprehensive History* is the high-water mark of studies produced before academic scholars undertook the writing of Church history after 1950. Roberts shows a faithfulness to documentary sources and rules of evidence. The six-volume set is a worthy monument to the Church's first century and still attracts serious attention.

BIBLIOGRAPHY

Bitton, Davis. "B. H. Roberts as Historian." *Dialogue* 4 (Winter 1968):25–44.

———, and Leonard Arrington. *Mormons and Their Historians*, pp. 69–86. Salt Lake City, 1988.

Madsen, Truman G. *Defender of the Faith: The B.H. Roberts Story*, pp. 357–66. Salt Lake City, 1980.

DOUGLAS D. ALDER

COMPUTER SYSTEMS

For many years The Church of Jesus Christ of Latter-day Saints used mechanical punched-card systems for accounting and other administrative purposes. These were replaced by modern computers. In 1962 the Church's computer systems were expanded to help provide names for temple work. They also were applied to managing the large and rapidly expanding genealogical information base. Church computer resources now serve every level, from general Church administration to the individual member.

In Church TEMPLES, computer systems are used to record biographical information of individuals, living and dead, who have received temple ORDINANCES. Family history computer systems maintain growing catalogs of worldwide genealogical records, a lineage-linked ANCESTRAL FILE, and an index of completed ordinances and other lists to help interested persons pursue family history work.

Computers also aid in the administration of various Church programs, including the international MISSIONARY program, where computers are used to track all missionaries and route individual requests for missionary visits. FINANCIAL CONTRIBUTIONS are recorded on computers by clerks at the WARD level, making possible regular reports to contributors and to the Church. All central budgeting and financial transactions are managed by computer. The Church maintains detailed membership records which are created on computers in the wards and are regularly updated and forwarded to central computers at Church headquarters or region/area offices (*see* RECORD KEEPING).

The Church uses computers to prepare, print, and distribute a wide range of materials through its DISTRIBUTION CENTERS in various parts of the world. SCRIPTURES, lesson manuals, handbooks, forms, and Church MAGAZINES are prepared with the use of computers. These materials are printed in as many as eighty-one languages, and computers are used extensively in the translation process.

PUBLIC COMMUNICATIONS uses computers to monitor public response to Church media. Computer systems also manage information in areas such as Church welfare, historical records, physical facilities, magazine subscriptions, and purchasing. The SEMINARIES and INSTITUTES track potential and enrolled students throughout the world by computer.

Large numbers of Latter-day Saints use personal computers in their homes to facilitate religious activities. Many use disk versions of the scriptures to enhance individual scripture research and study. Personal genealogical research has moved to a personal computer format that will allow exchanges of information with the large genealogical data bases in Salt Lake City.

DARWIN A. JOHN

CONDESCENSION OF GOD

The Book of Mormon prophet Nephi₁ (c. 600 B.C.) was asked by an angel, "Knowest thou the condescension of God?" (1 Ne. 11:16). Nephi was then shown in a vision a virgin who was to become "the mother of the Son of God, after the manner of the flesh" (verse 18). He next beheld the virgin with a child whom the angel identified as "the Lamb of God, yea, even the Son of the Eternal Father" (11:21). Then Nephi understood that the condescension of God is the ultimate manifestation of God's love through Jesus Christ (11:20–22). Such condescension denotes, first, the love of GOD THE FATHER, who deigned to sire a son, born of a mortal woman, and then allow this Son to suffer temptations and pain (Mosiah 3:5–7), "be judged of the world," and be "slain for the sins of the world" (1 Ne. 11:32–33). Second, it signifies the love and willingness of God the Son (Jesus Christ) to die for mankind.

The word "condescension" implies "voluntary descent," "submission," and "performing acts which strict justice does not require." This definition is particularly applicable to Jesus in the portrayal of him by prophets who lived before his birth and who affirmed: "God himself shall come down" to make an atonement (Mosiah 15:1); "the God of Abraham, and of Isaac, and the God of Jacob, yieldeth himself . . . into the hands of wicked men" (1 Ne. 19:10); "the great Creator . . . suffereth himself to become subject unto man in the flesh" (2 Ne. 9:5); and "he offereth himself a sacrifice for sin" (2 Ne. 2:7). "The Lord Omnipotent," said King Benjamin, "shall come down from heaven among the children of men, and shall dwell in a tabernacle of clay" (Mosiah 3:5).

In fulfillment of these prophecies, Jesus descended from the realms of glory for the purposes of experiencing mortal infirmities that he might have mercy and compassion according to the flesh and of taking upon himself the sins, transgressions, pains, and sicknesses of men in order to satisfy the demands of justice and gain victory over death, thereby redeeming his people (Mosiah 15:8–9; Alma 7:11–13). Christ's selfless sacrifice merits profound gratitude and endearing love from all who are recipients of his supernal offering.

BIBLIOGRAPHY

Bruce R. McConkie. "Behold the Condescension of God." *New Era* 14 (Dec. 1984):34–39.

BYRON R. MERRILL

CONFERENCE REPORTS

Since 1899, the Church has published official reports of its annual (April) and semiannual (October) General Conferences, commonly called *Conference Reports*. These reports are distributed in booklet form only to Church leaders (bishoprics and higher), Church employees, and libraries, but because other members of the Church wanted to study the conference addresses, the IMPROVEMENT ERA began in 1942 to devote two issues a year to conference reports. The *Ensign* has followed that pattern since replacing the *Era* in 1971. Those issues have made reports of conference addresses available to the world by subscription or single issue bookstore or newsstand purchase. The talks as printed in the Conference Report volumes (see below) and in the Church magazines have mostly been identical. Those publications are significant resources for the study of the theology, progress, and development of the Church.

When the Church first began holding conferences, many attending the meetings recorded in their private journals what was said and done. These personal records now constitute the primary sources available on the various conference addresses in the early years because no official Church publication printed much more than a list of conference events. It appears that the first full report of any Church conference address was published in the *Deseret News* in 1850, even though several partial reports were published in *Times and Seasons* from November 1839 to February 1846, in Nauvoo. The *Deseret News* was able to print word-for-word transcriptions because a young reporter, George D. Watt, had learned shorthand and transcribed the talks for publication. Watt and others thereafter transcribed a great many conference addresses and other talks for publication in the *Deseret News* and also in the *Journal of Discourses* (Liverpool and London, 1854–1886).

The conference report for the Church's fiftieth jubilee year (1880) was the first to be published as a separate booklet (110 pages) exclusively of general conference addresses. The next volume in that series contained the talks given at the October 1897 Semiannual General Conference (78 pages). Since 1899, the Church has published a Conference Report volume for each general conference.

CHARLES D. TATE, JR.

CONFERENCES

[*This entry is composed of three articles:*

Conferences
General Conference
Stake Conference

The first article explains the doctrinal concepts of holding conferences and the various types of conferences held by members of the Church. The second article focuses on the history of holding general conferences. The third article gives the background of holding stake conferences and their usual format.]

CONFERENCES

Latter-day Saints are counseled, as were the New Testament saints, to "meet together oft." Conferences are among the most frequent types of meeting. Because The Church of Jesus Christ of Latter-day Saints is administered by a constantly changing core of lay leaders, teachers, and officers, there is perpetual need for instruction, inspiration, and renewal. The scriptures state: "And now, behold, I give unto you a commandment, that when ye are assembled together ye shall instruct and edify each other, that ye may know how to act and direct my church, how to act upon the points of my law and commandments, which I have given" (D&C 43:8). The word "edify" means to enlighten, lift, or elevate spiritually. By "union of feeling," the Prophet Joseph SMITH taught the sisters of the RELIEF SOCIETY, "we obtain power with the heavens." Conferences contribute to building that union. In practice, Latter-day Saints often say to each other, "If you cannot come to receive, come to give." In conferences, as in other types of Church meetings, the "strong in the Spirit" may "take with him him that is weak" (D&C 84:106).

There are only general guidelines for conferences. For "it always has been given to the elders of my church from the beginning, and ever shall be, to conduct all meetings as they are directed and guided by the Holy Spirit" (D&C 46:2).

Specific objectives, scheduling, and activities of conferences vary according to the group being served and may vary from one conference to another of the same group. WARD conferences are held annually to bring the STAKE leaders, ward leaders, and ward members together in local congregations to "review the status of individuals and organizations and to plan for improvement" (*General Handbook of Instructions* 2-4). Stake conferences are held twice annually, and are administered by stake, regional, and GENERAL AUTHORITIES. YOUTH, young adult, and singles conferences are held annually; typically these conferences focus on inspirational experiences and social interchange. Women's conferences and Church women's FIRESIDES are also held each year.

The growth of the Church has led to area and regional conferences, which may involve thousands of participants in designated geographic areas. These conferences are planned, organized, conducted, and addressed by General Authorities.

Two general conferences are held each year, one in April (designated the "annual" conference) and the other in October (designated as a "semiannual" conference). These are the most far-reaching conferences of the Church and for many years have been held in the Salt Lake Tabernacle. They provide opportunities to share the common bonds of fellowship in an environment charged with spirituality and in a setting different from the local meeting places of the Church. Prayers, music, addresses by General Authorities and others, shared expressions of faith, meeting new acquaintances, and renewal of self and commitments combine to enrich the lives of all who attend or who experience the conferences on radio or television.

The Savior petitioned: "I pray not that thou shouldest take them out of the world, but that thou shouldest keep them from the evil" (John 17:15). Conferences of the Church serve an important purpose in aiding the members to be shielded from the evils of worldly influence and nurtured in discipleship.

BIBLIOGRAPHY

General Handbook of Instructions. Salt Lake City, 1989.

WILLIAM ROLFE KERR

GENERAL CONFERENCE

About two months after being organized on April 6, 1830, The Church of Jesus Christ of Latter-day Saints held its first general conference at the Peter Whitmer home in Fayette, Seneca County, New York. At that June 9 meeting about thirty members were in attendance and other people who were anxious to learn. This commenced a vital and enduring tradition (*see* CELEBRATIONS). Each April and October, members of the Church throughout the world assemble in Salt Lake City, Utah, for two days of meetings called general conference. For more than a century these meetings have been held in the 7,500-seat Salt Lake TABERNACLE located on TEMPLE SQUARE. Temple Square is virtually inseparable from the tradition of general conference and has been the site of nearly every one of them.

The April conferences of the Church are called annual conferences; those in October, semiannual conferences. Current practice includes four two-hour general sessions on Saturday and Sunday, with a special priesthood session Saturday night carried by satellite to thousands of priesthood bearers throughout the world. Prior to 1977, the conferences met for three days.

Through the years general conference has accommodated the needs of the Church in a variety of ways. In 1954 David O. MCKAY, President of the Church from 1951 to 1970, listed the following twentieth-century objectives:

(1) to inform the membership of general conditions of the Church—including whether it is progressing or retrogressing, and of its economic, ecclesiastic, and spiritual status; (2) to commend true merit; (3) to express gratitude for divine guidance; (4) to give instruction in principles, in doctrine, in the law of the gospel; (5) to proclaim the restoration, with divine authority to administer in all the ordinances of the gospel of Jesus Christ, and to declare, quoting the Apostle Peter, that there is none other name under heaven given among men than Jesus Christ

whereby we may be saved (Acts 4:12); (6) to admonish and inspire to continue in greater activity [*IE* (Dec. 1954), p. 872].

From a historical perspective, the conferences from 1830 to 1837 were called as needed by the Prophet Joseph SMITH, the first President of the Church. Those attending early conferences conducted the Church's business, heard announcements of new REVELATIONS, and exercised the principle of COMMON CONSENT in approving leaders and doctrine.

From 1838 to 1844 the concept of a regular general conference for the Church was set firmly in place and the precedents were established for the annual and semiannual conferences in April and October. Although the business of the Church was still transacted, emphasis was placed on expounding and teaching the doctrines of the Church. A significant body of doctrine was reviewed and revealed during this period.

One researcher has identified six major issues addressed in the conferences prior to 1845 that demonstrate flexibility and sensitivity to timely issues: (1) emergence and development of common consent; (2) initial experiment with a Zion concept and its temporary suspension; (3) teaching and expounding the doctrines of the Church, including new revelations; (4) institutionalizing of the conference system itself; (5) development of a temple-oriented worship, including COVENANTS and principles associated with the preparing of a people worthy to inherit Zion; and (6) exodus of the Church from organized society into the wilderness (Lowe, p. 398).

Clashes with tradition, tensions with neighbors of other faiths, and preparations for the westward movement all imposed adaptation on the general conferences of the Church just prior to the exodus to the Great Basin in 1847.

Conferences continued during the exodus and into the permanent settlement in Utah, although there was no general conference in October 1846, which occurred during the transition period after the Latter-day Saints had been driven from Nauvoo, Illinois, and before the first company of settlers arrived in the Salt Lake Valley in July 1847.

The conferences from 1848 to 1877 considered pressing needs such as emigration from the east and foreign countries, colonization, and missionary work. Assignments to colonize and calls to serve missions were frequently announced from the conference pulpit without prior notice. Leonard J. Arrington has characterized these conferences as "the cement which held together the Mormon Commonwealth. . . . It was through the instrumentality of the conference that church leaders were able to effect the central planning and direction of the manifold temporal and spiritual interests of their followers. It was in the conference that Latter-day Saints experienced most keenly the sense of belonging to a whole—a worshipping, building, expanding Kingdom" (p. 32).

The last two decades of the nineteenth century were troubled times for the Church because federal legislation against PLURAL MARRIAGE brought a financial and societal crisis. General conferences reflected those concerns. From 1885 to 1887, five conferences were held outside of Salt Lake City, and many of the GENERAL AUTHORITIES were in exile.

In the twentieth century because of technology and the Church's improving image, conference sessions began reaching beyond the Tabernacle and to peoples other than Latter-day Saints. In October 1924, KSL RADIO began broadcasting conferences. Coverage was extended in 1938 to other radio stations that wished to carry all or part of the sessions. In 1949 the conference was televised by KSL Television. Satellite transmission to interested television stations and cable systems in other parts of the United States was initiated in 1975, and in 1980 the conference sessions were first carried by satellite to Church centers outside of Utah. More than 2,600 Church satellite dishes in North America now receive general conference twice each year (see SATELLITE COMMUNICATION SYSTEM).

Conference sessions were first translated simultaneously into other languages in 1962, and by 1990 they were being translated into twenty-nine languages. Conferences can now be heard in multiple languages on Temple Square. As a result of the worldwide broadcasting and translation of conferences, the sessions are more structured and planned than they were in earlier years. Most of the speakers are presiding authorities of the Church, although on occasion other men and women are asked to participate.

General conference of The Church of Jesus Christ of Latter-day Saints continues today as a vital doctrinal and social institution. It touches the lives of hundreds of thousands of Latter-day Saints worldwide. The conference sermons are printed in the Church magazines and are recorded on video tapes.

[See also Celebrations.]

BIBLIOGRAPHY

Arrington, Leonard J. Great Basin Kingdom. Cambridge, Mass., 1958.

Godfrey, Kenneth W. "150 Years of General Conference." Ensign 11 (Feb. 1981):66.

Lowe, Jay R. "A Study of the General Conferences of the Church of Jesus Christ of Latter-day Saints, 1830–1901." Ph.D. diss., Brigham Young University, 1972.

McKay, David O. "Seek Ye First the Kingdom of God." IE (Dec. 1954):872–74.

M. DALLAS BURNETT

STAKE CONFERENCE

In the revelation on Church organization and government received by the Prophet Joseph Smith in April 1830, Church members were instructed to "meet in conference once in three months, or from time to time as said conferences shall direct or appoint; and said conferences are to do whatever church business is necessary to be done at the time" (D&C 20:61–62).

Once STAKES were organized, the Saints began meeting in stake conferences every three months. The practice of quarterly stake conferences continued from the mid-1800s until 1979, when the frequency was reduced to two per year. GENERAL AUTHORITIES of the Church presided at most stake conferences until the mid-1980s, when the growth in Church membership and the number of stakes made it impossible for an authority to attend each conference. In 1986, General Authorities were assigned to preside at one of the stake conferences, and the STAKE PRESIDENT was authorized to preside at the other. In 1990 General Authorities were assigned to visit each stake for a conference only once every other year.

Stake conferences bring together members and friends who reside within the geographical boundaries of a stake. At least four sessions are held during a two-day period: (1) the first meeting is with the stake presidency and the visiting authorities, if any, to review the activity and progress of the stake during the last six months; (2) a priesthood leadership meeting to train stake and WARD priesthood leaders in Church doctrine and principles; (3) a general assembly of all adults (eighteen years of age and over) where the presiding authority and invited stake members speak; and (4) a Sabbath general session for all stake members, including children and interested friends of the Church. The Sabbath general session features congregational hymns, specially arranged choir selections, stake business, and sermons from the presiding authority, stake leaders, and other invited speakers.

The major purposes of stake conference are: (1) sustaining general and stake officers; (2) releasing stake officers; and (3) approving ordinations to the MELCHIZEDEK PRIESTHOOD, and also enhancing the faith and testimony of the members through leadership training, music, sermons, and the fellowship of the Saints. The meetings are often considered a spiritual feast. The General Authority and stake leaders are well versed in the scriptures, are excellent teachers, and present strong witness to the divinity of Jesus Christ.

MERRILL J. BATEMAN

CONFESSION OF SINS

Confession of sins is a necessary beginning step in the process of repenting and gaining forgiveness. It is a test of true repentance: "By this ye may know if a man repenteth of his sins—behold, he will confess them and forsake them" (D&C 58:43).

The need for repentance has existed from the time of ADAM. The Lord instructed Adam: "Wherefore teach it unto your children, that all men, everywhere, must repent, or they can in nowise inherit the Kingdom of God, for no unclean thing can dwell there, or dwell in his presence" (Moses 6:57). The Bible states that "if we say that we have no sin, we deceive ourselves, and the truth is not in us" (1 Jn. 1:8). There are two categories of sin, those of commission and those of omission: "All unrighteousness is sin" (1 Jn. 5:17), and "To him that knoweth to do good, and doeth it not, to him it is sin" (James 4:17). Except for Jesus Christ, everyone who has lived past early childhood has sinned (1 Jn. 3:5; 2 Cor. 5:21).

At least three confessions may need to be made to help the sinner repent: To the Lord, to proper ecclesiastical officers, and to the injured party. Latter-day Saint doctrine holds that all must confess their sins to the Lord, from whom alone ultimate forgiveness can come. In addition, major

sins (such as adultery, fornication, robbery, embezzlement, fraud, false swearing, and comparable transgressions), which may have a bearing upon Church membership, must be confessed to ecclesiastical officers such as BISHOPS. Church officers are counseled to respond to confessions with confidentiality and understanding, and also to encourage members to seek the Lord's forgiveness, forsake transgression, and make restitution. Transgressors are taught to make proper reconciliation with and restitution to those they have injured. Effective confession requires a "broken heart and contrite spirit" (D&C 59:8) and a willingness to humble oneself and do all that is required for complete forgiveness.

Transgressions of lesser gravity that have offended others, such as marital or social differences, minor outbursts of anger, petty disagreements, and the like, are to be confessed to the injured party often resolving the matter without involving ecclesiastical authority. Public confession is not required unless the transgression has been against the public (D&C 42:88–93).

The Church has no set time or stated formula as to when confession takes place. Periodic interviews with ecclesiastical officers may be suitable occasions, or a special appointment can be made.

Confession helps lift the burden and leads toward peace, freedom, and happiness. After warning his hearers of excruciating pain and punishments that follow unrepented sins, the Lord said: "Confess your sins, lest you suffer these punishments" (D&C 19:20). Repentant persons find substantial psychological as well as spiritual strength in proper confession.

BIBLIOGRAPHY

Kimball, Spencer W. *The Miracle of Forgiveness*, pp. 177–89. Salt Lake City, 1989.

DONG SULL CHOI

CONFIDENTIAL RECORDS

Latter-day Saints have developed a long tradition of keeping detailed records about Church activities and their own lives (*see* RECORD KEEPING). As is true for the working files of most private institutions, the current records of the Church are not generally available to outside researchers. Undeterred public access to everyday work files would disrupt the organization's work flow and impinge on the privacy of individual Church members. The current membership records of the Church maintained by the Finance and Records Department are kept confidential, as are records of voluntary FINANCIAL CONTRIBUTIONS. The Missionary Department keeps the applications it receives from prospective missionaries confidential because they contain private information about the applicants' health and personal life. Similarly, the Personnel Department does not make employee files available.

Despite the general restriction of access to these current records, the Church allows exceptions in extraordinary cases that promise substantial benefits to mankind. For instance, Church officials have provided extensive membership data to cancer researchers and others who have established a legitimate need for such information (Lyon, pp. 129–33).

Most of the noncurrent records of the Church are stored in the Historical Department, one of the world's largest religious archival institutions. Besides housing institutional records, the department also accepts donations of personal historical materials, such as the diaries and papers of individual Church members.

The majority of the thousands of collections in the Historical Department are open and available to most members of the public. Like other major archival institutions, however, the Historical Department restricts access to some of its collections for several legal and ethical reasons. Some other materials are restricted by the terms of their donation. Some of these donor-imposed restrictions eventually expire, making the donated materials more accessible to the public.

The Historical Department restricts some materials to protect the privacy of persons mentioned in them. Experts on archival law have written that "privacy is by far the most pervasive consideration in restricting materials in archives" (Peterson and Peterson, p. 39). The Church's view of privacy embraces more than the legal principle that recognizes persons' privacy until death. "In addition," Dallin H. Oaks explained, "our belief in life after death causes us to extend this principle to respect the privacy of persons who have left mortality but live beyond the veil" (p. 65). Examples of materials restricted for privacy reasons include the records of Church disciplinary proceedings, confidential minutes of Church councils, and journals of

Church officials who record confidential information disclosed to them by Church members.

The Historical Department restricts other records because they are sacred. Examples of such records include transcripts of PATRIARCHAL BLESSINGS. Generally, researchers are given access only to their own blessing transcripts, those of their spouses, and their direct-line descendants and deceased ancestors.

BIBLIOGRAPHY

Clark, James R. *MFP* 2:315–20.

Lyon, Joseph L., et al. "Cancer Incidence in Mormons and Non-Mormons in Utah, 1966–1970." *New England Journal of Medicine* 294 (1976):129–33.

Oaks, Dallin H. "Recent Events Involving Church History and Forged Documents." *Ensign* 17 (Oct. 1987):63–69.

Peterson, Gary M., and Trudy Huskamp Peterson. *Archives & Manuscripts: Law.* Chicago, 1985.

RICHARD E. TURLEY, JR.

CONFIRMATION

Confirmation in The Church of Jesus Christ of Latter-day Saints is a sacred ORDINANCE essential for salvation. This ordinance follows baptism by immersion for the remission of sins and is efficacious only through faith in the Lord Jesus Christ and repentance. It is administered by the laying on of hands by men having AUTHORITY, one of whom performs the ordinance and blesses the candidate. By this process one becomes a member of the Church and is given the gift of the Holy Ghost (Acts 2:37–38; 19:1–7). Baptism and confirmation are administered to persons at least eight years of age, the age of ACCOUNTABILITY (D&C 68:25–27).

The scriptures attest to the administering of the ordinance of confirmation in New Testament times. When Peter and John went to Samaria and found certain disciples who had received John's baptism in water, they "laid their hands on them, and they received the Holy Ghost" (Acts 8:17; see also verses 14–22).

Confirmation may be performed only by those holding the MELCHIZEDEK PRIESTHOOD. The Book of Mormon records that Jesus "touched with his hand the disciples whom he had chosen, one by one, even until he had touched them all, and spake unto them as he touched them. [Thereby] he gave them power to give the Holy Ghost" (3 Ne. 18:36–37; Moro. 2:1–3). The Doctrine and Covenants specifies: "And whoso having faith you shall confirm in my church, by the laying on of the hands, and I will bestow the gift of the Holy Ghost upon them" (D&C 33:15).

The ordinance of confirmation is usually performed at a baptismal service or fast and testimony meeting. One or more bearers of the Melchizedek Priesthood lay their hands upon the head of the newly baptized person, and the one who is "voice," calling the person by name, says words to this effect: "In the name of Jesus Christ, and by the authority of the holy Melchizedek Priesthood, I confirm you a member of The Church of Jesus Christ of Latter-day Saints and say unto you, 'receive the Holy Ghost.'" Words of blessing follow as the Spirit of the Lord may dictate, invoking divine guidance, comfort, admonition, instruction, or promise. The initiates are often reminded that through this gift they will discern right from wrong and that the Spirit will be, as it were, a lamp to their feet.

The receiving of the gift of the Holy Ghost may or may not be apparent immediately, although the *right* to receive this gift is conferred at confirmation. The admonition to receive the Holy Ghost is interpreted to include living in a receptive way for the enlightenment of the Spirit. Joseph Smith taught, "No man can receive the Holy Ghost without receiving revelations. The Holy Ghost is a revelator" (*TPJS*, p. 328). One is admonished likewise to seek earnestly for spiritual gifts (1 Cor. 12:1–11, 31; D&C 46:9–26) and the "fruits of the Spirit," including love, joy, peace, and longsuffering (Gal. 5; Moro. 7:45–48).

The scriptures sometimes refer to the sanctifying influence of the Holy Ghost as the "baptism of fire" (Matt. 3:11; 3 Ne. 19:13; Morm. 7:10). Confirmation begins that process. It is seen as a lifetime quest formally renewed each Sabbath in the partaking of the SACRAMENT, whose prayers end with the plea that those who have taken upon themselves the name of Jesus Christ "may always have his Spirit to be with them" (Moro. 4:3).

Once individuals have been confirmed as members of the Church and have received the gift of the Holy Ghost, they may retain this gift by maintaining a state of worthiness with corrections as needed, through an ongoing process of repentance and discipleship.

A girl is confirmed a member of The Church of Jesus Christ of Latter-day Saints (Philippines, 1986). Confirmation is a priesthood ordinance performed after baptism, inviting the person to receive the Holy Ghost. Courtesy Floyd Holdman.

BIBLIOGRAPHY

Talmage, James E. *AF*, pp. 156–57. Salt Lake City, 1968.

RULON G. CRAVEN

CONSCIENTIOUS OBJECTION

While any member of the Church is free to object to military combat service because of conscience, simply holding membership in the Church in and of itself is not a justification. Church leaders have discouraged conscientious objection in every conflict of the twentieth century. Although it is opposed to war and recognizes that going to war is a very poor alternative means of resolving conflicts, the Church considers it the loyal duty of citizenship for members to answer the call of their various countries for military service.

At the same time, it recognizes the right of individual members to determine for themselves whether their deep, spiritual consciences will allow them to serve in combat or require them to request assignment to alternate service. The

Church will not support a member in that request until he or she has consulted with the appropriate bishop and stake president and has spiritual confirmation that the way decided upon by the member concerned is acceptable to the Lord.

BIBLIOGRAPHY

Boone, Joseph F. "The Roles of The Church of Jesus Christ of Latter-day Saints in Relation to the United States Military, 1900–1975." Ph.D. diss., Brigham Young University, 1975.

CHARLES D. TATE, JR.

CONSECRATION

[*The following two articles deal with the LDS concept of consecration.* Law of Consecration *offers an overview of the origin and extended practice of the principles of consecration among Latter-day Saints. The article* Consecration in Ohio and Missouri *specifically addresses both LDS efforts to live such principles and the resulting economic impact on LDS communities that flourished in these states between 1832 and 1846.*]

LAW OF CONSECRATION

The law of consecration was introduced through revelations given to the Prophet Joseph SMITH. As early as 1829, he was directed by the Lord to "seek to bring forth and establish the cause of Zion" (D&C 6:6; 11:6; 12:6; 14:6). Anciently, the ZION of ENOCH was made up of people who "were of one heart and one mind, and dwelt in righteousness; and there was no poor among them" (Moses 7:18). These features have characterized the Lord's people who have accepted and applied the fulness of the gospel in their lives, such as the people of the city of Enoch (Moses 7:17–18) and the Nephite golden era (4 Ne. 1:2–3, 15–17) and some of the early Christians (Acts 4:32–37). Latter-day Saints have also been given the law of consecration as an ideal and a challenge and promise for the future (D&C 42:32–39).

The level of dedication required to live the law of consecration has many ancient echoes. The Bible records acts of consecration expressly connected with instituting COVENANTS with God (e.g., Gen. 9:8–17; Num. 6). The willingness to sacrifice Isaac signified the complete dedication of Abraham to God's commands (Gen. 22:1–18). Exodus and Leviticus also disclose various sacrificial acts involving consecration to God, principally by AARON and his sons (cf. Ex. 40:12–16; Lev. 1–7). The New Testament records that early Christians were called upon to set their hearts first on the KINGDOM OF GOD and to have "all things in common" (Acts 2, 4, 5).

After the risen Jesus established his Church in the Western Hemisphere about A.D. 34, the Book of Mormon people followed the practice of consecration for nearly 200 years. "The people were all converted unto the Lord, upon all the face of the land, both Nephites and Lamanites, and there were no contentions and disputations among them, and every man did deal justly one with another. And they had all things common among them; therefore there were not rich and poor, bond and free, but they were all made free, and partakers of the heavenly gift" (4 Ne. 1:2–3).

On January 2, 1831, the Lord revealed to the Prophet Joseph SMITH in Fayette, New York, that anciently he had taken the Zion of Enoch to himself and then commanded him to go to Ohio to receive the law (D&C 38:4, 32; cf. Moses 7:21). When Joseph Smith arrived at Kirtland, Ohio, in February, he found the Saints organized in a communal society called "the family." He persuaded them to abandon this practice for "the more perfect law of the Lord." On February 9, while in the presence of twelve elders, he received the revelation that embraced "the law of the Church" (*HC* 1:146–48; D&C 42). This revelation presented the laws of Church government and of moral conduct for members and established the basic principles of consecration (D&C 42:32–39).

The key principles given in the revelations are consistent with those required for celestial living: all things belong to God, and his people are stewards (D&C 38:17; 104:11–14); individuals are to esteem others as themselves (D&C 38:24–27; 51:3, 9; 70:14; 78:6; 82:17); mankind must retain free AGENCY (D&C 104:17); men and women are made equal according to their wants, needs, and family situations (D&C 51:3); and there must be ACCOUNTABILITY (D&C 72:3; 104:13–18). Although the implementation of the law of consecration of property as revealed in the early 1830s was temporarily suspended (cf. *HC* 4:93), the principles themselves were not discontinued.

THE COVENANTS OF CONSECRATION TODAY. The Lord revealed several purposes for the law of consecration: to bring the Church to stand independent of all other institutions (D&C 78:14); to strengthen Zion, adorning her in beautiful garments, as a bride prepared and worthy of the bridegroom (D&C 33:17; 58:11; 65:3; 82:14, 18; etc.); and to prepare the Saints for a place in the CELESTIAL KINGDOM (D&C 78:7).

Commenting on this subject, President John TAYLOR stated that consecration is a celestial law and, when observed, its adherents become a celestial people (JD 17:177–81). Thus, men and women today can become like as those of Enoch's day, "of one heart and one mind, . . . with no poor among them" (Moses 7:18). Orson PRATT, an early apostle, observed that if the Lord's people aspire to the celestial kingdom, they must begin to learn the order of life that is there (JD 2:102–103).

IMPLEMENTATION OF THE LAW OF CONSECRATION. The law of consecration requires dedicating all of one's time, talents, and possessions to the Church and its purposes (D&C 82:19; 64:34; 88:67–68; 98:12–14). John A. Widtsoe, an apostle, noted that its operation was quite simple. Those who joined such an order were to place all their possessions in a common treasury—the rich their wealth, the poor their pittance. Then each member was to receive a sufficient portion—called an "inheritance"—from the common treasury to enable that person to continue in trade, business, or profession as desired. The farmer would receive land and implements; the tradesman, tools and materials; the merchant, necessary capital; the professional person, instruments, books, and the like. Members working for others would receive proportionate interests in the enterprises they served. No one would be without property. All would have an inheritance (Widtsoe, pp. 302–303).

A person's inheritance was to consist of personal property, to be operated permanently and freely for the benefit of the person and the family. Should the person withdraw from the order, the inheritance could be taken with him, but the person would have no claim upon surplus donations or possessions initially placed in the common treasury (D&C 51:3–6). At the end of a year or set period, the member who had earned more than needed for his family would voluntarily place the surplus in the common treasury. Substantial profits were to be administered by the group rather than by one individual. Men and women who, despite diligence, had a loss from their operations would have the loss made up by the general treasury for another start, or they might—with consent—be

placed in some activity better suited to their gifts. In short, the general treasury was to establish every person in a preferred field and was to care for those unable to profit from their inheritance. The general treasury, holding members' surpluses, would also finance public works and make possible all community enterprises decided upon by the group (D&C 104:60–77).

President J. Reuben Clark, Jr., counselor in the First Presidency, explained that the law of consecration as practiced was not a fully communal life. There was no common table. Each family lived as a unit. Property that was not turned back to the donor by mutual consent of the donor and the BISHOP became the property of the Church and was placed in the storehouse. Every member of the Church had equal access to the contents of the storehouse according to personal needs, circumstances, and needs of the family (Clark, p. 3).

EFFORTS TO LIVE THE LAW OF CONSECRATION. An early effort to live the law of consecration was first tried at Thompson, Ohio, in May 1831 by the members from the Colesville Branch who had moved there from New York. Complications arose when one of the participants withdrew his land and some of the members left for Missouri to help establish the center place of Zion before the practice could take root (Stewart, p. 125). Continued efforts to make necessary refinements in practicing the law in Ohio ultimately failed. A similar attempt was also made at this same time to institute the law of consecration and stewardship in Missouri, but intolerance and bickering among some of the Saints and the lack of any surplus to consecrate rendered the attempt unsuccessful (see CONSECRATION IN OHIO AND MISSOURI below).

After these early failures, the Lord adapted the requirements of the law of consecration to the capacities of the Saints and revealed the law of TITHING as a practice to follow (HC 3:44; D&C 119). Although tithing does not require the giving of everything to the Lord, it teaches the fundamental elements upon which the character of a Zion people rests: self-control, generosity, love of fellow humans, love for God, and a desire to build the kingdom of God. Giving tithing for over a century, as the Saints proved their ability to live this commandment, prepared them to accept also the welfare program, introduced in 1936 by Church President Heber J. GRANT (CR [Oct. 1936]:3). Five years later, President J. Reuben Clark, Jr., observed that the practices of tithing, FAST OFFERINGS, and Church welfare had brought Church members closer to the original principles of the UNITED ORDER and law of consecration (*CR* [Oct. 1942]:57).

Concerning the future, Zion can be redeemed only by obedience to the law of consecration. At the proper time, the Lord's leaders will implement the program. While it is not clear what procedures will be revealed, Latter-day Saints anticipate that the principles of stewardship, equality, agency, and accountability will eventually be subscribed to by all participants and that the goals originally envisioned will be reached (D&C 78:7, 14; 82:14).

BIBLIOGRAPHY

Clark, J. Reuben, Jr. "Testimony of Divine Origin of Welfare Plan." *Deseret News*, Church Section, Aug. 8, 1951, p. 3.

Cook, Lyndon W. *Joseph Smith and the Law of Consecration*. Provo, Utah, 1985.

Nelson, William O. "To Prepare a People." *Ensign* 9 (Jan. 1979):18–23.

Stewart, George, et al. *Priesthood and Church Welfare*. Salt Lake City, 1939.

Widtsoe, John A. *Evidences and Reconciliations*. Salt Lake City, 1943.

FRANK W. HIRSCHI

CONSECRATION IN OHIO AND MISSOURI

The principles of consecration were implemented in various forms in Ohio and Missouri in the 1830s to provide for the needs of the poor and of a financially struggling Church (*see* KIRTLAND, OHIO; KIRTLAND ECONOMY). Many of the Latter-day Saints migrating to Ohio and Missouri lacked the means to support themselves, and the Church had few resources to construct buildings such as the temple or to finance publications. The various implementations of the law of consecration helped to meet these practical needs as well as to teach participants to live a celestial law.

The law of consecration was never fully practiced in Ohio but was implemented in Missouri in several forms between 1831 and 1839. In its 1831 form, the law of consecration required all participants, or "stewards," to consecrate or convey their possessions to the Church storehouse. The bishop would then give back to each individual or family a "stewardship" of land, money, and other possessions according to just wants and needs. Surplus profits generated from these stewardships were contributed to the storehouse to assist the poor and

serve other general purposes. To administer the system, separate bishops and storehouses were established in the two Church centers of Kirtland and Missouri.

In 1833, the practice of consecration was modified to provide for private ownership of stewardships, and in 1838, the principle of tithing introduced another change. The law of tithing required the Saints to give "all their surplus property" to the bishop, and subsequently "one-tenth of all their interest [increase] annually" (D&C 119:1, 4).

Implementation of consecration was difficult for the early Latter-day Saints and occurred only intermittently. The impoverished Missouri Saints, were driven and persecuted by mobs, and repeatedly lost personal possessions, lands, and crops. Church property was often taken or destroyed (*see* MISSOURI CONFLICT). Under such circumstances, most members required more for their stewardships than they could contribute to the pool of resources. Others were reluctant to donate their surpluses, and some who left the Church pursued legal means to recover consecrated properties. In the face of such obstacles, the sincere efforts of some faithful Saints to implement the law are all the more remarkable.

The United Firm, more commonly known as the United Order, a corporate enterprise based on consecration principles, was a second and more limited implementation of consecration, which operated in Kirtland with a branch in Missouri from March 1832 to April 1834. About twelve men consecrated their possessions and received stewardships in this business venture. Surpluses were to go into the storehouse for printing the revelations and for meeting other Church needs. The firm dissolved when loan payments could not be made.

The Literary Firm, a third implementation of consecration principles, continued longer than the other two. Established in November 1831 to print the revelations and other publications for the Church, it operated in several forms until August 1837. Following the 1833 Missouri mob actions, printing operations were moved from Independence to Kirtland. Up to eight men were made stewards over the revelations and consecrated their efforts to manage publication. Although constantly beset by problems, the firm published the DOCTRINE AND COVENANTS (1st ed.), the BOOK OF MORMON (2nd ed.), and other Church books and periodicals.

BIBLIOGRAPHY

Arrington, Leonard J.; Feramorz Y. Fox; and Dean L. May. *Building the City of God: Community and Cooperation Among the Mormons.* Salt Lake City, 1976.

Cook, Lyndon W. *Joseph Smith and the Law of Consecration.* Salt Lake City, 1985.

KARL RICKS ANDERSON

CONSTITUTIONAL LAW

As a people, the Latter-day Saints are committed to sustaining constitutional government as the best instrument for maintaining peace, individual freedom, and community life in modern society. This commitment is reinforced by their scriptures, which affirm that constitutional law "supporting that principle of freedom in maintaining rights and privileges, belongs to all mankind, and is justifiable before [the Lord]" (D&C 98:5). The scripture cited further explains that not only has God made people free by giving them AGENCY, but "the law also maketh you free" (verse 8). Furthermore, any standard other than constitutional law "cometh of evil" (verse 10). This principle applies not only in the UNITED STATES OF AMERICA, but wherever Latter-day Saints might live throughout the world. However, Latter-day Saints everywhere believe also "in being subject to kings, presidents, rulers, and magistrates, in obeying, honoring, and sustaining the law" (A of F 12).

Latter-day Saints have both contributed to, and benefited from, laws and American constitutional law. The Constitution of the United States of America made the RESTORATION of the gospel possible because it limits governmental power, protects individual rights, and sets a moral tone tolerating controversial religious views and rights of expression and assembly. LDS belief in the divine origin of the Constitution contributes to respect for the document.

The majority of the main events associated with the restoration of the Church occurred in the United States. Its message was controversial and provocative, and without the protections of the United States Constitution, the Church likely would not have survived. President Wilford WOODRUFF taught that at that time the United States of America was the only place where the Lord could have established his Church and kingdom (*JD* 25:211). President David O. McKAY, in the dedicatory prayer for the Los Angeles Temple, expressed gratitude for the Constitution and for the fact that it made the establishment of the Church possible (*IE* 59 [Apr. 1956]:226). This idea is expressed frequently by Latter-day Saints and is more than patriotic rhetoric; a brief examination of the U.S. Constitution shows why.

The United States was especially hospitable to the restoration of the Church because its Constitution limits governments, both state and federal, thereby protecting individual rights. It limits governmental power in two ways: through two structural features commonly referred to as the separation of powers and federalism and through a series of express prohibitions.

The separation of powers refers to the division of governmental power on a horizontal plane among the three distinct branches of the federal government—legislative, executive, and judicial. Federalism divides governmental power on a vertical plane between the national government and the state governments. The separation of powers and federalism, by allocating governmental powers among several entities and by making each of these entities a competitor with the others, minimize the likelihood that government will trample individual rights.

The most famous of the express prohibitions against governmental action are contained in the first eight of the ten amendments to the Constitution that make up the Bill of Rights. By themselves, these provisions had been interpreted to apply only to the federal government, but the Fourteenth Amendment has now been held by the U.S. Supreme Court to make most of those Bill of Rights guarantees binding on state governments as well (*see* CIVIL RIGHTS). Because the Bill of Rights and the structural provisions of the Constitution protect individual rights against government intrusions, Latter-day Saints and other religious groups have been its distinct and identifiable beneficiaries.

Beyond its limitations on government, the Constitution sets a moral tone tolerating controversial religious views and rights of expression in general. This tone extends beyond its immediate impact on government. Without it, the public opposition to the Church, combined with the zeal of its adherents, might have brought about its demise. That Joseph SMITH was born soon after the adoption and ratification of the Constitution is no coincidence in the LDS view.

On November 28, 1843, the Church petitioned the United States government to help members obtain relief from their unconstitutional losses of property at the hands of mobs and the Missouri state militia, partly as a result of an executive order. This petition was signed by 3,419 people, including Joseph Smith, Hyrum Smith, Brigham Young, John Taylor, Orson Pratt, and Heber C. Kimball as Nauvoo city officials. The federal government took no action in what was then considered a matter outside federal jurisdiction.

Latter-day Saints have participated significantly in the development of American law dealing with constitutional protections of civil rights. The starting point for modern constitutional analysis of First Amendment freedoms—including not only the free exercise of religion but all First Amendment rights—is provided by REYNOLDS V. UNITED STATES (98 U.S. 145 [1879]), which involved the prosecution of a nineteenth-century Church leader for practicing polygamy. *Reynolds* was the first Supreme Court interpretation of the First Amendment. It draws a distinction between beliefs, which it holds are absolutely protected by the First Amendment, and conduct, which it says enjoys no protection.

That distinction between belief and conduct is still the cornerstone of First Amendment analysis. The first half of it (absolute protection for belief) is still good law, though the second half (no protection for conduct) is not. The present rule for religiously motivated conduct, which was not clearly developed until almost a century after the *Reynolds* decision was handed down, is that government actions adversely affecting religious behavior are prohibited by the First Amendment's free exercise clause unless government can show that its actions are based on a compelling state interest and that its regulation or other infringement is narrowly tailored to the achievement of that objective (*Wisconsin v. Yoder et al.*, 406 U.S. 205 [1972]). The test strongly favors individual rights over government interests and is therefore conducive to RELIGIOUS FREEDOM. It is also a test from which the Church has benefited.

As a group, Latter-day Saints in the United States are deeply patriotic. They sustained the Constitution even when, in times of severe persecution, some of its protections were denied them. Partly because of the Church's history and partly because of their unique understanding of the nation's origins, most Latter-day Saints in the United States accept the responsibility to study and understand their Constitution as being rooted not only in patriotism but in religion as well. The devotion of the Church and its leaders to the Constitution can be traced to early times. Doctrine and Covenants 134, "A Declaration of Belief Regarding Governments and Laws," adopted by unanimous vote at a general assembly of the Church held at Kirtland, Ohio, on August 17, 1835, is a vigorous statement on the importance of preserving individual rights, particularly those relating to religious and other expressive freedoms. As expressed by one Church President, Latter-day Saints "have a tremendous obligation to be good citizens, to uphold the Constitution of this land, to adhere to its basic concepts" (Benson, pp. 615–16; *see also* POLITICS: POLITICAL TEACHINGS).

Another aspect of the LDS understanding of the Constitution is the belief gained from scripture concerning its divine origins, which enhances Latter-day Saints' respect and even reverence for the document, particularly in the United States. The Lord revealed to Joseph Smith, "And for this purpose have I established the Constitution of this land, by the hands of wise men whom I raised up unto this very purpose" (D&C 101:80; cf. 3 Ne. 21:4). Some Church members espouse a view which goes beyond this scriptural language, esteeming the Constitution beyond criticism and as near scriptural. What the scripture in fact says is simple, informative, and understandable: this remarkably successful document did not emerge by chance or human wisdom alone. God had a hand in its creation—not in the same, direct, revelatory way that he creates scripture, but by assembling and inspiring, at the one crucial point in American history when it was sorely needed, probably the most talented collection of statesmen with which any nation has ever been blessed.

BIBLIOGRAPHY

Benson, Ezra Taft. *Teachings of Ezra Taft Benson.* Salt Lake City, 1988.

Lee, Rex E. *A Lawyer Looks at the Constitution.* Provo, Utah, 1980.

Mangrum, R. Collin. "Mormonism, Philosophical Liberalism, and the Constitution." *BYU Studies* 27 (Summer 1987):119–37.

Reynolds, Noel B. "The Doctrine of an Inspired Constitution." *BYU Studies* 16 (Spring 1976):315–40.

REX E. LEE

CONSTITUTION OF THE UNITED STATES OF AMERICA

While LDS scripture reinforces the traditional Christian duty of "respect and deference" to civil laws and governments in general as "instituted of God for the benefit of man" (D&C 134:1, 6), Latter-day Saints attach special significance to the Constitution of the UNITED STATES OF AMERICA. They believe that the Lord "established the Constitution of this land, by the hands of wise men whom [he] raised up unto this very purpose" (D&C 101:80). The Prophet Joseph SMITH once described himself as "the greatest advocate of the Constitution of the United States there is on the earth" (*HC* 6:56–57). All of his successors as President of the Church have reaffirmed the doctrine of an inspired Constitution. This consistent endorsement is notable, for basic LDS teachings are far removed from the premises of American liberalism, and largely as a result of these differences, Latter-day Saints suffered considerable persecution before achieving an accommodation with mainstream America.

The idea of an inspired Constitution is rare in contemporary public discourse and wholly absent from contemporary constitutional and historical scholarship. Seeking to discern the hand of divinity in America's beginnings, however, was once common not only in popular rhetoric but also among eminent nineteenth-century historians such as George Bancroft. Perhaps even more important is the repeated acknowledgment of divine aid by America's founding fathers. Notably, George Washington frequently expressed gratitude to God for felicitous circumstances surrounding the rise of the United States and chose the occasion of his first inaugural address to recognize the providential character of the framing of the Constitution:

> No people can be bound to acknowledge and adore the invisible hand which conducts the affairs of men, more than the People of the United States. Every step by which they have advanced to the character of an independent nation seems to have been distinguished by some token of providential agency. And in the important revolution just accomplished in the system of their united government, the tranquil deliberations and voluntary consent of so many distinct communities, from which the event has resulted, cannot be compared with the means by which most governments have been established, without some return of pious gratitude, along with an humble anticipation of the future blessings which the past [blessings] seem to presage [W. Allen, ed., *George Washington: A Collection,* p. 461. Indianapolis, Ind., 1988].

LDS teaching and revelation are in harmony with this self-understanding of the founding generation. Latter-day Saints believe that the Lord established the Constitution, not by communicating specific measures through oracles, but by raising up and inspiring wise men to this purpose (see D&C 101:80). This emphasis on the extraordinary character of the American founders—and perhaps, more generally, on the founding generation as a whole—accords with assessments by contemporaries, as well as by later students of the period. Thomas Jefferson, then U.S. ambassador to France, described the Constitutional Convention of 1787 as "an assembly of demigods." More than forty years later, Alexis de Tocqueville, the noted French observer of American society, included the American people as a whole in his praise of the founding:

> That which is new in the history of societies is to see a great people, warned by its lawgivers that the wheels of government are stopping, turn its attention on itself without haste or fear, sound the depth of the ill, and then wait for two years to find the remedy at leisure, and then finally, when the remedy has been indicated, submit to it voluntarily without its costing humanity a single tear or drop of blood [Vol. 1, p. 113].

This understanding of the divine inspiration of the Constitution as mediated through the human wisdom of the founders and the founding generation invites the inference that new needs and circumstances might require the continued exercise of inspired human wisdom by statesmen and citizens alike. LDS leaders have taught that the Constitution is not to be considered perfect and complete in every detail (as evidenced most clearly by its accommodation with slavery, contrary to modern scripture; e.g., D&C 101:79) but as subject to development and adaptation. It was part of the wisdom of the founders to forbear from attempting to decide too much; they therefore provided constitutional means for constitutional amendment. President Brigham YOUNG explained that the Constitution "is a progressive—a gradual work"; the founders "laid the foundation, and it was for after generations to rear the superstructure upon it" (JD 7:13–15).

If the wisdom embodied in the Constitution is considered open to future development, so must it be understood as rooted in the past. J. Reuben Clark, Jr., perhaps the most thorough expositor of the Constitution among past LDS Church leaders, emphasized the dependence of the founders' wisdom on "the wisdom of the long generations that had gone before and which had been transmitted

to them through tradition and the pages of history" (1962, p. 3). He saw the Constitution as the product of Englishmen's centuries-long struggle for self-government. This historical perspective fits well with the account of the Book of Mormon, according to which the Lord guided the discovery, colonization, and struggle for independence of America (1 Ne. 13:12–13), in order to establish it as a "land of liberty" (2 Ne. 10:11). Latter-day Saint teaching differs from the traditional providential view of the founding chiefly in holding this liberty not only a blessing in itself but also a condition for the restoration of the fulness of the gospel of Jesus Christ.

LDS teaching about the wisdom of the founders readily acknowledges that it was both conditioned by the past and open to the future. But there can be no question of completely reducing the Constitution to its historical conditions. If the document framed in 1787 remains a touchstone today, this is because, in some admittedly imperfect way, it aims at "the rights and protection of all flesh, according to just and holy principles" (D&C 101:77). Church President David O. MCKAY affirmed that "there are some fundamental principles of this republic which, like eternal truths, never get out of date. . . . Such are the underlying principles of the Constitution" (p. 319).

The scriptural reference to "just and holy principles" appears to locate these fundamentals in certain "rights." Section 98 of the Doctrine and Covenants recommends friendship to constitutional law based on the harmony between FREEDOM under its law and freedom under God (D&C 98:6, 8). Similarly, revelation links human "rights" with the opportunity to "act in doctrine and principle pertaining to futurity, according to the moral agency which I have given unto him, that every man may be accountable for his own sins in the day of judgment" (D&C 101:78). In this way, the reverence of Latter-day Saints for the Constitution is anchored in the fundamental doctrine of free AGENCY, or the idea that God makes possible people's progress toward eternal life in part by exposing them to the consequences, good or bad, of their choices. LDS scholars who have examined the Constitution from the standpoint of this fundamental interest in moral freedom have exhibited its connection with the basic principles of the rule of law (Reynolds, in Hillam) and of the separation of powers (Hickman, in Hillam), both of which concepts are connected with the ideal of limited government.

If "moral agency" stands at the core of the doctrine of an inspired Constitution, then one might say that whereas LDS teaching in the nineteenth century emphasized the agency, Church leaders in the twentieth century have increasingly stressed the moral foundations of the Constitution, echoing the prophet Mosiah$_2$ in the Book of Mormon: "If the time comes that the voice of the people doth choose iniquity, then is the time that the judgments of God will come upon you" (Mosiah 29:26–7; cf. Ether 2:8–12). Their praise of the Constitution has often been paired with warnings against the evils of Marxist communism, a system opposed to the Constitution and moral freedom.

LDS attachment to the Constitution has been further encouraged by an important oral tradition deriving from a statement attributed to Joseph Smith, according to which the Constitution would "hang by a thread" and be rescued, if at all, only with the help of the Saints. Church President John Taylor seemed to go further when he prophesied, "When the people shall have torn to shreds the Constitution of the United States the Elders of Israel will be found holding it up to the nations of the earth and proclaiming liberty and equal rights to all men" (*JD* 21:8). To defend the principles of the Constitution under circumstances where the "iniquity," or moral decay, of the people has torn it to shreds might well require wisdom at least equal to that of the men raised up to found it. In particular, it would require great insight into the relationship between freedom and virtue in a political embodiment of moral agency.

BIBLIOGRAPHY

Benson, Ezra Taft. *The Constitution: A Heavenly Banner*. Salt Lake City, 1986.

———. *The Teachings of Ezra Taft Benson*. Salt Lake City, 1988. Part 5, "Country," collects many statements relative to the Constitution by a Mormon apostle and Church President and former U.S. secretary of agriculture.

Cannon, Donald Q. *Latter-day Prophets and the United States Constitution*. Provo, Utah, 1991.

Clark, J. Reuben, Jr. *Stand Fast by Our Constitution*. Salt Lake City, 1962.

Hillam, Ray C., ed. *"By the Hands of Wise Men": Essays on the U.S. Constitution*. Provo, Utah, 1979. See in particular Richard L. Bushman, "Virtue and the Constitution," pp. 29–38; Martin B. Hickman, "J. Reuben Clark, Jr.: The Constitution and the Great Fundamentals," pp. 39–57, reprinted from *BYU Studies* 13 (Spring 1973):255–72; and Noel B. Reynolds, "The Doctrine of an Inspired Constitution," pp. 1–28, reprinted from *BYU Studies* 16 (Spring 1976):315–40.

Lee, Rex E. *A Lawyer Looks at the Constitution*. Provo, Utah, 1980.

Mangrum, R. Collin. "Mormonism, Philosophical Liberalism, and the Constitution." *BYU Studies* 27 (Summer 1987):119–37. Seeks a justification for Mormon celebration of the Constitution in a compatibility between Mormon theology and the liberal idea that "each individual is entitled to pursue whatever his or her individual *nomos* requires, subject to the equal right of others to do the same."

Vetterli, Richard. *The Constitution by a Thread*. Salt Lake City, 1967. Advocates an interpretation of the U.S. Constitution as consistent with the fundamentals of "Mormon political and religious philosophy" and opposed to the philosophies of Marx, Freud, and the "new liberal intellectual."

RALPH C. HANCOCK

CONTENTION

Ranging from hostile words spoken at home to international conflicts, contention is so prevalent in the world that people tend to think of it as normal, inevitable, and perhaps even necessary. In the Book of Mormon, however, Jesus states, "He that hath the spirit of contention is not of me, but is of the devil, who is the father of contention, and he stirreth up the hearts of men to contend with anger, one with another" (3 Ne. 11:29). Whether at home, at church, in business, or in the community, "such things should be done away" (3 Ne. 11:30). This is fundamental to the teachings of Jesus Christ.

Latter-day Saints place great value on directing their energy in positive ways: "Use boldness, but not overbearance; and also see that ye bridle all your passions, that ye may be filled with love" (Alma 38:12). Thus, scriptures admonish the faithful to "contend for the faith" (Jude 1:3; 1 Thes. 2:2), but not to the point of quarreling or arguing. Contention is especially detrimental at home (Mosiah 4:14) and over doctrine (1 Cor. 11:16; 3 Ne. 11:28).

Jesus taught not only that contention should cease, but anger too, along with derision, contempt, and scorn. Having such feelings place a person in danger of the judgments of the Church and of God (see Matt. 5:22; see also 3 Ne. 12:22, where the phrase "without a cause" is absent).

When people get into difficulties and disagreements with one another, the scriptures furnish wise counsel. If a person feels bad feelings, or discovers that someone has bad feelings against him or her, it is that person's responsibility to go "quickly" and be reconciled (3 Ne. 12:23–25). Implicit in this injunction is the recognition that "we are members one of another" (Eph. 4:25). A troubled relationship is shared by all persons involved and is not just the responsibility of the one who feels hurt or angry. The nature of the reconciliation depends upon the specifics of each situation. Rather than relying on human understanding or formulaic solutions, the Saints are taught to seek divine counsel and to trust the direction of the Lord, the reconciler of all (Prov. 3:5–6; D&C 112:10).

Standing in the way of most solutions to contention is pride: "Only by pride cometh contention" (Prov. 13:10). "The central feature of pride," declared Ezra Taft BENSON, "is enmity—enmity toward God and . . . [toward] our fellowmen." Underlying the solution to contention must be the desire for harmony between people which can come only as a person "yields to the enticings of the Holy Spirit . . . and becometh a saint through the atonement of Christ the Lord" (Mosiah 3:19). Atonement and reconciliation with God allow and evoke forgiveness and reconciliation among people.

BIBLIOGRAPHY

Ashton, Marvin J. "No Time for Contention." *Ensign* 8 (May 1978):7–9.

Benson, Ezra T. "Beware of Pride." *Ensign* 19 (May 1989):4–7.

Thornock, A. Lavar. "Contention—and How to Eliminate It." *Ensign* 10 (Aug. 1980):11–15.

CELIA HOKANSON

CONTRIBUTOR

Edited and published independently by Junius F. WELLS, the founder of the Young Men's Mutual Improvement Association (YMMIA; renamed YOUNG MEN in 1977), the *Contributor* (1879–1896) proposed "to represent the Mutual Improvement Associations, and to furnish a publication of peculiar interest to their members and to the mature youth of our people" ("Salutation," p. 12). One of its purposes was to encourage and foster the development of literary talents among the young men and young women in the Church. It contained articles on such subjects as travel, philosophy, history, biography, and gospel topics. There were also letters from the General Authorities, conference reports, lesson outlines for the youth weekly meetings, hymns, fiction, and a little poetry.

The Contributor Company was formed on January 11, 1886, and Wells continued as editor,

publisher, and business manager. But when it was purchased by the Cannon Publishing Company in 1892, Abraham H. Cannon became the editor and publisher. Cannon died suddenly in July 1896, and the *Contributor* ceased publication with the October issue.

In November 1897 the general board of the YMMIA launched an official magazine, the IMPROVEMENT ERA (1897–1970).

BIBLIOGRAPHY

Anderson, Edward H. "The Past of Mutual Improvement." *IE* 1 (Dec. 1897):85–93.

Wells, Junius F. "Salutation." *Contributor* 1 (Oct. 1879):12.

PETREA GILLESPIE KELLY

CONVERSION

From its beginnings to the present day, the Church has had a strong missionary orientation. It teaches that conversion is essentially a process of REPENTANCE and personal spiritual experience (*see* TESTIMONY; RELIGIOUS EXPERIENCE; JOINING THE CHURCH).

THE NATURE OF CONVERSION. A number of theories have been advanced by sociologists to explain why people are likely to convert to another religious denomination. Glenn M. Vernon indicated that conversion involves several subprocesses, which must be accounted for, including (1) the manner in which the convert becomes aware of the group possessing the ideology; (2) the acceptance of new religious definitions; and (3) the integration of the new convert into the group. John Lofland and Rodney Stark proposed that conversion is a problem-solving process in which the individual uses organizational facilities, programs, and ideologies to resolve various life problems. More recently, David A. Snow, Louis A. Zurcher, and Sheldon Ekland-Olson have emphasized structural proximity, availability, and affective interaction with members of the new denomination as the most powerful influences in determining who will join. Roger A. Straus has proposed that religious conversion is an active accomplishment by the person who converts. Straus thinks that previous theories focus too heavily on the idea that conversion is something which happens to a person as a result of circumstances external to himself. Similarly, C.

David Gartrell and Zane K. Shannon propose that conversion should be characterized as a rational choice based on the recruit's evaluation of the social and cognitive outcomes of converting or not converting.

Recovery from crisis, social proximity to members of the Church, and personal problem solving are certainly involved to some extent in at least some conversions. However, research about people who have converted to many churches, (Snow and Phillips; Heirich) including The Church of Jesus Christ of Latter-day Saints (Seggar and Kunz), has failed to provide much support for the problem-solving theory of Lofland and Stark. Research by David A. Snow and Cynthia L. Phillips and by Max Heirich provides more evidence of the influence of social networks in conversion.

Most scientific theories, however, lack any significant reference to the influence of the HOLY SPIRIT in conversion, which is the dominant element in the Latter-day Saint understanding of conversion. The visitation of Jesus Christ to Paul on the road to Damascus (Acts 9:1–9) does not fit into any secular theoretical categories. Paul was not seeking a new faith to solve problems in his life. He did not begin to serve Christ in order to be accepted by his friends. He persecuted Christians because he thought they had fallen away from the true faith. As a religious man, he recognized the voice of God when it spoke to him.

Similar conversion stories are told in the Book of Mormon. For example, as Alma$_2$ and the sons of King Mosiah$_2$ were going about teaching that the religion of their fathers was not true, they were stopped by the angel of the Lord, who asked why they persecuted the believers. Alma$_2$ was struck dumb and fell to the ground unable to move. While his father and others fasted and prayed in his behalf for two days and two nights, Alma$_2$ suffered excruciating pains and torment and finally called upon Jesus Christ for mercy to take away his sins. Immediately, the pain left and his soul was filled with exquisite joy (Alma 36:6–22). Alma arose and proclaimed that he had been reborn through the spirit of the Lord. Alma and the sons of Mosiah spent the rest of their lives preaching of Christ and doing many good works (Mosiah 27:8–31; cf. the spiritual rebirth of the people of Zarahemla at the time of King BENJAMIN in Mosiah 4–5).

Most conversions are not as dramatic as those of Paul and Alma$_2$ and the sons of Mosiah. The conversion of Alma$_1$ is closer to the kind experienced by most people who join the Church (Mosiah 17:2–4; 18:1). When Abinadi called him and the other priests of the wicked king Noah to repentance, Alma$_1$ knew in his heart that Abinadi spoke the truth. He repented of his sins and began to keep the commandments, with which he was already basically familiar. This wrought a significant change in his life.

From these and other scriptural accounts of the conversion process, it is evident that conversion "implies not merely mental acceptance of Jesus and his teaching but also a motivating faith in him and his gospel—a faith which works a transformation, an actual *change* in one's understanding of life's meaning and in his allegiance to God—in interest, in thought, and in conduct" (Romney, p. 1065). Conversion involves a newness of life, which is effected by receiving divine forgiveness that remits sins (*see* BORN OF GOD). It is characterized by a determination to do good continually, forsaking all sins, and by the healing of the soul by the power of the Holy Spirit, being filled with peace and joy (cf. Romney, p. 1066).

THE PROCESS OF CONVERSION TO THE CHURCH OF JESUS CHRIST OF LATTER-DAY SAINTS. The three subprocesses proposed by Vernon fit quite well the three most obvious aspects of conversion to the Church. The first is "the manner in which the convert becomes aware of the group possessing the ideology." This corresponds to what is referred to in LDS missionary circles as "finding." People come into contact with missionaries in many ways. The most effective source is referral by current Church members who invite friends or family relatives to meet with the missionaries to be taught about the gospel. A second way is for missionaries to knock on doors to invite people to learn about the Church. They also may talk with people they meet on the street or in any other form of normal social contact. Missionaries occasionally set up booths at fairs or expositions. The Church has advertised through the broadcast and print media, offering Church literature. It also operates several VISITORS CENTERS, usually associated with a Church temple or historical site. Two of the best known are Temple Square in Salt Lake City, Utah, and at historic Nauvoo, Illinois. All these visitors centers offer interested people the opportunity to accept teaching visits by missionaries.

The second of Vernon's subprocesses—acceptance of new religious definitions—corresponds to the second major missionary activity, teaching. Missionaries teach the basic principles of God's plan of salvation. They invite those they teach to learn more by studying the Bible and the Book of Mormon on their own. They encourage, inform, teach, and testify. Study is an important part of the conversion process, for the mind plays a role as the investigator learns to understand and ponder the wisdom, logic, and ethic of gospel principles. As B. H. Roberts once stated, "It is frequently the case that a proper setting-forth of a subject makes its truth self-evident. . . . To be known, the truth must be stated and the clearer and more complete the statement is, the better opportunity will the Holy Spirit have for testifying to the souls of men that the work is true" (Vol. 2, pp. vi–vii).

Prospective converts are invited to seek through prayer a spiritual witness from the Holy Ghost to let them know the truth. As Roberts stated regarding the Book of Mormon, "[The Holy Ghost] must ever be the chief source of evidence for the truth of the Book of Mormon. All other evidence is secondary to this, the primary and infallible. No arrangement of evidence, however skillfully ordered; no argument, however adroitly made, can ever take its place" (pp. vi–vii). A quotation from the Book of Mormon is generally used to invite the prospective convert to seek this spiritual manifestation of the truthfulness of the Book of Mormon and of the gospel message: "And when ye shall receive these things, I would exhort you that ye would ask God, the Eternal Father, in the name of Christ, if these things are not true; and if ye shall ask with a sincere heart, with real intent, having faith in Christ, he will manifest the truth of it unto you, by the power of the Holy Ghost" (Moro. 10:4).

Most converts to the Church do not seem to have personal characteristics that predispose them to conversion. While those who begin looking into the Church tend to be younger than the average population and tend somewhat more often to be women, these factors do not predict who will ultimately accept BAPTISM. Those who seek baptism do not tend to have more personal problems than those who do not, nor do they differ significantly from others in personality traits or personal dispositions.

Conversion to the Church is usually not precipitous. The process begins with the first signs of interest, and may continue for many years, even after baptism. It is not simply a matter of accepting and believing the teachings of the Church. Many who do accept baptism indicate that they do not fully understand the teachings, but that they have come to feel that accepting baptism is the right thing to do. Most of them achieve a more complete understanding and acceptance of Church doctrine as they become integrated into membership. Such integration is the third process mentioned by Vernon (see FELLOWSHIPPING).

Becoming a member of the Church has broader implications than simply adopting a new set of religious beliefs. For many new members it means adopting a new lifestyle quite different from the one to which they were accustomed. For nearly all new members, it also means that they become part of a new social network of friends and acquaintances. In some cases, the new Church member is rejected and ostracized by family and former friends. This social transition is made easier if the new convert has previously developed friends and acquaintances among members of the Church.

MISSIONARY WORK IN THE CHURCH. Those who have been converted usually want to share their newfound understanding with others (cf. Perry, pp. 16–18). Paul, Alma₁, and Alma₂ passionately taught the truth of Christ's saving mission throughout the remainder of their lives following their conversions. To the convert who loves people, there is a balance to be achieved between having genuine tolerance for the beliefs of others and fulfilling the desire and obligation to share with them the joy of conversion. The major Jewish and Christian religions have gone through phases when the proselytizing spirit was dominant and other periods when the desire to proselytize was restrained (Marty and Greenspahn).

The Church of Jesus Christ of Latter-day Saints has actively proselytized from its beginnings. Its leaders and members have accepted a mandate to proclaim the restored gospel to "every nation, and kindred, and tongue, and people" (Rev. 14:6; D&C 133:37), to all who will listen. Soon after the formal organization of the Church, Samuel Smith, a brother of Joseph Smith, traveled from place to place offering the Book of Mormon to any who would receive it. Missionaries were soon bringing in converts from the United States, Canada, England, Scandinavia, and Western Europe.

After the main body of members moved to the Intermountain West, the missionary work continued. Increasingly the missionary responsibility was given to young men who had not yet married. Their converts continued to migrate to the American West until well into the twentieth century, in spite of the fact that around the turn of the century Church leaders began to encourage converts to remain where they were and to build up the Church in their homelands.

The Church growth rate since 1860 has never been less than 30 percent for any ten-year period. Since 1950, Church growth has accelerated (*see* VITAL STATISTICS), advancing to more than 50 percent in each ten-year period from 1950 to 1980 (Cowan).

In recent years the Church has become less and less a church confined to the western United States. As late as 1960, more than half of Church members were located in the Intermountain West, with only 10 percent outside the United States. In 1980, nearly one-third of Church members lived outside the United States, with only about 40 percent in the Intermountain West. In 1989 less than one convert in four was an American citizen.

By far the greatest convert growth outside the United States has been in Latin America, particularly in Mexico, Brazil, Chile, Peru, and Argentina (*see* SOUTH AMERICA). There has also been considerable increase in the number of baptisms in Asia and the Philippines. In 1979 there were three missions in the Philippines; this increased to twelve by 1990, and the number of convert baptisms per year tripled in that same period (*see* ASIA). New missions were opened in eastern Europe in 1989 and 1990. In 1990 the Church had more than 40,000 full-time missionaries in 257 missions around the world.

Latter-day Saints believe, as stated by President Marion G. Romney: it may be that "relatively few among the billions of earth's inhabitants will be converted. Nevertheless . . . there is no other means by which the sin-sick souls of men can be healed or for a troubled world to find peace" (p. 1067).

BIBLIOGRAPHY

Burton, Theodore M. "Convince or Convert?" In *BYU Speeches of the Year.* Provo, Utah, 1964.

Cowan, Richard O. *The Church in the Twentieth Century.* Salt Lake City, 1985.

Gartrell, C. David, and Zane K. Shannon. "Contacts, Cognitions, and Conversion: A Rational Choice Approach." *Review of Religious Research* 27 (Sept. 1985):32–48.

Heirich, Max. "Change of Heart: A Test of Some Widely Held Theories About Religious Conversion." *American Journal of Sociology* 83 (Nov. 1977):653–80.

Lofland, John, and Rodney Stark. "Becoming a World-Saver: A Theory of Conversion to a Deviant Perspective." *American Sociological Review* 30 (1965):862–75.

Marty, Martin E., and Frederick E. Greenspahn, eds. *Pushing the Faith: Proselytism and Civility in a Pluralistic World.* New York, 1988.

Perry, L. Tom. "When Thou Art Converted, Strengthen Thy Brethren," *Ensign* 4 (Nov. 1974):16–18.

Roberts, B. H. *New Witnesses for God*, Vol. 2, pp. vi–vii. Salt Lake City, 1926.

Romney, Marion G. "Conversion." *IE* 66 (1963):1065–67.

Seggar, John, and Phillip Kunz. "Conversion: Evaluation of a Step-like Process for Problem-solving." *Review of Religious Research* 13 (Spring, 1972):178–84.

Snow, David A., and Cynthia L. Phillips. "The Lofland-Stark Conversion Model: A Critical Reassessment." *Social Problems* 27 (Apr. 1980):430–47.

Snow, David A.; Louis A. Zurcher, Jr.; and Sheldon Ekland-Olson. "Social Networks and Social Movements: A Microstructural Approach to Differential Recruitment." *American Sociological Review* 45 (Oct. 1980):787–801.

Straus, Roger A. "Religious Conversion as a Personal and Collective Accomplishment." *Sociological Analysis* 40 (Summer, 1979):158–65.

Vernon, Glenn M. *Sociology of Religion*, pp. 101–112. New York, 1962.

KAY H. SMITH

COOPERATIVE MOVEMENT

See: Economic History of the Church

CORRELATION OF THE CHURCH, ADMINISTRATION

Correlation is the process of identifying the role of each part of the Church, placing each in its proper relationship to the others, and ensuring that each functions properly. The parts include doctrines and ordinances, organizations and agencies, programs and activities, meetings, and printed and audiovisual materials. All of these parts should be "fitly framed together" (Eph. 2:21). They function properly when they are connected systematically and operate in harmony and unity. Like the parts of a human body, each has its function, none is sufficient of itself, and none can usurp the tasks of others (cf. 1 Cor. 12:12–28; D&C 84:108–110).

Correlation is a unifying process in which each organization of the Church subordinates limited views to the good of the whole Church. It is not censorship in the sense of inhibiting or channeling free expression and creativity. Rather, it is the way the Church ensures suitable and effective use of its resources.

Correlation serves under the direction of the First Presidency and the Twelve. It provides order to the many parts of the Church (cf. 1 Cor. 14:40; D&C 28:13; 107:84; 132:8) and systematic reviews of proposed action (cf. Matt. 18:16; D&C 6:28). It helps organizations avoid unnecessary duplication. Correlation ensures that Church programs, materials, and activities

• Support and strengthen families in learning and living the gospel.
• Are directed by the PRIESTHOOD.
• Use the scriptures and the words of the prophets as the basis for teaching.
• Comply with policies and meet standards approved by the COUNCIL OF THE FIRST PRESIDENCY and QUORUM OF THE TWELVE APOSTLES.
• Are simple to comprehend and use.
• Conserve demands in effort, time, or money on Church members.
• Encourage people to use local resources whenever appropriate and authorized, rather than to make them totally dependent on Church headquarters.

When the Church was organized in 1830, its structure and operation were relatively simple. However, as the RESTORATION of the gospel unfolded, the Church grew rapidly in numbers and organizational complexity. Various Church Presidents created or adopted the following auxiliary organizations: RELIEF SOCIETY in 1842 (for women), SUNDAY SCHOOL in 1849, Young Ladies' RETRENCHMENT ASSOCIATION in 1869 (which developed into the Young Women's Mutual Improvement Association for teaching YOUNG WOMEN), Young Men's Mutual Improvement Association in 1875 (for teaching YOUNG MEN), and PRIMARY in 1878 (for children). (See also AUXILIARY ORGANIZATIONS.) Church leaders also organized priesthood quorums, expanded missionary work into many countries, acquired family records to

identify ancestors, constructed temples and meetinghouses, held religion classes, established schools, and implemented a program for assisting needy people.

As the programs and activities of Church organizations expanded in number and complexity, they came to have their own general and local officers, curricula, reporting systems, meetings, magazines, funding, and lines of communication.

Part of the role of correlation was to maintain order among these organizations. In 1907, the First Presidency appointed the Committee of Correlation and Adjustments; in 1908, the Correlation Committee and the General Priesthood Committee on Outlines; in 1916, the Social Advisory Committee (combined with the Correlation Committee in 1920); in 1939, the Committee of Correlation and Coordination; and in 1940, the Union Board of the Auxiliaries. Relying on the mandates found in latter-day scripture, these groups were to correlate Church organizations in their structures, curricula, activities, and meetings.

In 1960, the First Presidency directed a committee of General Authorities to review the purposes and courses of study of the priesthood and auxiliaries. The work of this committee laid the foundation for present-day correlation efforts. The committee identified the purposes of each organization from its inception, traced its expansions and changes, and reviewed its courses of study and activities. On the basis of the committee's recommendations, the First Presidency established three coordinating committees in 1961—one for children, one for youth, and one for adults—and a coordinating council that directed the activities of the three committees. The council and committees, each headed by a member of the Quorum of the Twelve Apostles, were to correlate the instructional and activity programs of priesthood quorums, auxiliaries, and other Church agencies.

By 1962, the Church had organized its curricula and activities around three groups: children, youth, and adults. In 1965, it introduced a FAMILY HOME EVENING program with a study manual for families to learn gospel principles and values in their homes. By 1971, the Church had reformatted its magazines by age group rather than by organization—Ensign for adults, New Era for youth, and Friend for children.

In 1972, the First Presidency created the Department of Internal Communications to plan, correlate, prepare, translate, print, and distribute instructional materials and periodicals. As part of this reorganization, the First Presidency created the Correlation Department and placed all organizations, curricula, and periodicals under the direction of the priesthood.

In 1979 the Church published its own edition of the Bible in English, using the text of the King James Version. New editions of the Book of Mormon, the Doctrine and Covenants, and the Pearl of Great Price were published in 1981.

The Church instituted a consolidated meeting schedule in 1980 to decrease the time required for meetings and allow more time for family instruction and activities, placing most local Sabbath meetings within a three-hour period.

Strengthening priesthood direction, the First Presidency organized the First Quorum of the SEVENTY in 1975 and, in 1980, assigned its Presidents to be executive directors of departments at Church headquarters. In 1984, the First Presidency appointed AREA PRESIDENCIES from the Quorums of the Seventy to supervise the affairs of the Church in assigned areas of the world.

In 1987, the First Presidency restated the role of correlation: All proposed official Churchwide materials, programs, and activities must be submitted for evaluation by the Correlation Department. Moreover, no proposed item could be developed under Church auspices or placed in formally authorized use without written direction to do so from the Council of the First Presidency and Quorum of the Twelve.

During the 1990s, the focus of Church correlation shifted from maintaining order among Church entities to simplifying and reducing programs and materials, and to limiting volume, complexity, and cost.

Church leaders have determined that excessively complex and expensive programs and materials can impede taking the gospel to "all nations, kindreds, tongues and people" (D&C 42:58). As the Church grows in developing areas of the world, it will include many members who have limited education and resources.

The present (1990) correlation process at Church headquarters permits representatives of departments and auxiliaries to propose annually the materials, programs, and activities they want to have considered. An originator proceeds with a proposed item only after it has appropriate concept and final production approval.

From Church headquarters, all communica-tions are transmitted through a single priesthood line from the First Presidency and Council of the Twelve to STAKES and WARDS and thereby to families and individuals.

In local stakes and wards (congregations), leaders correlate programs and activities through councils whose members represent everyone within stake or ward boundaries. These councils ensure that Church programs and resources are available to the people to help them learn and live the principles of the gospel.

BIBLIOGRAPHY

Church News. Oct. 21, 1961, p. 3; Jan. 20, 1962, pp. 6, 14; Dec. 5, 1970, p. 3; Jan. 8, 1972, p. 3.

Cowan, Richard O. *Priesthood Programs of the Twentieth Century.* Salt Lake City, 1974.

First Presidency letters. June 7, 1922; Mar. 24, 1960; Apr. 10, 1973; Jan. 15, 1976; June 7, 1978; Apr. 15, 1981; June 30, 1987; June 15, 1989.

Lee, Harold B. "The Plan of Coordination Explained." *IE* 65 (Jan. 1962):34–37.

———. "Report from the Correlation Committee." *IE* 65 (Dec. 1962):936–41.

FRANK O. MAY, JR.

COUNCIL BLUFFS (KANESVILLE), IOWA

Between 1846 and 1852, Council Bluffs, then known as Kanesville, was the headquarters for a substantial LDS presence in western Iowa. During the exodus from Illinois to the Rocky Mountains in the late 1840s, thousands of Latter-day Saints wintered at the Missouri River. After many proceeded westward, WINTER QUARTERS, their original headquarters on the western bank, was abandoned in early 1848 in response to governmental pressure to leave Indian lands. Latter-day Saints who had not gone west relocated on the east bank of the river, in Iowa.

The new townsite was laid out in December 1847, on what originally had been Henry W. Miller's encampment on Indian Creek, in a hollow below the east bluffs of the Missouri River. That same month, Brigham YOUNG was sustained as PRESIDENT OF THE CHURCH in a reorganization of the FIRST PRESIDENCY in Kanesville. The new town of Kanesville took its name from a non-Mormon emissary of U.S. President James K.

Polk, Colonel Thomas L. KANE, who had proven himself a friend of the Latter-day Saints.

President Brigham Young assigned Orson HYDE of the Quorum of the Twelve Apostles to remain in Kanesville to supervise the movement of Latter-day Saints to the West as quickly as possible. The town's location on the Missouri River was particularly advantageous for several thousand British converts who had postponed their migration to America until a new gathering place and headquarters in the West had been established. By sailing to New Orleans, steamboating to St. Louis, and then upriver to Kanesville, these immigrants were spared the rigors of overland travel at least that far.

At one time, as many as thirty-one small encampments were clustered in and about Kanesville. At its height, Kanesville consisted of 350 log cabins, two log tabernacles, a post office, and numerous shops, stores, and other business establishments. Wheat, corn, and many vegetables thrived then, as they do today, in the rich riverbed soil near the bluffs. The town's most pressing problem, to provide adequate food, shelter, employment, and wagon outfits for large numbers of poor immigrants "passing through," was made easier by the California Gold Rush of 1849–1851, which resulted in a boom for Kanesville and other outfitting towns. The gold rush greatly expedited LDS migration while transforming Kanesville from a Mormon into a "Gentile" town.

By the summer of 1852, more than 12,000 Latter-day Saints—6,100 from Great Britain alone—had traveled west via Kanesville, ending the period of concentrated LDS presence in the area. In December 1853, non-LDS residents incorporated Kanesville and renamed it Council Bluffs, in memory of Lewis and Clark's council with the Indians in 1804 on or near the city site.

Kanesville is also remembered as the place where Oliver COWDERY was rebaptized by Orson Hyde in November 1848, ending years of estrangement from the Church he had helped organize in 1830.

BIBLIOGRAPHY

Aitchison, Clyde B. "The Mormon Settlements in the Missouri Valley." *The Quarterly of the Oregon Historical Society* 8 (1907):276–89.

Bennett, Richard E. *Mormons at the Missouri 1846–1852.* Norman, Okla., 1987.

Webb, Lynn Robert. "The Contributions of the Temporary Settlements Garden Grove, Mount Pisgah and Kanesville, Iowa, to Mormon Emigration, 1846–1852." Master's thesis, Brigham Young University, 1954.

Wyman, Walker D. "Council Bluffs and the Westward Movement." *Iowa Journal of History* 47 (Apr. 1949):99–118.

RICHARD E. BENNETT

COUNCIL OF FIFTY

The Council of Fifty, a council formed in Nauvoo in 1844, provided a pattern of political government under PRIESTHOOD and REVELATION. It was, to its members, the nucleus or focus of God's latter-day kingdom.

Old Testament prophecy speaks of a stone "cut out of the mountain without hands" that will roll forth to fill the whole earth (Dan. 2:44–45). Joseph Smith and his associates believed that the "little stone" represented in part a political kingdom similar to the other kingdoms referred to by DANIEL. Joseph Smith taught that in this, the DISPENSATION OF THE FULNESS OF TIMES, "all things" would be set in place for Christ's return, including the basic principles and organization for a system that would govern the earth during the MILLENNIUM (*JD* 1:202–203; 2:189; 17:156–57).

On April 7, 1842, Joseph Smith received a revelation giving the formal name of the "Living Constitution"—or, as it came to be known by the number of its members, the Council of Fifty—and indicating that the nucleus of a government of God would be organized. Two years later, in the spring of 1844, after a small group of faithful Church leaders and members had received their TEMPLE ENDOWMENT, the Prophet formally established the Council of Fifty.

Members of the council understood its principles to be consistent with the ethics of scripture and with the protections and responsibilities of the CONSTITUTION OF THE UNITED STATES. Non-Latter-day Saints could be members (three were among the founding members), but all were to follow God's law and seek to know his will. The PRESIDENT OF THE CHURCH sat as council president, with others seated according to age, beginning with the oldest. Revealed rules governed proceedings, including one that required that decisions be unanimous.

The council had some practical responsibilities for organizing Joseph Smith's presidential campaign in 1844, the exodus from Nauvoo in 1845–1846 (*see* WESTWARD MIGRATION), and early government in the Great Basin. But what interested council members most was, not their specific duties, but the expectation that the council represented something much larger: it was a working demonstration of the principles and pattern for a future KINGDOM OF GOD on earth. The Church already had a well-developed apocalyptic outlook, including belief in the latter-day collapse of existing governments before Christ's return. In this framework, the Council of Fifty was viewed as the seed of a new political order that would rule, under Christ, following the prophesied cataclysmic events of the last days.

The council, therefore, did not challenge existing systems of law and government (even in Nauvoo), but functioned more as a private organization learning to operate in a pluralistic society. Its exercise of actual political power was modest, but provided a symbol of the future theocratic kingdom of God. Always, the Fifty functioned under the FIRST PRESIDENCY and the QUORUM OF THE TWELVE APOSTLES, who were also members of the council.

After the westward migration and the early pioneer period, the Council of Fifty largely disappeared as a functioning body, except for a brief resurgence during John TAYLOR's presidency when the Church again faced intense political challenges. Still, the Saints found consolation in the belief that one day, when the Savior returned, the Council of Fifty, or a council based on its principles, would rise again to govern the world under the King of Kings.

BIBLIOGRAPHY

Andrus, Hyrum L. *Joseph Smith and World Government*. Salt Lake City, 1958.

Ehat, Andrew F. "It Seems Like Heaven Began on Earth: Joseph Smith and the Constitution of the Kingdom of God." *BYU Studies* 20 (Spring 1980):253–79.

Hansen, Klaus J. *Quest for Empire*. East Lansing, Mich., 1967.

Quinn, D. Michael. "The Council of Fifty and Its Members, 1844 to 1945." *BYU Studies* 20 (Winter 1980):163–97.

KENNETH W. GODFREY

COUNCIL OF THE FIRST PRESIDENCY AND THE QUORUM OF THE TWELVE APOSTLES

Each week the two presiding quorums of The Church of Jesus Christ of Latter-day Saints meet jointly as the Council of the First Presidency and the Quorum of the Twelve Apostles. Meeting in a room in the Salt Lake Temple, this council discusses and decides all major Church appointments and policy matters.

The presiding members in this council are the FIRST PRESIDENCY, consisting of the PRESIDENT OF THE CHURCH, who has ultimate authority for all matters in the Church, and his counselors, who assist him in directing the affairs of the Church. The Council also includes the QUORUM OF THE TWELVE APOSTLES. The members of these two quorums are the only men on earth who hold all the KEYS, or authorization, of the priesthood, and only they are sustained as prophets, seers, and revelators for the Church.

N. Eldon Tanner, counselor to four Church Presidents, said, "It is in this body [the Council] that any change in administration or policy is considered and approved, and it then becomes the official policy of the Church" (Tanner, 1979, p. 47). Responsibilities of the Council include such matters as approval of new bishops; changes in ward, stake, mission, and temple boundaries and organizations; and approval of general officers and central administration of the auxiliary organizations of the Church, such as the Primary, Sunday School, and Relief Society.

The order and procedure of the Council are rarely discussed in public, but can be inferred from published accounts of the process by which a revelation was announced in 1978. After a considerable period of prayer and discussion among the General Authorities, President Spencer W. KIMBALL felt inspired to extend eligibility for the priesthood to all worthy male members of the Church. He first presented it to his counselors, who accepted and approved it, and then to the Quorum of the Twelve Apostles in the Council of the First Presidency and the Quorum of the Twelve Apostles. The same inspiration came to the members of the Council, who then approved it unanimously (McConkie, p. 128). After the Council had sustained the President in this action, the revelation was subsequently presented to all other GENERAL AUTHORITIES and to the general membership of the Church, who approved it unanimously (Tanner, 1978).

BIBLIOGRAPHY

McConkie, Bruce R. "The New Revelation on Priesthood." In *Priesthood*. Salt Lake City, 1981.

The Council of the First Presidency and the Quorum of the Twelve Apostles (as of 1898–1901). On floor: Matthias F. Cowley, Abraham O. Woodruff. Seated (left to right): Brigham Young, Jr., George Q. Cannon, President Lorenzo Snow, Joseph F. Smith, Franklin D. Richards. Standing (left to right): Anthon H. Lund, John W. Taylor, John Henry Smith, Heber J. Grant, Francis M. Lyman, George Teasdale, Marriner W. Merrill.

Tanner, N. Eldon. "Revelation on Priesthood Accepted, Church Officers Sustained." *Ensign* 8 (Nov. 1978):16–17.

———. "The Administration of the Church." *Ensign* 9 (Nov. 1979):42–48.

W. KEITH WARNER

COUNCIL IN HEAVEN

The Council in Heaven, sometimes called the Grand Council, refers to a meeting of God the Father with his spirit sons and daughters to discuss the terms and conditions by which these spirits could come to earth as physical beings. The terms "Council in Heaven" and "Grand Council" do not appear in the scriptures, but are used by the Prophet Joseph SMITH in referring to these premortal activities, allusions to which are found in many scriptures (Job 38:4–7; Jer. 1:5; Rev. 12:3–7; Alma 13:3–9; D&C 29:36–38; 76:25–29; Moses 4:1–4; Abr. 3:23–28; cf. *TPJS*, pp. 348–49, 357, 365; *T&S* 4 [Feb. 1, 1843]:82).

One purpose of the heavenly council was to allow the spirits the opportunity to accept or reject the Father's PLAN OF SALVATION, which proposed that an earth be created whereon his spirit children could dwell, each in a PHYSICAL BODY. Such a life would serve as a probationary state "to see if they [would] do all things whatsoever the Lord their God shall command them" (Abr. 3:25). The spirits of all mankind were free to accept or reject the Father's plan but they were also responsible for their choice. The Creation, the Fall, mortality, the Atonement, the Resurrection, and the Final Judgment were contemplated and explained in the council (*TPJS*, p. 220, 348–50; *MD*, pp. 163–64; *see also* FIRST ESTATE). The plan anticipated mistakes from inexperience and sin and provided remedies. Many spirits were foreordained to specific roles and missions during their mortal experience, conditional upon their willingness and faithfulness in the premortal sphere and their promised continued faithfulness upon the earth. The Prophet Joseph Smith explained, "Every man who has a calling to minister to the inhabitants of the world was ordained to that very purpose in the Grand Council of heaven before this world was. I suppose I was ordained to this very office in that Grand Council" (*TPJS*, p. 365; cf. 1 Pet. 1:20; Jer. 1:5; Abr. 3:22–23).

Although spoken of as a single council, there may have been multiple meetings where the gospel was taught and appointments were made. Jesus and the prophets were foreordained in the council. A redeemer was to perform a twofold mission in redeeming mankind from the physical and spiritual deaths brought about by the FALL OF ADAM and also in providing redemption, upon repentance, for sins committed by individuals. At a certain point in the council, the Father asked, "Whom shall I send [as the Redeemer]?" Jesus Christ, known then as the great I AM and as Jehovah, answered, "Here am I, send me," and agreed to follow the Father's plan (Moses 4:1–4; Abr. 3:27). As a counter-measure, Lucifer offered himself and an amendment to the Father's plan of saving mankind that would not respect their AGENCY. The substitute proposal was also designed to exalt Lucifer above the throne of God. The Father's response was, "I will send the first" (meaning Jehovah). Lucifer rebelled and became Satan, or "the devil." A division developed among the spirits, and no spirits were neutral (*DS* 1:65–66). There was WAR IN HEAVEN (Rev. 12:7–8), and the third of the hosts who followed Lucifer were cast out (Rev. 12:4; D&C 29:36). These rebellious spirits, along with Lucifer, were thrust down to the earth without physical bodies (Rev. 12:9; cf. Isa. 14:12–17). The Prophet Joseph Smith explained: "The contention in heaven was—Jesus said there would be certain souls that would not be saved; and the devil said he could save them all, and laid his plans before the grand council, who gave their vote in favor of Jesus

Christ. So the devil rose up in rebellion against God, and was cast down, with all who put up their heads for him" (*TPJS*, p. 357). Heavenly Father and the faithful spirits in heaven wept over them (D&C 76:25–29). Satan and his followers are still at war with those spirits who have been born into mortality (Rev. 12:9; cf. "War in Heaven," p. 788).

BIBLIOGRAPHY

Bible Dictionary. "War in Heaven." In LDS Edition of the King James Version of the Bible, p. 788. Salt Lake City, 1977.

McConkie, Joseph F. "Premortal Existence, Foreordinations and Heavenly Councils." In *Apocryphal Writings and the Latter-day Saints*, ed. W. Griggs, pp. 173–98. Provo, Utah, 1986.

JOHN L. LUND

COURTS

See: Disciplinary Procedures

COURTS, ECCLESIASTICAL, NINETEENTH-CENTURY

In the nineteenth century, the LDS court system functioned in adjudicating virtually all kinds of legal disputes among Church members. Since the late 1800s, however, the Church courts, now entitled disciplinary councils, have not been used for the arbitration of private disputes.

The scriptural basis for Church courts originated in the early 1830s. At first, elders conducted trials for determining membership status. In 1831, a bishop, designated as a "judge in Israel" (D&C 58:17), and his counselors were authorized to function as a bishop's court. In 1834, Doctrine and Covenants 102 established the HIGH COUNCIL court and its procedures for hearing original cases and appeals from bishop's courts. The high council court consists of a STAKE PRESIDENT, his two counselors, and the twelve members of the stake high council. The FIRST PRESIDENCY court is the highest available for considering appeals from high council courts (D&C 102:27).

The roles of these courts have varied. In the 1830s, years marked by rapid expansion in Church membership and extensive migration to escape persecution in Ohio and Missouri, Church courts usually provided members an easy, appropriate, and friendly forum for settling non-Church related disputes. Then for several years prior to the NAUVOO CHARTER, and again in the westward migration until 1850, Church courts pronounced, enforced, and adjudicated a full range of civil and criminal ordinances. Thereafter, until the passage of the Poland Act (1874), Church courts continued to handle civil disputes even though alternative courts were available through the federal territorial government (judges appointed by the president of the United States) and through the county probate judges (appointed by the territorial legislature). Probate judges were almost always Mormon PRIESTHOOD leaders, including local stake presidents and bishops, and the probate courts had broad powers over all criminal and civil court matters in addition to normal probate functions. During this period, however, Church courts handled most disputes between members of the Church. Latter-day Saints turned to the county probate courts mostly in criminal actions, in actions against non-Mormons, and when it was important to obtain a formal court decree.

With passage in 1874 of the Poland Act and with the Supreme Court decision in *Reynolds v. United States* (1879), the federal assault on Mormon polygamy intensified, and the Church courts provided the only forum to assist wives and children in settling disputes with their polygamous husbands and fathers. Government courts could offer little assistance because polygamous marriages were outside the law.

In the nineteenth century members used Church courts in private disputes largely because of the principle of exclusive jurisdiction widely enforced by the Church. Applying this principle, leaders used sermons and scripture to encourage members to avoid the civil courts; they also imposed disfellowshipment or excommunication on members who sued another member in the civil courts. Thus non-Mormons initiated most of the cases in the civil courts of the UTAH TERRITORY even though the population was overwhelmingly Mormon.

After Utah acquired statehood in 1896, a regular state court system was instituted. Thereafter the Church court system ceased to consider temporal disputes.

Historically, at all times, many Church court cases have involved sexual offenses. In the early Utah decades land disputes were adjudicated by Church courts because the bishops had allocated land holdings to members according to their needs and abilities to put the land into productive use. In deciding contract matters, the main objective was reconciliation of brothers and sisters in the gospel. In such cases, Church courts gave weight to the likely outcome of a similar dispute in civil court. However, they never felt strictly bound by common law precedents; they used inspiration, custom, scripture, and ecclesiastical instructions to reach equitable solutions with reconciliation and benefit to the entire community as the guiding objectives.

BIBLIOGRAPHY

Firmage, Edwin B., and Richard C. Mangrum. *Zion in the Courts: A Legal History of The Church of Jesus Christ of Latter-day Saints, 1830–1900.* Chicago, 1988.

Leone, Mark P. "Ecclesiastical Courts: Inventing Labels and Enforcing Definitions." *Roots of Modern Mormonism.* Cambridge, Mass., 1979.

Swenson, Raymond T. "Resolution of Civil Disputes by Mormon Ecclesiastical Courts." *Utah Law Review* (1978):573–95.

JAMES H. BACKMAN

COVENANT ISRAEL, LATTER-DAY

God established a COVENANT with ABRAHAM, reaffirming it with Isaac and Jacob and then with the children of Israel. In the LDS view, this covenant has been renewed repeatedly and then breached, largely because God's people, after receiving his COMMANDMENTS and promises, have fallen into APOSTASY and disbelief. Today, as prophesied anciently, this covenant has been restored through the Prophet Joseph SMITH and is included in the NEW AND EVERLASTING COVENANT of the gospel (D&C 22:1; cf. Jer. 31:31–34; 32:36–40).

The term "Covenant Israel" refers to ancient Israel, to the New Testament era, and to modern times. Anciently God stated, "I will establish my covenant between me and thee [Abraham] and thy seed after thee . . . for an everlasting covenant, to be a God unto thee, and to thy seed" (Gen. 17:7). Yet this covenant was conditional. Those who would be "his people" had to prove themselves through obedience and faithful commitment to the laws and ORDINANCES of the covenant (cf. Abr. 2:6–11). Later, Jehovah said through Moses, "If ye will obey my voice indeed, and keep my covenant, then ye shall be a peculiar treasure unto me above all people. . . . And ye shall be unto me a kingdom of priests, and an holy nation" (Ex. 19:5–6).

Because ancient Israel rejected God's word and thereby lost his promises, the prophet Hosea warned:

> The Lord hath a controversy with the inhabitants of the land, because there is no truth, nor mercy, nor knowledge of God in the land. By swearing, and lying, and killing, and stealing, and committing adultery, . . . my people are destroyed. . . . I will also reject thee, that thou shalt be no priest to me: seeing thou hast forgotten the law of thy God, I will also forget thy children [Hosea 4:1–6; cf. Amos 8:11–12; Isa. 24:1–6; Jer. 2:11–13].

In New Testament times, Jesus Christ lamented a similar apostasy: "O Jerusalem, Jerusalem, thou that killest the prophets, and stonest them which are sent unto thee, how often would I have gathered thy children together, even as a hen gathereth her chickens, . . . and ye would not!" (Matt. 23:37–38; cf. 3 Ne. 10:4–6). Covenant Israel was meant to be expanded in Old Testament times (Abr. 2:9–11; 1 Ne. 17:36–40), and again in the New Testament era, to include all followers of Christ, both literal descendants of Abraham and GENTILES who became part of Abraham's lineage by adoption. "Know ye therefore that they which are of faith, the same are the children of Abraham . . . . For as many of you as have been baptized into Christ have put on Christ. There is neither Jew nor Greek, . . . for ye are all one in Christ Jesus. And if ye be Christ's, then are ye Abraham's seed, and heirs according to the promise" (Gal. 3:7, 27–29; cf. Rom. 4:12–13; Eph. 2:11–12).

The same doctrine applies today: Membership in latter-day covenant Israel, The Church of Jesus Christ of Latter-day Saints, is not limited to a certain lineage but is open to all who willingly accept and abide by its covenantal terms through the LAW OF ADOPTION. Latter-day Saints accept God's covenant with Abraham and his lineage, a covenant reestablished at the time of Joseph Smith (D&C 110:12). Known as the "new and everlasting covenant" (D&C 22:1; Jer. 31:31–34; 32:36–40), it is included in the fulness of the gospel of Jesus Christ. It is considered "new" in each age when it is given to God's people, yet it is "everlasting" because the conditions and promises never change. Further, covenant Israel implies a community willing to accept God's complete law, which is based in latter-day revelation of the same covenant that was revealed in the Old and New Testaments. This requires an acknowledgment that God has spoken to both ancient and latter-day prophets and continues to do so.

Covenants and accompanying ordinances of the gospel of Jesus Christ are the essence of religious life. LDS teaching holds that all of God's commandments are based in covenant. Thus the ordinances of BAPTISM, receiving the GIFT OF THE HOLY GHOST, and the SACRAMENT, as well as keeping the SABBATH DAY holy and TEMPLE WORSHIP—including eternal marriage—embody covenants with promises, obligations, and opportunities for blessings. These covenants are mutual promises between God in heaven and men and women on earth. Those willing to abide by such agreements are considered part of covenant Israel, with all the attendant blessings and opportunities. Thus the Church teaches that any law or commandment from God to his children, that helps ensure their SALVATION and ETERNAL LIFE is part of the "everlasting covenant."

The Prophet Joseph Smith taught that "the ancients . . . obtained from God promises of such weight and glory, that our hearts are often filled with gratitude that we are even permitted to look upon them. . . . If we are the children of the Most High, . . . and embrace the same covenant that they embraced, and are faithful to the testimony of our Lord as they were, we can approach the Father in the name of Christ as they approached Him, and for ourselves obtain the same promises" (*TPJS*, pp. 65–66).

[*See also* Abrahamic Covenant.]

JAMES B. MAYFIELD

COVENANTS

The word "covenant" in the Bible is a translation of the Hebrew *berith* and of the Greek *diathēkē*. The Book of Mormon concept seems close to the Hebrew indication of any formalized relation between two parties, such as a bond, pact, or agreement. As such, the term is used for nonaggression pacts between nations (Gen. 26:26–31), a promise of landownership (Gen. 15:18–21), a bond for free slaves (Jer. 34:8–9), or an oath of secrecy (2 Kgs. 11:4). The Greek *diathēkē* is a more legalistic term, implying a formal will, a legal bequest (Gal. 3:17). In the New Testament the term is often translated as "testament," but clearly is used for the same kind of bond as "covenant" (cf. Heb. 7:22; 8:6; Anderson, p. 5). This legal aspect is also clear in the Doctrine and Covenants (e.g., D&C 132:7), where certain organizational issues are couched in covenantal terms (e.g., D&C 82:11–12). The English term "covenant," meaning "coming together," stresses the relational aspect. In other languages the terms used may have more legal connotations.

Members of The Church of Jesus Christ of Latter-day Saints speak of themselves as a "covenant people," both collectively and individually. Entering into righteous and authorized covenants with God is one of the most important aspects of their lives. They see their covenants as modern counterparts of covenant making in biblical times.

Most covenants mentioned in scripture are made by God with mankind, either with individuals or a group. In a group covenant, like that of ancient Israel or of the NEPHITES, the leader or king "cuts the covenant" (as it is said in Hebrew) for, and in behalf of, his people, who in turn affirm their entrance into the covenant by a collective oath or by REPENTANCE (for example, 2 Chr. 34:29–32). This covenant may be reaffirmed and reestablished, as occurs in King Benjamin's speech (Mosiah 1–6; see Ricks, 1984). When such covenants are established, the collective bond with God holds as long as people are obedient to the commandments stated or implied in the covenant. Yet a gradual shift of emphasis from collective toward individual covenant making is discernible from the Old to the New Testament. It is also within the Book of Mormon and in the teachings of the Church. Some tension between the association with the "elect" (Ps. 89:3–4; D&C 88:130–133) and the more general covenant for all mankind (Isa. 55:3) remains. Individual covenants, in any event, are essential in LDS doctrine and religion, both in sacred history and in present practice.

In covenant making, God takes the initiative with a conditional promise, specifying attainable blessings and setting the terms for people to receive them. Sometimes a sign is given to commemorate the pact, like the tables of the covenant (Deut. 9:9–11). Revelations (Jer. 11:1–5) and miracles (Deut. 5:1–6) sometimes accompany covenants. One enters the covenant, usually through a ritual, a visible sign. Blood sacrifices ("the blood of the covenant," Ex. 24:8), the "salt covenant" (Num. 18:19; 2 Chr. 13:5), the circumcision of boys (Acts 7:8), baptism (D&C 22:1; Mosiah 18:7–11),

the sacrament (Heb. 8:6; 3 Ne. 18:1–14), the conferral of the priesthood with its "oath and covenant" (D&C 84:33–42), marriage (D&C 132) and other temple rites, all these revealed rituals are called sacraments or ORDINANCES, which have been given as covenants. They serve as a signal that individuals enter into or reaffirm personal covenants with the Lord. As God is bound by his promises (D&C 82:10), covenant making has to be guided by revelation and performed through the AUTHORITY of the priesthood. Otherwise, God is not truly made party to the accord and agreement. Since covenant rites are essential for man's salvation and EXALTATION, the role of the priesthood in administering these covenantal sacraments is crucial. Without priesthood authority, there are no everlasting covenants. Still, these overt covenant obligations are always directly related to the general commandment of loving God and one's neighbor, called the "covenant of the heart" (Heb. 10:16; Jer. 31:31–34; Isa. 55:3).

The Lord's covenants essentially cover the whole PLAN OF SALVATION. God's promise is to send a Savior for all humans, asking on their part for their obedience to the will of the Lord. Each covenant reflects aspects of the "fulness of his gospel" (D&C 133:57). Though various DISPENSATIONS may have their specific focus, such as Israel's "covenant of works" and Paul's "covenant of grace," Latter-day Saints categorize all divine covenants under the unity of one gospel. As a consequence, all covenants are always new, everlasting, and continually renewed.

Latter-day Saints enter into an eternal covenant with God at baptism, wherein they promise to take upon them the name of Jesus Christ, to keep his commandments, to bear one another's burdens, to stand as a witness of God at all times, to repent, and to serve and remember Christ always (see BAPTISMAL COVENANT; Mosiah 18:8–10; D&C 20:37). They renew this covenant by partaking of the sacrament of the Lord's Supper. Other covenants involving obligations of faithfulness, magnifying one's calling, sacrifice, obedience, righteousness, chastity, and consecration are made when one is ordained to the MELCHIZEDEK PRIESTHOOD (see OATH AND COVENANT OF THE PRIESTHOOD), when one receives the temple ENDOWMENT, and when a man and woman enter into eternal marriage (see MARRIAGE: ETERNAL).

Many commentaries stress the one-sidedness of scriptural covenants. Since the Lord's promises greatly exceed human obligations, the blessings of deity significantly overshadow the efforts demanded (see Mosiah 2:21), even though a notion of reciprocity is always present. Something is demanded in return, as a covenant is essentially two-sided; before anything else, it is a relation, the means by which God and man become reconciled in the atonement afforded to all by Jesus Christ.

A covenant is a special relationship with the Lord into which a person or a group may enter. The terms have been set by the Lord both for the rewards (blessings, salvation, exaltation) and the efforts demanded (obedience to rules and commandments). A covenant is fulfilled when people keep their promises and endure to the end in faith, with the Lord giving blessings during life, and salvation and exaltation upon completion.

A broken covenant results from a willful breach of promise, that is, transgression of commandments. By breaking this relationship, a person forfeits blessings. These can be restored in full only by repentance and reentering the covenant. Covenants comfort the righteous (Dan. 9:4) and lift the hearts of the oppressed (Ps. 74:20–21), but shame the unrepentant (Ezek. 16:60–63).

Latter-day Saints hold that the first personal covenants were made in PREMORTAL LIFE, later to be taken again on earth. In the sacred history of the earth, covenants have been made by God with Adam and Eve and with all the ancient patriarchs and prophets and their wives. For example, God made covenants of various kinds with Enoch; Abraham and Sarah; Moses; the kings of Israel and Judah, including David, Solomon, and Josiah (2 Chr. 34:29–32); and many of the prophets. Jesus Christ instituted the sacrament as a covenant establishing a personal relationship with his individual followers (Heb. 8:6), his blood replacing the old sacrificial "blood of the everlasting covenant" (Heb. 13:20). Through Joseph Smith, the everlasting covenants were established anew (see NEW AND EVERLASTING COVENANT; D&C 1:15, 22; 22:1; 132).

For each respective group of covenant people, this meaningful relation with the deity is also an identity marker, singling out people or a group from among their peers. Often outward signs are used: circumcision (Gen. 17:2–14), the SABBATH DAY (Ex. 31:12–17), endogamy or prohibitions on marriage outside the group (Ezra 10:3), greetings (D&C 88:131–133), and dietary proscriptions, such as the food taboos of Leviticus or the latter-day health code of the WORD OF WISDOM (D&C 89).

Among Christian churches historically, the focus on making covenants has risen since the Reformation. In John Calvin's Geneva the notion of covenant was crucial (Lillback, 1987), a tradition that was passed on to many Protestant denominations, including the Puritans (van Pohr, 1986). In early American ecclesiastical history, covenants were also crucial, and the New England Puritans clearly saw themselves as the covenant people of the Lord (Miller, 1966). This concept has remained important in American culture and is a vital and essential part of LDS religion.

BIBLIOGRAPHY

Anderson, Richard L. "Religious Validity: The Sacramental Covenants in 3 Nephi." In *By Study and Also by Faith*, ed. J. Lundquist and S. Ricks, Vol. 2, pp. 1–51. Salt Lake City, 1990.

Cooper, Rex E. *Promises Made to the Fathers: Mormon Covenant Organization*. Salt Lake City, 1990.

Lillback, P. A. *The Binding of God: Calvin's Role in the Development of Covenant Theology*. Ann Arbor, Mich., 1987.

Miller, P. *Life of the Mind in America from the Revolution to the Civil War*. London, 1966.

Pohr, J. van. *The Covenant of Grace in Puritan Thought*. AAR Studies in Religion 45. Atlanta, Georgia, 1986.

Ricks, Stephen D. "The Treaty/Covenant Pattern in King Benjamin's Address (Mosiah 1–6)." *BYU Studies* 24 (Spring 1984):151–62.

WOUTER VAN BEEK

COVENANTS IN BIBLICAL TIMES

The idea of making and keeping covenants is essential to Latter-day Saints, who would readily agree "that the central message of the Bible is God's covenant with men" (Bruce, p. 139). The "covenant theme pervades Old Testament teachings" and all scripture (Ludlow). A consistent and enduring pattern in God's dealings with mankind from the beginning of the earth's history down to present time is that sacred covenants are used to unite individuals to God and to each other.

Bringing extrabiblical revelations to bear on their understanding of biblical covenants, Latter-day Saints consider the history of God's dealings with mankind to be arranged according to DISPENSATIONS OF THE GOSPEL, in which the gospel (including the priesthood and all the necessary ordinances) is bestowed by God upon man, and received by covenant. Each dispensation is presided over by priesthood leaders who hold KEYS entitling them to put people under covenantal obligations that are bound in heaven as well as on earth. Thus, Moses (Deut. 29:10–15), Joshua (Josh. 24:14–28), and Peter (Matt. 16:19) were among those having authority to act on behalf of God in making and renewing binding covenants between God and his people.

God's covenant relationship with mankind began with Adam and Eve. Texts in the PEARL OF GREAT PRICE show that Adam and Eve were the first after the Fall to enter into a covenant relationship with God—through sacrifice, baptism (Moses 6:64–66), and receiving the priesthood and ordinances associated with the temple: "Thus all things were confirmed unto Adam, by an holy ordinance" (Moses 5:59; see also 4:4–5, 8, 10–12). Adam and Eve were promised a savior and were instructed to be obedient, to be repentant, and to do all things in the name of the Son of God (Moses 5:6–8).

Whereas the Bible first uses the term "covenant" in conjunction with Noah (Gen. 6:18; 9:9–17), its first use in other LDS scriptures is with Enoch (Moses 7:51; 8:2). Non-LDS Bible scholars (e.g., Fensham) usually arrange the principal biblical covenants into a fivefold sequence (Noah, Abraham, Moses, David, and the New Testament covenant), but Latter-day Saints follow a sequence of seven main dispensations (Adam, Enoch, Noah, Abraham, Moses, Christ and his apostles, and Joseph SMITH), and recognize those also of the brother of Jared, Lehi, and Alma in Book of Mormon history. Where non-LDS scholars explore both connections and distinctions between the covenants mentioned in the Bible (e.g., the patriarchal covenant of Abraham continued even when the covenant at Sinai was broken), Latter-day Saints see general uniformity of the principal covenant occurrences, all of them reflecting the same underlying principles of the gospel of Jesus Christ.

Central as they are to subsequent biblical references to covenants (e.g., Ex. 2:24; Luke 1:72–73; Acts 3:25; Gal. 3:13–14), the promises made explicit in the ABRAHAMIC COVENANT receive particular emphasis in LDS teachings (Ricks, 1985; Nyman). The BOOK OF ABRAHAM in the Pearl of Great Price adds to the understanding of the promises to Abraham and Sarah. To the promises of a land of inheritance (Gen. 15:18; 17:8; cf. Abr. 2:6) and of innumerable posterity (Gen. 15:5; 17:2–6;

cf. Abr. 2:9; 3:14), the book of Abraham adds priesthood blessings (Abr. 1:3–4, 18) and the promise that Abraham's seed will be the means whereby the gospel will be ministered throughout the earth so that all people might receive the gospel and obtain salvation (Abr. 2:10–11). Latter-day Saints believe that the power to give these ancient promises by way of covenant was reinstated on April 3, 1836, when Elijah, Elias, Moses, and other ancient prophets restored to Joseph Smith and Oliver COWDERY the keys of "the dispensation of the gospel of Abraham, saying that in us and our seed all generations after us should be blessed" (D&C 110:12; 124:58; 132:30–31).

In biblical times, political and legal covenants were made in various ways. Religious covenants often drew upon these secular practices by way of analogy. For example, in the language of the Bible, one "cuts" a covenant, reminiscent of the legal procedure of cutting a small animal in a ceremony when solemnizing a contract or treaty (Gen. 15:10; Hillers, pp. 40–45).

The process of renewing covenants, individually and communally, was also an important part of religious life in biblical times. Just as individual Latter-day Saints "renew" their covenant of baptism by partaking of the sacrament of the Lord's Supper, so there are scriptural instances of communal rites of covenant renewal (e.g., Deut. 31:10–13; Josh. 1:16–18). Covenant renewals are also found in the Book of Mormon, where Near Eastern (especially Hittite) analogues are evident (Ricks, 1984, 1990).

Despite such renewals, it is clear that the old covenant, or Mosaic law, was to be replaced by a new one, as Jeremiah prophesied (Jer. 31:31). Latter-day Saints believe that this prophecy was fulfilled in the New Testament (or, more exactly, the New Covenant). Christ "is the mediator of a better covenant, which was established upon better promises" (Heb. 8:6). The recurring symbol of renewal in the new covenant is the sacrament, instituted at the Last Supper and centered in the commitment to remember Christ always, evoking the Passover imagery of the old covenant and the covenantal cry of the prophets to know God (Hosea 4:6).

BIBLIOGRAPHY

Bruce, F. F. "Bible." In *The New Bible Dictionary*, 2nd ed., ed. J. D. Douglas et al., pp. 137–40. Wheaton, Ill., 1982.

Fensham, F. C., "Covenant, Alliance." In *The New Bible Dictionary*, 2nd ed., ed. J. D. Douglas et al., pp. 137–40. Wheaton, Ill., 1982.

Hillers, Delbert R. *Covenant: The History of a Biblical Idea.* Baltimore, 1969.

Ludlow, Victor L. "Unlocking the Covenant Teachings in the Scriptures." *Religious Studies Center Newsletter, Brigham Young University* 4, no. 2 (1990):1, 4.

Nyman, Monte S. "The Covenant of Abraham." In *The Pearl of Great Price: Revelations from God*, pp. 155–70, ed. H. Donl Peterson and C. Tate. Provo, Utah, 1989.

Ricks, Stephen D. "The Treaty/Covenant Pattern in King Benjamin's Address (Mosiah 1–6)." *BYU Studies* 25 (Spring 1984):151–62.

———. "The Early Ministry of Abraham." In *Studies in Scripture*, ed. R. Millet and K. Jackson, Vol. 2, pp. 217–24. Salt Lake City, 1985.

———. "Deuteronomy: A Covenant of Love." *Ensign* 20 (Apr. 1990):55–59.

Whittaker, David J. "A Covenant People: Old Testament Light on Modern Covenants." *Ensign* 10 (Aug. 1980):36–40.

GEORGE S. TATE

COWDERY, OLIVER

Oliver Cowdery (1806–1850) was next in authority to Joseph SMITH in 1830 (D&C 21:10–12), and was a second witness of many critical events in the restoration of the gospel. As one of the three BOOK OF MORMON WITNESSES, Oliver Cowdery testified that an angel displayed the GOLD PLATES and that the voice of God proclaimed them correctly translated. He was with Joseph Smith when John the Baptist restored to them the AARONIC PRIESTHOOD and when Peter, James, and John ordained them to the MELCHIZEDEK PRIESTHOOD and the apostleship, and again during the momentous KIRTLAND TEMPLE visions (D&C 110).

Oliver came from a New England family with strong traditions of patriotism, individuality, learning, and religion. He was born at Wells, Vermont, on October 3, 1806. His younger sister gave the only reliable information about his youth: "Oliver was brought up in Poultney, Rutland County, Vermont, and when he arrived at the age of twenty, he went to the state of New York, where his older brothers were married and settled. . . . Oliver's occupation was clerking in a store until 1829, when he taught the district school in the town of Manchester" (Lucy Cowdery Young to Andrew Jenson, March 7, 1887, Church Archives).

While boarding with Joseph Smith's parents,

he learned of their convictions about the ancient record that their son was again translating after Martin HARRIS had lost the manuscript in 1828. The young teacher prayed and received answers that Joseph Smith mentioned in a revelation (D&C 6:14–24). The Prophet's first history states the "Lord appeared unto . . . Oliver Cowdery and shewed unto him the plates in a vision and . . . what the Lord was about to do through me, his unworthy servant. Therefore he was desirous to come and write for me to translate" (*PJS* 1:10).

From April 7 through the end of June 1829, when they finished the translation, Joseph dictated while Oliver wrote, with "utmost gratitude" for the privilege (*Messenger and Advocate* 1:14). Oliver penned a letter then, expressing deep love for

Oliver Cowdery (1806–1850), scribe to Joseph Smith and witness of the Book of Mormon (1829), Second Elder of the Church (1830), and Assistant President of the Church (1834), editor, and lawyer. Cowdery was with Joseph Smith when the Aaronic and Melchizedek priesthoods and keys were restored. After ten years of separation from the Church, he was rebaptized. He died at age forty-three, faithful to his testimony. Photograph, c. 1848, C. W. Carter Collection.

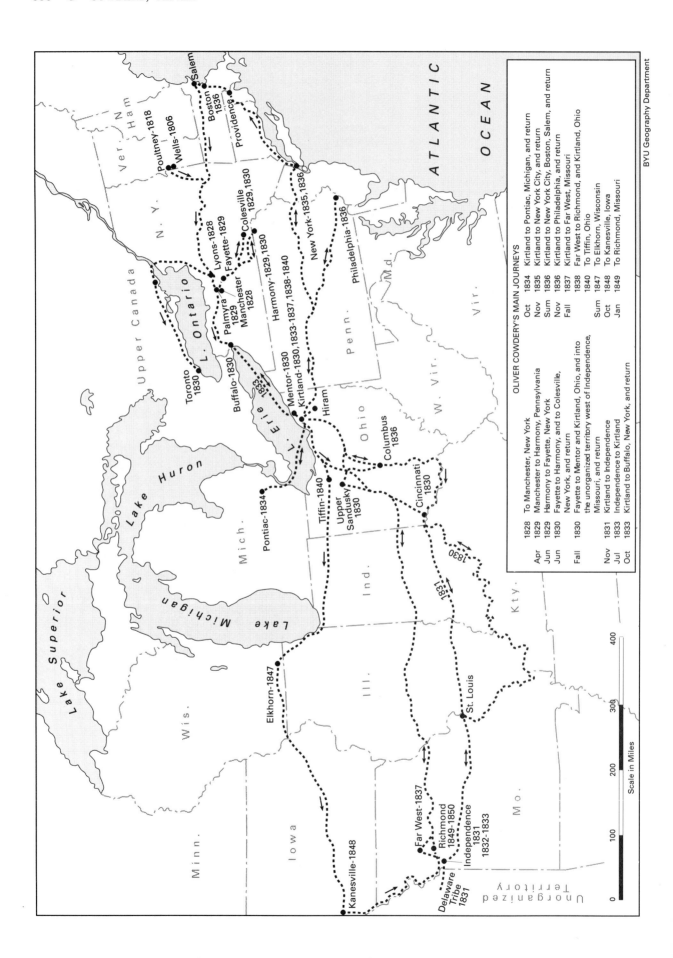

OLIVER COWDERY'S MAIN JOURNEYS

Apr	1828	To Manchester, New York
Jun	1829	Manchester to Harmony, Pennsylvania
Jun	1829	Harmony to Fayette, New York
	1830	Fayette to Harmony, and to Colesville, New York, and return
Fall	1830	Fayette to Mentor and Kirtland, Ohio, and into the unorganized territory west of Independence, Missouri, and return
Nov	1831	Kirtland to Independence
Jul	1833	Independence to Kirtland
Oct	1833	Kirtland to Buffalo, New York, and return
Oct	1834	Kirtland to Pontiac, Michigan, and return
Nov	1835	Kirtland to New York City, and return
Sum	1836	Kirtland to New York City, Boston, Salem, and return
Nov	1836	Kirtland to Philadelphia, and return
Fall	1837	Kirtland to Far West, Missouri
	1838	Far West to Richmond, and Kirtland, Ohio
	1840	To Tiffin, Ohio
Sum	1847	To Elkhorn, Wisconsin
Oct	1848	To Kanesville, Iowa
Jan	1849	To Richmond, Missouri

Christ, a lifetime theme. He later told how he and Joseph interrupted their work as they were translating the record of the Savior's post-resurrection American ministry, and how, as they prayed about baptism, they heard the "voice of the Redeemer" and were ministered to by John the Baptist, who gave them authority to baptize (JS—H 1:71, note).

In 1835 Oliver helped Joseph Smith correct and publish the revelations for the DOCTRINE AND COVENANTS. Section 27 lists the major priesthood messengers of the restoration: John the Baptist, whom "I have sent unto you, my servants, Joseph Smith, Jr., and Oliver Cowdery, to ordain you unto this first priesthood" (D&C 27:8); and "Peter, James, and John, whom I have sent unto you, by whom I have ordained you and confirmed you to be apostles and especial witnesses of my name, and bear the keys of your ministry" (D&C 27:12).

The lesser priesthood was restored on May 15, 1829, two weeks before the Prophet and Cowdery moved to the Whitmers' in New York to complete the translation of the Book of Mormon (HC 1:39–41, 48–49). The higher priesthood also came before this move; David Whitmer remembered he was ordained as an elder only weeks after their first arrival at his upstate farm (Whitmer, p. 32). The ancient apostles appeared with priesthood KEYS as Joseph and Oliver traveled between their Pennsylvania home and Colesville, New York (D&C 128:20), where Joseph Knight, Sr., lived. Knight remembered their seeking help to sustain them while translating in April or May (Jessee, p. 36).

After the move to the Whitmer farm, the angel showed the plates to Joseph Smith and the Three Witnesses in June 1829. Oliver supervised the printing of the Book of Mormon that fall and winter. After the publication of the book on March 26, the Church was organized on April 6, 1830. Oliver spoke in meeting the next Sunday, which was "the first public discourse that was delivered by any of our number" (HC 1:81).

Few exceeded Cowdery in logical argument and elevated style. Moreover, his speeches and writings carry the tone of personal knowledge. Generally serving as editor or associate editor in the first publications of the Church, Oliver wrote with unusual consistency through two decades of published writings and personal letters. He insisted that a relationship with God required constant contact: "Whenever [God] has had a people on earth, he always has revealed himself to them by the Holy Ghost, the ministering of angels, or his own voice" (Messenger and Advocate 1:2). Oliver Cowdery led the LAMANITE MISSION, the first major mission of the Church (D&C 28:8; 30:5), which doubled Church membership and took the Book of Mormon to Native Americans. After the temple site was designated in Jackson County in 1831, he traveled there with copies of the revelations for their first printing. Because publishing was vital for spreading the gospel and instructing members, Oliver was called to work with William W. Phelps, an experienced editor (D&C 55:4; 57:11–13). After Missouri ruffians destroyed the press, Cowdery returned to Ohio to counsel with Church leaders, who assigned him to relocate Church publications there. Because of the importance of accurate information, he and Sidney RIGDON remained in Ohio in 1834 when many faithful men marched to Missouri with ZION'S CAMP to assist the Saints in returning to their homes and land in Jackson County.

In 1830–1831, Oliver Cowdery served as the first Church Recorder, a calling he again resumed between 1835 and 1837 (see HISTORIANS, CHURCH). Even in other years, he often kept the official minutes of meetings, and was often editor and contributor for the first Church newspapers. He wrote articles for the MESSENGER AND ADVOCATE that help document early LDS history. From June to October 1830, Oliver served as scribe while the Prophet completed important portions of the JOSEPH SMITH TRANSLATION OF THE BIBLE.

An 1830 revelation named Oliver Cowdery next only to Joseph Smith in priesthood leadership (D&C 20:2–3), a status formalized in December 1834, when he was ranked above Sidney RIGDON, who had long served as Joseph's first counselor. Each would "officiate in the absence of the President, according to his rank and appointment, viz.: President Cowdery first; President Rigdon second, and President Williams third" (PJS 1:21). Cowdery wrote that this calling was foretold in the first heavenly ordination, though Missouri printing duties had intervened: "This promise was made by the angel while in company with President Smith, at the time they received the office of the lesser

←——Oliver Cowdery's journeys, 1806–1850.

priesthood" (*PJS* 1:21; cf. *HC* 1:40–41). His office next to the Prophet—sometimes called "associate president"—was given to Hyrum SMITH in 1841 (D&C 124: 194–6), after Cowdery's excommunication (*see* FIRST PRESIDENCY).

Oliver's Church career peaked from 1834 to 1836. Minutes and letters picture him as a highly effective preacher, writer, and administrator. His 1836 journal survives, showing his devotion to religion and family, his political activities, his study of Hebrew, and the spiritual power he shared at the completion of the Kirtland Temple. Cowdery's last entry in this journal, penned the day of the temple dedication, says of the evening meeting: "I saw the glory of God, like a great cloud, come down and rest upon the house. . . . I also saw cloven tongues like as of fire rest upon many . . . while they spake with other tongues and prophesied" (Arrington, p. 426).

Oliver also alluded to more. A year later he penned an editorial "Valedictory." After mentioning "my mission from the holy messenger" prior to the organization of the Church, he wrote that such manifestations were to be expected, since the Old Testament promised that God would "reveal his glorious arm" in the latter days "and talk with his people *face to face*" (*Messenger and Advocate* 3:548). The words he italicized match his recent temple vision of Christ on April 3, 1836, which he experienced in company with the Prophet (D&C 110:1–10). This was also the time that these first priesthood leaders received special priesthood keys from Moses, Elias, and Elijah, completing restoration of the "keys of the kingdom" (D&C 27:6–13) and completing Cowdery's mission as "second witness" to such restoration. Oliver had deep confidence in divine appearances. In 1835 he charged the newly appointed Twelve: "Never cease striving until you have seen God face to face" (*HC* 2:195).

Despite these profound spiritual experiences, Oliver's letters reveal a crisis of personal and family estrangement from Joseph Smith by early 1838. The Three Witnesses had seen an angel with Joseph Smith, but later they tended to compete rather than cooperate with his leadership. Cowdery disagreed with the Prophet's economic and political program and sought a personal financial independence that ran counter to the cooperative economics essential to the Zion society that Joseph Smith envisioned. Nonetheless, when Oliver was tried for his membership, he sent a resignation let-

ter in which he insisted that the truth of modern revelation was not at issue: "Take no view of the foregoing remarks, other than my belief on the outward government of this Church" (*Far West Record*, pp. 165–66).

This trial was related to the excommunications of Oliver's brothers-in-law John Whitmer and David Whitmer, also at this time; this paralleled Oliver's earlier support of the Whitmer family in the matter of Hiram Page's competing revelations (D&C 28:11–13). The Church court considered five charges against Cowdery: inactivity, accusing the Prophet of adultery, and three charges of beginning law practice and seeking to collect debts after the Kirtland bank failure (*see* KIRTLAND ECONOMY).

Oliver's charge of adultery against the Prophet was simplistic, for Oliver already knew about the principle of PLURAL MARRIAGE. Rather than deny the charge, the Prophet testified that because Oliver had been his "bosom friend," he had "intrusted him with many things" (*Far West Record*, 168). Brigham YOUNG later said that the doctrine was revealed to Joseph and Oliver during the Book of Mormon translation (cf. Jacob 2:30); clearly a fuller understanding of the principle of plural marriage came by 1832, in connection with Joseph Smith's translation of Genesis (cf. D&C 130:1–2). Brigham Young added that Oliver impetuously proceeded without Joseph's permission, not knowing "the order and pattern and the results" (Charles Walker Journal, July 26, 1872, Church Archives). Oliver married Elizabeth Ann Whitmer in 1832, and problems with polygamy apparently influenced him and the Whitmer family to oppose the principle later.

In 1838, following his excommunication, Oliver returned to Ohio, though he did not, as a fictitious deed states, then pay Bishop Edward Partridge $1,000 for the temple lot in Independence on behalf of his children, John, Jane, and Joseph Cowdery. Such children never existed; Oliver had no such money and showed no interest in Jackson County then or later. In fact, he continued law study and practiced in Kirtland, but in 1840 he moved to Tiffin, Ohio, where he became a prominent civic leader as an ardent Democrat. His law notices and public service regularly appeared in local newspapers, and he was personally sketched in the warm recollections of the prominent Ohio lawyer William Lang, who apprenticed under Cowdery and described him as being of slight build, about five and a half feet tall, clean, and courteous. Professionally, Cowdery was characterized as "an able lawyer," well informed, with "brilliant" speaking ability; yet "he was modest and reserved, never spoke ill of anyone, never complained" (Anderson, 1981, p. 41).

In 1847 Oliver moved to Wisconsin, where he continued his law practice and was almost elected to the first state legislature, in spite of newspaper accounts ridiculing his published declaration of seeing the angel and the plates. In his ten years outside the Church, Cowdery never succumbed to the considerable pressure to deny his Book of Mormon testimony. Indeed, letters to his LDS relatives show that he was hurt at the Church's rejection but remained a deep believer. Feeling that his character had been slandered, he asked for public exoneration, explaining that anyone would be sensitive about reputation "had you stood in the presence of John with our departed Brother Joseph, to receive the Lesser Priesthood, and in the presence of Peter, to receive the Greater" (Gunn, pp. 250–51).

These statements contradict a pamphlet that Oliver was alleged to have published in 1839 as a "Defense" for leaving the Church (see FORGERIES). Surfacing in 1906, it portrays Oliver as confused about seeing John the Baptist. But no original exists, nor does any reference to it in Cowdery's century. Its style borrows published Cowdery phrases but rearranges his conclusions. A clumsier forgery is the "Confession of Oliver Overstreet," which claims that the author was bribed to impersonate Cowdery and return to the Church. Abundant documents show that Oliver returned to Council Bluffs, Iowa, in 1848 with his wife and young daughter.

Diaries and official minutes record Oliver Cowdery's words in rejoining the Church. He sought only rebaptism and fellowship, not office. He publicly declared that he had seen and handled the Book of Mormon plates, and that he was present with Joseph Smith on the occasions when "holy angels" restored the two priesthoods (Anderson, *BYU Studies*, 1968, p. 278). The High Council questioned him closely about his published letter (to David Whitmer) in which Oliver claimed that he retained the keys of priesthood leadership after Joseph Smith's death. That was his opinion, Oliver said, before seeing the Nauvoo revelation giving all powers to Hyrum Smith "that once were put upon him that was my servant Oliver Cowdery" (D&C

124:95). "It was that revelation which changed my views on this subject" (Anderson, *IE*, Nov. 1968, p. 19).

Because they had started for Council Bluffs late in the season, the Cowdery family were forced to winter in Richmond, Missouri, where most of the Whitmer family lived. Letters throughout 1849 repeat Oliver's hope to move west and also disclose his lack of means. They speak of his coughing up blood, a long-term respiratory condition that finally took his life March 3, 1850. The circuit court recorded a resolution of fellow lawyers that in the death of "Oliver Cowdery, his profession has lost an accomplished member, and the community a valuable and worthy citizen" (Anderson, 1981, p. 46).

David Whitmer and other relatives living near Oliver Cowdery in his final year later claimed that he disagreed with many Kirtland and Nauvoo doctrines, but Oliver's documented criticisms at this time concern only intolerance and a continuing concern about polygamy. Although David Whitmer considered Joseph a fallen prophet, in 1848 Cowdery said publicly and privately "that Joseph Smith had fulfilled his mission faithfully before God until death" (Geo. A. Smith to Orson Pratt, *MS* 11 [Oct. 20, 1848]:14), and "that the priesthood was with this people, and the 'Twelve' were the only men that could lead the Church after the death of Joseph" (Anderson, *IE*, Nov. 1968, p. 18). In his last known letter, Oliver accepted an assignment from the Twelve to lobby in Washington, and acknowledged the leadership of the "good brethren of the [Salt Lake] valley" (Gunn, p. 261).

Oliver's wife, Elizabeth Ann Whitmer Cowdery (1815–1892), had known him when he was taking dictation during the translation of the Book of Mormon, before their marriage. Said she of his lifelong commitment: "He always without one doubt . . . affirmed the divinity and truth of the Book of Mormon" (Anderson, 1981, p. 63). This confidence stood the test of persecution, poverty, loss of status, failing health, and the tragic deaths of five of his six children. Dying at forty-three, Oliver was surrounded by family members who told how he reaffirmed the divinity of the Book of Mormon and the restored priesthood—and voiced total trust in Christ. Just before rejoining the Church, he penned his inner hopes to fellow witness David Whitmer: "Let the Lord vindicate our characters, and cause our testimony to shine, and then will men be saved in his kingdom" (Oliver

Cowdery to David Whitmer, July 28, 1847, *Ensign of Liberty*, 1:92).

BIBLIOGRAPHY

Anderson, Richard L. "Reuben Miller, Recorder of Oliver Cowdery's Reaffirmations." *BYU Studies* 8 (Spring 1968):277–93.

———. "The Second Witness of Priesthood Restoration." *IE* 71 (Sept. 1968):15–24; and 71 (Nov. 1968):14–20.

———. *Investigating the Book of Mormon Witnesses*. Salt Lake City, 1981.

Arrington, Leonard J. "Oliver Cowdery's Kirtland, Ohio, 'Sketch Book.'" *BYU Studies* 12 (Summer 1972):410–26.

Cannon, Donald Q., and Lyndon W. Cook. *Far West Record*. Salt Lake City, 1983.

Gunn, Stanley R. *Oliver Cowdery, Second Elder and Scribe*. Salt Lake City, 1962.

Jessee, Dean C. "Joseph Knight's Recollection of Early Mormon History." *BYU Studies* 17 [1976]:36.

Porter, Larry C. "Dating the Restoration of the Melchizedek Priesthood." *Ensign* 9 (June 1979):5–10.

Whitmer, David. *Address to All Believers in Christ*. Richmond, Mo., 1887.

RICHARD LLOYD ANDERSON

CREATION, CREATION ACCOUNTS

Latter-day Saints have, in addition to the biblical Genesis, two modern restorations of ancient scriptural accounts of the Creation in the BOOK OF MOSES and the BOOK OF ABRAHAM. Related authoritative information also appears in the Book of Mormon, the Doctrine and Covenants, and the LDS temple ceremony. Drawing on this wealth of creation literature, Latter-day Saints understand that Jesus Christ, acting under the direction of God the Father, created this and other worlds to make possible the immortality and eternal life of human beings who already existed as spirit children of the Father. This understanding differs from both scientific and traditional Christian accounts in that it affirms God's purpose and role, while recognizing creation as organization of pre-existing materials, and not as an ex nihilo event (creation from nothing). Furthermore, these accounts describe an active role for God's spirit children in the Creation and include a more detailed version of the origins of EVIL.

The frequent occurrence of creation accounts in LDS scriptures and sacred ceremonies reflects a pattern of the ancient world generally, and ancient Israel in particular, where the Creation was regularly recited or reenacted. The Creation—including its ritual recitation and reenactment—was viewed by the Israelites and other peoples of the ancient Near East as possessing a dynamic, not a static, quality. According to Raffaele Pettazzoni, a noted historian of religions, "What happened in the beginning has an exemplary and defining value for what is happening today and what will happen in the future" (p. 26).

Creation plays a central theological role in the Book of Mormon. The events surrounding creation are linked with the fall of that angel who became the DEVIL (2 Ne. 2:17; 9:8). His fall, in turn, led to the FALL OF ADAM; opposition as a feature of mortal existence; and, ultimately, the need for a divine redemption of mankind (2 Ne. 2:18–27). Book of Mormon prophets invoked the Creation as a symbol of God's goodness and a touchstone of human stewardship: "The Lord hath created the earth that it should be inhabited; and he hath created his children that they should possess it" (1 Ne. 17:36). Those who reject God's goodness, as symbolized by the Creation (and the Atonement), will inevitably be judged and punished (cf. 2 Ne. 1:10).

The creation account in the book of Moses (revealed in 1830 as the beginning of the JOSEPH SMITH TRANSLATION OF THE BIBLE) provides several insights in addition to those found in Genesis.

First, the book of Moses establishes Mosaic authorship of its creation account indicating explicitly that it resulted from a revelation given to Moses sometime between the time of the burning bush and the exodus (Moses 1:17, 25).

Second, it clarifies the role of Jesus Christ in the Creation: "By the word of my power have I created [these lands and their inhabitants], which is mine Only Begotten Son" (Moses 1:32–33); "I, God, said unto mine Only Begotten, which was with me from the beginning: Let us make man in our image" (Moses 2:26–27); "And I, the Lord God, said unto mine Only Begotten: Behold, the man is become as one of us to know good and evil" (Moses 4:28). This is consistent with the teachings of John and Paul in the New Testament (John 1:3, 10; Eph. 3:9; Col. 1:13–16; Heb. 1:2, 10).

Third, the Creation is placed in a much larger context of ongoing creations of innumerable inhabited earths with their respective heavens (in all of which Christ played a central role): "And worlds without number have I created . . . for mine own purpose; and by the Son I created them, which is mine Only Begotten. . . . And as one earth shall pass away, and the heavens thereof even so shall another come; and there is no end to my works" (Moses 1:33, 38; *see also* WORLDS). Moses is given details of the creation of "this heaven, and this earth" only (Moses 2:1; cf. 1:35).

Fourth, the origin of evil is traced back to the rebellion of Satan, who sought (1) to replace God's Beloved Son, who had been "chosen from the beginning," and (2) to receive and use God's own power to redeem all humans by destroying their agency (Moses 4:1–4). The importance of human agency is reaffirmed in the command to ADAM and EVE concerning the tree of knowledge of good and evil: "Thou shalt not eat of it, nevertheless, thou mayest choose for thyself, for it is given unto thee; but remember that I forbid it, for in the day thou eatest thereof thou shalt surely die" (Moses 3:17).

Fifth, the account in Moses makes clear that there was a spirit creation of all living things in heaven before they were created physically upon the earth: "I, the Lord God, created all things, of which I have spoken, spiritually, before they were naturally upon the face of the earth. . . . And I, the Lord God, had created all the children of men; and not yet a man to till the ground; for in heaven created I them; and there was not yet flesh upon the earth, neither in the water, neither in the air" (Moses 3:5).

Certain LDS commentators have explored the possibility that the Moses account could resolve the apparent conflict in the order of God's creative acts between Genesis 1 and Genesis 2 by treating the first as a spirit creation (O. Pratt, pp. 21–22; Roberts, pp. 264–68; cf. *DS* 1:74–76, which explains a different view). Later revelations make it clear that mankind's spirit creation had taken place long before the events described in any of the accounts of the earth's creation. God, our Heavenly Father, is literally the "Father of spirits" (Heb. 12:9). "Man as a spirit was begotten and born of heavenly parents, and reared to maturity in the eternal mansions of the Father, prior to coming upon the earth in a temporal body" (*see* First Presidency, "The Origin of Man," Nov. 1909 [Appendix]; *see also* SPIRIT BODY).

The Abrahamic account is distinctive among creation accounts. It describes a structured cosmos, with many stars, one above another, with their different periods and orders of government (Abr. 3:1–10). Within this context Abraham also learns about eternally existing SPIRITS, one above

the other in intelligence, all the way up to "the Lord thy God," who is "more intelligent than they all" (Abr. 3:19; see speeches cited in bibliography). He is shown a group of organized intelligences (or spirits, or souls—the words are here used interchangeably), over whom God rules and among whom he dwells, and is taught that "in the beginning" God came down in the midst of them, and said of some who were "noble and great": "These I will make my rulers. . . . And he said unto me: Abraham, thou art one of them; thou wast chosen before thou wast born" (Abr. 3:18–23). A purpose of this premortal assembly in heaven is explained by "one among them that was like unto God," who says to those who are with him, "We will go down . . . and we will make an earth whereon these may dwell; and we will prove them herewith, to see if they will do all things whatsoever the Lord their God shall command them" (Abr. 3:24–25). This is followed by a pronouncement of the glory to come upon those who prove worthy, the choosing of one "like unto the Son of Man" (who is to be sent to bring this about), and the rejection of Satan—all done by "the Lord," who is identified elsewhere as Jehovah (Abr. 3:25–28; cf. Abr. 1:15–16; 2:7–8). Thereafter, "the Lord said: Let us go down," whereupon the Gods "organized and formed the heavens and the earth" (Abr. 4:1). A significant feature of this revealed account is that both the space and the materials for the earth explicitly existed before its creation.

Within this context of the divine assembly, or COUNCIL IN HEAVEN, Abraham's account of the Creation proceeds, generally following the structural outline of Genesis. By the time Joseph Smith published this "translation" in 1842, he had gained a much deeper understanding both through additional revelation and some through study of Hebrew. In light of the doctrine of the council in heaven, Joseph Smith had pointed out that the Hebrew term *Elohim*, a plural form, should be rendered the "Gods" in the creation account, not as the traditional "God" (*WJS*, p. 379). It is so rendered throughout Abraham's account. In light of the doctrine of the eternal nature of matter, the word traditionally translated as "created" becomes "organized." The phrase "without form and void" (Hebrew *tohu wa-bohu*) is rendered, quite properly, "empty and desolate" and describes the condition of the earth after it was organized, not before (Abr. 4:2).

The term "day" (Hebrew *yom*) for the seven

"days" of creation is given as "time," a permissible alternative in both Hebrew and English; and it is explicitly pointed out that the "time" in which Adam should die if he partook of the forbidden fruit "was after the Lord's time, which was after the time of Kolob [a great star that Abraham had seen nearest to the throne of God, whose revolution, one thousand years by our reckoning, is a day unto the Lord]; for as yet the Gods had not appointed unto Adam his reckoning" (Abr. 5:13; 3:2–4).

On the basis of the above passage, which clearly excludes the possibility of earthly twenty-four-hour days being the "days" or "times" of creation, some Latter-day Saint commentators have argued for one-thousand-year periods as the "times" of creation as well as the "time" of Adam's earthly life after the fall; others have argued for indefinite periods of time, as long as it would take to accomplish the work involved. Abraham's account does contain the interesting passage, in connection with the "organizing" of the lights in the "expanse" of heaven, "The Gods watched those things which they had ordered until they obeyed" (Abr. 4:14–18). Abraham's account actually includes twelve different "labors" of the Gods, divided up among the "days" in the manner of Genesis. The later temple account of creation gives an abbreviated version of those labors, divided up differently among the seven days while retaining the same order, suggesting that it may not be significant which labor is assigned to which day.

Abraham connects the seemingly differing accounts of Genesis 1 and 2 within the context of the council in heaven. Abraham's seven-day account proceeds through the work of the first five creative times and part of the sixth as the physical creation of the earth and its preparation to support life before life was actually placed upon it. Thus, during the third time, "the Gods organized the earth *to bring forth* grass . . . and the earth *to bring forth* the tree from its own seed" (Abr. 4:12; emphasis added). And during the fifth time, the Gods "prepared the waters that they might bring forth great whales, and every living creature, . . . and every winged fowl after their kind" (Abr. 4:21). Similarly, on the sixth time "the Gods prepared the earth *to bring forth* the living creature after his kind. . . . And the Gods saw they would obey" (Abr. 4:24–25). Then upon the sixth time, the Gods again took counsel among themselves and determined to form man, and to give them dominion over the plants and animals that should come

upon the earth (Abr. 4:26–29). "And the Gods said among themselves: On the seventh time we will end our work, which we have counseled; and we will rest. . . . And thus were their decisions at the time that they counseled among themselves" (Abr. 5:2–3). The account paralleling Genesis 2 then follows smoothly as an account of the actual placing of life upon the earth: "And the Gods came down and formed these the generations of the heavens and of the earth, when they were formed in the day that the Gods formed the earth and the heavens, according to all that which they had said concerning every plant of the field before it was in the earth" (Abr. 5:4–5).

Several themes in other ancient creation accounts—premortal conflict in heaven, divine victory over the opposing powers of chaos, and the promulgation of law at the time of creation—are also familiar from creation accounts in LDS scripture and theology (2 Ne. 2:17; 9:8; Moses 4:3–4; Abr. 3:27–28; *see also* WAR IN HEAVEN; PREEXISTENCE). These ideas are alluded to in several places in the Bible (cf. Ex. 15; Job 38–41; Isa. 40–42; Ps. 18; 19; 24; 33; 68; 93; 104; Prov. 8:22–33; Hab. 3:8; Rev. 12:7–12). From the early Christian era until the end of the nineteenth century, traditional Christian interpretation has generally treated these biblical texts allegorically or has not considered them at all in discussions of the Creation. A profound transformation in the Christian interpretation of these passages took place during the latter part of the nineteenth century with the discovery and translation of creation accounts from ancient Mesopotamia and Egypt. While these accounts vary considerably in detail, they usually mention premortal combats, the establishment of the divine order before creation, and creation from chaos. The biblical passages mentioned above are now often understood in light of these descriptions of extrabiblical accounts.

The doctrine of ex nihilo creation has been the traditional Christian explanation. In recent discussion of the subject, many Jewish scholars agreed that the belief in an ex nihilo creation is not to be found before the Hellenistic period, while Christian scholars see no evidence of this doctrine in the Christian church until the end of the second century A.D. The rejection of ex nihilo creation in the teaching of the Latter-day Saints thus accords with the evidence of the earliest understanding of the Creation in ancient Israel and in early Christianity. Similarly, Latter-day Saints have understood such biblical passages as John 9:2 and Jeremiah 1:4–5 to refer to individual premortal existence, with implications for subsequent earthly existence. In support of this, it may be pointed out that various Christians and Christian groups in the early Christian centuries taught the same doctrine (cf. Origen, *De principiis* 1:7; 2:8; 4:1), and that it is also to be found in Jewish belief of the same period, including Philo (*De mutatione nominum* 39; *De opificio mundi* 51; *De cherubim* 32); in some apocryphal writings (Wisdom of Solomon 8:19–20; 15:3); and among the Essenes (Josephus, *Jewish War* 2.8.11, as well as in the Jewish Talmud and Midrash).

BIBLIOGRAPHY

Anderson, Bernhard W. "Creation." In *Interpreter's Dictionary of the Bible*, Vol. 1, pp. 725–32. New York, 1962.

Eliade, Mircea. "The Prestige of the Cosmogonic Myth." *Diogenes* 23 (Fall 1958):1–13.

Goldstein, Jonathan A. "The Origins of the Doctrine of Creation *Ex Nihilo.*" *Journal of Jewish Studies* 35 (Autumn 1984):127–35.

McConkie, Bruce R. "Christ and the Creation." *Ensign* 12 (June 1982):9–15.

Pettazzoni, Raffaele. "Myths of Beginnings and Creation-Myths." In Pettazzoni, *Essays on the History of Religions*, H. J. Rose, trans., Vol. 1, pp. 24–36. Leiden, 1954.

Pratt, Orson. "The Pre-existence of Man." Serialized in *The Seer* (1853–1854). Photo repr., Salt Lake City, 1990.

Pratt, Parley P. "Origin of the Universe." In Pratt, *The Key to the Science of Theology*, pp. 26–32. Salt Lake City, 1978.

Roberts, B. H. *The Gospel and Man's Relationship to Deity*, pp. 256–73. Salt Lake City, 1966.

Salisbury, Frank B. *The Creation.* Salt Lake City, 1976.

Smith, Joseph. See speeches reported in *WJS*, pp. 9, 33, 60, 341, 346, 351–52, and 359 and their contexts.

Smith, Joseph Fielding. *Man, His Origin and Destiny.* Salt Lake City, 1954.

Winston, David. "Creation Ex Nihilo Revisited: A Reply to Jonathan Goldstein." *Journal of Jewish Studies* 37 (Spring 1986):88–91.

Young, Brigham. *Discourses of Brigham Young*, chaps. 2, 4, 9. Salt Lake City, 1954.

F. KENT NIELSEN
STEPHEN D. RICKS

CREEDS

The Church of Jesus Christ of Latter-day Saints has no creed, as that term is understood in traditional theology. Truth and the things of God are comprehended by study, faith, reason, science, experience, personal revelation, and revelation received through the prophets of God. Creeds, on the other hand, tend to delimit this process.

From the beginning of the Church until the present, its view has always been that such formulas are incompatible with the gospel's inclusive commitment to truth and continual revelation. The Doctrine and Covenants states, "He that receiveth light, and continueth in God, receiveth more light and that light groweth brighter and brighter until the perfect day" (D&C 50:24). In his FIRST VISION in 1820, the young Prophet Joseph SMITH was told that the creeds of the competing churches around him "were an abomination in [God's] sight" (*HC* 1:19). These sweeping words were clarified in his WENTWORTH LETTER (1842): "all were teaching incorrect doctrines." During the April 1843 conference of the Church, the Prophet said: "It does not prove that a man is not a good man because he errs in doctrine" (*HC* 5:340), and later he elaborated: "I cannot believe in any of the creeds of the different denominations, though all of them have some truth. I want to come up into the presence of God, and learn all things, but the creeds set up stakes, and say, 'Hitherto shalt thou come, and no further,' which I cannot subscribe to" (*HC* 6:67).

Since Joseph Smith's day, the Christian world has moved in this direction by acknowledging that creeds are "historically conditioned," and that confessions of faith are to be seen as "guidelines" rather than as final pronouncements.

Authoritative statements found in LDS literature are not viewed as elements in a creed. For example, although its thirteen ARTICLES OF FAITH are scriptural, they are open-ended. One of them says, "We believe all that God has revealed, all that He does now reveal, and we believe that He will yet reveal many great and important things pertaining to the Kingdom of God" (A of F 9). During fast and testimony meetings, usually on the first Sunday of each month, the conviction is often expressed by members that they know that God lives, that Jesus is the Christ, the Son of the Living God, and that Joseph Smith and the living prophets are true prophets of God. These words in some respects parallel the Islamic confession of faith, or Shahadah, which is also not considered a creed.

BIBLIOGRAPHY

Gerrish, B. A. "Creeds." In *Encyclopedia of Religion*, ed. Mircea Eliade. New York, 1987.

McConkie, Bruce R. *MD*, pp. 170–72. Salt Lake City, 1966.

GARY P. GILLUM

CREMATION

Since the organization of the Church in 1830, Latter-day Saints have been encouraged by their leaders to avoid cremation, unless it is required by law, and, wherever possible, to consign the body to burial in the earth and leave the dissolution of the body to nature, "for dust thou art, and unto dust shalt thou return" (Gen. 3:19). President Spencer W. KIMBALL wrote, "The meaning of death has not changed. It releases a spirit for growth and development and places a body in . . . Mother Earth" (p. 45). In due time the mortal body returns to native element, and whether it is laid away in a family-selected site or buried in the depths of the sea, every essential part will be restored in the Resurrection: "Every limb and joint shall be restored to its body; yea, even a hair of the head shall not be lost; but all things shall be restored to their proper and perfect frame" (Alma 40:23).

To understand the LDS feeling about cremation, it is essential to understand the doctrine of the Church regarding the body. In a general conference Elder James E. Talmage, an apostle, stated, "It is peculiar to the theology of the Latter-day Saints that we regard the body as an essential part of the soul. Read your dictionaries, the lexicons, and encyclopedias, and you will find that nowhere, outside of The Church of Jesus Christ, is the solemn and eternal truth taught that the soul of man is the body and the spirit combined" (*CR*, Oct. 1913, p. 117).

BIBLIOGRAPHY

Kimball, Edward L., ed. *The Teachings of Spencer W. Kimball*, p. 45. Salt Lake City, 1982.

Lockhart, Barbara. "The Body: A Burden or a Blessing?" *Ensign* 15 (Feb. 1985):57–60.

Nelson, Russell M. "The Magnificence of Man." *Ensign* 18 (Jan. 1988):64–69.

BRUCE L. OLSEN

CROSS

The cross, a traditional symbol of Christianity, is displayed extensively in Catholicism, Eastern Orthodoxy, and Protestantism. In each tradition, the symbol of the cross focuses the worshiper's attention on central elements of the Christian faith.

The Crucifixion, by Carl Heinrich Bloch (1834–1890; oil on copper plate; 20″ × 30″). The Savior Jesus Christ is crucified on Calvary, offering himself as a sacrifice for mankind. Courtesy the Frederiksborg Museum, Hillerød, Denmark.

However, different theological points may be emphasized. For example, in Catholicism the crucifix (the cross with the dead Christ hanging on it) symbolizes the crucifixion of Christ and invites meditation on the Atonement. In contrast, the plain cross used by Protestants symbolizes not only the crucifixion but also the RESURRECTION of Christ, for the cross is empty. The Eastern Orthodox crucifix is a symbolic concept somewhere between those of Catholicism and Protestantism: Christ hangs on the cross, but as the living Lord, his head not bowed in death but raised in triumph. Thus, the crucifixion, the atonement, the resurrection, and the Lordship of Christ are all graphically presented in the Orthodox crucifix.

Latter-day Saints do not use the symbol of the cross in their ARCHITECTURE or in their chapels. They, like the earliest Christians, are reluctant to display the cross because they view the "good news" of the gospel as Christ's resurrection more than his crucifixion.

The LDS conception of the PLAN OF SALVATION is comprehensive. It encompasses a COUNCIL IN HEAVEN; JEHOVAH's (Jesus') acceptance of his role as Savior; the VIRGIN BIRTH; Jesus' life and ministry; his saving suffering, beginning in Gethsemane and ending with his death at Golgotha; his burial; his preaching to the spirits of the righteous dead; his physical resurrection; and his exaltation to the right hand of the Father. No one symbol is sufficient to convey all this. Moreover, the cross, with its focus on the death of Christ, does not symbolize the message of a living, risen, exalted Lord who changes the lives of his followers. Thus, President Gordon B. Hinckley, counselor in the First Presidency, stated that the lives of people must become a "meaningful expression of our faith and, in fact, therefore, the symbol of our worship" (p. 92).

While the symbol of the cross is not visually displayed among the Latter-day Saints, the centrality of the Atonement is ever present in their observance of BAPTISM, the SACRAMENT of the Lord's Supper, and the temple ordinances, and in their hymns and TESTIMONIES. Without the atonement of Jesus Christ, there is no hope for the human family. Scripture is replete with the admonition that disciples of Christ must "take up their cross," yielding themselves in humility to their Heavenly Father (D&C 56:2, 14–16; 112:14–15), releasing themselves from the ties of WORLDLINESS (3 Ne. 12:20), and submitting themselves to PERSECUTION and even martyrdom for the gospel of Jesus Christ (2 Ne. 9:18; Jacob 1:8).

BIBLIOGRAPHY

Hinckley, Gordon B. "The Symbol of Christ." *Ensign* 5 (May 1975):92–94.

Pocknee, Cyril E. *Cross and Crucifix*. London, 1962.

ROGER R. KELLER

CULT

The word "cult" has usages that range from neutral to pejorative. It derives from the Latin *cultus*, meaning "care" or "adoration." A neutral usage of the word refers to the system of beliefs and rituals connected to the worship of a deity. By this definition, virtually all religions, including The Church of Jesus Christ of Latter-day Saints, exhibit some cultic aspects.

However, the term "cult" more commonly refers to a minority religion that is regarded as unorthodox or spurious and that requires great or even excessive devotion. While the term is commonly used by the mass media and anticult movement in the late twentieth century as a negative label for such recently formed groups as the Unification Church and the International Society for Krishna Consciousness (the Hare Krishna movement), it has also been used to describe Pauline Christianity, Islam during the life of Muhammad, and MORMONISM in the nineteenth century.

The most common social-scientific definition identifies a cult as the beginning phase of an entirely new religion. As defined by this approach, a cult's central characteristic is that it provides a radical break from existing religious traditions (Roberts). The LDS Church's self-understanding of being a restoration movement that restored divine truths, rather than a reformation movement that purified existing truths, is consistent with the social-scientific understanding that nineteenth-century Mormonism was a cult due to its break from the existing religious traditions.

References to cult and other organizational classifications describe the characteristics of religious groups at particular moments in their history. Social scientists use these classifications to describe the normal process of religious evolution. Most groups that start as cults fail to survive more than a single generation; very few evolve into a developed new religion recognized by nonadherents as legitimate or conventional. Obviously, both Christianity and Islam successfully survived the transition from cult to new religion. Social scientists generally agree that The Church of Jesus Christ of Latter-day Saints is no longer properly classified as a cult and should instead be viewed as a new religion. For example, sociologist Rodney Stark identified the LDS Church as the single most important case on the agenda of the scientific study of religion because it demonstrates how a successful new religious movement differs from the thousands of cults that fail to survive or develop into new religions.

[*See also* SECT.]

BIBLIOGRAPHY

Roberts, Keith A. *Religion in Sociological Perspective*, 2nd ed. Belmont, Calif., 1990.

Stark, Rodney. "The Rise of a New World Faith." *Review of Religious Research* 26, no. 1 (1984):18–27.

———. "How New Religions Succeed: A Theoretical Model." In *The Future of New Religious Movements*, ed. D. Bromley and P. Hammond, pp. 11–29. Macon, Ga., 1987.

LAWRENCE A. YOUNG

CUMORAH

Cumorah in the Book of Mormon refers to a hill and surrounding area where the final battle between the NEPHITES and LAMANITES took place, resulting in the annihilation of the Nephite people (*see* BOOK OF MORMON PEOPLES). Sensing the impending destruction of his people, Mormon records that he concealed the plates of Nephi₁ and all the other records entrusted to him in a hill called Cumorah to prevent them from falling into the hands of the Lamanites (*see* BOOK OF MORMON PLATES AND RECORDS). He delivered his own abridgment of these records, called the plates of

The north end of the hill Cumorah, near Palmyra, New York, as it appeared c. 1900. More than thirty years after the final Nephite battle in A.D. 385, Moroni deposited the gold plates on the west side of this hill not far from the top. In 1827, the angel Moroni here entrusted those Book of Mormon plates to Joseph Smith, who translated them into English. The hill is a drumlin, a long hill with steep sides and a sloping end formed under an advancing continental ice sheet. Courtesy Rare Books and Manuscripts, Brigham Young University.

Mormon, and the small plates of Nephi, which he placed with them, to his son MORONI₂ (W of M 1:5; Morm. 6:6), who continued writing on them before burying them in an unmentioned site more than thirty-six years later (Moro. 10:1–2).

The Book of Mormon mentions a number of separate records that would have been part of Mormon's final record repository in the hill Cumorah. Though the contents of these can be known to us only to the extent that they are summarized or mentioned in the Book of Mormon, Latter-day Saints expect them someday to become available. Alma₂ prophesied to his son Helaman that the brass plates of Laban (the Nephites' version of the Old Testament) would be "kept and preserved by the hand of the Lord until they should go forth unto every nation" (Alma 37:4; cf. 1 Ne. 5:17–19). He further explained that "all the plates" containing scripture are the "small and simple" means by which "great things are brought to pass" and by which the Lord will "show forth his power . . . unto future generations" (Alma 37:5–6, 19).

Cumorah had also been the site of the destruction of the JAREDITES roughly 900 years earlier. Moroni states in the book of Ether that the Jaredites gathered for battle near "the hill Ramah," the same hill where his father, Mormon, hid up "the records unto the Lord, which were sacred" (Ether 15:11). It was near the first landing site of the people of Mulek (Alma 22:30), just north of the land Bountiful and a narrow neck of land (Alma 22:32).

The more common reference to Cumorah among Latter-day Saints is to the hill near present-day Palmyra and Manchester, New York, where the plates from which the Prophet Joseph SMITH translated the Book of Mormon were found. During the night of September 21, 1823, Moroni₂ appeared to Joseph Smith as an angel sent from God to show him where these plates were deposited (JS—H 1:29–47).

In 1928 the Church purchased the western New York hill and in 1935 erected a monument recognizing the visit of the angel Moroni (*see* ANGEL MORONI STATUE). A visitors center was later built at the base of the hill. Each summer since 1937, the Church has staged the CUMORAH PAGEANT at this site. Entitled *America's Witness for Christ,* it depicts important events from Book of Mormon history. This annual pageant has reinforced the common assumption that Moroni buried the plates of Mormon in the same hill where his father had buried the other plates, thus equating this New York hill with the Book of Mormon Cumorah. Because the New York site does not readily fit the Book of Mormon description of BOOK OF MORMON GEOGRAPHY, some Latter-day Saints have looked for other possible explanations and locations, including Mesoamerica. Although some have identified possible sites that may seem to fit better (Palmer), there are no conclusive connections between the Book of Mormon text and any specific site that has been suggested.

BIBLIOGRAPHY

Clark, John. "A Key for Evaluating Nephite Geographies." *Review of Books on the Book of Mormon* 1 (1989):20–70.

Palmer, David A. *In Search of Cumorah: New Evidences for the Book of Mormon from Ancient Mexico.* Bountiful, Utah, 1981.

Sorenson, John L. "Digging into the Book of Mormon: Part One." *Ensign* 14 (1984):26–37.

DAVID A. PALMER

CUMORAH PAGEANT

America's Witness for Christ has been presented at the hill CUMORAH in upstate New York nearly every summer since 1937. Recognized as one of America's largest and most spectacular outdoor theatrical events, it attracts an annual audience of almost 100,000 visitors to its seven performances.

This tradition dates back to 1917, when B. H. Roberts and a group of missionaries went to the Joseph Smith farm outside Palmyra, New York, to celebrate PIONEER DAY. Commencing in 1922, the "Palmyra Celebration" became an annual missionary conference for the Eastern States Mission. In July 1935, as part of the dedicatory exercises for the Angel Moroni Monument, trumpeters at the crest of the hill heralded the commencement of the first production at Cumorah. The next year a pageant, "Truth from the Earth," was presented, and plans were announced to make a pageant at the hill Cumorah an annual event.

Two pageants were presented in 1937: a play about the Mormon pioneer handcart companies, *The Builders* by Oliver R. Smith, on July 24, and *America's Witness For Christ* by H. Wayne Driggs on July 23 and 25. The latter script, with occasional revisions, was then presented annually for fifty years (excluding 1943–47). Harold I. Hansen, a

missionary with theatrical training, was named codirector and thereafter continued as director for forty years, overseeing the installation of a sound system built by stereophonic sound pioneer Harvey Fletcher, the expansion of the all-volunteer cast and crew to almost six hundred participants, and the run extended to seven performances. In 1957 the pageant was recorded with original music by Crawford Gates.

On July 22, 1988, a new *America's Witness for Christ*, written by Orson Scott Card with music again by Crawford Gates, premiered. Its major theme—the reality of Christ's atonement, resurrection, and ministry to the Nephites—is boldly portrayed through events recorded in the Book of Mormon. The visual aspects of the pageant were also updated, with new stages, seating, properties, costumes, and special effects, and a recontoured and landscaped hill.

BIBLIOGRAPHY

Argetsinger, Gerald S. "Palmyra: A Look at 40 Years of Pageant." *Ensign* 7 (Dec. 1977):70–71.

Armstrong, Richard N., and Gerald S. Argetsinger. "The Hill Cumorah Pageant: Religious Pageantry as Suasive Form." *Text and Performance Quarterly* 2 (1989):153–64.

Whitman, Charles W. "A History of the Hill Cumorah Pageant, 1937–1964." Ph.D. diss., University of Minnesota, 1967.

GERALD S. ARGETSINGER

CURRICULUM

The Church provides a standard set of curricular materials to all of its units throughout the world. Some matters of basic curriculum had been formatted and distributed to the Church membership since the early days of the Church, but as the AUXILIARY ORGANIZATIONS were formed, such as the Sunday School, Primary, Relief Society, and the Young Men and Young Women, each developed its own curriculum to help teach members. Eventually it became desirable to coordinate curriculum materials among these auxiliary organizations to avoid undesirable duplication and to ensure the coverage of important topics at all age levels.

At present, over 200 topics are considered annually in the lesson manuals prepared for the courses included in the Church curriculum. These topics are in the general areas of gospel principles and doctrines, home and family relationships, priesthood and Church government, historical study of the scriptures and the Church, development of individual talents and abilities, community relations, development of leadership abilities, teaching skills and talents, recreational and social activities, and fellowshipping and service activities (Table 1).

TABLE 1

1. HOME AND FAMILY RELATIONSHIPS
  1.1 Maintaining a spiritual atmosphere in the home
    1.1.1 Having regular family and individual prayers
    1.1.2 Keeping the Sabbath Day holy
    1.1.3 Establishing the home as the center for gospel study
    1.1.4 Seeking the inspiration of the Holy Ghost in all family affairs
  1.2 Building right relationships with other family members
  1.3 Building confidence and trust in the lives of members of the family
  1.4 Developing and fostering individual talents and abilities within the family circle
  1.5 Settling family problems harmoniously
  1.6 Managing family finances according to gospel principles
  1.7 Developing self-discipline and proper conduct in the home
  1.8 Promoting respect for the property of other family members
  1.9 Learning about human maturation and the process of procreation in the family circle
  1.10 Conducting an eternal courtship
  1.11 Honoring the priesthood and the patriarchal order in the home
  1.12 Honoring womanhood and the distinctive role of girls and women
  1.13 Honoring manhood and the distinctive role of men and boys
  1.14 Developing modesty and virtue in the home
  1.15 Playing together and having fun as a family
  1.16 Sharing in the family work schedule
  1.17 Appreciating and loving relatives
  1.18 Developing parental skills
  1.19 Learning to use time wisely
  1.20 Being responsible for the temporal well-being of family members
2. GOSPEL PRINCIPLES AND DOCTRINES
  2.1 Developing an understanding of and a love for the members of the Godhead
    2.1.1 The Father
    2.1.2 The Son
    2.1.3 The Holy Ghost
  2.2 Learning the true nature of man and his relationship to the Godhead
    2.1.1 As an intelligence
    2.2.2 As a spirit child of Heavenly Father
    2.2.3 As spirit brothers and sisters of Jesus Christ
    2.2.4 The potential to become like Heavenly Father
      2.2.4.1 Understanding oneself and developing self-esteem
  2.3 Gaining an understanding and testimony of the Plan of Salvation
    2.3.1 The premortal existence of man
      2.3.1.1 The grand council in heaven
      2.3.1.2 The principle of agency in the pre-existence
      2.3.1.3 Lucifer
      2.3.1.4 Jehovah and his followers
      2.3.1.5 The doctrine of foreordination
    2.3.2 The nature and purpose of mortal life
      2.3.2.1 The earth, its creation and destiny
      2.3.2.2 The need for a body of flesh and bone
      2.3.2.3 The fall of Adam and Eve and all mankind (the spiritual and physical deaths)
      2.3.2.4 Probation of man: personal accountability and free agency
      2.3.2.5 Universal faith
      2.3.2.6 Faith in the Godhead
        2.3.2.6.1 Faith in God the Father
        2.3.2.6.2 Faith in Jesus Christ
      2.3.2.7 Repentance
      2.3.2.8 Baptism
      2.3.2.9 Obedience: enduring to the end
      2.3.2.10 The mission and atonement of Jesus Christ
      2.3.2.11 Forgiveness
      2.3.2.12 Gift of the Holy Ghost
      2.3.2.13 Obtaining and building a testimony
      2.3.2.14 Covenants
      2.3.2.15 Light of Christ
      2.3.2.16 Need for opposition
      2.3.2.17 Birth of the spirit
      2.3.2.18 Revelation
      2.3.2.19 Continuing study of the gospel and the scriptures
      2.3.2.20 Prayer and meditation
      2.3.2.21 Fasting
      2.3.2.22 Word of Wisdom

4.4 An overview of the New Testament
    4.4.1 The life and mission of Jesus Christ (The four Gospels)
    4.4.2 The Early Church (Acts, the Epistles, and Revelation)
4.5 The Apostasy
    4.5.1 The Reformation period
4.6 An overview of the Book of Mormon
    4.6.1 God establishes a covenant people in the New World (1 Nephi through Omni)
    4.6.2 God's dealings with the ancient Americans before Christ (Words of Mormon through Helaman)
    4.6.3 The Church of Jesus Christ in ancient America (3 Nephi through Moroni)
4.7 The Restoration, an overview of early modern Church history and the Doctrine and Covenants
    4.7.1 Organization and establishment of the Latter-day Church (Doctrine and Covenants, Joseph Smith, Documentary History of the Church)
4.8 Modern prophets and Church growth
    4.8.1 A study of later modern Church history and Church expansion (Conference Reports and other official documents)

5. **DEVELOPMENT OF INDIVIDUAL TALENTS AND ABILITIES**
5.1 Understanding and applying the simple social graces
5.2 Appreciating and participating in things of cultural value
    5.2.1 Drama
    5.2.2 Music
    5.2.3 Literature
    5.2.4 Dance
    5.2.5 Art and handicraft
    5.2.6 Speech
5.3 Continuing with formal or informal education in secular and religious fields
5.4 Improving employment and career planning skills
5.5 Improving homemaking and household maintenance skills
5.6 Keeping physically fit and active
5.7 Gaining an appreciation for nature and the creations of God
5.8 Knowing the skills of outdoor living and survival
5.9 Knowing the values of good health care
5.10 Knowing the values of work and of being self-sustaining
5.11 Knowing how to handle health emergencies

6. **COMMUNITY RELATIONS**
6.1 Fulfilling our responsibilities in civil government and community affairs
6.2 Maintaining high community standards
6.3 Making appropriate use of community facilities and institutions
6.4 Taking appropriate part in community social and service organizations
6.5 Building a positive community image for the Church and Church members
6.6 Balancing involvement in community and Church activity
6.7 Being obedient to civil laws
6.8 Being a good friend and neighbor

7. **DEVELOPMENT OF LEADERSHIP ABILITIES**
7.1 Developing effective communication skills
7.2 Delegating responsibility
7.3 Following up on delegated responsibility
7.4 Learning the duties of our callings
7.5 Utilizing problem-solving techniques
7.6 Using inspiration in decision making
7.7 Conducting effective meetings
7.8 Setting and achieving goals
7.9 Keeping and using adequate minutes and records
7.10 Following line and staff organizational patterns
7.11 Recognizing and developing the leadership potential in others
7.12 Sustaining and using the help and counsel of those who preside over us
7.13 Working with committees and groups
7.14 Keeping an eye single to the glory of God
7.15 Observing the stewardship principle
7.16 Motivating ourselves and others
7.17 Evaluating progress and recovering from temporary setbacks
7.18 Accepting responsibility and being personally accountable
7.19 Using Church organizations and programs to accomplish objectives
7.20 Effective planning

8. **DEVELOPMENT OF TEACHING SKILLS AND TALENTS**
8.1 Identifying student needs and interests
8.2 Teaching for understanding of ideas and concepts
8.3 Teaching for reinforcement of or change in behavior
8.4 Reaching individual needs of class members
8.5 Making proper preparation to teach
8.6 Seeking qualified help to improve teaching skills
8.7 Practicing in a teaching situation
8.8 Teaching with testimony and with the power and influence of the Holy Spirit
8.9 Using a variety of methods and techniques
8.10 Maintaining order and reverence in the classroom

8.11 Setting a proper example for those whom we teach

8.12 Evaluating the progress of students

8.13 Establishing effective communication with and among students

9. RECREATION AND SOCIAL ACTIVITIES

9.1 Participating in sports and competitive athletics on ward, stake, region, and multi-region levels

9.2 Participating in camping and nature study activities

9.3 Participating in dancing, parties, outings, and other social activities

10. FELLOWSHIPPING AND SERVICE ACTIVITIES

10.1 Orienting new members to Church programs and activities

10.2 Using Church programs, resources, and activities to fellowship members and nonmembers

10.3 Fellowshipping those from varying racial, national, cultural, and language backgrounds

10.4 Participating in service activities and projects

10.4.1 In families

10.4.2 In priesthood quorums

10.4.3 In girls' and women's groups

10.4.4 In ward, stake, and regional groups

10.5 Sharing individual resources with those in need

10.5.1 Material goods

10.5.2 Skills and talents

10.6 Brotherhood and sisterhood

The GOSPEL OF JESUS CHRIST, as expounded in the scriptures and supplemented and interpreted by living prophets, forms the basis of LDS curriculum. The purpose of the curriculum was defined by the Prophet Joseph SMITH: "The fundamental principles of our religion are the testimony of the Apostles and Prophets concerning Jesus Christ, that He died, was buried, and rose again the third day, and ascended into heaven; and all other things which pertain to our religion are only appendages to it" (*TPJS*, p. 121). In support of this purpose, . . . LDS curriculum centers on the scriptures, and focuses on the nature of the Godhead, the nature and purpose of mortal life, the commandments God has given to his children, and the virtues they should develop. A master plan provides the necessary coordination to assure that all members are taught these principles several times throughout their lives at different levels of understanding and experience.

Although the curriculum is highly coordinated, there are still variations in content and its application. Local units and teachers adapt the materials sent from Church headquarters to meet the local needs and fit the local culture. In areas where literacy is limited or members have had little prior instruction in gospel principles, a simplified curriculum may be used at the discretion of local leaders. Materials for the use of members with disabilities are also provided.

In addition to the lesson materials, the Church has supportive materials to aid both teachers and members. Libraries in most meetinghouses contain illustrations, audio recordings, video presentations, motion pictures, maps, and other aids for both teacher and member use. Satellite broadcasts are also periodically available. The Church also produces three monthly MAGAZINES for English-speaking children, youth, and adults, and an INTERNATIONAL MAGAZINE in several different languages to supplement the curriculum of the Church for teachers and to support scripture study by members.

In 1961, Elder Harold B. LEE, then of the Quorum of the Twelve, described the objective of the Church curriculum as "building up a knowledge of the gospel, a power to promulgate the same, a promotion of the growth, faith, and stronger testimony of the principles of the gospel" (Lee, p. 79). He also announced a new emphasis on correlation, citing a need for better coordination among the courses of study and for a reduction in new courses of study each year. The outcome of this charge was an all-Church coordinating council, three coordinating committees (one each for children, youth, and adults), and an extensive curricular planning guide.

In 1972, the Church formed the Internal Communications Department and gave it the responsibility for curriculum planning and writing. All the curricular materials were examined, and from that assessment developed Curriculum Planning Charts. The purposes of the charts were twofold: to measure existing materials, and from the measurement to plan a well-balanced future offering. The actions resulted in the formation of an Instructional Development Department and the establishment of numerous writing committees, whose responsibility is to plan lesson content and methodology for courses in all age groups within the priesthood and auxiliary organizations. Once again, the primary curricular resources are the scriptures, supplemented by quotations from modern prophets. Computer technology discloses the extent of the distribution of the topics throughout the curriculum. The planning charts track not only the number of times a topic is considered, but where the topic has a primary or secondary focus. Instrumental in the development of the present overall curricular plan, the planning charts continue to guide instructional decision making and to produce a unified, balanced, and standardized curriculum, marked by stability and expansiveness.

BIBLIOGRAPHY

Lee, Harold B. *CR* (Oct. 1961):79.

WAYNE B. LYNN

CURSINGS

Cursings are the opposite of BLESSINGS and may be expressed as (1) the use of vulgar or profane language by people; (2) words or actions by God or his representatives expressing divine displeasure with or warning against wickedness; or (3) God's chastisement of mankind.

Cursing in the form of profane language employing names of deity literally "in vain" has been present in most societies. Since thought is expressed in language, vulgar and blasphemous language corrupts its user by establishing vulgar or profane thought patterns. The statement "Among the wicked, men shall lift up their voices and curse God and die" (D&C 45:32) illustrates both a cause and a consequence regarding profane language, with its effect on and relationship to spiritual life. Cursing that invokes the name of deity is a form of BLASPHEMY and, in biblical times, was punishable by stoning (Lev. 24:16). Cursing of parents was also cause for offenders to be put to death in ancient Israel (Ex. 21:17; Matt. 15:4).

Cursing may be the expression of divine displeasure, warning, or exclusion from God's blessing. Just as blessings are obtained by RIGHTEOUSNESS, cursings result from breaking God's law and failing to keep his commandments (Deut. 11:26–28; D&C 104:1–8; 124:48). Intelligent human beings are largely responsible for their own circumstances, and President Brigham YOUNG

said the most severe cursings come upon "those who know their Master's will, and do it not" (JD 1:248). Sinning against light and knowledge has more serious consequences than sinning in ignorance (see Mosiah 2:36–37; cf. Alma 32:19–20; 39:6). ALMA$_2$ gives an example wherein the same land was simultaneously blessed for those who acted righteously and cursed for those who did not (Alma 45:16).

Curses may be pronounced by God, or they may be invoked by his authorized servants, as was the case with Moses (Deut. 27–30); Elijah (1 Kgs. 17:1; 21:20–24); Peter (Acts 5:1–10); Paul (Acts 13:9–12); and Joseph Smith (D&C 103:25; cf. 124:93). However, the Lord's earthly agents are sent forth primarily to bless and not to curse (Matt. 5:44; Rom. 12:14).

Not all curses have totally negative consequences. As God only does good, his cursings are for "the sake" of improving the person cursed (Gen. 3:17; Deut. 23:5), even though the immediate consequence may be extremely unpleasant. When there is need for correction, the Lord has instructed his servants to reprove "with sharpness," but afterward to show forth an "increase of love" (D&C 121:43).

Some cursings are given first as warnings rather than a more severe immediate chastisement (2 Ne. 1:21, 22); and, like blessings, they sometimes require a long time for their full consequences to be realized. After being invoked, cursings may often be lessened or lifted entirely by subsequent righteousness. Mormon describes an experience of the LAMANITES: "And they began to be a very industrious people; yea, and they were friendly with the Nephites; therefore, they did open a correspondence with them, and the curse of God did no more follow them" (Alma 23:18).

Cursings may affect all temporal and spiritual aspects of our lives because all things are governed by law. Lands, crops, handiwork, employment, children, missionary endeavor, interpersonal relationships, and relationships with God are all subject to both cursing and blessing—depending upon individual and collective righteousness or lack of it.

SHERWIN W. HOWARD

D

DAMNATION

"Damnation" is a term derived from the Latin *damnum*, meaning "injury" and "loss," and often connotes deprivation of what should have been possessed. Just as there are varying degrees and types of SALVATION, coupled with ETERNAL PROGRESSION in some areas (D&C 76:96–98; 131:1–4), so are there varying degrees and types of damnation. In LDS doctrine, to be damned means to be stopped, blocked, or limited in one's progress. Individuals are damned whenever they are prevented from reaching their full potential as children of God. Damnation is falling short of what one might have enjoyed if one had received and been faithful to the whole law of the gospel. In this sense, all who do not achieve the highest degree of the CELESTIAL KINGDOM are damned, even though they are saved in some degree of glory. They are damned in the sense that they will not enjoy an ETERNAL INCREASE or the continuation of the family unit in eternity (D&C 132:4, 19). In this context, damnation does not necessarily refer to eternal suffering in hell with the devil, for loss of blessings is in itself a type of hell and damnation. LDS perspectives on this subject include biblical scriptures enriched and clarified by additional revelation; hence, damnation has a wider application than may seem apparent in modern usage (*see* DEGREES OF GLORY; EXALTATION; HEIRS).

In the scriptures, damnation usually refers to the judgment or condemnation that will be pronounced by Jesus Christ on the wicked at the end of the world (Matt. 25:41–46). "Damnation" is an English equivalent of the Hebrew *rasha*, which implies being wicked, impious, ungodly, or guilty, and the Greek *krino*, which implies being put under condemnation. While the word "damnation" appears regularly in the King James Version of the Bible, (i.e., in the New Testament) it is not found in several modern versions, which use words like "doom" or "condemnation" instead.

Many Jews and Christians reject the idea of damnation as an outmoded theological concept, but some Orthodox Jews and conservative Christians hold to a belief in final and eternal damnation. Conservative Christians generally believe that God himself will condemn unrepentant sinners based on justice as merited by the recipients (Matt. 12:41–42; John 12:48; Rom. 3:8). They hold, further, that Christ, the Redeemer, came to save rather than to condemn (John 3:17) and that he alone frees the individual from final damnation (Rom. 8:1–2).

Damnation comes as the result of not believing in the gospel (Mark 16:16), of not accepting additional light and knowledge (Alma 12:9–11), of believing in false doctrines (2 Pet. 2:1), of being slothful and having to be commanded in all things (D&C 58:26–29), and of refusing to humble oneself, repent, and live according to gospel principles. The Prophet Joseph SMITH explained, "God had decreed that all who will not obey His voice shall not escape the damnation of hell. What is the damnation of hell? To go with that society who have not obeyed His commands" (*TPJS*, p. 198; cf. pp. 322–23).

Damnation also results from partaking of the Lord's sacrament unworthily (1 Cor. 11:29), taking pleasure in unrighteousness (2 Thes. 2:12), engaging in adulterous relationships (1 Tim. 5:11–12), rejecting the law of the Church (D&C 42:60), neglecting the covenant of eternal marriage (D&C 132:4), altering the holy word of God (Morm. 8:33), and rejecting Jesus Christ (D&C 49:5). If persons do these things and do not repent, they are left without the protection of the law of God and without the spiritual nourishment that they could have enjoyed, and as a result they suffer damnation.

Damnation is not to be equated with neverending torment or punishment. An early revelation to Joseph Smith explains, "It is not written that there shall be no end to this torment, but it is written *endless torment*. Again, it is written *eternal damnation*; wherefore it is more express than other scriptures, that it might work upon the hearts of the children of men" (D&C 19:6–7; *see also* ENDLESS AND ETERNAL). President Brigham YOUNG explained, "We believe that all will be damned who do not receive the gospel of Jesus Christ; but we do not believe that they will go into a lake which burns with brimstone and fire, and suffer unnamed and unheard of torments, inflicted by cruel and malicious devils to all eternity. The sectarian doctrine of final rewards and punishments is as strange to me as their bodiless, partless, and passionless God. Every man will receive according to the deeds done in the body, whether they be good or bad. All men, excepting those who sin against the Holy Ghost, who shed innocent blood or who consent thereto, will be saved in some kingdom; for in my father's house, says Jesus, are many mansions" (*JD* 11:125–26).

Ultimate and total damnation comes only to the devil and his angels, who rebelled in the FIRST ESTATE, and to the SONS OF PERDITION, who are damned eternally and denied entrance into any kingdom of glory hereafter (D&C 76:32–34). The sons of perdition are those guilty of unpardonable sin against the Holy Ghost (D&C 132:27; cf. Mark 3:29), which includes the willful denial of the "Only Begotten Son of the Father, having crucified him unto themselves and put him to an open shame" (D&C 76:35).

BIBLIOGRAPHY

Kimball, Spencer W. "Marriage and Divorce." In *1976 Speeches of the Year*, p. 154. Provo, Utah, 1977.

Lee, Harold B. "Spiritual Rebirth and Death." *IE* 50 (Nov. 1947):716, 752, 754.

Stuy, Brian, ed. Discourse by George Q. Cannon. In *Collected Discourses*, 3 vols.; Vol. 2, pp. 64–76. Sandy, Utah, 1987–1989.

RICHARD NEITZEL HOLZAPFEL

DANCE

In 1830 when the Church was organized, many Christian denominations were hostile toward recreation and play, particularly dance. However, the Prophet Joseph SMITH and his successors advocated dance and participated in recreational dancing. Joseph Smith was a skillful dancer and enjoyed hosting dances in his home (Holbrook, p. 122). Brigham YOUNG and the Quorum of the Twelve "danced before the Lord" to the music of a small orchestra in the Nauvoo Temple after long days of joyous participation in temple ordinances (*HC* 7:557, 566; Holbrook, p. 123).

The revealed doctrine that the body and spirit together comprise the soul tends to encourage physical activity (D&C 88:15). Early Latter-day Saints commended dancing as healthful to body and mind, but only when conducted in accordance with Church principles. Emphasis was on propriety, good company, and the spirit of praising the Lord. During their difficult trek west, the pioneers danced as "camps of Israel." President Brigham Young said "I want you to sing and dance and forget your troubles. . . . Let's have some music and all of you dance" (Holbrook, p. 125). Around the campfires they danced polkas, Scotch reels, quadrilles, French fours, and other figures.

In the West, the Saints continued to enjoy dancing. Brigham Young emphasized that fiddling and dancing were not to be part of formal worship (Holbrook, p. 131), and he counseled that those who cannot serve God with a pure heart in the dance should not dance. Under these guidelines, dance continued as an integral part of Mormon culture.

The Deseret Musical and Dramatic Society was organized in 1862, and theatrical dance soon became a favorite attraction. Worship services and social activities were usually held in the same place, although at separate times. This practice, which prevailed in the frontier "brush bowery," continues today in LDS meetinghouses, which typically feature a cultural-recreation hall, complete with stage, adjacent to the chapel.

In the early and mid-twentieth century, the Mutual Improvement Association sponsored recreational and theatrical dance training and exhibitions (*see* YOUNG MEN and YOUNG WOMEN). Gold and Green Balls were annual social events in each WARD and STAKE. All-Church dance festivals held in Salt Lake City from 1922 to 1973 gained national recognition. After 8,000 dancers in bright costumes participated at the festival in 1959, a national news magazine described the Church as the "dancingest denomination" (Arrington, p. 31). In 1985, 13,000 dancers performed in the Southern California Regional Dance Festival with more than 100,000 viewing the two performances. Dance festivals continued at local levels from 1973 to 1990, when they were finally discontinued as major performances.

Dancing, however, continues as an integral part of youth and adult activities in the Church. It permeates many facets of campus life, entertainment, and performing arts programs at Church-sponsored schools. For example, more than 12,000 Brigham Young University students enroll annually for academic credit in ballet, ballroom, folk, modern, jazz, tap, aerobic, and precision dance courses. Student performing companies in ballet, ballroom, folk, and modern dance have gained national and international recognition.

BIBLIOGRAPHY

Arrington, Georganne Ballif. "Dance in Mormonism." In *Focus on Dance X: Religion and Dance*, ed. Dennis J. Fallon and Mary Jane Wolbers. Reston, Va., 1982.

Holbrook, Leona. "Dancing as an Aspect of Early Mormon and Utah Culture." *BYU Studies* 16 (Autumn 1975):117–38.

PHYLLIS C. JACOBSON

DANIEL, PROPHECIES OF

The Church of Jesus Christ of Latter-day Saints regards the book of Daniel as the writings of Daniel, who was deported from Jerusalem to Babylon (c. 606 B.C.), and accepts the work as SCRIPTURE. It sees in the work significant PROPHECIES about the latter days, including the APOSTASY from and RESTORATION of the GOSPEL OF JESUS CHRIST.

According to Wilford WOODRUFF, the angel Moroni quoted to the Prophet Joseph SMITH from Daniel chapter two which features a prophecy of the latter-day restoration of the gospel in Nebuchadnezzar's dream concerning "what shall be in the latter days" (Dan. 2:28; Whittaker, p. 159). Daniel identified the "head of gold" in the dream as a symbol of Nebuchadnezzar's empire, and latter-day PROPHETS have specified that the stone "cut out without hands" (Dan. 2:34) represents the latter-day KINGDOM OF GOD (D&C 65:2; HC 1:xxxiv–xl). The remaining symbols have been interpreted as follows: The "breast and arms of silver" represent the Persian realm that superseded Babylon. The "belly and thighs of brass" prefigure the succeeding Hellenistic states. The two "legs of iron" point to the Roman Empire, foreshadowing the division between Rome and Constantinople. The feet of the image, "part of iron and part of clay," symbolize the European kingdoms that grew out of the dissolving Roman Empire, beginning in the fifth century. Those kingdoms merged the culture of Rome with that of northern and eastern European tribes; hence, the symbolic mixing of iron and clay.

In the days of those kingdoms, Daniel predicted, "the God of heaven [will] set up a kingdom, which . . . shall stand for ever" (2:44). This final kingdom, represented by the stone "cut out without hands," is The Church of Jesus Christ of Latter-day Saints, restored to the earth in 1830, when European monarchs still ruled. That the Church would spread throughout the world is seen when "the stone that smote the image became a great mountain, and filled the whole earth" (2:34–35; Kimball, p. 8).

Daniel's vision in chapter seven is also interpreted in the context of the LAST DAYS. The "four great beasts" (Dan. 7:3) seem to represent successive empires of Babylon, Persia, Macedonia, and Rome; and the "ten horns" (7:7) of the fourth beast appear to symbolize again the kingdoms that succeeded the Roman Empire. Latter-day prophets identify the "Ancient of Days" (7:22) as Adam, who will preside at a gathering to be held at ADAM-ONDI-AHMAN in Missouri before Jesus' second coming (D&C 116). At that assembly, Jesus, "the

Son of Man," will appear. Acting for PRIESTHOOD leaders in all DISPENSATIONS, Adam will return to the risen Jesus the priesthood KEYS which represent everlasting dominion.

The prophecy of the "seventy weeks" in chapter nine interests Latter-day Saints because it suggests that the New Testament church would fall into apostasy. The sixty-nine weeks (Dan. 9:24–26) may be symbolic of the period between the Jews' return to Jerusalem (537 B.C.) and the coming of Jesus the MESSIAH, who would atone ("be cut off") for his people. Verse 27 reports that the Lord would "confirm the covenant with many for one week." This seventieth week may typify the decades that Christ's true church endured, led then by living apostles and prophets, ending shortly after A.D. 100, following the ministry of John the Apostle. The prophecy also notes that Jerusalem and its temple would be destroyed "in the midst of the week" (A.D. 70), mentioning the abomination of desolation and the cessation of temple SACRIFICE (cf. Mark 13:14).

BIBLIOGRAPHY

Kimball, Spencer W. "A Stone Cut Without Hands." *Ensign* 6 (May 1976):4–9.

McConkie, Bruce R. *The Millennial Messiah*, chap. 11, 47. Salt Lake City, 1982.

Sperry, Sidney B. *The Voice of Israel's Prophets*. Salt Lake City, 1952.

Whittaker, David J. "The Book of Daniel in Early Mormon Thought." In *By Study and Also by Faith*, ed. J. Lundquist and S. Ricks, Vol. 1, pp. 155–201. Salt Lake City, 1990.

JEFFREY R. CHADWICK

DANITES

Following the violence in northwestern Missouri in 1838, the Mormon dissident Sampson Avard, star witness in a court of inquiry weighing evidence against LDS leaders, charged that the Church had organized a band of armed men bound by secret oaths who had engaged in illegal activities against non-Mormon neighbors (*Document*, pp. 97–108). With the 1841 publication of the court proceedings, Avard's account became the foundation for all subsequent non-Mormon "Danite" accounts. Thus was born the legend of the Danites.

Though no Danite organization was known in Nauvoo or in Utah, the stereotype persisted, be-

coming a part of national discussion about Utah and the Latter-day Saints and for decades a staple of dime novels (*see* MORMONS, IMAGE OF: IN FICTION). By 1900 at least fifty novels had been published in English using the Avard-type Danite to develop story lines of murder, pillage, and conspiracy against common citizens. Arthur Conan Doyle (*A Study in Scarlet*) created Sherlock Holmes to solve a murder committed by Danites. Zane Grey (*Riders of the Purple Sage*) and Robert Louis Stevenson (*The Dynamiter*) were among the authors who found the image of the evil Danites well suited for popular reading audiences who delighted in sensationalism (Cornwall and Arrington). The image became so pervasive that few readers were willing to question the accuracy of such portrayals.

The reality of Danites in Missouri in 1838 is both less and more than the stereotype. Contemporary records suggest something fundamentally different. In October 1838, Albert Perry Rockwood, an LDS resident of Far West, Missouri, wrote in his journal of a *public* Danite organization that involved the whole Latter-day Saint community. He described in biblical terms companies of tens, fifties, and hundreds (cf. Ex. 18:13–26)—similar to the organization the pioneers later used during the migration to the Great Basin. Here the Danite organization encompassed the full range of activities of a covenant community that viewed itself as a restoration of ancient Israel. Working in groups, with some assigned to defense, others to securing provisions, and still others to constructing dwellings, these Danites served the interests of the whole. This was not the secret organization Avard spoke of; in fact, Rockwood's letters to friends and family were even more descriptive than his journal (Jessee and Whittaker).

In the fall of 1838, with old settlers in Missouri swearing to drive the Mormons out rather than permit them to become a political majority and with LDS leaders declaring that they would fight before again seeing their rights trampled, northwestern Missouri was in a state of war (*see* MISSOURI CONFLICT). Sparked by an effort to prevent LDS voting, violence erupted in August and soon spread. On both sides, skirmishes involved members of state-authorized militias. Evidence suggests that during this time of fear, clashes, and confusion, Sampson Avard, probably a captain within the public Danite structure and a militia officer, subverted the ideals of both by persuading his men to undertake the criminal activities he later argued were the authorized actions of the whole community. Encouraged perhaps by the firmly stated intentions of leaders to meet force with force but apparently without their approval, Avard used his Danite and military positions to mold a covert renegade band to avenge anti-Mormon outrages. He succeeded because after weeks of responding to violence with strictly defensive measures, Avard was not alone in feeling that the time for forbearance had passed. Others of the time in late reminiscences recalled that clandestine meetings were held, which were subsequently reported to Joseph SMITH, who then denounced Avard, removed him from his official command, and disbanded the maverick body. Though short-lived and unauthorized, this covert organization, thanks to Avard's distorted and widely publicized testimony, usurped the former usage of "Danites," and the once honorable appellation became a synonym for officially sanctioned secret lawlessness.

In contrast, when five hundred men in the Caldwell County (Mormon) militia later took the offensive in response to two months of unrelenting violence and depredations, there was nothing secretive about it. In mid-October, with supplies running low, they left defensive positions to forage and to punish enemies—a very public effort to improve security by preemptive forays. Two weeks later, facing increasing numbers of volunteers and a militia emboldened by the governor's EXTERMINATION ORDER, they surrendered their arms in defeat.

The reality, then, behind the supposed secretive, lawless Danites of legend was this renegade band formed briefly in 1838 in the midst of war. There is no evidence of any such band later, and even in 1838, the Latter-day Saint community as a whole did not deserve blame for the unauthorized actions of a few. As Parley P. Pratt, an apostle, wrote to his family after hearing Avard's court testimony, "They accuse us of things that never entered into our hearts." From LIBERTY JAIL on December 16, 1838, Joseph Smith summarized the situation as he then understood it: "We have learned also since we have been in prison that many false and pernicious things which were calculated to lead the saints far astray and to do great injury have been taught by Dr. Avard as coming from the Presidency . . . which the presidency never knew of being taught in the church by any

body untill after they were made prisoners . . . the presidency were ignorant as well as innocent of these things" (*PWJS*, p. 380).

Unfortunately, in an age when Latter-day Saints were hated and persecuted, Avard's story provided a ready explanation for anyone who wanted to believe the worst. The reality was far less sensational.

BIBLIOGRAPHY

Cornwall, Rebecca Foster, and Leonard J. Arrington. "Perpetuation of a Myth: Mormon Danites in Five Western Novels, 1840–90." *BYU Studies* 23 (Spring 1983):147–65.

Document Containing the Correspondence, Orders, Etc. in Relation to the Disturbances with the Mormons; and the Evidence Given before the Hon. Austin A. King. Fayette, Mo., 1841.

Gentry, Leland H. "The Danite Band of 1838." *BYU Studies* 14 (Summer 1974):421–50.

Jessee, Dean C., and David J. Whittaker, eds. "The Last Months of Mormonism in Missouri: The Albert Perry Rockwood Journal." *BYU Studies* 28 (Winter 1988):5–41.

Whittaker, David J. "The Book of Daniel in Early Mormon Thought." In *By Study and Also by Faith: Essays in Honor of Hugh W. Nibley on the Occasion of His Eightieth Birthday,* Vol. 1, pp. 155–201. Salt Lake City, 1990.

DAVID J. WHITTAKER

DATING AND COURTSHIP

Members of the Church are somewhat distinctive in their dating and courtship practices, but they are also influenced by broader cultural patterns. In some cultures, parents still closely supervise courtship and arrange children's marriages, but youth worldwide have increasing choices in dating and mate selection. For most young people in the United States outside the Church, dating begins at an early age (about age thirteen during the 1980s); it has no set pattern of progression, and is often informal and unsupervised. These contemporary dating patterns form a social context that influences somewhat the majority of LDS youth.

However, although courtship patterns change and vary across cultures, there is quite a conservative pattern for dating and courtship among Latter-day Saints in Western nations. It is expected that LDS youth will not begin dating until the age of sixteen. Serious, steady dating and marriage-oriented courtship are expected to be delayed longer, perhaps until after a MISSION for males and after completing high school for females. A chaste courtship is expected to lead to a temple MARRIAGE, in which a couple make binding commitments to each other for all time and eternity.

Two doctrinally based principles guide the dating and courtship of LDS youth: first, because of the religious significance of marriage, virtually everyone who can is expected to marry; second, because of the spiritual and social importance of CHASTITY, sexual relations must wait until after marriage.

Latter-day Saints place an unusually strong emphasis on marriage, believing that marriage is ordained of God (D&C 49:15) and is a prerequisite for obtaining the highest heavenly state after mortality (D&C 131:1–4; *see* EXALTATION). Because of the belief that people should be married and the doctrine that they can maintain marital ties throughout eternity, Latter-day Saints take dating and courtship more seriously than those for whom marriage has less religious significance.

Latter-day Saints believe that premarital chastity is a scriptural commandment reaffirmed by current revelation. From the New Testament: "Flee fornication. . . . He that committeth fornication sinneth against his own body" (1 Cor. 6:18). From a modern Church leader: "Chastity should be the dominant virtue among young people" (McKay, p. 458). LDS youth are also taught that they should not participate in sexual activities that often precede sexual intercourse: "Among the most common sexual sins our young people commit are necking and petting. Not only do these improper relations often lead to fornication, pregnancy, and abortions—all ugly sins—but in and of themselves they are pernicious evils, and it is often difficult for youth to distinguish where one ends and another begins" (Kimball, 1969, p. 65). Although Latter-day Saints consider sexual relationships outside of marriage to be sinful, sexual relations within marriage are not only right and proper but are considered sacred and beautiful (*see* SEXUALITY).

Like most of their non-Mormon peers in dating cultures, LDS youth date to have fun as they participate in social activities with other boys and girls. As plainly stated by prominent leaders of the Church, "It is natural to date. Every right-thinking young person has a native desire to become acquainted with the opposite sex, looking eventually to pairing off in honorable marriage" (Petersen, p. 37). "Dating has become the accepted form of so-cial recreation for the purpose of getting acquainted before young people can safely have a serious interest in each other. Because the selection of a mate in life is so extremely important, we should intelligently seek the experiences which will help us to make that great decision" (Hunter, pp. 101–102). Typical of the advice given to LDS youth is the following counsel about dating:

Who? Only those whose standards are high, like your own.

Where? Clean places, decent places, proper places where you can be proud to be.

Why? Associating with others under wholesome circumstances helps develop friendships and permits you to learn about qualities and characteristics in others, to get to know them, to have fun together, to widen areas of choice, to achieve a wider and wiser vision of what one may seek in an eternal companion.

When? Not too young, not too often, not on school nights as a rule, not too expensively.

What? Fun things, wholesome things, good and useful things— . . . things pleasing to you, to parents, to God.

How? With others, in groups, chaperoned when proper, appropriately dressed, cheerfully, courteously, modestly, wisely, prayerfully. And let parents know where you are, with whom, doing what, and when you will return. Have a happy time! [Hanks, pp. 134–35]

While dating and courtship patterns among LDS reflect broader societal patterns, there are several age-graded characteristics of dating and courtship in the Church that are special.

Age twelve is a line of demarcation in the life of a young member of the Church. At this age LDS boys and girls leave PRIMARY, the Church's organization for children, and enter the YOUNG WOMEN and YOUNG MEN organizations. Here, young people participate, usually once a week, in gender-segregated activities designed with an adult adviser for their particular age group. Occasionally, joint activities are planned that include boys and girls together. These are structured and well-supervised social and religious activities that bring teenage boys and girls together to help them develop appropriate social relationships.

While the Church sponsors joint social activities, its leaders have strongly discouraged early dating. "Young men and women, not yet ready for marriage, should be friends with many others, but they should not engage in courting. . . . Friendship, not courtship, should be the relationship of teenagers. . . . The change of this one pattern of social activities of our youth would immediately eliminate a majority of the sins of our young folks" (Kimball, 1986, pp. 287–88). Steady dating is further discouraged until youth are ready for courtship.

In the past, LDS youth were basically counseled not to begin dating, especially steady dating, until they were "old enough and mature enough" to consider marriage. During the 1970s the age of sixteen took on special significance in this regard when Spencer W. KIMBALL, as President of the Church, said: "When you get in the teen years, your social associations should still be a general acquaintance with both boys and girls. Any dating or pairing off in social contacts should be postponed until at least the age of 16 or older, and even then there should be much judgment used in the selections and in the seriousness" (Kimball, 1975, p. 4). As a consequence of this teaching, the age of sixteen has become the acceptable age when dating can begin.

Nineteen is an especially pivotal age in the social and religious life of late adolescent LDS youth. The males are expected to leave home for a two-year Church mission. Many young women upon reaching twenty-one will serve missions. Missionaries leave romantic relationships behind and are counseled not to worry about or telephone girlfriends or boyfriends. They are restricted from all dating activities during their missionary service. Although many boyfriend-girlfriend relationships do not last through the mission separation, the mission experience frequently brings a maturity that better prepares young men and women for eventual marriage.

Despite the postponing effect of missions on dating activities, LDS men tend to marry at an age younger than national averages, while LDS women marry at about the norm. Presumably, the value placed on marriage makes LDS youth less likely to postpone marriage for education and career advancement; they are certainly less likely to cohabit instead of marrying, and the customary pattern is to continue courting until the time of marriage (see SINGLE ADULTS). LDS prophets have consistently instructed young Mormon men that it is wrong to delay marriage unnecessarily (Benson; Kimball, 1975).

Because marrying a person of the same faith is important to Latter-day Saints, families that live away from the concentrations of Church popula-

tion often encourage the children to attend BRIGHAM YOUNG UNIVERSITY or RICKS COLLEGE or to participate in the programs of the INSTITUTES OF RELIGION at other colleges or universities, where they are more likely to find a suitable partner of their own faith. Also, units of the Church specifically for young adults are organized throughout the world, where numbers allow, to facilitate social opportunities. Because of the religious significance of mate selection to Latter-day Saints, a variety of common practices has developed. Couples seriously considering marriage are likely to pray for heavenly confirmation in their marriage decision. The choice of a partner is usually discussed with parents, and young couples planning to marry often go together to seek the advice of their Church leaders.

BIBLIOGRAPHY

Benson, Ezra Taft. "To the Single Adult Brethren of the Church." *Ensign* 18 (May 1988):51–53.

Hanks, Marion D. "The Six." *IE* 70 (June 1967):134–35.

Hunter, Howard W. *Youth of the Noble Birthright*, pp. 101–109. Salt Lake City, 1960.

Kimball, Spencer W. "Marriage and Divorce." In *1976 Speeches of the Year*. Provo, Utah, 1977.

———. "The Marriage Decision." *Ensign* 5 (Feb. 1975):2–6.

———. *The Miracle of Forgiveness*. Salt Lake City, 1969.

———. *The Teachings of Spencer W. Kimball*, ed. Edward L. Kimball. Salt Lake City, 1986.

McKay, David O. *Gospel Ideals*. pp. 458–64. Salt Lake City, 1953.

Petersen, Mark E. *Live It Up!* Salt Lake City, 1971.

BRENT C. MILLER
H. WALLACE GODDARD

DAVID, KING

David, king of ISRAEL, was the youngest of eight brothers, sons of Jesse (1 Sam. 16:6–12), a descendent of Boaz and RUTH (Ruth 4:21–22) and an ancestor to Jesus Christ (Matt. 1:6–17; Luke 3:23–31). He was born at Bethlehem and died in Jerusalem c. 1015 B.C., after reigning over Judah for seven years and the united kingdom of Israel for an additional thirty-three (1 Kgs. 2:11). He was buried in the ancestral home, in Bethlehem (1 Kgs. 2:10). He was perhaps the greatest king of Israel, once called "a man after [God's] own heart" (1 Sam. 13:14). Mormon interests in David have often dwelt on the issues of his plural marriages and his status in the AFTERLIFE.

While the scriptures relate different stories of his introduction at Saul's court (1 Sam. 16:14–23; 17:55–58), David's vault from obscurity to national awareness seems to have come as a result of his courageous defeat of the giant Goliath (1 Sam. 17:49).

David's strength and reliance on the Lord marked him as an exceptional leader and the epitome of Israelite heroism (2 Sam. 5:1–3; 22:2–51). Subsequent rulers were measured against his stature (cf. 1 Kgs. 15:3–5, 11), and his name was linked with that of the awaited MESSIAH (Mark 12:35; Luke 1:32; Rom. 1:3). Scripture indicates that David's blessings, including his wives, were given to him as a result of God's favor (2 Sam. 5:12–13; 12:8; D&C 132:39).

But when David also acquired wives and concubines, apparently under his own authority, he was condemned by God (Jacob 2:23–24). Certainly David lost divine approval as a result of his adulterous union with Bathsheba and the subsequent contrived murder of her husband, Uriah (2 Sam. 12:1–12; D&C 132:38–39).

Because of David's transgressions, his eternal blessings were taken from him (*TPJS*, pp. 188–89). The Lord granted David a continuation of life for another twenty-one years, perhaps because of his immediate and deep remorse (cf. Ps. 51), his acts of repentance, and his continued faithfulness to JEHOVAH (2 Sam. 12:13, 16; cf. *WJS*, p. 335). However, he must await in the SPIRIT PRISON the redemption promised to him (Acts 2:34; *WJS*, p. 74). Even with the assurance of the Lord's ultimate mercy (Ps. 86:13), David lost much that God had given him on earth, he fell "from his exaltation" and his wives were given unto another" (D&C 132:39). Yet his personal integrity appears in his insistence that he be punished in place of his people, whom he saw in vision being destroyed (2 Sam. 24:15–17).

BIBLIOGRAPHY

Bright, John. *A History of Israel*. 3rd ed., pp. 184–228. Philadelphia, 1981.

McCarter, P. Kyle. *Second Samuel. Anchor Bible*. New York, 1984.

NORMAN J. BARLOW

DAVID, PROPHETIC FIGURE OF LAST DAYS

King David (c. 1000 B.C.) remains today one of the most renowned Old Testament figures. His personality, spiritual sensitivity, creative abilities, military victories, and leadership carried him to the pinnacle of popularity. He had the potential to become an ideal king, but his kingship deteriorated after his adultery with Bathsheba and his involvement in Uriah's death. However, prophecy states that a model ruler in the last days will be "raised up" from David's lineage.

The Prophet Joseph SMITH taught that "the throne and kingdom of David is to be taken from him and given to another by the name of David in the last days, raised up out of his lineage" (*TPJS*, p. 339). Elder Orson Hyde, in his dedicatory prayer on the Mount of Olives, October 24, 1841, prophesied that the Jews would return to Jerusalem and that in time a leader called David, "even a descendant from the loins of ancient David, [would] be their king" (*HC* 4:457).

This predicted figure corresponds to a promised messianic servant. Hosea, speaking shortly before the loss of northern Israel, foretold that Israelites would return in the latter days "and seek the LORD their God, and David their king" (Hosea 3:5). JEREMIAH prophesied of Israel and Judah's future righteousness, and of "David their king, whom I [the LORD] will raise up unto them" (Jer. 30:9; cf. 23:5; 33:15–22). And in Ezekiel it is written, "And I will set up one shepherd over them, and he shall feed them, even my servant David; he shall feed them, and he shall be their shepherd. And I the LORD will be their God, and my servant David a prince among them" (Ezek. 34:23–24; cf. also 44:1-3).

Speaking to Joseph Smith, the angel MORONI₂ cited Old Testament passages telling of significant figures who would be involved with Christ's millennial reign (JS—H 1:40). As prophesied in Isaiah, it appears that two persons are spoken of, a "rod" and a "root" (11:1, 10)—one a leader "on whom there is laid much power," the other a person with special priesthood keys (D&C 113:3–6). These leaders are believed by some to be among the "messianic figures" spoken of in the Dead Sea Scrolls and in rabbinic literature (*Encyclopedia Judaica*, 11: 1409–1411).

Although noble attributes and spiritual powers characterize such messianic servants, Jesus Christ exemplifies these qualities perfectly (D&C 113:1–2). Jesus is the exemplar prophet, priest, and king. He identified himself as the PROPHET "like unto Moses" (Deut. 18:15; Acts 3:22–23; 3 Ne. 20:23) and was a HIGH PRIEST after the order of MELCHIZEDEK (Heb. 5:9–10; 7:15–22). Jesus is King of Kings (Rev. 19:16), greater than all other leaders of all time. Some see in Jesus Christ the complete fulfillment of the prophecy of a future David. Others feel that, while the titles and functions of the future Davidic king apply to Jesus, there will also be another righteous king by the name of David in the last days, a leader from the loins of Jesse (and thus of Judah).

VICTOR L. LUDLOW

DEACON, AARONIC PRIESTHOOD

Twelve-year-old LDS males usually receive the AARONIC PRIESTHOOD and are ordained deacons, continuing in that PRIESTHOOD OFFICE until age fourteen. Deacons receive assignments from their BISHOPS that may include distributing the SACRAMENT to the congregation, serving as messengers, collecting FAST OFFERINGS, providing assistance to the elderly or disabled, and caring for the meetinghouse and grounds.

Although the exact role of deacons (from the Greek *diakonos*, or "servant") in the Christian church of the New Testament is not known, tradition indicates that they were ordained to their positions and were ranked below bishops and elders. Their duties apparently involved collecting and distributing alms and waiting on tables. Also, relatively early in the Catholic tradition, deacons may have assisted in the administration of communion and taken the sacrament to the homes of those who could not attend church. They also maintained church properties and read the gospel lection in Eucharist assembly. While closely associated with bishops in their service at the sacrament table, deacons were younger and were understood to be in schooling for greater service upon reaching maturity (Shepherd, Vol. 1, pp. 785–86).

The office of deacon was introduced by Joseph Smith at least as early as the Church conference held on June 9, 1830 (D&C 20:39). Some deacons may have been ordained at the organizational

meeting on April 6, 1830 (*HC* 1:79), but the records are not specific.

Latter-day scriptures provide that teachers and deacons are "to warn, expound, exhort, and teach, and invite all to come unto Christ" (D&C 20:59) and are to edify one another (D&C 20:85). Deacons may be ordained by any elder or priest at the direction of the local bishop, contingent on a worthiness interview and the sustaining vote of the congregation (D&C 20:39, 48).

Deacons are organized into quorums of twelve or fewer members, with one called as president, two as counselors, and another as secretary (*see* PRIESTHOOD QUORUMS). The BISHOPRIC assigns an adult adviser to teach and help train the quorum members to emulate the example of Jesus Christ in word and deed and helps prepare them for ordination to the Melchizedek Priesthood and for missionary service.

Church-sponsored Boy Scout troops provide the major activity program for deacons in the United States and Canada, and give them important learning and leadership experiences (*see* SCOUTING).

BIBLIOGRAPHY

Lowrie, Walter. *The Church and its Organization in Primitive and Catholic Times: An Interpretation of Rudolph Sohm's KIRCHENRECHT.* New York, 1904.

Palmer, Lee A. *The Aaronic Priesthood Through the Centuries.* Salt Lake City, 1964.

Shepherd, M. "Deacon." In *Interpreter's Dictionary of the Bible*, Vol. 1. Nashville, Tenn., 1962.

RONALD L. BRAMBLE

DEAD SEA SCROLLS

[*This entry has two parts:*

Overview

LDS Perspective.]

OVERVIEW

The major corpus of the Dead Sea scrolls, about 600 manuscripts, dates from c. 250 B.C.E. to 68 C.E. Others works from the Southern Jordan Rift, Nahal Hever and Nahal Seelim chiefly, date from 131 to 135 C.E. Masada produced materials from the first century B.C. to A.D. 73.

The manuscripts include segments of all the Hebrew scriptures (except Esther; *see* OLD TESTAMENT), and more than one variant of many. For example, the three Samuel manuscripts from Qumran are much fuller texts than those of the Masoretic Bible (the traditional text). Also found were fragments of apocryphal and pseudepigraphical books, as well as manuscripts of previously unknown religious works, including a Temple Scroll, a Manual of Discipline, and a Thanksgiving Scroll.

The scrolls have required reappraisal of understanding in three categories: (1) the development of Hebrew scriptures before the formation of the CANON; (2) the dating and pervasive influence of APOCALYPTIC thinking; and (3) the religious milieu of the New Testament.

1. The "biblical" library of Qumran represents a fluid stage of the biblical text. Those documents show no influence of the rabbinic recension of the canon, the direct ancestor of the traditional Hebrew Bible. The scrolls help to place both the Pharisaic text and the canon in the era of Hillel, roughly the time of Jesus. In their selection of canonical books, the rabbis excluded those attributed to prophets or patriarchs before MOSES (e.g., the ENOCH literature, works written in the name of ABRAHAM and other patriarchs). They traced the succession of prophets from Moses to figures of the Persian period. Late works were excluded, with the exception of Daniel, which, the rabbis presumably, attributed to the Persian period.

2. The literature of Qumran includes apocalypses and works colored by apocalyptic. The writers saw world history in the grip of a final war between the Spirit of truth and the Spirit of evil; this conflict is at once cosmic and earthly. They considered themselves proper heirs of Israel and placed themselves under a new covenant as Sons of Light to contend with Sons of Darkness. They had a strict reading of the law, lived in daily self-denial, practiced ablutions, and had ceremonial meals. Their Manual of Discipline reflects the expectation of the immediate coming of the heavenly kingdom. A "Teacher of Righteousness" was apparently the priestly head of the earthly community of God; the forces of good were also led by a cosmic power or holy spirit called the "Prince of Light." The writers saw their own age as the age of consummation. The Messiah was about to appear, "bringing the sword." Collapse of other social structures was imminent before the new age. The people at Qumran, probably

Essenes, expected that the Davidic or royal Messiah would appear to defeat the earthly and cosmic powers of wickedness. Commentaries on the biblical materials, found in the same area, treat traditional prophecies in this eschatological setting. Theirs was a church of anticipation.

The Temple Scroll shows that these Jewish priests were separatists, maintaining that the Temple cultus was defunct. They replaced the lunar with a solar calendar for the festivals and introduced feasts of oil and wine mentioned nowhere in the Pentateuch. Considering themselves warriors in the last holy war, fighting alongside holy angels, they forbade all uncleanness (which in their view included the lame, blind, or diseased) both in the anticipated temple and in the temple city. At least for the duration of the war they were celibate.

Apocalypticism is now to be seen as a major element in the complex matrix that formed the background for the development of both Tannaitic Judaism and early Christianity. Gershom Scholem shocked scholars of this generation by demonstrating the existence and importance of apocalyptic mysticism in the era of Rabbi Akiba. It is now necessary to place apocalyptic thinking as beginning earlier than scholars had previously supposed, perhaps as early as the fourth century B.C.E. and lasting half a millennium.

3. The New Testament reflects these apocalyptic theological tendencies that scholars heretofore passed over lightly. For example, it now appears that the thought and teachings of John the Baptist and Jesus of Nazareth are more apocalyptic than prophetic in their essential character. The dualistic, apocalyptic, and eschatological framework marks John as the most Jewish of the four Gospels. In John's Gospel the spirit of truth is called the Paraclete or Advocate. He is the Holy Spirit, but as at Qumran he is not precisely identical with God's own spirit, which explains why he does not speak on his own authority (John 16:13). The emphasis on light and darkness, unity, community, and love is reiterated and expanded. The theme of religious knowing in an eschatological sense is comparable to statements in the epistles of Paul and the Gospel of Matthew. The Gospel of Luke quotes almost verbatim a pre-Christian apocalypse of Daniel, found in Cave 4, which refers to an eschatological king, whom we take to be the royal Messiah, from the titles "Son of God" and "Son of the Most High." In the parable of the banquet in

Luke 14:15–24, Jesus condemns those who seek places of rank in his kingdom, perhaps in polemic response to the Essene exclusion from their banquet of all except the elite of the desert who shared their goods and were "men of renown."

For the Essenes, the New Age was still anticipated. For early Christians, Jesus had been resurrected as the Messiah who brought the New Age. Both communities lived in anticipation of the full coming of redemption or the consummation of the kingdom of God. The Essenes formed a community of priestly apocalyptists. The early Christian movement was made up largely of lay apocalyptists, much like the Pharisaic party. Both searched the prophets for allusions to the events of their times, which they understood to be the "last times," and both spoke in language pervaded by the terminology of Jewish apocalyptic.

FRANK MOORE CROSS, JR.

LDS PERSPECTIVE

Like many Jews and like other Christians, Latter-day Saints were deeply interested in the announcement that ancient manuscripts from New Testament times were discovered in Palestine in 1947. Initial zeal led to some superficial treatments, sensationalism, and misunderstandings. But in the decades since the initial finds, Latter-day Saints who have followed the more careful analyses have come to appreciate several contributions of the Dead Sea Scrolls, including insights into the literary and sectarian diversity of Judaism at the time of Jesus, new evidence relating to the history and preservation of the biblical text, advances in the science of dating Hebrew and Aramaic documents based on changing styles of script, and valuable additions to the corpus of Jewish texts and text genres.

Certain aspects of the scrolls have particularly interested Latter-day Saints. For example, the Essenes of Qumran accepted the concepts of continuing REVELATION and open CANON much as Latter-day Saints do, in contrast to the current teaching of most Christians and Jews. Qumran commentaries on the books of Habakkuk, Nahum, and other prophets from the Old Testament contain new Essene prophetic interpretations of world events of the LAST DAYS, and the Qumran Temple Scroll claims to be a direct revelation to Moses. Similarly, Latter-day Saints believe that the Bible does not contain all of God's word, but that he has

revealed his will to prophets in the Book of Mormon and to Joseph SMITH, and he continues to reveal new truths to modern prophets.

Latter-day Saints point out that the Bible does not require or demand its own uniqueness. Now the Qumran library has shown that some of the most pious and observant Jews around the time of Christ consulted not only extrabiblical texts but also a variety of differing texts of the biblical books. For the Essenes, the sacredness of scripture did not impose a fixed or standard text. For example, their library contains several versions of the book of Isaiah, with minor differences in wording. They used both long and short versions of Jeremiah. They had varying collections of the Psalms. This open-mindedness about scriptural words and editions is similar to LDS views (see, for example, various LDS accounts of the CREATION). The Dead Sea Scrolls provide evidence that the successive theological concepts of (1) an authoritative text, (2) a fixed text, and ultimately (3) an inerrant text originated with Pharisaic or rabbinic Judaism.

Some people have made much of comparisons between Essene practices and those of the New Testament church, or between both of these and elements of Mormonism. For example, Essene cleansing rituals are in some ways similar to New Testament baptisms, and Essene ritual meals can be interpreted as sacramental. Some see the Christian idea of conversion in the Essene doctrine that an individual is elected to the community by deliberate choice and initiation rather than by birth and infant CIRCUMCISION. Some relate the Essene communal council, with its twelve men and three priests, to Jesus' calling of twelve apostles and favoring among them PETER, JAMES, and JOHN, or to the Latter-day Saint organization with twelve apostles and a three-member FIRST PRESIDENCY. The role of New Testament or modern LDS BISHOPS seems to correspond to many of the functions of the Qumranic *maskil*, or "guardian."

For Latter-day Saints, the emergence of such parallels is not surprising. The covenants of the Old and New Testaments are more alike than different (see DISPENSATIONS OF THE GOSPEL). They proceed from the same God. However, the similarities are counterbalanced by radical differences between Essene practices and the teachings of Jesus Christ, of Paul, or of the Church in modern times. Notably, the Essenes taught their adherents to hate their enemies. Their sect was strict and exclusive. Their ideas of ritual cleanness effectively barred women from the temple and from the temple city of Jerusalem. Such Essene doctrines are opposite to later Christian and LDS teachings. Similarities between Essenism and Christian or LDS concepts should therefore be explained as a dispersion of ideas among groups that share ancient connections rather than as evidences of more intrinsic relationships.

Much is still to be learned from the Dead Sea Scrolls. Many fragments and some scrolls remain unpublished or are not yet fully understood. Much light may yet be shed on ancient Jewish worship patterns, apocalyptic literature, angelology, and sectarianism beyond what is available in biblical accounts.

BIBLIOGRAPHY

For a more ample general statement, see S. Kent Brown, "The Dead Sea Scrolls: A Mormon Perspective," *BYU Studies* 23 (Winter 1983):49–66. Hugh Nibley discusses broad patterns in *An Approach to the Book of Mormon, Since Cumorah,* and *The Prophetic Book of Mormon,* in CWHN, Vols. 6–8. For a listing of editions of the scrolls, see Robert A. Cloward, *The Old Testament Apocrypha and Pseudepigrapha and the Dead Sea Scrolls: A Selected Bibliography of Text Editions and English Translations,* Provo, Utah, 1988.

ROBERT A. CLOWARD

DEAF, MATERIALS FOR THE

The Church makes a serious effort to serve the hearing impaired with gospel materials in formats they can understand. These formats include simplified versions, signed inserts (interpreters superimposed on film who sign conversations and sounds), closed captions (words that show on the screen only when decoded), printed signs, productions with all-deaf casts, and Church manuals translated into signing for the deaf on videocassettes. Each Church film is signed or closed-captioned. All satellite broadcasts and special programs are closed-captioned. To use closed-captioned videos requires a decoder, which the Church provides to units serving the hearing impaired.

All general conference sessions are signed and closed-captioned. The deaf and hearing impaired who attend general conference in SALT LAKE CITY, UTAH, are invited to the Church Office's auditorium to view the proceedings with an interpreter. Those who do not attend in person may participate via closed captions on the Church's satellite network at their local meetinghouses. The sessions are also recorded on videos, with sign language inserts, and made available on loan. TEMPLE ORDINANCES are also presented in formats understandable by the hearing impaired.

A handbook for interpreters and a dictionary of words and phrases peculiar to the Church are available in print and on videocassettes. The Book of Mormon is being translated into American Sign Language (ASL) on videocassette targeted for completion in 1994. A current list of all materials, including their costs and how to order, is available on request from the Special Curriculum Department of the Church.

In a meetinghouse serving the hearing impaired, the Church provides a Com Tek System which amplifies the spoken language. The Church participates in supplying TTY/TDDs (telecommunication devices) for the deaf and hearing-impaired members to carry on Church functions.

DOUGLAS L. HIND

DEATH AND DYING

At death, the spirit and body separate and "the spirits of all men, whether they be good or evil, are taken home to that God who gave them life" (Alma 40:11; cf. Eccl. 12:7). ALMA₂ describes how the spirits of the "righteous are received into a state of happiness, which is called paradise, a state of rest, a state of peace, where they shall rest from all their troubles and from all care, and sorrow" (Alma 40:12; *see* PARADISE; SPIRIT WORLD). In contrast, the wicked, who "chose evil works rather than good," suffer fear of the wrath of God (Alma 40:13; *see* SPIRIT PRISON). Both those who reside in paradise and those in the spirit prison await the RESURRECTION and the judgment of God (*see* JUDGMENT DAY, FINAL).

RESURRECTION FROM DEATH. Through the atonement of Christ, all mortals will be resurrected irrespective of personal righteousness. Their spirits will have their PHYSICAL BODIES restored to them, and thus there will be a permanent unity of the spirit with an immortal, incorruptible body (John 5:28–29; Alma 11:42–45). Except for the resurrection of Christ, "this flesh must have laid down to rot and to crumble to its mother earth, to rise no more," and the spirits of men would have become devils, subject to Satan for eternity (2 Ne. 9:7–9).

NATURE OF DEATH. The scriptures teach that death does not change one's personality (Alma 34:34). Individual identities are eternal (D&C 18:10; 93:29). Thus all those who have been obedient to God's commandments in any time of the world can look forward to reunions with loved ones and associations with ancestors and descendants. Latter-day Saints believe that death need not terminate personal awareness or interpersonal relationships. For the righteous, family ties can continue beyond death because of SEALINGS in the temple. Thus, family members who have received the gospel in mortality conduct FAMILY HISTORY research and perform necessary vicarious ordinances in the temple for deceased family members (see TEMPLE ORDINANCES). Many Latter-day Saints feel a closeness to ancestors from generations past because they have studied their lives, and some have served as proxies for them in temple ordinances (see Moses 6:45–46). Grieving parents know that children who die before reaching the age of ACCOUNTABILITY, and others such as the mentally disabled, receive eternal love and salvation through the grace of Christ and are restored to a completeness to continue in familial relationships (Moro. 8:17, 22; D&C 137:10).

Nevertheless, Latter-day Saints do not embrace death willingly, nor do they seek it (see PROLONGING LIFE). SUICIDE is condemned but judgment of it is left with the Lord (Ballard, pp. 6–9). ABORTION also is considered a serious sin under most circumstances and can cause much sorrow.

The best preparation for death is to repent and live righteously. Those who feel that their lives are in jeopardy with sickness may receive BLESSINGS from the ELDERS of the Church, who, holding the priesthood of God, "shall pray for and lay their hands upon them in my name; and if they die they shall die unto me, and if they live they shall live unto me" (D&C 42:44; see also SICK, BLESSING THE). Those who face extreme suffering in a terminal illness may call upon the Lord for comfort or relief from pain, and rely upon him to prolong or shorten their days upon the earth. To allow a person who is terminally ill to pass away, rather than maintaining a vegetative existence through artificial systems of support, is not the spiritual equivalent of failing to save the life of a person facing death under other circumstances. The Lord is, however, the ultimate giver and taker of life.

To Latter-day Saints, as to all people, death can be tragic, unexpected, or even a blessed release from suffering. The loss of loved ones is an occasion for mourning. However, in LDS doctrine, death is also an occasion for hope, a birth into the next life, a step in the PLAN OF SALVATION that began in the premortal existence and leads, if one is righteous, to eternal life with God in the CELESTIAL KINGDOM. The grieving of the faithful is appropriately marked by sorrow and hope, not despair and depression. Yet the loss of a loved one is to be taken neither lightly nor coldly. Grief and love are compatible—if not essential—emotions of the faithful. And Latter-day Saints who face death themselves, while experiencing uncertainty and concern for those left behind, can find hope in the plan of salvation and the Lord's promise that "those that die in me shall not taste of death, for it shall be sweet unto them" (D&C 42:46).

DEATH OF INFANTS. Joseph and Emma SMITH struggled with personal losses, including the death of several of their children. Joseph wrote: "I have meditated upon the subject, and asked the question, why it is that infants, innocent children, are taken away from us, especially those that seem to be the most intelligent and interesting. The strongest reasons that present themselves to my mind are these: . . . they were too pure, too lovely, to live on earth . . . [but] we shall soon have them again" (TPJS, pp. 196–97).

DEATH OF YOUTH. Joseph Smith commented on the untimely death of youth at the funeral of young Ephraim Marks: "[This occasion] calls to mind the death of my oldest brother, Alvin, who died in New York, and my youngest brother, Don Carlos Smith, who died in Nauvoo. It has been hard for me to live on earth and see these young men upon whom we have leaned for support and comfort taken from us in the midst of their youth. Yes, it has been hard to be reconciled to these things. . . . Yet I know we ought to be still and know it is of God" (TPJS, p. 215). The Prophet also found great comfort in the gospel's affirmation of the relationship of mortality to eternity: "We have reason to have the greatest hope and consolations for our dead of any people on the earth; for we have seen them walk worthily in our midst, and seen them sink asleep in the arms of Jesus; and those who have died in the faith are now in the celestial kingdom of God" (*TPJS*, p. 359).

Mourning not only is appropriate; it is also one of the deepest expressions of pure love: "Thou shalt live together in love, insomuch that thou shalt weep for the loss of them that die" (D&C 42:45). ALMA₁ taught that as part of the BAPTISMAL COVENANT the saints are "to mourn with those that mourn; yea, and comfort those that stand in need of comfort" (Mosiah 18:9). Mourning can heighten our faith and our hopes. The Prophet Joseph Smith said, "The expectation of seeing my friends in the morning of the resurrection cheers my soul and makes me bear up against the evils of life. It is like their taking a long journey, and on their return we meet them with increased joy" (*TPJS*, p. 296).

FUNERALS. LDS FUNERALS are solemn and grieving occasions but also project a spirit of hope based on anticipation of reunion with the deceased after this life. They are usually held in an LDS chapel or a mortuary under the direction of the BISHOP of the ward (Packer, p. 18). Funerals open and close with sacred music and prayer, sometimes involving congregational singing or a choir (Packer, p. 19). Some LDS hymns describe life after death as a return to the presence of God (*Hymns*, p. 292), or as a condition of rest from mortal cares, and often include a reminder of the travails of mortality as temporary: "And should we die before our journey's through, happy day, all is well. We then are free from toil and sorrow too; with the saints we shall dwell" (*Hymns*, p. 30).

The funeral includes reminiscences and eulogies as well as talks about the ATONEMENT, the Resurrection, life after death, and related doctrines that comfort and inspire the bereaved. Some families choose to have members or friends of the family talk about the life of the deceased or sing an appropriate hymn. A prayer on behalf of the family by one of its members before the public service begins is customary.

GRAVESIDE SERVICES. Following the funeral, a simple graveside dedication service traditionally is held, attended only by family and intimate friends. One who holds the MELCHIZEDEK PRIESTHOOD, usually a member or close friend of the family, dedicates the grave, asking God to protect it from the elements or other disturbance as a hallowed resting place until the resurrection.

Local law in some countries may dictate CREMATION rather than burial, but in the absence of such a law, burial is preferred because of its doctrinal symbolism (Packer, p. 19). Circumstances also may dictate a memorial service or a graveside service only. Bishops are counseled to show regard for family wishes in keeping with the spiritual and reverent nature of the occasion (Packer, pp. 19–20).

SUMMARY. Even as death began with the Fall, it will end with the Atonement, through which all are resurrected and the earth itself becomes immortal (D&C 29:22–29; 1 Cor. 15:19–26; Rev. 21:1–4). The hope engendered in Latter-day Saints by this long-range view of the loving Savior, triumphant over death, was reflected in a letter from Joseph Smith to the Church in 1842: "Now what do we hear in the gospel which we have received? A voice of gladness! A voice of mercy from heaven: and a voice of truth out of the earth; glad tidings for the dead; a voice of gladness for the living and the dead; glad tidings of great joy" (D&C 128:19). Although it brings grief to those left behind, death is part of "the merciful plan of the great Creator (2 Ne. 9:6), it is "a mechanism of rescue" (Packer, p. 21)—an essential step in the Lord's "great plan of happiness" (Alma 42:8).

[*See also* Afterlife; Autopsies; Burial; Cremation.]

BIBLIOGRAPHY

Ballard, M. Russell. "Suicide: Some Things We Know, and Some We Do Not." *Ensign* 17 [Oct. 1987]:6–9.

Barlow, Brent A. *Understanding Death.* Salt Lake City, 1979.

Hinckley, Gordon B. "The Empty Tomb Bore Testimony." *Ensign* 18 (May, 1988):65–68.

Hymns of the Church of Jesus Christ of Latter-day Saints. Salt Lake City, 1985.

Kimball, Spencer W. "Tragedy or Destiny?" *IE* 69 (Mar. 1966):178–80, 210–14, 216–17.

Madsen, Truman G. "Distinctions in the Mormon Approach to Death and Dying." In *Deity and Death*, ed. Spencer J. Palmer, pp. 61–74. Provo, Utah.

Packer, Boyd K. "Funerals—A Time for Reverence." *Ensign* 18 (Nov. 1988):18–21.

L. KAY GILLESPIE

DEATH RATES

See: Vital Statistics

DEDICATIONS

Dedication is the act of devoting or consecrating something to the Lord, or "setting apart" something for a specific purpose in building the KINGDOM OF GOD. It is a PRIESTHOOD function performed through an official and formal act of prayer.

For members of The Church of Jesus Christ of Latter-day Saints, dedications serve at least two clear functions. First, they call down the powers of heaven to establish a sacred space or time in the furthering of the desired purpose. Second, they consecrate the participants, focusing their souls upon the meaning of the dedicated object or act. In this way the secular is brought into sacred relationships, and the blessings of God are invoked so that the powers of heaven and earth are joined to bring about works of righteousness.

LDS church buildings are always dedicated to the Lord, usually after all indebtedness is removed. In the Bible the first recorded dedicatory prayer is that of the Temple of Solomon (1 Kgs. 8:22–53), at which time the glory of the Lord filled the temple, in divine approval. The first temple dedication in this dispensation was on March 27, 1836, when the Prophet Joseph SMITH dedicated the KIRTLAND TEMPLE as "a house of prayer, a house of fasting, a house of faith, a house of learning, a house of glory, a house of order, a house of God" (D&C 109:8). Since then many LDS temples and thousands of MEETINGHOUSES around the world have been similarly dedicated to the Lord. Church buildings such as schools, VISITORS CENTERS, storehouses, office buildings, and HISTORICAL SITES are also dedicated to the Lord for their intended uses. Schools may be dedicated as institutions of learning and character development, while bishop's storehouses are dedicated to provide welfare and physical supplies for the needy.

Lands and countries may be dedicated, sometimes more than once, for divinely appointed purposes. On October 24, 1841, Elder Orson Hyde ascended the Mount of Olives and dedicated the land of Palestine for the return of the Jews and the rearing of a temple. It was rededicated on several other occasions. More than thirty-two countries and entire continents have been dedicated for the preaching of the gospel.

Homes of the SAINTS, whether or not they are free of debt, may be dedicated "as sacred edifices where the Holy Spirit can reside, and as sanctuar-ies where family members can worship, find safety from the world, grow spiritually, and prepare for eternal family relationships" (*General Handbook of Instructions*, 11–2, 1989). On some occasions it has been deemed appropriate to dedicate business places or enterprises to accomplish righteous and divine purposes. It is customary in the Church to dedicate graves as the final resting place for the deceased, asking that the ground be hallowed and protected until the day of resurrection.

Olive OIL is also consecrated by a dedicatory prayer. It is thus set apart by the power of the priesthood for the divinely prescribed purposes of blessing the sick and anointing in the temple (James 5:14; D&C 109:35; 124:39).

TAD R. CALLISTER

DEGREES OF GLORY

The Church of Jesus Christ of Latter-day Saints has an optimistic view of the eternal rewards awaiting mankind in the hereafter. Members of the Church believe that there are "many mansions" (John 14:2) and that Christ's ATONEMENT and RESURRECTION will save all mankind from death, and eventually will reclaim from hell all except the SONS OF PERDITION (D&C 76:43–44). The saved, however, are not placed into a monolithic state called HEAVEN. In the resurrection of the body, they are assigned to different degrees of glory commensurate with the law they have obeyed. There are three kingdoms of glory: the celestial, the terrestrial, and the telestial. The apostle Paul spoke of three glories, differing from one another as the sun, moon, and stars differ in brilliance. He called the first two glories celestial and terrestrial, but the third is not named in the Bible (1 Cor. 15:40–41; cf. D&C 76:70–81, 96–98.) The word "telestial" is an LDS term, first used by the Prophet Joseph SMITH and Sidney RIGDON in reporting a vision they received on February 16, 1832 (D&C 76; *Webster's Third New International Dictionary* defines telestial glory as "the lowest of three Mormon degrees or kingdoms of glory attainable in heaven"; *see also* CELESTIAL KINGDOM; TERRESTRIAL KINGDOM; TELESTIAL KINGDOM).

At the final JUDGMENT, all except the DEVIL, his ANGELS, and those who become sons of perdition during mortal life will be assigned to one of the three kingdoms of glory. The devil and his fol-

Kingdoms, by Charlotte Warr Anderson (1987, pieced quilt, 95″ × 85″). "There is one glory of the sun, and another glory of the moon, and another glory of the stars. . . . So also is the resurrection of the dead" (1 Cor. 15:41–42; cf. D&C 76). Church Museum of History and Art.

lowers will be assigned a kingdom without glory (D&C 76:25–39; 88:24, 32–35).

LDS SCRIPTURE SOURCES. Although the Bible contains references to varying levels of resurrection and heaven (1 Cor. 15:39–58; 2 Cor. 12:2), LDS understanding of the subject comes mainly through revelations given to the Prophet Joseph Smith. The first revelation dealing directly with this matter was received February 16, 1832, and is called "The Vision" (D&C 76). Concerning the circumstances of receiving this revelation, Joseph Smith explained:

> Upon my return from Amherst [Ohio] conference, I resumed the translation of the Scriptures. From sundry revelations which had been received, it was apparent that many important points touching the salvation of man, had been taken from the Bible, or lost before it was compiled. It appeared self-evident from what truths were left, that if God rewarded every one according to the deeds done in the body the term "Heaven," as intended for the Saints' eternal home, must include more kingdoms than one. Accordingly . . . while translating St. John's Gospel, myself and Elder Rigdon saw the following vision"

[*HC* 1:245; *see also* JOSEPH SMITH TRANSLATION OF THE BIBLE (JST)].

Later revelations, especially Doctrine and Covenants 88, 131, 132, 137, and 138, have added information on this subject.

THE CELESTIAL GLORY. The celestial kingdom is reserved for those who receive a testimony of Jesus and fully embrace the gospel; that is, they have faith in Jesus Christ, repent of their sins, are baptized by immersion by one having authority, receive the HOLY GHOST by the LAYING ON OF HANDS, and endure in RIGHTEOUSNESS. All who attain this kingdom "shall dwell in the presence of God and his Christ forever and ever" (D&C 76:62). There are, however, different privileges and powers within this kingdom. "In the celestial glory there are three heavens or degrees; and in order to obtain the highest, a man must enter into this order of the priesthood (meaning the new and everlasting covenant of marriage); and if he does not, he cannot obtain it. He may enter into the other, but that is the end of his kingdom; he cannot have an increase" (D&C 131:1–4). "Increase" in this instance means the bearing of spirit children after mortal life (*see* ETERNAL LIVES). Joseph Smith explained, "Except a man and his wife enter into an everlasting covenant and be married for eternity . . . by the power and authority of the Holy Priesthood, they will cease to increase when they die; that is, they will not have any children after the resurrection" (*TPJS*, pp. 300–301). Latter-day Saints believe that those who attain the highest level in the celestial kingdom become gods, receive exaltation, and are joint heirs with Christ of all that the Father has (cf. Rom. 8:14–17; D&C 76:50–70; 84:33–39; 132:19–25).

There is no scriptural explanation of those who go to the two lower categories of the celestial kingdom except that they "are not gods, but are angels of God forever and ever," ministering servants who "remain separately and singly, without exaltation, in their saved condition, to all eternity" (D&C 132:16–17).

THE TERRESTRIAL GLORY. The inhabitants of the terrestrial kingdom are described as the honorable people of the earth who received a testimony of Jesus but were not sufficiently valiant in that testimony to obey all the principles and ordinances of the gospel (D&C 76:71–80). Also, those of "the heathen nations" who "died without law," who are honorable but who do not accept the fulness of the gospel in the postearthly spirit world, are candidates for the terrestrial glory (D&C 45:54; 76:72). In the hereafter, they receive the presence of the Son, but not the fulness of the Father. The glory of the terrestrial kingdom differs from the celestial as the light we see from the moon differs from that of the sun in glory. There is no mention of different degrees or levels in the terrestrial kingdom, but it is reasonable that there, as in the celestial and telestial kingdoms, individuals will differ from one another in glory (see D&C 76:97–98).

THE TELESTIAL GLORY. Those who on earth are liars, sorcerers, whoremongers, and adulterers, who receive not the gospel, or the testimony of Jesus, or the prophets, go to the telestial kingdom. They are judged unworthy of being resurrected at the SECOND COMING of Christ and are given additional time in "hell" to repent and prepare themselves for a later resurrection and placement into a kingdom of lesser glory. During this period, they learn to abide by laws they once rejected. They bow the knee and confess their dependence on Jesus Christ, but they still do not receive the fulness of the gospel. At the end of the MILLENNIUM, they are brought out of hell and are resurrected to a telestial glory. There "they shall be servants of the Most High; but where God and Christ dwell they cannot come, worlds without end" (D&C 76:112). However, they do receive "of the Holy Spirit through the ministration of the terrestrial" (verse 86). Though differing in glory from the terrestrial and celestial kingdoms as the light we perceive from the stars differs from that from the moon and the sun, the glory of the telestial kingdom still "surpasses all understanding" (verse 89; see D&C 76:81–90, 98–112; 88:100–101).

OPPORTUNITY FOR ALL. The Church holds that all mankind, except the sons of perdition, will find a place in one of the kingdoms of glory in the hereafter and that they themselves choose the place by the lives they live here on earth and in the postearthly spirit world. Even the lowest glory surpasses all mortal understanding. Everyone is granted AGENCY (D&C 93:30–32). All have access to the revelatory power of the LIGHT OF CHRIST, which, if followed, will lead them to the truth of the gospel (John 1:1–13; Alma 12:9–11; Moro. 7:14–19; D&C 84:45–48). Everyone will hear the gospel of Jesus Christ, either on earth or in the postearthly spirit world, and have ample opportu-

nity to demonstrate the extent of their acceptance (D&C 138; cf. 1 Pet. 4:6). Those who do not have a chance to receive the gospel on this earth, but who would have fully accepted it had they been able to hear it, and who therefore do receive it in the spirit world, are heirs of the celestial kingdom of God (D&C 137:7–8). They will accept the saving ordinances performed for them by proxy in a TEMPLE on the earth (see SALVATION OF THE DEAD). Christ, victorious and gracious, grants to all the desires of their hearts, allowing them to choose their eternal reward according to the law they are willing and able to abide.

BIBLIOGRAPHY

Dahl, Larry E. "The Vision of the Glories." In Studies in Scripture, ed. R. L. Millet and K. P. Jackson, Vol. 1, pp. 279–308. Sandy, Utah, 1984.

Smith, Joseph Fielding. DS, Vol. 2, pp. 20–24. Salt Lake City, 1955.

Talmage, James E. AF, pp. 375–94. Salt Lake City, 1968.

LARRY E. DAHL

DEIFICATION, EARLY CHRISTIAN

From the second to eighth centuries, the standard Christian term for SALVATION was *theopoiesis* or *theosis*, literally, "being made God," or deification. Such language survived sporadically in the mystical tradition of the West and is still used in Eastern Orthodoxy. LDS doctrines on ETERNAL PROGRESSION and EXALTATION to godhood reflect a similar view of salvation.

In its classical form, particularly in the works of Athanasius (fourth-century bishop of Alexandria), deification was built upon the concept of the incarnation of Christ. The Council of Nicaea (A.D. 325) defined the Son as *homoousios* (of the same substance) with the Father, and thus fully God. By taking upon himself our flesh through birth, Jesus as God united the essence of humanity to the divine nature. Eventually Christ's divinity overcame the limits of the flesh through RESURRECTION and glorification, transforming and raising his body to the full level of godhood. As Athanasius summarized, "God was made man that we might be made God" (*On the Incarnation of the Logos* 54).

Although the doctrine has been dismissed by later scholars as a mere "physical theory of redemption" focused on the Resurrection, deification is more than a synonym for IMMORTALITY. Church Fathers argued that deification not only restores the image of God that was lost in the Fall, but also enables mankind to transcend human nature so as to possess the attributes of God. "I may become God as far as he became man," declared Gregory of Nazianzus in the late fourth century (*Orations* 29.19). Descriptions of deification included physical incorruptibility, immunity from suffering, perfect virtue, purity, fullness of knowledge and joy, eternal progression, communion with God, inheritance of divine glory, and joint rulership with Christ in the KINGDOM OF GOD in heaven forever.

The roots of the Christian doctrine of deification are primarily biblical. Beginning with the creation of humanity in the image of God (Gen. 1:26–27), the church fathers developed aspects of deification from such concepts as the command to moral perfection and holiness (e.g., Lev. 19:1–2; Matt. 5:48; 1 Jn. 3:2; 1 Cor. 11:1; 2 Pet. 1:3–7), adoption as heirs of God (Rom. 8:15–17; Gal. 4:4–7), unification with God in Christ (John 17:11–23), and partaking in Christ's sufferings in order to be elevated with him in glory (e.g., Rom. 8:16–18; 2 Cor. 3:18; 4:16–18; Philip. 3:20–21; 2 Tim. 2:10–12). They also pointed to examples of humans described as "gods" in scripture (Ex. 4:16; 7:1; Ps. 82:6; John 10:34–36).

Jewish thought, particularly in response to developing CHRISTOLOGY and its perceived threat to monotheism, was more reticent to speak of humans attaining divinity. Nevertheless, Jews shared some of the crucial biblical texts underlying deification. Talmudic Judaism tended to stress humanity's obligation to imitate God's holiness in consequence of being created in the divine image. Moses and other prophets were spoken of as sharing God's glory and becoming "secondary gods" in relation to other mortals (Meeks, pp. 234–35). Philo described Moses' glorification as "a prototype . . . of the ascent to heaven which every disciple hoped to be granted" (Meeks, p. 244).

Due to its incongruity with the doctrine of God in Western Christianity, deification fell out of favor as the preferred way of describing salvation. Catholic theology increasingly stressed the transcendence of God, who alone was self-existent and eternal. All other beings were created ex nihilo, "out of nothing," having only contingent being. This theological development culminated in Augustine. For him, God's absolute oneness and otherness was so different from humanity's created status and dependence on divine grace that salvation could not bridge the gap between the eternal Creator and the creatures contingent upon him. Ever since, talk of deification has been suspect or heretical in Western Christianity and has formed a major point of objection among traditional Christians to the teachings of Latter-day Saints on the subject.

BIBLIOGRAPHY

Barlow, Philip L. "Unorthodox Orthodoxy: The Idea of Deification in Christian History." *Sunstone* 8 (Sept.–Oct. 1983):13–18.

Benz, Ernst W. "Imago Dei: Man in the Image of God." In *Reflections on Mormonism*, ed. T. Madsen, pp. 201–219. Provo, Utah, 1978.

Gross, Jules. *La divinisation du chrétien d'après les pères grecs.* Paris, 1938.

Meeks, Wayne A. *The Prophet-King: Moses Tradition and the Johannine Christology.* Leiden, 1967.

Norman, Keith E. "Deification: The Content of Athanasian Soteriology." Ph.D. diss. Duke University, 1980.

———. "Divinization: The Forgotten Teaching of Early Christianity." *Sunstone* 1 (1975):15–19.

Pelikan, Jaroslav. *The Christian Tradition*, Vols. 1 and 2. Chicago, 1971–1974.

KEITH E. NORMAN

DEMOGRAPHICS

See: Vital Statistics

DESERET

The word deseret is found in the most ancient book in the Book of Mormon, "And they did also carry with them deseret, which, by interpretation, is a honey bee" (Ether 2:3).

Because the Book of Mormon was written in "reformed Egyptian" (Mormon 9:32), Hugh Nibley has suggested that the etymology of the word deseret is related to the ancient Egyptian word ▱ ◯ ⸗ *dšrt*, read by Egyptologists as desheret. In Egyptian, *dšrt* means the red crown (of the king of Lower Egypt). The Egyptian word for bee is 🐝 ◯ | *bt*. In the discussion of the sign ꝱ *dšrt*, Alan Gardiner, in *Egyptian Grammar*, states that ꝱ was used to replace 🐝 in two Egyptian titles where 🐝 was used to mean the *bty* King of Lower Egypt. Thus, the title ⌓⌓ *n-sw-bt* was sometimes written as ⌓⌓ *n-sw-bt*, which literally means "He who belongs to the sedge plant (of Upper Egypt) and to the bee (of Lower Egypt)," normally translated "The King of Upper and Lower Egypt." This substitution of ꝱ for 🐝 has led Nibley to associate the Egyptian word *dšrt* and the Book of Mormon word deseret.

The beehive and the word deseret have been used variously throughout the history of the Church. The territory settled by the Mormon PIONEERS was called the State of Deseret. The emblem of the beehive is used in the seal of the State of Utah and is a common decoration in Utah architecture, symbolizing industriousness. Brigham YOUNG's house in Salt Lake City is called the Beehive House. Early Sunday schools were part of the Deseret Sunday School Union. A vital part of the Church Welfare Program carries the name Deseret Industries.

BIBLIOGRAPHY

Gardiner, Alan. *Egyptian Grammar*, 3rd ed., pp. 73-74, and signs L2 and S3. Oxford, 1982.

Nibley, Hugh. *Abraham in Egypt*, pp. 225-45. Salt Lake City, 1981.

———. *Lehi in the Desert and The World of the Jaredites, There Were Jaredites*. CWHN 5:189-94, 319-22.

STEPHEN PARKER

DESERET, STATE OF

On February 2, 1848, by the Treaty of Guadalupe Hidalgo, Mexico ceded to the United States an extensive area that included the Great Basin, where Mormon PIONEERS had begun settlement six months earlier. Even before the treaty was signed, Church leaders began discussing petitioning the U.S. government for recognition as a state or asking for territorial privileges. In July 1849 a committee wrote a constitution. It used as models the U.S. Constitution and the Iowa Constitution of 1846, from which the committee took fifty-seven of the sixty-seven sections of the new constitution. The committee requested that the state be named DESERET and that the boundaries be Oregon on the north, the Green River on the east, Mexico on the south, and the Sierra Nevada on the west, including a portion of the Southern California seacoast. "Deseret," a word from the Book of Mormon, means "honeybee" (Ether 2:3) and is symbolic of work and industry. A slate of officers was approved, with Brigham YOUNG as governor. Almon W. Babbitt, appointed representative to Congress, was instructed to carry the plea for statehood to Washington, D.C.

This effort by Latter-day Saint settlers to organize themselves into a provisional government was much like the attempt made in the 1780s by settlers in Tennessee, who organized the state of Franklin when they felt neglected by North Carolina, and the settlers of Oregon, who established a

The word "Deseret" appears twice on the Utah stone at the Washington Monument (1978; replica of the cornerstone of the Salt Lake Temple, 1853). The interior of the monument contains 190 stones representing individuals, cities, states, and nations. "Deseret" was a name often used in the territory colonized by the Mormon pioneers. Photographer: Robert L. Palmer.

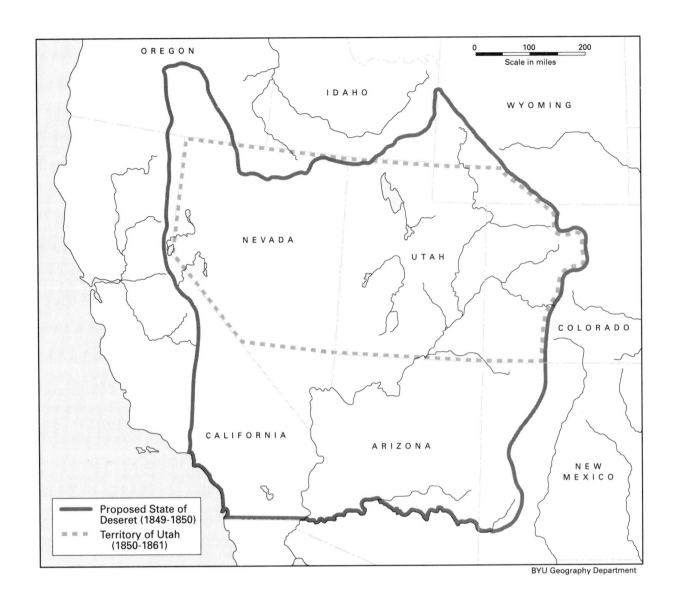

Proposed State of
Deseret (1849-1850)

Territory of Utah
(1850-1861)

BYU Geography Department

local government that functioned without recognition from the U.S. government until they were given territorial status in 1848.

The State of Deseret General Assembly met in regular session from December 1849 to March 1850. After special sessions during the summer, the members assembled for their second regular session in December 1850. Earlier, on September 9, U.S. President Millard Fillmore had signed an act to create a much smaller UTAH TERRITORY and appointed Brigham Young the first territorial governor. After word of the creation of the territory reached Utah, the tentative state of Deseret was dissolved on March 28, 1851. The provisional government had lasted only about a year and a half.

The territorial status did not provide the self-government Latter-day Saints desired, and even though Brigham Young was appointed first governor, Church leaders and the territorial legislature continued efforts to obtain statehood. In 1856, delegates met to again write a constitution and propose the state of Deseret, an effort rejected by Congress. As a part of a third effort in 1862, Brigham Young called the State of Deseret General Assembly into session for the first time since 1851. Thereafter it met each year until 1870, each session lasting only a few days and focusing on winning statehood on the basis of the proposed constitution of 1849 with only minor changes.

In the meantime, Brigham Young had been replaced as territorial governor by a series of outside appointees, who became progressively more hostile to the meetings of the General Assembly and complained about this "ghost government," as they called it. In 1872 a constitutional convention drew up a new constitution and dropped the name Deseret from the petition. This petition also failed, and hope for the state of Deseret came to an end.

[*See also* History of the Church, 1844–1877; Utah Statehood.]

BIBLIOGRAPHY

Constitution of the State of Deseret. Kanesville, Iowa, 1849.

Crawley, Peter. "The Constitution of the State of Deseret." *BYU Studies* 29 (Fall 1989):7–22.

Morgan, Dale L. "The State of Deseret." *Utah Historical Quarterly* 8 (1940):65–251. Reprinted as *The State of Deseret.* Logan, Utah, 1987.

JEFFERY OGDEN JOHNSON

DESERET ALPHABET

On April 8, 1852, Brigham YOUNG announced that the Board of Regents of the UNIVERSITY OF DESERET was preparing a new method of writing English. The idea was to develop a sort of universal system, especially so that foreign-language-speaking converts could learn to read English more easily.

The final version of the Deseret Alphabet utilized thirty-eight characters corresponding to sounds of English. Like Noah Webster and other early Americans who studied language, Brigham Young objected to sounding the letter *a* differently in the spellings of mate, father, fall, man, and many. In this, he was apparently influenced by studying shorthand with his secretary George D. Watt, who had studied systems of shorthand and spelling reform based on phonemes, the significant sounds of English, under Isaac Pitman.

The Regents discussed letter forms and sounds to be represented. The forms finally adopted were unfamiliar and unadaptable to cursive writing. The range of basic English sounds was close to present-day analyses, but the schwa (the unaccented, reduced vowel in ideA, tradEd, ratIfy, biolOgy, Upon) was omitted, leading to respellings based upon traditional spelling.

Learning the Deseret phonetic system was easy. A previously illiterate missionary wrote letters home after only six lessons. Hosea Stout, Thales Haskell, and others kept diaries in Deseret.

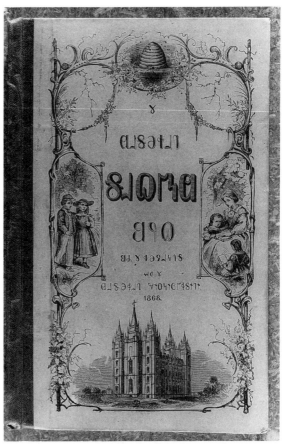

This reader was published in 1868 in the Deseret alphabet. Its title reads "The Deseret Second Book by the Regents of the Deseret University." Development of the Deseret Alphabet was begun in October 1853, and a few books, including the Book of Mormon, were published in this phonetic script before 1870. Courtesy Rare Books and Manuscripts, Brigham Young University.

However, since pronunciation, which varies, determined spelling, many words might appear more than one way in the same individual's usage, resulting in some confusion.

Scriptural passages written in the Deseret Alphabet appeared in the *Deseret News* in 1859. Orson Pratt transcribed further materials that were published in New York City, printed with type designed and cast there, at a total cost of $18,500. These included first and second school readers in 1868 and the Book of Mormon and a third reader of excerpts from it in 1869. Although few of these books were sold, some SUNDAY SCHOOLS as well as territorial schools used them.

In 1873 Pratt estimated the cost of printing a meager library of 1,000 titles at $5 million—

𐐜 𐐔𐐇𐐝𐐀𐐡𐐀𐐓 𐐈𐐢𐐙𐐆𐐒𐐇𐐓.

The thirty-eight symbols used in the Deseret Alphabet and their phonetic values. The top line reads "The Deseret Alphabet."

prohibitively expensive for a sparse population in a subsistence economy. Those already literate had little incentive to learn the Deseret Alphabet, while illiterates would have had very little to read. The death of President Young in 1877 marked the end of efforts on its behalf.

BIBLIOGRAPHY

Ivins, Stanley S. "The Deseret Alphabet." *Utah Humanities Review* 1 (1947):223–39.

Monson, Samuel C. "The Deseret Alphabet." Master's thesis, Columbia University, 1948.

SAMUEL C. MONSON

DESERET BOOK COMPANY

The Deseret Book Company had its beginnings in George Q. Cannon and Sons, a retail bookstore and publishing company established in Salt Lake City in 1866. Cannon was an apostle and a counselor in the FIRST PRESIDENCY of The Church of Jesus Christ of Latter-day Saints. After his death in 1901, the company was purchased by the Church's *Deseret News* and renamed the Deseret News Bookstore. Meanwhile, the Church SUNDAY SCHOOL organization began publishing its own lesson manuals and supplementary instructional materials in the early 1870s and later included book publishing and a retail bookstore. The two companies were merged in 1919 and subsequently named the Deseret Book Company.

A subsidiary of the Church's Deseret Management Corporation, the Deseret Book Company has three divisions: retail, publishing, and wholesale. The retail division operates stores in several states in the western United States: Mormon Handicraft, which is a Salt Lake City consignment shop for handmade goods; a book club; an audio- and videotape club; and a mail- and telephone-order shopping service. The publishing division produces books related to family life, history, biography, LDS doctrine and theology, fiction, and inspiration for both children and adults. It also produces audio- and videotapes and compact discs. The wholesale division distributes Deseret Book titles and books from other publishers to retailers throughout the world.

ELEANOR KNOWLES

DESERET HOSPITAL

With increasing evidence that home care of the sick and injured was no longer adequate, the women of the RELIEF SOCIETY, with the support of the First Presidency, opened Deseret Hospital in Salt Lake City on July 17, 1882. Though Roman Catholics and Episcopalians already sponsored hospitals in Utah, this was the first official endorsement of allopathic medicine by The Church of Jesus Christ of Latter-day Saints (*see* MEDICAL PRACTICES). A desire to have a place where spiritual ministrations could accompany medical treatment (*see* SICK, BLESSING THE) was among the motivations for the institution, and staff members were blessed and SET APART by Church leaders for their tasks. The hospital also specialized in obstetrics, both in providing care and in training midwives and others.

Deseret Hospital was originally located in downtown Salt Lake City in a building vacated when the Catholics moved their hospital to larger

Deseret Hospital Board of Directors. Top row: Ellis R. Shipp, MD; Bathsheba W. Smith; Elizabeth Howard; Romania B. Pratt Penrose, MD. Second row: Phebe C. Woodruff; Mary Isabella Horne; Eliza R. Snow; Zina D. H. Young; Marinda N. Hyde. Bottom row: Jane S. Richards; Emmeline B. Wells. Courtesy Utah State Historical Society.

quarters. In July 1884, Deseret Hospital moved to a larger building that could accommodate forty to fifty patients, though it seldom had more than sixteen at a time.

Deseret Hospital featured a homelike atmosphere, the latest surgical equipment from New York, and a staff of dedicated, well-trained, mostly female physicians, including Ellen B. Ferguson, Ellis R. Shipp, and Romania B. Pratt. Long before its doors opened, the women of the Church, led by Eliza R. SNOW, raised funds for the hospital. Though these efforts continued, support was never adequate to pay for the treatment of the many "free" patients, and the hospital was forced to close in 1894. The hospital kept its nursing and midwifery schools operating until the opening of the Groves Latter-day Saints Hospital in 1905 (*see* HOSPITALS).

BIBLIOGRAPHY

Arrington, Leonard J. "The Economic Role of Pioneer Mormon Women." *Western Humanities Review* 9 (Spring 1955):161–63.

Noall, Claire Wilcox. "Utah's Pioneer Women Doctors: The Story of the Deseret Hospital." *IE* 42 (May 1939):274–75, 308–309.

SCOTT PARKER

DESERET INDUSTRIES

Toward the end of the Great Depression, in August 1938, Deseret Industries was established "to help Church members help themselves" through a program of donated household items, volunteer labor, and vocational training.

In a letter to LDS congregations in Utah's Salt Lake Valley dated August 11, 1938, the FIRST PRESIDENCY and PRESIDING BISHOPRIC called for "contributions of clothing, papers, magazines, articles of furniture, electrical fixtures, metal and glassware" from each household. The letter explained that the project would be known as Deseret Industries, and that the organization would make "periodic collections of these materials from homes . . . and employ men and women to sort, process, and repair the articles collected for sale and distribution among those who desire to obtain usable articles . . . at a minimum cost."

Since then, goods have been sold at thrift stores bearing the Deseret Industries name. Local Church congregations continue donation drives, during which volunteer workers collect goods from the homes of members. Anyone can donate items at any Deseret Industries store as well.

This donation bag from the 1940s features the beehive, symbol of industry for the Church Welfare plan, as well as one of the stated goals of the Deseret Industries, "Help others to help themselves." Photographer: Holger Marius Larsen.

The Deseret Industries program was implemented specifically for the benefit of members who could not obtain employment elsewhere, and its initial work force consisted primarily of the unemployed and elderly. It was operated under the umbrella of the Church Security Plan—now Church WELFARE SERVICES—and continues as an integral part of the Church welfare system. Church leaders use Deseret Industries not only for employment training but as a resource for clothing and household items for needy members.

There were more than a dozen Deseret Industries stores in Salt Lake County and five in the Los Angeles area before World War II. Most of those were closed during the war, and operations were consolidated. By 1948 there were six stores, and growth continued slowly but steadily into the 1950s.

Deseret Industries started a rug-making operation in 1954 and acquired a woolen mill in 1957. The plants not only provided additional jobs but also goods to be distributed to needy Church members through the welfare program. Many elderly and handicapped members found work at Deseret Industries, and those who were sufficiently able were trained and moved into private industry.

As the program moved through the 1960s and into the 1970s, the emphasis on rehabilitation increased. Preparing people to enter the private workplace became a forte of Deseret Industries. Stores and equipment were upgraded through the mid-1970s and early 1980s to compare favorably with any of their kind.

Deseret Industries outlets have followed large concentrations of Church members. At the beginning of the 1990s there were forty-six Deseret Industries retail stores in cities of the western United States.

The Deseret Industries program still focuses on those with disabilities and those who have other social, employment, and economic challenges and obstacles to overcome. An estimated 60–70 percent of the people in the program are somewhat limited physically, mentally, emotionally, or socially. In 1980, Deseret Industries placed about 240 people into jobs with private companies. In 1989, it placed more than 700.

People needing training are usually referred to Deseret Industries by a Church leader. A program for each person is written with the individual's supervisors and rehabilitation workers. It incorporates personal and work-related goals and is closely monitored. Local Church members sometimes receive CALLINGS to help with training and rehabilitation.

Most Deseret Industries programs are more closely related to work adjustment than to skills training. Trainees get the experience of entering the workplace every day, being on time, learning to get along with coworkers, and taking directions from supervisors. Deseret Industries is not set up to train people to be journeymen plumbers or electricians, for example, though people may get experience doing these types of things.

Employment or career development is one of six standards of personal and family EMERGENCY PREPAREDNESS outlined by the Church, the others being literacy and education, financial and resource management, home production and storage, physical health, and social-emotional and spiritual strength.

The mission of Deseret Industries parallels the mission of Church Welfare Services. A 1936 statement by the Church's First Presidency explains the philosophy of the welfare program:

Our primary purpose was to set up, in so far as it might be possible, a system under which the curse of idleness would be done away with, the evils of a dole abolished, and independence, industry, thrift and self-respect be once more established amongst our people. The aim of the Church is to help the people help themselves. Work is to be re-enthroned as the ruling principle of the lives of our Church membership [*CR*, Oct. 1936].

BIBLIOGRAPHY

Searle, Don. "Deseret Industries at 50." *Ensign* 18 (July 1988):32–37.

Cannon, Michael. "Deseret Industries Commemorates 50 Years." *Church News*, Aug. 13, 1988, pp. 8–9, 12.

Lloyd, R. Scott. "Finding Dignity Through Work." *Church News*, Sept. 23, 1989, pp. 8–9.

MICHAEL C. CANNON

DESERET NEWS

The *Deseret News* began as a weekly newspaper in Salt Lake City on June 15, 1850, just three years after the Mormon pioneers founded the city. Established by the Church under the direction of Brigham YOUNG, the *News* has had uninterrupted publication to the present. It became a daily on November 21, 1867. From the beginning, the *Deseret News* has championed the U.S. Constitution and "truth and liberty." Editorially it has promoted free enterprise, the work ethic, and high moral values.

The early pioneers launched a newspaper against great odds. Because paper had to be brought in from California or Missouri by oxcart, they tried to make their own locally from rags in 1854. The result was a thick, gray paper that was often streaked with colors from the old shirts, pants, and dresses from which it was made.

The first editor of the *Deseret News* was Willard Richards (1850–1854), who was also a counselor in the FIRST PRESIDENCY of the Church. George Q. Cannon was the editor from 1867 to 1873 and from 1877 to 1879. As a youth, he had worked in the *Times and Seasons* printing office in Nauvoo, Illinois, and had edited the *Millennial Star* in Great Britain. He was mentioned by Charles Dickens in *The Uncommercial Traveler* in connection with his work in Church emigration.

As editor from 1880 to 1892 and again from 1899 to 1907, Charles W. Penrose was a tireless editorial defender of the Church. He fought over many topics, particularly polygamy, and was fond of referring to an opposing editor as "my friend, the enemy." Horace G. (Bud) Whitney, as business manager of the *Deseret News* from 1899 to 1920, increased circulation nearly 500 percent, doubled the number of pages, and left the *News* a substantial financial surplus.

Mark E. Petersen became editor of the *Deseret News* in 1946 after working as a reporter, news editor, and manager. Called to be an apostle in the Church in 1944, he handled both full-time jobs for several years. He wrote editorials for the *Church News*, a weekly supplement, until his death in January 1984.

In 1952 Elder Petersen brought the *Deseret News* into a newspaper agency arrangement with its competitor paper, the Salt Lake *Tribune*.

The Deseret News building, c. 1899, in the background, stood at that time on the corner of Main and South Temple Streets in Salt Lake City, the site of the former Hotel Utah. The Brigham Young Monument in the foreground was designed by Cyrus E. Dallin and dedicated in a five-day celebration, July 20–24, 1897, the fiftieth anniversary of the pioneers' arrival in Salt Lake Valley.

Under the Federal Newspaper Preservation Act, the two newspapers combined their printing, circulation, and advertising departments but remained independent in editorial and news areas. The *Tribune* was the morning newspaper, and the *News* the evening one. Since the partial merger, both papers have shown an annual profit, and circulation at the *News* was increasing as it entered the 1990s.

BIBLIOGRAPHY

Alter, J. Cecil. *Early Utah Journalism*. Salt Lake City, 1938.

Ashton, Wendell J. *Voice in the West: Biography of a Pioneer Newspaper*. New York, 1950.

WENDELL J. ASHTON

DEUTERONOMY

Deuteronomy (Greek for "duplication of the law") is the fifth book of the Old Testament. Latter-day Saints have specific interests in this work. It distinctively teaches that those who inherit a PROMISED LAND do so on condition that they remain faithful to the Lord, pure in heart, generous to the poor, and devoted to God's Law. In a formula that appears several times, the people are promised that they will receive blessings for obedience to God and punishment for disobedience (Deut. 27–30). Book of Mormon prophets taught similar doctrines, and they also indicated that such principles were divinely given long before Moses. Latter-day scriptures are replete with deuteronomic teachings. Significantly, Jesus Christ quoted Deuteronomy regularly.

JESUS' USE OF DEUTERONOMY. When Satan tempted Jesus, saying that if he were the Son of God he would turn stones to bread, leap from the temple's pinnacle to test God's care, and gain worldly kingdoms and glory by worshiping Satan, the Savior responded with quotations from Deuteronomy (Matt. 4:1–10; cf. Deut. 8:3; 6:16, 13). He cited Deuteronomy regarding the law of witnesses and levirate marriage (John 8:17; Luke 20:28; cf. Deut. 19:15; 25:5). Twice he quoted the law on loving God (Deut. 6:4–5), calling it "the first and great commandment" (Matt. 22:35–38; cf. Luke 10:25–27). Many of Jesus' teachings admonishing good and warning against evil reiterate the deuteronomic principle of human action and divine response. Indeed, the Book of Mormon teaches that the premortal Jesus gave the law of Moses (3 Ne. 11:14; 12:17–18; 15:4–6).

DEUTERONOMIC TEACHINGS IN THE BOOK OF MORMON. The Jerusalem emigrants who became a BOOK OF MORMON PEOPLE retained a copy of the five books of Moses on plates of brass (1 Ne. 4:38; 5:11–16). They were taught the law of Moses and were promised security and happiness if they obeyed it (e.g., 2 Ne. 1:16–20). Retention of their promised land depended upon continued obedience (e.g., 1 Ne. 2:20–23; 4:14; 7:13; 14:1–2; cf. Deut. 18:9–13). Just as deuteronomic teachings were a stimulus for righteous commitment in King Josiah's Jerusalem (2 Kgs. 23:2–8), so were they in the Book of Mormon (e.g., 1 Ne. 17:33–38; 2 Ne. 5:10; Omni 1:2; Mosiah 1:1–7; Alma 8:17). Certain summary statements in the Book of Mormon may also reflect deuteronomic law (e.g., Alma 58:40; Hel. 3:20; 6:34; 15:5; 3 Ne. 25:4). Further, the prophecy of God's raising up a prophet in Deuteronomy 18:15–19 is declared by the Book of Mormon to be fulfilled in Jesus Christ (1 Ne. 22:20; 3 Ne. 20:23; cf. John 6:14; Acts 3:22; 7:37).

Book of Mormon writers observed that the prophet ALMA₂ may have been taken up by God as Moses was, reflecting a possible variant in their copy of Deuteronomy 34:5–6: "The scriptures saith the Lord took Moses unto himself" (Alma 45:19).

The book of Ether describes a people from the time of "the great tower" of Babel (Ether 1:3), with whom God covenanted that they could escape the fate of the wicked and be blessed in their land of promise if they would serve him in righteousness. This account from an epoch long before Moses is nevertheless in harmony with deuteronomic principles (Ether 2:6–10; 7:23; 9:20; 10:28; 11:6). When their descendants became wicked, they destroyed each other in successive wars (Ether 11:13, 20–21; 15:19).

DEUTERONOMIC IDEAS IN OTHER LDS SCRIPTURES. As recorded in the PEARL OF GREAT PRICE, Adam and Eve were taught about choices and consequences in the beginning (Moses 3:15–17; 4:8–9, 22–25, 28). Generations of their descendants taught others righteousness and warned them about wickedness (Moses 6:22–23; 7:10, 15, 17–18). Noah taught the same doctrines; and the deluge followed rejection of his divine counsel (Moses 8:16–20).

The Doctrine and Covenants contains scores

of passages about keeping the commandments of God (e.g., D&C 5:22; 6:6, 9, 37; 8:5; 11:6, 9, 18, 20). Those who keep them are promised blessings (e.g., D&C 14:7; 63:23; 76:52–55; 89:18–21; 93:19–20). Violators, of course, will suffer negative consequences (e.g., D&C 10:56; 18:46; 56:2–3). Thus, so-called deuteronomic precepts persist as divinely ordained principles.

[*See also* Covenants in Biblical Times; Law of Moses; Obedience; Old Testament.]

BIBLIOGRAPHY

Nibley, Hugh. "How to Get Rich." *CWHN*, Vol. 9, pp. 178–201.

Rasmussen, Ellis T. "The Unchanging Gospel of Two Testaments." *Ensign* 3 (Oct. 1973):34–35.

Sperry, Sidney B. *The Spirit of the Old Testament.* 2nd ed., chaps. 5, 12, 13. Salt Lake City, 1970.

ELLIS T. RASMUSSEN

DEVILS

In LDS discourse, the term "devil" denotes anyone who promotes the cause of EVIL, but it is especially applied to those unembodied spirits who rebelled against God in the PREMORTAL LIFE and were cast down from HEAVEN to this earth. The devil, who leads them, is also known by the personal names of Lucifer in the premortal existence and Satan since being cast down.

The name Lucifer means "light bearer" in Latin and is a translation of the Hebrew *Heylel ben Shakhar,* which means "herald son of dawn" or "morning star." In the PREMORTAL LIFE, Lucifer was an ANGEL having authority in the presence of God. He played a prominent role in the COUNCIL IN HEAVEN. After the Father in Heaven offered the plan of righteousness to help his children become as he is, Lucifer countered with an alternative plan.

The Father's plan was to save and exalt all of his obedient children. To be obedient, they must keep his commandments and do good. In the Father's plan, it was foreknown that many would reject exaltation and therefore would receive lesser glories.

Lucifer's plan proposed to "save" all of the Father's children by forcing each to obey the Father's law in all things. Lucifer desired that he be rewarded for this great feat of saving everyone by having the Father's honor and glory given to him personally. Because mortals can be saved only in their own freely chosen repentance, Lucifer's proposal was rejected. In the ensuing WAR IN HEAVEN, he gained the allegiance of a third of the Father's spirit children. Lucifer and his followers were then cast out of heaven to earth, where he became Satan and they all became devils (Moses 4:1–3; D&C 29:36–37; 76:25–38).

The name Satan comes from a Hebrew root meaning "to oppose, be adverse," hence "to attack or to accuse" (see Rev. 12:10). On this earth the role of Satan and his fellow devils is to attack the working of righteousness and to destroy it wherever possible (Moses 4:4; D&C 10:20–23; 93:39).

Righteousness is the condition or action of accomplishing the greatest possible happiness for all beings affected. The attainment of full righteousness is possible only with the help of an omniscient and omnipotent being. This full righteousness is the special order of the celestial kingdom where the Father dwells. When the Father's will is done and his order is in place, every person and every thing attains, or is attaining, the potential he, she, or it has for development and happiness. This righteousness is the good of "good and evil." It is to be contrasted with those human desires that are contrary to the Father's order and will.

A good (righteous) person is an agentive being who chooses and accomplishes only righteousness. No mortal is intrinsically and perfectly good, nor can a mortal alone rise to that standard (Matt. 19:17). But mortals can do righteous acts and become righteous through the salvation provided by Jesus Christ. Christ is the fountain of all righteousness (Ether 12:28). The children of God can achieve the Father's order of righteousness through Christ if they choose that order in explicit rejection of evil.

Evil is any order of existence that is not righteous. A state of affairs, an act, or a person not in the order of righteousness is thus evil. Letting one's neighbor languish in abject poverty while one has plenty, or stealing, or desiring harm for another person are all evils. Satan promotes evil everywhere he can, to thwart the righteousness of God (see D&C 10:27). Thus, Satan tempts people to do evil instead of the Father's will. Satan himself is not necessary to evil, but he hastens and abets evil wherever he can.

Satan's first targets on earth were Adam and Eve in the GARDEN OF EDEN. Knowing that the Father had commanded Adam and Eve not to partake of the forbidden fruit on penalty of death, Satan sought to destroy the Father's work by enticing Adam and Eve to partake of it anyway. Satan's success marked the beginning of the world (as distinct from the creation of the earth), of Satan's kingdom on this earth (see JST, Matt. 1:55).

By obeying Satan, Adam and Eve opened the way for him to have partial dominion over them, over the earth, and over all of their children (*see* FALL OF ADAM). Examples of his partial dominion over the earth granted by the Father are his ability to possess the bodies of animals (Matt. 8:28–32) and to use water to destroy people (D&C 61:14–19). Satan gained the power to tempt those who are accountable to do evil (D&C 29:39), to communicate with individuals to teach them things (usually but not always lies), to possess their bodies, to foster illness and disease, and to cause mortal death. He promotes sin, the doing of evil, which brings SPIRITUAL DEATH to the sinner and misery to all those affected. In each of these opportunities, Satan's power is limited: He can do only what he has specific permission from God to do (D&C 121:4; Luke 8:30–33). His power may be taken away by individuals as they hearken to God and as they correctly use the holy priesthood to limit his operations (D&C 50:13–35).

What Satan did not realize in Eden was that what he did in attempting to destroy the Father's work was actually the very thing needed to fulfill the Father's plan (Moses 4:6). People could not demonstrate their love of God and their willingness to do the work of righteousness sufficiently to qualify them for exaltation unless they were subject to, and able to overcome, evil *and* devil adversaries, such as Satan and his hosts (2 Ne. 2:11–22).

On earth Satan is thus the father of deception, lies, and sin—of all evils—for he promotes them with vigor. He may appear as a counterfeit angel of light or as the prince of darkness, but his usual manifestations to mortals come as either evil revelation to one's heart and mind or indirectly through other persons. His mission is to tempt everyone to choose evil so that each accountable human being's choices can serve as an adequate basis for a final judgment.

This earth life is a mortal probation for all those who have the opportunity to accept and live by the new and everlasting covenant while in the mortal flesh. Those who do not have a full opportunity in this earth life will have their probation extended through the SPIRIT WORLD existence that

follows it. By the time of RESURRECTION, each of the Father's children will have made a final choice between good and evil, and each will be rewarded with the good or the evil chosen during the probation (Alma 41:10–15).

When Satan tempts a person to do evil, there are limits to what Satan can accomplish. He can put before a person any kind of evil opportunity, but that evil is enticing only if the person tempted already desires that thing. When people are tempted, it is actually by their own lusts (James 1:12–15).

Satan has power on earth only as individual persons give it to him by succumbing to his TEMPTATIONS (*TPJS*, p. 187). The agency of human beings is to choose righteousness through the Holy Spirit of God or to choose selfishness through the flesh by succumbing to Satan's temptations (2 Ne. 2:26–29). (Human flesh is not evil, but Satan may tempt humans through their flesh.) Individuals who repent in this life are nevertheless tempted by Satan until their death; then Satan has no power over them ever again. Those who die unrepentant are still in Satan's power in the SPIRIT PRISON (Alma 34:34–35). All except the SONS OF PERDITION will eventually accept Christ and obey him, and thereby escape the dominion of Satan (D&C 76:110). Thus is the Father's plan of agency fulfilled.

Satan's three temptations of the Savior may be seen as paradigmatic of all human temptation (see David O. McKay, *Gospel Ideals*, p. 154, Salt Lake City, 1953). The temptation to create bread and eat it when he should not represents the human temptation of the flesh, to sate the senses unrighteously. The temptation to cast himself down from the temple and to be saved by angels when he should not represents the human temptation of social acclaim. The temptation to receive the kingdoms of this world when he should not represents the temptation to have unrighteous dominion or power over others. The Savior did not yield to any of these temptations because his heart was pure and he knew that the way of righteousness lay only in doing the Father's will in all things.

All accountable mortals are tempted, even as our Savior was tempted. As mortals succumb, Satan gains power and earth life becomes a hell. Every person may resist temptation by choosing good over evil. But misinformation, evil cultural traditions (D&C 93:39), despair, and desperate human need all make the choosing of good difficult, even if the person does not particularly desire a given evil (cf. 2 Ne. 28 for an extensive description of the ploys of Satan).

Through Jesus Christ and the partaking of his new and everlasting covenant, mortals have the opportunity to gain power to choose good over evil unerringly and always. As they do so, they are able to establish the righteousness of God and thus heaven on earth (Moses 7:18; D&C 50:34–35; *see also* ZION).

Human beings resist Satan and evil by controlling their desires—that is, (1) by not desiring the evil that Satan proffers; (2) by gaining more knowledge so that they will be able to see that Satan's temptations are not what they really want; and (3) by having their hearts purified by Jesus Christ so that they will no longer desire any evil but desire instead to do the Father's will in all things (Moro. 7:48; cf. the Savior's answers in Matt. 4:1–10).

The great help in resisting temptation is the HOLY SPIRIT. It is Satan's business to dwell in and with all individuals who do not have the Holy Spirit with them, sometimes even gaining total possession of a person's body, so that he or she loses agency for a time. Partial possession may also occur, for whenever a human being becomes angry, he or she is at least partially possessed by Satan (James 1:20).

In his role as the destroyer, Satan can cause illness and death, but only with permission from God. He cannot take people before their time unless they disobey God and thus forfeit their mission (Job 1:6–12).

As the father of lies, Satan has a disinformation campaign. He spreads false notions about himself, about God, about people, about salvation—all for the purpose of defeating acts of faith in Jesus Christ. Mortals believe his lies because the lies are pleasing to the carnal mind and because they promote or support the selfish desires of the individual who believes them. About himself, Satan tells people that there is no devil, that such an idea is wild imagination (2 Ne. 28:22). About God, Satan desires human beings to believe either that he does not exist or that he is some distant, unknowable, or forbidding being. He tells people that they are to conquer in this world according to their strength and that whatever anyone does is no crime (Alma 30:17). Favorite lies about salvation are either that it comes to everyone in spite of anything one does (Alma 21:6) or that it is reserved only for a special few insiders (Alma 31:17). These erroneous creeds of the fathers, fastened upon their children in the form of false creeds, are called in the scriptures "the chains of hell" (Alma 12:11; D&C 123:7–8).

SECRET COMBINATIONS are another devilish device for spreading misery and obstructing the cause of righteousness (Ether 8:16–26; Hel. 6:16–32). Satan tempts selfish individuals to use others to their own oppressive advantage. Secrecy is essential to prevent retaliation by the victims and just execution of the laws against such combinations. Secret combinations involve personal, economic, educational, political, or military power that controls or enslaves some persons for the pleasure and profit of others.

Satan also has influence over the spirits of wicked persons who have passed from mortality by death and who inhabit the spirit prison (sometimes called Hades). The inhabitants of this prison do not yet suffer cleansing pain, which will later come, but continue to be subject to Satan's lies and temptations (Alma 40–41). They also have the opportunity to hear the servants of Christ (D&C 138:28–37), and if they did not have the opportunity on earth, they now may repent unto exaltation. If they did have the opportunity on earth but did not use it, the spirit prison opportunity again allows them to reject Satan and his lies and temptations, but with the reward of a lesser glory (D&C 76:71–79).

During the MILLENNIUM, Satan will be bound (Rev. 20:2). He will still be on earth, attempting to tempt every person, as he has since the fall of Adam, but he will be bound because no one will hearken to his temptations (1 Ne. 22:26).

Toward the end of the Millennium, Satan will be loosed (D&C 88:110–15) because people will again hearken to him. But he will be vanquished and sent from this earth to outer darkness, where he and his followers, both spirits and resurrected sons of perdition (Satan is Perdition, "the lost one"), will dwell in the misery and darkness of selfishness and isolation forever.

BIBLIOGRAPHY

For a more complete treatment of the concept of the devil from an LDS point of view, see LaMar E. Garrard, "A Study of the Problem of a Personal Devil and Its Relationship to Latter-day Saint Beliefs" (Master's thesis, Brigham Young University, 1955). Especially valuable is his compilation of quotations from early General Authorities of the LDS Church concerning the topic. Jeffrey Burton Russell's four companion works *The*

Devil: Perceptions of Evil from Antiquity to Primitive Christianity (Ithaca, N.Y., 1977), *Satan: The Early Christian Tradition* (Ithaca, N.Y., 1981), *Lucifer: The Devil in the Middle Ages* (Ithaca, N.Y., 1984), and *Mephistopheles: The Devil in the Modern World* (Ithaca, N.Y., 1986) constitute a comprehensive history of the concept of the devil traced through literature, art, and philosophy from ancient times to the modern day. The presentation is a thorough and scholarly treatment but does not derive from an LDS frame of thought.

CHAUNCEY C. RIDDLE

DIPLOMATIC RELATIONS

Joseph SMITH undertook his first diplomatic mission for the Church when he journeyed to Washington, D.C., in 1839 and met with President Martin Van Buren to seek federal intervention on behalf of Church members who had lost their lives or property during the Missouri persecutions. Since then, the diplomatic contacts of the Church with the governments of the world have been aimed mostly at securing legal recognition for the Church and freedom for its members to preach the gospel to others, meet together for religious worship, and live according to their religious precepts.

For a century and a half the Church had no formal diplomatic office; mission presidents or General Authorities on special assignment were responsible for creating a favorable climate for the Church's missionary effort and for resolving problems with host governments. In 1842, Lorenzo SNOW, an apostle, sought to establish a favorable impression of Latter-day Saints by presenting a handsome bound copy of the first British edition of the Book of Mormon to Queen Victoria and Albert, the Prince Consort. As the Church began practicing plural marriage, the task of maintaining a favorable public image became more difficult. That effort was not helped by a note sent by the U.S. government in 1887 to the governments of Great Britain and Scandinavia asking them to curtail immigration of Latter-day Saints to the United States—a move intended to stem the growth of polygamy. Since the Scandinavian countries did little and the note was ridiculed by the British press, the Church found it unnecessary to take any diplomatic initiative.

Fifty years later, a statute adopted by the legislature of Tonga barring entry of LDS missionaries was the subject of a diplomatic protest by the Church to the British government. The matter landed on the desk of Winston Churchill, who was then colonial secretary. He took no action because the British government could not veto a Tongan statute, and the Foreign Office informed him that the U.S. government would not protest if the statute did not apply retroactively to missionaries in the country but only to those subsequently applying for entry. The Church took no further action, since the mission president was able to convince the Tongan legislature to repeal the measure.

The rather limited extent of the Church's diplomatic relations with the governments of northern Europe, where the Church's missionary effort was concentrated in the nineteenth century, gave way in the twentieth to more extensive contacts as the Church became more ambitious in the reach of its missionary program. In many countries the right to proselytize was limited not only by statute but also by informal practice and tradition, stemming in part from the influence of an established state church with a special legal status. Moreover, the spread of communism had raised ideological barriers to missionary work in general. Still the Church maintained its policy of leaving the conduct of any needed diplomatic relations in the hands of mission presidents or General Authorities either permanently or temporarily in the country. That policy changed after 1975 when Spencer W. KIMBALL became President of the Church. He was determined to increase the Church's missionary effort, including gaining legal recognition in the countries where such recognition had been denied either as a matter of government policy or through the opposition of the established state church. The decision resulted in a policy that required organizational changes at Church headquarters. Such changes had been discussed during the tenure of President Harold B. LEE, but no steps had been taken before his death. N. Eldon Tanner, who served as first counselor to both President Lee and President Kimball, reviewed with President Kimball those previous discussions. They decided to appoint a special representative responsible to the First Presidency who would negotiate with governments outside the United States for removal of restrictive visa policies and for legal recognition of the Church where it had been denied. The special representative would also serve as liaison between the Church and U.S. embassies in foreign countries.

President Kimball appointed David M. Kennedy as the special representative of the First

Presidency. Kennedy had extensive experience working with international governments and leaders as an international banker, as U.S. secretary of the treasury under U.S. President Richard M. Nixon, as ambassador-at-large, and as ambassador to the North Atlantic Treaty Organization (NATO).

Since the Church wanted to gain legal recognition as rapidly as possible, the First Presidency and its special representative examined countries one by one, exploring the possibilities each offered. Barriers existed in each country. Some had statutes limiting freedom of religion. There were long-standing religious and cultural barriers in others. In some, legal recognition was possible, but statutes severely limited the right to proselytize. When President Kimball decided that legal recognition should be the first goal, he sent Kennedy to Greece, where recognition had long been withheld despite the vigorous efforts of Church leaders. Kennedy learned from his contacts in the Greek government and the U.S. embassy there that the key to recognition as "a house of prayer" required the approval of the Archbishop of Athens and All Greece, His Beatitude Seraphim. In a crucial interview, Kennedy pointed out that the Greek Orthodox Church enjoyed full freedom of religion in the United States, that the Greek government had honored President David O. MCKAY for the aid the Church had sent to Greece after the devastating earthquake of 1953, and that the Church was fully recognized by most of the other countries of Western Europe. Greece eventually gave legal recognition to the Church. Other countries where recognition would be sought and eventually granted included Yugoslavia, Portugal, and Poland.

When it became known that the Church was seeking recognition from communist countries, representatives of the media began asking how such action could be reconciled with the Church's ideological opposition to communism. Kennedy responded to those queries by referring to the Church's belief in "being subject to kings, presidents, rulers, and magistrates, in obeying, honoring, and sustaining the law" (A of F 12). The essential reality, Kennedy emphasized, is that the Church could enter, and prosper in, any country that would "permit us to offer our sacraments, . . . permit us in our homes to have our family organization and live within our religious patterns" (Hickman, p. 340). These minimal freedoms were all Latter-day Saints needed to live consistently with their general beliefs. Kennedy also drew a distinction between the economic and political systems that Church members preferred as private citizens and those restrictions on individual freedoms that would make it impossible for the Church to exist as an institution or prevent its members from following its fundamental precepts. Through Kennedy, the Church reemphasized that its mission was to preach the restored gospel to all the world and to help its members' lives to be marked by moral and spiritual growth—not to import the American political and economic systems.

In every country visited, the Church's first goal was to gain recognition that included the right to open a mission, entry rights for missionaries, the right to proselytize openly, and the right to hold public worship meetings. The most notable success in reaching these goals was achieved in Portugal, where the 1974 revolution had resulted in the adoption of a statute granting freedom of religion. In other countries, notably Poland, the Church was successful in gaining legal recognition permitting it to own property, to hold religious meetings, and to send Church representatives to the country, but the right to proselytize was refused. Despite that limitation, Church leaders believed that legal recognition was a significant step forward and that the Polish government's offer should be accepted even though it did not contain the right to proselytize. The Church was granted legal recognition in Yugoslavia on essentially the same terms. In each country where the Church undertook negotiations, Kennedy, as special representative of the First Presidency, emphasized that the Church was recognized in many countries of the world and that in the United States members held important positions in government, education, and business. He also stressed that Church members were recognized in the United States for their honesty, reliability, and work ethic.

In recent years there have occurred several changes that have improved the diplomatic relations of the Church. Changes in Eastern Europe have made it easier for the Church to gain recognition than it was in 1975, and restrictions on proselytizing are also being removed. The revelation announced by President Kimball in 1978 granting the priesthood to every worthy male member of the Church has been followed by the establishment of more missions in Africa (see AFRICA, THE CHURCH IN; DOCTRINE AND COVENANTS: OFFICIAL DECLARATION–2). Because of these changes, the First Presidency decided that the task assigned to its special representative had been achieved; hence, in 1990, Kennedy was released from that calling, and no replacement was named. The responsibilities of the special representative were assumed by the AREA presidencies and mission presidents.

BIBLIOGRAPHY

Hickman, Martin B. *David Matthew Kennedy: Banker, Statesman, Churchman*, pp. 334–65. Salt Lake City, 1987.

Kimball, Edward L., and Andrew E. Kimball. *Spencer W. Kimball.* Salt Lake City, 1977.

Palmer, Spencer J., ed. *The Expanding Church.* Salt Lake City, 1978.

MARTIN B. HICKMAN

DISCERNMENT, GIFT OF

The gift of discernment consists of the spiritual quality or skill of being able to see or understand, especially that which is hidden or obscure. This ability is shared in a general way by all of God's children, but "discerning of spirits" is one of the GIFTS OF THE SPIRIT that comes, under certain circumstances, specially from God (1 Cor. 12:10; D&C 46:23). The fuller gift of discerning in all spiritual matters—to know whether their occurrence is of God or not—is given by the Lord to "such as God shall appoint and ordain to watch over the church" (D&C 46:27). To possess this gift is to receive divinely revealed understanding of opposing spirits—the spirit of God and the spirit of the DEVIL. Persons possessing such a gift also correctly perceive the right course of action (D&C 63:41).

Not only can the power of discernment distinguish good from evil (Moro. 7:12–18), the righteous from the wicked (D&C 101:95), and false spirits from divine (D&C 46:23), but its more sensitive operation can also make known even "the thoughts and intents of the heart" of other persons (Heb. 4:12; D&C 33:1). "The gift of discernment [embodies] the power to discriminate . . . between right and wrong . . . [and] arises largely out of an acute sensitivity to . . . spiritual impressions . . . to detect hidden evil, and more importantly to find the good that may be concealed. The highest type of discernment . . . uncovers [in others] . . . their better natures, the good inherent within them" (Richards, p. 371).

Every Latter-day Saint has spiritual leaders who, by virtue of their CALLINGS, are entitled to the gift of discernment to enable them to lead and counsel correctly. "The gift of discernment is essential to the leadership of the Church [of Jesus Christ of Latter-day Saints]. I never ordain a bishop or set apart a president of a stake without invoking upon him this divine blessing, that he may read the lives and hearts of his people and call forth the best within them. The gift and power of discernment . . . [are] essential equipment for every son and daughter of God. . . . The true gift of discernment is often premonitory. A sense of danger should be heeded to be of value" (Richards, p. 371).

BIBLIOGRAPHY

Richards, Stephen L. "The Gifts of the Spirit." *IE* 53 [May 1950]:371.

Smith, Joseph Fielding, ed. *TPJS*, pp. 202–215. Salt Lake City, 1938.

LEON R. HARTSHORN

DISCIPLESHIP

Like many other Christians, Latter-day Saints believe that only the transformational discipleship of those who believe in and follow Jesus Christ leads to a fulness of joy and peace in this life and ETERNAL LIFE in the world to come. Hence, true disciples are those who make the resurrected, revealing Christ the center of their lives, as did the faithful referred to in the New Testament who sat at the feet, followed in the footsteps, mourned the death, and rejoiced in the resurrection of Christ.

"Faith in the Lord Jesus Christ"—the first principle of the GOSPEL as stated in the fourth ARTICLE OF FAITH—is the explicit foundation of discipleship. From this principle all other principles and ORDINANCES of the gospel derive their efficacy, power, and harmony.

Through his perfect earthly life and infinite atoning sacrifice, Jesus Christ became not only the model and mentor but also the Savior and Redeemer and mankind's advocate with the Father. The atonement, meaning "at-one-ment," empowered the plan whereby all men and women can eventually become like FATHER IN HEAVEN and MOTHER IN HEAVEN. Through the atonement, Christ took upon himself not only the original transgression of Adam and Eve but also the personal sins of mankind, as well as the consequences of weaknesses and mistakes—including those transmitted through the generations—that are manifested in the lives even of individuals trying to follow in his footsteps. As the savior of mankind, Jesus sets the example and lovingly makes the blessings of the atonement and personal guidance available to anyone who comes to him with a broken (teachable) heart and a contrite (repentant) spirit (3 Ne. 9:20–22; 12:19–20).

The commitment to become a disciple of Christ is an unconditional one of "heart, might, mind and strength" (D&C 4:2). It centers a person's life on Christ, making Jesus the supreme lawgiver, the frame of reference through which all else is viewed. Christ's influence then begins to direct a person's words, acts, and even thoughts, enabling that individual to become a partaker of the divine nature (2 Pet. 1:4), line upon line, precept upon precept.

While some believe that full discipleship comes about almost instantaneously, Latter-day Saints view the commitment at baptism as the beginning of a lifelong process that involves an upward spiral of learning, committing, and doing on increasingly higher planes. The heart of this process is learning to educate and obey the conscience, the repository of the Spirit of Christ given to every person (John 1:9; Moro. 7:16). As individuals obey the general commandments given through his appointed prophets, they become more attuned to hear the "still small voice" of the Holy Ghost (1 Ne. 17:45) that communicates specific personal direction and leads individuals to full discipleship.

The educated conscience, schooled by prayerful study of the scriptures, selfless service, and the making and keeping of God's COVENANTS, becomes a growing source of intrinsic security and well-being, the basis for decision making, the essence of personal FREEDOM. "If ye continue in my word," said Christ, "then are ye my disciples indeed; And ye shall know the truth, and the truth shall make you free" (John 8:31–32). As a person begins to see more as the Lord sees, to acquire more of the "mind of Christ" (1 Cor. 2:16), that individual is empowered to become independent of all other influences and to rise above childhood, genetic, and environmental tendencies.

The fruits that naturally grow out of this divine center are described as characteristics of disciples in both ancient and modern scripture. Disci-

ples receive and obey the Lord's commandments (D&C 41:5); they are "submissive, meek, humble, patient, full of love, willing to submit to all things which the Lord seeth fit to inflict upon [them]" (Mosiah 3:19); they remember the poor and needy, the sick and afflicted (D&C 52:40); they act as a light to others (3 Ne. 15:12), love others as Christ loves (John 13:34–35), and are willing to forsake all to follow him (Luke 14:33) and to lay down their lives for his sake (D&C 103:28).

The role of The Church of Jesus Christ of Latter-day Saints in the process of discipleship is, as PAUL observed of the former-day Church, "for the perfecting of the saints" (Eph. 4:12), and for helping members bridge the gap between theory and practice in becoming true disciples.

While one can go to church without being active in the gospel, for Latter-day Saints it is not possible to be a full disciple of Christ without being active in his Church. The Church teaches the GOSPEL, administers its ordinances, and provides opportunities to bring both temporal and spiritual blessings to others. The Church is the KINGDOM OF GOD on earth for which the disciple prays and works while seeking to unify it with God's kingdom in Heaven (Matt. 6:10). Gospel principles and ordinances empower the disciple of Christ, line upon line, to become even as he is.

BIBLIOGRAPHY

Covey, Stephen R. *The Divine Center*. Salt Lake City, 1987.

Hafen, Bruce C. *The Broken Heart*. Salt Lake City, 1989.

Maxwell, Neal A. *Deposition of a Disciple*. Salt Lake City, 1976.

———. *Even As I Am*. Salt Lake City, 1982.

STEPHEN R. COVEY

DISCIPLINARY PROCEDURES

To aid the spiritual development of its members, The Church of Jesus Christ of Latter-day Saints has developed a system of counseling, rehabilitation, and, where needed, disciplinary action.

Members are accountable to the Lord for the way they conduct their lives, and personal worthiness is requisite for enjoying the full blessings of Church MEMBERSHIP. The judge of such worthiness is in most cases the BISHOP of the WARD, who is appointed "to be a judge in Israel" (D&C 107:72) and is "to judge his people by the testimony of the just, and by the assistance of his counselors, according to the laws of the kingdom which are given by the prophets of God" (D&C 58:18). General Authorities and stake, mission, district, and branch presidents may, in some circumstances, also exercise judicial responsibilities. The term "bishop" in this article usually refers to any Church officer acting in such a judicial role.

Bishops function as judges and also as counselors when they hear voluntary, private confessions from members. They must also determine a member's worthiness before signing the temple recommend that permits a member to participate in temple ordinances. Moreover, bishops judge worthiness before recommending persons to serve as full-time missionaries, before calling officers or teachers to serve in Church organizations, or before a member enrolls at a Church-owned college or university. Although required standards of worthiness vary somewhat in these different situations, most worthiness interviews focus on conduct-oriented questions concerning personal MORALITY and CHASTITY, payment of tithes, observance of the WORD OF WISDOM, sustaining local and general Church leadership, obedience to gospel commandments, and general activity in the Church.

Because bishops are primarily concerned with the spiritual development of each member, they have wide discretion to make judgments and to give the counsel most likely to assist the member's spiritual progress and, where needed, the member's REPENTANCE. A bishop may simply accept a confession from a repentant person without imposing a penalty, may decide not to extend a proposed call for Church service, or may temporarily withhold other privileges of membership. In the most serious cases, bishops may impose disciplinary sanctions ranging from informal, probationary restrictions to formal proceedings that can result in disfellowshipment or EXCOMMUNICATION from the Church.

Church discipline may proceed from any or all of three purposes:

1. To aid the transgressors' repentance, thereby helping them receive the Savior's ATONEMENT for personal SINS (*see* JUSTICE AND MERCY). The Lord has said, "Whosoever transgresseth against me, him shall ye judge according to the sins which he has committed; and if he confess his sins before thee and me, and repenteth in the sincerity of his heart, him shall ye forgive, and I will forgive him also. . . . And whosoever will not repent of his sins the same shall not be numbered among my people" (Mosiah 26:29, 32; see also D&C 64:12–13). Toward this end, bishops often encourage repentance without the necessity of formal disciplinary proceedings. However, in certain cases, unless a bishop invokes formal discipline, a transgressor may be unable to experience the change of heart and behavior necessary to achieve complete repentance.

2. To identify unrepentant predators and hostile apostates and thereby protect innocent persons from harm they might inflict. "But if he repent not he shall not be numbered among my people, that he may not destroy my people" (3 Ne. 18:31).

3. To safeguard the integrity of the Church.

Standard guidelines for conducting disciplinary proceedings are provided to Church officers in the GENERAL HANDBOOK OF INSTRUCTIONS. Disciplinary councils are not normally convened to resolve civil disputes among members (see D&C 134:10), nor are they convened simply because a member does not attend Church meetings or is similarly neglectful. Furthermore, members who request to have their names removed from Church membership records for reasons of personal choice unrelated to serious misconduct need not appear before a disciplinary council to have their request honored.

When there has been transgression, bishops must decide each case according to its unique circumstances, including the extent of the member's repentance. Therefore, the Church does not impose rigid requirements on bishops; rather, they are instructed to weigh all relevant factors and to seek spiritual guidance to accomplish the purposes of Church discipline as the individual case requires. When a bishop imposes discipline informally, the proceedings are strictly confidential and no official Church record is made.

Formal proceedings may involve a three-member ward BISHOPRIC or a fifteen-member STAKE PRESIDENCY and high council. Formal disciplinary councils are typically convened only for such extraordinary behavior as murder or other serious crimes, incest, open and harmful APOSTASY, and flagrant or highly visible transgressions against the law of chastity. Members for whom a formal disciplinary council is convened are given advance notice of the reasons for the council and an opportunity for a hearing. Although legal procedures do not govern the proceedings, the Church observes basic standards of fairness. The proceedings are officially recorded by written minutes. Both the hearing and the formal record are treated as confidential information, and disciplinary penalties are announced only to those Church officers who have a need to know, except when the offender poses serious risks to uninformed Church members. Those subjected to disciplinary sanctions have a right of appeal.

A formal disciplinary council can result in four possible outcomes: (1) no action; (2) a formal probation involving restricted privileges; (3) disfellowshipment; or (4) excommunication. Disfellowshipment is a temporary suspension of membership privileges. A disfellowshipped person remains a Church member but may not enter Church temples, hold Church callings, exercise the priesthood, partake of the sacrament, or participate openly in public meetings. An excommunicated person is no longer a member of the Church, and all priesthood ordinances and temple blessings previously received are suspended. Excommunicants may not pay tithing and, if previously endowed in a temple, may not wear temple garments. They may attend Church meetings. Excommunicants may later qualify for REBAPTISM after lengthy and full repentance and still later may apply for a formal restoration of their original priesthood and temple blessings.

Authorization to reinstate disfellowshipped persons or to rebaptize excommunicated persons must be given by a disciplinary council in the area where the applicant resides. In some cases, clearance by the FIRST PRESIDENCY is required. The ordinance of restoration of temple blessings may be authorized only by the First Presidency.

The isolation of the Latter-day Saints during the settlement era in the Great Basin gave a broader jurisdiction to Church judicial courts than is presently the case, in part because of the absence of a developed state court system. In addition, Church policy has in recent years given greater protection to the confidentiality of disciplinary decisions. For example, until the 1970s, decisions of excommunication and disfellowshipment were announced openly in ward Melchizedek Priesthood meetings, although the nature of the transgression was usually not announced.

Because the fundamental purpose of Church discipline has always been to save souls rather than only to punish, formal disciplinary councils are considered "courts of love," marking the first step back to full harmony with the Lord and his Church, rather than the last step on the way out of the Church.

BIBLIOGRAPHY

Ballard, M. Russell. "A Chance to Start Over: Church Disciplinary Councils and the Restoration of Blessings." *Ensign* 20 (Sept. 1990):12–19.

"The Church Judicial System." In *Seek to Obtain My Word: Melchizedek Priesthood Personal Study Guide 1989*, pp. 29–36. Salt Lake City, 1988.

Firmage, Edwin Brown, and Richard Collin Mangrum. *Zion in the Courts: A Legal History of the Church of Jesus Christ of Latter-day Saints, 1830–1900.* Urbana, Ill., 1988.

Kimball, Spencer W. "The Church Will Forgive." *The Miracle of Forgiveness*, pp. 323–37. Salt Lake City, 1969.

Moss, James R. "The Historical Development of the Church Court System." Church History Symposium Paper, 1977. Abstract published in *First Annual Church Educational System Religious Educators Symposium*, pp. 75–77. Salt Lake City, 1977.

Preston, James J. "Expulsion." *ER* 5:233–36.

Simpson, Robert L. "Courts of Love." *Ensign* 2 (July 1972):48–49.

BRUCE C. HAFEN

DISFELLOWSHIPMENT

See: Disciplinary Procedures

DISPENSATION OF THE FULNESS OF TIMES

The Dispensation of the Fulness of Times is the final dispensation for this earth. Dispensations are periods of time in which the gospel of Jesus Christ is administered by holy PROPHETS called and ordained by God to deliver his message to the inhabitants of the world. The central work of the "dispensation of the fulness of times" consists of bringing together all gospel ordinances and truths of past dispensations and some items unique to the last days. Paul spoke of a future time when all things that are in heaven and on earth would at last be gathered together, and he called it the "dispensation of the fulness of times" (Eph. 1:10).

This dispensation began with the Prophet Joseph Smith's FIRST VISION, and all revelations and divine gifts of former dispensations continually flow into it. Concerning this, Joseph Smith wrote on September 6, 1842: "It is necessary in the ushering in of the dispensation of the fulness of times, which dispensation is now beginning to usher in, that a whole and complete and perfect union, and welding together of dispensations, and keys, and powers, and glories should take place, and be revealed from the days of Adam even to the present time" (D&C 128:18).

David W. PATTEN, a member of the QUORUM OF THE TWELVE APOSTLES, said in 1838: "The dispensation of the fullness of times is made up of all the dispensations that ever have been since the world began, until this time. . . . All [the prophets] received in their time a dispensation by revelation from God, to accomplish the great scheme of restoration, . . . the end of which is the dispensation of the fulness of times, in the which all things shall be fulfilled that have been spoken of since the earth was made" (*HC* 3:51).

Revelation and restoration characterize the fulness of times. Priesthood, keys (authorization to act), ordinances, covenants, and teachings of past dispensations have been, or will yet be, restored, and this can occur only by revelation. Heavenly messengers ministered to Joseph Smith and Oliver COWDERY, giving them authority, keys, doctrines, and ordinances of past dispensations that had been lost to the world because of fragmentation, abuse, and APOSTASY. The Doctrine and Covenants records several instances in which these two men saw, talked with, and received authority from resurrected ancient prophets. On May 15, 1829, John the Baptist ordained them to the AARONIC PRIESTHOOD (D&C 13). Shortly thereafter, Peter, James, and John, three of Christ's original APOSTLES, conferred the MELCHIZEDEK PRIESTHOOD on them (D&C 27:12). On April 3, 1836, in the KIRTLAND TEMPLE, Moses gave them "the keys of the gathering of Israel from the four parts of the earth, and the leading of the ten tribes from the land of the north" (D&C 110:11); ELIAS committed the keys of the dispensation of the GOSPEL OF ABRAHAM (D&C 110:12); and ELIJAH fulfilled the promise of Malachi 4:5–6 by bestowing on them the SEALING power to "turn the hearts of the . . . children to the fathers" and make available the saving gospel ordinances to all who have lived on earth (D&C 110:13–15). As part of the restoration, the Book of Mormon, a scriptural witness of Jesus Christ and his dealings with ancient people of the Western Hemisphere, was translated by Joseph Smith by divine power. These events were part of the gathering "together in one all things in Christ" (Eph. 1:10; D&C 27:7–13; *see also* RESTORATION OF ALL THINGS). The priesthood has been revealed "for the last time," and those who now hold the keys do so "in connection with all those who have received a dispensation at any time from the beginning of the creation" (D&C 112:30–31).

Of things unique to the Dispensation of the Fulness of Times, the Prophet Joseph Smith wrote, "Those things which never have been revealed from the foundation of the world, but have been kept hid from the wise and prudent, shall be revealed unto babes and sucklings in this, the dispensation of the fulness of times" (D&C 128:18). Although the PLAN OF SALVATION is the same in every dispensation, the fulness of times will see the accomplishment of specific and unique events, including the rebuilding of the old Jerusalem; building the NEW JERUSALEM; preaching the gospel to every nation, kindred, tongue, and people; the gathering of Israel; and the SECOND COMING of Jesus Christ. Everything necessary to usher in the MILLENNIUM comes under the purview of the dispensation of the fulness of times, which will continue until Christ has subdued all his enemies and has perfected his work (D&C 76:106; *TPJS*, pp. 231–32).

BIBLIOGRAPHY

Matthews, Robert J. "The Fulness of Times." *Ensign* 19 (Dec. 1989):46–51.

McConkie, Bruce R. *A New Witness for the Articles of Faith*, pp. 137, 320. Salt Lake City, 1985.

RAND H. PACKER

DISPENSATIONS OF THE GOSPEL

The term "dispensation" is translated in the New Testament from the Greek *oikonomia*, denoting an idea of STEWARDSHIP and of ordering affairs of a household. "Dispensations" are also time periods in which the Lord placed on the earth the necessary knowledge, PRIESTHOOD, and KEYS of authority to implement his PLAN OF SALVATION for his children. This plan, along with priesthood, was first given to ADAM (Moses 5:4–12; 6:62–68; D&C 84:16–18; *TPJS*, pp. 157, 167), but as a consequence of later APOSTASY and fragmentation among his descendants, it did not remain constantly upon the earth. Hence, from time to time the Lord called new prophets and again revealed the plan and bestowed the necessary priesthood authority, creating a new dispensation.

Each new dispensation, or period of restored truth, presents men and women with a divine stewardship in performing the Lord's work on earth. The recipients become custodians and co-workers with God in bringing to pass his purposes. They work according to his orderly and revealed design. His plan takes into account human weaknesses and provides for times of renewal following apostasy, just as it provides for a redemption from individual failings through repentance and obedience (D&C 121:31–32). The concepts of stewardship and orderliness are important themes in LDS theology.

Prophets are stewards who preach and organize the work of redemption in each dispensation. It has become traditional in some unofficial LDS commentaries to refer to seven major dispensations named after the principal prophet of each: Adam, Enoch, Noah, Abraham, Moses, Jesus Christ (who led the dispensation of the MERIDIAN OF TIME), and Joseph SMITH (who introduced the DISPENSATION OF THE FULNESS OF TIMES; see Acts 3:21.) However, this list does not take into account other dispensations, such as those among the Jaredites, the Nephites, and the ten lost tribes of Israel.

Rarely have gospel dispensations been universal, reaching all nations, although that is the ideal (e.g., Abr. 2:11). More often, one people has been responsive, while other nations have languished in ignorance and unbelief. However, the Adamic dispensation would at first have been communicated to the entire family of Adam early in his time (see Moses 5:12), and again in the final dispensation, the fulness of times, the gospel "shall be preached unto every nation, and kindred, and tongue, and people" (see D&C 133:37; cf. 90:9–11). The meridian of time was given the same mandate (Matt. 28:19–20), but we have no record that the gospel reached every nation in that period.

Several fundamentals are common to all dispensations: priesthood authority, BAPTISM by immersion and the LAYING ON OF HANDS for the GIFT OF THE HOLY GHOST, the SEALING power (D&C 128:9–11), and TEMPLE worship. Basic gospel doctrines, including the FALL OF ADAM, faith in Jesus Christ, repentance, and the need for an infinite ATONEMENT, were taught in each era from Adam's day onward whenever there were living prophets selected by the Lord (Moses 5:4–12; D&C 112:29–32).

Some prophets have been given keys and responsibility over specific aspects of God's plan for this earth. In the sense of dispensation or stewardship, each of these assignments could with propriety be called a special dispensation. Joseph Smith taught that Adam, as "the father of all living," stands as the head of the patriarchal order of priesthood for this earth under Christ (TPJS, p. 158; D&C 78:16) and holds the keys from generation to generation. Whenever the gospel is revealed anew, it is under the direction of Adam. Noah, the "father of all living" after Adam, is also known as Gabriel and stands next to Adam in priesthood authority (TPJS, pp. 157, 167). Moses holds keys of the gathering of Israel (D&C 110:11); and Elijah, of sealing the generations (D&C 2; 110:13–16; JS—H 1:38–39). John the Baptist had a special role of messianic preparation (JST Matt. 11:13–15; 17:10–14). Peter, James, and John received the keys of the MELCHIZEDEK PRIESTHOOD (TPJS, p. 158) from Jesus, Moses, and Elias (Elijah). Moroni holds responsibility for the Book of Mormon (D&C 27:5). Each of these prophets has received a dispensation of keys for which he holds a stewardship and will give an account to the Lord (D&C 27:5–13). In a future gathering, all who hold keys will give a stewardship report to Adam, and he, to Christ (TPJS, p. 157; cf. JST Luke 3:8–9).

In establishing the final dispensation, the Lord prepared Joseph Smith by sending prophets from previous dispensations to confer their keys upon him (see D&C 110; 112:32; 128:20–21). Thus, in the dispensation of the fulness of times, all things will be "gathered together into one" (Eph. 1:10; D&C 27:13). Since the final dispensation is a culmination of all that has come before, Joseph Smith is revered as a preeminent figure under Jesus Christ (D&C 128:18; 135:3).

Every dispensation, beginning with Adam's, has been a dispensation of the gospel of salvation through Jesus Christ. That is, in each dispensation the same plan of redemption through the Savior and the necessary holy priesthood have been revealed by God in a similar and consistent manner.

The general consistency of the plan does not preclude differences in revealed counsel and direction appropriate to the diversity in times and cultures of different dispensations. CIRCUMCISION, for example, important in previous dispensations as a sign of a covenant, was not essential in later dispensations. Blood SACRIFICES required in Old Testament times to anticipate the Atonement were fulfilled in Christ, with new redemptive emblems of bread and wine being prescribed by Jesus. Latter-day Saints have a strong recognition of change and progress in sacred history. Personal growth and its implications for the development of a perfected Zion society are essential in LDS eschatology (*see* ETERNAL PROGRESSION). This view of progress is evidenced in the concept that the final dispensation builds upon previous ones and achieves the goals of all of them with the celestialization of the earth. The earth then will become a glorious residence for those of all dispensations who have been resurrected and perfected in Christ (D&C 88:17–26).

A definite priesthood line of authority is an essential component of the LDS understanding of dispensations. Thus, Moses and Elijah visited Peter, James, and John at the MOUNT OF TRANSFIGURATION to restore certain keys of authority, and as already noted, these and many other ancient prophets visited Joseph Smith to give him the same authority (*see* RESTORATION OF THE GOSPEL).

Although the Lord's Church in successive dispensations ceased to function on earth because of apostasy, the work of the Lord in each dispensation is open-ended, leading to the final dispensation. The Lord's work that was not completed in an earlier dispensation will continue into the final dispensation, which is appropriately called "the fulness of times." In this last dispensation, some ideals never before reached on the earth will be accomplished (i.e., GATHERING of Israel, the SECOND COMING OF JESUS CHRIST, and the MILLENNIUM).

BIBLIOGRAPHY

Arrington, F. L. "Dispensationalism." In *Dictionary of Pentecostal and Charismatic Movements*, ed. Stanley M. Burgess and Gary B. McGee. Grand Rapids, Mich., 1988.

Hunter, Milton R. *The Gospel Through the Ages*. Salt Lake City, 1945.

Matthews, Robert J. "The Fulness of Times." *Ensign* 19 (Dec. 1989):46–51.

Roberts, B. H., ed. *A Comprehensive History of The Church of Jesus Christ of Latter-day Saints*, Introduction. Salt Lake City, 1930.

COURTNEY J. LASSETTER

DISTRIBUTION CENTERS

In order to make standardized administrative and teaching materials available to its members, The Church of Jesus Christ of Latter-day Saints has developed a system of distribution centers around the world. These distribute authorized Church literature and CURRICULUM materials to Church units, members, and officers in approximately one hundred languages. Such materials include scriptures, lesson manuals, teaching aids, handbooks, forms, reports, supplies, and video and cassette tapes.

The item in greatest demand is the Book of Mormon, with over four million copies distributed annually. Since 1989 the majority of these copies are in languages other than English. Some centers also coordinate local printing and distribution of Church magazines in their areas. Each center offers services geared to the particular proselytizing, teaching, and administrative needs of Church programs in its area. Some centers are equipped to print many of the materials they distribute, thus reducing the expense of shipping from Salt Lake City. Materials required in large quantities and hardbound books are often produced by commercial vendors. Wherever printed and regardless of language, all materials are uniform in their content.

BIBLIOGRAPHY

"A Conversation about the Church's Distribution Centers." *Ensign* 16 (Oct. 1986):78–79.

"Family Resources from the Church's Distribution Center." *Ensign* 15 (Mar. 1985): unnumbered insert opposite p. 40.

JOHN E. CARR

DISTRICT, DISTRICT PRESIDENT

A "district" is an ecclesiastical unit similar in function to a STAKE. Districts are found within missions in developing areas of the Church mostly outside the United States and Canada. Districts are meant to be transitional. Once membership in a district has grown to an average of 250–300 members per BRANCH, with 10 percent or more of these members holding the MELCHIZEDEK PRIESTHOOD, the district will normally be made into a stake and the qualifying branches within the district made into WARDS. Insofar as possible and practical, all

Church programs are made available to members living within districts.

Until recent years, there were more districts in the Church than stakes. But Church growth from 1965 to 1990 has changed that ratio. As of January 1, 1991, there were 1,784 stakes and 482 districts in the Church (457 of these districts were outside the United States and Canada).

A district is presided over by a district president, who must hold the Melchizedek Priesthood (either elder or high priest). The district president is nominated by the mission president, approved by the AREA PRESIDENCY, called and set apart by the mission president, and sustained by a vote at district conference or district general priesthood meeting. He serves with two counselors and generally serves with a district council of twelve Melchizedek Priesthood holders.

The word "district" is also used to describe certain other Church geographical divisions. For example, a temple district is made up of a number of stakes and/or missions whose members are encouraged to perform their TEMPLE ORDINANCES in a designated temple.

WILLIAM S. EVANS

DIVORCE

The Church of Jesus Christ of Latter-day Saints officially disapproves of divorce but does permit both divorce (the legal dissolution of a marriage bond) and annulment (a decree that a marriage was illegal or invalid) in civil marriages and "cancellation of sealing" in temple marriages.

Latter-day Saints believe that God intended marriage to be an eternal union when he commanded that a man and woman "shall be one flesh" (Gen. 2:24). However, under Jewish interpretation of the LAW OF MOSES, a man had the right to divorce his wife if she found disfavor in his eyes or for "uncleanness" (adultery or other reasons). The man was required to give his wife a written bill of divorcement, which freed her to remarry (Deut. 24:1–2), although in some cases he was not allowed to "put away" his wife (Deut. 22:29).

Jesus Christ condemned divorce under most circumstances, saying, "What therefore God hath joined together, let not man put asunder" (Matt. 19:6). He explained that Moses had permitted divorce only "because of the hardness of your hearts" and because the people could not live the higher law of eternal marriage, "but from the beginning it was not so" (Matt. 19:8). To this he added, speaking in the Sermon on the Mount to those who would strive to be the light of the world and the children of God, "Whosoever putteth away his wife, and marrieth another, committeth adultery: and whosoever marrieth her that is put away from her husband committeth adultery" (Luke 16:18; Matt. 5:31–32; 3 Ne. 12:31–32).

The Doctrine and Covenants reiterates the teaching that marriage is ordained of God (D&C 49:15–16). The Church distinguishes between (1) civil marriages, which are valid for "time" (until divorce or the death of one spouse), and (2) temple marriages, or sealings, solemnized by proper ecclesiastical authority, which are binding for "time and all eternity" if the participants are obedient to the gospel (see MARRIAGE: ETERNAL). Legal annulments and divorces free the individuals married civilly for remarriage. Only the President of the Church can authorize a "cancellation of sealing" in temple marriages to free a worthy member to remarry in the temple. Without a cancellation of sealing, divorced members may remarry for time only (see SEALING: CANCELLATION OF).

For nineteenth-century Latter-day Saints, feelings about divorce were mixed. President Brigham Young did not approve of men divorcing their wives, but women were relatively free to dissolve an unhappy marriage, especially a polygamous union (see PLURAL MARRIAGE). Such divorces were handled in ecclesiastical COURTS because polygamous marriages were not considered legal by the government. Records of the number of divorces granted between 1847 and 1877 show a relatively high rate of divorce for polygamous marriages. This rate was high, not so much because polygamy was difficult, but because LDS society had not developed clear rules and expectations for the practice or the participants (Campbell and Campbell, p. 22).

Early Utah laws reflected general LDS beliefs and may have influenced the incidence of divorce. An 1851 territorial divorce law had lenient residency requirements and allowed divorce when it was clear "that the parties cannot live in peace and union together, and that their welfare requires a separation" (First Legislative Assembly of the Territory of Utah, 1851, p. 83).

Current Church statistics on divorces among Latter-day Saints show somewhat fewer divorces among U.S. Mormons than among the general U.S. population. Data from a 1981 Church membership survey in the United States show that 16 percent of members (as compared to 23 percent of U.S. whites, statistically the most comparable group) had been divorced (Goodman and Heaton, p. 93). Latter-day Saints in Canada, Great Britain, Mexico, and Japan were more likely than their respective national populations to be divorced. However, converts who had divorced before joining the Church contributed to the relatively high proportion of divorced members outside the United States.

Recent U.S. data from the National Survey of Families and Households indicate that about 26 percent of both Latter-day Saints and non-LDS have experienced a divorce (Heaton et al., Table 2). If these trends continue, researchers project that about one-third of recent U.S. LDS marriages may end in divorce (Goodman and Heaton, p. 92). Nationally, experts predict that 50–60 percent of recent marriages will end in divorce or separation (Cherlin, p. 148).

Societal pressures and individual characteristics affect the likelihood of divorce. There will be a higher incidence of divorce among Latter-day Saints if they marry younger than age twenty or older than age thirty, have less than a college education, or marry outside the faith. These factors correlate with factors influencing divorce among U.S. citizens generally. In addition, divorce is more common when Latter-day Saints marry within the faith but do not have the marriage sealed in the temple. Goodman and Heaton found that such marriages are five times more likely to end in divorce than are temple marriages (p. 94). Those who choose a temple marriage usually are more committed to the Church and are required to comply with strict behavioral standards of chastity and fidelity to qualify for the temple marriage.

Severe personal and economic consequences usually accompany divorce among Latter-day Saints. LDS women are often not well prepared to support themselves and their children, and men may pay little in child support or alimony. About one-third of female-headed LDS households, a majority of which were the result of divorce, are living in poverty, despite a high rate of employment among single mothers (Goodman and Heaton, pp. 101, 104).

Divorced Latter-day Saints have lower religious participation than married members. They attend Church less often, and they pray, pay tithing, and hold Church callings less frequently than married members. These may be symptomatic of both the causes and the consequences of divorce.

Divorced Latter-day Saints are also more likely to remarry than the general divorced U.S. population. More than three-fourths of divorced Mormons probably will remarry (Goodman and Heaton).

After the divorce of their parents, most LDS children live with their mothers. They attend Church less frequently than children in two-parent households, even when the custodial parent attends regularly. Church researchers estimate that one-third of LDS children in the United States will live with a single or remarried parent.

Twentieth-century Church leaders speak of divorce as a threat to the family. In the April 1969 general conference, President David O. MCKAY declared, "Christ's ideal pertaining to marriage is the unbroken home, and conditions that cause divorce are violations of his divine teachings. Except in cases of infidelity or other extreme conditions, the Church frowns upon divorce" (IE 72 [June 1969]:2–5). President Spencer W. KIMBALL said that relatively few divorces are justifiable. He also told members that divorce frequently results from selfishness and other sins of one or both spouses (Kimball, 1975, p. 6). Other Church leaders also emphasize selfishness and mention additional causes of divorce, such as poor choice of a marriage partner, infidelity, lack of understanding of the divine nature of marriage, poor financial management, and lack of continued marital enrichment. "The current philosophy—get a divorce if it doesn't work out—handicaps a marriage from the beginning" (Haight, p. 12).

Church leaders urge members to prepare for marriage, marry within the faith, marry in the temple, live righteously and nurture their marriage relationships, pray for guidance, and counsel with each other and with priesthood leaders to resolve differences and deter divorce. Priesthood leaders are advised to help members strengthen their marriages but, when necessary, to permit divorce and to determine whether disciplinary action should be taken against any spouse guilty of moral transgression, such as infidelity or abuse. Priesthood leaders are to "cast out" (i.e., excommunicate) unrepentant adulterers from among the Saints, but to accept the victims of divorce (D&C 42:74–77).

Church members who are divorced and the children of divorced parents sometimes report feelings of isolation or lack of acceptance because of the strong orientation toward two-parent families in the Church (Hulse, p. 17). Church leaders admonish all members to be sensitive to the needs of people in difficult circumstances and to offer help and appropriate encouragement and compassionate service wherever possible.

BIBLIOGRAPHY

Campbell, Eugene E., and Bruce L. Campbell. "Divorce Among Mormon Polygamists: Extent and Explanations." *Utah Historical Quarterly* 46 (Winter 1978):4–23.

Cherlin, Andrew. "Recent Changes in American Fertility, Marriage and Divorce." *ANNALS, AAPSS* 510 [July 1990]:148.

Foster, Lawrence. "A Little-Known Defense of Polygamy from the Mormon Press in 1842." *Dialogue* 9 (Winter 1974):21–34.

———. *Religion and Sexuality: Three American Communal Experiments of the Nineteenth Century.* New York, 1981.

Goodman, Kristen L., and Tim B. Heaton. "LDS Church Members in the U.S. and Canada: A Demographic Profile." *AMCAP Journal* 12 (1986):88–107.

Haight, David B. "Marriage and Divorce." *Ensign* 14 (May 1984):12.

Heaton, Tim B., and Kristen L. Goodman. "Religion and Family Formation." *Review of Religious Research* 26 (June 1985):343–59.

Heaton, Tim B., et al. "In Search of a Peculiar People: Are Mormon Families Really Different?" Meeting of the Society for the Scientific Study of Religion, October 1989, Table 2.

Hulse, Cathy. "On Being Divorced." *Ensign* 16 (Mar. 1986):17.

Kimball, Spencer W. "The Time to Labor is Now." *Ensign* 5 (Nov. 1975):6.

———. *Marriage.* Salt Lake City, 1978.

KRISTEN L. GOODMAN

DOCTRINE

[*This entry consists of five articles:*

For related articles, see, generally, Articles of Faith; Gospel; Jesus Christ; *and* Plan of Salvation. *See also* Intellectual History *and* Smith, Joseph: Teachings of. *For articles of a philosophical nature, see* Epistemology; Ethics; Knowledge; Metaphysics; Philosophy; Reason and Revelation; Theology; *and* Truth, *among others.*]

MEANING, SOURCE, AND HISTORY OF DOCTRINE

MEANING OF DOCTRINE.   The word "doctrine" in the scriptures means "a teaching" as well as "that which is taught." Most often in the Church it refers to the teachings or doctrine of Jesus Christ, understood in a rather specific sense. Scripturally, then, the term "doctrine" means the core message of Jesus Christ—that Jesus is the Messiah, the Redeemer. All other teachings are subordinate to those by which all people "know how to come unto Christ and be saved"—that is, to the "points of doctrine," such as faith, repentance, baptism, and receiving the gift of the Holy Ghost. At one time, stressing the preeminence and foundational nature of this message, Jesus taught, "And whoso shall declare more or less than this, and establish it for my doctrine, the same cometh of evil, and is not built upon my rock" (3 Ne. 11:40).

In the King James Version (KJV) of the Old Testament, the word "doctrine" occurs six times (Deut. 32:2; Job 11:4; Prov. 4:2; Isa. 28:9, 29:24; Jer. 10:8), usually as a translation of the Hebrew word *leqakh,* meaning "instruction" or, more literally, "what is to be received." In the KJV New Testament it is used some fifty times, most often in reference to the teaching or instruction of Jesus Christ, less frequently to the teachings of others.

The "doctrine of Jesus Christ," which the Savior's listeners found "astonishing" (Matt. 7:28) and "new" (Mark 1:27) and which he attributed to the Father (John 7:16–19), is synonymous with his central message, the GOSPEL OF JESUS CHRIST. In Paul's words, it was the good news that the kingdom of God is at hand and that God "hath reconciled us to himself by Jesus Christ" (2 Cor. 5:18).

The apostles, following the death and resurrection of the Savior, continued to teach this essential message (Acts 13:12; 1 Tim. 6:1). They used the word "doctrine" most often in reference to what a person must believe and do in order to be saved (Acts 2:41–47; 1 Tim. 4:16; Heb. 6:1–3).

Most occurrences of the term "doctrine" in the New Testament are in the singular and refer to the "doctrine of Jesus Christ." The plural "doctrines" usually refers to the teachings of men and devils, false and vain teachings contrary to or denying the Savior's "doctrine." Jesus' message comes from the Father and has its content in Jesus Christ, the Messiah and Redeemer, the way of salvation. The "doctrine" of Jesus Christ is the foundation upon which all other teachings, principles, and practices rest.

The Book of Mormon and the Doctrine and Covenants use the word "doctrine" in the same way. In the singular it always refers to the "doctrine of Jesus Christ" or to the "points of his doctrine" and means "that which will ensure the salvation of those who accept and act upon it." In the plural, it refers to the false teachings of devils or others (2 Ne. 3:12; 28:9; D&C 46:7). The Book of Mormon uses "doctrine" in this special sense as the "doctrine of Jesus Christ" or the gospel (twenty-eight times). Jesus attributed his teaching to the Father: "This is my doctrine, . . . that the Father commandeth all men, everywhere, to repent and believe in me. And whoso believeth in me, and is baptized, the same shall be saved; and they are they who shall inherit the kingdom of God" (3 Ne. 11:32–33). Later he declared, "This is the gospel which I have given unto you—that I came into the world to do the will of the Father, . . . and my Father sent me that I might be lifted up upon the cross; . . . that whoso repenteth and is baptized in my name shall be filled; and if he endureth to the end, behold, him will I hold guiltless before the Father at that day when I shall stand to judge the world" (3 Ne. 27:13–16; cf. D&C 76:40–42).

Thus, the "doctrine of Jesus Christ" is the only teaching that can properly be called "doctrine." It is fixed and unchanging. It cannot be modified or contradicted, but merely amplified as additional truths that deepen understanding and appreciation of its meaning are revealed. It is the basis on which the test of faith is made, and the rock or foundation of all other revealed teachings, principles, and practices.

Some of these other teachings comprise what is sometimes referred to as the PLAN OF SALVATION, which is understood as the larger historical setting in which the "doctrine of Jesus Christ" is situated and hence best understood. This is the plan worked out by the Father from the beginning, centering on the ATONEMENT of Jesus Christ as the necessary means by which all individuals are saved and exalted. All other revealed teachings are either aspects of the doctrine of Jesus Christ or extensions, elaborations, or appendages of it. The Prophet Joseph SMITH taught, "The fundamental principles of our religion are the testimony of the Apostles and Prophets, concerning Jesus Christ, that He died, was buried, and rose again the third day, and ascended unto heaven; and all other things which pertain to our religion are only appendages to it" (TPJS, p. 121).

Some of the "appendages" that are explicitly identified in the scriptures as part of the doctrine of Jesus Christ are (1) faith in the Lord Jesus Christ, the Son of God; (2) repentance of all sins; (3) baptism by immersion for the remission of sins; (4) the gift of the Holy Ghost by the laying-on of hands by those in AUTHORITY; (5) enduring in righteousness to the end; and (6) the resurrection of all human beings to be judged by Christ (3 Ne. 9:1–16; 11:23–39; 19:7–28; 27:13–21; D&C 10:62–69; 33:10–15; 39:5–6; 76:40–43). Additional teachings, or "things we know" (D&C 20:17), that are closely associated with this foundation include knowledge about the nature of GOD, the CREATION and the FALL OF ADAM, AGENCY, continuing REVELATION, an open CANON and the continual search for the truth of all things, PREMORTAL LIFE, the GATHERING OF ISRAEL, the role of a COVENANT people, sharing the gospel, HOPE and CHARITY, the establishment of ZION, the second coming of Christ, Christ's reign on earth for a thousand years, TEMPLE ORDINANCES for the living and the dead, the preaching of the gospel in the postearth SPIRIT WORLD, the need for PRIESTHOOD, degrees of glory in the hereafter, ETERNAL MARRIAGE, and the concept of ultimate EXALTATION in the presence of God to share his glory and life.

In addition to its scriptural use, the word "doctrine" has a broad meaning in Mormon vernacular, where it is used to mean virtually everything that is, or has been, taught or believed by the Latter-day Saints. In this sense, doctrinal teachings answer a host of questions. Some relate closely to the core message of the gospel of Jesus Christ; others are farther removed and unsystematically lap over into such disciplines as history, psychology, philosophy, science, politics, business, and economics. Some of these beliefs qualify as official doctrine and are given to the Saints as counsel, exhortation, reproof, and instruction (2 Tim. 3:16). Continual effort is made to harmonize and implement these principles and doctrine into a righteous life. Other teachings, ones that lack official or authoritative standing, may also be widespread among Church members at any given time.

SOURCE OF DOCTRINE.   God is the source of doctrine. It is not devised or developed by man. It is based on eternal truth and is revealed by God to man. It can be properly understood only by revelation through the Spirit of God (1 Cor. 2:11–14; Jacob 4:8).

God dispenses eternal truths "line upon line, precept upon precept" (2 Ne. 28:30). At times, he has revealed the fulness of the gospel, and those who have accepted and lived it were received into his presence. When people have ignored or rejected his gospel, God has on occasion withheld his Spirit, and people have had to live in a state of spiritual darkness (see APOSTASY).

God reveals as much light as humankind is willing to abide. Hence, varying amounts of true doctrine have existed on the earth at different periods of time, and people on earth during the same era have enjoyed differing amounts of truth. In this sense, there can be said to be a history of doctrine— that is, an account of how, over time, humankind has either grown or declined in the knowledge of the things of God, man, and the world. Joseph Smith taught, "This is the principle on which the government of heaven is conducted—by revelation adapted to the circumstances in which the children of the kingdom are placed" (*TPJS*, p. 256).

Many factors influence how much God reveals, to whom, and under what circumstances. These include (1) who takes the opportunity to ask the Father in the name of Christ; (2) how much faith those seeking knowledge have; (3) what they ask for; (4) what is good for them to receive (D&C 18:18); (5) how willing they are to obey what is given (Alma 12:9–11); (6) what the will and wisdom of God require, for he gives "all that he seeth fit that they should have" (Alma 29:8); (7) whether the faith of people needs to be tested (Mormon was about to write more, but "the Lord forbade it, saying: I will try the faith of my people" [3 Ne. 26:8– 11]); and (8) how spiritually prepared people are to receive the revelation (for example, Jesus taught through PARABLES in order to protect those who were not ready to understand [Luke 8:10; D&C 19:22]). The eternal truths constituting the gospel do not change, and eventually all who are exalted in the kingdom of God will understand them and apply them fully. However, mankind's knowledge and understanding of these truths change, as do the policies and practices appropriate to concurrent levels of understanding and obedience.

Inasmuch as God's house "is a house of order . . . and not a house of confusion" (D&C 132:8), there must be one who can speak for God for the whole Church and also settle differences. In The Church of Jesus Christ of Latter-day Saints, the living prophet is the only one authorized to "receive revelations and commandments" binding on the entire Church (D&C 28:1–7; 43:1–7; 128:11). From the time the Church was organized, there has been—and always will be—"a prophet, recognized of God and his people, who will continue to interpret the mind and will of the Lord" (Spencer W. Kimball, *Ensign* 7 [May 1977]:78). Ordinarily, the prophet acts in concert with his counselors in the FIRST PRESIDENCY and the QUORUM OF THE TWELVE APOSTLES—those who hold, with the Prophet, the "keys of the kingdom" (D&C 81:2; 112:30)—with the principle of quorum unanimity and COMMON CONSENT of the members of the Church giving power and validity to their decisions (D&C 26:2; 107:27–31). Acting collectively and under the inspiration of God, these leaders are authorized to determine the position of the Church at any given time on matters of doctrine, policy, and practice. This is the proper channel through which changes come. Latter-day Saints believe that God "will yet reveal many great and important things pertaining to the Kingdom of God" (A of F 9). It is expected that such revelations will involve an expanded understanding of doctrine.

Many individuals write or preach their views. Some, by study and obedience, may learn truths that go beyond the stated position of the Church, but this does not authorize them to speak officially for the Church or to present their views as binding on the Church. There are many subjects about which the scriptures are not clear and about which the Church has made no official pronouncements. In such matters, one can find differences of opinion among Church members and leaders. Until the truth of these matters is made known by revelation, there is room for different levels of understanding and interpretation of unsettled issues.

HISTORY OF DOCTRINE. The doctrine of the Church was revealed principally through the Prophet Joseph Smith, though subsequent additions and clarifications have been made. These truths are part of the fulness of the gospel of Jesus Christ, known on earth in earlier times but now lost, necessitating a restoration by revelation.

The Prophet Joseph Smith received and shared his doctrinal understanding line upon line, from the time of his FIRST VISION in 1820 to his death in 1844. In many instances, his own understanding was progressively enhanced. In other matters, he learned certain principles early but only taught them as his followers were able and willing to accept them. Concerning the hereafter, for example, he said, "I could explain a hundred fold more than I ever have of the glories of the kingdoms manifested to me in the vision, were I permitted, and were the people prepared to receive them" (*TPJS*, p. 305).

There is no simple pattern or predictable sequence in the growth of Joseph Smith's knowledge. Much of his doctrinal understanding gradually unfolded through revelations that he received in response to various contemporary issues and circumstances facing the infant but quickly expanding Church. Other teachings emerged quite spontaneously. His perceptions grew in completeness and detail, but they did not lose their historical footing in past dispensations or their undeviating goal of bringing people to Christ.

One important catalyst in this process was Joseph Smith's systematic examination of the Bible (*see* JOSEPH SMITH TRANSLATION OF THE BIBLE [JST]), which yielded inspired biblical interpretations and textual restorations. Also, many sections of the Doctrine and Covenants are revelations answering questions that arose in this process (e.g., D&C 76, 91, 132).

Joseph's teachings about the Godhead illustrate the previous points. At first, he simply taught that God the Father and the Son were separate personages, without mentioning explicitly the nature of their bodies, even though 3 Nephi 11:15 (translated in 1829) made it clear that Jesus' resurrected body was tangible. Later, in Nauvoo, Joseph declared that "there is no other God in heaven but that God who has flesh and bones" (*TPJS*, p. 181, a comment made in 1841 on the biblical text in John 5:26), and that both the Father and the Son have bodies of "flesh and bones as tangible as man's" (D&C 130:22). Two months before his death, Joseph, for the first time in a recorded public sermon—indeed, in his crowning sermon about the nature of God, the KING FOLLETT DISCOURSE—taught that God is an exalted man. And two weeks before his death he spoke of a "plurality of Gods," expanding one's understanding in Genesis 1 of the Hebrew plural *elohim*, or "gods" (Joseph had studied Hebrew in 1835), explaining that "there are Gods many and Lords many, but to us only one, and we are to be in subjection to that one," and declaring that for

fifteen years he had always preached "the plurality of Gods" (*TPJS*, pp. 370-71; cf. 1 Cor. 8:5–6).

Similarly, Joseph's teachings relating to such things as the nature of man, his premortal existence, his agency, and his eternal potential of GODHOOD also gradually unfolded to him and to those around him. He learned in December 1830 that "all the children of men" were created "spiritually, before they were naturally upon the face of the earth" (Moses 3:5). A revelation in 1833 indicated that a component of each individual existed before his or her spiritual creation, a component called INTELLIGENCE, which "was not created or made, neither indeed can be" (D&C 93:29). During the period 1835–1842, while translating the book of Abraham, Joseph Smith learned that Abraham had seen into the premortal world and beheld myriads of "intelligences that were organized before the world was," in the presence of God (Abr. 3:22). Many were "noble and great" and chose to follow Christ. To this was added in 1841 that "at the first organization in heaven we were all present, and saw the Savior chosen and appointed and the plan of salvation made, and we sanctioned it" (*TPJS*, p. 181).

The Prophet's teachings on the atonement of Jesus Christ, creation, foreordination, salvation for the dead, priesthood, temple ordinances, eternal marriage, exaltation, and many other subjects can all be shown to have followed similar courses of development during his ministry (Cannon, Dahl, and Welch).

By 1844, the basic doctrinal structure of the Church was in place. Since that time, however, there have been official pronouncements clarifying doctrinal understanding or adapting doctrinal applications to particular circumstances. Some are now included in the Doctrine and Covenants; others are published as official messages of the First Presidency (cf. *MFP*). Over the years, various procedures and practices have received greater or lesser emphasis as changes have occurred in economic conditions (*see* CONSECRATION; TITHING; UNITED ORDER; WELFARE), political circumstances (*see* CHURCH AND STATE; POLITICS; WAR AND PEACE), intellectual atmosphere (*see* INTELLECTUAL HISTORY), Church growth (*see* ORGANIZATION), and many other areas. The essential doctrine of the Church, however, has remained constant amid such change.

Certain Church leaders have written extensively of their understanding of the doctrines of the

Church and, as a consequence, have had a significant influence on what many members believe (*see* TREATISES ON DOCTRINE below). These have included Parley P. Pratt, Orson Pratt, James E. Talmage, John A. Widtsoe, B. H. Roberts, Joseph Fielding Smith, and Bruce R. McConkie. Their writings evidence some differences of opinion on unsettled issues, just as different schools of thought exist among Church members in general on certain issues. Examples include efforts to reconcile current scientific teachings and revealed truths, to ponder the nature of uncreated intelligence, and to define eternal progression. Latter-day Saints have faith that answers will eventually be revealed, and are urged, in the meantime, to seek knowledge by all available means and to show tolerance toward those espousing differing opinions on such subjects.

BIBLIOGRAPHY

Cannon, Donald Q.; Larry E. Dahl; and John W. Welch. "The Restoration of Major Doctrines Through Joseph Smith: The Godhead, Mankind, and the Creation." *Ensign* 19 (Jan. l989):27–33; and "The Restoration of Major Doctrines Through Joseph Smith: Priesthood, the Word of God, and the Temple." *Ensign* 19 (Feb. 1989):7–13.

Lyon, T. Edgar. "Doctrinal Development of the Church During the Nauvoo Sojourn, 1839–1846." *BYU Studies* 15 (Summer 1975):435–46.

M. GERALD BRADFORD
LARRY E. DAHL

DISTINCTIVE TEACHINGS

Few religious doctrines are unique in the strict sense, but many are rare enough to be considered distinctive features of this or that religion or denomination. Several doctrines of the Latter-day Saints are distinctive in this sense, although in most cases other Christians have at some time held identical or similar beliefs. Latter-day Saints insist that their distinctive doctrines were revealed by God in earlier DISPENSATIONS headed by Adam, Enoch, Noah, and so forth down to the time of Christ. Thus, while they may be distinct among modern denominations, these newly revealed doctrines were shared with the one true Church of Jesus Christ in ancient times.

Unique to LDS theology in modern times is a view of the GODHEAD as consisting of three separate beings, two possessing bodies of flesh and bone and one possessing a spirit body. An official declaration concerning the Godhead states: "The Father has a body of flesh and bones as tangible as man's; the Son also; but the Holy Ghost has not a body of flesh and bones, but is a personage of Spirit" (D&C 130:22). Latter-day Saints take the Bible, both Old and New Testaments, in a literal, anthropomorphic sense, attributing to God both a human form and emotions. They accept both a "oneness" and "threeness" of the Godhead as taught in the Bible. However, they reject the traditional doctrine of the Trinity, and believe instead that the Godhead is one in mind, purpose, and testimony, but three in number. Thus, they believe that God is spirit in the sense that he is infused with spirit, and in the sense that the Holy Ghost is a spirit, but they do not limit the Father or the Son to incorporeality.

Latter-day Saints identify Jehovah, the God of the Old Testament, specifically as Jesus Christ. They believe that the God of Abraham, Isaac, and Jacob, the God who walked with Enoch and who talked with Moses on Mount Sinai, was the premortal Jesus Christ, or God the Son, acting as the agent of his Father.

Latter-day Saints also have distinct doctrines about the nature of the universe and how it began. Because they believe that spirit and matter are actually the same thing in different degrees of refinement (see D&C 131:2), Latter-day Saints perceive the universe in terms of two realms, the physical and the spiritual, but these are not antithetical. They deny the spirit/matter dichotomy and insist that both spirit and matter make up a single eternal universe.

Moreover, Latter-day Saints understand "in the beginning" to mean "in the beginning of our part of the story," or in the premortal state "when God began to create our world." They do not believe in an absolute beginning, for in LDS theology spirit, matter, and element are all eternal. Creations may progress from lower to higher orders, and it is God's work and glory to bring this development about (Moses 1:39), but there never was a time when matter did not exist. Latter-day Saints reject the common idea of an ex nihilo creation—that God made everything that exists out of nonexistence. They teach instead that God created everything out of pre-existing but unorganized materials. He organized pre-existing elements to create worlds, and he organized pre-existing intelligence to beget spirits. The spirits of all human beings existed as God's spirit children before their mortal birth on earth.

LDS eschatology also offers several distinct doctrines. For example, Latter-day Saints believe in a temporary state between DEATH and RESURRECTION that the scriptures call the spirit world. This temporary spirit world includes Paradise, where the spirits of the righteous await their glorious resurrection, and Hell, where the spirits of the wicked suffer for their sins while they await resurrection to a lesser degree of glory (Alma 40:11–14; cf. Luke 16:22–23). LDS doctrine teaches that every human being will be resurrected. Many were resurrected soon after Jesus' resurrection; the remaining righteous will be resurrected at the second coming of Christ, and the wicked at the end of Christ's one-thousand-year reign on earth. Hell is a temporary condition, which will yield up its captive spirits at the Resurrection, just as death will yield up its bodies (2 Ne. 9:10–14; cf. Rev. 20:13–14). In the Resurrection all suffering comes to an end (D&C 76:84, 88–89), and all human beings except the sons of perdition will be saved in one of three kingdoms, or degrees of glory: the celestial, the terrestrial, or the telestial (D&C 76:1–19; 88:29–32; cf. 1 Cor. 15:4–42).

Distinctive LDS doctrines concerning the nature of the Church include the belief that the Church of Jesus Christ has been on earth many times, beginning with father Adam, in much the same form it has now and with the same doctrines. The Church and gospel of Jesus Christ are eternal. They were revealed to the people of Adam, Enoch, Noah, Abraham, Moses, Jared, Lehi, and others. Adam knew the gospel, was baptized by immersion in the name of Jesus Christ, and received the gift of the Holy Ghost, just as the Saints in all other dispensations. At times humanity has rejected or distorted the gospel and fallen into apostasy. But eventually the gospel has been restored to its original purity through prophets called to begin a new dispensation. Most recently this same eternal gospel has been restored through the modern Prophet Joseph SMITH. Thus the establishment of The Church of Jesus Christ of Latter-day Saints was not the result of a long religious evolution, nor was it merely the restoration of primitive Christianity, but it was the final restoration to earth of an eternal gospel of Jesus Christ revealed to humanity many times since the beginning.

What distinguishes "the true and living Church" from all other churches is possession of the priesthood keys of the kingdom of heaven (see Matt. 16:19). The belief that possession of the apostolic keys is necessary in the true Church is not unique to Latter-day Saints, but the insistence that one of those keys necessarily bestows the gifts of prophecy and revelation is. To hold the keys of the kingdom as Peter did is to be a prophet, seer, and revelator like Peter. And in order to be "true and living" a church must receive these apostolic keys as exercised and transmitted through the hands of its living prophets. As a tree is alive only when its branches are connected to its trunk and roots, so a church is alive only when it is connected by an open channel of revelation to its divine source. Where ecclesiastical leaders have no such prophetic link with the heavens, a church may even teach true doctrines, but it can not be "true and living" (see D&C 1:30; 27:12–13), for it lacks the necessary communication with its own divine roots.

With such emphasis placed on the need for living prophets, it follows that the word of God is primarily the word as spoken to and communicated by the prophets. The written words, the scriptures, are always important as historical precedent and as a record of what the Lord has said to his people in the past, but they are supplemental and secondary to what he may say now through his living prophet. Since Latter-day Saints believe in the genuine gift of prophecy, it follows that the revelations received by modern prophets should be esteemed as highly as those received by ancient ones. Hence, the LDS canon of scripture can never be closed: "We believe all that God has revealed, all that He does now reveal, and we believe that He will yet reveal many great and important things pertaining to the Kingdom of God" (A of F 9).

The Latter-day Saints are also unique in several aspects of their concept of salvation. While most of the LDS doctrines would be familiar to other Christians—for example, the doctrines of the Atonement, justification, sanctification, and grace—there are several distinct features found among the Latter-day Saints. They make a distinction between generic "salvation," which to them means that through the atonement of Christ one is delivered from the grave and from the power of Satan and hell to enter a degree of glory, and "exaltation," which means that through the atonement of Christ and personal obedience to the principles and ordinances of the gospel of Jesus Christ one is raised to the highest degree of glory to share the powers and privileges of God, to sit on his throne and reign in eternity (see D&C 76:1–119; 88:22–23; cf. Rev. 1:6; 3:21). To be exalted is to become like God (*see* DEIFICATION).

Faithful Latter-day Saints receive in the LDS temples the ordinances and knowledge necessary for celestial exaltation. One part of these sacred rites is called the temple ENDOWMENT because it constitutes a major part of the overwhelming gift extended to humanity through the atonement of Christ. Another temple ordinance is the SEALING of husbands and wives, parents and children into families that will endure for time and for eternity. The celestial kingdom will consist of God's heavenly family linked together in love as husbands and wives, parents and children, and brothers and sisters forever. As single individuals, human beings may be saved in lesser degrees of glory, but only families can be exalted.

Not everyone has had the opportunity in mortal life to hear the gospel of Christ and receive all the ordinances of exaltation. Latter-day Saints teach that God has provided for all to hear the gospel so they can accept or reject its blessings. Those who do not have that opportunity in mortality will receive it in the spirit world. The New Testament teaches that Jesus himself visited the spirit world after his death on the cross and preached to the spirits there: "For Christ also hath once suffered for sins, the just for the unjust, that he might bring us to God, being put to death in the flesh, but quickened by the Spirit: By which also he went and preached unto the spirits in prison" (1 Pet. 3:18–19). The purpose of his preaching ministry to the spirits is revealed in the next chapter: "For this cause was the gospel preached also to them that are dead, that they might be judged according to men in the flesh, but live according to God in the spirit" (1 Pet. 4:6). This doctrine has been amplified and explained in latter-day revelation (D&C 137, 138; *see* SALVATION FOR THE DEAD).

Other areas in which the views of the Latter-day Saints differ noticeably from those of the contemporary religious world are the concepts of TIME AND ETERNITY, the LIGHT OF CHRIST, the GIFT OF THE HOLY GHOST, the positive estimate of the CREATION and of the physical EARTH, the eternal necessity of ORDINANCES, the centrality of the ABRAHAMIC COVENANT for modern Christians, and

the concept of heaven as a CELESTIAL KINGDOM located upon this renewed and glorified earth.

BIBLIOGRAPHY

Keller, Roger R. *Reformed Christians and Mormon Christians: Let's Talk.* Ann Arbor, Mich., 1986.

Madsen, Truman G. "Are Christians Mormon?" *BYU Studies* 15 (Autumn 1974):73–94.

McConkie, Bruce R. *MD.* Salt Lake City, 1966.

Robinson, Stephen E. *Are Mormons Christians?*, chaps. 6-8. Salt Lake City, 1991.

Talmage, James E. *AF.* Salt Lake City, 1924.

ALMA P. BURTON

LDS DOCTRINE COMPARED WITH OTHER CHRISTIAN DOCTRINES

As biblical scholar W. D. Davies once pointed out, LDS doctrine can be described as biblical Christianity separated from hellenized Christianity, a conjunction of first-century Judaism and Christianity. Latter-day Saints accept the BIBLE and its apostolic teachings as God's word, but reject many later interpretations of the Bible that express Greek philosophical concerns—they accept John and Paul but reject Augustine. For example, Latter-day Saints accept both the threeness of God and the oneness of God as biblical teachings. The Father, Son, and Holy Spirit are three divine personages who together constitute one GODHEAD. But Mormons reject the attempts of postbiblical, nonapostolic Christianity to define how the oneness and the threeness of God are related. They accept the biblical doctrine of the Trinity, but reject the philosophical doctrine of the Trinity as defined at the Council of Nicaea and later. In short, Latter-day Saints reject the AUTHORITY and conclusions of theologians and philosophers to define or interpret what the Bible, apostles, or prophets have not. They accept biblical Christianity, but not its extension in extrabiblical CREEDS and traditions.

To those Christians who have welded the Bible to its later interpretation and cannot separate Plato and Augustine from Peter and Paul, and cannot think of "true" Christianity in first-century categories, LDS doctrine may seem iconoclastic in separating biblical texts from their later "traditional" interpretation. Nevertheless, Latter-day Saints feel that New Testament Saints would have been just as uncomfortable with the philosophical creeds of later Christianity as they themselves are.

LDS rejection of much postbiblical Christianity is based on belief in an ancient APOSTASY that is both predicted and chronicled in the New Testament (e.g., 2 Thes. 2:1–5; 3 Jn. 9–10). Apostolic authority ceased just after the New Testament period, and without apostolic leadership and authority the Church was soon overwhelmed by alien intellectual and cultural pressures. The simple affirmations of biblical faith were turned into the complex propositions of THEOLOGY. Though subsequent churches were still "Christian," in the LDS view they no longer possessed the *fulness* of the GOSPEL OF JESUS CHRIST or apostolic authority. Latter-day Saints would agree with Catholics and "high church" Protestants that apostolic authority is essential in the true church but would also agree with other Protestants that apostolic authority was lacking in medieval orthodoxy. A close parallel is presented by Protestant rejection of Roman Catholic claims to binding apostolic authority. While Latter-day Saints trace the Apostasy to roughly the second century and reject subsequent orthodoxy, most Protestants would place it somewhere nearer the fifteenth century and then reject subsequent Catholicism.

Protestants who denied the necessity of apostolic succession, or who did not believe its links were severed by the Reformation, generally held that the fulness of the gospel could be achieved by reforming the Roman Church. Latter-day Saints, who insist on the necessity of apostolic succession but believe its links were severed early, see a reformation as inadequate for recovering the fulness of the gospel and reestablishing original Christianity. Only a total restoration of apostolic doctrines and authority could reestablish the pure Christianity of the first century. The Church of Jesus Christ of Latter-day Saints sees itself as constituting this Restoration.

LDS rejection of hellenistic philosophy in matters of doctrine accounts for many characteristic differences between Latter-day Saints and other Christians. For example, Latter-day Saints reject the Platonic spirit–matter dichotomy, which holds that spirit and matter are opposed and inimical to each other. They believe instead that spirit is refined matter and that both spirit and matter are eternal, being neither created nor destroyed. The Prophet Joseph SMITH taught that "there is no such thing as immaterial matter. All spirit is mat-

ter, but it is more fine or pure, and can only be discerned by purer eyes" (D&C 131:7).

Thus, for Latter-day Saints there is no ultimate incompatibility between spirit and matter or between the spiritual and the physical realms. In LDS theology, the physical elements are coeternal with God. The idea that physical matter is transitory, corrupt, or incompatible with spiritual or eternal life is rejected. Latter-day Saints usually define "spiritual" as "infused with spirit" rather than as "nonphysical." This unitary understanding of spirit and matter allows them to accept the Father and the Son as the concrete, anthropomorphic beings represented in scripture and reject the definition of God as the abstract, "totally other" nonbeing of philosophical theology. For Latter-day Saints, God *exists* in the normal sense in association with time and space, rather than in the abstract Platonic sense of beyond time and space. The traditional disparagement of matter and of the physical state of being is not well grounded biblically, and Latter-day Saints believe it is a product of hellenistic thought. They also think the concept of a God "without body, parts or passions" dismisses too much of the biblical data or allegorizes it excessively.

Since Mormons believe that the elements are eternal, it follows that they deny the ex nihilo creation. Rather, the universe was created (organized) out of preexisting elements that God organized by imposing physical laws. The Prophet Joseph Smith also taught that intelligence is also eternal and uncreated: "The intelligence of spirits had no beginning, neither will it have an end. . . . Intelligence is eternal and exists upon a self-existent principle" (*TPJS*, pp. 353–54).

Just as God organized preexisting matter to create the universe, so he organized preexisting intelligence to create the spirits that eventually became human beings. Consequently, Latter-day Saints do not view God as the *total* cause of what human beings are. Human intelligence is uncreated by God, and therefore independent of his control. Thus Mormons insist that human beings are free agents in the fullest sense, and deny both the doctrines of prevenient and irresistible grace, which make God's choice determinative for SALVATION or damnation. God will not coerce independent, self-existent wills. Though he desires the exaltation of all, and offers it equally to all, its achievement requires individual cooperation, a covenant relationship. In this way, LDS theology escapes the classical dilemma of predestination and theodicy imposed by believing that God created all things from nothing and is therefore solely responsible for the final products. Their radical doctrine of individual free agency also allows the Latter-day Saints to deny the theory of human depravity. The fall of Adam did not totally incapacitate humans from doing any good thing—they remain able to choose and to perform either good or evil. Moreover, Latter-day Saints accept the concept of the "fortunate Fall" (*mea culpa*). The Fall was a necessary step in the progress of humanity: "Adam fell that men might be; and men are, that they might have joy" (2 Ne. 2:25).

A positive view of the physical universe and of man also allows Latter-day Saints to anticipate a physical afterlife, the CELESTIAL KINGDOM, a community of physically resurrected beings transformed and perfected. Unlike many ancient church fathers, they do not long to escape the realm of the flesh, but rather to sanctify it. Hence, in the LDS view, even the physical relationships of FAMILY and MARRIAGE can continue in the eternities in a sanctified state. Thus there is little asceticism and no CELIBACY in LDS theology, which sees in both of these tendencies a denial of the goodness of God's physical creation (Gen. 1:31); and LDS theology avoids the traditional disparagement of the human body and the contempt for human SEXUALITY that are largely due to the neoplatonism of late antiquity.

While common ground for Latter-day Saints and other Christians is an acceptance of the Bible and its teachings, issues of interpretation aside, Mormonism agrees with "high church" orthodoxy against conservative Protestantism on the doctrine of the sufficiency of scripture. Though they accept the Bible, Latter-day Saints, like Roman Catholics and the Eastern Orthodox, for example, do not believe that the biblical text alone is sufficient for salvation. Biblical teaching, while true and accepted, has been imperfectly preserved and can be fully reconstituted only through supplemental REVELATION. This is not because New Testament Christianity was defective, but because New Testament Christianity is only partially preserved in the modern Bible. Those doctrines that were not preserved must be *restored*; consequently, Mormons deny both biblical inerrancy and sufficiency. Since the apostles and prophets of earliest Christianity received direct revelation from God (see, e.g., Acts 10:9–16, 28), Latter-day Saints believe that

any church claiming the fulness of the gospel must also enjoy this gift.

This crucial principle of continuing revelation is illustrated in the experience of the Prophet Joseph Smith, whose visions and revelations form the foundation of LDS doctrine. As the *magisterium* of the church is fundamental for Roman Catholics, and the scriptures are the *fontes* for Protestants, for Latter-day Saints the highest authority in religious matters is continuing revelation from God given through the living APOSTLES and prophets of his Church, beginning with Joseph Smith and continuing to the present leadership.

Latter-day Saints insist that both the CANON of SCRIPTURE and the structure of theology are always open-ended, and can always be added upon by God through revelation to his PROPHETS (A of F 9). Through this means they have received clarification of biblical doctrines that are disputed in other denominations, for example, Christ's ministry to the dead in 1 Peter 3:18 and 4:6 (see D&C 128; 137; 138). Also through modern revelation Latter-day Saints have received some distinctive doctrines that are not explicitly found in the Bible. In these cases modern revelation has not rehabilitated a doctrine that is unclear, but has restored a doctrine that was entirely lost.

Latter-day Saints share with most Christians the conviction that salvation comes only through the ATONEMENT of Jesus Christ, which is representative, exemplary, and substitutionary in nature. Christ is the mediator of humanity to the Father instead of fallen Adam; he sets an example for humans to emulate; and he takes mankind's place in suffering for sins.

Latter-day Saints are monophysite in their CHRISTOLOGY; that is, they believe Christ has only one nature, which is simultaneously both human and divine. This is possible because the human and the divine are not mutually exclusive categories in LDS thought, as in the duophysite christology of much orthodoxy. As Lorenzo SNOW said, "As man now is, God once was: As God now is, man may be" (Snow, p. 46). Most Christians would agree with the first half of this couplet as applied to the person of Christ, but Latter-day Saints apply it also to the Father. The second half of the couplet is more orthodox in the denominational sense than either Protestants or Catholics, for Latter-day Saints share the ancient biblical doctrine of DEIFICATION (*apotheosis*) with Eastern Orthodoxy. Several of early Christianity's theologians said essentially the same thing as Lorenzo Snow. Irenaeus said, "If the word became a man, it was so men may become gods" (Against Heresies, 4. Pref), and Athanasius maintained that "[Christ] became man that we might be made divine" (On the Incarnation, 54). Yet Latter-day Saints combine both halves of the couplet to reach what they feel is the only possible conclusion—human and divine are not mutually exclusive categories. Mormons insist that the two categories are one: Humans are of the lineage of the gods. Latter-day Saints would agree entirely with C. S. Lewis in *Mere Christianity*:

> He said (in the Bible) that we were "gods" and He is going to make good His words. If we let Him—for we can prevent Him, if we choose—He will make the feeblest and filthiest of us into a god or goddess, dazzling, radiant, immortal creature, pulsating all through with such energy and joy and wisdom and love as we cannot now imagine [p. 175].

BIBLIOGRAPHY

Dodds, Erwin. *Pagan and Christian in an Age of Anxiety.* New York, 1970.

Keller, Roger. *Reformed Christians and Mormon Christians: Let's Talk.* Ann Arbor, Mich., 1986.

Lash, Symeon. "Deification." In *The Westminster Dictionary of Christian Theology*, ed. A. Richardson and J. Bowden. Philadelphia, 1983.

Madsen, Truman, ed. *Reflections on Mormonism: Judaeo-Christian Parallels.* Salt Lake City, 1978.

Robinson, Stephen E. *Are the Mormons Christians?* Salt Lake City, 1991.

Snow, Eliza R. *Biography and Family Record of Lorenzo Snow.* Salt Lake City, 1884.

STEPHEN E. ROBINSON

HARMONIZATION OF PARADOX

Because Latter-day Saints reject the influences of Neoplatonism on original Christian theology, they are not on the horns of the dilemmas posed by some of the paradoxes in traditional Christian theology. This is not to say, however, that LDS ethical life and religious thought are free of paradox. LDS perspective tends to harmonize many paradoxes through its views that opposition is necessary in all things and that God and mankind are in the same order of reality but at different stages of knowledge and progression.

As used in ordinary discourse, "paradox" usually refers to a statement that on its face is unbelievable because it is apparently self-contradictory or is contrary to well-established facts, common sense, or generally received belief. While many paradoxes are no doubt false, not all necessarily are. Indeed, in the history of human thought, many brash paradoxes have overthrown a generally received but false belief, eventually to become widely accepted themselves —"some time a paradox, but now time gives it proof" (*Hamlet* 3.1.115).

Classical Christian theology is in many ways paradoxical. This is often the result of the unstable theological blending that occurred in the early centuries of Christianity when (a) insights that came from personal Judeo-Christian revelation were (b) interpretatively recast within an impersonal Neoplatonic view of reality. To mention a few:

1. (a) The loving God who is profoundly touched by the feelings of our infirmities is (b) without passions or outside influences.
2. (a) The God who acts in human history and responds to personal prayers is (b) timeless and unchangeable.
3. (b) The God without body or parts became (a) embodied in the person of Jesus of Nazareth.
4. The God who is (b) absolutely unlimited and good, and who created all things out of nothing (a) created a world abounding with evils.
5. (a) The Godhead consists of three perfect and separate persons who (b) collectively constitute one metaphysical substance.

Latter-day Saint doctrine, while affirming (a) the Judeo-Christian dimensions of the foregoing propositions regarding God, rejects (b) the Neoplatonic framework and metaphysic within which Judeo-Christian revelation has historically been interpreted. Accordingly, LDS understanding of Christian doctrine does not manifest those paradoxes that are generated by the union of these two incompatible sets of beliefs.

Latter-day Saint thought builds bridges between entities and quantities that are normally thought to be incongruous (*see* METAPHYSICS). Reality is not seen as a dichotomy but as a graded continuum: Thus, SPIRIT is understood to be a form of MATTER, but a highly refined form; and TIME is part of eternity. A corporeal God is omnipresent through the light that emanates from him and that is in and through all things (D&C 88: 12–13).

In ethical discourse, the axiomatic and eternal principle of AGENCY demands that there be "an opposition in all things" (2 Ne. 2:11) to ensure that meaningful choices can be made—not only between good and evil but also from among an array of righteous alternatives (see ETHICS; EVIL; SUFFERING IN THE WORLD; THEODICY). Weakness exists that it may bring strength (Ether 12:27). Thus, Latter-day Saint moral life ranges between options that are often paradoxical: the imperatives of improving oneself or serving other people; spending time at home or rendering Church service; favoring individuality or institutionality; obtaining wealth or giving to the poor; finding one's life by losing it in service to others (Matt. 10:39).

Such tensions, however, do not impede LDS action, nor are they transcended through mysticism, irony, or resignation (whether optimistically or pessimistically). They are embraced in a series of interrelated gospel principles that guide LDS life, including

• personal revelation (by the Holy Ghost each individual can tell what leads to Christ [Moro. 7:12–13; 10:5–6])

• the mandate to act (knowledge of what is right comes by doing it [John 7:17])

• the making of voluntary covenants (people obligate themselves by what they agree to do)

• an extended concept of self (helping others is tantamount to helping oneself)

• the atonement of Jesus Christ (his judgment will encompass both divine grace and human works, retributive justice and compassionate mercy)

• the eternal relativity of kingdoms and progression (with all their differences, all people are on the same pathway to perfection).

For Latter-day Saints, the paradoxes of knowledge are generally resolved under the concept of "continuing revelation" (see EPISTEMOLOGY; REVELATION). While Latter-day Saints are inclined to hold that each truth is self-consistent and coherent with all other truth, they also acknowledge the imperfection of human understanding. Mortal attempts to comprehend or express divine truths are inherently liable to error for at least two reasons: (1) the linguistic-conceptual frameworks within which such facts are expressed and interpreted are culturally conditioned and manifestly inadequate; and (2) mankind's awareness of the facts is fragmentary and incomplete, "for as the heavens are higher than the earth, so are my ways higher than your ways, and my thoughts than your thoughts" (Isa. 55:8–9), and in mortality "man doth not comprehend all the things which the Lord can comprehend" (Mosiah 4:9). But by revelation, human knowledge may increase: "No man knoweth of [God's] ways save it be revealed unto him" (Jacob 4:8). "The natural man receiveth not the things of the Spirit of God, . . . neither can he know them, because they are spiritually discerned" (1 Cor. 2:14).

Thus where definitively clear revelation appears to contradict generally received opinion, common sense, or well-established facts, Latter-day Saints give priority to revelation and trust that time will give proof to what now seems paradoxical or that within God's more complete comprehension of things there may be mediating principles by which two apparently conflicting partial truths may be reconciled. This trust and hope for further revelation quiet such unsearchable paradoxes as how God's complete knowledge can be reconciled with mankind's agency, how scriptural and scientific accounts of creation can be harmonized, or how, in general, study and faith, REASON AND REVELATION, symbolic vision and practical literal-mindedness can all be accommodated concurrently. LDS doctrine is resistant to extremes: Its authoritativeness has not been transformed into abstractions or absolutes; nor have its revelations wandered into mysticism or vagueness. In such ways, the doctrines of the eternal gospel maintain their own set of tensions in a mortal world.

BIBLIOGRAPHY

Hafen, Bruce C. "Love Is Not Blind: Some Thoughts for College Students on Faith and Ambiguity." In *BYU Speeches of the Year*, pp. 8–17. Provo, Utah, 1979.

DAVID L. PAULSEN

TREATISES ON DOCTRINE

Doctrinal works—that is, periodicals, tracts, and books—have been numerous in the LDS tradition, reflecting the lay character of the ministry, the large corpus of scripture, and continuing concern with right belief as well as right conduct.

Official letters, including doctrinal expositions, of the First Presidency are published in *Messages of the First Presidency*, ed. James R. Clark, 6 vols. (Salt Lake City, 1965–1975). Influential tracts and pamphlets have been compiled in *Handbook of the Restoration* and in *Scrapbook of Mormon*

Literature, comp. Ben E. Rich, 2 vols. (Chicago, n.d.).

In addition to volumes on Joseph Smith's teachings (*TPJS, WJS*), there are doctrinal statements in *Journal of Discourses* (1980). Compilations of discourses of the Presidents of the Church, all published in Salt Lake City, include Brigham Young, *Discourses of Brigham Young*, ed. John A. Widtsoe (1954); John Taylor, *The Gospel Kingdom*, ed. G. Homer Durham (1987); *Discourses of Wilford Woodruff*, ed. G. Homer Durham (1946); *Teachings of Lorenzo Snow*, comp. Clyde J. Williams (1984); Joseph F. Smith, *Gospel Doctrine* (1939); Heber J. Grant, *Gospel Standards* (1941); George Albert Smith, *Sharing the Gospel with Others* (1948); David O. McKay, *Gospel Ideals* (1953); Joseph Fielding Smith, *Doctrines of Salvation*, comp. Bruce R. McConkie, 3 vols. (1954–1956); Harold B. Lee, *Stand Ye in Holy Places* and *Ye Are the Light of the World* (1974); *Teachings of Spencer W. Kimball*, ed. Edward L. Kimball (1982); and *Teachings of Ezra Taft Benson* (1988).

Following is a list of books that have made significant contributions to the understanding of doctrine (unless otherwise noted, these works were published in Salt Lake City): Parley P. Pratt, *A Voice of Warning* (New York, 1837) and *Key to Theology* (1856); Orson Pratt, *An Interesting Account of Several Remarkable Visions and of the Late Discovery of Ancient American Records* (Edinburgh, 1840); Orson Spencer, *Spencer's Letters* (Liverpool and London, 1852); John Taylor, *Mediation and Atonement* (1882) and *The Government of God* (1884); Franklin D. Richards and James Little, *A Compendium of the Doctrines of the Gospel* (1882); B. H. Roberts, *The Gospel* (Liverpool, 1888), *Mormon Doctrine of Deity* and *Jesus Christ: The Revelation of God* (1903) and *The Seventy's Course in Theology*, 5 vols. (1907–1912); James E. Talmage, *Articles of Faith* (1899) and *Jesus the Christ* (1915); Orson F. Whitney, *Gospel Themes* (1914) and *Saturday Night Thoughts* (1921); Joseph F. Smith, *Gospel Doctrine* (1919); Brigham Young, *Discourses of Brigham Young*, ed. John A. Widtsoe (1926); John A. Widtsoe, *Priesthood and Church Government* (1939), *A Rational Theology* (1945), and *Evidences and Reconciliations*, 3 vols. in 1 (1960); Joseph Smith, *Teachings of the Prophet Joseph Smith*, comp. by Joseph Fielding Smith (1938); Orson Pratt, *Orson Pratt's Works*, ed. Parker P. Robison (1945), and *Masterful Discourses of Orson Pratt*, ed. N. B. Lundwall (1946); Milton R.

Hunter, *The Gospel Through the Ages* (1945); Daniel H. Ludlow, ed., *Latter-day Prophets Speak* (1948); J. Reuben Clark, Jr., *On the Way to Immortality and Eternal Life* (1949); *Writings of Parley P. Pratt*, ed. Parker P. Robison (1952); Bruce R. McConkie, *Mormon Doctrine* (1958, rev. 1966); Spencer W. Kimball, *The Miracle of Forgiveness* (1969); and George Q. Cannon, *Gospel Truth*, ed. Jerreld Newquist, 2 vols. (1972, 1974).

Shorter treatises include Oliver Cowdery, "General Charge to the Twelve" (1835); Quorum of the Twelve, "A Proclamation to the World" (1845); Lorenzo Snow, "Law of Tithing" (1899); James E. Talmage, "The Honor and Dignity of the Priesthood" (1914); J. Reuben Clark, Jr., "The Charted Course of the Church in Education" (1938) and "When Are the Writings or Sermons of Church Leaders Entitled to the Claim of Scripture?" (1954); Harold B. Lee, "Priesthood . . . Core of All Activity" (1961) and "Priesthood Correlation" (1961); Spencer W. Kimball, "When the World Will Be Converted" (1974), "Lengthening Our Stride" (1974), and "Becoming Pure in Heart" (1978); N. Eldon Tanner, "Church Administration" (1979).

ELEANOR KNOWLES

DOCTRINE AND COVENANTS

[This entry consists of twenty articles:

Sections 131–132
Sections 137–138
Official Declaration—2

The first article is an introduction to the Latter-day Saint scripture known as the Doctrine and Covenants, its meaning, significance, and use in The Church of Jesus Christ of Latter-day Saints. The second article summarizes the main contents of this collection of revelations and official statements of the Church. A series of individual articles follows on selected sections of the Doctrine and Covenants, summarizing their contents and importance. For Official Declaration—1, see MANIFESTO. *Commentaries on, editions of, and literary features of the Doctrine and Covenants are also discussed in the separate articles.*]

OVERVIEW

The Doctrine and Covenants is a compilation of REVELATIONS, most of which were received by the Prophet Joseph SMITH for the establishment and governance of the KINGDOM OF GOD in the latter days. It is a STANDARD WORK of the Church and functions as its open, ever-expanding, ecclesiastical constitution. Its main focus is to build up the Church of Jesus Christ and to bring people into harmony with Christ's kingdom. It is viewed as the capstone of the Church; its companion volume, the Book of Mormon, is seen as the keystone (Benson, pp. 83–85). The Book of Mormon was written to convince all individuals that Jesus is the Christ (*see* BOOK OF MORMON: OVERVIEW); the Doctrine and Covenants was given to organize and orient them according to God's mind and kingdom.

Of the 138 sections and 2 declarations presently in this collection, 133 were received principally through Joseph SMITH, the first prophet and President of the Church. The seven remaining sections were received or written by or under the direction of Oliver COWDERY (sections 102 and 134), John TAYLOR (section 135), Brigham YOUNG (section 136), Joseph F. SMITH (section 138), Wilford WOODRUFF (Official Declaration—1), and Spencer W. KIMBALL (Official Declaration—2).

While most passages in the Doctrine and Covenants have a specific historical setting, virtually every verse is one of wisdom, general instruction, religious principle, or doctrine. Most of the revelations were received in answer to specific prayerful requests. Although many were given for the benefit of particular individuals, by and large their guidance has universal application, making these revelations as relevant today as when first received.

They were given to the servants of the Lord "in their weakness, after the manner of their language, that they might come to understanding" (1:24). They are recognized by Latter-day Saints as "the will of the Lord, . . . the mind of the Lord, . . . the word of the Lord, . . . the voice of the Lord, and the power of God unto salvation" (68:4).

The revelations in the Doctrine and Covenants were received by various methods. Some were received by INSPIRATION, the mind being enlightened by the Holy Spirit (e.g., sections 20–22); others came from an ANGEL (sections 2, 13, 27, 110); in VISIONS, or sight-knowledge, usually through the spiritual eyes of the prophet (sections 76, 137–138); by the still small voice, a voice that comes into the mind (section 85); or by an audible voice (section 130:12–13). At times, other people were present and shared the spiritual manifestations (*see* VISIONS OF JOSEPH SMITH).

The sections are of many types, containing various kinds of materials and historical docu-

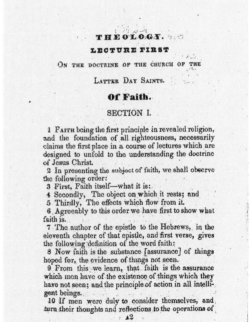

After a short preface, this was the first page in the 1835 edition of the Doctrine and Covenants. It is the first of seventy pages of lectures on the doctrine of the Church, the origin of the word "doctrine" in the title of this book of scripture.

ments. For example, section 102 contains the minutes of a high council meeting; section 113 answers questions on the writings of Isaiah; sections 121–23 are part of a letter written by Joseph Smith in relation to persecution; sections 127–28 are epistles on baptisms for the dead; section 134 is an article on government and laws; and section 135 reports the martyrdom of Joseph and Hyrum Smith. Section 7 is a translation of a record written and hidden up by the Apostle John; sections 65 and 109 are prayers; other sections are items of instruction (sections 130–31) and prophecies (sections 87 and 121). Section 1 is the Lord's Preface to the other revelations. Section 133 is known as the Appendix; it was given two days after the Preface and contains eschatological information. Both sections 1 and 133 were provided in preparation for the publication of the revelations.

The first compilation of the revelations given to Joseph Smith was printed in 1833 and was known as *A Book of Commandments, for the Government of the Church of Christ* (*see* BOOK OF COMMANDMENTS). It contained sixty-five chapters. This collection was submitted to a priesthood conference of the Church on November 1, 1831, for approval prior to publication. Because of the unpolished language of the revelations, one member doubted their authenticity. A revelation, section 67 in modern editions, challenged any person to write a revelation; when the doubter confessed that he was unable to do so, the compilation was approved by those assembled. Because the printing office of the Church in Independence, Missouri, was destroyed by a mob in July 1833 while the book was in production, only a few copies of this first compilation have survived.

Over the years after the first printing, other revelations were received and some earlier materials were deleted. An 1835 edition, published in Kirtland, Ohio, was entitled *Doctrine and Covenants of the Church of the Latter Day Saints* and contained 103 sections. In subsequent editions, more sections were added (*see* DOCTRINE AND COVENANTS EDITIONS). The most recent additions were sections 137 (1836) and 138 (1918) on salvation of the dead, and the Official Declaration—2 announcing the PRIESTHOOD available to every worthy male member of the Church (1978). An article on marriage written by Oliver Cowdery in 1835 was deleted from the 1876 edition. Beginning with the 1921 edition, a set of lessons called the LECTURES ON FAITH have not been included.

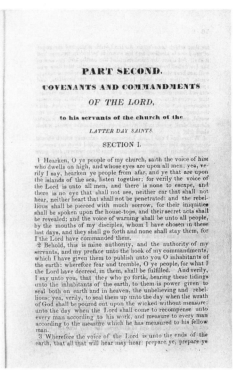

The beginning of the second part of the 1835 edition of the Doctrine and Covenants, containing the "Covenants and Commandments of the Lord to his servants."

One hundred of the revelations were received before 1834, during the early, formative years of the Church. Many of them were addressed to specific individuals who sought wisdom from the Prophet. Gospel doctrines were often not revealed in their fulness at first, but were received progressively from time to time. As the Church grew and relocated, questions regarding Church administration, duties of officers, guidance for the members of the Church, and events of the future became the subjects of further revelations.

Not all the revelations received by Joseph Smith are included in the Doctrine and Covenants (*see* UNPUBLISHED REVELATIONS). Some are contained in the *History of the Church*, giving counsel and instruction to individuals (*HC* 1:229), concerning the Saints being driven to the Rocky Mountains (*HC* 5:85), and a prophecy about Stephen A. Douglas (*HC* 5:393–94).

Deciding which revelations to include in the Doctrine and Covenants is a prerogative of the FIRST PRESIDENCY and the QUORUM OF THE

TWELVE APOSTLES. The selection is then affirmed by the COMMON CONSENT of Church members.

The Doctrine and Covenants is directed to the people of this generation. To the Latter-day Saints it is the voice of the Lord Jesus Christ confirming and revealing the way of salvation and instruction for the government of his Church. It warns individuals and nations of impending destruction if they do not repent. It witnesses to the reality of life beyond the grave.

Prominent among its teachings are the specific principles, covenants, and ordinances that lead to eternal life. It prescribes priesthood ordinances from baptism to marriage sealed for eternity. Salvation of the dead also is made known by revelations concerning baptism for the dead and visions of preaching to the spirits who are awaiting resurrection.

Its emphasis upon the spiritual nature of temporal matters heightens one's appreciation of and respect for this life. For example, its code of health, known as the WORD OF WISDOM, promises both spiritual and physical health to those who obey it (section 89).

The Doctrine and Covenants contains numerous teachings and pithy sayings that powerfully influence the daily lives and feelings of Latter-day Saints, which set the tone of Church service and instill vitality into the work. Among its frequently quoted lines are the following maxims and words of counsel and divine assurance: "If ye are prepared ye shall not fear" (D&C 38:30); "Seek not for riches but for wisdom" (11:7); "He who doeth the works of righteousness shall receive his reward, even peace in this world, and eternal life in the world to come" (59:23); "Seek ye out of the best books words of wisdom; seek learning, even by study and also by faith" (88:118); "Without faith you can do nothing" (8:10); "Of you it is required to forgive all men" (64:10); "Men should be anxiously engaged in a good cause, and do many things of their own free will" (58:27); "All these things shall give thee experience, and shall be for thy good" (122:7); "For I will raise up unto myself a pure people, that will serve me in righteousness" (100:16); "Be not weary in well-doing" (64:32); "Search diligently, pray always, and be believing, and all things shall work together for your good" (90:24); and "Now what do we hear in the gospel which we have received? A voice of gladness! A voice of mercy from heaven; and a voice of truth out of the earth; glad tidings for the dead; a voice of gladness for the living and the dead; glad tidings of great joy" (128:19).

BIBLIOGRAPHY

Benson, Ezra Taft. "The Book of Mormon and Doctrine and Covenants." *Ensign* 17 (May 1987):83–85.

Doxey, Roy W. *The Latter-day Prophets and the Doctrine and Covenants*, 4 vols. Salt Lake City, 1963–1970.

———. *The Doctrine and Covenants Speaks*, 2 vols. Salt Lake City, 1969–1970.

Ludlow, Daniel H. *A Companion to Your Study of the Doctrine and Covenants*, 2 vols. Salt Lake City, 1978.

Millet, Robert L., and Larry E. Dahl, eds. *The Capstone of Our Religion*. Salt Lake City, 1989.

ROY W. DOXEY

CONTENTS

The revelations compiled in the Doctrine and Covenants contain directions and doctrine needed to inspire, organize, and administer the affairs of the Church. They were not received or written as a textbook, treatise, or organized curriculum of lesson plans, but were received intermittently when the Prophet Joseph SMITH and others sought divine guidance in various circumstances.

Despite the fact that many of these revelations are personally directed to certain individuals or groups in nineteenth-century times and places, they contain principles that have eternal application and thus current value. The revelations include warnings of divine judgments upon the wicked; teachings about the progression of human souls toward exaltation and eternal life through the gospel of Jesus Christ; information about scripture, including the coming forth of the Book of Mormon and the translation of the Bible by Joseph Smith; instructions about the priesthood, its restoration, functions, offices, and ordinances; commandments and instructions to people of the Church regarding personal behavior, education, lands and property, buildings, and caring for the poor; and callings and counsel to preach and live the gospel.

Section 1 is the Preface, given at a conference of the Church on November 1, 1831. It came in response to Joseph Smith's request for authority from the Lord to publish some of the revelations that he had previously received. In it, the Lord authorized the request and issued the following challenge and declaration to all who would read it: "Search these commandments, for they are true and faithful, and the prophecies and promises which are in them shall all be fulfilled" (D&C 1:37).

Sections 2–19 are revelations received prior to the organization of the Church in 1830. In them,

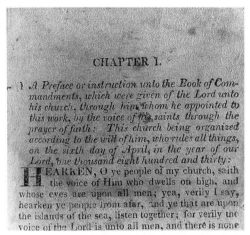

The first page of the Book of Commandments (1833), predecessor to the Doctrine and Covenants. "A Preface or instruction" to the commandments "given of the Lord unto his church." Courtesy Rare Books and Manuscripts, Brigham Young University.

the Lord instructed Joseph Smith and his companions on many subjects, especially the translation, publication, and value of the Book of Mormon, and the need to trust completely in the Lord and to safeguard sacred things (sections 3, 5, 10, 17, 20). Joseph SMITH, Sr.; Hyrum SMITH; Joseph Knight, Sr.; John, Peter, and David WHITMER; Oliver COWDERY; and Martin HARRIS were taught how they might be a part of the work that was about to come forth and were instructed about its sacredness (sections 4, 6, 8–9, 11–12, 14–19). They were also counseled to become worthy to receive the Lord's Spirit so that they might recognize God's revelations and carry out his will (sections 6, 8–9, 11).

Also during this time, the authority to act in the name of the Lord was restored (*see* PRIESTHOOD), and the purpose and scope of that authority were explained (sections 13, 18, 20; cf. 27). The Lord gave counsel concerning the value of individual souls and encouraged his servants to labor for one another's salvation by teaching the restored gospel and bringing people to repentance (section 18). The value of and need for the ATONEMENT OF JESUS CHRIST were revealed, and people were directed to come to him for forgiveness and spiritual strength (section 19).

Sections 20–40 gave instructions in 1830 to the newly organized Church in New York. The basic doctrines of the Church as contained in the Bible and the Book of Mormon and the criteria for establishing COVENANTS with the Lord were summarized, and the responsibilities of members and priesthood holders in the Church were established (section 20).

The Lord gave a revelation concerning the relationship of the Prophet to the Lord and of Church members to the word of the Lord through his Prophet (section 21). This is a major topic in the Doctrine and Covenants and provides the basis for understanding the process of continuing revelation through the PRESIDENT OF THE CHURCH (section 28; cf. 43, 68, 81, 90, 124).

Further revelations were received for the benefit of various individuals and for the Church in general, in which many doctrinal insights were provided on such subjects as BAPTISM (section 22); following counsel (sections 23–24, 31); music, and counsel to the Prophet's wife, Emma SMITH (section 25); COMMON CONSENT (section 26); the SACRAMENT (section 27); the HOLY SPIRIT (sections 29–30, 34, cf. 46, 50, 75, 79); preaching to the American Indians, or Lamanites (section 30, 32); proclaiming the gospel to all the world in the last days (sections 29, 33, 35, 38; cf. 43, 45, 86–87, 90, 101, 116, 133); and Joseph Smith's work on translating the Bible and other records (sections 35, 37; cf. 41–42, 45, 73–74, 76–77, 86, 91, 93–94, 124:89). It was through this translation activity that many of the doctrines of the Church were revealed to Joseph Smith (*see* Matthews).

The Lord directed members of the Church to gather to Ohio, where he promised that he would give them his law, establish Zion, and endow them with power from on high (sections 37–38, 42). The making and keeping of covenants are identified as the basis for individuals becoming God's people or his disciples (sections 39–41).

Sections 41–123 were given during the Ohio and Missouri periods of the Church (1831–1839) and contain various instructions concerning the affairs of the Church. During these years many doctrines and principles of the gospel were revealed that helped to build a vital doctrinal framework for the Church. The first revelation recorded by Joseph Smith in Ohio called Edward Partridge to serve as the first BISHOP of the Church (section 41). As promised, the Saints were given the Lord's laws by which members of the Church are governed, including the law of teaching (sections 42, 68, 88, 93, 100); moral laws (sections 42, 58–59); the law of CONSECRATION (sections 42, 51, 54, 70, 78, 82–83,

104); the law of labor (sections 42, 60, 68, 75; *see* WORK); instructions concerning administration to the sick (sections 42, 46, 63); laws of remuneration for goods and services (sections 42, 43, 70, 106); and laws pertaining to transgressors (sections 42, 58, 102, 107). Joseph Smith also received instruction concerning the importance of marriage and the family (section 49; cf. 131–32), and the Lord revealed information by which counterfeit and evil practices might be detected and avoided (sections 43, 46, 50, 52; cf. 129).

A major theme of the Doctrine and Covenants is the establishment and building of ZION, both as a place (*see* NEW JERUSALEM) and as a condition of the people (the pure in heart; D&C 97:21). Joseph Smith was instructed to go to Missouri, where the site for the city of Zion would be made known (section 52). While there, he received guidance from the Lord concerning the establishment of Zion and its people (sections 57–59). The Saints began to gather in Missouri to fulfill the Lord's requirements, and additional revelations were received pertaining to their various responsibilities (sections 63–64). They were taught the necessity of building and having a TEMPLE, or house of the Lord, in connection with becoming a people of Zion (sections 57, 84, 88, 97, 101, 109–110; cf. 124). Since some members did not reach levels of consecrated faith and obedience reflective of a Zion society, they failed to establish Zion at that time. They were expelled from Missouri, and the building of Zion in that place was temporarily suspended (sections 101, 103, 105).

During this same time and later, other insightful revelations were provided concerning health rules (sections 49, 89); the life, light, spirit, and power of Christ (sections 50, 84, 88, 93); missionary work (sections 75, 79–80, 84, 99); the SABBATH (section 59); obedience and sacrifice (sections 58–59, 82, 97, 117–18); obtaining and extending forgiveness (sections 58, 64, 82, 98); the PLAN OF SALVATION for all humankind (sections 76, 93; cf. 131, 137–38); priesthood functions and quorums (sections 81, 84, 90, 107, 112, 121; cf. 124; and Official Declaration—2 of 1978); impending wars (section 87); biblical texts (sections 74, 77, 113); and TITHING (sections 119–20).

Sections 124–135 were recorded in Nauvoo during the last years of Joseph Smith's life (1839–1844). They include directions to the Church regarding the NAUVOO TEMPLE, the first full-ordinance temple (section 124); ordinances and SALVATION FOR THE DEAD (sections 124, 127–128); the nature of the GODHEAD and exalted beings (sections 130, 132); eternal and PLURAL MARRIAGE (sections 131–32; *see also* Official Declaration—1); political laws and governments (section 134); and a statement of the contributions of Joseph Smith and of his testimony at the time of his martyrdom (sections 135–36).

BIBLIOGRAPHY

Berrett, William E. *Teachings of the Doctrine and Covenants.* Salt Lake City, 1956.

Cook, Lyndon W. *The Revelations of Joseph Smith.* Provo, Utah, 1981.

Matthews, Robert J. "The Joseph Smith Translation and The Doctrine and Covenants: Historical and Doctrinal Companions." In *The Capstone of Our Religion: Insights into the Doctrine and Covenants,* ed. Robert L. Millet and Larry E. Dahl. Salt Lake City, 1989.

Otten, Leaun G., and C. Max Caldwell. *Sacred Truths of the Doctrine and Covenants,* 2 vols. Springville, Utah, 1983.

Smith, Hyrum M., and Janne M. Sjodahl. *Doctrine and Covenants Commentary.* Salt Lake City, 1954.

Smith, Joseph Fielding. *Church History and Modern Revelation,* 2 vols. Salt Lake City, 1946.

Welch, John W., and Jeannie Welch. *The Doctrine and Covenants by Themes.* Salt Lake City, 1986.

Widtsoe, John A. *The Message of the Doctrine and Covenants,* ed. G. Homer Durham. Salt Lake City, 1969.

Woodford, Robert J. "The Historical Development of the Doctrine and Covenants," 3 vols. Ph.D. diss., Brigham Young University, 1974.

C. MAX CALDWELL

SECTION 1

Section 1 of the Doctrine and Covenants is called the "Preface." It was a revelation received by Joseph SMITH between sessions of a conference in Hiram, Ohio, on November 1, 1831. The conference had been convened to consider publishing sixty-three of the revelations Joseph Smith had received (*see* BOOK OF COMMANDMENTS). The conference voted unanimously to publish them as the word of the Lord. In accordance with the Lord's declaration, this section was published as "my preface unto the book of my commandments" (D&C 1:6). It sets an urgent tone for the entire Doctrine and Covenants.

Like the revelations it introduces, section 1 is written predominantly in the first person as the word of the Lord: "What I the Lord have spoken, I have spoken" (verse 38). It proclaims to the world that through the RESTORATION of his Church, God has set his hand the last time to redeem his children and prepare the earth for the Savior's return.

Section 1 is a bold declaration that God sees all things and speaks to all people, that his words will go to all nations through his chosen disciples, that every person eventually will hear the gospel in his or her own language so that each may understand, and that weak things of the world will break down the mighty and strong and the Church will be brought out of obscurity by the power of God (see also the revelation given two days later, D&C 133).

Section 1 balances judgment and relief. It is a voice of warning of impending judgments: "Prepare ye, prepare ye" (verse 12). It warns that those who do not repent will suffer much sorrow, for worldwide sin has kindled the "anger of the Lord" and people "have strayed from [his] ordinances and have broken [his] everlasting covenant" (verses 13–15). Those who hearken, however, are promised instruction, chastening, correction, knowledge, and blessings from God.

The section ends with the certification of the Lord that all his prophecies and promises, though given to men in their weakness, are true and will be fulfilled.

GEORGE W. PACE

SECTIONS 20–22

Sections 20–22 of the Doctrine and Covenants are fundamental, formative documents in early Church history. They continue to serve as a definitive statement of beliefs and PRIESTHOOD functions. Originally sections 20 and 22 were published together as "Articles and Covenants of the Church of Christ." They were first published in the *Painesville* (Ohio) *Telegraph* in April 1831 and later on the first page of the first issue of *The Evening and the Morning Star* in June 1832. The earliest known version of section 20 is dated June 1829. Many early copies were made of a draft in Oliver COWDERY's hand.

Sections 20–22 were officially adopted as doctrinal revelations by the Church at its first conference on June 9, 1830, and were the first sections of the Doctrine and Covenants to be thus approved. Later, missionaries often would read manuscript copies of these "Articles" at public meetings and conferences because they had been instructed to include the "Church Articles" in their teachings

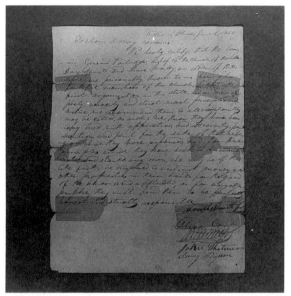

Section 20 was known originally as the Articles and Covenants of the Church, setting forth basic beliefs and duties. Pictured here is an 1835 letter, or license, indicating that Edward Partridge was the authorized bishop of the Church (cf. D&C 20:63–64, 84). It is signed by Joseph Smith, Oliver Cowdery, W. W. Phelps, John Whitmer, and Sidney Rigdon.

(D&C 42:13). Section 20 was Chapter II in the 1835 edition of the Doctrine and Covenants, right after the revealed Preface. The present order was established in the 1876 edition.

Section 20 is a composite text that divides into a historical prologue (verses 1–16), a statement of beliefs (verses 17–36), and a collection of policies and procedures (verses 37–84). While its principles continue to guide Latter-day Saints today, its provisions also provide glimpses of Church life in its initial years. The prologue contains the earliest published references to the ordination of Joseph Smith and Oliver Cowdery as APOSTLES (verses 2–3) and to Joseph Smith's FIRST VISION: "It was truly manifested unto this first elder that he had received a remission of his sins" (verse 5). The personal dimension of this account is consistent with Joseph's 1832 and 1835 accounts of his First Vision.

Section 20 also contains the Church's earliest known declaration of faith. It affirms basic Christian doctrines, following the sequence common to most Protestant confessions, beginning with the nature of God (verse 17), the Creation (verses 18–19), the Fall (verse 20), Jesus Christ, the Atonement, and the plan of salvation (verses 21–28).

Additional comments discuss the possibility of "falling from grace" and the nature of sanctification, which were lively issues in the 1820s. Sensitivity to the surrounding Christian world is shown in verse 35, which assures that these articles are "neither adding to, nor diminishing from the prophecy of [John's] book, the holy scriptures, or the revelations of God that will come hereafter."

Most of section 20 gives guidelines for Church government. Drawing partly upon texts from the Book of Mormon, it explains the ordinances of BAPTISM and the SACRAMENT, and the duties of baptized members. Originally, priests, teachers, and deacons were local adult priesthood leaders, which explains the significant pastoral charge given them (verses 46–59) and their role in signing certificates of worthiness for members moving from one branch of the Church to another (verse 84). The AARONIC PRIESTHOOD had a public ministry to "preach, teach, expound, exhort" (verse 46) and needed to be properly "licensed" (verse 64).

Received on the day the Church was incorporated, section 21 defines Joseph Smith's leadership of the new Church as "a seer, a translator, a prophet, an apostle of Jesus Christ" (verse 1), with Oliver Cowdery as an elder "under his hand" (verse 11). Church members are counseled to keep records and to receive Joseph's words "as if from mine own mouth" (verses 1, 5).

Section 22, received the same month, requires all people, even those previously baptized, to be baptized into "a new and an everlasting covenant" (verse 1).

Together, these three sections provide a firm organizational foundation for the restored Church of Christ.

BIBLIOGRAPHY

Anderson, Richard L. "The Organization Revelations: D&C 20, 21, and 22." In *Studies in Scripture*, Vol. 1, pp. 109–123, ed. R. Millet and K. Jackson. Sandy, Utah, 1984.

Woodford, Robert J. "The Articles and Covenants of the Church of Christ and the Book of Mormon." In *Doctrines for Exaltation*, pp. 262–73. Salt Lake City, 1989.

GRANT UNDERWOOD

SECTION 25

This revelation was given in HARMONY, PENNSYLVANIA, in July 1830, three months after the organization of the Church. It was first printed in the BOOK OF COMMANDMENTS in 1833 as Chapter

XXVI. It is addressed to Emma SMITH, wife of the Prophet Joseph Smith. In the earliest version, Emma Smith is addressed as "my daughter in Zion." Joseph Smith later expanded this verse to add, "All those who receive my Gospel are sons and daughters in my kingdom."

The section has five main components:

1. Emma is designated as an "elect lady" (verse 3). Later, on March 17, 1842, when Emma Smith became the first president of the RELIEF SOCIETY and the women were organized in the order of the priesthood, Joseph explained that this was the office of her "elect" calling. The benevolent organization that she led had grown to more than 3 million women by 1990.

2. Emma is admonished to unity with her husband to "be unto him for a scribe" and to "go with him at the time of his going" (verse 6). She accepted these callings, though she was later required to abandon home and security.

3. Emma is called to "be ordained under [Joseph's] hand to expound scriptures, and exhort the church," as "given thee by my Spirit" (verse 7). She is also commanded to study and devote her time "to writing, and to learning much" (verse 8). In the course of her life, she taught, expounded, exhorted, presided, and served in many Church organizations. The mandate has remained with LDS women: to master the scriptures, thus the more powerfully to lead, teach, minister, and serve.

4. Emma is charged to select sacred hymns, and a manifesto is given of the spiritual power of music: "The song of the righteous is a prayer unto me" (verse 12). Her hymnal was first published in 1836 (although 1835 appears on the title page). This collection utilizes many classical Christian words and melodies but also embodies songs related to most of the unique events and teachings of the RESTORATION (*see* HYMNS AND HYMNODY; MUSIC).

5. Emma is counseled against murmuring, putting her public ministry before her role as companion of her husband, seeking "the things of this world" (verse 10), and pride. "Let thy soul delight in thy husband" (verse 14). She is to glorify her husband while involved in a public ministry. Emma fulfilled each of these callings, endured the loss of five children, and stood by Joseph until his martyrdom.

This inclusion of women in leading roles of the Church, presiding in some organizations and over certain sacral functions, was a marked departure from nineteenth-century patterns. Church leaders, both men and women, continue to cite passages from this inspired calling of Emma to exemplify some of the potentials of women and facilitate their full participation in all spiritual callings and blessings of the Gospel.

BIBLIOGRAPHY

Hinckley, Gordon B. "If Thou Art Faithful." *Ensign* 14 (Nov. 84):89–92.

KLIS HALE VOLKENING

SECTION 42

This section is called the "law of Christ" and the "law of the Church," and receiving it fulfilled a promise made on January 2, 1831, in Doctrine and Covenants 38:32, that the law would be given to the Church in Ohio. As a precondition (see D&C 41:2–3), the ELDERS were to unite in the prayer of faith. The first seventy verses of section 42 were given February 9, 1831, while twelve elders were, as the record states, "united in mighty prayer." Verses 71–93 were received two weeks later in similar circumstances. The revelation was first published in *The Evening and The Morning Star*, in July and October 1832, and was included as chapters 44 and 47 of the BOOK OF COMMANDMENTS in 1833.

High requirements were here imposed on the infant Church, with a small and scattered membership and little instruction and experience. They can be divided into six main segments:

1. A missionary commission to travel to the West (verses 1–17). Its members were to go two by two, under proper ordination and authority, to teach the principles of the gospel from the Bible and Book of Mormon and to teach only "by the Spirit."

2. A reaffirmation of the TEN COMMANDMENTS (verses 18–29). The ancient decalogue of Moses stressed the laws of behavior. The New Testament, especially the SERMON ON THE MOUNT, and a similar sermon in 3 Nephi emphasize both the act and the inner condition, letter and spirit. Section 42 also affirms the more inclusive expectations and aspirations of the NEW AND EVERLASTING COVENANT. Additions include "Thou shalt not lie . . . [nor] speak evil of thy neighbor, nor do him any harm" and "Thou shalt love thy wife with all thy heart, and shalt cleave unto her and none else." Violators, it is said, "shall not have the Spirit" and shall fear.

3. A statement on the laws of STEWARDSHIP and CONSECRATION (verses 30–39). Properties were to be consecrated by a covenant "which cannot be broken," for support of the poor, each person acting as a steward over his own property, and a HIGH COUNCIL and BISHOP as stewards over the Church storehouse. The storehouse, replenished by "residues," would administer to the poor and needy. "Inasmuch as ye do it unto the least of these, ye do it unto me." Through these principles, the Church was to procure land, build houses of worship, and eventually establish the NEW JERUSALEM.

4. Warnings against pride of heart, ostentation, idleness, and uncleanness (verses 40–42).

5. Admonitions to compassionate care for the sick who are without the gift of faith unto HEALING (verses 43–52). Signs, including healing, will follow specific gifts of faith, but the highest form of faith is to "have power to become my sons." Reassurance is given those who die unto the Lord, for their death "shall be sweet unto them" (verse 46).

6. Instructions on Church procedures regarding transgressors, trials, witnesses, Church discipline in relation to the laws of the land, and patterns of confession and reconciliation (verses 53–93).

[*See also* DISCIPLINARY COUNCILS.]

BIBLIOGRAPHY

Otten, L. G., and C. M. Caldwell. *Sacred Truths of the Doctrine and Covenants*, Vol. 1, pp. 195–206. Springville, Utah, 1982.

VICTOR L. BROWN, SR.

SECTION 45

This revelation of the Doctrine and Covenants was received in early March 1831, a time when "many false reports, lies, and foolish stories, were published in the newspapers, and circulated in every direction, to prevent people from investigating the work, or embracing the faith" (*HC* 1:158). In it the Lord called the Saints to hearken to his voice, and noted that he was pleading unto the Father for them (D&C 45:1–7). He then told them he would "prophesy, as unto men in days of old," and gave them what he had given his disciples in Jerusalem concerning events that would take place in that day, in the last days, and at his second coming.

Three events would take place during the time of the Savior's own generation: (1) the temple in Jerusalem would be destroyed (verses 18–20); (2) the Jewish nation would be desolated and destroyed (verse 21); and (3) the Jews would be scattered among all nations (verse 24). History shows that these prophecies were fulfilled. Before the end of first century, Roman conquests brought about a literal and exact fulfillment of all that Jesus had described. Some who heard him prophesy lived to witness those events.

Many events would happen in the last days preceding the Lord's second coming:

1. The Jews shall be gathered to Jerusalem (verse 25).
2. There shall be wars and rumors of wars (verse 26).
3. Men's hearts shall fail them (verse 26).
4. There shall be claims of a delay in Christ's coming (verse 26).
5. The love of men shall wax cold (verse 27).
6. Iniquity shall abound (verse 27).
7. The fulness of the gospel shall be restored (verse 28).
8. Times of the Gentiles shall be fulfilled (verse 30).
9. There shall be an overflowing scourge and desolating sickness (verse 31).
10. The wicked shall curse God (verse 32).
11. There shall be earthquakes and many desolations (verse 33).
12. There shall be displays of heavenly phenomena—sun, moon, stars (verses 40–44).

The Times of the Gentiles referred to in item 8 began with the taking of the gospel to the Gentiles by the apostles after the death of Christ. The second opportunity for the Gentiles came with the restoration of the gospel through Joseph Smith, to be preached first to the Gentiles and then to the Jews.

When the Savior comes a second time, he will make at least three general appearances:

1. He will appear to the Saints or covenant members of his church (verses 45–46, 56–57). The Savior likened those faithful members to the five wise virgins who had taken the Holy Spirit to be their guide (cf. Matt. 25:1–13).

2. He will appear to the Jews at Jerusalem (verses 47–53). When the Jews are engaged in a battle for survival, the Savior will appear and intervene in their behalf and they will recognize him as their Messiah.

3. He will appear to the world (verses 74–75). This appearance will not be to a select group, but rather will be of such magnitude that the wicked will be destroyed, leaving only the righteous to enjoy the millennial reign of the Savior. The second coming of the Savior will coincide with the resurrection of faithful covenant members of his Church who shall be caught up to meet him when he comes in his glory (verse 45). And the heathen who lived without the law will be resurrected, and also "they that knew no law" (verse 54).

The revelation known as section 45 then focuses on Joseph Smith's work on the Bible translation (verses 60–62), and also mentions wars abroad and at home (verse 63). The last verses call the Saints to gather "with one heart and with one mind . . . [to build] the New Jerusalem, a land of peace, a city of refuge, a place of safety" (verses 65–66).

BIBLIOGRAPHY

Church Educational System. *The Doctrine and Covenants Student Manual.* Salt Lake City, 1981.

Cook, Lyndon W. *The Revelations of the Prophet Joseph Smith.* Provo, 1981.

Otten, Leaun G., and C. Max Caldwell. *Sacred Truths of the Doctrine and Covenants,* Vol. 1. Springville, Utah, 1982.

C. MAX CALDWELL

SECTION 76

Section 76 presents a vision about the PLAN OF SALVATION, particularly the nature of the three kingdoms or heavens of glory that mankind may inherit following the Resurrection, depending on their personal faithfulness (*see* DEGREES OF GLORY).

As Joseph SMITH and Sidney RIGDON were working on the JOSEPH SMITH TRANSLATION OF THE BIBLE (JST) on February 16, 1832, they came to John 5:29, concerning the resurrection of the just and the unjust. Of that experience, Joseph explained, "It appeared self-evident that . . . if God rewarded every one according to the deeds done in the body, the term 'Heaven,' as intended for the Saints' eternal home must include more kingdoms than one. . . . While translating St. John's Gospel, myself and Elder Rigdon saw the following vision" (*HC* 1:245). At least ten people were in the room when this revelation was received. One of them, Philo Dibble, sixty years later recalled how Joseph and Sidney, almost motionless for about one hour, would alternately relate and confirm to each other what they were concurrently seeing in the vision (Cannon, pp. 303–304).

The revelation contains a series of six visions: They see the Son of God on the right hand of God (verses 1–24); they see how the devil and his followers rebelled and were cast down (25–49); they see the CELESTIAL KINGDOM (50–70), TERRESTRIAL KINGDOM (71–80), and TELESTIAL KINGDOM (81-90), and those who will inherit each of these degrees of glory; and they see the three kingdoms of glory compared (91–119). The text was first published in *The Evening and the Morning Star* in July 1832 and was included as section 91 in the 1835 edition of the Doctrine and Covenants.

Because this section, called "The Vision," departed significantly from the mainstream Christian view of one heaven and one hell, it was not easily received by some at first. Brigham YOUNG said, "My traditions were such, that when the Vision came first to me, it was so directly contrary and opposed to my former education, I said, wait a little; I did not reject it, but I could not understand it" (*Deseret News, Extra*, September 14, 1852, p. 24). Entire BRANCHES of the Church had the same problem. John Murdock and Orson Pratt, serving missions in Ohio at the time, struggled to help Church members there accept these new outlooks on eternity. Soon, however, most members believed and understood the concepts, and came to revere this vision as one of the most beautiful and awe-inspiring ever given.

Joseph Smith himself rejoiced in "the light which burst upon the world through the foregoing vision" (*PJS* 1:372), which he said was "a transcript from the records of the eternal world. The sublimity of the ideas; the purity of the language; the scope for action; the continued duration for completion, in order that the heirs of salvation may confess the Lord and bow the knee; the rewards for faithfulness, and the punishments for sins; are so much beyond the narrow-mindedness of men, that every man is constrained to exclaim: 'It came from God'" (*TPJS*, p. 11).

BIBLIOGRAPHY

Cannon, George Q., ed. "Recollections of the Prophet Joseph Smith." *Juvenile Instructor*, 27 (May 15, 1892):302–304.

Cook, Lyndon W. *The Revelations of the Prophet Joseph Smith*, pp. 157–66, 311–12. Provo, Utah, 1981.

Dahl, Larry E. "The Vision of the Glories." In *Studies in Scripture*, Vol. 1, pp. 279–308. Sandy, Utah, 1984.

DONALD Q. CANNON

SECTION 84

Given on September 22–23, 1832, at KIRTLAND, OHIO, section 84 was first published as Chapter IV in the 1835 edition of the Doctrine and Covenants. It is called a revelation on priesthood and was given in the presence of six ELDERS who had just returned from their MISSIONS to the eastern states. The revelation has four main themes.

ZION. Earlier, the establishment of ZION and the need for a TEMPLE as its center had been revealed (D&C 57:1–3). Section 84 makes the Church responsible for assembling the Saints and building the NEW JERUSALEM (Zion), beginning with the temple. Both undertakings are to be completed in a "generation." Zion is to be established through the power and authority of the MELCHIZEDEK PRIESTHOOD (verses 1–5).

PRIESTHOOD. Priesthood is the power and authority delegated to man to act for God in saving souls, and it cannot be assumed, but must be passed on from one who already has it. Section 84 clearly distinguishes two priesthoods, namely, the Melchizedek and Aaronic. Moses, for example, received the Melchizedek Priesthood from Jethro, who received it through rightful heirs back to "Adam, who was the first man" (verses 6–17). The Melchizedek Priesthood administers the GOSPEL and holds the KEYS of the mysteries of the kingdom and knowledge of God. Through the ORDINANCES administered by this priesthood, men and women partake of the powers of godliness. Only thus may they behold his face and endure his presence (verses 19–22).

The AARONIC PRIESTHOOD holds the keys of the ministering of ANGELS and the preparatory gospel. It continued in an unbroken line from Aaron and was the priesthood of the law of Moses. It was also the priesthood held by John the Baptist. This preparatory gospel includes FAITH, REPENTANCE, and BAPTISM, and leads to the Melchizedek Priesthood and its ordinances (verses 26–27).

OATH AND COVENANT OF THE PRIESTHOOD. When worthy men receive the Melchizedek Priesthood, they enter into a covenant relationship with the Lord. They covenant that in faithfulness and OBEDIENCE they will magnify their priesthood CALLINGS—that is, wholeheartedly honor and fulfill their stewardships. By keeping this covenant, the priesthood holder receives the oath of the Father, which leads to receiving the Father's kingdom and "all that [the] Father hath" (verse 38). Those who violate or break this covenant and altogether turn from it "shall not have forgiveness of sins in this world nor in the world to come" (verse 41; see also OATH AND COVENANT OF THE PRIESTHOOD).

The elders of the Church are told that because of "vanity and unbelief" they and all the children of Zion have been spiritually darkened and are under condemnation before the Lord. They are to repent and remember the "new covenant," even the Book of Mormon. Through obeying this counsel, they will be forgiven their sins and bring forth fruit worthy for the kingdom (verses 54–61).

MISSIONARY COUNSEL. Section 84 gives instruction and promises to those who are emissaries of Jesus Christ. Under their direction, the gospel is to be taken to all the world. Those who desire to enter into the kingdom of Christ are to be baptized and receive the GIFT OF THE HOLY GHOST. Signs will follow those who believe. The missionaries are promised protection as well as necessities of life (verses 62–119, cf. Matt. 10).

In summary, priesthood bearers are counseled to learn their duties and faithfully function in their offices and callings. Each calling is essential within the kingdom of Christ (verses 109–110).

BIBLIOGRAPHY

Otten, Leaun G., and C. Max Caldwell. *Sacred Truths of the Doctrine and Covenants*, 2 vols. Springville, Utah, 1983.

Smith, Hyrum M., and Janne M. Sjodahl. *Doctrine and Covenants Commentary*, rev. ed. Salt Lake City, 1978.

LEAUN G. OTTEN

SECTION 88

Section 88 was given through Joseph Smith in the "translating room" of the WHITNEY STORE in KIRTLAND, OHIO. Verses 1–126 were given on December 27 and 28, 1832, and verses 127–141 on January 3, 1833. The revelation was recorded in the Kirtland Council Minute Book, and portions of it were published in *The Evening and the Morning Star* in February and March 1833. It was printed as section 7 in the 1835 edition of the Doctrine and Covenants.

On Christmas Day 1832, Joseph Smith received what has become known as the prophecy on war (D&C 87), which predicted "the death and misery of many souls." His brethren were troubled at this. They united in FASTING AND PRAYER before the Lord, seeking his will concerning the upbuilding of Zion. The Prophet designated the subsequent revelation (D&C 88) the "olive leaf" and "the Lord's message of peace to us" (HC 1:316).

The section opens with an intimate promise "even upon you my friends," which is given of God through Jesus Christ, his Son (D&C 88:3–5) and is comparable with the promise of John 14 of the Comforter and the HOLY SPIRIT OF PROMISE.

Passages follow on the pervasive immanence of divine light: THE LIGHT OF CHRIST enlightens the eyes and quickens the understanding (see LIGHT AND DARKNESS). It is in and through all things, the very light of the sun, moon, and stars. It "proceedeth forth from the presence of God to fill the immensity of space" (verse 12). It is equated with the life, the law, and the power of God.

In this context the following doctrines are clarified:

The SPIRIT and BODY are the SOUL of man. There are three DEGREES OF GLORY and three orders of glorified bodies. One receives a resurrected body according to the law by which one abides while in this world: "Your glory shall be that glory by which your bodies are quickened" (verse 28). In the resurrection one receives in full what in this world one has had only in part. A fourth order of resurrected bodies pertains to the Sons of Perdition, who, though resurrected, receive no glory (verses 32–33).

The earth itself is alive. It will die and be glorified, and the bodies who are quickened by a celestial spirit will inherit; "for this intent was it made and created, and for this intent are they sanctified" (verse 20).

There are multiple worlds, multiple creations, all governed by law. "Unto every kingdom is given a law; and unto every law there are certain bounds also and conditions" (verse 38). Law includes appointed cosmic times, seasons, and orders, as well as the divine attributes and powers of mercy, justice, and judgment. "All beings who abide not in those conditions are not justified" (verse 39; *see* JUSTIFICATION). Those who seek to become a law unto themselves will not, and cannot, be sanctified.

A parable of laborers in a field teaches the magnitude of the Lord's creations (verses 46–61), that glorification comes only in appointed time and sequence, "every man in his own order" (verse 60).

The call is given to build a TEMPLE and hold a SOLEMN ASSEMBLY. The temple is to become a house of God: of prayer, fasting, faith, learning, glory, and order. All incomings, outgoings, and salutations will be in the name of the Lord. The Saints are commanded to "organize yourselves, and prepare yourselves, and sanctify yourselves" (verse 74) through solemnity and sober study, to be ready for the temple experience. (*See* KIRTLAND TEMPLE; TEMPLE DEDICATIONS.)

A comprehensive curriculum for the SCHOOL OF THE PROPHETS is introduced. It includes languages, history, and a study of "the wars and the perplexities of the nations, . . . and a knowledge also of countries and of kingdoms" (verse 79).

Prophecies are reiterated concerning the changes, earthquakes, tempests, and commotion in the earth and the heavens that will precede the second coming of Christ. Six periods or epochs of one thousand years each are designated. These are to culminate in the seventh or millennial era. An angel and an angelic trump symbolize each period.

The revelation concludes with specific instructions on the conduct of meetings, the duties of the presidency, admission into the School of the Prophets, and WASHING OF FEET, in the pattern of John 13, as an initiatory and purifying ordinance for members of the school.

BIBLIOGRAPHY

Cook, Lyndon W. *The Revelations of the Prophet Joseph Smith.* Provo, Utah, 1981.

BARBARA R. CARTER

SECTION 89

This section, known as the WORD OF WISDOM from its first words, was received at a meeting of the SCHOOL OF THE PROPHETS in the upper level of the Whitney store on February 27, 1833, in Kirtland, Ohio. According to Zebedee Coltrin, one of twenty-two Church leaders in attendance, Joseph Smith received the revelation in an adjoining room in the presence of two or three brethren, walked in with the document in hand, and read the contents to the assembled school members. The revelation was first printed in December 1833 or January 1834 on a broadsheet and was included in the 1835 edition of the Doctrine and Covenants.

The Word of Wisdom was given "in consequence of evils and designs which do and will exist in the hearts of conspiring men in the last days" (verse 4). As some of these designs pertain to what people eat and drink, the Word of Wisdom gives basic directions on what is good and not good, and posits a strong relationship between what individuals take into their bodies and their physical and spiritual well-being. The revelation prohibits three things: tobacco, strong drinks, and hot drinks (verses 5–9). "Strong drinks" were understood as alcoholic beverages; "hot drinks" were defined by early Church leaders as tea and coffee. Church leaders have traditionally confined relevant worthiness requirements to the prohibited items. The revelation also recommends the prudent use of herbs and fruits, the sparing consumption of meat, and the use of "all grain," but especially "wheat for man" (verses 10–17). Saints who obey the admonitions are promised health and strength, wisdom and knowledge, and protection from the destroying angel (verses 18–21).

The Word of Wisdom was an inspired response to specific problems or paradoxes within the Church and to pressing social issues in contemporary American society. Brigham Young recalled in 1868 that Joseph Smith was bothered by the seeming incongruity of discussing spiritual matters in a cloud of tobacco smoke and that Joseph's wife, Emma Smith, was bothered at having to clean the quid-littered floor. It is also probable that the Prophet was sensitive to, and supportive of, the widespread temperance sentiment of the 1830s. As was his custom, the Prophet went to the Lord for instructions, and section 89 is distinctive in the sense that it is a divinely approved code of health.

Interpretations and applications of the Word of Wisdom have gradually changed through the years. In part, this change is consistent with the Church's belief in continuing revelation through living PROPHETS. With regard to this particular section, the varied interpretations also reflect some ambiguity in verse 2, which states that the revelation was given "not by commandment or constraint." Since verses 1–4 were part of the introduction to this section in the 1835 edition of the Doctrine and Covenants, through the years there have been differences of opinion as to whether the Word of Wisdom is a commandment in the sense that observance is obligatory to enjoy full Church fellowship as well as whether observance implies abstinence or merely moderation.

In the mid-1830s, many Church members felt that abstinence from alcohol, tobacco, tea, and coffee was a criterion for fellowship. The one possible exception to this otherwise strict interpretation was wine, which some early Church leaders may not have considered "strong drink." This early emphasis on abstinence or near abstinence failed to gain Church-wide or official acceptance, although Joseph Smith said no member "is worthy to hold an office" who has been taught the word of wisdom and fails "to comply with and obey it" (*TPJS*, p.117, fn.). Even so, the early statement gradually gave way to an emphasis on moderation. President Joseph F. Smith later taught that the Lord did not insist on strict compliance in these early years in order to allow a generation addicted to noxious substances some years to discard bad habits. This early pattern of moderation, observable by the 1840s, continued throughout the nineteenth century. President John TAYLOR initiated a reform in the early 1880s in which he stressed that all Church officers should abstain from the prohibited items, but his efforts were cut short by the social disruption caused by federal antipolygamy raids. While Church leaders did not require abstinence in the nineteenth century, they stressed moderation, counseled strongly against drunkenness, and opposed or carefully regulated the establishment of distilleries and grog shops. The numerous observations by visitors in UTAH TERRITORY attest to the prevailing orderliness and sobriety of Mormon communities and evidence the effectiveness of such preaching.

The path leading to the present position on the Word of Wisdom began with the presidency of Joseph F. Smith (1901–1918) and culminated in the administration of Heber J. Grant (1918–1945), who, more than any other Church leader, preached strict compliance with frequency and fervor. By the early 1930s, abstinence from alcohol, tobacco, tea, and coffee had become an established test of Church fellowship. There was no known specific revelation that brought this about. It resulted from Church leaders' long-term concern over the deleterious physical and spiritual effects of alcohol, tobacco, tea, and coffee on both individuals and communities. National and local agitation over prohibition and the mounting scientific evidence attesting to the harmful effects of certain substances intensified that concern.

The Word of Wisdom has resulted in, among other things, better physical health among LDS people (see VITAL STATISTICS) and physical affirmations of truths received through revelation. It has also brought about a distinguishing separateness that reminds Latter-day Saints of their religious commitments and responsibilities.

BIBLIOGRAPHY

Alexander, Thomas G. *Mormonism in Transition*, pp. 258–71. Urbana, Ill., 1986.

Bush, Lester E., Jr. "The Word of Wisdom in Early Nineteenth-Century Perspective." *Dialogue* 14 (Fall 1981):47–65.

PAUL H. PETERSON

SECTION 93

Section 93 is a revelation received through the Prophet Joseph SMITH on May 6, 1833, during a conference of high priests at KIRTLAND, OHIO. It was first printed as chapter 82 of the 1835 edition of the Doctrine and Covenants. The insights of this revelation pervade LDS understanding of the nature and relationship of God and man.

It begins with the divine promise that every soul who forsakes sin, comes unto Christ, calls upon his name, obeys his voice, and keeps his commandments shall see his face "and know that I am, and that I am the true light that lighteth every man that cometh into the world" (verses 1–2).

The next verses refer to sayings from a record of John yet to be revealed in full. They are reminiscent of the prologue to John's Gospel, but they also witness to Jesus' baptism by John the Baptist.

Christ is called the Father and is one with the Father because "he gave me of his fulness" (verse 4). He is called the Word because he is the "messenger of salvation" (verse 8). In him is "the life of men and the light of men" (verse 9). "The worlds were made by him; men were made by him; all things were made by him, and through him, and of him" (verse 10).

In contrast with theologies of static being, several verses affirm Christ's becoming. Three times they reiterate that Christ did not receive a fulness at the beginning but continued "from grace to grace" until he received a fulness of the glory of the Father (verses 12, 13, 14; cf. Luke 2:40; Heb. 5:8–9). Christ became like the Father in the exalted sense only after his resurrection and glorification (cf. Rev. 5:12–13). An understanding of this process is the foundation of authentic worship.

The revelation denies the notion of *ex nihilo* creation. The intelligence of man, "the light of truth," (verse 29), is not created but is self-existent. Man, like Christ himself, "was . . . in the beginning with God" (verse 29). Furthermore, "The elements are eternal" (verse 33).

Truth is "knowledge of things as they are, and as they were, and as they are to come" (verse 24). Truth and intelligence are independent in the spheres in which God has placed them (verse 30). The spirit of man is native to the spirit of truth, which is "plainly manifest" from the beginning (verse 31). This is the basis of AGENCY and ACCOUNTABILITY. "Every man whose spirit receiveth not the light is under condemnation" (verse 32).

Christ is the exemplar in all things. All may "come unto the Father in my name" (verse 19) and, in due time, "be glorified in me as I am in the Father" (verse 20). Man is a temple and a defiled temple will be destroyed. "Spirit and element" inseparably connected (resurrected) can receive a fulness of joy. "The glory of God is intelligence" defined as "light and truth." One who receives light and truth forsakes the evil one (verse 37).

"Every spirit of man was innocent in the beginning; and God having redeemed man from the fall, men became again, in their infant state, innocent before God" (verse 38). Through disobedience men become sinful, "light and truth" taken as they embrace the "traditions of their fathers" (verse 39).

The revelation closes with admonitions to the assembled high priests to set their houses in order by teaching the gospel more fully to their families (verses 42–50). Sidney Rigdon is to proclaim "the gospel of salvation" (verse 51) and the brethren are to "hasten to translate my scriptures" (Bible) and "to obtain a knowledge of history, and of countries, and of kingdoms, of laws of God and man," all "for the salvation of Zion" (verse 53).

DAN J. WORKMAN

SECTION 107

Section 107 is one of the most important statements in latter-day scripture on the divisions, offices, quorums, and councils of the PRIESTHOOD. Section 107 establishes an orderly arrangement of lay priesthood responsibilities at several levels. It was first published as Chapter III in the 1835 edition of the Doctrine and Covenants and was entitled "On Priesthood." Over the years it has been accepted as a major document and has been viewed as a wise and effective charter on priesthood keys and offices. It is the foundation of the priesthood administration of the Church (*see* ORGANIZATION).

On March 28, 1835, in Kirtland, Ohio, the recently organized QUORUM OF THE TWELVE APOSTLES met in preparation for their mission to the eastern United States. Feeling a sense of inadequacy in their new callings as special witnesses for Christ, the quorum drafted a letter to the Prophet Joseph SMITH requesting a revelation on their behalf: "The time when we are about to separate is near; and when we shall meet again, God only knows; we therefore feel to ask of him whom we have acknowledged to be our Prophet and Seer, that he inquire of God for us, and obtain a revelation, (if consistent) that we may look upon it when we are separated, that our hearts may be comforted" (*HC* 2:209–210).

Joseph "inquired of the Lord" and received section 107:1–57. The document distinguishes the MELCHIZEDEK PRIESTHOOD from the AARONIC PRIESTHOOD and defines which offices fall under each: The FIRST PRESIDENCY, and under it the twelve apostles, HIGH PRIESTS, and ELDERS, officiate in the Melchizedek Priesthood and function in all "spiritual things" (verses 1–12, 18–19, 21–26); the BISHOP, with his counselors, serves in the Aaronic Priesthood, which administers the "outward ordinances" of the Church, including baptism (verses 13–17, 20). The First Presidency presides over the Church; the Twelve are "special witnesses of the name of Christ in all the world" (verse 23); and the SEVENTY are called to preach the gospel abroad (verse 25).

The principles of priesthood organization established by this revelation combine democratic and hierarchic elements. "Of necessity there are presidents" over the several offices (verse 21), but every decision of one of the three governing quorums of the Church "must be by the unanimous voice of the same" (verse 27), made "in all righteousness, in holiness, and lowliness of heart" (verse 30). These quorums—the First Presidency, the Quorum of the Twelve, and the quorums of the Seventy—are "equal in authority" but function under the priesthood keys of the First Presidency, or of the Quorum of the Twelve when the presidency is dissolved on the death of the President (verses 22–26). The revelation also traces the lineage of the patriarchal priesthood in ancient times from Adam to Noah (verses 39–57).

With few exceptions, verses 58–100 were excerpted from an earlier revelation and vision that Joseph Smith had received. It declared that the President of the High Priesthood is "to preside over the whole Church, . . . like unto Moses" (verse 91), and defined the duties, presidencies, and membership limits for quorums of elders, priests, teachers, and deacons. It also specified the duties of the bishop as a judge in Zion and gave the procedures for trying the conduct of a general officer of the Church.

BIBLIOGRAPHY

Cook, Lyndon W. *The Revelations of the Prophet Joseph Smith*, pp. 215–16, 326–29. Provo, Utah, 1981.

WALTER D. BOWEN

SECTIONS 109–110

Section 109 is the dedicatory prayer for the KIRTLAND TEMPLE. Joseph Smith records that he received this prayer under the spirit of revelation (*HC* 2:420). The prayer contains some temple language repeated from Doctrine and Covenants 88 (see verses 119–21), and some passages in it pertaining to the redemption of Jerusalem are paralleled in the Orson Hyde prayer given on the Mount of Olives five years later.

Section 109 is Hebraic in tone and reminiscent of the Solomonic dedication of the first temple and the temple-related benedictions of Jewish tradition (cf. 1 Kgs. 8).

It begins with thanksgiving, "Thanks be to thy name, O Lord God of Israel, who keepest covenant and showest mercy"; seeks divine acceptance and visible manifestation of divine glory upon the temple and the faithful; petitions that God accept what has been done in the spirit of sacrifice; designates the building as a house of God, of prayer, fasting, faith, learning, glory, and order (verse 8; cf. verse 16), where the divine name may be put upon his

servants; asks forgiveness and the blotting out of sin; pleads for emissaries of truth to go forth in power and seal their witness with power; pleads for protection from enemies and deliverance from the calamities in Missouri; and prays for mercy on the nations of the earth, for expansion of stakes, for the gathering of scattered Jacob and Judah, for the redemption of Jerusalem "from this hour" (verse 62), and finally for blessings on the homes and families of the leaders of the Church. It ends with "O hear, O hear, O hear us, O Lord . . . that we may mingle our voices with those bright, shining seraphs around thy throne" and an "Amen, and Amen" (verses 78, 80).

Section 110 is the record of events following the temple dedication on April 3, 1836. The account (not canonical in the RLDS church) was recorded by Joseph's scribe Warren Cowdery, and first published one week after the events it describes in the *Messenger and Advocate*, and later was included in the 1876 edition of the Doctrine and Covenants (see headnote). After partaking of the sacrament and bowing in "solemn and silent prayer," Joseph Smith and Oliver Cowdery received a shared vision. The Savior appeared and accepted the temple, saying, "My name shall be here; and I will manifest myself to my people in mercy in this house" (verse 7). MOSES next appeared to restore the "keys of the gathering of Israel from the four parts of the earth" (verse 11) preparatory to the renewal of temples and temple worship (see ISRAEL: GATHERING OF ISRAEL; TEMPLE ORDINANCES). Elias "committed the dispensation of the Gospel of Abraham" (verse 12) to restore the covenant promise made to Abraham that through him and his seed all generations would be blessed (see COVENANT OF ABRAHAM; GOSPEL OF ABRAHAM). Finally Elijah appeared and bestowed the keys of SEALING for all priesthood ordinances, including the sealing of families, and announced the imminence of the second coming of the Messiah (verses 13–16). This was in keeping with the final prophecy of Malachi that Elijah would come to turn the hearts of the children to the fathers before the great and dreadful day of the Lord (Mal. 4:5–6; see ELIJAH, SPIRIT OF).

BIBLIOGRAPHY

Sperry, Sidney B. *Doctrine and Covenants Compendium*. Salt Lake City, 1960.

S. MICHAEL WILCOX

SECTIONS 121–123

These sections are selections from a long letter written by Joseph Smith in LIBERTY JAIL, Missouri, on March 20, 1839, addressed "To the Church of Latter-day Saints at Quincy, Illinois and scattered abroad and to Bishop Partridge in particular" (*HC* 3:289). The power and richness of the letter, both its doctrinal content and its literary images, may have resulted from the Prophet's personal suffering.

Section 121 begins with a prayer, a cry of "O God, where art thou?" a plea that God will recognize the sufferings of the Saints, punish their enemies, and avenge their wrongs (verses 1–6). In the next verse, the Prophet hears the consoling voice of inspiration saying, "My son, peace be unto thy soul; thine adversity and thine afflictions shall be but a small moment" (verse 7). He is reminded "Thy friends do stand by thee," and promised "They shall hail thee again with warm hearts and friendly hands" (verse 9). "Thou art not yet as Job" (verse 10). The righteousness of the Saints' actions

Interior of the Liberty Jail, restored. Joseph Smith and his companions were held in the dark, low-ceilinged basement of this building from December 1838 to April 1839. D&C 121–123 were written in March, beginning with the prayer, "O God, where art thou?"

is confirmed; in the Lord's time those who have afflicted the Saints will be punished (verses 11–25).

Verses 26–33 promise blessings of knowledge that will soon be poured out upon the Latter-day Saints by the Holy Spirit, including a knowledge of all God's dominions and the laws by which they operate. The last part of section 121 includes some of the most sensitive and powerful verses in LDS scripture. Here the Prophet teaches against all forms of unrighteous dominion. True authority, he writes, is always linked to love. "No power or influence can or ought to be maintained by virtue of the priesthood, only by persuasion, by long-suffering, by gentleness and meekness, and by love unfeigned" (verse 41).

Section 122 is a revelation directed specifically to Joseph Smith, to help him understand the trials he is suffering. It assures him that he will be known for good among the noble and virtuous of the earth, and that his own people will never be turned against him by "the testimony of traitors" (verse 3). The verses graphically name perils and betrayals he has suffered or has yet to suffer, and then continues "Know thou, my son, that all these things shall give thee experience, and shall be for thy good" (verse 7). The section ends by reminding the young prophet that "the Son of Man hath descended below them all" (verse 8).

Section 123 instructs the Saints in the steps they should take to seek redress for their persecution and losses in Missouri. They are admonished to compile lists of property damages and character and personal injuries, to take affidavits, and to gather libelous publications so that they may present their case before government officials. This course of action is explained as the last duty they owe to God, to their families, and to the rising generation. The section ends by assuring the Saints that these efforts, although they may not understand their value, will be important to the Church in the future (verse 15).

BIBLIOGRAPHY

Christianson, James R. "A Ray of Light in an Hour of Darkness." In *Studies in Scripture*, ed. R. Millett and K. Jackson 1:463–75. Salt Lake City, 1984.

Maxwell, Neal A. *But for a Small Moment.* Salt Lake City, 1986.

SUSAN HOWE

SECTION 124

Section 124, given January 19, 1841, to the Prophet Joseph SMITH, is the longest revelation in the Doctrine and Covenants. It was the first section received at NAUVOO, Illinois, and was first printed in the 1844 edition of the Doctrine and Covenants as number 103.

Church members had fled from Missouri to Illinois in 1839 to escape the EXTERMINATION ORDER of Governor Lilburn W. Boggs. The eastern banks of the Mississippi River became a place of refuge and the Church headquarters. By 1841, Nauvoo had been established there and the village had grown to approximately 3,000 inhabitants. In that setting, section 124 served as an important inaugural, a kind of constitution for further development of Nauvoo and the Church. It provided instruction on temporal, doctrinal, and organizational matters, and gave assignments and counsel to fifty-five individuals.

Section 124 includes the following:

- A charge to Joseph Smith to "make a solemn proclamation" of the gospel to rulers of all nations (verses 2–14, 16–17, 107).

- Directions to build the NAUVOO HOUSE, a hotel where "the weary traveler may find health and safety" while contemplating the word of the Lord (verses 22–24, 56–82).

- A commandment to members to assist in building the NAUVOO TEMPLE, begun three months earlier. It was to be a place for the Lord to restore the fulness of the PRIESTHOOD and reveal "things which have been kept hid from before the foundation of the world" pertaining to the DISPENSATION OF THE FULNESS OF TIMES (verses 25–28, 40–44; see also TEMPLE ORDINANCES).

- A promise that if members would hearken unto the voice of God and his servants, "they shall not be moved out of their place" (verses 45–46).

- A clarification on BAPTISM FOR THE DEAD, defined as a temple ordinance. The revelation said Moses had received a similar charge to build a tabernacle for ordinance work (verses 25–48).

- A declaration that efforts of the Saints to establish a city and temple in Missouri were accepted by the Lord, even though persecutions prevented their establishment at that time (verses 49–54).

- Callings and confirmations of various positions in the Church, including a listing of some new officers and a reiteration of some previous callings. For example, Hyrum SMITH was named as PATRIARCH, replacing his father, who had died September 14, 1840. Joseph Smith, Sidney RIGDON, and William Law were appointed to the FIRST PRESIDENCY. Brigham YOUNG was renamed President of the QUORUM OF THE TWELVE APOSTLES (he had been sustained in this position on April 14, 1840), and assignments were made to that quorum. Twelve members were named for a stake HIGH COUNCIL, and others were called to serve in the presidencies of the high priests, elders, seventies, two bishoprics, and priests. Teachers, deacons, and stake organizations were mentioned, but no leadership assignments in these were made (verses 20–21, 123–42).

PAUL C. RICHARDS

SECTIONS 127–128

Sections 127 and 128 constitute two doctrinal letters dictated by the Prophet Joseph SMITH while "in exile" near Nauvoo, Illinois, during the first week of September 1842. His scribe was William Clayton. The sections were first published in the TIMES AND SEASONS on September 14 and October 1, 1842, and first appeared in the Doctrine and Covenants in 1844 as numbers 105 and 106.

These documents clarified and formalized the LDS doctrine and practice of BAPTISM FOR THE DEAD, a practice attested to in the first century at Corinth (1 Cor. 15:29). Two years earlier, while speaking at a funeral on August 15, 1840, Joseph Smith first publicly announced the privilege and the responsibility of Church members to perform baptisms for the dead (TPJS, p. 179). "It presents the Gospel of Christ in probably a more enlarged scale than some have imagined it" (TPJS, p. 180). Immediately thereafter, Church members began performing proxy baptisms in the Mississippi River. A year later, Joseph Smith declared, "There shall be no more baptism for the dead, until the ordinance can be attended to in the Lord's House" (HC 4:426). When the baptismal font in the Nauvoo Temple was completed November 21, 1841, baptisms for the dead were performed there (HC 4:454).

Sections 127 and 128 stress the requirement for eyewitnesses and a recorder at all such baptismal services. Without authenticated records on earth and in heaven, a baptism is not deemed valid (D&C 127:6–9; 128:3–10).

In Section 128, the Prophet expounded on Malachi 4:5–6 and explained that baptism for the dead is "a welding link" between parents and children (D&C 128:18). He further explained that unless children are sealed by temple ordinances to their deceased forebears, who are in turn sealed to each other in God's family, neither can be fully saved and exalted (verses 14, 15, 18). "They without us cannot be made perfect—neither can we without our dead be made perfect" (verse 15; cf. Hebrews 11:40).

Baptisms and other temple ordinances for the dead continue as a vital part of Church doctrine and practice.

GEORGE D. DURRANT

SECTIONS 131–132

These sections discuss the principle of eternal marriage as a requirement for obtaining the highest degree of glory in the celestial kingdom (D&C 131:1–4; cf. 76:50–70). In that exalted state, men and women become gods (*see* GODHOOD), continue to have children (*see* ETERNAL INCREASE), and come to know God fully (D&C 132:23–24).

Section 131 contains selected statements made by Joseph SMITH on May 16–17, 1843, during a visit to members of the Church in Ramus, Illinois, 22 miles east of Nauvoo (*HC* 5:391–93). They were recorded by William Clayton in his diary. In addition to its teachings on eternal marriage, section 131 also defines the phrase "more sure word of prophecy," declares that no one can be saved in ignorance (cf. *TPJS*, p. 217), and explains that spirit is purified matter.

Section 132 contains the doctrinal basis of the practice of PLURAL MARRIAGE. Although some were distressed by it, others found plural marriage "the most holy and important doctrine ever revealed" (W. Clayton, in A. Jenson, *Historical Record* 6:226). This revelation was recorded on July 12, 1843, in the brick store in Nauvoo. At the urging of Hyrum SMITH so that Emma Smith might be convinced of its truth, the Prophet Joseph Smith dictated it sentence by sentence. Clayton reported that "after the whole was written Joseph asked me to read it through, slowly and carefully, which I did, and he pronounced it correct" (*CHC* 2:106–

107). That evening, Bishop Newel K. Whitney received permission to copy the revelation. The next day, his clerk, Joseph C. Kingsbury, copied the document, which Whitney and Kingsbury proofread against the original. This copy was given to Brigham YOUNG in March 1847; it was officially adopted as revelation at a general conference in Salt Lake City in August 1852, and was first published for public review in a *Deseret News Extra* of September 14, 1852.

The doctrines in this revelation were probably received sometime in 1831 while the Prophet was translating the Bible. In response to questions about the legitimacy of the ancient prophets' plural marriages, the Lord revealed to Joseph Smith the conditions and requirements under which plural marriage was to be observed. Lyman Johnson told Orson Pratt that "Joseph had made known to him [Johnson] as early as 1831, that plural marriage was a correct principle," but had said it was not yet time to teach and practice it (*MS* 40 [1878]:788). That date was later confirmed in various statements and affidavits collected by Joseph F. SMITH and others from those who had been close to Joseph Smith in Nauvoo.

Section 132 states that all covenants must be made in the proper manner, by proper authority, and be sealed by the Holy Spirit of Promise in order to be valid eternally (verses 7–19), and that through faithfulness eternal blessings are guaranteed to those who marry by this new and everlasting covenant: "Then shall they be gods, because they have no end; therefore shall they be from everlasting to everlasting, because they continue" (verse 20). This law was ordained before the world was, and through it Abraham received the promise of eternal lives through his seed (verses 28–37). Strict prohibitions against adultery accompany the law of eternal marriage (verses 38–44, 61–63). In concluding verses, Joseph Smith received divine affirmation of his eternal standing with God and acceptance of his labors (verses 45–50); and admonitions were given to Emma and others to observe this law and to multiply and replenish the earth so that God may be glorified (verses 51–66).

BIBLIOGRAPHY

Danel W. Bachman. "New Light on an Old Hypothesis: The Ohio Origins of the Revelation on Eternal Marriage." *Journal of Mormon History* 5 (1978):19–32.

PAUL G. GRANT

SECTIONS 137–138

Section 137 reports a vision of the CELESTIAL KINGDOM recorded in the diary of Joseph SMITH. On January 21, 1836, he and several other Church leaders gathered in the Kirtland Temple for the ordinances of washing and anointing. Joseph blessed and anointed his aged father, Joseph SMITH, Sr., who in turn anointed the members of the Church presidency and sealed blessings upon the Prophet. Joseph recorded that as the presidency laid their hands on his head and prophesied, "the heavens were opened upon us and I beheld the celestial kingdom of God, and the glory thereof" (verse 1). He saw its streets as if paved with gold. The Father and the Son sat on a blazing throne. ADAM and ABRAHAM were there; so were Joseph's parents, who were still alive at the time of the vision, and his brother Alvin, who had died before the priesthood was restored and hence had not been baptized for the remission of sins. The vision continued beyond that which is included in section 137 (*HC* 2:380–81; *PWJS*, pp. 145–46). Many present received visions and witnessed the glory of God fill the room.

Joseph's vision was the first doctrinal revelation to the Church disclosing that the Lord will provide all who die without hearing the gospel an opportunity to hear and accept it in the SPIRIT WORLD so they can enter the celestial kingdom (D&C 137:8–9; clarifying 76:72) and that children who die before the age of accountability (eight years) will be heirs of the celestial kingdom (D&C 137:10).

Section 138 is the record of a vision received by President Joseph F. SMITH on October 3, 1918, as he was pondering the universal nature of the atonement of Jesus Christ and wondering how the Savior taught the spirits in prison in the brief time between his death and resurrection (D&C 138:1–11; cf. 1 Pet. 3:19; 4:6). He saw the visit of the Savior to the righteous spirits in PARADISE. He also observed that Jesus did not go in person among the wicked and disobedient but organized representatives from among the righteous spirits to carry the gospel to "all the spirits of men" (D&C 138:30). Those who were not taught the gospel on earth will be given the opportunity to hear it and accept its exalting fulness when taught by Christ's authorized representatives in the spirit world; those spirits who are "in darkness and under the bondage of sin . . . who repent will be redeemed" (verses 138:57–58; cf. 76:74).

The accounts of these two visions were canonized in the general conference of April 1976 as additions to the Pearl of Great Price. They became sections in the Doctrine and Covenants in 1981.

BIBLIOGRAPHY

Millet, Robert L. "Salvation Beyond the Grave (D&C 137 and 138)." In *Studies in Scripture*, Vol. 1, pp. 549–63, ed. R. Millet and K. Jackson. Sandy, Utah, 1984.

LEON R. HARTSHORN

OFFICIAL DECLARATION—2

Declaration—2 revealed that the "long-promised day has come when every faithful, worthy man in the Church may receive the holy priesthood." This "priesthood revelation" made it possible for all worthy males to be ordained to all levels of the PRIESTHOOD. Previously black members of the Church had been denied the priesthood, which precluded their holding priesthood CALLINGS and participation in most TEMPLE ORDINANCES.

The revelation was received by President Spencer W. KIMBALL "after extended meditation and prayer" in the SALT LAKE TEMPLE. That same revelation came to his counselors and to the QUORUM OF THE TWELVE APOSTLES in the temple, and then it was presented to all of the other GENERAL AUTHORITIES, who approved it unanimously. It was announced by letter to all priesthood officers of the Church and to the press on June 8, 1978. Declaration—2 contains the text of that letter and records its presentation and acceptance on September 30, 1978, in general conference by the COMMON CONSENT of the members of the Church. The revelation resolved problems for many members who had agonized over the prior practice (Bush and Mauss), the historical origins and ramifications of which had become the subject of considerable debate and reflection.

Since the announcement, missionaries have actively proselytized in many nations with large black populations, where thousands have become members of the Church. Dallin H. Oaks, an apostle, noted this growth in the LDS Afro-American Symposium held at BRIGHAM YOUNG UNIVERSITY on the occasion of the tenth anniversary of the revelation (Oaks). In particular, he pointed to the rapid growth in black converts in the Caribbean islands, West Africa, and Brazil.

BIBLIOGRAPHY

Bush, Lester E., and Armand L. Mauss, eds. *Neither White nor Black: Mormon Scholars Confront the Race Issue in a Universal Church.* Midvale, Utah, 1984.

Grover, Mark L. "The Mormon Priesthood Revelation and the São Paulo Brazil Temple." *Dialogue* 23 (Spring 1990):39–53.

McConkie, Bruce R. "All Are Alike unto God." In *Second Annual CES Symposium*, pp. 3–5. Salt Lake City, 1978.

Oaks, Dallin H. "For the Blessing of All His Children." Address, LDS Afro-American Symposium. Provo, June 8, 1988.

CARDELL JACOBSON

DOCTRINE AND COVENANTS COMMENTARIES

Commentaries on the Doctrine and Covenants follow the pattern of many biblical commentaries, supplying the historical context, that is, the time, circumstances, and situation of the REVELATIONS. In the most recent (1981) edition of the Doctrine and Covenants, headnotes for each section have been added or enlarged, with a brief synopsis of the historical setting. Additional notes and explanations are provided by the various separately published commentaries discussed here. Commentaries written by members of the Quorum of the Twelve Apostles are given special consideration. Others are recommended as helps to the membership of the Church to provide historical insight to their study of the scriptures.

An early (1916) and still useful one-volume commentary was written by Hyrum M. Smith, a member of the Quorum of the Twelve Apostles, and Janne M. Sjodahl. *Doctrine and Covenants Commentary* contains the text of the Doctrine and Covenants and gives historical background and commentary for each section. It is extensively footnoted with exegetical notes. The volume was later supplemented and expanded under the direction of Joseph Fielding SMITH, Harold B. LEE, and Marion G. Romney of the Quorum of the Twelve.

The Message of the Doctrine and Covenants (1969, edited by G. Homer Durham) is a published version of a series of lectures delivered at the University of Southern California by John A. Widtsoe, also of the Quorum of the Twelve. The author's scientific background is apparent in his references to nineteenth- and twentieth-century scientific theory.

T. Edgar Lyon, former director of the INSTITUTE OF RELIGION adjacent to the University of Utah in Salt Lake City, published his *Introduction to the Doctrine and Covenants and Pearl of Great Price* in 1948. He treats the work as a "connected message" and emphasizes the functional aspects of many topics, including priesthood, missionary work, Zion, gathering, ordinances, Christian teachings, economics, millennium, unique revelations, and literary value.

From 1947 through 1949 the Church published a series of manuals titled *Church History and Modern Revelation*, written by Joseph Fielding SMITH of the Quorum of the Twelve. It was a study course for the MELCHIZEDEK PRIESTHOOD quorums of the Church. These volumes integrated each section of the Doctrine and Covenants with the life and times of the Prophet Joseph Smith. A more concise attempt at this approach was that of E. Cecil McGavin in a volume titled *The Historical Background of the Doctrine and Covenants*, published in 1949.

Sidney B. Sperry, longtime professor of Hebrew and ancient scripture at Brigham Young University, published *A Doctrine and Covenants Compendium* in 1960, which considered linguistic and doctrinal issues in detail.

A four-volume work titled *The Latter-day Prophets and the Doctrine and Covenants* (1963), by Roy W. Doxey, former dean of the College of Religious Instruction at Brigham Young University, includes statements of General Authorities on each section of the Doctrine and Covenants. It demonstrates applications of Doctrine and Covenants texts in homiletic settings.

A historical account is *The Revelations of the Prophet Joseph Smith* by Lyndon W. Cook (1981), providing a compilation of background facts relevant to each section. Documented biographical profiles of the personalities mentioned in the text are included.

A commentary titled *The Edwards Commentary on the Doctrine and Covenants* was written by F. Henry Edwards of the REORGANIZED CHURCH OF JESUS CHRIST OF LATTER DAY SAINTS and published in 1946. This book provides a brief historical overview for each section and commentary on the major themes of the sections, as these relate and apply to the problems of that church.

A critical analysis of the earliest texts and publication of the Doctrine and Covenants is Robert J. Woodford's *The Historical Development of the Doctrine and Covenants*, a Ph.D. dissertation, Brigham Young University, 1974. Other studies are those by William E. Berrett, *Teachings of the Doctrine and Covenants*, 1961; Roy W. Doxey, *Doctrine and Covenants Speaks*, 2 vols., 1970; Richard O. Cowan, *The Doctrine and Covenants, Our Modern Scripture*, 1978; Daniel H. Ludlow, *A Companion to Your Study of the Doctrine and Covenants*, 1978; Leaun G. Otten and C. Max Caldwell, *Sacred Truths of the Doctrine and Covenants*, 2 vols., 1982; and Robert L. Millet and Kent P. Jackson, eds., *Studies in Scripture, the Doctrine and Covenants*, 1985.

H. DEAN GARRETT

DOCTRINE AND COVENANTS EDITIONS

The Doctrine and Covenants contains revelations from God as given to the Prophet Joseph SMITH and later Presidents of The Church of Jesus Christ of Latter-day Saints and includes other inspired writings and doctrinal declarations accepted as scripture by the Latter-day Saints. The first edition appeared in 1835. Later editions incorporated additional revelations and reference aids. The Doctrine and Covenants has been translated into many languages, though the English edition is the official version.

By the fall of 1831, Joseph Smith had recorded seventy or more revelations, most of which contained instructions to Church members. In a special conference held November 1, 1831, in Hiram, Ohio, the Church decided to publish a selection of these revelations, or "commandments." A new revelation was received on that occasion as "my preface unto the book of my commandments," from which the title of the 1833 compilation, the Book of Commandments, may have been taken (D&C 1:6). This publication was never completed; a mob destroyed the Independence, Missouri, press and all but about a hundred unfinished copies in July 1833. These few copies of the Book of Commandments were circulated within the Church and were often called the "Book of Covenants," in reference to the lead section, which had circulated widely in handwritten versions as "The Articles and Covenants of the Church." Received the day the Church was organized, this revelation is now section 20 of the Doctrine and Covenants.

THE 1835 EDITION. Shortly after the unsuccessful 1833 effort to print the Book of Commandments

was stopped, plans were made to publish the revelations in Kirtland, Ohio. Renamed the *Doctrine and Covenants of the Church of the Latter Day Saints*, the book was presented to, and accepted by, the members of the Church in an August 1835 conference as the word of God. The change in name to Doctrine and Covenants reflected a change in content. Unlike the Book of Commandments, which contained revelations only, the Doctrine and Covenants was divided into two parts. The new first part consisted of seven theological presentations now known as the LECTURES ON FAITH but then titled "On the Doctrine of the Church of the Latter Day Saints." The part including the revelations published previously, the original preface, and a number of new revelations not in the 1833 compilation, were titled "Part Second, Covenants and Commandments." The title of the Doctrine and Covenants reflects the subtitles of these two parts.

In preparing the 1835 edition, Joseph Smith and a committee appointed to the task on September 24, 1834 (*HC* 2:165, 243–44) edited the revelations that had formerly appeared in the Book of Commandments. They corrected scribal and printing errors and occasionally clarified the text. They added explanations of the duties of officers that were new in the Church organization since the earlier revelations were received. They also combined some of the revelations to simplify publication and corrected grammatical problems.

The 1835 edition of the Doctrine and Covenants contained 103 sections, though two sections were inadvertently numbered 66, so that the last one's number was printed 102. Sections 1–100 were revelations to Joseph Smith. Section 101 prescribed practices for MARRIAGE. Section 102 stated the appropriate relationship of the Church to governments (*see* POLITICS: POLITICAL TEACHINGS). These two sections were not revelations but were included as expressions of belief of the Church at that time. Oliver COWDERY (and possibly W. W. Phelps) wrote them, probably in response to critics of the doctrines and activities of the Church. Although Joseph Smith subsequently endorsed the statement on government, there is evidence that he opposed including the statement on marriage from the beginning, and it was eventually removed (see Cook, pp. 348–49, n. 11).

THE 1844 NAUVOO EDITION. By 1840 the Church needed a new edition of the Doctrine and

Covenants. The 1835 edition had sold out, and Joseph Smith had received additional revelations. The new edition appeared in Nauvoo shortly after the death of Joseph Smith in 1844. The eight newly added revelations are numbered sections 103, 105, 112, 119, 124, 127, 128, and 135 in the 1981 edition. The metal printing plates from the 1844 edition were used in the 1845 and 1846 reprintings.

THE 1845 LIVERPOOL, ENGLAND, EDITION. In 1847, Brigham YOUNG led the members of the Church to the Salt Lake Valley, where they had no facilities to print books. In 1845 Wilford Woodruff printed 3,000 copies of the Doctrine and Covenants in England for the growing LDS population in the British Isles. This edition included the new revelations published in the 1844 Nauvoo edition. Other Church representatives arranged reprintings in England in 1849, 1852, 1854, 1866, and 1869 and shipped most of the 1854 printing to Salt Lake City because of very limited facilities for printing there.

THE 1876 EDITION. In 1876 Orson Pratt, a member of the QUORUM OF THE TWELVE APOSTLES and Church historian, acting under the direction of President Brigham Young, prepared a new edition of the Doctrine and Covenants in Salt Lake City. He divided each revelation into verses and added twenty-six revelations not previously included. They are now sections 2, 13, 77, 85, 87, 108–11, 113–18, 120–23, 125, 126, 129–32, and 136. Since section 132 contained information about PLURAL MARRIAGE inconsistent with the 1835 article on marriage, the latter was eliminated.

THE 1879 EDITION. Three years later, Pratt published another edition in England in which he added footnotes to the text. He also requested permission from President John Taylor to drop the "Lectures on Faith," but was instructed that, though the time might come to do this, it was not yet. This edition was published in 1879 in England and in 1880 in Salt Lake City from duplicate plates. President George Q. Cannon, a counselor in the FIRST PRESIDENCY, presented this edition to the members of the Church in a fiftieth jubilee conference held in October 1880; they accepted the book as scripture.

From 1880 to 1920 the Church published at least twenty-eight printings from this edition. Beginning in 1908, each printing included a concordance and excerpts from President of the Church

Wilford Woodruff's "Manifesto," an official declaration ending plural marriage.

THE 1921 EDITION. In 1920, President Heber J. GRANT assigned a committee of six members of the Council of the Twelve to prepare a new edition of the Doctrine and Covenants. The major change in the 1921 edition was the removal of the "Lectures on Faith," which were not considered to be revelations. The committee also revised the footnotes and divided the pages into double columns. Even though the name of the collection had been changed in the 1835 edition to signal the addition of the "Lectures on Faith," it was not changed back when the lectures were deleted. The 1921 edition was the standard until 1981.

THE 1981 EDITION. A committee appointed by the First Presidency of the Church directed the publication of a new edition of the Doctrine and Covenants in 1981. New features included completely revised footnotes and rewritten introductory headings for each section. Two additional sections and a second official declaration were also incorporated. Section 137 is a portion of a vision of the celestial kingdom given to Joseph Smith in the Kirtland Temple on January 21, 1836. Section 138 is a vision about the redemption of the dead given to Joseph F. SMITH, sixth President of the Church, in 1918. OFFICIAL DECLARATION—2 is the 1978 announcement by the First Presidency that all worthy male members of the Church can be ordained to the priesthood.

FOREIGN-LANGUAGE EDITIONS. The Church has also published the Doctrine and Covenants in many languages other than English. Beginning in 1851 with the Welsh edition, the Doctrine and Covenants has been translated and published in its entirety in a score or more languages and selections from it in many others.

BIBLIOGRAPHY

Cook, Lyndon W. *The Revelations of the Prophet Joseph Smith: A Historical and Bibliographical Commentary of the Doctrine and Covenants.* Salt Lake City, 1985.

Gentry, Leland H. "What of the Lectures on Faith?" *BYU Studies* 19 (Fall 1978):5–19.

Lambert, A. C. *The Published Editions of the Book of Doctrine and Covenants of the Church of Jesus Christ of Latter-day Saints in All Languages, 1833–1950.* Provo, Utah, 1950.

Woodford, Robert J. "The Historical Development of the Doctrine and Covenants." 3 vols. Ph.D. diss., Brigham Young University, 1974.

———. "The Doctrine and Covenants: A Historical Overview." In *Studies in Scripture*, ed. R. Millet and K. Jackson, Vol. 1, pp. 3–22. Sandy, Utah, 1984.

ROBERT J. WOODFORD

DOCTRINE AND COVENANTS AS LITERATURE

The literary quality of the Doctrine and Covenants can best be seen in its similarities to a near literary relation—that "noblest monument of English prose," the King James Version of the BIBLE. Although a truly unique religious text, the Doctrine and Covenants contains more than 2,000 close parallels to biblical passages, and the literary manner of the book is similar to the Bible in subject matter. Like earlier scripture, the Doctrine and Covenants offers a rainbow of literary genres. The collection of revelations ranges from forms as transcendent as VISIONS (sections 3, 76, 110), angelic annunciations (sections 2, 13, 27), and PROPHECIES (sections 87, 121); through such ecclesiastical proclamations as PRAYERS (sections 109, 121), epistles (sections 127, 128), scriptural explanations (sections 74, 77, 86), COMMANDMENTS (section 19), and official declarations; to down-to-earth instructions (sections 130, 131) and minutes of meetings (section 102).

The literary kinship of the Doctrine and Covenants with the Bible is more apparent in tone than in style. The Doctrine and Covenants, for instance, is impressive for a simple, condensed straightforwardness that lends itself to statements remarkably rich in implication. The following two examples are from a single section: "Truth is knowledge of things as they are, and as they were, and as they are to come" (D&C 93:24). "The glory of God is intelligence, or in other words, light and truth" (93:36). These lines are not set in contexts that illuminate them so much as they are parts of a sorites—conclusions without the use of thesis and antithesis.

Tonal richness sometimes expresses itself in vivid metaphor. A single section of the Doctrine and Covenants, for example, displays a sensitive sequence of images of water—progress like "rolling waters" that cannot "remain impure" (D&C 121:33), evil prospects that shall "melt away as the hoar frost melteth before the burning rays of the rising sun" (121:11), and DOCTRINE that will "distil upon thy soul as the dews from heaven" (121:45).

As the most recent compilation of divine prophecy of The Church of Jesus Christ of Latter-day Saints, the Doctrine and Covenants provides the invaluable literary benefit of immediacy; divinity can be approached by modern readers through this book naturally and directly. It locates the reader not in the distant past of Ophir or Tarsus but in the recent history of such familiar landscapes as New York and Boston, where God reveals himself in close proximity. That closeness is apparent in his manner of address; he refers to recipients of his revelations a half dozen times in the book as "friends" (D&C 84:63; 84:77; 94:1; 98:1; 100:1; 104:1).

That is how the voice of the God of ABRAHAM and Isaac and of PETER and PAUL addresses readers in the Doctrine and Covenants—as friends. The most striking literary characteristic of the book is the directness of its access to God. When Joseph Smith cries out in a long and painful prayer of reproach, "O God, where art thou?" the Father's response is as immediately comforting to present readers as it was to the Prophet: "My son, peace be unto thy soul" (D&C 121:1, 7). The Doctrine and Covenants speaks with biblical power to the immediate conditions of modern life. In the most difficult moments of current circumstance, the Doctrine and Covenants lifts readers' eyes above mortal disappointments toward eternal hopes: "All these things shall give thee experience, and shall be for thy good" (122:7).

BIBLIOGRAPHY

Sperry, Sidney B. *Doctrine and Covenants Compendium.* Salt Lake City, 1960.

Walker, Steven C. "The Voice of the Prophet." *BYU Studies* 10 (Autumn 1969):95–106.

STEVEN C. WALKER

DOVE, SIGN OF THE

All four Gospel writers indicate that at the baptism of Jesus, JOHN THE BAPTIST saw the Spirit descend upon Jesus like a dove (Matt. 3:16; Mark 1:10; Luke 3:22; John 1:32). The JOSEPH SMITH TRANSLATION OF THE BIBLE, John 1:31-33, reads: "And John bare record, saying: When he was baptized of me, I saw the Spirit descending from heaven like a dove, and it abode upon him. And I knew him; for he who sent me to baptize with water, the same said unto me: Upon whom thou shalt see the Spirit descending, and remaining on him, the same is he who baptizeth with the Holy Ghost. And I saw, and bare record that this is the Son of God" (see also JST Matt. 3:45–46).

The HOLY GHOST is a spirit person in the form of man (D&C 130:22) and does not transform himself into a dove or any other form. The Prophet Joseph SMITH explained: "The sign of the dove was instituted before the creation of the world, a witness for the Holy Ghost, and the devil cannot come in the sign of a dove. The Holy Ghost is a personage [a man], and is in the form of a personage [a man]. It does not confine itself to the *form* of the dove, but in *sign* [symbol or representation] of the dove. The Holy Ghost cannot be transformed into a dove; but the sign of a dove was given to John to signify the truth of the deed, as the dove is an emblem or token of truth and innocence" (*TPJS*, p. 276). The dove was a supernatural sign given to John to witness the identity of the MESSIAH. Some non-LDS scholars have entertained differing opinions as to whether or not a real dove was present. Joseph Smith's explanation leads toward a conclusion that the dove was not literally present (*see* JESUS CHRIST: BAPTISM).

Other references to the sign of the dove are 1 Nephi 11:27; 2 Nephi 31:8 and Doctrine and Covenants 93:15. The BOOK OF ABRAHAM states that to Abraham also was revealed "the sign of the Holy Ghost in the form of a dove" (Facsimile 2, Fig. 7).

ROBERT L. MARROTT

DRAMA

Latter-day Saints have supported and participated in theatrical activities throughout their history. Members of the Church established one of the first community theaters in America at Nauvoo, Illinois, in the 1840s. The Prophet Joseph SMITH directed that a home dramatic company be established. He taught the Saints to seek after all things "virtuous, lovely, or of good report, or praiseworthy" (A of F 13). These included theater, drama, and the related arts—music, dance, painting, singing, acting, and writing. Theatrical activity in Nauvoo did not cease until 1846, when the city was besieged and the Saints were driven out.

Soon after arriving in Salt Lake Valley in 1847, the Latter-day Saints erected what they call a bowery (a temporary shelter made from placing tree boughs on a frame structure) on the southeast cor-

LDS wards use drama or "roadshows" for entertainment, celebration, and instruction. This pioneer pageant was presented in the Logan, Utah, Fourth Ward in 1979. Courtesy Craig Law.

ner of what became TEMPLE SQUARE. Three successively larger boweries replaced the first. Concerts, plays, and dances were performed there. President Brigham Young observed, "If I were placed on a cannibal island and given a task of civilizing its people, I should straightway build a theatre" (Skidmore, p. 47).

Social Hall in Salt Lake City was formally dedicated in 1853, scarcely more than five years after the arrival of the Mormon pioneers in the valley. In *Utah and the Mormons*, Benjamin G. Ferris described the presentations held there: "During the winter they keep up theatrical exhibitions in Social Hall, and generally the performances are better sustained in all their parts than in theatres of Atlantic cities" (quoted in Maughan, p. 5).

The SALT LAKE THEATRE, one of the finest theater buildings of its time, was dedicated in 1862. Brigham Young believed that it had been created for an ennobling purpose. During the dedicatory service, he said, "On the stage of a theatre can be represented in character evil and its consequences, good and its happy results and rewards, the weaknesses and follies of man and the magnanimity of the virtuous life" (quoted in Maughan, p. 84).

The tradition of theater continues in the Church today. Latter-day Saints write and produce plays, musicals, and roadshows. Roadshows are original mini-musicals, locally created and produced under the sponsorship of WARD and STAKE activities committees. The Church also sponsors religious pageants, including those presented annually in Palmyra-Manchester, New York; Nauvoo, Illinois; Independence, MISSOURI; Temple View, New Zealand; Calgary, Canada; Oakland, California; Mesa, Arizona; and Manti and Clarkston, Utah (*see* PAGEANTS).

BRIGHAM YOUNG UNIVERSITY in Utah and RICKS COLLEGE in Idaho have theater departments that train playwrights, actors, directors, and designers. The Promised Valley Playhouse in Salt Lake City is owned and operated by the Church. It stages its own productions, and its facilities are also available for stake and ward performances.

BIBLIOGRAPHY

Clinger, Morris M. "A History of Theatre in Mormon Colleges and Universities." Ph.D. diss., University of Minnesota, 1963.

Gledhill, Preston R. "Mormon Dramatic Activities." Ph.D. diss., University of Wisconsin, 1950.

Maughan, Ila Fisher. *Pioneer Theatre in the Desert*. Salt Lake City, 1961.

Skidmore, Rex A. "Mormon Recreation in Theory and Practice: A Study of Social Change." Ph.D. diss., University of Pennsylvania, 1941.

CHARLES L. METTEN

DRUGS, ABUSE OF

The abuse of drugs is contrary to the teachings of the Church. Leaders have frequently cautioned members against using narcotics such as marijuana, heroin, LSD, and crack-cocaine, as well as misusing prescription medication or over-the-counter drugs. In the October 1974 General Conference, President Spencer W. KIMBALL stated, "We hope our people will eliminate from their lives all kinds of drugs so far as possible. Too many depend upon drugs as tranquilizers and sleep helps, which is not always necessary. Certainly numerous young people have been damaged or destroyed by the use of marijuana and other deadly drugs. We deplore such" (*Ensign* 4 [Nov. 1974]:6).

Latter-day Saints view drug abuse as harmful to both the physical and spiritual health of the individual. Drug abuse frequently results in substance addiction, which severely limits personal freedom. That AGENCY is vital and has eternal consequences is reason enough to avoid abuse and addiction. Furthermore, the impact on one's health and general well-being is often severe. Though not explicitly mentioned in the WORD OF WISDOM, the Church's health code revealed in 1833 (*see* DOCTRINE AND COVENANTS: SECTION 89), drug abuse is nonetheless viewed as contrary to its precepts. President Joseph Fielding SMITH explained that additional revelation in regard to drugs was unnecessary because if members "sincerely follow what is written with the aid of the Spirit of the Lord, [they] need no further counsel" (*IE* 59 [Feb. 1956]:78).

Bishops counsel drug addicts to seek professional treatment to help them overcome their addiction, and offer assistance as appropriate through LDS SOCIAL SERVICES.

BIBLIOGRAPHY

Swinyard, Ewart A. "Wisdom in All Things." *New Era* 4 (Sept. 1974):44–49.

RAY G. SCHWARTZ